THE
ALL ENGLAND
LAW REPORTS
1983

Volume 3

Editor
PETER HUTCHESSON LL M
Barrister, New Zealand

Assistant Editor
BROOK WATSON
of Lincoln's Inn, Barrister
and of the New South Wales Bar

Consulting Editor
WENDY SHOCKETT
of Gray's Inn, Barrister

London
BUTTERWORTHS

ENGLAND	Butterworth & Co (Publishers) Ltd 88 Kingsway, **London** WC2B 6AB
AUSTRALIA	Butterworths Pty Ltd, **Sydney, Melbourne, Brisbane, Adelaide** and **Perth**
CANADA	Butterworth & Co (Canada) Ltd, **Toronto** Butterworth & Co (Western Canada) Ltd, **Vancouver**
NEW ZEALAND	Butterworths of New Zealand Ltd, **Wellington**
SINGAPORE	Butterworth & Co (Asia) Pte Ltd, **Singapore**
SOUTH AFRICA	Butterworth Publishers (Pty) Ltd, **Durban**
USA	Mason Publishing Co, **St Paul**, Minnesota Butterworth Legal Publishers, **Seattle**, Washington, **Boston**, Massachusetts and **Austin**, Texas D & S Publishers, **Clearwater**, Florida

©

Butterworth & Co (Publishers) Ltd

1983

ISBN 0 406 85149 2

Typeset by CCC, printed and bound in Great Britain by William Clowes Limited, Beccles and London

House of Lords

The Lord High Chancellor: Lord Hailsham of St Marylebone

Lords of Appeal in Ordinary

Lord Diplock
Lord Fraser of Tullybelton
Lord Keith of Kinkel
Lord Scarman
Lord Roskill

Lord Bridge of Harwich
Lord Brandon of Oakbrook
Lord Brightman
Lord Templeman

Court of Appeal

The Lord High Chancellor

The Lord Chief Justice of England: Lord Lane
(President of the Criminal Division)

The Master of the Rolls: Sir John Francis Donaldson
(President of the Civil Division)

The President of the Family Division: Sir John Lewis Arnold

The Vice-Chancellor: Sir Robert Edgar Megarry

Lords Justices of Appeal

Sir John Frederick Eustace Stephenson
Sir Frederick Horace Lawton
Sir George Stanley Waller
Sir James Roualeyn Hovell-Thurlow-
    Cumming-Bruce
Sir Edward Walter Eveleigh
Sir Desmond James Conrad Ackner
Sir Robin Horace Walford Dunn
Sir Peter Raymond Oliver
Sir Tasker Watkins VC
Sir Patrick McCarthy O'Connor
Sir William Hugh Griffiths
Sir Michael John Fox

Sir Michael Robert Emanuel Kerr
Sir John Douglas May
Sir Christopher John Slade
Sir Francis Brooks Purchas
Sir Robert Lionel Archibald Goff
Sir George Brian Hugh Dillon
Sir Stephen Brown
    (appointed 22 November 1983)
Sir Roger Jocelyn Parker
    (appointed 22 November 1983)
Sir Nicolas Christopher Henry Browne-
    Wilkinson
    (appointed 22 November 1983)

Chancery Division

The Lord High Chancellor

The Vice-Chancellor

Sir Peter Harry Batson Woodroffe Foster
   (retired 30 September 1983)
Sir John Norman Keates Whitford
Sir Ernest Irvine Goulding
Sir Raymond Henry Walton
Sir Nicolas Christopher Henry Browne-
   Wilkinson
   (appointed Lord Justice of Appeal,
   22 November 1983)
Sir John Evelyn Vinelott

Sir Martin Charles Nourse
Sir Douglas William Falconer
Sir Jean-Pierre Frank Eugene Warner
Sir Peter Leslie Gibson
Sir David Herbert Mervyn Davies
Sir Jeremiah LeRoy Harman
Sir Donald James Nicholls
   (appointed 1 October 1983)
Sir Richard Rashleigh Folliott Scott
   (appointed 23 November 1983)

Queen's Bench Division

The Lord Chief Justice of England

Sir Joseph Donaldson Cantley
Sir Hugh Eames Park
Sir Bernard Caulfield
Sir Hilary Gwynne Talbot
   (retired 30 September 1983)
Sir William Lloyd Mars-Jones
Sir Ralph Kilner Brown
Sir Peter Henry Rowley Bristow
Sir Hugh Harry Valentine Forbes
Sir David Powell Croom-Johnson
Sir Leslie Kenneth Edward Boreham
Sir Alfred William Michael Davies
Sir John Dexter Stocker
Sir Kenneth George Illtyd Jones
Sir Haydn Tudor Evans
Sir Peter Richard Pain
Sir Kenneth Graham Jupp
Sir Stephen Brown
   (appointed Lord Justice of Appeal,
   22 November 1983)
Sir Roger Jocelyn Parker
   (appointed Lord Justice of Appeal,
   22 November 1983)
Sir Ralph Brian Gibson
Sir Walter Derek Thornley Hodgson
Sir James Peter Comyn
Sir Anthony John Leslie Lloyd
Sir Frederick Maurice Drake
Sir Brian Thomas Neill
Sir Michael John Mustill
Sir Barry Cross Sheen

Sir David Bruce McNeill
Sir Harry Kenneth Woolf
Sir Christopher James Saunders French
Sir Thomas Patrick Russell
Sir Peter Edlin Webster
Sir Thomas Henry Bingham
Sir Iain Derek Laing Glidewell
Sir Henry Albert Skinner
Sir Peter Murray Taylor
Sir Murray Stuart-Smith
Sir Christopher Stephen Thomas Jonathan
   Thayer Staughton
Sir Donald Henry Farquharson
Sir Anthony James Denys McCowan
Sir Iain Charles Robert McCullough
Sir Hamilton John Leonard
Sir Alexander Roy Asplan Beldam
Sir David Cozens-Hardy Hirst
Sir John Stewart Hobhouse
Sir Michael Mann
Sir Andrew Peter Leggatt
Sir Michael Patrick Nolan
Sir Oliver Bury Popplewell
Sir William Alan Macpherson
Sir Philip Howard Otton
   (appointed 1 October 1983)
Sir Paul Joseph Morrow Kennedy
   (appointed 23 November 1983)
Sir Michael Hutchison
   (appointed 23 November 1983)

Family Division

The President of the Family Division

Sir John Brinsmead Latey
Sir Alfred Kenneth Hollings
Sir Charles Trevor Reeve
Dame Rose Heilbron
Sir Brian Drex Bush
Sir Alfred John Balcombe
Sir John Kember Wood
Sir Ronald Gough Waterhouse

Sir John Gervase Kensington Sheldon
Sir Thomas Michael Eastham
Dame Margaret Myfanwy Wood Booth
Sir Anthony Leslie Julian Lincoln
Dame Ann Elizabeth Oldfield Butler-Sloss
Sir Anthony Bruce Ewbank
Sir John Douglas Waite
Sir Anthony Barnard Hollis

CITATION

These reports are cited thus:

[1983] 3 All ER

REFERENCES

These reports contain references to the following major works of legal reference described in the manner indicated below.

Halsbury's Laws of England

The reference 39 Halsbury's Laws (3rd edn) 860, para 1303 refers to paragraph 1303 on page 860 of volume 39 of the third edition, and the reference 26 Halsbury's Laws (4th edn) para 577 refers to paragraph 577 on page 296 of volume 26 of the fourth edition of Halsbury's Laws of England.

Halsbury's Statutes of England

The reference 5 Halsbury's Statutes (3rd edn) 302 refers to page 302 of volume 5 of the third edition of Halsbury's Statutes of England.

The Digest

References are to the blue band replacement volumes and the green band reissue volumes of The Digest (formerly the English and Empire Digest), and to the continuation volumes.

The reference 47 Digest (Repl) 781, 25 refers to case number 25 on page 781 of Digest Blue Band Replacement Volume 47.

The reference 36(2) Digest (Reissue) 764, 1398 refers to case number 1398 on page 764 of Digest Green Band Reissue Volume 36(2).

The reference Digest (Cont Vol E) 640, 2392a refers to case number 2392a on page 640 of Digest Continuation Volume E.

Halsbury's Statutory Instruments

The reference 20 Halsbury's Statutory Instruments (4th reissue) 302 refers to page 302 of the fourth reissue of volume 20 of Halsbury's Statutory Instruments; references to other reissues are similar.

Cases reported in volume 3

Digest of cases reported in volume 3

CORRIGENDA

[1983] 2 All ER

p 657. **R v Ewing.** For lines *g*3 to *g*5 substitute:

'29 June. The court refused leave to appeal to the House of Lords but certified, under s 33(2) of the Criminal Appeal Act 1968, that the following point of law of general public importance was involved in the decision: whether, in cases where the details of a bank account were held in a computer, a print-out of those details was admissible in evidence under the Criminal Evidence Act 1965 to prove those details.

20 October. The Appeal Committee of the House of Lords (Lord Roskill, Lord Brandon of Oakbrook and Lord Brightman) dismissed a petition by the appellant for leave to appeal.'

p 833. **Dove v Banhams Patent Locks Ltd.** Line *f*1 should read '. . . damages for the loss . . .'

p 1066. **R v Seymour.** Solicitors for the appellant should read *'Sharpe Pritchard & Co,* agents for *Keith Turner & Galpin*, Northampton'.

[1983] 3 All ER

p 118. **London and South of England Building Society v Stone.** Line *f*2 should read '. . . full amount *of* the borrowers' personal liabilities . . .'

p 187. **R v Miller (Raymond).** Counsel for Mr Glennie should read *'Alastair Hill QC* and *Anthony Clover'*.

R v Kent

COURT OF APPEAL, CRIMINAL DIVISION

LORD LANE CJ, McCULLOUGH AND LEONARD JJ

12 MAY 1983

Road traffic – Penalty points – Disqualification – Endorsement of licence – Endorsement with penalty points – Whether endorsement of penalty points can be ordered at same time as disqualification imposed – Road Traffic Act 1972, s 101(1) – Transport Act 1981, s 19(1), Sch 7.

Road traffic – Penalty points – Disqualification – Endorsement of licence – Endorsement with particulars of offence – Endorsement with penalty points – Guidance on disqualification and endorsement of licence.

The appellant pleaded guilty at a magistrates' court to offences of burglary, taking away a vehicle without the owner's consent contrary to s 12(1) of the Theft Act 1968, driving while disqualified contrary to s 99(b) of the Road Traffic Act 1972 and driving while uninsured contrary to s 143 of the 1972 Act. He was committed for sentence to the Crown Court, where the judge sentenced him to a total of 18 months' imprisonment for the burglary offences. In relation to the motor vehicle offences (ie those arising under the 1968 and 1972 Acts) the judge erroneously believed that disqualification from driving was in the circumstances obligatory and not discretionary. He therefore disqualified the appellant from driving for 12 months, and ordered that his licence be endorsed with particulars of the offences and be further endorsed with a total of eight penalty points pursuant to s 19(1)[a] of and Sch 7[b] to the Transport Act 1981. The appellant appealed against the disqualification and the endorsement of penalty points.

Held – Where an offender was disqualified for holding or obtaining a driver's licence for an offence which attracted obligatory or discretionary disqualification it was contrary to s 19(1) of the 1981 Act and s 101(1)[c] of the 1972 Act to order at the same time the endorsement of penalty points on the offender's licence, and the judge had been wrong

---

a Section 19(1) provides: 'Where a person is convicted of an offence involving obligatory or discretionary disqualification and the court does not order him to be disqualified (whether on that or any other conviction) but orders particulars of the conviction to be endorsed under section 101 of the 1972 Act, the endorsement ordered shall include—(a) particulars of the offence, including the date when it was committed; and (b) the number of penalty points shown in respect of the offence in Schedule 7 to this Act (or, where a range of numbers is so shown, a number falling within the range); but if a person is convicted of two or more such offences the number of penalty points to be endorsed in respect of those of them that were committed on the same occasion shall be the number or highest number that would be endorsed on a conviction of one of those offences.'

b Schedule 7, provides, inter alia, that an offence under s 12 of the Theft Act 1968 carries eight penalty points, that an offence under s 99(b) of the Road Traffic Act 1972 carries six penalty points and that an offence under s 143 of the 1972 Act carries four to eight penalty points.

c Section 101(1), so far as material, provides: ' . . . where a person is convicted of an offence—(a) under a provision of this Act specified in . . . Part I of Schedule 4 to this Act in relation to which there appears in . . . that Part the word "obligatory" or the word "obligatory" qualified by conditions relating to the offence; and (b) where the said word "obligatory" is so qualified, the conditions are satisfied in the case of the offence of which he is convicted; or where a person is convicted of an offence specified in Part II or Part III of that Schedule (any such offence being in this section

(Continued on p 2)

to do so. Since the judge had a discretion whether to disqualify the appellant he could
either have disqualified the appellant and ordered that his licence be endorsed with *a*
particulars of the offences or he could have ordered that his licence be both endorsed
with the particulars and endorsed with penalty points but without disqualification. In
the circumstances the appellant's disqualification would be allowed to stand while the
endorsement of penalty points would be quashed, and to that extent the appeal would be
allowed (see p 3 *d e*, p 4 *h* and p 5 *d* to *h*, post).

Guidance on imposing disqualification, and on endorsing a licence with particulars of *b*
offences and with penalty points (see p 4 *c* to p 5 *d* and *g h*, post).

Notes

For statutory disqualification for road traffic offences, see Supplement to 33 Halsbury's
Laws (3rd edn) para 1061A.

  For the imposition of penalty points, see ibid para 1087.   *c*
  For the Theft Act 1968, s 12, see 8 Halsbury's Statutes (3rd edn) 790.
  For the Road Traffic Act 1972, ss 99, 101, 143, see 42 ibid 1751, 1752, 1786.
  For the Transport Act 1981, s 19, Sch 7, see 51 ibid 1413, 1426, 1439.

Appeal against sentence

On 16 October 1982 the appellant, Michael Peter Kent, pleaded guilty, at Marlborough *d*
Street Magistrates' Court to two offences of burglary, taking a vehicle without the owner's
consent contrary to s 12(1) of the Theft Act 1968, driving while disqualified contrary to
s 99(b) of the Road Traffic Act 1972 and driving while uninsured contrary to s 143 of the
1972 Act. He was committed for sentence to the Crown Court. On 5 November 1982 in
the Crown Court at Knightsbridge before his Honour Judge Friend the appellant was
sentenced to: 18 months' imprisonment for each burglary offence; 9 months' *e*
imprisonment, disqualification from driving for 12 months and endorsement of eight
penalty points on his licence for taking a vehicle without the owner's consent; 6 months'
imprisonment, disqualification from driving for 12 months and endorsement of six
penalty points on his licence for driving while disqualified; and a fine of £50 (or one
day's imprisonment) and endorsement of six penalty points on his licence for driving
while uninsured. All the terms of imprisonment and all the periods of disqualification *f*
were to run concurrently. The appellant appealed against sentence with leave of the
single judge on the grounds that the period of disqualification was too long and that
endorsement of his licence with penalty points ought not to have been ordered. The facts
are set out in the judgment of the court.

Ayoob Oozeer (assigned by the Registrar of Criminal Appeals) for the appellant. *g*
Judith Rowe for the Crown.

LORD LANE CJ delivered the following judgment of the court. On 15 October 1982
the appellant pleaded guilty at a magistrates' court and was committed for sentence to
the Crown Court at Knightsbridge where, on 5 November, sentences were imposed on
him as follows: for two offences of burglary, 18 months' imprisonment for each offence, *h*
to run concurrently; for taking a vehicle without the owner's consent, 9 months'
imprisonment, disqualified from driving for 12 months, and eight penalty points
endorsed on his licence; for driving while disqualified, 6 months' imprisonment,
disqualified from driving for 12 months, and six penalty points endorsed on his licence;
for driving while uninsured, fined £50 or one day's imprisonment, and six penalty

j

(Continued from p 1)
referred to as an "offence involving obligatory endorsement"), the court shall order that there shall
be endorsed on any licence held by him particulars of the conviction and, if the court orders him
to be disqualified, particulars of the disqualification, and, if the court does not order him to be
disqualified, the particulars and penalty points required by section 19(1) of the Transport Act 1981
. . .'

a points endorsed on his licence. All the terms of imprisonment and all the periods of disqualification were to run concurrently.

The facts were these. In October 1982 he took a car in Woodford in order to commit a burglary in central London. He was both disqualified from driving at that time and also uninsured. He effected entry into the premises through a door at the top of the fire escape up which he climbed. He stole property in the building and also cash to the value of something just over £1,100.

b A police officer found him crouching under the fire escape. He was wearing gloves. He threw these away when he saw the policeman. When the policeman asked him, 'What are you doing?' he said, 'Oh, come on, it's obvious. I have done the place.' He handed over a builder's bolster and a torch and the officer saw four plastic bags alongside in which was the stolen property. The appellant said he needed money and had stolen the goods to sell.

c He is aged 39, divorced and unemployed. He has no permanent place of residence. He has, regrettably, a long criminal record behind him.

It is only the question of disqualification about which complaint is made. What counsel on his behalf has asked us to do is to so reorganise the disqualification as to allow him his licence when he comes out of prison.

The appellant himself seems to think that the disqualification imposed on him was *d* one of 18 months. The mistake was understandable. When one reads the way the sentence was passed, although it was passed quite properly by the judge, it may very well have left the impression in the appellant's mind that he was disqualified for 18 months. In fact it was only 12 months.

If one examines the dates it is apparent that if he earns his full remission, and we have no reason to suppose that he will not, he will be released only a matter of three weeks *e* before the disqualification expires. That means it will only be three weeks of disqualification imposed on him when he leaves prison. In those circumstances it seems to us that it would really be tinkering with the disqualification if we were to interfere with it. Consequently that part of the appeal fails. The 12 months' disqualification stands.

In this case, as in the three cases which follow, it is apparent that difficulties are being encountered and have been encountered by the Crown Court in relation to the system of *f* penalty points which were introduced by s 19 of the Transport Act 1981. That came into force on 1 November 1982. May we say immediately that this court sympathises with courts which have to grapple with this sort of legislation. It may be said that it would be very surprising if judges did not make mistakes in this branch of their work.

In order to illustrate the sort of difficulty which courts face, we would like to take three relevant offences which are likely to give rise to the imposition of penalty points, *g* and to say first of all that in many cases all three of the offences will have been committed.

First of all, taking and driving a motor vehicle without the consent of the owner. The statute creating the offence is the Theft Act 1968, s 12(1). The punishment is in s 12(2) of that Act. The question of disqualification or endorsement is to be found in Sch 4 to the Road Traffic Act 1972. The power to disqualify for the offence itself is to be found in s 93 of the 1972 Act. The power to disqualify for repeated offences is in s 19(2) of the *h* Transport Act 1981. The power to endorse is to be found in s 101 of the Road Traffic Act 1972. The power to impose penalty points is in s 19(1) of the Transport Act 1981. The number of points to be imposed is in Sch 7 to the 1981 Act. Thus there are three Acts, comprising four sections and three schedules to be considered.

We now turn to driving while disqualified. The statute creating the offence is the Road Traffic Act, 1972, s 99. The punishment is to be found in Sch 4 to the 1972 Act. So *j* is the question of disqualification or endorsement. The power to disqualify for the offence itself is in s 93 of the 1972 Act as amended by Sch 9 to the Transport Act 1981. The power to disqualify for repeated offences is in s 19(2) of the 1981 Act. The power to endorse is in s 101 of the 1972 Act as amended by Sch 9 to the 1981 Act. The power to impose penalty points is in s 19(1) of the 1981 Act and the number of points to be imposed is in Sch 7 to the 1981 Act. That is, in summary, two Acts, comprising four sections and three schedules.

We now turn to driving while uninsured. The statute which creates the offence is s 143 of the Road Traffic Act 1972. The punishment is to be found in Sch 4 to the 1972 Act and so is the question of disqualification and endorsement. The power to disqualify for the offence itself is in s 93 of the 1972 Act. The power to disqualify for repeated offences is s 19(2) of the 1972 Act. The power to endorse is to be found in s 101 of the 1972 Act. The power to impose penalty points is to be found in s 19(1) of the Transport Act 1981 and the number of points is to be found in Sch 7 to the 1981 Act. That is two Acts, comprising four sections and three schedules.

We would like, if we may, in the hope that it may assist courts in the future, to point out one or two practical problems by way of clarification. We add, however, that most courts, much to their credit, now seem to have overcome most of the difficulties which face them in this mass of legislation.

1. *Disqualification*

A person appearing before a court may be disqualified for the following reasons. (a) Because the offence of which he is convicted attracts obligatory or discretionary disqualification. Such offences are set out in Sch 4 to the Road Traffic Act 1972. The power to disqualify is in s 93(1) and (2) of that Act. Disqualifications run from the time of sentence and cannot be consecutive to one another. Or (b) because the court is satisfied that a motor vehicle was used by the person convicted or anyone else for the purpose of committing or facilitating the commission of the offence in question: that is found in s 44 of the Powers of Criminal Courts Act 1973. Or (c) because he has committed repeated offences attracting obligatory or discretionary disqualification ('totting up'); the power to disqualify is set out in s 19(2) of the Transport Act 1981. If the offender is liable to be disqualified under s 19(2) for several offences, the disqualification is allocated to one offence only (see s 19(5)(*a*)), although for the purposes of an appeal the disqualification is treated as an order made on the conviction of each offence (see s 19(5)(*c*)). Or (d) for both (a) and (c) or (b) and (c) above; all disqualifications now run concurrently since the repeal of s 93(5) of the Road Traffic Act 1972, which used to make disqualification for repeated offences consecutive to any other disqualification.

2. *Endorsement*

All offences attracting obligatory or discretionary disqualification must be endorsed on the offender's driving licence, unless there are special reasons for not doing so. This is irrespective of whether he is disqualified or not: see s 101(1) of the Road Traffic Act 1972 as amended by Sch 9 to the Transport Act 1981.

3. *Penalty points*

This is a matter which has caused the most difficulty, as can be observed from the cases which we are dealing with this morning. If a court does not disqualify an offender for an offence attracting obligatory disqualification (where there are special reasons: see s 93(1) of the 1972 Act) or discretionary disqualification, it is bound to endorse his driving licence with penalty points as set out in Sch 7 to the Transport Act 1981, unless there are special reasons for not doing so: s 19(1) of the 1981 Act. Conversely, if the court does disqualify from driving, it may not on the same occasion order penalty points to be endorsed: s 101(1) of the Road Traffic Act 1972 as amended by Sch 9 to the 1981 Act. There is a catch here. If the court's power to disqualify derives solely from s 44 of the Powers of Criminal Courts Act 1973 (that is a vehicle being used for the commission of the offence in question) and the court decides not to disqualify, it cannot order the offender's licence to be endorsed either generally or with penalty points. That provision is to be found in s 19(9) of the 1981 Act.

Crown Court record sheets

Judges in the Crown Court have been making mistakes resulting in illegal sentences. The following are some of the examples which should be looked for.

(1) Ordering consecutive periods of disqualification.

a   (2) Disqualifying and at the same time ordering penalty points to be endorsed on a licence.

(3) Awarding the incorrect number of penalty points.

(4) Disqualifying for repeated offences without allocating the disqualification to a single offence: see s 19(5)(a) of the Transport Act 1981.

(5) Ordering penalty points to be endorsed for more than one offence committed on
b the same occasion. The correct procedure is to allocate a number of points for the most serious of the offences.

(6) Failing to disqualify when the points exceed 12 points when there are no mitigating circumstances.

(7) Failure to state 'special reasons' or 'mitigating circumstances' (a) when not ordering disqualification, or ordering disqualification less than the minimum or (b) when not
c ordering endorsement on the licence: see s 105 of the Road Traffic Act 1972.

There have been further difficulties arising in the following way. There have on occasions been, understandably, efforts made by court staff to prevent mistakes arising. This has resulted in discrepancies being observed between the sentence pronounced by the judge and that appearing on the record sheet. We wish to make these matters clear. First of all, the order of the court is that pronounced by the judge in open court. Second,
d the responsibility of the court staff is to make a record which accurately reflects that pronouncement. Third, if the court staff are in doubt as to the pronouncement, the judge must be consulted where the staff are not clear what it was the judge said, or where they think that the judge's order may be faulty.

Turning then to the present case, the judge took the view that the disqualification in the present case was mandatory. In fact the offences to which the appellant here pleaded
e guilty involved only discretionary disqualification by virtue of s 93 of the 1972 Act and Sch 4 to that Act. He was not liable to totting up. Consequently the judge's direction that the appellant's driving licence be endorsed with penalty points when he was at the same time imposing a disqualification was contrary to the terms, as we have already observed, of s 101(1) of the 1972 Act.

In those circumstances there are two alternative courses open to this court: either to
f confirm the disqualification and the general endorsement and quash the direction of penalty points to be endorsed on the licence, or to quash the disqualification, announce the penalty points and order that the licence be endorsed with eight points, that number being the highest of those attributable to the three offences of taking and driving away, (eight points), driving while disqualified (six points), and driving while uninsured (four to eight points). As already indicated, and for the reasons already indicated, we prefer the
g former course, that is to leave the disqualification standing and quash the endorsement of the penalty points on the licence.

There is a further complication here, namely that is that the court staff observed the error which had been made in the present case. They notified the authorities at Swansea of the disqualification and the endorsement but not of the penalty points. The proper course would have been to inform the judge and to allow him to make the necessary
h alteration in open court in accordance with his powers under s 47(2) of the Supreme Court Act 1981.

For the reasons indicated, and in the way indicated, to that extent this appeal is allowed.

Appeal allowed in part.

Solicitors: *D M O'Shea* (for the Crown).

N P Metcalfe Esq   Barrister.

British Airports Authority v Ashton and others

QUEEN'S BENCH DIVISION
ROBERT GOFF LJ AND MANN J
19, 20 APRIL, 12 MAY 1983

Aerodrome – British Airports Authority – Statutory powers – Byelaws regulating use and operation of aerodrome – Right of peaceful picketing on aerodrome in furtherance of trade dispute – Employees mounting picket at control post within aerodrome – Byelaw prohibiting 'public demonstrations' interfering with use of airport – Employees refusing constable's request to leave aerodrome – Whether employees entitled to exercise right of peaceful picketing within airport – Whether picketing constituting 'public demonstration' – Whether constable's request to employees to leave aerodrome reasonable – Trade Union and Labour Relations Act 1974, s 15.

Trade dispute – Picketing – Right of peaceful picketing – Whether right exercisable against will of owner of land and regardless of byelaws affecting land – Trade Union and Labour Relations Act 1974, s 15.

In the course of a trade dispute between an airline company and its employees at an airport owned and operated by the British Airports Authority, some of the employees mounted a union picket at a control post situated within the airport and used to control the entry of vehicles to the airport. From time to time the employees stopped vehicles as they approached the control post and spoke to the drivers. A constable requested the employees to leave the airport but they refused to do so. The constable arrested them. The employees were charged with remaining on the airport after being requested to leave by a constable and taking part in a 'public demonstration' likely to interfere with the proper use of the aerodrome, contrary to byelaws regulating the use of the airport. The magistrates dismissed the information, on the grounds (i) that in mounting the picket the employees were acting within s 15ᵃ of the Trade Union and Labour Relations Act 1974, which permitted peaceful picketing in furtherance of a trade dispute at or near an employee's place of work, and that therefore the byelaws prohibiting public demonstrations could not render their action unlawful, and (ii) that the employees were not taking part in a 'public demonstration' within that byelaw. The airport authority appealed.

Held – (1) Although the airport authority's ownership of the airport was subject to the public's right of access, that right of access was for the purpose of taking advantage of the services and facilities provided at the airport and did not extend to a right of access for the purposes of peaceful picketing pursuant to s 15 of the 1974 Act, since s 15 did not authorise picketing on land against the owner's will and did not affect the operation of any byelaws regulating the use and operation of the land. Accordingly, s 15 was irrelevant in considering whether the employees' picket was in breach of the airport byelaws (see p 14 b to d and f, post); Larkin v Belfast Harbour Comrs [1908] 2 IR 214 applied.

(2) Although for the purposes of the byelaws a 'public' demonstration was merely one which occurred in public, as the employees' picketing had done, their picketing was not a 'demonstration' in the sense of a public manifestation of feeling such as a procession or mass meeting. Accordingly, the employees had not contravened the byelaw restricting public demonstrations (see p 12 d to f, post).

(3) Although the airport authority's byelaws did not require that there should have been a previous breach of another byelaw before a constable could request someone to leave the airport, a request to leave the airport had to be fair and reasonable in the circumstances, having regard to the need to secure the efficient, economic and safe

---

ᵃ Section 15, so far as material, is set out at p 11 j, post

a operation of the services and facilities provided at the airport. Since the magistrates had not considered whether the constable's request to the employees to leave the airport was fair and reasonable in that sense, the case would be remitted to the magistrates for a further hearing (see p 12 *g h*, p 13 *b* to *d* and p 14 *e* to *h*, post); dictum of Lord Denning MR in *Cinnamond v British Airports Authority* [1980] 2 All ER at 372 applied.

Notes

b For the British Airports Authority's duty in relation to aerodromes, see 2 Halsbury's Laws (4th edn) para 1021, and for the control of aerodromes by byelaws, see ibid para 1032.

For the Trade Union and Labour Relations Act 1974, s 15 (as substituted by the Employment Act 1980, s 16), see 50(2) Halsbury's Statutes (3rd edn) 2634.

Cases referred to in judgment

c *Associated Provincial Picture Houses Ltd v Wednesbury Corp* [1947] 2 All ER 680, [1948] 1 KB 223, CA.

Broome v DPP [1974] 1 All ER 314, [1974] AC 587, [1974] 2 WLR 58, HL.

Cinnamond v British Airports Authority [1980] 2 All ER 368, [1980] 1 WLR 582, CA.

Ferguson (L L) Ltd v O'Gorman [1937] IR 620.

Kavanagh v Hiscock [1974] 2 All ER 177, [1974] QB 600, [1974] 2 WLR 421, DC.

d *Larkin v Belfast Harbour Comrs* [1908] 2 IR 214.

Appeal

The British Airports Authority (BAA) appealed by way of case stated by the justices for the Middlesex Area of Greater London acting in and for the Petty Sessional Division of Uxbridge in respect of their adjudication on 24 June 1982, as a magistrates' court sitting at Uxbridge, dismissing informations laid on behalf of the Commissioner of Police of the

e Metropolis against the respondents, Anthony John Ashton, Alwyne Patrick Street, Mike Le Cornu, William Robert Doe, Paul Joseph Burrell, Kenneth James Gallagher and Thomas Patrick McGrath that (i) they on 31 March 1982 at Heathrow Airport remained on the aerodrome after having been requested to leave by a constable, contrary to byelaw 5(58) of the Heathrow Airport–London Byelaws 1972, and (ii) they on 31 March 1982 at Heathrow Airport took part in a public demonstration likely to interfere with the proper

f use of the aerodrome, contrary to byelaw 5(34) of the 1972 byelaws. The questions for the opinion of the High Court were as follows. (a) Was attendance for the purposes provided for in s 15 of the Trade Union and Labour Relations Act 1974 as amended lawful on any part of Heathrow Airport owned by the BAA and if so on which part and in what circumstances? (b) Were acts which were contrary to the 1972 byelaws lawful if they were done at Heathrow Airport within the terms of s 15 of the 1974 Act? (c) On the

g facts of the case did the police have power in law to require the respondents to leave the aerodrome? (d) Could persons who were attending on land owned by the BAA at Heathrow Airport for the purposes provided in s 15 of the 1974 Act lawfully be required to leave the airport and if so in what circumstances? (e) Was each of the respondents 'at or near his place of work' or 'an official of a trade union, at or near the place of work of a member of that union whom he is accompanying and whom he represents' within s 15

h of the 1974 Act, and in the circumstances of Heathrow Airport what was meant in law by 'at or near his own place of work' in s 15? (f) Did byelaw 5(58) of the 1972 byelaws give an absolute right to a constable to require a person to leave the aerodrome? The facts are set out in the judgment of the court.

j *Timothy Walker* for BAA.
Timothy Nash for the respondents.

Cur adv vult

12 May. The following judgment of the court was delivered.

MANN J. There is before the court a case stated by the justices for the Middlesex Area

of Greater London acting in and for the Petty Sessional Division of Uxbridge in respect
of adjudications made by them as a magistrates' court sitting at Uxbridge. The a
adjudications were made on 24 June 1982. On that date the seven respondents appeared
charged on informations laid on behalf of the Commissioner of Police of the Metropolis
to the effect that (i) they on 31 March 1982 at Heathrow Airport, London, remained on
the aerodrome after having been requested to leave by a constable contrary to byelaw
5(58) of the Heathrow Airport–London Byelaws 1972 and (ii) they on 31 March 1982 at
Heathrow Airport, London did take part in a public demonstration likely to interfere b
with the proper use of the aerodrome contrary to byelaw 5(34) of the Heathrow Airport–
London Byelaws 1972.

Each of the respondents pleaded not guilty to both informations. The justices dismissed
all of the informations. Their opinion as recorded in the case stated was:

'We were of opinion that the Respondents had acted within the terms of Section
15 of the [Trade Union and Labour Relations Act 1974] and that Regulation 5(34) c
of the Byelaws could not render this action unlawful. We also decided that even if
Section 15 of the 1974 Act did not apply, the Respondents had not been taking part
in a public demonstration within the terms of Regulation 5(34). We considered
Section 4(1) of the Policing of Airports Act 1974 and noticed that authority had been
conferred by that statute to include in any Byelaws a requirement that a constable
may require any person to leave the aerodrome. We decided that in view of our d
findings in relation to Regulation 5(34) it would be incongruous to convict under
Regulation 5(58).'

As has been said, the informations were laid on behalf of the Commissioner of Police
of the Metropolis. The case stated was applied for by the British Airports Authority
(BAA) and that corporation has prosecuted the appeal before this court. The respondents
conceded that BAA was able so to do as being a person aggrieved by the determination of e
the justices.

The facts found by the justices were as follows:

'4. Heathrow Airport, London is sited on land owned by the Appellants and in
March 1982 some 280 companies and organisations operated at Heathrow employing
50,000 people. There are three passenger terminals at Heathrow and ramp workers f
are employed for the loading and off-loading of aircraft, the handling of baggage
and mail, catering deliveries and the towing of aircraft.
5. British Airways employed 1500 ramp workers at Terminal 1 and 400 at
Terminal 2. British Airways handled 90–95% of flights at Terminal 1 and although
Terminal 2 was entirely for foreign carriers, 21 of the 38 airlines involved used
British Airways handling. At Terminal 3 British Airways were responsible for about g
4 million of the 10 million passengers each year and for about 50% of the aircraft. A
copy of a plan of the airport exhibited at the hearing is attached to this case.
6. The respondents were all employed by British Airways as ramp workers. The
Respondents Ashton, Le Cornu, Doe and McGrath were employed at Terminal 1
and the Respondent Street at Terminal 2. The Respondents Gallagher and Burrell
were employed at the Cargo Centre on the South Side of the Airport and they were h
required to drive vehicles between this Cargo Centre and Terminals 1 and 2. Mr.
Burrell could also be required to work in the Airmail Unit adjacent to Control Post
8. All of the Respondents with the exception of Mr. Burrell were officials of the
Transport and General Workers Union.
7. When a trade dispute arose at Heathrow an officer of the Metropolitan Police
sought a meeting with the officials of the trade union involved and if the intention j
was to picket, an agreement was reached on the number and location of pickets with
reference to the Code of Practice on picketing issued by the Department of
Employment. Picketing was not permitted at the twelve Control Posts sited within
the Airport perimeter forming access points between the airside and the landside of
the Airport. A presence of up to three persons was permitted at the Control Posts in

order that Trade Union Officials may communicate with their members and monitor a trade dispute. These persons were not permitted to display armbands or to display banners or to indicate that they were a picket. Picketing was not permitted inside or immediately outside the Terminal Buildings nor airside. Picketing at other locations within the perimeter of the Airport was permitted provided it was within the terms of the Code of Practice and at or near the place of work of those involved. Normally this applied to locations occupied by a single tenant. Picketing was also permitted at the seven entrances to the Airport provided that the picket line was outside the Airport perimeter. The Police informed the Appellants of their decision in each case but did not normally consult with the Appellants.

8. On the 8th February 1982 the Respondents Le Cornu and Street, Transport and General Workers Union Shop Stewards of British Airways Ramp Workers at Terminals 1 and 2 informed the Police that they anticipated an industrial dispute with their employers when new work rosters were introduced the following day. An agreement was reached that they could have a presence at the Control Posts on the understanding that there would not be any armbands or other indication of a picket and that no persons or vehicles would be stopped.

9. On the 9th February 1982 the dispute commenced and from 7 a.m. there was a presence of three persons at most of the Control Posts. There were also 3 trade union representatives at the entrance to the British Airways Catering Building, North Side and although this was not part of the agreement, the Police acquiesced as they were aware that a number of catering loader drivers involved in the dispute worked from this building.

10. On the 12th February 1982 the Respondent Street informed the Police that the Shop Stewards intended to organise a picket at every entrance to the Airport. The Police agreed that up to four pickets identified by armbands could picket the seven Airport entrances with placards provided that they were outside the Airport perimeter.

11. On the 17th February 1982 the Police informed the Respondent, Le Cornu, that in view of the picket lines at the Airport entrances, the presence within the Airport perimeter was no longer justified.

12. On the 2nd March 1982 there was a 24 hour strike by catering workers employed by British Airways at the South Side Catering Centre in support of the ramp dispute. The Police permitted a presence of four trade union members at the entrance to the building. It was police policy to allow picketing within the Airport perimeter at premises occupied by workers, so long as this did not interfere with other workers or the smooth running of the Airport.

13. On the 12th March 1982 a number of trade union members appeared at a Control Post as a picket but left when requested to do so by the Police. The Respondent, Gallagher, was advised that picketing could take place outside the Airport perimeter otherwise they faced prosecution under the Heathrow Byelaws. He stated that the pickets may consider returning to test the law and establish a point of principle.

14. Control Post 8 was adjacent to Terminal 3 Arrivals Building and was a point of access to the aircraft aprons. It was effectively the only entrance for the B.P., Shell and Esso fuel tankers. These three companies supplied over 60% of all the fuel supplied for aircraft at Heathrow, with more than 20% of this fuel carried by fuel lorries. A majority of this fuel went to British Airways operations. The road leading to Control Post 8 was an access way to the coach station at Terminal 3 Arrivals Building. The Control Post itself provided access to the Airmail Unit and was a through route for various personnel and vehicles. Ramp workers were under no restriction of movement either landside or airside.

15. In February 1982 the Appellants carried out a survey and found that an average of 160 vehicles per hour used Control Post 8 at peak periods. Control Posts 8 and 4 were the busiest at the Airport.

16. At 2.10 p.m. on the 31st March 1982 the Respondents were part of a group, varying in estimation between 8 and 12 persons seen at Control Post 8. A sign was affixed to the Control Post gate which read "Official Picket TGWU". Other posters were resting against a fence but these were curled over.

17. At 2.15 p.m. a Post Office van approached the open barrier, a man stood in the road in front of the van and held his hand up. The van stopped and another man spoke to the driver who then continued to drive through the Control Post. At 2.35 p.m. a Shell tanker approached the Control Post and stopped. Three men were in the road and two of them spoke to the driver. The driver turned his vehicle round and drove away. Another tanker approached the Control Post and when a man raised his arm the tanker continued and went through the Control Post. A British Airways van then approached the Control Post and stopped at the barrier. After the driver had spoken to someone he drove away without passing through the Control Post.

18. The Respondents were all requested by a Constable to leave the Airport and they refused. They were arrested.'

The questions raised in the case stated are as follows:

'(a) Is attendance for the purposes provided for in S. 15(1) Trade Union and Labour Relations Act 1974 as amended—(TULRA 1974) lawful on any part of Heathrow Airport owned by the British Airports Authority and if so on which part and in what circumstances? (b) Are acts which are contrary to the Heathrow Airport London Byelaws 1972 lawful if they are done at Heathrow Airport within the terms of S. 15 of TULRA 1974 as amended? (c) On the facts of this case did the police have the power in law to require the defendants to leave the aerodrome? (d) Can persons who are attending on land owned by the Authority at Heathrow Airport for the purposes provided for in S. 15 TULRA 1974 as amended lawfully be required to leave the airport and if so in what circumstances? (e) Were each of the Defendants at or near their place of work, or an official of a trade union at or near the place of work of a member of that union whom he was accompanying and whom he represented, within the meaning of S. 15 TULRA 1974 as amended and in the circumstances of Heathrow Airport what is meant in law by "at or near his own place of work" in the said S. 15? . . . (f) Does Regulation 5(58) of the Heathrow Airport London Byelaws give an absolute right to a constable to require a person to leave the aerodrome?'

The statutory provisions which are material for the purpose of answering the questions raised can be stated under four heads.

1. *BAA's constitution and functions.* BAA was constituted by the Airports Authority Act 1965. Section 1 of that Act provided that:

'There shall be a body corporate to be called the British Airports Authority . . . to which shall be transferred the . . . aerodromes at Heathrow, Gatwick, Stansted and Prestwick and which shall manage those aerodromes and any other aerodrome provided or acquired by it under the following provisions of this Act.'

The functions of BAA were set out in s 2, of which sub-ss (1), (2) and (3) provided:

'(1) It shall be the duty of the Authority to provide at its aerodromes such services and facilities as are in its opinion necessary or desirable for their operation, but the Authority shall not provide any navigation services except with the consent in writing of the Minister.
(2) In carrying out that duty the Authority shall have regard to the development of air transport and to efficiency, economy and safety of operation.
(3) The Authority shall have power to do anything which is calculated to facilitate the discharge of its duty under this Act.'

The 1965 Act was repealed and replaced by a consolidating enactment entitled the
Airports Authority Act 1975. The new sections corresponding to ss 1 and 2 of the 1965
Act have the same numbers.

2. *BAA's byelaw-making power*. Section 9(1) of the 1965 Act provided:

> 'The Authority may, in respect of any aerodrome owned or managed by it, make
> byelaws for regulating the use and operation of the aerodrome and the conduct of
> all persons while within the aerodrome, and in particular byelaws—(a) for securing
> the safety of aircraft, vehicles and persons using the aerodrome and preventing
> danger to the public arising from the use and operation of the aerodrome; (b) for
> preventing obstruction within the aerodrome; (c) for regulating vehicular traffic
> anywhere within the aerodrome except on roads therein to which the road traffic
> enactments apply, and in particular (with that exception) for imposing speed limits
> on vehicles therein and for restricting or regulating the parking of vehicles or their
> use for any purpose or in any manner specified in the byelaws; (d) for prohibiting
> waiting by hackney carriages except at standings appointed by the Authority; (e) for
> prohibiting or restricting access to any part of the aerodrome; (f) for preserving
> order within the aerodrome and preventing damage to property therein; (g) for
> regulating or restricting advertising within the aerodrome; (h) for requiring any
> person, if so requested by a constable appointed under this Act, to leave the
> aerodrome or any particular part of it; (i) for restricting the area which is to be taken
> as constituting the aerodrome for the purposes of the byelaws.'

Byelaws made by BAA under this power did not have effect until confirmed by the
Secretary of State (see s 9(4)). The Heathrow Airport–London Byelaws 1972 were made
on 18 May 1972 and confirmed on 15 August 1972. The powers to make and confirm
byelaws are now contained in identical terms in s 9 of the 1975 Act and byelaws made
under the 1965 Act have since 12 December 1975 had effect as if made under the new
provision (see ss 25(7) and 26(2) of the 1975 Act).

There is an additional byelaw-making power in s 4(1) of the Policing of Airports Act
1974, but the additional power is not material to the present case.

3. *The policing of BAA's aerodromes*. Section 10 of the 1965 Act empowered BAA to
appoint persons to be constables. A person so appointed had 'the powers and privileges'
and was 'liable to the duties and responsibilities of a constable' on each of the aerodromes
owned or managed by BAA. BAA established a constabulary at Heathrow under the
powers so conferred. However, the Policing of Airports Act 1974 (s 1(1)) empowers the
Secretary of State to designate an aerodrome if he considers the policing of that aerodrome
should—

> 'in the interests of the preservation of the peace and the prevention of crime, be
> undertaken by constables under the direction and control of the chief officer of
> police for the police area in which the aerodrome is wholly or mainly situated.'

The Secretary of State made the Policing of Airports (Heathrow) Order 1974, SI 1974/
1671, which designated Heathrow. After the coming into force of that order on 1
November 1974 the BAA constabulary was replaced at Heathrow by the Metropolitan
Police Force (to which the BAA constables were transferred) acting under the direction
and control of the Commissioner of Police of the Metropolis.

4. *The Trade Union and Labour Relations Act 1974 as amended by the Employment Act 1980*.
The relevant provision of the 1974 Act is s 15(1) (as substituted by s 16 of the Employment
Act 1980) which provides:

> 'It shall be lawful for a person in contemplation or furtherance of a trade dispute
> to attend—(a) at or near his own place of work, or (b) if he is an official of a trade
> union, at or near the place of work of a member of that union whom he is
> accompanying and whom he represents, for the purpose only of peacefully obtaining
> or communicating information, or peacefully persuading any person to work or
> abstain from working.'

In our judgment the case stated requires an examination of three questions. Those questions are as follows. (1) Were the acts of the respondents in mounting a picket at *a* control post 8 on 31 March 1982 a contravention of byelaw 5(34)? (2) In remaining on the aerodrome on 31 March 1982 after being requested to leave by a constable, were the respondents in contravention of byelaw 5(58)? (3) Is the position affected by s 15(1) of the 1974 Act?

As to the first question, byelaw 5(34) provides:

'No person shall organise or take part in any public assembly, demonstration or *b* procession likely to obstruct or interfere with the proper use of the aerodrome or cause serious public disorder or obstruct or interfere with the comfort and convenience or safety of passengers or persons using the aerodrome.'

Whether or not there was a contravention of this byelaw depends on the establishment, inter alia, of there having been a 'public . . . demonstration'. The justices appear to have *c* thought that 'public . . . demonstration' meant a demonstration involving the public. We cannot agree to such a construction. It is one which would lead to a curious consequence in that a demonstration in public by numerous members of a society or organisation would not constitute a 'public . . . demonstration' within the meaning of the byelaw. In our view the prefatory word 'public' is to be construed as indicating that the demonstration must be one which occurs in public. In that sense what the respondents *d* did was 'public'. Was it, however, a 'demonstration'? The researches of counsel did not reveal any decision on that word. We were referred to the *Shorter Oxford English Dictionary* (3rd edn), which gives as the seventh variant of the word the meaning 'a public manifestation of feeling; often taking the form of a procession and mass meeting'.

We find this an acceptable description in the present context. Accordingly, we ask ourselves whether the action of the respondents in mounting a picket at control post 8 *e* on 31 March 1982 was a demonstration within that description. We are of the opinion that no properly instructed and reasonable bench of magistrates could have found that the action as described in findings of fact (16) and (17) was a 'demonstration'. Accordingly, we decide (albeit for a reason which differs from that of the justices) that there was not a contravention of byelaw 5(34).

As to the second question, byelaw 5(58) provides: *f*

'No person shall remain on the aerodrome, or any part thereof, after having been requested by a constable to leave.'

The word 'constable' means a constable under the direction and control of the Commissioner of Police of the Metropolis (see the Policing of Airports (Heathrow) (First Supplementary) Order 1974, SI 1974/1672, art 8(2)). The byelaw is plainly intra vires in *g* that it mirrors the statutory language which authorised its making (see s 9(1)(h) of the 1965 Act). It is also plain that byelaw 5(58) does not require there to be a previous breach of another byelaw as a condition precedent to a request to leave the aerodrome. However, it was conceded on behalf of BAA that there must be an implied limitation on the power of request in that a request to leave made capriciously would not support a prosecution for failure to leave. We agree that there must be an implied limitation. *h*

In considering what is that limitation we have had regard to the decision of the Court of Appeal in *Cinnamond v British Airports Authority* [1980] 2 All ER 368, [1980] 1 WLR 582. In that case the court had to consider the power of the corporation itself to prohibit entry on Heathrow aerodrome. Lord Denning MR said ([1980] 2 All ER 368 at 372, [1980] 1 WLR 582 at 588):

'On a proper interpretation of [s 2(3) of the 1975 Act], I think that the airport *j* authority can turn a passenger back, and others too, if the circumstances are such as fairly and reasonably to warrant it. By "reasonably" I take the ordinary meaning of the word and not the extraordinary meaning which some have placed on it, and which counsel for the airport authority asked us to adopt following *Associated Provincial Picture Houses Ltd v Wednesbury Corp* [1947] 2 All ER 680, [1948] 1 KB

a
223. If that is the position, as I believe it to be, then the airport authority has power
to forbid entry if the circumstances fairly and reasonably warrant that step being
taken.'

(See also [1980] 2 All ER 368 at 375, 376, [1980] 1 WLR 582 at 591, 592 per Shaw and
Brandon LJJ.)

b
In the light of Lord Denning MR's observations, it is our judgment that a request to
leave which can found a prosecution under byelaw 5(58) is one which is fair and (in the
ordinary sense) reasonable in the particular circumstances in which the request is made.
The question at once arises, fair and reasonable having regard to what? We return the
answer, fair and reasonable having regard to securing the efficient, economic and safe
operation of the services and facilities provided by BAA at Heathrow aerodrome. We
return that answer (which embodies words drawn from what is now s 2 of the 1975 Act)
because BAA's byelaws must be regarded as operating (and as operating only) in order to
c
secure the proper achievement of the mandate conferred on BAA by Parliament.

Whether or not the request made by the constable on 31 March 1982 was fair and
reasonable in the circumstances was a question to which the justices did not address
themselves. They decided that in view of their conclusion on byelaw 5(34) it would be
'incongruous' to convict under byelaw 5(58). What, if anything, is now to be done we
shall state as our conclusion.

d
As to the third question, s 15 of the 1974 Act does not in terms confer a right to attend
on land against the will of the owner of that land. It would be astonishing if Parliament
intended that such a right should be implied. There is no direct English authority on
whether or not the implication should be made. There is, however, an Irish authority
which we regard as of persuasive assistance. The case is *Larkin v Belfast Harbour Comrs*
[1908] 2 IR 214. The decision was in regard to s 2 of the Trade Disputes Act 1906. That
e
section was materially similar to s 15 of the 1974 Act, and no effective difference between
the two texts was suggested to us (see also *Broome v DPP* [1974] 1 All ER 314 at 317,
[1974] AC 587 at 595 and *Kavanagh v Hiscock* [1974] 2 All ER 177 at 185, [1974] QB 600
at 612). The headnote to the report of *Larkin* reads:

f
'The Belfast Harbour Commissioners had made a by-law, under their statutory
powers, prohibiting persons from addressing a crowd on any quay, &c., the property
of the Commissioners, without permission in writing from the secretary. L.,
without such permission, addressed a crowd of workmen on a quay, the property of
the respondents, advising the workmen who were on strike to go back to work. L.
was prosecuted by the Commissioners under the by-law. No direct evidence was
given on behalf of the Commissioners that the permission of the secretary had not
g
been obtained; but it was proved that L. had been warned previously against
addressing meetings on the quay, and evidence was given of a statement by L. at the
time of the alleged offence, that he knew that what he was doing was a violation of
the by-laws. L. having been convicted of an offence against the by-law:—*Held*, that
the by-law in question was not repealed by sect. 2 of the Trade Disputes Act, 1906(2),
and that the conviction was right.'

h
O'Brien LCJ said (at 221):

'The great object of the 2nd section of the Trade Disputes Act was to define what
should *not* be considered intimidation, namely peacefully acquiring information, or
peacefully communicating with workmen, or endeavouring peacefully to persuade
them. In fact, the intention of Parliament was to define what was before a subject of
j
acute controversy, namely, peaceful picketing, and to take what they considered
peaceful picketing out of the category of intimidation. It was never intended to
authorize as a matter of right an invasion into a man's house, or entry against the
will of the owner into a place of business, no matter how busy that place might be,
or in any way to repeal or modify the by-laws of the Belfast Harbour Commissioners,
which, made pursuant to power conferred by statute, clearly defined what should

be considered an unauthorized intrusion into their property; and of this intrusion the defendant, even on his own admission, was guilty.'

a

The decision was twice followed in Ireland and the latest decision, *L L Ferguson Ltd v O'Gorman* [1937] IR 620 was cited without disapproval by Lord Reid in *Broome v DPP* [1974] 1 All ER 314 at 318, [1974] AC 587 at 596.

We accept the reasoning in *Larkin v Belfast Harbour Comrs* [1908] 2 IR 214. In our judgment s 15 of the 1974 Act neither gives a right to attend on land against the will of its owner (or the will of a person to whom the owner has granted exclusive occupation), nor does it affect the operation of any byelaws by which the use and operation of that land is regulated. BAA owns every part of Heathrow Aerodrome including all of the roads within the aerodrome perimeter (none of which is a highway). BAA had not (on the facts as found) granted exclusive occupation of any part of the aerodrome with which we are concerned to another person. BAA's byelaws regulate the operation and use of the aerodrome. BAA's ownership (unlike that of the private landowner) is subject to the right of the public to have access for the purpose of taking advantage of the services and facilities provided by BAA in pursuance of its statutory duty: see *Cinnamond v British Airports Authority* [1980] 2 All ER 368, [1980] 1 WLR 582. However, access for the purpose of picketing is not a right to which BAA's ownership is subject. In regard to access for that purpose, BAA's ownership and the status of its byelaws is indistinguishable from those of the Belfast Harbour Commissioners which were considered in *Larkin*. Accordingly, in our judgment s 15 of the 1974 Act is irrelevant in the context of a prosecution under byelaw 5(58).

b

c

d

Other arguments were advanced to us by counsel in the course of his submissions on behalf of BAA in regard to all three questions and to other questions, but we do not find it necessary to advert to them. We record that other arguments were advanced, should this case be taken elsewhere.

e

Conclusion. Our conclusion is that we remit to the justices the question whether the request referred to in para 18 of the statement of case was, in the circumstances in which it was made, fair and reasonable having regard to securing the efficient, economic and safe operation of the services and facilities provided by BAA at Heathrow aerodrome. If the justices should be of the opinion that it was, they must convict the respondents of a contravention of byelaw 5(58).

f

In regard to the six specific questions raised in the case stated we give answers as follows. (a) Section 15(1) of the 1974 Act gives no right to attend on any part of the aerodrome at Heathrow against the will of the owner and occupier (BAA), or (where apposite) of a person to whom BAA has granted exclusive occupation. (b) No. (c) This question is remitted to the justices in order that they may make a finding whether the request referred to in para 18 of the statement of case was, in the circumstances in which it was made, fair and reasonable having regard to the considerations to which we have referred. (d) Yes. (e) BAA conceded before us that, should it be relevant, the respondent's picket was 'at or near' their own place of work for the purposes of s 15 of the 1974 Act; as will have appeared, we regard the point as irrelevant. (f) No; the request must in the circumstances in which it is made be fair and reasonable, having regard to the considerations to which we have referred.

g

h

Order accordingly.

Solicitors: *M W T Nott*, Gatwick (for BAA); *John L Williams* (for the respondents).

Sepala Munasinghe Esq   Barrister.

a

Hart and others v Emelkirk Ltd
Howroyd and others v Emelkirk Ltd

CHANCERY DIVISION
GOULDING J
30 NOVEMBER 1982

b

Receiver – Appointed by court – Protection or preservation of property – Landlord failing to collect rents or to repair – Whether court will appoint receiver to collect rents and to effect repairs – Supreme Court Act 1981, s 37.

In the exercise of the court's power under s 37[a] of the Supreme Court Act 1981 to 'appoint
c   a receiver [where] it appears to the court to be just and convenient to do so' and its power
to invest the receiver with such powers as the court, in its discretion, thinks necessary for
the preservation of property, the court may appoint a receiver to receive and give a good
receipt for the rents, profits and all other moneys payable under a lease of a property and
to manage the property in accordance with the rights and obligations of the reversioner
in a case where the landlord refuses or neglects to collect the rents due under the lease
d   and refuses or neglects to perform the covenants in the lease to repair and insure the
property (see p 16 *j* to p 17 *b*, post).
   Riches v Owen (1868) LR 3 Ch App 820 considered.

Notes
For the appointment of a receiver for the protection or preservation of property, see 39
e   Halsbury's Laws (4th edn) para 827, and for cases on the subject, see 39 Digest (Repl) 25–
42, 293–488.
   For the Supreme Court Act 1981, s 37, see 51 Halsbury's Statutes (3rd edn) 632.

Case referred to in judgment
Riches v Owen (1868) LR 3 Ch App 820, LJJ.

f

Cases also cited
Leney & Sons Ltd v Callingham [1908] 1 KB 79, CA.
S v S (1973) 117 SJ 649.

Motions
g   In an action between the plaintiffs, (1) Prudence Jane Hart, (2) Carole Angela Lennox, (3)
Richard Charles Standish Pollock, (4) Colin Gordon Maitland and (5) Ivor Anthony
Snowden, and the defendants, Emelkirk Ltd, the first, second, fourth and fifth plaintiffs
by motion sought, inter alia, (1) an order that John Clifford Trevor FRICS of 58 Grosvenor
Street, London W1, chartered surveyor, or some other fit and proper person be appointed
without security (i) to receive the rents and profits of the block of flats known as 11–20
h   Cambridge Mansions, Cambridge Road in the London Borough of Wandsworth and all
other moneys payable under any lease of any part of the block of flats and (ii) to manage
the block of flats in accordance with the rights and obligations of the person entitled to
the reversion expectant on the leases of the first, second, fourth and fifth plaintiffs of flats
in the block of flats in each case until trial or further order in the mean time, (2) an order
that the person so appointed be at liberty so to act at once and (3) an order that the person
j   so appointed might give to Richard Charles Murr a good receipt for the sum of £3,493·21
in his hands together with interest accrued but not credited and have resort thereto in his
management of the block of flats. In an action between the plaintiffs, (1) Kathleen Nicole
Howroyd, (2) Sally Diana Price, (3) James Anthony Hume Greenfield, (4) Christine

---

a   Section 37, so far as material, is set out at p 16 *h*, post

Theresa Murr, (5) Richard Charles Murr, (6) Anne Katherine Somerville, (7) Brian John
Mack, (8) Caroline Helen Clare Jenkins, (9) Gwyn Desmond Tew, (10) Gareth George   *a*
Stephens, (11) Francis Patrick Harrigan and (12) Robin John Blunt, and the defendants,
Emelkirk Ltd, the first to eleventh plaintiffs sought similar relief in respect of the block
of flats known as 41–60 Cambridge Mansions, Cambridge Road in the London Borough
of Wandsworth and in respect of the sum of £7,133·29 together with interest accrued
but not credited in the hands of the fifth plaintiff. The facts are set out in the judgment.

b

Alastair Norris for the plaintiffs.
Roger A Cooke for the defendant company.

GOULDING J. These are motions in two actions relating to blocks of flats in Battersea.
A situation has arisen which I believe is not, by any means, unprecedented in the suburbs
of London but which does not seem before to have been, so far as reported cases go, the   *c*
subject matter of a similar application to what I have today.

The several flats in each block are let under separate long leases, not expiring until far
into the next century, made by a freeholder who was the predecessor in title of the
defendant company. For two or three years past, the reversioner has neither attempted
to collect the rent and the contributions to maintenance and services provided for by the
leases, nor performed the covenants by the landlord contained in the leases to keep the   *d*
property in repair, or even to effect insurance. The evidence adduced by the plaintiffs
shows that the properties are now in a condition where serious deterioration is taking
place and where, in more than one of the flats, reasonably comfortable occupation is
threatened by the incursion of damp and the propagation of moulds and rots.

The defendant company says by counsel, as it has already alleged in correspondence,
that in 1979 it sold the freehold reversion and completed the sale by transfer but the   *e*
purchaser has neither registered his title nor sought, as I have said, to exercise any of the
rights attached to the reversion. It is, indeed, suggested on the defendant's behalf that the
purchaser may have sold on to yet a further party.

The action is brought to obtain a mandatory injunction against the defendant company
to comply with the landlord's covenants and also for damages, and counsel for the
defendant company tells me that third party proceedings are likely. But what I am asked   *f*
to do today by the plaintiffs in each of the two actions dealing with adjoining blocks of
flats is to appoint a named surveyor to receive the rents and profits of each property and
all other moneys payable under any lease of any part thereof and to manage the property
in accordance with the rights and obligations of the reversioner until trial or further
order. I am asked to say that the person so appointed may give a good receipt for certain
sums of money which one of the plaintiffs in each case has received as representing (or   *g*
apparently representing) what remains of a reserve fund, intended under the leases to be
built up by tenants' contributions, and that he (the receiver) may have resort to those
funds in course of management.

Now, I know of no precedent for such relief but I also know of no authority that
forbids it under the provisions of the Judicature Acts now represented by the Supreme
Court Act 1981, s 37:   *h*

> '(1) The High Court may by order (whether interlocutory or final) . . . appoint a
> receiver in all cases in which it appears to the court to be just and convenient to do
> so . . .'

It clearly appears to me to be just to appoint a receiver in this case because it is done to
support the enforcement by the court of covenants affecting property: cf *Riches v Owen*   *j*
(1868) LR 3 Ch App 820. It is also convenient because, as I said, the properties are in a
condition that demands urgent action.

I propose, therefore, in each action to appoint Mr Trevor the nominated surveyor, in
respect of whom an affidavit of fitness has been provided. I am assuming, of course, that
his formal consent to act will be forthcoming. I will appoint him to receive the rents and

a profits and other moneys payable under the leases in the form of the notice of motion and to manage, in accordance with the rights and obligations of the reversioner, again as stated in the notice of motion, until trial or further order. I think the court has a wide jurisdiction to invest a receiver with such powers as the court, in its discretion, thinks necessary for the preservation of the property the income of which he is to receive.

I see no reason to dispense with security. I think the order should be that he be appointed on giving security, and subject to such security I will include a direction that

b he may give a good receipt to the plaintiff Mr Murr for the two sums that are in his hands.

As regards the position of the defendant company, whose legal advisers appear not yet to be fully instructed in the matter, I think I can safeguard that and also assist generally if I direct that the parties be at liberty to apply as they may be advised in the most general terms. The costs of the motions are reserved to trial.

c
Order accordingly.

Solicitors: *Parlett Kent & Co* (for the plaintiffs); *Bernstein & Co*, Stamford Hill (for the defendant company).

d
                                            Evelyn M C Budd   Barrister.

Hargreaves and others v Church Commissioners for England

e

PRIVY COUNCIL
LORD KEITH OF KINKEL, LORD SCARMAN AND LORD BRIGHTMAN
22 FEBRUARY, 12 APRIL 1983

f *Ecclesiastical law – Appeal – Pastoral scheme – Scheme providing for union of two benefices and that incumbent of united benefice should reside in the smaller parish – Whether church authorities making error of judgment in selecting the smaller parish – Pastoral Measure 1968, s 8(2).*

The Church Commissioners published a draft scheme under the Pastoral Measure 1968 which provided for the union of two adjacent parishes, the larger of which had a thriving and growing population while the smaller parish had an elderly and static or diminishing

g population. The draft scheme provided for the incumbent of the united benefice to reside in the smaller parish. The appellants and other parishioners of the larger parish objected to the scheme and organised a campaign against it. The Church Commissioners considered both written and oral representations made to them by the objectors and then made the scheme in which they selected the smaller parish as the residence of the

h incumbent because it contained a homogeneous village of which the church and parsonage were an integral part, the community was supportive and the incumbent would be able to carry out his ministry efficiently and contentedly if housed there. The appellants appealed to the Privy Council under s 8(2)[a] of the 1968 Measure contending, inter alia, that the Church Commissioners were guilty of an error of judgment in selecting the smaller parish as the residence of the incumbent of the united benefice

j having regard to the fact that most of the activity, business or otherwise, would be in the

_____

a Section 8(2) provides: 'Any person who has duly made written representations with respect to the scheme may appeal to Her Majesty in Council against the scheme or any provisions thereof by lodging notice of appeal with the Clerk of the Privy Council before the expiration of a period of twenty-eight days beginning with the day immediately after the date of the first publication of the notice of the submission of the scheme as aforesaid.'

larger parish, and requesting that the scheme be returned to the Church Commissioners for reconsideration of the residence of the incumbent.

Held – The exercise of the right of appeal against a pastoral scheme given by s 8(2) of the 1968 Measure gave rise to a genuine appeal process rather than mere judicial review and therefore an appellant was entitled to have his appeal heard on its merits. Accordingly, change of circumstances or the emergence of fresh evidence could in a proper case constitute grounds for allowing an appeal even though there was no question of any erroneous judgment by the Church authorities at the time they made the scheme. Although the evidence gathered after the publication of the draft scheme showed that there was a reasonable case for selecting the larger parish as the residence of the new incumbent, the Church authorities had weighed up the respective merits of the two places of residence and had for cogent reasons chosen the smaller parish. Moreover, in selecting the smaller parish they were entitled to take into account the welfare of the clergy as well as that of the inhabitants. They could not therefore be said to have been guilty of an error of judgment. The appeal would accordingly be dismissed and the scheme confirmed (see p 19 c d, p 20 b j, p 21 a and p 22 b c and e to p 23 a, post).

Notes
For appeals against pastoral schemes, see 14 Halsbury's Laws (4th edn) para 881.
    For the Pastoral Measure 1968, s 8, see 10 Halsbury's Statutes (3rd edn) 771.

Cases referred to in judgment
Elphick v Church Comrs [1974] AC 562, [1974] 2 WLR 756, PC.
Holy Trinity, Birkenhead, Parochial Church Council v Church Comrs (6 May 1974, unreported), PC.
Little Leigh Parochial Church Council v Church Comrs [1960] 1 WLR 567, PC.
Pim v Church Comrs (1975) Times, 8 May, PC.
Rogers v Church Comrs (11 February 1980, unreported), PC.

Appeal
Captain Geoffrey Hargreaves, Ted Puntis, David Hornsby and Roy Farmers, acting on behalf of themselves and some 400 other parishioners of the benefice of St Mary, North Eling (otherwise known as Copythorne) in the diocese of Winchester, appealed against a pastoral scheme made by the respondents, the Church Commissioners for England, on 2 June 1981 for the union of the benefice of Copythorne with that of Minstead in so far as the scheme provided that the residence of the incumbent of the new benefice should be at Minstead and not at Copythorne. The facts are set out in the judgment of the Board.

The appellants appeared in person.
Spencer G Maurice for the respondents.

12 April. The following judgment of the Board was delivered.

LORD SCARMAN. The pastoral scheme against which this appeal is brought was made by the Church Commissioners on 2 June 1981 and relates to the two parishes and benefices of St Mary, North Eling (otherwise known and now generally referred to as Copythorne) and Minstead in the diocese of Winchester. The scheme provides for the union of the two benefices but the two parishes 'shall continue distinct'. The new benefice is to be named 'The Benefice of Copythorne and Minstead'. The scheme further provides that the parsonage house of Minstead shall be the place of residence of the incumbent of the new benefice and that the parsonage house of Copythorne shall be transferred to the Diocesan Board of Finance for disposal.
    Petitions of appeal against the scheme have been duly lodged with the Clerk of the Privy Council by Captain Geoffrey Hargreaves, Mr Ted Puntis, Mr David Hornsby and

a Mr Roy Farmers acting on behalf of themselves and some 400 other parishioners of Copythorne. They petition not that the scheme shall be of no effect but only that Her Majesty be graciously pleased to return it to the commissioners for reconsideration. Their real objection is to that part of the scheme wherein it is proposed that the incumbent of the new benefice shall reside not in Copythorne but at Minstead.

b Much of the very full and carefully prepared evidence presented by the appellants to the Board is, however, concerned with other matters, which plainly have caused concern among some of the parishioners of Copythorne. Protest has been voiced and a campaign 'Save the Parish of St Mary's' was developed against the union of the benefices. The fact that the two parishes are to remain distinct has not dissuaded some from believing that the parish of St Mary, Copythorne is in danger of extinction. But this is now in the past. Wisely, albeit reluctantly, the appellants accept the union of the two benefices. Their Lordships do not, therefore, review the arguments for and against the union.

c A very considerable volume of evidence and argument has been directed to the proposition that there has been on the part of the Church authorities inadequate consultation between them and the parishioners of Copythorne. Their Lordships are, for the reasons which they will briefly outline, satisfied that the Church authorities have complied with the requirements of the Pastoral Measure 1968; indeed, they have done more than the minimum required by the Measure.

d Under the Measure it is the duty of the diocesan pastoral committee from time to time to review the arrangements for pastoral supervision and to make recommendations to the bishop: see s 2(1). Before deciding to make recommendations, the committee shall 'so far as may be practicable ascertain the views of the interested parties': see s 3(1). The interested parties are the incumbents of any benefices affected, the patrons, the parochial church councils affected, the archdeacon, the rural dean and the local planning authority:

e see s 3(2). This was done. Before the committee made its recommendations, the Bishop of Southampton and the Archdeacon of Winchester met the Copythorne parochial church council on 24 April 1980. On 24 July 1980 a sub-committee of the diocesan pastoral committee met the Copythorne parochial church council when two votes were taken which at the very least revealed that a majority of the council (as then constituted) objected neither to the union of the benefices nor to the residence of the incumbent

f being at Minstead. The figures of the two votes were: (a) union of the benefices: 11 in favour (or, at least, not objecting), 4 against, 1 abstention; (b) incumbent at Minstead: 10 in favour, 4 against, 2 abstentions. When, therefore, the Bishop of Winchester submitted his proposals, based on the committee's recommendations, to the commissioners on 19 September 1980, the requirement of s 3 of the 1968 Measure that the committee do ascertain the view of the parochial church council of Copythorne had been met.

g The Church Commissioners accepted the bishop's proposals and published the draft of the scheme on 24 October 1980. A campaign to oppose it was organised and attracted considerable support. One of the victories of the campaign was to secure a majority on the parochial church council against it. Undoubtedly many believe or were persuaded into thinking that the future of St Mary's as a parish was in danger. And there was a powerfully voiced opposition to the new vicar residing in Minstead. On 24 November

h 1980 the campaign committee submitted to the commissioners its 'Original Case', a formidable document covering with its annexures 27 pages. It was the duty of the commissioners to consider the representations contained in this document: see s 5(4). They also had the power, though there was no obligation, to afford an opportunity to its signatories and also to other persons to make oral representations to them: see s 5(4). This they did in March 1981 when a sub-committee of the diocesan pastoral committee

j attended an open meeting at Copythorne Parish Hall and later met the parochial church councils of the two parishes affected by the draft scheme. Their Lordships do not doubt the commissioners were fully informed and well aware of the arguments of the appellants and their supporters in the parish of Copythorne before they made the scheme, which they did on 2 June 1981. Any conceivable doubt that there could have been on this score was, or ought to have been, dispelled by their very full written statement of 1 June 1981 in which they gave their reasons for making the scheme. Accordingly, their Lordships reject the submission that there was inadequate consultation before the scheme was *a* made.

Before turning to the real issue between the parties their Lordships think it may be helpful to review the relevant law. A right of appeal against a pastoral scheme is given by s 8(2) of the 1968 Measure to any person who has made written representations. The exercise of the right leads to a genuine appeal process, that is to say it is not to be compared with judicial review under RSC Ord 53, notwithstanding certain superficial *b* similarities. It follows that an appellant is entitled to have his appeal heard on its merits. Their Lordships would repeat, and respectfully indorse, what Lord Wilberforce, delivering the opinion of the Board, said in *Pim v Church Comrs* (1975) Times, 8 May, of which we have seen the transcript:

> 'If objections are genuinely brought forward and supported by factual evidence,
> their Lordships must take them into account. They will not lose sight of the fact, as *c*
> underlined above, that the scheme has the support of responsible bodies within the
> Church of England, which, in some cases, may well have considered the very
> objections now urged and weighed them up. But it is not enough, their Lordships
> would venture to state, for the Church Commissioners to rest on general assertions
> in the face of specific objections, where these seem to be of a concrete and relevant *d*
> character.'

Nevertheless, the elaborate process of making a scheme set out in ss 3 to 7 of the 1968 Measure, a process which begins with a review by the pastoral committee of the diocese, requires the approval by the bishop of the committee's recommendations, and the decision of the Church Commissioners first to prepare a draft scheme and later, after considering any written representations made to them, to make the scheme itself, *e* underlines the very careful consideration demanded of the Church authorities throughout all its stages. By the time a scheme is brought to the attention of the Judicial Committee on appeal it will represent, unless there has been some irregularity or departure from the statutory process, the fully considered view of those charged by law with providing for the cure of souls in the diocese and with protecting, so far as practicable, the traditions, needs and characteristics of individual parishes, which are the two matters to which the *f* Measure requires the pastoral committee to have regard 'at all times': see s 2(2). In this process the bishop of the diocese has the vital role: no scheme can go forward without his approval.

It is not surprising, therefore, that successive Boards have emphasised the importance to be attached to the view of the Church authorities. In *Elphick v Church Comrs* [1974] AC 562 at 566 Lord Diplock, delivering the opinion of the Board, quoted with approval the *g* warning given in an earlier case under the legislation which preceded the Pastoral Measure of 1968:

> 'This does not, however, mean that their Lordships should not be slow to dissent,
> save for the most cogent reasons, from the recommendations embodied in a scheme
> regularly brought into existence with the concurrent approval of the pastoral *h*
> committee, the bishop and the Church Commissioners . . .'

(See *Little Leigh Parochial Church Council v Church Comrs* [1960] 1 WLR 567 at 568.)

The adjective 'cogent' has assuredly become part of the case law in this field; 'repeated to the point of tedium' according to Lord Lane in *Rogers v Church Comrs* (11 February 1980, unreported). But important though the word is, it should not be allowed to mask *j* the truth, namely that appeal to the Judicial Committee is an appeal on the merits. And in some contexts it can be misleading. For instance, frequent reference is made in the cases to a dictum to be found in the Board's opinion in *Holy Trinity, Birkenhead, Parochial Church Council v Church Comrs* (6 May 1974, unreported) to the effect that their Lordships

will not refuse to confirm a scheme 'unless for irregularity of procedure, for excess of
a jurisdiction, or on cogent evidence of erroneous judgment'. This is helpful, so far as it
goes. But it is not, nor no doubt was it intended to be, a complete statement of the law.
Change of circumstances, or the emergence of fresh evidence, can in a proper case
constitute grounds for allowing an appeal, even though there was no question of any
erroneous judgment by the Church authorities at the time they made the scheme.
Rogers's case was one in which there was shown to have been a sufficiently significant
b change of circumstance (the provision by voluntary contributions of the finance necessary
to maintain a second church, which the scheme had declared redundant). And, if the
appellants are right, it must be part of their case that the gathering of evidence and the
growth of hostile parish opinion since the publication of the draft scheme should cause
the Church Commissioners, if the scheme be returned to them, to consider it afresh so
far as the residence of the incumbent is concerned.

c   The appellants argued their case in person. Captain Hargreaves accepted the suggestion
put to him by one of their Lordships that the most effective formulation of their case was
that they were able to show that, in selecting Minstead Rectory as the place of residence
of the new incumbent, the Church authorities had made a serious error of judgment and
that this view was strongly reinforced by the evidence which, after publication of the
draft scheme, the campaign committee had succeeded in gathering together. It is not,
d however, enough to show that a reasonable person, or body of people, could reasonably
have reached the conclusion that Copythorne Vicarage was better suited than Minstead
Rectory as the residence of the vicar of the two parishes. If there is room for two
reasonable opinions, the fact that the Church authorities have adopted one will almost
always be decisive against the other. In the present case their Lordships accept that two
views were and are possible. There is a reasonable case, as will emerge when their
e Lordships outline the facts, for selecting Copythorne; but is the evidence such as to
ground an inference that it would be an error of judgment to select Minstead? That is
the true issue. The appeal cannot succeed unless it can be shown either that it was an
error of ecclesiastical judgment to choose Minstead or that circumstances have changed
so significantly since Minstead was chosen that the commissioners and the bishop ought
to reconsider this part of the scheme.

f   Their Lordships propose now to outline the salient features of the appellants' factual
case. Copythorne is a parish of scattered settlements in a rural setting lying close to the
northern perambulation of the New Forest and only a few miles west of the centre of
Southampton. Its eastern boundary is adjacent to the largely suburban Totton. The
parish is divided into two parts by the M27 motorway. North of the motorway the parish
consists of farm and park land and two villages. Newbridge and Ower (with Wigley).
g South of the motorway are the townships of Cadnam and Bartley, which grew up as a
ribbon development along the A336. St Mary's Church and, at a little distance from it,
Copythorne Vicarage, are somewhat isolated, being a mile or so to the north-east of
Cadnam. The south-west boundary of the parish marches with the perambulation of the
New Forest. The population of Copythorne is about 2,700 and growing.

Minstead is a small parish adjacent to the south-west boundary of Copythorne. Part of
h the New Forest lies between Cadnam and Bartley in Copythorne, and Minstead village
where the church (a historic and beautiful building) and the rectory are to be found. The
distance between the village and the developed area of Copythorne is between $2\frac{1}{2}$ and 3
miles. The parish's population is 710 and static (or diminishing).

The two parishes are very different in character, in size and in the age structure of their
populations. Minstead tends to be elderly; but it is admitted to be a compact little
j community supportive of its church and vicar. And the rectory is close to the historic
church, which in summer attracts many visitors.

Copythorne parish, particularly south of the motorway, is an active bustling place.
Community activities, with clubs for young and old, abound. There is a vigorous scout
movement. There are two good Church of England schools. The church is well

supported: and the vicarage was built some thirteen years ago with the aid of voluntary contributions. Some parishioners feel this gives them a claim on it for meetings. *a* Although this cannot be so, it is the fact that it has been the practice of the vicar until recently to allow it to be used for church and other meetings.

The foregoing is the barest summary of the very full and helpful evidence prepared by the appellant, Mr Hornsby, himself a professional surveyor. The evidence justifies his conclusion that the great preponderance (he put a figure on it of 90% to 95%) of activity, business, industrial, social and religious of the new benefice will be in the parish of *b* Copythorne. He thought it totally illogical that the vicar should reside elsewhere than in the parish and at the Copythorne Vicarage. This short, and by no means complete, outline of the facts presented to their Lordships by the appellants is certainly sufficient to show that there exists a reasonable case for selecting Copythorne as the place of residence of the new incumbent.

The Church authorities, however, rejected it. They accepted the differences in structure *c* and population of the two parishes. Of the parish of Minstead they said, correctly, that it contains a homogeneous village of which the church and the parsonage house form an integral part. Copythorne they described, also accurately, as consisting of six scattered settlements with no identifiable centre. They were satisfied that one priest, whether his residence be at Minstead or Copythorne, would not have too difficult a task in ministering to two parishes consisting of some seven settlements. They concluded (and this was the *d* firm opinion of the bishop of the diocese) that the incumbent should be housed at Minstead where there was a supportive community and where he would be able to carry out his ministry efficiently and contentedly.

In their Lordships' view it cannot be said that the Church authorities were guilty of any error of judgment. They plainly weighed up the respective merits of the two places of residence and chose Minstead for reasons which their Lordships think were cogent. *e* Inevitably the new incumbent will have to travel daily if he is to minister effectually to the scattered inhabitant of the two parishes. It will make little difference to the time and money spent on travel whether his home be at the Copythorne Vicarage or the Minstead Rectory. Both are some distance from the centres of habitation, though Copythorne is nearer. It is, however, very important that the incumbent should be housed agreeably so that he may minister to his parishioners 'efficiently and contentedly'. The Copythorne *f* house is, no doubt, entirely suitable. But the Minstead house has the edge for the reasons given by the Bishop of Winchester. In his affidavit he listed four reasons: (*a*) the parsonages committee thought Minstead was marginally the 'nicer' house; (*b*) the Minstead house is more pleasantly situated; (*c*) the Copythorne house is 'rather isolated', whereas the house at Minstead is next door to the church, with which and the village it forms a compact entity; (*d*) the Minstead church attracts many visitors who, though the *g* duty owed to parishioners comes first, represent an opportunity for extending the incumbent's ministry. The bishop concluded this part of his evidence with these words:

> 'I regard it as of considerable importance that any Incumbent should have in the place where he resides a friendly and supportive community amongst whom he and his family feel happy.'

h

In their Lordships' view the bishop is not to be criticised for bearing in mind the welfare of his clergy as well as that of the inhabitants of his diocese or for his reasons in choosing Minstead.

Their Lordships fully understand the feelings of the appellants and their supporters. They have shown that genuine grounds for wishing their vicar to be in Copythorne exist. It is not an unreasonable view. But they have shown no error of judgment on the part of *j* the Church authorities. Had the two opposing views been evenly balanced, their Lordships would have thought it right to uphold the view of the Church authorities for the reasons earlier developed. But the balance is, in their Lordships' considered opinion, in favour of the bishop's firmly expressed choice of Minstead.

a Accordingly, their Lordships will humbly advise Her Majesty that the appeal should be dismissed and the scheme confirmed. The commissioners have, very properly, withdrawn their claim to costs. There will, therefore, be no order as to costs.

Appeal dismissed. No order as to costs.

Solicitors: *Radcliffes & Co* (for the respondents).

b

Mary Rose Plummer   Barrister.

R v Birmingham Justices, ex parte Lamb

c # and another application

QUEEN'S BENCH DIVISION
McNEILL AND WOOLF JJ
26 NOVEMBER 1982

d *Magistrates – Proceedings – Control by judicial review – Magistrates dismissing charge without giving prosecution opportunity to present case – Whether magistrates having power to dismiss charge without hearing any evidence on ground that unjust or prejudicial to defendant for hearing to continue.*

In the first case the defendant was charged with obtaining by deception a meal at a hotel *e* valued at £6·75. On two occasions he attempted to plead guilty to the charge before the magistrates but on each occasion the magistrates refused to accept his plea and entered a plea of not guilty because the defendant said he honestly believed a third party was going to pay for the meal and he was thus denying any criminal intent. On the second occasion the magistrates indicated to the prosecution that it would not be in the interests of justice to proceed with the charge because in their view the defendant was the innocent victim *f* of circumstances, it would be difficult for the prosecution to prove criminal intent and the sum involved was minimal, and they invited the prosecution not to offer any evidence. The prosecution declined the invitation, pointing out that there was a prima facie case against the defendant. The magistrates then insisted that the case should be heard that morning and when the prosecution were unable to produce their witnesses the magistrates refused an adjournment and dismissed the information.
g In the second case the defendant was charged with careless driving and pleaded not guilty. When the case came on for hearing before the magistrates they indicated that because of the length of the hearing it was probable that the case would not be completed that day and that they did not wish to part-hear the case because of the inconvenience to witnesses of having to attend court on another day. The prosecution then applied for an adjournment of the hearing. It was unlikely that an adjourned hearing could take place *h* before some 14 months would have elapsed since the commission of the alleged offence, and when the defendant objected to an adjournment the magistrates refused the application for an adjournment and, on the basis that it would be unjust to part-hear the case that day, dismissed the charge.
In each case the prosecutor applied for judicial review of the magistrates' decision by way of orders of certiorari to quash the justices' decision dismissing the charges and for *j* mandamus directing them to hear the case.

Held – (1) Magistrates had no power to dismiss a charge without hearing any evidence simply because in their view it would be unjust or prejudicial to the defendant to continue the hearing; they could only reflect their sense of any injustice to the defendant by deciding that the charge had not been made out at the end of the prosecution's case, or by acquitting the defendant after they had heard the whole of the evidence or by imposing a penalty which reflected their sense of the injustice (see p 28 *a* to *c* and *g h*, post).

(2) Accordingly, in each case the application for judicial review was well founded because the magistrates had abused their powers. However, as a matter of discretion, the court would not in all the circumstances grant the relief sought, particularly as the defendants were entitled to take the view that they had been acquitted by the dismissal of the charges against them and that they should not be put in jeopardy a second time. There would therefore be no order on the applications for judicial review (see p 28 *c* to *h*, post).

Notes

For control of justices' proceedings by judicial review, see 11 Halsbury's Laws (4th edn) para 1529 and 29 ibid para 474.

Applications for judicial review

R v Birmingham Justices, ex parte Lamb

Robert Edgar Lamb, a chief inspector of police at Birmingham, applied, with the leave of Glidewell J granted on 19 August 1982, for (i) an order of certiorari to quash an order of justices sitting at Birmingham Magistrates' Court, made on 23 June 1982, dismissing an information against Paul Martin Raitt alleging that he dishonestly obtained goods by deception and (ii) an order of mandamus directing the justices to hear the information. The grounds on which the relief was sought was that the justices acted in disregard of the principles of natural justice in insisting on 23 June 1982 that the case should proceed that morning and when after a short adjournment the prosecution was unable to offer any evidence, in dismissing the information. The facts are set out in the judgment of McNeill J.

R v Birmingham Justices, ex parte Lamb

Robert Edgar Lamb, a chief inspector of police at Birmingham, applied, with the leave of Glidewell J granted on 19 August 1982, for (i) an order of certiorari to quash an order of justices sitting at Birmingham Magistrates' Court, made on 3 June 1982, dismissing an information against Sheila O'Regan that she drove a motor car without due care and attention and (ii) an order of mandamus directing the justices to hear the information. The grounds on which the relief was sought was that the justices acted in disregard of the principles of natural justice when having announced that in view of the probable length of the hearing there was not enough time to hear the case that day (3 June), they refused to grant the prosecution's application for an adjournment, or to sit late on that day in order to hear the case and instead decided to dismiss the information forthwith before the hearing had commenced. The facts are set out in the judgment of McNeill J.

R D H Smith for the prosecutor in both applications.
Malcolm Lee for the justices in the first application.
The justices in the second application did not appear.

McNEILL J. These are two applications for judicial review of decisions made by the magistrates in Birmingham. The relief sought in each case is orders of certiorari and mandamus. In each case, the magistrates purported to dismiss informations laid against Paul Martin Raitt and Sheila O'Regan. The relevant dismissals occurred on 23 June 1982 in the case of Mr Raitt and on 3 June 1982 in the case of Mrs O'Regan.

The facts in each case require summarising. Mr Raitt first appeared before the justices on 5 May 1982 to answer an information alleging that on 27 April 1982 he committed an offence contrary to s 15(1) of the Theft Act 1968, namely that at the Grand Hotel, Birmingham, he consumed a meal without having the funds to pay for that meal and dishonestly obtained from Grand Metropolitan Hotels Ltd one meal belonging to them a with the intention of permanently depriving them of it. The total cost of the meal was £6·75. Although it is not expressed in the information, the offence was also charged against a man named Marston. It would appear that the total cost of the food consumed by the two of them was £6·75.

On 5 May the case was adjourned and both Mr Raitt and Mr Marston were remanded on bail to 9 June. On that date, Mr Raitt appeared but Mr Marston did not. A bench warrant was issued to procure his appearance. Mr Raitt was further remanded on bail to
b 23 June. Mr Marston was arrested in pursuance of the bench warrant. He was brought before the court on 15 June. He was remanded until 7 July.

Apparently, it is the practice at the Birmingham Magistrates' Court for the prosecutor to ascertain the plea at an early hearing. If a plea of not guilty is anticipated or intimated, the prosecuting solicitor's department prepare a full file and an application is made to the court for the date of the hearing of the contested matter. That is why, in the case of Mr
c Marston, it was not until 7 July that a date was to be fixed for the hearing of the charge against him.

So far as Mr Raitt is concerned, he asked to plead guilty at his first appearance. The prosecuting solicitor opened the facts of the offence to the justices and Mr Raitt, who was not represented, spoke in mitigation. As a consequence of what he said, namely that although he had consumed the meal in question, he had expected that it would be paid
d for by a guest in the hotel, the magistrates very properly took the view that that was not an unequivocal plea of guilty and directed that a plea of not guilty be entered.

When Mr Raitt came before the justices on 23 June, he said that he wished to plead guilty. He was not represented and according to the affidavit of the solicitor who was then conducting the prosecution, he denied any criminal intent, stating that he honestly believed that a third party would buy the food and that he was only pleading guilty in
e order to save any further worry. According to that affidavit, the magistrates discussed the matter with the clerk and indicated that a not guilty plea should be entered. Then, according to the solicitor, the magistrates suggested that it would not be in the interests of justice for the case to proceed in any event and he was invited to offer no evidence. He declined that invitation, pointing out that there was a prima facie case and that the defendant would be entitled to be acquitted if the prosecution evidence 'did not come up
f to scratch.' The solicitor said that the delay was not the fault of the prosecutor but was the fault of Mr Marston, who jumped his bail. He was ready to fix a special court for the hearing. He was then advised by the Bench that the matter had to proceed at once. He explained that he had no witnesses warned and that the court was straying from its invariable practice. However, the Bench insisted and he requested a short adjournment.

The prosecutor made some inquiries. He tried to contact the manager of the hotel but
g 20 minutes later, he heard that the manager was away in Uxbridge and the case was called on again without witnesses. He was unable to offer any evidence in the case of Mr Raitt. The prosecutor annexed to his affidavit a copy of the entry in the register of the Birmingham Magistrates' Court relating to the proceedings in this matter.

There was an affidavit by the chairman of the justices who was sitting on that date. He canvassed certain facts. He said:

h
'. . . On the basis that we felt that the defendant had been the innocent victim of circumstances, and in view of the fact that two benches had declined to accept his plea of guilty, we were of opinion that it would be difficult for the prosecution to prove criminal intent, and therefore invited the prosecuting solicitor to take fresh instructions regarding the continuation of the case. We felt that it would be unjust
j to prolong the distress if there was a doubt . . . I indicated that we wished to hear the case that morning, and that enquiries should be made regarding the availability of witnesses . . . At no stage did I announce that the case must proceed at once . . . The Bench were not at any time informed that the main prosecution witness was out of Birmingham and unable to give evidence. My impression was that the Manager of the Hotel would not deign to cross the road to give evidence . . . The impression created is that the prosecution were only given twenty minutes to

produce their witness, whereas the matter was not further heard until the end of
the morning, in excess of two hours later.   *a*

6. It was not sufficiently clear that Mr. Raitt and Mr. Marston were each alleged
to have consumed a meal to the value of £6·75, which led the court to believe the
value at stake was minimal.

7. We were impressed by the sincerity of the defendant, and were concerned that
the defendant persisted in admitting the offence as a means to have the charge dealt
with quickly.   *b*

8. The defendant, who was not represented, pressed us quite stongly to deal with
the matter as this was the third appearance and the prolongation would cause further
distress to his immediate family.

9. We were of opinion that the prosecution would not be able to prove criminal
intent and that the continuation of the proceedings was prejudicial to the defendant.
In the absence of any reasonable explanation from the prosecution for the non-   *c*
appearance of their principal witness we dismissed the information.'

I would only add this point to the recital of the facts. The information laid against the
defendant was under s 15(1) of the Theft Act 1968. Without having had the matter fully
argued, the view can properly be taken that the offence properly charged against this
defendant, on the facts, should have been one under s 3 of the Theft Act 1970. Counsel
for the justices was expressly instructed to indicate on that point that, whatever the other   *d*
aspects of the case may be, the justices were, or would have been advised, that the
information as framed was not one on which the prosecution could or were likely to
proceed. In those circumstances, whether the prosecuting solicitor would have applied
to amend or taken whatever course was open to him we know not. Counsel for the
justices recognised that the chairman, in his affidavit, said that that was only drawn to
his attention after the decision had been made and it played no part in their deliberations.   *e*
Therefore, the decision to dismiss the information was based on the reasons which I have.
read from his affidavit.

In the case of Mrs O'Regan the situation was this. She was charged with careless
driving. It was alleged against here that she had been guilty of careless driving on 21
November 1981. She had, from the beginning, intimated that she proposed to plead not
guilty and the case was listed for trial before a differently constituted magistrates' court   *f*
on 3 June 1982. On that date Mrs O'Regan and the witnesses on both sides attended.

The case was estimated to take about one and a half hours. It was not the only case in
the list and according to the affidavit of Mr Coleman, who was the prosecuting solicitor
on that day, the court dealt with a number of other cases, one of which included charges
against six defendants. Evidently, that took some little time. He had arranged, with the   ·
consent of the defendant and her advisers, that Mrs O'Regan's case should follow.   *g*
However, the Bench was persuaded to take what was described as a quick guilty plea. As
sometimes happens with a quick guilty plea, it took 25 minutes. It was not until
11.55 am that the court could take Mrs O'Regan's case.

In his affidavit, Mr Coleman says:

'. . . The Court enquired as to the probable length of the hearing of the case and I   *h*
gave them my estimate of 1½ hours. I was then asked why the case had not been
called on earlier and I replied that although at 10.00 am one of the police officer
witnesses had not arrived at Court this witness did subsequently arrive during the
case which involved the six defendants. This case had lasted longer than had been
anticipated and I told the Magistrates that I had arranged with the Clerk of the Court
for Mrs. O'Regan's case to be called on at approximately 11.30 am but that another   *j*
case had been called instead.

7. The Clerk then asked the Respondent, Mrs O'Regan to confirm her plea and
whether she wished the case to proceed. She confirmed her "not guilty" plea and
said that she wanted the matter to be dealt with.

8. The Court then announced that there was not enough time left to deal with
the case and I accordingly asked for the matter to be adjourned to a "Special Court."'

a   After considering this request, the clerk indicated to the solicitor that the court was not minded to adjourn the hearing. The solicitor said that everyone was there and that the witnesses were ready. He said that it was no fault of the prosecution that the case had not been called on earlier. However, the court dismissed the case. The solicitor asked the clerk for the reason for the dismissal and he was informed that it was on general grounds. He also produced a copy of the register of the Birmingham Magistrates' Court for 3 June 1982, showing the entry relating to the information concerning Mrs O'Regan. On the

b   register, there appear to be a number of pieces of writing. The relevant passage says:

   'Case Dismissed (due to a lot of tenuous circumstances, ie time factor, witnesses, JPs, prosecution, etc. etc.)'

   The chairman of the magistrates on that occasion made an affidavit. He dealt with the position at 12 o'clock when Mrs O'Regan's case came on. An inquiry was made as to the

c   length of the case. He thought that it was likely to take three hours. In his affidavit he continues:

   '9. It was readily apparent that we would not complete the case in its entirety by 1.00 pm, and as I myself was required in the juvenile Court at 2.00 pm and my colleagues and the clerk allocated to three different afternoon courts, there was no prospect of part hearing the case in the morning and completing it that same day,

d   neither, I was told, would it have been practicable to have relisted the matter to be heard by a different bench in the afternoon. We felt it unjust to part hear the case and require certainly the defence witnesses, and possibly some of the prosecution witnesses, to reattend at some distance of time in the future.

   10. Having announced this, the prosecutor applied for the adjournment of the case to a special hearing. Again, because of the pressure of business within these

e   courts, and bearing in mind the likely duration of the case, it was unlikely that the matter would be heard before January 1983, some fourteen months after the commission of the alleged offence. The defendant, who was not represented, objected to the adjournment of the case, having been on the court premises since 9.45 am.

f   11. Bearing in mind all of these matters, we felt that the prosecution had been at fault in not acquainting the court earlier, of the fact that a case of this length fell to be dealt with, the reason for this failure apparently being the absence of one of their witnesses. Indeed, had the case been called on earlier by the court, the prosecution may not have been in a position to proceed. As it was, the delay in calling the matter on, due to the fault of the prosecution, effectively prevented a hearing of the case taking place and would have necessitated a long adjournment of the case. Our first

g   reaction was of anger, and we therefore allowed a "cooling-off" period to elapse before discussing the matter. After consultation, my colleagues and I were of opinion that the application for an adjournment in the circumstances amounted almost to an abuse of the process of the court, and was prejudicial to the defendant as the matter depended on recollection of witnesses.

h   12. Accordingly we refused the application for the adjournment and on the grounds above dismissed the allegation on the basis that it would have been unjust to continue.'

   I have set out the facts in those two cases in some considerable detail because, in the end, it is necessary to analyse and discover the basis on which the justices dismissed the information in the first case and the summons in the second case. In each case, the court

j   is conscious of the frustration that justices must feel in a busy court such as the Birmingham court, when their work is not so arranged that it is capable of speedy and convenient disposal. No doubt the justices are conscious of the public pressure and criticism. It may well be that the justices felt a sense of frustration at the practice which is operated in the prosecuting solicitor's office which requires a case which, in terms of time and comparative importance, is short and small, to be adjourned so that a full file can be prepared. Speaking for myself, I would have thought that the case of Mr Raitt could have been disposed of by competent magistrates in something like 30 minutes. I would have thought that Mrs O'Regan's case could have been dealt with in something ***a*** like one and a half to two hours.

At the end of the day, the law does not permit cases, on grounds of supposed injustice, to be dismissed out of hand without hearing any evidence. The justices can reflect their sense of injustice at the end of the prosecution case if they are not satisfied that the offence has been made out. They can reflect it at the end of the whole of the evidence by acquitting the defendant or, if they feel obliged to convict, they can reflect it by imposing ***b*** such a penalty as reflects their view of the case.

In the magistrates' court, there is no power which enables the magistrates to dismiss a summons simply on the basis that it would be, in the words of one of the chairmen, 'unjust to let it continue' and, in the words of the other, 'that the continuation of the proceedings was prejudicial to the defendant'.

In the latter of the two cases, the matter was, in a sense, made worse because the ***c*** magistrates themselves prejudged an issue which they had not heard, namely that the prosecution would not be able to prove the elements of the offence. That being so, the basis for judicial review in each of these cases is, in my view, well founded. However, the remaining question is whether or not, on the facts of these cases, it would be right, as a matter of discretion, to send it back.

In the case of Mr Raitt, the matter which he had hoped to dispose of by his plea of ***d*** guilty was as long ago as May 1982. If sent back, and if the material in the affidavits is correct, it is unlikely to be tried until some time in 1983. This means that there is a real likelihood that the recollections of the witnesses will be less reliable than they are now. One also has to bear in mind that in this matter, the total amount gained from his alleged criminal activity was just under £4. Using my discretion, I would not sent this case back and would not let the order go in the case of Mr Raitt. ***e***

In the case of Mrs O'Regan, I am of the same view. In that case, the offence was committed a year ago. If it was tried again, it would not be tried until well into 1983 and the same considerations as to the recollections of the witnesses apply in her case. I also bear in mind this fact. The expense of the trial in June was estimated to be over £200 on one side. It would be even greater if this matter was contested.

Finally, in both cases, it seems to me that both Mr Raitt and Mrs O'Regan might ***f*** properly feel that they have been acquitted and it would be wrong to allow them to feel, however erroneously, that they would be put in jeopardy for a second time. Accordingly, although in my view the grounds for mandamus and certiorari in each case are established, using my discretion I would not make the orders sought.

WOOLF J. I entirely agree. The explanation for what has happened is no doubt to be ***g*** found in the fact that the pressure on the Bench in the Birmingham Magistrates' Court, which is the largest magistrates' court in the country, is extreme. However, when exercising the discretion which they have whether or not to adjourn cases, the justices have to exercise their discretion judicially. Doing that, they must be just not only to the defendants but to the prosecution as well. They must not use their powers to refuse an adjournment to give a semblance of justification for their decision to dismiss prosecutions ***h*** when the refusal of the adjournment means that that is an inevitable consequence.

No order on the applications.

Solicitors: *I S Manson*, Birmingham (for the prosecutor in both applications); *M A Walker*, Birmingham (for the justices in the first application).

Sepala Munasinghe Esq   Barrister.

a

R v Dorking Justices, ex parte Harrington

QUEEN'S BENCH DIVISION
ROBERT GOFF LJ AND GLIDEWELL J
4, 20 MAY 1983

b
Magistrates – Proceedings – Control by judicial review – Magistrates dismissing charge without giving prosecution opportunity to present case – Breach of natural justice – Magistrates dismissing information because date of adjournment sought by prosecution not covenient for defence – Prosecutor applying for certiorari to quash dismissal and mandamus directing justices to hear prosecution evidence against defendant – Whether on application for judicial review court has power to interfere with magistrates' dismissal of charge.

c
The defendant was charged with assaulting a police constable and using threatening behaviour likely to cause a breach of the peace. On 13 August 1982, the date fixed for the hearing of the charges, he appeared in a magistrates' court. Both he and the prosecutor were legally represented. At the start of the hearing the prosecutor applied for an adjournment because the constable alleged to have been assaulted was away on holiday. The defence raised no objection to an adjournment. The magistrates decided to adjourn

d
the case until 24 August. The defence then asked for an adjournment to another date because the defendant would be away on holiday on 24 August. The magistrates refused to allocate another date for the hearing of the case and instead, without asking the prosecution if they were in a position to proceed forthwith, decided to dismiss the charges. The prosecutor applied for judicial review of the magistrates' decision by way of orders of certiorari to quash the decision to dismiss the informations and mandamus to

e
direct the magistrates to hear the evidence against the defendant. On the hearing of the application the defendant conceded that the magistrates had acted in breach of natural justice in dismissing the informations without giving the prosecution an opportunity to present their case but submitted that the decision to dismiss the informations amounted to an acquittal and that therefore the Divisional Court could not reopen the case.

f
Held – Although the court had statutory power under ss 111 and 112 of the Magistrates' Courts Act 1980 to quash the magistrates' dismissal of a charge against the defendant when the prosecutor brought the appeal by way of a case stated, the court had no statutory power to quash the dismissal when the proper mode of proceeding in respect of the magistrates' decision was by an application for judicial review, as, for example,

g
where it was alleged that the dismissal was in breach of natural justice. In such a case the rule applicable to jury trial applied, namely that where a defendant had been put in jeopardy of being convicted and had been acquitted the court would not interfere with the dismissal by prerogative order however improperly the acquittal had been obtained. Since the defendant had been in jeopardy of being convicted when he appeared before the magistrates on 13 August 1982 the court would not interfere with the dismissal of

h
the charges against him. The prosecutor's application would therefore be dismissed (see p 31 *d e* and *g* to p 32 *e*, post).

R v Simpson [1914] 1 KB 66 and *R v Middlesex Justices, ex p DPP* [1952] 2 All ER 312 applied.

Per curiam. The procedure for appeals by way of case stated constitutes in reality, if not in form, a recognition that superior courts may review decisions of justices to acquit

j
defendants, and that the procedure may result in the conviction of the defendant (see p 32 *e* to *g*, post).

Notes
For control of justices' proceedings by judicial review, see 11 Halsbury's Laws (4th edn) para 1529 and 29 ibid para 474.

For the Magistrates' Courts Act 1980, ss 111, 112, see 50(2) Halsbury's Statutes (3rd edn) 1538, 1541.

a

Cases referred to in judgment
R v Birmingham Justices, ex p Lamb [1983] 3 All ER 23, [1983] 1 WLR 339, DC.
R v Middlesex Justices, ex p DPP [1952] 2 All ER 312, [1952] 2 QB 758, DC.
R v Simpson [1914] 1 KB 66, DC.
R v Wandsworth Justices, ex p Read [1942] 1 All ER 56, [1942] 1 KB 281, DC.

b

Application for judicial review
John Alfred Harrington, a police officer, applied, with the leave of McCullough J given on 10 November 1982, for (1) an order of certiorari to quash an order made by Dorking justices sitting at Dorking Magistrates' Court on 13 August 1982 that two informations laid against the respondent, Peter Arnold Roots, be dismissed and (2) an order of mandamus requiring the justices to hear the evidence against the respondent. The facts are set out in the judgment of the court.

c

Howard Vagg for the applicant.
Roger Bull for the respondent.

d

Cur adv vult

20 May. The following judgment of the court was delivered.

ROBERT GOFF LJ. There is before the court an application for judicial review by John Alfred Harrington. The applicant is a police sergeant of the Surrey constabulary, and he was the supervising courts' officer in the Dorking Magistrates' Court on 13 August 1982 when the magistrates made the decision which is the subject of the present application.

e

The matter arises as follows. Peter Arnold Roots appeared at the Dorking Magistrates' Court on 13 August 1982 charged with (1) assaulting Simon Lane a constable in the execution of his duty at Dorking on 2 July 1982, contrary to s 51(1) of the Police Act 1961, and (2) using threatening behaviour whereby a breach of the peace was likely to be occasioned at Dorking on 2 July 1982, contrary to s 5 of the Public Order Act 1936. There were in fact four other defendants, all charged with similar offences, though only the case of Roots appears to have been dealt with by the Dorking magistrates on 13 August in the manner in which we will now set out.

f

The prosecution and the defendant were both legally represented. At the start of the case, counsel for the prosecution made an application for an adjournment in the case of Roots on the basis that Pc Lane was on annual leave, the defence and the court having been previously informed that such an application would be made. Counsel for the defence raised no objection. Following a retirement by the justices, they decided to adjourn the case until 24 August 1982.

g

This date was not suitable for Roots, because he had already booked his holiday for a period within which that date fell; indeed, we were informed that the justices had been informed of the dates of Roots's holiday booking before they retired. Accordingly, counsel for the defence asked the magistrates for another date. After some discussion, the magistrates decided not to allocate another date.

h

Counsel for the defence thereupon pursued the matter with the magistrates, pointing out that his client would lose both his holiday and the money paid for his holiday if the rearranged date stood, and submitting that the same courtesy should be shown to the defendant as had been shown to the prosecution. Counsel for the prosecution did not oppose this application. The chairman then stated that they were in a difficult position and for that reason the magistrates had decided that the case should be dismissed.

j

Counsel for the prosecution then invited the bench to reconsider that decision, because at no time had he stated that he could not present the prosecution case; on the contrary,

a he was able to proceed with the case on such evidence as was then available, there being
present in court another police officer, Pc Campbell, who had witnessed the assault on Pc
Lane. He submitted that, if the justices decided contrary to their previous decision not to
adjourn, their proper course was to inform the prosecution; and it would then be for the
prosecution either to offer no evidence, or to proceed with the case calling such evidence
as was available.

The justices then retired to consider the situation. On their return, it was stated that
b they had obtained advice from another court's senior clerk, and that their decision to
dismiss the case against Roots would have to stand. At no stage did the magistrates ask
counsel for the prosecution if the prosecution was in a position to proceed without Pc
Lane, before they purported to dismiss the charge.

In these circumstances, the applicant has applied for an order of certiorari removing
the decision of the magistrates into this court for the purpose of its being quashed, and
c for an order of mandamus directing the Dorking justices to hear the evidence against
Roots. The basis of the application is that the magistrates were in breach of the rules of
natural justice.

It is plain to us that there indeed was, in these circumstances, a breach of the rules of
natural justice by the Dorking magistrates in dismissing the charge without giving the
prosecution an opportunity to present their case. Counsel for the respondent Roots before
d this court found it impossible to contend otherwise. If authority is needed for the
proposition, it is to be found in the decision of this court in *R v Birmingham Justices, ex p
Lamb* [1983] 3 All ER 23, [1983] 1 WLR 339. Prima facie, therefore, it would appear that
this is an appropriate case to make the orders asked for by the applicant. But it was
submitted by counsel for the respondent that we should not make any such orders.
Founding his argument on authority, to which we will refer in a moment, he submitted
e that the decision of the magistrates to dismiss the charge against his client amounted to
an acquittal; and that in such circumstances the court has no power to reopen the matter
by quashing the acquittal and remitting the matter to the justices to hear the evidence.

We have come to the conclusion that we are bound by authority to accept the
submission advanced on behalf of the respondent. The authorities were reviewed by this
court, consisting of five judges presided over by Lord Goddard CJ, in *R v Middlesex
f Justices, ex p DPP* [1952] 2 All ER 312, [1952] 2 QB 758. In that case there had been the
most flagrant misconduct by the chairman of quarter sessions of a trial by jury of a
defendant charged with driving a motor car when under the influence of drink. After
counsel for the prosecution had opened the case the chairman, who had read the
depositions, expressed the obviously unjustified opinion that it would be a waste of time
for the jury to hear any evidence, and in effect directed the jury to enter a verdict of not
g guilty, thereby depriving the prosecution of their right to present the case to the jury.
The Director of Public Prosecutions applied for an order of certiorari to quash the
acquittal, and an order of mandamus directing the quarter sessions to try the defendant
of the charge. Lord Goddard CJ, in delivering the judgment of the Divisional Court,
expressed the gravest disapprobation of the conduct of the chairman, but concluded that
it was impossible for the court to interfere. Where a defendant has been in jeopardy and
h has been acquitted, the court cannot interfere to quash the acquittal and order a new
trial, however improperly the verdict may have been obtained. The matter will however
be different if there has been such a mistrial as to render the proceedings a nullity,
because if they are a nullity the defendant will not have been lawfully liable to suffer
judgment for the offence charged against him and so will not have been in jeopardy.

The case before the Divisional Court on that occasion was concerned with a trial by
j jury; but we can see no reason why the same principle should not apply where a charge
has been dismissed by justices. Indeed, in *R v Simpson* [1914] 1 KB 66 at 75 Scrutton J
said: ' . . . There never has been a case in which an acquittal by a Court of summary
jurisdiction has been quashed by certiorari . . .' At first sight, the situation appears to be
anomalous, because on appeal by way of case stated this court frequently allows appeals
brought by the prosecution, quashes the order of the justices dismissing the charge
against the respondent and directs that the respondent shall be convicted of the charge in

question. However, the jurisdiction so to do arises under statute, now ss 111 and 112 of
the Magistrates' Courts Act 1980. Under those provisions, a complainant who is aggrieved
by an order dismissing his complaint may apply for a case to be stated by the justices;
and if he does so, and a case is stated, this court has power to review the decision of the
justices by answering the questions posed for decision on the facts stated in the case, and
making the appropriate order consequent on the answering of those questions. However,
where the allegation is (as here) that the justices failed to comply with the rules of natural
justice, it is established by authority that the proper mode of proceeding is not by an
appeal by way of case stated but by an application for judicial review, because the facts
have to be placed before the superior court, and 'the only way in which that denial of
justice can be brought to the knowledge of this court is by way of affidavit' (see *R v
Wandsworth Justices, ex p Read* [1942] 1 All ER 56 at 57, [1942] 1 KB 281 at 283 per
Viscount Caldecote CJ).

Apart possibly from anxiety to expedite the matter, that was no doubt the reason why
the present case was brought before this court by way of an application for judicial
review. In such a case, there is no statutory power for the court to quash an order
dismissing a charge against the respondent; and, for the reasons already stated, the court
cannot interfere where the respondent has been in jeopardy and has been acquitted.

In the present case, it is plain to us that the respondent was in jeopardy. He had been
charged with the offence before the justices and, on the date fixed for the hearing, that
charge had been dismissed. In our view, the fact that there had been no trial on the
merits does not in these circumstances affect the matter. The case was no different in that
respect from a case where the prosecution had offered no evidence on a charge, and the
charge had in consequence been dismissed; in such a case, it could not be said that the
defendant had never been in jeopardy, so that the prosecution was free to commence
fresh proceedings for the same offence. Furthermore, it cannot be said, and indeed it was
not argued, that the breach of the rules of natural justice which occurred in the present
case rendered the proceedings a nullity. In these circumstances, we have no option but to
dismiss the application before the court.

We wish to record our disquiet at the anomaly which appears to us to be revealed by
the present case in the procedure for reviewing decisions of justices. Of course, the policy
underlying the pleas of autrefois acquit and autrefois convict is well understood; but the
procedure for appeals by way of case stated constitutes in reality, if not in form, a
recognition that superior courts may review decisions of justices under which they acquit
defendants, and that the procedure of review may result in conviction of the defendant,
despite the earlier decision by the justices to acquit him. It must appear strange to
complainants that, when the basis of their case is so serious a matter as a breach of the
rules of natural justice, they are bound to adopt a procedure under which, if there has
been an acquittal, this court has no power to intervene; although in less serious matters
an appeal may lie by way of case stated, in which event the court has power to interfere
despite the decision of the justices to acquit the respondent. However, that is, as we see
it, the effect of the law as it now stands, which we have been bound to apply in the
present case.

Application dismissed.

2 June. *The court refused leave to appeal to the House of Lords but certified, under s 1(2) of the
Administration of Justice Act 1960, that the following point of law of general public importance
was involved in its decision: whether on the dismissal by justices of an information as a result of a
breach of the rules of natural justice the Divisional Court of the Queen's Bench Division had power
on an application by the prosecutor for judicial review to quash the acquittal and remit the matter
to the justices for rehearing.*

Solicitors: *Wontner & Sons* (for the applicant); *Downs*, Dorking (for the respondent).

Sepala Munasinghe Esq   Barrister.

Practice Note

a

COURT OF APPEAL, CRIMINAL DIVISION
LORD LANE CJ AND BINGHAM J
21 JULY 1983

b   *Practice – Affidavits, exhibits, documents – Court of Appeal and High Court – Marking – Binding – Sequence – Pagination – Copies – Bundles of documents generally – Effect of failure to comply with rules – RSC Ord 41.*

LORD LANE CJ gave the following direction at the sitting of the court. This Practice
c Direction applies to the Court of Appeal and to all divisions of the High Court. Any affidavit, exhibit or bundle of documents which does not comply with RSC Ord 41 and this direction may be rejected by the court or made the subject for an order for costs.

Affidavits
d   1. *Marking*   At the top right-hand corner of the first page of every affidavit, and also on the backsheet, there must be written in clear permanent dark blue or black marking (i) the party on whose behalf it is filed, (ii) the initials and surname of the deponent, (iii) the number of the affidavit in relation to the deponent and (iv) the date when sworn. For example: '2nd Dft: E W Jones: 3rd: 24.7.82.'
  2. *Binding*   Affidavits must not be bound with thick plastic strips or anything else
e which would hamper filing.

Exhibits
  3. *Marking generally*   Where space allows, the directions under para 1 above apply to the first page of every exhibit.
f   4. *Documents other than letters*   (i) Clearly legible photographic copies of original documents may be exhibited instead of the originals, provided the originals are made available for inspection by the other parties before the hearing and by the judge at the hearing. (ii) Any document which the court is being asked to construe or enforce, or the trusts of which it is being asked to vary, should be separately exhibited, and should not be included in a bundle with other documents. Any such document should bear the
g exhibit mark directly, and not on a flysheet attached to it. (iii) Court documents, such as probates, letters of administration, orders, affidavits or pleadings should never be exhibited. Office copies of such documents prove themselves. (iv) Where a number of documents are contained in one exhibit, a front page must be attached setting out a list of the documents with dates which the exhibit contains, and the bundle must be securely fastened. The traditional method of securing is by tape, with the knot sealed (under the
h modern practice) by means of wafers; but any means of securing the bundle (except by staples) is acceptable, provided that it does not interfere with the perusal of the documents and it cannot readily be undone. (v) This direction does not affect the current practice in relation to scripts in probate matters, or to an affidavit of due execution of a will.
  5. *Letters*   (i) Copies of individual letters should not be made separate exhibits, but they should be collected together and exhibited in a bundle or bundles. The letters must
j be arranged in correct sequence, with the earliest at the top, and properly paged in accordance with para 6 below. They must be firmly secured together in the manner indicated in para 4 above. (ii) When original letters, or original letters and copies of replies, are exhibited as one bundle, the exhibit must have a front page attached, stating that the bundle consists of so many original letters and so many copies. As before, the letters and copies must be arranged in correct sequence and properly paged.

6. *Paging of documentary exhibits*   Any exhibit containing several pages must be paged consecutively at centre bottom.   *a*

7. *Copies of documents generally*   It is the responsibility of the solicitor by whom any affidavit is filed to ensure that every page of every exhibit is fully and easily legible. In many cases photocopies of documents, particularly of telex messages, are not. In all cases of difficulty, typed copies of the illegible document (paged with 'a' numbers) should be included.

8. *Exhibits bound up with affidavit*   Exhibits must not be bound up with, or otherwise   *b* attached to, the affidavit itself.

9. *Exhibits other than documents*   The principles are as follows: (i) the exhibit must be clearly marked with the exhibit mark in such a manner that there is no likelihood of the contents being separated; and (ii) where the exhibit itself consists of more than one item (e g a cassette in a plastic box), each and every separate part of the exhibit must similarly be separately marked with at least enough of the usual exhibit mark to ensure precise   *c* identification. This is particularly important in cases where there are a number of similar exhibits which fall to be compared. Accordingly, (a) the formal exhibit marking should, so far as practicable, be written on the article itself in an appropriate manner (e g many fabrics can be directly marked with an indelible pen) or, if this is not possible, on a separate slip which is securely attached to the article in such a manner that it is not easily removable (NB items attached by sellotape or similar means are readily removable). If the   *d* article is then enclosed in a container, the number of the exhibit should appear on the outside of the container unless it is transparent and the number is readily visible. Alternatively, the formal exhibit marking may be written on the container or, if this is not possible, on a separate slip securely attached to the container. If this is done, then either (i) the number of the exhibit and, if there is room, the short name and number of the case, the name of the deponent and the date of the affidavit must be written on the   *e* exhibit itself and on each separate part thereof or (ii) all these particulars must appear on a slip securely attached to the article itself and to each separate part thereof; (b) if the article, or part of the article, is too small to be marked in accordance with the foregoing provisions, it must be enclosed in a sealed transparent container of such a nature that it could not be reconstituted once opened, and the relevant slip containing the exhibit mark must be inserted in such container so as to be plainly visible. An enlarged   *f* photograph or photographs showing the relevant characteristics of each such exhibit will usually be required to be separately exhibited.

10. *Numbering*   Where a deponent deposes to more than one affidavit to which there are exhibits in any one matter, the numbering of such exhibits should run consecutively throughout, and not begin again with each affidavit.

11. *Reference to documents already forming part of an exhibit*   Where a deponent wishes   *g* to refer to a document already exhibited to some other deponent's affidavit, he should not also exhibit it to his own affidavit.

12. *Multiplicity of documents*   Where, by the time of the hearing, exhibits or affidavit have become numerous, they should be put in a consolidated bundle, or file or files, and be paged consecutively throughout in the top right-hand corner, affidavits and exhibits being in separate bundles or files.   *h*

Bundles of documents generally

13. The directions under paras 5, 6 and 7 above apply to all bundles of documents. Accordingly they must be (i) firmly secured together, (ii) arranged in chronological order, beginning with the earliest, (iii) paged consecutively at centre bottom and (iv) fully and easily legible.   *j*

14. Transcripts of judgments and evidence must not be bound up with any other documents, but must be kept separate.

15. In cases for trial where the parties will seek to place before the trial judge bundles of documents (apart from pleadings) comprising more than 100 pages, it is the responsibility of the solicitors for all parties to prepare and agree one single additional

a bundle containing the principal documents to which the parties will refer (including in particular the documents referred to in the pleadings), and to lodge such bundle with the court at least two working days before the date fixed for the hearing.

N P Metcalfe Esq   Barrister.

b

Petrofina (UK) Ltd and others v Magnaload Ltd and others

c QUEEN'S BENCH DIVISION (COMMERCIAL COURT)
LLOYD J
15, 16, 17 FEBRUARY, I MARCH 1983

Insurance – All risks insurance – Contractors' all risk policy – Construction – Policy to indemnify insured including contractors and sub-contractors – Insurance policy taken by head contractors to
d *cover risk to all contractors and sub-contractors – Loss resulting from negligence of defendants engaged by sub-contractors of head contractor – Insurers seeking to exercise right of subrogation against defendants – Whether defendants acting as sub-contractors – Whether sub-contractors insured in respect of whole contract works or only in respect of own property – Whether nature of interest insured insurance of property or only insurance against liability in respect of other parties on site.*

e The plaintiffs owned and operated an oil refinery which they wished to extend. In the course of the construction of the extension, the lifting of equipment was sub-contracted to G, who in turn engaged a Dutch company to provide specialist lifting equipment to lift the heaviest items of equipment. G and the Dutch company agreed that the Dutch company would remain responsible for the lifting operation but that for administrative
f purposes the actual contract for the supply of lifting equipment and services would be in the name of an English subsidiary of the Dutch company. The contract works were insured under a 'contractors' all risks' policy which defined the insured persons as, inter alios, the owners and 'Contractors and/or Sub-contractors' and the insured property as 'The works and temporary works erected . . . in performance of the . . . Construction erection and testing of an extension to [the refinery]'. The definition was later extended
g to include 'The erection operation and subsequent dismantlement of . . . items of plant' used on G's sub-contract, including the lifting equipment supplied by the Dutch company. The policy also provided third party liability cover in respect of sums which the insured persons were liable to pay as damages resulting from, inter alia, 'Accidental loss of or damage to property occurring . . . as a result of and solely due to the performance of the insured contract happening on . . . the contract site'. An exception to the third
h party cover excluded property forming the subject matter of the insured contract. There was also a general exception in the policy excluding liability which was insured under policies with other companies. In the course of dismantling the equipment supplied by the Dutch company, after the lifting had been successfully completed, part of the equipment fell to the ground causing extensive damage to the refinery. The owners claimed under the insurance policy for physical damage to the contract works and,
j having settled the claim, the insurers sought to exercise their right of subrogation by suing the defendants (the Dutch company and their English subsidiary), on the grounds that they were negligent. The defendants contended that they were sub-contractors and therefore fully insured under the policy and that accordingly the insurers had no right of subrogation which they could exercise against the defendants. The insurers contended (i) that the defendants were not 'sub-contractors' within the meaning of the policy, and

furthermore there was nothing to show that the Dutch company, as distinct from the
English subsidiary, were contractors at all, (ii) that a contractors' all risks policy was to be   *a*
read distributively as only insuring each insured person in respect of his own property or
that for which he was responsible and did not insure each insured person in respect of
the whole of the contract works and therefore did not cover damage caused by the
defendants to the owners' property, (iii) that, alternatively, the policy was a composite
policy which covered each of the insured persons in respect of his own particular property
and his liability only in respect of loss of or damage to property of the insured persons   *b*
and therefore the defendants could not recover in respect of the damage caused to the
owner's property unless it was shown that the defendants were liable for such damage,
and (iv) that the fact that the defendants had liability policies with other insurance
companies meant that under the general exception in the policy the insurers were not
liable or were liable only for the excess over the amounts covered by other policies. On
the preliminary issue whether the defendants were covered by the policy,   *c*

Held – The insurers were not entitled to recover from the defendants under the principle
of subrogation, for the following reasons—
(1) On the true construction of the insurance policy, the English subsidiary, although
technically sub-sub-contractors, were 'sub-contractors' for the purposes of the policy.
Furthermore, a contract was to be implied between the Dutch company and their English   *d*
subsidiary under which the Dutch company also became 'sub-contractors' on terms that
they would carry out the lifting operations for an agreed price (see p 39 *j* to p 40 *d* and p
45 *j*, post).
(2) On the ordinary meaning of the policy, each insured person, including all sub-
contractors, was insured in respect of the whole contract works, since there were no
words of severance to indicate that each insured person was only insured in respect of his   *e*
own property, and there was no business necessity to imply words of severance.
Accordingly each insured person was insured in respect of the entire contract works,
including property belonging to any of the other insured persons or for which any of the
other insured persons were responsible (see p 40 *e f* and p 45 *j*, post).
(3) Furthermore, the nature of the interest insured was an insurance of property and
not merely an insurance against liability in respect of the property of other persons on   *f*
the site. By analogy with a bailee's right to insure and recover the full value of bailed
goods, the head contractor under a building or engineering contract who took out a
contractors' all risks policy was entitled to take out a single policy covering the whole
risk, including cover for all contractors and sub-contractors in respect of loss of or damage
to the entire contract works, since it was commercially convenient for one policy to cover
the whole risk. It followed that a sub-contractor was entitled under such a policy to   *g*
recover in respect of the entire contract works as well as his own property. Accordingly
the insurers could have no right of subrogation against the defendants, since an insurer
was not entitled to sue one co-insured in the name of another (see p 40 *g h*, p 42 *c d f g*
and p 44 *c d* and *j* to p 45 *b* and *j*, post); *Waters v Monarch Fire and Life Assurance Co* [1843–
60] All ER Rep 654 and *Hepburn v A Tomlinson (Hauliers) Ltd* [1966] 1 All ER 418 applied;
Commonwealth Construction Co Ltd v Imperial Oil Ltd (1976) 69 DLR (3d) 558 adopted; *The*   *h*
Yasin [1979] 2 Lloyd's Rep 45 considered.
(4) The fact that the defendants had liability policies with other companies did not
affect the position, because the other policies were liability policies and not policies on
property and there was not, therefore, double insurance on the same property in respect
of the same risk (see p 45 *e* to *g* and *j*, post).

    j

Notes
For the nature and right of subrogation, see 25 Halsbury's Laws (4th edn) paras 523–524,
and for cases on the subject, see 29 Digest (Reissue) 500–502, 4273–4281.

Cases referred to in judgment
Commonwealth Construction Co Ltd v Imperial Oil Ltd (1976) 69 DLR (3d) 558.

Hepburn v A Tomlinson (Hauliers) Ltd [1966] 1 All ER 418, [1966] AC 451, [1966] 2 WLR
a   453, HL; *affg* [1965] 1 All ER 284, [1966] 1 QB 21, [1965] 2 WLR 634, CA.
North British and Mercantile Insurance Co v London, Liverpool and Globe Insurance Co (1877)
     5 Ch D 569, CA.
Simpson & Co v Thompson, Burrell (1877) 3 App Cas 279, HL.
Waters v Monarch Fire and Life Assurance Co (1856) 5 E & B 870, [1843–60] All ER Rep
     654, 119 ER 705.
b   *Yasin, The* [1979] 2 Lloyd's Rep 45.

Preliminary issue
By a writ issued on 13 June 1980, the plaintiffs, Petrofina (UK) Ltd, Total Oil Great
Britain Ltd, Lindsey Oil Refinery Ltd and a consortium of companies trading under the
name of Omnium Leasing Ltd, claimed against the defendants, Magnaload Ltd and
Mammoet Stoof BV, damages for negligence. The defendants contended that they were
c   sub-contractors employed to carry out the contract works and that any claim against
them was covered by a contractor's all risks policy taken out by the head contractors,
Foster Wheeler Ltd, to cover all risks arising out of any acts or negligence of the
contractors and the sub-contractors in respect of the construction, erection and extension
to the Lindsey Oil Refinery. The defendants also issued third party notices on Greenham
d   (Plant Hire) Ltd, who were sub-contractors of the head contractors, and on the New
Hampshire Insurance Co, the insurers of the policy taken out by the head contractors.
The insurers having settled the plaintiffs' claim under the policy, sought to exercise their
right of subrogation against the defendants. The defendants claimed that since they were
sub-contractors and therefore fully insured under the policy, the insurers had no right of
subrogation. On 5 February 1982 Parker J ordered the trial of a preliminary issue, namely
e   whether the defendants were covered by the insurance policy. The facts are set out in the
judgment.

Michael Wright QC and *Crawford Lindsay* for the plaintiffs.
Adrian Hamilton QC and *Robert Glancy* for the defendants.

Cur adv vult
f
1 March. The following judgment was delivered.

LLOYD J. This is a preliminary issue tried by order of Parker J dated 5 February 1982.
The claim arises out of an accident which occurred on 2 September 1978 in the course of
carrying out a major extension to an oil refinery at Killingholme, South Humberside.
g   Two men lost their lives in the accident and there was extensive damage to property.
     Lindsey Oil Refinery Co Ltd, the third plaintiffs, are the owners of the refinery. They
operate it for the benefit of the first and second plaintiffs. The fourth plaintiffs are a
consortium of companies carrying on business under the name Omnium Leasing Co.
They have put up the money for the extension, including the manufacture and
installation of a new catalytic cracking unit. The fourth plaintiffs are the owners of the
h   unit. There is a contract under which the unit is leased by the fourth plaintiffs to the
third plaintiffs.
     The head contractors, Foster Wheeler Ltd, were appointed under a contract which was
eventually reduced to writing on 31 January 1979. Foster Wheeler sub-contracted the
heavy lifting operation to Greenham (Plant Hire) Ltd. The catalytic cracking unit or 'cat-
cracker' consists of or includes eight large cylindrical vessels, weighing up to 380 tons.
j   The lifting of the two heaviest vessels required specialist lifting equipment, which was
provided by a Dutch company, Mammoet Stoof BV, the second defendants. The
equipment, known as the hydrajack system, comprises two vertical masts, 67 m high
and 30 m apart, with a gantry beam across the top. In the course of dismantling the
hydrajack, after the lifting had been successfully completed, the gantry became displaced.
It crashed to the ground, bringing the masts with it, and causing much damage to the
works below.

The first defendants, Magnaload Ltd, are an English company which is owned as to
50% by the second defendants, Mammoet. The part played in these events by the *a*
employees of Magnaload, Mammoet and Greenhams Ltd who have been joined as the
first third parties in the proceedings, will have to be investigated at the trial. For the
purposes of the preliminary issue I have to assume in favour of the plaintiffs that the
defendants, Magnaload and Mammoet were both negligent, and that their negligence
caused the accident.

The contract works were insured with the second third party, New Hampshire *b*
Insurance Co for £50m, subsequently increased to £92m. There was a claim on the
policy for physical damage to the contract works brought by Lindsey. I was not told the
amount of the claim, but I understand it has been settled for about £1,250,000. Having
paid that claim, the insurers now seek to exercise their right of subrogation by suing the
defendants. The defendants' answer, put very briefly, is that the insurers have no right
of subrogation, because the defendants are themselves fully insured under the same *c*
policy. The question I have to determine on this preliminary issue is whether that
contention is correct.

Counsel for the defendants told me that it is a question of great importance for the
construction industry generally; for policies such as the one I have to consider are in
common use. I am sure he is right. The answer in the present case turns on the
construction of this particular policy, and on general principles of law. The policy is a *d*
'contractors' all risks insurance policy'. By section 1 it provides:

> 'The insurers will indemnify the insured against loss of or damage to the insured
> property whilst at the contract site from any cause not hereinafter excluded
> occurring during the period of insurance.'

'The insured' are defined in the schedule as—   *e*

> 'Omnium Leasing (Owner) and/or Lindsey Oil Refinery and/or Foster Wheeler
> Ltd. and/or Contractors and/or Sub-contractors.'

'The insured property' is defined as—

> Item No. 1. The works and temporary works erected . . . in performance of the *f*
> insured contract and the materials . . . for use in connection therewith belonging to
> the insured or for which they are responsible brought on to the contract site for the
> purpose of the said contract . . .
> Item No. 2. Constructional plant comprising plant and equipment . . . if and
> insofar as not otherwise insured belonging to the insured and for which they are
> responsible brought on to the contract site for the purpose of the insured contract. *g*

'The insured contract' is defined as: 'Construction erection and testing of an extension to
the Lindsey Oil Refinery at South Humberside.'

By an indorsement dated 23 April 1978 the policy was extended to include—

> 'The erection operation and subsequent dismantlement of the following items of
> plant which are being used on the Greenham (Plant Hire) Ltd. sub-contract for the *h*
> erection of eight large vessels: (1) . . .£600,000; (2) . . . £250,000; (3) Hydrajack
> system £2,150,000'

giving a total of £3,000,000. The minimum premium was increased by £9,000.

The policy also provides in section 3, third party liability cover in standard terms,
whereby the insurers agree to indemnify the insured—   *j*

> 'Against all sums for which the insured shall become legally liable to pay as
> damages consequent upon (a) Accidental bodily injury to or illness or disease of any
> person (b) Accidental loss of or damage to property occurring . . . as a result of and
> solely due to the performance of the insured contract happening on or in the
> immediate vicinity of the contract site.'

There is an exception to the third party liability cover which excludes property forming
a the subject of the insured contract.

The first point taken by the insurers is that the defendants are not 'sub-contractors'
within the meaning of the policy, and are therefore not insured at all. If they are right
about that, then none of the other points arise. At an early stage of the argument counsel
for the plaintiffs very properly accepted, though he never formally conceded, that the
first defendants, Magnaload, must be sub-contractors; but he maintained the argument
b in relation to the second defendants, Mammoet.

The facts are that in the initial stages of the negotiations it was contemplated that
Mammoet would enter into a contract with Greenhams for carrying out the specialist
lifting operation with their hydrajack. At the end of June there was a change of direction.
At a meeting which took place between Magnaload and Mammoet on 27 June 1978 it
was agreed that, for administrative reasons, the contract would be in the name of
c Magnaload, not Mammoet. Mammoet would, however, remain responsible for the
operation itself. The reasons for this change do not matter. The sub-contract price had
already been agreed between Greenhams and Mammoet at £185,000. It was agreed that
Mammoet would reimburse Magnaload out of that sum for any services which
Magnaload performed or any costs which they incurred. On 13 July 1978 there was a
meeting between Magnaload, Mammoet and Greenhams at which Greenhams agreed
d that the contract would be with Magnaload provided they received '100 per cent support'
from Mammoet. On 24 July Greenhams sent a telex to Magnaload as follows:

> 'Please find the draft of the purchase order for Foster Wheeler job at Immingham.
> Could we have your comments as soon as possible. "*Order on Magnaload*. For supply
> of lifting equipment and services in order to carry out the erection of heavy vessels
> at the Lindsey Oil Refinery expansion project, Killingholme, South Humberside.
e > All as more fully described in the attached scope of work and conditions of order.
> For the lump sum price of £185,000."'

Then, under the heading scope of work and conditions of order, I will quote two
paragraphs:

f > 'Erection of vessels at Lindsey Oil Refinery expansion project, Killingholme,
> South Humberside. Main contractor: Foster Wheeler Ltd. Heavy lifting sub-
> contractor: Greenham Plant Hire Ltd. Specialist lifting contractor: Magnaload Ltd.
> ... General conditions of contract in line with those which Greenham Plant Hire
> have accepted from Foster Wheeler are understood to apply to this order.'

That telex is signed by Greenham Plant Hire.
g The same day a copy of that telex was sent on by Magnaload to Mammoet. Mammoet
came back with certain comments, which were sent on to Greenhams. According to Mr
Wignall, who gave evidence at the hearing, and who had taken an active part in the
negotiations as commercial director of Magnaload, all three parties reached agreement
on all points of substance.

The term 'sub-contractor' is defined in the head contract as meaning—

h > 'Any person to whom the preparation of any design the supply of any plant or the
> execution of any part of the works is sub-contracted, irrespective of whether the
> contractor is in direct contract with such person.'

There is a similar definition in the sub-contract between Foster Wheeler and Greenhams.
On the facts which I have set out, there was clearly a contract between Greenhams and
j Magnaload, as, indeed, counsel for the plaintiffs accepted. Strictly speaking Magnaload
were not sub-contractors but sub-sub-contractors. But I would hold that they were
nevertheless sub-contractors within the definition contained in the contracts and within
the ordinary meaning of the word 'sub-contractors' as contained in the policy. To my
mind the word 'sub-contractors' in the context of the policy must include sub-sub-
contractors as well as sub-contractors.

Turning to Mammoet, counsel for the plaintiffs argued that there is nothing in the documents to show that Mammoet, as distinct from Magnaload, were contractors at all; *a* if so, they could not be sub-contractors. I cannot accept that argument. It frequently happens that businessmen do not tie up their contracts in ways which seem satisfactory to lawyers, particularly where the parties are companies which, though not members of the same group in the strict sense, are nevertheless as closely associated as these were. I would require a great deal of persuasion before holding that Mammoet had no contractual claim to remuneration from anyone. It seems to me that a contract must be implied *b* between Magnaload and Mammoet, under which Mammoet became sub-contractors of Greenhams, on terms that Mammoet would carry out the operation for the agreed price.

In passing I may mention the parallel proceedings which have been brought by Magnaload and Mammoet against the insurers under this very policy. By their points of claim, they claimed just under 1,200,000 Dutch florins for damage to the hydrajack and various other items of equipment. I understand that the insurers have settled that claim *c* for 800,000 Dutch florins. If the defendants are not sub-contractors within the meaning of the policy, the insurers would have had a complete defence. On the true construction of the policy I would hold that Magnaload and Mammoet were both sub-contractors and were both insured under the policy.

The next question relates to the property insured. Counsel for the defendants submits that a 'contractors' all risk' policy in this form is an insurance on property, namely the *d* works and temporary works belonging to the insured, or for which the insured are responsible. Counsel for the plaintiffs accepts that it is an insurance on property, but submits that the property insured must be read distributively, in other words, each insured is only insured in respect of his own property, or property for which he is responsible. I do not accept that construction. It seems to me that on the ordinary meaning of the words which I have quoted, each of the named insured, including all the *e* sub-contractors, are insured in respect of the whole of the contract works. There are no words of severance, if I may use that term in this connection, to require me to hold that each of the named insured is only insured in respect of his own property. Nor is there any business necessity to imply words of severance. On the contrary, as I shall mention later, business convenience, if not business necessity, would require me to reach the opposite conclusion. I would hold, as a matter of construction, that each of the named *f* insured is insured in respect of the entire contract works, including property belonging to any other of the insured, or for which any other of the insured were responsible.

But then comes the question: what is the nature of the interest insured? Counsel for the plaintiffs submits that the only possible insurable interest which one insured could have in property belonging to another, is in respect of his potential liability for loss of or damage to that property. Accordingly section 1 of the present policy is, he submits, a *g* composite insurance. It is an insurance on property so far as it relates to property belonging to any particular insured; it is a liability insurance so far as it relates to all other property comprised in 'contract works'.

Counsel for the defendants, on the other hand, submits that section 1 of the policy is a policy on property, pure and simple.

In my judgment the submission of counsel for the defendants is correct. A very similar *h* question arose in *Hepburn v A Tomlinson (Hauliers) Ltd* [1966] 1 All ER 418, [1966] AC 451, HL; *affg* [1965] 1 All ER 284, [1966] 1 QB 21, CA. In that case a firm of carriers took out a policy of insurance of goods in transit, on a form known as 'Form J'. A quantity of cigarettes were stolen while the goods were still in transit, by reason of the negligence of the owners, Imperial Tobacco Co. It was common ground that the carriers were not liable to the owners. On the carriers making a claim under the policy, for the benefit of *j* the owners, it was argued that the policy was a liability policy, and since the carriers were not liable to the owners, they could not recover from the insurers. The argument was rejected by Roskill J, and his judgment was upheld by the Court of Appeal and the House of Lords.

It appears that underwriters had always regarded an insurance on 'Form J' as being a liability policy, and not a policy on goods. But Lord Reid said that the language of the

policy showed conclusively that the policy was a policy on goods. I can find no relevant
distinction between the language of the present policy and the language in *Hepburn v
Tomlinson*. Section 1 of the present policy covers 'all risks of loss or damage to the insured
property'. It excludes the cost of replacing or rectifying insured property which is
defective in material or workmanship, and so on. There is nothing in section 1 of the
policy which is appropriate to an insurance against liability, whereas everything is
appropriate to a policy on property. Section 2 of the policy covers the contractual liability
of the contractors to maintain the contract works during the maintenance period. Section
3 covers third party liability. The very fact that third party liability is covered in a
separate section, which expressly excludes liability for damage to property forming part
of the contract works, shows to my mind that s 1 of the policy is an insurance on
property, and not an insurance against liability.

There is a passage in Jessel MR's judgment in *North British and Mercantile Insurance Co
v London, Liverpool and Globe Insurance Co* (1877) 5 Ch D 569 at 578 which points in the
other direction. For he refers to a wharfinger's insurance on goods held in trust, or for
which they are responsible, as being in terms an insurance against liability. But that
dictum (for it was no more) cannot now stand against the decision of the House of Lords
in *Hepburn v Tomlinson*.

That brings me to the central question in the case. In *Hepburn v Tomlinson* it was held,
indeed it was conceded, that if the policy was an insurance on goods, then the carriers
could, as bailees, insure for their full value, holding the proceeds in trust for the owners.
In the present case the defendants could not be regarded as being in any sense bailees of
the property insured under the policy. Does that make any difference? Can the
defendants recover the full value of the property insured, even though they are not
bailees? It is here that one leaves the construction of the policy, and enters, hesitatingly,
the realm of legal principle.

What are the reasons why it has been held ever since *Waters v Monarch Fire and Life
Assurance Co* (1856) 5 E & B 870, [1843–60] All ER Rep 654 that a bailee is entitled to
insure and recover the full value of goods bailed? Do those reasons apply in the case of a
sub-contractor?

One reason is historical: the bailee could always sue a wrongdoer in trover. If his
possessory interest in the goods was sufficient to enable him to recover the full value of
the goods in trover, why should he not be able to insure that interest?

Another reason was that, as bailee, he was 'responsible' for the goods. Responsibility is
here used in a different sense from legal liability. A bailee might by contract exclude his
legal liability for loss of or damage to the goods in particular circumstances, e g by fire.
But he would still be 'responsible' for the goods in a more general sense, sufficient, at any
rate, to entitle him to insure the full value.

It is clear that neither of these reasons apply in the case of a sub-contractor.

But there is a third reason which is frequently mentioned in connection with a bailee's
right to insure the full value of the goods. From a commercial point of view it was always
regarded as highly convenient. Thus in *Waters v Monarch Fire and Life Assurance* (1856) 5
E & B 870 at 880, [1843–60] All ER Rep 654 at 655 itself Lord Campbell CJ said:

> 'What is meant in these policies by the words "goods in trust"? I think that means
> goods with which the assured were entrusted; not goods held in trust in the strict
> technical sense . . . but goods with which they were entrusted in the ordinary sense
> of the word. They were so entrusted with the goods deposited on their wharfs: I
> cannot doubt the policy was intended to protect such goods: and it would be very
> inconvenient if wharfingers could not protect such goods by a floating policy.'

Similarly Lord Pearce in *Hepburn v Tomlinson* [1966] 1 All ER 418 at 431, [1966] AC 451
at 481 said:

> 'A bailee or mortgagee, therefore, (or others in analogous positions) has, by virtue
> of his position and his interest in the property, a right to insure for the whole of its

value, holding in trust for the owner or mortgagor the amount attributable to their
interest. To hold otherwise would be commercially inconvenient and would have *a*
no justification in common sense.'

In the case of a building or engineering contract, where numerous different sub-
contractors may be engaged, there can be no doubt about the convenience from
everybody's point of view, including, I would think, the insurers, of allowing the head
contractor to take out a single policy covering the whole risk, that is to say covering all *b*
contractors and sub-contractors in respect of loss of or damage to the entire contract
works. Otherwise each sub-contractor would be compelled to take out his own separate
policy. This would mean, at the very least, extra paperwork; at worst it could lead to
overlapping claims and cross claims in the event of an accident. Furthermore, as Mr
Wignall pointed out in the course of his evidence, the cost of insuring his liability might,
in the case of a small sub-contractor, be uneconomic. The premium might be out of all *c*
proportion to the value of the sub-contract. If the sub-contractor had to insure his liability
in respect of the entire works, he might well have to decline the contract.

For all these reasons I would hold that a head contractor ought to be able to insure the
entire contract works in his own name and the name of all his sub-contractors, just like a
bailee or mortgagee, and that a sub-contractor ought to be able to recover the whole of
the loss insured, holding the excess over his own interest in trust for the others. *d*

If that is the result which convenience dictates, is there anything which makes it illegal
for a sub-contractor to insure the entire contract works in his own name? This was a
question which was much discussed in the early cases on bailment. But it was never
illegal at common law for a bailee to insure goods in excess of his interest. As for statute,
the Marine Insurance Acts obviously do not apply. It is true that the Life Assurance Act
1774 by s 3 prohibited an insured from recovering more than his interest on the *e*
happening of an insured event. But policies on goods were specifically excluded by s 4 of
the Act. Accordingly it was held that neither at common law nor by statute was there
anything to prevent the bailee from insuring in excess of his interest.

What about a sub-contractor? 'Goods' in s 4 of the 1774 Act has always been given a
wide interpretation, and would clearly cover contract works until they became part of
the realty. Whether the works would remain 'goods' thereafter, and if so for how long, *f*
may be more difficult. But it was not suggested that the insurers would have any defence
here under the Life Assurance Act, so I say no more about it. I would hold that the
position of a sub-contractor in relation to contract works as a whole is sufficiently similar
to that of a bailee in relation to goods bailed to enable me to hold, by analogy, that he is
entitled to insure the entire contract works, and in the event of a loss to recover the full
value of those works in his own name. *g*

Turning from principle to authority, there is, so far as I know, no English decision
covering the present case. But there is an important decision of the Supreme Court of
Canada. In *Commonwealth Construction Co Ltd v Imperial Oil Ltd* (1976) 69 DLR (3d) 558,
the facts were that Imperial Oil Ltd entered into a building contract for the construction
of a fertiliser plant with Wellman Lord Ltd as main contractor. Wellman Lord Ltd
entered into a sub-contract with Commonwealth Construction Co Ltd for the construction *h*
of the pipework. Imperial took out a policy known as a 'course of construction policy'.
The policy was in the name of Imperial, together with their contractors and sub-
contractors. It covered—

'all materials ... and other property of any nature whatsoever owned by the
insured or in which the insured may have an interest or responsibility or for which *j*
the insured may be liable or assume liability prior to loss or damage ...'

There was a fire at the site which was said to have been due to the negligence of
Commonwealth. The insurers paid the loss to Imperial, and then sought to recover in
the name of Imperial from Commonwealth under their right of subrogation. It will be
seen that the facts are thus almost identical to those in the present case.

The matter came before the court on a preliminary issue. The court at first instance
a rejected the claim on the ground that Commonwealth were fully insured under the
policy. The Court of Appeal reversed the trial judge, holding that Commonwealth could
only claim to be indemnified under the policy to the extent of that part of the work
performed under the sub-contract, ie property belonging to Commonwealth and
property for which it was responsible before the loss occurred. The Supreme Court,
consisting of the Chief Justice and eight judges, restored the judgment of the trial judge.
b The Supreme Court stated the main issue as follows (at 560):

> 'Did Commonwealth, in addition to its obvious interest in its own work, have an
> insurable interest in the entire project so that in principle the insurers were not
> entitled to subrogation against that firm for the reason that it was all assured with a
> pervasive interest in the whole of the works?'

c There was a preliminary question whether the policy was to be regarded as an
insurance on property at all or whether it was an insurance against liability. The Supreme
Court held that it was property insurance. Indeed there seems to have been no real
argument to the contrary. At the beginning of their judgment the court described the
policy as a 'multi-peril subscription policy stated to be property insurance which it clearly
is'. Later the court said (at 560): '. . . given the fact that the policy is property insurance
d and not liability coverage the reasoning of the Court of Appeal may be summarised thus
. . .'

Having decided that preliminary question in favour of Commonwealth, the court
went on to consider whether Commonwealth had a 'pervasive interest' in the entire
property. The judgment referred to *Waters v Monarch Fire and Life Assurance Co, Tomlinson
v Hepburn*, and other bailment cases, including a number of American cases, and then
e said (at 562–563):

> 'In all these cases, there existed an underlying contract whereby the owner of the
> goods had given possession thereof to the party claiming full insurable interest in
> them based on the special relationship therewith. Although in the case at bar
> Commonwealth was not given the possession of the works as a whole, does the
> concept apply here? I believe so. On any construction site, and especially when the
f > building being erected is a complex chemical plant, there is ever present the
> possibility of damage by one tradesman to the property of another and to the
> construction as a whole. Should this possibility become reality, the question of
> negligence in the absence of complete property coverage would have to be debated
> in Court. By recognising in all tradesmen an insurable interest based on that very
> real possibility, which itself has its source in the contractual arrangements opening
g > the doors of the job site to the tradesman, the Courts would apply to the construction
> field the principle expressed so long ago in the area of bailment. Thus all the parties
> whose joint efforts have one common goal, *e.g.*, the completion of the construction,
> would be spared the necessity of fighting between themselves should an accident
> occur involving the possible responsibility of one of them.'

h The *Commonwealth Construction* case is, in my view, indistinguishable from the present
case, and is highly persuasive authority. Even if I had thought it wrongly decided, which
I do not, I should have hesitated long before declining to follow it.

Counsel for the plaintiffs sought to extract comfort from the following passage (at
563):

j
> 'In the description of the property insured, the words "assume liability prior to
> loss" are sufficient to define the general contractor. The words "may be liable" add
> another dimension and are wide enough, in my eyes, to recognise in all contractors
> (which term I underline again includes subcontractors) an insurable interest having
> its source in the very real possibility ("may") of liability, considering the close inter-
> relationship of the labour performed by the various trades under their respective
> agreements. Of course, that very real possibility exists prior to the loss.'

Counsel for the plaintiffs argued that there are no equivalent words to 'assume liability prior to loss' in the present case, and that the words show that the policy was in truth a *a* liability policy. Alternatively he argued that while Foster Wheeler and Greenhams 'assumed liability' in the present case under cl 31 of their respective contracts, the defendants did not. There is nothing in either of these points. I have already drawn attention to the passages in which the Supreme Court quite clearly decided or assumed that the policy was a policy on property, and not a liability policy. As for the words 'assume liability' I would myself have doubted whether they added anything to the word *b* 'responsibility'. They are not, I think, intended to refer to legal liability towards others taking part in the joint project, and they are certainly not confined to contractual assumption of liability, a question which, as the court said, 'may well remain unanswered'. There is therefore no ground of distinction, either between the present case and the *Commonwealth Construction* case, or between Foster Wheeler and Greenhams on the one hand and the defendants on the other.   *c*

For the reasons which I have mentioned, I would hold, both on principle and on the authority of the *Commonwealth Construction* case, that a sub-contractor who is engaged on contract works may insure the entire contract works as well as his own property, and that the defendants in this case were each so insured.

That brings me to the next question: does the fact that the defendants are fully insured under the present policy defeat the insurer's right of subrogation? In the *Commonwealth* *d* *Construction* case, and in the American cases there referred to, it was assumed that it followed automatically that the insurers could have no right of subrogation. In the *Commonwealth Construction* case it was described as being a 'basic principle'. In one of the American cases it was said that the rule was too well established to require citation. In none of the cases is there any discussion as to the reason for the rule, except for a brief reference in the *Commonwealth Construction* case (1976) 69 DLR (3d) 558 at 561 to *Simpson* *e* *& Co v Thompson, Burrell* (1877) 3 App Cas 279 as follows:

'The starting point of that submission is the basic principle that subrogation cannot be obtained against the insured himself. The classic example is, of course, to be found in *Simpson & Co et al v. Thompson Burrell et al*. In the case of true joint insurance there is, of course, no problem; the interests of the joint insured are so inseparably connected that the several insureds are to be considered as one with the *f* obvious result that subrogation is impossible. In the case of several insurance, if the different interests are pervasive and if each relates to the entire property, albeit from different angles, again there is no question that the several insureds must be regarded as one and that no subrogation is possible.'

The question whether there is a fundamental principle of the law of insurance that *g* insurers can never sue one co-insured in the name of another came up in *The Yasin* [1979] 2 Lloyd's Rep 45. In that case I said that I was not satisfied that there was any such fundamental principle as had been suggested; the reason for the rule seemed to me to rest on ordinary principles of circuity. This idea has since been adopted by the current editors of *MacGillivray and Parkington on Insurance Law* (7th edn, 1981) at para 1214. In para 1215 the editors say: *h*

'The crucial question therefore in any case involving joint assured is whether the liability of one co-assured to the other is one of the matters covered by the policy . . .'

Thus where a bailee is insured against liability to the bailor, and the bailor is insured under the same insurance, it is obvious that the insurer could not exercise a right of *j* subrogation against the bailee; circuity would be a complete answer. But in *The Yasin* I went on to contrast the position where the bailee had insured, not his liability to the bailor, but the goods themselves. Now that the matter has been argued again, I have come to the conclusion that the contrast I was seeking to draw is fallacious. Whatever be the reason why an insurer cannot sue one co-insured in the name of another (and I am still inclined to think that the reason is circuity) it seems to me now that it must apply *a*   equally in every case of bailment, whether it is the goods which the bailee has insured, or his liability in respect of the goods. The same would also apply in the case of contractors and sub-contractors engaged on a common enterprise under a building or engineering contract. Even if I still had reservations of the kind which I tried to voice in *The Yasin*, I would feel obliged to bury them in the light of the decision of the Supreme Court of Canada in the *Commonwealth Construction* case, a decision which was not cited in *The Yasin* and for the reference to which in the present case I am very grateful to counsel.

b   Lastly I come to a point which was raised by a late amendment to the points of reply. The policy provides by general exception (2)—

'The insurer shall not be liable in respect of loss damage or liability which at the time of happening of such loss damage or liability is insured by or would but for the existence of this policy be insured by any other policy or policies except in respect of any excess beyond the amount which would have been payable under such other policy or policies had this insurance not been effected.'

c

The defendants admit that at all material times they had in force liability policies with the Royal Insurance and other insurers. Some at least of these other policies have a provision similar in effect to general exception (2). Counsel for the plaintiffs submits that the existence of these other liability policies brings exception (2) into effect, with the result that the insurers are either not liable at all, or only for the excess over the amounts

d   covered by the other policies.

Counsel for the defendants submits that general exception (2) is, on its true construction, intended to take effect only in the case of true double insurance. There cannot be double insurance unless the same insured is covered in respect of the same property against the same risks. Thus if in the present case there were, in addition to the

e   New Hampshire policy, another policy on the contract works, covering the same risks, then that would be a true case of double insurance. But here the other policies, so counsel for the defendants submits, are not policies on property, but liability policies. Counsel argues that there cannot be double insurance in those circumstances.

I agree with the argument of counsel for the defendants. It is true that general exception (2) refers to 'liability' as well as 'loss and damage'. But that is because the

f   general exceptions are intended to apply to section 3 of the policy, which covers third party liability, as well as sections 1 and 2. Since I agree with the submission of counsel for the defendants it is unnecessary to investigate the terms of the Royal Insurance policy and the other policies in any detail, or indeed at all, for they are admittedly liability policies, whereas the insurance under section 1 is, as I have already held, an insurance on property. The insurances are not therefore insurances on the same property and against

g   the same risk and it follows that there is here no possibility of double insurance in the true sense, and general exception (2) does not apply.

Counsel for the defendants had an alternative argument, should he be wrong on everything else. He submitted that having regard to Foster Wheeler's obligation under cl 32 of the main contract to take out insurance in the joint names of all parties, including the sub-contractors, and having regard in particular to the indorsement under which the

h   policy was specifically extended to include the erection operation and subsequent dismantlement of the hydrajack system, a contract is to be implied between the plaintiffs and the defendants that the plaintiffs would not hold the defendants liable in the event of loss or damage to the contract works resulting from the defendant's negligence. There is much to be said for that argument: but having already decided in favour of the defendants on the main ground, I need say no more about it.

j   It follows from all I have said, that the issue directed by Parker J will be decided in favour of the defendants.

Order on preliminary issue for the defendants. Leave to appeal.

Solicitors: *Herbert Smith & Co* (for the plaintiffs); *Elborne Mitchell & Co* (for the defendants).

K Mydeen Esq   Barrister.

The Abidin Daver

a

COURT OF APPEAL, CIVIL DIVISION
SIR JOHN DONALDSON MR, DUNN AND PURCHAS LJJ
17 MAY 1983

Practice – Stay of proceedings – Foreign defendant – Action in rem – Action by foreign plaintiff against defendant's vessel whilst vessel visiting in English port – Grounds for justifying stay – Proceedings pending in foreign court commenced by defendants – Whether existence of foreign proceedings sufficient ground for granting stay of proceedings – Whether existence of foreign proceedings a factor to be taken into account in weighing balance of convenience.

As a result of a collision in the Bosphorus between the plaintiffs' vessel and the defendants' vessel, the Turkish defendants commenced proceedings in Turkey for damages against the Cuban plaintiffs. Subsequently the plaintiffs served a writ on a sister ship of the defendants' vessel in England and brought an action in rem in the Admiralty Court against the defendants for damages in respect of the collision. The defendants applied for a stay of the proceedings in the Admiralty Court on the ground that there were in existence other proceedings in the Turkish court. The judge stayed the proceedings on the grounds that the litigation between the parties could be more conveniently tried in the Turkish court and that the plaintiffs would not be deprived of any juridical advantage if the proceedings in the English court were stayed. The plaintiffs appealed.

Held – A mere balance of convenience was not a sufficient ground for depriving a plaintiff of the advantage of pursuing his action in the English courts and the fact that there was a claim by the defendant against the plaintiff pending abroad was not of itself a bar to the plaintiff claiming in England against the defendant for damages arising out of the same cause of action. The existence of proceedings abroad was a factor to be taken into account but it was not a factor which, of itself, save in exceptional circumstances, was of sufficient weight to displace the right of a plaintiff to choose his own forum, or to weigh the balance of convenience in favour of the defendant. It followed that, since the plaintiffs were entitled to litigate their claim in the English courts and since there were no other factors to weigh the balance in favour of the defendants, the fact that there were in existence other proceedings in Turkey did not deprive the plaintiffs of their right to bring proceedings in the English courts. Furthermore (per Dunn and Purchas LJJ) the defendants had not shown that the Turkish court was a forum to whose jurisdiction the defendants were amenable and in which justice could be done between the parties at substantially less inconvenience or expense so far as the plaintiffs' claim in the action was concerned (see p 51 *f* to *j*, p 52 *a b* and p 53 *c* to *g*, post).

Dictum of Scott LJ in *St Pierre v South American Stores (Gath & Chaves) Ltd* [1935] All ER Rep at 414, *The Tillie Lykes* [1977] 1 Lloyd's Rep 124 and *MacShannon v Rockware Glass Ltd* [1978] 1 All ER 625 applied.

Cases referred to in judgments

Atlantic Star, The, Atlantic Star (owners) v Bona Spes (owners) [1973] 2 All ER 175, [1974] AC 436, [1973] 2 WLR 795, HL.
Gulf Oil Belgian SA v Finland Steamship Co Ltd, The Wellamo [1980] 2 Lloyd's Rep 229.
MacShannon v Rockware Glass Ltd, Fyfe v Redpath Dorman Long Ltd [1978] 1 All ER 625, [1978] AC 795, [1978] 2 WLR 362, HL.
St Pierre v South American Stores (Gath & Chaves) Ltd [1936] 1 KB 382, [1935] All ER Rep 408, CA.
Tillie Lykes, The [1977] 1 Lloyd's Rep 124.

Cases also cited

Trendtex Trading Corp v Crédit Suisse [1981] 3 All ER 520, [1982] AC 679, HL.
Wladyslaw Lokietek, The [1978] 2 Lloyd's Rep 520.

Notes

a For general principles governing stay of proceedings, see 8 Halsbury's Laws (4th edn) paras 407, 787–788, and for cases on the subject, see 11 Digest (Reissue) 631–633, 1696–1689.

Appeal

b The plaintiffs, the owners of the vessel Las Mercedes, appealed with leave of the Court of Appeal granted on 17 May 1983, against the judgment of Sheen J made on 4 May 1983, whereby he ordered that the plaintiffs' action against the defendants, the owners of the vessel Abidin Daver, be stayed. The facts are set out in the judgment of Sir John Donaldson MR.

c *Elizabeth Blackburn* for the plaintiffs.
Nigel Teare for the defendants.

SIR JOHN DONALDSON MR. On 23 March 1982 high winds and strong tidal streams were experienced by those who were at sea in the Bosphorus. One result of that situation was that there was a collision between the Cuban vessel Las Mercedes and the *d* Turkish vessel Abidin Daver.

If the evidence of both sides is to be accepted, we have at last met the classic case of a collision between two anchored and immovable ships which were at least one mile apart. If the evidence of both sides is not to be accepted, then a choice has to be made between one version, that the Cuban vessel dragged her anchor and was pushed down onto the Turkish vessel, and the alternative version, that the Turkish vessel weighed anchor and, *e* moving to windward, struck the anchored Cuban vessel. For the purposes of these proceedings no such choice need be made.

The next event after the collision was that the Cuban vessel was arrested in Turkish waters at the suit of the owners of the Turkish vessel with a view to beginning an action in the Turkish courts. Nothing further happened of materiality for two months until the Turkish owners, in the ordinary course of their business, ordered a sister ship to go to *f* England. On arrival in England, she was arrested by the Cuban shipowners with a view to starting a second action, in which of course the Cubans would be the plaintiffs, claiming damages for the collision on the basis that the Turks were at fault.

The Turks, not unnaturally, applied for a stay of those proceedings. The motion came before Sheen J, who on 4 May 1983 granted the application. We have dealt with the matter today, 17 May, as a matter of urgency because it is said that further steps are about *g* to be taken in the action in Turkey, and it is a cardinal principle in this court, as in others, that within the limits of possibility matters will be dealt with within such time as is necessary, and it is necessary that this appeal should be dealt with before then.

In granting the application, Sheen J began by saying:

> 'On this motion counsel for the defendants moves for an order that this action be stayed on the ground that there is another forum to whose jurisdiction the
> *h* defendants are amenable, namely the Sariyer District Court at Buyukdere in Turkey, in which justice can be done between the parties at substantially less inconvenience and expense and that a stay of this action will not deprive the plaintiffs of a legitimate personal or juridical advantage available to them in this court.'

He did not in fact put that part of his judgment in quotation marks, but he could have *j* done so because it is quite clear from the speech of Lord Diplock in *MacShannon v Rockware Glass Ltd* [1978] 1 All ER 625 at 630, [1978] AC 795 at 812 that this, virtually word for word, is the second part of the test which has to be applied according to that decision. The first part, taken from the historic judgment of Scott LJ in *St Pierre v South American Stores (Gath & Chaves) Ltd* [1936] 1 KB 382 at 398, [1935] All ER Rep 408 at 414, is set out in an earlier passage in Lord Diplock's speech (see [1978] 1 All ER 625 at 628, [1978] AC 795 at 810). The first part reads:

'(1.) A mere balance of convenience is not a sufficient ground for depriving a
plaintiff of the advantages of prosecuting his action in an English Court if it is
otherwise properly brought. The right of access to the King's Court must not be
lightly refused.'

The second part which, as I say, is quoted by the judge is a modification of Scott LJ's
formulation. That test is also subscribed to by Lord Salmon and by Lord Fraser (see
[1978] 1 All ER 625 at 636–637, 639, [1978] AC 795 at 819, 823). The only voice which
was raised in a manner which might cast some doubt what the test meant was that of
Lord Keith where he said ([1978] 1 All ER 625 at 645, [1978] AC 795 at 829):

'Where however, the defendant shows that England is not the natural forum and
that if the action were continued there he would be involved in substantial (ie more
than de minimis) inconvenience and unnecessary expense, or in some other
disadvantages, which would not affect him in the natural forum, he has made out a
prima facie case for a stay, and if nothing follows it may properly be granted.'

It was argued, of course, in this appeal that that meant that in the test set out in Lord
Diplock's speech, supported by Lord Salmon and Lord Fraser, 'substantially' must be read
as 'more than de minimis'. For my part, I do not accept that argument; I think the word
means what it says, 'substantially'.

The argument has shown that this test appears to contain a lacuna in that it does not
tell the court seeking to apply it whether and to what extent account is to be taken of the
fact that other proceedings have been begun earlier elsewhere: in this case that other
proceedings have previously been begun in Turkey. As will appear, in my judgment that
makes a considerable difference.

The factors which we have to balance are the following.

(1) The collision occurred in Turkish waters. That has to be qualified to this extent,
that the Bosphorus is an international waterway akin to the high seas, and the vessel was
not proceeding to Turkey, but was merely sheltering in Turkish waters. It is much the
same as a vessel proceeding up-Channel to the Low Countries which, for reasons of
weather, shelters in the Downs. Technically it is English territorial waters, but in reality
it is still in one of the main international shipping waterways.

(2) One of the ships was Turkish. That has to be seen in the context that the Admiralty
jurisdiction of all countries is essentially international because the high seas themselves
are extra-territorial. Accordingly the nationality of the vessels involved is not normally a
factor of any great relevance.

(3) There was a Turkish crew on one of the ships, and it is said, and rightly said, that
if the dispute is tried in the Turkish court, they would have less of a language problem
than would be the case if the dispute were tried in any other court. It could equally be
said that the Cubans would have less trouble if the matter were tried in a Spanish
speaking court than if it were tried in a Turkish or English court. Perhaps it may not
unfairly be said that while English may not be a language with which either party is
familiar, it is the lingua franca and may represent an acceptable compromise between
the competing linguistic needs of the parties.

(4) It is said that the cost of litigation is a factor of which account has to be taken. It
would undoubtedly be less for the Turks in Turkey, and possibly more for the Cubans
(comparing litigation in Turkey with litigation in England), purely in terms of the travel
involved. On the other hand, if the litigation were to be in England, the increase in travel
costs for the Turks might perhaps be redressed by a reduction in costs to the Cubans, I
know not, but for my part I would not regard the difference as being very startling. It is
right to take account of the fact that there may perhaps be more Turkish evidence than
Cuban evidence because there was a Turkish pilot who was on board the Cuban vessel
some time before the collision occurred, and it is suggested that he may be able to
contribute materially towards the evidence. But I doubt whether it is significant.

(5) Turkish court surveyors have already made a report on the incident and the
damage to the vessels, but it is accepted by counsel for the plaintiffs that this ought to be

a made available to the English court, and she is prepared to waive any technical rules as to admissibility to enable it to be produced before an English court, subject of course to all questions of weight.

(6) It is said that account should be taken of the local knowledge of the Turkish court. By a curious coincidence it is true that, if his bench is facing in the right direction and there is an appropriate window, the Turkish judge could look out at the scene of the collision. However, it was not clear to me on the evidence that there was anything

b peculiar about this particular area of the Bosphorus which could not as well be conveyed to an English Admiralty judge as to a Turkish Admiralty judge, or of which a Turkish Admiralty judge would necessarily be aware in the absence of evidence.

(7) It is said that the Cubans would have to provide 15% deposit, the amount of the counterclaim, before making a claim in Turkey. By contrast to that, it is said that the English court fees are wholly inadequate, and there would therefore be a substantial

c saving in coming to England. As to the court fees being inadequate, that is beyond argument, but it is only fair to take account of the fact that some order for security of costs might well be made in this country. Probably the deposit and the security for costs would be of the same order of magnitude.

(8) It is said that the Turkish shipowners would be more familiar with Turkish courts and Turkish procedure. That undoubtedly is true, but both parties will be equally

d familiar (or unfamiliar) with the English courts, and it may be that there is something to be said for equality of opportunity and equality of sacrifice in the determination of disputes of this nature.

(9) It is said that the English Admiralty Court is a court which is superior to the Turkish court. I share entirely the reluctance of Sheen and Brandon JJ to express any view as to the relative merits of particular courts. That must be a matter of subjective

e judgment which I, as a judge of an English court, and an ex-Admiralty judge, do not feel that I should make.

What I think can be said, and I doubt whether it would be controverted by anybody, is that the English Admiralty Court has a vast amount of international maritime experience in this field going back over the centuries. While I do not doubt for one moment that the Turkish courts have long maritime experience, I doubt very much

f whether it is as international or extensive. That is not a criticism, and should not be taken as a criticism, of the Turkish courts; it is an accident of geography. The English courts are situated on an island off Europe. That has led, as a matter of history, to their being involved in far more maritime disputes than Turkey or any country similarly situated.

Those are the factors. Ignoring the fact that there is already an action on foot in

g Turkey, if I were to ask myself whether the Turkish shipowners could show that there is another jurisdiction to which they are amenable and one in which the matter can be dealt with at substantially less inconvenience or expense, I should say that they could not. It seems to me that, ignoring the fact that an action is already on foot, the factors, as I have indicated them, would be fairly evenly balanced.

But if I look again at those factors, taking account of the existence of the Turkish

h action, then I think that the answer is different. The Turkish courts have assumed jurisdiction. It is true that they will require the Cubans to pay a deposit before prosecuting a counterclaim but that they might not have to give security for costs. The decisive factor would be the saving in costs in having only one set of proceedings. Furthermore, if account is to be taken of the existence of the Turkish proceedings, staying the English action would remove the theoretical risk of wholly inconsistent findings of fact, which

j must be desirable. So it seems to me that this appeal really turns on the issue of to what extent an English court shall take account of the fact that there are prior proceedings in another jurisdiction.

That was dealt with by Brandon J in *The Tillie Lykes* [1977] 1 Lloyd's Rep 124. For the purposes of this judgment I would like to refer to two somewhat lengthy passages. The first passage begins where the judge says (at 126):

'It was conceded by Counsel for the defendants that, but for *The Atlantic Star*, ([1973] 2 All ER 175, [1974] AC 436) he could not hope to succeed on this *a* application. But he said that in the light of that decision a different view should be taken of this kind of case and a stay should be granted. I think it is important to appreciate that *The Atlantic Star* was a very special case on its facts. There were in that case many powerful circumstances making the Belgian Court a more convenient forum for the trial of the relevant dispute than the English Court. Circumstances of that kind are not present in this case. What this case involves, mainly at any rate, is *b* the inherent disadvantage of having two sets of proceedings in two different countries in respect of the same subject-matter. The disadvantages involved in that situation, by themselves, have never hitherto been considered sufficient to justify a stay. The question is whether the decision of the House of Lords in *The Atlantic Star* alters that position. In order to answer that question it seems to me to be necessary to examine more closely what was said in the House of Lords about the factor of *c* multiplicity of proceedings, and, in order to do that, I shall read certain passages from the speech of Lord Wilberforce in which he refers to that matter . . . he says ([1973] 2 All ER 175 at 194, [1974] AC 436 at 468): "Secondly, in considering whether a stay should be granted the court must take into account (i) any advantage to the plaintiff; (ii) any disadvantage to the defendant: this is the critical equation, and in some cases it will be a difficult one to establish. Generally this is done by an *d* instinctive process—that is what discretion, in its essence, is. But there are perhaps some elements which it is possible to disengage and make explicit." Lord Wilberforce goes on to consider what sort of advantage to the plaintiff ought to be taken into account, and then he turns to the other half of the equation, the disadvantage to the defendant, and he says this: "Then the disadvantage to the defendant: to be taken into account at all this must be serious, more than mere disadvantage of multiple *e* suits; to prevail against the plaintiff's advantage, still more substantial—how much more depending how great the latter may be. The words 'oppressive' or 'vexatious' point this up as indicative of the degree and character of the prejudice that must be shown. I think too that there must be a relative element in assessing both advantage and disadvantage—relative to the individual circumstances of the plaintiff and defendant." Later, he deals specifically with the group of cases before *The Atlantic* *f* *Star*, to which I referred earlier. He says this ([1973] 2 All ER 175 at 195, [1974] AC 436 at 469): "Secondly, there has not been brought to notice any case—at least of an action in rem—where, in a case where foreign proceedings are pending and the plaintiff in one suit is defendant in the other, a stay has been granted. A list of cases to the contrary includes well-known cases [—and then he refers to the decisions that I have mentioned. He goes on—] These instances are impressive, but they are *g* instances. More than one of them recognises the existence of the discretion to stay. I do not find either in their facts or in any statement of principle in them a general rule which would cover this case. But they do vouch the proposition that a very clear case is needed to justify a stay, where a plaintiff is (properly as to jurisdiction) suing here and that the mere fact that there are proceedings abroad is not enough." The effect of those passages seems to me to be that the mere existence of other *h* proceedings abroad, the mere existence of a multiplicity of proceedings, is not to be taken into account at all as a disadvantage to the defendant. There has to be something more than that, and, depending on the extent of the advantages to the plaintiff of suing here, there may have to be much more than that. *The Atlantic Star* requires me to weigh on the one hand the advantage to the plaintiffs, and, on the other hand, the disadvantage to the defendants. As regards the advantage to the *j* plaintiffs it was not suggested in this case that the plaintiffs had any special advantage in suing in England, besides the advantage of being able to bring an action in the country of their choice. On that advantage, the right to choose the forum, Lord Wilberforce said in *The Atlantic Star* ([1973] 2 All ER 175 at 196, [1974] AC 436 at 470, that this right was an initial fact "which always requires displacement". In

a
other words, he was recognizing that a plaintiff need say no more to establish some advantage than that he has preferred to sue here where he is entitled to sue.'

In order that it should not be said that I am taking a passage which does not reflect the true balance of the judge's judgment, I would also refer to a passage where he says ([1977] 1 Lloyd's Rep 124 at 128):

b
'There might be cases, of course, where it could be shown not only that there was the extra cost and expense of a second action but that, having regard to the particular circumstances of the case, that cost and expense would be excessive and an unusual hardship to a particular defendant. No such case has sought to be made here. It was not suggested that the expense or the difficulty of fighting a second action here was so great as to constitute oppression on the defendants in this case.'

c
Counsel for the defendants submits that that decision no longer reflects the law following *The Atlantic Star* [1973] 2 All ER 175, [1974] AC 436 and *MacShannon v Rockware Glass Ltd*, to which I have already referred.

It is reasonably clear to me that Sheen J took the same view because in his judgment, having recorded that counsel for the plaintiffs had relied on *The Tillie Lykes* [1977] 1 Lloyd's Rep 124, he said:

d
'That case was heard and decided before the House of Lords gave judgment in *MacShannon v Rockware Glass Ltd* [1978] 1 All ER 625, [1978] AC 795 which lays down the principles to be applied on a motion such as this.'

Further, I think it is clear that the judge, in balancing the various factors, was giving very full weight, as, indeed, he was entitled to do on the view he took of the law, to the

e
fact that there were already proceedings on foot in Turkey. But I have come to the conclusion that in that the judge erred in principle. I see no reason for disagreeing with the judgment of Brandon J save in one minor respect. He said, after quoting Lord Wilberforce ([1977] 1 Lloyd's Rep 124 at 127):

'The effect of those passages seems to me to be that the mere existence of other proceedings abroad, the mere existence of a multiplicity of proceedings, is not to be

f
taken into account at all as a disadvantage to the defendant.'

That seems to me to be putting it too high. It is a factor of which account should be taken, but it is not a factor which, of itself, is of sufficient weight to displace the right of a plaintiff to choose his own forum and, of itself, to create a tilt in the other direction. But it is not weightless. If there are other factors, it will add some weight to those other factors. But in the light of the fact that it will not itself displace the right of a plaintiff to

g
choose his own forum, it is clearly a factor to which, save in exceptional circumstances, relatively little weight should be given. The exceptional circumstances are the circumstances to which Brandon J adverted in the second passage to which I referred (see [1977] 1 Lloyd's Rep 124 at 128).

I cannot see any situation here which would enable me to say that the fact that the

h
Turkish proceedings are in existence tilts the balance. The Cubans are entitled to come to this country. They are entitled to litigate their claim in this country. In the English proceedings it is a claim and not a counterclaim. If there is any serious inconvenience to the Turkish shipowners in being involved in two sets of proceedings, they have their remedy. They can transfer their claim here where it will be dealt with in the same proceedings as that of the Cubans.

For those reasons I would allow the appeal.

j

DUNN LJ. I agree. At the outset of his judgment the judge asked himself the question whether the Turkish court or the English court was the more appropriate forum for the trial of this action, and held on a balance of convenience that the Turkish court was clearly the more appropriate.

With respect to the judge, that was the wrong question to ask. *The Atlantic Star* [1973] 2 All ER 175, [1974] AC 436 and *MacShannon v Rockware Glass Ltd* [1978] 1 All ER 625, *a* [1978] AC 795 show that the English Court of Admiralty, whose jurisdiction has been invoked in rem, is prima facie the natural and appropriate forum in which to bring an action of this kind, and is recognised as such by international convention.

A mere balance of convenience is not a sufficient ground for depriving the plaintiffs of the advantages of pursuing their action in the Admiralty Court. The fact that there is a claim by the defendants against the plaintiffs already pending in Turkey is not of itself a *b* bar to the plaintiffs claiming in this country against the defendants for damages arising out of the same collision as is being litigated in Turkey: see *The Tillie Lykes* [1977] 1 Lloyd's Rep 124.

The judge suggested that, since the *Rockware Glass* case, *The Tillie Lykes* was no longer good law. Like Sir John Donaldson MR, I cannot accept that. *The Tillie Lykes* was decided after *The Atlantic Star*, and Brandon J, in considering the application for a stay, adopted *c* the test laid down in *St Pierre v South American Stores (Gath and Chaves) Ltd* [1936] KB 382 at 398, [1935] All ER Rep 408 at 414 by Scott LJ and explained in *The Atlantic Star*. The *Rockware Glass* case did no more than restate the second limb of Scott LJ's test, and in no way invalidated the judgment of Brandon J in *The Tillie Lykes*.

However, I can conceive that the fact that proceedings are pending in a foreign court might provide evidence that justice could be done between the parties in the foreign *d* court at substantially less inconvenience and expense than in the Admiralty Court in England. It seems to me that notwithstanding the apparently unequivocal statement of Brandon J, to which Sir John Donaldson MR has referred, in *The Tillie Lykes* [1977] 1 Lloyd's Rep 124 at 127, he accepted that possibility in the passage which Sir John Donaldson MR has cited. For clarity, it is quite short, I will cite it again (at 128):

'There might be cases, of course, where it could be shown not only that there was *e* the extra cost and expense of a second action but that, having regard to the particular circumstances of the case, that cost and expense would be excessive and an unusual hardship to a particular defendant. No such case has sought to be made here. It was not suggested that the expense or the difficulty of fighting a second action here was so great as to constitute oppression on the defendants in this case.'
f

That passage seems to me to stand as an accurate statement of the law if the word 'oppression' is deleted and replaced by appropriate words in accordance with the test now to be applied following the *Rockware Glass* case in deciding whether there is another forum to whose jurisdiction the defendant is amenable.

That may indeed be the case here so far as the defendants' claim against the plaintiffs is concerned, but it is certainly not so as far as the plaintiffs' claim is concerned, and that *g* seems to me to be the point of *The Tillie Lykes* because Brandon J concluded his judgment by saying this (at 128):

'It would no doubt be possible to have a doctrine of law under which the Court would regard the avoidance of a multiplicity of proceedings as something to be secured at all costs. You might have a system under which the Court always stayed the second of two actions brought in respect of the same subject-matter. I can see *h* advantages in such a doctrine. I can also see considerable disadvantages in it. In particular (as was pointed out in the course of the argument) the date on which a party begins an action may be a matter of luck without great significance. But whether it would be desirable to have such a doctrine of law or not, I am quite satisfied that such a doctrine is no part of the law of England. It was no part of the law of England before the House of Lords decided *The Atlantic Star* and in my *j* judgment it is no part of the law of England since the House of Lords decided *The Atlantic Star*.'

And I would add that it is no part of the law of England since the House of Lords decided *MacShannon v Rockware Glass Ltd*.

It is certainly true that this collision occurred in Turkish territorial waters, and in *The*
a *Atlantic Star* and *Gulf Oil Belgian SA v Finland Steamship Co Ltd, The Wellamo* [1980] 2
Lloyd's Rep 229, the only two collision cases in which stays have been granted in respect
of proceedings in the Admiralty Court, the collisions both occurred in territorial waters,
one in Belgian territorial waters in the River Schelde, and the other in Swedish territorial
waters when one of the vessels was approaching Stockholm. But that does not seem to
have been a decisive factor in the reasons which were given by the court for coming to
b the conclusion that another forum was available to the defendants and so a stay should
be granted.

In any event, I agree with Sir John Donaldson MR that the situation is distinguishable
in this case because the Bosphorus is an international waterway. The vessel was not
proceeding to Turkey, but she was using the Bosphorus pursuant to international
convention.

c So in my view the defendants do not fulfil the first condition which must be satisfied
before a stay is granted, the positive condition that there is another forum to whose
jurisdiction the defendants are amenable and in which justice can be done between the
parties at substantially less inconvenience or expense so far as the plaintiffs' claim in this
action is concerned.

But there is still the second condition, namely that the stay must not deprive the
d plaintiff of a legitimate juridical advantage which would be available to him if he invoked
the jurisdiction of the English courts.

The judge held that the plaintiffs would not be deprived of any juridical advantage if
the stay were granted. Once again, I cannot agree with that. The plaintiffs would lose the
juridical advantage of pursuing their claim as plaintiffs here in the Admiralty Court, and
having control of the action, rather than counterclaiming as defendants in Turkey. They
e also have the juridical advantage of not having to pay a deposit of 15% of the amount
claimed by way of counterclaim which they would have to pay if they counterclaimed
in the Turkish proceedings. There is a question as to how real that juridical advantage is
since they might be required to give security for costs in this country; but, at any rate,
on the first ground, namely that they can pursue their claim as plaintiffs here, I think
that they would be deprived of that juridical advantage.

f I agree with Sir John Donaldson MR that this appeal should be allowed and the stay
lifted.

PURCHAS LJ. I agree that this appeal should be allowed for the reasons that have
fallen from Sir John Donaldson MR and Dunn LJ. There is nothing that I feel I can
usefully add to the judgments which have already been delivered.

g
Appeal allowed.

7 July. The Appeal Committee of the House of Lords granted the defendants leave to appeal.

Solicitors: *Richards Butler & Co* (for the plaintiffs); *Holman Fenwick & Willan* (for the
defendants).

Frances Rustin   Barrister.

Tse Kwong Lam v Wong Chit Sen and others

PRIVY COUNCIL

LORD FRASER OF TULLYBELTON, LORD BRANDON OF OAKBROOK, LORD BRIGHTMAN, LORD TEMPLEMAN AND SIR JOHN MEGAW

9, 10, 11, 12, 16 MAY, 25 JULY 1983

Mortgage – Sale – Duty of mortgagee – Standard of duty in exercising power of sale – Duty to take reasonable care to obtain price equal to market value – Sale by auction – Sale to company in which mortgagee has an interest – Reserve price fixed by mortgagee – Advertisements announcing bare fact of auction with minimum description of property – Conditions of sale containing bare legal requirements – Mortgagee not obtaining expert or independent advice about sale – Property purchased by family company of mortgagee for reserve price – No competitive bidding at auction – Mortgagee providing interest-free loan to company to enable it to purchase property – Whether sale valid.

In 1963 the appellant arranged for the construction of a 15-storey building, containing 90 shop, office and flat units, on land leased by him in Hong Kong. He financed the construction partly by advance sales and partly by borrowing some $HK1·4m on the security of a mortgage over the remainder of the building under a legal charge which contained the usual power of sale. By 28 February 1966, 54 of the units remained unsold despite a considerable reduction in price and arrears of interest under the mortgage amounted to some $76,500. On 28 April the mortgagee required payment of all principal and interest due under the mortgage and gave notice of his intention to exercise his power of sale if payment was not made by 29 May. When the appellant failed to make payment the mortgagee arranged for the mortgaged property to be sold at public auction on 24 June and placed advertisements in three newspapers on three separate days giving notice of the auction and a minimum description of the property. The particulars and conditions of sale contained only the bare legal requirements and disclosed that there would be a reserve price and that the vendor reserved to himself the right to bid generally or withdraw the property at any time. The prospective purchaser was required to pay 20% of the purchase price on the date of the auction and the balance on or before 23 July 1966, time being of the essence. The mortgagee, without consulting the auctioneer or other estate agents about the sale or the reserve, fixed the reserve at $1·2m. On 20 June 1966 at a board meeting of a company which was financed entirely by the mortgagee and the directors of which were the mortgagee, his wife and his son, it was resolved that the mortgagee's wife should bid up to $1·2m for the property at the auction on behalf of the company. At the auction the auctioneer introduced the property, announced the reserve price (which he had been given shortly before the auction) and invited bids. The only bid came from the mortgagee's wife who bid the reserve price of $1·2m. The property was knocked down to her. Subsequently the mortgagee advanced $1·2m to the company by way of an interest-free loan and the company paid that sum to the mortgagee in return for an assignment of the property. The mortgagee then claimed some $400,000 from the appellant, being the amount alleged to be still outstanding in respect of principal and interest under the mortgage after payment of the $1·2m for the property. The appellant disputed the sum claimed and also counterclaimed to set aside the sale to the company on the ground that the sale to the company had been improper and at an undervalue. The mortgagee's claim was referred to an arbitrator, who found that the amount owed by the appellant was some $239,000. Judgment was given for that amount in favour of the mortgagee but execution was suspended pending determination of the appellant's counterclaim. In May 1979 judgment was given for the appellant on the counterclaim, the judge finding that the price paid by the company was not a proper price. However, the judge refused to set aside the sale to the company because of the lapse of time and instead awarded the appellant damages. On appeal by the mortgagee

and cross-appeal by the appellant, the Hong Kong Court of Appeal set aside the judgment.
a The appellant appealed to the Privy Council.

Held – (1) There was no inflexible rule that a mortgagee exercising his power of sale under a mortgage could not sell to a company in which he had an interest. However, the mortgagee and the company had to show that the sale was made in good faith and that the mortgagee had taken reasonable precautions to obtain the best price reasonably
b obtainable at the time, namely by taking expert advice as to the method of sale, the steps which ought reasonably to be taken to make the sale a success and the amount of the reserve. The mortgagee was not bound to postpone the sale in the hope of obtaining a better price or to adopt a piecemeal method of sale which could only be carried out over a substantial period or at some risk of loss, but sale by auction did not necessarily prove the validity of a transaction, since the price obtainable at an auction which produced only
c one bid might be less than the true market value (see p 59 *b c g h*, p 60 *h j* and p 63 *a b*, post); *York Buildings Co v Mackenzie* (1795) 3 Cr S & P 378, dictum of Kay J in *Warner v Jacob* (1882) 20 Ch D at 224, *Farrar v Farrars Ltd* (1888) 40 Ch D 395, *Kennedy v De Trafford* [1895–9] All ER Rep 408, *Hodson v Deans* [1903] 2 Ch 647 and dictum of Salmon LJ in *Cuckmere Brick Co Ltd v Mutual Finance Ltd* [1971] 2 All ER at 646 applied.

(2) Applying those principles, the company was not barred by law from purchasing
d the mortgaged property, but, in view of the close relationship between the company and the mortgagee and in particular the conflict of duty and interest to which the mortgagee was subject, the sale to the company could not be supported unless the mortgagee proved that he had taken all reasonable steps to obtain the best price reasonably obtainable. On the evidence, the mortgagee had failed to establish that. However, because the appellant had been guilty of inexcusable delay in prosecuting his counterclaim, he was not entitled
e to have the sale set aside but only to the alternative remedy of damages. It followed, therefore, that to that extent the appellant's appeal would be allowed (see p 60 *g*, p 62 *c* and p 63 *c d f g* and *j* to p 64 *a c d* and *f g*, post).

Notes
f For the mode of exercise of a power of sale in a mortgage and who may purchase, see 32 Halsbury's Laws (4th edn) paras 726–735, and for cases on the subject, see 35 Digest (Repl) 569–570, 2444–2466.

Cases referred to in judgment
Cuckmere Brick Co Ltd v Mutual Finance Ltd [1971] 2 All ER 633, [1971] Ch 949, [1971] 2
g   WLR 1207, CA.
Farrar v Farrars Ltd (1888) 40 ChD 395, CA.
Hodson v Deans [1903] 2 Ch 647.
Kennedy v De Trafford [1897] AC 180, [1895–9] All ER Rep 408, HL.
McHugh v Union Bank of Canada [1913] AC 299, PC.
Martinson v Clowes (1882) 21 Ch D 857.
h *Warner v Jacob* (1882) 20 Ch D 220.
York Buildings Co v Mackenzie (1795) 3 Cr S & P 378, HL.

Appeal
By a writ issued on 31 October 1966 the plaintiff, Wong Chit Sen (the mortgagee), claimed against the defendant, Tse Kwong Lam (the borrower), the sum of
j $HK382,855·70, the balance alleged to be outstanding in respect of principal and interest owing under a building mortgage, following the mortgagee's exercise of his power of sale. The borrower counterclaimed against the mortgagee and against Ching Wai Shork or Shook the mortgagee's wife and Chit Sen Co Ltd, the company, for an order, inter alia, to have the sale to the company set aside and for an account of rents and profits derived from the property or, alternatively, an account based on the true value of the property at

the material time, and damages. On 15 May 1979 Zimmern J sitting in the High Court of Hong Kong refused to set aside the sale to the company, gave judgment for the *a* borrower against the mortgagee for $950,000 and interest thereon at 1·2% as from 1 July 1966 and dismissed the appellant's claim against the mortgagee's wife and the company. The mortgagee appealed to the Court of Appeal of Hong Kong (Huggins, McMullin JJA and Garcia J), which allowed his appeal on 26 November 1980 and dismissed the borrower's cross-appeal which sought to have the sale declared void or set aside. The borrower appealed to the Privy Council with leave of the Court of Appeal. The facts are *b* set out in the judgment of the Board.

Donald Rattee QC and *Peter Crampin* for the borrower.
Richard Scott QC and *Oliver Albery* for the mortgagee, the mortgagee's wife and the company.

c

25 July. The following judgment of the Board was delivered.

LORD TEMPLEMAN. This appeal concerns the rights and obligations of a mortgagee in the exercise of his power of sale.

In 1963 the appellant borrower, Tse Kwong Lam, arranged for the construction of a building to be known as Kwong Hing Building on two sections of land at Kowloon held *d* by the borrower under a Crown lease for the residue of a term expiring in 1973 but with the right of renewal until 1997. The building was duly constructed of 15 storeys containing 90 units consisting of 6 shops on the ground floor, 12 offices on the first and second floor and 72 flats on the third to the fourteenth floors. The borrower financed the building construction partly by borrowing on the security of the property and partly by advance sales of the units. The borrower underestimated the cost of the building and *e* overestimated the prices obtainable for the units.

By 28 February 1966 the Kwong Hing Building had been completed and 36 units had been sold but 54 units remained to be sold notwithstanding that the original asking prices had been considerably reduced.

The building, save for the 36 units which had been sold, was by 28 February 1966 mortgaged to the first respondent, the mortgagee Wong Chit Sen, for a principal sum *f* and arrears of interest amounting to some $HK1·4m. These sums were secured on the terms of a legal charge dated 30 November 1963 which contained the usual power for the mortgagee to sell the mortgaged property as a whole or in lots by public auction or by private treaty. By notice dated 28 February 1966 the mortgagee informed the borrower that unless certain arrears of interest amounting to $76,548 were paid on or before 29 March 1966 the mortgagee would exercise his power of sale without further *g* notice. By a notice dated 28 April 1966 the mortgagee required payment of all the principal moneys and interest secured by the mortgage and warned that in default of payment on 29 May 1966 the mortgagee would exercise his power of sale. The mortgagee arranged for the mortgaged property to be sold by Messrs Lammert Bros by public auction at their auction room in Pedder Building, Victoria, Hong Kong on 24 June 1966 and placed advertisements of the auction in three newpapers circulating in Hong Kong *h* for publication in those newspapers on 9, 16 and 24 June. Particulars and conditions of sale were prepared by the mortgagee's solicitors and were dated 9 June. The property was described as being 54/90 parts of the building know as 52 and 54 Cheung Sha Wan Road, registered in the Land Office together with the sole and exclusive right and privilege to hold, use, occupy and enjoy the numbered shops, offices and flats of the building which remained unsold. The conditions of sale gave notice that there would be a reserve price *j* and that the vendor reserved the right to bid generally by himself or his agents or to withdraw the property at any time. The purchaser was to pay 20% of his purchase price on the date of the auction and was to pay the balance on or before 23 July 1966 and time was made of the essence.

On 20 June 1966 the mortgagee and his wife, the second respondent, Wong Cheng

Wai Shuk, held a meeting of the directors of the third respondent company, Chit Sen Co
Ltd, at which it was resolved, inter alia, that the mortgagee's wife—

> 'be appointed to attend at the office of the Lammert Brothers before 3 p.m. on
> the 26th June [sic] of this year to take part in the auction of Kwong Hing building
> but in principle the bidding price shall not exceed 1·2m dollars'.

At that time the directors of the company were three in number, namely the
mortgagee, the mortgagee's wife and the mortgagee's eldest son. The board meeting held
on 20 June 1966 was not attended by the eldest son who was abroad. The issued shares of
the company were held as to 50 by the mortgagee, 50 by the mortgagee's wife, 50 by the
eldest son and 40 by three infant children of the mortgagee. The company was financed
by non-interest bearing loans from the mortgagee.

On 24 June the mortgagee accompanied by his wife, his solicitor and his solicitor's
managing clerk attended the auction and informed the auctioneer that the reserve price
for the Kwong Hing Building was $1·2m. The mortgagee and his wife occupied seats in
the front row which, according to the managing clerk, usually were occupied by the
mortgagee and his advisers. The auctioneer introduced the property, announced that the
reserve price was $1·2m and invited bids from the 30 to 40 persons present. There was
no bid until the mortgagee's wife bid $1·2m and the property was knocked down to her.
Subsequently, the mortgagee advanced $1·2m to the company by way of interest free
loan and the company paid $1·2m to the mortgagee for an assignment of the Kwong
Hing Building dated 23 July 1966.

The mortgagee then claimed payment by the borrower of some $400,000 being the
difference alleged to be outstanding in respect of principal and interest owing under the
mortgage less the sum of $1·2m paid by the company for the Kwong Hing Building.
The borrower disputed the amount claimed and counterclaimed to set aside the sale to
the company on the grounds that the sale to the company was improper and that the
purchase price was an undervalue. It was subsequently found by an arbitrator's report
dated 26 February 1968 that the amount owing by the borrower to the mortgagee after
taking into account the sale price of $1·2m paid by the company and including interest
up to 29 June 1966 amounted to $238,933·39. Judgment was given for that amount but
execution was suspended pending determination of the borrower's counterclaim. That
counterclaim in which the borrower alleged impropriety, fraud and undervalue in the
sale to the company was dated 15 December 1966, but the borrower did not succeed in
obtaining judgment on the counterclaim until 15 May 1979 when Zimmern J found
that the price of $1·2m paid by the company was not a proper price but refused to set
aside the sale to the company after a lapse of 13 years and awarded the borrower damages
payable by the mortgagee of $950,000 and interest at 1·2% per month from 1 July 1966
until payment. By judgment dated 26 November 1980 the Court of Appeal of Hong
Kong (Huggins, McMullin JJA and Garcia J) allowed an appeal by the mortgagee, set
aside the judgment of Zimmern J and dismissed the borrower's cross-appeal which asked
for the sale to the company to be set aside. The borrower appeals to Her Majesty in
Council.

Counsel for the borrower submitted that the sale to the company should be set aside
because the mortgagee who sold the property was interested in the company which
bought the property. There was a conflict between the interest of the mortgagee as
vendor in obtaining the highest price and the interest of the mortgagee in the company
as purchaser to pay the lowest price. A sale by a mortgagee to a company in which he
was interested would only be upheld if the sale was at arm's length and the mortgagee
played no part in the decision of the company to buy or in the implementation of that
decision.

Counsel for the mortgagee submitted that a mortgagee may exercise his power of sale
in favour of a company in which the mortgagee is interested but must satisfy the
mortgagor or the court that the mortgagee took reasonable steps to obtain the true
market value. In the present case the mortgaged property was purchased by the company

at an auction which the courts below described as 'unimpeachable' or 'impeccable'. The price bid by the company and accepted by the auctioneer represented the true market value because no higher bid was received. Both counsel relied on authority for their submissions.

In *Warner v Jacob* (1882) 20 Ch D 220 at 224 Kay J after considering the authorities concluded:

> '. . . a mortgagee is strictly speaking not a trustee of the power of sale. It is a power given to him for his own benefit, to enable him the better to realize his debt. If he exercises it *bonâ fide* for that purpose, without corruption or collusion with the purchaser, the Court will not interfere even though the sale be very disadvantageous, unless indeed the price is so low as in itself to be evidence of fraud.'

In *Martinson v Clowes* (1882) 21 Ch D 857 at 860 North J said:

> 'It is quite clear that a mortgagee exercising his power of sale cannot purchase the property on his own account, and I think it clear also that the solicitor or agent of such mortgagee acting for him in the matter of the sale cannot do so either.'

Counsel for the borrower submitted that a mortgagee, his solicitor or agent cannot be allowed to purchase because they cannot resolve the conflict between their interest to buy for the lowest price with their duties to sell for the highest price. Therefore, he says, whenever there is such a conflict, the sale will not be upheld. In the present case there was clearly a conflict between the interest of the mortgagee in securing that the company secured the mortgaged property at the lowest price and the duty of the mortgagee to sell for the highest price. Counsel for the borrower admits that there can be no general rule that a company in which a mortgagee is interested cannot purchase the mortgaged property. He submits that the company can only do so where the sale is negotiated at arm's length and where it is clear that the mortgagee had no influence on the decision of the company to purchase or on the implementation of that decision.

In *Farrar v Farrars Ltd* (1888) 40 Ch D 395 a solicitor who was one of three mortgagees and acted for the mortgagees negotiated a sale in principle and agreed a price at the time when he had no connection with the purchasers. He subsequently took shares in a company formed by the purchasers to carry the sale into effect. Lindley LJ said (at 409):

> 'The plaintiffs on appeal did not question the view of the Judge that there was no fraudulent sale at an undervalue, but they contended that fraud or no fraud, undervalue or no undervalue, the sale could not stand, inasmuch as it was in substance a sale by a mortgagee to himself and others under the guise of a sale to a limited company.'

That submission was rejected. Lindley LJ also said (at 409–411):

> 'A sale by a person to a corporation of which he is a member is not, either in form or in substance, a sale by a person to himself . . . There is no authority for saying that such a sale is not warranted by an ordinary power of sale . . . But although this is true, it is obvious that a sale by a person to an incorporated company of which he is a member may be invalid upon various grounds, although it may not be reached by the rule which prevents a man from selling to himself or to a trustee for himself. Such a sale may, for example, be fraudulent and at an undervalue or it may be made under circumstances which throw upon the purchasing company the burden of proving the validity of the transaction, and the company may be unable to prove it . . . A mortgagee with a power of sale, though often called a trustee, is in a very different position from a trustee for sale. A mortgagee is under obligations to the mortgagor, but he has rights of his own which he is entitled to exercise adversely to the mortgagor. A trustee for sale has no business to place himself in such a position as to give rise to a conflict of interest and duty. But every mortgage confers upon the mortgagee the right to realize his security and to find a purchaser if he can, and

a
if in exercise of his power he acts *bonâ fide* and takes reasonable precautions to obtain a proper price, the mortgagor has no redress, even although more might have been obtained for the property if the sale had been postponed . . .'

The Court of Appeal concluded (at 415):

b
'The sale here impeached having been made honestly and at a fair value, ought, in our opinion, to be allowed to stand, and there is no hard and fast rule which compels us to hold the contrary.'

In the view of this Board on authority and on principle there is no hard and fast rule that a mortgagee may not sell to a company in which he is interested. The mortgagee and the company seeking to uphold the transaction must show that the sale was in good faith and that the mortgagee took reasonable precautions to obtain the best price reasonably obtainable at the time. The mortgagee is not however bound to postpone the
c
sale in the hope of obtaining a better price or to adopt a piecemeal method of sale which could only be carried out over a substantial period or at some risk of loss. This view of the matter is consistent with the decision of the House of Lords in the *York Buildings Co v MacKenzie* (1795) 3 Cr S & P 378. In that case an agent for creditors purchased an estate of the insolvent at auction. The sale was set aside although 11 years elapsed before the sale was impugned. Lord Loughborough LC referred to two extreme arguments (at 398),
d
first that 'the quality of common agent, barred his exercising any right as a purchaser', and second, that—

'if he was not disabled absolutely in point of law from purchasing, he must stand in the position of all the rest of mankind, and might purchase as advantageously as he could, provided there was no gross practice or direct fraud.'

e
The Lord Chancellor rejected both extremes and held that agents were entitled to purchase but—

'The bargain must be perfectly fair and equal, at the best price, because they are placed in a situation which they are bound, in the first instance, to act against their own advantage, and for the advantage of their employers; and if they sacrifice that
f
interest and advantage, with view of profiting and taking the interest of it to themselves, the purchase will be liable to be set aside, the advantage will not come to themselves, and the breach of confidence will not avail them.'

(See 3 Cr S & P 378 at 398–399.)

In the present case in which the mortgagee held a large beneficial interest in the shares of the purchasing company, was a director of the company and was entirely responsible
g
for financing the company, the other shareholders being his wife and children, the sale must be closely examined and a heavy onus lies on the mortgagee to show that in all respects he acted fairly to the borrower and used his best endeavours to obtain the best price reasonably obtainable for the mortgaged property.

Sale by auction does not necessarily prove the validity of a transaction. In *Hodson v Deans* [1903] 2 Ch 647, at a sale by auction by a friendly society in exercise of their power
h
of sale as mortgagees, the secretary of the committee which fixed the reserve and instructed the auctioneer bought the property for himself having '. . . conceived the idea of buying . . . and making a profit for himself out of the transaction' (see per Joyce J at 651). The judge found (at 653) that—

'the property was sold at an undervalue, not of itself so great as to invalidate the
j
sale, but still at an undervalue. The investment committee could not have sold privately to themselves either as representing the society or as individuals at a price fixed by themselves, nor could they, I think, have so sold to one or more of their number. It is said that any such objection is cured by the fact that the sale was by auction. I do not think so. At all events . . . the onus is on the defendant to shew that everything was done fairly and *bonâ fide*.'

In *Kennedy v De Trafford* [1897] AC 180, [1895–9] All ER Rep 408 a mortgagee sold
the mortgaged property to one of two mortgagors who were entitled to the equity of   *a*
redemption as tenants in common for a sum equal to the mortgage debt. Lord Herschell
was—

> 'disposed to think that if a mortgagee in exercising his power of sale exercises it
> in good faith, without any intention of dealing unfairly by his mortgagor, it would
> be very difficult indeed, if not impossible, to establish that he had been guilty of any   *b*
> breach of duty towards the mortgagor.'

But in that case he advised the House that—

> 'if you were to accept the definition . . . for which the appellant contends, namely,
> that the mortgagee is bound to take reasonable precautions in the exercise of his
> power of sale, as well as to act in good faith, still in this case he did take reasonable
> precautions. Of course all the circumstances of the case must be looked at.'   *c*

(See [1897] AC 180 at 185, [1895–9] All ER Rep 408 at 411.)

The circumstances there were that the mortgagee had told each of the mortgagors that
he wished to sell and was willing to take a sum sufficient to discharge the mortgage. No
offer or objection was made by the mortgagor who subsequently sought to impugn the
sale.   *d*

In *McHugh v Union Bank of Canada* [1913] AC 299 at 311 Lord Moulton in tendering
the advice of the Privy Council said:

> 'It is well settled law that it is the duty of a mortgagee when realizing the
> mortgaged property by sale to behave in conducting such realization as a reasonable
> man would behave in the realization of his own property, so that the mortgagor
> may receive credit for the fair value of the property sold.'   *e*

Finally, in *Cuckmere Brick Co Ltd v Mutual Finance Ltd* [1971] 2 All ER 633 at 646,
[1971] Ch 949 at 968 Salmon LJ, after considering all the relevant authorities including
the views expressed in *Kennedy v De Trafford*, concluded, with the subsequent agreement
of Cross and Cairns LJJ, that—

> 'both on principle and authority, that the mortgagee in exercising his power of   *f*
> sale does owe a duty to take reasonable precautions to obtain the true market value
> of the mortgaged property at the date on which he decides to sell it.'

In the result their Lordships consider that in the present case the company was not
debarred from purchasing the mortgaged property but, in view of the close relationship
between the company and the mortgagee and in view in particular of the conflict of duty   *g*
and interest to which the mortgagee was subject, the sale to the company for $1·2m can
only be supported if the mortgagee proves that he took reasonable precautions to obtain
the best price reasonably obtainable at the time of sale.

On behalf of the mortgagee it was submitted that all reasonable steps were taken when
the mortgagee, with adequate advertisement, sold the property at a properly conducted
auction to the highest bidder. The submission assumes that such an auction must produce   *h*
the best price reasonably obtainable or, as Salmon LJ expressed the test, the true market
value. But the price obtained at any particular auction may be less than the price
obtainable by private treaty and may depend on the steps taken to encourage bidders to
attend. An auction which only produces one bid is not necessarily an indication that the
true market value has been achieved.

In the present case, the mortgagee threatened on 28 February 1966 to sell the property   *j*
if certain arrears of interest was not paid; it was then obvious that the borrower was in
difficulties. On 28 April the mortgagee called in the principal and gave notice of his
intention to sell the property if the principal and interest, which the mortgagee alleged
to amount to $1·6m, were not paid by 29 May 1966. The mortgagee had ample
opportunity to consult and instruct estate agents. The property could have been offered

for sale by auction or by private treaty or by announcing that the property would be sold
a by public auction if not previously sold by private treaty. The property could have been
sold as a whole or in units. The mortgagee might have been advised that, as happened, a
sale by auction might not produce any independent bidders; that the number of potential
purchasers able and willing in 1966 to pay over $1m for this building was limited; that,
to obtain a purchaser by private treaty or to obtain sufficient interest to justify an auction,
it would be necessary for the estate agents to approach their clients and other persons
b known to be interested in property purchase, investment and speculation and to provide
them with full information about the construction of the building, the terms on which
parts had already been sold, the provisions for sharing expenses and maintenance, the
existing condition of the building, its advantages and prospects. The auctioneers to be
employed in selling the property by auction, if this was necessary or desirable, could have
been instructed to seek out potential purchasers and bidders and to arouse interest in the
c property. The mortgagee was advised by his solicitor's managing clerk that a sale by
auction was 'fairer' but the mortgagee does not appear to have considered the possibility
that a higher price could be obtained by a sale by private treaty to an independent third
party at a price recommended by an estate agent as being the best obtainable after the
agent had had an opportunity to explore the market. Moreover, the mortgagee does not
appear to have taken any step to secure any interest in the auction. The mortgagee's
d solicitors prepared particulars and conditions of sale which were dated 9 June. On the
same day the sale was advertised in three newspapers. There is no evidence that the
advertisement did more than give notice of the bare fact of the auction coupled with a
minimum description of the property. The particulars and conditions of sale contained
only the legal requirements. There was no evidence that anyone requested a copy of the
particulars and conditions or asked to inspect the property. The conditions of sale
e disclosed that there was a reserve price, that the vendor reserved the right to bid, that
20% of the purchase price was payable after the auction and that the balance was payable
one month thereafter, time being of the essence. A reader of the first advertisement had
just 15 days in which to make detailed inquiries and investigations and to organise his
finances so that he was prepared to engage in competitive bidding possibly with a vendor
and with a borrower who knew all about the property and might be puffing the sale.
f There was no evidence that anyone took the elementary precautions which a purchaser
of a building for a sum in excess of $1m would expect to take before venturing to bid at
an auction.

The mortgagee could have consulted estate agents about the method of sale and about
the method of securing the best price. At the very least he could have consulted an estate
agent about the level of the reserve price. The auctioneer was not informed of the reserve
g price until immediately before the auction and in evidence he very properly declined to
comment on the reserve because he had not valued the property.

This confirms the impression that the auctioneers were not instructed to do more than
put the property under the hammer, a procedure which may be appropriate to the sale
of secondhand furniture but is not necessarily conducive to the attainment of the best
price for freehold or leasehold property. It was not of course in the interests of the
h company that enthusiasm for the sale should be stimulated or that the reserve should be
settled by anyone other than the mortgagee.

The reserve of $1·2m was fixed by the mortgagee and was the price at which he
advised and intended that the company should purchase. The mortgagee was a property
investor and speculator. The company was his family company and he held shares in and
financed the company. The mortgagee would not have advised the company to bid
j $1·2m for the property unless he thought that was an advantageous price for the
company to pay.

The company, unlike an independent bidder, knew all about the property through the
mortgagee and knew the amount of the reserve in advance. The company and the
mortgagee did not have to arrange finance. The company bought the property for $1·2m
provided by the mortgagee who received back that sum in reduction of his mortgage

debt. The sale transferred from the borrower to the mortgagee's family company at a
price advised by the mortgagee the chance of making a profit which the mortgagee could   *a*
not acquire for himself. The borrower was exposed to an action for $200,000 being the
difference between $1·2m, the price paid by the company and $1·4m the amount of the
mortgage debt. That left the mortgagee with a hold over the borrower which he exercised
when the borrower complained about the sale. If, as appeared probable, the borrower
could not pay $200,000 the mortgagee would suffer a loss which he could have prevented
by advising the company to bid $1·4m for the property. No doubt the mortgagee did   *b*
what was best for himself and the company.

The only indication that $1·2m represented the market value of the property was the
fact that no one at the auction bid more than $1·2m. But the fact that no one bid more
than $1·2m at this auction does not necessarily mean that the property could not have
been sold for more than $1·2m if the mortgagee had consulted estate agents about the
method of sale and the amount of the reserve and had instructed them to try to interest   *c*
the investing public in the property. There was no competitive bidding and the company
purchased the property at a price fixed by the mortgagee. There is no sufficient evidence
that this particular auction produced the true market value.

On behalf of the mortgagee, counsel objected that the pleadings did not allege that the
mortgagee should have taken more precautions than he in fact took to obtain the best
price. At the trial the mortgagee was not asked why he had not consulted the auctioneers   *d*
or other estate agents about the sale or about the reserve. Their Lordships were impressed
with counsel's forceful arguments and with his submission that the judges of Hong Kong
are the best judges as to the propriety and effectiveness of steps taken in local conditions
to procure the best price reasonably obtainable at the sale of a Crown lease. But counsel
for the mortgagee rightly accepted that in the circumstances the mortgagee must
shoulder the burden of proving that the mortgagee took all reasonable steps to obtain the   *e*
best price reasonably obtainable. The mortgagee made no effect to discharge that burden
but relied simply on the fact that, fortified by the vague approval of a solicitor's managing
clerk, he submitted the property to auction after proper advertisement.

The auction took place on 24 June 1966 and by December 1966 the borrower had filed
a counterclaim alleging, inter alia, that the auction price of $1·2m was a gross undervalue.
The borrower sought an account on the basis of what was the true value of the building   *f*
at the date of the auction and damages equal to the diffence between the true value and
the price realised. Despite these allegations the mortgagee came to trial without any
contemporaneous or other evidence as to the value of the building at the date of the
auction. At the trial the judge was asked to determine 'agreed issues' which included the
question whether the auction sale should be set aside or damages awarded for 'collusion
and bad faith (equitable fraud) and or negligence in relation to the sale'. The mortgagee   *g*
did not proffer any evidence seeking to justify the steps which he took to sell the building
or any expert evidence that any other steps would have been futile. The mortgagee gave
evidence that his solicitor's managing clerk advised that an auction sale was 'fairer'. Even
this vague advice shows that the mortgagee realised that he ought to seek some advice
about the method of sale; he ought to have realised that a solicitor's managing clerk was
not the best person to give such advice. It is impossible to imagine any sound reason why   *h*
the mortgagee did not consult the auctioneers about the method of sale or about the
possibility of stimulating interest in the auction. In any event the advice of the managing
clerk did not explain or justify the failure of the mortgagee to consult the auctioneers
about the reserve price. There being no relevant cross-examination the court could not
assume that the mortgagee thought that the advice of or valuation by the auctioneers or
some other expert might prove an embarrassment. But in the circumstances in which   *j*
the building came to be sold without any bid save the bid of the company made on the
advice of the mortgagee and in the absence of any contemporaneous and expert
independent advice whatsoever, the price paid by the company proved nothing about
the value of the building. At the trial and on this appeal the mortgagee adopted the
attitude that a mortgagee exercising his power of sale is entitled to secure the mortgaged

a property for a company in which he is interested at a price advised by the mortgagee provided that the property is properly advertised and sold by auction. A decision to this effect would expose borrowers to greater perils than those to which they are now subject as a result of decisions which enable a mortgagee to chose the date of the exercise of his power. A mortgagee who wishes to secure the mortgaged property for a company in which he is interested ought to show that he protected the interests of the borrower by taking expert advice as to the method of sale, as to the steps which ought reasonably be

b taken to make the sale a success and as to the amount of the reserve. There was no difficulty in obtaining such advice orally and in writing and no good reason why a mortgagee, concerned to act fairly towards his borrower, should fail or neglect to obtain or act on such advice in all respects as if the mortgagee were desirous of realising the best price reasonably obtainable at the date of the sale for property belonging to the mortgagee himself.

c   Where a mortgagee fails to satisfy the court that he took all reasonable steps to obtain the best price reasonably obtainable and that his company bought at the best price, the court will, as a general rule, set aside the sale and restore to the borrower the equity of redemption of which he has been unjustly deprived. But the borrower will be left to his remedy in damages against the mortgagee for the failure of the mortgagee to secure the best price if it will be inequitable as between the borrower and the purchaser for the sale

d to be set aside. In the present case it is submitted on behalf of the mortgagee and the company that the borrower is debarred by the terms of his mortgage from any remedy save damages. Alternatively, the mortgagee and the company submit that the delay on the part of the borrower in pursuing his counterclaim has rendered it unjust for the building to be restored to the borrower.

        By the legal charge dated 30 November 1963 the mortgagee agreed not to exercise his

e power of sale or other powers in relation to the building until he gave notice in writing or unless the borrower defaulted in the payment of interest or in the observance of his covenants. The legal charge also provided that—

        'the remedy of the Mortgagor in respect of any breach of the clauses or provisions hereinbefore contained with respect to the letting, leasing or sale of the premises shall be in damages only . . .'

f
But, in the view of the Board, there is nothing in the legal charge that enables or could enable the mortgagee to uphold a sale which is defective because the mortgagee failed to fulfil the duty imposed on him by the law to take all reasonable steps to obtain the best price reasonably obtainable. The borrower is not therefore debarred by the terms of the legal charge from seeking to set aside the sale to the company.

g   The borrower has however been guilty of inexcusable delay in prosecuting his counterclaim. The mortgagee's writ was issued on 31 October 1966, the borrower's defence and counterclaim were filed on 17 December 1966 and the mortgagee obtained judgment on his claim on 16 November 1968. The successive delays which took place thereafter were the responsibility of the borrower. In particular two years elapsed between the date in 1970 when the borrower filed an amended counterclaim and the

h date in 1972 when the borrower took out a summons for directions. A further five years elapsed between the date in 1972 when the court ordered that the action should be set down for trail within 40 days and the date in 1977 when the action was in fact set down for trial. The borrower contends that these delays have not been prejudicial to the mortgagee who will receive principal and interest. But the borrower also seeks an account from the mortgagee on the basis of wilful default. Moreover, either the mortgagee or

j the company must have been put to expense in maintenance and repairs of the building and may have laid out moneys on other matters which could have been better employed elsewhere. The borrower by his delay achieved a favourable position; if the property decreased in value he could either abandon his action or seek damages in setting aside the sale. If the property increased in value he could persist with his claim to set aside the sale. In the circumstances the Board consider that the borrower is not entitled to have the sale

set aside but is entitled to the alternative remedy of damages. That was the view taken
by the trial judge.   *a*

The measure of damages must be the difference between the best price reasonably
obtainable on 24 June 1966 and the price of $1·2m paid by the company. The trial judge
assessed these damages at $950,000. The Court of Appeal in Hong Kong strongly
criticised the evidence on which this assessment was made. The oral evidence of a valuer
who gave evidence for the borrower was vitiated by the fact that the valuer was supplied
with insufficient information and assumed a sale of individual parts of the building over   *b*
a period. There was more cogent evidence in the form of a letter from the Wing On Life
Assurance Co dated 26 April 1966 whereby the insurance company agreed in principle
to advance $1·5m on the security of the building. There was evidence that the insurance
company would not normally advance more than 70% of the value of a security thus
valuing the building at nearly $2·15m. This was cogent evidence, save that there was no
direct evidence from the representative of the insurance company who valued the   *c*
building for the purpose of making the offer. More particularly, there was no evidence
of the amount by which the building declined in value between April and June 1966.
The Court of Appeal recognised and identified a general fall in the value of real property
in Hong Kong between April and June 1966. In these circumstances the Board consider
that the action must be remitted to the Court of Appeal of Hong Kong for that court to
make such directions as may be considered necessary for the assessment of damages.   *d*

Counsel for the borrower and the respondents have very helpfully agreed the form of
the order which is appropriate in the light of the conclusions reached by the Board. The
draft minutes of order settled by counsel are attached to this judgment. The respondents
object to the award of interest on the damages payable to the borrower as provided by
the order, but their Lordships consider the mortgage rate of interest which was payable
to the mortgagee pursuant to the terms of the mortgage should be paid to the borrower   *e*
as from 24 June 1966.

In all the circumstances of the present case, however, taking into account the delays
for which the borrower was responsible and the deficiencies of the pleadings and evidence
and cross-examination their Lordships consider that the borrower is only entitled to
receive from the mortgagee and the company jointly and severally 50% of the costs of
the trial, the appeal to the Court of Appeal and the appeal to the Board. The respondents   *f*
must pay their own costs.

Their Lordships will accordingly humbly advise Her Majesty that this appeal should
be allowed in accordance with the terms set out in their Lordships' judgment and the
draft minutes of order settled by counsel and that the action ought to be remitted to the
Court of Appeal of Hong Kong for that court to make such directions as may be
considered necessary for the assessment of damages by the High Court.   *g*

Appeal allowed. Order accordingly.

Solicitors: *Stephenson Harwood* (for the borrower); *Norton Rose Botterell & Roche* (for the
mortgagee, the mortgagee's wife and the company).

Mary Rose Plummer   Barrister.

a   # Western Heritable Investment Co Ltd v Husband

HOUSE OF LORDS

LORD FRASER OF TULLYBELTON, LORD KEITH OF KINKEL, LORD ROSKILL, LORD BRIGHTMAN AND LORD TEMPLEMAN

b   27, 28 JUNE, 27 JULY 1983

Rent restriction – Fair rent – Scarcity element – Assumption that number of persons seeking to rent houses in a locality does not outnumber houses available for rent – Whether deduction to be made in assessing fair rent on account of scarcity element – Rent (Scotland) Act 1971, s 42(2).

c *Rent restriction – Fair rent – Scarcity element – Evidence of capital value not conclusive basis of fair rent – Whether yield on invested capital an essential ingredient in determining fair rent – Whether rent of comparable properties discounting scarcity value best guide to fair rent – Rent (Scotland) Act 1971, s 42(2).*

The landlords applied to a rent officer for the determination of a fair rent for an
d unfurnished house which was let under a regulated tenancy. The house was in an area of Scotland where there was a scarcity of houses available to rent. When the landlords objected to the fair rent determined by the rent officer the matter was referred to a rent assessment committee, which determined the fair rent by comparing the property with 80 similar houses the fair rent for which had been fixed by another rent assessment committee three months earlier. That committee had made its determination by first
e ascertaining the capital value of the houses with vacant possession, then taking 6% of that value as being a fair return for the landlord, then deducting certain sums representing repairs and other expenses and further deducting 40% of the landlord's notional return because the houses were in an area of relatively high scarcity. The landlords appealed to the Court of Session, contending that the rent assessment committee had erred in law in following the previous committee's decision to make a deduction for scarcity value,
f because s 42(2)[a] of the Rent (Scotland) Act 1971 required the rent officer and rent assessment committee to assume that the number of persons seeking to rent houses in a locality did not outnumber the number of houses available for rent in that locality and therefore created an irrebuttable presumption that there was no scarcity of houses available for rent regardless of the real situation and that accordingly the actual rents being paid in the market were to be presumed to be the rents which would be paid in a
g balanced market. The Court of Session allowed the landlords' appeal. The tenant appealed to the House of Lords.

Held – Since the purpose of the 1971 Act was to favour tenants by protecting them from any increases of rent which would otherwise be caused by demand exceeding supply, the effect of s 42(2) of the 1971 Act was that the fair rent was to be determined on the
h hypothetical basis that there was no scarcity of accommodation to let. Therefore, if there was in fact such a scarcity, then, depending on the circumstances, some allowance or deduction had to be made if the actual rent or the return on actual capital value was used to determine the fair rent. Furthermore, yield on invested capital was not an essential ingredient in determining a 'fair rent', since the best guide to the fair rent was the rent, if available, of comparable properties which did not reflect scarcity value or which was
j discounted so as not to reflect scarcity value. Since there was evidence before both committees that the capital value was enhanced by the scarcity of accommodation and since both committees had correctly discounted the scarcity value, the tenant's appeal would be allowed (see p 66 e f, p 67 c to f, p 68 f to j, p 70 b to f and p 71 b to d and f to j, post).

---

a   Section 42(2) is set out at p 67 h j, post

Notes
For determination of fair rent, see 27 Halsbury's Laws (4th edn) para 731.

Section 70(1) and (2) of the Rent Act 1977 corresponds to s 42(1) and (2) of the Rent *a*
(Scotland) Act 1971. For s 70 of the 1977 Act, see 47 Halsbury's Statutes (3rd edn) 476.

Case referred to in opinions
Skilling v Arcari's Executors 1974 SC(HL) 42.

Appeal   *b*
Janet Boyd Husband (the tenant) appealed with leave of the Appeal Committee of the
House of Lords granted on 24 February 1983 against an interlocutor of the Extra Division
of the Court of Session in Scotland (Lord Avonside and Lord Kincraig, Lord Dunpark
dissenting) dated 18 November 1982 allowing an appeal by the landlords, Western
Heritable Investment Co Ltd, against a decision of a rent assessment committee sitting in   *c*
Glasgow dated 29 October 1980 in respect of the registration of a fair rent for an
unfurnished dwelling house situated at 49 Burnfoot Drive, Glasgow let under a regulated
tenancy on a reference by a rent officer at the instance of the landlords. The facts are set
out in the opinion of Lord Keith.

Brian Gill QC and *Jonathan Mitchell* (both of the Scottish Bar) for the tenant.
Peter K Vandore QC and *D I Mackay* (both of the Scottish Bar) for the landords.   *d*

Their Lordships took time for consideration.

27 July. The following opinions were delivered.

LORD FRASER OF TULLYBELTON. My Lords, I have had the advantage of *e*
reading in advance the speeches prepared by my noble and learned friends Lord Keith
and Lord Brightman, and I entirely agree with them. I add a few comments of my own
only because we are differing from the majority of the court below.

The rent assessment committee in the present case determined the fair rent of the
house occupied by the appellant, by relying on the comparative method, using for   *f*
comparison the rents determined for 80 similar houses on 28 July 1980 by another
committee, the chairman of which was a Mr Kennedy. The Kennedy committee made
their determination by first finding the capital values of the houses, with vacant
possession. They then applied to the capital value a rate of 6% to represent a reasonable
return to the landlord. From the resulting figure they made deductions for repairs and
other expenses, and also a deduction of 40% because the houses were in an area of
relatively high scarcity. The question at issue in the present appeal is whether that   *g*
deduction of 40% for scarcity was one that the Kennedy committee were entitled to
make in accordance with s 42 of the Rent (Scotland) Act 1971 or not. The majority of the
Extra Division of the Court of Session (Lord Avonside and Lord Kincraig, with Lord
Dunpark dissenting) held that the scarcity deduction ought not to have been made and
that the Kennedy committee's computation of fair rents was vitiated by their error in   *h*
making the deduction and ought not to have been relied on by the committee in the
present case. Section 42 of the 1971 Act is quoted by Lord Keith and I need not repeat it.

Lord Avonside expressed the view that to make a deduction for scarcity in a calculation
such as that made by the Kennedy committee was 'plainly wrong and ignores the
provision of s 42(2) of the Act.' The final words of his opinion were that the case should
be sent back to the committee to proceed as accords 'under direction that their use of a   *j*
"scarcity" element in their determination is *wrong in law*' (my emphasis). His Lordship
thus reached his decision on the basis that the issue was one of law, not depending on
evidence. Lord Kincraig reached the same conclusion as Lord Avonside, partly on the
same ground. Thus, Lord Kincraig said that the assessment committee, by making a
deduction because of the scarcity of houses to let, had 'made an assumption which is not
warranted by s 42(2) of the Act. Indeed, the subsection requires them to make the very

opposite assumption, that there is no scarcity of houses to let'. Lord Kincraig relied also
a on a second ground, which was that, in his view, there was no evidence that the capital
value of houses was influenced by any scarcity of houses to let. I shall return to that point
in a moment.

With regard to the issue of law, on which both Lord Avonside and Lord Kincraig
relied, they seem to have read the proviso in s 42(2) that 'it shall be assumed that the
number of persons seeking to become tenants . . . is not substantially greater than the
b number of . . . dwelling-houses' as creating an irrebuttable presumption of fact that there
is no scarcity, whatever the true facts may be. With the utmost respect that impresses me
as a most improbable construction of the subsection, especially considering that the main
reason why the 1971 Act, and the various Acts thereby consolidated, were passed, was
the notorious shortage of accommodation to let, particularly by private landlords. If the
effect of s 42(2) was to create such an irrebuttable presumption, I do not understand why
c the fair rent should be different from the market rent, or why the system of registration
of rents, introduced by the Rent Act 1965, and now contained in Pt IV of the 1971 Act
was necessary at all.

In my opinion, the effect of s 42(2) is to direct that the fair rent is to be determined on
the assumption that there is no scarcity of accommodation to let. Accordingly, if there is
such scarcity in fact, some allowance or deduction may have to be made for it when
d actual rents (or the return on actual capital values) are used for determining fair rents.
Whether any allowance or deduction should be made, and, if so, how much it should be,
are questions of fact to be determined on the evidence, mainly of experts in valuation.
Lord Kincraig, in the second ground of his opinion, accepted that proposition but he
held that in none of the appeals before the court was there 'any evidence' that the capital
value of the houses taken for the purposes of comparison had been influenced 'at all' by
e any shortage of houses to let within the area. I infer from that if he had been satisfied on
the evidence that the capital value of the houses was influenced by the shortage of houses
to let, he would have thought it right to make some allowance for the effect of such
influence. That appears to me to be the correct approach although I am, with respect,
unable to agree that there is no evidence to show that the capital value was affected by
the shortage of houses let. On that matter I am in full agreement with the views
f expressed by Lord Keith. I agree also with the opinion of Lord Dunpark.

I would allow the appeal and restore the finding of the committee.

LORD KEITH OF KINKEL. My Lords, this appeal arises out of a determination by
a rent assessment committee sitting in Glasgow, dealing with a reference by a rent officer
at the instance of the landlords relating to the fair rents for certain dwelling houses
g subject to regulated tenancies under the Rent (Scotland) Act 1971.

The issue in the appeal is concerned with the provisions of s 42(1) and (2) of the 1971
Act, which at the material time were in these terms:

'(1) In determining for the purposes of this Part of this Act what rent is or would
be a fair rent under a regulated tenancy of a dwelling-house, regard shall be had,
subject to the following provisions of this section, to all the circumstances (other
h than personal circumstances) and in particular to the age, character and locality of
the dwelling-house and to its state of repair.

(2) For the purposes of the determination it shall be assumed that the number of
persons seeking to become tenants of similar dwelling-houses in the locality on the
terms (other than those relating to rent) of the regulated tenancy is not substantially
greater than the number of such dwelling-houses in the locality which are available
j for letting on such terms.'

Before the committee the landlords put forward, through the evidence of a surveyor,
certain figures of rent based on the decision of another committee made as at mid-1976,
adjusted to take into account an allowance for insurance and management and also for
the increase in the cost of repairs and the effect of inflation since that time. This brought
out a rent of £855 for a four-apartment house and one of £950 for a five-apartment

house. In support of these figures the surveyor submitted a calculation based on a fair
return on capital value. He estimated the capital value of a typical house at £15,200, and *a*
a fair return at 6%. From this he deducted 35% for scarcity (bringing out £593), while
maintaining that no such deduction ought properly to be made, and added to the
resultant figure certain sums for repairs, insurance and management, making a total of
£905 for a four-apartment house.

The committee did not accept the surveyor's computation based on the mid-1976
registered rents, nor his estimate of £15,200 for capital value. They took the view that *b*
there was insufficient evidence to enable them to proceed on the basis of present-day
market rents, and preferred to rely on the fair rents fixed for 80 comparable houses by
the determination of another committee (the Kennedy committee) given about three
months previously. In the result, they fixed the fair rent for a four-apartment house at
£725 and for a five-apartment house at £750, which represented a modest increase on
those fixed by the rent officer. *c*

Before the Kennedy committee, the landlords' witness had put forward a computation
of fair rent based on a vacant possession capital value for a four-apartment house of
£15,500, reduced by 33⅓% in respect of 'scarcity', a fair return of 7%, and additions in
respect of repairs, insurance and management, bringing out a final figure of £946. The
committee took the view that the vacant possession capital value was properly to be
estimated at £14,000, that a figure of 6% was appropriate for a fair return, and that 40% *d*
should be deducted as being what they regarded as appropriate for an area of 'relatively
high scarcity'. They accepted the landlords' figures for repairs etc, and in the result
brought out a figure of £727.

The landlords appealed to the Court of Session under s 13 of the Tribunals and
Inquiries Act 1958, their principal contention being that the committee had erred in law
by failing to form any conclusion on the propriety of making a deduction in respect of *e*
'scarcity' from vacant possession capital value, and in relying on the decision of the
Kennedy committee, which was arrived at by making a deduction of that character.

The appeal came before an Extra Division of the Inner House which by a majority
(Lord Avonside and Lord Kincraig, Lord Dunpark dissenting) allowed the appeal and
remitted back to the committee to reassess the fair rents in the light of their opinions.

The first matter for consideration is the true intendment of s 42(2) of the 1971 Act. In *f*
my opinion it is clear that on a proper construction s 42(2) requires fair rents to be
determined on the hypothetical basis that the house-letting market in the locality is in a
state of equilibrium, in respect that the number of comparable houses available for
letting does not substantially exceed the number of persons seeking to become tenants.
If the actual state of affairs is that the market is unbalanced, in respect that the demand
for houses to let substantially exceeds the supply, then the rents actually paid in the *g*
market will reflect the imbalance, being higher than they would be in a balanced market.
In that situation it will be necessary for the rent officer and the rent assessment
committee, in so far as in striking a fair rent they rely on the rents actually being paid in
the market, to apply to these rents a discounting procedure in order to eliminate from
them the element which is attributable to the relative scarcity of houses available for
letting. Where some method of valuation other than comparison with market rents is *h*
adopted, the exercise will be less straightforward. But it will be necessary to proceed in
such a way that the resultant figure of fair rent accords with the statutory hypothesis.
The purpose of the enactment is plain. It is to secure that when market rents have been
pushed up by a shortage of houses to let, tenants do not have to bear the burden of the
increase over what would otherwise be fair which is attributable to that shortage.

In the opinions of the majority of the Extra Division there are indications of a view *j*
that what s 42(2) requires is that, whatever the actual state of the house-letting market, it
must be assumed to be in balance, so that the rents actually being paid in the market
represent what would be expected to be paid in such a balanced market. If that is what
the majority intended to hold, it is clearly incorrect, and indeed counsel for the
respondent landlords did not seek to support it.

a What the respondents did seek to argue was that, since there was no evidence before the committee whose determination was the subject of appeal, or before the Kennedy committee on whose decision the former relied, tending to show that a shortage of houses to let had the effect of inflating the prices paid for houses for sale, it was erroneous to make any 'scarcity' deduction from vacant possession capital values in the process of determining fair rents on the basis of a fair return to the landlord. It was not disputed that both the present committee and the Kennedy committee had before them cogent

b evidence of a serious scarcity of houses to let in the relevant locality.

As Lord Dunpark said in the course of his dissenting opinion, there would appear to be three main guidelines available in the calculation of a fair rent under the Act. The first is to have regard to fair market rents for similar properties. The second is to compare registered rents for other similar protected tenancy properties. The third is to ascertain what would be a fair return to the landlord on the capital value of his house. I would

c observe that the third method, which represents some sort of application of what is known as the contractor's principle of valuation, seems to have gained considerable currency before Glasgow rent assessment committees. The contractor's principle is a notoriously unreliable method of valuation, normally used only as a last resort. It is also to be observed that not only in this case, but also in the Kennedy committee's case and others which have been drawn to our attention, the valuer appearing for the landlords

d did not seek to support a figure of fair rent derived from a straight application of a suitable percentage return to his estimate of vacant possession capital value. A deduction of at least $33\frac{1}{3}\%$ was invariably made. This tends to suggest that in the valuer's professional opinion the resultant figure would be unreasonably high if such a deduction was not made. The figure which would have resulted from the valuer's calculations in the present case would, in the absence of such a deduction, have amounted to about £1,200, as

e against the figure of £855 which he actually put forward as being a proper estimate of the fair rent.

Whether or not a shortage of houses for letting has the effect of inflating the price paid for houses with vacant possession may not be capable of being precisely demonstrated, though it would appear not unreasonable to infer that such an effect is a likely one. Inability to find a house to let might well turn many persons seeking accommodation

f onto the house purchase market, and thus tend to create an upward trend in prices. However that may be, it would, in my opinion, be bad valuation practice to proceed on a rigid rule of thumb basis of applying an assumed fair rate of return to vacant possession capital value. There are many factors which the valuer should keep in mind in order to arrive at a reasonable result. In *Skilling v Arcari's Executors* 1974 SC(HL) 42 at 53 Lord Morris said:

g 'A purchaser might be willing to pay a high price in order to have a house for his own personal occupation. That would be a personal circumstance which would have to be disregarded. Alternatively, a purchaser might have bought with vacant possession and with the intention of letting. He would know that, whatever was the sum that he had paid, a tenant under a regulated tenancy could seek a determination as to what, having regard to all the circumstances (except personal ones), was the fair

h rent. On the other hand, a purchaser might have bought a house with a sitting tenant and have paid a purchase price based upon his hope or expectation of receiving some particular sum (being either the then existing rent or some other sum) by way of rent. He would, however, always have to contemplate that under a regulated tenancy an assessment as to the fair rent could be sought.'

j This passage is of importance as illustrating the need, where the art of valuation is being exercised in the present context, to avoid rigidity of approach and have regard to all relevant circumstances. A list of prices paid for comparable houses with vacant possession may, without more, be an uncertain guide. There is no evidence either in this case or in the Kennedy committee's case to indicate whether the houses, the purchase prices of which were adduced in evidence, were bought for personal occupation or for investment purposes. The former may well be regarded as the more probable. The material must be handled with caution. As has been mentioned, it is apparent that many professional *a* valuers acting for landlords have, in their application of this variant of the contractor's principle to the exercise of determining a fair rent, consistently made a substantial deduction from their estimates of vacant possession capital values. This shows that in practice they have indeed treated the raw material with caution. These deductions have been made because the valuers concerned considered them necessary, in the exercise of their professional skill, in order to arrive at a figure of fair rent which corresponded to *b* the statutory requirements of s 42(1) and (2) of the 1971 Act. The deductions have been described as having been made to discount the 'scarcity' element. It seems to me that this is no more than a compendious manner of describing the valuer's recognition that his figure of fair rent had to take into account the statutory hypothesis postulated by s 42(2). The attempt to erect this recognition into a breach of some supposed rule of law is misconceived. We are here concerned not with any rule of law but with an exercise of *c* the valuer's professional skill.

In all the circumstances I consider it to be clear that neither the committee in the present case nor the Kennedy committee fell into any error of law, and that both committees had evidence before them on which they were entitled to reach the determinations they did. The committees were well qualified to assess the effect of the evidence, including among their membership, as each of them did, a chartered surveyor. *d* I am of opinion, for reasons I have indicated, that there are no grounds on which a court of law could properly interfere with the determinations.

I would therefore allow the appeal and sustain the determination of the rent assessment committee. The appellant is entitled to her expenses before this House and in the Court of Session.

e

LORD ROSKILL. My Lords, I have had the advantage of reading in draft the speeches prepared by my noble and learned friends Lord Fraser, Lord Keith and Lord Brightman. I entirely agree with them and for the reasons therein given I too would allow this appeal and restore the finding of the committee.

LORD BRIGHTMAN. My Lords, I am in entire agreement with the views expressed *f* by my noble and learned friends Lord Fraser and Lord Keith.

The appeal before your Lordships is concerned with an application dated 17 August 1979 by the landlords for the registration of the rent of an unfurnished house, 49 Burnfoot Drive, Glasgow, which is let under a regulated tenancy to the appellant, Janet Boyd Husband. At the date of the application the rent payable was the equivalent of £420 a year. The new rent proposed by the landlords was £900. On 14 January 1980, *g* the rent officer determined a fair rent of £680 a year, following which there was a reference to the rent assessment committee at the instance of the landlords. At the hearing, which took place before the committee in September 1980, the landlords' surveyor, Mr McNeill, submitted, in a written proof of his evidence, that 'having in regard to all the circumstances I consider that the fair rent as at August and September 1979 can be fairly stated at £855 . . .' In fact, the proof had originally specified £900 as *h* in the application, but Mr McNeill deleted this and inserted £855 after, no doubt, more mature consideration. The committee did not accept the rent officer's determination, and raised the rent of 49 Burnfoot Drive (and other similar houses comprised in concurrent applications) to £725. In reaching that conclusion, the committee expressed themselves as determining the fair rent by reference to 80 comparables which had been the subject matter of a decision of another rent assessment committee (the Kennedy *j* committee) on 28 July 1980, to which I shall refer as 'the Kennedy comparables'.

The landlords appealed to the Court of Session on three grounds (shortly stated). Ground (1): the committee erred by 'failing to take into account consideration of a fair return on capital, basing their decision exclusively upon comparison with a previous determination'. Ground (2): the committee erred by 'failing to come to any concluded

view on the appellant's argument as to the propriety of making a deduction for scarcity
a from capital value with vacant possession for the purposes of assessing a fair return on
capital'. Ground (3): 'That in any event the Committee was not entitled to rely upon a
comparison with the said previous determination . . . The said previous determinations
were criticised for making a scarcity deduction.'

There is, I think, implicit in grounds (1) and (2) the proposition that the requirement
in sub-s (1) of s 42 to have regard to 'all the circumstances' imposes on an assessment
b committee the duty to take into consideration 'a fair return on capital' as one of the 'the
circumstances'. I disagree. I accept that there may be the exceptional case in which a
committee are justified in taking into consideration what would be a 'fair return on
capital', leaving aside the precise definition of 'capital' in this context. I do not accept that
a committee's decision can be challenged as erroneous in law merely because the
committee have failed to take into consideration a 'fair return on capital' but have based
c their decision exclusively on comparables. The 1971 Act is concerned with the
determination of a 'fair rent', that is to say a rent which is fair to the landlord and fair to
the tenant, and yield on invested capital is not an essential ingredient of that
determination. If comparables are available which do not reflect, or are discounted so as
not to reflect, scarcity value, such comparables are the best guide to a fair rent.

Ground (3) appears to be that to which argument in the Court of Session was principally
d directed; the argument being that the Kennedy comparables were not true comparables
because they were based on a 'fair return on capital' from which a deduction of 40% was
made for 'scarcity value'. Lord Avonside, with whom Lord Kincraig concurred, expressed
the opinion that (at least in the context of a 'capital value' approach) such a deduction—

> **e** 'is plainly wrong and ignores the provision of section 42(2) of the Act . . . My
> understanding [of the argument of counsel] was that it was said that the Act was
> designed to favour tenants. That suggestion is insupportable, looking to the
> provisions of the Act.'

Lord Avonside concluded his opinion by recommending that the five cases before the
Court of Session 'should be sent back to the committees to proceed as accords, under
direction that their use of a "scarcity" element in their determination is wrong in law'.
f One matter which seems to me to be clear beyond a peradventure is that the 1971 Act
was designed to favour tenants by protecting them from any increase of rent which
would otherwise have been caused by demand exceeding supply. The Act requires the
rent to be determined on the hypothetical basis of an equilibrium, ie there are X dwelling
houses of the particular sort in question which landlords are desirous of letting, and there
are X tenants who are desirous of renting accommodation of that sort; what in those
g circumstances is the 'fair rent' for the landlords to demand and for the tenants to pay? In
an area of scarcity that hypothesis inevitably favours tenants and disadvantages landlords,
as s 42 of the 1971 Act intended, as also did its predecessor, s 27 of the Rent Act 1965. If
scarcity of accommodation causes the sale value of dwelling houses with vacant possession
to be inflated, it seems to me that the use of that inflated value as a touchstone for a 'fair
rent' which has to be determined as if no scarcity of accommodation existed, would
h deprive s 42(2) of its obvious purpose. I find myself in complete agreement with the
reasoning of Lord Dunpark.

In so far as Lord Kincraig rested his opinion on the alternative ground that there was
no evidence in the Kennedy case that the 'capital value' of the Kennedy comparables was
enhanced by scarcity of accommodation and that therefore the Kennedy comparables
were not true comparables, I think that there was ample such evidence.
j I would allow this appeal.

LORD TEMPLEMAN. My Lords, for the reasons given by my noble and learned
friends Lord Fraser, Lord Keith and Lord Brightman, I agree that this appeal must be
allowed.

Appeal allowed.

Solicitors: *Denton Hall & Burgin*, agents for *Balfour & Manson*, Edinburgh, agents for *Bird*   a
Semple & Crawford Herron, Glasgow (for the tenant); *Nabarro Nathanson*, agents for *Gray
Muirhead & Carmichael WS*, Edinburgh, agents for *Breeze Paterson & Chapman*, Glasgow
(for the landlords).

Mary Rose Plummer   Barrister.   b

R v Cripps, ex parte Muldoon and others

QUEEN'S BENCH DIVISION

ROBERT GOFF LJ AND MANN J

21, 26, 27 APRIL, 27 MAY 1983

  c

*Judgment – Order – Correction – Accidental slip or omission – Election court for local election –
Correction of order for costs – Whether correction permissible – RSC Ord 20, r 11.*

Elections – Election court – Election court for local election – Election court making ultra vires   d
*direction as to costs – Application for judicial review – Jurisdiction of High Court to grant judicial
review – Whether election court an 'inferior court' – Representation of the People Act 1949, ss
110(2), 115(6).*

After the respondent had been elected as a councillor at a local government election, the
petitioners presented a petition under the Representation of the People Act 1949 alleging   e
that the respondent had been guilty of certain illegal practices in respect of the election,
namely overspending and making an untrue return and declaration of expenses. In
accordance with s 115(1)[a] of the 1949 Act, the petition was tried by an election court
consisting of a barrister (the commissioner) who for the purposes of the trial had, by
virtue of ss 115(6) and 110(2)[b], the same powers and privileges as a High Court judge on
the trial of a parliamentary election petition. The commissioner held that the respondent   f
had been substantially responsible for the petition being brought and ordered the
respondent to pay the petitioners 'three quarters (75%) of their costs properly incurred in
relation to the Petition'. The petitioners and the respondent failed to agree on the
meaning of the order and the respondent asked the commissioner to clarify it. The
commissioner sat again and stated that he had intended to include in the order only those
costs relevant to the two matters on which the petitioners had succeeded and that he had
not intended to include the whole of the petitioners' costs. He issued a direction to that   g
effect. The petitioners applied to the High Court for an order of certiorari to quash the
direction on the ground that it was ultra vires because the commissioner was functus
officio once the trial of the petition had been concluded and that therefore he had had no
jurisdiction to vary the order for costs. At the hearing of the application the respondent
contended (i) that the commissioner had merely clarified the order, and ought to be   h
regarded as having exercised his powers under ss 115(6) and 110(2) to act under the 'slip
rule' in RSC Ord 20, r 11, and (ii) that an election court was to be regarded as a 'superior
court' and accordingly the High Court had no jurisdiction to grant relief by way of
judicial review.

Held – (1) The commissioner had no jurisdiction to make the direction varying his order   j
for costs because in doing so he was purporting not merely to clarify the costs order but
to make a fundamental variation to it, and even if he had had power to act under the 'slip

---

a   Section 115, so far as material, is set out at p 79 *a* and *c*, post
b   Section 110(2) is set out at p 79 *b*, post

rule' (which was doubtful) that rule did not enable him to make an amendment of such
a a radical nature (see p 76 j to p 77 a and j, p 78 c to g and p 84 f to h, post).

(2) Despite the wide powers conferred on a local election court by ss 115(6) and 110(2)
of the 1949 Act such a court was, having regard to its constitution, powers and
relationship with the High Court, an 'inferior court' for the purposes of judicial review.
It followed that the High Court could and in the circumstances would grant an order of
certiorari to quash the commissioner's direction (see p 83 b c and j to p 84 d and f to h,
b post); Colonial Bank of Australasia v Willan (1874) LR 5 PC 417, Skinner v Northallerton
County Court Judge [1895-9] All ER Rep 1288, R v Central Criminal Court Justices, ex p
London County Council [1925] All ER Rep 429, R v St Edmundsbury and Ipswich Diocese
(Chancellor), ex p White [1947] 2 All ER 170 and Baldwin & Francis Ltd v Patents Appeal
Tribunal [1959] 2 All ER 433 considered.

Per curiam. The mere fact that a court consists of a High Court judge is not conclusive
c of the question whether such a court is a superior court (see p 83 h j, post); dictum of
Lord Widgery CJ in R v An Election Court, ex p Sheppard [1975] 2 All ER at 725-726
doubted.

Notes
For the jurisdiction, status and practice of the election court, see 15 Halsbury's Laws (4th
d edn) paras 834, 855.
For the Representation of the People Act 1949, ss 110, 115, see 11 Halsbury's Statutes
(4th edn) 648, 653.
As from 15 March 1983, ss 110 and 115 of the 1949 Act were replaced by ss 123 and
130 of the Representation of the People Act 1983.

Cases referred to in judgment
e Baldwin & Francis Ltd v Patents Appeal Tribunal [1959] 2 All ER 433, [1959] AC 663,
[1959] 2 WLR 826, HL.
Colonial Bank of Australasia v Willan (1874) LR 5 PC 417.
Peart v Stewart [1983] 1 All ER 859, [1983] AC 109, [1983] 2 WLR 451, HL.
R v An Election Court, ex p Sheppard [1975] 2 All ER 723, [1975] 1 WLR 1319, DC.
R v Central Criminal Court Justices, ex p London County Council [1925] 2 KB 43, [1925] All
f ER Rep 429, DC.
R v Glamorganshire (Inhabitants) (1700) 1 Ld Raym 580, 91 ER 1287.
R v Hurst (Judge Sir Donald), ex p Smith, R v Oxford Electoral Registration Officer, ex p Smith
[1960] 2 All ER 385, [1960] 2 QB 133, [1960] 2 WLR 961, DC.
R v St Edmundsbury and Ipswich Diocese (Chancellor), ex p White [1947] 2 All ER 170, [1948]
1 KB 195, CA.
g Skinner v Northallerton County Court Judge [1898] 2 QB 680, CA; affd [1899] AC 439,
[1895-9] All ER Rep 1288, HL.

Application for judicial review
Denis Muldoon, Christopher Nigel Pearson Lewis, Richard Martin Cantor and Solomon
Jacques Green applied, with the leave of McNeill J granted on 21 December 1982, for (i)
an order of certiorari to remove into the High Court and to quash a direction given on 3
h November 1982 by Mr Anthony Cripps QC, (ii) a declaration that the taxing master was
bound to proceed with the taxation of the costs of the applicants pursuant to an order of
the election court dated 26 March 1982 without regard to the direction given on 3
November 1982 and (iii) a declaration that on the true construction of the order dated 26
March 1982 the applicants' costs were to be taxed on a party and party basis in accordance
with RSC Ord 62, r 28, and the applicants were to be paid by Adrian Carnegie Slade
j three-quarters of their costs in accordance with RSC Ord 62, r 9(4)(a). The facts are set
out in the judgment of the court.

Michael Tugendhat for the applicants.
Timothy Barnes for the respondents.

Cur adv vult

27 May. The following judgment of the court was delivered.

ROBERT GOFF LJ. There is before the court an application for judicial review. The
matter arises out of an election petition presented by four petitioners, Mr Muldoon, Mr
Lewis, Mr Cantor and Mr Green against Mr Adrian Slade, who was the candidate elected
for the Greater London Council for the area of Richmond-upon-Thames at the election
held on 7 May 1981. The petition was tried by an election court, consisting of Mr
Anthony Cripps QC. The hearing before Mr Cripps lasted for no less than 13 days,
between 1 and 19 March 1982. He gave his judgment on 23 March 1982. In their
petition, the petitioners had alleged that the return and declaration of election expenses
made on behalf of Mr Slade were untrue, and they further alleged overspending under
13 heads. Mr Cripps upheld the first of these allegations, relating to the return and
declaration of election expenses; but of the heads of alleged overspending he held that
only one had been established, in an amount of £19 which resulted in a net overspending
of less than £1. In his judgment, Mr Cripps made some severe comments about the
return, stating that no serious attempt had been made to complete the return adequately,
and that time, trouble and expense would have been saved if proper records had been
kept and retained by Mrs Wainwright (Mr Slade's agent). He also criticised the declaration,
as failing to comply with s 70 of the Representation of the People Act 1949 in stating
that certain sums had been paid by the agent, which were never paid, and in incorrectly
stating the return to be correct. Mr Cripps commented:

> 'The respondent himself and by his agent in this careless conduct has thus been
> substantially responsible for this petition ever being brought by these obvious
> errors.'

He therefore held that illegal practices on the part of the respondent in regard to the
return and the declaration were established. However, he concluded that none of these
illegal practices could reasonably be supposed to have affected the result of the election,
and he therefore granted relief to the respondent.

After the judgment had been given, there was extensive argument about costs, which
were obviously substantial. Leading counsel for the petitioners asked for the whole of
their costs, relying on the facts that (1) the petition had succeeded, (2) in so far as there
had been adverse findings of fact, they related to matters which the respondent and his
agent had brought on themselves, (3) the respondent had fought a strenuous rearguard
action to prevent examination of such documents as there were and (4) it was reasonable
and sensible that all the matters should be investigated. Counsel for the respondent
submitted that the bulk of the case had been occupied with issues which had been
resolved in the respondent's favour and on that basis it would be right for the respondent
to recover at least a part of his costs. Mr Cripps expressed his conclusion as follows:

> 'It is clear to me that the respondent ought not to have any costs. The respondent
> has really brought the case on himself in the manner I have indicated. Therefore,
> there will be no order for any costs to be paid to the respondent. As far as the
> petition is concerned, I also bear that in mind and I bear in mind the fact that the
> petitioner has succeeded and has succeeded on matters which were raised and were
> important, but in my judgment the petitioner has certainly taken up more time
> than was necessary, even in view of the way in which the respondent has refused at
> earlier stages to co-operate what appears to be reasonably in producing the
> documents. The order, therefore, is that the respondent has to pay three-quarters of
> the petitioner's costs, including the reamendment, to be taxed if not agreed.'

The order was then drawn up in the usual way, and included the following order relating
to costs:

> 'IT IS FURTHER ORDERED that i the Respondent Adrian Carnegie Slade do pay to the
> Petitioners three quarters (75%) of their costs properly incurred in relation to the

a   Petition including the costs reserved by this Court on 8 March, 1982 in dealing with
the Petitioners' application to re-amend their petition and that such costs be taxed
by a Taxing Master if not agreed. *ii* Adrian Carnegie Slade and Patricia Mary
Wainwright the Applicants for Relief do pay to the Petitioners their costs properly
incurred in relation to the Application for Relief and that such costs should be taxed
by a Taxing Master if not agreed.'

b   The petitioners' solicitors accordingly prepared and lodged their bill for costs, which
totalled over £42,000. The taxation was fixed for 28 October 1982. However on 25
October the respondent's solicitors asked for an adjournment because they wished to
refer the order for costs back to Mr Cripps on the ground that the order meant that the
bill of costs ought to have been drawn so as to distinguish between those costs incurred
in respect of issues on which the petitioners had succeeded and those incurred in respect
of issues on which they had not succeeded. The taxing master (the Chief Taxing Master,
c   Master Matthews) expressed the opinion that the order did not require him to apportion
costs to issues, the order being therefore in accordance with the general rules discouraging
the making of any such apportionment. However, he adjourned the matter, on the terms
that the respondent consent that an interim certificate be issued in the sum of £10,000
plus value added tax of £1,500. The respondent did so consent and that sum has in fact
been paid. The master also ordered the costs of the adjournment to be paid by the
d   respondent.
The parties went before Mr Cripps on 3 November 1982. The petitioners, we were
told by counsel, considered that the order was perfectly clear, and that Mr Cripps had no
jurisdiction to vary it; however they also attended by leading and junior counsel,
confident that their attendance could not, by waiver, create any jurisdiction where none
existed. Having heard submissions from counsel on both sides, Mr Cripps expressed
e   himself as follows:

'The application before me raises a point under the order made at the end of the
local government election petition heard earlier this year. The point concerns costs.
The actual order . . . which is now before me, was "that . . . the Respondent . . . do
pay to the Petitioners three quarters (75%) of their costs properly incurred in relation
f   to the Petition including the costs reserved by this Court on 8 March, 1982 in
dealing with the Petitioners' application to re-amend their petition and that such
costs be taxed by a Taxing Master if not agreed . . . " I am certainly not going to seek
to usurp any of the functions of a taxing master, for which I would be unqualified,
nor am I going to seek in any way to vary the order which was made but merely to
seek to clarify it. The main points about this lengthy matter were, first, that on the
g   petition itself the respondent succeeded technically, in the sense that there were
illegal but not corrupt practices found. On the subsequent application the petitioners
succeeded and it was clear that on any probable result of the evidence as it came out
that there would be relief to the respondent on all the matters on which the
petitioners succeeded. I therefore regarded the petitioners' result as being a success
of what one might call to some extent a technical kind. It was for that reason that
h   the 75% was imported into the order. That was one restriction on the costs to be
paid. But there was also a completely separate restriction on the costs to be paid,
namely those "properly incurred". In those properly incurred I intended to be
included the costs relevant to the two matters on which the petitioners were
successful, namely in relation to the return itself and in relation to the Young
Liberals' letter, items 1 and 6 of the 15 headings mentioned in the judgment. I did
j   not intend to be included any costs referable to any of the other items in those 15
headings, items 2, 3, 4, 5, 7, 8, 9, 10, 11, 12, 13, 14 and 15, because it seems to me
that on those matters, bearing in mind that there had only been as it were a technical
success, on the other matters there was not even a technical success, but complete
failure. Therefore what the order means is that the taxing master as best he can is to
tax the costs which were incurred in relation to the two matters I have mentioned,

the return itself and the Young Liberals' letter, and in addition to that the costs of the petitioners in relation to the application to reamend the petition. Having arrived *a* at that total sum the order requires 75% only of that to be paid. In other words there were two restrictions: one, as regards the percentage of the amount and, two, as regards what headings should be included in the amount . . .'

The matter came again before the Chief Taxing Master on 5 November 1982. We have been told that he expressed astonishment at the judgment or direction give by Mr Cripps on 3 November, but indicated that he would feel bound to follow it and that a new bill *b* would have to be drawn if the taxation was to proceed.

So the petitioners found themselves in this position. They considered that Mr Cripps's original order was perfectly clear, and that by his 'direction' of 3 November he had purported to vary that order, which he had no jurisdiction to do. However, if they took no steps to quash that direction, the taxation of costs would proceed on the basis stated by Mr Cripps in his direction, and only on a review of that taxation, after considerable *c* further costs had been expended, could they challenge the basis on which the Chief Taxing Master felt, following Mr Cripps's direction, that he ought to proceed. They therefore decided to apply for judicial review, which they now do by leave of the single judge. The relief sought by them is as follows:

'(a) an order of certiorari to remove into the High Court and to quash the said *d* direction and (b) judicial review by way of a declaration that the Taxing Master is bound to proceed with the taxation of the costs of the Petitioners pursuant to the order of the Election Court dated 26th March 1982 without regard to the directions or judgment given on 3rd November 1982 and (c) judicial review by way of a declaration that on the true construction of the said order dated 26th March 1982 the Petitioners' costs are to be taxed on a party and party basis in accordance with *e* Order 62 rule 28 of the Rules of the Supreme Court and the Petitioners are to be paid three quarters of their costs so taxed in accordance with Order 62 rule 9(4)(*a*) of the said Rules.'

The grounds on which they seek relief are these:

'(a) that Mr Cripps was on 3rd November 1982 no longer constituting the *f* election court to whom the trial of the said election petition was assigned pursuant to section 115 of the Representation of the People Act 1949, the trial thereof having been concluded in accordance with section 125 of the said Act upon the determination thereof on 23rd March, 1982, or the certification in writing of the said determination on or about 26th March, 1982. (b) that the said directions or judgment of 3rd November 1982 would, if effective, constitute a variation of the *g* order as to costs made on 23rd March 1982 and drawn up on 26th March, 1982.'

We have to say that the resulting situation is most unfortunate. If the order as drawn up is perfectly clear as the petitioners (whom we shall refer to as 'the applicants') submit it to be, and as the Chief Taxing Master thought, then the petitioners will consider themselves aggrieved if they are deprived of the benefit of that order. On the other hand, *h* if we quash Mr Cripps's direction of 3 November, the respondent will consider himself aggrieved, since he has been told by Mr Cripps that he intended to order him to pay no more than 75% of the applicants' costs on the two issues on which they have succeeded. We have, however, simply to consider this application in the ordinary way irrespective of such considerations. We agree with counsel who appeared before us on behalf of the applicants that two questions arise on the application. (1) Did Mr Cripps have jurisdiction to make his direction of 3 November 1982? That question resolves itself into this form: *j* was the direction a variation of the order drawn up after the hearing on 23 March 1982? (2) If Mr Cripps did not have jurisdiction to make his direction, has this court jurisdiction to grant relief by way of judicial review, having regard to the fact that this matter relates to an election court?

We turn then to the first of these questions. In our judgment, it is plain that Mr

Cripps's direction of 3 November was one which, if effective, did indeed operate as a
variation of the order as drawn.

We look first at the order as drawn. In our judgment the ordinary meaning of the
words 'three quarters (75%) of their costs properly incurred in relation to the Petition . . .
such costs [to] be taxed by a Taxing Master if not agreed' is that the taxing master's task
is to ascertain the total amount of the costs properly incurred by the applicants in relation
to the petition, and then to ascertain three-quarters of those costs. The words 'properly
incurred in relation to the Petition' mean, on their ordinary meaning, the costs incurred
by the applicants in relation to the whole petition, but only such costs as were properly
so incurred. We understand that the word 'properly' is not ordinarily included in orders
for costs drawn up in the High Court, though it is ordinarily included in orders for costs
drawn up in election courts, as is evidenced by the fact that, although Mr Cripps (contrary
to his recollection seven months later) did not use the word 'properly' when making his
order, that word was incorporated as a matter of form when the order was drawn up.
Internal evidence in support of this view is to be found in the particular order: the words
'properly incurred' appear in both limbs of the order, and there can be no question of
those words as used in the second limb of the order bearing any meaning other than that
which we have described, because Mr Cripps cannot possibly have intended that there
should be an apportionment of the costs incurred by the applicants in relation to the
application for relief by reference to the issues decided on the petition.

We reach this conclusion purely as a matter of construction of the order; but the
construction which we prefer is, we consider, consistent with certain other matters. First,
an award of 75% of the costs incurred by the applicants, limited to those issues on which
they have succeeded, would be a most remarkable order, when there appears to be no
material on which Mr Cripps could properly have limited the costs recoverable by the
applicants on those issues. Second, the factual context in which the order is set appears to
us to support this construction. It appears from observations which Mr Cripps made in
the course of his judgment that he considered the respondent himself and his agents in
their careless conduct to have been substantially responsible for the petition ever being
brought, a view which he repeated when making his order as to costs, saying that the
respondent had really brought the case on himself. Furthermore, Mr Cripps, when
making his order as to costs, stated that he bore in mind that the petitioners had
succeeded and had succeeded on matters which were raised and were important, though
the petitioner had certainly taken up more time than was necessary. Lastly, orders for
costs related to specific issues are strongly discouraged (see *The Supreme Court Practice
1982* vol 1, p 999, para 62/2/62), and very much more specific words than those used in
this order would be needed to achieve an order in that form.

In all circumstances, we entertain no doubt that the order bears the construction which
we have indicated.

Faced with these formidable points, counsel for the respondent submitted first that all
that Mr Cripps did was to clarify his order; but he recognised, quite rightly, that if what
Mr Cripps directed was inconsistent with his order it could not amount simply to a
clarification. Next he submitted that Mr Cripps was trying to give effect to what he
believed that he had intended to order, and must be regarded as having acted under the
slip rule in RSC Ord 20, r 11. Now, under s 115(6) of the Representation of the People
Act 1949, the election court consisting of Mr Cripps had 'for the purposes of the trial' the
same powers and privileges as a judge on the trial of a parliamentary election petition;
the court therefore had, subject to the provisions of the 1949 Act, the same powers,
jurisdiction and authority as a judge of the High Court (see s 110(2) of the Act). We
accept that the powers of a judge of the High Court include the power to operate the slip
rule. However, there must be doubt whether this power was conferred on Mr Cripps
under s 115(6) of the 1949 Act for the purpose in question. For, once he had made his
order, the election court which consisted of him was functus officio and had ceased to
exist. Of course, where a High Court judge sitting in the High Court exercises his power
under the slip rule to correct accidental errors, he can do so because, although his order
has been drawn up, the High Court has not ceased to exist. He can therefore exercise the

jurisdiction under Ord 20, r 11, which is vested in the High Court as such; indeed, it appears to us that, if in any particular case the trial judge was not available (for example, because he had died) after the drawing up of the order, another judge of the High Court could exercise the power of the High Court under the slip rule to correct an accidental error. It appears that when an election court has ceased to exist the exercise of powers under the slip rule to correct accidental errors should be made not by the barrister who formerly constituted the election court but by the High Court by virtue of its powers under s 137(3) of the 1949 Act, which provides:

> 'The High Court shall, subject to the provisions of this Act, have the same powers, jurisdiction and authority with respect to an election petition and the proceedings thereon as if the petition were an ordinary action within its jurisdiction.'

However, even if we are wrong in that view, we do not consider that what Mr Cripps purported to do in the present case could be described as falling within the slip rule. Order 20, r 11 provides:

> 'Clerical mistakes in judgments or orders, or errors arising therein from any accidental slip or omission, may at any time be corrected by the Court on motion or summons without an appeal.'

Plainly, this is not a case where there was a clerical mistake. Nor do we think that this can be described as a case where there was an error arising in the order from any accidental slip or omission. We appreciate that Mr Cripps has now said that he intended the order to have a different meaning from that which, on a true construction, it must in our judgment bear. But to vary an order in the fundamental manner now directed by Mr Cripps cannot be described as the correction of a slip, still less as the correction of an accidental slip, in the ordinary meaning of those words. This is not a case where the error was an error in expressing the manifest intention of the court; on the contrary, the proposed correction was one which was not only disputed but constituted a radical departure from an order which, when made, appeared to be consistent with the expressed intention of Mr Cripps when sitting as the election court, in the light of his judgment and of his observations when making his order as to costs. For these reasons, we are unable to accept counsel for the respondent's submission that Mr Cripps should be regarded as having acted under the slip rule, even if he had power to do so.

It follows that we hold that Mr Cripps had no jurisdiction to make the direction of 3 November 1982.

We turn, therefore, to the question whether this court has jurisdiction to grant the relief for which the applicants now ask. It was common ground, in argument before us, that the answer to that question depends on whether an election court should, for the purposes of judicial review be regarded as an inferior court; and whether it should, for such purposes, be so regarded, was a matter which really depended on the relevant provisions of the Representation of the People Act 1949.

An election court is an unusual court. It may take one of two forms: a court for the trial of a parliamentary election petition and a court for the trial of a petition questioning an election in England or Wales under the Local Government Act 1972. The provisions of the 1949 Act dealing with such courts are to be found in ss 107ff of that Act. We are concerned in the present case with the consitution of such a court, its jurisdiction and powers, and its relationship with the High Court. The constitution of a court for the trial of a parliamentary election petition (which for convenience we will refer to as a parliamentary election court) is provided for by s 110(1) of the 1949 Act, which provides:

> 'A parliamentary election petition shall be tried by two judges on the rota for the trial of parliamentary election petitions and the judges for the time being on that rota shall, unless they otherwise agree, try the election petitions standing for trial according to their seniority. The judges presiding at the trial of a parliamentary election petition are hereinafter referred to as the election court.'

The constitution of a court for the trial of a petition questioning an election in England
a or Wales under the Local Government Act 1972 (which for convenience we will refer to
as a local election court) is provided for by s 115(1) of the 1949 Act, which provides:

> 'A petition questioning an election in England or Wales under the local
> government Act shall be tried by an election court consisting of a barrister qualified
> and appointed as provided by this section.'

b As to the powers of a parliamentary election court, s 110(2) provides:

> 'This election court shall, subject to the provisions of this Act, have the same
> powers, jurisdiction and authority as a judge of the High Court (or, in Scotland, a
> judge of the Court of Session presiding at the trial of a civil cause without a jury)
> and shall be a court of record.'

c And, for local election courts, s 115(6) provides:

> 'The election court shall for the purposes of the trial have the same powers and
> privileges as a judge on the trial of a parliamentary election petition.'

These were provisions on which counsel for the respondent placed some reliance. But
there are other provisions of the Act, to which we must now refer, on which counsel for
d the applicants relied.

First, there are a number of provisions conferring on the High Court power to deal
with certain interlocutory matters in relation to election courts, such as amendment of
the petition (s 114(6)), place of trial (ss 110(3) and 115(7)), security for costs (s 119(2)),
consolidation of petitions (s 121(4)), and withdrawal of an election petition (s 127(1)).
We should also refer to s 111, which makes detailed provision for the reception of, and
e attendance on, judges of parliamentary election courts, and shows that they should be
treated in the same way, so far as circumstances permit, as judges of the High Court on
assize.

We do not however regard any of these provisions as being of more than peripheral
importance. They simply show the High Court exercising powers in election petitions
where it is impracticable for an election court to deal with them; and they require High
f Court judges trying Parliamentary election petitions to be treated in the same way as
High Court judges on assize.

There are however other provisions to which we must refer. First, ss 124 and 125 deal
with the conclusion of trials on parliamentary and local election petitions respectively.
In respect of the former, s 124(1) provides that the election court shall certify its
determination in writing to the Speaker of the House of Commons, and s 124(3) provides
g for the sending of any special report to the Speaker. However, in respect of local election
petitions, s 125(2) provides that the election court shall certify its determination in
writing to the High Court, and s 125(4) provides for any special report to be made to the
High Court; under s 125(5) a copy of any certificate or report made to the High Court
shall be sent by the High Court to the Secretary of State. It is difficult, however, to
envisage the High Court exercising more than a ministerial function under this section.
h More important than the above provisions is s 126, which applies to both parliamentary
and local election petitions. It provides as follows:

> '*Special case for determination of High Court.*—(1) If, on the application of any party
> to a petition made in the prescribed manner to the High Court, it appears to the
> High Court that the case raised by the petition can be conveniently stated as a special
> case, the High Court may direct it to be stated accordingly and the special case shall
j > be heard before the High Court. In the case of a parliamenary election petition, the
> High Court shall certify to the Speaker its decision in reference to the special case.
> In the case of a petition questioning an election in England or Wales under the local
> government Act, a statement of the decision on the special case shall be sent by the
> High Court to the Secretary of State and shall also be certified by the High Court

under the hands of two or more judges thereof to the clerk of the authority for which the election was held.

(2) If it appears to the election court on the trial of an election petition that any question of law as to the admissibility of evidence or otherwise requires further consideration by the High Court, the election court may postpone the granting of a certificate until the question has been determined by the High Court, and for this purpose may reserve the question by stating a case for the decision of the High Court . . .'

So s 126(1) confers power on the High Court to assume jurisdiction over election petitions, no doubt in cases not involving a factual inquiry, in place of an election court; and s 126(2) envisages an election court reserving a question of law for the determination of the High Court. In either case, an appeal may go (with leave of the High Court) to the Court of Appeal, but no further: see s 137(1). Section 126 was strongly relied on by counsel for the applicants. In this connection he also referred us to the Corrupt Practices (Municipal Elections) Act 1872, which was a statute under which election courts for local elections were first established. In that Act, 'superior court' is defined as the Court of Common Pleas at Westminster. In s 15(6) and (7) we find (in terms which are very similar) the same powers conferred on the 'superior court' as are now by s 126 of the 1949 Act conferred on the High Court, though of course relating only to local government petitions. The 1872 Act also provided (in s 14(5)):

'The court shall for the purposes of the trial of a petition have all the same powers and privileges which a judge may have on the trial of an election petition under the provisions of the Parliamentary Elections Act, 1868, with this modification, that any fine or order of committal by the court may upon motion by the person aggrieved be discharged or varied by the superior court, or in vacation by a judge thereof, upon such terms, if any, as such superior court or judge thinks fit.'

No such modification is now to be found in s 115(6) of the 1949 Act. But it was present in the 1949 Act until 1960, when repealed by s 19(2) of and Sch 4 to the Administration of Justice Act 1960, instituting the new procedure in respect of contempt of court under that Act. We shall be referring to that new procedure later in this judgment.

Finally, we refer to s 137(3) of the 1949 Act, which we have already mentioned and which provides:

'The High Court shall, subject to the provisions of this Act, have the same powers, jurisdiction and authority with respect to an election petition and the proceedings thereon as if the petition were an ordinary action within its jurisdiction.'

We understand this provision to be a supplementary provision enabling the High Court to deal with any matter not expressly reserved to an election court.

Such are for present purposes the relevant provisions of the 1949 Act.

We now can turn to consider other tribunals, in respect of which the same problem either may arise or has arisen; and we find that the conclusion must on each occasion depend on the precise nature and powers of the particular tribunal. To take first two simple examples, the statutes causing the Courts-Martial Appeal Court and the Restrictive Practices Court to continue in existence each provide that the court shall be a 'superior court of record': see the Courts-Martial (Appeals) Act 1968, s 1(2), and the Restrictive Practices Court Act 1976, s 1(1). There could, we think, in any event be no doubt that these courts are superior courts. One fact to be taken into account appears to be whether High Court judges sit in the court in question, because it may be inappropriate that a Divisional Court of the Queen's Bench Division should exercise powers of judicial review over courts consisting of or including High Court judges. But that is merely one factor to be taken into account; it is not conclusive. So for example the Patents Appeal Tribunal, by virtue of s 85(2) of the Patents Act 1949, consists of 'a judge of the High Court nominated for the purpose by the Lord Chancellor'; and yet the view has been expressed

in the House of Lords that, having regard to various provisions of the Patents Act 1949,
a 'the Appeal Tribunal is an inferior tribunal and that the only remedy of persons aggrieved
by a decision of that tribunal is by way of order of certiorari' (see *Baldwin & Francis Ltd v
Patents Appeal Tribunal* [1959] 2 All ER 433 at 437, [1959] AC 663 at 678 per Lord
Morton). A similar conclusion was reached by the Privy Council in 1874 in respect of
courts of mines created by Acts of the local legislature of the old colony of Victoria; these
too were held to be inferior courts, although the Chief Judge of the Court of Mines was
b to be one of the judges of the Supreme Court (see *Colonial Bank of Australasia v Willan*
(1874) LR 5 PC 417). In that case the court invoked the authority of the ancient decision
of Holt CJ in *R v Glamorganshire (Inhabitants)* (1700) 1 Ld Raym 580 at 581, 91 ER 1287
at 1288, in which he stated that it was 'the constant practice to grant certioraris into
Wales, as also into the Counties Palatine of Durham and Lancaster, which yet had original
jurisdiction', the implication being that the Court of King's Bench would readily exercise
c its power to issue prerogative writs directed towards courts with extensive, even
comprehensive jurisdiction, within limited geographical areas. In *Willan's* case Sir James
W Colvile, in delivering the advice of the Privy Council, said (at 440):

> '. . . these Courts of Mines, which have been created by Acts of the local
> Legislature, and with a jurisdiction which, however wide, is limited both as to the
> persons and the matters within the colony over which it is to be exercised, must, on
d > the principle laid down by Lord *Holt* in *Rex* v. *Inhabitants of —*, in *Glamorganshire*, be
> taken to stand in relation to the Supreme Courts on the footing of inferior Courts . . .'

However, in *R v Central Criminal Court Justices, ex p London County Council* [1925] 2 KB 43,
[1925] All ER Rep 429, Lord Hewart CJ appears to have been sufficiently impressed by
the powers of judges of the Central Criminal Court to hold that the court was a superior
e court. He said after referring to several cases ([1925] 2 KB 43 at 56 57, [1925] All ER
Rep 429 at 432):

> 'To put these judgments together and to consider them in the light of s. 16 of the
> Judicature Act, 1873 . . . one may express the conclusion which they support in this
> way: judges of assize exercise powers upon the same plane with the powers exercised
f > by judges of the High Court in that Court; the Central Criminal Court is a Court of
> not less authority than a Court of assize; the Central Criminal Court is, therefore, a
> superior Court, and a writ of certiorari from the King's Bench Division does not lie
> to it for the purpose of quashing its order.'

In *R v St Edmundsbury and Ipswich Diocese (Chancellor), ex p White* [1947] 2 All ER 170,
[1948] 1 KB 195 the Court of Appeal held that, although prohibition lay to an ecclesiastical
g court, certiorari would not lie. It is plain from the judgment of the court that it was
considered right that what we now call judicial review should be exercised over such
courts for the purposes of curbing acts in excess of jurisdiction; but that such jurisdiction
should not be exercised to review any errors of law by those courts, since they were
concerned not with questions of common law, but with questions of canon law with
which the High Court was unfamiliar. Furthermore, historically the writ of certiorari
h had never lain to an ecclesiastical court; and it was considered that the writ of prohibition
was effective to prevent any excess of jurisdiction. It was therefore held that, whereas
prohibition would lie, certiorari would not. There are however observations made in the
course of the judgment of the Court of Appeal which indicate that the decision depends
on the somewhat unusual jurisdiction exercised by the ecclesiastical courts, and should
not be regarded as detracting from the general application of powers exercisable by the
j High Court by means of judicial review. For example, Evershed LJ said ([1947] 2 All ER
170 at 181, [1948] 1 KB 195 at 222–223):

> 'Whenever, as a result of the establishment by Act of Parliament of some new
> jurisdiction or some new tribunal exercising judicial or quasi-judicial functions, it
> is necesary to consider the application thereto of well established forms of remedy,
> the court will not be afraid to extend the older principles to new circumstances. But

the present case is not, in my judgment, of that character. We are considering, not
the application of established principle to a new jurisdiction, but the scope of the
principle itself in regard to a jurisdiction no less ancient than the principle.'

The position of the Crown Court and the county courts is a little more complicated.
Under s 4(2) of the Courts Act 1971 it is provided:

'The jurisdiction and powers of the Crown Court shall be exercised by—(a) any
judge of the High Court, or (b) any Circuit judge or Recorder, or (c) subject to and
in accordance with the provisions of the next following section, a judge of the High
Court, Circuit judge or Recorder sitting with justices of the peace, and any such
person when exercising the jurisdiction and powers of the Crown Court shall be
judges of the Crown Court.'

Section 10(5) of the Act, however, provides:

'In relation to the jurisdiction of the Crown Court, other than its jurisdiction in
matters relating to trial on indictment, the High Court shall have all such jurisdiction
to make orders of mandamus, prohibition or certiorari as the High Court possesses
in relation to the jurisdiction of an inferior court.'

It thus appears that the Crown Court is treated as an inferior court, except when it is
exercising its jurisdiction in matters relating to trial on indictment. It is therefore
something of a hybrid. Since however it is difficult to imagine a High Court judge sitting
in the Crown Court otherwise than on a trial on indictment, it appears improbable that
the actions of the Crown Court when a High Court judge is sitting will be subject to a
judicial review.

At first sight the position of a county court is simple. Sections 115 to 119 of the County
Courts Act 1959 make it plain that a county court is an inferior court: see also *R v His
Honour Judge Sir Donald Hurst, ex p Smith* [1960] 2 All ER 385, [1960] 2 QB 133. But there
have been occasions when a county court has performed functions which resulted in the
court being treated as a superior court. This occurred when a county court exercised
bankruptcy jurisdiction under the Bankruptcy Acts 1883 and 1890. It was provided by
s 100 of the 1883 Act:

'A county court shall, for the purposes of its bankruptcy jurisdiction, in addition
to the ordinary powers of the Court, have all the powers and jurisdiction of the High
Court, and the orders of the Court may be enforced accordingly in manner
prescribed.'

It was further provided by s 102(2):

'A Court having jurisdiction in bankruptcy under this Act shall not be subject to
be restrained in the execution of its powers under this Act by the order of any other
court, nor shall any appeal lie from its decisions except in manner directed by this
Act.'

Having regard in particular to these provisions, it was held by the Court of Appeal that a
county court, exercising that jurisdiction, was not subject to what we now call judicial
review (see *Skinner v Northallerton County Court Judge* [1898] 2 QB 680). A L Smith LJ said
(at 684):

'In my judgment, the result of these sections is that the position of a county court
judge sitting in Bankruptcy and exercising bankruptcy jurisdiction, and acting
within that jurisdiction, is a position similar to that of a judge of the High Court
exercising his jurisdiction, and that so long as a county court judge is exercising
bankruptcy jurisdiction the remedy by which to question an order made by such a
judge, when exercising such jurisdiction, if such order requires alteration or
amendment, is by application to the judge himself sitting in Bankruptcy, and then
possibly by appeal, and not by certiorari to bring up the order into the Queen's
Bench Division.'

The decision of the Court of Appeal was affirmed by the House of Lords. The Earl of
a Halsbury LC put the position in characteristically forthright terms ([1899] AC 439 at
441, [1895–9] All ER Rep 1288 at 1289):

> '. . . the statute itself has made the county court the High Court for this purpose.
> You might just as well argue that a warrant, defective in form, issued by the Court
> of Queen's Bench can be set right by certiorari. Of course that is absurd. This is the
> High Court for this purpose.'
b

From these cases, it is difficult to extract any precise principle. The most that can be
said is that it is necessary to look at all the relevant features of the tribunal in question,
including its constitution, jurisdiction and powers and its relationship with the High
Court, in order to decide whether the tribunal should properly be regarded as inferior to
the High Court, so that its activities may appropriately be the subject of judicial review
c by the High Court. As we have already indicated, in considering that question the fact (if
it be the case) that the tribunal is presided over by a High Court judge is a relevant factor,
though not conclusive against the tribunal being classified as an inferior court; just as
relevant are the powers of the tribunal and its relationship with the High Court, which
can ordinarily be ascertained from the statute under which the tribunal is set up. But, as
is demonstrated in particular by the approach adopted by the Court of Appeal in R v St
d Edmundsbury and Ipswich Diocese (Chancellor), ex p White [1949] 2 All ER 170, [1948] 1 KB
195 and by the Privy Council in Willan's case (1874) LR 5 PC 417 at 440 (following and
adopting the view of Holt CJ in the Glamorganshire case (1700) 1 Ld Raym 580 at 581, 91
ER 1287 at 1288), there is an underlying policy in the case of tribunals of limited
jurisdiction, whether limited by area, subject matter or otherwise, that, unless the
tribunal in question should properly be regarded in all the circumstances as having a
e status so closely equivalent to the High Court that the exercise of power of judicial review
by the High Court is for that reason inappropriate, it is in the public interest that
remedies by way of judicial review by the High Court should be available to persons
aggrieved, although in some cases there may be special reasons why such remedy should
be available only to curb an excess of jurisdiction but not to review and correct an error
of law committed within the jurisdiction.
f   With this guidance we turn to the election court. The matter here is complicated by
the fact that, as we have seen, there are two types of election court. We are only concerned
with what we have called a local election court; and we do not think it would be right in
this judgment to express any opinion on the position of a parliamentary election court.
We recognise that it might perhaps be thought anomalous if one type of election court
should be subject to judicial review, and the other not. That was, however, the conclusion
g contemplated by Lord Widgery CJ in R v An Election Court, ex p Sheppard [1975] 2 All ER
723 at 725–726, [1975] 1 WLR 1319 at 1323. In his unreserved judgment in that case he
expressed the opinion, obiter, that—

> 'It is quite clear that the election court which deals with parliamentary elections,
> consisting, as it will do, of a Queen's Bench judge, is a superior court and it is clear
> that no question of the prerogative orders could be available there. But it is not so
h > clear whether the same applies to a barrister appointed under s 115 as the election
> court for a local government election.'

While expressing no opinion about the status of a parliamentary election court, we think
it right to comment that, having (we believe) heard fuller argument and a more copious
citation of authority than did the Divisional Court in that case, we doubt whether the
j mere fact that such a court consists of a High Court judge is conclusive of the question.
However, we are concerned only with the position of an election court which hears
petitions in respect of local elections. As to this, looking at all the relevant circumstances,
we have reached the conclusion that such a court should be regarded as an inferior court,
at least for the purpose of review of any excess of jurisdiction. It is true that, by virtue of
ss 115(6) and 110(2) of the 1949 Act, the court has for the purposes of the trial the same
powers, jurisdiction and authority as a judge of the High Court; but there are other

factors which, in our judgment, nevertheless tilt the balance towards the conclusion that the court is an inferior court. First, there is the fact that the court consists of a barrister, and not of a High Court judge. Second, there is the fact that, by virtue of s 126 of the 1949 Act, the High Court may deal with the matter itself if the case raised by the petition can conveniently be stated as a special case, and may also deal with any question of law on a case stated by the election court. Third, there is the historical fact that such an election court was treated as an inferior court under the terms of the statute (the 1872 Act) by which it was created; and we do not think that the present legislation under which both types of election court are treated in the same Act has materially altered its status. We have of course to look at the matter as a whole; and we note that, despite the wide powers conferred on the court by ss 115(6) and 110(2) of the 1949 Act, it could not possibly be regarded as 'the High Court for this purpose' (to quote again the Earl of Halsbury LC's words in *Skinner v Northallerton County Court Judge* [1899] AC 439 at 441, [1895–9] All ER Rep 1288 at 1289), so as to make it absurd that judicial review over an election court of this type should be exercised by the Queen's Bench Division of the High Court. Looking at the matter as whole, we reach the conclusion that a local election court is an inferior court, at least for the purposes of dealing with excess of jurisdiction.

There is however one particular matter to which we should refer. Under the 1872 Act, under which election courts of this type were established, one matter on which the superior court (then the Court of Common Pleas) had jurisdiction related to orders for committal by the election court (see s 14(5) of the 1872 Act), to which we have already referred. As we have stated, that provision was retained in s 115(6) of the 1949 Act, although the High Court was for this purpose substituted for the superior court; that provision as re-enacted therefore lends force to the conclusion that an election court of this type is an inferior court. It is true that this part of s 115(6) was repealed by the Administration of Justice Act 1960, under which the new procedure relating to contempt of court was introduced; and indeed that, in *Peart v Stewart* [1983] 1 All ER 859 at 863, [1983] AC 109 at 117, Lord Diplock expressed the opinion that an election court, having the same powers, jurisdiction and authority as a judge of the High Court, fell within the definition of a superior court in s 19 of the 1960 Act. We do not however think that it can be right that a statute concerned to reform the law relating to contempt of court was intended to alter the pre-existing status of a particular tribunal in respect of the power of the High Court to exercise judicial review over the activities of that tribunal. We do not therefore regard the 1960 Act as casting light on the question we have to decide.

In the result, we have reached the conclusion that Mr Cripps, by purporting to vary the order which he made, acted in excess of the powers conferred on him as election court in this matter; and we are satisfied that this court has jurisdiction to correct this excess of jurisdiction by judicial review. The mere fact that his purported variation of his order as to costs was a nullity is immaterial, because it is well established that this will not of itself inhibit the court from exercising its power of judicial review in appropriate circumstances. We consider that we should exercise our power to quash the direction made by Mr Cripps; indeed, if we did not do so, further substantial legal costs would be wasted by both parties. We shall accordingly grant the first head of relief sought by the applicants, viz an order of certiorari removing Mr Cripps's direction into this court in order that it may be quashed.

Certiorari to issue to quash the direction of 3 November 1982.

Solicitors: *Penningtons* (for the applicants); *Frere Cholmeley* (for the respondents).

Sepala Munasinghe Esq   Barrister.

a # National Westminster Bank plc v Morgan

COURT OF APPEAL, CIVIL DIVISION
DUNN AND SLADE LJJ
15, 16, 29 JUNE 1983

b *Equity – Undue influence – Presumption of undue influence – Banker and customer – Customer relying on bank's advice – Fiduciary duty of bank – Duty to advise customer to obtain independent legal advice – Wife executing mortgage to bank over her and husband's home – Wife concerned that mortgage not securing business loans made to husband – Bank manager incorrectly advising wife that mortgage limited to securing mortgage advance – Bank manager not advising wife to obtain independent legal advice – Bank suing to recover possession of home for mortgage arrears*
c *– Husband dying without business indebtedness to bank – Wife seeking to set aside mortgage – Whether transaction concluded having to be manifestly disadvantageous before court can set it aside – Whether transaction should be set aside for undue influence.*

The husband, who was an unreliable and improvident businessman, was unable to meet the repayments due under a mortgage secured over the home which he owned jointly d with his wife. As a result the then mortgagee commenced proceedings to take possession of the home, and to avert that the husband made refinancing arrangements with a bank. The bank was made aware of the urgency of the matter and, after the husband executed a legal charge in favour of the bank, the bank manager, at the husband's request, called at the home to get the wife to execute it. Unlike the previous occasion when she executed a mortgage over the home, independent legal advice was not given to her before she e signed the mortgage. The husband was present at the brief meeting between the bank manager and the wife at the home although she made it clear she would have preferred him to be absent. The wife told the bank manager that she had little faith in her husband's business ventures and that she did not want the legal charge to cover his business liabilities. The bank manager assured her in good faith but incorrectly that the charge only secured the amount advanced to refinance the mortgage. In fact the charge f did extend to business advances. The bank obtained an order for possession of the home after the husband and wife fell into arrears with payments. Soon afterwards the husband died without any indebtedness owing to the bank for business advances. The wife appealed against the order for possession contending that she had signed the mortgage because of undue influence from the bank and that therefore the legal charge should be set aside. The bank argued that a defence of undue influence could only be raised when g a defendant had entered into a transaction which was manifestly disadvantageous to him and, since the husband had died without business debts owing to the bank, the wife was not manifestly disadvantaged but instead had benefited under the transaction because it had averted the proceedings by the prior mortgagee for possession.

Held – A presumption of undue influence arose whenever a transaction was concluded h between persons who enjoyed or who were bound in a relationship of confidentiality. That relationship was not circumscribed by reference to defined limits but could exist in a wide variety of situations whenever, first, one party relied on the guidance or advice of another party who not only was aware of that reliance but also stood to obtain a benefit from the transaction or had some other interest in it being concluded, and, second, when there also existed between the parties an element of confidentiality that went beyond j that which might be present between normally trustworthy persons dealing with each other in a business transaction at arm's length. Once the relationship was established and the presumption was raised the court, for reasons of public policy, would set aside the transaction unless the party who gave the advice or guidance could rebut the presumption by showing that he had discharged his fiduciary duty by ensuring that the party liable to be influenced had formed an independent judgment after full, free and informed

thought. The party relying on the other's guidance did not have to show that he had
concluded a transaction which was manifestly disadvantageous to himself before he   *a*
could invoke the presumption. Although the relationship of bank manager and customer
did not normally of itself create the relationship of confidentiality, the circumstances of
the execution of the legal charge by the wife showed that the special relationship had
been created and that raised a presumption of undue influence which the bank could not
rebut, since it had failed to advise the wife to obtain independent legal advice. The appeal
would accordingly be allowed and the legal charge would be set aside in respect of the   *b*
wife's interest in the property (see p 90 *b* to p 91 *j*, p 92 *a* to *h*, p 93 *d* to *g* and p 94 *a*,
post).

Dictum of Cotton LJ in *Allcard v Skinner* [1886–90] All ER Rep at 93 and *Lloyds Bank
Ltd v Bundy* [1974] 3 All ER 757 applied.

Notes   *c*
For the relation of banker and customer, see 3 Halsbury's Laws (4th edn) para 40, and for
cases on the subject, see 3 Digest (Reissue) 553–561, 3587–3625.

For persons in a confidential relationship, see 16 Halsbury's Laws (4th edn) para 1454.

Cases referred to in judgments
Allcard v Skinner (1887) 36 Ch D 145, [1886–90] All ER Rep 90, CA.   *d*
Craig, Re, Meneces v Middleton [1970] 2 All ER 390, [1971] Ch 95, [1970] 2 WLR 1219.
Inche Noriah v Shaik Allie Bin Omar [1929] AC 127, [1928] All ER Rep 189, PC.
Lloyds Bank Ltd v Bundy [1974] 3 All ER 757, [1975] 1 QB 326, [1974] 3 WLR 501, CA.
Morley v Loughnan [1893] 1 Ch 736.
Tate v Williamson (1866) LR 2 Ch App 55.
Tufton v Sperni [1952] 2 TLR 516, CA.   *e*

Appeal
By notice of appeal dated 25 January 1983 Janet Morgan (the wife) appealed against an
order made by Mr C S Rawlins sitting as an assistant recorder in the Bridgwater County
Court on 5 November 1982 whereby he adjudged that the respondent, National
Westminster Bank plc (the bank), was entitled to recover possession of the property   *f*
known as Crossmoor Meadows, East Lyng, Taunton, Somerset from the wife and ordered
her to deliver up possession of the property within 28 days. The facts are set out in the
judgment of Dunn LJ.

Jack Hames QC and *Peter St J Langan QC* for the wife.
Charles Falconer for the bank.
                                                                                           g

                                                              Cur adv vult
29 June. The following judgments were delivered.

DUNN LJ. This is an appeal from an order for possession, made by Mr C S Rawlins
sitting as an assistant recorder in the Bridgwater County Court on 5 November 1982, of   *h*
a house, Crossmoor Meadows, East Lyng, Taunton, in an action on a mortgage dated
8 March 1978 between National Westminster Bank plc (the bank) and Mr and Mrs
Morgan (the husband and the wife). The defence was that the wife's signature was
procured by the undue influence of the manager of the Taunton branch of the bank, a
Mr Barrow. The assistant recorder rejected the allegation of undue influence and, there
being no dispute that the wife had executed the mortgage, and had failed to pay the sums   *j*
due thereunder which were demanded by notice dated 16 May 1979, he made the order
for possession.

It was not suggested in this court that any express influence was used by the manager.
The allegation is that the relations between the bank and the wife were such as to raise a
presumption that the manager had influence over her. In particular reliance was placed

a on the decision of this court in *Lloyds Bank Ltd v Bundy* [1974] 3 All ER 757, [1975] 1 QB 326. The principal question in the appeal is whether a confidential relationship existed between the bank and the wife, which in the circumstances of the case gave rise to a fiduciary duty.

The circumstances of the case are set out in the careful judgment of the assistant recorder, whose findings of fact were not seriously disputed in this court. The terms of the charge were as follows:

b 'The Mortgagor as beneficial owner charges by way of legal mortgage and as a continuing security the property referred to in the Schedule hereto (the Mortgaged Property) with the payment to the Bank on demand by the Bank on the Mortgagor of all present or future actual or contingent liabilities of [the husband] (the debtor) to the Bank whether on account of monies advanced bills of exchange promissory notes guarantees indemnities interest commission banking charges and whether c incurred solely severally or jointly and all legal or other expenses (on a full indemnity basis) howsoever incurred by the Bank in connection therewith . . .'

The husband and the wife purchased the property on 17 September 1974 with the benefit of two mortgages. The first was a charge by way of legal mortgage to the Abbey National Building Society for a capital sum lent of £12,800. The second was a legal d charge for a capital sum of £4,200 lent by the Standard Property Investment Co Ltd. The total capital sum borrowed to purchase the property was £17,000 which was probably most of the value of the property. By those two mortgages the husband and the wife undertook a substantial liability of mortgage repayments which they were unable in the event to meet. The husband was an earth moving contractor, and the history shows that he was in continual financial difficulties, and was unable to meet his financial obligations e in particular with regard to the repayments of the mortgage. The assistant recorder described him in this way:

f 'The husband may be an experienced civil engineer, although he has no technical qualifications, but he is undoubtedly incapable of handling his business affairs in a sensible way. I got the impression that he is one of the world's optimists. Every time he gets into financial difficulties he thinks that better times are around the corner. Every time his financial difficulty was put right and things looked rosy he was determined to expand so that his business activities became bigger and bigger on a shoestring budget. So it is hardly surprising that there were huge variations in his cash flow and in his fortunes resulting in continual financial worries. The picture is that he tended to shrug off his worries and keep them from his wife as far as possible but of course she was aware of them.'

g From 1975 until 1977, when his personal and business accounts were transferred from the bank's branch at Basingstoke to Taunton, the husband was in constant touch with his bank manager, and the bank's interview notes show the position clearly. In 1977 the husband was minded to redeem the second mortgage, and sought a loan from the bank to enable him to do so. The bank agreed in principle, subject to taking a second charge on the house. The charge was drawn up, and the wife went to the bank to sign it. Mr h Barrow was not the manager at the time, but all these matters are recorded in the bank's interview notes. Before the wife signed she was given the opportunity by the then manager of taking legal advice from a solicitor. The charge was a general charge in the same terms as the charge of 8 March 1978, ie on one of the bank's standard forms. Having seen the solicitor the wife decided to limit the amounts secured by the mortgage j to £6,000, and this amendment was made in manuscript on the document itself. The advice of the solicitor was paid for by the bank as appears from the bank's records. The second mortgage was discharged on 30 June 1977 and the liability transferred to the bank under its second charge. Shortly after that the bank obtained an unlimited personal guarantee from the husband as collateral security for the borrowing of his company. This is relevant because of the specific reference to 'guarantees' in the charge to which I

have referred, and which is the subject of this action. According to an affidavit sworn by
the wife—

'A few months later my husband again fell into financial difficulties and I
understand from him and verily believe that he went into the bank at 25 Fore Street,
Taunton to discuss raising a further loan. A few days later I went with my husband
to the bank. After some discussion I was asked by a bank official whose identity I do
not know what I felt about taking a further loan and I indicated my unwillingness
to do so. I was then told as I had been on the previous occasion that I must take
independent legal advice. On that occasion I saw Mr. David White, a solicitor with
Clarke Willmott & Clarke, and as a result of what he told me I decided not to sign
the mortgage. Consequently the bank declined to help my husband further and he
was furious with me and there was a terrible argument between him and me on the
way home which left me very shaken.'

Meanwhile the Abbey National Building Society were pressing for the repayments due
under the first mortgage. Although no details appear in the evidence, the arrears must
have been substantial because, on 27 October 1977, the Abbey National wrote to the
bank stating that they were commencing proceedings for possession as their debt stood
at over £13,000, that is to say the whole capital sum and interest. On 12 December 1977
the wife opened her own account in her own name at the North Street branch of the
bank in Taunton of which Mr Barrow was the manager. On 30 January 1978 the husband
approached the manager for a loan to refinance the Abbey National Building Society
loan. The urgency of refinancing was indicated by him. He said that a possession order
had been made in favour of the society (it is doubtful whether this was correct), and he
stated that he wanted short term refinancing arrangements only, because he asserted that
his company could provide funds to repay the loan within about five weeks. The manager
accepted the loan and proposed to the bank's area office that a loan should be granted by
way of bridging finance, to take over the building society mortgage of £14,500 and
would be repaid by remortgaging or refinancing from the company within five weeks.
This recommendation was accepted by the area office on 31 January 1978. It is against
that background that the circumstances in which the wife signed the mortgage in
question fall to be considered.

The husband signed the mortgage at the manager's office of the bank probably on
1 February 1978, although it was dated 5 March. Unusually, instead of inviting the wife
to the office, the manager took the document to her house in the early evening of that
day. He said he did so because the husband had asked him to, although the husband did
not give him a reason. When the manager got to the house both the husband and the
wife were there. According to the assistant recorder's full note of the evidence of the
manager, whose evidence of the interview the assistant recorder accepted in preference
to that of the wife—

'She was concerned and quite rightly so that the document might enable her
husband to borrow from the bank for his business purposes. I advised her that she
was only signing the document to cover the house mortgage and not to cover any
business liability. I cannot recall any other matters being discussed. She did say that
she had little confidence in his business succeeding and that was why she did not
want the mortgage to cover business liabilities. She signed it. During this
conversation [the husband] was in the same room.'

And the manager then went on to describe that it was an L shaped room, and he and
the wife were at one end and the husband was at the other. He said that his visit lasted
perhaps 15 to 20 minutes, only five minutes of which was spent in talking to the wife.
He said:

'I was quite certain she understood the effect of what she was signing. Her mind
seemed quite clear. She seemed quite grateful. She thanked me for doing it, for
keeping them in the house. She thought she was going to lose their home.'

a As a result of that document the Abbey National mortgage was redeemed, and replaced by the mortgage in favour of the bank. The assistant recorder found as follows:

'I wish to emphasise that the predicament which faced the defendants was in no way caused by facts emanating from the bank. I am satisfied that the bank was not seeking to obtain any advantage for itself but to provide at extremely short notice a short term rescue operation for the defendants. It is true that the wife had on the occasion when she signed the previous mortgage been recommended to take legal
b advice. It is true that on another occasion she was invited to sign a mortgage but declined to do so. On the occasion when she signed the document on which the bank sues she was not invited to take independent legal advice or other advice. I think she was desperately anxious to obtain the enormous advantage of time to pay off the Abbey National Building Society borrowing. I conclude that it came as an enormous relief to her and her husband that the bank was coming to their rescue. I
c reject any suggestion that she had any misgivings about signing the document on the basis that she would prefer the house to be sold.'

On those findings the assistant recorder rejected the allegation in the defence of undue influence.

Shortly after these events the husband tragically died; he had no liability to the bank
d except in respect of the debt transferred from the Abbey National with interest, and the bank's demand was limited to that amount.

In those circumstances the first submission made by counsel for the bank in the course of his able argument was that as the transaction was not disadvantageous to the wife, there could be no relationship of confidence between her and the bank. He relied in particular on a statement by Ungoed-Thomas J in *Re Craig, Meneces v Middleton* [1970] 2
e All ER 390, [1971] Ch 95. Counsel submitted that the first requirement before the presumption of undue influence could arise was that the transaction should be one that was manifestly disadvantageous to the person influenced, and which called for an explanation by the person influencing. He said that in this case the transaction was not manifestly disadvantageous to the wife. On the contrary, on balance it was to her advantage, because it was the only way in which she could avoid her house being sold on
f the application of the Abbey National. The admitted fact that the manager gave her wrong advice as to the effect of the charge, ie that it only covered the amount of the loan and interest from the Abbey National, whereas in truth it covered all borrowing and other liabilities of the husband to the bank, was immaterial to the question of undue influence. Those matters might amount to negligent advice, if the bank had sought (which it did not) to recover more than the amount of the Abbey National loan, in which
g case the wife would have had a complete defence and counterclaim for damages for negligence. But that provided no ground for setting aside the whole transaction.

This point was referred to by Sir Eric Sachs in *Lloyds Bank Ltd v Bundy* [1974] 3 All ER 757 at 768, [1975] 1 QB 326 at 342. He first cited a passage from the judgment of Cotton LJ in *Allcard v Skinner* (1887) 36 Ch D 145 at 171, [1886–90] All ER Rep 90 at 93:

'"In the second class of cases the Court interferes, not on the ground that any
h wrongful act has in fact been committed by the donee, but on the ground of public policy, and to prevent the relations which existed between the parties and the influence arising therefrom being abused." . . . Stress was placed in argument for the bank on the effect of the word 'abused' as it appears in the above cited passage in the judgments of Cotton LJ and in other judgments and text books. As regards the second class of undue influence, however, that word in the context means no more
j than that once the existence of the special relationship has been established, then any possible use of the relevant influence is, irrespective of the intentions of the person possessing it, regarded in relation to the transaction under consideration as an abuse—unless and until the duty of fiduciary care has been shown to be fulfilled or the transaction is shown to be truly for the benefit of the person influenced. This approach is a matter of public policy.'

Counsel for the bank submitted that this transaction was truly for the benefit of the wife, but the passage to which I have referred shows that this does not prevent the existence of the confidential relationship arising in the first place. Slade LJ posed the case in argument of a solicitor who bought his client's house at a full and fair valuation. No doubt the relationship of confidence would exist, and there would be a presumption of undue influence. Only if the solicitor could show that the client had formed an independent and informed judgment could the transaction be upheld, and the mere fact that the price was fair would not be enough to discharge this. There might be all sorts of reasons, apart from the price, why the client did not want to sell his house.

It is true that in all the reported cases of undue influence to which we were referred the transactions were disadvantageous to the person influenced, otherwise they would not have sought to set them aside. As Sir Eric Sachs said in the passage I have cited, it is a matter of public policy which requires that once the relationship of confidence is established, then any possible use of the influence is regarded as an abuse. In this case the terms of the mortgage deed itself constituted a possible abuse of the confidential relationship, because they rendered the wife liable for the very thing she did not wish to accept, namely an open-ended liability for the debts of her husband. That was a possible abuse of the relationship, and in the light of it it cannot be said that the transaction was truly for the benefit of the wife. It is right to say that it was conceded before the assistant recorder that there could be no presumption of undue influence unless the transaction was manifestly disadvantageous to the person influenced. If this concession had not been made, the assistant recorder's conclusion might well have been different.

Counsel for the bank accepted that, if contrary to his submission the above proposition was correct and the transaction need not be disadvantageous to the person influenced, then he could not establish that the bank had performed its fiduciary duty, because the wife had not been given the opportunity of obtaining independent legal advice.

That brings me to the nub of the appeal, namely whether a confidential relationship existed. The relevant law is set out in the judgment of Sir Eric Sachs, with which Cairns LJ agreed, in *Lloyds Bank Ltd v Bundy* [1974] 3 All ER 757 at 766–767, [1975] 1 QB 326 at 341. Sir Eric Sachs said:

'As was pointed out in *Tufton v Sperni* [1952] 2 TLR 516 at 522, the relationships which result in such a duty must not be circumscribed by reference to defined limits; it is necessary to "refute the suggestion that, to create the relationship of confidence, the person owing a duty must be found clothed in the recognizable garb of a guardian, trustee, solicitor, priest, doctor, manager, or the like." Everything depends on the particular facts, and such a relationship has been held to exist in unusual circumstances as between purchaser and vendor, as between great uncle and adult nephew, and in other widely differing sets of circumstances. Moreover, it is neither feasible nor desirable to attempt closely to define the relationship, or its characteristics, or the demarcation line showing the exact transition point where a relationship that does not entail that duty passes into one that does (cf Ungoed-Thomas J in *Re Craig* [1970] 2 All ER 390 at 395–396, [1971] Ch 95 at 104). On the other hand, whilst disclaiming any intention of seeking to catalogue the elements of such a special relationship, it is perhaps of a little assistance to note some of those which have in the past frequently been found to exist where the court had been led to decide that this relationship existed as between adults of sound mind. Such cases tend to arise where someone relies on the guidance or advice of another, where the other is aware of that reliance and where the person on whom reliance is placed obtains, or may well obtain, a benefit from the transaction or has some other interest in it being concluded. In addition, there must, of course, be shown to exist a vital element which in this judgment will for convenience be referred to as confidentiality. It is this element which is so impossible to define and which is a matter for the judgment of the court on the facts of any particular case. Confidentiality, a relatively little used word, is being here adopted, albeit with some hesitation, to avoid the

a

b

c

possible confusion that can arise through referring to "confidence". Reliance on advice can in many circumstances be said to import that type of confidence which only results in a common law duty to take care—a duty which may co-exist with but is not coterminous with that of fiduciary care. "Confidentiality" is intended to convey that extra quality in the relevant confidence that is implicit in the phrase "confidential relationship" (cf per Lord Chelmsford LC in *Tate v Williamson* (1866) LR 2 Ch App 55 at 62, Lindley LJ in *Allcard v Skinner* (1887) 36 Ch D 145 at 181, [1886–90] All ER 90 at 98 and Wright J in *Morley v Loughnan* [1893] 1 Ch 736 at 751) and may perhaps have something in common with "confiding" and also "confidant", when, for instance, referring to someone's 'man of affairs'. It imports some quality beyond that inherent in the confidence that can well exist between trustworthy persons who in business affairs deal with each other at arm's length. It is one of the features of this element that once it exists, influence naturally grows out of it (cf Evershed MR in *Tufton v Sperni* [1952] 2 TLR 516 at 523, following Lord Chelmsford LC in *Tate v Willamson* LR 2 Ch App 55 at 61).'

d

There can be no doubt that in this case the bank obtained a benefit from the transaction. Banks are not charitable institutions, and the area office would not have approved the transaction unless it considered it to be for the benefit of the bank and its shareholders. So far as the bank was concerned it was a transaction whereby money was lent at commercial rates on ample security. The house was valued at £26,000 and the Abbey National debt with interest stood at £15,600.

e

Counsel for the bank submitted that this was no more than a transaction at arm's length between trustworthy persons, and did not involve the additional 'indefinable' element of confidentiality. He pointed out that the wife had never used the bank or the manager as her 'man of business', and that the only relationship between them was that of banker and customer, which did not of itself give rise to a confidential relationship. Further the meeting only lasted five minutes, which was insufficient to give rise to the confidential relationship.

f

In my view the fact that the manager took the document to the wife's house indicates something more than the relationship of banker and customer. When he arrived the wife explained to him that she did not wish to discuss the document in the presence of her husband. On the evidence of the manager himself, the wife was relying on his guidance and advice whether or not she should sign the document. She explained her fears to him in circumstances which, despite the shortness of the interview, must have shown him that she was relying on his advice. Everything that happened during the meeting showed that she was treating the manager as a confidant.

g

As Sir Eric Sachs said in *Lloyds Bank Ltd v Bundy* each case turns on its own facts. I am not to be taken as saying that every time a bank manager puts a document before a customer to sign, the confidential relationship arises. That would be contrary to the decided cases. But, on the unusual and special facts of this case in my judgment the confidential relationship did exist between the manager, representing the bank, and the wife immediately before she signed the document. Accordingly, the bank having failed to prove that it had fulfilled its fiduciary duty by recommending the wife to take independent legal advice, the presumption of undue influence prevails and the mortgage must be set aside. For those reasons I would allow the appeal.

h

SLADE LJ. I have had the advantage of reading in draft the judgment of Dunn LJ. I respectfully agree with it, but will add something of my own, both because we are differing from the assistant recorder and out of deference to counsel's excellent argument for the respondent bank.

j

The crucial question in this case is whether the circumstances in which the legal mortgage of 8 March 1978 came to be executed give rise to a presumption (albeit rebuttable) that the wife executed it by reason of the undue influence of the manager of the bank.

Counsel for the bank, as his first submission, contended that as a matter of law the
presumption is not capable of arising in relation to this transaction, on the grounds that *a*
the mortgage contract was not a manifestly disadvantageous one so far as the wife was
concerned. It appears to have been common ground in the county court that the contract
had to be shown to be manifestly disadvantageous to her if the presumption was to arise.
However, no such concession was made on her behalf in this court, and in my judgment
rightly so. No doubt the obviously disadvantageous nature of a particular transaction
may make it easier for a party to assert, in particular circumstances, that the presumption *b*
of law arises and, if it does arise, to show that it has not been rebutted. Nevertheless
nothing in *Lloyds Bank Ltd v Bundy* [1974] 3 All ER 757, [1975] 1 QB 326, or other cases
which have been cited to us, in my opinion establishes that it is always incumbent on a
party to a transaction to show that it is manifestly disadvantageous to him before he can
invoke the presumption. The purpose of the court in applying the presumption in
appropriate cases, as I understand it, is, as a matter of public policy, to mitigate the risk *c*
of a particular relationship existing between two parties and the influence arising
therefrom from being abused: see *Allcard v Skinner* (1887) 36 Ch D 145 at 171, [1886–
90] All ER Rep 90 at 93 per Cotton LJ. Where a transaction has been entered into
between two parties who stand in the relevant relationship to one another, it is still
possible that the relationship and influence arising therefrom has been abused, even
though the transaction is, on the face of it, one which, in commercial terms, provides *d*
reasonably equal benefits for both parties.

By the time when she came to execute the legal mortgage, the wife was already a
customer of the Taunton branch of the bank, where she had opened an account a few
weeks before. Mr Barrow was manager at that bank. Nevertheless, neither these, nor any
other facts in evidence, suffice to show that, before the manager came to see the wife at
the beginning of February for the purpose of procuring her signature to the proposed *e*
legal charge, there existed between him and her a relationship such as to give rise to the
relevant presumption. The mere existence of a banker-customer relationship does not,
in my opinion, by itself give rise to it.

I therefore accept the submission of course for the bank that everything turns on
whether there arose *at that meeting in early February* a relationship of what Sir Eric Sachs
in *Lloyds Bank Ltd v Bundy Ltd* [1974] 3 All ER 757 at 766–767, [1975] 1 QB 326 at 340– *f*
341 termed 'confidentiality', such as to give rise to what he called a duty of 'fiduciary
care' on the part of the bank.

In the latter case, Sir Eric Sachs expressed the view, with which I respectfully agree,
that the relationships which result in such a duty must not be circumscribed by reference
to defined limits and—

'it is neither feasible nor desirable to attempt closely to define the relationship, or *g*
its characteristics, or the demarcation line showing the exact transition point where
a relationship that does not entail that duty passes into one that does.'

(See [1974] 3 All ER 757 at 767, [1975] 1 QB 326 at 341.)

Nevertheless, like Dunn LJ, I have come to the conclusion that, on the particular facts
of this case, the meeting between the manager and the wife marked a transition point, *h*
where their relationship passed into one that entailed the duty of fiduciary care on the
part of the manager towards her. In this context among the points to which I attach
particular significance (though in no particular order) are the following. (1) As at
February 1978, as the wife and the manager both realised, the wife was in a vulnerable
situation, because the Abbey National Building Society had taken, or was threatening to
take, proceedings for possession of her home, but the wife was nevertheless reluctant to *j*
sign a new mortgage in favour of the bank. (2) Against this background, the manager,
instead of seeing her in his bank in the usual way, went to her house with a view to
procuring her signature to the document. (3) It was not the wife but her husband who
had suggested that the manager should go to their house in this way for this purpose. (4)
The manager knew that the husband was a somewhat improvident and unreliable

business man. (5) Shortly after the start of her conversation with the manager, the wife
a made it clear to him that she had no confidence in her husband's ability to manage his
business affairs, and specifically asked him for an assurance that the proposed mortgage
would not cover her husband's mortgage liabilities. (6) As the manager accepted in his
evidence, while the husband hovered around during the conversation, the wife made it
plain that she did not want him there. The inevitable inference to be drawn by the
manager was, in my opinion, that she did not want her husband there because she was
b looking to the manager for advice and considered that both she and he might be restricted
in seeking and giving advice if her husband was present. (7) The manager in answer to
the wife's specific question as to the scope of the mortgage, took it on himself to advise
her in what I infer must have been the full knowledge that she reposed confidence in
him, and that she was relying on his advice on a matter as to which she attached great
importance. (8) While the proposed transaction may or may not, on balance, have been a
c potentially beneficial one to the wife, it must be assumed that the bank considered it also
beneficial to itself because, as Dunn LJ has observed, banks are not charitable institutions.

No attack has been made in these proceedings on the manager's personal honesty and
integrity and I, of course, accept that he was throughout acting in entire good faith.
Nevertheless, I am of the opinion that the eight factors to which I have referred, taken
cumulatively, are amply sufficient to have given rise to a duty of fiduciary care on the
d part of the bank and to a presumption of undue influence.

If, as I have concluded, the duty of fiduciary care existed, it is, in my opinion, quite
clear on the evidence that it was not discharged. The duty in question is, broadly, to
ensure that the person liable to be influenced has formed an independent and informed
judgment after full, free and informed thought: see *Lloyds Bank Ltd v Bundy* [1974] 3 All
ER 757 at 768 [1975] 1 QB 326 at 342. No doubt in good faith, the manager unfortunately
e gave the wife entirely incorrect advice on the matter on which she had particularly
sought his guidance. He told her that the proposed mortgage would not cover her
husband's business liabilities, and as a result she signed the document under a complete
misapprehension. The decision in *Inche Noriah v Shaik Allie Bin Omar* [1929] AC 127,
[1928] All ER Rep 189 shows that independent legal advice is not necessarily in all cases
the only way in which a presumption of undue influence can be rebutted (see [1929] AC
f 127 at 135, [1928] All ER Rep 189 at 193 per Lord Hailsham LC). Nevertheless, I think
it clear that the prudent course for the manager to have adopted, when asked to advise
the wife as to the legal effect of this legal charge proposed to be executed by her in favour
of the bank, must have been to recommend her to seek legal advice on her own behalf.
This was the course which other representatives of the bank had very properly taken on
two previous occasions when the proposed execution of mortgages in its favour by the
g wife was under discussion.

In conclusion, I would make two unconnected comments. First, while I have thought
it unnecessary to deal with the point, I must not be taken as necessarily accepting the
view that the relevant transaction, in the form which it took, was not, on balance, a
manifestly disadvantageous transaction so far as the wife was concerned. The inference
from the manager's evidence seems to be that, if the wife had asked for the mortgage to
h be amended so as to exclude her husband's business liabilities, the bank would probably
have agreed to the amendment sought.

Second, I have already accepted that a banker-customer relationship does not by itself
give rise to a presumption of undue influence. Nevertheless, the present case illustrates
that, at least in my opinion, it is prudent for a bank to exercise a degree of caution before
volunteering legal advice to a customer in relation to a contract to which it and the
j customer are to be the parties. Though it may have a worthy desire to spare the customer
the trouble and expense of taking legal advice of his own, it has to bear in mind that, in
assuming the mantle of adviser, it may be placing itself in a position where the customer
is manifestly looking to it for protection, but its own interest and duty conflict. In such
circumstances the presumption of undue influence is, in my judgment, quite capable of
arising, though everything must depend on the facts of the particular case.

For these reasons, and the further reasons given by Dunn LJ, I would allow this appeal.

Appeal allowed; declaration that legal charge of 8 March 1978 not a good and subsisting charge in respect of the legal interest in the property or in respect of the wife's interest therein on 8 March 1978; respondents' application for leave to appeal to House of Lords refused.

Solicitors: *Clarke Willmott & Clarke*, Taunton (for the wife); *Osborne Clarke*, Bristol (for the bank).

Diana Brahams   Barrister.

C & P Haulage (a firm) v Middleton

COURT OF APPEAL, CIVIL DIVISION

ACKNER AND FOX LJJ

27 JUNE 1983

Contract – Damages for breach – Licence – Licence to occupy premises – Contractual licence – Terms of licence providing that fixtures not to be removed at end of licence – Licensee expending money on fixtures – Licensor ejecting licensee in breach of contract – Licensee moving to rent-free premises until after licence would have expired – Licensee claiming cost of fixtures as damages – Whether licensee entitled to be put in same position as if contract never made – Whether licensee only entitled to be put in position he would have been in if contract performed.

The appellant, a self-employed engineer, was granted a contractual licence to occupy premises on a renewable six-monthly basis. He expended money in making the premises suitable for the purposes of his work even though it was expressly provided that fixtures put in by him were not to be removed at the expiry of the licence. Ten weeks before the end of a six months' term he was unlawfully ejected from the premises by the licensor after a disagreement. As a temporary measure the appellant obtained permission from the local authority to use his own home for his work, which he did until well after the six months' term would have expired. The appellant claimed against the licensor for the cost of the improvements effected by him in the premises. The judge held that, although the licensor was in breach of contract by ejecting the appellant before the expiry of the term, the appellant had suffered no loss since he had been able to move to his home rent free and the expenditure on improvements to the premises would still have been lost even if the licence had been validly terminated at the end of the six months. The appellant appealed, contending that he was entitled to recover his expenditure on the premises by way of damages for breach of contract.

Held – In assessing damages for breach of contract the court had to endeavour to put a plaintiff in the position he would have been in had the contract been performed. The appellant had not suffered any loss as a result of the licensor's breach since, in the circumstances, he was no worse off than if the contract had been fully performed. He was not entitled to claim the expenses incurred as a result of making the contract so as to return him to the position he had been in before he entered into the contract, since that would compensate him at the licensor's expense for the bad bargain he had made and would leave him better off than he would have been had the contract been wholly performed. The appeal would accordingly be dismissed save that judgment would be entered for nominal damages of £10 (see p 99 g to p 100 b and e f, post).

Bowlay Logging Ltd v Domtar Ltd [1978] 4 WWR 105 applied.

Lloyd v Stanbury [1971] 2 All ER 267 and *Anglia Television Ltd v Reed* [1971] 3 All ER 690 distinguished.

Notes

a For the assessment of damages, see 12 Halsbury's Laws (4th edn) paras 1174–1185, and for cases on the subject, see 17 Digest (Reissue) 101–112, 109–167.

Cases referred to in judgments

Albert (L) & Son v Armstrong Rubber Co (1949) 178 F 2d 182.
Anglia Television Ltd v Reed [1971] 3 All ER 690, [1972] 1 QB 60, [1971] 3 WLR 528, CA.
b *Bowlay Logging Ltd v Domtar Ltd* [1978] 4 WWR 105.
Cullinane v British 'Rema' Manufacturing Co Ltd [1953] 2 All ER 1257, [1954] 1 QB 292, [1953] 3 WLR 923, CA.
Hodges v Earl of Litchfield (1835) 1 Bing NC 492, [1835–42] All ER Rep 551.
Lloyd v Stanbury [1971] 2 All ER 267, [1971] 1 WLR 535.
Perestrello & Cia Ltda v United Paint Co Ltd (No 2) (1969) 113 SJ 324.
c *Wallington v Townsend* [1939] 2 All ER 225, [1939] Ch 588.

Cases also cited

Collins v Howard [1949] 2 All ER 324, CA.
Pelosi v Newcastle Arms Brewery (Nottingham) Ltd (1982) 43 P & CR 18.
Ponte Naya (CIA) Maritima SA v Liberty Marine Inc (18 February 1983, unreported), QBD.
d *Saint Line Ltd v Richardsons Westgarth & Co Ltd* [1940] 2 KB 99.
Spedding v Nevell (1869) LR 4 CP 212.

Appeal

Gordon Middleton appealed against the decision of his Honour Judge Eric Stockdale in Watford County Court on 13 September 1982 whereby judgment was entered for the
e respondents, C & P Haulage (a firm), on the appellant's counterclaim for the sum of £1,767·51. The facts are set out in the judgment of Ackner LJ.

Andrew Keogh for the appellant.
David Lamming for the respondents.

f **ACKNER LJ.** This appeal, which has been admirably argued on both sides, arises out of these facts. The appellant is an automobile engineer and repairer. He had been up to the end of 1978 working from a garage, part of his own home. The local authority, however, objected to this use being made of domestic property, and they gave him the appropriate notice to desist. He thereupon urgently looked round for other accommodation.

g C & P Haulage, the respondents in this case, a firm which carried on the business of plant hire, were well known to the appellant, he having done work for them and they having hired machinery to him. Knowing one of the partners, he discussed with him the terms on which he might use a yard they had, which had a covered workshop, and which was only used for storage. Eventually they entered, on or about 15 December 1978, into an agreement. This is essentially contained in a document which emanated
h from the respondents, the material terms of which read as follows:

'Before offering you the use of our yard at Winton Approach we would like you to agree to the following: 1) The use of the yard to be reviewed every six months. 2) We require spare keys to any locks which you may wish to fix on outer doors. 3) We require to know whom besides yourself will be working in the yard. 4) We would not except [sic] any liability for any injury or accident while on our premises.
j 5) Any fixtures you put in are left. 6) The rates and electricity to be paid by you via C & P. The bills will be seen by you.'

The agreement itself does not in fact refer to what payment should be made, but the judge in the county court accepted that there would in due course be an agreement as to the payment. The judge concluded (and this is not challenged; in fact it was accepted

before him) that the agreement amounted in law to a licence. It was not a lease. The
payment had still to be discussed.

The appellant moved in and began to use the premises for commercial purposes but
not until towards the end of 1978. He had to carry out quite a considerable amount of
work to make the premises suitable for his purpose. A wall had to be built enclosing the
premises, locks had to be fitted, and electricity had to be laid on.

On 16 June he was still in occupation. The judge concluded, and again this is not
challenged, that the licence was for six months with renewal every six months. It could
thus be terminated every six months, and he took the view, and this has not been
challenged, that a reasonable notice prior to its termination of one month at least would
have been necessary.

Accordingly, when 16 June went by, no notice having been given, a second period of
six months then started, with the result that the appellant was at least sure of the licence
continuing until 15 December 1979.

Unfortunately there was some misunderstanding or trouble on 5 October, by which
time the premises were completed and were being used for the garage work, when the
senior partner of the firm had some difficulty in getting oil from a drum which had been
moved without his permission. He became very angry, and told the appellant to get out.
The locks were changed. The appellant did not take the sensible course of consulting
solicitors, who undoubtedly would have advised him to apply for an injunction and
appropriate further relief. He accepted the position. He managed to climb in and, with
help, moved his essential equipment out of the premises. He went back to his own
garage. He told the council about his predicament, and they were very sympathetic. He
was allowed to stay where he was, which meant of course he did not pay any rent because
it was his property, and he was allowed to remain using the premises, despite the council's
previous objection, for a period of a year. The council clearly behaved both generously
and reasonably.

The proceedings in this case were in fact begun by the respondents. They brought
proceedings on the basis of a cheque which had been provided by the appellant and
which had not been paid. The appellant had stopped payment because of his grievance
with regard to being summarily ejected from the premises after paying a considerable
amount on effecting the improvements of which I have made mention. That of course
was no answer to the claim on the cheque, and judgment was duly signed.

A defence and counterclaim had been put in which contained the appellant's claim for
the reimbursement of his expenditure on the premises, and it is in relation to that
counterclaim that this appeal arises from the decision of his Honour Judge Eric Stockdale
given on 13 September 1982 at the Watford County Court. In those proceedings, of
course, the appellant was in effect the plaintiff suing the respondents, the firm, for
damages for breach of contract, the contract being the licence agreement to which I have
referred. His claim amounted to £1,767·51, which covered labour and material used in
building the wall, to which I have referred, laying on the electricity and moving or
transferring a telephone.

There is no dispute, and counsel for the appellant frankly accepted that at the outset of
this appeal, that under the agreement the appellant could not take out of the premises at
the termination of the agreement any fixtures. There was the specific provision in para 5
that they were to be left. He secondly accepted that the agreement could have been
lawfully terminated ten weeks later, on 15 December 1979, than the date on which it
was unlawfully and summarily determined on 5 October.

The judge concluded that, since in those ten weeks the appellant had been able to
return to his own garage and pay no rent, he had suffered no damage, and he accordingly
gave judgment against the appellant. The judge accepted that in putting new locks on
the premises on 5 October and making it impossible for the appellant to return and use
the yard and premises that was a breach of contract by the respondents.

At the outset of this appeal we raised the point that, having established a breach of
contract, the appellant was entitled to judgment. If he could prove no damages beyond

nominal damages, then the judgment would have to be limited to nominal damages.
a Accordingly, when this matter was further considered, the notice of appeal was amended
to take this point, and counsel for the respondents very sensibly accepted that there was
no answer to the proposition that the judge should in fact have entered judgment for the
appellant, although, on the basis of the judge's decision, only for nominal damages of
£10.

The appeal here has not been concerned with that criticism of the judge. The
b submissions made by counsel for the appellant are essentially the same submissions
which he made before the judge. They are to the effect that the appellant, having
expended this sum of money, was entitled to recover that sum of money back by way of
damages for breach of contract.

The judge approached the case essentially on this basis, that the accepted principle in
relation to the assessment of damages for breach of contract was to put the plaintiff in the
c same position, as far as one could, as he would have been in if the contract had been
performed; and, in order to evaluate whether if the contract had been performed what
was the nature, if any, of the damage that he should be entitled to claim, one had to look
at the consequences of the breach of contract.

The consequences of this breach of contract were that, so far from the appellant
suffering any damage as a result of being excluded from the premises ten weeks earlier
d than would lawfully have been the case, thanks to the tolerance of the planning
authorities, he had in effect been saved the payment which was likely to be between £60
and £100 a week which he would have, had to have paid for the use of the respondents'
premises. He accordingly came to the conclusion that if he was to award the damages
claimed he would be putting the appellant in a better position than would have been the
case if the contract had been lawfully determined.

The case which was at the forefront of counsel for the appellant's submissions before
e the judge and before us as well is *Anglia Television Ltd v Reed* [1971] 3 All ER 690, [1972]
1 QB 60. There the defendant, a well-known actor, contracted with the plaintiffs, Anglia
Television Ltd, to play the leading man's part in a television play which they were
producing. A few days afterwards the defendant repudiated the contract. Anglia
Television could not get a substitute, accepted his repudiation and abandoned the
f production. They sued him for nearly £3,000 total wasted expenditure. In his judgment
Lord Denning MR said ([1971] 3 All ER 690 at 691–692, [1972] 1 QB 60 at 63–64):

> 'Counsel for Mr Reed [the actor] has referred us to the recent unreported case of
> *Perestrello & Compania Limitada v United Paint Co Ltd (No 2)* (1969) 113 SJ 324, in
> which Thesiger J quoted the words of Lord Tindal CJ in 1835 in *Hodges v Earl of
> Litchfield* 1 Bing NC 492 at 498, [1835–42] All ER Rep 551 at 552–553: "The
> g expenses preliminary to the contract ought not to be allowed. The party enters into
> them for his own benefit at a time when it is uncertain whether there will be any
> contract or not." Thesiger J applied those words, saying: "In my judgment pre-
> contract expenditure, though thrown away, is not recoverable . . ." I cannot accept
> the proposition as stated. It seems to me that a plaintiff in such a case as this has an
> election: he can either claim for his loss of profits; or for his wasted expenditure.
> h But he must elect between them. He cannot claim both. If he has not suffered any
> loss of profits—or if he cannot prove what his profits would have been—he can
> claim in the alternative the expenditure which has been thrown away, that is,
> wasted, by reason of the breach. That is shown by *Cullinane v British 'Rema'
> Manufacturing Co Ltd* [1953] 2 All ER 1257 at 1261, 1264–1265, [1954] 1 QB 292 at
> 303, 308.'

j Lord Denning MR was not contemplating what has been referred to subsequently as
the 'bad bargain' case, a case in which a plaintiff has entered into a loss-making contract
or, I would include, an otherwise disadvantageous contract. He was considering a case
where it would not be possible to establish any loss of profits because the situation could
not be prophesied had the defendant complied with his contractual obligations. Mr Reed

in the *Anglia Television* case had not taken part in the film: the film had never been made. It was therefore quite impossible to assess whether the film, had it been made, would have been a success and would have earned a profit. Therefore Anglia Television were thrown back on limiting their claim to the expense thrown away.

As I have indicated from the excerpt from the judgment of Lord Denning MR, he referred to and relied on the *Cullinane* case [1953] 2 All ER 1257 at 1264, [1954] 1 QB 292 at 308. Lord Denning MR made reference to this statement in the judgment of Jenkins LJ:

'The general principle applicable to the case is, I apprehend, this. The plant having been supplied in contemplation by both parties that it should be used by the plaintiff in the commercial production of pulverised clay, the case is one in which the plaintiff can claim as damages for the breach of warranty the loss of the profit he can show that he would have made if the plant had been as warranted. Where damages are awarded on that basis the object in view (as, indeed, in any other assessment of damages) is to put the plaintiff in the same position (so far as money can put him in the same position) as if the contract had been duly complied with or the subject-matter of the contract had conformed to any warranty given.'

That is not the approach which the appellant seeks. He is not claiming for the loss of his bargain, which would involve being put in the position that he would have been in if the contract had been performed. He is not asking to be put in that position. He is asking to be put in the position he would have been in if the contract had never been made at all. If the contract had never been made at all, then he would not have incurred these expenses, and that is the essential approach he adopts in mounting this claim; because, if the right approach is that he should be put in the position in which he would have been had the contract been performed, then it follows that he suffered no damage. He lost his entitlement to a further ten weeks of occupation after 5 October, and during that period he involved himself in no loss of profit, because he found other accommodation, and in no increased expense, in fact the contrary, because he returned immediately to his own garage, thereby saving whatever would have been the agreed figure which he would have to have paid the respondents.

We have had our attention invited to two cases which deal with the sale and purchase of land, and, speaking for myself, I do not think they bear on the particular question which we have to consider. Those cases were *Wallington v Townsend* [1939] 2 All ER 225, [1939] Ch 588 and *Lloyd v Stanbury* [1971] 2 All ER 267, [1971] 1 WLR 535.

The case which I have found of assistance, and I am grateful to counsel for their research, is *Bowlay Logging Ltd v Domtar Ltd* [1978] 4 WWR 105. It is a case in the British Columbia Supreme Court. Berger J, in a very careful and detailed judgment, goes through various English and American authorities and refers to the leading textbook writers, and I will only quote a small part of his judgment. He refers (at 116) to the work of Professor L L Fuller and William R Perdue Jr in 'The Reliance Interest in Contract Damages' (1936) 46 Yale LJ 52 at 79:

'We will not in a suit for reimbursement for losses incurred in reliance on a contract knowingly put the plaintiff in a better position than he would have occupied had the contract been fully performed.'

Berger J then refers to a case in 1949, *L Albert & Son v Armstrong Rubber Co* 178 F 2d 182, in which Learned Hand CJ, speaking for the Circuit Court of Appeals, Second Circuit, 'held that on a claim for compensation for expenses in part performance the defendant was entitled to deduct whatever he could prove the plaintiff would have lost if the contract had been fully performed'.

What Berger J had to consider was this (at 105):

'The parties entered into a contract whereby the plaintiff would cut timber under the defendant's timber sale, and the defendant would be responsible for hauling the a timber away from the site of the timber sale. The plaintiff claimed the defendant was in breach of the contract as the defendant had not supplied sufficient trucks to make the plaintiff's operation, which was losing money, viable, and claimed not for loss of profits but for compensation for expenditures. The defendant argued that the plaintiff's operation lost money not because of a lack of trucks but because of the plaintiff's inefficiency, and, further, that even if the defendant had breached the contract the plaintiff should not be awarded damages because its operation would

b have lost money in any case.'

This submission was clearly accepted because the plaintiff was awarded only nominal damages, and Berger J said (at 117):

'The law of contract compensates a plaintiff for damages resulting from the defendant's breach ; it does not compensate a plaintiff for damages resulting from his making a bad bargain. Where it can be seen that the plaintiff would have

c incurred a loss on the contract as a whole, the expenses he has incurred are losses flowing from entering into the contract, not losses flowing from the defendant's breach. In these circumstances, the true consequence of the defendant's breach is that the plaintiff is released from his obligation to complete the contract—or in other words, he is saved from incurring further losses. If the law of contract were to

d move from compensating for the consequences of breach to compensating for the consequences of entering into contracts, the law would run contrary to the normal expectations of the world of commerce. The burden of risk would be shifted from the plaintiff to the defendant. The defendant would become the insurer of the plaintiff's enterprise. Moreover, the amount of the damages would increase not in relation to the gravity or consequences of the breach but in relation to the inefficiency with which the plaintiff carried out the contract. The greater his expenses owing to

e inefficiency, the greater the damages. The fundamental principle upon which damages are measured under the law of contract is restitutio in integrum. The principle contended for here by the plaintiff would entail the award of damages not to compensate the plaintiff but to punish the defendant.'

It is urged here that the garage itself was merely an element in the appellant's business:

f it was not a profit-making entity on its own. Nevertheless, if as a result of being kept out of these premises the appellant had found no other premises to go to for a period of time, his claim would clearly have been a claim for such loss of profit as he could establish his business suffered.

In my judgment, the approach of Berger J is the correct one. It is not the function of the courts where there is a breach of contract knowingly, as this would be the case, to put

g the plaintiff in a better financial position than if the contract had been properly performed. In this case the appellant, if he was right in his claim, would indeed be in a better position because, as I have already indicated, had the contract been lawfully determined, as it could have been in the middle of December, there would have been no question of his recovering these expenses.

This is a case, let it be stressed, where there was no question ultimately of the appellant

h being able to establish that he was a tenant; but, had he been a tenant, then the compensation for the improvements which he had carried out would have been regulated by the Landlord and Tenant Act 1927. That would have involved him in complying with the various conditions which that Act lays down before a valid claim for compensation for improvements can be made; but, even when such a claim is open to a tenant, there is a ceiling put to what can be recovered, namely the net addition to the

j value of the holding, which may be far less than the money actually expended on the improvements.

So the approach which the judge was asked to follow, and which we have also been invited to follow, would not only put this licensee in a better position as a result of the breach than if the licence had been lawfully determined but would put him in a better position than if he had achieved the superior status in law of being a tenant and not a licensee.

I do not consider that the plaintiff is entitled in an action for damages for breach of contract to ask to be put in the position in which he would have been if the contract had never been made where it is easy to assess what his position would have been if the contract had been performed.

Accordingly, save in the respect to which I have already made reference, namely that there should be judgment for the appellant for nominal damages of £10, I would dismiss the appeal.

FOX LJ. I agree. We were referred on behalf of the appellant to *Lloyd v Stanbury* [1971] 2 All ER 267, [1971] 1 WLR 535 and to the comments on it by Lord Denning MR in *Anglia Television Ltd v Reed* [1971] 3 All ER 690, [1972] 1 QB 60. In *Lloyd v Stanbury* there was a contract for the sale of land. In anticipation of the contract and before it was actually concluded the purchaser incurred expense in moving his caravan onto the site and of getting his furniture there as well. The seller broke the contract and failed to convey. The land had not increased in value, so the purchaser could not claim a loss of profit. It was held that he could recover the cost of moving his caravan and his furniture onto the site. Lord Denning MR in the *Anglia Television* case [1971] 3 All ER 690 at 692, [1972] QB 60 at 64 said this of *Lloyd v Stanbury*:

'That decision is in accord with the correct principle, namely, that wasted expenditure can be recovered when it is wasted by reason of the defendant's breach of contract.'

The present case seems to me to be quite different both from *Anglia Television Ltd v Reed* and from *Lloyd v Stanbury* in that, while it is true that the expenditure could in a sense be said to be wasted in consequence of the breach of contract, it was equally likely to be wasted if there had been no breach, because the respondents wanted to get the appellant out and could terminate the licence at quite short notice. A high risk of waste was from the very first inherent in the nature of the contract itself, breach or no breach. The reality of the matter is that the waste resulted from what was, on the appellant's side, a very unsatisfactory and dangerous bargain.

I agree with Ackner LJ that the appeal must be dismissed.

Appeal dismissed save that judgment be entered for the appellant for nominal damages of £10. Costs in Court of Appeal but no order for costs below.

Solicitors: *Hanbury Gery Brooks & Weston*, Rickmansworth (for the appellant); *Woolley & Weston*, St Albans (for the respondents).

Frances Rustin   Barrister.

R v Watts

a

COURT OF APPEAL, CRIMINAL DIVISION
LORD LANE CJ, McCULLOUGH AND LEONARD JJ
6 MAY 1983

b *Criminal evidence – Character of accused – Previous conviction – Cross-examination as to previous conviction – Imputation on character of prosecutor or witness – Police – Confession – Allegation that police witness fabricated confession – Whether cross-examination as to previous convictions permissible – Criminal Evidence Act 1898, s 1(f)(ii).*

The appellant, who was of low intelligence and had two previous convictions for sexual offences against children, was interviewed by the police after a young married woman was indecently assaulted near his home by a man whose description fitted the appellant.
c The appellant made plain admissions to the police both orally and in a statement and he was later charged with the indecent assault. At his trial he advanced an alibi defence and in effect claimed that the police had fabricated the admission evidence. The prosecution then sought, and was granted, leave pursuant to s 1(f)(ii)[a] of the Criminal Evidence Act 1898 to cross-examine him as to his previous convictions. The jury found him guilty of
d the offence. The appellant appealed, contending that the judge had wrongly exercised his discretion by allowing the cross-examination as to previous convictions.

Held – The sole reason for admitting evidence of a defendant's previous convictions pursuant to s 1(f) of the 1898 Act was to establish the extent of his credibility; such evidence was not admissible to enable a jury to infer that a defendant was guilty of the
e offence charged. The fact of the previous sexual offences added little if anything to the issue of the appellant's credibility, especially as those past offences did not involve dishonesty, but their prejudicial effect was considerable because, although they were not sufficiently similar to be admitted as similar fact evidence on the issue of identity, they would lead the jury to conclude that the appellant had committed the offence charged. It followed that the judge had failed properly to exercise his discretion in permitting
f cross-examination as to the appellant's previous convictions. The appeal would accordingly be allowed and the conviction quashed (see p 103 j, to p 104 a and e to j and p 105 a b, post).
Dictum of Viscount Sankey LC in *Maxwell v DPP* [1934] All ER Rep at 174 applied.

Notes
g For cross-examination of defendant as to character, see 11 Halsbury's Laws (4th edn) paras 388–391, and for cases on the subject, see 14(2) Digest (Reissue) 499–503, 4074–4125.
For the Criminal Evidence Act 1898, s 1, see 12 Halsbury's Statutes (3rd edn) 865.

Cases referred to in judgment
Maxwell v DPP [1935] AC 309, [1934] All ER Rep 168, HL.
h *R v Duncalf* [1979] 2 All ER 1116, [1979] 1 WLR 918, CA.
R v France [1979] Crim LR 48, CA.

Appeal
On 21 September 1982 in the Crown Court at Swansea before his Honour Judge Howells and a jury the appellant, William Winston Idwal Watts, was convicted of indecent assault
j and sentenced to 18 months' imprisonment. In addition a suspended sentence of two years' imprisonment was activated and ordered to run concurrently. The appellant appealed against conviction on the ground that the judge erred in the exercise of his

a Section 1, so far as material, is set out at, p 102 *h j*, post discretion in permitting the prosecution to elicit in cross-examination of the appellant details of his previous convictions. The facts are set out in the judgment of the court.

a

Frank Phillips (assigned by the Registrar of Criminal Appeals) for the appellant.
Rameshwar Singh for the Crown.

LORD LANE CJ delivered the following judgment of the court. On 21 September 1982 in the Crown Court at Swansea, the appellant was convicted of indecent assault on a woman and was sentenced to 18 months' imprisonment. He was the subject of a suspended sentence of two years which was passed on him in August 1981, and that sentence was ordered to take effect concurrently. He now appeals against conviction by leave of the single judge.

b

The facts of the case were these. The complainant was a young married woman. Her statement was read. She said that shortly after midday on Monday, 19 April 1982 she was in an underpass in the centre of Swansea walking along pushing her baby in a push chair. A man rushed up behind her, put one hand over her mouth and the other hand up her skirt and indecently assaulted her. She cried out and he ran off. She did not see his face, but she described him as follows: 5 ft 7 in, slim, dark wispy curly hair, balding on top but full and collar length at the back, and wearing black trousers and a black jumper.

c

It so happens that the appellant lived only two or three minutes away from the scene of that incident. As he had convictions for sexual offences and appeared to match the description which the victim had given, two police officers went to his home to interview him on 12 May, about three weeks after the incident in question. It is right to say immediately that he is a man of low intelligence with a history of epileptic fits.

d

They said they were making inquiries into an indecent assault which had taken place at the place on the date I have already indicated, and asked him if he could help. The first thing he said was 'Don't say any more in front of my wife'. That was not a remark which implicated him at all. An innocent person might well have said that. Eventually he went with them to the police station, where, according to Woman Det Con Brain and Det Con Mages, he made plain admissions both orally and later in a statement which they took down at his dictation and he signed.

e

The appellant gave evidence. He denied committing the assault. He said that on the day in question he had been to a speech clinic with his young son who had some impediment or defect in speaking, that his wife was with him and that he never left them. At the time when the offence was committed, said he, he was at home and was nowhere near the underpass. He said, if not in terms, that the police had fabricated the oral admissions and had written down the statement not at his dictation but by making it appear that he had spoken the words in the statement when he had done nothing of the sort.

f

g

The prosecution asked the judge for leave to take action under the terms of s 1(f)(ii) of the Criminal Evidence Act 1898, which reads, so far as material, as follows:

'A person charged and called as a witness in pursuance of this Act [that is what the appellant was] shall not be asked, and if asked shall not be required to answer, any question tending to show that he has committed or been convicted of or been charged with any offence other than that wherewith he is then charged, or is of bad character, unless . . . (ii) he has personally or by his advocate asked questions of the witnesses for the prosecution with a view to establish his own good character, or has given evidence of his good character, or the nature or conduct of the defence is such as to involve imputations on the character of the prosecutor or the witnesses for the prosecution . . .'

h

j

Plainly in this case the nature and conduct of the defence was such as to involve imputations on the character of the two police officers who, it was alleged by the appellant, had made up the statement which they attributed to him.

The passage in the transcript where Mr Singh, as counsel for the prosecution, raised
a this point, which occurred during the course of the cross-examination of the appellant,
and was in the presence of the jury, runs as follows:

> 'Mr Singh. Your Honour, I have an application to make. It would involve a matter
> of law.
> Judge Howells. Well, I apprehend the nature of the application, and I canvassed it
> in an indirect manner on a few occasions with Mr Phillips [who was counsel for the
b appellant], who indicated he would not be in a sense resisting. Mr Phillips. Well,
> your Honour, the only thing I can say is to invite your Honour's discretion in the
> matter. It does fall within the pattern.
> Judge Howells. No. I grant you leave. Mr Singh. I am grateful.'

With that Mr Singh put to the appellant his previous convictions in the following way:
c

> 'Q. It is right that on 6 July 1979 you were convicted by the Swansea Magistrates
> for indecent assault? A. Yes.
> Q. And you were placed on probation for two years, Mr Watts? A. Yes.'

Then Mr Singh started to go into the detail in this way: 'It is right that on that occasion
at about 4 pm you had . . .' Mr Phillips then interposed:
d

> 'Mr Phillips. Your Honour, if my learned friend is going to deal with the details of
> that, I would object to that, because it is not in my submission within the terms of
> the statute.
> Judge Howells. I think that is right, is it not, Mr Singh? You are entitled, now that
> I have given you leave to do so, and you would not otherwise be entitled, to cross-
e examine about previous convictions, but you are not entitled to cross-examine about
> the actual circumstances of the convictions, are you? Mr Singh. Your Honour, I will
> accept that ruling.'

Mr Singh went on:

> 'Q. Were you again convicted at this court on 24 August 1981 of attempting to
f have sexual intercourse and indecent assault . . .
> Judge Howells. Well, there is no such offence as attempted sexual intercourse,
> unless it be attempted rape, or attempted sexual intercourse with a girl under the
> age of 16 years, the age of consent. What was the actual offence? Mr Singh. I am
> grateful, your Honour. I will deal with that.'

Then he went on:
g

> 'Q. It is right that you were convicted of attempting to have sexual intercourse
> with a child of five years of age, that was your sister-in-law's daughter? A. Yes.
> Q. And you indecently assaulted a three year old niece of yours? A. Yes.
> Q. And you were sentenced by this court to two years' imprisonment, suspended
> for two years? A. Yes.
h Q. And you were also dealt with for breach of the probation, when you were
> given six months' imprisonment, suspended for two years? A. Yes.'

So before the jury there was evidence that he had in the past committed a number of
indecent assaults on young girls when the charge before the jury was indecent assault on
a woman.
j Counsel for the appellant submits that the judge was wrong to exercise his discretion
to allow these convictions to be put to the appellant.
There is no doubt that the law on this particular topic is in an unhappy state. There
are numerous decisions of this court and of the House of Lords to the effect that the only
relevance of the previous convictions of the defendant, admitted by virtue of s 1 of the
Criminal Evidence Act 1898, is as to the credibility of the prisoner, and that the jury

must not be asked to infer guilt from such convictions. This in many cases requires the
jury to perform difficult feats of intellectual acrobatics. In the view of this court the   *a*
present case is a good example.

We have been referred to a number of authorities, amongst them *R v France* [1979]
Crim LR 48 and a further decision of this court, *R v Duncalf* [1979] 2 All ER 1116, [1979]
1 WLR 918. We have had the opportunity of seeing a transcript of the judgment in *R v
France* and it is quite plain that the text is corrupt. There are a number of obvious
misprints and mistakes. The transcript was not apparently approved by the judge who   *b*
delivered the judgment, and we view *R v France* therefore with considerable suspicion.

In any event it seems to us that where the exercise of discretion is concerned, which is
the problem here, each case is a case on its own and has to be considered on its own
particular facts.

The jury in the present case was charged with deciding the guilt or innocence of a man
against whom an allegation of indecent assault on a woman was made. They were told   *c*
that he had previous convictions for indecent assaults of a more serious kind on young
girls. They were warned that such evidence was not to be taken as making it more likely
that he was guilty of the offence charged, which it seems it plainly did, but only as
affecting his credibility, which it almost certainly did not.

The passage in which the judge directed the jury to that effect runs as follows:

> 'And then his previous offences were put to him, members of the jury. And of   *d*
> course you will not use that knowledge in any way as being evidence against him of
> committing this offence. It is not. The fact that a person has committed an offence
> on a previous occasion does not make him any more or less likely to be guilty of
> committing an offence on a subsequent occasion. It is not evidence. It was only
> allowed to be brought to your knowledge because of the serious allegations of
> misconduct which are made by the defendant, albeit he is a man of low intelligence,   *e*
> against the police. You are entitled to know that a person has previous offences
> when such assertions are made, but not as evidence against him.'

The direction was, of itself, sound in law but in the circumstances of this case it would
have been extremely difficult, if not practically impossible, for the jury to have done
what the judge was suggesting. The prejudice which the appellant must have suffered in   *f*
the eyes of the jury when it was disclosed that he had previous convictions for offences
against young children could hardly have been greater. The probative value of the
convictions, on the sole issue on which they were admissible, was, at best, slight. The
previous offences did not involve dishonesty. Nor were they so similar to the offence
which the jury were trying that they could have been admitted as evidence of similar
facts on the issue of identity. In short, their prejudicial effect far outweighed their   *g*
probative value. We would not have allowed this particular man to have been cross-
examined about these particular convictions in these particular circumstances. That is
not, however, the end of the matter. This court will not simply substitute its own
discretion for that of the judge. But in the present case it seems to us that the judge was
not given an opportunity to exercise his discretion on a proper basis. In fairness to him
neither counsel placed all the relevant considerations before him. It was all done in a   *h*
hurry and in the presence of the jury. We cannot help feeling that if the matter had been
argued before him in the absence of the jury and in the same care as that with which we
have examined the case today, he would have exercised his discretion differently.

There is a passage in the opinion of their Lordships in *Maxwell v DPP* [1935] AC 309
at 321, [1934] All ER Rep 168 at 174 which seems to us to be appropriate. It is in the
speech of Viscount Sankey LC. It relates, inter alia, to the exercise of the judge's discretion   *j*
and reads as follows:

> '... the question whether a man has been convicted ... ought not to be admitted
> ... if there is any risk of the jury being misled into thinking that it goes not to
> credibility but to the probability of his having committed the offence of which he
> is charged.'

a That exactly fits the present circumstances, and, for the reasons which we have endeavoured to indicate, this grave risk was overlooked by the judge. In those circumstances the only matter which remains to be considered is whether this is an appropriate case for the application of the proviso. We think that it is not. It is quite impossible to say what might have been the result of this case had these previous convictions not been put before the jury. Accordingly we allow this appeal and quash the conviction.

b Other matters have been argued before us. First of all, the question what detail about his previous convictions the prosecution is allowed to elicit from a defendant in these circumstances and, secondly, whether the directions which the judge gave about corroboration were adequate. Those are matters into which we do not have to inquire, because the first point is decided in favour of the appellant.

c *Appeal allowed. Conviction quashed.*

Solicitors: J M Timmons, Cardiff (for the Crown).

N P Metcalfe Esq   Barrister.

d
London and South of England Building Society v Stone

COURT OF APPEAL, CIVIL DIVISION
STEPHENSON, O'CONNOR LJJ AND SIR DENYS BUCKLEY
e 25, 26, 27, 28 APRIL, 27 MAY 1983

Damages – Measure of damages – Negligence – Valuer – Valuer negligently recommending property to lender as security for mortgage advance – Lender making advance in reliance on valuation – Subsidence rendering property valueless – Subsidence not discovered until after purchase completed by borrowers – Lender expending more than amount of original advance to
f *repair property to prevent its collapse – Lender electing not to recover costs of repairs from borrowers – Borrowers selling property and repaying advance – Lender suing valuer for negligent valuation – Whether lender acting reasonably in undertaking repairs – Whether damages limited to difference between amount of advance and amount which would have been lent on a proper valuation – Whether all direct loss and expense recoverable as damages – Whether lender acting unreasonably in electing not to recover from borrowers under their personal covenant – Whether*
g *value of personal covenant to be deducted from award of damages.*

Damages – Mitigation of loss – Benefit accruing to plaintiff – Defendant valuer negligently recommending property as security for mortgage advance – Lender making advance in reliance on valuation – Subsidence rendering property valueless – Subsidence not discovered until after purchase completed – Lender electing not to seek repayment from borrowers under personal
h *covenant in order to protect commercial reputation – Lender suing valuer for amount of mortgage advance – Whether lender acting unreasonably in not enforcing personal covenant – Whether lender under a duty to mitigate loss by enforcing covenant.*

In 1976 the lender, a building society, instructed a valuer to carry out a valuation of a property for the purpose of making a mortgage advance to prospective purchasers (the
j borrowers). The valuer recommended the property as being suitable security for the requested loan and consequently the lender advanced £11,880 to the borrowers, the advance being secured by a legal charge on the property on completion of the purchase. By the terms of the legal charge the borrowers convenanted, inter alia, 'to keep any buildings on the Property in good and tenantable repair', in default of which the lender could effect necessary repairs to the property, the expenditure of doing so being a charge

on the property until repaid. The valuer's survey failed to disclose that the dwelling suffered from serious subsidence which rendered it valueless and which had the lender *a* known of it would have caused the lender not to advance any money on the security of the property. The subsidence became apparent soon after the purchase was completed and in order to avert the collapse of the dwelling the lender, as a gesture of goodwill and being mindful of its commercial reputation and the fact that the borrowers were fully committed with their existing repayments, undertook repairs at a cost to itself of £29,000 (being far greater than the original estimate) rather than seeking to rely on the repair *b* clause in the charge. In 1978 the lender sued the valuer for breach of contract and negligence. The borrowers made regular payments pursuant to the legal charge, including at least one small payment in reduction of capital, until 1981, when they sold the property and repaid the advance. At the trial of the lender's action shortly after the sale the judge held, inter alia, (i) that the valuer had been negligent, (ii) that the lender had acted unreasonably in expending so much in repairs, (iii) that the lender was not *c* unreasonable in not seeking to recover from the borrowers the full extent of their contractual obligations, although a partial recovery of the outstanding sum would be reasonable, and (iv) that the proper measure of damages was the difference between the amount originally lent and the amount that would have been lent on a proper valuation, less £3,000 (being the value which the judge placed on the borrowers' personal covenant to repay the advance). The lender appealed, contending that the £3,000 should not have *d* been deducted.

Held (Sir Denys Buckley dissenting) – The appeal would be allowed for the following reasons—

(1) In a successful action by a lender against a valuer for loss arising from a negligent valuation of a property intended as a security for a loan to a borrower damages were not *e* limited to the difference between the amount lent in reliance on the negligent valuation and the amount which would have been lent on a proper valuation; the correct measure of damages was the amount of expense and loss sustained by the lender as a result of the negligent valuation (see p 110 *j*, p 111 *d e* and *j* to p 112 *b*, p 115 *j* to p 116 *b e f* and *j*, p 119 *e* to *h* and p 122 *e*, post); *Scholes v Brook* (1891) 64 LT 674, *Baxter v F W Gapp & Co Ltd* [1939] 2 All ER 752 and dictum of Morris LJ in *Philips v Ward* [1956] 1 All ER at *f* 878–879 applied; *Eagle Star Insurance Co Ltd v Gale & Power (a firm)* (1955) 166 EG 37 overruled.

(2) (Per Stephenson LJ) There was a distinction between a defendant claiming credit for a benefit obtained by a plaintiff under a contract with another so as to reduce the loss suffered by the plaintiff due to the defendant's wrongful act and a defendant claiming the value of the possibility of a contractual benefit which a plaintiff had chosen not to *g* pursue. In the latter case the defendant could only claim the benefit if it could be shown that the plaintiff's refusal to pursue it was an unreasonable refusal to mitigate the damage flowing from the defendant's wrongful act. In all the circumstances the lender's refusal to enforce the borrowers' personal covenant was not unreasonable, and accordingly the judge was wrong to deduct a sum representing the value of the personal covenant from the assessed damages (see p 121 *c* to p 122 *e*, post); *James Finlay & Co Ltd v NV Kwik Hoo* *h* *Tung Handel Maatschappij* [1928] All ER Rep 110, *Banco de Portugal v Waterlow & Sons Ltd* [1932] All ER Rep 181, *Pilkington v Wood* [1953] 2 All ER 810 and *The Liverpool (No 2)* [1963] P 64 applied; *Eagle Star Insurance Co Ltd v Gale & Power (a firm)* (1955) 166 EG 37 overruled.

(3) (Per O'Connor LJ) It was clear that, regardless of whether the lender had elected to expend the additional sums in repairs or had simply allowed the dwelling to collapse, it *j* had lost at least the whole of the advance as a result of the valuer's negligence and that loss had not been diminished by the small repayment of capital by the borrowers. Furthermore, the lender was not under a duty to mitigate the loss by trying to extract money from the borrowers (see p 116 *f* to *j*, post); *Baxter v F W Gapp & Co Ltd* [1939] 2 All ER 752 applied.

Notes

a For the measure of damages, see 12 Halsbury's Laws (4th edn) paras 1127–1144, and for cases on the subject, see 17 Digest (Reissue) 101–119, 109–208.

For the duty to mitigate, see 12 Halsbury's Laws (4th edn) paras 1193–1196, and for cases on the subject, see 17 Digest (Reissue) 124–133, 242–302.

b **Cases referred to in judgments**

Banco de Portugal v Waterlow & Sons Ltd [1932] AC 452, [1932] All ER Rep 181, HL.

Baxter v F W Gapp & Co Ltd [1939] 2 All ER 752, [1939] 2 KB 271, CA; *affg* [1938] 4 All ER 457.

Cash v Brinsley (1888) 5 TLR 14.

Corisand Investments Ltd v Druce & Co (1978) 248 EG 215.

Eagle Star Insurance Co Ltd v Gale & Power (a firm) (1955) 166 EG 37.

c *Finlay (James) & Co Ltd v NV Kwik Hoo Tung Handel Maatschappij* [1929] 1 KB 400, [1928] All ER Rep 110, CA.

Liverpool, The (No 2) [1963] P 64.

Lowenburg Harris & Co v Wooley (1895) 25 SCR 51, Can SC.

Parry v Cleaver [1969] 1 All ER 555, [1970] AC 1, [1969] 2 WLR 821, HL.

d *Perry v Sidney Phillips & Son (a firm)* [1982] 3 All ER 705, [1982] 1 WLR 1297, CA.

Philips v Ward [1956] 1 All ER 874, [1956] 1 WLR 471, CA.

Pilkington v Wood [1953] 2 All ER 810, [1953] Ch 770, [1953] 3 WLR 522.

Scholes v Brook (1891) 64 LT 674, CA; *affg* 63 LT 837.

Simple Simon Catering Ltd v Binstock Miller & Co (1973) 228 EG 527, CA.

Singer & Friedlander Ltd v John D Wood & Co (1977) 243 EG 212.

e *Yianni v Edwin Evans & Sons (a firm)* [1981] 3 All ER 592, [1982] QB 438, [1981] 3 WLR 843.

Appeal

The plaintiff, London and South of England Building Society (the lender), appealed against the order of Russell J made on 13 November 1981 at the trial of the action

f brought by the lender against the defendant, Barrie Stone (the valuer), seeking damages for breach of contract and negligence for loss arising from a survey and valuation carried out by the valuer on the property Lane End in Corsham, Wiltshire on instructions from the lender. The judge held that the valuer had been negligent and ordered him to pay the sum of £9,133·13 plus interest being the lender's costs of investigation and the amount of the mortgage advance of £11,880 less the sum of £3,000 which the judge

g deducted as the value of the borrowers' personal covenant to repay the mortgage advance. The facts are set out in the judgment of O'Connor LJ.

Patrick Twigg for the lender.
John Slater and *Jane Davies* for the valuer.

h   *Cur adv vult*

27 May. The following judgments were delivered.

j **O'CONNOR LJ** (giving the first judgment at the invitation of Stephenson LJ). This appeal raises an important question on the measure of damages in a case where a building society has lent money on mortgage in reliance on a valuation that has been made in breach of the valuer's duty to his employer.

The facts of the case are unusual. In March 1976 Mr Robinson, aged 42, a salesman earning £3,250 per annum, and his fiancée Mrs Hurd, aged 37, a school teacher earning

£4,000 pa (the borrowers), were negotiating for the purchase of a semi-detatched house
in Corsham, Wiltshire (Lane End). They approached the appellant building society (the
lender) for a mortgage to finance the purchase. After the lender had received satisfactory
references a formal request for an advance of £12,800 repayable in 25 years against a
purchase price of £14,850 was made by the borrowers to the lender on 25 May 1976; on
24 May the lender instructed the respondent, a qualified surveyor and valuer (the valuer),
to value the property. The lender has a printed form which goes to the valuer for him to
complete but in part has already been filled in by the lender. Paragraph 1(11) stated that
the advance required was £12,800 repayable over 25 years. Paragraph 1(12) stated that
the agreed purchase price was £14,850. The valuer inspected the property and made his
report to the lender on 27 May. He gave the house a clean bill of health and at para 14(1)
stated that the gross value for mortgage was £14,850. By para 15(2) the valuer certified
that he had valued the property, and prepared his report in accordance with the provisions
of s 25 of the Building Societies Act 1962. Lastly, by para 13(2), the valuer recommended
the property as a suitable security for the advance and term requested in para 1(11).

Although the borrowers and the property had been cleared for a loan of £12,800, the
lender found that they were still bound by an in-house rule not to lend more than 80%
of the purchase price so it offered a loan of £11,880 which was accepted and in due course
the purchase of the property went through on that basis on 23 September 1976. By a
legal charge of even date the borrowers charged the house to the lender. By cl 1(a) the
borrowers covenanted:

> 'to pay monthly to the Society the sum stated in Part 5 of the First Schedule (or
> such other sum or sums as may hereafter at any time be agreed in writing by the
> parties hereto or may be determined by the Board of Directors of the Society ("the
> Board") hereunder) until the Principal Sum and any further advances or any re-
> advances that may be made to the Borrower by the Society with interest thereon as
> hereinafter provided and all other monies payable by the Borrower to the Society
> hereunder or by the Rules shall have been repaid the first of such payments to made
> on the date stated in Part 6 of the First Schedule and subsequent payments to be
> made on the day in the month stated in Part 7 of the First Schedule.'

By cl 4(d) of the legal charge the borrowers entered into further covenants with the
lender, namely:

> 'at all times to keep any buildings on the Property in good and tenantable repair
> to the satisfaction of the [lender] and to give to the [lender] on demand such
> information about and such opportunity to inspect or repair the Property as it may
> require.'

By cl 5 it was mutually agreed and declared that—

> '(a) . . . the Borrower shall not let or part with possession of the Property or any
> part thereof without the written consent of the Society first had and obtained . . .
> (h) That if default be made by the Borrower in payment of any one or more of
> the said monthly payments and other payments hereby covenanted to be made or
> in the observance and performance of any of the Borrower's covenants or obligations
> herein expressed or implied or if the Borrower or the Guarantor (if any) shall become
> bankrupt or being a limited company shall go into liquidation other than voluntary
> liquidation for the purpose of reconstruction or shall have a winding up order made
> against it or in case the Property shall be compulsorily acquired or demolished by
> order of any competent authority the whole of the money payable or to become
> payable hereunder shall be deemed to be forthwith due and owing and the Society
> may without any previous notice to or concurrence by the Borrower: (i) Appoint a
> Receiver under the statutory power and eject from the Property the Borrower his
> tenants and workmen and all other persons then in possession or occupation thereof
> (ii) Complete any unfinished buildings and effect and carry out upon the Property
> any such repairs amendments alterations or additions as the Society shall consider

a necessary or desirable for the improvement of the Property or the security hereby
created (iii) In exercise of the statutory power sell or let all or any part of the
Property.

(i) That all money paid by the Society in completing repairing amending altering
improving or insuring the Property or in making any payments for outgoings in
relation thereto or for the protection or improvement of the security hereby created
shall carry interest at the rate of interest herein provided for and shall be repayable
b by the Borrower on demand and in the meantime shall be a charge on the Property
...'

The borrowers moved into their new home but despite the charm of the view from
the windows soon found that all was not well with their house; cracks appeared and the
doors ceased to fit, the sure tell-tales that the property was subject to subsidence. The
borrowers became alarmed and called in consulting engineers who reported in September
c 1977 that the house was built on the site of an old quarry in the hillside which had been
indifferently filled, that not only was the whole hillside gradually moving downward,
but that the fill in the quarry was sliding downhill, lubricated by water, and was taking
the foundations of the house with it. They said:

'We consider that, although the house is not likely to collapse within the next few
d months, if there is another long period of wet weather then there is every possibility
of the filled material beneath the foundations slipping away and the downhill corner
of the house collapsing.'

They recommended underpinning, but could give no estimate of the cost until the depth
of the quarry floor below the house had been ascertained. The borrowers applied to the
insurance company but the insurance company would have nothing to do with the
e claim, for they said that this condition existed before the policy was effected and indeed
they had a report from a valuer as late as February 1976 including a photograph showing
a great big crack and reporting the true condition of this house.

The borrowers turned to the lender for help and Mr Stoughton-Harris, its managing
director, who gave evidence at the trial, agreed to get an estimate for the repair of the
house, and on 9 February he wrote to the valuer, warning him that he proposed to take
f proceedings on the grounds that the valuer's inspection of the property in May 1976
should have disclosed the evidence of the subsidence. By September 1978 the lender had
received an estimate for the repair of the house in the sum of £14,000. The borrowers
could not afford to pay any more than they were already paying; they were fully stretched
financially. There were only two alternatives, either to repair the house or to pull it down
and incur the further expense of shoring up the party wall of the other half of the semi-
g detached building; the lender decided to repair the house. Unfortunately the estimate
for carrying out the work proved wholly insufficient. It is unnecessary to go into any
details as to what was wrong with it, but in the end it cost £29,000 to repair the house.
In June 1979 Mr Stoughton-Harris, on behalf of the lender, wrote to the borrowers:

'I am writing to tell you that after giving the matter considerable thought I have
h decided not to ask you to make up any deficiency which may arise as a result of this
unfortunate affair. On behalf of the Society I shall be pursuing Barrie Stone for
negligence and I hope to recover the total costs which amount to approximately
£20,000, but any deficiency that may arise will be paid for by the Society. In
agreeing to do this I am not in any way accepting liability on behalf of the building
society. It is a gesture of goodwill on the part of the Society for what has been a most
j difficult and frightening experience for you and your wife.'

Following the finding of Russell J to that effect, the valuer accepts that he was guilty
of negligence in his valuation. I shall confine myself to tracing the history of the claim
for damages. The particulars of damage in the statement of claim originally delivered in
August 1978 read:

'The value of the Plaintiff's security has been reduced. To put the property into a

state where the Plaintiff's security would be of such value as the Defendant reported
will cost £7,462 plus provisional sums of £2,150 in each case plus V.A.T.'   *a*

In July 1980 the particulars were amended to read:

'The value of the Plaintiff's security has been reduced ... Had the property
conformed with the Defendant's description and valuation the advance made by the
Plaintiff as above would have been fully secured. In order to put the property into a
state where such advance is fully secured the Plaintiff has expended the sum of   *b*
£29,909·93 as follows ...'

and then details of how the sum was made up are given.

During the trial the particulars were further amended by adding the following
paragraph:

'The property was worthless. Had the Plaintiffs realised or sought to realise their   *c*
security, they would have got nothing thereby suffering a loss of £11,880 and
interest thereon which loss would not otherwise have been diminished.'

The purpose of this amendment was to put into the pleading a foundation for the
submission being made for the lender that if the true measure of damage was the
difference between the sum lent and that which would have been lent had the valuation
been a proper one they were not required to make any reduction in the resulting figure   *d*
by reason of the personal covenants of the borrowers.

Russell J dealt with this submission by ruling that a deduction had to be made and,
fixing the deduction at £3,000, he said:

'Should I make any discount from the figure of £11,880 claimed in the
amendment? At one stage counsel for the valuer argued that because the Society   *e*
had received this sum on the resale of the property there had in fact been no loss as
a result of the valuer's negligence, but that submission was not pursued. I have to
look at the situation at the date of the report. The lender was left without any
security in the house but the lender had the continuing personal covenants of the
borrowers. I bear in mind those factors to which I have already alluded. Despite the
difficulties that would have been encountered by the borrowers in the event of their   *f*
having to leave I think that their personal covenants must be something more than
an illusory factor. As time went on, their income rose (they are now earning
something like £15,000 per annum; their precise financial position was not
investigated in any great depth). But doing the best I can on the evidence before me
I do not think that it would have been commercial good sense on the part of the
lender simply to have waived all their rights under the mortgage deed. It would   *g*
probably have been both honourable and commercial good sense for the lender not
to have pursued the borrowers to the *full* extent of their contractual obligations. I
do not think to have done so would have been a necessary or reasonable mitigation
of the loss and I do not think that the lenders were under any duty to do so.
Accordingly to take account of the borrowers' covenants and the other facts to which
I have referred, I shall make a deduction which reduces the claim from £11,880 to   *h*
£8,880; to this must be added, by agreement, the reasonable costs incurred by the
lender in investigating the matter. That sum I understand to be £253·13.
Accordingly there will be judgment for the lender in the sum of £9,133·13.'

It is accepted by the lender that Russell J was right in holding that the measure of
damages was the difference between the amount lent, and the amount that would have
been lent on a proper valuation. There is no dispute that the relevant figures are £11,800   *j*
and nil. The only issue in this appeal is whether the judge was right in deducting £3,000
from that sum. Before I consider that issue there is a little more history. From the
beginning the borrowers kept up their repayments due under the agreement with the
lender, and in August 1981 they sold the house for £26,500. The whole of the original
advance was repaid at that stage, but that transaction is to be disregarded in the present

a   case, because in effect the lender was being repaid with its own money. The actual amount outstanding at the date when the debt was paid off was £11,912. We have details of the repayments made by the borrowers down to the end of March 1980, and these show that one payment of £127·50 was allocated to repayment of capital; that is sufficient to raise the problem whether credit must be given for it, and it would follow that if it must be given it must also be given for any allocation to capital between March 1980 and August 1981 when the house was sold and the debt paid off.

b   In deciding that some deduction had to be made for the value of the borrowers' personal covenant to repay the loan the judge followed a decision of Devlin J in *Eagle Star Insurance Co Ltd v Gale & Power (a firm)* (1955) 166 EG 37. I shall have to deal with that decision later in this judgment.

I start by considering the nature of the agreement between a building society and a valuer asked to value a house as security for a proposed loan of £12,800. The valuer does not warrant the accuracy or sufficiency of his valuation; he fulfills his part of the bargain
c   if in making his valuation he exercises the care and skill reasonably to be expected from a member of his profession. If a valuer fails to exercise that skill and care in making his valuation he is in breach of his duty and liable in damages. Broadly speaking, his failure will be in one of two categories. The first category is the case where he negligently makes a wholly erroneous valuation of the property, for example to value building land on a
d   negligently mistaken density figure. The second category is where the valuer has negligently failed to discover defects in the property, as in the present case.

If the duty is broken what is the damage and how is it to be assessed? The fundamental rule is that the measure of damages is that sum of money which will put the injured party in the same position as that in which he would have been if he had not sustained the injury. Where the injured party is the purchaser or vendor of property who has acted
e   on the negligent valuation, the measure of damages is the difference in the valuation figure and the market value of the property at the date of the transaction, that is in cases where the valuation and purchase or sale are reasonably contemporaneous. *Perry v Sidney Phillips & Son (a firm)* [1982] 3 All ER 705 at 708, [1982] 1 WLR 1297 at 1301–1302 was a purchaser case. Lord Denning MR said:

f   '... where there is a contract by a prospective buyer with a surveyor under which the surveyor agrees to survey a house and make a report on it, and he makes it negligently and the client buys the house on the faith of the report, then the damages are to be assessed at the time of the breach, according to the difference in price which the buyer would have given if the report had been carefully made from that which he in fact gave owing to the negligence of the surveyor. The surveyor gives no warranty that there are no defects other than those in his report. There is
g   no question of specific performance. The contract has already been performed, albeit negligently. The buyer is not entitled to remedy the defects and charge the cost to the surveyor. He is only entitled to damages for the breach of contract or for negligence. That was so decided by this court in *Philips v Ward* [1956] 1 All ER 874, [1956] 1 WLR 471, followed in *Simple Simon Catering Ltd v Binstock Miller & Co*, (1973) 228 EG 527.'

h   In that case the plaintiffs submitted that the damages should be the difference between the value of the house at the date of trial, and the value it would have had if it had been in the condition it would have been in on the basis of the surveyor's report. The Court of Appeal rejected the submission.

The position of a mortgagee who has lent money on the faith of the valuation is
j   different. This was recognised by Morris LJ in his judgment in *Philips v Ward* [1956] 1 All ER 874 at 878–879, [1956] 1 WLR 471 at 476–477. That was another purchaser case; the official referee had refused to award the cost of repairs but awarded the difference between the purchase price and the actual value of the house. Morris LJ said:

'The present case differs from *Baxter v. Gapp & Co., Ltd.* ([1939] 2 All ER 752, [1939] 2 KB 271) where a negligently given valuation caused the plaintiff to advance

money on mortgage to an unsatisfactory borrower, with the result that the plaintiff
as mortgagee was put to expense and loss. The amount of such expense and loss was
in that case the measure of the damage sustained by the plaintiff. In the present case,
the plaintiff, being mindful to purchase a property and seeking advice as to its
condition, paid £25,000 for it, which would have been its value if it had been in the
condition described by the defendant, whereas its real value in its actual condition
as it should have been described by the defendant was £21,000. In those
circumstances, it seems to me that the figure of £4,000 represented the proper
measure of the damage sustained by the plaintiff, and I see no error of law in the
approach of the learned Official Refereee.'

Baxter v F W Gapp & Co Ltd is a decision which is binding on us. In that case the
defendant valuers valued the property at £1,800 and reported that it was a reliable
trusteee security for an advance of £1,200. In August 1935 the plaintiff advanced the
£1,200 to the owner of the property by way of first mortgage; the mortgagor paid to the
plaintiff one half year's interest in February 1936 but thereafter she failed to pay any
interest, and abandoned the property; in April 1937 the plaintiff obtained possession of
the property. He made various abortive attempts to sell it, including putting it up for
auction, and in June 1938 he succeeded in disposing of it at a price of £850. Goddard LJ
tried the case at first instance and assessed the damages at £742 16s 7d. That figure
included the difference between the sum advanced by the plaintiff and the proceeds of
the sale of the property, the amount of the interest which the mortgagor had failed to
pay, the cost of insuring the property and of maintaining it in repair while it was in the
plaintiff's possession, legal charges during that period, expenses of abortive attempts to
sell the property, estate agents' commission on the eventual sale price of the property,
and legal charges in connection with the sale. The Court of Appeal dismissed the
defendant's appeal. I must set out the judgments in full. MacKinnon LJ said ([1939] 2
All ER 752 at 757–758; cf [1939] 2 KB 271 at 273–275):

'The judge has assessed them on the basis of the fact that, by reason of this
excessive valuation, the plaintiff was induced to enter upon this enterprise of lending
this money, which he would not have done but for the valuation. As a result of
lending this money upon this mortgage, he has sustained a certain pecuniary loss—
namely, the loss of his interest during 2 years and the loss of his capital, so far as it
has not been repaid by the price paid by Mrs. Rapozo. That resulting figure—
amounting to £720, I think—the judge has awarded the plaintiff as damages. In
principle, apart from any authority, it seems to me that that is the right basis on
which to assess the damages. Curiously enough, there is no very clear authority.
There is one case, *Scholes* v. *Brook* ((1891) 63 LT 837), which was a similar claim
against valuers for negligence. ROMER, J., as he then was, gave judgment for the
plaintiff, and awarded damages. In the report of the case before ROMER, J., the basis
upon which he assessed the damages is not clearly shown, because the report merely
ends as follows (at 838): "His Lordship reviewed the evidence, and, having decided
that the valuation by Messrs. Brook and Dransfield was not carried out with proper
care and skill, gave judgment against them for damages." In the Court of Appeal
((1891) 64 LT 674), so far as the judgment goes, LINDLEY, L.J., is only reported as
saying: ". . . he was therefore of opinion that the mode of estimating the damages
adopted by the judge was correct." One can only infer and discover the basis so
approved and adopted by the judge below from a passage in the body of the report
and the argument for the appellants. The statement of facts in the body of the report
is as follows (at 674): "His Lordship gave damages to the plaintiff, representing the
whole loss he had sustained through the deficiency of the security. The defendants
appealed. *Haldane, Q.C.,* and *Oswald,* for the appellants, contended on the evidence
that the appellants were not employed by the plaintiff; and also that the measure of
damages (if any) ought to be the difference between the value of the estate as stated
by the valuers and the real value at that time." That seems to indicate that ROMER,
J., had adopted the same basis of assessing the damages as that employed by

GODDARD, L.J., in this case. That was approved by LINDLEY, L.J., as the proper
a   measure of damages. Therefore, as I have said, I think that the principle is right,
and, as far as authority is available, that seems to confirm it. We were referred by
counsel for the appellants to the only case when he has been able to find, the
discovery of which indicates great industry on his part. It is a decision of the
Supreme Court of Canada in *Lowenburg, Harris & Co. v. Wolley* ((1895) 25 SCR 51).
That was a similar claim. The headnote is as follows: "The measure of damages in
b   such a case is not the amount loaned with interest, but the difference between that
amount and the actual value of the land." It is obvious that in that case the
mortgagee, having got into possession, was still in possession, and had been quite
unable to sell the property at all. Therefore, when the court said that the measure of
damages is the difference between the amount loaned and the actual value of the
land, supposing that the amount lent was £1,000 and the actual value, which he
c   had not been able to ascertain, because he had been unable to sell, was £500, he
would get the difference—namely, half of what he had lent. That, in effect, is the
same basis of assessing the damages as that adopted by the judge in this case, the
only difference being that in this case the value of the land to the plaintiff has been
ascertained by his sale to Mrs. Rapozo. That the same basis of assessment—namely,
what the plaintiff has lost by being led into this disastrous investment—should be
d   employed is shown by the fact that the judge in the court below, whose judgment
was affirmed by the Court of Appeal, had said that the plaintiff should recover the
whole amount of his advance, and should assign to the defendants the land, so that
they could do what they could to realise its value and so mitigate the loss. That
would be a process which would achieve the same result as that which, as a matter
of principle, the Court of Appeal was laying down as the proper basis of damages,
e   and the same result as that which, I think, GODDARD, L.J., rightly applied, and which
should be applied, in the present case. In the result, I think that this appeal fails, and
must be dismissed with costs.'

Du Parcq LJ said ([1939] 2 All ER 752 at 760; cf [1939] 2 KB 271 at 275):

'I have nothing to add on the question of the measure of damages, as to which it
seems to me that we are bound by the decision of this court in *Scholes v Brook* ((1891)
f   64 LT 674), a decision which, if I may say so, seems to be in accordance with
principle. I agree that this appeal should be dismissed.'

Macnaghten J said ([1939] 2 All ER 752 at 760, [1939] 2 KB 271 at 275):

'I agree that the appeal must be dismissed. As to the damages, I think that they
were rightly assessed by the judge.'

g   The trial judge, Goddard LJ, said ([1938] 4 All ER 457 at 465):

'I now turn to the question of what damages the plaintiff is entitled to recover.
The plaintiff says: "My measure of damages is this: if you had given me careful
information, made a careful valuation, this property would have been valued at a
considerably lower sum. I should never have entered into this transaction at all."
h   That is to say (I ignore the £150 for this purpose): "I should never have entered into
that first mortgage transaction under which I advanced £1,200. Whether I should
have entered into another transaction advancing £1,000 or whether I should have
advanced £800, I do not know, but I should never have advanced this £1,200. I
therefore entered into a transaction into which, but for your advice, I should never
have entered. Therefore, if I show that I have a cause of action, my damage is the
j   damage I have sustained through entering into this transaction." That seems to be
right, unless, of course, some different measure has to be applied in ascertaining the
actual damage he has sustained through the negligent valuation. Therefore, I think
that one has to examine rather carefully the facts and the law with regard to this,
because this matter is a question of law, and, if I am wrong on this question of law,
I can be put right in another court.'

I need make no further reference to *Scholes v Brook* because an examination of the reports reveals nothing beyond the matter referred to by MacKinnon LJ in his judgment in *Baxter*.

Counsel for the valuer submits that *Baxter* is authority only in cases where the borrower has defaulted, and he relies on *Eagle Star Insurance Co Ltd v Gale & Power (a firm)* (1955) 166 EG 37; alternatively that the Court of Appeal in *Baxter* misunderstood the effect of the Canadian case *Lowenburg Harris & Co v Wolley* (1895) 25 SCR 51, and as MacKinnon LJ relied on his reading of that case as authority to support his decision we are free to say that the decision was reached per incuriam and is not binding on us.

In the *Eagle Star* case the plaintiffs advanced £3,015 on a house owned and occupied by the defendant with a mortgage on the house as security relying on a valuation of £3,350 by the defendants in 1952. The defendants had failed to discover defects in the house which as a result was worth only £1,600. It was agreed that the cost of the repairs to put the house in the condition spoken to in the defendants' report was £950 in 1952, and £1,030 at the date of trial, July 1955. The report of the judgment of Devlin J in the Estates Gazette is sparse; I quote the relevant passages of the report in full:

'Mr William Thomas Lovett, manager of plaintiffs' mortgage department, said their prime security for Mr. Curtis's loan was the property he was buying and the value of the property governed the amount of the advance. If the company had known the true value and condition of the property, they would not have made such a large loan. Any damages the company might recover would be used, subject to Mr. Curtis's approval, in carrying out repairs or reducing Mr. Curtis's loan. Mr. Adelbert Percy Curtis, a head schoolmaster, said that when he bought the property he believed it to be perfectly sound. The house was so bad that for 18 months he and his wife had to live in the kitchen. The insurance company had offered him a further loan of £1,000 to put the house in good order but, in view of his impending retirement, he could not further commit himself . . . Mr. Lawson, for defendants, submitted that in assessing any damages one had to consider what the plaintiffs would get out of the transaction with Mr. Curtis, if it ran its normal course. It was evident that Mr. Curtis intended to fulfil his obligations to the plaintiffs and the probabilities of the plaintiffs sustaining any actual damages were very small. Counsel agreed that plaintiffs were entitled to nominal damages for the defendants' breach of contract. For plaintiffs, Mr. Marnan submitted that plaintiffs were entitled to at least sufficient damages to enable them to restore the house to the state which was wrongly reported to them by defendants. Giving judgment, his Lordship said that defendants, if they were competent surveyors, ought to have seen the signs of subsidence and advised plaintiffs that this was a property on which money should not be advanced. "I cannot help feeling that this is a situation which need not have arisen at all", continued his Lordship. "If building societies and insurance companies were to make arrangements for their clients to have the benefit of the surveyor's report, for which the clients have to pay, the clients would then have a right of action against the surveyor. It is a situation which is a trap, though innocently set, which makes people think that in paying for the surveyor's report they can rely on it in law. It is distressing to see people who have invested all their savings in their homes being treated in this way. This is the second case of this type I have dealt with in the past two years and I feel that there must be many more cases where this sort of hardship goes without remedy." His Lordship said plaintiffs had done their best to assist Mr. Curtis in his predicament and deserved every credit. Any damages they got would be used to put the house in good order. The judge said that the only way of assessing damages was to calculate what plaintiffs would have got had they realised their securities. The fact that they had not done this could not influence his judgment. The two main items of security were the house, which his Lordship estimated as being worth £1,600, and Mr. Curtis's personal covenant to repay £1,500 out of his retirement gratuity in August, 1956. Together these amounted to £3,100 without counting the other personal covenants. "I cannot, therefore, say that by any method of calculation, plaintiffs have lost any of the money they

advanced. I cannot accept defendants' submission that this is a case for nominal
damages, and I think £100 would indemnify plaintiffs against the possibilities of
their not being able to recover their money from Mr. Curtis. Plaintiffs are also
entitled to £52 10s., the cost of the surveys and reports made on the house
subsequently. There will be judgment for plaintiffs for £152 10s." Mr. Lawson said
defendants had paid £800 11s. 11d. into Court, and his Lordship ordered that
plaintiffs should have their costs of the action up to date of the payment in of the
money, and the balance should be paid out to defendants, who would also have their
costs after the date of payment into Court.'

Baxter v Gapp was not cited and as a result in my judgment that case was wrongly
decided. I will assume that the legal charge contained similar provisions to cll 4(d) and
5(h) and (i) of the legal charge in the present case set out earlier in this judgment.

The contract between the Eagle Star and Mr Curtis must have contained some special
term as to the repayment of £1,500 out of his retirement gratuity but we do not know
the terms for the repayment of the balance of the loan. In my judgment both are
irrelevant. If the Eagle Star had spent £950 on repairing the house in 1952 they would
have been entitled to say that they had entered into a transaction on the faith of the
defendants' report which they would not have entered into had they reported the true
state of affairs; and as a result they had suffered loss in that Mr Curtis had defaulted on
his obligation to keep the house in good repair and he could not repay the whole loan
forthwith so they could have sold the house for £1,600, and recovered the balance of
£1,415 from the defendants but in mitigation of damage they had repaired the house
for £950. In my judgment it should have made no difference that the £950 had not in
fact been spent, but even if the decision could be defended on that narrow ground it
would not avail the valuer in the present case. Further I am clear that it simply would
not have been open to the defendants to assert that the Eagle Star should have added the
£950 to the mortgage of Mr Curtis and that their own liability should have been reduced
by such sum as might have been wrung out of him.

I think that the criticism that in Baxter v Gapp MacKinnon LJ misapprehended the
effect of the judgment of the Supreme Court in the Canadian Lowenburg Harris case is
well founded. I have no doubt that this is because the headnote from that case cited is
itself misleading. In the Canadian case the mortgagee was in possession; after the valuer
had been found negligent the trial judge ordered that the valuer repay the whole amount
of the advance together with interest but that the mortgagees should transfer the land to
the valuer who could realise what he could on it. By a majority that decision was upheld
in the British Columbia Court of Appeal. In the Supreme Court that assessment was set
aside; Strong CJ, giving the judgment of the majority, said (25 SCR 51 at 56–57):

'I am of opinion that this was not a correct disposition of the case. The effect of
this judgment would be to make the appellants not only responsible for such
damages as were caused by the negligent performance of their duty as the
respondent's agents, in over-valuing the mortgaged property, but also for any
depreciation (if any there has been) in the actual value of the property subsequent to
the loan. It is manifest that any loss in this respect should be borne by the respondent
himself in as much as it cannot be attributed to the neglect of the appellants. All
that the appellants can possibly be liable for is the loss occasioned by the over-
valuation adopted and acted on by them.'

So the Supreme Court was substituting the value of the land at the date of the loan for
the value of the land at the date of trial or at any time in between. There is no doubt that
the effect of the Lowenburg Harris case was fairly and squarely put to the court by counsel
for the valuers (see the report of the argument ([1939] 2 KB 271 at 272) and also the full
report of the extempore judgment ([1939] 2 All ER 752 at 753)). But the whole point of
the decision in Baxter v Gapp is that the Court of Appeal rejected the submission that
damages were limited to the difference between the sum loaned and the true value of the

property at the date of the transaction. It would seem from a passage of the report of
Baxter [1938] 4 All ER 457 at 463 at first instance that the value of the house at the time   *a*
of the loan was about £1,000.

I am quite unable to say that the decision of the Court of Appeal was reached per
incuriam, and it is binding on us.

We were referred to two further decisions at first instance. First the case of *Singer &*
Friedlander Ltd v John D Wood & Co 243 EG 212, decided by Watkins J in June 1977. In
that case the bank lent £1½m on building land to developers against a valuation of £2m.   *b*
This was in 1972. In 1975 the developers went into liquidation with liabilities of £50m
and the bank were left with the building land then valued at £600,000. There was
evidence, which the judge accepted, that at the date of the loan the true value was
£1,500,000. He held that the valuers were guilty of negligence, and counsel concerned
had agreed that the correct measure of damages was the difference between 75% of the
negligent valuation, namely the amount loaned, and 75% of the true value, and the judge   *c*
agreed that that was the proper figure for damages. The agreed amount contained an
element for interest.

In *Corisand Investments Ltd v Druce & Co* (1978) 248 EG 215 the plaintiffs in 1973
advanced £60,000 on four properties together valued by the defendants at £662,000,
already charged with £375,000 to first mortgagees. The loan was on the basis that the
total borrowing on the properties should not exceed 70% of their value. The loan was for   *d*
one year with interest at 30%, payable monthly. The property boom burst, the borrowers
went into liquidation, and when the properties were realised there was not enough to
pay off the first mortgagees. The plaintiffs lost their money and interest, less £9,000
which had been paid. The defendants had negligently over-valued one of the properties
in the sum of £55,000, and applying the 70% rule Gibson J held that if the valuation had
been in a true figure the plaintiffs would have lent £22,000, not £60,000, so that their   *e*
loss was £38,000 under this head. For some reason which is not clear to me, Gibson J
rejected the plaintiffs' claim for interest on that sum.

I do not think that any help is to be derived from these property boom and collapse
cases; in each case the lender would have suffered loss on the sums which the court found
he would have lent against a proper valuation and it was appropriate to assess that loss as
the difference between the sum lent and that which would have been lent. It is not a   *f*
formula to govern all cases where money is lent on the faith of a negligent valuation.

I return to the facts of the present case and apply the reasoning in *Baxter v Gapp* to
them in the same way as I have applied that case in theory to the facts in the *Eagle Star*
case. The actual loss to the lender was £29,000. The judge has held that it was
unreasonable to spend so much money on repairing the house. It is not suggested that
the house could have been repaired for less than £11,800. What then is it suggested that   *g*
the lender should have done? The judge did not ask himself this question, and as a result
did not answer it. Something had to be done, for the evidence was that the house was
about to fall down. The borrowers could not afford to put the house into repair; what
then should the lender have done? Should it have called in the loan for breach of
covenant and repossessed the property? That would have been a pointless exercise, as the
house was worthless and indeed a liability, for it either had to be repaired or pulled down   *h*
and the neighbouring premises shored up.

The truth is that however one looks at this case the lender has lost the whole of its
advance at the very least. This loss has been caused by the negligence of the valuer, for it
is quite certain that but for the negligent valuation the lender would not have embarked
on the transaction at all; it would have lent nothing. That loss has not been diminished
by the small repayment of capital.   *j*

I can see no justification for the suggestion that the lender was under any duty to the
valuer to mitigate this loss by trying to extract money from the borrowers. Let me test
the proposition in a simple way: assume that the borrowers had agreed to contribute
£5,000 towards these repairs, could the valuer have claimed credit for this or any part of
this sum on the facts of this case? I am quite clear that he could not have done so. I would
allow this appeal and enter judgment for the lender in the full sum of £11,800.

a   It will be obvious that in my judgment the valuer's cross-appeal asking that more than £3,000 should be deducted from the £11,800 must be dismissed.

SIR DENYS BUCKLEY. In this appeal we are concerned only with the quantum of the damages which the plaintiff building society (the lender) is entitled to recover. Liability is no longer in issue. It is common ground in this court that at 27 May 1976, when the defendant (the valuer) reported to the lender that he valued Lane End at
b   £14,850, the property was, on account of its physical state, commercially valueless. In reliance on that report the lender advanced £11,880 to Mr and Mrs Robinson (the borrowers) on the security of the legal charge dated 23 September 1976. The lender's cause of action thereupon came into existence. The writ was issued on 12 August 1978, by which date the physical condition of the property had at least partially come to light, which demonstrated the defective character of the valuer's valuation, and the lender's
c   insurers had disclaimed all liability. Experts' estimates at that time indicated that necessary remedial work would cost about £14,000 which might, it was thought, render the property of a value in excess of £20,000.

Matters stood thus at about the time of the issue of the writ, but as the remedial work progressed the cost escalated steeply, amounting eventually to £27,187·79. It is not in dispute that that was a reasonable sum for the necessary works, which did no more than
d   put the property in a condition such as was described in the valuer's valuation report.

The borrowers, who had had to vacate the house during the works, returned to occupy it, but in August 1981 the property was sold because Mr Robinson had to move for business reasons. It fetched £26,500. Accordingly the remedial works did not mitigate any loss occasioned to the lender by the valuer's negligent valuation, for the cost of the works exceeded the resulting value of the property.
e   The lender's loan of £11,880 to the borrowers was secured by the legal charge with interest at 11·1% per annum and made payable by monthly payments of £121 over a term of 25 years. When the property was sold, the outstanding amount of the advance was repaid. The borrowers, as I understand, had paid all the monthly instalments down to that date.

Under cl 5(1) of the legal charge all the expenditure by the lender on the remedial
f   works was to carry interest, be repayable on demand and in the meantime be a charge on the property. In June 1979, however, the lender decided as a gesture of goodwill not to require the borrowers to meet any of the repair costs, and they have not done so.

How, in these circumstances, are the damages which the lender is entitled to recover against the valuer to be assessed? The formula for such assessment must, in my judgment, have been the same at whatever date after accrual of the cause of action the assessment
g   might have been made, notwithstanding that the relevant data may have varied from time to time. Obviously, if the assessment had been made at, or shortly after, the accrual of the cause of action or the issue of the writ, there would have been likely to be a much greater element of estimate than would be the case if it were made at some later date when supervening facts had become known. The kind of damage with which we are concerned is pecuniary. The primary question is: what loss in terms of money did the
h   lender suffer in consequence of the valuer's tort or breach of contract? A second question may be: to what extent has the lender succeeded in reducing that loss by taking any steps available to him to do so, or to what extent could he have reduced that loss by taking steps which have been available to him but which he has failed unreasonably to take? The amount recoverable by the lender will be the excess of the loss over the actual mitigation (if any) plus any available mitigation which the lender has unreasonably failed
j   to achieve. Any reduction of the loss which should properly find its place in the calculation of the primary loss cannot come into the calculation a second time in the form of mitigation.

What, then, was the extent of the monetary loss suffered in the present case in consequence of the valuer's negligent valuation? It is clear from the documentation that the valuer was aware, when he made his valuation, that the lender's object in obtaining it was to satisfy itself that the property would be a sufficient and satisfactory security for repayment of an advance of up to £12,800 repayable with interest over 25 years and secured by a mortgage of the property. It was in reliance on the valuer's valuation that the lender made the loan of £11,880 which was secured by the legal charge. By that legal charge the lender obtained the following concurrent remedies for the recovery of the loan with interest: (a) the personal covenants of the borrowers contained in cl 2(a) thereof and (b) the rights of enforcement of the charge contained in cl 3 thereof. These were concurrent remedies in respect of one and the same loan liability. If the valuer had made a proper valuation, disclosing that the property had no commercial value, the lender would have realised that it could not safely lend any money on the security of Lane End and that the proposed charge would be a valueless security. If the lender had recovered, and could recover, no part of the loan, it would have lost £11,880 in consequence of the negligent act of the defendant. *Baxter v F W Gapp & Co Ltd* [1939] 2 All ER 752, [1939] 2 KB 271, *Singer & Friedlander Ltd v John D Wood & Co* (1977) 243 EG 212 and *Corisand Investments Ltd v Druce & Co* (1978) 248 EG 215 were all cases in which nothing could be recovered under any personal covenant or guarantee. That is, in my opinion, a distinction from the present case of fundamental importance.

The lender did in fact recover at least £127, being the amount of one instalment of capital repaid by the borrowers in the year ended 4 April 1978. I understood the lender to concede (and in my view rightly) that that sum at least should be credited in favour of the valuer in calculating the lender's loss. So must any other instalments of capital which were repaid before the mortgage was paid off.

The obligations of the borrowers under their personal covenants remained intact, unaffected by the valuer's negligence. Indeed, as I understand, they were duly performed down to the time when the loan was paid off. What impact, if any, does the continued subsistence of the borrowers' obligations under their covenants have on the measure of the lender's loss?

If the borrowers had been so amply endowed with wealth that there was no real likelihood of their being unable to fulfil their covenants fully and punctually or, if they failed to do so, no real likelihood of the lender's being unable to recover in full any claim for damages for breach of covenant, the lender could not, in my opinion, have successfully asserted that it had suffered any financial loss in consequence of the valuer's negligence; or, since there can be no absolute certitude about the future solvency of even a very wealthy covenantor, the court might take the view that the lender should be allowed some moderate discount on the full amount on the borrowers' personal liabilities in order to compensate the lender for any risk of the lender's proving to be unable to recover whatever sums might become due from the borrowers in full. This was the course adopted by Devlin J in *Eagle Star Insurance Co Ltd v Gale & Power* (1955) 166 EG 37 where the learned judge took into account the value of a personal covenant by a Mr Curtis at its full face value of £1,500 subject to a discount of £100 to indemnify the plaintiffs against the possibility of their not being able to recover the full sum payable under the covenant. This appears to me to be an entirely logical and satisfactory way of approaching the problem of assessing damages in such a case. It does not involve, in my opinion, the operation of any doctrine of mitigation of damage by the plaintiff, for it proceeds on the basis that the covenantor is likely fully and punctually to discharge his obligations without any act on the part of the plaintiff. In other words, it does not depend on mitigation by the plaintiff of his primary loss, but on a reduction in the amount of that primary loss by the expected performance by the covenantor of his covenant. The discount is a measure of the possible risk that the loan will not be repaid in full. The amount of the loan less the discount is the measure of the extent to which it has been established on a balance of probability that the loan will be repaid notwithstanding the loss of any security in consequence of the negligence. It is part of the process referred to by Morris LJ in *Philips v Ward* [1956] 1 All ER 874 at 878, [1956] 1 WLR 471 at 475 of assessing the damage which could fairly and reasonably be considered as resulting from the failure of the defendant to report as he should have done, that is, it is part of the process of assessing the loss to the plaintiff resulting from the defendant's negligence, not a part of the assessment of any mitigation which the plaintiff ought reasonably to have effected.

If this analysis is sound, this method of valuation is, in my judgment, just as applicable to a case in which a covenantor is not shown to be certain, or virtually certain, to be able to discharge his covenanted liabilities in full but is likely to do so to some extent as to a case in which he is shown to be certain, or virtually certain, to be able to do so in full.

b In the present case the borrowers were not wealthy but there was at least a possibility, although no certainty, that they would be able to continue to fulfil their covenanted obligation for so long as the legal charge remained on foot, and that they would in fact do so for at least some part of that period.

The judge in his judgment proceeded on the same lines as those adopted by Devlin J in the *Eagle Star* case. He held that he must look at the situation as at the date of the defendant's report. In my judgment, the relevant date at which to look is the date when c the cause of action arose (that it, when the advance was made on the faith of the report) but this substitution makes no significant difference. In substance I think the judge pursued the appropriate method of measuring the damages in the present case. Although he was not very explicit about his method of arriving at his figure of £3,000 discount, he appears to me to have taken the appropriate circumstances into account in doing so, and I can see no cogent reason for saying that he was wrong in his estimate. I apprehend that d the £3,000 should be regarded as including any instalments of capital repaid before the loan was paid off out of the proceeds of sale of the property.

For these reasons, and with diffidence as I find myself in a minority, I would dismiss this appeal.

STEPHENSON LJ. It has been agreed by both counsel, who have so ably and helpfully e addressed us, that the true measure of damages for the breach of a defendant surveyor's duty to value a property mortgaged to a plaintiff building society is the difference between the sum the building society advanced on the false valuation, which the surveyor carelessly and unskilfully put on the property, and the sum the building society would have advanced on the true valuation, which a careful and skilful surveyor would have put on it. And that is the true measure of damages resulting from the breach, whether f the property should have been valued as worth something less than the false valuation or worth nothing at all, as was this property.

The decision of this court in *Baxter v F W Gapp & Co Ltd* [1939] 2 All ER 752, [1939] 2 KB 271 binds us, in my opinion, to hold that that difference may not always be the true measure of the lender's actual loss: the loss of the money advanced may be increased by expenses and reduced by receipts. In that case the expenses allowed by Goddard LJ and g approved by this court were costs of insurance and maintenance, legal charges and expenses of unsuccessful attempts to sell and the ultimate sale of the mortgaged property; the receipt, which may be a guide to the excess of the negligent valuation, was the sale price set off against the interest and capital which the borrower had failed to pay; these factors giving the whole loss sustained through the deficiency of the security in line with the imperfectly reported decision of the court in *Scholes v Brook* (1891) 63 LT 837 and 64 h LT 674.

I would add a reference to *Cash v Brinsley* (1888) 5 TLR 14, where a special jury awarded a mortgagee £1,500, the full amount of a second advance made on a negligent valuation of property over-valued at £2,000 and sold for £410. The jury found that the valuer was not negligent in valuing the property at £2,000 for a first advance of £1,500, but was negligent in so valuing it for the further advance. The argument on damages is not j reported, but presumably the figure awarded was in accordance with the directions of Denman J.

In none of these cases does it appear to have been considered that the lender's loss should be reduced by what the borrowers had not paid but might be able to pay. That is the question, and the only question, raised by this appeal and cross-appeal. Should the judges have discounted the repayment of the £11,800 which the lender advanced on his

worthless property by £3,000 or any sum for the borrowers' obligation to repay it with
interest under their personal covenant?

I have been attracted by the first argument of counsel for the lender that the difference
between what would have been advanced but for the new valuation and what was
advanced in reliance on it is always recoverable without regard to the borrowers, what he
may have paid in performance of his covenanted obligation under the mortgage deed, or
may be liable to pay, or to the value of the chance that he might pay if called on by the
lender to do so. What has been agreed between lender and borrowers is res inter alios
acta, a transaction completely collateral to the transaction between lender and valuer, and
too remote to be taken into account in measuring the lender's loss through the valuer's
negligent valuation. By dismissing from consideration the borrowers' covenant to repay
the loan the court is saved from the difficult task of estimating chances and the invidious
task of penalising a lender who has refused to add to the financial embarrassment of an
innocent borrower already suffering loss from the negligent valuation, and thereby to
endanger the lender's own good relations with other potential customers and so damage
the lender's commercial reputation.

But counsel for the valuer has, I think, given the answer in the special nature of the
valuer's valuation. It was not a valuation for an unspecified purpose but for the particular
purpose of securing an advance by the lender to the borrowers of £12,800, repayable
over 25 years; and it was coupled with a recommendation by the valuer that the property
was a suitable security for that advance and term, as the valuer's report and valuation of
27 May 1976 shows. Though the identity of the borrowers was of no interest or relevance
to the valuer or his duty to the lender, the amount of the advance and the length of time
for repayment were. Though the mortgage deed by way of legal charge gave the lender
a right to foreclose for other breaches of covenant, the object of securing the loan by
charging the property was to secure repayment of the sum lent with interest under the
covenant to repay. The borrowers' obligation to repay was therefore not so collateral or
remote as to be disregarded altogether in measuring the lender's loss, and although the
valuer was not a party to the mortgage, and the mortgage was literally res inter alios acta,
it was a transaction with which the valuer's report and valuation and breach of duty were
closely connected, as now demonstrated by the decision of Park J in *Yianni v Edwin Evans*
& Sons (a firm) [1981] 3 All ER 592, [1982] 1 QB 438. If, therefore, the borrowers had
suddenly found themselves in sufficient funds to repay the lender's advance, and had
repaid it in full before the valuer's liability was established, I do not see how the lender
could have recovered more than nominal damages, or perhaps some expenses in
investigating the condition of the property, because the lender would have suffered no
loss in consequence of the valuer's breach of duty. There are, of course, cases in which
the lender can recover damages from a wrongdoer for tort and breach of contract,
notwithstanding that he has been already compensated,eg by benevolence, private or
public, or by insurance (though he had paid premiums for that), and the wrongdoer
cannot get out of paying compensation himself by relying on the uncovenanted benefit
conferred on the plaintiff by another: see *Parry v Cleaver* [1969] 1 All ER 555 at 557–
558, [1970] AC 1 at 14 per Lord Reid. But if an advance secured by the borrowers'
reliance on a false valuation of a property becomes in fact an advance which needs no
security, but is repaid without recourse to the property, then in my judgment the valuer
may be fortunate enough to be able to rely on the borrowers' repayment in diminution
of the lender's loss and of the compensation he is legally liable to pay for it.

There may be circumstances in which the lender who has been repaid by the borrowers
some of the principal advanced will nevertheless be entitled to be paid by the valuer the
full amount of the difference between what he would have lent and what he did lend.
However, on the assumption that it would be permissible for the valuer to claim credit
for any repayment of capital by the borrowers before action, can he also claim credit for
what the borrowers have not repaid if the lender could have insisted on repayment in
full or in part and could, if the borrowers refused, have sued them with a reasonable
prospect of some success? The judge did that in this case and, I think, valued the
borrowers' covenant to pay, or the chances of a partially successful recovery, by demand,

or action if the demand was refused, at £3,000, or roughly 25% of the principal sum
a advanced. In that he was following the decision of Devlin J in *Eagle Star Insurance Co Ltd
v Gale & Power* (1955) 166 EG 37.

With considerable hesitation I have, however, come to the conclusion that counsel for
the lender is right in his second submission and in contending that the view of these
judges can only be justified if it was reasonable for the respective plaintiff to enforce the
borrowers' covenants to pay; for what the borrowers might pay could only be taken into
b account in mitigation of the plaintiff's damage if the plaintiff ought to have mitigated
that loss and damage by enforcing the borrowers' covenants. That was, I think, the view
of Russell J (though not of Devlin J, who seems to have treated the valuer as if he were a
guarantor), and it leaves open the question, and indeed demands an answer to the
question, whether the lender acted reasonably in not seeking to enforce the borrowers'
covenant, or rather whether the valuer has proved that the lender had acted unreasonably.
c For the valuer is not merely asking the court to take account of what has actually been
paid to the lender; he is requiring the lender to have taken action in claiming payment
from the borrowers; and it is one thing for a wrongdoer to claim the benefit of a benefit
obtained by the wronged party under a contract with another; it is quite another thing
(and, in my judgment, a far stronger thing) to claim the valuation of the chance of such
a benefit which the wronged party has deliberately chosen not to take. In that case it
d seems to me the wrongdoer must show that the wronged party's reasoned choice to waive
his contractual rights against the third party is unreasonable in the ordinary course of
events in the particular field of commercial business and in all the circumstances (it may
be something special) of the particular case.

What the valuer is contending is that the lender ought to have done something and
that must, in my opinion, be an assertion that they should have mitigated the damage
e flowing from the worthlessness of the security. They should have had recourse to what
Devlin J regarded as another item of security than the mortgaged property, but surely a
security in a different sense not by itself securing the loan, namely the borrowers'
contractual obligation under the first covenant in the deed. If, as I think and the judge
thought, that is only available to the valuer as mitigation, the valuer must prove it was
reasonable and when the court has to decide that question of fact, the lender's conduct in
f not taking steps to reduce the loss will not be weighed in nice scales at the instance of the
party who has occasioned the loss: see what Lord Macmillan said of the plaintiff's conduct
in taking positive steps to reduce his loss in *Banco de Portugal v Waterlow & Sons Ltd*
[1932] AC 452 at 506, [1932] All ER Rep 181 at 204. I bear in mind the illustrations
given in *McGregor on Damages* (14th edn, 1980) paras 234–241, of which counsel for the
lender relies on paras 236, 238, 239 and 240; and I accept these principles as established
g by authority and applicable to this case: (1) a plaintiff need not take the risk of starting an
uncertain litigation against a third party, for which *Pilkington v Wood* [1953] 2 All ER
810, [1953] Ch 770 is authority, and that includes litigation which may be reasonably
certain to result in judgment for the plaintiff but there is no certainty that the judgment
will be satisfied; (2) a plaintiff need not take steps to recover compensation for his loss
from parties who, in addition to the defendant, are liable to him, for which *The Liverpool*
h (No 2) [1963] P 64 is authority. There the other party was a tortfeasor, unlike the
borrowers in this case; but (3) a plaintiff need not act so as to injure innocent persons;
and (4) need not prejudice its commercial reputation.

For both (3) and (4) the *Banco de Portugal* case is authority; (3) is illustrated also by *James
Finlay & Co Ltd v NV Kwick Hoo Tung Handel Maatschappij* [1929] 1 KB 400, [1928] All
ER Rep 110, where this court held that buyers were entitled to refuse to enforce their
i legal rights against a sub-buyer, thereby wiping out their loss on their contract to
purchase from the defendant, but injuring their commercial reputation.

Where, as here, there was evidence from Mr Robinson, one of the borrowers, that he
was unable to provide additional payments and, more important, credible and indeed
unchallenged evidence from the lender's managing director, Mr Stoughton-Harris, that
the lender felt morally responsible for the loss of the borrowers' home and that
enforcement of the covenant to pay would injure the lender's public relations, I find it

hard to see how the valuer had proved the lender's refusal to enforce the covenant
unreasonable. Was it unreasonable, as the judge held, to refuse to enforce it all? Would a   *a*
prudent lender in the lender's position have enforced three-quarters of the covenanted
obligation or some part of it? Counsel for the lender has convinced me, with all the
respect due to those who think differently, that the judge's answer was wrong and he
should not have discounted the amount now claimed by £3,000 or any amount. If a
mortgagor's unperformed covenant to repay principal and interest is to be taken into
account in assessing a mortgagee's primary loss through a negligent valuation, it seems   *b*
to me that there will be some discount, however small and however hard to assess, in
every case, whether or not there is any connection between the inadequacy of the
mortgaged property to secure the loan and the mortgagor's failure to pay. In this case I
would regard the application of that view of the law to be unfair to the lender. It would
be surprising if the benefit of the covenant, 'uncovenanted' so far as the valuer is
concerned, were available to save him from the natural consequences of his breach of   *c*
duty to the lender when the lender had such reasons as Mr Stoughton-Harris put forward
in justification of such honourable and understandable conduct towards the innocent
borrowers, even though they may have a right of action against the valuer and even
though their inability to pay may have been less complete than the evidence of Mr
Robinson suggested. I can see nothing unreasonable in the lender's waiver of their
contractual right to recover their loss from the borrowers on the evidence and in the   *d*
circumstances of this case.

Counsel for the valuer has not satisfied me that the lender's total refusal to enforce the
covenant was an act of unreasonable benevolence or forgiveness, and I would accordingly
allow the appeal.

Two of the judgments which have been handed down are in favour of allowing the
appeal; the judgment of Sir Denys Buckley which has been handed down is for dismissing   *e*
it. Accordingly, the appeal will be allowed.

*Appeal allowed; damages increased to £12,133·13. Valuer given leave to appeal to the House of
Lords.*

Solicitors: *Lawrance Messer & Co* (for the lender); *Barlow Lyde & Gilbert* (for the valuer).   *f*

Diana Brahams   Barrister.

g

Governors of the Peabody Donation Fund v Higgins and another

COURT OF APPEAL, CIVIL DIVISION
CUMMING-BRUCE AND MAY LJJ   *h*
20 JUNE 1983

*Landlord and tenant – Forfeiture of lease – Breach of covenant prohibiting assignment – Secure
tenancy – Tenant assigning secure tenancy in breach of lease – Statute preserving secure tenancy
on assignment if assignee meeting statutory requirements – Whether assignment in breach of lease
of no effect – Whether statutory provisions preserving secure tenancy on assignment only   *j*
applicable to assignments not in breach of lease – Whether landlord required to comply with
statutory notice requirements for possession proceedings against tenant – Housing Act 1980,
s 37(1).*

In 1971 the landlords granted the father a weekly tenancy of a flat on terms which
included an absolute prohibition on assignment. In 1980 the tenancy became a secure

tenancy by virtue of s 28^a of the Housing Act 1980. On 16 September 1982 the father
a executed an assignment of the tenancy to his daughter in breach of the tenancy and on
17 September he vacated the premises in favour of the daughter. Section 37^b of the 1980
Act provided that if a secure tenancy was assigned it ceased to be a secure tenancy unless,
inter alia, the assignee could have qualified under s 30^c of that Act to succeed the tenant
had he died immediately before the assignment. The daughter would have so qualified
under s 30 to succeed her father as the tenant immediately prior to the assignment. The
b landlords considered that the assignment in breach of the tenancy agreement was of no
effect and that the provisions of the 1980 Act preserving the secure tenancy on assignment
only applied when the assignment was not made in breach of any condition in the lease.
They regarded the daughter as a trespasser and obtained an order for possession against
the father and the daughter without complying with the requirements of s 33^d of the
1980 Act for proceedings for possession or termination against a tenant under a secure
c tenancy. The father and the daughter appealed.

Held – Although the tenancy agreement contained a prohibition on assignment, the
assignment had validly passed the father's interest to the daughter. Moreover, on its true
construction, s 37 of the 1980 Act applied to any assignment whether or not it was in
breach of the terms of the particular tenancy agreement. It followed that the daughter
d enjoyed a secure tenancy. The appeal would therefore be allowed, although it remained
open to the landlords to commence new proceedings for possession in accordance with
s 33 of the 1980 Act on the basis of the father's breach of covenant (see p 126 f, p 127 b d
e and g to j and p 128 c d f g, post).
    Old Grovebury Manor Farm Ltd v W Seymour Plant Sales and Hire Ltd (No 2) [1979] 3 All
ER 504 applied.

e **Notes**
For sub-letting and assignment under a secure tenancy, see 27 Halsbury's Laws (4th edn)
para 880.
    For the Housing Act 1980, ss 28, 30, 33, 37, see 50(1) Halsbury's Statutes (3rd edn) 920,
923, 925, 928.

f **Case referred to in judgments**
    Old Grovebury Manor Farm Ltd v W Seymour Plant Sales and Hire Ltd (No 2) [1979] 3 All
    ER 504, [1979] 1 WLR 1397, CA.

---

a Section 28, so far as material, is set out at p 124 j to p 125 b, post
b Section 37, so far as material, is set out at p 126 b, post
g c Section 30, so far as material, is set out at p 125 f g, post
d Section 33 provides:
    '(1) The court shall not entertain proceedings for the possession of a dwelling-house let under a
    secure tenancy or for the termination of a secure tenancy, unless the landlord has served on the
    tenant a notice complying with the provisions of this section and, if the tenancy is a periodic
    tenancy—(a) the proceedings are begun after the date specified in the notice; and (b) the notice is
    still in force at the time the proceedings are begun.
h   (2) A notice under this section must be in a form prescribed by regulations made by the
    Secretary of State and must specify the ground on which the court will be asked to make an order
    for the possession of the dwelling-house or for the termination of the tenancy and give particulars
    of that ground.
      (3) If the secure tenancy is a periodic tenancy the notice—(a) must also specify a date after
    which proceedings for the possession of the dwelling-house may be begun; and (b) ceases to be in
    force twelve months after the date specified in it; and the date specified in it must not be earlier
j than the date on which the tenancy could, apart from this Act, be brought to an end by notice to
    quit given by the landlord if the notice to quit were given on the same date as the notice under
    this section.
      (4) Where a notice under this section is served with respect to a secure tenancy for a term certain
    it has effect also with respect to any periodic tenancy arising by virtue of section 29 above on the
    termination of that tenancy, and paragraphs (a) and (b) of subsection (1) and subsection (3) above
    do not apply to the notice.'

Appeal

The first defendant, William Higgins (the father), and the second defendant, Marion *a*
Higgins (the daughter), appealed against the decision of his Honour Judge Harris QC
made at the hearing of the action on 28 February 1983 in the West London County
Court whereby he ordered, inter alia, the father and daughter to deliver up possession of
the premises known as 66 The Square, Peabody Estate, Fulham Palace Road, London
within 28 days to the plaintiffs, the Governors of the Peabody Donation Fund (the
landlords), and further ordered the father and daughter to pay the landlords rent arrears *b*
of £138·40 and £179·82 respectively. The facts are set out in the judgment of Cumming-
Bruce LJ.

Anthony Radevsky for the father and the daughter.
Michael Bloch for the landlords.

CUMMING-BRUCE LJ. This is an appeal against an order made by his Honour Judge *c*
Harris QC on 28 February 1983 whereby he ordered that the plaintiffs, the Governors of
the Peabody Donation Fund (the landlords), do have possession of the premises at 66 The
Square, Peabody Estate, Fulham Palace Road (the premises), as against the first defendant
(the father), who had become their tenant pursuant to a grant in 1971. The judge further
ordered that the father should pay rent arrears in the sum of £138 and proceeded to
order that the landlords should have possession of the premises as against the second *d*
defendant, the daughter of the first defendant (the daughter), and rent arrears in the sum
of £179.

The appeal raises a short but important point on the construction and effect of s 37 of
the Housing Act 1980. It arises in this way. By a lease in 1971 the landlords granted to
the father a weekly unfurnished tenancy of the premises at a rent of £13·84 per week. It
was a condition of the tenancy, pursuant to cl 10 of the conditions of tenancy, that the *e*
father was not permitted to assign or sublet or, without special permission, to take in
lodgers. That condition comes within the category, described for the purposes of the law
of landlord and tenant, of an absolute prohibition on assignment as compared to a
qualified permission to assign, such permission not to be refused save on reasonable
grounds.

By a statement of agreed facts the following facts are agreed: (1) the landlords fall *f*
within s 28(2) of the Housing Act 1980; (2) the father fell within s 28(3) of the Act until
he vacated the premises on 17 September 1982; (3) the daughter is an individual and
occupies the premises as her only or principal home; (4) the document headed 'Peabody
Trust Conditions of Tenancy for flats' dated 13 December 1971 applies to the tenancy;
(5) the father by deed executed on 16 September 1982 assigned or purported to assign
the tenancy to the daughter; (6) the father vacated the premises on 17 September 1982; *g*
(7) the daughter falls within s 30(2)(*b*); (8) no notice complying with s 33 of the Act has
been served.

The short point of the case I would summarise as follows. By the grant to the father
there was an absolute prohibition of assignment. On 17 September 1982 the father
executed an assignment, or purported assignment, of the tenancy to his daughter. He
then vacated the premises. The daughter was an individual who had been occupying the *h*
premises as her only or principal home for a long period of years.

On those facts the landlords brought proceedings against the father and the daughter
in which they claimed possession against the father and the daughter, and arrears of rent
and mesne profits.

Between the date of the grant of the lease to the father in 1971 and the purported
assignment of the premises in 1982, there had intervened the 1980 Act and by Ch II of *j*
that statute Parliament made new provision for security of tenure and rights of people
described as 'secure tenants'.

By s 28(1), the first section in that chapter, it is provided:

'A tenancy under which a dwelling-house is let as a separate dwelling is a secure a   tenancy at any time when the conditions described below as the landlord condition and the tenant condition are satisfied, but subject to the exceptions in Schedule 3 to this Act and to subsection (5) below and sections 37 and 49 of this Act.'

The relevant landlord condition is s 28(2)(*b*):

'the interest of the landlord belongs to a housing association falling within subsection (3) of section 15 of the 1977 Act.'

b   The tenant condition in sub-s (3) provides:

'The tenant condition is that the tenant is an individual and occupies the dwelling-house as his only or principal home . . .'

As one peruses the provisions of Ch II, one finds that it clothes the relevant tenant, who is clad with the appropriate qualification against a landlord who comes within the
c   category of compliance with the landlord conditions in sub-s (2), with a quite new and immensely valuable security of tenure because, before this section, tenants of local authorities, tenants of housing associations, and so on, were at the mercy of their landlords who were entitled to terminate the lease on short notice at will. Of course, the background of that was that local authorities were trusted to behave in a humanitarian
d   way and the housing associations, who historically have been charities motivated by an interest to provide housing for the poorer classes, could be trusted to exercise their discretion, again in a social and humanitarian manner.

The background of the 1980 Act was that Parliament had decided that, in the case of persons falling within the description of the statutory landlord and tenant conditions, the tenant should be given the security of tenure indicated in Ch II. One of the provisions of Ch II was to the effect that the provisions of the chapter should apply to tenancies
e   granted before, as well as after, the date when the Act came into operation.

The question posed by this appeal is the effect of the impact of Ch II of the 1980 Act on a tenancy granted nine years before the 1980 Act came before the statute book having, by its terms, an absolute prohibition of assignment.

One of the new provisions of Ch II was to provide for succession on the death of the
f   tenant and by s 30(1) it was provided:

'Where a secure tenant is a periodic tenancy and, on the death of the tenant, there is a person qualified to succeed him, the tenancy vests by virtue of this section in that person or, if there is more than one such person, in the one who is to be preferred in accordance with subsection (3) below, unless the tenant was a successor.'

g   The persons qualified to succeed the tenant were enacted in sub-s (2):

'A person is qualified to succeed the tenant under a secure tenancy if he occupied the dwelling-house as his only or principal home at the time of the tenant's death and either—(*a*) he is the tenant's spouse; or (*b*) he is another member of the tenant's family and has resided with the tenant throughout the period of twelve months ending with the tenant's death.'

h   It is unnecessary to deal, for the purposes of this appeal, with sub-s (3).

One of the features of the situation, to wit the impact of the Housing Act 1980, on the father's tenancy granted by the landlords was that the father became a secure tenant and if he had died in September 1982 his daughter, the second defendant, who had been occupying the premises as her sole premises for a long period of time, would have been
j   able to claim succession to the father's secure tenancy by virtue of the provisions of s 30. Fortunately, however, the father is not dead. He decided to leave. We are told from the bar that he has gone back to Ireland. He wanted to do the right thing by his daughter. He consulted solicitors. What I would venture to call an ingenious instrument came into existence, designed to enable the father to avail himself of the provisions of s 37 of the 1980 Act and, without the consent of the landlords, to assign his interest in the land to

his daughter, and by doing so to enable her to avail herself of her condition whereby she could claim on assignment to succeed herself as a secure tenant to the previous secure *a* tenancy.

Section 37(1) provides:

'If a secure tenancy is assigned it ceases to be a secure tenancy, unless—(a) the assignment is made in pursuance of an order under section 24 of the Matrimonial Causes Act 1973; or (b) the assignment is to a person in whom the tenancy would or *b* might have vested by virtue of section 30 above had the tenant died immediately before the assignment, or in whom it would or might have so vested had the tenancy been a periodic tenancy.'

So, if the effect of the instrument purporting to be an assignment was to create a valid assignment, albeit in breach of prohibition by virtue of cl 10 of the lease, then the daughter is entitled to claim that, by virtue of that assignment, she by her condition can *c* claim a secure tenancy. Of course, that will not be the end of the story if the landlords wish to pursue against her a right of possession by reason of a ground appearing in Sch 4 to the 1980 Act. They could claim possession on the ground that an obligation of the tenancy had been broken, to wit assignment in breach of the covenant not to assign. In such proceedings, if they were instituted, it would be necessary for the landlords to comply with the procedural provisions of the 1980 Act and then to pray the county court *d* to grant them possession and the daughter would present her case why a possession order should not be made.

The crunch turns on the words in s 37(1): 'If a secure tenancy is assigned it ceases to be a secure tenancy . . .' The landlords submit, and the judge accepted, that that phrase in the statute was intended to mean a lawful assignment, that is to say an assignment which was not in breach of any condition of the lease but an assignment in exercise of the lawful *e* rights of a tenant, and it was submitted (and the judge held) that the effect of a prohibition against an assignment was that the purported assignment had no effect in law. The judge found that it was illegal and did not operate as a valid assignment. Therefore, the father having vacated the premises and the daughter having no right to be there, being a trespasser, the judge made the orders for which the landlords prayed.

With respect to the judge I am unable to accept that the draftsman of s 37(1) intended *f* to express Parliamentary intention limited only to lawful assignment, that is to say excluding assignments in breach of a covenant or condition prohibiting assignment. I cannot distinguish the ratio of this court in *Old Grovebury Manor Farm Ltd v W Seymour Plant Sales and Hire Ltd (No 2)* [1979] 3 All ER 504, [1979] 1 WLR 1397. That case dealt with the lease of business premises containing a covenant not to assign without the lessor's written consent. In breach of that covenant the second defendant executed an *g* assignment of the remainder of the term to the first defendant. The plaintiff served a notice under s 146 of the Law of Property Act 1925 on the assignor prior to commencing forfeiture proceedings. This court held ([1979] 1 WLR 1397)—

'that the assignment, though made in breach of covenant, operated to vest the remainder of the term in the first defendant . . . and that, as, accordingly, the first *h* defendant was the person concerned to avoid forfeiture and, therefore, to receive the notice under section 146 of the Law of Property Act 1925 and as "lessee" in section 146 included an assignee, the first defendant was "the lessee" within the meaning of section 146 and the person on whom the notice should have been served.'

If the ratio of the judgment of Lord Russell, with which Browne LJ agreed, cannot be *j* distinguished from the instant case, then the law to be applied is as follows. Although there was a prohibition on assignment, the effect of the purported assignment was that the interest of the assignor validly passed to the assignee, and if the landlords wished to terminate it their duty then was to serve a s 146 notice on the assignee and proceed against the assignee for forfeiture on the grounds of breach of a covenant in the lease. It was submitted before us that that case could be distinguished because, on the facts, it was dealing with a lease for a term certain of three years and in his judgment Lord Russell described the interest of the lessee as a property right.

For my part I am unable to accept that the distinction is, for this purpose, a valid distinction. This was a periodical tenancy, but as long as it survived the fath.: had an interest in the land which may reasonably be described as a legal right of prope.ty. The attempt of counsel for the landlords to persuade me that, in spite of the terms of the particulars of claim, this was a licence and not a lease did not appear to me to have any force. I would regard the principle in the *Old Grovebury Manor Farm* case as applying in the instant case and although the assignment was in breach of a condition of the lease, its effect was to transfer the father's interest to the daughter.

One comes to the next question. Was the draftsman, when he used the phrase 'if a secure tenancy is assigned', contemplating only lawful assignments? In spite of the argument of counsel for the landlords and the view taken by the judge, I am unable to take that view of the construction of the subsection. And I am influenced by the fact that, in the Rent Act 1977, in provisions dealing with sublettings, the draftsman used the expression 'lawfully sublet'. One has to be extremely careful, particularly perhaps in relation to the chequered history of the Rent Acts, in using the draftsman's technique in the Rent Act legislation as applied to the meaning of the draftsman's language in a Housing Act, Housing Acts having a rather different history to the Rent Acts.

I recognise the importance of that caution but I would have thought that in this field of property law, including housing law, it is to be expected that, if it was the intention of the draftsman in s 37 to restrict the operation of the subsection to assignments which comply with the lawful rights of the tenant, the language would have been explicit and the probability is that the phrase would have read 'if a secure tenancy is lawfully assigned' or 'is assigned in accordance with the tenant's rights under his contract of tenancy'. I would construe the phrase selected by the draftsman in s 37 as applying to all assignments whether lawful or unlawful.

It was submitted on behalf of the landlords that a scrutiny of s 35 in the same chapter points to a different construction, because in that section Parliament provided for the reading of statutory implied terms into the terms of existing leases, and it was submitted by counsel for the landlords that the inference to be drawn from s 35 is that, if Parliament had intended to modify existing leases by enacting a statutory implied term that prohibitions against assignment were only to have effect subject to certain provisions, a section or subsection would have been included in Ch II to that express effect.

I accept that there is force in that submission, but it does not seem to me strong enough to prevail against the clear express words of the first line of s 37. There does not seem to be any ambiguity. The words are quite clear. Their legal meaning is well known, and where Parliament has used the phrase 'if a secure tenancy is assigned' I think it would need some strong indication of a different intention to place quite a drastic limitation on the clear words used. For those reasons my conclusion is, with respect to the judge, that the words mean what they say; no more, no less. Here there was an assignment and that assignment enables the provisions of s 37 to be applied. The daughter (the assignee) comes within the provisions of Ch II and is entitled to claim a secure tenancy. Subject, of course, to this. There has been a breach of cl 10. It is open to the landlords to seek possession on the grounds of the first ground in Sch 4 to the 1980 Act. In order to do so it is necessary for them to comply with the procedural provisions of the 1980 Act and it is necessary for them, if they are so minded, to take the necessary action against her in accordance with the provisions of that Act.

For those reasons I would hold that the judge was wrong, that the landlords, in the proceedings that they brought, were not entitled to an order for possession against the father because he had, by assignment, divested himself of right to possession and that they were not entitled to an order for possession against the daughter because they had not complied with the provisions of the 1980 Act of taking the necessary action to claim forfeiture against her in reliance on ground 1 of Sch 4 to the 1980 Act.

For those reasons I would allow the appeal.

MAY LJ. In the context of the background to the Housing Act 1980, to which Cumming Bruce LJ referred, it is interesting also to refer to a part of the long title to the Act, which provides as follows: 'An Act to give security of tenure, and the right to buy their homes, to tenants of local authorities and other bodies . . .' In my view it is quite apparent that the object of the 1980 Act was to give such tenants greater security in their dwellings, either by purchase or the acquisition of a long lease under Ch I of the 1980 Act, or at least substantial protection as secure tenants under Ch II of the 1980 Act. The crucial point in this case, as Cumming-Bruce LJ has said and as I respectfully agree, is whether the deed of 16 September 1982 was valid to pass the legal interest of the first defendant (the father) as tenant of the relevant flat to his daughter, the second defendant. If it was not, then she became a trespasser and the landlords were entitled to possession. If it was, then she became a secure tenant under the 1980 Act, subject always, of course, to the rights of the landlords to take such steps thereunder as they saw fit and lay within their powers.

The deed could be, and was, attacked by counsel for the landlords in his submission on two bases. First, that as the assignment was in breach of the terms of the tenancy precluding assignments, it did not have the effect of transferring the legal title. This appears to have been the basis on which the judge came to his conclusion that the plaintiffs succeeded in this case. With respect, I cannot agree. The principle to which Cumming-Bruce LJ has referred and which was relied on in *Old Grovebury Manor Farm Ltd v W Seymour Plant Sales and Hire Ltd (No 2)* [1979] 3 All ER 504, [1979] 1 WLR 1397 is, I think, of substantially greater antiquity than 1979 and, in my judgment, the judge was wrong in law in reaching the conclusion which he did.

The second basis on which it was sought to say that the deed did not pass a legal interest for the purposes of the 1980 Act was, as Cumming-Bruce LJ has mentioned, that on its proper construction s 37(1) of the Act only comprehends assignments which can be said to be lawful in this sense, that they are not in breach of the terms of the particular tenancy.

The subsection does not say so. I see no reason why it could not have said so. I see less reason to read into the subsection any words to give that effect. In this particular field I have no doubt that the draftsman of the 1980 Act was well aware of the references to lawful sublettings and the like in the Rent Act 1977 and other ancillary legislation.

In the result I do not accept that the deed of 16 December 1982 was invalid to pass the legal interest in the tenancy of the flat on either of the two grounds. The result must be that the daughter has become the secure tenant of the flat but, of course, she is at the risk of the landlords seeking possession on the basis of her father's breach of covenant if the landlords take appropriate steps under s 33 of the 1980 Act and proceed in the county court. That, however, is for the future. For the present I agree that this appeal succeeds.

Appeal allowed.

Solicitors: *Sheridan & Stretton*, Hammersmith (for the father and the daughter); *Bridges Sawtell & Adams* (for the landlords).

Bebe Chua   Barrister.

Israel Discount Bank of New York v Hadjipateras and another

COURT OF APPEAL, CIVIL DIVISION
STEPHENSON, O'CONNOR AND ROBERT GOFF LJJ
24, 25 MAY 1983

Conflict of laws – Foreign judgment – Enforcement – Public policy – Plaintiff commencing proceedings in New York court for repayment of moneys under guarantee – Defendant taking no steps to defend action in New York – Plaintiff obtaining judgment in New York court and seeking summary judgment in England – Defendant contending that enforcement of New York judgment would be contrary to public policy on ground that guarantee obtained by undue influence – Whether fact that agreement obtained by undue influence ground for English court refusing to enforce foreign judgment based on agreement – Whether defendant can rely on public policy to assert that foreign judgment should not be recognised if defendant failed to raise public policy defence available to him in foreign court.

In July 1981 the defendant and his father each executed a guarantee in favour of a bank whereby each of them guaranteed the repayment of large sums of money lent by the bank to two Liberian companies. Those guarantees replaced earlier guarantees given by the defendant and his father when the defendant was 20 years old. The guarantees contained clauses whereby the defendant and his father submitted to the jurisdiction of the New York courts and whereby the proper law of the guarantee was to be New York law. In August 1981 the bank brought an action in the United States District Court, Southern District of New York, against the defendant and his father on their guarantees. In December 1981 the defendant swore an affidavit in another action setting up a defence of undue influence by his father in connection with the execution of the guarantee but did not raise that defence in the New York action. In October 1982 the New York court gave judgment in favour of the bank for a sum in excess of $US9m. The bank then issued a writ against the defendant in England for judgment under RSC Ord 14 for the sum awarded in the New York action. The respondent opposed the bank's application contending that he had an arguable case against the bank on the grounds, inter alia, that the enforcement of the New York judgment in England would be contrary to public policy since it was based on a transaction obtained by undue influence. The judge gave the defendant leave to defend on the basis that he had an arguable case that the New York judgment should not be enforced as a matter of public policy. The bank appealed.

Held – The fact that an agreement was obtained by undue influence, duress or coercion was a reason for an English court to treat a foreign judgment based on that agreement as being invalid or to refuse to enforce the foreign judgment as being contrary to English public policy. However, the refusal to enforce a foreign judgment because it was contrary to English public policy arose out of the fact that the law or practice of the foreign country differed from English public policy, and a defendant could therefore not rely on public policy to assert that a foreign judgment should not be recognised if the law and practice of the foreign country was the same as that in England and he had failed to raise a 'public policy' defence, such as undue influence, duress or coercion, which had been available to him in the foreign court. On the facts, New York law was to be assumed to be the same as English law, namely that undue influence was a defence to the agreements which the defendant claimed were invalid, and since the defendant had deliberately chosen not to argue that defence in the New York court because he thought he could do better defending the bank's claim in England he could not thereafter set up such a defence in England and claim that the foreign judgment was contrary to public policy. It followed that it would not be contrary to English public policy to enforce the judgment of the New York court. The appeal would accordingly be allowed (see p 131 d to j, p 133 c d, p 134 a to d and g to j and p 135 g to p 136 c and e f, post).

Dictum of Bovill CJ in *Ellis v M'Henry* (1871) LR 6 CP at 238 followed.
Rousillon v Rousillon (1880) 14 Ch D 351, *Re Macartney, Macfarlane v Macartney* [1921] ***a***
1 Ch 522 and *Meyer v Meyer* [1971] 1 All ER 378 distinguished.

Notes
For injunctions to restrain foreign proceedings, see 8 Halsbury's Laws (4th edn) paras
730, 787, and for cases on the subject, see 11 Digest (Reissue) 637–642, 1713–1753.
For the means by which a defendant may resist an application for summary judgment ***b***
under RSC Ord 14, see 37 Halsbury's Laws (4th edn) paras 413–415, and for cases on the
subject, see 50 Digest (Repl) 410–414, 1183–1227.

Cases referred to in judgments
Cow v Casey [1949] 1 All ER 197, [1949] 1 KB 474, CA.
Ellis v M'Henry (1871) LR 6 CP 228.   ***c***
European Asian Bank AG v Punjab and Sind Bank [1983] 2 All ER 508, [1983] 1 WLR 642,
CA.
Kaufman v Gerson [1904] 1 KB 591, [1904–7] All ER Rep 896, CA.
Kempson v Ashbee (1874) LR 10 Ch App 15.
Lloyds Bank plc v Ellis-Fewster [1983] 2 All ER 424, [1983] 1 WLR 559, CA.
Macartney, Re, Macfarlane v Macartney [1921] 1 Ch 522.   ***d***
Meyer v Meyer [1971] 1 All ER 378, [1971] P 298, [1971] 2 WLR 401.
Rousillon v Rousillon (1880) 14 Ch D 351.
Tracomin SA v Sudan Oil Seeds Co Ltd (No 2) [1983] 2 All ER 129.
Verrall v Great Yarmouth BC [1980] 1 All ER 839, [1981] 1 QB 202, [1980] 3 WLR 258,
CA.
        e
Appeal
The plaintiff, Israel Discount Bank of New York (the bank), appealed against the order of
Neill J made on 4 February 1983 giving the second defendant, George C Hadjipateras,
unconditional leave to defend an action commenced by writ issued on 29 October 1982.
Judgment was entered against the first defendant, Costas A Hadjipateras, on 4 February
1982. The facts are set out in the judgment of Stephenson LJ.   ***f***

Gavin Lightman QC and *Nicholas Chambers* for the bank.
Simon Crookenden for the second defendant.

STEPHENSON LJ. This is an appeal by the plaintiff bank from an order of Neill J of 4
February 1983, giving the second defendant, Mr George Hadjipateras, unconditional   ***g***
leave to defend an action brought against him and his father, the first defendant, on
guarantees.
    On or about 23 July 1981 the second defendant and his father each executed a
guarantee in favour of the bank whereby each of them guaranteed the repayment of
large sums of money lent by the bank to two Liberian companies, Seabound Shipping
Corp and Seaport Shipping Corp. These guarantees replaced earlier guarantees given by ***h***
the second defendant and his father in 1980, when the second defendant was 20 years of
age. In August 1981 Seabound and Seaport failed to make certain payments in accordance
with the terms of the agreements between them and the bank. The bank demanded
repayment of the loans; Seabound and Seaport failed to pay and the bank instituted legal
proceedings.
    The guarantees contained clauses whereby the guarantors, father and son, irrevocably ***j***
submitted to the jurisdiction of the New York courts and whereby the proper law of the
contracts was New York law. Accordingly, on 31 August 1981 the bank brought an
action against the second defendant and his father on their guarantees in the United
States District Court, Southern District of New York (the New York action). But on 11
September 1981 the bank also brought an action here in the High Court of Justice,

a
Queen's Bench Division, for recovery of the loan moneys and on the guarantees against
the second defendant and his father among others (the English action).

On 1 October 1981 the second defendant and his father filed a short answer in the
New York action denying liability. On 21 October that answer was amended. Fourteen
affirmative defences were set up, including defences that the court lacked jurisdiction.
In addition, certain counterclaims were made, which included a charge of fraud. The
relief sought included a claim for punitive damages in the sum of $US20m.

b
On 10 December 1981 the second defendant swore an affidavit in the English action
setting up a defence of undue influence in connection with the execution of the
guarantee.

The only question raised by the bank's appeal is whether the second defendant has an
arguable defence in law: might he, in the English action, successfully resist the claim
under the guarantee with his plea of undue influence? That question is divided by the

c
second defendant's notice into two parts: first, a plea that in July 1981 he signed the
guarantee, including the clause giving jurisdiction to the New York court, under the
undue influence of his father; and, second, that he submitted to the jurisdiction of the
New York court later by serving an answer to the bank's claim in the New York action in
October 1981 under the same influence.

It is conceded that for the purposes of these RSC Ord 14 proceedings (a) it was arguable

d
that the guarantee signed by the second defendant in July 1981 was given in circumstances
which amounted to undue influence by his father and (b) it was therefore arguable that
the contractual submission to the jurisdiction of the New York courts contained in the
guarantee was ineffective. There is no evidence as to the law of New York on undue
influence, so it must be assumed to be the same as English law. The second defendant
could therefore have raised it in the New York action unless he was prevented by the

e
continuing undue influence of his father from doing so. Even if that influence must be
presumed to have continued from July until October, it is conceded on the second
defendant's behalf that it had terminated by 10 December 1981 when he swore the
affidavit to which I have referred. Thereafter the second defendant took no steps to raise
the plea of undue influence in the New York action; on the contrary, he took out a
summons for a stay of the Ord 14 proceedings in the English action on 10 February

f
1982, on the ground that the New York action was lis alibi pendens, and his leading
counsel on the hearing of that summons on 15 and 16 February recognised that any
judgment obtained in the New York action might be enforceable, though he would not
go so far as to concede it; and leading counsel for the bank then gave an undertaking not
to proceed with the Ord 14 summons except on 7 days' notice.

The second defendant did nothing, except to join his father in failing to comply with

g
orders of the New York Court of Appeals and in moving the New York district court
unsuccessfully to dismiss the New York action for lack of subject matter of jurisdiction.
On 19 October 1982 judgment in default was given against both the father and the
second defendant. On 29 October 1982 the bank claimed in the second English action
the sum of $US10,720,477·07 and judgment for that sum, which consisted of the amount
of the New York judgment and some further interest. On 23 December 1982 the

h
summons under Ord 14 was restored. The defendant's father did not oppose the bank's
application for summary judgment, and on 4 February 1983 summary judgment was
given against the father.

On those facts, can the second defendant raise with any hope of success in the English
action the defence that he was not bound by the guarantee or by submission to the
jurisdiction of the New York court because he agreed to both through the undue

j
influence, not of the bank but of his father? I am clearly of the opinion that he cannot.

Neill J in the court below stated the general rule as to the enforcement of foreign
judgments shortly and correctly thus:

'A foreign judgment in personam made by a court of competent jurisdiction is
enforceable by action in England provided that it is for a definite sum of money and
is final and conclusive. To this general rule there is an exception in the case of sums

payable in respect of taxes or penalties. Furthermore, a foreign judgment can be impeached (a) if the judgment was obtained by fraud or (b) if the registration or the enforcement of the judgment would be contrary to English public policy or (c) if the proceedings in which the judgment was obtained were contrary to natural justice.'

The judgment of 19 October 1982 is admittedly enforceable in this jurisdiction unless the second defendant can establish (i) that it was made without jurisdiction or (ii) that its enforcement would be contrary to public policy. Counsel on behalf of the second defendant has sought to raise further grounds for claiming that this judgment is unenforceable and should not be acted on by the courts of this country, but we have not allowed him to go beyond the two defences which were alleged below to be arguable defences entitling him to unconditional leave to defend.

The judge decided that the second defendant had no arguable case on jurisdiction but on public policy he said this:

'As at present advised, I feel bound to say that I regard the defence as unconvincing, but I do not feel able to say it is unarguable. With considerable hesitation, therefore, having regard to the history of this matter, I have finally come to the conclusion that it would not be right for me to give judgment for the bank against the second defendant on this summons. In other circumstances a conditional order might be appropriate, but the sum claimed here is in excess of $US10m. There will therefore be unconditional leave to defend . . .'

On jurisdiction, I agree with the judge. In the light of the bank's concessions this question, which I deal with first as the judge did, is whether, apart from the jurisdiction clause in the guarantee, the New York court acquired jurisdiction because the respondent voluntarily appeared and took part in the New York action. What the second defendant swore on 1 February 1983 relating to that was this; I will read paras 18, 19 and 20 of his affidavit:

'18. I was advised that my chances of defending the proceedings in England were far greater than defending the proceedings in New York. Although I was advised that there was a potential conflict of interest between my father and myself, at no juncture was it suggested to me that I could defend the proceedings in New York on the grounds of undue influence. The decision not to defend the proceedings in New York was taken by my father.

19. I was advised by Elborne Mitchell [a firm of solicitors] in January that they were unable to represent both my father and myself. I had made no decision about separate representation before because firstly, I understood that it was better to try and run both cases together, secondly, my father took all the decisions on what steps should be taken and thirdly, I neither have nor had any financial means and I had to discuss the case and seek financial help from other relatives.

20. I have to say that were it not for my respect for my father and the control he exercised over my actions and also that, as his youngest son, I was considerably under his influence, I would not have acted in the manner in which I did.'

Counsel for the second defendant submits on his behalf, first, that those steps by the second defendant stem directly from the signing of the guarantee by him when he was only 21, and cannot be regarded as an independent voluntary submission to the jurisdiction of the New York court, and, second, that the conduct of the New York proceedings was in his father's hands; the second defendant himself did what he was told by his father, so that the bank cannot take advantage of the submission, procured as it was by the undue influence of the father. Until discovery produces positive evidence, we should presume that the bank's knowledge of the undue influence exerted by the father, assumed to exist in July 1981, extended to knowledge of the father's influence over the conduct of the proceedings taken so soon after July 1981. Counsel relies on *Kempson v Ashbee* (1874) LR 10 Ch App 15, a case in which a young woman was held not to be

bound by a bond entered into under the influence of her stepfather six years after
a entering into a similar bond under his influence, because she had not become aware that
the first bond might be invalid. I am afraid that I do not get help from that case, or from
speculating on what discovery might fish out of the bank's files. The judge did not
consider the evidence in the affidavit of the second defendant, which I have read,
sufficient to raise an arguable case of undue influence in the conduct of the New York
proceedings, and thought it fanciful to suggest that the bank, as plaintiff in those
b proceedings, was privy to, or had knowledge of, undue influence exerted by the father
on the second defendant in those proceedings. He also accepted the bank's argument that
it was inconsistent with the action taken in the English proceedings and the inaction in
the New York proceedings to raise the defence of no voluntary submission or appearance.
I agree that the submission and appearance cannot now be challenged by the second
defendant, for the reasons given by the judge.
c   On public policy, I regret that I have to differ from the judge, my regret tempered by
the hesitation which he expressed on deciding this point in the second defendant's
favour. There is authority for holding that it would be contrary to public policy for our
courts to enforce a judgment based on a transaction which may have been tainted by
undue influence. In *Rousillon v Rousillon* (1880) 14 Ch D 351 it was held that if an
agreement contrary to the policy of English law is entered into in a country by the law
d of which it is valid, an English court will not enforce it, and Fry J said (at 369):

> '[Counsel] has insisted that, even if the contract was void by the law of *England* as
> against public policy, yet, inasmuch as the contract was made in *France*, it must be
> good here, because the law of *France* knows no such principle as that by which
> unreasonable contracts in restraint of trade are held to be void in this country. It
e > appears to me, however, plain on general principles that this Court will not enforce
> a contract against the public policy of this country, wherever it may be made. It
> seems to me almost absurd to suppose that the Courts of this country should enforce
> a contract which they consider to be against public policy simply because it happens
> to have been made somewhere else.'

In *Re Macartney, Macfarlane v Macartney* [1921] 1 Ch D 522 at 528 Astbury J, having
f cited that passage from the judgment of Fry J in *Rousillon v Rousillon*, said that it 'applies
directly to the non-enforceability of foreign judgments founded on contracts contrary to
public policy or rights of that character' and he refused to enforce a judgment of the
Court of Appeal in Malta condemning a putative father's estate to provide an allowance
for his natural daughter—

g   'because the general recognition of the permanent rights of illegitimate children
and their spinster mothers as recognised in Malta is contrary to the established policy
of this country, especially having regard to the fact that the child's interest is not
confined to minority.'

In *Kaufman v Gerson* [1904] 1 KB 591, [1904–7] All ER Rep 896 this court refused to
h enforce a contract, valid in France where it was made, against a woman who had been
coerced into making it by threats that her husband would be prosecuted if she did not
pay the balance of what he had criminally misappropriated from the plaintiff. She had
undertaken to pay a considerable sum, and had already paid most of it by instalments.
The Court of Appeal refused to enforce the contract obtained by means of such coercion,
variously stating that it violated a moral principle which ought to be universally
recognised, or that it contravened what the law of this country deemed an essential moral
j interest. There was in that case no French judgment, and the decision has not lacked
critics.
In *Meyer v Meyer* [1971] 1 All ER 378, [1971] P 298 Bagnall J granted a wife forced to
petition in a German court for the dissolution of her marriage to a Jew, a declaration that
the resulting German decree of divorce was invalid as obtained by duress, and was
contrary to natural justice.

I do not doubt that an agreement obtained by undue influence, like an agreement obtained by duress or coercion, may be treated by our courts as invalidating a foreign *a* judgment based on the agreement, or as a ground for not enforcing it as contrary to the distinctive public policy of this country. We have to assume that the original guarantee and its jurisdiction clause were arguably so obtained, presumably by the bank or with the bank's connivance or knowledge, though not that the agreement to take part in the New York action was arguably so obtained. But what is plain here is that in those cases to which we have been referred the public policy involved was what English courts *b* considered to be the distinctive public policy of this country, and it was only because the law or practice of the foreign country (Malta or France or Germany) differed from that policy that the question of the validity of the contract or judgment was raised in the court of this country. It was out of this conflict that those cases arose.

Counsel in his courageous argument for the second defendant has submitted that none of the judgments in those cases stresses the fact that the foreign law differed from our *c* own; but there was no reason why they should. But for that fact, the judges would not have had the cases to consider or any question of public policy to decide. It is that fact which distinguishes those cases from the present case, because the law of New York must be assumed to allow undue influence as a defence to the agreements which the second defendant wants to argue are invalid; and, because he thinks he can do better defending the bank's claim in England, he has deliberately chosen not to argue that defence in the *d* New York court, where it was available. But a defendant must take all available defences in a foreign court. The judgment of the Court of Common Pleas in *Ellis v M'Henry* (1871) LR 6 CP 228 at 238 is old authority for this rule, and the judgment of Leggatt J in *Tracomin SA v Sudan Oil Seeds Co Ltd (No 2)* [1983] 2 All ER 129[1] is a very recent illustration of it.

In *Ellis v M'Henry* Bovill CJ, giving the judgment of the court which consisted of *e* himself, Willes, Keating and Brett JJ, said (LR 6 CP 228 at 238):

'The first action, however, is upon a judgment which was recovered after the deed was completed. In the view that we take of this case, the deed might have been set up as a defence to the action brought in Upper Canada; and it is averred, as a matter of fact, in the third replication, and not denied, that it might have been so pleaded. The question then arises, whether it can now be brought forward in the proceedings *f* as an answer to the judgment. When a party having a defence omits to avail himself of it, or having relied upon it, it is determined against him, and a judgment is thereupon given, he is not allowed afterwards to set up such matters of defence as an answer to the judgment, which is considered final and conclusive between the parties.'

g

That is not, it is true, a judgment dealing with public policy, but it seems to me that that statement of the law, which is plainly good sense and in line with considerations of comity and the duty of the courts to put an end to litigation, is conclusive of this case.

It is impossible for the second defendant, who is at fault in not raising this defence in the New York court, to impeach the court's judgment. That failure, in my opinion, destroys both the defences which he wishes to argue, and it would not be contrary to *h* public policy to enforce the judgment in the New York action or the agreement of guarantee and submission to the jurisdiction of the New York court on which that judgment is based. The law is clearly against the second defendant, and in my judgment this court should say so now by giving judgment against him.

We are not, in so doing, interfering with the judge's decision in what is essentially a matter for his discretion. When the judge thinks that there is a triable issue on evidence *j* as opposed to law, it is not the intention of the new right of appeal given by the Supreme Court Act 1981, against a grant of unconditional leave to defend, that this court should often dissent from the judge's view that there is a triable issue of fact: see *Lloyds Bank plc*

---

1   Subsequently reversed on a different point: see [1983] 3 All ER 140

a
v Ellis-Fewster [1983] 2 All ER 424 at 426, [1983] 1 WLR 559 at 562 per Sir John
Donaldson MR. Changes in economic circumstances rendering it more likely that
defendants will have recourse to delaying tactics and changes in the relevant rules of
court reducing the number of appellate courts before finality is reached, as well as the
wording of Ord 14, r 3(1), indicate that these interlocutory appeals are by way of
rehearing, and the discretionary aspect of an appeal against an order giving unconditional
leave to defend is reduced to vanishing point. This is expounded in an illuminating
b judgment of this court (Slade and Robert Goff LJJ) given by Robert Goff LJ in *European
Asian Bank AG v Punjab and Sind Bank* [1983] 2 All ER 508 at 515–516, [1983] 1 WLR 642
at 654, which concludes its comments on the new statutory jurisdiction with these
words:

c
'If the judge has already decided, on the evidence, that there is a triable issue on a
question of fact, it must in the very nature of things be unlikely that this court will
interfere with his decision and decide that no trial should take place; because, where
such a conclusion has already been reached by a judge, this court will be very
reluctant to hold that there is no issue or question which ought to be tried. But
where the appeal raises a question of law, this court may be more ready to interfere.
Moreover, at least since *Cow v Casey* [1949] 1 All ER 197, [1949] 1 KB 474, this court
has made it plain that it will not hesitate, in an appropriate case, to decide questions
d of law under Ord 14, even if the question of law is at first blush of some complexity
and therefore takes 'a little longer to understand'. It may offend against the whole
purpose of Ord 14 not to decide a case which raises a clear-cut issue, when full
argument has been addressed to the court, and the only result of not deciding it will
be that the case will go for trial and the argument will be rehearsed all over again
before a judge, with the possibility of yet another appeal (see *Verrall v Great Yarmouth
e   BC* [1980] 1 All ER 839 at 843, 845–846, [1981] 1 QB 202 at 215, 218 per Lord
Denning MR and Roskill LJ). The policy of Ord 14 is to prevent delay in cases where
there is no defence; and this policy is, if anything, reinforced in a case such as the
present, concerned as it is with a claim by a negotiating bank under a letter of credit
...'

f   Whatever the approach of this court to a judge's decision as to a triable issue of fact, it is
(and I quote from the judgment of Sir John Donaldson MR in the *Lloyds Bank* case [1983]
2 All ER 424 at 426, [1983] 1 WLR 559 at 562) 'quite different if you are dealing with a
triable issue which arises as a matter of law'.
I am clearly of opinion that there is no reason why we should not respect the judgment
of the New York court and treat it as deciding the second defendant's liability to the bank
g on the guarantee, and put an end to this litigation now. I would accordingly allow the
appeal, set aside the judge's order and give summary judgment for the bank against the
second defendant.

O'CONNOR LJ. I agree that this appeal should be allowed. The appellant bank
obtained judgment in the New York action for some $US10,700,000 on 19 October 1982.
h It commenced these proceedings on 29 October 1982 to enforce the judgment against
the two Hadjipateras, father and son, Costas and George. Costas, the first defendant,
submitted to the judgment under RSC Ord 14; George, the second defendant, sought
leave to defend the English action enforcing the New York judgment. He sought leave
on two grounds, submitting that to the knowledge of the bank he had been under the
undue influence of his father at the time when the guarantees were entered into, and
j that in the result the submission to the New York jurisdiction contained in the guarantees
was void, and that there had been no voluntary submission to the jurisdiction in New
York.
The judge dismissed the idea that there had been no voluntary submission to the New
York court. On the facts before him there quite plainly had been, but he gave
unconditional leave to defend on the plea that the second defendant was at all times
under the undue influence of his father, to the knowledge of the bank, and that in the

result the courts in this country would not enforce the New York judgment because it would be against public policy to enforce a judgment which had been obtained wrongly, *a* according to the second defendant, because the guarantee was void as having been obtained when he was under the undue influence of his father. In my judgment there is a very short answer to that plea: it is that the point was never taken in the New York proceedings. We have no evidence in this case as to the law of New York; it is therefore the same as our own, and as at 10 October 1981, a year before judgment was entered in New York, the second defendant swore an affidavit in proceedings in this country raising *b* the defence of undue influence. He never raised it in the New York action, though it was open to him to do so. In those circumstances he cannot complain that the judgment in New York is bad.

I can see no grounds for refusing to enforce the judgment here. The judge was influenced by a decision of this court in *Kaufman v Gerson* [1904] 1 KB 591, [1904–7] All ER Rep 896. That was a very extraordinary case. What had happened was that the *c* plaintiff had provided Gerson with money in France for a particular purpose. Gerson had misappropriated the money to his own purposes; the plaintiff obtained an agreement by his wife to repay the money. She had in fact repaid some £800 of £1,000; he brought an action for the balance in this country. It was said that that agreement had been obtained by means which were against public policy in this country and that therefore it could not be enforced. It was a very exceptional case; it was said that the wife had been *d* threatened that her husband would be prosecuted if she did not enter into the agreement. It is wholly different from the present case; the ratio of it was straightforward. The court in this country held that the agreement, according to French law, was a valid agreement, and they must have held that the English defence of coercion or duress could not have been raised in France. Be that as it may, it has no bearing on the facts of the present case; that problem simply does not arise, and in my judgment the judge in the present case *e* fell into error in thinking that *Kaufman v Gerson* was of any help to the second defendant in the present proceedings.

I agree with Stephenson LJ that if this court comes to the conclusion that the law is clear and that the only defence is one of law, and the law is against the second defendant, we should interfere with the judge's ruling and order that judgment be entered for the bank. *f*

ROBERT GOFF LJ. I agree.

Appeal allowed. Order of judge set aside and summary judgment entered for plaintiff in sums of principal and interest to be agreed. Leave to appeal to House of Lords refused. Execution stayed on terms. *g*

Solicitors: *Cameron Markby* (for the bank); *McHale & Co* (for the second defendant).

Diana Brahams   Barrister.

Tracomin SA v Sudan Oil Seeds Co Ltd (No 1)

a

COURT OF APPEAL, CIVIL DIVISION
SIR JOHN DONALDSON MR, ACKNER AND FOX LJJ
23 JUNE 1983

b

Conflict of laws – Foreign judgment – Enforcement or recognition – Jurisdiction of foreign court – Submission to jurisdiction by defendant – Sudanese company contracting to sell goods to Swiss company – Contract evidenced by sold note – Sold note stating that conditions of contract 'as per' standard form – Standard form providing that disputes to be referred to arbitration in London – Buyers bringing action in Swiss court for damages for breach of contract – Sellers entering plea in

c *Swiss court requesting stay of proceedings on ground that dispute should be settled under arbitration clause incorporated into contract – Swiss court dismissing plea – Sellers asking arbitrators to proceed with arbitration in London – Buyers seeking order of English court to restrain arbitration – Whether Swiss judgment could be recognised or enforced by English court – Civil Jurisdiction and Judgments Act 1982, ss 32, 33(1), Sch 13, Pt II, para 8(1).*

d A dispute arose between Swiss buyers and Sudanese sellers in respect of a contract of sale which was evidenced by a sold note stating that the conditions of the contract were to be 'as per' a trade association's standard form of contract, which provided that such a contract was to be governed by English law, that any dispute arising under it was to be submitted to arbitration in London and that neither party was to take legal proceedings until the dispute had been determined by arbitration. The buyers, however, brought an action in

e a Swiss court claiming damages for breach of contract. The sellers entered what was in effect a plea in bar in the Swiss court asking for a stay of proceedings on the ground that the dispute should be settled under the arbitration clause incorporated in the contract. The Swiss court dismissed the sellers' application, holding that the arbitration clause was not to be regarded as having been incorporated into the contract. The sellers then requested arbitrators to proceed with arbitration in London. The buyers brought an

f action in England applying for an order to restrain the sellers from proceeding with the arbitration. During the course of the hearing ss 32*a* and 33*b* of the Civil Jurisdiction and Judgments Act 1982 came into force and the question arose what effect, if any, that Act had on the buyers' application. Section 32(1) provided that a judgment of a court of an overseas country was not to be recognised or enforced in the United Kingdom if the bringing of the proceedings in the overseas court was contrary to an agreement for the

g settlement of the dispute, if the other party did not agree to the proceedings being brought in the overseas court and if the other party did not submit to that court's jurisdiction. Section 33(1) provided that the person against whom judgment was given was not to be regarded as 'having submitted to the jurisdiction of the court' by reason only of the fact that he had appeared in the proceedings for the purpose of, inter alia, requesting a stay of proceedings on the ground that the dispute should be submitted to

h arbitration. Under the transitional provisions contained in para 8(1)*c* of Pt II of Sch 13 to the 1982 Act the provisions of s 32 were not to apply to judgments which had been registered under certain statutes relating to the reciprocal enforcement of foreign judgments before s 32 came into force or where 'proceedings at common law for [the] enforcement' of a foreign judgment had been finally determined before s 32 came into force. The judge refused the buyers' application on the grounds that para 8(1) did not

j have the effect that s 32 was not to apply to the judgment obtained in the Swiss court by the buyers, and furthermore that, by virtue of s 33(1), the sellers were to be deemed not

---

a   Section 32, so far as material, is set out at p 139 *a* to *c*, post
b   Section 33, so far as material, is set out at p 139 *d*, post
c   Paragraph 8(1) is set out at p 139 *g*, post

to have submitted to the jurisdiction of the Swiss court merely because they had entered a plea requesting a stay of proceedings on the grounds that the dispute should be decided *a* under the arbitration agreement. Accordingly, the judge held that s 32 applied and that the English court could not recognise or enforce the judgment of the Swiss court. The buyers appealed.

Held – On its true construction s 32 of the 1982 Act applied to all foreign judgments, other than those specifically excluded by para 8(1) of Pt II of Sch 13, which came before *b* the court after s 32 came into operation, regardless of when the foreign judgment was given, and accordingly s 32 applied to the judgment of the Swiss court. Similarly, by virtue of s 33(1) of the 1982 Act the sellers were not to be regarded as having submitted to the jurisdiction of the Swiss court by reason only of the fact that they had appeared in the proceedings in Switzerland for the purpose of seeking a stay of proceedings on the ground that the dispute should be submitted to arbitration. It followed that the court *c* could not recognise or enforce the judgment of the Swiss court because under English law there was a valid arbitration agreement and the proceedings in Switzerland had been brought contrary to that agreement and without the agreement of the sellers. The buyer's appeal would therefore be dismissed (see p 140 *a* to *d*, post).

Decision of Staughton J [1983] 1 All ER 404 affirmed.

Notes   *d*
For recognition of foreign judgments, see 8 Halsbury's Laws (4th edn) para 767, and for cases on the subject, see 11 Digest (Reissue) 606–617, 1505–1599.

For the Civil Jurisdiction and Judgments Act 1982, ss 32, 33, Sch 13, Pt II, para 8, see 52 Halsbury's Statutes (3rd edn) 408, 409, 471.

Case cited   *e*
Henry v Geopresco International Ltd [1975] 2 All ER 702, [1976] QB 726, CA.

Appeal
The plaintiffs, Tracomin SA (the buyers), appealed against the judgment of Staughton J ([1983] 1 All ER 404) dated 6 October 1982 whereby he refused the buyers' application *f* for (i) a declaration that Mr A P Beaton and Mr George J Bridge had no jurisdiction as arbitrators to determine any dispute between the buyers and the defendants, Sudan Oil Seeds Co Ltd (the sellers), arising out of a contract dated 6 December 1980 because the parties had never agreed, in that contract or elsewhere, to refer such disputes to arbitration, and (ii) an order restraining the sellers, by themselves, their servants or agents, from proceeding with or taking any step in a reference (or purported reference) to the arbitration of A P Beaton and G Bridge made under the Rules of Arbitration and *g* Appeal of the Federation of Oils, Seeds and Fats Association Ltd of disputes arising under the contract made between the buyers and the sellers. The facts are set out in the judgment of Sir John Donaldson MR.

David Grace for the buyers.   *h*
Nicholas Merriman for the sellers.

SIR JOHN DONALDSON MR. The previous history of this appeal appears in a report of the judgment of Staughton J (see [1983] 1 All ER 404). That being so, I can come immediately to the point of the appeal. Tracomin SA, the buyers, appeal against that decision of the judge, given on 6 October 1982, whereby he held that a judgment of *j* a Swiss court could not be recognised in this country. The basis of the judge's decision was that the judgment was affected by ss 32 and 33 of the Civil Jurisdiction and Judgments Act 1982. That Act had come into force during the course of the hearing, and the whole issue in the appeal is whether it took effect so as to bear on a foreign judgment given before the date when the particular provisions came into force. Section 32 provides:

'(1) Subject to the following provisions of this section, a judgment given by a court of an overseas country in any proceedings shall not be recognised or enforced in the United Kingdom if—(a) the bringing of those proceedings in that court was contrary to an agreement under which the dispute was to be settled otherwise than by proceedings in the courts of that country; and (b) those proceedings were not brought in that court by, or with the agreement of, the person against whom the judgment was given; and (c) that person did not counterclaim in the proceedings or otherwise submit to the jurisdiction of that court.

(2) Subsection (1) does not apply where the agreement referred to in paragraph (a) of that subsection was illegal, void or unenforceable or was incapable of being performed for reasons not attributable to the fault of the party bringing the proceedings in which the judgment was given.

(3) In determining whether a judgment given by a court of an overseas country should be recognised or enforced in the United Kingdom, a court in the United Kingdom shall not be bound by any decision of the overseas court relating to any of the matters mentioned in subsection (1) or (2) . . .'

Similarly s 33 provides:

'(1) For the purposes of determining whether a judgment given by a court of an overseas country should be recognised or enforced in England and Wales or Northern Ireland, the person against whom the judgment was given shall not be treated as having submitted to the jurisdiction [and then it goes on to define what is meant by submission to the jurisdiction] . . .'

Counsel for the buyers has submitted that prima facie provisions of this nature have no effect on substantive law, although he accepts that they would affect procedural law, and the judge held that this was a procedural provision. But that is subject to another rule, namely that, if Parliament wishes to enact retrospectively, it can do so provided it uses sufficiently plain words. The intention to legislate retrospectively need not be expressed provided that there is a very clear implication to that effect.

To find out what Parliament's intention was in this case it is necessary to look at Sch 13, which deals with 'Commencement, Transitional Provisions and Savings'. Paragraph 2 of Pt I of that schedule indicates the dates on which particular sections are to come into force. Sections 32 and 33 came into force six weeks after the day on which the Act was passed, and that six weeks in fact expired on 24 August 1982. But Sch 13 does not stop there, and it contains this provision in para 8(1) of Pt II:

'Section 32 shall not apply to any judgment—(a) which has been registered under Part II of the Administration of Justice Act 1920, Part I of the Foreign Judgments (Reciprocal Enforcement) Act 1933 or Part I of the Maintenance Orders (Reciprocal Enforcement) Act 1972 before the time when that section comes into force; or (b) in respect of which proceedings at common law for its enforcement have been finally determined before that time.'

Counsel for the buyers concedes that he is not within either para (a) or para (b). He also concedes that, if ss 32 and 33 are intended to have retrospective effect, then this appeal fails.

So we have to look at Sch 13 and answer the question: what was Parliament's intention? In my judgment, it is quite clear that Parliament was making provision in para 8 for delineating the retrospective extent of s 32, and was saying that it would not have retrospective effect in relation to any judgment in respect of which enforcement proceedings had been taken, as indicated in paras (a) and (b). But in setting out precisely the extent to which s 32 should not have retrospective effect Parliament impliedly indicated that in all other respects it should have retrospective effect. Counsel for the buyers says that the opening words of para 8(1), 'Section 32 shall not apply to any judgment', properly construed mean that s 32 shall not apply in relation to the *enforcement* of any judgment in paras (a) and (b), but have no reference to *recognition*.

I do not so construe it. If I did so construe it, there would still be a question in my mind whether, Parliament having made express provisions in relation to the enforcement of judgments, it did not follow on the ordinary principles of expressio unius est exclusio alterius that there was to be a retrospective effect in relation to recognition. As I say, I do not so construe it. I think that the paragraph means precisely what it says. It says that s 32 shall not apply to particular categories of judgments, and by necessary implication it shall apply to all other judgments. The Swiss judgment in this case was one of those other judgments, and accordingly in my judgment s 32 applies. There are equivalent provisions for s 33 contained in para 9 of Pt II of Sch 13, and the same arguments apply.

Accordingly, I would dismiss the appeal.

I should have added that I very much appreciate the extent to which counsel for the buyers has refined his submissions, and has made every concession he possibly could make with a view to saving time and cost.

ACKNER LJ. I agree.

FOX LJ. I also agree.

Appeal dismissed.

Solicitors: *Richards Butler & Co* (for the buyers); *William A Crump & Son* (for the sellers).

Frances Rustin   Barrister.

Tracomin SA v Sudan Oil Seeds Co Ltd and another (No 2)

COURT OF APPEAL, CIVIL DIVISION
SIR JOHN DONALDSON MR, ACKNER AND FOX LJJ
23, 24 JUNE 1983

Conflict of laws – Foreign proceedings – Restraint of foreign proceedings – Circumstances in which court will restrain foreign proceedings – Contract providing for arbitration in London – Contract between Swiss buyers and Sudanese sellers – Buyers commencing proceedings in Swiss court for breach of contract – Seller asking Swiss court to stay proceedings in view of arbitration agreement – Swiss court giving judgment for buyers on basis of Swiss law following failure of sellers to adduce evidence of English law – Sellers seeking injunction from English court to restrain buyers from proceeding further with Swiss proceedings – Whether court having jurisdiction to restrain buyers from instituting or maintaining foreign proceedings in breach of arbitration agreement – Whether sellers' failure to inform Swiss court of relevant English law a reason for English court to refuse injunction – Whether duplicity of proceedings sufficient reason to restrain buyers from proceeding in Swiss court.

A dispute arose between Swiss buyers and Sudanese sellers in respect of a contract of sale which was evidenced by a sold note stating that the conditions of the contract were to be 'as per' a trade association's standard form of contract, which provided that such a contract was to be governed by English law, that any dispute arising under it was to be submitted to arbitration in London and that neither party was to take legal proceedings until the dispute had been determined by arbitration. The buyers, however, brought an action in a Swiss court claiming damages for breach of contract. The sellers entered what was in effect a plea in bar in the Swiss court asking for a stay of proceedings on the ground that the dispute should be settled under the arbitration clause incorporated in the contract. The Swiss court dismissed the sellers' application because, in the absence of the citation

of English law by either party, the court assumed English law to be the same as Swiss law
a and held that the arbitration clause was not to be regarded as having been incorporated
into the contract. The sellers then requested arbitrators to proceed with arbitration in
London. The buyers brought an action in England seeking an order to restrain the sellers
from proceeding with the arbitration, while the sellers counterclaimed for an order
restraining the buyers from proceeding further with the Swiss action. On the
counterclaim, the judge held that, although the English court had jurisdiction to grant
b an injunction restraining either party from instituting or maintaining proceedings
abroad in breach of the arbitration agreement, the sellers had to submit to the
consequences of their own negligence, even though that might result in duplicity of
proceedings, because the Swiss court had reached its conclusion on account of the sellers'
negligence in failing to cite English law. He accordingly dismissed the counterclaim.
The sellers appealed.

c
Held – (1) Notwithstanding that the buyers were a foreign national who did not carry
on business within the jurisdiction of the English court, the fact that they had agreed to
submit disputes to English arbitration amounted to a sufficient submission to the
jurisdiction of the English courts, or alternatively created a sufficiently close nexus
between the buyers and the jurisdiction of the English courts to entitle the court to
d exercise its jurisdiction (see p 144 *b c* and p 146 *d e*, post); *Pena Copper Mines Ltd v Rio
Tinto Co Ltd* [1911–13] All ER Rep 209 applied.
    (2) Although the sellers had been negligent in failing to plead the relevant English
law before the Swiss court, that was not a balancing factor of equal weight which
cancelled out the blameworthiness of the conduct of the buyers in seeking to deny their
own covenant to arbitrate. The judge, in refusing to exercise his discretion, had erred in
e principle, beyond a mere difference of opinion as to the weight to be accorded to the
conduct of the respective parties, and had failed to give sufficient weight to the possibility
of inconsistency between the judgments of the Swiss court and the arbitrators and had
failed to take into account the fact that, because the sellers could still resort to arbitration
in England, the arbitrators would be in a position to assume an appellate role over the
findings of the Swiss court. It followed that the injunction would be granted restraining
f the buyers from continuing their action in the Swiss court and the sellers' appeal would
accordingly be allowed (see p 144 *j* to p 145 *j* and p 146 *d e*, post); dictum of Dunn LJ in
Mike Trading and Transport Ltd v R Pagnan & Flli, The Lisboa [1980] 2 Lloyd's Rep at 551
applied.
    Decision of Leggatt J [1983] 2 All ER 129 reversed.

g **Notes**
For injunctions to restrain foreign proceedings, see 8 Halsbury's Laws (4th edn) paras
730, 787, and for cases on the subject, see 11 Digest (Reissue) 637–642, 1713–1753.

Cases referred to in judgments
Castanho v Brown & Root (UK) Ltd [1980] 3 All ER 72, [1980] 1 WLR 833, CA; *varied*
h   [1981] 1 All ER 143, [1981] AC 557, [1980] 3 WLR 991, HL.
Cohen v Rothfield [1919] 1 KB 410, [1918–19] All ER Rep 260, CA.
Mike Trading and Transport Ltd v R Pagnan & Flli, The Lisboa [1980] 2 Lloyd's Rep 546,
    CA.
Pena Copper Mines Ltd v Rio Tinto Co Ltd (1911) 105 LT 846, [1911–13] All ER Rep 209,
    CA.
j *Tracomin SA v Sudan Oil Seeds Co Ltd (No 1)* [1983] 1 All ER 404.

Cases also cited
Godard v Gray (1870) LR 6 QB 139.
Henry v Geopresco International Ltd [1975] 2 All ER 702, [1976] QB 726, CA.
Settlement Corp v Hochschild [1965] 3 All ER 486, [1966] Ch 10.
West (Richard) & Partners (Inverness) Ltd v Dick [1969] 1 All ER 943, [1969] 2 Ch 424, CA.

Appeal

The defendants, Sudan Oil Seeds Co Ltd (the sellers), appealed against the judgment of a
Leggatt J ([1983] 2 All ER 129) on 17 February 1983 whereby he refused the sellers'
counterclaim for an order that, inter alia, the plaintiffs, Tracomin SA (the buyers), their
directors, officers, solicitors, advocates, servants or agents be restrained from continuing
or prosecuting proceedings commenced by the buyers against the sellers in the canton of
Vaud, Switzerland, or from commencing any further or other proceedings there or
elsewhere, directed to obtaining an order for the payment of moneys alleged to be due or b
damages or compensation for breach of contract or otherwise concerning or arising from
or in relation to a contract no 4–80/81 dated 30 November 1980 by which the sellers
agreed to sell to the buyers 2,000 tonnes, 5% more or less, Sudanese HPS groundnut
kernels (Spanish type) 70/80 count per ounce 1980–81 crop pure basis. The second
defendant, George J Bridge, one of two arbitrators in references to arbitration pursuant
to arbitration agreements contained in the contract took no part in the counterclaim. c
The facts are set out in the judgment of Sir John Donaldson MR.

Nicholas Merriman for the sellers.
David Grace for the buyers.

SIR JOHN DONALDSON MR. Sudan Oil Seeds Co Ltd (the sellers), as their name d
implies, are a Sudanese company. Tracomin SA (the buyers) are a Swiss corporation. On
30 November 1980 the sellers agreed to sell 2,000 tonnes of groundnuts to the buyers to
form the subject matter of three separate shipments in the spring of 1981. A week later,
on 6 December, they entered into a further contract with the buyers for another 2,000
tonnes of the same commodity to form the subject matter of four separate shipments in
1981. e
    The contract notes for both these contracts contained the clause: 'OTHER CONDITIONS:
As per F.O.S.F.A. Contract No. 20.' The material clause in FOSFA contract no 20 which
has given rise to the present litigation is the arbitration clause, cl no 20, which was in the
following terms:

   'Any dispute arising out of this contract, including any question of law arising in
   connection therewith, shall be referred to arbitration in London (or elsewhere if so f
   agreed) in accordance with the Rules of Arbitration and Appeal of the Federation of
   Oils, Seeds and Fats Associations Limited, in force at the date of this contract and of
   which both parties hereto shall be deemed to be cognizant. Neither party hereto,
   nor any persons claiming under either of them shall bring any action or other legal
   proceedings against the other of them in respect of any such dispute until such
   dispute shall first have been heard and determined by the arbitrators, umpire or g
   Board of Appeal (as the case may be), in accordance with the Rules of Arbitration
   and Appeal of the Federation, and it is hereby expressly agreed and declared that the
   obtaining of an Award from the arbitrators, umpire or Board of Appeal (as the case
   may be), shall be a condition precedent to the right of either party hereto or of any
   person claiming under either of them to bring any action or other legal proceedings
   against the other of them in respect of any such dispute.' h

    In February, March and April 1981 shipments were made under the first contract, and
the buyers were highly dissatisfied with the quality and condition of the commodity
shipped. I think it is right, although it is immaterial, that in respect of the first two
shipments the allegations primarily concerned the quality of the groundnuts, whereas in
respect of the third shipment there was a suggestion of an admixture of a poisonous j
substance.
    Thus far nothing very unusual had happened. One would have expected the dispute
between the parties to have been referred to arbitration and dealt with in the usual way.
Indeed in May 1981 both parties appointed arbitrators in relation to those shipments.
But in addition the buyers sequestrated the documents relating to the second and third

shipments, those documents being in Switzerland. That procedure was the equivalent of
a saissie conservatoire or a Mareva type of proceeding.

In July 1981 the sellers claimed that the buyers had repudiated the remaining
shipments under the second contract. So we then had the position that the parties were
in dispute in respect of all contracts, albeit the nature of the disputes was slightly
different.

In August 1981 an application was made to the Swiss courts by the buyers seeking
b confirmation of the sequestration procedure, and that led to the sellers applying to the
Swiss courts for what is described as a 'requête en déclinatoire', which can be treated as
equivalent to an application for a stay.

Thereafter things took a rather surprising turn, because in the Swiss proceedings the
buyers denied the validity of the arbitration clause. They did so on the basis of Swiss law,
which apparently requires that an arbitration clause, in order to be effective, shall be
c reproduced in extensio in the contract document, whereas in the bought and sold notes
in this case it was incorporated simply by reference.

I say that that is surprising, if not astonishing, because the buyers are members of
FOSFA. Indeed, we were told that their managing director is a member of the council of
FOSFA. One of the proudest traditions of the City, and those who trade in and through
the City of London, is that their word is their bond. To enter into a FOSFA contract
d containing not only an arbitration clause but an express covenant not to litigate elsewhere,
and then to appear in another court and deny the validity of the contract, seems to me
not to be in accordance with the traditions of the market. However, that is what they
did.

The sellers had a remedy open to them. They could apply to the Swiss courts asserting
the arbitration clause. They availed themselves of that remedy, but for reasons which
e have never been explained (they are largely incomprehensible except on the basis of an
error of judgment) they failed to draw the attention of the Swiss court to the fact that the
contracts which formed the basis of the dispute in this case were governed by English
law. It is reasonably clear from the judgment given by the Cantonal Appeal Court that
had that matter been raised and English law been proved, the Swiss courts might well
have imposed a stay requiring the buyers to arbitrate their disputes in London. But the
f Swiss courts were faced with this problem, that there was no evidence of English law
and, although they may have appreciated that the contract was governed by English law,
in the absence of any such evidence they had to apply the rules which the English courts
would have applied in similar circumstances, namely to assume that the English law was
the same as the Swiss law. That being so, they held that the arbitration clause was of no
effect and dismissed the sellers' application for a stay. The original application was
g appealed to the Cantonal Appeal Court and on to the Federal Supreme Court of
Switzerland. We are told that the English law point could have been raised in the
Cantonal Appeal Court, although it certainly could not have been raised in the Supreme
Court. Not having been raised by the sellers, we now have the position in which the
Swiss courts have held that the arbitration clause is a nullity.

The scene then moves to England where the buyers, even more surprisingly, sought
h an injunction restraining the sellers from arbitrating. The sellers, not to be outdone, then
began proceedings seeking an injunction to prevent the buyers litigating in Switzerland.

The basis of the buyers' claim for an injunction prohibiting further proceedings by
the arbitrators was that the Swiss decision had produced an estoppel per rem judicatam,
as a result of which it was no longer open to the sellers to claim that there was an effective
arbitration in England.

j Staughton J considered that matter, and held that the Swiss decision did not have that
effect because of the provisions of ss 32 and 33 of the Civil Jurisdiction and Judgments
Act 1982 (see Tracomin SA v Sudan Oil Seeds Co Ltd (No 1) [1983] 1 All ER 404). An appeal
from Staughton J's decision was heard by this court yesterday, and that appeal was
dismissed (see [1983] 3 All ER 137). Counsel on behalf of the buyers has expressly
disclaimed any wish to take the matter further.

The basis of the sellers' claim that the buyers should be enjoined from litigating in Switzerland is, of course, the express terms of the covenant contained in the arbitration *a* clause, and in addition, although perhaps not quite so important, the Scott v Avery provision in that clause.

That claim was considered by Leggatt J, who refused to issue an injunction against the buyers (see [1983] 2 All ER 129). His judgment was given on 17 February 1983, and it is from that judgment that the sellers now appeal.

The judge held that he had jurisdiction to grant such an injunction, and on the *b* authority of *Pena Copper Mines Ltd v Rio Tinto Co Ltd* (1911) 105 LT 846, [1911–13] All ER Rep 209 he was plainly right so to hold, and indeed it is not challenged in this court that he had the jurisdiction to do so. The basis of that jurisdiction, which all the cases stress should be used sparingly, is that, notwithstanding that the buyers are a foreign national not carrying on business within the jurisdiction of this court, the fact that they have agreed to submit disputes to English arbitration amounts either to a sufficient *c* submission to the English courts or, alternatively, the creation of a sufficiently close nexus between them and the jurisdiction of the English courts to entitle us to exercise that jurisdiction.

I said that the jurisdiction should be used sparingly on the authorities, and I would make that good by a brief extract from a judgment of Dunn LJ in *Mike Trading and Transport Ltd v R Pagnan & Flli, The Lisboa* [1980] 2 Lloyd's Rep 546 at 551, which was in *d* fact cited by Leggatt J. Dunn LJ said:

'Although the English Court has jurisdiction to restrain a party to English proceedings from proceeding in a foreign Court, the jurisdiction will be exercised with great caution especially when the defendant to the English proceedings is plaintiff in the foreign proceedings, and the injunction should not normally be granted unless the foreign proceedings are vexatious or oppressive [and he cites *e* *Cohen v Rothfield* [1919] 1 KB 410, [1918–19] All ER Rep 260 and *Castanho v Brown & Root (UK) Ltd* [1980] 3 All ER 72, [1980] 1 WLR 833].'

The judge in refusing relief did so in the exercise of his discretion, and I think it is right that I should refer to the passage in his judgment where he deals with that aspect. He said ([1983] 2 All ER 129 at 137): *f*

'In my judgment the sellers have forfeited their right to expect that the English court would intervene to protect their interests. At the outset they would have had the opportunity of applying for an injunction if they had had any reason to doubt the availability of the remedy they sought in Switzerland, or if they had been able to point to any prospective deficiency in the administration of justice in the foreign court. Their alternative was to apply for a stay in the foreign court. They chose that *g* alternative course. If the foreign court had, without fault on the sellers' part, reached a palpably wrong conclusion then this court might have been justified in intervening. But, where, as here, the foreign court has behaved with perfect propriety and has only reached what to an English lawyer was the wrong conclusion on account of the negligence of the sellers, it seems to me that they no longer merit the assistance of the English court. True it is that this may result in duplicity of proceedings, but *h* that is not a sufficient reason in my judgment for the court to attempt to restrain the plaintiffs from proceeding in their own court, even if the defendants continue to pursue the contractual remedy of arbitration.'

For my part, I entirely agree with the judge's criticism of the sellers for failing to take the point before the Swiss courts at the appropriate time. But I part company with the *j* judge if, as I think is the case, he was treating the negligence, as he described it, of the sellers in failing to take the point before the Swiss courts as being a balancing factor of equal weight which, as it were, cancels out the blameworthiness and conduct of the buyers in seeking to deny their own covenant to arbitrate. I would not seek to criticise the buyers for trying to take security in Switzerland. It is when they go on to deny the

existence of the arbitration clause, and above all when they then start proceedings in this
a country to restrain the arbitration, trying to rely on a judgment which they entirely
adventitiously obtained in the Swiss court, that I think the scales dropped very heavily
against the sellers.

This decision was a decision by the judge in the exercise of the discretion which is
given to him, and it would be quite wrong for us to intervene unless we are satisfied that
he has erred in principle. For my part I think there was an error of principle beyond a
b mere difference of opinion as to weight in the equality of treatment which he seems to
have accorded to the conduct of these two parties. But I think there are more important
errors than that. He says in the passage to which I have referred: 'True it is that this may
result in duplicity of proceedings, but that is not a sufficient reason in my judgment for
the court to attempt to restrain the plaintiffs . . .' In saying that, I think that the judge
must have contemplated that the result of duplicity of proceedings would be, as it were,
c the ordinary result of such duplicity, namely that two courts might, and I stress the word
'might', reach inconsistent findings of fact. Counsel for the buyers has stressed that that
may not even be a real possibility, in his submission, since the claims are different in
nature. The claim by the buyers is that they had defective goods tendered to them; the
claim by the sellers is that there was a repudiation of later shipments under a different
contract.

d For my part I would not accept the submission of counsel for the buyers. In form it is
correct that the claims are different, but they are linked, and must be linked, because,
whatever special defences there may be to the sellers' claim, there must also be the
defence linked to the defective quality of the earlier shipment.

Accepting that there is a possibility of inconsistent judgments and that the judge took
account of that fact, there is no trace in his judgment of consideration of a further and,
e to my mind, decisive factor. That factor is this, that if and in so far as the Swiss courts
were to give any judgment against the sellers the sellers would have an unanswerable
claim against the buyers in arbitration alleging that that judgment had been obtained in
breach of cl 20 of the FOSFA contract. The question which would then arise would be
whether they were entitled to more than nominal damages. That would depend on
whether the Swiss court had reached the same conclusion as would FOSFA arbitrators if
f the claim which formed the basis of the Swiss judgment had been submitted to
arbitration. So we should have the position that, in so far as the Swiss courts gave any
judgment against the sellers, there would then be a claim in arbitration which would
have to be fully investigated and adjudicated on by the FOSFA arbitrators, and on appeal
by the FOSFA Board of Appeal, in order to decide whether FOSFA agreed with the Swiss
courts. If FOSFA would have reached the same conclusion, the sellers would have been
g entitled only to nominal damages. If FOSFA decided that they would have reached a
different conclusion, and one which would have been less adverse to the sellers, they
would have to make an award in favour of the sellers representing the difference between
the two.

That seems to me to be a very special factor, and one which neither these courts, nor
the Swiss courts if they were in a position to consider the matter, could contemplate with
h any degree of equanimity whatsoever. The Swiss courts, owing to the negligence of the
sellers, have been put into the position in which they have given a judgment which is
wrong in terms of English law. It is no fault of the Swiss courts whatsoever, but it is
going to have these consequences, and I cannot believe that the Swiss courts will be
unduly perturbed at the English courts intervening to avoid the rather unseemly
spectacle, if I may say so with respect to FOSFA, of trade arbitrators considering a Swiss
j judgment and deciding whether it is right or wrong.

For my part I would therefore in principle allow the appeal and grant the injunction,
the exact terms of which will have to be worked out. I say 'in principle' because I would,
however, impose two conditions. The first is that the sellers should pay the costs thrown
away by the Swiss proceedings. In principle the costs which were thrown away were all
costs which were incurred beyond the court of first instance. The sellers had to go to the

court of first instance, and had they taken the point about English law that should have been the end of the matter; but, by failing to take that point and by appealing to the two higher courts, they did involve the buyers in unnecessary expense.

I would add one further condition. Under the arbitration rules of FOSFA, as opposed to the arbitration clause, there are the time bar provisions. I do not think I need refer to them in detail, but they do end with this clause:

> 'In the event of non-compliance with any of the preceding provisions of this Rule, claims shall be deemed to be waived and absolutely barred unless the arbitrators, umpire or Board of Appeal referred to in these Rules, shall, at their absolute discretion, otherwise determine.'

It would, in my judgment, be wholly wrong for the arbitrators to take a time point and treat any claims by the buyers as barred if, as a result of our enjoining them from carrying on with the Swiss proceedings, they wish with reasonable promptitude to put forward claims in arbitration which otherwise might have been dealt with by the Swiss courts. That of course does remain a matter for the arbitrators to decide, but I would make it a condition that the sellers should support any application by the buyers that the arbitrators should not exercise the discretion which they have under these rules, provided of course that the buyers act promptly. I am not suggesting for one moment that the buyers can just sit on their hands and bring forward claims at any time they like in the future, but starting as of now they should be entitled to do so provided they act promptly.

Subject to those points, I would allow the appeal.

ACKNER LJ. Notwithstanding the very able arguments put forward by counsel for the buyers, I too would allow the appeal and impose the conditions in relation to the grant of the relief sought specified by Sir John Donaldson MR and for the reasons which he has given.

FOX LJ. I agree.

Appeal allowed. Liberty to apply. Leave to appeal to the House of Lords refused.

Solicitors: *William A Crump & Son* (for the sellers); *Richards Butler & Co* (for the buyers).

Frances Rustin   Barrister.

a
Kirkup v British Rail Engineering Ltd and another appeal

COURT OF APPEAL, CIVIL DIVISION
LAWTON, KERR AND DILLON LJJ

b   15 JUNE 1983

Practice – Evidence – Expert evidence – Disclosure to other parties – Time for disclosure – Personal injuries action – Non-medical expert's reports – Court ordering disclosure of reports – Whether disclosure should be mutual – Whether court may order one party to disclose his expert's report first – RSC Ord 38, r 37.

c   *Discovery – Interrogatory – Amendment – Amendment to make interrogatories allowable – Whether court will interfere with master's order.*

The plaintiff brought an action against the defendants, his employers, claiming damages for personal injuries, alleging that, because of the negligence and breach of statutory duty of the defendants, he had become deaf as a result of being exposed since 1952 to excessive
d   noise in the course of his employment with the defendants at their railway engineering workshops. On the summons for directions the master ordered that the plaintiff disclose his non-medical expert's report not later than 28 days after setting down and that the defendants disclose their report within 42 days thereafter. The plaintiff appealed against the master's order contending that, in exercising his discretion under RSC Ord 38, r 37 to order disclosure of the reports, the master should have ordered mutual disclosure. The
e   judge dismissed the appeal and also refused to allow certain interrogatories to be delivered by the plaintiffs to the defendants on the ground that they were so vague as to be oppressive. The plaintiff appealed to the Court of Appeal. It was accepted by the plaintiff that there was a discretion in the court when the experts reports should be disclosed.

Held – The appeal would be dismissed for the following reasons—
(1) In the majority of cases, where the area of inquiry was comparatively limited, it
f   might be just and convenient that there should be simultaneous disclosure of non-medical expert's reports. In the plaintiff's case, however, the area of inquiry went back to 1952 and it was likely that at the trial the plaintiff's only witnesses would be the plaintiff himself and his expert witnesses and it would be for the plaintiff to say where and under what conditions he had been working. Until the plaintiff had given that evidence the defendants could not direct their minds either to the precautions which they had or
g   ought to have taken or to the degree of noise at any particular place at any particular time. In those circumstances, the fair way of dealing with the expert evidence was that there should be sequential exchange of reports as ordered by the judge (see p 151 g to p 152 d and g h, post).
(2) With respect to the interrogatories, there were no grounds for interfering with the judge's order by amending the interrogatories so as to make them allowable because,
h   where interrogatories were allowed, it was normally a matter for the master and not the judge, still less the Court of Appeal (see p 152 f to h, post).
Decision of Croom-Johnson J [1983] 1 All ER 855 affirmed.

Notes
For disclosure of expert evidence in the form of a report in actions for personal injuries,
j   see 37 Halsbury's Laws (4th edn) para 463.

Case referred to in judgments
Berry v Stone Manganese Marine Ltd (1971) 12 KIR 13.

Case also cited
Practice Direction [1974] 2 All ER 966, [1974] 1 WLR 904.

Interlocutory appeals

Kirkup v British Rail Engineering Ltd   a

By writ dated 27 July 1979 the plaintiff, Arthur Kirkup, brought an action against the defendants, British Rail Engineering Ltd, for damages for personal injuries and consequential loss as a result of contracting a hearing condition as a result of exposure to excessive noise in the course of his employment with the defendants at their premises at Shildon, Co Durham, owing to the negligence and/or breach of statutory duty of the defendants, their servants or agents. On 28 January 1982 Master Creightmore ordered, b inter alia, that the plaintiff disclose his engineer's report not later than 28 days after setting down and that the defendants disclose their engineer's report within 42 days thereafter. The plaintiff appealed against that part of the master's order and applied for the parties' engineers' reports to be mutually disclosed within 28 days after setting down. On 4 October 1982 Croom-Johnson J ([1983] 1 All ER 855, [1983] 1 WLR 190) dismissed the appeal and refused the plaintiff's application for leave to serve certain interrogatories c on the defendants. The plaintiff appealed to the Court of Appeal with leave of the judge against his refusal to order mutual disclosure of experts reports and applied for leave to appeal and appealed if leave should be granted, the judge having refused leave, against the judge's refusal to allow the interrogatories sought. The facts are set out in the judgment of Lawton LJ.

d

Priestley v British Rail Engineering Ltd

By writ dated 1 July 1980 the plaintiff, John Priestley, brought an action against the defendants, British Rail Engineering Ltd, for damages for personal injuries and consequential loss as a result of contracting a hearing condition as a result of exposure to excessive noise in the course of his employment with the defendants at their premises at Shildon, Co Durham, since 1965 owing to the negligence and/or breach of statutory duty e of the defendants, their servants or agents. On 29 January 1982 Master Elton adjourned an application by the defendants for an order that the plaintiff disclose his engineer's report first and that the defendants disclose their engineer's report after that to give the defendants an opportunity to file an affidavit in support of their application. By consent the question of disclosures was argued before the judge and a request for interrogatories was referred to him by the master. On 4 October 1982 Croom-Johnson J, having heard f argument, decided to leave the question of disclosure of the engineers' reports to the master on receipt of the defendant's affidavit and ordered that the plaintiff's application for leave to serve on the defendant's certain interrogatories be refused and referred back to the master (see [1983] 1 All ER 855, [1983] 1 WLR 190). The plaintiff applied to the Court of Appeal for leave to appeal and appealed if leave should be granted against the judge's refusal to allow the interrogatories sought. The facts are set out in the judgment g of Lawton LJ.

Christopher Rose QC and *K L May* for the plaintiffs.
William M Gage QC and *Edward Southwell* for the defendants.

LAWTON LJ. In these two cases the same points arise. They are these: whether it was h right for the judge, Croom-Johnson J, to make an order that the plaintiffs should first disclose an expert engineer's report and then the defendants should disclose their engineer's report, if they intended to call expert engineering evidence, 42 days after the disclosure of the plaintiffs' reports. The second point is a very short one and turns on the refusal of the judge to allow certain interrogatories to be delivered by the plaintiffs to the defendants.   j

The background of the case is surprising and to some extent worrying. In 1971 it was adjudged by Ashworth J that it was negligent for an employer to allow excessive noise in his factory so as to cause deafness amongst his employees (see *Berry v Stone Manganese Marine Ltd* (1971) 12 KIR 13). Since that judgment there have been a very large number of claims made by employees against their employers. The number runs into tens of

thousands. The British Railways Board, of whom the defendants in these two appeals are
a subsidiaries, have had 8,661 claims of this kind made against them. They have settled
4,552 and at the present time 4,059 claims are still being considered. The outstanding
claims involve no less than 20 different firms of plaintiffs' solicitors and relate to 15
different depots and workshops. The plaintiffs' solicitors, who are solicitors to a well-
known engineering union, either are dealing with or have dealt with no less than 3,200
claims. They have delivered about 2,000 statements of claims; 1,428 claims have been
b settled, some without any recourse to litigation. This plethora of claims has caused
considerable difficulties. It must be borne in mind that in each of these cases it is for the
plaintiffs to prove their cases. Second, it has to be remembered that almost inevitably the
majority of the claims depend on their own facts. Working conditions vary not only
from work place to work place, but from different parts of work places.

The two plaintiffs in this case, Mr Kirkup and Mr Priestley, were both employed by
c the defendants in the well-known railway workshops at Shildon in County Durham.
Both are still employed there. Mr Kirkup entered the defendants' employment in 1952,
and he has worked at Shildon in various capacities. He started as a fitter, then a
millwright, then a workshop assistant and more recently an industrial engineering
assistant. Counsel for the defendants has told us that the defendants have a general idea
of the parts of the workshops at Shildon where Mr Kirkup has been working, but they
d do not know the exact places where he has been working. This is understandable, because
when Mr Kirkup started his employment with the defendants it was as a fitter. If fitters
work at Shildon in the same way as they usually work in engineering workshops the
probabilities are that his places of work have changed from time to time. At one time he
may have been working in a noisy part of Shildon and at another time he may have been
working in one where there was much less noise. Mr Priestley started his work at Shildon
e in 1965. He too was employed as a fitter. The comments which I have made about Mr
Kirkup's places of work apply equally to Mr Priestley.

Another factor which has got to be borne in mind in these two cases is this. Following
a report which was made by the Wilson Committee in 1963 (Final Report of the
Committee on the Problem of Noise (Cmnd 2056)), by 1965 it was generally appreciated
in industry and indeed elsewhere that excessive noise could cause deafness amongst those
f who were subjected to it. Any employer who has subjected his workforce to excessive
noise since 1965 and has not taken adequate precautions to protect them from such noise
is likely nowadays to be found guilty of negligence. Different problems arise altogether
with the position which existed in industry before 1965. We have been told by counsel
for the defendants that an issue arises in this case as to the knowledge which the
defendants had or ought to have had about the likelihood of excessive noise causing
g deafness before 1965.

The plaintiffs have had engineering advice on a number of issues. We have been told
that they cover the following: first, the kind of noise levels which exist in workshops,
and in particular in the Shildon works; second, advice as to what before 1965 was known
in industry about the potentiality of the danger of excessive noise; third, what effective
steps could have been taken and are being taken nowadays to mitigate the consequences
h of excessive noise; fourth, what protective devices were available at different periods
during the times which will have to be investigated at the trial; and, finally, what could
have been done by the defendants to cut down the amount of noise which existed in the
works at Shildon. All these matters cover a very broad area of investigation.

The statement of claim in the *Kirkup* action, which I will take as a specimen (the
Priestley statement of claim is in substantially the same form) is in very general terms,
j and it is relevant, in my opinion, for me to set out in some detail what the relevant
allegations of negligence are. The statement of claim starts off with a reference to an
alleged breach of statutory duty. I say no more about that. The allegations of negligence
continue:

'(ii) Failing to ascertain the dangers of noise-induced deafness until the late 1970s.
(iii) Failing to warn the Plaintiff of the dangers of noise-induced deafness. (iv) Failing

to institute effective medical inspections. (v) Failing to survey noise levels in their premises. (vi) Failing to provide the Plaintiff with suitable ear protection. (vii) Failing to provide proper instruction and supervision. (viii) Failing to silence their plant and equipment. (ix) Failing to institute a safe system of work. (x) In the premises, failing to take proper care for the Plaintiff's safety and exposing him to unnecessary risk of injury.'

The defendants did not ask for particulars of those allegations. Counsel for the defendants told us the reason was this. When this series of claims against the defendants and British Rail and their subsidiaries first started, counsel was instructed to ask for further and better particulars, but when the flood of claims reached the level it did it became obvious that much the same issues were going to arise in many of the cases and it would be a waste of the railways' money to instruct counsel time and time again to settle the same kinds of request for particulars, and equally clearly it would have been a waste of the plaintiffs' money, and to their detriment if they failed in their claims. The result has been that the case has gone on without any further particulars of the statements of claim.

The plaintiffs, however, did ask for particulars of the defence and an order for particulars was made as long ago as 30 October 1981, and that order, through forgetfulness, so counsel for the defendants tells us, has never been complied with. But the particulars ordered have not got much to do with the main issue of liability in this case, because some of the particulars relate to the adequacy of protective measures which the defendants did take after they did become admittedly aware of the dangers of excessive noise and the other particulars relate to the issue of causation.

It is against that background of fact that the matters which we have to consider arise. There are further facts which are necessary to state in order to explain the basis on which counsel for the plaintiffs has submitted that the order made by the judge is wrong. These cases are coming to trial somewhat slowly. It is within the knowledge of counsel for the plaintiffs that there are nine cases which are likely to be heard at Newcastle-upon-Tyne at or about the beginning of the next Michaelmas sittings. Those cases arise out of the ship building and ship repairing industry. In all those cases, whether at first instance or on appeal, it matters not, there was a hearing about directions before Mustill J. We are told by counsel for the plaintiffs that that hearing lasted two days, but he is unable to remember exactly what were the matters which occupied the judge for so long. It suffices to say that he did make an order for the simultaneous exchange of engineers' reports. We are asked to infer, and I have no difficulty in inferring, that the allegations of negligence in those cases are the same as the allegations of negligence in the two cases before us. But, when the matter in these present two cases came before the master, he made an order not for simultaneous exchange of engineers' reports, but a sequential order. The plaintiffs were dissatisfied with that order and appealed to the judge in chambers. The judge in chambers considered the matter was of some importance and delivered a reserved judgment (see [1983] 1 All ER 855, [1983] 1 WLR 190). He examined carefully the Rules of the Supreme Court relating to the exchange of reports in personal injury actions. We have been told today that there was in fact no dispute between the parties before Croom-Johnson J about the proper construction of the rules, but he thought it right in order to make clear why he was making the order which he did to state the basis on which he made it. It suffices for the purposes of this judgment to repeat his approach to the problem as set out in the headnote ([1983] 1 WLR 190). His judgment is summarised in these terms:

'*Held*, that the discretion of the court to order disclosure of an expert's report, under R.S.C., Ord. 38, r. 37(2), was not limited by the terms of rule 37(3) and (4); that in a proper case, the court could exercise its discretion under rule 37(2) to order one party to disclose his expert's report first so that the expert consulted by the other party could address his mind specifically to the points raised in it; and that since it was not unreasonable in an appropriate case to require a plaintiff to disclose his

a   report first, the appeal from the master's order in the first case would be dismissed and the question of disclosure in the other cases would be referred back to the master.'

Counsel for the plaintiffs has submitted that although the judge's construction of the rules was right he exercised his discretion under them wrongly. The basis for his submission in that respect was twofold. He said, first, that Mustill J had exercised his discretion in a different way in the cases which are going to be heard in the near future b   at Newcastle-upon-Tyne and, second, that the judge had taken into account a factor which he really ought not to have taken into account, because it was an irrelevant one in all the circumstances of this case. I can deal with the point based on Mustill J's exercise of discretion very shortly indeed. We do not know on what grounds Mustill J exercised his discretion. He may have had reasons which are inappropriate to this case. He was dealing with different cases in a different industry. There is no substance in that criticism.

c   So far as the other complaint about the exercise of discretion is concerned, it turns on the following passage in the judge's judgment. He said ([1983] 1 All ER 855 at 858–859, [1983] 1 WLR 190 at 194):

'It would be unreasonable to expect the defendants to have one ready-made standard engineer's report available to be trotted out every time a claim is made d   against them. The pleadings in the three actions which I have seen are not in the least informative as to particularity. It would not be unreasonable, in appropriate circumstances, to require the plaintiff to show his hand by sending his expert's report so that the defendants may consider the issues raised by it and ask their own expert to deal with it.'

e   The complaint of counsel for the plaintiffs was that the reference to particularity was misconceived. It was the defendants' own fault that there were no further and better particulars and in any case the defendants had been ordered to deliver particulars and had not done so. As I have already said, the order is of no relevance so far as the main point in the case is concerned. Counsel for the plaintiffs went on to point out that under the provisions of RSC Ord 25, r 8 in the ordinary way nowadays the parties are encouraged f   to have a mutual exchange of reports without an order of the court. That clearly is a useful practice and is followed in the majority of cases where there is a claim for personal injuries. But claims for personal injuries vary greatly in their nature and complexity. If the parties do not want a mutual exchange of reports with a view to agreeing them, Ord 38 applies and has to be complied with strictly. This is now well known. Without an order of the court neither side can call expert witnesses. If expert witnesses are to be g   called, then reports have to be disclosed. But, as was accepted by counsel for the plaintiffs, there is undoubtedly a discretion in the court when they should be disclosed. In the majority of cases the probability is that it is convenient and just that there should be simultaneous disclosure of reports. The reason is obvious. In the case of expert opinions about a plaintiff's physical or mental condition the plaintiff is the subject matter of the reports. The experts' opinions will be concerned with his condition and the consequences h   of such injury as he has received. The area of inquiry and possible disagreement is comparatively limited. Where the case arises because of an alleged dangerous machine or an unsafe system of work, once again the area of inquiry and dispute is limited. The experts on both sides look, for example, at a machine and say whether it has been properly fenced, and if one of them says it has not been he can say why, and if the other one says it has been he too can say why. In those cases there is normally no problem.

j   But in this case there undoubtedly is a problem, because a great deal depends on a whole area of inquiry, in the case of Mr Kirkup going back to 1952. It is likely at the trial that the only witnesses to be called on behalf of the plaintiff will be the plaintiff himself and his expert witnesses. For the reasons I have already indicated, it will be for the plaintiff to say where he was working and under what conditions he was working. A great deal will depend on his evidence on those matters. It is only when the defendants know what he is saying about his work places that they can start directing their minds to the working conditions in them and the precautions, if any, which they took or, if they *a* took none, why they did not take any. The plaintiff no doubt will have supplied the consulting engineers who will support his case with particulars of that kind. The defendants at the moment have not got them. Another inquiry which will have to be made is the state of knowledge. It is said that British Rail have a chief medical officer who no doubt has kept every branch of the railway service, including the engineering branches, informed of what is the state of knowledge about excessive noise. But he could *b* not possibly have had in mind the degrees of noise at any particular place at any particular time. All these are matters of particularity. Until the defendants know exactly what it is that the plaintiffs are going to say on these matters they cannot start preparing their expert evidence. As Kerr LJ pointed out in the course of the submissions of counsel for the plaintiffs, there is a danger in a case of this kind that the defendants will be called on to write a thesis on noise generally in engineering workshops. That will not be of any *c* value to the plaintiffs and it certainly will not be of any value to the trial judge.

I am satisfied in the circumstances of this case that the fair way of dealing with this problem of expert evidence on the facts of this case is that there should be a sequential exchange of reports. I can see nothing wrong with the order made by Croom-Johnson J.

As to the interrogatories, he allowed four of them provided they were limited to the Shildon works. He would not allow the others for this reason, as taken down in counsel's *d* note:

'Interrogatories must be precise questions capable of precise answers. The person ordered to answer them must be capable of informing himself as to the answers. These Interrogatories are very widely drawn. They cover the whole of the Defendants' operations. By consent they are now limited to the Shildon Works. With this amendment I allow the first four. The others are, in my view, so vague as *e* to be oppressive.'

We have been told by counsel that he went on to say, but it did not get onto the note, that it was not for him to amend the interrogatories.

In the course of the submission of counsel for the plaintiffs, suggestions were made from the Bench how these interrogatories could be amended so as to make them *f* allowable. Perhaps they could have been. But, just as it was not the task of Croom-Johnson J to amend the interrogatories, so it is not the task of this court to amend them. It is said that interrogatories 5 and 6 in the draft are sufficiently precise. They are in very wide terms. Perhaps in some circumstances they could be allowed, but, as counsel for the defendants pointed out, where interrogatories are allowed it is almost always a matter for the master and it is seldom that the judge overrules the master about interrogatories. It *g* is even less seldom that this court overrules the judge in chambers about interrogatories.

I would dismiss the appeal.

KERR LJ. I agree and there is nothing that I would wish to add.

DILLON LJ. I also agree.   *h*

Appeals dismissed.

Solicitors: *Evill & Coleman*, Putney (for the plaintiffs); *Michael G Baker* (for the defendants).

Mary Rose Plummer   Barrister.

a # Computer Machinery Co Ltd v Drescher and others

CHANCERY DIVISION
SIR ROBERT MEGARRY V-C
8, 16, 17, 18 MARCH, 27 MAY 1983

b

Costs – Interlocutory application – Evidence – Admissibility – Motion for interlocutory relief – Documents obtained by plaintiff after hearing of motion – Plaintiff alleging that documents material to question of costs – Whether documents admissible in evidence on question of costs – Supreme Court Act 1981, s 51(1).

c *Compromise – Offer made before hearing – Injunction – Application by plaintiff for interlocutory injunction – Offer by defendant to submit to injunction – Offer made 'without prejudice' save as to costs – Effect of offer on court's discretion in awarding costs.*

The first two defendants left the plaintiff's employment and set up their own company (the third defendant). The plaintiff, believing that the first two defendants were
d wrongfully using confidential information obtained during their employment with the plaintiff, brought an action against the defendants seeking, inter alia, injunctions to restrain them from using the information and also substantial damages. The plaintiff also applied for interlocutory relief pending the hearing of the action, as did the third defendant. As a result of the interlocutory applications a consent order was made under which the defendants gave a number of undertakings until judgment or further order, the
e costs of each motion being reserved. Some time later the defendants notified the plaintiff that they were making a payment into court and in a letter stated to be 'without prejudice' save as to costs offered to submit to permanent injunctions in the same terms as those sought by the plaintiff 'with taxed costs relating thereto' as if RSC Ord 62, r 10(2) applied. The plaintiff accepted the offer and the money paid into court, and the action accordingly never proceeded to trial. The question whether the taxed costs included the
f costs reserved in respect of the interlocutory motions was, however, referred to the court. On the hearing of that question the plaintiff sought to adduce certain documents which it had obtained on discovery after the hearing of the motions in order to show that evidence relied on by the defendants in their affidavits on the motions was false. The defendants contended that the documents were not admissible because only evidence which had been used at the hearing of the motions could be admitted for the purpose of
g deciding the question of costs.

Held – There was no rule that on the issue of costs evidence was inadmissible, even though relevant, unless it had been previously adduced. Under s 51(1)[a] of the Supreme Court Act 1981 costs were in the discretion of the court, and if evidence tendered on costs was of little or no cogency on that issue the court could reflect that in the order for
h costs. Since the evidence which the plaintiff sought to adduce was relevant to the costs of the motion it would be admitted (see p 158 b to p 159 b, post).

Mayor of Bristol v Great Western Rly (1916) 14 LGR 756 distinguished.

Per curiam. In any proceedings where a defendant makes an offer to submit to an injunction, give an undertaking or afford other relief 'without prejudice' or 'without prejudice save as to costs', the court ought to enforce the terms on which the offer is
j made in order to encourage compromises and shorten litigation; and an offer 'without prejudice save as to costs' has the advantage of preventing the offer from being inadmissible on costs, thereby assisting the court towards justice in making the order as to costs, especially when relief other than money is sought (see p 156 b to h, post); dictum of Cairns LJ in *Calderbank v Calderbank* [1975] 3 All ER at 342 followed.

---

a   Section 51(1), so far as material, is set out at p 158 d e, post

Notes

For 'without prejudice' communications, see 17 Halsbury's Laws (4th edn) paras 212– 213, and for cases on the subject, see 22 Digest (Reissue) 407–410, 4082–4108.

For relevancy and admissibility of documents in general, see 17 Halsbury's Laws (4th edn) para 5, and for cases on the subject, see 22 Digest (Reissue) 52–53, 308–315.

For documentary evidence in affidavits, see 17 Halsbury's Laws (4th edn) para 196.

For the Supreme Court Act 1981, s 51, see 51 Halsbury's Statutes (3rd edn) 647.

Cases referred to in judgment

Bristol (Mayor) v Great Western Rly (1916) 14 LGR 756, [1916] WN 47.
Calderbank v Calderbank [1975] 3 All ER 333, [1976] Fam 93, [1975] 3 WLR 586, CA.
McDonnell v McDonnell [1977] 1 All ER 766, [1977] 1 WLR 34, CA.
Martin French (A) (a firm) v Kingswood Hill Ltd [1960] 2 All ER 251, [1961] 1 QB 96, [1960] 2 WLR 251, CA.
Stotesbury v Turner [1943] KB 370.
Stratford (J T) & Son Ltd v Lindley (No 2) [1969] 3 All ER 1122, [1969] 1 WLR 1547, CA.
Walker v Wilsher (1889) 23 QBD 335, CA.

Application as to costs

An action by the plaintiff, Computer Machinery Co Ltd, against the first three defendants, Nicholas A Drescher, Alan B Wilson and Universal Computers Ltd, was settled after three applications for interlocutory relief had been made to the court and a consent order, under which the question of how and by whom the costs of each of the three motions were to be borne and paid was reserved, had been made at the interlocutory stage. After the action had been settled the parties asked the court to determine the question as to the costs of the three motions. The facts are set out in the judgment.

Benet Hytner QC and Jeremy Davies for the plaintiff company.
Michael Lyndon-Stanford QC and Nicholas Asprey for the first three defendants.

Cur adv vult

27 May. The following judgment was delivered.

SIR ROBERT MEGARRY V-C. The dispute before me is as to the costs of three motions in an action which was subsequently terminated by payments into court by the defendant and acceptance of those payments by the plaintiff company. This has raised an apparently undecided point on the evidence that is admissible in resolving such disputes.

The plaintiff company is a wholly-owned subsidiary of an American corporation. The plaintiff company trades in computer hardware and software. The first two defendants, Mr Drescher and Mr Wilson, are former employees of the plaintiff company, and the third defendant, Universal Computers Ltd, is a rival company which they acquired. Mr Drescher was the manager of the plaintiff company's Croydon branch and Mr Wilson was a salesman there. The two major products of the plaintiff company are the 'Sovereign' system and the 'Reality' system. One of the main complaints by the plaintiff company against the first two defendants is that before they left the plaintiff company they embarked on a course of action which was designed to undermine the plaintiff company's relationship with its customers, and to promote and sell a rival system, the 'Ultimate' system, to those customers. A further complaint is that the first two defendants both took part in granting customers of the plaintiff company options to determine their hiring contracts with the plaintiff company before they had run their full course (which was usually some three or five years), that these options were neither authorised by nor reported to the head office of the plaintiff company, and that the first two defendants as a result had received larger commissions than they would have been entitled to if they had disclosed the options. The relief claimed against the first three defendants was for injunctions to restrain them from conspiring to defraud or injure the plaintiff company,

from defrauding the plaintiff company, from inducing breaches of contract, from
a disclosing confidential information, for damages for these matters and for conversion
and breach of contract, and for an order for delivery up of confidential documents; I put
the main claims very shortly. There were also three other defendants, but I need not
discuss them. The writ was issued on 13 March 1980. The statement of claim was not
served until 22 January 1981, and on 11 January 1983 this was amended, mainly in the
details of the alleged overpayments.

b   In the mean time, much had been happening. On 13 March 1980, the day when the
writ was issued, the plaintiff company issued a notice of motion. This sought an
injunction to restrain the defendants (a term that I shall use to mean the first three
defendants, unless otherwise indicated) from dealing with anyone whose name appeared
on the plaintiff company's customer list, and from using or disclosing any of the
information on the plaintiff company's customer list or price list, and other confidential
c information. On 18 March 1980 the motion was, by consent, stood over until 21 March,
on certain undertakings. By these, the defendants undertook over the adjournment not
to induce any breach of contract between the plaintiff company and its customers, and
not to solicit those whose name was on a certain list, with further undertakings as to
delivery up and not using or disclosing information. On 21 March 1980 the undertakings
were continued over 1 April 1980. On 25 March 1980 the third defendant issued a notice
d of motion against the plaintiff company, seeking to restrain it from representing that the
third defendant did not own or have a right to promote or sell the Ultimate system, or
that it was not a full operational computer system.

On 1 April 1980 the plaintiff company undertook not to proceed with the notice of
motion of 13 March 1980 but to serve a new notice of motion in certain terms by 4 pm
on 2 April. The motions were made motions by order, and the defendants gave various
e undertakings until the hearing or further order. These included undertakings not to
induce customers of the plaintiff company to exercise options to determine their contracts
with the plaintiff company where those options had been given by either Mr Drescher
or Mr Wilson, not to deal with those who had exercised such options, and not wrongfully
to induce breaches of contract between the plaintiff company and any of its customers.
On 2 April 1980 the plaintiff company duly served the new notice of motion. This
f sought interim injunctions against the defendants to restrain them from inducing a
breach of contract between the plaintiff company and its customers, inducing such
customers to exercise options of determination save those authorised by certain officers
of the plaintiff company, dealing with any who had exercised such an option, dealing
with any who had had the benefit of such an option, and using or disclosing information
in the plaintiff company's customer lists or price lists which had not been made public.

g   On 14 November 1980 the matter came before me, and an eight-page consent order
was made. The main provisions of this order consisted of a series of undertakings by the
defendants until judgment or further order. The only order made by the court was in
respect of the plaintiff company's motions under the notices of motion dated 13 March
1980 and 2 April 1980 (which I shall call 'motion no 1' and 'motion no 2' respectively) and
the third defendant's motion under the notice of motion dated 25 March 1980,
h which I shall call the 'defendant's motion'. The order was that 'The question of how and
by whom the costs of each of the said Motions are to be borne and paid be reserved'. By
this time, the parties had produced nearly 30 affidavits, which, with their exhibits, come
to over 750 pages; and it is common ground that the costs are very substantial. What is
before me for decision is what order for the costs thus reserved ought to be made; for the
action never proceeded to trial, but instead was disposed of in a manner which left the
j costs of the motions unresolved.

After the consent order of 14 November 1980, the parties proceeded with their
preparations for trial, with the exchange of pleadings, and so on. The case was fixed for
trial on 14 February 1983, but early in January 1983 the defendants' solicitors made
certain substantial payments into court, and on 6 January the plaintiff company's
solicitors received from the defendants' solicitors two letters and notices of the payments
into court. During the hearing these letters were referred to as Calderbank letters, the

reference being to *Calderbank v Calderbank* [1975] 3 All ER 333, [1976] Fam 93, a case
that was applied in *McDonnell v McDonnell* [1977] 1 All ER 766, [1977] 1 WLR 34. Each   a
letter referred to these cases, and stated that it was written 'without prejudice' but on the
basis that the right was reserved to bring the letter to the attention of the court after
judgment, on the question of costs.

For reasons that will appear, I think that I should pause in my recital of the facts in
order to say something about these two cases. For a long while it has been settled law that
if letters written 'without prejudice' do not result in an agreement, they cannot be looked   b
at by the court even on the question of costs, unless both parties consent: see, for example,
Walker v Wilsher (1889) 23 QBD 335; *Stotesbury v Turner* [1943] KB 370. Thus if in
'without prejudice' correspondence a defendant offers less than the plaintiff is claiming
but more than the plaintiff ultimately recovers at the trial, the defendant cannot use his
offer in support of a contention that the plaintiff should receive no costs for the period
subsequent to the offer. If the claim is purely a money claim, this causes no difficulty: c
the defendant may pay into court under RSC Ord 22 the sum that he is offering, and
although knowledge of this will be withheld from the court until both liability and
quantum have been decided, the fact of payment in is admissible, and usually highly
relevant, in deciding what order for costs should be made. If, however, the claim is not
solely a money claim, but some other relief is sought, such as an injunction, there was
formerly no comparable procedure. What was needed was some procedure whereby the   d
defendant could make an offer to submit to an injunction, give an undertaking or afford
other relief on the footing that the offer would be without prejudice until the case was
decided but with prejudice when it came to costs.

It was a procedure of this type which was suggested by Cairns LJ in *Calderbank v
Calderbank* [1975] 3 All ER 333 at 342, [1976] Fam 93 at 105–106 and was acted on in
McDonnell v McDonnell [1977] 1 All ER 766 at 770, [1977] 1 WLR 34 at 38. These were   e
both matrimonial appeals from the Family Division, however, and there has been some
uncertainty whether the procedure applies to other cases. Thus 17 Halsbury's Laws (4th
edn) para 213 cites *Calderbank v Calderbank* for the proposition that 'in matrimonial
proceedings relating to finance' a party may make this type of offer, and the 1983
cumulative supplement leaves it there. Nor do the cases appear to have been given the
prominence which they deserve. Thus leading books which discuss offers made 'without   f
prejudice' still leave unamended statements based on *Walker v Wilsher* (1889) 23 QBD
335, without any mention of either *Calderbank* or *McDonnell*: see, for example, *Phipson on
Evidence* (13th edn, 1982) p 374; *Cross on Evidence* (5th edn, 1979) p 301. Nor are the cases
mentioned in *The Supreme Court Practice 1982*.

In my view, the principle in question is one of perfectly general application which is
in no way confined to matrimonial cases. Whether an offer is made 'without prejudice'
or 'without prejudice save as to costs', the courts ought to enforce the terms on which the   g
offer was made as tending to encourage compromises and shorten litigation; and the
latter form of offer has the added advantage of preventing the offer from being
inadmissible on costs, thereby assisting the court towards justice in making the order as
to costs. I should say at once that no point on this arises for decision, as the parties have
very sensibly acted on this footing. What I have been saying is as obiter as what Cairns LJ   h
said (and Scarman LJ and Sir Gordon Willmer concurred with) in *Calderbank v Calderbank*;
but I hope that the attention of the profession (including authors and editors) will be
more generally directed to what seems to me to be a valuable procedural process that is
too little used.

I now return to the events in this case. As I have said, the *Calderbank* letters were sent
with notices of payment into court. One letter was sent on behalf of the first three
defendants and the other on behalf of the first five defendants; and the plaintiff company's   j
solicitors received the letters on 6 January 1983. The first three defendants offered to give
permanent undertakings (or to submit to permanent injunctions) in terms of the prayers
in the amended statement of claim for injunctions against defrauding the plaintiff
company, conspiracy to defraud or injure and inducing breaches of contract, and using
or disclosing confidential information, with an order for delivery up of confidential

documents, 'together with taxed costs relating thereto' as if RSC Ord 62, r 10(2) applied
a thereto. That rule applies to the taxation of costs after payment into court, and signing
judgment for the taxed costs. The sums paid into court were paid in by the first three
defendants in respect of the plaintiff company's claims for excess commission and all
other causes of action, and by the first five defendants in respect of a particular claim,
called the Eggar Forrester matter: the amounts were £24,000 and £43,000 respectively.
On 10 January the plaintiff company's solicitors wrote accepting the offers made by the
b defendants, with a modification that had been agreed on the telephone, namely that the
court should be asked to decide whether the taxed costs should include the costs reserved
by my order of 14 November 1980. In consequence, the Clerk of the Lists was duly
informed that the date fixed for the trial, 14 February 1983, was to be vacated.

On 8 March 1983 the matter again came before me. Minutes of order were submitted
which, as typed, recorded that the defendants were to pay to the plaintiff company the
c plaintiff company's costs of the issues identified by the notices of payment into court
down to the time when the plaintiff company received notice of the payment in, together
with certain other costs. Up to the last minute there had been a dispute between solicitors
about these costs. The plaintiff company had contended that they related only to the
plaintiff company's costs, and that they had not thought it arguable that there should be
any question of the plaintiff company paying the defendants' costs; but the plaintiff
d company then conceded this, and just before I sat the third defendant dropped a
contention that the disagreement meant that there had never been a binding agreement,
since the parties had not been ad idem. In the end, however, the minutes of order were
amended by agreement so as to give liberty to apply how and by whom (if at all) all or
any of the costs reserved by my order of 14 November 1980 were to be borne and paid;
and the minutes made it explicit that the costs in question were the costs of the plaintiff
e company against the first three defendants alone, and also the costs of those defendants.

It soon became plain that it would not be possible to decide any question of costs that
day. Counsel who appeared on behalf of the plaintiff company had that morning told
counsel who appeared for the first three defendants that he would be asserting that some
of the evidence in the defendants' affidavits on the motion had been shown to be false by
what had subsequently emerged on discovery, and that this was a material matter on the
f question of the costs of the motions. For this and other reasons I directed that the plaintiff
company should promptly deliver to the defendants a note of the submissions to be made
on the question of costs, and that the defendants should similarly give the plaintiff
company a note of their submissions. This was done promptly by the plaintiff company
and considerably less promptly by the defendants. The matter then came back before me
on 16 March and two subsequent days. The note of the plaintiff company's submissions
g was accompanied by a small bundle of supporting documents, just over 30 pages long,
which were mainly (but by no means exclusively) letters that had emerged on discovery.

It very soon became plain that there was in effect a preliminary point. Counsel for the
first three defendants contended that none of the documents obtained on discovery was
admissible on the issue of costs, and that nothing should be admitted unless it was in
evidence on the motions. His mainstay was *Mayor of Bristol v Great Western Rly* [1916]
h WN 47. There, Sargant J had decided a witness action on 17 January, and ordered it to be
mentioned on 21 January as to costs. On the latter date, counsel for the defendants sought
to call a witness to prove what had happened at an interview between representatives of
the parties prior to the issue of the writ; but the judge refused to hear him, and said that
it was 'quite contrary to the practice of the Court to admit such evidence after the case
had been heard and judgment given'. I was told that the report in Weekly Notes, which
j is very short, was the only report on the point; but after I had reserved judgment I found
a more ample report, with the judgment a page long instead of the mere four sentences
in the Weekly Notes' report (see 14 LGR 756 at 767). There, the most relevant sentence
is that it is 'quite contrary to the practice of the Court, after a case has been heard on
behalf of both parties and judgment given, to look, as regards the question of costs, at
anything except correspondence that may have passed between the agents of the parties
before action brought'. The judge then stated that he had listened to counsel's statement

as to the effect of the evidence that he proposed to tender, and said that it would not in any way have altered the conclusion that he had reached. It would be helpful if *The Supreme Court Practice 1982* were to cite the more ample and, I think, more accurate report in the Local Government Reports, which includes a report of the submissions of the elder Upjohn KC.

The *Bristol* case is plainly distinguishable. It was a decision on the adduction of viva voce evidence after there had been a trial and judgment had been given, whereas here the evidence is documentary, and there has been neither trial nor judgment. Further, I do not know whether the practice of the court has remained unchanged during the last 60 or 70 years. My recollection over the last 15 years is that it is common enough for the parties, without objection, to refer to correspondence and other documents when costs come to be argued after judgment has been given; and this has not been limited to correspondence before action brought, or to correspondence or other documents which have been put in evidence during the trial. It is far from uncommon for some document which has no probative value on what is in issue at the trial nevertheless to be of considerable relevance on costs. Furthermore, I cannot in principle see why all viva voce evidence should be excluded. If what is stated in correspondence is to be considered on the argument on costs, I do not see why something which orally falsifies or varies part of the correspondence should be excluded merely because it is oral. Of course, if this is put into an affidavit it then ceases to be presented orally: but the point cannot depend on the precise form in which the evidence is tendered.

Now s 51(1) of the Supreme Court Act 1981 provides that the costs of and incidental to all proceedings in the High Court 'shall be in the discretion of the court, and the court shall have full power to determine by whom and to what extent the costs are to be paid'. By RSC Ord 62, r 2(4) the powers and discretion of the court must be exercised in accordance with Ord 62; but neither in this nor in the 1981 Act can I see anything which prevents evidence relevant to costs from being considered if it has not already been admitted during the trial. The matter, I think, is one for determination by the judge when considering how to exercise his discretionary power to determine by whom and to what extent the costs are to be paid. I do not consider that the judge is fettered by any rule which would exclude evidence if it is oral, or if it consists of correspondence taking place after and not before action brought. If the evidence is admissible, why should it not be admitted? I do not think that such a rule would open the floodgates to the adduction of a mass of new evidence when arguing costs after judgment has been given. In most cases there will be little or nothing to add; but in those cases where something material is tendered I do not think that it ought to be shut out by any general rule. The matter is one for the judge who has to decide the issue, and if one party seeks to adduce evidence which is of little or no cogency in relation to costs the judge, if he admits it, may reflect his view of it in the order for costs that he makes.

Where the case has never been tried and what has to be decided is the order to be made in respect of the reserved costs of interlocutory proceedings, the case seems to me to be even stronger. The evidence which would have been given at the trial is not before the court, and the case has not been decided on the merits. Yet both that evidence and other evidence may well contain matter that is material to the costs of the interlocutory proceedings. The process of discovery, for instance, may have yielded documents which make it plain that evidence in the affidavits on the one side or the other is plainly wrong or highly questionable. The apparently inexplicable may have been convincingly explained, and a threatened loss may instead have yielded a profit. I cannot think that it would be right to exclude evidence of this sort. On the other hand, it would not be right to allow anything resembling a trial of the action to take place in the guise of an argument on costs. From first to last the one question is what order should be made on the interlocutory proceedings, and any evidence must be confined to that issue. Thus I doubt whether the court should consider evidence on matters which might have been raised in the interlocutory proceedings but were not, as contrasted with matters which were raised and have since proved to be unsound.

I do not attempt any comprehensive statement of the law. This will have to emerge as
a further cases on the point occur, though at the present rate of progress that will take a
long time. I have, however, said enough to explain why in the present case I reached the
conclusion that I should not exclude the evidence proffered by counsel for the plaintiff
company, even if it had not been in evidence on the motion. To some of the documents
in his bundle counsel for the first three defendants had no objection. To most of them he
objected on the grounds that they should not be admitted on costs, and to one of them
b he objected on the ground that it was not admissible at all. This last document I excluded;
but I admitted the others. If there had been any objection to their authenticity, I should
have required them to be proved; but as there was not, I admitted them purely on the
issue of costs.

That brings me to the question of the effect of these documents. The purpose of
counsel for the plaintiff company in producing them was to show that the first two
c defendants had sworn false affidavits on the motion, and that the defendants were so
untrustworthy that the plaintiff company was fully justified in seeking relief by motion.
Initially counsel for the plaintiff company said that he was content not to read or refer to
the documents unless counsel for the first three defendants sought costs against the
plaintiff company on anything, or made various other submissions on costs. However,
in the event counsel for the first three defendants contended that the plaintiff company
d should pay the defendants' costs on motion no 1, as well as making many other
submissions, and so the admissible documents were explored at some length in relation
to the affidavits.

I do not propose to discuss the documents or the submissions that were made on them
in any detail. In my judgment it would be entirely wrong to reach any conclusion that
the first two defendants have been guilty of perjury or the equivalent on the basis of
e documents such as these. It may well be said that the documents show that the three
defendants have something to explain. Nevertheless, if those documents were put to the
defendants in cross-examination, it may be that they would sufficiently explain them or
modify their effect. At all events, I feel no hesitation in saying that the hearing of an
application for costs is neither the time nor the place (if, indeed, there is one) in which to
conduct anything like a trial for perjury on affidavit evidence, or to conclude that there
f has been a deliberate or reckless lack of frankness.

On behalf of the defendants, counsel for the first three defendants put much reliance
on *J T Stratford & Son Ltd v Lindley (No 2)* [1969] 3 All ER 1122, [1969] 1 WLR 1547.
That was a case in which the House of Lords had restored an interlocutory injunction,
and had ordered that the costs all the way up were to be costs in the cause. Apart from
some discussions, the case then went to sleep for some four years, until the defendants
g took out a summons to dismiss the action for want of prosecution and the plaintiffs
replied by taking out a summons for leave to discontinue the action on such terms as the
court thought just. Neither side wished to continue the action, and neither side wanted
to pay the costs thus far incurred; and since there would be no judgment in the action,
the order of the House of Lords that the costs of the interlocutory proceedings were to be
costs in the cause could not be carried out. Lord Denning MR said that the court should
h deal with the order for costs to be costs in the cause as if it were 'costs reserved'; and he
said that the court could not try the actions at that stage, and that he put aside the
respective merits of the dispute [1969] 3 All ER 1122 at 1124, [1969] 1 WLR 1547 at
1554. The view of Winn LJ was similar. The court held that the master and the judge
had both exercised their discretion wisely in giving the plaintiffs leave to discontinue the
action on the footing that each party was to bear its own costs. That, said counsel for the
j first three defendants, should be the result in the present case, though as an alternative
he contended for certain cross-orders on the three motions in dispute.

It will be observed that the *Stratford* case never proceeded beyond the interlocutory
stage. There was no trial, and there was no termination of the action by a consent order
containing injunctions after payments into court by the defendants. For these reasons
alone, the *Stratford* case seems to me to be very different from the case before me. In his

argument and his written summary of submissions, counsel for the first three defendants
emphasised that the defendants denied and continued to deny the plaintiff company's   *a*
claims; and he said that payment into court implied no admission about the merits of
the cause of action (see, for example, *A Martin French (a firm) v Kingswood Hill Ltd* [1960]
2 All ER 251 at 252, [1961] 1 QB 96 at 102). He also pointed out that the sums paid into
court were much less than the sums claimed by the plaintiff company, and he contended
that the defendants had merely accepted advice that in view of the heavy costs of a trial,
it would be better to pay the money into court than to spend it on lawyers. Even if the   *b*
defendants won, a significant part of the costs would be irrecoverable on taxation.
Furthermore, in submitting to the injunctions, the defendants were merely submitting
to orders not to do certain acts which they had no intention of doing.

If one accepts all that, there remains the hard fact that the plaintiff company was suing
to obtain relief against the defendants, and has now obtained relief. True, the relief
obtained is not as great as the relief claimed, but it is very substantial, and there is nothing   *c*
to suggest that it could have been obtained without bringing proceedings. The plaintiff
company has not only obtained substantial relief but also has obtained a substantial order
for costs. True, the plaintiff company has obtained these benefits not by a judgment after
trial on the merits but by a compromise of the proceedings. Nevertheless, the result of
bringing the proceedings has been to give the plaintiff company this substantial relief. In
short, the proceedings have been successful. I cannot see that it matters to the plaintiff   *d*
company whether the defendants made the payments into court and submitted to the
order out of a sense of guilt or with a conviction of innocence and a desire to save costs.
Of course, a judgment in favour of the plaintiff company would create an estoppel,
whereas the payment into court does not; but the substance of the matter is not the
creation of an estoppel but the obtaining of relief.

When one turns to the motions in dispute, one does so against the background of the   *e*
substantive proceedings having ended in favour of the plaintiff company. The efforts by
the plaintiff company to obtain interlocutory relief seem to me to be entirely proper and
reasonable. Without making any findings on the merits of the plaintiff company's case, I
can say that nothing that I have seen or heard has impressed me with any sense of the
defendants being exposed to injustice or unwarrantable hardship if they have to bear the
costs of the motions in question.

That is the general aspect of the matter; but I must look separately at each of the   *f*
motions. Motion no 1 was the motion under the plaintiff company's notice of motion
dated 13 March 1980. This held sway for a little under three weeks, until on 1 April
1980 the plaintiff company undertook not to proceed further on it, but to replace it by a
new notice of motion. This was done on 2 April 1980, and the motion under the new
notice was motion no 2. Counsel for the plaintiff company accepted that as the plaintiff   *g*
company had not proceeded with no 1, he could not very well claim as against the
defendants the cost of drafting the notice of motion and issuing and serving it, though
he said that the costs of the affidavits should be paid by the defendants, since they were
all part of the process of obtaining the interlocutory relief that under motion no 2 was
given by the consent order. Nor would he accept that the costs of the hearing of motion
no 1 should not be borne by the defendants. Apart from this limitation of the costs in   *h*
respect of motion no 1, he contended that he should have the costs of all three motions.
He had succeeded on motion no 2, and the defendant's motion had in effect been
abandoned.

There seems to me to be an apparent lack of consistency in these submissions. They
come close to saying that when the defendants abandon a motion they must pay the
plaintiff company's costs, whereas when the plaintiff company abandons a motion,   *j*
the plaintiff company need not pay the defendants' costs, but can make the defendants
pay them, apart from the cost of drafting, issuing and serving the notice of motion.
However, to say this overlooks, I think, the fact that the defendant's abandoned motion
was not the forerunner of any successful motion but was simply an abandoned motion,
whereas the plaintiff company's motion no 1 was the precursor of the successful motion

no 2. Looking at the case as a whole, I think that, subject to anything further that counsel
a may say, the right order to make in respect of motion no 1 is that there should be no
order as to the costs of that motion except that any affidavits, exhibits and other material
which was of utility in motion no 2 should be treated as part of the costs of motion no 2.
On motion no 2 and the defendant's motion, I think that the first three defendants and
the third defendant respectively should pay the costs of the plaintiff company.

b The court then heard submissions by counsel for the first three defendants that the
plaintiff company's costs should be reduced because of the time spent in argument in
previous proceedings on the false evidence point.

SIR ROBERT MEGARRY V C. The order I propose to make is this: that the costs of
8 March should be included with the costs of 16–18 March 1983, and that the defendants
c should pay to the plaintiff company three-quarters of those costs.

Order accordingly. Leave to appeal refused.

Solicitors: *Linklaters & Paines* (for the plaintiff company); *Stoneham Langton & Passmore*
(for the first three defendants).

d
                                                            Vivian Horvath   Barrister.

e # P Perl (Exporters) Ltd v Camden London Borough Council

COURT OF APPEAL, CIVIL DIVISION
WALLER, OLIVER AND ROBERT GOFF LJJ
f 13, 14, 30 JUNE 1983

*Negligence – Duty to take care – Act of third party – Duty to adjacent occupier for act of third
party – Thieves gaining access to defendants' unoccupied and unsecured premises – Thieves then
making hole in common wall between defendants' and plaintiffs' premises in order to steal from
plaintiffs – Whether defendants owing duty to plaintiffs to act positively to prevent third party
g entering defendants' premises – Whether defendants liable for plaintiffs' loss.*

The appellant local authority owned a block of flats which included an unoccupied
basement flat. The respondent company occupied a neighbouring flat, which had a
basement which was separated from the appellants' basement flat by a common wall.
The appellants' unoccupied flat was not secured to prevent admission by intruders and
h vagrants had been seen near the entrance way. Other flats in the block had been burgled,
but despite complaints the appellants did nothing to improve security. In May 1977
thieves entered the unoccupied flat and knocked a hole in the common wall to gain
admission to the respondents' basement, from which they removed over 700 garments
which had been stored there. The respondents sued the appellants for the loss. The judge
held that the appellants had continuously neglected to supply a secure structure, that
j they should have foreseen that damage to property would ensue and that accordingly
there had been an absence of reasonable care. He therefore awarded damages to the
respondents. The appellants appealed, contending that they did not owe a duty of care to
the respondents as occupiers of the neighbouring property to act to avoid loss arising
from the actions of a third party, or alternatively, if there was such a duty, that they had
not been in breach of it.

Held – In the absence of any special relationship of control existing between the occupier of premises and a third party, the occupier did not owe a duty of care to an occupier of neighbouring premises to protect his own premises or to act to prevent the third party from gaining access to his own premises and from there gaining access to the adjoining premises where he could damage the neighbour's property. The appellants and the thieves were not connected by any such special relationship and the appellants had therefore not been negligent in failing to take steps to prevent the thieves from entering their premises for the purpose of breaking into the respondents' premises. Accordingly, the appellants were not liable for the consequent loss suffered by the respondents and the appeal would therefore be allowed (see p 164 h j, p 166 f g, p 167 e, p 168 g h j, p 170 j, p 171 c and p 172 c d and g, post).

Dicta of Lord Sumner in *Weld-Blundell v Stephens* [1920] All ER Rep at 47, of Dixon J in *Smith v Leurs* (1945) 70 CLR at 261–262, *Home Office v Dorset Yacht Co Ltd* [1970] 2 All ER 294 and dictum of Lord Wilberforce in *Anns v Merton London BC* [1977] 2 All ER at 498 applied.

Evans v Glasgow DC 1978 SLT 17 and *Hosie v Arbroath Football Club Ltd* 1978 SLT 122 distinguished.

Per Waller LJ. A very high degree of foreseeability is required if liability is to be imposed on a person for the acts of an independent third party (see p 165 h and p 166 d, post); dicta of Lord Morris and Lord Diplock in *Home Office v Dorset Yacht Co Ltd* [1970] 2 All ER at 303–304, 334 and of Oliver LJ in *Lamb v Camden London BC* [1981] 2 All ER at 418–419 applied.

Notes

For duty of care, see 34 Halsbury's Laws (4th edn) paras 18–52, and for cases on the subject, see 36(1) Digest (Reissue) 75–151, 299–577.

Cases referred to in judgments

A-G v Corke [1933] Ch 89, [1932] All ER Rep 711.
Anns v Merton London BC [1977] 2 All ER 492, [1978] AC 728, [1978] 2 WLR 1024, HL.
Donoghue (or M'Alister) v Stevenson [1932] AC 562, [1932] All ER Rep 1, HL.
Evans v Glasgow DC 1978 SLT 17.
Home Office v Dorset Yacht Co Ltd [1970] 2 All ER 294, [1970] AC 1004, [1970] 2 WLR 1140, HL.
Hosie v Arbroath Football Club Ltd 1978 SLT 122.
Lamb v Camden London BC [1981] 2 All ER 408, [1981] QB 625, [1981] 2 WLR 1038, CA.
Ontario Hospital Services Commission v Borsoski [1974] DLR (3d) 339.
Overseas Tankship (UK) Ltd v Morts Dock and Engineering Co Ltd, The Wagon Mound [1961] 1 All ER 404, [1961] AC 388, [1961] 2 WLR 126, PC.
Paterson Zochonis & Co Ltd v Merfarken Packaging Ltd [1983] FSR 273, CA.
Rylands v Fletcher (1868) LR 3 HL 330, [1861–73] All ER Rep 1, HL.
Scott's Trustees v Moss (1889) 17 R (Ct of Sess) 32.
Sedleigh-Denfield v O'Callagan (Trustees for St Joseph's Society for Foreign Missions) [1940] 3 All ER 349, [1940] AC 880, HL.
Smith v Leurs (1945) 70 CLR 256.
Stansbie v Troman [1948] 1 All ER 599, [1948] 2 KB 48, CA.
Weld-Blundell v Stephens [1920] AC 956, [1920] All ER Rep 32, HL.

Cases also cited

Bradburn v Lindsay [1983] 2 All ER 408.
Doughty v Turner Manufacturing Co Ltd [1964] 1 All ER 98, [1964] 1 QB 518, CA.
Hughes v Lord Advocate [1963] 1 All ER 705, [1963] AC 837, HL.

Appeal

The appellants, the Camden London Borough Council, appealed from the decision of Mr Barry Chedlow QC acting as a deputy judge of the High Court made on 25 March 1982

whereby he held that the appellants had been negligent and awarded the respondents,
a   P Perl (Exporters) Ltd, damages of £7,950 plus interest. The facts are set out in the
judgment of Waller LJ.

Michael Turner QC and John Trench for the appellants.
Desmond Browne for the respondents.

Cur adv vult
b

30 June. The following judgments were delivered.

WALLER LJ. This is an appeal from a decision of Mr Barry Chedlow, QC, sitting as a
deputy judge of the High Court and given on 25 March 1982. He awarded damages to
the plaintiffs of £12,338·93, arising out of a theft by unknown third parties at their
c   premises at 142 Southampton Row. The appellants own 142 Southampton Row and also
144 Southampton Row, no 144 being premises divided into flats. The respondent
company are the tenants of no 142. As part of the premises let to the respondents there
is a basement which was used by the respondents for the storage of clothing in connection
with their business and at the relevant time was used for the storage of a quantity of
d   Scottish sweaters. As part of no 144 one of the flats was an unoccupied basement flat
adjoining the basement of no 142 separated by an 18-inch wall and with no direct
communication with it. The entrance to no 144 was through a double doorway into a
lobby with another double door at the other side, then a short distance across the ground
floor and then down some stairs into a light well the floor of which was at basement
level. The access to the basement flat was up some steps at the opposite end of the light
well into a corridor branching off the main corridor. There were two windows from part
e   of the respondents' premises which looked on to the light well but these windows were
barred and wired with a burglar alarm.
    The evidence was that there were no locks on the front door at the time of the burglary,
that there had been no catch on the door at the top of the stairs leading to the bottom of
the light well and that the door leading into the basement flat was off its hinges.
f   Furthermore, tramps and vagrants had been seen in the light well. There had been a
number of complaints to the appellants about the lack of security at the flats and there
had also been several burglaries but little or nothing had been done about this up to 22
May 1977. Over the weekend of 21–22 May 1977 thieves knocked a hole into the
common wall between the vacant flat in the basement of no 144 and the basement of
no 142, the wall being an 18-inch thick brick wall, and through this hole a slim person
g   was able to climb and over 700 garments were stolen. The judge held that there was an
absence of reasonable care on the part of the respondents in that the appellants had
continuously neglected to supply a secure structure and should have known that vandals,
tramps and undesirables were continuously on their structure and therefore it should
have been foreseen that damage to property would ensue. He held that the simplest
inspection would have revealed a situation which any prudent landowner should not
h   have allowed to have continued. The judge accordingly held that there was an absence of
reasonable care and awarded damages to the respondents.
    Counsel for the appellants submitted that the judge had applied the wrong test in that
he had considered the landlord's duty towards those lawfully in their own premises and
had not distinguished that duty from the duty of the occupier of one set of premises to
the occupier of adjoining premises. He submitted that the appellants were not under any
j   duty to occupiers of adjoining property or alternatively if they were under a duty it
would be to refrain from doing acts which could be foreseen to be very likely to cause
damage and they were not in breach of such duty.
    Counsel for the respondents submitted that there was a duty of care and that the
appellants owed such duty even though the immediate cause of the damage was the act
of third parties. He submitted that the appellants' knowledge of the valuable goods held
by the respondent in his storeroom, the presence of unauthorised persons in no 144 and

the state of the doors and locks on the doors were such that the breaking in and stealing was foreseeable and accordingly the appellants were liable.

The facts of this case raise certain questions of principle. If the judgment is right the *a* appellants are liable for the acts of third parties whose identity is unknown. Furthermore, although on the facts of this case there was very considerable carelessness on the part of the appellants' staff, if the appellants are liable to the respondents it would follow that in many cases the duty of care imposed on householders to their neighbours would be very different from that which they have always been understood to be.

The first question to consider is in what circumstances a defendant will be responsible *b* for the acts of a third party. In *Home Office v Dorset Yacht Co Ltd* [1970] 2 All ER 294 at 321–322, [1970] AC 1004 at 1055 Lord Pearson considering this problem in relation to the facts of that case, the case being one where borstal boys escaped from their supervisors, said:

'*Act of third party*. In *Weld-Blundell v Stephens* [1920] AC 956 at 986, [1920] All ER *c* Rep 32 at 47 Lord Sumner said: "In general (apart from special contracts and relations and the maxim Respondeat superior), even though A. is in fault, he is not responsible for injury to C. which B., a stranger to him, deliberately chooses to do." In *Smith v Leurs* (1945) 70 CLR 256 at 261–262 Dixon J said: " . . . apart from vicarious responsibility, one man may be responsible to another for the harm done to the latter by a third person; he may be responsible on the ground that the act of *d* the third person could not have taken place but for his own fault or breach of duty. There is more than one description of duty the breach of which may produce this consequence. For instance, it may be a duty of care in reference to things involving special danger. It may even be a duty of care with reference to the control of actions or conduct of the third person. It is, however, exceptional to find in the law a duty to control another's actions to prevent harm to strangers. The general rule is that *e* one man is under no duty of controlling another to prevent his doing damage to a third. There are, however, special relations which are the source of a duty of this nature. It appears now to be recognised that it is incumbent upon a parent who maintains control over a young child to take reasonable care so to exercise that control as to avoid conduct on his part exposing the person or property of others to unreasonable danger. Parental control, where it exists, must be exercised with due *f* care to prevent the child inflicting intentional damage on others or causing damage by conduct involving unreasonable risk of injury to others." In my opinion, this case falls under the exception and not the rule, because there was a special relation. The borstal boys were under the control of the Home Office's officers, and control imports responsibility. The boys' interference with the boats appears to have been a direct result of the Home Office's officers' failure to exercise proper control and *g* supervision. Problems may arise in other cases as to the responsibility of the Home Office's officers for acts done by borstal boys when they have completed their escape from control and are fully at large and acting independently. No such problem faces the respondents in this case.'

We were also referred to the case of *Hosie v Arbroath Football Club Ltd* 1978 SLT 122, *h* where the football club were held liable for injuries caused when spectators broke through a defective gate and caused injury to one man. Thus parents may be responsible for the acts of their children, the relationship of borstal staff to borstal boys on an exercise on an island may make the staff responsible, or a football club may be responsible for the actions of spectators whom they have invited to their premises. But no case has been cited to us where a party has been held liable for the acts of a third party when there was *j* no element of control over the third party. While I do not take the view that there can never be such a case I do take the view that the absence of control must make the court approach the suggestion that there is liability for a third party who was not under the control of the defendant with caution.

The next question to consider is the nature of the duty of the appellants as occupiers of no 144 to the respondents as occupiers of the adjoining property, no 142. In *Home Office*

v Dorset Yacht Co Ltd, the case to which I have already referred, the House of Lords held
a that the Home Office were liable when seven borstal young offenders escaped and
damaged a yacht in trying to escape from Brownsea Island where they were. Lord Reid
said ([1970] 2 All ER 294 at 300, [1970] AC 1004 at 1030):

> 'These cases show that, where human action forms one of the links between the
> original wrongdoing of the defendant and the loss suffered by the plaintiff, that
> action must at least have been something very likely to happen if it is not to be
b > regarded as novus actus interveniens breaking the chain of causation. I do not think
> that a mere foreseeable possibility is or should be sufficient, for then the intervening
> human action can more properly be regarded as a new cause than as a consequence
> of the original wrongdoing. But if the intervening action was likely to happen I do
> not think that it can matter whether that action was innocent or tortious or criminal.
> Unfortunately tortious or criminal action by a third party is often the "very kind of
c > thing" which is likely to happen as a result of the wrongful or careless act of the
> defendant. And in the present case, on the facts which we must assume at this stage,
> I think that the taking of a boat by the escaping trainees and their unskilful
> navigation leading to damage to another vessel were the very kind of thing that
> these borstal officers ought to have seen to be likely.'

d It is not altogether clear from that passage what kind of possibility or probability Lord
Reid had in mind, but Lord Morris said ([1970] 2 All ER 294 at 303–304, [1970] AC
1004 at 1034):

> 'On these facts a normal or even modest measure of prescience and prevision
> must have led any ordinary person, but rather specially an officer in charge, to
> realise that the boys might wish to escape and might use a yacht if one was near at
e > hand to help them to do so. That is exactly what it is said that seven boys did. In my
> view, the officers must have appreciated that either in an escape attempt or by
> reason of some other prompting the boys might interfere with one of the yachts
> with consequent likelihood of doing some injury to it. The risk of such a happening
> was glaringly obvious. The possibilities of damage being done to one of the nearby
> yachts (assuming that they were nearby) were many and apparent. In that situation
f > and in those circumstances I consider that a duty of care was owed by the officers to
> the owners of the nearby yachts. The principle expressed in Lord Atkin's classic
> words in his speech in *Donoghue v Stevenson* [1932] AC 562 at 580, [1932] All ER Rep
> 1 at 11 would seem to be directly applicable. If the principle applied, then it was
> incumbent on the officers to avoid acts or omissions which they could reasonably
> foresee would be likely to injure the owners of yachts. They were persons so closely
g > and directly affected by what the officers did or failed to do that they ought
> reasonably to have been in the contemplation of the officers.'

And Lord Diplock said ([1970] 2 All ER 294 at 334, [1974] AC 1004 at 1070–1071):

> 'I should therefore hold that any duty of a borstal officer to use reasonable care to
> prevent a borstal trainee from escaping from his custody was owed only to persons
h > whom he could reasonably foresee had property situate in the vicinity of the place
> of detention of the detainee which the detainee was likely to steal or to appropriate
> and damage in the course of eluding immediate pursuit and recapture. Whether or
> not any person fell within this category would depend on the facts of the particular
> case including the previous criminal and escaping record of the individual trainee
> concerned and the nature of the place from which he escaped.'

j Lord Diplock, in the passage I have quoted, restricts the foreseeability and Lord Morris
describes the risk as glaringly obvious. These quotations do indicate that in circumstances
in which it is sought to make somebody liable for the actions of a third party it would
appear to require a fairly high degree of foreseeability.

This question was considered by the Court of Appeal in *Lamb v Camden London BC*
[1981] 2 All ER 408, [1981] QB 625. In that case the local council had broken a water

main and as a result the plaintiff's house subsided and the walls cracked. Sometime after
the house had become empty, squatters went into the house and did serious damage to   a
the house. The Court of Appeal had to consider whether or not that damage was too
remote and unanimously came to the conclusion that it was too remote. The reasoning
of each of the judges differed somewhat. I prefer that of Oliver LJ, who after quoting the
passage which I have already quoted from Lord Reid's speech, when considering precisely
what Lord Reid meant, said ([1981] 2 All ER 408 at 418–419, [1981] QB 625 at 642–
643):   b

> 'But the question is not what is foreseeable merely as a possibility but what would
> the reasonable man actually foresee if he thought about it, and all that Lord Reid
> seems to me to be saying is that the hypothetical reasonable man in the position of
> the tortfeasor cannot be said to foresee the behaviour of another person unless that
> behaviour is such as would, viewed objectively, be very likely to occur . . . The test
> of remoteness is said to be the same as the test of duty in negligence (see *The Wagon*   c
> *Mound (No 1)* [1961] 1 All ER 404, [1961] AC 388). If the instant case is approached
> as a case of negligence and one asks the question, did the defendants owe a duty not
> to break a water pipe so as to cause the plaintiffs' house to be invaded by squatters a
> year later, the tenuousness of the linkage between act and result becomes apparent.
> I confess that I find it inconceivable that the reasonable man, wielding his pick in
> the road in 1973, could be said reasonably to foresee that his puncturing of a water   d
> main would fill the plaintiffs' house with uninvited guests in 1974. Whilst,
> therefore, I am not altogether in accord with the official referee's reasoning, I think
> that he came to the right conclusion in the light of his finding of fact, which has not
> been challenged. Accordingly, the appeal should, in my judgment, be dismissed . . .
> There may, for instance, be circumstances in which the court would require a degree
> of likelihood amounting almost to inevitability before it fixes a defendant with   e
> responsibility for the act of a third party over whom he has and can have no control.'

I agree with Oliver LJ that the foreseeability required to impose a liability for the acts of
some independent third parties requires a very high degree of foreseeability. Adapting
the words of Lord Atkin, ought the appellants to have had the respondents, as occupiers
of no 142, in contemplation as being affected when directing their minds to the question   f
of repairing the doors and locks of no 144? It is not sought here to make the appellants
liable for any act, it is sought to make the appellants liable for an omission to act. Can it
be said that the appellants ought reasonably to have had in contemplation the fact that
third parties would go into the empty basement of no 144, make a hole in an 18-inch
wall large enough for somebody to climb through and steal a large number of articles of
clothing from within? I would unhesitatingly answer No. Whether or not an occupier
of a house can ever be liable to a neighbour for an omission to act is doubtful. I do not   g
however have to consider whether such a case may possibly arise. It is sufficient to say
that in this case I am satisfied that there was no breach of duty by the appellants to the
respondents and accordingly I would allow this appeal.

OLIVER LJ. The question raised by this appeal is solely one of the appellants' common   h
law liability to the respondents for the tort of negligence. No contractual duty is alleged
and the fact that, in addition to having the control of the common parts and the basement
flat in no 144 Southampton Row, the appellants were also the respondents' landlords in
respect of the premises at no 142 is irrelevant save in so far as it supports the suggestion
that the appellants were familiar with the geographical features of both premises and
that they were or should have been aware of the possible risk of intrusion into no 142 by
trespassers who had first entered no 144. Thus the question posed is a perfectly general   j
one: does a landowner owe any, and if so what, duty to an adjoining occupier to secure
his land against the entry of trespassers who may damage his neighbour's property? The
deputy judge held that there was, in the circumstances of this case, a duty in the
appellants to take reasonable care to ensure that their premises were secured against
trespassers and the basis of his decision was that since it would be reasonably foreseen

that trespassers entering the appellants' premises might include (as they evidently did in
a fact) thieves interested in securing illegal access to the adjoining premises, the case fell
squarely within the classic statement of Lord Atkin in *Donoghue v Stevenson* [1932] AC
562 at 580, [1932] All ER Rep 1 at 11: 'You must take reasonable care to avoid acts or
omissions which you can reasonably foresee would be likely to injure your neighbour.'

The appellants have, of course, done nothing; so the case is one, not of an act, but of an
omission. They simply omitted to keep and maintain an effective lock on the front door
b giving access to no 144 and they similarly omitted to keep and maintain effective internal
barriers such as would or might have prevented trespassers obtaining access to the rear
wall of the respondents' storeroom. It cannot be asserted that those omissions, by
themselves, caused any injury to anyone. They merely enabled some unknown third
party over whom the appellants had no control to effect an unlawful entry on the
appellants' premises and thence to effect an equally unlawful entry on the respondents'
c premises. It would, in fact, be more accurate to say that the omissions failed to impede
such an entry rather than that they enabled it to take place, for it is by no means certain
that even an effective lock on the outer door would have prevented an incursion by a
really determined gang of thieves. Thus the assertion that the appellants are liable for the
damage which the respondents sustained rests on the proposition that the breaking into
the respondents' premises was the natural and probable consequence of the appellants'
d failure to secure their own premises from invasion.

Counsel for the appellants has forcefully submitted that the deputy judge was wrong
in two essential respects. First, he submits that there was no foundation in law for the
duty attributed to the appellants: in broad terms a general common law duty to control
the acts of an independent third party cannot exist apart from some special relationship
with the third party, which does not exist here.

e Second, in the absence of such a relationship, a damage arising from the act of an
independent third party is, in any event, too remote. Speaking for myself, I think that
the question of the existence of a duty and that of whether the damage brought about by
the act of a third party is too remote are simply two facets of the same problem; for if
there be a duty to take reasonable care to prevent damage being caused by a third party
then I find it difficult to see how damage caused by the third party consequent on the
f failure to take such care can be too remote a consequence of the breach of duty. Essentially
the answer to both questions is to be found in answering the question: in what
circumstances is a defendant to be held responsible at common law for the independent
act of a third person which he knows or ought to know may injure his neighbour? The
deputy judge, as I read his judgment, deduced from the authorities the general
proposition that where the act of the third person of which A complains is something
g which is likely to occur if B does or omits to do a particular act then B owes a duty to A
to refrain from or to do that act. The foundation for the respondents' case and for the
deputy judge's conclusion is the speech of Lord Reid in *Home Office v Dorset Yacht Co Ltd*
[1970] 2 All ER 294 at 300, [1970] AC 1004 at 1030 and, in particular, this passage:

'These cases show that, where human action forms one of the links between the
original wrongdoing of the defendant and the loss suffered by the plaintiff, that
h action must at least have been something very likely to happen if it is not to be
regarded as novus actus interveniens breaking the chain of causation. I do not think
that a more foreseeable possibility is or should be sufficient, for then the intervening
human action can more properly be regarded as a new cause than as a consequence
of the original wrongdoing. But if the intervening action was likely to happen I do
not think that it can matter whether that action was innocent or tortious or criminal.
j Unfortunately, tortious or criminal action by a third party is often the "very kind of
thing" which is likely to happen as a result of the wrongful or careless act of the
defendant.'

In *Lamb v Camden London BC* [1981] 2 All ER 408, [1981] 1 QB 625 I ventured to
suggest that in this passage Lord Reid was seeking to do no more than to place a
qualification or limitation, in cases of third party intervention, on the more general

proposition that he who does or omits to do something is responsible for the reasonably foreseeable consequences of his act or omission, the suggestion, as I thought, being that in such a case a consequence should not be regarded as reasonably foreseeable unless it was something which was either likely or very likely to happen. Whether, however, that be right or wrong, the passage quoted does not appear to me, when read in its full context, to be authority for the more general proposition that wherever particular conduct of a third person is likely to take place if something is done or omitted there arises from that likelihood alone a duty to refrain from or to do, as the case may be, the relevant act. That is, as it seems to me, the general proposition which the deputy judge deduced from the authorities to which he referred and which led him to the conclusion that the appellants were liable for the damage which the respondents suffered in this case. He observed:

'I think that if the defendants continuously neglect to supply a secure structure and know, or should know, that vandals, tramps and undesirables are continuously on their structure it can fairly be foreseen that damage to property will ensue.'

It can be seen from this that the deputy judge is presupposing a duty 'to supply a secure structure'; and when the judgment is analysed it is found that there is, in fact, no support for the existence of the duty apart from the knowledge that the structure is frequented by trespassers. The foreseeability of damage to property is, by itself, being treated as the foundation of the duty. Thus the first question to be answered is whether the *Dorset Yacht* case is authority for the proposition. In my judgment, it clearly is not. All of their Lordships who constituted the majority recognised that there was, apart from special relationships, no general duty to avoid or inhibit conduct of third parties which foreseeably may lead to damage. Lord Reid [1970] 2 All ER 294 at 297–298, [1970] AC 1004 at 1027) observed that—

'when a person has done nothing to put himself in any relationship with another person in distress or with his property mere accidental propinquity does not require him to go to that person's assistance. There may be a moral duty to do so, but it is not practicable to make it a legal duty.'

Lord Morris observed ([1970] 2 All ER 294 at 304, [1970] AC 1004 at 1034):

'It cannot be, therefore, that in all circumstances where certain consequences can reasonably be foreseen a duty of care arises. A failure to take some preventive action or rescue operation does not of and by itself necessarily betoken any breach of a legal duty of care.'

(See also [1970] 2 All ER 294 at 321–322, 326, [1970] AC 1004 at 1054–1055, 1060 per Lord Pearson and Lord Diplock.)

What gave rise to the duty on the *Dorset Yacht* case was the special relationship which existed between the defendant and the third person who inflicted the damage, inasmuch as the defendants had both the statutory right and the statutory duty to exercise control over those persons. This was, I think implicit in the speech of Lord Reid, and it was expressed in the speeches of Lord Morris, Lord Pearson and Lord Diplock, all of whom quoted and relied on the judgment of Dixon J in *Smith v Leurs* (1945) 70 CLR 256 at 262, where he said:

'It is, however, exceptional to find in the law a duty to control another's action to prevent harm to strangers. The general rule is that one man is under no duty of controlling another man to prevent his doing damage to a third. There are, however, special relations which are the source of a duty of this nature.'

Lord Diplock, indeed, went further, in that he envisaged, at any rate on the facts of that case, a special relation also between the defendant and the person injured arising from the particular susceptibility of that person to risk of injury (see [1970] 2 All ER 294 at 334, [1970] AC 1004 at 1070).

The *Dorset Yacht* case does not, therefore, in my judgment support the conclusion at

which the deputy judge arrived, unless it can be said that there was here some special
a relation taking the case out of the general rule which excludes liability for the acts of
independent third parties. Counsel for the respondents has submitted that that special
relation is to be found from a number of factors combined that is to say (a) geographical
propinquity, (b) the appellants' knowledge that the respondents used their premises to
store goods which might be attractive to thieves, (c) the appellants' knowledge or means
of knowledge that there had been frequent incursions by trespassers (including burglaries
b in some of the flats in no 144) and (d) the relatively simple steps required to impede the
entry of trespassers by fitting an effective lock on the front door. These factors, however,
whilst they are, no doubt, relevant as regards remoteness of damage and may possibly be
said to give rise to a relation between the appellants and the respondents, go nowhere
towards establishing the sort of relation referred to by the majority in the *Dorset Yacht*
case and clearly envisaged by Dixon J in the passage from his judgment in *Smith v Leurs*
c referred to above, namely a relation between the defendant and the third party for whose
act he is said to be responsible. If, therefore, support is to be found for the deputy judge's
broad proposition it must, in my judgment, be looked for elsewhere. He relied, in
addition to the *Dorset Yacht* case, on *Hosie v Arbroath Football Club Ltd* 1978 SLT 122 and
Evans v Glasgow DC 1978 SLT 17. I do not, for my part, find the former of these of very
much assistance. It was a claim under the Occupiers' Liability (Scotland) Act 1960 and
d there was no question but that the defendants there owed a duty to the plaintiff to take
reasonable care to keep their football ground and its entry and exit facilities safe by, inter
alia, ensuring that the gates were sufficiently strong to withstand pressure from crowds.
The question at issue was whether that duty extended to deliberate interference by
unruly elements, the occurrence of which was clearly not only foreseeable but, having
regard to the known habits of football crowds, likely. The case does not, however, help
e in the present context because there clearly was there a special relation both between the
defendants and those who damaged the plaintiff and between the defendants and the
plaintiff, himself, inasmuch as both the plaintiff and his assailants were the defendants'
invitees for whom as occupiers of the ground the defendants had to assume responsibility.
The same may I think be said of *Scott's Trustees v Moss* (1889) 17 R (Ct of Sess) 32, referred
to by Lord Reid in the *Dorset Yacht* case. If, for your own commercial purpose, you invite
f or entice a crowd to assemble in circumstances where you can reasonably foresee that
they are likely to damage the plaintiff, it is not difficult to infer that the circumstances of
the enticement or invitation creates the special relation which grounds responsibility.
That however is a far cry from a case where the defendant does nothing in the way of
issuing an invitation but merely takes insufficient steps to protect himself from invasion
of his own rights. The proposition that because I have failed adequately to protect myself
g against X's wrongdoing I therefore become responsible for the further wrong which X
chooses to do to Y is one which is, on the face of it, startling. Counsel for the respondents,
however, submits that this consequence flows from the other case relied on by the deputy
judge: *Evans v Glasgow DC* 1978 SLT 17. There the defenders had demolished premises
which adjoined the pursuer's premises (also leased from the defenders) and in doing so
had damaged the locks securing the pursuer's doors, which they replaced with inadequate
h locks. The pursuer suffered loss by reason of (a) theft of goods by persons who broke the
new and inadequate locks, (b) fire caused by vandals dropping lighted material through
gaps left in the floorboards above the pursuer's premises and (c) escape of water from the
defenders' premises caused by vandals interfering with the plumbing thereon. The
question (expressed in terms of English law) was whether the allegation to this effect in
the pleading were demurrable. In fact the action was dismissed on other grounds, which
j turned on an exclusion clause in the pursuer's lease, but the defender's claim that the
allegations were irrelevant failed. Lord Wylie, the Lord Ordinary, observed (1978 SLT
17 at 19):

'... I accept the submission of senior counsel for the defenders that there is
accordingly a very strong presumption that no such duty exists in law. On the other
hand, in such a situation, I think that the court is thrown back on first principles,

and it cannot be ignored that, in the words of Lord Macmillan in *Donoghue* v. *Stevenson* ([1932] AC 562 at 619, [1932] All ER Rep 1 at 30): "The categories of negligence are never closed." In the circumstances of the present case, on averment, there is the all-important factor that the defenders were well aware that both the premises occupied by the pursuer were located in areas where vandalism was likely to take place ... In these circumstances ... it seems to me that it would be entirely in accordance with principle to hold that in such circumstances there was a general duty on owners or occupiers of property, particularly property of the tenement type, where they choose to leave it vacant for any material length of time, to take reasonable care to see that it was proof against the kind of vandalism which was calculated to affect adjoining property.'

The duty thus stated is, of course, extremely wide, but quite apart from the fact that the case is not binding on this court, I find some difficulty in following it. In the first place, it was decided before *Lamb*'s case, with which, as I think, it is in conflict. Moreover, perhaps somewhat surprisingly, it seems to have been decided without reference to all the *Dorset Yacht* case. Quite apart from this, however, the facts were very different. The defenders had actually altered the state of their adjoining premises in a way which had rendered the pursuer's premises more vulnerable than they would normally have been; they had done damage to the pursuer's premises which had not been properly repaired, and the fire and water damage, albeit created by trespassers, would (at any rate in English law) have prima facie given rise to a liability in nuisance in any event: see *Sedleigh-Denfield v O'Callaghan (Trustees for St Joseph's Society for Foreign Mission)* [1940] 3 All ER 349, [1940] AC 880. Furthermore, it has to be borne in mind that the application was, effectively, a striking-out application and the only question which the court had to decide was whether the case was sufficiently arguable to justify its going to trial. This indeed appears a little later in Lord Wylie's judgment, where he said (1978 SLT 17 at 19):

'Notwithstanding two substantial amendments, counsel for the pursuer did not seek to argue more than that enough had been averred to justify an inquiry into the facts and in my view the pleadings qualify for that.'

In the circumstances, therefore, I do not find in this case any substantial support for the wide proposition for which counsel for the respondents contends and on which the deputy judge appears to have relied. There are, of course, circumstances where, without any special relation between the defendant and the third party tortfeasor, a duty of care in relation to the acts of independent third parties may arise as a result of a relationship between the plaintiff and the defendant. Such a duty may be and frequently is assumed as a matter of contract: see for instance *Stansbie v Troman* [1948] 1 All ER 599, [1948] 2 KB 48, where the duty of care was an implied term of the defendant's engagement to decorate the plaintiff's house.

There are, however, no such circumstances that I can see in this case. Counsel for the respondents, in a final attempt to bring himself within the *Dorset Yacht* case, has submitted that there was indeed in this case the necessary special relationship arising from control and he arrives at this, as I understand his submission, by this process. A lock on the front door of no 144 would make entry by trespassers more difficult. The appellants could have fitted such a lock. If they had done, trespassers could not have entered without breaking the lock. Therefore the thieves who entered the respondents' premises could not have so entered without breaking the appellants' lock. Therefore the thieves were under the appellants' 'control'. The proposition has only to be thus stated to be seen to be fallacious and would ultimately lead to the further proposition that the borstal boys in the *Dorset Yacht* case were under the control of the yacht company because the yacht could have been made more secure against theft than in fact it was.

Speaking for myself, I am unable to see here any circumstances from which there could properly be inferred any duty on the appellants so to protect their own premises as to prevent trespassers from entering the respondents' premises beyond the fact that such entry was, as it plainly was, a foreseeable possibility. In my judgment that is not, by

itself, sufficient to raise the duty for which the respondent contends. Indeed the contrary
a position would, I think, lead to the most startling and far-reaching consequences. Not
only would every owner of a semi-detached or terrace house have a duty to every
adjoining owner to secure his premises against entry but the extent of the duty would
depend on the use that the adjoining owner chose to make of his premises. The more
valuable the contents, the greater the temptation and the greater the risk of entry. The
greater the risk of entry, the higher the standard of reasonable care. In fairness to the
b deputy judge he was, I think, put in a difficult position by a concession made in the court
below and to which he refers in his judgment, for it was, as I understand it, conceded
that if the thieves had entered the respondents' storeroom through the windows
overlooking the light well on the appellants' premises or through a door hypothetically
supposed to open onto that light well, the appellants would have been liable. If that
concession stood, then for my part I would find it difficult to say that the mere fact that
c entry was effected in a different and perhaps more unusual way could render the damage
too remote; and with that concession before him I regard it as not altogether surprising
that the deputy judge reached the conclusion that he did. Counsel for the appellants,
however, makes (and in my judgment rightly makes) no such concession in this court.
    For the reasons which I have endeavoured to state, I too would allow this appeal.

d **ROBERT GOFF LJ.** The facts of the present case, and the submissions of counsel,
have been set out by Waller LJ in his judgment; and I need not repeat them. The crucial
question in the case, as it seems to me, is whether an occupier of property owes a duty of
care to owners and users of neighbouring property to prevent third persons from entering
his property who might thereby obtain access to the neighbouring property and there
commit theft.
e   Nowadays, following the statement of principle by Lord Wilberforce in *Anns v Merton
London BC* [1977] 2 All ER 492 at 498, [1978] AC 728 at 751–752, the question has to be
approached in two stages:

      'First one has to ask whether, as between the alleged wrongdoer and the person
      who has suffered damage there is a sufficient relationship of proximity or
f   neighbourhood such that, in the reasonable contemplation of the former, carelessness
      on his part may be likely to cause damage to the latter, in which case a prima facie
      duty of care arises. Secondly, if the first question is answered affirmatively, it is
      necessary to consider whether there are any considerations which ought to negative,
      or to reduce or limit the scope of the duty or the class of person to whom it is owed
      or the damages to which a breach of it may give rise . . .'

g   There may well be cases in which it can be said that the occupier of property can
reasonably foresee that, if he leaves his property unprotected, thieves may enter and
thereby gain access to neighbouring property. For example, it may be notorious that
burglars are operating in a certain part of a town; and an occupier of premises may
reasonably foresee that, if he goes away for a weekend and leaves his house unprotected
(perhaps if it is empty or, to take an example considered in argument, if he always leaves
h a window open for his cat) a burglar may enter and thereby work unmolested over the
weekend to gain access to the house next door where there is a valuable collection of
pictures. Even so, in my judgment, there are considerations in such circumstances which
ought to negative the broad duty of care for which the respondents' counsel contended.
    The vital feature in the type of case under consideration is, as I see it, that the
respondents are seeking to render the appellants liable in negligence for the wrongdoing
j of a third party. Now there may indeed be circumstances where a person may be liable
for a third party's wrongdoing. He may of course be liable in contract (see *Stansbie v
Troman* [1948] 1 All ER 599, [1948] 2 KB 48); he may be liable under the Occupiers'
Liability Act 1959, for example, where he invites a crowd of persons onto his land and
part of his premises, designed to control the crowd, are unfit for that purpose and
collapse, with the result that the plaintiff is injured (see *Hosie v Arbroath Football Club Ltd*

1978 SLT 122); he may be liable in nuisance if he causes or permits persons to gather on his land, and they impair his neighbour's enjoyment of his land (cf *A-G v Corke* [1933] Ch 89, [1932] All ER Rep 711, though that case was expressed to be decided on the principle in *Rylands v Fletcher* (1868) LR 3 HL 330, [1861–73] All ER Rep 1); and he may be vicariously liable for the third party's wrongdoing. He may even be liable in negligence, when the wrongdoer is a person who, by virtue of a special relationship, is under his control: see *Home Office v Dorset Yacht Co Ltd* [1970] 2 All ER 294, [1970] AC 1004. Speaking for myself, I do not rule out the possibility that there are other circumstances in which a person may be liable in negligence for the wrongdoing of a third party. This is a matter which this court considered recently in *Paterson Zochonis & Co Ltd v Merfarken Packaging Ltd* [1983] FSR 273, and which I need not therefore dwell on in this judgment. In particular, I have in mind certain cases where the defendant presents the wrongdoer with the means to commit the wrong, in circumstances where it is obvious or very likely that he will do so, eg where he hands over a car to be driven by a person who is drunk, or plainly incompetent, who then runs over the plaintiff (cf *Ontario Hospital Services Commission v Borsoski* (1974) 54 DLR (3d) 339). But such cases are very different from the present case, where the allegation is that the appellants failed to exercise reasonable care to prevent a third party from causing damage to the respondents. In *Smith v Leurs* (1945) 70 CLR 256 at 261–262, in a passage which was cited with approval in *Home Office v Dorset Yacht Co Ltd*, Dixon J said: 'The general rule is that one man is under no duty of controlling another to prevent his doing damage to a third. There are, however, special relations which are the source of a duty of this nature.'

It is of course true that in the present case the respondents do not allege that the appellants should have controlled the thieves who broke into their storeroom. But they do allege that the appellants should have exercised reasonable care to prevent them from gaining access through their own premises; and in my judgment the statement of principle by Dixon J is equally apposite in such a case. I know of no case where it has been held, in the absence of a special relationship, that the defendant was liable in negligence for having failed to prevent a third party from wrongfully causing damage to the plaintiff. If the Scottish case of *Evans v Glasgow DC* 1978 SLT 17 is to be understood as reaching any such conclusion, then I (associating myself with the observations of Oliver LJ on that case) would, with all respect, not be prepared to follow it. Indeed, the consequences of accepting the respondents' submission in the present case are so startling, that I have no hesitation in rejecting the suggestion that there is a duty of care on occupiers of property to prevent persons from entering their property who might thereby obtain access to neighbouring property. Is every occupier of a terraced house under a duty to his neighbours to shut his windows or lock his door when he goes out, or to keep access to his cellars secure, or even to remove his fire escape, at the risk of being held liable in damages if thieves thereby obtain access to his own house and thence to his neighbour's house? I cannot think that the law imposes any such duty.

For these reasons, I too would allow the appeal.

Appeal allowed. Leave to appeal to the House of Lords refused.

Solicitors: *Barlow Lyde & Gilbert* (for the appellants); *David Alterman & Sewell* (for the respondents).

Sophie Craven   Barrister.

a # Secretary of State for Social Services v S and another

COURT OF APPEAL, CIVIL DIVISION
WALLER, FOX AND MAY LJJ
5, 6 MAY 1983

b

Social security – Guardian's allowance – Persons entitled to allowance – Parent of child not entitled to allowance – Parent – Illegitimate child adopted by grandmother – Child subsequently looked after by natural mother on death of grandmother – Natural mother claiming guardian's allowance – Whether natural mother ceasing to be a 'parent' once child adopted – Whether natural mother entitled to guardian's allowance – Social Security Act 1975, s 38(1)(2)(6) –
c *Children Act 1975, Sch 1, para 3(2)(5).*

In 1965 the claimant gave birth to an illegitimate child, which was legally adopted and looked after by the claimant's mother (the grandmother) until the grandmother died in May 1980. The child then went to live with the claimant, who applied for a guardian's allowance under s 38(1)*a* of the Social Security Act 1975. The insurance officer took the
d view that the claimant, being the child's natural mother, was a 'parent' of the child and that her claim was therefore barred by s 38(6)*b* of the Social Security Act, which provided that no person was entitled to a guardian's allowance in respect of a child 'of which he or she is the parent'. The claimant appealed unsuccessfully to a national insurance tribunal and then to the Social Security Commissioners, contending that she was not a 'parent' of the child for the purposes of s 38(6) because (i) once the child had been adopted by the
e grandmother the child was, by virtue of para 3(2)*c* of Sch 1 to the Children Act 1975, to be treated in law as if he was the grandmother's child, and (ii) although the Children Act was enacted after the Social Security Act nevertheless s 38(6) was to be construed in the light of para 3(2) since para 3(5) of Sch 1 to the Children Act stipulated that para 3 applied to the construction of enactments passed before the adoption 'subject to any contrary indication'. The commissioners held that s 38 of the Social Security Act drew an inherent
f distinction between adoptive and natural parents, which showed a 'contrary indication' so that para 3(2) did not apply to s 38(6). The commissioners therefore dismissed the claimant's appeal. The Secretary of State appealed to the Court of Appeal.

Held – On its true construction, s 38 of the Social Security Act 1975 was concerned with the circumstances in which a guardian's allowance could be paid to anyone who cared for
g a child after the person who had previously cared for the child had died, rather than with differentiating between natural and adoptive parents, they being merely two of the categories of persons whose death while caring for children meant that a guardian's allowance became payable to someone else if the requirements of s 38 were satisfied. Accordingly, s 38 did not indicate a 'contrary indication' that para 3 of Sch 1 to the Children Act 1975 was not to apply in construing s 38, and so construing s 38(6) in the
h light of para 3(2) the claimant was not a 'parent' for the purposes of s 38(6). She was therefore entitled to a guardian's allowance and the Secretary of State's appeal would accordingly be allowed (see p 177 *b c* and *f* and p 178 *a* to *h*, post).

Notes
For the status of an adopted child, see 24 Halsbury's Laws (4th edn) paras 549, 630.
j For the Social Security Act 1975, s 38, see 45 Halsbury's Statutes (3rd edn) 1126.
For the Children Act 1975, Sch 1, para 3, see ibid 753.

---

a   Section 38(1) is set out at p 174 *j* to p 175 *a*, post
b   Section 38(6), so far as material, is set out at p 175 *d e*, post
c   Paragraph 3, so far as material, is set out at p 175 *f*, post

As from a day to be appointed para 3(2) and (5) of Sch 1 to the 1975 Act is to be replaced
by s 39(2) and (6)(a) of the Adoption Act 1976.   *a*

Appeal
The Secretary of State for Social Services appealed, under s 14 of the Social Security Act
1980, against a decision of a tribunal of Social Security Commissioners (I O Griffiths QC
and M J Goodman, J G Monroe dissenting), dated 16 July 1982, whereby they dismissed
an appeal by the first respondent, Mrs S, against a decision of a local tribunal, sitting at   *b*
Liverpool on 4 September 1980, which upheld a decision by the second respondent, the
insurance officer, on 24 July 1980, that the first respondent was not entitled to be paid a
guardian's allowance in respect of a child known as C P W. The facts are set out in the
judgment of May LJ.

Simon D Brown for the Secretary of State.
David Latham for the second respondent.   *c*
The first respondent did not appear.

MAY LJ (delivering the first judgment at the invitation of Waller LJ). This is an appeal
from a majority decision of the Social Security Commissioners of 16 July 1982 concerning
the proper construction of s 38(6) of the Social Security Act 1975, in the light of the   *d*
provisions contained in para 3(2) and (5) of Sch 1 to the Children Act 1975. The appeal is
brought under s 14 of the Social Security Act 1980. The appropriate court under s 14,
and as specified by the commissioners is, by virtue of s 14(4), the Court of Appeal.
Although not a party to the proceedings below, the Secretary of State is entitled to appeal
by virtue of the provisions of s 14(3)(c) of the 1980 Act.
     The background facts can be briefly stated. On 19 July 1965 the claimant (the first   *e*
respondent to this appeal but who, for reasons which will become apparent, has taken no
part in the hearing of it) bore a son who has been referred to throughout the proceedings
by his initials, C P W. She was at that time, and still remains, married, but her husband
is not the natural father of the boy.
     On 19 April 1972 an adoption order was made in the magistrates' court in respect of
the child, in favour of the claimant's mother, the boy's grandmother. Unfortunately the   *f*
grandmother, the adoptive parent, died on 15 May 1980. Thereupon the claimant and
her husband immediately took the boy to live with them and their other children and
have since wholly maintained him.
     On 21 May 1980 the claimant claimed the social security benefit known as 'guardian's
allowance' in respect of the child C P W under s 38 of the Social Security Act 1975, which
I shall go into in more detail later.   *g*
     On 24 July 1980 the insurance officer, the second respondent to this appeal, decided
that the claimant was not entitled to a guardian's allowance. The claimant appealed to
the local tribunal but the tribunal upheld the insurance officer's decision and dismissed
the mother's appeal on 4 September 1980. The matter was then taken on appeal to the
commissioners and they gave their majority decision on 16 July 1982, upholding the
previous decisions of the local tribunal and the insurance officer. It is from that decision   *h*
that the Secretary of State now brings this appeal, leave having been granted by the
commissioners on 19 October 1982.
     The argument put before us on behalf of the Secretary of State was, to all intents and
purposes, the same as that put forward on behalf of the claimant before the commissioners
in July 1982. It was the argument which found favour with the commissioner, Mr
Monroe, who gave the minority judgment. He was in favour of allowing the appeal. The   *j*
relevant statutory provisions and the argument now need detailed consideration.
     The entitlement to guardian's allowance arises under s 38 of the Social Security Act
1975. Subsection (1) provides:

      'Subject to the provisions of this Act (and in particular to those of section 43
      imposing limitations on payment of benefit in respect of children), a person shall be

a
entitled to a guardian's allowance at the weekly rate specified in relation thereto in
Schedule 4, Part III, paragraph 4, in respect of a child where he is entitled to child
benefit in respect of that child and the circumstances are any of those specified in
subsection (2) below.'

Subsection (2) lists circumstances in which the entitlement to guardian's allowance
arises, subject to the other provisions in sub-s (1) being satisfied. In the present case we
are concerned only with the last few words of sub-s (1), namely those referring to the
b
circumstances specified in sub-s (2). It is not disputed that, subject to the matters with
which I shall deal, the present claimant otherwise comes within the provisions of sub-s
(1).

By s 38(4) the Secretary of State is given power to make regulations, among other
things, to modify the circumstances set out in sub-s (2) 'in relation to cases in which a
child has been adopted or is illegitimate, or the marriage of a child's parents has been
c
terminated by divorce . . .' Such regulations have been made. They are the Social Security
(Guardian's Allowances) Regulations 1975, SI 1975/515. By reg 2(b) it is provided that
the circumstances specified in s 38(2) of the Social Security Act 1975 are to be modified
in the case of an adopted child in this respect, that 'in the case of a child adopted by one
person only, as if the following circumstances were substituted for those in that
subsection, namely that that person is dead'.
d
As is apparent from the brief facts which I have outlined, this child C P W was adopted
by one person only, that person unfortunately is now dead, and accordingly the
circumstances in s 38(2), as modified by reg 2(b), obtain. Up to this point, therefore,
prima facie this claimant, so the argument runs, is entitled to a guardian's allowance.

But the contrary argument originates in s 38(6) which provides: 'No person shall be
entitled to a guardian's allowance in respect of a child of which he or she is the parent.'
e
The argument against the claimant's entitlement to guardian's allowance is obvious on
the wording of that subsection. It is to this effect: this claimant is the natural parent of
the child, and therefore she is not entitled to a guardian's allowance.

The argument raised against that contention is based on the provisions of para 3 of Sch
1 to the Children Act 1975. That was an Act which, among a substantial number of other
matters, dealt fully with the question of the adoption of children. Part II of Sch 1
f
contained provisions relating to the consequences of adoption orders in various respects.
By para 3(2) of Sch 1, it was provided that 'An adopted child shall be treated in law as if
he were not the child of any person other than the adopters or adopter', and by para 3(5):

'Subject to the provisions of this Part, this paragraph applies for the construction
of enactments or instruments passed or made before the adoption or later, and so
g
applies subject to any contrary indication.'

Thus the argument on behalf of the Secretary of State, repeating the argument of the
claimant below, in order to rebut the prima facie disentitlement to guardian's allowance
arising by virtue of s 38(6) of the Social Security Act 1975 is that, after the adoption by
the claimant's mother of the child, the latter was to be treated, by virtue of the provisions
of Sch 1 to the Children Act 1975, as if in law he were not the child of anyone except his
h
adopter, that is to say his grandmother, the claimant's mother. The relationship of parent
and child is, it is contended, a mutual one and therefore it necessarily follows from those
provisions that, in law and in respect of the construction of any enactment or instrument,
after the adoption the child in question had no parent except the adopter, i e the claimant's
mother, who has since died. Thus, when one construes s 38(6) the reference there to
'parent' in the circumstances of the present case, having regard to the provisions of the
j
Children Act 1975, does not include the present claimant and consequently, contrary to
the views taken by the tribunal below, she is entitled to a guardian's allowance in respect
of this child. That contention, it is submitted, is reinforced by the provisions of s 8(3)(a)(i)
of the Children Act 1975, which is in these terms:

'The making of the order [i e an adoption order] operates to extinguish—(a) any
parental right or duty relating to the child which—(i) is vested in a person (not

being one of the adopters) who was the parent or guardian of the child immediately before the making of the order . . .'

The submission emphasises the word 'was' in that provisions and suggests that the statute there clearly contemplates what counsel described as the concept of the extinct parent; that is to say that the making of an adoption order removes the natural parent from the original parent/child relationship. It is suggested also that the contention for which the Secretary of State contends is supported by the fact that, by s 108 of and Sch 4 to the Children Act 1975, s 24(3)(c) of the Child Benefit Act 1975 has been repealed: it is submitted that it was repealed as being superfluous.

Section 24(3) of the Child Benefit Act 1975, before its repeal, provided:

'References in this Act to a parent, father or mother of a child shall be construed . . . (c) as if a child that has been adopted in pursuance of an adoption order made in the United Kingdom, any of the Channel Islands or the Isle of Man, or by an overseas adoption within the meaning of section 4 of the Adoption Act 1968, were the child of the adopter and not of any person who (not being the adopter) was its parent at the time of the adoption.'

I have said that the contention is that, having regard to the provisions of para 3 of Sch 1 to the Children Act 1975, that provision in the Child Benefit Act 1975 was superfluous and it was for that reason that the section was repealed, unlike other provisions of the Social Security Act 1975 which were maintained in force.

Thus, having reached this point, so the argument proceeds, one is merely thrown back to see whether there is any 'contrary indication' in any of the relevant statutory provisions that s 38(6) of the Social Security Act 1975 is not to be construed in accordance with the provisions of para 3(2) and (5) of Sch 1.

The argument proceeds that one would in truth expect to find any contrary indication, if contrary indication there be, in the later of the two Acts passed in 1975, namely in the Children Act itself. When one looks through that Act for any such contrary indication, one finds none, so it is said; indeed one finds material to support the construction for which the Secretary of State contends, namely support in this way, that by para 7 of Sch 1 it is specifically provided in sub-paras (3), (4) and (5) that the provisions of para 3 are not to apply to certain sections of the Social Security Act 1975. Those sections there specified do not include s 38, and this, it is suggested, provides strong support for the contention that there is no contrary indication in the later Children Act 1975 against the construction which para 3 of the Schedule would otherwise require one to employ in relation to adopted children.

As I have said, that argument was one which received the support of the judgment of the single commissioner who was in the minority below. The other two commissioners in their judgment, taking it as shortly as I can, proceeded on this basis: in relation to any argument based on s 8(3) of the Children Act 1975 they took the view that that section went no further than similar provisions in earlier legislation, and in para 9 of their judgment they expressed their opinion that the extinguishment of the rights and duties of a parent in no way severs the natural relationship that exists between mother and child.

Put simply in that fashion, as a bald statement, it is no doubt correct, but the question which presently arises for decision is not that question. The question which arises in the course of this appeal is what is: the proper view in law of the effect of para 3(2) and (5) of Sch 1 to the Children Act 1975 on s 38(6) of the Social Security Act 1975.

In para 11 of their judgment the commissioners were not prepared to accept what I have described as the 'mutuality' of the relationship between parent and child. But the other side of the coin which makes nobody but the adopter the parent of the child, is one which makes the child the child of nobody else but the adoptive parents. For my part, with all respect to the commissioners, I am satisfied that there must be that mutuality of relationship and one must approach legislation relating to parent and child from that viewpoint. Consequently if, after an adoption, a child has in law to be treated as if the

child is no longer a child of anyone except the adopter, it can only follow that no one can
a   be treated as the parent of that child, after the adoption, except the person adopting him
or her.

Having considered the matter, counsel for the respondent insurance officer was
minded to accept that there was the mutuality to which I have referred, that there was
validity in the 'other side of the coin' argument and felt unable to support the view of
the majority of the commissioners on this point.

b   The commissioners proceeded to say that s 24(3)(c) of the Child Benefit Act 1975 was
more explicit than the provisions of paras 3(2) and (5) of Sch 1 to the Children Act 1975
and that consequently the repeal of the former could not be viewed merely as the
removal of superfluous matter, which, as I have said, is the argument which suggested
that that repeal supported the contention of the Secretary of State in this appeal. Again,
with respect to the commissioners, in my judgment the two provisions in effect, on their
c   proper construction, achieve exactly the same result and I am much more attracted by
the argument that the repeal was to remove superfluous matter than that the repeal was
to modify the existing situation which had been produced only a short while before by
the provisions of s 24(3)(c) of the Child Benefit Act 1975.

The judgment of the majority of the commissioners then proceeded to what is perhaps
the most important aspect of this case. In para 12 of their judgment they said that the
d   whole tenor of the legislation embodied in s 38 of the Social Security Act 1975 and in the
regulations to which I have referred 'is such as to draw a clear distinction between
adoptive parents and natural parents' on the one hand and 'not to substitute the one for
the other, or to equate the one with the other'. Thus it was their view that the whole
legislative scheme and its working did in itself show a clear contrary indication so as to
prevent the application of para 3(5) of Sch 1 to the Children Act 1975 to s 38(6) of the
e   Social Security Act 1975. It was this argument which was developed by counsel for the
respondent insurance officer, and I will deal with it shortly hereafter.

Before doing so, however, it is right to say that I understood counsel to accept the
correctness of the analysis of the statutory position and the construction of the complicated
interlocking subsections and regulations, which I have outlined as being the argument
on behalf of the Secretary of State on this appeal. The only point, as I understand it, at
f   which counsel for the insurance officer diverged from the Secretary of State was in his
contention that there was this real contrary indication embodied within s 38 of the Social
Security Act 1975.

For my part, subject to consideration of counsel's argument, I, too, take the view that
the result of such analysis of the relevant provisions is clear beyond a peradventure and
unless one could say and draw out of s 38 of the Social Security Act 1975 such a contrary
g   indication, my judgment would be that this appeal should succeed and that the claimant
is entitled to the guardian's allowance.

It therefore becomes necessary to consider carefully the argument to which I have
referred, which is said to raise the contrary contention. As I understood the argument, it
was to this effect. Section 38 of the Social Security Act 1975 contains a full code providing
for the circumstances in which a person becomes entitled to a guardian's allowance,
h   inherent in which is a clear distinction between natural parents on the one hand and
adoptive parents on the other. The fact that the code relating to guardian's allowance
contains such a distinction, that such a distinction is inherent in it is, it is contended,
itself a clear indication against the application of para 3(2) and (5) of Sch 1 to the Children
Act 1975. The argument proceeds in this way. When one looks at s 38(6) it is quite
apparent that it is empty of effect, that it has nothing to bite on if one is considering
j   whether the qualifying circumstances in s 38(2) are satisfied in the case of a child who
has not been adopted, and thus sub-s (6) can only have effect, it is submitted, where one
has to consider the case of a child who has been adopted. In such circumstances, the
'parent' referred to in sub-s (6) cannot include an adoptive parent. The purpose of sub-s
(6) in such circumstances, counsel for the insurance officer submits, is quite clearly to
prevent a natural parent from being entitled to guardian's allowance when a child has
been adopted and when the circumstances laid down in the regulations made under sub-

s (4) modifying the circumstances in sub-s (2) have been satisfied. It should be noted, counsel says in passing, that the power to make regulations under sub-s (4) does not *a* include any power to modify sub-s (6). Thus, suggests counsel, there is demonstrated a clear intent that the parent referred to in sub-s (6) must mean only a natural parent. This is inherent in the code laid down by s 38 which, in the way I have sought briefly to indicate, draws a distinction between natural and adoptive parents and thus in itself shows the clear indication to the contrary to which para 3(5) of Sch 1 to the Children Act 1975 refers. *b*

With all respect to counsel for the insurance officer, in my judgment the fallacy behind his argument is that it in truth starts from the express or implicit premise that s 38 of the Social Security Act 1975 is concerned only with, and only differentiates between, two classes of children, i e children who have not been adopted on the one hand, and children who have been adopted on the other. If you start from that premise, it is not difficult to demonstrate that s 38 has inherent within it a distinction between natural and adoptive *c* parents. But in my judgment s 38 is not concerned only with children who can be put into one or other of those two classes. It is not to be construed as if all children must be put into one or other of them. I think that s 38 is concerned, in short, with children who, as a result of the death of the person or persons who had previously looked after them, are now being looked after by, in effect, a stranger. The persons who one would normally expect to have been looking after the child in the majority of cases, of course, would be *d* the child's natural parents; but in other situations it may be that those looking after the child prior to the unfortunate deaths were either the child's adoptive parents or parent, or an illegitimate parent, or a parent who is divorced and has the custody, care and control of the child to the exclusion of the other parent. I take the view that s 38 is concerned with the circumstances in which a guardian's allowance comes to be payable to the stranger who assumes the care of the child after the death or deaths of the person *e* who previously cared for that child and who comes within the categories to which I have referred (natural, adoptive, illegitimate or divorced) provided that the circumstances specified in s 38(2) are satisfied, either unmodified, or alternatively, modified by the regulations to which I have referred.

By way of example it seems to me quite clear that the circumstances in s 38(2) are in no way apt to deal with a child who is being looked after by a single adoptive parent, or a *f* single parent who is divorced. The position of those two classes of person looking after a child is quite clearly clarified by the relevant regulations, to which I need not refer in detail. Viewed in this way, although s 38 of the Social Security Act 1975 may indeed contain a code (if that is the proper description) for ascertaining those who are entitled to receive a guardian's allowance, I do not think that it is one which contains the inherent distinction between natural parents on the one hand and adoptive parents on the other; *g* these are merely two of the categories of adults caring for children on whose death any guardian's allowance made thereafter becomes payable to a stranger.

I therefore take the view that there is no such contrary indication as that contended for. As I have indicated, in my judgment the argument, up to the suggested emergence of a contrary indication, on the construction of the relevant statutory provisions put forward on behalf of the appellant Secretary of State, is unanswerable. In those *h* circumstances I would allow this appeal.

FOX LJ. For the reasons which May LJ has given, I, too, would allow the appeal.

WALLER LJ. I also agree.

Appeal allowed. *j*

Solicitors: *Solicitor to the Department of Health and Social Security; Treasury Solicitor.*

Sophie Craven   Barrister.

a

Newland v Boardwell
MacDonald v Platt

COURT OF APPEAL, CIVIL DIVISION
CUMMING-BRUCE LJ AND SIR DENYS BUCKLEY
19 MAY, 1 JULY 1983

b

County court – Costs – Small claims procedure – Plaintiff making claim within limits of small claims procedure – Defendant admitting negligence but denying liability – Whether defence 'unreasonable' – Whether plaintiff's solicitor's charges incurred through defendant's unreasonable conduct – Whether plaintiff entitled to costs – CCR 1936 Ord 19, r 1(4)(11).

c

In two separate county court actions each plaintiff made a claim in negligence for damages and each defendant filed a defence admitting negligence but denying liability for the loss suffered by the plaintiff. Because the amounts claimed were within the limits for the small claim procedure the registrar automatically referred the claims to arbitration pursuant to CCR 1936, Ord 19, r 1(4)[a]. Order 19, r 1(11)[b] provided that solicitors' charges arising from the arbitration were not normally to be allowed between party and party but r 1(11)(c) allowed such costs as the arbitrator certified had been incurred through the unreasonable conduct of the opposite party to the proceedings. Each plaintiff accepted the sum which each defendant paid into court in full settlement of the actions and the registrar then certified and awarded costs to the plaintiffs pursuant to Ord 19, r 1(11)(c) after deciding that the defendants had filed the defences to take advantage of the no-costs rule (which would have applied if the issue of the quantum of damages had been arbitrated) instead of allowing judgment to be entered against them and having damages assessed at a separate hearing for which they would have been liable to pay the costs. Each defendant appealed unsuccessfully to the judge and then appealed to the Court of Appeal against the award of costs.

f

Held – The defence pleaded by the defendants had put liability at issue notwithstanding that they had no defence on liability and no real intention of disputing liability except as to quantum. That was a device calculated to get the protection of the no-costs rule under CCR 1936 Ord 19, r 1(11) and as such involved a misuse of the pleading process which justified a certificate of unreasonableness under Ord 19, r 1(11)(c). However, the solicitors' charges incurred between the date of the summons and the filing of the defence were not costs incurred 'through', ie in consequence of, the unreasonable conduct of the defendants. Furthermore, on the filing of the defence it had been open to the plaintiffs, who were aware of their position under the Ord 19, r 1(4) procedure, to terminate their solicitors' retainers, and charges incurred thereafter were therefore the consequence of their failure to do that and not of the defendants' unreasonable conduct. It followed that the exception to the no-costs rule contained in Ord 19, r 1(11)(c) did not apply to those subsequent charges, and the appeals would accordingly be allowed to that extent (see p 184 c to p 185 b, post).

Notes

For the discretion of a county court as to costs, see 10 Halsbury's Laws (4th edn) para 602, and for cases on the subject, see 13 Digest (Reissue) 494–498, 4087–4123.

j   As from 1 September 1982 CCR 1936 Ord 19, r 1(4) and (19) was replaced by CCR 1981 Ord 19, rr 2(3) and 6.

---

a   Rule 1(4), so far as material, is set out at p 181 a, post
b   Rule 1(11), so far as material, provides: 'No solicitor's charge shall be allowed as between party and party in respect of any proceedings referred to arbitration under Order 19, Rule 1(4), except for . . . (c) such costs as are certified by the arbitrator to have been incurred through the unreasonable conduct of the opposite party in relation to the proceedings or the claim therein.'

Cases cited

Meyer v Leanse [1958] 3 All ER 213, [1958] 2 QB 371, CA.
Pepper v Healey [1982] RTR 411, CA.
Rankine v Garton Sons & Co Ltd [1979] 2 All ER 1185, CA.

Appeals

Newland v Boardwell

The defendant, K Boardwell, appealed from the judgment of his Honour Judge Edward Jones sitting in Liverpool County Court, dated 18 June 1982, dismissing his appeal from the order of Mr Registrar Wilkinson dated 25 November 1981 whereby the defendant was ordered to pay the costs of the plaintiff, Mrs Jean Newland, to be taxed on new scale 1. The facts are set out in the judgment of the court.

MacDonald v Platt

The defendant, Mrs Sonja Platt, appealed from the judgment of his Honour Judge Edward Jones sitting in Liverpool County Court dated 18 June 1982, dismissing her appeal from the order of Mr Registrar Wilkinson dated 22 January 1982 whereby the defendant was ordered to pay the costs of the plaintiff, Kenneth Alfred Macdonald, assessed at £70 plus plaint fee of £32·00. The facts are set out in the judgment of the court.

Michael Wright QC and John Phipps for both defendants.
T R A King for both plaintiffs.

Cur adv vult

1 July. The following judgment of the court was delivered.

CUMMING-BRUCE LJ. These two appeals involve identical questions. Both cases were originally determined by Mr Registrar Wilkinson in the Liverpool County Court and on appeal by his Honour Judge Edward Jones, who heard the two appeals together and delivered a single judgment in both of them. They raise what appear to be questions of general interest and some importance. It will be convenient to deal with them in relation to the facts in Newland v Boardwell.

In May 1981 a collision occurred between a motor vehicle owned and driven by the plaintiff and another driven by the defendant. The plaintiff sued the defendant for damages in the county court. Her particulars of claim were in these terms:

'1. On the 14th may 1981 in Bedford Road at its junction with Stuart Road a collision occurred between a motor vehicle owned and driven by the Plaintiff and a motor vehicle driven by the Defendant and caused by the negligence of the Defendant.

2. The Defendant has stated that liability will not be in issue.

3. By reason of the premises the Plaintiff, who is aged about 45 years, suffered injury loss and damage and was deprived of the use and enjoyment of his [sic] said vehicle and suffered inconvenience thereby.

PARTICULARS OF INJURY

Shock and general shaking up.

PARTICULARS OF SPECIAL DAMAGE

Estimated cost of repairs   £296·07
And the Plaintiff claims damages in all not exceeding £500·00.'

The effect of that limitation on the amount of damages claimed was to bring the case within the scope of CCR 1936 Ord 19, r 1(4) which, so far as relevant, provides:

'Any proceedings in which the sum claimed or amount involved does not exceed
£500 shall stand referred for arbitration by the registrar upon the receipt by the
court of a defence of the claim . . .'

On 12 September 1981 the registrar issued a summons addressed to the defendant
enclosing a copy of the plaintiff's particulars of claim, stating that the costs already
accrued were court fee £28 and solicitors' charge £21, and summoning the defendant to
appear at the court office on 22 September 1981, when the registrar would consider
giving directions for securing the determination of the action. On 18 September the
defendant gave notice to the plaintiff and to her solicitors that he had paid into court the
sum of £350 in satisfaction of the plaintiff's claim. On 22 September before the pre-trial
review fixed for that day the defendant filed the following defence:

'1. The defendant admits paragraph 1 of the Particulars of Claim.

2. For the purpose of this action alone, the Defendant admits that he was
negligent.

3. The injuries, loss and damage alleged are not admitted.'

As a result, the proceedings were automatically referred to arbitration under CCR
1936 Ord 19, r 1(4). Mr Registrar Wilkinson gave directions for discovery, inspection
and expert witnesses and ordered the action to be set down for arbitration before a
registrar.

Before the action commenced the defendant's insurers had intimated to the plaintiff
or her advisers in open correspondence that liability was not in issue and that they would
meet any reasonable claim; but the effect of the defence, para 3, was to put liability in
issue notwithstanding the admission of negligence.

On 5 October the plaintiff's solicitors filed her list of documents, limited to special
damage, comprising only an estimate for motor vehicle repairs of £257·10 plus value
added tax. On 20 October the plaintiff gave notice of acceptance of the sum paid into
court in full satisfaction of her claim. On 25 November the registrar, after hearing
solicitors for both parties, made an order for costs (as drawn up) as follows:

'There be no order for costs save that the plaintiff's costs of this action be taxed on
new scale 1.'

It is, however, common ground that that order was wrongly drawn up. It appears clearly
from the written reasons of the registrar that he gave a certificate in favour of the plaintiff
under CCR 1936 Ord 19, r 1(11)(c) and ordered that her costs of the action taxed under
scale 1 should be paid by the defendant by reason of the defendant's unreasonable conduct
in defending the action.

Counsel for the plaintiff contended before the registrar that the defendant had no
other reason for refusing to submit to interlocutory judgment than the avoidance of the
payment of the plaintiff's costs. He argued that, if the registrar did not give a certificate
of unreasonableness, the plaintiff would have to bear her own solicitors' costs out of the
damages which she had recovered. Counsel for the defendant contended that the
defendant had every right to file a defence in order to preserve his position on the
assessment of damages.

It appears from the registrar's written reasons that counsel for the defendant conceded
in argument that the defendant had never sought to argue that no damage followed from
his negligence: he merely wanted to be heard on quantum. The registrar said that he
could think of no reason (other than costs) why the defendant did not consent to
interlocutory judgment with damages to be assessed, in which case he would have been
entitled to call witnesses and to cross-examine the plaintiff's witnesses as to the extent of
the damage. The registrar said:

'The small claims jurisdiction of the county court was never intended to operate
as an indemnity charter against the payment of costs for the benefit of insurance
companies in running-down cases . . . It seems to me to be fundamentally wrong to

leave a successful plaintiff (where liability has never been an issue) to pay his own
solicitor out of his own damages. Defendants who file specious defences solely for   *a*
the purpose of seeking the protection of the no-costs rule ought to be flushed out by
a certificate of unreasonableness.'

The defendant applied to the judge to set aside the registrar's award on the grounds
that the matter was subject to the provisions of Ord 19, r 1(11), that the registrar had
been wrong in law in certifying that the defendant had acted unreasonably or alternatively
that he had failed to exercise his discretion judicially. The defendant also submitted that   *b*
it was not unreasonable for the defendant to file a defence admitting negligence but not
admitting the alleged loss and damage.

That application was heard by the county court judge at the same time as the appeal in
the other case now before this court, *MacDonald v Platt*. He delivered a reserved judgment
covering both cases together. I will return to *MacDonald v Platt* later for its facts, but here
it should be stated that the plaintiff in each of the two cases employed a solicitor   *c*
throughout to conduct his or her case, and that in each case the effective defendant was
an insurance company.

The judge more than once in the course of his judgment indicated that what he had to
decide was whether the filing of a defence admitting negligence but putting the existence
of any loss or damage in issue was 'unreasonable' for the purposes of Ord 19, r 1(11) in
circumstances in which (as the judge found in respect of each of the two cases) the   *d*
defendants simply could not contend, and indeed did not contend, that it could ever have
been argued that no damage flowed from this negligence.

We confess that we do not find it easy to discover from his judgment just how the
judge resolved this problem, if indeed he ever did. After saying that on taxation a
registrar could hardly allow the cost of drafting such a defence as was filed in each of
these cases, he observed: *e*

'Hence the filing of a defence for such a purpose would not be proper and I should
have thought would have been regarded as unreasonable. Has it [which we take to
mean the filing of the defence] a wider consequence is, however, the real issue, as
the registrar has undoubtedly held it to have.'

f
He then embarked on a discussion of the effect of the words 'incurred through the
unreasonable conduct of the opposite party' in Ord 19, r 1(11)(c), and expressed the
opinion that no solicitor's charges could be said to have been incurred by either plaintiff
because of the filing of the relevant defence. The judge's view seems to have been that
either plaintiff, when initially retaining a solicitor, would have done so for the conduct
of the action from beginning to end, and would thereby and thereupon have 'incurred'
all the solicitor's charges for the entire conduct of the action before the occurrence of any   *g*
allegedly unreasonable conduct on the part of the defendant.

The judge then said that Ord 19, r 1(11)(c) does not exclude the recovery of costs by
the party in person, and that CCR 1936 Ord 47, r 2 contains special provisions for the
payment of costs to a litigant in person. On this ground it seems that the judge considered
that the registrar had power to award costs to the plaintiffs notwithstanding anything in   *h*
Ord 19, r 1(11), provided that the amount so awarded would not exceed the the amount
which could be awarded to a litigant in person.

In the result the judge declined to set aside either award.

Counsel for the respondents in this court has not sought to support the judge's last-
mentioned ground of decision, and we have heard little or no argument on it. It seems
to us, however, as at present advised, that the judge was mistaken on this point. Neither   *j*
plaintiff was at any time a litigant in person and Ord 47, r 2 has no application to either
of them. Costs may include court fees, disbursements and solicitors' charges. Order 19,
r 1(11) clearly only relates to such costs as consist of solicitors' charges, since it is only
solicitors' charges which are disallowed under the rule. Costs allowed to a litigant in
person under Ord 47, r 2 may be measured by reference to what would have been

a allowed if the work and disbursements to which such costs relate had been done or made
by a solicitor on the litigant's behalf, but they are clearly not solicitors' charges.
    Counsel for the plaintiffs seeks to support the judge's refusal to set aside either of the
awards on the grounds set out in the written reasons of Mr Registrar Wilkinson in
Newland v Boardwell.
    It may be convenient for us at this point to state shortly the facts in *MacDonald v Platt*.
The accident occurred in this case on 6 August 1981. The particulars of claim are dated
b 14 October 1981 and the summons was issued on that date. The costs already accrued
were stated in the summons to be court fee £32 and solicitor's charge £20. The
particulars of claim alleged negligence and that the plaintiff has suffered personal injury,
loss and inconvenience, particularised as severe shock and shaking up. Special damage
was particularised as hiring charges £276 and taxi fares £6. The plaintiff claimed
damages not exceeding £500. The defendant filed a defence on 13 November 1981
c admitting negligence, but not admitting any personal injury, loss or inconvenience, and
pleading that, if (which was not admitted) the plaintiff suffered the same, the said
personal injury, loss and inconvenience was not caused by the defendant's admitted
negligence. The plaintiff disclosed on discovery only an account for hiring charges in a
sum of £276. On 8 December 1981 the defendant paid £375 into court, which was
accepted on 22 December 1981. The pre-trial review took place on 17 November 1981,
d four days after delivery of the defence. On 21 January 1982 Mr Registrar Wilkinson
delivered his written judgment in *Newland v Boardwell* which has been referred to earlier.
On 22 January 1982 he made an order in *MacDonald v Platt* assessing the plaintiff's costs
in that case at £70 plus plaint fee £32. On 8 February 1982 the registrar by a letter
written on his behalf to the defendant's solicitors stated that he considered it unreasonable
that in a claim of under £500 a defence should be filed admitting negligence but denying
e loss. As £20 costs plus the plaint fee would have been allowable in any event, the registrar
had assessed an additional £50 in respect of the plaintiff's additional work which he, the
registrar, considered it was unreasonable for the plaintiff to bear in all these circumstances
in view of the defendant's admission of negligence. It is common ground in this court
that that letter imports the certification under Ord 19, r 1(11)(c) of the additional £50
costs awarded.
f   We think that there is no significant difference for present purposes between the two
cases. In each the first question is whether it was unreasonable conduct on the part of the
defendant for the purposes of Ord 19, r 1(11) to file a defence admitting negligence but
putting damage wholly in issue, thereby putting liability in issue, notwithstanding that
the defendant had in fact no defence on liability and no real intention to dispute liability
except as to quantum.
g   The defendants contend that in any action in which the plaintiff claims unliquidated
damages quantum is in issue, and that must be so; but in each of these cases the defendant
did more than put quantum in issue: he put liability in issue, notwithstanding that he
admitted negligence; in other words, each defendant put in issue the question whether
his negligence had occasioned any or all of the damage suffered by the plaintiff. In the
county court, where a plaintiff claims unliquidated damages, if the only issue is the
h quantum of those damages, the usual practice is for the registrar to enter interlocutory
judgment for the plaintiff for an amount of damages to be assessed. On the reference for
assessment each party can adduce evidence and cross-examine his opponent's witnesses.
There is a full opportunity to litigate the question of quantum. There can be no prejudice
to either party on the quantum being assessed in this way instead of being adjudicated in
a formal trial. There can consequently be no advantage in pleading issues of fact which
j go only to quantum: this would only be likely to occasion extra expense. This must be
otherwise, however, if the defendant puts in issue the entire question of liability by
pleading that whatever damage or loss the plaintiff may have suffered was not a
consequence of the alleged and admitted negligence of the defendant. Such an allegation
by a defendant could not be adjudicated on by means of an assessment of damages before
a registrar; it must necessitate a formal trial of the issue.

The function of pleadings in our mode of judicial proceedings is to define and clarify the issues between the parties. A party can properly make such allegations of fact as he *a* thinks he has some hope or chance of establishing, and can admit, refuse to admit, or deny such allegations of his opponent as he thinks fit. He can in this way compel his opponent to establish affirmatively any fact in respect of which the burden of truth rests on the opponent; but, if he ventures to put in issue some fact the truth of which can be demonstrated to have been known to the party purporting to put it in issue, he will be at risk of having his pleading in respect of it struck out as being frivolous, vexatious or an *b* abuse of the process of the court, or at the least he will be at risk as to the costs of that issue.

In *Newland v Boardwell* paras 1 and 2 of the defence consist only of admissions. The sole ground of defence pleaded in the document is contained in para 3. The position in *MacDonald v Platt* is similar. The judge found, as already mentioned (and indeed this was conceded), that on the facts the defendants 'simply cannot contend, and indeed do not *c* contend, that it could ever have been argued that no damage flowed from their negligence'. The denial of liability implicit in each defence is clearly a device to take advantage of Ord 19, r 1(4) and counsel for the defendants makes no bones about this. Indeed, he says that it was the duty of the defendants' solicitors to employ this device in order to protect their clients from liability for costs to which they would otherwise be exposed. The device, in our judgment, involves a misuse of the pleading process. So far *d* from clarifying the real issues between the parties, it obfuscated them. It speciously purported to raise an issue between the parties which the defendant in neither case genuinely intended to pursue. It was designed to exclude the plaintiff in each case from the benefit of the summary procedure of interlocutory judgment for damages to be assessed, while at the same time debarring the plaintiff from seeking the exercise of the court's discretion to award costs in his favour occasioned by a specious defence. *e*

In our judgment, there were sufficient grounds in each of these cases to justify certificates under CCR 1936 Ord 19, r 1(11)(c) and to the extent that 'through' the filing of the defences the plaintiffs respectively incurred solicitors' charges which they would not otherwise have incurred. 'Through' in this context must, in our opinion, have the meaning 'in consequence of'. The words 'to have been incurred through the unreasonable conduct of the opposite party' cannot affect any costs incurred before the occurrence of *f* the unreasonable conduct of the defendant. If either plaintiff incurred further solicitors' charges for services rendered between the date of the summons and the filing of the defence, those charges would seem to be made unrecoverable by para (11). But what about solicitors' charges incurred after the occurrence of the unreasonable conduct? Either plaintiff, as soon as he became aware that a defence had been filed in his or her action and as soon as he or she had been advised about the terms and effect of that defence *g* could have determined his solicitor's retainer so as to avoid further solicitors' charges occurring. Neither plaintiff did so. Can it be said in these circumstances that any solicitors' charges accruing thereafter have been incurred through the unreasonable conduct of the defendant in filing the defence? We think not. The plaintiff has expressly restricted his claim to the limit of the small claims procedure. He must be taken to have known that, if a defence were filed, the case would be automatically referred for *h* arbitration, in which event, if he continued to employ a solicitor, he would be prohibited from recovering any solicitors' charges from his opponent except under Ord 19, r 1(11)(c). If he does not protect himself by determining the solicitor's retainer, his liability to pay any solicitors' charges arising thereafter will, in our judgment, have been incurred as a consequence of his own failure to protect himself and not as a consequence of the reference to arbitration or to the filing of a defence which occasioned that reference. *j*

We should perhaps add that at no stage has either of the plaintiffs sought to get the defence in his or her action struck out, or to have the reference of his claim to arbitration made under Ord 19, r 1(4) rescinded under r 1(5) of that order. We accordingly express no view whether any application for either of these forms of relief could have succeeded at any stage.

a For these reasons, and with some regret, we allow all these appeals and set aside both
awards, since it seems to us (subject to anything that counsel may say) that no useful
purpose is likely to be served by remitting either arbitration to the registrar for
reconsideration in the light of this judgment. The consequence of this will be that each
plaintiff will only recover against the defendant in his or her action the solicitors' charges
referred to in the summons.

b We think there is room for doubt whether this result really accords with what the
rule-making authority intended to be a proper consequence of CCR 1936 Ord 19,
r 1(11)(c).

*Appeals allowed. Order for costs before the registrar varied. Costs before the judge varied to no
order for costs. No order for costs of appeal, save legal aid taxation where requisite.*

c Solicitors: *Davis Campbell & Co*, Liverpool (for the defendant Boardwell); *Weightmans*,
Liverpool (for the defendant Platt); *Morecrofts & Owen Dawson*, Liverpool (for the
plaintiff Newland); *E Rex Makin & Co*, Liverpool (for the plaintiff MacDonald).

Patricia Hargrove   Barrister.

R v Miller (Raymond) and another

QUEEN'S BENCH DIVISION

LLOYD J SITTING WITH THE CHIEF TAXING MASTER AND MR L J WATMORE AS ASSESSORS

3, 4, 5, 25 MAY 1983

Criminal law – Costs – Award out of central funds – Defendant acquitted – Costs 'incurred by' defendant – Defendant's employers undertaking to pay defendant's costs of defence – Order made for payment of defence costs out of central funds – Whether costs of defence 'incurred by' defendant – Costs in Criminal Cases Act 1973, s 3(3)(a).

The defendant was charged with causing an affray but was acquitted at his trial in the Crown Court, following which the trial judge ordered that the costs of the defence be paid out of central funds. The defendant's employers had undertaken to pay the costs of the defence but the defendant was aware that if they did not do so he would have to pay the costs himself. The taxing authority refused to certify that any part of the bill of costs submitted by the solicitors representing the defendant was payable out of central funds, on the ground that because it was almost certain that the defendant's employers would pay the defence costs it was never realistically anticipated that the defendant would bear any of the costs, and therefore for the purposes of s 3(3)(a)ᵃ of the Costs in Criminal Cases Act 1973 no costs had been 'incurred by him' in respect of the defence. The defendant appealed to the taxing master, who upheld the taxing authority and further held that the facts established that there was an agreement between the solicitors and the employers that the employers would be primarily liable for the costs of the defence. The defendant appealed from the taxing master's decision.

Held – Costs were 'incurred by' an accused within s 3(3)(a) of the 1973 Act if he, as the client, was responsible or liable to his solicitors for the costs of his defence, even if a third party, for example his employer, had in fact undertaken, or was also liable, to pay the costs. Furthermore, the fact that the accused was the client of the solicitors representing him raised a presumption that the accused was personally liable for the costs of his defence. It was only where there was an express or implied agreement which was binding on the accused's solicitors to the effect that in no circumstances would they seek to recover the costs from the accused that the costs ceased to be 'incurred by him' for the purposes of s 3(3)(a). On the facts, the realistic expectation that the employers would pay the defence costs was not conclusive, but merely a factor to be taken into account, in determining whether there was an implied agreement that the accused would not be liable for the costs in any event. Since the defendant was aware that he would be liable for the costs if the employers failed to pay them such an agreement could not be implied. The taxing master's decision had therefore been wrong and the appeal would accordingly be allowed (see p 188 j and p 190 f g and j to p 191 b and e to j, post).

Adams v London Improved Motor Coach Builders Ltd [1920] All ER Rep 340, *Davies v Taylor (No 2)* [1973] 1 All ER 959 and *Lewis v Averay (No 2)* [1973] 2 All ER 229 applied.

Notes

For the award of costs out of central funds in the Crown Court, see 11 Halsbury's Laws (4th edn) para 783.

For Costs in Criminal Cases Act 1973, s 3, see 43 Halsbury's Statutes (3rd edn) 269.

Cases referred to in judgment

Adams v London Improved Motor Coach Builders Ltd [1921] 1 KB 495, [1920] All ER Rep 340, CA.

ᵃ Section 3(3), so far as material, is set out at p 188 h, post

a
Berry v British Transport Commission [1961] 3 All ER 65, [1962] 1 QB 306, [1961] 3 WLR
450, CA.
Davies v Taylor (No 2) [1973] 1 All ER 959, [1974] AC 225, [1973] 2 WLR 610, HL.
Griffiths v Evans [1953] 2 All ER 1364, [1953] 1 WLR 1424, CA.
Gundry v Sainsbury [1910] 1 KB 645, CA.
Lewis v Averay (No 2) [1973] 2 All ER 229, [1973] 1 WLR 510, CA.
O'Brien v Robinson (No 2) [1973] 1 All ER 969, [1973] 1 WLR 515, HL.

b   Storer v Wright [1981] 1 All ER 1015, [1981] QB 336, [1981] 2 WLR 208, CA.

Appeal
On 21 November 1979 Raymond Karl Miller and the appellant, Alistair Kincaid Glennie,
were acquitted on the direction of the judge and a jury in the Central Criminal Court
before his Honour Judge Lawson QC of the offence of causing an affray. The judge,
c   pursuant to s 3(1)(b) of the Costs in Criminal Cases Act 1973, awarded Mr Glennie the
costs of his defence out of central funds. When Mr Glennie's solicitors submitted on 20
June 1980 their bill of costs to the taxing authority at the Central Criminal Court, the
taxing authority refused to allow any payment on the bill out of central funds on the
ground that it was never intended that Mr Glennie himself should meet the costs of his
defence and, instead it was intended that his employers should meet the costs. On 6
d   March 1980 Mr Glennie gave notice of appeal from the taxing authority's decision. On
24 July 1980 the Lord Chancellor gave notice of his intention to make oral representations
on the hearing of the appeal. On 20 April 1982 the taxing master, Master Horne,
dismissed the appeal and upheld the decision of the taxing authority but certified,
pursuant to the proviso to reg 5(1) of the Costs in Criminal Cases (Central Funds)
(Appeals) Regulations 1977, SI 1977/248, that his decision and that of the taxing authority
involved points of principle of general importance, namely (1) whether he was right in
e   holding as a matter of law that the liability of a client to his solicitor for payment of the
solicitor's costs, which was implied in the normal retainer of a solicitor by his client,
could be excluded where it was never realistically anticipated that the client would have
to bear any costs at all and (2) whether he was right in holding that when, pursuant to an
order made under s 3(1)(b) of the 1973 Act, the taxing authority was required under
f   s 3(3) of the 1973 Act to assess the costs of the successful defendant in such sum as appears
reasonably sufficient to compensate the defendant for the expenses properly 'incurred by
him' in carrying on the proceedings, it was for the successful defendant to satisfy the
taxing authority that any expenses so claimed by him had in fact been properly incurred
by him in carrying on the proceedings. Mr Glennie appealed to the High Court by way
of an originating summons dated 27 July 1982, seeking an order that Master Horne's
g   decision be reversed, that Mr Glennie's appeal from the decision of the taxing authority
be allowed and that the taxing authority should determine the sum which was to be paid
to Mr Glennie by way of costs out of central funds. The appeal was heard in chambers
but at the request of the parties judgment was given by Lloyd J in open court. The facts
are set out in the judgment.

h   Alastair Hill QC and Anthony Clover for Mr Glennie.
Andrew Collins for the Lord Chancellor.

Cur adv vult

25 May. The following judgment was delivered.

j
LLOYD J. This is an appeal to the High Court under reg 5 of the Costs in Criminal
Cases (Central Funds) (Appeals) Regulations 1977, SI 1977/248, from a decision of Master
Horne given on 20 April 1982, dismissing an appeal from a decision of Mr A C Johnson
as taxing authority at the Central Criminal Court. The master has certified in accordance
with reg 5 that there are questions to be decided which involve points of principle of

general importance. If I may summarise the essential point in my own words, it is
whether an employee, who is a successful defendant in a criminal trial, and who has been   *a*
awarded his costs out of central funds, can recover those costs when it is his employers
who are expected to pay the bill.

The points is of importance in itself. But it also has an importance outside the
relationship of employer and employee. For if a successful defendant cannot recover his
costs when he is supported by his employer, it is obviously arguable that he cannot
recover his costs when he is supported by his trade union or by an insurance company or   *b*
even by the legal aid fund.

These questions have now been fully argued by counsel on behalf of the appellant, Mr
Glennie and by counsel on behalf of the Lord Chancellor. At their request I am giving
this judgment in open court. I am indebted to them both, and also to the help I have
received from my assessors.

The facts are briefly as follows. In the early part of 1977 there was a dispute between   *c*
the owners of the Globtik Venus and her Philippine crew, as a result of which the vessel
was detained at Le Havre. The owners decided to replace the Philippine crew. On
1 March 1977 a relief crew boarded the vessel. The Philippine crew were removed and
eventually repatriated.

Mr Alastair Glennie was at the time chief accountant of Globtik Management Ltd, one
of the companies in the Globtik Group. He has since become a director. The chairman   *d*
of the group was and is Mr Ravi Tikkoo.

As a result of the incident on 1 March 1977 criminal proceedings were brought against
Mr Glennie and Mr Raymond Miller, a trawlerman from Grimsby. They were charged
with false imprisonment of members of the Philippine crew, and with causing an affray.
Mr Glennie was represented at the committal proceedings by leading and junior counsel.
That hearing took place in March 1979. The charge of false imprisonment was dismissed.   *e*
But Mr Glennie and Mr Miller were both committed for trial on the charge of causing
an affray. The trial took place before his Honour Judge Lawson QC and a jury at the Old
Bailey in November 1979.

At the conclusion of the prosecution case there was a submission of no case to answer.
The submission was upheld. The defendants were duly acquitted, and the judge ordered
that Mr Glennie should be paid his costs out of central funds.   *f*

The solicitors representing Mr Glennie were Messrs Richards Butler & Co. At one stage
there was a question whether they were in truth representing Mr Glennie, or his
employers. But it is now conceded that they were representing Mr Glennie. Whatever
may have been agreed between the parties as to the payment of Mr Glennie's costs, or as
to the conduct of his defence, it is accepted that Mr Glennie was himself the client.

Section 3 of the Costs in Criminal Cases Act 1973 provides: *g*

'(1) Subject to the provisions of this section, where a person is prosecuted or tried
on indictment before the Crown Court, the court may . . . (b) if the accused is
acquitted, order the payment out of central funds of the costs of the defence.
(3) The costs payable out of central funds under the preceding provisions of this
section shall be such sums as appear to the Crown Court reasonably sufficient—(a)
to compensate . . . the accused, for the expenses properly incurred by him in carrying   *h*
on the proceedings . . .'

It was common ground between the parties that the question in the present case
depends on the meaning of the words, 'incurred by him' in s 3(3). Counsel for the Lord
Chancellor argued that 'incurred by him' meant 'paid by him'; so that, if, for instance,
the successful defendant's costs are in fact paid by an insurance company or trade union,   *j*
then they are not recoverable out of central funds. He relied on the distinction between
costs, 'incurred by him' in s 3(3) and costs 'incurred in or about the defence' (and therefore
not necessarily incurred by him) in s 4(1)(b). I cannot accept so narrow a construction of
s 3(3).

A very similar point arose in *Adams v London Improved Motor Coach Builders Ltd* [1921]
1 KB 495, [1920] All ER Rep 340. In that case the plaintiff brought an action against his

employers for wrongful dismissal. His action succeeded, and he was awarded costs. It
a   was argued that the plaintiff was not entitled to recover anything by way of costs, as it
was the plaintiff's union who had retained the solicitors in the case, and it was the union
to which the solicitors looked for payment of their costs. The argument was rejected by
the Court of Appeal. Banks LJ said ([1921] 1 KB 495 at 501, [1920] All ER Rep 340 at
343):

b   'When once it is established that the solicitors were acting for the plaintiff with
his knowledge and assent, it seems to me that he became liable to the solicitors for
costs, and that liability would not be excluded merely because the Union also
undertook to pay the costs. It is necessary to go a step further and prove that there
was a bargain, either between the Union and the solicitors, or between the plaintiff
and the solicitors, that under no circumstances was the plaintiff to be liable for costs.'

c   Atkin LJ said ([1921] 1 KB 495 at 504, [1920] All ER Rep 340 at 344–345):

'. . . I think that it is highly probable, though the matter has not been discussed,
that the solicitors have a personal right against the trade union to receive a proper
remuneration for their services. It has not been discussed, and we do not know the
precise terms of the relation between the trade union and the solicitors, but I will
d   assume that there exists such an obligation. Nevertheless there is nothing
inconsistent in that obligation co-existing with an obligation on the part of the
plaintiff to remunerate the solicitors. Naturally, as a matter of business, the solicitors
would, I have no doubt, apply in the first instance to the trade union as being the
person ultimately liable to pay the costs as between all parties—that is to say, the
persons who would have to indemnify the plaintiff against the costs. But that does
e   not exclude the liability of the member, and it seems to me not in the least to affect
the position that the client may be liable, although there may be a third person to
indemnify the client.'

These judgments were cited with approval by Lord Dilhorne in *Davies v Taylor (No 2)*
[1973] 1 All ER 959, [1974] AC 225. That was a case under s 1 of the Legal Aid Act 1964.
Section 1(1) of the 1964 Act, now repealed, provided, in terms identical with s 13(1) of
f   the current Legal Aid Act 1974:

'Where a party receives legal aid in connection with any proceedings . . . and those
proceedings are finally decided in favour of the unassisted party, the court . . . may
. . . make an order for the payment to the unassisted party out of the legal aid fund
of the whole or any part of the costs incurred by him in those proceedings.'

g   It will thus be seen that the words, 'costs *incurred by him* in those proceedings' are the
very same words as 'expenses properly *incurred by him* in carrying on the proceedings' in
s 3(3) of the Costs in Criminal Cases Act 1973.
It was argued in *Davies v Taylor (No 2)*, as it has been argued here, that no costs had
been incurred by the successful defendant, as he was insured, and the insurance company
was bound to pay his costs. The argument was rejected. After citing *Adams v London
h   Improved Motor Coach Builders Ltd* Lord Dilhorne said ([1973] 1 All ER 959 at 962, [1974]
AC 225 at 230):

'In this case the solicitors, no doubt first instructed by the insurance company,
were the solicitors on the record as the solicitors for the respondent. They acted for
him, and in the absence of proof of an agreement between him and them or between
j   them and the insurance company that he would not pay their costs, they could look
to him for payment for the work done and his liability would not be excluded by
the fact that the insurance company had itself agreed to pay their costs. In my
opinion, the costs incurred were incurred by the respondent in the sense in which
those words are used in the Legal Aid Act 1964.'

Finally there is *Lewis v Averay (No 2)* [1973] 2 All ER 229, [1973] 1 WLR 510, another case under the Legal Aid Act 1964. This time it was the Automobile Association who undertook the successful defendant's appeal to the Court of Appeal. The solicitors in the *a* case wrote to the Law Society:

'... we ... made it clear that Mr. Averay was indemnified in all respects by the Automobile Association so that no part of the cost of the appeal has or would have fallen on him.'

Nevertheless it was held that the successful defendant's costs in the case could be recovered *b* from the legal aid fund. Lord Denning MR said ([1973] 2 All ER 229 at 231, [1973] 1 WLR 510 at 513):

'Counsel suggests that in this case the costs were not incurred by Mr Averay, but were incurred by the Automobile Association; because the Automobile Association undertook the appeal and instructed their solicitors and paid them. I cannot accept this suggestion. It is clear that Mr Averay was in law the party to the appeal. He was *c* the person responsible for the costs. If the appeal had failed, he would be the person ordered to pay the costs. If the costs had not been paid, execution would be levied against him and not against the Automobile Association. The truth is that the costs were incurred by Mr Averay, but the Automobile Association indemnify him against the costs ... That is sufficient to satisfy the requirements that the costs were, "incurred by him".' *d*

Counsel for the Lord Chancellor sought to distinguish this consistent line of authority on the ground that all the cases which I have mentioned were concerned with legal aid in civil proceedings. He argued that in criminal proceedings the rule is different. Costs are not awarded so freely. In this connection he relied on *Berry v British Transport Commission* [1961] 3 All ER 65, [1962] 1 QB 306. *e*

I do not accept counsel's suggested distinction. I can see no reason to differentiate between the meaning of the words, 'expenses properly incurred by him' in the 1973 Act, re-enacting s 1 of the Costs in Criminal Cases Act 1952, which itself re-enacted the Costs in Criminal Cases Act 1908 as amended by s 44 of the Criminal Justice Act 1948, and the same words in the Legal Aid Act 1964 and now the Legal Aid Act 1974.

It follows that I reject the main argument of counsel for the Lord Chancellor that 'costs *f* incurred by' means 'costs paid by'. I would hold, following *Adams v London Improved Motor Coach Builders Ltd* and the other cases I have mentioned, that costs are incurred by a party if he is responsible or liable for those costs, even though they are in fact paid by a third party, whether an employer, insurance company, motoring organisation or trade union, and even though the third party is also liable for those costs. It is only if it has been agreed that the client shall in no circumstances be liable for the costs that they cease *g* to be costs incurred by him, as happened in *Gundry v Sainsbury* [1910] 1 KB 645.

There was some discussion whether the agreement to relieve a client of costs must be made with the client himself, or whether it is sufficient that it is made with the third party. Banks LJ in *Adams v London Improved Motor Coach Builders Ltd* and Lord Dilhorne in *Davies v Taylor (No 2)* contemplated that an agreement with the third party would suffice. But Lord Cross in *Davies v Taylor (No 2)* [1973] 1 All ER 959 at 965–966, [1974] *h* AC 225 at 234–235 refers only to an agreement with the client, and it was Lord Cross's speech which was adopted by Lord Diplock in *O'Brien v Robinson (No 2)* [1973] 1 All ER 969, [1973] 1 WLR 515. On the facts of the present case it makes no difference, and I express no view.

There was also some discussion as to the burden of proof. The initial burden of proving that Richards Butler & Co were acting for Mr Glennie lay on Mr Glennie. But that *j* burden could be discharged, as it was in the present case, by showing that Mr Glennie was the party to the proceedings, and Richards Butler & Co the solicitors on the record. Once it was shown, as is now conceded, that Mr Glennie was indeed the client, then a presumption arose that he was to be personally liable for the costs. That presumption could, however, be rebutted if it were established that there was an express or implied

a agreement, binding on the solicitors, that Mr Glennie would not have to pay those costs
   in any circumstances.
        In practice, of course, the taxing officer will have before him on the taxation the whole
   of the solicitor's file. If it appears to the taxing officer that there is doubt whether there
   was an express or implied agreement, binding on the solicitors, not to seek to recover the
   costs from the client, the taxing officer should ask for further evidence. It must then be
   for the taxing officer to come to a conclusion on the whole of the facts presented to him.
b Unless those facts establish a firm agreement, express or implied, that in no circumstances
   will the solicitors seek to obtain payment from their client, then the basic presumption
   stands, and reasonable costs must be allowed on a taxation out of central funds.
        Nothing I have said on the burden of proof affects the general rule that where there is
   a dispute between solicitor and client as to the solicitor's retainer, then the burden is on
   the solicitor to establish the validity and extent of his retainer. The reason for the rule,
c which goes back a long way, is given by Denning LJ in *Griffiths v Evans* [1953] 2 All ER
   1364 at 1369, [1953] 1 WLR 1424 at 1428. But here there was no dispute between Mr
   Glennie and Richards Butler & Co. They were at one in asserting that there was no
   agreement whereby Mr Glennie was not to be liable for costs in any circumstances.
        I now turn to the facts of the present case. According to Master Horne's reasons, the
   ground on which the taxing authority decided the case was that it was never realistically
d anticipated that Mr Glennie would have to bear any costs at all. Master Horne's own
   decision is stated in the following paragraph:

        'Inevitably one is drawn to the conclusion that the particular facts of this
        exceptional case establish that there was an agreement between Richards Butler with
        Mr Tikkoo that he and or Globtik would be primarily liable for their costs incurred
        in the defence of Mr Glennie and that it was never realistically anticipated that Mr
e   Glennie would personally be liable for any such costs.'

        I find myself unable to agree with Master Horne's approach. The question is not who
   was *primarily* liable for the costs, whether Mr Tikkoo or Mr Glennie. The question is
   whether it was agreed that Mr Glennie should not be liable for those costs under any
   circumstances. The fact that it was never realistically anticipated that Mr Glennie would
f pay the costs was a factor to be taken into account in determining whether there was an
   implied agreement that he would not be liable for the costs in any event. But it was no
   more than a factor. It was not conclusive. Mr Glennie in his affidavit says that he was
   aware that he would be liable for Richards Butler & Co's costs if they were not paid by
   the Globtik group. If that evidence was accepted, then it was inconsistent with an implied
   agreement that Mr Glennie should not be liable in any event. The fact that Globtik had
g agreed to pay the costs, and that it was 99% certain that they would pay the costs, may
   make them *primarily* liable, in the sense that the solicitors would look to them in the first
   place. But that, as I have said, is not the question. The same was true in *Adams v London
   Improved Motor Coach Builders Ltd* and the other cases I have mentioned. In my judgment
   the evidence falls short of establishing that Mr Glennie was not to be liable in any
   circumstances.
h   For the reasons which I have given, I consider that Master Horne's approach was
   erroneous in law. The appeal will therefore be allowed. Question 1 will be answered No.
   It is not sufficient to exclude the normal liability of a client to pay his solicitors' costs that,
   'it was never realistically anticipated that the client would have to bear any costs at all'.
   Question 2 will be answered in the manner I have already indicated.
        The matter will now go back to the taxing authority for Richards Butler & Co's bill to
j be taxed in the normal way on a common fund basis. The bill submitted amounted to
   £68,391. How much of that will be allowed as reasonable compensation for expenses
   properly incurred will be for the taxing authority to decide. I hope that nothing I have
   said will be taken as supporting a suggestion that the whole of the bill should be allowed.
   On the contrary, there are on the face of it a number of substantial items which would
   be hard to justify. As Lord Denning MR pointed out in *Storer v Wright* [1981] 1 All ER

1015, [1981] QB 336, it is the duty of the taxing officer in legal aid taxations to bear the public interest in mind, and disallow any items which are unreasonable in amount or which are unreasonably incurred. He must act as a watchdog, since there is no one else to perform that function. In all the circumstances it would I think be preferable, that when this case goes back to the taxing authority, it should be considered by a fresh mind.

Appeal allowed. No order as to costs.

Solicitors: *Richards Butler & Co* (for Mr Glennie); *Treasury Solicitor.*

K Mydeen Esq   Barrister.

Practice Direction

COURT OF PROTECTION

Mental health – Court of Protection – Practice – Costs – Solicitors' costs – Fixed costs.

1. In place of the current practice of assessing costs in respect of certain Court of Protection work, fixed costs are to be introduced by agreement with the Law Society.
2. Fixed costs will be available as follows:

Category I   In respect of work up to and including completion of the directions contained in the First General Order £135

Category II   In respect of the preparation and lodgment of a receivership account £55

Category III   In respect of general management work in the second and subsequent years £165

Note: it will be possible to claim the second and third items together at a figure of £220.

3. In the case of the first category, solicitors will be advised by the court at the time the draft First General Order is sent out whether a bill is required for taxation or whether fixed costs will be authorised. It will remain open to solicitors to request a taxation in any event. In the second and third categories solicitors will claim the fixed costs or apply for taxation. It will remain open to the court either to allow the fixed costs or to order a taxation.

4. This Practice Direction applies to Court of Protection costs as follows:

Category I   All draft First General Orders sent out from the Court of Protection on or after 3 October 1983

Category II   All receivership accounts lodged on or after 3 October 1983

Category III   All general management costs in respect of years ended on or after 3 October 1983.

Issued with the concurrence of the Lord Chancellor.

A B MACFARLANE
Master, Court of Protection.

1 September 1983

Peco Arts Inc v Hazlitt Gallery Ltd

QUEEN'S BENCH DIVISION
WEBSTER J
25, 26, 27 MAY 1983

Limitation of action – Postponement of limitation period – Action for relief from consequences of mistake – Plaintiff buying from reputable art dealer drawing believed to be original – Drawing discovered to be reproduction ten years after purchase – Whether plaintiff's claim for rescission time-barred – Whether plaintiff could 'with reasonable diligence' have discovered mistake six years prior to institution of proceedings – What constitutes 'reasonable diligence' – Whether plaintiff obliged to have independent valuation of drawing soon after purchase – Whether plaintiff entitled to rely on reputation of art dealer – Limitation Act 1980, s 32(1)(c).

In 1970, on the recommendation of M, a specialist in nineteenth century drawings, the plaintiff bought from the defendants, a well-known and reputable art gallery, a drawing which both parties thought to be an original by a famous nineteenth century artist. The plaintiff paid $US18,000 for the drawing. It was an express term of the sale that the subject matter of the sale was an original drawing signed and inscribed by the artist. In 1976 the plaintiff had the drawing revalued for insurance purposes by an art expert, and on that occasion no doubts were cast on the authenticity of the drawing. In 1981 the plaintiff had the drawing revalued again and it was then discovered that the drawing was in fact a reproduction. The plaintiff brought an action against the defendants claiming, inter alia, (i) recovery of the purchase price and interest as money paid under a mutual mistake of fact and (ii) rescission of the contract in equity and return of the purchase price on the ground of a unilateral or common mistake of fact. The defendants contended that the action had accrued more than six years prior to the institution of the proceedings and that therefore the action was time-barred under ss 2[a] and 5[b] of the Limitation Act 1980. The plaintiff contended that, because the action was for relief from the consequences of a mistake, the period of limitation had not, by virtue of s 32(1)(c)[c] of the 1980 Act, begun to run until the plaintiff had discovered the mistake or 'could with reasonable diligence have discovered it', and that in the circumstances she could not with reasonable diligence have discovered the mistake six years prior to the institution of the proceedings. The defendants contended that the burden of proof lay on the plaintiff to show that she could not have discovered the mistake by exercising reasonable diligence and further that the plaintiff could not show that she had exercised reasonable diligence if there had been available to her a means of discovering the mistake which she had not used. They further contended that, particularly in the art world, public policy and the interests of finality and fair trading required that, unless a purchaser of a work of art verified its authenticity within a reasonable time, the purchaser took the risk of any false attribution that may have attached to it.

Held – (1) It was not possible to devise a meaning or construction to be put on the words 'reasonable diligence' in s 32 of the 1980 Act which could be applied generally to all contexts, because the precise meaning to be given to those words varied with the particular context in which they were to be applied. In the context of the plaintiff's action 'reasonable diligence' meant not the doing of everything possible, nor necessarily the use of any means at the plaintiff's disposal nor even necessarily the doing of anything at all, but simply the doing of that which an ordinarily prudent buyer and possessor of a

---

a   Section 2 provides: 'An action founded on tort shall not be brought after the expiration of six years from the date on which the cause of action accrued.'

b   Section 5 provides: 'An action founded on simple contract shall not be brought after the expiration of six years from the date on which the cause of action accrued.'

c   Section 32(1), so far as material, is set out at p 195 h and p 202 g, post

valuable work of art would do having regard to all the circumstances, including the circumstances of the purchase (see p 199 *g* to *j*, post); *Leaf v International Galleries* [1950] 1 **a** All ER 693 distinguished.

(2) On the facts, a prudent purchaser in the position of the plaintiff would not normally have obtained independent authentification in the circumstances of the sale because she was entitled to rely on the reputation and recommendation of M and on the reputation of the defendants, and to assume that both M and the defendants were satisfied as to the authenticity of the drawing and to expect the vendor who had sold the drawing **b** through the defendants to have had the drawing authenticated by them. Furthermore, the plaintiff was reasonably entitled to expect that on an ordinary competent revaluation in 1976 the valuers' suspicions would have been aroused and that the valuers would have informed her accordingly. It followed that nothing had happened between the purchase of the drawing by the plaintiff in 1970 and the discovery that it was a reproduction in 1981 to put the plaintiff on notice that it might be a reproduction, and in those **c** circumstances there was no lack of diligence on the part of the plaintiff. Furthermore, the act or omission of the valuers in 1976 was not a matter for which the plaintiff was responsible. It followed that the action was not time-barred and there would be judgment for the plaintiff accordingly (see p 201 *g h*, p 202 *b* to *d* and *f* to *h* and p 203 *b* to *e*, post).

Per curiam. Although the equitable remedy of rescission is to be pursued without laches and within a reasonable time, it does not follow that the limitation period is **d** extended by s 32(1)(*c*) of the 1980 Act whenever there is a bona fide mistake regarding the attribution of a picture. It may well be that where attribution of a picture forms a term of the contract, either as a condition or as a warranty, and the attribution is mistaken, s 32(1)(*c*) does not apply either because the attribution is not a 'mistake' within s 32(1)(*c*) or because, where goods are sold with a condition or warranty as to attribution which is broken because the vendor was under a mistake, the price paid is not to be **e** regarded as money paid in consequence of a mistake (see p 203 *e* to *g*, post). *Chetham v Hoare* (1870) LR 9 Eq 571.

Notes

For rescission of contract made under mistake of fact, see 32 Halsbury's Laws (4th edn) paras 43–45, and for cases on the subject, see 35 Digest (Repl) 130–135, 251–290. **f**

For postponement of limitation period for relief from consequences of mistake, see 28 Halsbury's Laws (4th edn) paras 923–924, and for cases on the subject, see 32 Digest (Reissue) 704, 5133–5138.

For the Limitation Act 1980, ss 2, 5, 32, see 50(1) Halsbury's Statutes (3rd edn) 1255, 1258, 1285.

Cases referred to in judgment

Baker v Courage & Co [1910] 1 KB 56, [1908–10] All ER Rep 65.
Betjemann v Betjemann [1895] 2 Ch 474, CA.
Chetham v Hoare (1870) LR 9 Eq 571.
Dean v Richards, The Europa (1863) 2 Moo PCCNS 1, 15 ER 803.
Ecclesiastical Comrs for England v North Eastern Rly Co (1877) 4 Ch D 845. **h**
Lawrance v Lord Norreys (1890) 15 App Cas 210, [1886–90] All ER Rep 858, HL.
Leaf v International Galleries [1950] 1 All ER 693, [1950] 2 KB 86, CA.

Action

By a writ issued on 6 April 1982 the plaintiffs, Peco Arts Inc, claimed as against the defendants, Hazlitt Gallery Ltd, (i) $US18,000 plus interest as damages for negligent **j** misrepresentation, (ii) for recovery of money paid under a mistake of fact and interest and (iii) for rescission of the agreement for common or unilateral mistake of fact and the repayment of the purchase price. The facts are set out in the judgment.

John Peppitt QC and *Peter Cresswell QC* for the plaintiffs.
Lord Rawlinson QC and *Richard Rampton* for the defendants.

WEBSTER J. In November 1970 the plaintiffs bought from the defendants what
a purported to be an original drawing in black chalk on paper 'Etudes Pour le Bain Turc'
by J A D Ingres for a price of $US18,000.

It was alleged, in the statement of claim in the proceedings that followed, and
admitted, that the following were express terms of the sale, namely that the subject
matter of the sale was an original drawing in black chalk by J A D Ingres signed and
inscribed lower left: 'J. Ingres a Monsieur Theop. Gauthier 1861'. In fact it was not an
b original drawing by Ingres, it was a reproduction worth virtually nothing. It was alleged
and admitted that the defendants were in breach of those express terms of the agreement.

It is common ground that at the time of the sale both parties, the defendant seller and
Mrs Curran who purchased on behalf of the plaintiffs, thought that the drawing was an
original drawing by Ingres but that they were both mistaken. The true nature of it
however was not discovered for some years. It was finally discovered in about June 1981
c when, for the second occasion between November 1970 and that date, it was professionally
revalued on behalf of Mrs Curran, or the plaintiffs, for insurance purposes; and it was on
that occasion in June 1981 that its true nature was discovered. Consequently, in April
1982 these proceedings were issued.

When the trial began, two days ago, the plaintiffs, through their counsel, if I understand
him correctly, relied on three causes of action: first of all, on a claim for the return of the
d purchase price and interest as money paid under a mutual mistake of fact; second, on a
claim for rescission of a contract in equity and a return of the purchase price on the
ground of a unilateral or common mistake of fact; and, third, on a claim for damages for
negligent misrepresentation under the Misrepresentation Act 1967, although, as I
understood counsel for the plaintiffs, the plaintiffs are not proposing to pursue any claim
for damages but prefer to rely on the claim for interest which would attach to their claim
e for the return of the purchase price.

Counsel for the plaintiffs accepted that the effect of ss 2, 5 and 9 of the Limitation Act
1980 is that causes of action founded on tort, or on simple contract, or actions to recover
a sum recoverable by virtue of any enactment, were all barred by limitation six years
after the date on which the cause of action arose, subject to the provisions of s 32 of the
1980 Act. By virtue of s 36(1) those time limits do not apply to a claim for equitable
f relief except in so far as any such time limit might be applied by analogy. Thus the
provisions of s 32 of the 1980 Act were, and are, central to the plaintiffs' case since the
action was not brought until nearly 11½ years after the case of action arose, assuming, as
is probably correct, that it arose on the date of the sale.

The particular provisions on which the plaintiffs rely are those of s 32(1)(c), which
provides:

g
  'Subject to subsection (3) below [which is not material], where in the case of any
  action for which a period of limitation is prescribed by this Act . . . (c) the action is
  for relief from the consequences of a mistake; the period of limitation shall not
  begin to run until the plaintiff has discovered the . . . mistake . . . or could with
  reasonable diligence have discovered it . . .'

h   The trial was adjourned half way through the first day to enable the parties, at their
own instance, to simplify the issues. As a result, by consent of both parties, I am now
asked to decide only the following matter and I quote the terms of the agreed question
that I am asked to decide: on the defendants agreeing for the purpose of these proceedings
that if it is found that (a) the plaintiffs did not discover the mistake relied on and (b)
could not with reasonable diligence have discovered it before a date six years prior to the
institution of such proceedings the plaintiffs shall be entitled to judgment for $18,000
j together with interest of $23,400 thereon as money paid under a common mistake of
fact. The plaintiffs in turn agree not to pursue further any other relief claimed in such
proceedings and unreservedly withdraw the allegations of negligence contained therein.
So that the only question or questions that I have to decide are first whether the plaintiffs
discovered the mistake relied on and second whether she could, with reasonable diligence,
have discovered it before a date six years prior to the institution of such proceedings?

Consequently, it is unnecessary for me to decide a number of questions of law which otherwise would or might have arisen including for instance: whether the sale was a sale by description; whether any representation made merged in any description or condition or other term included in the contract so that no reliance could be placed on the representation as such; whether the mistake was a mutual mistake; if so, what the effect of such a mutual mistake is on a contract of sale in these terms; and if it was a mutual mistake for the purposes of such a contract whether the provisions of s 32(1)(c) can apply in principle in such a case, in particular whether this would be a case in which money was paid in consequence of a mistake. So in deciding the largely factual issues which I now have to decide I am not purporting to decide, one way or the other, any of those other questions.

This agreement which the parties have made is consistent on the defendants' part with their attitude throughout these proceedings, and indeed before they began, which has been one in which, as it seems to me, they have not sought to shelter behind what some people might regard as legal technicalities. It is also in this particular case an agreement which in many ways must be in the interests of both parties in any event because if those points which I have just mentioned had been argued the length of the trial would almost certainly have been doubled, possibly more than doubled; it would certainly not have been concluded this term and the costs of it, consequently, would have been considerably increased. Consistently with that same attitude on the part of the defendants they, from an early stage, if not immediately the authenticity of the drawing was doubted then when it was known that the drawing was in fact a reproduction, have made and have kept open an open offer to Mrs Curran, or the plaintiffs, to repay the purchase price of $18,000; and this offer remains open whatever the outcome of the trial on this issue, that is to say whether the defendants win it or lose it.

So I turn now to the question that I have to decide and first of all to the history of the whole matter. I shall, for that purpose, refer extensively to the evidence of various witnesses all of whom I am quite satisfied have given wholly truthful evidence to the best of their recollections. Scarcely any of the evidence has been challenged and I am to be deemed to find facts in accordance with that evidence unless I expressly say otherwise.

Mrs Curran is a citizen of the United States but she has lived in this country for about 23 years, although she has an apartment and a summer cottage in the United States. She has always been interested in art and she is an assiduous collector owning, through the vehicle of the plaintiff company which she uses for this purpose, a very valuable and wide-ranging collection of works of art including drawings, pastels, old master drawings and paintings.

The defendants appear at the proceedings, in evidence, by Mr Baer, who is their managing director. Mr Baer has been in the art trade since 1946 and the defendant gallery has undergone various transformations but, for many years now, it has been a well-known and highly reputable gallery. Mr Baer himself has held many distinguished offices in the fine art world.

The circumstances in which the purchase came to be made, according to Mrs Curran, are these. She knew then, and knows now no doubt, a Mrs Stephanie Maison. Mrs Stephanie Maison has for many years been, and certainly was in 1970, a specialist in nineteenth century French drawings of which an original by Ingres would be a prime example. Mrs Curran's recollection of the events which led up to the sale was that she was recommended by Mrs Maison to buy two drawings, one by one of the Tiepolos and the other this particular drawing, for inclusion in her collection; and she was assured that they had both come from a good collection, that of Mr Villiers-David. She herself did not know Mr Villiers-David but she knew of his name. He had in fact been known to Mr Baer for some years both as a well-known collector and as a friend of his, Mr Baer's. Either when she first discussed the matter with Mrs Maison, or certainly later when she went to look at these two drawings at the defendant gallery, Mrs Curran was told that this drawing had been exhibited in Paris. She looked at it, and she decided to buy it for $18,000. She had no doubt that she was buying an authentic drawing.

When she was cross-examined her recollection was prompted a little bit further and
a she remembered looking at the drawing and discussing it at the gallery with Mr Baer
and Mrs Maison and she remembered them showing her the catalogue of the Paris
exhibition.

Mr Baer's account of how the transaction arose was as follows. Mr Villiers-David had
asked him some time before the sale took place if he would sell these two drawings for
him and Mr Baer had agreed to do so. He had seen both of them in Mr Villiers-David's
b flat on various occasions. At the time they were at a bank for safe keeping and so it was
arranged that they would be forwarded to Mr Baer's gallery in packing cases, which was
done. Mr Baer himself had been to the Ingres exhibition in Paris, although he could not
actually say that he saw this particular drawing there. He kept the two drawings in his
office but not for very long, and while they were there Mrs Maison called on him, as she
often did, and he mentioned them; and she told him, either then or later, about Mrs
c Curran and that she was a collector who might be interested in them. Consequently, a
few days later, Mrs Curran was brought to the gallery where, as I have said, as Mrs Curran
herself remembered, they all three spoke about and looked at the two drawings and
looked at the actual entry in the catalogue, which was at the gallery, relating specifically
to the Ingres.

So, having agreed to buy that and the other drawing she asked for the invoice to be
d sent to the plaintiffs. In addition to the terms of the inscription which I have already
mentioned and to the agreed express terms of the contract of sale that I have already
mentioned, the invoice made reference to the fact that the drawing had been exhibited
at that particular exhibition and contained a reference to the catalogue entry relevant to
it.

Mrs Curran took both drawings home. There she kept this particular drawing from
e then until 1981 in her bedroom on the wall near to the door as one of a group of other
paintings or drawings. During the period from November 1970 when she bought it
until the early summer of 1981 when its true nature was discovered, a large number,
about twelve, of distinguished and well-known members of the art world saw it from
time to time when they were visiting her. It is not suggested, she did not suggest, that
any of them inspected it, but they were all of them obviously interested in her collection
f and they looked at this drawing amongst others in that way; but none of them said
anything to suggest that it was not authentic.

One of the people who visited her in that way was Mr Andrew Somerville, to whose
evidence I shall return later, and he also remembered seeing it on the wall. He looked at
it there on a number of occasions although he had never examined it and he, on those
occasions, had never had any suspicions about its authenticity. In 1976 Mrs Curran,
g having insured the drawing for $18,000 after she bought it, decided that the time had
come to have it revalued for insurance purposes and she instructed Sotheby's to carry out
that valuation. A Mr Strauss was in charge of the overall valuation and he provided
experts from various departments to value particular items in which they had special
expertise. Nothing was said during that valuation to throw any doubt on the authenticity
of the drawing.

In 1981 Mrs Curran decided that it was time to have another valuation and on this
h occasion she instructed Mr Somerville, whom I have already briefly mentioned. He is a
director of Somerville & Simpson Ltd, the well-known gallery in Saville Row. Amongst
other things he is the valuer for the Paul Mellon Collection and he has been active in the
fine art world for many years. His speciality are prints and drawings. He had known Mrs
Curran for some time, since about 1974 or 1975, and so, when she asked him to carry
j out the valuation, he came along to her house to do so.

When he came to this particular drawing he took it off the wall to the window to get a
better light and when he took it into a better light he was immediately suspicious of it.
He examined first the inscription in the bottom left hand corner and that immediately
raised his suspicions; and he realised that that part of it at least was a reproduction, not
an original. He then examined the whole of the drawing without, I think, at that stage

removing it from its frame and concluded that it was most likely to be a reproduction. So he took it back to his gallery, removed it from the frame and discovered that in truth *a* it was a reproduction. He said that it was his special expertise which enabled him to come to that conclusion primarily because of his training in prints. But even with that special expertise he was not able to say precisely how it had been reproduced.

When he decided that it was a reproduction, no doubt with Mrs Curran's approval or authority, he took it along to the defendant gallery. It was at one stage, I understood from his evidence, examined by an expert on behalf of the defendants who said that he *b* could not confirm that it was a reproduction without a proper examination; but it is common ground that it was a reproduction. Mr Baer said that, having heard no more about this sale from November 1970 until the early summer of 1981 when Mr Somerville called on him and told him that he had suspicions that the drawing was a reproduction, he was very shocked, because he said he had had no suspicion of the kind at all until then. He looked at it again and, his suspicions having been aroused, he said it was not very *c* difficult to see that Mr Somerville was right and that it probably was a reproduction.

The value today, if it had been an original and not a reproduction, would, according to Mr Somerville, be something between £60,000 and £80,000 and possibly more.

So much for the history of the matter. I now turn to the law.

Section 32(1)(c) contains provisions which were formerly contained in s 26(1) and (5) of the Limitation Act 1939, as substituted by the Limitation Amendment Act 1980, s 7. *d* But the particular words which I have to construe and apply appeared in a statute as early as the Real Property Limitation Act 1833, s 26.

Counsel on behalf of the defendants made a number of submissions about the construction and application of those words. First, he submitted that in this context the burden of proof lies on the plaintiffs to show that Mrs Curran could not have discovered the mistake if she had exercised reasonable diligence; and counsel, on her behalf, accepts *e* that that is where the burden lies. I should add, however, that, when referring me to the authority on which he relied for his submission (which as I have said is common ground) that the burden of proof in a case such as this lies on the plaintiff, he cited the case of *Lawrance v Lord Norreys* (1890) 15 App Cas 210, [1886–90] All ER Rep 858, this also being a case concerned with the application of the same words although in a wholly different factual context. I note this passage where Lord Herschell in his speech said (15 *f* App Cas 210 at 215–216, [1886–90] All ER Rep 858 at 860) (and I am taking a sentence out of context only to draw attention to a few particular words):

'An heir-at-law of one who, as far as appeared to him, had died intestate (for if he knew nothing of any will he would naturally assume this) *would ordinarily be led to make inquiries* for the purpose of ascertaining what property his ancestor had died *g* possessed of . . .'

Counsel for the defendants relied on *Chetham v Hoare* (1870) LR 9 Eq 571, a case concerning the same words in the 1833 Act to which I have already referred, and in particular to a part of the judgment of Malins V-C which is to the effect that the provision should be strictly interpreted; and, as it seems to me, it is right that if there is a choice between a strict or a more relaxed interpretation it should, in the context in which it *h* appears, be given a strict interpretation.

But the substance of counsel for the defendants submission on the construction of these words is that the plaintiff cannot show that he or she has exercised due diligence if there is available a means of discovering the mistake which the plaintiff does not use. Here, submits counsel for the defendants, Mrs Curran had available means of discovering the mistake which she did not use because she could, very soon after she acquired the *j* drawing, have had it independently authenticated. He relies in support of that submission of law principally on two cases: first, *Betjemann v Betjemann* [1895] 2 Ch 474, another case concerned with the same words but in an action between partners not between a buyer and a seller, and, second, *Baker v Courage & Co* [1910] 1 KB 56, [1908–10] All ER Rep 65,

yet another case concerned with the same words. I bear in mind all those cases and the
a passages from them to which I have been referred.

Counsel for the plaintiffs for his part referred me to one case only concerned with these
words, that of *Ecclesiastical Comrs for England v North Eastern Rly Co* (1877) 4 Ch D 845.
Again, as is the case of all the other authorities to which I have been referred, the facts
were wholly different from the facts of this case, but counsel relied in this case on the
judgment of Malins V-C and particularly on a passage of it, where Malins V-C said (at
b 861) (and, again, I am omitting a number of, for this purpose, immaterial sentences from
the paragraph that I am about to refer to):

'Then it is said that in this case by reasonable diligence this fraud might have been
discovered in 1864 . . . Now this depends a great deal upon the inquiry a man is
bound to make . . . Now was there anything to lead them to believe or suspect, or
were they bound to suspect or to make inquiries as to whether these boundaries
c which had been so formally settled by the agents of the *West Hartlepool Company* in
1862, had been broken into or transgressed between 1862 and 1864?

He also referred me to the decision in *Dean v Richards, The Europa* (1863) 2 Moo PCCNS
1, 15 ER 803, not a case arising under this or any equivalent section but a case concerned
with a maritime lien for damages caused by a collision between ships where the possessor
d of the lien, it was held, is not entitled to enforce the lien unless he uses reasonable
diligence to discover the ship's whereabouts. Counsel for the plaintiffs relied in particular
on a passage from the judgment of Dr Lushington, at first instance, being a judgment
which was upheld on appeal, where Dr Lushington said (2 Moo PCCNS 1 at 15, 15 ER
803 at 808):

'However, what I have to decide is, whether what has been done constitutes
e reasonable diligence; and the meaning of such expression is not the doing of
everything possible, but the doing of that which, under ordinary circumstances and
with regard to expense and difficulty, could be reasonably required.'

Counsel for the plaintiffs' submission, in the light of all these authorities, is that there
is no rule of universal application that the exercise of reasonable diligence necessarily
f imports, as counsel for the defendants submits, the doing of something or that it
necessarily involves the using of any means available to discover a mistake.

Taking into account these authorities I conclude, first of all, that it is impossible to
devise a meaning or construction to be put on those words which can be generally applied
in all contexts because, as it seems to me, the precise meaning to be given to them must
vary with the particular context in which they are to be applied. In the context to which
g I have to apply them, in my judgment, I conclude that reasonable diligence means not
the doing of everything possible, not necessarily the using of any means at the plaintiff's
disposal, not even necessarily the doing of anything at all, but that it means the doing of
that which an ordinarily prudent buyer and possessor of a valuable work of art would do
having regard to all the circumstances, including the circumstances of the purchase.

Counsel for the defendants relied particularly on his submission that, particularly in
h the art world, public policy and the interests of finality and fair trading require that
unless a purchaser of a work of art verifies its authenticity within a reasonable time, by
which I think he means really months not years, then he takes the risk of any false
attribution that may have been attached to it. In support of that submission he relied on
three dicta of the Court of Appeal in *Leaf v International Galleries* [1950] 1 All ER 693,
[1950] 2 KB 86, where a picture, represented to have been painted by John Constable,
j was sold for £85. It turned out that the representation was untrue and the plaintiff
purchaser sought to have the sale rescinded on the ground of innocent misrepresentation
five years after the sale took place. In that case Denning LJ said ([1950] 1 All ER 693 at
695, [1950] 2 KB 86 at 90):

'In this case this buyer took the picture into his house, and five years passed before

he intimated any rejection. That, I need hardly say, is much more than a reasonable
time. It is far too late for him at the end of five years to reject this picture for breach
of any condition. His remedy after that length of time is for damages only, a claim
which he has not brought before the court.'

As will be seen in a moment, Denning LJ at that stage in the judgment was looking at
the position first of all as if the representation had constituted a condition of the contract.
Jenkins LJ said ([1950] 1 All ER 693 at 696, [1950] 2 KB 86 at 92):

'. . . in my judgment, contracts such as this cannot be kept open and subject to
the possibility of rescission indefinitely. Assuming that acceptance of delivery was
not fatal to his claim, at all events, I think it behoves the buyer either to verify, or,
as the case may be, disprove, the representation within a reasonable time or else to
stand or fall by the representation. If he is allowed to wait five, ten, or twenty years
and then re-open the bargain, there can be no finality.'

And finally, Evershed MR said, to very much the same effect ([1950] 1 All ER 693 at 697,
[1950] 2 KB 86 at 96):

'That leads me to suggest this matter for consideration. The attribution of works
of art to particular artists is often a matter of great' controversy and increasing
difficulty as time goes on. If the buyer is right in saying that he is entitled, perhaps
years after the purchase, to raise the question whether in truth a particular painting
was rightly attributed to a particular artist, it may result in most costly and difficult
litigation in which there will be found divergent views of artists and critics of great
eminence, and the prevailing view at one date may be quite different from that
which prevails at a later date . . . Those results, it seems to me, are undesirable. If a
man elects to buy a work of art or any other chattel on the faith of some
representation, innocently made, and delivery of the article is accepted, then it
seems to me that there is much to be said for the view that on acceptance there is an
end of that particular transaction, and that, if it were otherwise, business dealings in
these things would become hazardous, difficult, and uncertain.'

But, as is apparent from what I have already said about that case, it was concerned not
with any Limitation Act nor with the equivalent of s 32(1)(c) of the Limitation Act 1980;
nor was it concerned with the question whether the buyer had used reasonable diligence
to discover a mistake. The question, which the Court of Appeal had to decide, was simply
whether the buyer was entitled to rescind the sale on the ground of innocent
misrepresentation and in order to answer that question the court had to decide whether
there had been any laches, that is to say whether the buyer had sought to pursue the
equitable remedy of rescission within a reasonable time. Certainly, so far as Denning LJ
was concerned, the ratio decidendi of the decision was that if the representation had
constituted a condition the right to reject the picture, and so to call for repayment of its
price, would have been lost long before five years was up, and if the right to reject it for
breach of condition had been lost by then, a fortiori the buyer must have lost the right to
rescind in equity. Of course, that authority is wholly binding on me and, with respect, I
of course entirely accept it; but it is not this case at all. It is partly not this case because of
the very limited question which I have been asked to decide.

So, against the background of my conclusions about the law I turn to the evidence
which goes to the question whether Mrs Curran can satisfy me that she could not have
discovered the mistake with due diligence. First of all, as to her own expertise she said
that she would not have sufficient expertise to know just by looking at that or any similar
drawing whether it was authentic and that, until she was told that it was not by Mr
Somerville, she did not have any suspicions about it. Mr Somerville said of her that she
can be described as an enlightened amateur: someone who, in his opinion, would not
have been able to spot the lack of authenticity.

a   She was asked a number of questions about why she did not have it authenticated and similar questions. In my view these answers are important. She was asked whether it ever occurred to her to have it authenticated, and she said, 'Never.' She was asked whether she thought it would have been prudent to have it authenticated, and her answer to that was, 'I do not think that one does that in my position. You buy from particular people, and you assume that it has been authenticated before it has been sold.' She was asked whether she had had any of her other pictures authenticated, and she said, 'Only when

b   selling.' She was asked whether it was customary, to her knowledge, to have a picture authenticated by the buyer when it was bought, and all she could say was, 'It must be an individual thing; a matter for the individual to decide on.' She was asked what she relied on for the authentification of this picture, and she said she relied on the gallery's reputation, the provenance of the picture and its history, meaning the history which had been given to her by Mr Baer and Mrs Maison. Asked a further question about when she

c   has had pictures authenticated when she has sold them, she said that if she sells through a dealer or a sales-room then the picture will be examined for authenticity by that dealer or sales-room.

    Mr Somerville gave a little evidence on the same sort of matter. He said that he assumed that Mrs Maison, as the intermediary in the sale, also endorsed or confirmed the terms of the invoice and he said that he did not think it would be customary for a

d   purchaser to confirm its authenticity if the painting had come from a reputable dealer. He said that collectors do have their different ways: some would not dream of having a picture authenticated (in those circumstances they would trust the seller) although others might rush round asking the opinions of all and sundry, but usually asking them whether they liked it rather than whether they thought it was authentic or not.

    It is relevant in this context to consider the reputation of the defendants and of Mrs

e   Maison at that time. There is no doubt that the defendants at that time were specialists in Italian seventeenth and eighteenth century paintings and, though not holding themselves out to be experts in nineteenth century French drawings, that they were none the less a gallery of very considerable reputation; and there is no doubt that Mrs Maison herself was then, and was known as being, an expert in nineteenth century French drawings.

f   In the light of that evidence I conclude that a prudent purchaser in the position of Mrs Curran would not normally obtain independent authentification in the circumstances of a sale of this kind. I am satisfied that Mrs Curran was wholly entitled to rely on the reputation and recommendation of Mrs Maison and on the reputation of Mr Baer and the defendant gallery, and that she was entitled to assume, as was indeed the case, that both of them, Mrs Maison and Mr Baer, were satisfied as to the authenticity of the drawing. There was no challenge to her evidence that if she was selling a picture through

g   a dealer or a sales-room she would expect to have it authenticated by the dealer or the sales-room, meaning of course on her own behalf. In my judgment she was entitled to expect that Mr Villiers-David would take the same sort of course and for that reason, and the other reasons that I have mentioned, in my judgment she was entitled to rely on the defendants and Mrs Maison in that respect.

h   If, contrary to the conclusion I have reached about the law, in order to establish due diligence it is necessary for her to show that she did something, as counsel for the defendants submits, then none the less it seems to me that counsel for the plaintiffs is right in at least three out of the four of his submissions that, in fact, she did do something. He submitted that the things that she did which constituted the exercise of due diligence, if the submission of counsel for the defendants about those words is right, were first that

j   she confirmed for herself from the catalogue when she obtained it that it had been exhibited and that it was illustrated in the catalogue; and it is clear from her evidence that that is what she did. Second, he submitted that if independent appraisal was called for she had in effect obtained it from Mrs Maison herself: so far as she knew, and so far as she was concerned, Mrs Maison was an independent intermediary who had recommended the sale to her. Third, he submitted that showing her collection, including this drawing, to a wide collection of distinguished figures in the art world constituted some such action; that I have my doubts about. Fourth, he submitted that having it revalued with the rest of her collection by Sotheby's in March 1976 constituted an action sufficient to amount to due diligence. In my judgment, although on the evidence it seems that she would not be entitled to assume that they would necessarily test every picture for authenticity on such a revaluation none the less, if it be material, I would find that she would be reasonably entitled to expect them to tell her if their suspicions were aroused on a revaluation and that it would be reasonably likely that suspicions would be aroused on an ordinarily competent revaluation in those circumstances.

Nothing happened between the purchase by her in November 1970 and the discovery that it was a reproduction in 1981 to put Mrs Curran on notice that it might be a reproduction. In those circumstances, in my judgment, there was no lack on her part of reasonable diligence and I expressly reject the suggestion that, as a matter of reasonable diligence and despite the circumstances of the purchase, she ought to have had the drawing independently authenticated. So I am satisfied, treating the burden as being on her, that she has established that she could not have discovered the mistake with the exercise of reasonable diligence.

If counsel for the defendants was right in his submission that every buyer of a picture of any value must properly have it authenticated if he is to exercise reasonable diligence for the purpose of this subsection, even where the picture is sold by a highly reputable seller or dealer, on a sale of which the picture's attribution constitutes a term or condition, it would seem to follow that such a course of action would be necessary in very many cases. It may well be necessary to take this action if a buyer seeks to reject a picture for a breach of condition but that is not the question raised at this trial. I cannot think that it is a requirement of all buyers who, for any reason, have to satisfy a test of reasonable diligence and I would be surprised if the art market as a whole would expect them to comply with such a requirement.

There remains the question, however, which counsel for the defendants wants to keep open although he has not pressed it at all, whether there is any lack of reasonable diligence to be attributed to the plaintiff by virtue of the revaluation by Sotheby's in 1976. In my judgment that matter can be shortly dealt with as a matter of law, because, as it seems to me, as a matter of construction arising out of the express words contained in the last sentence of s 32(1) the acts or omissions of an agent of a plaintiff are not to be attributed to the plaintiff for the purposes of this section; that is because those last words are in these terms:

'References in this subsection to the defendant [I emphasise the word 'defendant'] include references to the defendant's agent and to any person through whom the defendant claims and his agent.'

By application of a well-known Latin maxim, which I shall not repeat, it would seem to me, as a matter of construction, that the act or omission on the part of Sotheby's is not to be attributed to Mrs Curran. Were that to be wrong, however, I will deal very shortly with the facts that would go to that issue were it to be a live one.

Mr Baer, when he gave evidence, said that a valuation depends very much on correct attribution and that you cannot put a value on an object unless you believe it to be genuine, in the sense both that the attributed author is indeed the author and that the object is what it purports to be, that is to say an original rather than a reproduction. Mr Somerville said that if he is asked to value for insurance he treats that request as including a request or instruction to test for authenticity, but he went on to say that he cannot say that that is the general practice in the trade. He added that anyone who had made a mistake in relation to this particular reproduction, on examining it, could not be regarded as an expert, in his view. It seems to me that at that stage in his evidence Mr Somerville was perhaps applying rather too high a test.

It has to be remembered that Mr Baer himself had sold the drawing as authentic and
a that the allegation that he or the defendants were negligent was abandoned; it would
clearly be repudiated if it were to be pursued. Mrs Maison also had recommended the
purchase to Mrs Curran, and I assume that both Mr Baer and Mrs Maison would repudiate
any suggestion that they had acted without reasonable diligence. Mr Baer said (I have no
doubt he is right and it was never challenged) that he and his gallery have a reputation
for integrity and expertise and that in order to uphold that reputation his gallery is
b required, as a responsible gallery, to use all diligence at their command to ensure that
what they sell as originals are not reproductions. Yet, as we know, no suspicion was
aroused in the mind of Mr Baer who sold the drawing to Mrs Curran or in the mind of
Mrs Maison, with her particular experience, who recommended it for sale. My conclusion,
therefore, as to the revaluation by Sotheby's is that, were the burden to lie on the
defendants to establish that Sotheby's had not exercised reasonable diligence, I would be
c unable to conclude that they had not done so in this respect when their suspicions were
not aroused during their 1976 valuation, but that, as the burden would lie on Mrs Curran
if the matter were a relevant one, I would be unable to find that they had exercised due
diligence in failing to discover that this was a reproduction when they carried out that
valuation.

I conclude, therefore, that the plaintiffs did not discover the mistake relied on and that
d Mrs Curran could not with reasonable diligence have discovered it before a date six years
prior to the institution of proceedings. I would add only this, that, contrary to the fears
of counsel for the defendants, there is in my view nothing in this judgment which need
necessarily alarm the art world. It is true that there is nothing that can abridge the
contractual limitation period of six years, except possibly indirectly where the only
remedy relied on is the equitable one of rescission which must be pursued without laches
e and within reasonable time; but conversely it does not follow from this decision that the
limitation period is extended by s 32(1)(c) whenever there is a bona fide mistake as to the
attribution of a picture. It may well be the case that, where attribution forms a term of
the contract, either as a condition or as a warranty, and where that attribution is mistaken,
then in those circumstances s 32(c) does not apply either because it is not a mistake within
the meaning of that subsection or because, where goods are sold with a condition or
f warranty as to attribution which is broken because the seller is under a mistake, the price
paid is not to be regarded as money paid in consequence of a mistake. If it is to be
regarded as money paid in consequence of a mistake then it would seem to follow that,
in many instances of sales of many kinds of goods, where a warranty or condition is
honestly but mistakenly given, the statutory limitation periods do not apply unless the
buyer has acted without reasonable diligence. That result, if right, might be regarded as
g surprising and would seem to be generally contrary to the interests of normal trading
where goods are often sold on, and some goods, such as works of art, often sold on more
than once in the years following the sale in question. These points which I have
mentioned have not been argued in this case and I have not had to decide them: all I have
had to do is to apply the words 'could with reasonable diligence have discovered the
mistake' to the facts of this case.

h
Judgment for the plaintiffs.

Solicitors: *William Easton & Sons* (for the plaintiffs); *Goodman Derrick & Co* (for the
defendants).

K Mydeen Esq   Barrister.

Re Peachdart Ltd

a

CHANCERY DIVISION
VINELOTT J
9, 10, 11 MARCH 1983

Sale of goods – Passing of property – Vendor retaining property in goods – Contract reserving property in goods to vendor after delivery until payment made in full – Vendor supplying leather *b* *used by purchaser in manufacture of handbags – Leather becoming inseparable part of handbags – Purchaser becoming insolvent – Whether vendor retaining property in unused leather – Whether vendor having property in unsold handbags – Whether fiduciary relationship existing between vendor and purchaser – Whether vendor entitled to trace and recover debt from proceeds of sale of handbags – Whether vendor limited to a charge over the goods – Whether charge void for non-registration – Companies Act 1948, s 95.* *c*

The respondents supplied a company with leather for the manufacture of handbags. The conditions of sale provided that property in the leather remained with the suppliers until payment was received in full and that the suppliers had the right to resell the leather when payment became overdue. Payment was due immediately on delivery. The conditions of sale also provided that pending payment in full the suppliers had property *d* in any products made from the leather until they were sold by the company and that a fiduciary relationship existed between the suppliers and the company which entitled the suppliers to trace the proceeds of sale of the handbags. The company got into financial difficulties and a receiver was appointed by a debenture holder. On a summons by the receiver to determine the priority of creditors' claims the unpaid sellers claimed priority ahead of the debenture holder, preferential creditors and unsecured creditors in respect *e* of the unused leather, completed and partly completed handbags, and amounts due from sales made before the receiver's appointment, because by the terms of the conditions of sale the suppliers remained bailors and the company merely the bailee of the leather until payment was made. The debenture holder and preferential creditors conceded that the suppliers had property in the unused leather but contended that at best the suppliers had a charge over the book debts and the completed or partly completed handbags which *f* was void for non-registration in accordance with s 95[a] of the Companies Act 1948.

Held – On the true construction of the conditions of sale the parties were to be presumed to have intended that once the company appropriated a piece of leather to the manufacture of a handbag and began work on it the leather ceased to be the exclusive property of the suppliers, whether as bailors or as unpaid vendors, but that instead the *g* suppliers had a charge on handbags, both in the course of manufacture and when completed, which could shift to the proceeds of sale. However, since the charge had not been registered it was void pursuant to s 95 of the 1948 Act and the suppliers therefore ranked only as unsecured creditors (see p 210 *d* to p 211 *c*, post).

Aluminium Industrie Vaassen BV v Romalpa Aluminium Ltd [1976] 2 All ER 552 and *h* *Borden (UK) Ltd v Scottish Timber Products Ltd* [1979] 3 All ER 961 considered.

---

a Section 95, so far as material, provides:
'(1) . . . every charge created . . . by a company registered in England and being a charge to which this section applies shall, so far as any security on the company's property or undertaking is *j* conferred thereby, be void against the liquidator and any creditor of the company, unless the prescribed particulars of the charge together with the instrument, if any, by which the charge is created or evidenced, are delivered to or received by the registrar of companies for registration . . '(2) This section applied to the following charges . . . (c) a charge created or evidenced by an instrument which, if executed by an individual, would require registration as a bill of sale . . . (f) a floating charge on the undertaking or property of the company . . .'

Notes

a For the right to follow and recover assets or the money into which they have been
converted, see 16 Halsbury's Laws (4th edn) para 1460.

For the Companies Act 1948, s 95, see 5 Halsbury's Statutes (3rd edn) 189.

Cases referred to in judgment

Aluminium Industrie Vaassen BV v Romalpa Aluminium Ltd [1976] 2 All ER 552, [1976] 1
b WLR 676, QBD and CA.

Bond Worth Ltd, Re [1979] 3 All ER 919, [1980] Ch 228, [1979] 3 WLR 629.

Borden (UK) Ltd v Scottish Timber Products Ltd [1979] 3 All ER 961, [1981] Ch 25, [1979] 3
WLR 672, CA; *rvsg* [1979] 2 Lloyd's Rep 168.

Hallett's Estate, Re, Knatchbull v Hallett (1880) 13 Ch D 696, [1874–80] All ER Rep 793,
CA.

c
Cases also cited

Bevington and Morris v Dale & Co Ltd (1902) 7 Com Cas 112.

Holroyd v Marshall (1862) 10 HL Cas 191, [1861–73] All ER Rep 414, 11 ER 999, HL.

Wait, Re [1927] 1 Ch 606, [1926] All ER Rep 433, CA.

d **Summons**

By an originating summons dated 6 August 1982 Nicholas Lyle, the receiver and
manager of Peachdart Ltd (the company), applied to the court to determine, inter alia,
(a) whether on the appointment of the receiver the respondents, Freudenberg Leather Co
Ltd (Freudenbergs), had, by virtue of their conditions of sale, an interest in or charge on
(i) unused leather supplied by Freudenbergs to the company at its premises at the date of
e the appointment of the receiver, (ii) handbags manufactured by the company at its
premises incorporating leather supplied by Freudenbergs and unsold at the date of the
appointment of the receiver, (iii) uncollected invoices payable to the company in respect
of handbags manufactured by the company incorporating leather supplied by
Freudenbergs, (b) whether any such interest or charge was valid and enforceable and/or
had priority against or over other creditors when it had not been registered against the
f company under s 95 of the Companies Act 1948, and (c) whether the receiver was
accountable to Freudenbergs for the unused leather, handbags and uncollected invoices.
The facts are set out in the judgment.

Simon Mortimore for the receiver.
Jeffrey Littman for Freudenbergs.

g
VINELOTT J. This is an application by the receiver of a company, Peachdart Ltd
(which I will call the company), which formerly carried on the business of manufacturing
handbags. The question is whether the respondent, Freudenberg Leather Co Ltd (which
I will call Freudenbergs), who supplied leather for the manufacture of the handbags is
entitled under a retention of title clause in the conditions of sale governing the supply of
h the leather to claim, in priority to the holder of the debenture under which the receiver
was appointed and to preferential creditors, first the proceeds of sale of a stock of unused
leather in the possession of the company when the receiver was appointed, second the
proceeds of sale of handbags, some completely and some partly manufactured when the
receiver was appointed and since sold by him, and third the proceeds of sale of handbags
which had been sold by the company before the receiver was appointed but for which
j the company had not been paid when he was appointed.

The facts which give rise to these questions are shortly as follows. On 21 January 1980
the company (which until December 1981, when the right to use its original name was
sold, was called S Launer & Co (London) Ltd) granted a debenture to Barclays Bank Ltd
to secure all moneys for the time being owed by the company to the bank. The debenture
was in the bank's standard form. By cl 3 of the debenture the company charged by way
of first fixed charge all freehold and leasehold property to become vested in the company,

together with all buildings, fixtures, fixed plant and machinery from time to time
thereon and its goodwill and uncalled capital, and also by way of first fixed charge all *a*
book debts and other debts then or from time to time becoming due to the company,
and by way of floating charge all other undertakings and assets of the company, 'but so
that the Company is not to be at liberty to create any mortgage or charge upon and so
that no lien shall in any case or in any manner arise on or affect any part of the premises
either in priority to or pari passu with the charge hereby created'.

The debenture contained the usual provision for the appointment of a receiver. The *b*
charge created by the debenture was duly registered pursuant to s 95 of the Companies
Act 1948 on 11 February 1980. The receiver was appointed on 10 August 1981. He duly
took possession of the assets of the company, which comprised trade debts owed to the
company under contracts for the supply of handbags which had been delivered
amounting to £27,317, leather and leather goods (the manufactured or partly
manufactured handbags) valued in the statement of affairs at £7,500, plant, machinery, *c*
furniture and fittings valued at £8,500 and a motor car valued at £1,200. The debt due
to the bank amounted to over £64,000. Debts owed to preferential creditors amounted
to nearly £50,000. The company owed Freudenbergs some £16,200, and other unsecured
creditors approximately £26,000. Freudenbergs claim to be entitled under the title
retention clause to the moneys recovered by the receiver from the trade debtors (all these
debts arose, as I have said, on the sale of handbags which had been delivered before the *d*
receiver was appointed) and to the proceeds of the sale by the receiver of the unused
leather and the completed or partly completed handbags in the possession of the company
when he was appointed. The receiver has in fact sold the unused stock of leather to
Freudenbergs for £1,400 on terms that that sum will be reimbursed to Freudenbergs if
they establish that they retained title to it under the retention of title clause, in which
event Freudenbergs will, of course, have purchased their own goods. The stock of *e*
manufactured and partly manufactured handbags has been sold and realised a little under
£1,500. The unused leather and the handbags and partly completed handbags were not,
of course, the subject of any fixed charge in the debenture and the proceeds of sale of
those items (if Freudenbergs cannot establish prior title under the title retention clause)
will be payable to the preferential creditors who will rank before the bank's floating
charge by virtue of s 94 of the 1948 Act. To save costs counsel who appeared for the *f*
receiver has in effect represented the interests of the bank, which relies on the first fixed
charge in cl 3(c) of the debenture as regards the book debts, and the preferential creditors
in opposing Freudenbergs' claim.

Freudenbergs supplied the company with substantially all its requirements of leather
for use in the manufacture of handbags. I should observe in passing that the company
manufactured only high quality leather handbags. In practice, Freudenbergs sold leather
to the company as and when required on the terms of their standard general conditions *g*
of sale. It is common ground that these terms were incorporated into each contract for
the supply of each parcel of leather.

The conditions of sale are printed on the reverse side of Freudenbergs' standard form
of invoice in microscopic print. I have fortunately been supplied with a typed copy
which in normal print runs to nearly eight foolscap pages. I need only refer to a few of *h*
the conditions. Clause 1(a) defines 'Seller' as Freudenbergs, 'The Products' as 'the products
to which this document relates' and 'Buyer' as the customer buying 'the Products'. Clause
2(a) provides that 'Unless otherwise agreed all payments are due immediately on delivery
without any deductions'. It was not 'otherwise agreed' in this case. Clause 10(a) provides
that the seller is to be entitled to interest at 2% over Bank of England minimum lending
rate on overdue payments. Part of the sums claimed by Freudenbergs represent interest. *j*
I shall read cl 11 in full:

> '(a) The risk in the Products shall pass to the Buyer (i) When the Seller delivers
> the Products in accordance with the terms to the Buyer or its Agent or other person
> to whom the Seller has been authorised by the Buyer to deliver the Products or (ii)
> If the Products are appropriated to the Buyer but kept at the Seller's premises at the

a Buyer's request AND the Seller shall have no responsibility in respect of the safety of the Products thereafter and accordingly the Buyer should insure the Products thereafter against such risks (if any) as it thinks appropriate.

(b) However the ownership of the Products shall remain with the Seller which reserves the right to dispose of the products until payment in full for all the Products has been received by it in accordance with the terms of this contract or until such time as the Buyer sells the Products to its customers by way of bona fide sale at full b market value. If such payment is overdue in whole or in part the Seller may (without prejudice to any of its other rights) recover or resell the Products or any of them and may enter upon the Buyer's premises by its servants or agents for that purpose. Such payment shall become due immediately upon the commencement of any act or proceeding in which the Buyer's solvency is involved. If any of the products are incorporated in or used as material for other goods before such payment the property c in the whole of such other goods shall be and remain with the Seller until such payment has been made or the other goods have been sold as aforesaid and all the Seller's rights hereunder in the Products shall extend to those other goods.

(c) Until the Seller is paid in full for all the Products the relationship of the Buyer to the Seller shall be fiduciary in respect of the Products or other goods in which they are incorporated or used and if the same are sold by the Buyer the Seller shall d have the right to trace the proceeds thereof according to the principles in *In re Hallett's Estate* ((1880) 13 Ch D 696, [1874–80] All ER Rep 793). A like right for the Seller shall apply where the Buyer uses the Products in any way so as to be entitled to payment from a third party.'

The effect of similar title retention clauses has been considered in a group of recent e cases. They are, in chronological order, the decisions of Mocatta J and the Court of Appeal in *Aluminium Industrie Vaassen BV v Romalpa Aluminium Ltd* [1976] 2 All ER 552, [1976] 1 WLR 676, the decision of Judge Rubin QC sitting as a judge of the High Court in *Borden (UK) Ltd v Scottish Timber Products Ltd* [1979] 2 Lloyd's Rep 168, the decision of Slade J in *Re Bond Worth Ltd* [1979] 3 All ER 919, [1980] Ch 228 and the decision of the Court of Appeal in the *Borden* case [1979] 3 All ER 961, [1981] Ch 25.

f None of the title retention clauses considered in those cases is in precisely the same terms as the title retention clause in cl 11 of Freudenbergs' general conditions of sale. The nearest is the clause considered by Mocatta J and the Court of Appeal in the *Romalpa* case. But there is this vital difference. In the *Romalpa* case the question was whether the vendor could recover from the receiver, first aluminium foil supplied by it which had not been used by Romalpa in any process of manufacture and which under the terms on g which it was supplied had to be stored in such a way that it was clearly the property of the vendor, and secondly the proceeds of sale of aluminium foil which similarly had not been used in any process of manufacture and which had been sold by Romalpa before the receiver was appointed. The receiver had received and paid the proceeds of sale into a separate account with Romalpa's bankers and the vendors claimed to be entitled to the moneys in the account which were less than the unpaid balance of the price of aluminium h supplied. There was a preliminary issue whether the title retention clause had been incorporated into the contract for the supply of the aluminium foil in question. It was conceded on behalf of the receiver that if, as was held by Mocatta J and the Court of Appeal, the retention of title clause was so incorporated then Romalpa became and remained a bailee of any aluminium foil delivered to it, pending payment in full of all moneys due from Romalpa under contracts for the supply of aluminium foil, and that j the vendor was accordingly entitled to recover the unused aluminium foil in the possession of the receiver. It was held in the Court of Appeal that Romalpa had an implied power to sell, as agent for the vendor, unused aluminium foil which remained the property of the vendor. It followed that Romalpa, and after his appointment the receiver, were accountable for the proceeds of sale. Roskill LJ said ([1976] 2 All ER 552 at 563–564, [1976] 1 WLR 676 at 690):

'I see no difficulty in the contractual concept that, as between the defendants and
their sub-purchasers, the defendants sold as principals, but that, as between   *a*
themselves and the plaintiffs, those goods which they were selling as principals
within their implied authority from the plaintiffs were the plaintiffs' goods which
they were selling as agents for the plaintiffs to whom they remained fully
accountable. If an agent lawfully sells his principal's goods, he stands in a fiduciary
relationship to his principal and remains accountable to his principal for those goods
and their proceeds. A bailee is in like position in relation to his bailor's goods. What, *b*
then, is there here to relieve the defendants from their obligation to account to the
plaintiffs for those goods of the plaintiffs which they lawfully sell to sub-purchasers?
The fact that they so sold them as principals does not, as I think, affect their
relationship with the plaintiffs; nor, as at present advised, do I think—contrary to
the argument of counsel for the defendants—that the sub-purchasers could on this
analysis have sued the plaintiffs on the sub-contracts as undisclosed principals for, *c*
say, breach of warranty of quality.'

It was argued before Mocatta J that if the vendor succeeded in its tracing claim it
would, in effect, have found a way of avoiding s 95 of the 1948 Act. Mocatta J held that
s 95(1) had no application, on the ground that if the property in the aluminium foil
never passed to Romalpa the proceeds of the sub-sales belonged in equity to the vendor
and were not the subject of any charge. On that analysis the vendor remained the legal *d*
owner of the goods supplied until payment for those goods and any goods supplied on
like terms; the title would pass only on payment of any outstanding balance and the
purchaser's right to claim the property in the goods would then be a contractual right
under the contract of sale and not an equity of redemption. No reference was made to
s 95 in the Court of Appeal.

In *Romalpa* the second part of the title retention clause (dealing with the title to mixed *e*
or manufactured goods and the sale of them in the ordinary course of business) was relied
on to support the implication of a power for Romalpa to sell the unused aluminium foil
as agent for the vendor. The question whether the vendor could claim to be entitled to,
or to a charge on, mixed or manufactured goods was not in issue. That was the question
in issue in *Borden*. But in that case the title retention clause provided only that the
property in goods supplied by the vendors (resin for use in making chipboard) under any *f*
given contract of sale for the supply of resin would pass only on payment in full for all
resin supplied under that or any other contract for the supply of resin. The claim by the
vendor was a bold claim to trace resin, which under the title retention clause remained
the property of the vendor up to the time when it was used in the manufacture of
chipboard, into the chipboard and the proceeds of sale of the chipboard. The purchaser
was clearly entitled to use the resin in the manufacture of chipboard and to do so *g*
notwithstanding that moneys were still due to the vendor of the resin and that the
property in the resin accordingly remained with the vendor. When used the resin ceased
to exist as a separate or separable constituent of the chipboard. The Court of Appeal
accordingly had little difficulty in holding that when the resin became an inseparable
ingredient of the chipboard the vendor no longer had any property in it and that the title
retention clause did not preclude the purchaser from selling the chipboard, receiving the *h*
purchase price and employing the proceeds of sale in its business. Templeman LJ said
([1979] 3 All ER 961 at 972–973, [1981] Ch 25 at 44):

'. . . the property in the resin could be retained by the sellers, and was retained,
only as security for the payment of the purchase price and other debts incurred, and
to be incurred, by the buyers to the sellers in respect of supplies of resin . . . When *j*
the resin was incorporated in the chipboard, the resin ceased to exist, the sellers' title
to the resin became meaningless and the sellers' security vanished. There was no
provision in the contract for the buyers to provide substituted or additional security.
The chipboard belonged to the buyers.'

Bridge LJ rejected the argument which had succeeded in the court below that the

purchaser was a bailee of the resin. He said ([1979] 3 All ER 961 at 965, [1981] Ch 25 at
a　3 *c*) that in circumstances where—

　'it was never intended that the resin should be recovered, either in its original or
　in its altered form at all, it seems to me quite impossible to say that this was a
　contract of bailment. The contract was essentially one of sale and purchase, subject
　only to the reservation of title clause, whatever its effect may have been.'

b　　That conclusion seems to me implicit also in the passage from the judgment of
Templeman LJ which I have read. Buckley LJ left open the question whether while the
resin remained in the possession of the purchaser in the state in which it was supplied
the purchaser was a bailee of it. He said ([1979] 3 All ER 961 at 974, [1981] Ch 25 at 46):

　'Common ownership of the chipboard at law is not asserted by the buyers; so the
　sellers must either have the entire ownership of the chipboard, which is not
c　suggested, or they must have some equitable interest in the chipboard, or an
　equitable charge of some kind on the chipboard. For my part, I find it quite
　impossible to spell out of this condition any provision properly to be implied to that
　effect. It was impossible for the sellers to reserve any property in the manufactured
　chipboard, because they never had any property in it; the property in that product
　originates in the buyers when the chipboard is manufactured. Any interest which
d　the sellers might have had in the chipboard must have arisen either by transfer of
　ownership or by some constructive trust or equitable charge, and, as I say, I find it
　impossible to spell out of this condition anything of that nature.'

　　In the instant case counsel for the receiver concedes that the property in the unused
stock of leather which came into the hands of the receiver when he was appointed
e　remained with Freudenbergs. He submits that the company was not strictly a bailee but
(like the purchaser in *Borden*'s case) a purchaser under an agreement to sell under the
terms of which agreement the property in each parcel of leather was to pass only on
payment of the price for that parcel. The company had implied authority to sell the
leather or to use it in the manufacture of handbags. On a sale of the unused leather the
sub-purchaser, of course, would obtain a good title under s 25(1) of the Sale of Goods Act
f　1979.
　　Counsel for Freudenbergs submitted that the company was a bailee of each parcel of
leather pending payment in full of the price of that parcel. He pointed out that the
concession by counsel for the defendants in the *Romalpa* case that Romalpa was a bailee
of the unused aluminium foil was accepted by the Court of Appeal as properly made,
and submitted that there was no material difference between the first part of the title
g　retention clause in the instant case and the first part of the title retention clause considered
in the *Romalpa* case. Indeed the instant case is in one respect even stronger than that
considered in the *Romalpa* case in that under cl 11(b) Freudenbergs have the right to
enter the premises of the company and to take away 'the Products' if not fully paid for.
The only other material difference is that in the instant case there is no specific provision
corresponding to the provision in the *Romalpa* case requiring the purchaser to store the
h　materials supplied in such a way that it was clearly the property of the vendor. Counsel
for Frendenbergs submitted that no such requirement was needed in a case where the
material supplied under each contract would inevitably remain separate and easily
identifiable. He informed me that in practice a person skilled in the leather trade could
identify without difficulty any given skin as that sold under a particular contract, and
indeed could do so even after it had been made into a handbag. However, for reasons
j　which will later appear, I do not find it necessary to decide whether in this case the
company was strictly a bailee of the unused leather.
　　Turning to the partly or wholly manufactured handbags and the proceeds of sale of
those sold before the receiver was appointed, the submission of counsel for Freudenbergs
was shortly as follows. It was said that under the terms of the bailment of each parcel of
leather supplied by Freudenbergs pending payment in full of the price for that parcel the

company as bailee was entitled to use the leather in the manufacture of handbags, a process which involved cutting and shaping and sewing a piece of leather and attaching   *a* to it hinges, handles, clasps and the like, in the course of which the piece of leather would remain identifiable throughout. The thread and attachments, which were, it was said (and I do not think it is disputed), of comparatively minor value, then became the property of Freudenbergs as accessories to the leather. Thus the company remained a bailee of a handbag throughout the process of manufacture, and when the company sold a handbag it sold it (as in *Romalpa*) as agent for Freudenbergs, and was accordingly   *b* accountable to Freudenbergs as owner for the entire proceeds of sale. Freudenbergs were not entitled to a mere charge. Counsel for Freudenbergs instanced as an analogy a sportsman who having shot a rare animal takes the skin to a leather worker and instructs him to make it into a game bag. There the property in the skin would remain with the sportsman notwithstanding that the skin would undergo many operations and would have thread and other material added to it. He distinguished the *Borden* case on the   *c* ground that in that case the resin was inevitably consumed and destroyed as a separate substance when used in the manufacture of chipboard. The title retention clause did not purport to vest the property in the chipboard in the vendor, and if it had done so the vesting could only have been by way of equitable transfer of something not in existence when the resin was sold.

To my mind it is impossible to suppose that in the instant case, even assuming in   *d* Freudenbergs' favour that the company became a bailee of the leather when it was first delivered to it, the parties intended that until a parcel of leather had been fully paid for the company would remain a bailee of each piece of leather comprised in the parcel throughout the whole process of manufacture, that Freudenbergs should have the right until the parcel had been fully paid for to enter the company's premises and identify and take away any partly or completely manufactured handbag derived from it, and that on   *e* the sale of a completed handbag the company would be under an obligation to pay the proceeds of sale into a separate interest-bearing account and to keep them apart from their other moneys and not employ them in the trade.

It may be that, as counsel for Freudenbergs asserts, an expert in the leather trade could identify each handbag, whether partly or completely manufactured, as made from a skin comprised in a particular parcel of leather. But after a handbag had been sold it would be   *f* impossible to do so. There is nothing in the conditions of sale which requires the company to keep a record of handbags sold so as to identify those of which it was a bailee and agent of Freudenbergs. No such records were in fact kept and there is nothing in the evidence which suggests that the parties contemplated that they would be. So, on the facts of this case it would be impossible for Freudenbergs now to prove that the handbags sold by the company but not paid for when the receiver was appointed were in fact made   *g* out of leather comprised in any of the parcels to which the unpaid invoices relied on by Freudenbergs relate. It seems to me that the parties must have intended that at least after a piece of leather had been appropriated to be manufactured into a handbag and work had started on it (when the leather would cease to have any significant value as raw material) the leather would cease to be the exclusive property of Freudenbergs (whether as bailor or as unpaid vendor) and that Freudenbergs would thereafter have a charge on   *h* handbags in the course of manufacture and on the distinctive products which would come into existence at the end of the process of manufacture (the value of which would be derived for the most part from Mr Launer's reputation and skill in design and the skill of his workforce). The charge would in due course shift to the proceeds of sale. That I accept does some violence to the language of cl 11(b) in so far as that clause provides that 'The property in the whole or such other goods shall be *and remain* with the Seller' (my   *j* emphasis). I do not think that those words compel the conclusion that the company was to be a mere bailee throughout the whole process of manufacture until the whole purchase price of the relevant parcel had been paid, and that on a sale before that time it would be no more than an agent for Freudenbergs. The language is, I think, consistent with the view that once the process of manufacture had started so that in the course of

manufacture work and materials provided by the company would result in the leather
a being converted into (that is incorporated in or used as material for) other goods of a
distinctive character the property in those other goods would vest in Freudenbergs only
as security for any outstanding balance of the price of the relevant parcel of leather. What
the draftsman has done is to elide and I think confuse two quite different relationships,
that of bailor and bailee, with a superimposed contract of sale (or of vendor and
purchaser), on the one hand and that of chargor and chargee on the other hand.

b Counsel for Freudenbergs conceded, and I think he must concede, that if Freudenbergs
had no more than a charge on the partly completed and completed handbags the charge
was void for want of registration. It may also have been void as regards the book debts
against the bank which under the debenture had a prior fixed charge (all the invoices on
which Freudenbergs rely are dated after January 1980) and as regards the completed or
partly completed handbags against the preferential creditors by virtue of s 94 of the 1948
c Act.

Order accordingly.

Solicitors: *David Elton & Wineman* (for the receiver); *Gamlens*, agents for *Max Engel & Co*,
Northampton (for Freudenbergs).

d   ·

                                        Jacqueline Metcalfe   Barrister.

e
Vasso (owners) v Vasso (cargo owners)
The Vasso

QUEEN'S BENCH DIVISION (COMMERCIAL COURT)
LLOYD J
f 17, 29 MARCH 1983

*Arbitration – Arbitrator – Jurisdiction – Inspection of property – Whether arbitrator having
power to make order for inspection of property which is subject of reference – Whether order for
inspection can be made only by High Court – Arbitration Act 1950, s 12(1)(6).*

g *Arbitration – Arbitrator – Jurisdiction – Salvage arbitration – Inspection of property – Inspection
of ship – Arbitration under Lloyd's form of salvage agreement – Application by cargo owners for
order for inspection of salved vessel – Whether arbitrator having power to make order for
inspection.*

A ship carrying a cargo of tiles was severely damaged by fire while at sea and was towed
h ashore pursuant to a salvage agreement on Lloyd's form. During the course of the salvage
arbitration which followed, the arbitrator, at the cargo owners' request, made an order
under s 12(1)[a] of the Arbitration Act 1950 directing the shipowners to allow the cargo
owners' surveyors to board the ship so that they could form an opinion, for the purposes
of the arbitration, as to the origin and path of the fire and to inspect her for any damage
which might affect the assessment of her value. The shipowners contended that the
j arbitrator had no power to make the order because s 12(6)(g)[b] of the 1950 Act conferred
on the High Court sole jurisdiction to make orders for the inspection of property which
was the subject of arbitration proceedings. On the questions whether an arbitrator had

---

a   Section 12(1) is set out at p 215 *fg*, post
b   Section 12(6), so far as material, is set out at p 215 *j* to p 216 *a* and *c*, post

power to make an order for the inspection of property and, if so, whether such an order
could be made in a salvage arbitration where the property in question was a ship and the   *a*
application for inspection was made not by the salvors but by the cargo owners,

Held – (1) On the true construction of s 12 of the 1950 Act an arbitrator had power to
make an order for the inspection of property belonging to one of the parties to an
arbitration because it enabled him to discharge his function properly and, as such, was to
be distinguished from those powers conferred on the High Court by s 12(6), such as the   *b*
power to make an order for security for costs or to grant an interim injunction, which
were collateral to the arbitrator's function and could be exercised only by a judge (see
p 216 *b* to *h* and p 217 *a* and *f*, post); *Barlow v Bailey* (1870) 22 LT 464, *Barnett v Aldridge
Colliery Co Ltd* (1887) 4 TLR 16 and *Kursell v Timber Operators and Contractors Ltd* [1923]
2 KB 202 considered.

(2) Although in a salvage arbitration the shipowner and the cargo owner had a   *c*
common interest in defeating the salvor or in securing the lowest award they could get,
and in that sense were on same side against the salvor, the interests of the shipowner and
the cargo owner were not identical, and there was nothing, either in the Lloyd's form or
elsewhere, to prevent the arbitrator from making an order for the inspection of the ship
at the request and for the benefit of the cargo owner as well as the salvor (see p 217 *a* to *d*
and *f*, post).
                                                                                          d

Notes
For the power of an arbitrator or umpire in respect of evidence and discovery in
arbitration proceedings, see 2 Halsbury's Laws (4th edn) para 597, and for cases on the
subject, see 3 Digest (Reissue) 153–154, 875–896.

For the Arbitration Act 1950, s 12, see 2 Halsbury's Statutes (3rd edn) 444.   *e*

Cases referred to in judgment
Barlow v Bailey (1870) 22 LT 464.
Barnett v Aldridge Colliery Ltd (1887) 4 TLR 16.
Kursell v Timber Operators and Contractors Ltd [1923] 2 KB 202, DC.
Pioneer Shipping Ltd v BTP Tioxide Ltd, The Nema [1981] 2 All ER 1030, [1982] AC 724,   *f*
   [1981] 3 WLR 292, HL.
Tor Line AB v Alltrans Group of Canada Ltd, The TFL Prosperity [1982] 1 Lloyd's Rep 167.

Cases also cited
East India Co v Kynaston (1821) 3 Bli 153, 4 ER 561, HL.
Oxford (Charles) Ltd v Gonshaw Ltd [1948] 2 All ER 229, CA.
Saxton (decd), Re [1962] 2 All ER 618, [1962] 1 WLR 859; *varied* [1962] 3 All ER 92,   *g*
   [1962] 1 WLR 968, CA.
Unione Stearinerie Lanza and Wiener, Re [1917] 2 KB 558, [1916–17] All ER Rep 1079, DC.

Interlocutory application
The owners of the ship Vasso applied to the High Court for the determination of certain   *h*
questions of law specified by the arbitrator, Mr Geoffrey Brice QC, in the course of a
salvage arbitration to which they and the owners of the cargo lately laden on the Vasso
were party, namely (1) whether an arbitrator had power to make an order for inspection
of property? (2) if so, whether an arbitrator had power to make such an order in a salvage
arbitration where the property in question was a ship and the application for inspection
of the ship was made not by the salvors but by the cargo owners? and (3) if so, whether   *j*
the order made by the arbitrator, at the request of the cargo owners, on 28 February
1983, and confirmed on 8 March 1983, was one which he could, in the exercise of his
discretion, properly make? The shipowners also or alternatively sought a declaration that
the arbitrator's order was not within the scope of his jurisdiction or powers and/or an
injunction restraining the cargo owners, by themselves, their servants or agents, or
howsoever otherwise, from boarding or attempting to board the Vasso without the

consent of the shipowners, and a declaration that the shipowners were entitled to refuse
a such permission notwithstanding the arbitrator's order. The facts are set out in the
judgment.

M N *Howard* for the shipowners.
Peter Gross for the cargo owners.

b   *Cur adv vult*

29 March. The following judgment was delivered.

LLOYD J. The substantive question for decision in this case is whether arbitrators have
power under s 12(1) of the Arbitration Act 1950 to order a party to an arbitration to
c permit inspection of his property where the property is the subject matter of the
reference. Both the leading textbooks on arbitration answer the question in the
affirmative: see Mustill and Boyd *Commercial Arbitration* (1982) p 294 and *Russell on
Arbitration* (20th edn, 1982) p 255. The question is whether they are right.

On 6 January 1983 the plaintiffs' vessel Vasso caught fire in the course of a voyage
from Valencia to Kuwait with a cargo of tiles. The vessel suffered substantial damage. It
d may be that she will prove a constructive total loss. She was towed first to Crete and
thence to Piraeus. These salvage services were performed pursuant to a salvage agreement
on Lloyd's form. In due course Mr Geoffrey Brice QC was appointed arbitrator by the
committee of Lloyd's. On 18 and 22 February 1983 the parties appeared before Mr Brice
on an application by the owners of the cargo that they be permitted to place two surveyors
on board the vessel, a fire expert and a hull surveyor. On 28 February the arbitrator made
e an order on the analogy of RSC Ord 75, r 28, which enables the court in Admiralty
proceedings to make an order for inspection—

    '... by the assessors (if the action is tried with assessors), or by any party or
    witness, of any ship or other property, whether real or personal, the inspection of
    which may be necessary or desirable for the purposes of obtaining full information
    or evidence in connection with any issue in the action.'

f On 8 March the arbitrator confirmed his order in writing as follows:

    '1. That the Ship Respondents do give reasonable access to a fire expert and a Hull
    surveyor (acting on behalf of Cargo Respondents . . .) in order to inspect such a space
    or spaces in the "VASSO" which will enable them to form an opinion for the purposes
    of this Arbitration as to (a) the place of origin of the fire (b) the path taken by the
g fire thereafter and (c) whether the fire might have spread to any other space or spaces
    in the absence of the firefighting services. 2. That the Ship Respondents do give
    reasonable access to a Hull surveyor (acting on behalf of the said Cargo Respondents
    . . .) in order to inspect the "VASSO" for any damage which may affect the assessment
    of the value of the vessel for the purpose of this salvage Arbitration.'

h The arbitrator was asked to give his reasons. This he did in a document of the same date.
In the course of giving his reasons the arbitrator helpfully identified three questions for
his decision, which I can paraphrase as follows. (1) Does an arbitrator have power to make
an order for inspection of property? (2) If so, does an arbitrator have power to make such
an order in a salvage arbitration, where the property in question is a ship, and the
application for inspection of the ship is made, not by the salvors, but by cargo? (3) If so,
j should the order be made on the facts of the present case?

The shipowners, being dissatisfied with the arbitrator's order for inspection, invited
him to consent to certain questions of law being raised for the consideration of the court
under s 2 of the Arbitration Act 1979. The arbitrator consented, and the questions which
I am asked to consider are substantially as I have set them out above, except that for
question (3) the arbitrator substituted: '(3) If so, was the order one which the arbitrator
could, in the exercise of his discretion, properly make?'.

The jurisdiction of the court to consider preliminary questions of law is set out in s 2 of the Arbitration Act 1979:

'(1) Subject to subsection (2) and section 3 below, on an application to the High Court made by any of the parties to a reference—(a) with the consent of an arbitrator who has entered on the reference or, if an umpire has entered on the reference, with his consent, or (b) with the consent of all the other parties, the High Court shall have the jurisdiction to determine any question of law arising in the course of the reference.

(2) The High Court shall not entertain an application under subsection (1)(a) above with respect to any question of law unless it is satisfied that—(a) the determination of the application might produce substantial savings in costs to the parties; and (b) the question of law is one in respect of which leave to appeal would be likely to be given under section 1(3)(b) above . . .'

I can dispose of question (3) at the outset. It does not raise any question of law at all, but a question for the decision of the arbitrator in his discretion. Even if I had been disposed to disagree with the way in which the arbitrator has exercised his discretion, which, on the material before me, I am not, I would have been unwilling to interfere.

The other questions are questions of law, and questions of some general interest and importance. There is no reported case on whether the arbitrator's powers under s 12(1) of the 1950 Act include a power to order an inspection of property. In the case of a salvage arbitration there is the added complication that the question arises, not only between ship and cargo on the one hand and the salvor on the other, but also between ship and cargo inter se.

But it is not enough under s 2 of the 1979 Act that one party wants a preliminary question or questions of law decided by the court, even if the arbitrator consents. I have to be satisfied that I have jurisdiction. My jurisdiction depends on two conditions being fulfilled: first, that the determination of the question might produce substantial savings in costs and, second, that the question is such that I would have been likely to give leave if the application had been for leave to appeal from an award under s 1 of the Act.

Counsel for the cargo owners submits that neither condition is fulfilled. Paradoxically, the question whether the conditions are fulfilled or not seems to me much more difficult than the substantive question under s 12(1) of the 1950 Act.

Normally a preliminary point of law will produce a saving in costs when, if decided one way, it will either determine the result altogether, or at least shorten the hearing. The fact that it may be decided the other way does not prevent the court having jurisdiction, because it is enough that the application might result in a substantial saving in costs. It is not easy to apply that analysis in the present case. Whichever way I may decide the question of law cannot determine the ultimate result or shorten the hearing. It may make it more difficult for the cargo owners to prepare their case, or even obtain justice if I decide against them, but it will not, so far as I can see, save costs.

Counsel for the shipowners seeks to meet this difficulty by arguing that if the arbitrator's order stands the shipowners will wish their own surveyors to be present when the inspection takes place. If I reverse the arbitrator's order, the expense of sending out their surveyors will be spared, and costs thereby saved. Counsel for the cargo owners replies that that argument does not lie in the shipowners' mouth, for the cargo owners had suggested that their surveyors be present when the shipowners' surveyors were originally on board, and they are happy to bear the expense of sending out their own surveyor now whatever the ultimate result of the arbitration.

I admire the ingenuity of the argument of counsel for the shipowners. But I doubt whether the saving in costs which would result from the shipowners not having to comply with an order, if wrong, is the sort of saving in costs which Parliament had in mind when enacting s 2 of the 1979 Act. In truth, the present application does not really fit the terms of s 2 at all. It would have been appropriate, perhaps, for the old form of consultative case. But the consultative case has been abolished. Instead, we have the

preliminary question of law. But we also have s 7(1)(a) of the 1979 Act, which provides,
a in effect, that the court can give leave to appeal on a question of law arising out of an
interim award. Although the parties, and the arbitrator, have approached this application
as being made under s 2 of the 1979 Act, it may be that they should have regarded the
arbitrator's order for inspection as an interim award, in which case, of course, there
would have been no need to show a substantial saving in costs as a condition of leave to
appeal.

b   The second condition also gives rise to difficulty. There is a difficulty on the facts of
the present case; there are difficulties in general. The difficulties in general are discussed
in *Mustill and Boyd* pp 579–581, and are described there as being intractable. The
difficulty on the facts of the present case is to see how questions (1) and (2) could ever
arise in connection with the arbitrator's final award. Since it is difficult to envisage them
as questions of law arising on the award at all, it is obviously difficult to say whether
c leave to appeal would be likely to be given. It may be that the solution again is that
which I have already suggested, that wherever a question of law arises in connection with
an interlocutory order of an arbitrator, the order should be treated as an interim award.
Meanwhile, all I can do is repeat what I have already said, that questions (1) and (2) seem
to me questions of some interest and importance. If they were questions arising on an
interim award, then, applying the principles in *Pioneer Shipping Ltd v BTP Tioxide Ltd, The*
d *Nema* [1981] 2 All ER 1030, [1982] AC 724, I would have been willing to grant leave to
appeal.
    At the conclusion of the application under s 2, it was obviously expected of me by the
parties that I would go on to determine the questions of law there and then. I decided to
do so having regard to the urgency of the matter. But I would echo in this case what was
said by Bingham J in *Tor Line AB v Alltrans Group of Canada Ltd, The TFL Prosperity* [1982]
e 1 Lloyd's Rep 617. Normally, the court will not determine questions of law under s
2(1)(a) immediately after a successful application, any more than it will hear an appeal
under s 1. It is important that applications, whether under s 1 or s 2(1)(a), should be dealt
with expeditiously, and should not become full-dress hearings as they would if the
application normally led straight on to the appeal.
    Turning now to the substantive question, it is convenient to start by setting out s 12(1)
f of the 1950 Act:

> 'Unless a contrary intention is expressed therein, every arbitration agreement
> shall, where such a provision is applicable to the reference, be deemed to contain a
> provision that the parties to the reference, and all persons claiming through them
> respectively, shall, subject to any legal objection, submit to be examined by the
> arbitrator or umpire, on oath or affirmation, in relation to the matters in dispute,
g and shall, subject as aforesaid, produce before the arbitrator or umpire all documents
> within their possession or power respectively which may be required or called for,
> and do all other things which during the proceedings on the reference the arbitrator
> or umpire may require.'

It will be seen that whereas s 12(1) covers the examination on oath of the parties
h themselves, and the production of their documents, it does not specifically cover the
inspection of their property. The question is whether an order for inspection of property
comes within the general words 'and do all other things which during the proceedings
on the reference the arbitrator or umpire may require'.
    Section 12(6) provides that the High Court shall have power to make the following
orders in relation to arbitrations:

j
> '... (a) security for costs; (b) discovery of documents ... (c) the giving of evidence
> by affidavit; (d) examination on oath of any witness before an officer of the High
> Court or any other person, and the issue of a commission or request for the
> examination of a witness out of the jurisdiction; (e) the preservation, interim custody
> or sale of any goods which are the subject matter of the reference; (f) securing the

amount in dispute in the reference; (g) the detention, preservation or inspection of
any property or thing which is the subject of the reference . . . and (h) interim   a
injunctions or the appointment of a receiver . . .'

The basic argument of counsel for the shipowners is simple. The power which the
arbitrator has purported to exercise is the power to make an order for the 'inspection of
. . . property . . . which is the subject of the reference'. This is a power which is given
specifically to the High Court under s 12(6)(g). Nobody has ever suggested that an
arbitrator has the power to make an order for security for costs or to grant an interim   b
injunction, which are covered by s 12(6)(a) and (h) respectively. No more has he power to
make an order for inspection of property, which is covered by s 12(6)(g).

Stated in that simple form the argument is unconvincing. There is a proviso to s 12(6)
as follows:

'Provided that nothing in this subsection shall be taken to prejudice any power   c
which may be vested in an arbitrator or umpire of making orders with respect to
any of the matters aforesaid.'

Thus the fact that the High Court has power to make an order of a particular kind does
not mean that the arbitrator may not also have power to make the same order. It has, for
example, been held that an arbitrator may make an order for discovery, even though
discovery is specifically covered by s 12(6)(b): see *Kursell v Timber Operators and Contractors*   d
Ltd [1923] 2 KB 202.

Counsel for the shipowners then seeks to refine his argument. A distinction must be
drawn between those powers which the arbitrator and the court can exercise, as it were,
concurrently, and those powers which belong exclusively to the court. The power to
order inspection of property belongs, he submits, exclusively to the court, first, because
it is analogous to the power to grant an injunction, both powers being contained in RSC   e
Ord 29, and, second, because it is a serious matter to allow a person to invade the property
of another against his will.

I agree with the first part of counsel's proposition. A similar distinction is drawn in
Kursell v Timber Operators and Contractors Ltd where Salter J (at 206) refers to the power
to order discovery as being of a kind to aid the arbitrator in discharge of his function, and
'not of a kind which only a judge can use'.   f

But I disagree with counsel's conclusion. It seems to me that the power to order
inspection of property is not 'of a kind which only a judge can use'. I say that for two
reasons. First, the property in question is the property of one of the parties to the
arbitration. If it had been the property of a third party, the result might well have been
different, though it is unnecessary so to decide. Where the property, as here, belongs to
one of the parties, I see no reason for holding that the power to inspect the property can   g
only be exercised by the court. Second, the property in question is the subject matter of
the reference. In order to enable the arbitrator to do his job properly, it is desirable, if not
essential, that he should have the benefit of expert evidence on *both* sides as to the matters
in dispute. The power is therefore necessary to enable the arbitrator 'to discharge his
function'; in that respect it is to be distinguished from, for instance, the power to order
security for costs, which is collateral to the arbitrator's functions.   h

It is common ground that the tailpiece to s 12(1) of the 1950 Act does not give the
arbitrator *all* the powers of the court. As already mentioned, an arbitrator cannot make
an order for security for costs or grant an interim injunction. Some limitation must
therefore be implied. The question is then: on which side of the line does the present
application fall? Having heard the arguments, I am satisfied, for the reasons already
mentioned, that it falls within the arbitrator's powers. Counsel for the cargo owners   j
referred me to *Barlow v Bailey* (1870) 22 LT 464, in which Stuart V-C drew an analogy
between an inspection of documents and an inspection of property. To my mind the
connection is not sufficiently close to afford any real assistance in the present case; nor do
I get much help from *Barnett v Aldridge Colliery Co Ltd* (1887) 4 TLR 16 decided before

a the Arbitration Act 1889 in which the Queen's Bench Division held on appeal that the power to order an inspection of a mine lay with the arbitrator and not with the court. I prefer to put my decision on what I take to be the true construction of s 12(1) as a whole.

I would therefore answer the first question in favour of the cargo owners.

I can deal with the second question very briefly. It is true that, in one sense, cargo and ship are on the same side in the salvage arbitration, and the salvor is on the other side. The ship and cargo have a common interest in defeating the salvor altogether, or in

b securing the lowest award they can get. But their interests are not identical.

When it comes to salved values, ship and cargo are in conflict. Moreover, I was told that, when the ship's salved value is low in relation to cargo, the ship may, and often does, settle independently with the salvor, and thereafter drop out of the arbitration altogether. In those circumstances it seems to me essential, in the interests of a fair hearing, that the arbitrator should be able to make an order for inspection of the ship at

c the instance of, and for the benefit of, cargo as well as the salvor.

The only argument the other way was that the cargo might use the inspection as an occasion for collecting evidence to support a claim against the ship, e g for breach of the warranty of seaworthiness. On the facts of the present case, the owners of the cargo say that they have no intention of using the inspection for any ulterior purpose. But even if the shipowners' suspicions were justified it would not be ground for saying that the

d arbitrator had no power to make such an order in favour of cargo in a salvage arbitration under Lloyd's form. At most, it would go to discretion. There is nothing in the language of the form itself to preclude the arbitrator making such an order. Accordingly, I answer the second question, like the first, in favour of cargo.

Finally, counsel for the shipowners applied to set aside the arbitrator's order on the ground of misconduct. He submitted that the arbitrator has exercised his discretion on a

e wholly wrong basis. The only ground for that submission seemed to be that the shipowners had offered the cargo the benefit of their own experts' report, or alternatively were willing to agree that the arbitrator should himself appoint an independent surveyor. I am unable to see how it followed that the arbitrator's discretion was, for either or both of those reasons, exercised on a wholly wrong basis; and even if it was I should not accept that the arbitrator had thereby misconducted himself. It cannot be said too often, or too

f emphatically, that error of law is not misconduct, nor is error of fact. The application to set aside is therefore dismissed.

In summary, the two questions of law which, rightly or wrongly, I have entertained under s 2 of the Arbitration Act 1979 are answered in favour of cargo. I have not been persuaded that I ought to put the cargo on terms, that they will use any information which they may obtain on the inspection for the purpose of the salvage arbitration only.

g I am unwilling to entertain the third question which I do not regard as a question of law. All other applications by the shipowners are refused. The cargo owners' cross-application does not arise.

Order accordingly.

Solicitors: *Coward Chance* (for the shipowners); *Clyde & Co*, Guildford (for the cargo owners)

K Mydeen Esq   Barrister.

Re Islington Metal and Plating Works Ltd a

CHANCERY DIVISION (COMPANIES COURT)

HARMAN J

14, 15, 23 MARCH, 3, 27 MAY 1983

Company – Winding up – Application of bankruptcy rules – Proof and ranking of claims – Unliquidated claim for damages in tort – Company in creditor's voluntary liquidation – Outstanding claims against company in tort – Claimants not obtaining judgment by date of commencement of winding up – Whether claims admissible to proof in winding up of insolvent company – Bankruptcy Act 1914, s 30 – Companies Act 1948, s 317.

Company – Winding up – Application of bankruptcy rules – Surplus assets after payment of debts – Company placed in creditor's voluntary liquidation on basis of insolvency – Unliquidated claims in tort outstanding against company but not admitted to proof – Prospect of liquidators recovering damages in action against directors for misfeasance – Whether on liquidators recovering damages in misfeasance action sufficient to leave a surplus after repaying all proven creditors surplus to be paid to tort claimants or to contributories – Companies Act 1948, ss 316, 317.

A company went into a creditor's voluntary liquidation on 20 June 1979. The liquidators realised assets which were likely to produce a dividend of 90p in the pound for unsecured creditors admitted to proof. It was also possible that all creditors could be repaid in full if further sums could be recovered in misfeasance proceedings against former directors who were also contributories. In addition to the unsecured creditors admitted to proof there were several likely claims against the company in tort although none of the possible claimants had obtained judgment against the company. In the case of the winding up of a solvent company s 316^a of the Companies Act 1948 provided that 'all' claims were admissible to proof, while in the case of an insolvent company s 30^b of the Bankruptcy Act 1914 (which was applied by s 317^c of the 1948 Act) provided that demands in the nature of unliquidated damages were not admissible to proof. The liquidators applied to the court by summons to determine, (i) whether the tort claims could be admitted to proof, given that the company was insolvent, and (ii) whether in the event of a claim against the directors for misfeasance succeeding and leaving a surplus after the unsecured creditors and costs of the liquidation were paid in full that surplus should be paid to the contributories or would be available to be paid to the tort claimants.

Held – (1) It was well established that a creditor's right to be admitted to proof was to be determined as at the date of the commencement of the winding up. Accordingly, because at the date of the commencement of the winding up the company was insolvent, s 30 of the 1914 Act governed the admission of claims to proof in the winding up and since at that date all the tort claims were for unliquidated amounts they were not admissible to proof (see p 222 h to p 223 c and f and p 224 d, post); Re Berkeley Securities (Property) Ltd [1980] 3 All ER 513 not followed.

(2) Where a company which was insolvent when winding-up proceedings commenced thereafter became solvent after payment both of creditors admitted to proof under s 317 of the 1948 Act and of the costs of the liquidation, s 316 of that Act applied to the admission to proof of claims for the surplus and accordingly 'all' claims became admissible even if they exceeded the apparent surplus thus making the company insolvent again. Accordingly, any surplus arising if the misfeasance claims proved to be

---

a Section 316, so far as material, is set out at p 220 h, post

b Section 30, so far as material, is set out at p 220 j, post

c Section 317, so far as material, is set out at p 220 h, post

successful would be available for distribution to the claimants instead of to the
a contributories (see p 224 *g* to *j* and p 225 *e* to *h*, post); *Re Milan Tramways Co* (1884) 25
Ch D 587 and *Re Rolls-Royce Ltd* [1974] 3 All ER 646 applied; *Government of India, Ministry
of Finance (Revenue Division) v Taylor* [1955] 1 All ER 292 distinguished.

Notes
For debts provable in a winding up, see 7 Halsbury's Laws (4th edn) paras 1259–1275,
b and for cases on the subject, see 10 Digest (Reissue) 1050–1062, 6451–6520.
   For application of bankruptcy rules, see 7 Halsbury's Laws (4th edn) paras 1276–1280,
and for cases on the subject, see 10 Digest (Reissue) 1063–1066, 6524–6544.
   For the Bankruptcy Act 1914, s 30, see 3 Halsbury's Statutes (3rd edn) 78.
   For the Companies Act 1948, ss 316, 317, see 5 ibid 344.

c **Cases referred to in judgments**
Berkeley Securities (Property) Ltd, Re [1980] 3 All ER 513, [1980] 1 WLR 1589.
Dynamics Corp of America, Re [1976] 2 All ER 669, [1976] 1 WLR 757.
Great Orme Tramways Co, Re (1934) 50 TLR 450.
Government of India, Ministry of Finance (Revenue Division) v Taylor [1955] 1 All ER 292,
   [1955] AC 491, [1955] 2 WLR 303, HL; *affg* sub nom *Re Delhi Electric Supply and
d   Traction Co Ltd* [1953] 2 All ER 1452, [1954] Ch 131, [1953] 3 WLR 1085, CA.
Humber Ironworks and Shipbuilding Co, Re (1869) LR 4 Ch App 643, CA.
Lines Bros Ltd, Re [1982] 2 All ER 183, [1983] Ch 1, [1982] 2 WLR 1010, CA.
Milan Tramways Co, Re (1884) 25 Ch D 587.
Parana Plantations Ltd, Re [1946] 2 All ER 214, CA.
Rolls-Royce Ltd, Re [1974] 3 All ER 646, [1974] 1 WLR 1584.
e

Cases also cited
Fryer v Ewart [1902] AC 187, HL.
Newman, Re, ex p Brooke (1876) 3 Ch D 494, CA.
Parana Plantations Ltd, Re [1948] 1 All ER 742.
R-R Realisations Ltd (formerly Rolls-Royce Ltd), Re [1980] 1 All ER 1019, [1980] 1 WLR
f   805.
Ward, Re, Hammond & Son v Official Receiver and the debtor [1942] 1 All ER 513, [1942] Ch
   294.

Summons
g By originating summons dated 29 September 1982 Malcolm Barry Harris and George
Albert Auger, the joint liquidators of Islington Metal and Plating Works Ltd, applied to
the court to determine the extent to which persons who at the commencement of the
winding up of the company had claims against the company for unliquidated damages
in tort were entitled to be admitted to proof in the winding up of the company and to
share in any distribution from the liquidated assets of the company. The joint liquidators
h also sought orders that the first respondent, the Department of Employment, represent
all unsecured creditors, that the second respondents Peter Wildridge and Leila Mary
Margaret Wildridge represent all tort claimants and that the third respondent, Henry
Herbst, represent all the contributories to the company. The facts are set out in the
judgment.

j *Alan Steinfeld* for the joint liquidators.
Philip Heslop for the Department of Employment.
Christopher G Russell for the tort claimants.
The third respondents did not appear.

Cur adv vult

23 March. The following judgment was delivered.

HARMAN J. By this summons issued on 29 September 1982 in the liquidation of Islington Metal and Plating Works Ltd (which I shall call 'the company') counsel for the joint liquidators, asked the court to answer questions as to who is entitled to be admitted to prove in the winding up. The application is supported by an affidavit by a well-known liquidator, Mr George Auger.

The evidence shows that the company went into creditors' voluntary liquidation on 20 June 1979. The company had assets and the liquidators are at present likely to be able to pay a dividend to unsecured creditors already admitted to proof of about 90p in the pound. It is possible that further assets will be recovered in misfeasance proceedings brought by the liquidators against former directors. If those proceedings succeed all creditors already admitted to prove will be paid in full and there may be a worthwhile surplus for whoever ranks next in order of claim. However, the liquidators' difficulty arises because there were at the date of liquidation claims in tort, largely the tort of nuisance, against the company. The total damages might, and I stress that the figure is highly speculative, amount to £300,000. If the claimants in the nuisance actions, who have been called (and whom I will call) 'the tort claimants', can get themselves admitted to proof, then there will certainly be a deficiency for creditors. The present funds available might provide a dividend of about 20p in the pound on those very approximate figures.

In those circumstances the liquidators, seeking to do their duty to all claimants, issued the summons herein joining, firstly, the Department of Employment, an undoubted unsecured creditor admitted to proof for £40,000-odd to represent all unsecured creditors admitted to proof. Counsel for the Department of Employment has argued that the tort claimants should not be admitted to proof, at all events while the company is insolvent as it is at present.

The second and third defendants are husband and wife, who are tort claimants. They were joined to represent all tort claimants. They have not brought any action against the company as yet but may well have a claim in nuisance for damage to their premises. They are represented by counsel and have argued that the tort claimants are entitled to prove and to rank for a distribution in the liquidation. I use that form of words because counsel for the tort claimants, labouring under great handicaps, was forced to argue that tort claimants should be admitted to proof when, but not until, they have recovered a judgment against the company.

The fourth defendant to the summons was a contributory. Despite the joint liquidators having very properly made clear that they would support payment of all parties' costs on this summons out of the assets of the company, the fourth defendant has not appeared before me. I have thus been deprived of assistance which I consider would have been of help to the court in deciding whether the tort claimants are entitled to some stake in the winding up or are entitled to nothing at all.

The relevant sections of the Companies Act 1948 are s 316, which provides that 'In every winding up (subject, in the case of insolvent companies, to the application in accordance with the provisions of this Act of the law of bankruptcy) . . . all claims against the company . . . shall be admissible to proof', and s 317, which provides that 'In the winding up of an insolvent company . . . the same rules shall prevail . . . with regard . . . to debts provable . . . as are in force . . . under the law of bankruptcy in England'. By s 30(1) of the Bankruptcy Act 1914 it is provided that 'Demands in the nature of unliquidated damages . . . shall not be provable in a bankruptcy'. Thus on the face of it the tort claimants whose only claim today is as tort claimants for unliquidated damages, and a fortiori had at date of the resolution to wind up no judgment or right to any liquidated sum, are not entitled to prove. What then has caused this problem to be raised before the court?

The difficulties in the matter arise from a recent decision of Vinelott J in *Re Berkeley Securities (Property) Ltd* [1980] 3 All ER 513, [1980] 1 WLR 1589. In that case Vinelott J

had before him an appeal against a refusal of Mr Registrar Bradburn to permit a claimant
a   to bring an action against a company in liquidation. The action was a claim in tort.
Vinelott J was urged not to give leave because the claim, being for unliquidated damages
in tort, was not capable, even if liquidated by a subsequent judgment, of being admitted
to proof (see [1980] 3 All ER 513 at 522, [1980] 1 WLR 1589 at 1601–1602). Vinelott J
decided that the claimant, if he obtained a judgment, would be entitled at that time to
be admitted to proof. He therefore gave leave to bring the action, but on very special
b   terms limiting its progress for various other reasons.

The decision was undoubtedly surprising since it had been assumed for many years by
company practitioners that an unliquidated claim for damages in tort could not be
proved in a liquidation (see eg the decision of that very experienced company judge Eve J
in Re Great Orme Tramways Co (1934) 50 TLR 450 and the statement in Palmer's Company
Law (22nd edn, 1976) vol 1, p 913, para 81-51. The decision however was not challenged
c   by appeal. However this circumstance, which might have had considerable significance
in some cases, was not in fact significant in the Berkeley case. Counsel for the department,
who was junior counsel for the unsuccessful party in Berkeley, pointed out to me the
terms of the judge's order which gave only a very limited right to proceed as far as service
of a statement of claim, a defence and third party notices, but permitted no further steps
in the action to be taken without further leave of the court (see [1980] 3 All ER 513 at
d   531–532, [1980] 1 WLR 1589 at 1613). The practical result (as counsel demonstrated)
was adequately satisfactory for the company and therefore no appeal was lodged against
the decision.

I have said that the decision in the Berkeley case was surprising to practitioners in
company law, and not easy to reconcile with the terms of s 30 of the 1914 Act, and so I
turn to consider the basic framework of the winding up of an insolvent company,
e   whether by the court or voluntarily.

Counsel for the department submitted that ever since at least 1869 it has been clear
that the theory of all liquidations is that the liquidation and the distribution are to be
treated as notionally simultaneous (see Re Humber Ironworks and Shipbuilding Co (1869) LR
4 Ch App 643 esp at 646–647 per Selwyn and Gifford LJJ; the rule was quoted and
applied by Oliver J in Re Dynamics Corp of America [1976] 2 All ER 669 at 673–674,
f   [1976] 1 WLR 757 at 762). I was informed by counsel for the department that this case
was mentioned to Vinelott J in the Berkeley case though not formally cited or read to him.
It plainly did not affect his reasoning and is not cited in the report. In my judgment the
submission of counsel for the department is correct and the law binding on this court
and the Court of Appeal is as stated. That basic principle of liquidation is cut across by
the decision in the Berkeley case. The principle has the convenient result that a line can be
g   ruled across a company's accounts at the date of liquidation. Creditors can be ascertained
and a committee of inspection formed from the creditors at that date. All debts are to be
computed as at that date, as the Court of Appeal held in Re Lines Bros Ltd [1982] 2 All ER
183, [1983] Ch 1. Foreign claims are converted into sterling at that date. Brightman LJ
analyses the authorities in detail (see [1982] 2 All ER 183 at 192–195, [1983] Ch 1 at 17–
21). His decision was that the date of liquidation was the date on which all the claims
h   had to be established and at which all claims had to be valued. He expressly approved the
decision in Re Dynamics Corp holding that the proposition that all claims must be as at
the date of winding up was axiomatic. Oliver LJ re-examined his own decision in Re
Dynamics Corp, but in the end firmly held that it was correct.

In my judgment this basic scheme is wholly inconsistent with the approach adopted
by Vinelott J in the Berkeley case. Further counsel for the joint liquidators pointed out
j   that the judge in that case thought that he was producing 'a sensible and workable
scheme' (see [1980] 3 All ER 513 at 529, [1980] 1 WLR 1589 at 1610). For the joint
liquidators who have to administer the scheme so produced their counsel submitted it
was quite unworkable and far from sensible. In the present case there are several notified
claims by tort claimants. None have been liquidated by a money judgment. Several have
not yet begun their actions. There is no machinery that can compel tort claimants to

proceed, and there are good reasons why they should not, in their own proper interest, be in any haste to do so. In the result the joint liquidators, faced with known claims of **a** unknown (and almost unascertainable at this date) amount, would be bound to await the eventual outcome of the tort claimant's proceedings, maybe several years ahead. No payment could safely be made to the undoubted creditors in the mean time, since if the tort claimants eventually obtained judgments for very large damages the liquidators might well be found to be short of assets to pay the proper dividend. Further, Vinelott J's exception to the rule that all claims must be established at the date of winding up was **b** based on the proposition that a judgment must be obtained. In the result the joint liquidators' right to make a fair estimation of the amount of the claims and to pay out dividends on that basis is wholly frustrated. No estimation is allowed, only a judgment will do. This plainly puts a powerful weapon in the hands of the tort claimants. Further, it has the oddity that whereas the basic rule is that all claims have to be valued as at the date of winding up (see *Re Parana Plantations Ltd* [1946] 2 All ER 214 at 218–219, a **c** decision of the Court of Appeal) the judgment in tort, especially in a claim in nuisance, must be based on the damages as at the date of judgment. Indeed in nuisance actions the date of winding up is obviously wholly irrelevant to the rights of the tort claimants. That must produce inequality between creditors.

In my judgment these criticisms by counsel for the joint liquidators are well founded, and, with all respect to Vinelott J, his scheme is not workable or sensible. It may none **d** the less be the law if the reasoning which leads to it is sound. I therefore return to the judgment in the *Berkeley* case. Vinelott J recited, as I have done, s 317 of the Companies Act 1948, which applies to the winding up of insolvent companies the same rules as apply in bankruptcy. He then referred to s 30 of the Bankruptcy Act 1914, by sub-s (1) of which 'Demands in the nature of unliquidated damages . . . shall not be provable in bankruptcy'. It will be seen that the claim by the tort claimants in this summons and of **e** the applicant in the *Berkeley* case were both for unliquidated damages. None the less, as I have said, Vinelott J allowed the claim to be made. He did so because he held that

'The consequences which flow from a literal application of the bankruptcy rules in the winding up of an insolvent company are so absurd as to compel the conclusion that the bankruptcy rules must be modified in some way if they are to fit into the scheme of the winding up of an insolvent company.'   **f**

(See [1980] 3 All ER 513 at 528, [1980] 1 WLR 1589 at 1609.)

With all respect to the judge, the addition of the adjective 'literal' adds merely a somewhat pejorative emphasis, but nothing else, to the statement that because the rules laid down by Parliament are absurd they must be modified. I find this a difficult process of reasoning to follow or adopt.   **g**

Vinelott J goes on to hold in the *Berkeley* case [1980] 3 All ER 513 at 529, [1980] 1 WLR 1589 at 1610 that 'The fallacy in the construction of counsel for the liquidators' was to equate a winding up order and a receiving order. I confess that I am quite unable to see any fallacy in this contention. It is of course true that a receiving order has to be followed by adjudication. None the less, in my judgment the two steps do equate and it was expressly conceded by counsel for the tort claimants before me (in my view correctly) **h** that the analogy between the two was complete. The judge goes on to hold that s 317 operates 'only to exclude from proof a claim for damages for tort which has not been liquidated by judgment *at the time when the claimant comes in to prove*' (see [1980] 3 All ER 513 at 529, [1980] 1 WLR 1589 at 1610; my emphasis).

With all respect, this is to confuse the fundamentals of winding-up procedures. It is in my judgment clear beyond doubt, and established by authorities (some of which I have **j** mentioned) binding on puisne judges and the Court of Appeal, that admission to proof is to be determined as at the commencement of the winding up. The time when the actual proof of debt is lodged and the date when it is admitted are frequently long after that time, but to confuse the issue whether a creditor has a claim admissible to proof with the detail of when the creditor actually lodges it is in my judgment fundamentally

unsound. In my judgment the decision in the *Berkeley* case is wrong and I refuse to follow
a it.

As counsel for the tort claimants felt compelled by the authorities to concede, the rules
in bankruptcy and winding up are closely assimilated. It is plain that in bankruptcy a
tort claimant such as counsel's clients could not be entitled to prove. The result of the
Berkeley case is to produce differing results in insolvency according to whether the
tortfeasor was a limited company or an individual. It was said by Vinelott J that he
b considered that it was difficult to justify tort claimants being excluded from proof in
bankruptcy (see [1980] 3 All ER 513 at 530, [1980] 1 WLR 1589 at 1611). That may or
may not be correct as a matter of moral attitude. There are plainly strong arguments of
convenience and fairness to other creditors in favour of the rule. But in my judgment,
whatever the morals may be, to produce differences between the two sorts of insolvency
is contrary to the express enactment of Parliament and undesirable in principle. It was
c said that after all a tort claimant in bankruptcy was better off than a tort claimant in a
company liquidation because, if the bankrupt obtained his discharge from bankruptcy
the tort claimant could then proceed to pursue his claim to judgment and obtain either
payment or a further, second, bankruptcy. That is of course factually true, but it is, with
all respect, nothing to do with the question whether a tort claimant who has no liquidated
judgment in his favour can be admitted to proof in the first insolvency to say that there
d may be a right to be admitted in a second insolvency when the circumstances have
changed. The difference in my judgment lies, and lies only, in the inevitable results on
the one hand of a liquidation. In a liquidation an insolvent company inevitably (as I said
in argument) dies; it is dissolved, to use more formal language. In a bankruptcy, a
bankrupt may, or may not according to ordinary human vicissitudes, die. If the bankrupt
does die while a bankrupt, and assuming that his estate does not receive some large
e bounty after his death, the claim of a tort claimant will be wholly prevented from
coming to any judgment in the end, because it will not have been admissible to proof in
the bankruptcy at the time of the bankrupt going bankrupt and it will not be capable of
pursuit, the bankrupt being undischarged and dead and his estate being insolvent. So
also in a winding up; it is not, in my judgment, admissible to proof in the winding up;
the company dies and the claim cannot be pursued thereafter. The analogy is complete.
f The difference which may arise because a bankrupt may survive his bankruptcy and
come back into the land of a normal person who can be sued for his debts to judgment
is, in my view, nothing whatever to do with the administration of the insolvency. It is a
wholly other and outside consideration. I therefore conclude that in this case the tort
claimants are not entitled to be admitted to proof in this liquidation at this stage.

g *Order to stand summons over to a date to be fixed in order to hear argument on behalf of the
contributories.*

3 May. The court heard argument on the question whether the tort claimants would be
entitled to be admitted to proof if the company were to become solvent.

h *Alan Steinfeld* for the joint liquidators.
M K I Kennedy for the contributories.
Christopher G Russell for the tort claimants.
The unsecured creditors did not appear.

Cur adv vult

j 27 May. The following judgment was delivered.

HARMAN J. In this originating summons I have already delivered judgment on 23
March on question 1. I shall not repeat the facts there set out. I decided that the tort
claimants as therein defined were not entitled to be admitted to proof in this liquidation
by reason of the terms of s 317 of the 1948 Act.

The matter was restored for further hearing and counsel again appeared for the liquidators. The undoubted unsecured creditors, being content with the judgment given, *a* in effect, in their favour, did not appear before me. Counsel appeared for the tort claimants and for the contributories. The contest on this occasion was whether once all the company's undoubted unsecured creditors and the costs of liquidation had been paid or secured any surplus moneys then in the hands of the liquidators should go to the tort claimants or to the contributories.

The importance of the matter to the liquidator, in a company where there is at present *b* in prospect a deficiency as to undoubted unsecured creditors, arises in this way. The liquidators have claims against former directors for misfeasance. These claims may be substantial and if fought to a conclusion might produce in the liquidators' hands enough money to pay in full the unsecured creditors and the proper costs of the liquidation to that date, and leave a surplus over. But the defendants to the misfeasance proceedings will certainly be some of the contributories. Accordingly, if any surplus would be *c* distributed to the contributories and a comparatively small payment now would discharge all the undoubted unsecured creditors and the liquidation costs, it may very well be sensible for both liquidators and the contributories who are also directors to settle the misfeasance proceedings speedily. If, on the other hand, the tort claimants rank for distribution of any surplus moneys, then the liquidators' duty plainly is not satisfied by accepting a comparatively small payment in settlement from the director/contributories. *d* Thus, the liquidators need to know now what the rights to claim in any surplus which may arise will be.

At present it is clear that this company is insolvent. It is for that reason that I held that s 317 of the 1948 Act applied and brought in s 30 of the Bankruptcy Act 1914, so as to exclude the tort claimants. It is plain that so long as my judgment stands and the company remains insolvent the liquidators need have no regard to the tort claimants. It *e* is also plain that on a company which is not insolvent going into liquidation s 316 of the 1948 Act applies and 'all claims' are admissible to proof. In such a case persons who were in the position of the present tort claimants against a solvent company would be able to prove in a winding up and the liquidator in such case would have to make a 'just estimate' of the value of the claim.

The difficult question that arises is what happens when a company is insolvent at the *f* outset of its liquidation but becomes solvent during that process? Such events do in fact occur, as is well shown by the affairs of the old Rolls-Royce company, which was put into liquidation when thought to be hopelessly insolvent, but which in the end paid all creditors in full and distributed some 46p per share to the contributories. It is found by the judgment of Pennycuick V-C in *Re Rolls-Royce Ltd* [1974] 3 All ER 646 at 652, [1974] 1 WLR 1584 at 1591 that a company in liquidation which moves from being insolvent *g* to being solvent also moves from the provisions of s 317 to those of s 316. As is shown by the quotation in that case from Lord Selborne LC's judgment in the Court of Appeal in *Re Milan Tramways Co* (1884) 25 Ch Div 587 at 591, a company in liquidation always starts under the terms of what is now s 317 and only moves to s 316 when a surplus has been proved (see [1974] 3 All ER 646 at 651–652, [1974] 1 WLR 1584 at 1590–1591).

The real difficulty arises when a liquidator, having paid a company's undoubted *h* creditors and provided for the costs of winding up, is left with moneys in his hand but on turning to 'all claims' under s 316 finds that there are now claimants (such as the tort claimants here) whose claims exceed the apparent surplus. The company is thus again 'insolvent'. Does s 317 again apply? If so, there being no undisputed creditors left, an eternal state of oscillation between the sections would be created. This might be the secret of perpetual motion, but I cannot believe it is the law. In my judgment, once a *j* company has passed from s 317 to s 316 *all* claims have to be admitted. I appreciate that this may result in some claims in an apparently solvent liquidation not being paid in full. But any other result seems to me a view that is impossible and, in my judgment, there is no legislative or authoritative compulsion enforcing such a result on me.

When counsel for the contributories argued this part of the summons he argued that

once claimants, such as the tort claimants here, were prevented from proving by s 317
a they were so prevented for all time. In particular the propositions which I found
compelling on question 1 of this summons (that is to say that a liquidation has to be
treated as if liquidation and distribution were simultaneous, that the committee of
inspection has to be formed from the creditors entitled to prove at the date of liquidation,
and that all debts have got to be valued as at that date) show that one cannot have
claimants who are not admitted at the date of liquidation but come in thereafter. He
b referred to *Re Delhi Electric Supply and Traction Co Ltd* [1953] 2 All ER 1452, [1954] Ch
131 in the Court of Appeal, and in the House of Lords under the name *Government of
India, Ministry of Finance (Revenue Division) v Taylor* [1955] 1 All ER 292, [1955] AC 491.
    It is to be noted that the argument in that case concerned the meaning and scope of
the word 'liabilities' in s 302 of the 1948 Act. The decision was that an undoubted debt
of the company which was unenforceable in England was not a 'liability' for the purposes
c of a winding up. The House was divided on precisely how the exclusion from proof
came about. The case concerned, however, an undoubtedly solvent company and one
within s 316 and not s 317. It appears to me that there is nothing in the speeches in the
House or in the decision of the Court of Appeal which was directed to considering the
position of a claim which was enforceable against the company in England while it was
a going concern but is, however, rendered incapable of proof in an insolvent situation,
d but which would plainly be a proper 'claim' to be dealt with in a solvent liquidation. In
my judgment, although the contributories were the successful party in *Government of
India v Taylor*, it does not follow that the contributories in this case should also be
successful, and nothing in that authority directly bears on the problem before me.
    Further, nothing in the speeches or judgments in that case go to deal with, or refer in
any way to, the question whether a company which had, as I put it, passed from s 317 to
e s 316 so passes as to bar all those prevented from proving by s 317 but who would be
admissible under s 316.
    In my judgment, the key to the whole problem lies in the concept that a company in
liquidation starts subject to s 317 but can then move to s 316. The tests for admission to
proof are different in the two sections. The fact that this shift of position may occur
demonstrates, in my judgment, that the theory of simultaneous dealing has to be
f modified to this limited extent.
    I confess to being glad to be able to reach this result. As Vinelott J rightly pointed out
in *Re Berkeley Securities (Property) Ltd* [1980] 3 All ER 513, [1980] 1 WLR 1589, the gross
injustice which would be caused by ruling out a claim, in a liquidation where all
'undoubted' creditors have been paid, by persons such as the tort claimants here is a
consideration such as must impel any judge to try and find a way of allowing them to
g prove. As I held earlier, I was forced to the conclusion that the decision of Vinelott J in
the *Berkeley* case was wrong. I am happy that his well justified desire to see justice fairly
applied can to some extent be achieved without the difficulties which the liquidators in
this case put before me as arising from the full scope of that decision.
    I therefore hold that in this liquidation if all the undoubted creditors are satisfied and
provision has been made for the costs and there is then a surplus the tort claimants are
h entitled to claim in that surplus notwithstanding that their claims exceed, or may exceed,
the amount available.

Order accordingly.

Solicitors: *Booth & Blackwell* (for the joint liquidators); *Treasury Solicitor* (for the
Department of Employment and for the contributories); *W R Bennett & Co* (for the tort
claimants).

Evelyn M C Budd   Barrister.

Coupland v Arabian Gulf Petroleum Co   a

COURT OF APPEAL, CIVIL DIVISION
WALLER, OLIVER AND ROBERT GOFF LJJ
20 JUNE 1983

Conflict of laws – Tort – Proper law of tort – Scottish plaintiff employed by Libyan company to **b**
work in Libya – Contract of employment governed by Libyan law – Plaintiff suffering personal
injuries in course of employment in Libya – Plaintiff bringing action for damages in tort in England
– Effect of contract on proper law – Whether proper law of tort English law or Libyan law –
Whether fact that contract governed by Libyan law having effect on claim in tort under English
law.

The plaintiff was a maintenance technician living and domiciled in Scotland. The   **c**
defendants were a nationalised oil company in Libya which was registered in England
under Pt X of the Companies Act 1948. In January 1978 the plaintiff was employed by
the defendants through agents in London to work for them in Libya. The contract of
employment having been duly made in London, the plaintiff worked in Libya until
December 1978, when he had a serious accident at work. The plaintiff began proceedings
against the defendants in England for damages for personal injuries. By their defence the   **d**
defendants claimed that the proper law applicable to the contract and/or to any obligation
owed by the defendants to the plaintiff was Libyan law. On the trial of a preliminary
issue regarding the proper law of the claim the judge held that the plaintiff's claim in
tort was not governed by Libyan law but by English law, and that because the claim was
actionable both under the law of the place where the action was brought (the lex fori,
which was English law) and under the law of the foreign country (the lex loci delicti,   **e**
which was Libyan law) the plaintiff was entitled to bring his claim in England. He
further held that the proper law of the contract was Libyan law, but that since it was
open to the plaintiff to proceed either in tort or in contract the fact that the proper law of
the contract was Libyan law was of no relevance to the claim in tort brought in England.
The defendants appealed, contending that since the contract was governed by Libyan law
the claim in tort could not be considered in isolation of Libyan law, which had to be   **f**
taken into account in determining the proper law of the tort. They further contended
that, in considering the question of the law applicable to the claim in tort, the court
ought to adopt a flexible approach and it would be wrong for the court to disregard the
fact that there was a Libyan contract under which there was an obligation on the plaintiff
to take reasonable care of his own safety since that was relevant to the claim in tort.
                                                                                                   g

Held – Applying ordinary principles the contract was only relevant to the claim in tort
in so far as, on its true construction in accordance with the proper law of the contract, it
had the effect of excluding or restricting the claim in tort. On the facts, there was no
clause in the contract which limited or restricted the plaintiff's right to claim damages
in tort, since the clause relating to the obligation on the plaintiff to take all reasonable
care for his own safety was relevant only to a claim in contract and had no bearing on the   **h**
claim in tort. Accordingly, there was nothing in the contract, regardless of whether it
was governed by Libyan law or by English law, which purported to have the effect of
excluding or restricting the claim in tort. Since that claim was actionable by English law
(the lex fori) and by Libyan law (the lex loci delicti) it followed that the trial could
proceed on the ordinary principles of common law negligence in England. The appeal
would accordingly be dismissed (see p 228 *j* to p 229 *a c* to *f*, post).   **j**
    Chaplin v Boys [1969] 2 All ER 1085 followed.
    Decision of Hodgson J [1983] 2 All ER 434 affirmed.

Notes

For the general rule as to foreign torts and actionability under English law and under the

a law of the place of the tort, see 8 Halsbury's Laws (4th edn) paras 617–618, and for cases on the subject, see 11 Digest (Reissue) 495–497, 943–953.
    For the Companies Act 1948, Pt X, see 5 Halsbury's Statutes (3rd edn) 404.

Case referred to in judgments
Chaplin v Boys [1969] 2 All ER 1085, [1971] AC 356, [1969] 3 WLR 322, HL.

b **Case also cited**
Sayers v International Drilling Co NV [1971] 3 All ER 163, [1971] 1 WLR 1176, CA.

Interlocutory Appeal
By a writ issued on 22 September 1980 the plaintiff, John Waugh Fraser Coupland, brought an action against the defendants, Arabian Gulf Oil Co (a Libyan nationalised
c corporation in amalgamation with Umm Al-Jawaby Petroleum Co SAL), for damages for personal injuries suffered by the plaintiff in the course of his employment with the defendants in Libya. On 7 November 1980 the defendants served their defence denying liability and claiming that the proper law of the contract of employment was that of Libya. By a summons dated 24 July 1981 the defendants applied, inter alia, to have the claim struck out on the grounds (i) that neither the cause of action nor the parties had
d any connection with English law and it would be unjust to permit the action to continue, (ii) that the claim was governed by Libyan law and had been satisfied under Libyan law and accordingly there was no actionable cause of action in Libya, and they further sought to have the question of the proper law of the claim determined as a preliminary issue. On 4 December 1981 Master Lubbock refused the defendants' application to strike out the claim but ordered, inter alia, that a preliminary issue be tried, namely whether the
e plaintiff's claim was governed by Libyan law and had been satisfied. By an order made on 21 January 1983 Hodgson J ([1983] 2 All ER 434) held, inter alia, (i) that the plaintiff's claim in tort was not governed by Libyan law but by English law and (ii) that the proper law of the contract was Libyan law. The defendants appealed, with leave of the Court of Appeal granted on 13 June 1983, against that part of the judge's decision which held that tortious liability should be governed by English law, on the grounds, inter alia, that it
f was inconsistent with the second determination that the proper law of the contract was Libyan law. The facts are set out in the judgment of Robert Goff LJ.

Raymond Croxon QC for the defendants.
Barry Mortimer QC and *V E Hartley Booth* for the plaintiff.

g **ROBERT GOFF LJ** (delivering the first judgment at the invitation of Waller LJ). There is before the court an appeal by the defendants, Arabian Gulf Oil Co, against a decision of Hodgson J ([1983] 2 All ER 434) made on 2 January 1983 on a preliminary point raised by the defendants in this action.
    The action takes the form of a claim by the plaintiff, Mr Coupland, who is the respondent before us, against the defendants for personal injuries suffered by him in the
h course of his employment by the defendants in Libya. It appears from the judgment, and I think it is common ground before us, that the plaintiff lives in Scotland and is domiciled there and that the defendants are a Libyan nationalised oil company. Like many other oil companies they have offices elsewhere in the world; and they have a registered office in this country, and are registered under Pt X of the Companies Act 1948.
j The plaintiff was recruited as one of the defendants' senior maintenance technicians. He entered into a contract with the defendants in March 1978; he went out to Libya in June of that year, and then began his employment with the defendants as a senior maintenance technician.
    At the end of that year, on 12 December, he unfortunately suffered a serious accident. He was involved in dismantling a substantial piece of machinery, and in the course of that operation he had to climb up the side of that piece of machinery and down again.

As he was climbing down, he went past a guard which took the form of a cross-mesh piece of wire in which there was, as has been shown in the photographs before us, a substantial hole. His foot unfortunately went through the hole; it became entangled with a fan and was seriously damaged, as a result of which in due course he suffered a below-knee amputation of his leg.

In simple terms, the issues in the action can be said to be whether the defendants were in breach of their duty towards the plaintiff (in other words, were they negligent) and whether the plaintiff himself was guilty of what we call contributory negligence with the result that he can recover nothing or only part of the damages he has claimed. The pleaded case of the plaintiff, as one would expect, put forward the claim on three grounds: first on the basis of negligence; second on the basis of breach of contract; and third on the basis of breach of statutory duty, which I understand to mean breach of Libyan statutory duty.

The judge had to consider certain preliminary points. One of the main points which was advanced before him was that under Libyan law the plaintiff's claim had been satisfied; that argument was considered by the judge and rejected by him, and there is no appeal on that point.

However, another matter considered by the judge related to the appropriate system of law applicable to the claim advanced in this case. The judge considered the matter both in respect of the claim in tort and the claim in contract, the greater part of his judgment being devoted to the claim in tort. Applying the principles stated by the House of Lords in *Chaplin v Boys* [1969] 2 All ER 1085, [1971] AC 356, he came to the conclusion that the plaintiff could succeed in an action in tort if he could show that the claim was actionable by the lex fori, which is the law of this country, and the lex loci delicti, which is the law of Libya. As far as the claim in contract was concerned, he came to the conclusion that the proper law of the contract was the law of Libya. But he considered, and so stated in his judgment, that it was open to the plaintiff to proceed either in tort or in contract, and that the fact that the proper law of the contract was Libyan was of no relevance to the claim in tort.

Before this court, counsel for the defendants has sought to challenge the judge's conclusion on that point. The way in which he put his case was this. Here you have a case of an employee who has gone to work for a Libyan company in Libya under a contract of employment governed by Libyan law. In those circumstances, said counsel, you cannot simply look at the tortious claim in isolation because the contract being governed by Libyan law must be taken into account in considering the tortious claim, or, as he put it, the two were interlinked. He further submitted that since the House of Lords in *Chaplin v Boys* has stated that nowadays, in considering the question of the applicable law in claim for tort, one had to adopt a flexible approach, it would be quite wrong to disregard the fact that there was a Libyan contract in considering the applicable law in regard to the claim in tort. In this connection he also referred to the fact that in their defence the defendants had pleaded that there was this contract and that under the contract there was an obligation on the plaintiff to take reasonable care of his own safety; and he submitted that for this reason too the terms of the contract must be relevant in considering the claim in tort.

Now I find myself unable to accept the submission of counsel for the defendants. It seems to me that the position is this. The plaintiff can advance his claim, as he wishes, either in contract or in tort; and no doubt he will, acting on advice, advance the claim on the basis which is most advantageous to him. It appears that he is likely to proceed primarily on the basis of his claim in tort, for reasons which I suspect are connected with the assessment of damages.

That being so, I ask myself: what impact does the existence of the contract have on the claim in tort? In my judgment, on ordinary principles the contract is only relevant to the claim in tort in so far as it does, on its true construction in accordance with the proper law of the contract, have the effect of excluding or restricting the tortious claim.

However this is not a case where an exclusion clause, or anything of that kind, is relied

on by the defence. There is in the contract no clause which limits or restricts the
plaintiff's right to claim damages in tort; and so that line of defence is not open to the
defendants. The only particular matter relied on by the defendants is to be found in para
6 of their defence, to which I have already referred, which states that under the contract
there was an obligation imposed on the plaintiff to take all reasonable care of his own
safety; but that matter is pleaded only on the basis that it is relevant in relation to the
claim in contract. For para 6 opens with the words:

> 'If, which is denied, there was an implied term of the contract in Paragraph 6 of
> the Statement of Claim, it will be averred that there was a concomitant obligation
> imposed on the Plaintiff to take all reasonable care of his own safety . . .'

It follows that this matter, as pleaded, relates only to the claim in contract. It has no
bearing on the claim in tort. I wish to add, however, that even if this point did have some
bearing on the claim in tort it would make no difference in practical terms because the
allegations of contributory negligence set out in the defence are said to be the same as the
allegations of breach of the so-called concomitant obligation in the contract. At all events,
so far as I can see on the case as pleaded, there is no term of the contract which, whether
the contract be governed by Libyan law or by English law, purports to have the effect of
either excluding or restricting the claim in tort. I find myself therefore in entire
agreement with the judge that even if the contract, as he held, is governed by Libyan
law, then that contract has no impact on the claim in tort.

That being so, we are left with the simple situation that the judge has held, applying
the principles in *Chaplin v Boys*, that the claim in tort must proceed on the basis that the
claim must be actionable by the lex fori and also actionable by the lex loci delicti. He has
held, having heard the evidence, that it is actionable under the lex loci delicti, and so that
requirement has been fulfilled. It follows, in my judgment, that for the claim in tort,
Libyan law falls out of the picture as being irrelevant, and so for that purpose the trial
can proceed on the basis of the ordinary principles of common law negligence.

For those reasons I would dismiss the appeal.

OLIVER LJ. I agree.

WALLER LJ. I also agree.

Appeal dismissed.

Solicitors: *Amhurst Brown Martin & Nicholson* (for the defendants); *Dibb & Clegg* (for the
plaintiff).

Sophie Craven   Barrister.

JJC (a minor) v Eisenhower

QUEEN'S BENCH DIVISION
ROBERT GOFF LJ AND MANN J
28 APRIL 1983

Criminal law – Wounding – Unlawful and malicious wounding – Wound – What constitutes a
wound – Injury consisting of internal rupture of blood vessels but without break in continuity of   **b**
whole skin – Whether constituting a wound – Offences against the Person Act 1861, s 20.

For the purposes of s 20[a] of the Offences against the Person Act 1861, which provides
that it is an offence unlawfully and maliciously to wound another person, a 'wound' is a
break in the continuity of the whole skin. Accordingly, an injury where there has merely
been internal rupturing of blood vessels is not a 'wound' for which a person may be   **c**
convicted under s 20 (see p 232 *a c d f* and p 233 *c* to *h*, post).

R v William Wood and James M'Mahon (1830) 1 Mood CC 278, *R v Shadbolt* (1833) 5 C
& P 504, *R v M'Loughlin* (1838) 8 C & P 635 and *R v Waltham* (1849) 3 Cox CC 442
applied.

R v Warman (1846) 1 Den 183 considered.

   d

Notes
For unlawful wounding and for what constitutes wounding, see 11 Halsbury's Laws (4th
edn) paras 1199–1200, and for cases on wounding, see 15 Digest (Repl) 1178, *10,030–*
10,040.

For the Offences against the Person Act 1861, s 20, see 8 Halsbury's Statutes (3rd edn)   **e**
154.

Cases referred to in judgments
R v M'Loughlin (1838) 8 C & P 635, 173 ER 651.
R v Shadbolt (1833) 5 C & P 504, 172 ER 1073.
R v Waltham (1849) 3 Cox CC 442.
R v Warman (1846) 1 Den 183, 169 ER 203, CCR.   **f**
R v Wood (William) and James M'Mahon (1830) 1 Mood CC 278, 168 ER 1271, CCR.

Cases also cited
Moriarty v Brooks (1834) 6 C & P 684, 172 ER 1419.
R v Beckett (1836) 1 Mood & R 526, 174 ER 181.
R v Jones (1849) 3 Cox CC 441.
R v Payne (1831) 4 C & P 558, 172 ER 824.   **g**
R v Smith (1837) 8 C & P 173, 173 ER 448.
R v Withers (1831) 1 Mood CC 294, 168 ER 1277, CCR.

Case stated
JJC (a minor) appealed by way of case stated by the justices for the Middlesex area of   **h**
Greater London acting in and for the petty sessional division of Edmonton in respect of
their adjudication as a juvenile court at Tottenham, London on 17 May 1982 whereby
they found the appellant guilty of unlawfully and maliciously wounding another,
contrary to s 20 of the Offences against the Person Act 1861, with which he was charged
in an information preferred by the respondent, Vincent Eisenhower. The appellant was
made the subject of a supervision order for a period of two years and also ordered to pay   **j**
compensation of £5 to the person injured. He appealed against the conviction on the

---

a   Section 20, so far as material, provides: 'Whosoever shall unlawfully and maliciously wound . . .
     any other person . . . shall be guilty of [an offence] . . .'

ground that the justices erred in law in concluding that the injuries suffered by the
a victim constituted a wound for the purpose of s 20 of the 1861 Act. The facts are set out
in the judgment of Robert Goff LJ.

Glen Brasse for the appellant.
Robert Rhodes for the respondent.

b **ROBERT GOFF LJ.** There is before the court a case stated by justices sitting at
Tottenham in respect of an information which came before them on 17 May 1982.
Under that information two young boys were charged with unlawfully and maliciously
wounding Martin Cook. The appellant is one of those two accused. The magistrates on
that occasion found the appellant guilty of the offence with which he was charged.
The offence arose in the following circumstances. These two boys were both 15 at the
c relevant time. The appellant's co-accused in company with the appellant, purchased an
air pistol and some pellets from a shop. A few days later, on 21 January 1982, they were
walking together along Flexmere Road, Tottenham, when they became aware of a young
man called Martin Cook, together with another young man and two girls, on the opposite
side of the road. As the appellant and his co-accused walked along, the co-accused aimed
the air pistol in the direction of those four young people. He fired once. A little later he
d fired again. Martin Cook was hit in the area of the left eye by a pellet from the air pistol.
The magistrates in the case found that the injuries sustained by Martin Cook amounted
to a bruise just below the left eyebrow and that fluid filling the front part of his left eye
for a time afterwards abnormally contained red blood cells.
At the trial before the magistrates, the matters primarily in issue were how far those
two boys were involved in the shooting of the air pistol, and how far in particular the
e appellant, who did not fire the gun, was involved. They also had to consider whether the
requirement of malice in the Offences against the Person Act 1861 had been complied
with. But the question also arose whether the injuries suffered by Martin Cook could be
described as a wound. It is that last question alone which has survived for argument
before this court on the question of law posed by the justices in the case.
The question stated by the justices is as follows:

f   'The question for the opinion of the High Court is whether in the light of the
    facts as we found them and the law applied to those facts we were right to find the
    Appellant guilty of the offence with which he had been charged.'

The only point argued before us was that the magistrates were not right to find the
appellant guilty of that offence because they were wrong to conclude that the injuries
g suffered by Martin Cook, which I have described, constituted a wound. The magistrates
gave their reason for concluding that it was a wound in the following sentence. They
said:

        'We considered that the abnormal presence of red blood cells in the fluid of the
    left eye of Martin Cook, after being hit by the air gun pellet, indicated at the least
    the rupturing of a blood vessel or vessels internally which was sufficient to constitute
h   a wound for the purposes of Section 20 of the Act.'

Before us counsel for the appellant submitted that those facts did not justify the
magistrates' conclusion that there was a wound for the purposes of s 20. Counsel for the
respondent submitted that the magistrates were justified in reaching their conclusion
that there was a wound on those facts.
j   We have been very helpfully taken through all the reported cases discovered by counsel
concerned with the meaning of the word 'wound'. We are indebted to counsel for the
respondent for having prepared a bundle of the relevant authorities. Those show that the
question of what constitutes a wound was considered in a number of cases over a period
of about 20 years between 1830 to 1850, but does not appear to have been considered
since that date. By 1850 the word 'wound' had acquired a meaning which appears to
have become the settled meaning. It is certainly true today that judges habitually address

juries on the question whether there has been a wounding within s 18 or s 20 of the 1861 Act, on the basis that there is a wound if the skin has been broken. In my judgment, the cases which have been cited to us by counsel support the view that the habitual direction nowadays given by judges to juries is founded on good authority.

The earliest case cited to us was *R v William Wood and James M'Mahon* (1830) 1 Mood CC 278, 168 ER 1271. After considering the matter it was concluded by all the judges (except Bailey B and Park J, who dissented) that there was no wound where the continuity of the skin had not been broken. That test appears to have been consistently applied thereafter.

In later cases the matter was refined in two ways, in particular in *R v M'Loughlin* (1838) 8 C & P 635, 173 ER 651. It was held in that case by Coleridge J, other judges being present, that it must be the whole skin that is broken. He, of course, was referring to the fact that the human skin has two layers, an outer layer called the epidermis or the cuticle, and the underlayer which is sometimes called the dermis or the true skin. In that case there was evidence of an abrasion of the skin, with blood issuing from it. It was made plain to the jury by Coleridge J that 'if it is necessary to constitute a wound, that the skin should be broken, it must be the whole skin, and it is not sufficient to shew a separation of the cuticle only.' It was therefore not enough that there had been an abrasion. There had to be a break in the continuity of the whole skin.

The second way in which the point was refined is to be found in two cases. The first is *R v Shadbolt* (1833) 5 C & P 504, 172 ER 1073; and the second is *R v Waltham* (1849) 3 Cox CC 442. These cases show that there can be a break in the continuity of the skin sufficient to constitute a wound if the skin which was broken is the skin of an internal cavity of the body, being a cavity from the outer surface of the body where the skin of the cavity is continuous with the outer skin of the body. So, for example, in *R v Shadbolt* it was held that it was sufficient if there had been a break in the skin of the internal surface of the lips inside the mouth. In *R v Waltham*, which is possibly the most extreme of the cases cited to us, it was held by Cresswell J that there would be a wounding if there had been a rupture of the lining membrane of the urethra causing a small flow of blood into the urine, because that membrane was of precisely the same character as that which lined the cheek and the external internal skin of the lip.

So we can see a picture emerging. There must be a break in the continuity of the skin. It must be a break in the continuity of the whole skin, but the skin may include not merely the outer skin of the body but the skin of an internal cavity of the body where the skin of the cavity is continuous with the outer skin of the body.

Counsel for the respondent has submitted to us that a wound should include the rupturing of an internal blood vessel. In support of this submission, he referred us in particular to *R v Warman* (1846) 1 Den 183, 169 ER 203. That was a somewhat unusual case. It appears that the case was tried by Alderson B at the spring assizes for the county of Hertford on a coroner's inquisition. The coroner's inquisition stated that Levi Warman attacked his wife with an instrument called a swingle (made of wood, iron and leather) and struck her with it on the right side of the head thereby causing her one mortal wound. The said mortal wound was such that she then and there instantly died of it. The evidence of the witnesses, in particular the surgeon, was to the effect that he found on examining the woman's head no external breach of the skin, but he found a collection of blood in the back part of her head. She died from an extravasation of blood which pressed on the brain. On examining and cutting the scalp he found a collection of blood between the scalp and the cranium, just above the spot where within the cranium he found the pressure on the brain. He described that as a contused wound with effusion of blood, which is the same thing as a bruise. He stated that the internal part of the skin was broken.

Alderson B reserved the question whether the mode of death was sufficiently proved by the evidence. He was there certainly referring to the use of the words 'one mortal wound' in the inquisition. The matter was considered by Lord Denman CJ, Tindal CJ, Pollock CB, and a number of other judges. Parke B's note runs (1 Den 183 at 184–185, 169 ER 203 at 204):

a
'All thought that this internal wound was a sufficient wound to support the allegation in the indictment, whether it would have been so or no in an indictment on the statute for cutting or wounding with intent to murder, &c.'

b
This, counsel for the respondent submitted, showed that they thought that there could be a wound where there had been no break in the continuity of the skin, but that they did not go on to consider whether technically there would in such circumstances be a wounding for the purposes of a charge of cutting or wounding with intent to murder. Speaking for myself, I am unable to accept that construction, because this was a most unusual case. What was considered by the judges was not the question whether there was a wound within the statute, but merely whether the words 'a mortal wound' used in the coroner's inquisition were proved on the evidence of the particular case. They were not concerned with the construction of the word 'wounding' in the statute, but simply with the common sense use of the word 'wound' on the facts of this particular case. I do

c
not therefore think that the case provides any guidance on the construction of the word 'wound' in the statute which we have to consider.

In my judgment, if one looks at the cases there is a continuous stream of authority (to which I myself can find no exception at all) which does establish that a wound is, as I have stated, a break in the continuity of the whole skin. I can see nothing in the authorities which persuades me to think otherwise. This has become such a well-

d
established meaning of the word 'wound' that in my judgment it would be very wrong for this court to depart from it.

We now turn to the case stated for our consideration by the magistrates. The magistrates concluded that there was a wound because, although they described the injury as a bruise just below the left eyebrow with fluid filling the front part of his left eye for a time afterwards which abnormally contained red blood cells, they thought that

e
the abnormal presence of red blood cells in the fluid in Martin Cook's left eye indicated at least the rupturing of a blood vessel or vessels internally; and this they thought was sufficient to constitute a wound for the purposes of s 20 of the Offences against the Person Act 1861.

In my judgment, that conclusion was not in accordance with the law. It is not enough that there has been a rupturing of blood vessel or vessels internally for there to be a

f
wound under the statute because it is impossible for a court to conclude from that evidence alone whether or not there has been any break in the continuity of the whole skin. There may have simply been internal bleeding of some kind or another, the cause of which is not established. Furthermore, even if there had been a break in some internal skin, there may not have been a break in the whole skin. In these circumstances, the evidence is not enough, in my judgment, to establish a wound within the statute. In my

g
judgment, the magistrates erred in their conclusion on the evidence before them. The question posed for the opinion of this court is whether, in the light of the facts found by the magistrates and the law applied to those facts, they were right to find the appellant guilty of the offence with which he had been charged, namely the unlawful and malicious wounding of Martin Cook contrary to s 20 of the Offences against the Person

h
Act 1861. I would answer that question in the negative.

MANN J. I agree.

Appeal allowed; conviction quashed.

Solicitors: *J G Daultry & Co*, Enfield (for the appellant); *Paul E Nicholls*, Tottenham (for the respondent).

Raina Levy   Barrister.

West Yorkshire Metropolitan County Council v MFI Furniture Centre Ltd and another appeal

QUEEN'S BENCH DIVISION
ROBERT GOFF LJ AND McNEILL J
15 MARCH 1983

Consumer protection – Price marking – Bargain offers relating to goods – Prohibition on statements implying that advertised price lower than another price for sale of goods of same description – Test to be applied in determining meaning of words used in offer – Price Marking (Bargain Offers) Order 1979, arts 2(1)(a), 3(1)(b).

Consumer protection – Price marking – Bargain offers relating to goods – Prohibition on statements implying that advertised price lower than another price for sale of goods of same description – Goods of same description – Company offering for sale one item at 'special clearance price' – Whether offence committed – Whether prohibition applying only where comparison invited between advertised goods and other goods of same description – Whether prohibition covering one item marked down as against itself – Price Marking (Bargain Offers) Order 1979, arts 2(1)(a), 3(1)(b).

A furniture company inserted two advertisements in the press. One stated that it was selling a six-drawer chest at £24·95, which it described as a 'bargain price' and 'Britain's lowest price'. The other stated that it was selling a Welsh dresser at £69·95, which it described as a 'special clearance price'. The company was charged and convicted in respect of both advertisements as contravening arts 2(1)(a)[a] and 3(1)(b)[b] of the Price Marking (Bargain Offers) Order 1979 by indicating that the price of the goods was 'lower than . . . the amount of another price for the sale of goods of the same description'. The company appealed to the Crown Court, contending (i) that in the first advertisement the words 'bargain price' and 'Britain's lowest price' did not inevitably imply that the goods were cheaper than elsewhere, and (ii) that in the second advertisement the words 'special clearance price' did not contravene art 3(1)(b) because they merely invited comparison between the advertised price of the goods and another price for the sale of the same goods and did not invite comparison with the price for the sale of other goods of the same description. The Crown Court allowed the appeals because in respect of the first advertisement it was not satisfied beyond reasonable doubt that an ordinary shopper would infer from the advertisement that he was getting a preferential price and not just a bargain (ie good value for money), and in respect of the second advertisement it had not been established that the words 'special clearance price' contravened the terms of art 3(1)(b). The prosecutor appealed.

Held – (1) The court would not interfere with the Crown Court's decision regarding the first advertisement because it was a question of fact rather than law whether, in the context of the advertisement, the words 'bargain price' and 'Britain's lowest price' contravened arts 2 and 3 of the 1979 order, and the Crown Court had adopted the correct approach of looking at the advertisement through the eyes of an ordinary shopper and applying the criminal standard of proof. The appeal in respect of the first advertisement would accordingly be dismissed (see p 239 c to h and p 241 b, post); Doble v David Greig Ltd [1972] 2 All ER 195, R v Clarksons Holidays Ltd (1972) 57 Cr App R 38 and R v Sunair Holidays Ltd [1973] 2 All ER 1233 considered.

---

a   Article 2(1) is set out at p 236 g, post
b   Article 3(1) is set out at p 236 h j, post

(2) The second advertisement infringed the terms of art 3(1)(b) of the 1979 order
a because on the true construction of that article the words 'goods of the same description'
included a particular item of goods which was marked down as against itself. The appeal
in respect of the second advertisement would accordingly be allowed (see p 240 *f* to p 241
c, post).

Notes
b For price marking, see 41 Halsbury's Laws (4th edn) para 624.

Cases referred to in judgments
Doble v David Greig Ltd [1972] 2 All ER 195, [1972] 1 WLR 703, DC.
R v Clarksons Holidays Ltd (1972) 57 Cr App R 38, CA.
R v Sunair Holidays Ltd [1973] 2 All ER 1233, [1973] 1 WLR 1105, CA.

c

Cases stated

West Yorkshire Metropolitan County Council v MFI Furniture Centre Ltd

West Yorkshire Metropolitan County Council appealed, by way of case stated by the
Crown Court at Bradford, against a decision of that court before Mr Recorder G Barr
d Young and justices on 13 November 1981 whereby it allowed an appeal by the
respondents, MFI Furniture Ltd, against their conviction in Bradford Magistrates' Court
on 15 April 1981 of 25 offences under ss 4 and 7 of, and para 5 of the schedule to, the
Prices Act 1974 and arts 2(1)(a) and 3(1)(b) of the Price Marking (Bargain Offers) Order
1979, SI 1979/364, as amended. The questions of law for the opinion of the High Court
were: (1) whether, on the true construction of arts 2(1)(a) and 3(1)(b) of the 1979 order
e the words 'bargain price' in relation to the price of goods offered for sale by retail were a
statement that the price indicated was lower than the amount of another price for the
sale of goods of the same description; (2) whether a contravention of arts 2(1)(a) and
3(1)(b) of the 1979 order was established on a finding that some persons would reasonably
conclude that the statement complained of was an assertion that the price indicated was
lower than the amount of another price for the sale of goods of the same description;
f (3) whether, in relation to exhibit 3 and the advertisement of a '6-drawer chest', it was
open to the Crown Court to find that the statement 'bargain price' in conjunction with
the words 'Britain's lowest price' and/or the words 'Britain's lowest bargain prices right
across Britain's biggest bedroom choice' did not amount to a contravention of arts 2(1)(a)
and 3(1)(b) of the 1979 order. The facts are set out in the judgment of Robert Goff LJ.

g   *West Yorkshire Metropolitan County Council v MFI Furniture Centre Ltd*

West Yorkshire Metropolitan County Council also appealed by way of case stated by the
Crown Court at Bradford against another decision of that court before Mr Recorder
G Barr Young and justices on 13 November 1981 whereby it allowed an appeal by the
respondents, MFI Furniture Centre Ltd, against their conviction in Bradford Magistrates'
h Court on another occasion of certain offences under ss 4 and 7 of, and para 5 of the
schedule to, the Prices Act 1974 and arts 2(1)(a) and 3(1)(b) of the Price Marking (Bargain
Offers) Order 1979, SI 1979/364, as amended. The questions of law for the opinion of the
High Court were: (1) whether, in relation to exhibit 1 and the advertisement of a 'Welsh
solid pine dresser', it was open to the Crown Court to conclude that the statement 'end of
range clearance price' did not amount to a contravention of the 1979 order; (2) whether,
j in relation to exhibit 2 and the advertisement of a 'Welsh dresser', it was open to the
Crown Court to conclude that the statement 'special clearance offer' did not amount to a
contravention of the 1979 order; (3) whether a statement, within the meaning of art 3(1)
of the 1979 order, that the indicated price of goods was lower than the amount of another
price for the sale of the same goods was a statement that the price indicated was lower
than the amount of another price for the sale of goods of the same description within the

meaning of art 3(1)(b) of the 1979 order. The facts are set out in the judgment of Robert
Goff LJ.   *a*

R M *Harrison* for the appellants.
Anthony *Scrivener* QC and Ian *Croxford* for the respondents.

ROBERT GOFF LJ. There are before the courts two cases stated by the Crown Court
at Bradford. Each case arises between the same parties, the appellants being the West   *b*
Yorkshire Metropolitan County Council and the respondents being a company called
MFI Furniture Centre Ltd. In each case complaints had been made under the Price
Marking (Bargain Offers) Order 1979, SI 1979/364, against the respondent company
which carries on business in the sale of furniture. This they do, to some extent at least,
through advertising their products in the press. The complaints were concerned with the
description of the prices given in relation to certain products advertised by the   *c*
respondents in the press.
     I will take, first of all, what we have called the first case. There were no less than 25
charges advanced against the respondents under the order, but only three are the subject
matter of this case stated. All three are similar except for one matter which I shall refer
to in a moment. The first charge was concerned with certain goods described as a 'Pastelle
nesting set', which was apparently a nest of tables. The price of those goods was stated to *d*
be £9·95 and it was described as a 'bargain price'. The second charge was concerned with
an item advertised in the Sunday Express, which was an 'Aquarius two door wardrobe';
the price was £27·95 and again was stated to be a 'bargain price'. The third charge was
concerned with an item advertised in the Telegraph and Argus. That was a 'Nicole six
drawer chest'; the price was stated to be £24·95, again called a 'bargain price'; but in
addition, alongside the words 'bargain price' were written the words 'Britain's lowest   *e*
price'.
     In the second case stated there were two matters complained of. One related to an
advertisement (unillustrated) in the Sunday Express, advertising for sale a 'Welsh solid
pine dresser, end of range clearance, price £69·95'. The other related to an advertisement
for sale of a 'Welsh dresser, £69·95' described as a 'special clearance price'.
     The complaint made in relation to all these descriptions of prices is that they offended *f*
against arts 2 and 3 of the Price Marking (Bargain Offers) Order 1979. The relevant part
of art 2 of the order, headed 'Regulation of bargain offers', reads:

     '(1) Subject to paragraph 2 below, a person who indicates that—(a) any goods are
     or may be for sale by retail; or (b) any services (except services which he indicates are
     or may be provided only for the purposes of businesses carried on by other persons)
     are or may be provided, shall not, on or in relation to those goods, indicate a price   *g*
     for their sale . . . in such a manner that the indication includes a statement to which
     this article applies . . .'

We then turn to art 3, headed 'Bargain offers relating to goods', para (1) of which reads:

     'Subject to the following provisions of this Order, article 2 above applies, in   *h*
     relation to a price, to any statement (however framed and whether express or
     implied) that the price indicated is lower than—(a) a value ascribed to goods, not
     being the amount of such a price as is mentioned in sub-paragraph (b) below; or (b)
     [and I pause to say that this is the most relevant sub-paragraph for the purposes of
     this case] the amount of another price for the sale of goods of the same description
     (whether that price is, or is not, specified or quantified or is, or is not, a price which *j*
     has been charged, indicated or proposed by any person).'

     In respect of every one of the matters referred to in the two cases, the respondents were
charged with offending against that provision. Article 3(2) then cites cases to which art
3(1)(b) does not apply. There are three of these exceptions, which are as follows:

'(2) Sub-paragraph (b) of paragraph (1) above does not apply—(a) to a particular
price which the person giving the indication—(i) proposes to charge or has charged
in the ordinary course of business on the same or on other identified premises, or
(ii) has reasonable cause for believing has been charged in the ordinary course of
business by another identified person in identified circumstances and has no reason
for believing has ceased to be a price at which that person is prepared to do business
in those circumstances, including in each case a price for the sale of goods of the
same description in a specified different condition or quantity; (b) to a particular
price applicable to the sale by the person giving the indication of goods of the same
description—(i) upon specified different terms as to the time or manner of payment
(including the provision of credit by any person either generally or to persons of a
specified class or description), (ii) in specified different circumstances, (iii) in a
specified different condition or quantity, or (iv) to any person who is not within a
class or description of persons for sales to whom the indicated price is expressed to
apply; or (c) in a case where the indicated price applies to goods when supplied with
other specified goods or with specified services, to a particular price for the sale of
the goods without those other goods or services or with other specified goods or
services.'

Against that background, I turn to the first case. I have already set out the terms of the
advertisements which in that case were said to have offended against art 3(1)(b). The
court below approached the matters as follows, as is set out in para 7 of the special case:

'We placed ourselves in the position of the ordinary shopper, and found as follows:
(1) That the words "bargain price" do relate to the price of the goods offered for sale;
(2) That a shopper would not necessarily come to the view that "bargain price"
meant the price offered was lower than another price for something of the same
description; he might feel that he was getting an advantageous price in the sense of
good or excellent value for money; we could not be sure that a shopper's
interpretation would be one that would put the Respondents in contravention of
the Order; (3) As to charge (1) paragraph 3 above, some shoppers might interpret
"bargain price £9·95" as meaning there is some other price, but not necessarily an
ordinary shopper in this context; (4) As to charge (2) paragraph 3 above, there was
nothing in exhibit 1 to indicate that somewhere else the "Aquarius 2 door wardrobe"
might have been offered at another price; (5) As to charge (3) paragraph 3 above,
exhibit 3, we felt that the Respondents came close to contravening the Order; in the
context, the ordinary shopper looking at the whole advertisement would not think
he was getting a preferential price, merely a bargain.'

So on that basis, they dismissed the charges against the respondents with regard to all
the three items which are the subject of the case stated. Counsel for the appellants
approached the matter as follows. He said that the question whether on a true
construction these advertisements offended against art 3(1)(b) of the order was a question
of law, and depended on the construction to be placed on these documents. He next
referred us to the Shorter Oxford English Dictionary and relied on a passage which appeared
to indicate that, on one view of the matter, a 'bargain price' could be construed as
indicating a difference between that price and another higher price. He then submitted
that that was the true construction to be placed on these particular advertisements. He
further submitted, in relation to the third advertisement, that where there were in the
advertisement the additional words 'Britain's lowest price', those words added force to
the submission that the word 'bargain price' should be read as indicating a comparison
between the advertised price and another higher price. Therefore, he submitted that,
contrary to the view taken by the court below, there had been a contravention of the
order in respect of these three advertisements.

Counsel for the respondents, on the other hand, submitted that the question whether
these advertisements contravened the order was essentially a question of fact. He indorsed

the approach adopted by the Crown Court below when they placed themselves in the
position of the ordinary shopper. That, he said, was precisely what had to be done. In *a*
cases, such as these, he submitted, when the court is placing itself in the position of an
ordinary shopper, the question how an advertisement should be understood, although it
could be called a question of construction, is essentially a question of fact. Accordingly,
he submitted, this is not a case in which this court should interfere with the conclusion
of the Crown Court.

Certain authorities were cited to us. We were referred first to *R v Sunair Holidays Ltd* *b*
[1973] 2 All ER 1233, [1973] 1 WLR 1105. That was a case concerned with the Trade
Descriptions Act 1968 as applied to a brochure about holidays. In the course of the
judgment of the court which was given by MacKenna J he referred to the question how
the construction of these brochures should be considered. He said ([1973] 2 All ER 1233
at 1240, [1973] 1 WLR 1105 at 1113–1114):

> 'Somebody had to construe the brochure to answer those questions of construction *c*
> and the question whether the words about the swimming pool related to the present
> or the future. Both parties were agreed in the court below and before us that it was
> for the jury to construe the document as it would be in proceedings for libel. That
> was the view taken in the earlier case of *R v Clarksons Holidays Ltd* (1972) 57 Cr App
> R 38 and tacitly approved by this court to which the case was brought on appeal.
> Following that precedent we shall assume that this is the right course, observing *d*
> only that if it is right statements in books on evidence which treat libel proceedings
> as the only exception to a rule that the construction of documents is for the judge
> may need to be revised . . .'

We were referred also to *R v Clarksons Holidays Ltd* (1972) 57 Cr App R 38. That was a
decision of the Court of Appeal, Criminal Division, and was concerned with an alleged *e*
offence under the Trade Descriptions Act 1968, once again in relation to holiday
brochures. In giving the judgment of the court Roskill LJ said (at 53–54):

> 'The question of what this written representation meant was essentially a question
> of fact for the jury, subject only to this, that if the words [in the brochure] relied
> upon by the Crown were upon their true construction incapable of bearing the *f*
> meaning which the Crown sought to attribute to them, then, of course, the learned
> Recorder ought to have withdrawn the case from the jury.'

So it is plain in that case that the matter was being treated, in the context of a criminal
case, as one of fact for the jury.

Counsel for the appellants urged that we should not treat those cases as binding on us
in the present case. He relied on the general principle that a question of construction of a *g*
written document is a question of law. He referred us to another case, *Doble v David Greig
Ltd* [1972] 2 All ER 195, [1972] 1 WLR 703, which was a decision of the Divisional
Court. That again was a case under the Trade Descriptions Act 1968, in that case under
s 11(2) which provides as follows:

> 'If any person offering to supply any goods gives, by whatever means, any *h*
> indication likely to be taken as an indication that the goods are being offered at a
> price less than that at which they are in fact being offered he shall, subject to the
> provisions of this Act, be guilty of an offence.'

Counsel for the appellants referred us to various passages in the judgment of
Ashworth J, who delivered the leading judgment in that case, as indicating that generally *j*
speaking the question of how one looks at a document for the purposes of this Act is a
question of construction. He further submitted that in relation to words such as 'likely
to be taken as an indication', the matter can properly be regarded as a question of fact for
a jury; but such words should be contrasted with an order like the present case which
does not use words of that kind, where the matter should be approached as a question of

pure construction, i e as a question of law. I am bound to say that, having been referred
by counsel for the appellants and by counsel for the respondents to the relevant passages
a in the judgments in that case, I do not so construe them. I refer in particular to the
judgment of Ashworth J where he says ([1972] 2 All ER 195 at 199–200, [1972] 1 WLR
703 at 708):

'. . . the principle that persons must not be convicted on an ambiguity should be
upheld, but at the same time I venture to repeat what I have already said, that this
b section was so worded as to cater for cases where possibly the wording, strictly
construed, might admit of two constructions.'

We find a similar passage in the judgment of Forbes J. In other words, what the judge is
saying is that the breadth of words here used is not designed to change what would
otherwise be a question of law to a question of fact, but widens the ambit of cases where
c a conviction may be secured to cases where more than one meaning is possible.

In my judgment, taking these three cases as a whole, it seems to me that it would be
proper for us, in the light of the approach adopted by the Court of Appeal in the *Clarksons
Holidays* case and assumed to be correct in the *Sunair Holidays* case, to say that in a case of
this kind the question of the meaning to be placed on the advertisement should be
approached as a question of fact, as a jury question, looking at the matter through the
d eyes of the ordinary shopper. This seems to me also to be in accordance with common
sense, because the question can indeed be properly described as a jury question. For my
part I would reject the submission of counsel for the appellants that this question is one
of law.

It follows, therefore, that, the question being one of fact and the court below (which
consisted of a recorder sitting with two magistrates) having reached the conclusion as a
e question of fact on the meaning to be placed on the words 'bargain price' and 'Britain's
lowest price' as used in the relevant advertisements, viz that these words did not offend
against the relevant provision, then this court should not interfere.

I shall now refer to the three questions of law set out in the stated case. Question (1)
relates to the effect of the words 'bargain price' which, as I have already indicated, is a
question of fact and does not raise a question of law at all. The same applies to question
f (3), although it refers also to the words 'Britain's lowest price'. Question (2) is as follows:

'Whether a contravention of Articles 2(1)(*a*) and 3(1)(*b*) of the said Order, is
established upon a finding that some persons would reasonably conclude that the
Statement complained of was an assertion that the price indicated is lower than the
amount of another price for the sale of goods of the same description.'

g The answer to that question, in my judgment, is this. In this case the approach of the
court below, which was to apply the criminal burden of proof, was quite right, this being
a criminal case. So if, when they placed themselves in the position of the ordinary
shopper, they could not be sure that from that point of view the interpretation to be
placed on the words complained of led to there having been a contravention of the order,
they should not convict. For these reasons I would for my part answer question (2) in the
h negative.

I turn, therefore, to the second of the two cases. This raises a different question, which
is one of construction of the order. There is no doubt that this question is one of law. I
have already set out the matters complained of. The words used in one case were 'Special
clearance offer' and in the other were 'End of range clearance price'. The approach urged
on us by counsel on behalf of the appellants is a very simple one. If you use those words,
j you must be indicating that the price is lower than the amount of another price for the
same goods of the same description. Therefore the case is caught by art 3(1)(*b*).
Furthermore he submits, and this is accepted by counsel for the respondents, that the
case does not fall within any of the exceptional cases in art 3(2), so this is a case where
plainly the court below should have convicted.

But they did not. They set out their reasons in para 5 of the case stated. This is what they said:

> 'The Appellants argued, and the Respondents conceded, that the statements "Special Clearance Offer" and "End of range clearance price" meant that the price at which the particular goods were offered for sale had been purposely reduced to clear the stock, and so amounted to statements that the price indicated was lower than the amount of another price, namely the price for the goods before the reduction.'

Pausing there, 'So far so good', said counsel for the appellants. Then the case continues:

> 'The Appellants contended that, accordingly, the offences had been proved. The Respondents argued that the offences were not made out because the statements complained of referred to the amount of another price *for the sale of the same goods*, not "for the sale of goods of the same description" within the terms of the Order.' (My emphasis.)

In para 6 the court below said:

> 'We were not convinced that the statements complained of offended the Order. On the facts agreed, it offended our common sense to say there had been an infringement in these circumstances. Accordingly, we allowed the appeal and quashed the convictions.'

It is possible to feel considerable sympathy with the reaction of the court below. It can be argued that, as a matter of common sense, there was nothing wrong in what the respondents were doing, because they were indicating quite plainly that this was a clearance sale and there can be nothing wrong in indicating that fact to the general public. But I fear that, in a case of this kind, we are not concerned just with common sense. We have to apply the order. There may be reasons of policy which explain why the order was drafted in its present form. It would have been perfectly possible for Parliament, if it thought right, to have included in the exceptions in art 3(2) a fourth exception to deal with this very point with which we are now concerned. They have, however, not done so, which I find very striking. So counsel for the respondents was compelled to fall back on the general words and submit that as a matter of construction, the present case does not fall within the order.

May I refer again to the relevant words of the order. The offence is committed if 'the price indicated is lower than . . . the amount of another price for the sale of goods of the same description . . .' Counsel for the respondents says: 'This was not such a case, because these were the very same goods, not goods of the same description.' In my judgment, such a submission really flies in the face of reality. Let me take the case of a vendor of goods who has 30 articles of the same description, all of which are sitting in his basement because he has not been able to sell them. He puts them up for sale as a special clearance offer. Clearly he would be indicating that the price of those goods or each of them was lower than the amount of another price for the sale of goods of the same description. That would be an almost classic example of a case where the statute applies. I cannot see how the situation would be any different if there was only one article of goods in the basement to which the offending words were applied. The same principle would apply. In other words, the words 'goods of the same description' embrace in this context a particular item of goods which is marked down, so to speak, as against itself.

So I find myself differing from the court below on the construction placed by them on art 3(1)(b) of the order in relation to these particular advertisements. The questions posed for our consideration are as follows:

> '(1) Whether, in relation to exhibit 1 and the advertisement of a "Welsh Solid Pine Dresser", it was open to the Crown Court to conclude that the statement "End of range clearance price" did not amount to a contravention of the said Order.'

I would answer that question No.

The next question is:

a

'(2) Whether, in relation to exhibit 2 and the advertisement of a "Welsh Dresser", it was open to the Crown Court to conclude that the statement "Special Clearance Offer" did not amount to a contravention of the said Order.'

Again I would answer that question No.

Question (3) reads:

b

'Whether a statement, within the meaning of Article 3(1) of the said Order, that the indicated price of goods is lower than the amount of another price for the sale of the same goods is a statement that the price indicated is lower than the amount of another price for the sale of goods of the same description within the meaning of Article 3(1)(b) of the said Order.'

c   I would answer that question Yes.

McNEILL J. I agree. I would only add that my answer to the last of the three questions would be the same on the basis that, having regard to the concession made by the respondents in para 5 of the case stated, no reasonable tribunal could have come to the conclusion on the facts that there had not been an infringement even though they may

d   have thought that the infringement was a minimal infringement. In those circumstances, the proper course would have been to convict and impose no penalty if that was what they thought all the facts disclosed.

Appeal dismissed in the first case. Appeal allowed in the second case.

Solicitors: *Hewitt Woollacott & Chown* (for the appellants); *Cripps & Shone*, Marlow (for the respondents).

April Weiss   Barrister.

Harris and another v Goddard and others   a

COURT OF APPEAL, CIVIL DIVISION
LAWTON, KERR AND DILLON LJJ
23, 24 JUNE, 25 JULY 1983

Joint tenancy – Means of effecting severance – Notice in writing of desire to sever joint tenancy in
equity – Prayer in divorce petition – Prayer for transfer of or settlement or variation of settlement   b
of former matrimonial home – Whether effective to constitute severance of joint tenancy in equity
– Law of Property Act 1925, s 36(2).

A husband and his second wife were joint tenants in equity of a property which they
used partly as a residence and partly as shop premises. In 1979 the wife petitioned for
divorce and in para 3 of the prayer of her petition she sought relief in the terms of s 24 of   c
the Matrimonial Causes Act 1973 asking 'That such order may be made by way of
transfer of property and/or settlement of property and/or variation of settlement in
respect of the former matrimonial home . . . and otherwise as may be just'. Shortly
before the date fixed for the hearing of the petition the husband was seriously injured in
a car accident and he died a few weeks later. The plaintiffs, the husband's executors and
children of his first marriage, sought a declaration that the joint tenancy had been severed   d
under s 36(2)[a] of the Law of Property Act 1925 by the prayer in the divorce petition and
that they were entitled to half of the proceeds of sale of the property. The wife
counterclaimed, seeking a declaration that she was entitled to the whole of the proceeds
by right of survivorship on her husband's death. The judge held that para 3 of the prayer
in the divorce petition did not take effect as a severance notice and he dismissed the
plaintiffs' claim and allowed the wife's counterclaim. The plaintiffs appealed.   e

Held – A notice in writing of a desire to sever a joint tenancy in equity served pursuant
to s 36(2) of the 1925 Act took effect forthwith and accordingly a desire to sever had to
evince an intention to bring about the wanted result immediately. Furthermore, the
notice had to be one which showed an intention to bring about the consequences set out   f
in s 36(2), i e that the net proceeds of the statutory trust for sale 'be held upon the trust
which would have been requisite for giving effect to the beneficial interests if there had
been an actual severance'. Paragraph 3 of the prayer of the petition did no more than
invite the court to consider at some future time whether to exercise its jurisdiction under
s 24 of the 1973 Act and, if it did, to do so in one or more of three different ways. It
followed therefore that para 3 of the prayer of the petition did not operate as a notice in
writing to sever the joint tenancy in equity and the wife was entitled to the whole of the   g
proceeds of sale of the property. The appeal would accordingly be dismissed (see p 246 a
to e and j and p 247 e f, post).
Re Draper's Conveyance, Nihan v Porter [1967] 3 All ER 853 approved.
Bedson v Bedson [1965] 3 All ER 307 considered.
Re Wilks, Child v Bulmer [1891] 3 Ch 59 not followed.   h

Notes
For severance of joint tenancies, see 32 Halsbury's Laws (3rd edn) 334–337, paras 522–
528, and for cases on the subject, see 38 Digest (Reissue) 606–619, 5071–5120.
For the Law of Property Act 1925, s 36, see 27 Halsbury's Statutes (3rd edn) 393.
For the Matrimonial Causes Act 1973, s 24, see 43 ibid 566.   j

Cases referred to in judgments
Bedson v Bedson [1965] 3 All ER 307, [1965] 2 QB 666, [1965] 3 WLR 891, CA.

---

a   Section 36(2) is set out at p 243 j to p 244 c, post

Burgess v Rawnsley [1975] 3 All ER 142, [1975] Ch 429, [1975] 3 WLR 99, CA.

a   *Draper's Conveyance, Re, Nihan v Porter* [1967] 3 All ER 853, [1969] 1 Ch 486, [1968] 2 WLR 166.

Nielson-Jones v Fedden [1974] 3 All ER 38, [1975] Ch 222, [1974] 3 WLR 583.

Wilks, Re, Child v Bulmer [1891] 3 Ch 59.

Williams v Hensman (1861) John & H 546, 70 ER 862.

b   **Cases also cited**

Gould v Kemp (1834) 2 My & K 304, 39 ER 959, LC.

Jackson v Jackson [1971] 3 All ER 774, [1971] 1 WLR 1539, CA.

Radziej (orse Sierkowska) v Radziej [1967] 1 All ER 944, [1967] 1 WLR 659; *affd* [1968] 3 All ER 624, [1968] 1 WLR 1928, CA.

c   **Appeal**

The plaintiffs, Duncan Gregory Harris and Sandra Fenn Smith, the executors of the will of Dudley Jack Watson Harris deceased (the testator), appealed against the judgment of Mr Gerald Godfrey QC sitting as a deputy judge of the High Court on 21 January 1983 whereby (1) he dismissed the plaintiffs' action against the first and second defendants, George Kelsey Goddard and Peter Donald Richardson Brown, the trustees of the proceeds

d   of sale of a property known as 93–95 The Street, Fetcham, Surrey, and against the third defendant, Alaide Harris, the widow of the testator, seeking (a) a declaration that the equitable joint tenancy formerly subsisting between the testator and the third defendant in respect of the property and the proceeds of sale thereof was validly and effectively severed prior to the death of the testator and (b) as against the first and second defendants, an account of the proceeds of sale of the property and an order for payment by them to

e   the plaintiffs, as executors of the testator, of the amount found to be due on the taking of an account, and (2) he made a declaration on a counterclaim by the third defendant that the beneficial joint tenancy of the testator and the third defendant in the property was not severed prior to his death and that she was entitled to give good receipt to the first and second defendants for the proceeds of sale of the property. The facts are set out in the judgment of Lawton LJ.

f   *Simon Berry* for the plaintiffs.
David Iwi for the defendants.

Cur adv vult

g   25 July. The following judgments were delivered.

LAWTON LJ. This appeal from a judgment of Mr Gerald Godfrey QC, sitting as a deputy judge of the High Court in the Chancery Division, given on 21 January 1983, raises this question: does a divorce petition which, when served, includes in its prayer a request in general terms for the exercise of the jurisdiction given to the court by s 24 of

h   the Matrimonial Causes Act 1973 constitute a notice in writing of a desire to sever a joint tenancy in equity within the meaning of s 36(2) of the Law of Property Act 1925? Answering this question has required the court to construe the word 'sever' as used in that section. Section 36 provides as follows:

'(1) Where a legal estate (not being settled land) is beneficially limited to or held in trust for any persons as joint tenants, the same shall be held on trust for sale, in

j   like manner as if the persons beneficially entitled were tenants in common, but not so as to sever their joint tenancy in equity.

(2) No severance of a joint tenancy of a legal estate, so as to create a tenancy in common in land, shall be permissible, whether by operation of law or otherwise, but this subsection does not affect the right of a joint tenant to release his interest to

the other joint tenants, or the right to sever a joint tenancy in an equitable interest
whether or not the legal estate is vested in the joint tenants: Provided that, where a
legal estate (not being settled land) is vested in joint tenants beneficially, and any
tenant desires to sever the joint tenancy in equity, he shall give to the other joint
tenants a notice in writing of such desire or do such other acts or things as would, in
the case of personal estate, have been effectual to sever the tenancy in equity, and
thereupon under the trust for sale affecting the land the net proceeds of sale, and the
net rents and profits until sale, shall be held upon the trusts which would have been
requisite for giving effect to the beneficial interests if there had been an actual
severance. Nothing in this Act affects the right of a survivor of joint tenants, who is
solely and beneficially interested, to deal with his legal estate as if it were not held
on trust for sale.

(3) Without prejudice to the right of a joint tenant to release his interest to the
other joint tenants no severance of a mortgage term or trust estate, so as to create a
tenancy in common, shall be permissible.'

The plaintiffs are the executors and children by his first marriage of Dudley Jack
Watson Harris (Mr Harris) who died on 24 September 1980. The third defendant, Alaide
Harris (Mrs Harris), was his second wife. He married her on 17 August 1972. The first
and second defendants are the trustees of a fund which has come into existence following
the sale of a property known as 93–95 The Street, Fetcham in Surrey. That property had
on purchase been conveyed into the joint names of Mr and Mrs Harris. It was admitted
at the trial that they held it as joint tenants in equity. The first and second defendants
want to know how to distribute the fund. The plaintiffs claimed that they, as Mr Harris's
executors, were entitled to be paid half the fund. Mrs Harris counterclaimed that she was
entitled to the whole of it by the right of survivorship on her husband's death.

Mrs Harris at all material times after the marriage had been employed by a bank. She
had been paid a modest salary which had provided the greater part of the family income.
Mr Harris had worked as a photographer but his earnings had been small and irregular.
For a short time after their marriage this couple lived in rented accommodation. They
then in their joint names bought a house at River Lane, Fetcham, with the help of a loan,
secured by a mortgage, made to them by Mrs Harris's employers. The loan was protected
by a life policy on the life of Mr Harris. The interest on the loan and the premiums on
the policy were deducted by Mrs Harris's employers from her salary. The trial judge
accepted Mrs Harris's evidence that she regarded this property as providing some security
for her if her husband died before she did, which seemed a likely possibility because of
the difference in their ages. In 1978 Mr and Mrs Harris decided to sell the River Lane
property and buy 93–95 The Street, Fetcham. Part of it was to be used as their residence,
part as shop premises for Mr Harris's photographic business. The further money required
for this purchase was once again provided by Mrs Harris's employers by way of a loan
secured by a mortgage and protected by a policy on Mr Harris's life; and once again the
property was conveyed to them in their joint names. It was agreed by all parties at the
trial that they held it as joint tenants in equity. As with the River Lane property Mrs
Harris regarded it as providing some security for her if her husband died first.

About 1979 the marriage began to break down. Mrs Harris told her husband that she
wanted a divorce. He did not want one. She left him on or about 22 June 1979 and
consulted solicitors. By letter dated 8 August 1979 her solicitors told Mr Harris that in
due course she wanted to petition for divorce. They raised the problem presented by the
joint ownership of 93–95 The Street and the fact that she was paying the interest on the
bank loan and the premiums on the life policy. At that time the equity in the property
after repayment of the loan was estimated to be worth about £13,500. The letter
contained this sentence: 'The property is in joint names and it would appear therefore
that you are entitled to half each of the balance left over.' Before this court it was accepted
by counsel for the plaintiffs that this letter did not amount to a severance notice for the
purposes of s 36(2) of the Law of Property Act 1925.

On or about 28 December 1979 Mrs Harris's solicitors caused a divorce petition of that
a date to be served on Mr Harris. It was alleged that the marriage had broken down
irretrievably and that Mrs Harris could not reasonably be expected to live with her
husband. The prayer of this petition asked for the dissolution of the marriage and
maintenance, and, in para 3, included the words which the plaintiffs have submitted
should be construed as a notice of a desire to sever the joint tenancy. They were as
follows:

b   'That such order may be made by way of transfer of property and/or settlement
     of property and/or variation of settlement in respect of the former matrimonial
     home at 95 The Street, Fetcham aforesaid and otherwise as may be just.'

They echo the words of s 24(1)(a), (b) and (c) of the Matrimonial Causes Act 1973.

On 18 August 1980, three days before the date fixed for the hearing of the petition,
c Mr Harris was injured in a car accident. He was rendered unconscious and remained in a
coma until his death on 24 September 1980. On 22 August 1980 Mr Harris's solicitors
sent Mrs Harris's solicitors what purported to be a notice of severance of the joint tenancy
in equity of 93–95 The Street. They did so on the instructions of Mr Harris's accountant.
Having regard to the trial judge's findings that the accountant had no authority from Mr
Harris to give the instructions he did, the plaintiffs accepted in this court that this notice
d had no effect in law and that Mrs Harris on her husband's death took the whole interest
in the fund which represented the balance of the sale price of 93–95 The Street after the
repayment of the loan unless para 3 of the prayer of the divorce petition took effect as a
severance notice. In a long and careful judgment, and after discussion of a number of
authorities, the trial judge decided that it did not.

Counsel on both sides in this court went through the authorities again, starting with
e *Blackstone's Commentaries* (2 Bl Com (8th edn) p 185). I did not find them of much help.
The question to be decided in this appeal is the correct construction of the proviso to
s 36(2) of the Law of Property Act 1925. Parliament intended this Act to define rights of
property. It made radical changes in the law. I can see no good reason for looking behind
the words of the 1925 Act unless they are capable of more than one meaning or the
meaning is obscure.

f   I start with s 36. It dealt with beneficial joint tenancies, which must mean all joint
tenancies, including those held by husbands and wives. The section makes no special
provisions by way of giving extra rights or raising presumptions in favour of spouses.
When severance is said to arise under s 36(2), not from the giving of a notice in writing,
but from '[doing] . . . other acts or things' which would, in the case of personal estate,
have been effectual to sever a joint tenancy in equity, the fact that the parties were
g married may make the drawing of inferences easier. It is, in my judgment, only in this
limited evidential context that the existence of the married state has any relevance. In
reaching this conclusion I have followed what Russell LJ said in *Bedson v Bedson* [1965] 3
All ER 307 at 318–319, [1965] 2 QB 666 at 689–690 rather than the obiter statement of
Lord Denning MR in the same case (see [1965] 3 All ER 307 at 311, [1965] 2 QB 666 at
677). Lord Denning MR said that spouses holding as beneficial joint tenants cannot sever
h their interests so as to convert them into tenancies in common. The trial judge seems to
have been influenced to some extent by what Lord Denning MR said. Since in this case
severance is said to have come about by a notice in writing the sole question is whether
that which is said to be the notice did show that Mrs Harris desired to sever the joint
tenancy.

In *Williams v Hensman* (1861) John & H 546, 70 ER 862 Page Wood V-C said that a
j joint tenancy could be severed in three ways, that is by disposal of one of the interests, by
mutual agreement and 'by any course of dealing sufficient to intimate that the interests
of all were mutually treated as constituting a tenancy in common'. The words in s 36(2)
'do such other acts or things as would . . . have been effectual to sever the tenancy' put
into statutory language the other ways of effecting severance to which Page Wood V-C
referred in *Williams v Hensman*. The words 'and any tenant desires to sever the joint

tenancy in equity, he shall give to the other joint tenants a notice in writing of such
desire' operate to extend the mutual agreement concept of severance referred to in a
Williams v Hensman. Unilateral action to sever a joint tenancy is now possible. Before
1925 severance by unilateral action was only possible when one joint tenant disposed of
his interest to a third party. When a notice in writing of a desire to sever is served
pursuant to s 36(2) it takes effect forthwith. It follows that a desire to sever must evince
an intention to bring about the wanted result immediately. A notice in writing which
expresses a desire to bring about the wanted result at some time in the future is not, in b
my judgment, a notice in writing within s 36(2). Further the notice must be one which
shows an intent to bring about the consequences set out in s 36(2), namely that the net
proceeds of the statutory trust for sale 'shall be held upon the trust which would have
been requisite for giving effect to the beneficial interests if there had been an actual
severance'. I am unable to accept the submission of counsel for the plaintiffs that a notice
in writing which shows no more than a desire to bring the existing interest to an end is a c
good notice. It must be a desire to sever which is intended to have the statutory
consequences. Paragraph 3 of the prayer of the petition does no more than invite the
court to consider at some future time whether to exercise its jurisdiction under s 24 of
the 1973 Act and, if it does, to do so in one or more of three different ways. Orders under
s 24(1)(a) and (b) could bring co-ownership to an end by ways other than by severance. It
follows, in my judgment, that para 3 of the prayer of the petition did not operate as a d
notice in writing to sever the joint tenancy in equity. This tenancy had not been severed
when Mr Harris died, with the consequence that Mrs Harris is entitled to the whole of
the fund held by the first and second defendants as trustees. I wish to stress that all I am
saying is that para 3 in the petition under consideration in this case did not operate as a
notice of severance.

Perhaps this case should be a cautionary tale for those who draft divorce petitions e
when the spouses hold property as joint tenants in equity. The decision of Plowman J in
Re Draper's Conveyance, Nihan v Porter [1967] 3 All ER 853, [1969] 1 Ch 486 is an example
of how starting legal proceedings can sever a joint tenancy. In that case a wife, after a
decree nisi but before a decree absolute, issued a summons under s 17 of the Married
Women's Property Act 1882 asking for an order that a house in the joint names of herself
and her husband be sold and the proceeds of sale distributed in accordance with the f
parties' respective interests therein. An affidavit sworn by the wife in support of the
summons contained this paragraph:

> 'In the premises I humbly ask that the said property may be sold and that the
> proceeds of sale thereof may be distributed equally; alternatively that the Respondent
> pay me one half of the value of the said property with vacant possession . . .'

Plowman J adjudged that the summons and the affidavit together effected a severance g
during the lifetime of the husband. I agree that it did; but it is not clear from the
judgment whether the judge regarded the summons or the affidavit or both as notices in
writing or whether the service of the summons and the filing of the affidavit were acts
which were effectual to sever the joint tenancy. I do not share the doubts about the
correctness of this judgment on this point which Walton J expressed in *Nielson-Jones v
Fedden* [1974] 3 All ER 38 at 50, [1975] Ch 222 at 236 relying on *Re Wilks, Child v Bulmer* h
[1891] 3 Ch 59. The fact that the wife in *Re Draper's Conveyance* could have withdrawn
the summons is a factor which could have been taken into account in deciding whether
what was done was effectual to sever the joint tenancy in equity. The weight of that
factor would have depended on all the other circumstances and was in that case clearly
negligible.

I would dismiss the appeal. j

KERR LJ. I have read the judgments to be delivered by Lawton and Dillon LJJ. I
respectfully agree with both of them and have nothing that I wish to add.

DILLON LJ. I agree that this appeal should be dismissed for the reasons given by
Lawton LJ. I agree also that *Re Draper's Conveyance, Nihan v Porter* [1967] 3 All ER 853,

[1969] 1 Ch 486 was correctly decided in so far as Plowman J based his judgment on s 36
a   of the Law of Property Act 1925. *Re Wilks, Child v Bulmer* [1891] 3 Ch 59, though no
doubt correct in its time, would be decided differently now because of s 36.

I desire to add a few words on the concept of severance, as I understand it, and to
emphasise the difference between the relief claimed in *Re Draper's Conveyance* and the
relief claimed by para 3 of the prayer in the divorce petition in the present case.

Joint tenancy is a form of co-ownership, or concurrent ownership, of property. Its
b   special feature is the right of survivorship, whereby the right to the whole of the property
accrues automatically to the surviving joint tenants or joint tenant on the death of any
one joint tenant. Severance is, as I understand it, the process of separating off the share of
a joint tenant, so that the concurrent ownership will continue but the right of
survivorship will no longer apply. The parties will hold separate shares as tenants in
common. The joint tenancy may come to an end through other acts which destroy the
c   whole concurrent ownership, e g if one joint tenant acquires the entire beneficial interest
of the other joint tenants, so as to become solely and absolutely entitled beneficially to
the property, or by all the joint tenants joining in resettling the property on other trusts
not involving concurrent ownership; but such acts do not involve severance and would
not be called severance of the joint tenancy.

In *Re Draper's Conveyance* the relief claimed by the originating summons which had
d   been issued and by the affidavit in support included, as Lawton LJ has pointed out, a
claim that the property might be sold and the proceeds be distributed equally in
accordance with the rights of the parties. This plainly involved severance of the beneficial
joint tenancy as I understand the term 'severance'.

In the present case, however, para 3 of the prayer in the petition merely seeks relief in
the most general and unparticularised terms under s 24 of the Matrimonial Causes Act
e   1973. Apart from the fact that any relief for Mrs Harris under s 24 lay in the future and
was contingent on the court's exercising its discretion under the section in her favour,
she had not yet specified what she desired by the time Mr Harris died, and the general
prayer in her petition could have been satisfied by relief which did not involve severance,
e g an order extinguishing Mr Harris's interest in the property and directing that the
property be vested in Mrs Harris as sole absolute beneficial owner, or an order directing
f   a resettlement of the property on Mr and Mrs Harris successively and not as concurrent
owners. Therefore the petition in this case cannot be notice of a desire to sever the joint
tenancy.

I should add that we have had the benefit, in the course of the excellent argument by
counsel for the plaintiffs, of being referred to *Burgess v Rawnsley* [1975] 3 All ER 142,
[1975] Ch 429, the most recent decision of this court where s 36 has been considered in
g   relation to the law of severance of joint tenancies. I have found the observations of Sir
John Pennycuick, in particular, most helpful.

Appeal dismissed. Leave to appeal to the House of Lords refused. Application for stay refused.

Solicitors: *Gilmours* (for the plaintiffs); *Heald Nickinson* (for the defendants).

                                                          Mary Rose Plummer   Barrister.

Re Rapley's Estate
Rapley v Rapley

CHANCERY DIVISION

HIS HONOUR JUDGE FINLAY QC SITTING AS A JUDGE OF THE HIGH COURT

14, 15 MARCH 1983

Will – Soldier's or mariner's privileged will – Seaman at sea – Document made in contemplation of voyage – Seaman ashore on leave not under orders to sail – Seaman executing document while a minor and without attestation – Whether seaman in contemplation of voyage when orders merely expected – Whether seaman 'mariner or seaman . . . at sea' – Wills Act 1837, s 11.

On 22 October 1960 the deceased, who was then apprenticed to a shipping company and was on leave in England pending the receipt of orders to join a ship's crew for a further voyage, purported to execute a will which made his mother the principal beneficiary of his estate. The deceased was a minor at that time and s 7[a] of the Wills Act 1837 provided that wills made by minors were invalid. The deceased also failed to have the document attested as required by s 9[b] of the 1837 Act. However, s 11[c] of the 1837 Act exempted 'any mariner or seaman being at sea' from the provisions of that Act, including the prohibition on minors making valid testamentary dispositions. The deceased died in 1980 and the plaintiff, the deceased's mother, was granted letters of administration on the basis that the deceased had died intestate. The plaintiff then issued a writ against the defendant, the deceased's father, who was the only other person interested in the estate, seeking orders that the document was a valid mariner's will, that she be granted letters of administration with will annexed, and that the existing grant be revoked.

Held – Section 11 of the 1837 Act exempted any mariner or seaman at sea from the formal requirements imposed by that Act for the valid execution of a will because those who were at sea were without legal assistance and also faced a greater risk of death. For those reasons the words 'at sea' included a mariner or seaman who was in a state of preparation being under orders to go to sea but did not apply to the deceased who, although he was at the relevant time a mariner or seaman, had not by the time he executed the document received instructions to join a ship. It followed that the document was not a valid testamentary disposition and the plaintiff's action would accordingly be dismissed (see p 254 *b* to *j*, post).

Re Hale's Goods [1915] 2 IR 362, *Re Newland's Estate* [1952] 1 All ER 841 and *Re Wilson's Estate, Wilson v Coleclough* [1952] 1 All ER 852 distinguished.

Notes

For privileged wills, see 17 Halsbury's Laws (4th edn) paras 825–829, and for cases on the subject, see 39 Digest (Repl) 399–406, 196–260.

For the Wills Act 1837, ss 7, 9, 11, see 39 Halsbury's Statutes (3rd edn) 859, 862.

As from 1 January 1983 s 9 of the 1837 Act was substituted by s 17 of the Administration of Justice Act 1982, but the substitution does not affect the will of any testator who died before that date.

---

a Section 7 is set out at p 250 *b c*, post

b Section 9 provides: 'No will shall be valid unless it shall be in writing, and executed in manner herein-after mentioned; (that is to say), it shall be signed at the foot or end thereof by the testator, or by some other person in his presence and by his direction; and such signature shall be made or acknowledged by the testator in the presence of two or more witnesses present at the same time, and such witnesses shall attest and shall subscribe the will in the presence of the testator, but no form of attestation shall be necessary.'

c Section 11 is set out at p 250 *c d*, post

Cases referred to in judgment

a *Barnard v Birch* [1919] 2 IR 404.
Corby's Goods, Re (1854) 1 Ecc & Ad 292, 164 ER 169.
Euston (Earl) v Lord Seymour (1802) cited 2 Curt 339, 163 ER 432.
Hale's Goods, Re [1915] 2 IR 362.
Hayes's Goods, Re (1839) 2 Curt 338, 163 ER 431.
Lay's Goods, Re (1840) 2 Curt 375, 163 ER 444.
b *M'Murdo's Goods, Re* (1868) LR 1 P & D 540.
Newland's Estate, Re [1952] 1 All ER 841, [1952] P 71.
Patterson's Goods, Re (1898) 79 LT 123.
Wernher, Re, Wernher v Beit [1918] 2 Ch 82, CA; *affg* [1918] 1 Ch 339.
Wilson's Estate, Re, Wilson v Coleclough [1952] 1 All ER 852, [1952] P 92.

c **Action**
By a writ issued on 22 January 1982 the plaintiff, Nettie Rapley, sought as against the defendant, Albert William Alfred Rapley, orders (i) that the document executed by the deceased, Clive William Rapley, on 22 October 1960 was a valid testamentary disposition, (ii) that letters of administration with the will annexed be granted to the plaintiff and (iii) that, so far as necessary, letters of administration granted to the plaintiff on 8 January d 1981 be revoked. The facts are set out in the judgment.

Ian Romer for the plaintiff.
The defendant appeared in person.

HIS HONOUR JUDGE FINLAY QC. In this action the plaintiff, Nettie Rapley, e propounds a will in the form of what is often referred to as a seaman's will made by her son in October 1960, and the document, which is signed by the deceased, but not attested and was made by him when under the age of 21, is valid as a testamentary document only if it is so validated by the application of s 11 of the Wills Act 1837.

The deceased died on or after 9 September 1980 when the ship in which he was then serving foundered in a typhoon in the Pacific Ocean. He was then aged about 39 years.
f At the time when he signed the document the effect of which is in question in these proceedings he was apprenticed to the Ellerman & Bucknell Steamship Co. By an apprentice's indenture dated 13 May 1959 he bound himself apprentice to that company for a term of three years from that date. The schedule of his voyages' record shows that, having served in the ship City of London from May 1959 until February 1960, a period of some eight months or more, he then joined the ship City of Ely and served for a period g of two months and fifteen days, when he had apparently a period of leave or furlough, from 19 April 1960 until 19 May in that year, when he rejoined the City of Ely and served in her until 7 October 1960. On the day following he went on leave to his family home in St Leonards-on-Sea, and there on 22 October 1960 he signed the document which the plaintiff in this action seeks to propound.

By that document the deceased expressed himself as follows:
h
'I, the undersigned Clive William Rapley, at present residing at 349 London Road in the town of St Leonards-on-Sea in the County of Sussex do hereby bequeath and bequest all that I die possessed of to my mother, Mrs Nettie Rapley, nee Pemberton, to be used as she feels fit.'

He then made provision for the event, which did not happen, of his mother j predeceasing him, and finally made this disposition:

'Such of my possessions as are used by me in my career, viz. my uniforms, books, instruments, etc., are to be sent to the Captain Superintendent, The Thames Nautical Training College, Greenhithe, Kent, for disposal of amongst its pupils as he thinks fit.'

Then there follows the words: 'Signed this 22nd day of October in the year of our Lord 1960', and the signature of the deceased with his name typed thereunder. The whole *a* document, I should say, apart from that signature, is in typescript.

On 8 January 1981 letters of administration of the estate of the deceased were granted out of the District Probate Registry, Brighton, to his mother, the plaintiff, on the basis that he had died on or after 9 September 1980 domiciled in England and Wales and intestate. It appears that the document of 22 October 1960 was known to the plaintiff at the time she obtained the grant of letters of administration, but it may be some view as *b* to its operation and effect was taken at that time. The document, it has emerged in evidence, was among the deceased's papers lodged at his bank. These proceedings were instituted by a writ dated 22 January 1982, and the defendant, Albert William Alfred Rapley, is the father of the deceased and the only other person interested in any estate in respect of which he died intestate.

The Wills Act 1837, s 7, provides: 'No will made by any person under the age of *c* twenty-one years shall be valid.' The subsequent amendment of that section to substitute 'eighteen' for 'twenty-one' is immaterial to this case. Section 9 contains the provisions that require a will to be in writing signed by the testator in the presence of two witnesses. Section 11 of the 1837 Act is in these terms:

'Provided always, that any soldier being in actual military service, or any mariner or seaman being at sea, may dispose of his personal estate as he might have done *d* before the making of this Act.'

By reason of doubts that had been expressed in *Re Wernher, Wernher v Beit* [1918] 1 Ch 339 it was enacted by the Wills (Soldiers and Sailors) Act 1918, s 1:

'In order to remove doubts as to the construction of the Wills Act, 1837, it is hereby declared and enacted that section eleven of that Act authorises and always *e* has authorised any soldier being in actual military service, or any mariner or seaman being at sea, to dispose of his personal estate as he might have done before the passing of that Act, though under the age of twenty-one years.'

The issue, therefore, which arises on the facts of this case is whether at the time when he signed this document on 22 October 1960 the deceased can be regarded as being a *f* 'mariner or seaman being at sea' within the meaning of s 11 of the 1837 Act, because if he was not then the document is clearly invalid as a testamentary disposition both by reason of s 7 of the 1837 Act in that he was under age and by reason of the provisions of s 9 in that it was not duly attested.

I have already indicated the record of voyages of the deceased up to the point where he went on leave, having been discharged from the City of Ely on 7 October 1960. On 29 *g* November of that year he joined another ship of the Ellerman Line, namely the City of Melbourne. It is pleaded by the defendant in his defence that at the time when the deceased signed the typed document dated 22 October 1960 he had not been given notice by his employer that he was required to join another vessel in the immediate future; and in the reply it is expressly admitted that that was the case.

I have heard evidence from William Reed Strachan, an insurance manager for *h* Ellerman City Lines, the company which I understand is the company to which the deceased was bound apprentice, or the successor of that company, as to the practice of what I will call Ellerman City Lines in relation to granting leave to apprentices and notifying them of their instructions as to joining or rejoining any ship after a period of leave, and Mr Strachan gave that evidence in the light of the fact that he had been employed by that company since 1945 and was familiar with their mode of operation. *j* In brief his evidence was that for every month on board ship an apprentice would have about four days' leave and that although not the whole of that leave was always given at the conclusion of a voyage some of it might be put, as it were, in a leave bank (I think that was his phrase) to be used at some later date, nevertheless the apprentice would normally have at least 50% of the leave due to him at the end of any voyage when leave was granted. On that footing it would appear that since, from the time of his last

preceding leave prior to October 1960, he had been at sea for some four to five months
a he would have been due for something like 20 days' leave or thereabouts, and that he
was not likely to be recalled to duty until half of that period, that is to say some ten days,
had expired. It is submitted that in those circumstances he must have regarded it as
likely, once 18 October was passed, that at any time he might be recalled to duty. In fact
the recall, as appears from his record, did not come until he was told to join the City of
Melbourne, and it is common ground, as I have said, that those instructions were given
b at some date after 22 October 1960.

The most recent authority on this not easy subject is Re Newland's Estate [1952] 1 All
ER 841, [1952] P 71 and Re Wilson's Estate, Wilson v Coleclough [1952] 1 All ER 852,
[1952] P 92, both being decisions of Havers J. In the former case, Newland, Havers J
considered not only the authorities on the meaning of 'mariner or seaman being at sea'
but also those concerning a soldier on active military service, and he said ([1952] 1 All ER
c 841 at 843, [1952] P 71 at 75):

'I have examined the various authorities which have been cited to me to see
whether I could extract from them some principle of universal application, but I
have been unable to find such a principle.'

The conclusion that it is not possible to find a unifying principle is one with which I am
d constrained respectfully to agree, but nevertheless there does appear to me to be a
measure of consistency to be found in the authorities on the significance and meaning of
the words 'a seaman being at sea'.

In those cases, where it has been held that the maker of the testamentary document of
a nuncupative type (and for convenience I will refer to the maker in each case as 'the
testator') was a seaman being at sea in circumstances where that was not in any obvious
e and ordinary sense the case, there appear to be the following features. In the first place,
one finds that there is material that justified a finding that the testator was a mariner or
seaman. The evidence in short has to show that the testator was serving either in the
Royal Navy or the Merchant Navy. It matters not whether he be a man or a woman, nor
in what capacity he or she served or was employed, provided that the nature of the service
is sea service. Second, the evidence, it appears to me, must also justify a finding that the
f testator is 'on maritime service' in the sense that the testator either (a) is already (that is at
the time of signing the document in question or making the nuncupative will) in post as
a ship's officer (see, for example, Re M'Murdo's Goods (1868) LR 1 P & D 540, where the
testator was the mate in HMS Excellent, and Re Lay's Goods (1840) 2 Curt 375, 163 ER
444, where the testator was the mate of HMS Calliope and made a will when on shore
leave from that vessel), or (b) is already a member of a particular ship's company serving
g in that ship (and an instance of that is Re Patterson's Goods (1898) 79 LT 123), or on shore
leave (an example of that is Re Lay's Goods) or on long leave ashore (of which Re Newland's
Estate itself is an instance), or (c) being employed by owners of a fleet of ships and having
been discharged from one such is already under orders to join another ship in that fleet
(and examples of that are Re Hale's Goods [1915] 2 IR 362 and Re Wilson's Estate).

In the cases where a grant was refused one or other of these features is, I think, always
h found to be lacking. For example, in Re Corby's Goods (1854) 1 Ecc & Ad 292, 164 ER
169, the first of the cases which Havers J examined in Re Newland's Estate, Dr Lushington
appears to have doubted whether the resident of Melbourne who shipped as an able
seaman for passage to England could be regarded on the day he did so as a mariner or
seaman, although he decided the case on the basis that as the vessel was in Melbourne
harbour at the relevant time, that is at the time when the document was signed, and not
j at sea, the propositus was not 'a mariner or seaman being at sea'.

In Earl of Euston v Lord Seymour (1802), which is referred to in the report of Re Hayes's
Goods (1839) 2 Curt 338 at 339, 163 ER 431 at 432, the admiral made a nuncupative
codicil when he was in the admiral's house ashore. Sir William Wynn, it appears, would
have held that the admiral was 'a mariner or seaman', but was not willing to hold that he
was at sea. It will be noted that the admiral, even assuming that ordinarily he hoisted his
flag in one particular ship, could not be regarded as appointed to that ship or as a member

of its complement in any of the senses I have instanced in setting out the features which I find in those cases where the seaman's will has been upheld.

The fact that the features I have indicated have to be found, if it is to be held that the testator falls within the sense of the words 'being at sea' when he is in fact ashore at the relevant time does not imply that he must be regarded as being at sea if those features are established. In *Barnard v Birch* [1919] 2 IR 404, the deceased was a captain in the Royal Mail service and commanded the SS Leinster during its cross-channel voyages between Holyhead and Kingston, and he was actually at sea for the time each day that was spent in transit. He had a house in Holyhead, and the document purporting to be a will was signed by him when he was at that house, and Dodd J held that he was sitting in his house when he made the will and that 'he was a seaman on shore and not a seaman being at sea'. Nevertheless that was a case where the necessary features which I have enunciated were clearly to be found but where the conclusion on the facts was that the captain of the SS Leinster was not a 'seaman being at sea'.

Now in the present case the deceased was, in my judgment, clearly a mariner or seaman by calling. He was an apprentice indentured for training as a sea officer. It is further clear that he made and signed the questioned document when he was ashore. Is he then to be treated as a mariner or seaman being at sea within the meaning of the section bearing in mind that he had not, at the time when he signed the document, been posted to a seagoing ship? I have already referred to how that matter stands on the pleadings.

Counsel for the plaintiff submits that in *Re Newland's Estate* [1952] 1 All ER 841, [1952] P 71 is authority that it is enough if the testator makes a will in contemplation of sailing on a fresh voyage. The facts in *Re Newland's Estate* were that the deceased was an apprentice in the Merchant Navy and he executed a testamentary document shortly before rejoining his ship, which sailed a day or two later. The document was executed in compliance with the formalities of the 1837 Act in that it was attested by two witnesses but, as he was then a minor, it was only a valid will if it was validated by virtue of s 11 on the basis that he was a mariner or seaman being at sea at the time when he executed it. He was an apprentice serving in the SS Strathmore. He had joined that ship in April 1944 and continued to serve in her until 24 October 1944. In July of that year, while the Strathmore was docked in Liverpool, the deceased went on shore leave, and at Walton-on-Thames in Surrey he executed the will in the presence of two witnesses. It appears from the facts as stated in the judgment that Havers J inferred that he had received instructions to rejoin the Strathmore before he wrote and executed the document in question.

Havers J referred to various cases, most of which I think I have already mentioned in passing, that is to say *Corby, Lay, Lord Seymour, Patterson, M'Murdo* and certain other cases which I need not, I think, refer to, bearing in mind the very full manner in which they are dealt with in the judgment of Havers J. He said ([1952] 1 All ER 841 at 850–851, [1952] P 71 at 88–89):

'Counsel for the applicants argued before me that, whether I approach this matter from the angle of *In the Goods of Lay* ((1840) 2 Curt 375, 163 ER 444), or from the angle of *In the Goods of Hale* ([1915] IR 362), I ought to decide this case in favour of the applicants. He pointed out that the deceased was throughout in continuous maritime service in this ship. He joined the ship when it was engaged in this service and he had commenced and carried out completed voyages in it, he was an apprentice bound to serve where ordered, and throughout the whole of the relevant period the ship was engaged as a troopship on a series of voyages between England and India. If, for instance, while the ship was in dock at some port in India at the end of the voyage from England, the deceased had been given temporary shore leave for a day or two and while he was on such leave in India he had made this document, I think there would be great force in the argument that, following the decision in *In the Goods of Lay* ((1840) 2 Curt 375, 163 ER 444), that document would have been made by him while he was a seaman at sea. I cannot see any distinction in principle between the instance which I have just given and a case where, while the ship is in dock in England for the necessary period of time for refitting and so on, the deceased in temporarily on leave ashore in England, and I see no reason why I should not similarly hold that he was during that period a seaman "at sea". If one approaches the matter in the light of *In the Goods of Hale* ([1915] IR 362), I find that the deceased was in the service of this shipping company at the time of the writing of this document, that the document was written in contemplation of sailing in the Strathmore on a fresh voyage within a very few days, and that therefore, he was a "seaman at sea" when he made this will on July 25 1944.'

Re Hale's Goods was a case where the deceased was a typist in the employ of the Cunard Steamship Co, and she was employed as a typist on the ocean liners of that company sailing between Liverpool and New York, and in the periods between voyages she worked in the company's offices in Liverpool. She executed an allegedly testamentary document on 14 January 1915, and the judgment makes it clear that the judge, Madden J, found that at that date she was under orders to sail in the Lusitania on 16 January, and she in fact did so. The judge decided that the lady was a seaman within the meaning of the section and the question arose: was she to be treated as being at sea on 14 January 1915? It will be noted that in that case the deceased was under orders to sail at the time when she executed the relevant document; and the same was the case according to the inferences drawn by Havers J in *Re Newland's Estate*.

In my judgment *Re Newland* is a case distinguishable from the present. There the testator was on leave from the Strathmore, he had not been discharged from one ship and gone on leave awaiting a posting to another. He was at all times, when on leave, one of the complement of the Strathmore. Here the deceased had been discharged from the City of Ely on 7 October 1960 and at some time after 22 October 1960 he was posted to or received orders to join the City of Melbourne.

The other case decided by Havers J was *Re Wilson's Estate, Wilson v Coleclough* [1952] 1 All ER 852, [1952] P 92. There the deceased made a declaration which was held in the event to be a nuncupative will, and he did so at a time when he was under orders to join a ship other than that from which he had been discharged and from which he went on furlough in January 1946. He was on furlough on 25 April when he received instructions to join another ship belonging to the company who were his employers, and two days later he made the nuncupative will. Havers J said ([1952] 1 All ER 852 at 852–853, [1952] P 92 at 93):

'The plaintiff has to satisfy me that at the time the deceased made this nuncupative will he was a seaman at sea. It is unnecessary for me again to review the authorities which I have reviewed in *Newland's* case. The facts which seem to me to be decisive in this case are that at all material times the deceased was a chief officer in the Anglo-Saxon Petroleum Company's fleet of merchant ships, that prior to the furlough he had been at sea in one of the company's ships, that at the end of the furlough he was awaiting re-appointment to another of the company's ships, and that, at the time he made this nuncupative will, he had been ordered to join a ship for a specific voyage. I find that he made this nuncupative will in contemplation of sailing in that ship on that particular voyage, and I find that he was preparing for the voyage. In those circumstances, following the decision of *In the Goods of Hale* ([1915] IR 362), I hold that he was a seaman at sea.'

Now that case of *Re Wilson's Estate* is in my view the one which comes nearest to the facts of the present case. In the present case the deceased was employed as an apprentice of the Ellerman City Lines, he went on furlough having left one of the ships of that company in which he had been serving, and during the time of his furlough he was reappointed to another of the company's ships. The point of distinction is that at the time the deceased signed the document of 22 October 1960 he had not yet received orders to join a ship, or to join a ship for a specific voyage. Counsel for the plaintiff, however, submits that the question is whether, when he signed the document on 22 October, he did so in contemplation of a voyage, and he invites me to hold that, having regard to the numerous authorities which he has taken me to (and I may say that, the defendant here appearing in person, counsel has drawn my attention to both those cases which assist and those which are against the submissions which he is making, and done so in a very fair and ample manner), I am entitled to hold that the deceased signed this document in contemplation of his being appointed to another ship of his employer company, and that in signing it in that contemplation he is to be regarded as being at sea for the purposes of s 11 of the 1837 Act.

I find that none of the authorities which have been cited to me goes so far as to decide that when one who is a mariner or seaman by calling and employment makes a will when on shore on leave and is not at that time a member of the complement of a particular ship and has not at that time been posted to a ship, he is yet to be treated as being at sea. To extend the meaning of s 11 to such a case would appear to me to result in according no significance to the words 'at sea' in the section, because it would make the section applicable to anyone who at the relevant time was a mariner or seaman, since any mariner or seaman must always be in contemplation of another voyage until in fact he gives up the sea, retires from the marine service and so ceases from that point to be a mariner or seaman.

The cases have gone very far to extend the meaning of 'at sea' to include those who are in a state of preparation for going to sea, being under orders to do so, but to go beyond that and to extend the ambit of the section to cover the case where a mariner or seaman is on furlough or leave, knows well that he may at any time be instructed to join another ship but has not at the moment received such instructions is, I think, to extend the operation of the section beyond the circumstances which were no doubt in the contemplation of the legislature when this provision was originally enacted and when it was re-enacted in 1837. The ground and justification for this privilege is no doubt the circumstance that those who are at sea are both without the advantage of legal assistance and also the justification for the privilege is no doubt the danger of the calling and the fact that to those who follow the sea death is an always present likelihood and not the remote certainty which it is for others.

I do not think that, considering the basis for this privilege, I can find any ground in that for extending the operation of the section to the extent that counsel invites me now to do.

The defendant, who made his submissions to the contrary with becoming brevity, made the submission that there was not a single case in the books of a will being treated as a privileged will of a seaman who was not a member of a ship's crew. In one sense that is no doubt well founded, but it is quite clear, of course, that the cases do cover the situation of the mariner or seaman who has orders to join a ship and treat him as being at sea even before he has actually done so. The defendant also submitted, on the basis of a sentence which he had found in a publication which unhappily has not been found in the Supreme Court Library, that in times of peace the privilege only applies from the time the seaman joins the ship until he is paid off. I am quite satisfied that that proposition is not well founded, and the latest case on the matter is the complete answer to it, and that is *Re Wilson's Estate*, to which I have already referred.

In these circumstances I am unable to grant the relief which the plaintiff seeks. She has already obtained letters of administration, and no further order in that regard appears to be necessary.

Action dismissed.

Solicitors: *Percy Walker & Co*, Hastings (for the plaintiff).

Hazel Hartman   Barrister.

Practice Direction

COURT OF PROTECTION

Mental health – Patient's property – Settlements and gifts – Application normally to be heard and determined by master – Parties – Evidence – Mental Health Act 1983, s 96(1)(d) – Court of Protection Rules 1982, rr 21, 4).

Mental health – Patient's property – Execution of will – Application – Parties – Evidence – Evidence of lack of testamentary capacity – Execution and attestation – Evidence of patient's domicile and situation of immovable property affected by proposed will – Mental Health Act 1983, ss 96(4), 97 – Court of Protection Rules 1982, r 21.

This note refers to applications for settlements and gifts under s 96(1)(d) of the Mental Health Act 1983, which comes into effect on 30 September 1983. The note is intended for the general guidance of solicitors as to the practice of the court and supersedes the Practice Direction of 27 November 1969 ([1970] 1 All ER 15, [1970] 1 WLR 228).

Applications will be heard and determined by the master unless the master decides, in accordance with r 45 of the Court of Protection Rules 1982, SI 1982/322, to refer the application, or any question arising in the proceedings, to one of the nominated judges.

By reason of s 17(2)(b) of the Interpretation Act 1978, the 1982 rules (which were made under the Mental Health Act 1959) continue to have effect as if made under the 1983 Act.

1. SETTLEMENTS AND GIFTS

Parties

Under r 21 of the 1982 rules, the application should be made by one or more of the persons who seek to benefit from the proposed settlement or gift. The receiver, if not the applicant or one of the applicants, should be joined as respondent. Otherwise, no person should be made a respondent until the master has so directed.

If the receiver is personally interested in the relief sought, or if there is some other reason for having the interests of the patient separately represented, the master will probably direct that the patient be added as a respondent and that he be represented by the Official Solicitor.

In general, all persons whose interests will be materially affected by proposals should be parties, but the discretion as to parties is a wide one and will be exercised according to the particular facts of each case.

Evidence

The only evidence before the master will be the evidence filed or referred to on the summons. Accordingly, this evidence should give all relevant information necessary for the disposal of the application; full particulars as to the family, property, needs and general circumstances of the patient and the general background of his affairs should be set out, as well as those facts directly giving rise to the application.

2. THE EXECUTION OF WILLS AND CODICILS

In general the same procedure, mutatis mutandis, will be followed as in applications *a* for settlements and gifts. Rule 21 above referred to applies also to applications for the execution of wills, and the same principles as to parties and evidence will be followed. Attention is called to the following matters.

(a) Section 96(4) of the 1983 Act requires that the court must have reason to believe that the patient is incapable of making a valid will for himself. It can be assumed that in most cases the court will require recent evidence of lack of testamentary capacity. If *b* recent evidence is not available, the court may decide to adjourn the application and (if no other evidence can be obtained) call for a report from one of the Lord Chancellor's visitors on this question.

(b) Section 97 of the 1983 Act directs how a statutory will is to be executed and attested, and solicitors should consider and submit a suitable form of attestation clause. Statutory wills will not be sealed by the court until they have been correctly executed *c* and attested.

(c) Having regard to s 97(4) of the 1983 Act the evidence on the summons should state the patient's domicile, whether any immovable property will be affected by the proposed will and, if so, the situation of that property if already belonging to the patient.

A B MACFARLANE
September 1983   Master of the Court of Protection.

R v Epping and Harlow General Commissioners, ex parte Goldstraw

QUEEN'S BENCH DIVISION (CROWN OFFICE LIST)
STEPHEN BROWN J
18 FEBRUARY 1983

COURT OF APPEAL, CIVIL DIVISION
SIR JOHN DONALDSON MR AND PURCHAS LJ
11 MAY 1983

Income tax – Appeal – Decision of commissioners – Finality – Commissioners' clerk advising commissioners that they had no power to reopen determination – Taxpayer alleging that clerk gave advice maliciously – Relevance of maliciousness if advice correct – Taxes Management Act 1970, s 46(2).

Judicial review – Availability of remedy – Alternative remedy available – Alternative remedy not pursued – Whether appropriate to grant leave to apply for judicial review.

The applicant appealed against estimated assessments to income tax. After an adjournment at the request of the applicant, the appeals came on for hearing before the General Commissioners on 11 November 1980. At that hearing the applicant did not appear and was not represented and the commissioners, after hearing the evidence adduced by the Crown, determined the assessments in the figures which the applicant's accountants had previously put forward to the inspector of taxes for the settlement of his liability to tax. The following day, the clerk to the commissioners sent a letter to the applicant informing him of the commissioners' decision. On 12 January 1981 the Crown applied to the commissioners for an interest certificate under s 70 of the Taxes Management Act 1970. At that hearing the applicant sought to reopen the appeal determined on 11 November. The clerk to the commissioners advised them that they had no power to reopen the appeal and the commissioners refused to accede to the applicant's application. Thereupon the applicant sought the leave of the court to apply for judicial review of the commissioners' decision, seeking a declaration that the assessments confirmed by the commissioners were not final and binding on him and an order that the commissioners should hear and determine afresh his appeal against the assessments. The applicant alleged that the commissioners had refused to reopen his appeal because they had acted on advice given maliciously by their clerk.

Held – (1) Under s 46(2)[a] of the 1970 Act the commissioners had no power to reopen their determination and the advice given to the commissioners by their clerk was therefore correct. In those circumstances, the question whether the clerk had acted maliciously in giving that advice was immaterial (see p 262 a b and p 263 a b, post).

(2) The application for judicial review was within the residual jurisdiction of the court but, save in exceptional circumstances, that jurisdiction would not be exercised where other remedies were available and had not been used. Since the applicant could, within 30 days after the determination, have asked the commissioners to state a case for the opinion of the court under s 56[b] of the 1970 Act, raising as a question of law the way in which the hearing had been conducted, and since the applicant had not done that, the application for leave would be refused (see p 262 j to p 263 b, post).

---

a   Section 46(2) is set out at p 262 b, post
b   Section 56, so far as material, is set out at p 262 d e, post

Notes
For the finality of determinations by General Commissioners, see 23 Halsbury's Laws _a_
(4th edn) para 1585.
For judicial review, see 37 ibid paras 567–583.
For the Taxes Management Act 1970 ss 46, 56, 70, see 34 Halsbury's Statutes (3rd edn)
1293, 1302, 1315.

Cases referred to in judgments
_b_
IRC v Pearlberg [1953] 1 All ER 388, [1953] 1 WLR 331, CA.
IRC v Soul (1976) 51 TC 86, CA.
McKerron (R & D) Ltd v IRC [1979] STC 815, CS.
R v Morleston and Litchurch General Comrs, ex p G R Turner Ltd (1951) 32 TC 335, DC.
Rutherford v Lord Advocate (1931) 16 TC 145, CS.

_c_
Application for judicial review
The applicant, Ralph Hudson Goldstraw, sought leave to apply for judicial review seeking
(1) a declaration that purported assessments confirmed by the General Commissioners of
Income Tax for the Division of Epping and Harlow were not final or binding on him
and (2) an order that the commissioners should hear and determine afresh the applicant's
request that his appeal against the assessments be reopened and reheard. The facts are set _d_
out in the judgment.

Andrew Goodman for the applicant
David Griffith-Jones for the Crown

STEPHEN BROWN J. This is an application for leave to apply for judicial review by _e_
Mr Ralph Hudson Goldstraw (the applicant). By his notice of motion he seeks, firstly, a
declaration that the purported assessments confirmed by the General Commissioners of
Income Tax for Epping and Harlow on 11 November 1980 are not final or binding on
him; secondly, he seeks an order that the General Commissioners do hear and determine
afresh his request that his appeal against the said assessments be reopened and reheard.
The applicant's tax affairs have a long history, so it would appear from the affidavits _f_
which he has filed and the documents annexed to his affidavits. The history is
conveniently set out in an affidavit of Barbara Rae, a member of the office of the Solicitor
of Inland Revenue, sworn on 18 November 1982, which is annexed to the applicant's
affidavit. It appears that the applicant has been involved in extensive purchases and sales
of properties and that no income tax return was completed by him for a period of over
15 years from August 1967. As a result, assessments were raised by the inspector of taxes _g_
on 14 December 1976 in sums estimated in the absence of returns, and appeals against
those assessments were entered by the applicant in December 1976.
Following investigations into his tax situation and after considerable interviews with
the applicant he was asked to make proposals for the settlement of his tax liability. His
accountants made certain counter-proposals to those put forward by the Inland Revenue
on 20 February 1980. Following that, appeals which had been entered in 1976 were _h_
listed for hearing before the General Commissioners of Income Tax for the Harlow
Division on 5 August 1980. At that hearing the applicant was represented by counsel
and the hearing was also attended by his solicitor and his accountant on his behalf.
An application was made on behalf of the applicant for an adjournment to enable
counsel to familiarise himself with the case, and that was not opposed by the inspector;
accordingly, the commissioners adjourned the hearing on that occasion to the fixed date _j_
of 11 November 1980. It appears that they determined that some portion of the tax due
should no longer be postponed from payment pending determination of the appeals and
it was agreed by or on behalf of the applicant that he should pay the amount in question;
but he did not in fact do so.
The adjourned hearing was held on 11 November 1980, but the applicant did not

attend and nobody attended on his behalf. It appears that the commissioners heard
a evidence from the inspector of taxes and they determined the appeals on the basis of the
figures previously submitted as a proposal by the applicant's accountants on 20 February
1980. To that extent the commissioners indorsed the applicant's accountants' counter-
proposals. On 12 November, the day following, a letter was sent by the clerk to the
General Commissioners formally notifying him of the details of the commissioners'
determination. In addition full details of the revised assessments and computations of
b tax due were forwarded to him on the same date by the inspector of taxes.

The next event occurred on 12 January 1981, when the inspector of taxes applied to
the General Commissioners for an interest certificate under s 70 of the Taxes Management
Act 1970. The applicant appeared on that occasion, and he then sought to reopen the
appeals which had been determined on 11 November 1980. He alleged that he was not
able to attend on that day due to sickness. He did not however produce satisfactory
c evidence of sickness at the relevant time and the commissioners declined to reopen their
previous determination.

The applicant has submitted through his counsel that the commissioners on that
occasion were wrong in refusing to reopen the determination of the appeals which they
had in fact determined on 11 November 1980. The applicant, through his counsel,
submits that they had power to do so and, furthermore, that they acted in bad faith
d because their clerk was ill-disposed towards the applicant due to some previous dispute
(this is the allegation) and had maliciously advised the commissioners that they had no
power to reopen their determination of 11 November 1980. The applicant has submitted
details of a history of medical problems, depression and amnesia over the years, but none
of these details actually covers 11 November 1980.

In this application the applicant seeks a declaration that the assessments confirmed on
e 11 November 1980 are not final or binding. In point of fact, the grounds on which the
relief is sought (both in writing and as developed in argument) relate entirely to the
proceedings of 12 January 1981. He has not in fact appealed against or sought to apply
for judicial review of the determination of the appeals on 11 November 1980. However,
quite apart from that, s 46(2) of the Taxes Management Act 1970 provides: 'Save as
otherwise provided in the Taxes Acts, the determination of the General Commissioners
f or the Special Commissioners in any proceedings under the Taxes Acts shall be final and
conclusive.'

Counsel for the Crown submits that the effect of that section is to prevent the
commissioners from reopening their own determination on a subsequent occasion in
circumstances such as are alleged to obtain in this particular case. This is not a case of the
possible application of the slip rule, the kind of situation which was envisaged in R v
g Morleston and Litchurch General Comrs, ex p G R Turner Ltd (1951) 32 TC 335. That was a
case where a clerk, rather aged so it would appear, misheard the decision of his
commissioners and it was sought subsequently to put it right.

Another case cited by counsel for the applicant was that of R & D McKerron Ltd v IRC
[1979] STC 815, where the Scottish Court of Session allowed an appeal in a case where a
solicitor had been absent at the very moment that the case was called on before the
h commissioners but actually appeared before they had finished their sitting. The
commissioners refused to allow him to present the appeal. Those seem to me to be
entirely different situations from that in the present case.

In the present case counsel for the Crown cites the decision of the Court of Appeal in
IRC v Soul (1976) 51 TC 86, in which Bridge LJ considered the machinery for appealing
from a notice of assessment. The facts were different and one need not refer to them in
j any detail. But Bridge LJ said (at 87):

'The material on which [the taxpayer] relies to establish that proposition factually
is sparse in the extreme. But, quite apart from that consideration, the short answer
to [the taxpayer's] point is that it is not now open to him in the present proceedings
to raise any issue by way of challenge to the assessments raised against him by the

Commissioners of Inland Revenue, in the first place, and confirmed by the General
Commissioners on appeal. That is the clear result of the decision of this Court in the   *a*
case of the *Commissioners of Inland Revenue* v. *Pearlberg* ([1953] 1 All ER 388, [1953]
1 WLR 331). The statutory machinery for an appeal from a notice of assessment is
exclusive machinery, and when it has been exhausted to the point of appeal to the
General Commissioners, and notwithstanding that there is a Case stated to the High
Court pending it is not open to the taxpayer to dispute his liability in proceedings
brought by the Commissioners to enforce the assessments against him.'   *b*

In *Rutherford v Lord Advocate* (1931) 16 TC 145 at 156, a case in the Court of Session in
Scotland, the question of setting aside a determination of the commissioners was
considered by Lord Fleming. He said:

'In my opinion, it is essential to the Complainer's case that he must somehow or
other get rid of the determination of the Commissioners which has a statutory   *c*
finality. The only operative order which I can pronounce in this process is to grant
or refuse the prayer of the Note. If the Complainer's contentions in fact and law are
well founded, the Commissioners' determination should be set aside and they ought
to hear his appeal, and, if satisfied on the merits, should alter the assessment made
upon him. It seems to me that nothing but an express order from a court of
competent jurisdiction reducing or setting aside the determination of the   *d*
Commissioners and authorising them to meet and hear the Complainer's appeal in
accordance with the statute would be a sufficient warrant to the Commissioners
disregarding their previous determination. I do not think that a mere expression of
judicial opinion would justify the Commissioners acting in apparent disregard of
the statutory provision.'
                                                                                          e
It is that passage to which counsel for the Crown specifically draws the attention of the
court. He submits that s 46(2) of the Taxes Management Act 1970 has the effect of
preventing the commissioners from reopening their previous determination, which had
been made final. There was no question of exercise of discretion. So far as the
determinations were concerned, they were functus officio. Furthermore the applicant
has not sought to appeal in any effective way from their determination of his appeals.   *f*
    The applicant has added to the grounds on which he seeks relief the very serious
suggestion, indeed allegation, that the clerk was affected by animosity towards the
applicant personally, and it was on that ground, suggests the applicant, that he advised
the commissioners that they had no power to reopen the matter on 12 January 1981.
    I am quite satisfied that the General Commissioners did not have any power on 12
January 1981 to reconsider or to reopen their determination which they had effectively   *g*
made on 11 November 1980. Accordingly, even if there was any question of bad faith
on the part of the clerk, it would be irrelevant. I think, in fairness to the clerk, one should
say that the evidence of bad faith is merely a suggestion which is quite unsupported by
evidence and it springs solely from the applicant's suggestion that because of previous
differences in matters not related to his tax affairs this man might tend to behave in a
hostile way towards him. This is, of course, a very serious allegation to make against   *h*
someone in his position. In my judgment it cannot afford any ground for granting leave
on this occasion.
    It should be stated that this application relates to matters which occurred in 1980 and
at the beginning of 1981. The reason for that is said on behalf of the applicant to be that
he was concerned in proceedings in the High Court between himself and the Inland
Revenue. The Inland Revenue were seeking to enforce by writ and action in the High   *j*
Court tax liabilities alleged to be due from him. He had delivered a defence and
counterclaim in which similar allegations to those made on this application were being
made. Those proceedings have now been adjourned since yesterday, I understand. I
understand that judgment initially had been entered in the proceedings under RSC Ord
14 and he was seeking to appeal against that order.

a Counsel for the applicant has said that following a recent decision of the House of
Lords he now realises that the application which is now sought to be brought before the
court should more properly proceed by way of judicial review than by action in the High
Court. He does not consider that it is now open to the applicant to succeed in gaining the
kind of relief that he seeks in the proceedings in the High Court. So he has turned his
attention to this jurisdiction.

I am quite satisfied that leave should not be granted in this case. I am satisfied that the
b commissioners on 12 January 1981 had no power to reconsider the decision which they
had arrived at quite properly in November 1980. I am further satisfied that the applicant
has not sought in these proceedings by his notice of motion to appeal against the
assessments made on 11 November 1980. He seeks merely a declaration that those
assessments are not final or binding on him and an order of the court that the General
Commissioners should hear and determine afresh his request that his appeal against the
c assessments be reopened and reheard.

Furthermore I find that there is no ground for the submission that there has been a
denial of natural justice in this case in the refusal of the General Commissioners to hear
the applicant's further submissions on his appeals. The question of course is whether he
was given an opportunity to be heard. It is quite plain on the facts that he was. The
adjournment was at his request and the date was fixed at the hearing which was then
d adjourned at his request. He did not attend on the adjourned hearing and had made no
approach for an adjournment and gave no explanation for his failure to attend until, at
the further hearing on a different aspect of that matter, on 12 January 1981 he put
forward the excuse that he was medically unfit to attend on the earlier occasion.

I am quite satisfied that this is a case where leave should be refused and that is the
order that I make.

e
Application refused

Solicitors: *Landau Cohen*, Edgware (for the applicant); *Solicitor of Inland Revenue*.

Application
f The applicant renewed his application by applying to the Court of Appeal.

The applicant appeared in person
David Griffith-Jones for the Crown

SIR JOHN DONALDSON MR. This is an application by Ralph Hudson Goldstraw
g (the applicant) for leave to apply for judicial review in respect of a decision reached by
the General Commissioners of Income Tax on 12 January 1981 when they declined to
reopen a decision which they had reached in his absence on 11 November 1980. The
history of the matter is very fully set out in a judgment of Stephen Brown J given on 18
February 1983, before whom the matter came at the request of the applicant, who was
not prepared to accept the refusal of Glidewell J to give leave to apply.

h Suffice it for present purposes to say that the applicant's tax matters were under
consideration by the General Commissioners in August 1980, at which time the applicant
was represented by solicitors and counsel. Counsel had had inadequate time in which to
master the various matters, and accordingly a hearing date in August was adjourned at
the request of the applicant's professional advisers and the date of 11 November 1980 was
fixed for the resumed hearing. Shortly before that date the solicitors wrote to the General
j Commissioners saying that they could no longer get instructions from the applicant and
should be deemed no longer to be acting on his behalf. On 11 November the applicant
was not present in person, nor was he represented, and the commissioners made certain
determinations.

The matter came back before them on 12 January 1981 in connection with interest,
and the applicant then applied for the determination of 11 November 1980 to be

reopened. The clerk advised the commissioners that they had no power to do so, and the applicant complains that that advice was given maliciously. For my part, without for one *a* moment finding that the advice was malicious, I find it important to remember that any malice by the clerk is entirely immaterial if the advice given was correct. So I have looked to see whether the advice given was correct, and, in my judgment, it was abundantly correct.

The relevant statutory provisions are ss 46, 50 and 56 of the Taxes Management Act 1970. Section 46(2) provides: *b*

'Save as otherwise provided in the Taxes Acts, the determination of the General Commissioners or the Special Commissioners in any proceedings under the Taxes Acts shall be final and conclusive.'

The other provisions in the Act which are relevant and to which that subsection refers are s 50(4), which provides: *c*

'If it is shown to the satisfaction of the Commissioners that owing to absence, sickness or other reasonable cause any person has been prevented from attending at the hearing of an appeal on the day fixed for that purpose, they may postpone the hearing of his appeal for such reasonable time as they think necessary, or may admit the appeal to be made by any agent, clerk or servant on his behalf.'

d
And s 56, which provides:

'(1) Immediately after the determination of an appeal by the Commissioners, the appellant or the inspector or other officer of the Board, if dissatisfied with the determination as being erroneous in point of law, may declare his dissatisfaction to the Commissioners who heard the appeal.
(2) The appellant or the inspector or other officer of the Board, as the case may *e* be, having declared his dissatisfaction, may, within thirty days after the determination, by notice in writing addressed to the clerk to the Commissioners, require the Commissioners to state and sign a case for the opinion of the High Court thereon . . .'

So we have the position that if the applicant or anybody else on his behalf had informed *f* the commissioners at the time of the 11 November hearing that he was unable to attend by reason of illness they could then have adjourned. But it is not suggested by the applicant that anybody did do that. The highest he puts it is that shortly after their determination there was some communication to the General Commissioners explaining why the applicant had not attended, and he further suggests that the inspector of taxes knew that the applicant was unable to attend. But neither of those facts, even if proved, *g* would have entitled the commissioners to act under s 50. So that left the applicant with another remedy which he could have exercised, though whether he would have been successful is another matter. He could have applied within 30 days to the commissioners asking them to state a case for the opinion of the High Court. He did not do so. That period had already elapsed by 12 January 1981, and accordingly that avenue was also closed.   *h*

The applicant referred us to the Scottish case of *R & D McKerron Ltd v IRC* [1979] STC 815, where, owing to a misunderstanding, a solicitor representing a taxpayer was prevented from addressing the commissioners and the commissioners nevertheless adhered to their decision. That was an appeal under s 56 by case stated and shows nothing other than that it is possible to mount an appeal by case stated raising as a question of law the way in which the hearing was conducted, as distinct from a question of law going to *j* the merits of the particular dispute. That accordingly does not help the applicant.

That only leaves the residual jurisdiction of the Divisional Court, which of course is that which we are being asked to allow to be exercised. But it is a cardinal principle that, save in the most exceptional circumstances, that jurisdiction will not be exercised where other remedies were available and have not been used.

Taking all the matters which the applicant urges into account, not least the fact that

a the evidence to support his allegation that he was quite unable to attend to his business
affairs on 11 November is slender in the extreme, I would refuse this application.

PURCHAS LJ. I agree with everything that has fallen from Sir John Donaldson MR,
and there is nothing that I can usefully add. I agree that this application should be
refused.

b *Application refused.*

Solicitors: *Solicitor of Inland Revenue.*

Clare Mainprice   Barrister.

c

R v Gibson

COURT OF APPEAL, CRIMINAL DIVISION
WATKINS LJ, DRAKE AND BELDAM JJ
d 21 FEBRUARY, 16 MAY 1983

*Legal aid – Criminal cases – Appeal – Application for leave to appeal – Application to full court
when single judge refuses leave to appeal – Scope of legal aid certificate – Assistance in preparation
of application for leave to appeal – Certificate also covering assistance regarding application to
full court where single judge refuses leave – No need for court to amend certificate – Criminal*
e *Appeal Act 1968, s 31(3) – Legal Aid Act 1974, ss 28(7), 30(1)(7)(9), 31(3) – Criminal Appeal
Rules 1968, r 12.*

*Criminal law – Verdict – Record – Formal record – Necessity for record of proceedings to show
verdict given by jury and any directions given by court concerning counts in respect of which jury
discharged from giving verdict.*

f
*Legal aid – Criminal cases – Amendment – Retrospective amendment – Power of court – Court
of Appeal – Power of Court of Appeal to amend legal aid order made by single judge when giving
leave to appeal – Legal Aid Act 1974, s 31 – Legal Aid in Criminal Proceedings (General)
Regulations 1968, reg 12.*

g On the true construction of s 30(7)[a] of the Legal Aid Act 1974 a legal aid certificate
granted under ss 28(7)[b] and 30(7) of that Act to a defendant for the purpose of proceedings
in the Crown Court covers not only advice or assistance given by counsel or a solicitor (or
both) assigned to him by the court in the preparation of an application to the single judge
for leave to appeal against conviction or sentence but also, where the application is refused
by the single judge, advice or assistance regarding the making of a renewed application
h under s 31(3)[c] of the Criminal Appeal Act 1968 and r 12[d] of the Criminal Appeal Rules
1968 to the full court of the Court of Appeal for leave to appeal. Accordingly, it is not
necessary for the certificate to be amended under s 30(9)[e] of the 1974 Act to cover the
work done in respect of the renewed application, but merely for a bill of costs to be
submitted to the taxing authority, who will then decide whether to allow the costs and
disbursements (see p 265 g to j and p 266 b to e, post).

j
a Section 30(7) is set out at p 265 f g, post
b Section 28(7) set set out at p 265 e, post
c Section 31(3) provides: 'If the single judge refuses an application on the part of an appellant to
   exercise in his favour any of the powers above specified, the appellant shall be entitled to have the
   application determined by the Court of Appeal.'
d Rule 12, so far as material, is set out at p 266 a b, post
e Section 30(9) is set out at p 267 e, post

It is of the highest importance that the record of proceedings in a criminal trial reflects
what is said in open court in the presence of the defendant and the jury when it delivers   *a*
its verdict or verdicts. Where the jury intimates that it has reached a verdict on the lesser
of two counts in an indictment, it is incumbent on the clerk of the court to put the other
count to the jury and to take a verdict on it, since the defendant is entitled to have the
jury's verdict on all counts in respect of which he has been placed in the charge of the
jury; and where the court discharges the jury from giving a verdict on a count and the
court directs that it is not to be proceeded with without leave, that direction should   *b*
likewise be given in open court so that a record of it appears for all to see (see p 269 *d* and
g to *j*, post).

Observations on the powers of the court under s 30(9) of the 1974 Act and reg 12 *f* of
the Legal Aid in Criminal Proceedings (General) Regulations 1968 to make legal aid
orders retrospective and the power under s 31 *g* of the 1974 Act to amend legal aid orders
made by the single judge when giving leave to appeal (see p 267 *c e* to *j* and p 268 *d* to *h*,   *c*
post).

Notes

For legal aid in criminal proceedings, see 11 Halsbury's Laws (4th edn) paras 755–758.
　For the Criminal Appeal Act 1968, s 31, see 8 Halsbury's Statutes (3rd edn) 711.
　For the Legal Aid Act 1974, ss 28, 30, 31, see 44 ibid 127, 130, 133.   *d*
　For the Legal Aid in Criminal Proceedings (General) Regulations 1968, reg 12, see 6
Halsbury's Statutory Instruments (4th reissue) 34.
　For the Criminal Appeal Rules 1968, r 12, see ibid 58.

Cases referred to in judgment

R v Bennett (28 October 1982, unreported), CA.
R v Rogers [1979] 1 All ER 693.   *e*

Application

Ivano Gibson appealed, with the leave of the full court of the Court of Appeal granted on
9 December 1982, against his conviction on 25 May 1982 in the Crown Court at Wood
Green, before Mr Recorder Hart-Leverton QC and a jury, of wounding, contrary to s 20
of the Offences against the Person Act 1861. The appeal was heard on 21 February 1983.   *f*
The court quashed the conviction and then went on to hear argument in respect of a
matter which had been adjourned on 9 December 1982 for their consideration at the
hearing of the appeal, namely an application by the solicitors who had assisted the
appellant in the preparation of his application on 9 December 1982 to the full court for
leave to appeal for an order extending the legal aid certificate, which he had been granted
by the Crown Court, to cover work done by them in respect of his application. The facts   *g*
are set out in the judgment of the court.

Michael Hucker (who did not appear below and who was assigned by the Registrar of
　Criminal Appeals) for the appellant.
K Maitland Davies for the Crown.

Cur adv vult   *h*

16 May. The following judgment of the court was delivered.

WATKINS LJ. When on 9 December 1982 the full court gave the appellant leave to
appeal after refusal by the single judge, Parker J in giving the judgment of the court
stated: *j*

　'There are also applications for legal aid and bail. The application for bail is
　refused. The application for legal aid is granted (counsel only) but there is one
　further matter which requires to be mentioned. The solicitors acting for the

---

f　Regulation 12 is set out at p 267 *g*, post
g　Section 31 is set out at p 267 *j* to p 268 *c*, post

applicant have indicated that they would wish to have included in the legal aid some
form of retrospective legal aid to cover the work done in preparing for the renewal
of the application for leave after refusal by the single judge. That is a matter which
is not presently included in the legal aid which we grant, but it is not rejected. The
application is adjourned to be heard with the substantive hearing of the appeal,
when it may be fully argued and the necessary authorities cited. It is a point of some
importance which requires full argument, for, on one view, there may be a lacuna
in the legal aid provisions.'

We have heard full argument on the point referred to, from counsel for the appellant
and counsel for the Crown, and have taken time to consider their helpful submissions on
what is undoubtedly a matter of some consequence to solicitors and others.

The relevant facts are that on 28 October 1982 the single judge refused leave to appeal
and the appellant was notified of that decision. On 12 November 1982 his solicitors gave
notice on his behalf of his wish to have his application for leave to appeal determined by
the full court. In other words, as is customarily said, he renewed his application. On 17
November 1982 the solicitors wrote to the Registrar of Criminal Appeals explaining
what they contended was the main ground of appeal, namely that the judge had made
observations which amounted to a direction to convict, and asserting that counsel in
drafting the grounds of appeal and the judge when considering the application, as his
reasons for refusal show, had missed this vital point. In the final passage of the letter they
stated with regard to legal aid that, if the full court granted leave to appeal, then legal aid
should be granted retrospectively to cover the work done by them for the appellant from
the time of the single judge's refusal and the hearing of the appeal.

The solicitors appear to have assumed that they were no longer covered by the legal
aid certificate granted in the Crown Court at Wood Green in accordance with, inter alia,
ss 28(7) and 30(7) of the Legal Aid Act 1974, which are in the following terms:

'**28** . . . (7) Where a person is committed to or appears before the Crown Court
for trial or sentence, or appears or is brought before the Crown Court to be dealt
with, the court which commits him or the Crown Court may order that he shall be
given legal aid for the purpose of the trial or other proceedings before the Crown
Court . . .

30 . . . (7) Legal aid which may be ordered to be given to any person for the
purpose of any proceedings by a legal aid order under section 28(7) above shall, in
the event of his being convicted or sentenced in those proceedings, include advice
on the question whether there appear to be reasonable grounds of appeal and—(a) if
such grounds appear to exist, assistance in the preparation of an application for leave
to appeal or in the giving of a notice of appeal; (b) while that question is being
considered, assistance in the making of a provisional application or the giving of a
provisional notice . . .'

One of the issues we have to determine is whether the solicitors' assumption is correct.
If it is not, and the legal aid certificate covers work done on behalf of the appellant in
renewing his application to the full court, the solicitor can properly invite the taxing
authority to consider allowance of his costs and disbursement under that certificate. In
that event it would follow that no order in that regard should be made by this court,
even if it possessed the power to make it.

Counsel for the Crown argued that, although the expression 'renewal of the application'
is a useful and convenient form of describing the procedure for inviting the full court to
consider an application after refusal by the single judge, the renewal, so called, is part of
one indivisible application. Support for this contention, he says, is to be found in s 31 of
the Criminal Appeal Act 1968, as amended, which, having provided for the powers of
the Court of Appeal to be exercised with regard to, inter alia, giving leave to appeal by a
single judge, by sub-s (3) further provides that if the single judge refuses to grant leave to
appeal the appellant shall be entitled to have 'the application' determined by the Court of
Appeal. 'The application' is also expressly referred to in r 12(1) and (4) of the Criminal
Appeal Rules 1968, SI 1968/1262, viz:

'(1) Where a judge of the court has refused an application on the part of the
appellant to exercise in his favour any of the powers referred to in section 31(2) of   *a*
the [1968] Act, the appellant may have the application determined by the court by
serving a notice in Form 15 on the Registrar within fourteen days, or such longer
period as a judge of the court may fix, from the date on which notice of the refusal
was served on him by the Registrar . . .
(4) If such a notice is not served on the Registrar within the said 14 days or such
longer period as a judge of the court may fix, the application shall be treated as   *b*
having been refused by the court.'

We are impressed by this argument and therefore are of the view that the renewal to
the full court is but a further step in the making of an application, which is not finally
dealt with until it is (a) granted by the single judge, or (b) refused by the single judge, or
(c) renewed to the full court and either granted or refused. Until one of those events has
occurred 'the application' is in being and attracts the provisions of s 30(7) of the 1974 Act.   *c*
Thus, in our opinion, assistance given in the preparation of the application for leave to
appeal, provided by counsel or solicitors or both, either originally or when consideration
is being given to renewal of a refused application, is covered by the original legal aid
certificate.

In our experience, assistance, which of course includes advice whether an application
should be renewed and if so whether it requires amendment in any respect, is very   *d*
seldom required. When it is given it will be for the taxing authority, the registrar, to
decide whether it would be right to take this additional work into account by applying
s 30(7). We appreciate that our view does not accord with that expressed in para 14.3 of
the pamphlet *Preparation for Proceedings in the Court of Appeal Criminal Division* issued by
the registrar on 4 June 1974 with the approval of the Court of Appeal: see *Practice Note*
[1974] 2 All ER 805, [1974] 1 WLR 774. That paragraph is worth setting out here in full   *e*
for the valuable assistance which it provides on certain consequences flowing from a
refusal by a single judge. To conform with this judgment it will of course have to be
suitably amended to state that the registrar's power on taxation will, in this context, be
derived from s 30(7), and not s 30(9) applied retrospectively. The paragraph reads:

'14. *Refusal by single Judge*   *f*
14.1 Where the single Judge refuses an application for leave to appeal, the
Registrar sends a notification of the refusal to the applicant, who is informed that he
may require the application to be considered by the Court. He is also informed that
he must send his "renewal" within 14 days.
14.2 Where notification of the refusal by a single Judge of an application for
leave to appeal is sent to an applicant who was assisted under the provisions of the   *g*
Legal Aid Act, 1974, s. 30(7), the Registrar will send a copy of the notification to the
solicitor who assisted the applicant. The notification includes observations by the
single Judge.
14.3 When the solicitor receives the copy of the notification he may consider it
right to give advice to the applicant as to whether he should renew his application
or abandon it. The provisions of the Legal Aid Act, 1974, s. 30(7) do not extend to   *h*
the giving of such advice, but the Registrar will consider on taxation whether it
would be right for him to take the additional work into account by applying the
provisions of s. 30(9) of the 1974 Act. Under these provisions legal aid may be
granted retrospectively for work done in giving advice or assistance on appeal. Such
legal aid will not be granted unless it was reasonable to undertake the work at this
stage. A letter from the solicitor to the applicant, perhaps after informal consultation   *j*
with counsel, may well be justified if sent within the time allowed.'

For these reasons we are not called on in the present case to decide the solicitors'
application. The registrar will deal with it as he thinks fit under s 30(7), and we do not
presume to advise him how he should act in the matter.
That is sufficient to dispose of the solicitors' application, but not of the whole of the

submissions addressed to us, the remainder of which were devoted to the power of the
a court, if any, when granting an application for leave to appeal with legal aid, to order
that legal aid be applied retrospectively. Since we were expressly invited to do so we give
our opinion on this point.

We do not think that there is in the legal aid provisions a lacuna inhibiting the Court
of Appeal from ensuring that an applicant is assisted by legal aid from when it can fairly
and justly be said that he needed it. The scope of legal aid is set out in s 30(1) of the 1974
b Act:

> 'For the purposes of this Part of this Act legal aid, in relation to any proceedings
> to which a person is a party, shall be taken, subject to the following provisions of
> this section, as consisting of representation by a solicitor and counsel assigned by the
> court, including advice on the preparation of that person's case for those proceedings.'

c Having regard to that subsection it cannot, we think, be too strongly emphasised that
neither counsel nor solicitor can claim to be recompensed for work done for an assisted
person unless he has been assigned by the court to represent that person. Once assigned
he may thereafter safely act in accordance with the terms of s 30(8), viz:

> 'Legal aid which may be ordered to be given to any person for the purpose of any
> appeal by a legal aid order under section 28(8) or (9) above may, without prejudice
d > to subsection (1) above, consist in the first instance of advice, by counsel or a solicitor
> assigned by the court, on the question whether there appear to be reasonable grounds
> of appeal and assistance by that solicitor in the preparation of an application for leave
> to appeal or in the giving of a notice of appeal.'

If counsel or a solicitor does work before a legal aid order is made, and becomes
e assigned when or after it is made, providing the work done is of the kind referred to in
s 30(9), the court may make a deeming order under that section, the terms of which are:

> 'A legal aid order under section 28(8) or (9) above may, if the court thinks fit,
> include provision that the legal aid ordered to be given shall be deemed to include
> the like advice and assistance previously given by counsel or a solicitor not then
> assigned by the court.'
f
The deeming order is the only retrospective power which Pt II of the 1974 Act gives the
court. This was the view expressed by Master Matthews in *R v Rogers* [1979] 1 All ER
693, with which we entirely agree.

Considerable additional power to act retrospectively is, however, as it appears to us,
given to the court by reg 12 of the Legal Aid in Criminal Proceedings (General)
g Regulations 1968, SI 1968/1231, which provides:

> '*Commencement of legal aid order.* In making a legal aid order in respect of
> proceedings in the Court of Appeal, the court, a judge of the court or the Registrar,
> as the case may be, may specify the stage of the proceedings at which the legal aid
> shall commence.'

h In our view, this enables the court to order that the legal aid order that it makes shall
commence at any time prior to, or on or after, the day on which it is applied for.
Accordingly, all work done by counsel or a solicitor, or both, assigned by the court may
be governed by the provisions of s 30(8) from that date. Whether the court chooses to
backdate an order will obviously depend on the whole of the circumstances, including
the need for work to have been done and its value in promoting the interests of an
j assisted person.

Finally, we comment on the power of the court to amend a legal aid order made by a
single judge when giving leave to appeal. This power is set out in s 31 of the 1974 Act,
which provides:

> '(1) A court having power to make a legal aid order may on the application of the
> legally assisted person or otherwise amend any such order by substituting for any

legal representative or representatives previously assigned to him any legal representative or representatives whom the court could have assigned to him if it *a* had then been making the legal aid order.

(2) A court having power to make a legal aid order may revoke any such order— (*a*) on the application of the legally assisted person; or (*b*) if the only legal representative or all the legal representatives for the time being assigned to him withdraws or withdraw from the case and it appears to the court that, because of his conduct, it is not desirable to amend the order under subsection (1) above.   *b*

(3) The amendment or revocation of a legal aid order under this section shall not affect the right of any legal representative previously assigned to the legally assisted person to remuneration for work done before the date of the amendment or revocation, as the case may be, but where a court revokes such an order, the court may make a legal aid contribution order under section 32 below as if it had disposed of the case.'   *c*

We take this to mean that, if the single judge has given legal aid for counsel only, the Court of Appeal may amend the representation by assigning counsel (who may be the one already assigned) and *solicitor* to represent the legally assisted person. This dual representation will then take effect from such time and for such purpose as the court orders. Here too the court, in considering amendment, will have regard to the merits of the application, which is likely to succeed, we think, but rarely.   *d*

The following extract from the transcript in *R v Bennett* (28 October 1982, unreported) is an example of how this kind of application has been dealt with, and it may be regarded as a useful guide to disposal of it:

'*Counsel for the appellant.* Might I trouble your Lordships with one further matter. Throughout my activities in this case after trial and sentence, I have been assisted greatly, particularly in attending two conferences, by the solicitors who had acted *e* for [the appellant] at the trial. I have omitted to approach the registrar to extend legal aid to cover their assistance and they have acted, as it were, at their own risk because of their concern about this case. They have facilitated communications with the family, which has been most helpful to me, and attended two conferences. Would your Lordships consider at this late stage making that extension to the legal aid in this case?.   *f*

Watkins LJ. The court must issue a cautionary warning about applications of this kind made at this stage on behalf of solicitors who have volunteered themselves to continue to act for persons who come here on appeal. It is only in very rare instances indeed that an application of this kind would be acceded to. If you give us a moment . . . we will think about whether or not this is such a case, and consider the actual merits of your application. [After consideration his Lordship continued:] We have *g* considered the merits of your application. In doing so, we have examined the documents. We find that your solicitors received notification of the single judge's decision early in August 1982. Among those decisions was an order that this appeal be conducted by counsel only, with legal aid for counsel only. Any solicitor who goes on in the face of that does so at his own peril. We see no good reason therefore *h* in this case why we should extend the legal aid certificate.'

Since first preparing this judgment we have been informed by the registrar that a new publication, entitled *A Guide to Proceedings in the Court of Appeal Criminal Division*, will be issued shortly, superseding the pamphlet *Preparation for Proceedings in the Court of Appeal Criminal Division*. The new guide, like its predecessor, will contain information valuable to all who practise in this court, and we take this opportunity of commending it to the *j* profession.

Paragraph 14 of the pamphlet has, in the new guide, been recast in the following terms to accord with the terms of this judgment:

'8. *Refusal by the single judge*

8.1 Where the single judge refuses leave to appeal, the Registrar sends a notification of the refusal, including any observations which the judge may have

a made, to the appellant who is informed that he may require the application to be
   considered by the Court. He is also informed that he must send any notice of
   renewal within 14 days of receipt of the notification . . .
     8.2 A refused application which is not renewed within 14 days is treated as
   having been refused by the Court—Rule 12(4) Criminal Appeal Rules 1968.
     8.3 Where solicitors have lodged grounds a copy of the single judge's decision is
   also sent to those solicitors.

b   8.4 When the solicitor receives the copy of the notification he may wish to
   consider, in cases of unusual difficulty, whether to give advice to the appellant as to
   whether he should renew his application, amend it or abandon it. Such advice is
   however seldom likely to be required. When given it will be for the Registrar, as
   taxing authority, to decide if such additional work should be taken into account by
   applying the provisions of section 30(7) Legal Aid Act 1974. A letter or message
c from the solicitor to the appellant, perhaps after informal consultation with counsel,
   may be justified. In any event such advice should be given within such time as to
   enable the appellant to renew his application within 14 days of notice of the single
   judge's decision . . .'

     We desire to add a word or two to this judgment in respect of a point of practice or
   procedure. It is of the highest importance that the record of proceedings reflects what
d was said in open court in the presence of the defendant and the jury which has just
   delivered its verdict or verdicts. Whether this is so or not can of course be discovered
   from an examination of the transcript. As has been said in the main body of the
   judgment, the indictment contained two counts, namely an offence under s 18 of the
   Offences against the Person Act 1861 and an alternative offence under s 20 of the same
   Act.

e   When the jury returned to the courtroom the clerk, having asked the foreman to stand
   and to confine herself to answering his first question Yes or No, invited her to say whether
   or not a verdict on which at least ten members of the jury agreed had been reached. She
   said that it had. In the transcript this interchange is recorded as having then ensued:

       '*Clerk.* Do you find him guilty on either counts one or two? *Foreman.* Yes.
       Clerk. On what count do you find him guilty, on count one? *Foreman.* We find
f   him guilty on count one. No, sorry, two.
       Clerk. You find the defendant guilty on count two of wounding? *Foreman.* Yes.
       Clerk. Is this the verdict of you all or by a majority? *Foreman.* By majority.'

     There is no indication in the transcript of what happened to count 1. The jury having
   been placed in charge of the appellant on it, he was entitled to have their verdict on that
g count, but there were not invited to provide it. That was an error.
     In such a situation, when the jury has given an intimation that it has come to a verdict
   on the lesser of two counts in an indictment, it is incumbent on the clerk of the court to
   put the more serious of the counts to the jury and to take a verdict on that. In the
   circumstances of the present case it may be (we cannot be sure of this, of course) that the
   jury would have found the appellant not guilty on count 1. If that be right, he was
h entitled to be so found. Having obtained that verdict, or a plain indication that the jury
   could not agree on that count, the clerk should have proceeded, as is customary, to put
   count 2 to the jury and to obtain their verdict on that.
     The court record, which we have seen, has this entry on it in relation to count 1:

       'Verdict—Jury discharged from giving a verdict; not to be proceeded with
       without the leave of the court or the Court of Appeal, Criminal Division.'

j   If it was right to give that direction it should have been given, but apparently was not,
   in open court so that a record of it appeared on the shorthand note for all to see.

   No order.

   Solicitors: *D M O'Shea* (for the Crown).

                                                   N P Metcalfe Esq   Barrister.

R v Kearney

COURT OF APPEAL, CRIMINAL DIVISION
LORD LANE CJ, MUSTILL AND SKINNER JJ
5, 15 JULY 1983

Legal aid – Criminal cases – Appeal – Application for leave to appeal – Application to full court when single judge refuses leave to appeal – Whether grant of legal aid for purposes of appeal covers legal representation at hearing of application before full court – Whether full court can grant legal aid to cover legal representation at hearing – Legal Aid Act 1974, ss 28(8), 30(7)(a), (9) – Legal Aid in Criminal Proceedings (General) Regulations 1968, reg 12.

Where a defendant applies to the full court of the Court of Appeal, Criminal Division, for leave to appeal against conviction or sentence after having been refused leave by the single judge and does so after having applied for and, under s 28(8)^a of the Legal Aid Act 1974, been granted legal aid for the purpose of his application for leave to appeal then, by virtue of s 30(7)(a)^b of the 1974 Act, the legal aid order covers merely legal 'assistance in the preparation of the application' to the full court and not legal representation at the hearing of the application. However, the full court can at the invitation of the registrar grant legal aid for the hearing prior to the hearing and can of its own motion grant legal aid for the hearing at any time, and where necessary may make a retrospective grant of legal aid under s 30(9)^c of the 1974 Act and reg 12^d of the Legal Aid in Criminal Proceedings (General) Regulations 1968 see p 272 e to g, post).

R v Gibson [1983] 3 All ER 263 considered.

Notes
For legal aid in the Crown Court and for legal aid for an appeal from the Crown Court, see 11 Halsbury's Laws (4th edn) paras 755, 756.

For the Legal Aid Act 1974, ss 28, 30, see 44 Halsbury's Statutes (3rd edn) 127, 130.

Case referred to in judgment
R v Gibson [1983] 3 All ER 263, CA.

Application for leave to appeal against sentence
On 22 March 1983 in the Crown Court at Willesden the applicant, William Christopher Kearney, pleaded guilty to two counts of burglary. On 23 March in the Crown Court at Acton sitting at Willesden before his Honour Judge Worthington the applicant was sentenced to consecutive terms of 12 months' imprisonment on each count. He had been granted legal aid for the trial under s 28(7) of the Legal Aid Act 1974. The applicant applied to the single judge for leave to appeal against sentence and, pursuant to s 28(8) of the 1974 Act, applied for legal aid for the purpose of the appeal. The single judge refused leave to appeal. The applicant renewed his application for leave to appeal to the full court. The facts are set out in the judgment of the court.

Philip Shears for the applicant.
Peter Caton for the Crown.

---

a   Section 28(8) is set out at p 271 *f*, post
b   Section 30(7), so far as material, is set out at p 271 *h*, post
c   Section 30(9), so far as material, provides: 'A legal aid order under setion 28(8) . . . may, if the court thinks fit, include provision that the legal aid ordered to be given shall be deemed to include the like advice and assistance previously given by counsel or a solicitor not then assigned by the court.'
d   Regulation 12 provides: 'In making a legal aid order in respect of proceedings in the Court of Appeal, the court, a judge of the court or the Registrar, as the case may be, may specify the stage of the proceedings at which the legal aid shall commence.'

At the conclusion of the argument the court announced that the application for leave to appeal against sentence would be refused, but on a question which arose on the hearing of the application, namely whether under s 30(7) of the Legal Aid Act 1974 the legal aid order covered legal aid not only for legal assistance in preparation for the hearing of the renewed application before the full court but also for the hearing itself, the court reserved its decision for reasons to be given later.

15 July. The following judgment of the court was delivered.

LORD LANE CJ. We have already dismissed an application by this applicant for leave to appeal against a sentence of imprisonment imposed in the Crown Court at Acton on 23 March 1983.

Counsel on his behalf now raises a further point under the Legal Aid Act 1974, and the regulations made thereunder. The point arises in this way. Legal aid was granted for the trial. Under the provisions of s 30(7) of the 1974 Act, counsel for the applicant drafted grounds of appeal and wrote an advice. The notice of application for leave to appeal included notice of application for legal aid under the provisions of s 28(8) of the Act. After refusal by the single judge, counsel specifically advised renewal of the application before the full court. The applicant's solicitors took the view that, in consequence of the decision of this court in *R v Gibson* [1983] 3 All ER 263, the original legal aid order extended to cover their instructions to counsel to appear before this court to make the application.

Counsel for the applicant therefore submits that where a defendant has been granted legal aid for the purpose of the trial in the Crown Court, that legal aid serves to cover not only the trial in the Crown Court and assistance in the preparation of an application to this court for leave to appeal or in the giving of a notice of appeal, but also covers representations before this court on the hearing of such application.

The relevant provisions of the 1974 Act as amended are in s 28 and are as follows:

'(7) Where a person is committed to or appears before the Crown Court for trial or sentence, or appears or is brought before the Crown Court to be dealt with, the Court which commits him or the Crown Court may order that he shall be given legal aid for the purpose of the trial or other proceedings before the Crown Court.

(8) Where a person desires to appeal to the Court of Appeal under Part I of the Criminal Appeal Act 1968, or to appeal to that court under section 13 of the Administration of Justice Act 1960 against an order or decision of the Crown Court, the criminal division of the Court of Appeal may order that he shall be given legal aid for the purpose of the appeal and any proceedings preliminary or incidental thereto.'

Section 30, so far as relevant, provides as follows:

'(7) Legal aid which may be ordered to be given to any person for the purpose of any proceedings by a legal aid order under section 28(7) above shall, in the event of his being convicted or sentenced in those proceedings, include advice on the question whether there appear to be reasonable grounds of appeal and—(a) if such grounds appear to exist, assistance in the preparation of an application for leave to appeal or in the giving of a notice of appeal . . .

(8) Legal aid which may be ordered to be given to any person for the purpose of any appeal by a legal aid order under section 28(8) or (9) above may, without prejudice to subsection (1) above, consist in the first instance of advice, by counsel or a solicitor assigned by the court, on the question whether there appear to be reasonable grounds of appeal and assistance by that solicitor in the preparation of an application for leave to appeal or in the giving of a notice of appeal.'

The submission of counsel for the applicant depends very largely on the decision of this Court in *R v Gibson*. In that case the single judge refused leave to appeal and the

applicant then renewed his application. His solicitors wrote to the registrar asking, inter
alia, that if leave to appeal was granted by the full court, legal aid should also be granted
retrospectively to cover the work done by them for the applicant from the time of the
single judge's refusal. They assumed apparently that they were no longer covered by the
legal aid certificate granted in the Crown Court at Wood Green in accordance with
ss 28(7) and 30(7) set out above.

The main issue which the court had to decide in that case was whether the solicitors'
assumption was correct. The court came to the conclusion that the renewal of the
application to the full court was merely a further step in the making of an application
which is not finally dealt with until it is (a) granted by the single judge, or (b) refused by
the single judge and not renewed, or (c) renewed to the full court and either granted or
refused. Until one of those events has occurred the application is in being and attracts the
provisions of s 30 of the 1974 Act. The court held accordingly that assistance in the
preparation of the application for leave to appeal provided by counsel or solicitor or both,
either originally or when consideration was being given to renewal of a refused
application, is covered by the original legal aid certificate.

The submission of counsel for the applicant is that the logical result of that judgment
is that the legal aid order covers not only the preparation for the hearing of the renewed
application before the court, but also the application to the court itself. In our judgment
that conclusion is not justified by the words of s 30(7). The words 'in the preparation of
an application for leave to appeal' quite plainly exclude the application in court itself.
That is enough to defeat the submission made by counsel.

However he contends that the result of such a decision would be in effect that there is
no proper provision under legal aid for what may turn out to be a meritorious renewal.

In fact in some cases the court, having considered the papers, either of its own motion
or at the invitation of the registrar, grants legal aid before the hearing. In any event the
court at the hearing may grant legal aid and proceed with the case if counsel is already
present, or adjourn the case to enable counsel to be instructed. The court has ample
power under the law as it stands to prevent any injustice arising. Indeed in addition to
the above there are the provisions under s 30(9) and reg 12 of the Legal Aid in Criminal
Proceedings (General) Regulations 1968, SI 1968/1231, which enable the court to make a
retrospective order where the situation requires.

As Watkins LJ pointed out in *Gibson's* case, whether the court chooses to back date an
order will depend on the whole of the circumstances, including the need for the work to
have been done.

In the result counsel for the applicant's submission that his appearance before us on
this application was covered by the legal aid order granted by the Crown Court fails.

Order accordingly.

Solicitors: *Powell Magrath & Spencer*, Kilburn (for the applicant); *D M O'Shea* (for the
Crown).

N P Metcalfe Esq   Barrister.

a Department of Transport v North West Water Authority

HOUSE OF LORDS

LORD FRASER OF TULLYBELTON, LORD EDMUND-DAVIES, LORD ROSKILL, LORD BRANDON OF OAKBROOK AND LORD BRIGHTMAN

b 25, 26, 27 JULY, 13 OCTOBER 1983

Nuisance – Defence – Statutory authority – Action for damages for nuisance arising from escape of water from burst water main under street – Water main laid by water authority under statutory duty to supply water – Street authority claiming cost of repairs to street from water authority – Whether water authority liable for nuisance caused without negligence – Public
c *Utilities Street Works Act 1950, s 18(2).*

The appellants, a water authority who were under a statutory duty to supply water within their area, were responsible for a water main running underneath a street which was under the control of the respondents, a street authority. In 1978 the main burst and as a result damage was caused to part of the street. There had been no negligence on the
d part of the appellants or their predecessors and the appellants used all reasonable diligence to prevent the main becoming a nuisance. Section 18(2)(b)[a] of the Public Utilities Street Works Act 1950 provided that if a nuisance was caused by the discharge of water from apparatus which statutory undertakers, such as a water authority, had power to place or maintain without the consent of the street authority then 'nothing in the enactment which confers the relevant power [to execute works in the street] shall exonerate the
e undertakers from any action or other proceedings at the suit . . . of the street authority'. The respondents carried out the necessary repairs to the street and claimed reimbursement of the cost of the repairs from the appellants, who disputed liability for damage to the street caused by the escape of the water. The appellants conceded that the escape of water constituted a nuisance which would have been actionable at common law at the suit of the repondents but they contended that s 18(2)(b) absolved them from liability because
f (i) s 18(2)(b) did not impose in clear terms a strict or absolute liability, and in the absence of negligence they were not liable for a nuisance attributable to the exercise of a duty to supply water imposed by statute, or (ii) even if s 18(2)(b) did create strict or absolute liability it did so in terms only where the nuisance was attributable to the exercise of a statutory 'power' and not where it was attributable to the exercise of a statutory duty such as that imposed on the appellants. The judge held that the escape of the water was
g attributable to the appellants' performance of their statutory duty to supply water rather than the exercise of any statutory power, but went on to hold that even so the effect of s 18(2)(b) was to create liability on the part of the appellants by removing any exoneration which the appellants might otherwise have had arising out of the fact that the nuisance was attributable to the exercise of a power. The appellants appealed direct to the House of Lords.
h

Held – Section 18(2) of the 1950 Act was merely a non-exoneration clause which applied generally to statutory undertakers and which made uniform provision for their liability when a nuisance was caused which was attributable to their carrying out street works in the exercise of their statutory powers. However, when the nuisance was attributable to the performance of a statutory duty by an undertaker the ordinary common law rules,
j rather than s 18(2), applied and the undertaker was not liable for the nuisance in the absence of negligence even if the statute expressly made it liable or did not exempt it from liability for nuisance. Since the damage to the street was attributable to the

---

a   Section 18(2), so far as material, is set out at p 275 c, post

appellants' performance of a statutory duty they were, applying the common law rules, not liable for the damage in the absence of negligence (see p 277 *a* to *j*, post).

Decision of Webster J [1983] 1 All ER 892 reversed.

Notes
For the defence of statutory immunity in actions for nuisance, see 34 Halsbury's Laws (4th edn) para 375.

For the liability of public bodies for nuisance, see ibid para 368, and for cases on nuisance caused in the exercise of a statutory power, see 36(1) Digest (Reissue) 416, 86–87.

For the Public Utilities Street Works Act 1950, s 18, see 15 Halsbury's Statutes (3rd edn) 89.

Cases referred to in opinions
Allen v Gulf Oil Refining Ltd [1981] 1 All ER 353, [1981] AC 1001, [1981] 2 WLR 188, HL.
Charing Cross Electricity Supply Co v Hydraulic Power Co [1914] 3 KB 772, [1914–15] All ER Rep 85, CA.
Hammond v St Pancras Vestry (1874) LR 9 CP 316.
Smeaton v Ilford Corp [1954] 1 All ER 923, [1954] Ch 450, [1954] 2 WLR 668.
Stretton's Derby Brewery Co v Derby Corp [1894] 1 Ch 431, [1891–4] All ER Rep 731.

Appeal
The North West Water Authority appealed direct to the House of Lords pursuant to a certificate granted by Webster J under s 12 of the Administration of Justice Act 1969 and with leave of the House granted on 26 January 1983 against the order of Webster J ([1983] 1 All ER 892, [1983] 3 WLR 105) giving judgment in the sum of £555·24 for the respondents, the Department of Transport, in the respondents' action against the appellants in which the respondents claimed damages of £1,014·87 representing the cost of repairs to a street which were necessary following the escape of water from a burst water main under the control of the appellants. The appellants admitted liability to the extent of £459·66. The facts are set out in the opinion of Lord Fraser.

John Roch QC and *G W Wingate-Saul QC* for the appellants.
John Davies QC and *Simon D Brown* for the respondents.

Their Lordships took time for consideration.

13 October. The following opinions were delivered

LORD FRASER OF TULLYBELTON. My Lords, this appeal is solely concerned with the proper construction of s 18(2) of the Public Utilities Street Works Act 1950.

On 7 September 1978 a water main laid under the A57 trunk road outside 746 Warrington Road, Rainhill, burst. The appellants are, and at all material times have been, the regional water authority responsible for the main. They were established by the Water Act 1973, s 2 and Sch 1. The respondents were at the material time the highway authority for the stretch of the A57 trunk road where the burst occurred. That part of the road was a 'street' and the respondents were a 'street authority', as both terms are defined in s 39(1) of the 1950 Act. That stretch of the A57 road is now no longer a trunk road. As a result of the bursting of the main, water escaped from it and caused damage to the road outside no 746. The parties are agreed that the burst was not caused by any negligence on the part of the appellants, or those for whom they are responsible. They are also agreed that the appellants used all reasonable diligence to prevent the main becoming a nuisance.

The damage to the road caused an appreciable obstruction of the public highway. The total cost to the respondents of the work carried out in making good the damage to the road was £1,014·87. Of that total, the sum of £459·66 is accepted by the appellants as

representing the cost which would have been incurred in any event in obtaining access
a through the highway to repair the broken water main. The appellants admitted liability
for that sum and have paid it, but they dispute any liability in respect of the remainder
of the total, amounting to £555·21. That sum represents the cost of repairing the damage
due to the escape of water from the burst main.

The issue between the parties accordingly is whether or not the appellants are liable to
pay damages to the respondents to compensate them for the cost of repairing the damage
b to the highway caused by the escape of water from the burst main. The solution to that
issue depends on the construction of s 18(2) of the 1950 Act. That subsection provides as
follows:

'If any nuisance is caused—(a) by the execution of code-regulated works, or (b) by
explosion, ignition or discharge of, or any other event occurring to, gas, electricity,
c water or any other thing required for the purposes of a supply or service afforded by
any undertakers which at the time of or immediately before the event in question
was in apparatus of those undertakers the placing or maintenance of which was or
is a code-regulated work . . . nothing in the enactment which confers the relevant
power to which section one of this Act applies or in any enactment which regulates
the exercise of that power . . . shall exonerate the undertakers from any action or
d other proceeding at the suit either—(i) of the street authority or street managers . . .'

'Code-regulated works' is defined in s 1(5) of the 1950 Act. It concerns works executed
by undertakers under statutory powers, and to which the street works code applies. For
present purposes, it is enough to note that the work of laying the appellants' water main
in the street where the burst occurred would have been a code-regulated work. Counsel
e for the appellants conceded that the escape of water from the main would have
constituted a nuisance at common law and would have been actionable at the instance of
the respondents, if the appellants had not been acting in discharge of a statutory duty.
Counsel for the respondents conceded that the appellants, in maintaining water under
pressure in the main, were acting in the discharge of a statutory duty. The duty is
imposed by the Water Act 1973, s 11(1) and (7)(b), incorporating Pt IX of Sch 3 to the
f Water Act 1945. Counsel for the respondents further conceded that the respondents
could not succeed in their present claim unless the law as it stood before the passing of
s 18(2) of the 1950 Act was amended. Thus he attributed to s 18(2) the effect of imposing
on the appellants a liability to which they would not otherwise have been subject.

Before Webster J there was some argument whether the escape of water was due to the
performance by the appellants of their statutory duty to supply water under pressure or
g to their exercise of the statutory power to lay water pipes in the highway. Webster J held
that the escape was attributable to the performance of a statutory duty and that the burst
occurred because of the pressure of water in the main. In my opinion that is clearly
correct. The importance of this finding will appear in what follows.

The question at issue therefore comes to be whether, as the respondents contend,
s 18(2) has the effect of imposing strict liability on the appellants as the water authority
h for a nuisance caused by them in the course of performing their statutory duty, so that
they are liable for the nuisance notwithstanding that they were not negligent and that
they took all reasonable care to avoid it. Their liability could, according to the respondents'
contention, be avoided only if the nuisance was attributable to act of God or of a third
party. Webster J decided that the respondents' contention was correct and he gave
judgment in their favour for the sum of £555·21 (see [1983] 1 All ER 892, [1983] 3
j WLR 105). This appeal comes direct to your Lordships' House under the leap-frog
procedure of s 12 of the Administration of Justice Act 1969.

The general law on this subject is well established and is not in dispute between the
parties. It was correctly summarised by the judge ([1983] 1 All ER 892 at 895, [1983] 3
WLR 105 at 109) in four propositions, the first two of which are directly relevant to this
case, in which the nuisance was attributable to the performance of a statutory duty.
These propositions are:

'1. In the absence of negligence, a body is not liable for a nuisance which is attributable to the [performance] by it of a duty imposed on it by statute: see *Hammond v St Pancras Vestry* (1874) LR 9 CP 316.

2. It is not liable in those circumstances even if by statute it is expressly made liable, or not exempted from liability, for nuisance: see *Stretton's Derby Brewery Co v Derby Corp* [1894] 1 Ch 431, [1891–4] All ER Rep 731 and *Smeaton v Ilford Corp* [1954] 1 All ER 923, [1954] Ch 450.'

Where the nuisance is attributable to the exercise of a power, the position is different. The contrast was brought out in the fourth of the judge's propositions, which was as follows:

'4. A body is liable for a nuisance by it attributable to the exercise of a power conferred by statute, even without negligence, if by statute it is expressly either made liable, or not exempted from liability, for nuisance: see *Charing Cross Electricity Supply Co v Hydraulic Power Co* [1914] 3 KB 772, [1914–15] All ER Rep 85.'

The word 'negligence' is used in these propositions in the special sense explained by Lord Wilberforce in *Allen v Gulf Oil Refining Ltd* [1981] 1 All ER 353 at 356, [1981] AC 1001 at 1011 of requiring the undertaker, as a condition of obtaining immunity from action, 'to carry out the work and conduct the operation with all reasonable regard and care for the interests of other persons'.

Having regard to the judge's finding that the nuisance in this case was attributable to the performance of a statutory duty, the respondents have to show that s 18(2) of the 1950 Act made a substantial change in the previously established law, by in effect superseding proposition 2 and making proposition 4 apply to a nuisance attributable to performance of a statutory duty as well as to one attributable to exercise of a statutory power. The judge held that the respondents had succeeded in showing that. In considering whether he was right, the first point to be observed is that s 18(2) does not in terms purport to impose any new liability. All it provides is that 'nothing in the enactment which confers the relevant power . . . shall exonerate the undertakers'. Those words are in marked contrast to the words of ss 18(1) and 19(1), both of which expressly impose on undertakers absolute liability in certain circumstances. The contrast with s 19(1)(b) is particularly striking. Sections 18 and 19 are parallel sections, the former dealing with liability of undertakers to street authorities and the latter with liability to transport authorities, such as railway or harbour authorities. Section 19(1) provides that if damage is caused to a bridge or other property of a transport authority, by any such event as is mentioned in s 18(2)(b) (viz explosion, ignition etc) occurring in code-regulated works in a street, the undertakers 'shall indemnify' the transport authority against expense reasonably incurred by them in making good the damage. If the draftsman intended by s 18(2) to impose a similar liability to indemnify the street authority for the events of explosion, ignition etc I do not understand why he did not use similarly clear and direct language. Webster J recognised that s 18(2), if literally construed, did not impose strict liability for nuisance, but he was disposed to read into it additional words, which I have emphasised in the following passage and which would have the effect of making it read as follows:

'Nothing in the enactment which confers the relevant power . . . or in any enactment which regulates the exercise of that power *nor the fact that the nuisance is attributable to the exercise of such a power* . . . shall exonerate the undertakers . . .'

His reason for reading in the additional words was that he considered they were necessary to make s 18(2) consistent with the provisions of ss 18(1) and 19(1). My Lords, I am bound to say that the reading in of additional words in that way seems to me unjustifiable. No doubt s 18(2) should, if possible, be construed in a way that would be consistent with the scheme of the Act as a whole, and especially of other subsections dealing with similar subject matter. But that is not to say that the subsection should be extended by adding a new provision which the draftsman has not included. That is especially true where, as here, the subsection as it stands can be given a sensible meaning. In my opinion the

a subsection is simply a non-exoneration clause of general application to undertakers acting in the exercise of a power (but not in the performance of a duty), and its effect is to make a uniform provision for their liability to replace the various differing provisions in different enactments which confer power on authorities such as the Post Office and electricity boards to lay cables and gas boards and statutory water and sewerage authorities to lay pipes in public streets. It makes a useful amendment to the law, but one which is

b much more limited than the complete reversal of the general rule contended for by the respondents. Such a limited effect is entirely consistent with the purpose of the 1950 Act as stated in the first part of the long title which is as follows: 'An Act to enact *uniform provisions* for regulating relations as to apparatus in streets between authorities . . . having statutory powers to place and deal with apparatus therein and those having the control or management of streets . . .' (my emphasis). It is not necessary to construe the subsection

c as having any wider effect in order to give content to it or to make it consistent with the purpose of the Act as a whole. I am therefore of opinion that the judge erred in his construction of the subsection.

An additional reason why I reject the respondents' construction is that s 18(2) provides for non-exoneration by anything in 'the enactment which confers the relevant *power* to which section 1 of this Act applies'. The power referred to must be 'any statutory power

d to execute undertakers' works in a street' (see s 1(1)). But the judge's finding that the bursting of a pipe in the present case was attributable to the appellants' performance of a duty to supply water under pressure, and not to their exercise of their power to lay the pipe, makes the provision of any enactment conferring a mere power to lay pipes irrelevant. It also makes the words which the judge was willing to add to s 18(2) (viz 'nor the fact that the nuisance is attributable to the exercise of such a *power*') irrelevant. Even

e if they were read in they would not have the effect for which the respondents contend. In order to produce that effect it would be necessary to include a reference to the nuisance being attributable to the performance of a statutory duty. But such a reference would be quite out of place in s 18(2) which provides that nothing in the enactment which confers the relevant 'power' or which regulates the exercise of 'that power' shall exonerate the undertakers from liability.

f For these reasons I am of the opinion that the respondents' contention is not well founded and I would allow the appeal.

LORD EDMUND-DAVIES. My Lords, I am in respectful agreement with the speech prepared by my noble and learned friend Lord Fraser, and accordingly concur that this appeal should be allowed.

g

LORD ROSKILL. My Lords, I have had the advantage of reading in draft the speech to be delivered by my noble and learned friend Lord Fraser. For the reasons he gives I too would allow this appeal.

h **LORD BRANDON OF OAKBROOK.** My Lords, I have had the advantage of reading in draft the speech prepared by my noble and learned friend Lord Fraser. I agree with it, and for the reasons which he gives I would allow the appeal.

LORD BRIGHTMAN. My Lords, I would allow this appeal for the reasons given by my noble and learned friend Lord Fraser.

j
Appeal allowed.

Solicitors: *Hextall Erskine & Co*, agents for *Keogh Ritson & Co*, Bolton (for the appellants); Treasury Solicitor.

Mary Rose Plummer   Barrister.

Davy v Spelthorne Borough Council   a

HOUSE OF LORDS

LORD FRASER OF TULLYBELTON, LORD WILBERFORCE, LORD ROSKILL, LORD BRANDON OF
OAKBROOK AND LORD BRIGHTMAN

18, 19 JULY, 13 OCTOBER 1983

Town and country planning − Enforcement notice − Appeal against notice − Grounds − Local b
authority agreeing not to enforce notice for three years if plaintiff not appealing against notice −
Plaintiff agreeing not to appeal on advice of local authority − Time for appeal elapsing − Plaintiff
bringing action for damages for negligent advice of local authority in respect to plaintiff's rights
under notice − Local authority seeking to strike out claim on ground that claim for damages
involving challenge to validity of enforcement notice and accordingly statute−barred − Whether
enforcement notice could be challenged on grounds not specified in statute − Town and Country c
Planning Act 1971, ss 88(2), 243(1)(a).

Judicial review − Availability of remedy − Circumvention of procedure for application for judicial
review − Plaintiff bringing action for damages in negligence against local authority for advice
given in respect of enforcement notice − Local authority seeking to strike out statement of claim on
ground that it was an abuse of the process of the court − Whether claim in negligence involving d
public or private rights − Whether plaintiff entitled to protection of public law and therefore
unable to defend right by way of ordinary action.

The plaintiff was the owner of premises used to produce precast concrete. The council
were the local planning authority for the district within which the premises were
situated. In November 1979, as a result of discussions with the council's officers, the e
plaintiff entered into an agreement with the council whereby he undertook not to appeal
against an enforcement notice in respect of the use of the premises provided that the
notice was not enforced by the council for a period of three years from the date of its
service. The council served an enforcement notice on the plaintiff in October 1980, in
accordance with the agreement, requiring the plaintiff to cease using the land for the
manufacture of concrete products and to remove from it all buildings and works within f
three years of the notice taking effect. The plaintiff did not appeal against the notice and
the time for appealing against it expired. In August 1982 the plaintiff issued a writ
against the council alleging that the agreement of November 1979 was ultra vires and
void and claiming damages against the council on the ground that they had negligently
advised him as to his rights under the Town and Country Planning Act 1971. The
council denied liability and applied to have the writ and statement of claim struck out g
on the ground that the proceedings were an abuse of the process of the court. Their
application was dismissed and they appealed to the Court of Appeal. The Court of Appeal
struck out part of the claim on the ground that it raised questions of public law which
could only be raised by way of judicial review under RSC Ord 53, but allowed the
plaintiff's claim for damages for negligence to stand. The council appealed to the House
of Lords, contending (i) that the plaintiff's claim for damages involved a challenge to the h
enforcement notice which was in substance a challenge to its validity and was therefore
barred by s 243(1)(a)[a] of the 1971 Act, which provided that the validity of an enforcement
notice could not 'except by way of an appeal under [that] Act, be questioned in any
proceedings whatsoever on any of the grounds on which such an appeal may be brought',
and (ii) that, when the plaintiff alleged that he had had a good defence to the enforcement
notice, he was asserting a right to which he was entitled to protection under public law j
and accordingly he could not be permitted to defend by way of an ordinary action.
Section 88[b] of the 1971 Act provided that appeals against enforcement notices were to be

---

a Section 243(1), so far as material, is set out at p 281 j, post
b Section 88, so far as material, is set out at p 282 b c, post

made to the Secretary of State and set out the grounds on which such appeals might be
a brought.

Held – The appeal would be dismissed for the following reasons—
(1) The enforcement notice was not itself being questioned in the proposed action,
but, in any event, the words 'any of the grounds on which such an appeal may be
brought' in s 243(1)(a) of the 1971 Act referred only to an appeal on any of the grounds
b specified in s 88(2) of that Act. Accordingly, even if the enforcement notice was being
challenged, it was not being challenged on any of the grounds specified in s 88(2) and
therefore s 243(1)(a) did not apply to bar the plaintiff's action (see p 282 *e* to *j*, p 284 *j*,
p 285 *c d* and p 287 *h* to p 288 *a*, post).
(2) The plaintiff's action was not an abuse of the process of the court because—
(a) (Per Lord Fraser, Lord Roskill, Lord Brandon and Lord Brightman) The plaintiff's
c claim for damages in negligence was an ordinary action in tort concerning his rights at
common law and did not raise any issue of public law. Accordingly, the rights concerned
were not rights to which the plaintiff was entitled to protection under public law, and
the general rule that a plaintiff was not entitled to defend by way of an ordinary action a
right to which he was entitled to protection under public law did not apply. Furthermore,
if the claim based in negligence was struck out the only way in which the plaintiff could
d bring his claim for damages before the court would be by obtaining leave to seek judicial
review and then relying on RSC Ord 53, r 7(1)ᶜ to attach a claim for damages to his claim
for judicial review, and that would be an awkward and uncertain process to which the
plaintiff ought not to be subjected unless it was required by statute (see p 283 *e* to *g*,
p 284 *d* to *f* and *j* and p 287 *j* to p 288 *a*, post); dictum of Viscount Simonds in *Pyx Granite
Co Ltd v Ministry of Housing and Local Government* [1959] 3 All ER at 6 followed; *O'Reilly v*
e *Mackman* [1982] 3 All ER 1124 distinguished.
(b) (Per Lord Wilberforce) In order for the plaintiff's proceedings, which were
proceedings at common law, to be an abuse of the process of the court, it had to be shown
that the plaintiff's claim both could and should be brought by way of judicial review.
However, since no prerogative writ or order could be sought in relation to the claim and
consequently no declaration or injunction could be asked for, no right to judicial review
f existed under Ord 53, r 1ᵈ and consequently no claim for damages could be made under
Ord 53, r 7 since a claim to damages under that rule was linked to a claim for judicial
review. Furthermore, even if a claim could be brought under the procedure for judicial
review, Ord 53 did not state that the procedure which it authorised was the only
procedure which could be followed, and accordingly the plaintiff could prima facie
choose the court and the procedure which suited him best, the onus being on the council
g to show that in doing so the plaintiff was abusing the court's procedure (see p 286 *b c h j*
and p 287 *c* to *h*, post).

Notes
For the general principles relating to judicial review, see 37 Halsbury's Laws (4th edn)
paras 567–583.
h For the Town and Country Planning Act 1971, s 243, see 41 Halsbury's Statutes (3rd
edn) 1856, and for s 88 of that Act (as substituted by the Local Government and Planning
(Amendment) Act 1981, s 1, Sch, para 1), see 51 ibid 2020.

c Rule 7(1), so far as material, provides: 'On an application for judicial review the Court may . . .
award damages to the applicant if—(a) he has included in the statement in support of his
j application for leave under rule 3 a claim for damages arising from any matter to which the
application relates, and (b) the Court is satisfied that, if the claim had been made in an action begun
by the applicant at the time of his making his application, he could have been awarded damages.'
d Rule 1, so fas material, provides:
'(1) An application for—(a) an order of mandamus, prohibition or certiorari . . . shall be made
by way of an application for judicial review in accordance with the provisions of this Order.
(2) An application for a declaration or an injunction . . . may be made by way of an application
for judicial review . . .'

Cases referred to in opinions

Anns v Merton London Borough [1977] 2 All ER 492, [1978] AC 728, [1977] 2 WLR 1024, *a*
HL.

Cocks v Thanet DC [1982] 3 All ER 1135, [1983] 2 AC 286, [1982] 3 WLR 1121, HL.

Home Office v Dorset Yacht Co Ltd [1970] 2 All ER 294, [1970] AC 1004, [1970] 2 WLR
1140, HL.

IRC v National Federation of Self-Employed and Small Businesses Ltd [1981] 2 All ER 93,
[1982] AC 617, [1981] 2 WLR 722, HL. *b*

O'Reilly v Mackman [1982] 3 All ER 1124, [1983] 2 AC 237, [1982] 3 WLR 1096, HL.

Pyx Granite Co Ltd v Ministry of Housing and Local Government [1959] 3 All ER 1, [1960]
AC 260, [1959] 3 WLR 346, HL.

Square Meals Frozen Foods Ltd v Dunstable BC [1974] 1 All ER 441, [1974] 1 WLR 59, CA.

c

Interlocutory appeal

The defendants, Spelthorne Borough Council, appealed with leave of the Appeal
Committee of the House of Lords granted on 28 March 1983 against that part of the
judgment of the Court of Appeal (Cumming-Bruce, Fox LJJ and Bush J) dated 9 February
1983 dismissing the appellants' appeal against the order of Sir Robert Megarry V-C on 11 *d*
October 1982 refusing to make an order on the appellants' motion that the writ of
summons and statement of claim of the plaintiff respondent, Arthur James Davy, be
struck out or that the action be transferred to the Queen's Bench Division (Crown Office
list). The facts are set out in the opinion of Lord Fraser.

Jeremy M Sullivan QC and David Mole for the appellants.
Kenneth Bagnall QC and Erica Foggin for the respondent. *e*

Their Lordships took time for consideration.

13 October. The following opinions were delivered.

LORD FRASER OF TULLYBELTON. My Lords, this appeal is a sequel to the *f*
decision of this House in O'Reilly v Mackman [1982] 3 All ER 1124, [1983] 2 AC 237. The
issue of most general importance raised in the appeal relates to the circumstances in
which a person with a cause of action against a public authority, which is connected with
the performance of its public duty, is entitled to proceed against the authority by way of
an ordinary action, as distinct from an application for judicial review.

The respondent is the owner of premises known as Riverside Works, Nutty Lane, *g*
Shepperton. The appellants are the local planning authority for the district within which
those premises are situated. On 28 September 1977 the respondent made a planning
application for the retention for a period of ten years of the existing buildings and the
continued use of the premises as a precast concrete works. Thereafter, the respondent
made another planning application, which was later withdrawn, and amended his
original application, which was refused, and he met officers of the appellants on several *h*
occasions, when he discussed with them the future use of the premises. The respondent
alleges that eventually, as a result of the discussions and correspondence with the
appellants' officers, on or about 6 November 1979 he entered into an agreement with the
appellants whereby he undertook not to appeal against an enforcement notice to be
served by the appellants on him in respect of the use of the premises, provided that the
notice would not be enforced by the appellants for a period of three years from the date *j*
of its service. The appellants served an enforcement notice on 15 October 1980 which,
the respondent alleges, was in accordance with that agreement. The enforcement notice
stated that the appellants required the respondent, within three years of the date when
the notice took effect, to cease using the land for the manufacture of concrete products
and to remove from it all buildings and works. The respondent did not appeal against
the enforcement notice and the time for so doing has long since expired. The notice took

effect 35 days after the date of service, 15 October 1980, and the time for appealing
against it expired when it took effect. The respondent alleges that he refrained from
appealing against the enforcement notice in pursuance of the agreement of 6 November
1979 and that he entered into that agreement on the advice of the appellants' officers.

On 24 August 1982 the respondent issued a writ against the appellants. In his
statement of claim he made allegations including those which I have summarised. He
also alleged that the agreement of 6 November 1979 was ultra vires the appellants and
void on several grounds which I need not now particularise. He claimed damages from
the appellants on the ground that the appellants, or their officers, had purported to advise
him as to his rights under the Town and Country Planning Act 1971, and that their
advice had been negligent. The appellants deny that there was any legally enforceable
agreement between the respondent and themselves. They also deny that they, or their
officers, purported to advise the respondent on his rights, and they say that if they did
give any such advice it was not given negligently. For the purposes of the present appeal
the respondent's allegations must be taken to be true.

The relief claimed by the respondent was as follows: (1) an injunction ordering the
appellants not to implement the enforcement notice; (2) damages; (3) an order that the
enforcement notice be set aside.

The appellants applied to have the writ and statement of claim struck out under RSC
Ord 19, r 1, or under the inherent jurisdiction, on the ground that they were an abuse of
the process of the court. Their application was rejected by Sir Robert Megarry V-C on 11
October 1982, before the decision of this House in *O'Reilly v Mackman*, and the Vice-
Chancellor's reasons have been largely superseded by that decision. The appellants
appealed and the Court of Appeal (Cumming-Bruce, Fox LJJ and Bush J), with the
decision of your Lordships' House in *O'Reilly* before it, ordered that claims 1 and 3, and
certain portions of the statement of claim relating to them, be struck out, on the ground
that they raised questions of public law which could only be raised by way of judicial
review under RSC Ord 53. The Court of Appeal left the respondent's claim for damages
for negligence alive. In the instant appeal, the appellants seek to have that, the only
remaining claim, struck out.

The first contention of the appellants is that the respondent's claim for damages
involves a challenge of the enforcement notice which is, in substance, a challenge of its
validity, and which is therefore barred by s 243 of the 1971 Act. In order that the
respondent may succeed in his claim for damages, he must establish three things, viz (1)
that the appellants, or their officers, advised him on his rights under the 1971 Act and
that they owed him a duty of care when they did so, (2) that they were in breach of that
duty by negligently advising him not to appeal against the enforcement notice and (3)
that he has suffered damage flowing from the breach. The damages are claimed because,
according to the respondent, he had a good defence to the enforcement notice which he
could, or at least might, have established, if he had appealed against the notice timeously,
but which he lost the chance of establishing when he acted on the appellants' advice and,
in accordance with the agreement of 6 November 1979, did not appeal. It is thus a
necessary step in the respondent's case for him to show that he had a good defence, good
enough to give him at least a chance of successfully challenging the enforcement notice,
if he had appealed against it in time. The amount of damages to which he would be
entitled will, of course, depend largely on the prospects of success if he had appealed. The
appellants maintain that the respondent is not entitled to have the merits of his defence
investigated in these proceedings because the defence is in substance a challenge of the
validity of the enforcement notice, and is therefore barred by s 243 of the 1971 Act.
Section 243(1) (as amended by the Local Government and Planning (Amendment) Act
1981) provides as follows:

> 'Subject to the provisions of this section—(a) the validity of an enforcement notice
> shall not, except by way of an appeal under Part V of this Act, be questioned in any
> proceedings whatsoever on any of the grounds on which such an appeal may be
> brought . . .'

Part V of the 1971 Act deals with enforcement of planning control. The first section
in Pt V is s 87 which (as substituted by the 1981 Act) provides that a local planning   *a*
authority shall have power to serve an enforcement notice in cases where there has been
a breach of planning control. Section 88 (as substituted by the 1981 Act) provides:

'(1) A person having an interest in the land to which an enforcement notice
relates may, at any time before the date specified in the notice as the date on which
it is to take effect, appeal to the Secretary of State against the notice, whether or not
a copy of it has been served on him.   *b*

(2) An appeal may be brought on any of the following grounds—(a) that planning
permission ought to be granted for the development to which the notice relates or,
as the case may be, that a condition or limitation alleged in the enforcement notice
not to have been complied with ought to be discharged; (b) that the matters alleged
in the notice do not constitute a breach of planning control; (c) that the breach of
planning control alleged in the notice has not taken place; (d) in the case of a notice   *c*
which, by virtue of section 87(4) of this Act, may be issued only within the period
of four years from the date of the breach of planning control to which the notice
relates, that that period had elapsed at the date when the notice was issued . . .'

The defence on which the respondent would have relied would have been under para
(d) of sub-s (2) of that section. The effect of s 243(1)(a) is to prohibit the bringing of   *d*
appeals on any of the grounds to which it relates before the High Court and, in accordance
with s 88(1), to substitute the Secretary of State as the forum for deciding such appeals.
Section 88(1) also limits the time for appealing to the period before the date on which
the enforcement notice is to take effect. Accordingly, the appellants say that the present
proceedings, being in substance an appeal against the enforcement order, are incompetent
because they are brought before the wrong tribunal and also, although I did not   *e*
understand this to be relied on as a separate point, because they are out of time.

I note in passing that, although s 243(1)(a) provides that the 'validity' of an enforcement
notice is not to be questioned except as therein provided, the word 'validity' is evidently
not intended to be understood in its strict sense. It is used to mean merely enforceability.
That appears from a consideration of the grounds on which an appeal may be brought
under Pt V of the 1971 Act, which are not limited to matters affecting the validity of the   *f*
notice. The relevant grounds are set out in s 88(2), part of which I have already quoted,
and it is apparent that para (a) (at least) goes to the merits rather than to the validity (in
the strict sense) of the notice. Accordingly, the fact that the respondent is not questioning
the 'validity' of the notice is immaterial. In fact, of course, the respondent now accepts
the notice as perfectly valid and, as at the date of instituting the present proceedings,
unappealable; indeed, that is the essential basis of his claim for damages.   *g*

But, in my opinion, the respondent's claim for damages is not barred by s 243(1)(a).
That paragraph provides that the validity of an enforcement notice shall not be questioned
in any proceedings whatsoever 'on any of the grounds on which such an appeal may be
brought'. The words 'such an appeal' are a reference back to an appeal under Pt V of the
1971 Act, and they mean in effect the grounds specified in s 88(2). But s 243(1)(a) does
not prohibit questioning the validity of the notice on other grounds. If, for example, the   *h*
respondent had alleged that the enforcement notice had been vitiated by fraud, because
one of the appellants' officers had been bribed to issue it, or had been served without the
appellants' authority, he would indeed have been questioning its validity, but not on any
of the grounds on which an appeal may be brought under Pt V. So here, the respondent's
complaint that he acquiesced in the enforcement notice because of negligent advice from
the appellants is not one of the grounds specified in s 88(2), and it would not have entitled   *j*
him to appeal to the Secretary of State under Pt V of the 1971 Act. Accordingly, even on
the assumption that the validity of the enforcement notice is being questioned in the
present proceedings (an assumption which in my opinion is open to serious doubt), it is
certainly not being questioned on any of the grounds referred to in s 243(1)(a) and the
proceedings are not barred by that subsection. In my opinion, therefore, the appellants'
first contention fails.

Their second contention is that, when the respondent alleges that he had a good
a defence to the enforcement order, he is asserting a right to which he is entitled to
protection under public law, and one which therefore he cannot be permitted to defend
by way of an ordinary action. The contention was based on the speech of Lord Diplock
in *O'Reilly v Mackman* [1982] 3 All ER 1124 at 1134, [1983] 2 AC 237 at 285:

> '. . . it would in my view as a general rule be contrary to public policy, and as such
> an abuse of the process of the court, to permit a person seeking to establish that a
> *b* decision of a public authority infringed rights to which he was entitled to protection
> under public law to proceed by way of an ordinary action and by this means to
> evade the provisions of Ord 53 for the protection of such authorities.'

The appellants accept that there are, of course, many claims against public authorities
which involve asserting rights purely of private law, and which can be pursued in an
c ordinary action. They accept also that, if a question as to the validity of the enforcement
notice had arisen incidentally in an action to which they, the appellants, were not parties,
it could properly have been decided in the High Court, for example, if it had arisen as a
preliminary issue in an action by the respondent against his solicitors for negligence. But
counsel for the appellants maintained that, when there is an issue between a citizen and
a public authority which involves determining whether the citizen can challenge a public
d notice or order, the only way to decide the issue is by way of procedure under Ord 53.
He maintained further that it makes no difference whether the issue concerns a present
right or a past right to challenge the notice or order. The only relevant distinction, he
said, between a past right and a present right is that investigating a past right tends to be
more difficult, and more burdensome to the public authority, than investigating a
present right, so that the authority's need for the protection of Ord 53 will be all the
e greater in the former case.

Although the argument was presented most persuasively, it is in my view not well
founded. The present proceedings, so far as they consist of a claim for damages for
negligence, appear to me to be simply an ordinary action for tort. They do not raise any
issue of public law as a live issue. I cannot improve on the words of Fox LJ, in the Court
of Appeal, when he said:

f > '. . . I do not think that the negligence claim is concerned with "the infringement
> of rights to which [the plaintiff] was entitled to protection under public law", to use
> Lord Diplock's words in *O'Reilly v Mackman*. The claim, in my opinion, is concerned
> with the alleged infringement of the plaintiff's rights at common law. Those rights
> are not even peripheral to a public law claim. They are the essence of the entire
> claim (so far as negligence is concerned).'

g
It follows that in my opinion they do not fall within the scope of the general rule laid
down in *O'Reilly*. The present proceedings may be contrasted with *Cocks v Thanet DC*
[1982] 3 All ER 1135, [1983] 2 AC 286, which was decided in this House on the same
day as *O'Reilly*. In *Cocks* the House held that the general rule stated in *O'Reilly* applied
(and I quote the headnote ([1983] 2 AC 286 at 287)) 'where a plaintiff was obliged to
h impugn a public authority's determination as a condition precedent to enforcing a
statutory private law right'. In that case the plaintiff had to impugn a decision of the
housing authority, to the effect that he was intentionally homeless, as a condition
precedent to establishing the existence of a private law right to be provided with
accommodation. It is quite clear from the speech of Lord Bridge, with which all the
other members of the House agreed, that the plaintiff was asserting a present right to
j impugn or overturn the decision ('the decision of the public authority *which the litigant
wishes to overturn*' (see [1983] 3 All ER 1135 at 1139, [1983] 2 AC 286 at 294; my
emphasis)). In the present case, on the other hand, the respondent does not impugn or
wish to overturn the enforcement order. His whole case on negligence depends on the
fact that he has lost his chance to impugn it. In my opinion therefore the general rule
stated in *O'Reilly* is inapplicable. The circumstances in which the procedure under Ord
53 is appropriate were described in some detail by Lord Diplock in *O'Reilly*. He

mentioned the fact that in that case no claim for damages would lie against the
defendants, and that the only relief sought was for a declaration, a form of relief that is   a
discretionary only (see [1982] 3 All ER 1124 at 1126, [1983] 2 AC 237 at 275). He
explained that one of the reasons why the procedure under Ord 53 is appropriate in
certain cases is that it provides 'a very speedy means, available in urgent cases within a
matter of days rather than months, for determining whether a disputed decision was
valid in law or not' (see [1982] 3 All ER 1124 at 1131, [1983] 2 AC 237 at 281). The
importance of obtaining a speedy decision is that—   b

'The public interest in good administration requires that public authorities and
third parties should not be kept in suspense as to the legal validity of a decision the
authority has reached in purported exercise of decision-making powers for any
longer period than is absolutely necessary in fairness to the person affected by the
decision.'

c

(See [1982] 3 All ER 1124 at 1131, [1983] 2 AC 237 at 280–281.)
    That explanation points the contrast with the present case, where the validity of the
enforcement order is not now challenged, and no public authority or third party is being
kept in suspense on that matter. Procedure under Ord 53 would in my view be entirely
inappropriate in this case.
    A further consideration is that if the claim based on negligence, which is the only one   d
of the original three claims now surviving, were to be struck out, the blow to the
respondent's chances of recovering damages might well be mortal. The court has no
power to order the proceedings for damages to continue as if they had been made under
Ord 53. The converse power under Ord 53, r 9 operates in one direction only: see *O'Reilly
v Mackman* [1982] 3 All ER 1124 at 1133, [1983] 2 AC 237 at 284. So, if the present
appeal were to succeed, the respondent's only chance of bringing his claim for damages   e
before the court would be by obtaining leave to start proceedings for judicial review
(now long out of time) and then by relying on Ord 53, r 7 to attach a claim for damages
to his claim for judicial review. That would be an awkward and uncertain process to
which the respondent ought not to be subjected unless it is required by statute: see *Pyx
Granite Co Ltd v Ministry of Housing and Local Government* [1959] 3 All ER 1 at 6, [1960]
AC 260 at 286 per Viscount Simonds. In my view it is not.   f
    The third contention for the appellants was that the claim for damages had the same
purpose and would have the same effect as the other reliefs claimed, namely injunction
and setting aside. My Lords, this contention seems to me entirely without justification.
The ostensible purpose of the claim for damages is clearly different from the purpose of
the other claims, and, for all that your Lordships can tell, the respondent may at this date
prefer to receive a payment in cash rather than to have the enforcement order set aside.   g
It seems to me quite impossible to hold that the true purpose of the claim for damages is
only to put pressure on the appellants not to enforce the order. As regards the effect of
the claim for damages being allowed to proceed, the suggestion was that the threat of the
claim hanging over the head of the appellants would be likely to cause them to refrain
from enforcing the order, if the respondent has not complied with it when the three-
year period expires in November 1983. I have some doubt whether it would be proper   h
for the appellants to allow their decision to be influenced by such a threat, but, assuming
that the threat would be a legitimate and proper consideration, it could only operate by
affecting the exercise of the appellants' discretion in deciding whether to prosecute the
respondent for failing to obey the enforcement notice, and it would in my opinion be
something much less compelling than an injunction or an order to quash. I have no
hesitation therefore in rejecting the appellants' third contention.   j
    For these reasons I would dismiss this appeal.

LORD WILBERFORCE. My Lords, although, with one qualification which I shall
state, I agree with the judgments in the Court of Appeal, I will make some observations

on this appeal both from respect to the attractive argument of counsel for the appellants
and because this case may be of some general importance.

The issue as it reaches this House, after other matters have been disposed of without
cross-appeal, is simply whether a common law action for damages against the appellant
council arising from alleged negligence should be struck out as an abuse of the process of
the court. There are two grounds on which this is sought to be done. The first is that the
claim is precluded by s 243(1)(a) of the Town and Country Planning Act 1971 (as
amended), which reads:

'Subject to the provisions of this section—(a) the validity of an enforcement notice
shall not, except by way of an appeal under Part V of this Act, be questioned in any
proceedings whatsoever on any of the grounds on which such an appeal may be
brought . . .'

I agree with the Court of Appeal that this section does not apply. In my opinion the
enforcement notice is not questioned in the proposed action, and, even if it is, it is not
questioned on the grounds specified. Although there may be some warrant for not giving
to this subsection a restricted meaning (see *Square Meals Frozen Foods Ltd v Dunstable BC*
[1974] 1 All ER 441, [1974] 1 WLR 59), to extend it so as to cover a claim such as that we
are concerned with would amount to a reconstruction too radical to be contemplated. I
need add no more on the point to what has been said by my noble and learned friend
Lord Fraser.

The second point is the substantial one. For proper appreciation it is necessary to define
the claim to which it relates. As pleaded (and for the purpose of this appeal we are only
concerned with the pleading and not with its substance or merits) it is that the appellants
owed to the respondent plaintiff a duty of care in, through its officers, advising him as to
his planning application, that the appellants were negligent in so advising him, that by
reason of this negligence he suffered damage, namely the loss of a chance of successfully
appealing against the enforcement notice served on him by the appellants. Though this
was initially one of several claims, it now stands on its own, and should be judged as an
independent and separate action.

To say that such a claim, so formulated, ought to be, or indeed can be, struck out as an
abuse of the process of the court seems on the face of it a remarkable proposition. There
is no doubt that, side by side with their statutory duties, local authorities may in certain
limited circumstances become liable for negligence at common law in the performance
of their duties (see for example *Home Office v Dorset Yacht Co Ltd* [1970] 2 All ER 294,
[1970] AC 1004, *Anns v Merton London Borough* [1977] 2 All ER 492 at 502, 503, [1978]
AC 728 at 756, 758). In what circumstances then can it be said to be an abuse of process
to sue them for negligence in the common law courts?

It is said that, in this case, the right should be denied because the claim involves
consideration of a question not of 'private law' but of 'public law', namely whether the
respondent had or would have had a defence against the enforcement notice, that this
consideration cannot take place in an ordinary action but can only take place in a
proceeding of what is now called 'judicial review' under the provisions of RSC Ord 53.

The expressions 'private law' and 'public law' have recently been imported into the law
of England from countries which, unlike our own, have separate systems concerning
public law and private law. No doubt they are convenient expressions for descriptive
purposes. In this country they must be used with caution, for, typically, English law
fastens not on principles but on remedies. The principle remains intact that public
authorities and public servants are, unless clearly exempted, answerable in the ordinary
courts for wrongs done to individuals. But by an extension of remedies and a flexible
procedure it can be said that something resembling a system of public law is being
developed. Before the expression 'public law' can be used to deny a subject a right of
action in the court of his choice it must be related to a positive prescription of law, by
statute or by statutory rules. We have not yet reached the point at which mere

characterisation of a claim as a claim in public law is sufficient to exclude it from consideration by the ordinary courts: to permit this would be to create a dual system of law with the rigidity and procedural hardship for plaintiffs which it was the purpose of the recent reforms to remove.

The relevant statute to the present case is the Supreme Court Act 1981, s 31, and the relevant statutory rules those contained in RSC Ord 53 dating from 1977. These lay down the conditions under the procedure by which the courts can be asked to review the actions or omissions of, inter alia, statutory bodies, persons acting under statute and inferior courts. Before a proceeding at common law can be said to be an abuse of process, it must, at least, be shown (1) that the claim in question *could* be brought by way of judicial review, (2) that it *should* be brought by way of judicial review.

O'Reilly v Mackman [1982] 3 All ER 1124, [1983] 2 AC 237 illustrates this in the clearest manner, and goes no distance towards supporting the appellants' case in this appeal. It was not contested there that the appellants, seeking directly to attack the board's decisions, would have had a remedy by way of judicial review (see [1982] 3 All ER 1124 at 1126, [1983] 2 AC 237 at 274); indeed, as I understand the case, they would not have had a remedy in private law at all. The only question, which Lord Diplock was able to put in a single sentence, was whether it was an abuse of process to apply for declarations by using the procedure laid down by the rules for proceedings begun by writ or originating summons instead of using the procedure laid down by RSC Ord 53 (see [1982] 3 All ER 1124 at 1126, [1983] 2 AC 237 at 274–275). It was decided that it would be such an abuse of process. The statements of law laid down in the single opinion must be related to that issue, the foundation of which was that the claims in question could have been brought by way of judicial review. Even when this requirement was satisfied, Lord Diplock was careful to make it clear that he was stating no universal rule that such claims could only be brought by this procedure (see [1982] 3 All ER 1124 at 1134, [1983] 2 AC 237 at 284–285). And he expressly stated that, though there should be a general rule of public policy against permitting a person seeking to establish that a decision of a public authority infringed rights to which he was entitled to protection under public law to proceed by way of ordinary action, there might be exceptions, particularly where the invalidity of the decision arises as a collateral issue in a claim for infringement of a right of the plaintiff arising under private law, and in other instances on a case to case basis. (The contemporaneous case of *Cocks v Thanet DC* [1982] 3 All ER 1135, [1982] 2 AC 286 may be regarded as one where a direct issue of public law arose at one remove.)

It is indeed plain enough that issues which could be characterised as issues of 'public law' may arise in a number of contexts besides those where an attack on, or review of, actions or omissions of public bodies is involved, cases, for example, where the invalidity of such action is set up by way of defence or where the validity of such action arises collaterally in actions against third parties. The Law Commission in its recommendations of 1971 (Remedies in Administrative Law (working paper no 40)) suggested that the procedure of judicial review should cover such cases, but this suggestion was not accepted and the reforms of 1977–81 were of a more limited character. So we must judge a contention of 'abuse of process' according to normal principle.

In fact neither of the requirements which I have mentioned above is met.

First (and it is here that I venture to differ to some extent from the judgment of Cumming-Bruce LJ in the Court of Appeal), this claim, treated as it must be as a claim for damages for negligence, could not, in my opinion, be pursued by way of judicial review under RSC Ord 53.

This proposition can be established in two steps. First, the right to award damages conferred by Ord 53, r 7 is by its terms linked to an application for judicial review. Unless judicial review would lie, damages cannot be given. Second, an action for judicial review in respect of alleged negligence is not 'appropriate' within the meaning of Ord 53, r 1. I quote the words of Lord Scarman in *IRC v National Federation of Self-Employed and Small Businesses Ltd* [1981] 2 All ER 93 at 109, [1982] AC 617 at 647–648:

'The application for judicial review was introduced by rules of court in 1977. The

new RSC Ord 53 is a procedural reform of great importance in the field of public
law, but it does not, indeed cannot, either extend or diminish the substantive law.
Its function is limited to ensuring "ubi jus ibi remedium". The new procedure is
more flexible than that which it supersedes. An applicant for relief will no longer
be defeated merely because he has chosen to apply for the wrong remedy. Not only
has the court a complete discretion to select and grant the appropriate remedy, but
it now may grant remedies which were not previously available. Rule 1(2) enables
the court to grant a declaration or injunction instead of, or in addition to, a
prerogative order where to do so would be just and convenient. This is a procedural
innovation of great consequence, but it neither extends nor diminishes the
substantive law. For the two remedies (borrowed from the private law) are put in
harness with the prerogative remedies. They may be granted only in circumstances
in which one or other of the prerogative orders can issue. I so interpret Ord 53,
r 1(2) because to do otherwise would be to condemn the rule as ultra vires.'

(See also [1981] 2 All ER 93 at 103, [1982] AC 617 at 639 per Lord Diplock.)

So, since no prerogative writ, or order, in relation to the present claim could be sought,
since, consequently, no declaration or injuction could be asked for, no right to judicial
review exists under r 1, and no consequential claim for damages can be made under r 7.

Second, and even assuming that this claim could in some way be brought under the
procedure of judicial review, there is no ground, in my opinion, on which it can be said
that it should only be so brought. Order 53 does not state that the procedure which it
authorised was the only procedure which could be followed in cases where it applied. (In
this it followed the recommendation of the Law Commission.) So prima facie the rule
applies that the plaintiff may choose the court and the procedure which suits him best.
The onus lies on the defendant to show that in doing so he is abusing the court's
procedure. In O'Reilly v Mackman [1982] 3 All ER 1124, [1983] 2 AC 237 it was possible
to show that the plaintiffs were improperly and flagrantly seeking to evade the protection
which the rule confers on public authorities. There is nothing of that sort here. The only
'public law' element involved in the present claim is that which may require the court,
after it has decided the issue of duty of care and of negligence, in assessing damages to
estimate, as best it can, the value of the chance which the respondent lost of resisting
enforcement of the appellants' notice. The presence of this element is in my opinion
quite insufficient to justify the court, on public policy grounds, from preventing the
respondent from proceedings by action in the ordinary way in the court of his choice,
particularly when one has regard to the serious procedural obstacles which he would find
if compelled to seek judicial review. If he had been suing his solicitor for negligent
advice, exactly the same problem in assessing damages would have arisen and nobody
could contend that the action would not proceed. I cannot see that it makes any difference
that the defendant is a public authority: the claim remains one the essence of which is a
claim at common law; any 'public law' element is peripheral. On the same line of
reasoning, but a fortiori, I reject the appellants' argument that any award of damages
against the appellants might inhibit them in the performance of their statutory duty or
might have the same effect, in practice, as granting an injunction, an argument which
logically would apply to any 'private law' claim against public authorities.

In my opinion the decision of the Court of Appeal was right and I would dismiss the
appeal.

LORD ROSKILL. My Lords, I have had the advantage of reading in draft the speech
delivered by my noble and learned friend Lord Fraser. For the reasons he gives I too
would dismiss this appeal.

LORD BRANDON OF OAKBROOK. My Lords, I have had the advantage of
reading in draft the speech prepared by my noble and learned friend Lord Fraser. I agree
with it, and for the reasons which he gives I would dismiss the appeal.

LORD BRIGHTMAN. My Lords, I would dismiss this appeal for the reasons given by my noble and learned friend Lord Fraser.

Appeal dismissed.

Solicitors: *Sherwood & Co* (for the appellants); *Sharpe Pritchard & Co* (for the respondent).

Mary Rose Plummer   Barrister.

R v Morris
Anderton v Burnside

HOUSE OF LORDS

LORD FRASER OF TULLYBELTON, LORD EDMUND-DAVIES, LORD ROSKILL, LORD BRANDON OF OAKBROOK AND LORD BRIGHTMAN

20, 21 JULY, 13 OCTOBER 1983

Criminal law – Theft – Appropriation – Defendants taking articles from shelf in self-service store and attaching price labels taken from lower-priced articles – One defendant arrested after paying lower price for articles at check-out point – Other defendant arrested at check-out but before he paid lower price – Whether appropriation of articles at any stage before arrest – Theft Act 1968, ss 1(1), 3(1).

Criminal law – Obtaining property by deception – Defendant dishonestly switching price labels on goods in store and thereby deceiving cashier into charging too low a price – Whether defendant guilty of both theft and obtaining property by deception – Whether if both offences committed both should be charged – Theft Act 1968, ss 1(1), 15(1).

The appellants in two cases each took articles from the shelves in a self-service store and substituted for the price labels attached to those articles labels taken from lower-priced articles in the store. At the check-out point one of the appellants was asked for and paid the lower prices indicated on the substituted labels; he was then arrested. The other appellant's dishonesty was detected at the check-out point but before he had paid the lesser price for the articles; he was then arrested. The appellants were both convicted of theft contrary to s 1(1)[a] of the Theft Act 1968 on the basis that the switching of price labels amounted to an 'appropriation' of the articles within s 3(1)[b] of that Act. The appellants' appeals against their convictions were dismissed. The appellants appealed to the House of Lords.

Held – On the true construction of s 3(1) of the 1968 Act 'appropriation' involved an element of adverse interference with or usurpation of some right of the owner. Accordingly, there was a dishonest appropriation where, by the substitution of a price label showing a lesser price on goods for one showing a greater price, a defendant either by that act alone or by that act in conjunction with another or other acts (which did not necessarily have to be overt acts), whether done before or after the substitution of the labels, adversely interfered with or usurped the right of the owner to ensure that the goods concerned were sold and paid for at that greater price. It followed that the appellants had been rightly convicted of theft and the appeals would therefore be dismissed (see p 290 f g, p 293 d to j, p 294 g h and p 295 f to h, post).

---

a   Section 1(1) is set out at p 292 a, post
b   Section 3(1) is set out at p 292 d, post

a *Lawrence v Comr of Police for the Metropolis* [1971] 2 All ER 1253, *R v McPherson* [1973] Crim LR 191, *Anderton v Wish* (1980) 72 Cr App R 23 and *Eddy v Niman* (1981) 73 Cr App R 237 approved.
Dictum of Webster J in *Eddy v Niman* (1981) 73 Cr App R at 241 criticised.
Dip Kaur v Chief Constable of Hampshire [1981] 2 All ER 430 doubted.
Per curiam. (1) A person who dishonestly appropriates goods by switching price labels and thereby deceives the cashier at the check-out point into charging too low a price for
b the goods commits the offences of theft under s 1(1) of the 1968 Act and obtaining property by deception under s 15(1)^c of that Act. In principle there is no reason why, when there is clear evidence of both offences being committed, both offences should not be charged. However, where the shoplifter has passed the check-out point and clearly has, by deception, obtained goods either without paying or by paying only a lesser price than he should, it may be preferable in the interests of simplicity for prosecutors to
c charge only an offence against s 15(1). When the dishonesty has been detected before the defendant has reached the check-out point and he has been arrested before that point (so that no property has been obtained by deception), then theft is properly charged and will be established if appropriation and the other ingredients of the offence are proved (see p 290 *f g* and p 294 *j* to p 295 *a c* to *e* and *g h*, post).
(2) Questions whether particular contracts are void or voidable on the ground of
d mistake or fraud or whether mistake is sufficiently fundamental to vitiate a contract should be confined to those fields of law to which they are immediately relevant and are not relevant to questions under the 1968 Act (see p 290 *f g*, p 294 *h j* and p 295 *g h*, post).
Decision of the Court of Appeal, Criminal Division [1983] 2 All ER 448 affirmed.

Notes
e For theft, see 11 Halsbury's Laws (4th edn) para 1262, and for what amounts to appropriation, see ibid para 1264.
For obtaining property by deception, see ibid para 1278.
For cases on appropriation in theft, see 15 Digest (Reissue) 1264, 1282, *10831–10832*, *11029–11030*.
For the Theft Act 1968, ss 1, 3, 15, see 8 Halsbury's Statutes (3rd edn) 783, 784, 792.

f **Cases referred to in opinions**
Anderton v Wish (1980) 72 Cr App R 23, DC.
Dip Kaur v Chief Constable of Hampshire [1981] 2 All ER 430, [1981] 1 WLR 578, DC.
Eddy v Niman (1981) 73 Cr App R 237, DC.
Lawrence v Comr of Police for the Metropolis [1971] 2 All ER 1253, [1972] AC 626, [1971] 3
g WLR 225, HL; *affg* sub nom *R v Lawrence* [1970] 3 All ER 933, [1971] 1 QB 373, [1970] 3 WLR 1103, CA.
R v McPherson [1973] Crim LR 191, CA.
R v Meech [1973] 3 All ER 939, [1974] QB 549, [1973] 3 WLR 507, CA.
R v Skipp [1975] Crim LR 114, CA.

h **Consolidated appeals**

R v Morris

On 23 April 1982 in the Crown Court at Acton before Mr W Thomas sitting as an assistant recorder and a jury the appellant, David Alan Morris, was convicted on two counts of theft contrary to s 1(1) of the Theft Act 1968 and was fined £50 on each count.
j He appealed against his conviction to the Court of Appeal, Criminal Division (Lord Lane CJ, O'Connor LJ and Talbot J), which dismissed his appeal on 8 March 1983 ([1983] 2 All ER 448, [1983] 2 WLR 768). On 24 March 1983 the Court of Appeal certified, under

---

c Section 15(1), so far as material, provides: 'A person who by any deception dishonestly obtains property belonging to another, with the intention of permanently depriving the other of it, shall on conviction on indictment be liable to imprisonment . . .'

s 33(2) of the Criminal Appeal Act 1968, on the application of the appellant, that a point
of law of general public importance was involved in the decision to dismiss the appeal *a*
and refused leave to appeal to the House of Lords. On 5 May 1983 the Appeal Committee
of the House of Lords granted the appellant leave to appeal. The facts are set out in the
opinion of Lord Roskill.

Anderton v Burnside

On 27 January 1982 the appellant, James Burnside, was convicted by the justices for the *b*
county of Greater Manchester, acting in and for the petty sessional division of the City of
Manchester as a magistrates' court sitting at Crown Square, Manchester, on a single
charge of theft contrary to s 1(1) of the Theft Act 1968 on an information preferred
against the appellant by the respondent, Cyril James Anderton, the Chief Constable of
Manchester. The appellant appealed by way of case stated against his conviction to the
Divisional Court of the Queen's Bench Division (Ackner LJ and Webster J), which *c*
dismissed his appeal on 5 November 1982. The Divisional Court, on the appellant's
application, certified, under s 1(2) of the Administration of Justice Act 1960, that a point
of law of general public importance was involved in the decision but refused leave to
appeal to the House of Lords. On 5 May 1983 the Appeal Committee of the House of
Lords granted the appellant leave to appeal and ordered that his appeal be consolidated
with the appeal of David Alan Morris. The facts are set out in the opinion of Lord Roskill. *d*

Neil Denison QC and *Philippa Jessel* for the appellants.
David Jeffreys QC and *Laura Harris* for the prosecution.

Their Lordships took time for consideration.
                                                                                              e
13 October. The following opinions were delivered.

LORD FRASER OF TULLYBELTON. My Lords, I have had the advantage of
reading in draft the speech prepared by my noble and learned friend Lord Roskill. I
entirely agree with it, and for the reasons given by him I would answer the certified
questions in the way he proposes, and I would dismiss both appeals. *f*

LORD EDMUND-DAVIES. My Lords, having had the advantage of reading in draft
form the speech prepared by my noble and learned friend Lord Roskill, I too would
answer the questions certified in these appeals in the manner indicated by him and
dismiss both appeals.
                                                                                              g

LORD ROSKILL. My Lords, these two consolidated appeals, one from the Court of
Appeal, Criminal Division, the other from the Divisional Court, have been brought by
leave of your Lordships' House in order that controversial questions of law arising from
the dishonest practice of label-switching in connection with shoplifting in supermarkets
may be finally decided. These matters have been in controversy for some time and have *h*
been the subject of judicial decisions which are not always easy to reconcile as well as
disagreement between distinguished academic lawyers.

The facts giving rise to these appeals are simple. Morris, the appellant from the Court
of Appeal, Criminal Division, on 30 October 1981 took goods from the shelves of a
supermarket. He replaced the price labels attached to them with labels showing a lesser
price than the originals. At the check-out point he was asked for and paid those lesser *j*
prices. He was then arrested. Burnside, the appellant from the Divisional Court, was seen
to remove a price label from a joint of pork in the supermarket and attach it to a second
joint. This action was detected at the check-out point but before he had paid for that
second joint which at that moment bore a price label showing a price of £2·73 where as
the label should have shown a price of £6·91½. Burnside was then arrested.

a
The only relevant difference between the two cases is that Burnside was arrested before he had dishonestly paid the lesser price for the joint of pork. Morris was arrested after he had paid the relevant lesser prices. Morris was tried in the Crown Court at Acton on two charges of theft contrary to s 1(1) of the Theft Act 1968. A third count of obtaining property by deception contrary to s 15 of that Act appeared in the indictment but the assistant recorder did not take a verdict on it and ordered that count to remain on the file. Morris appealed. The Court of Appeal, Criminal Division (Lord Lane CJ, O'Connor
b
LJ and Talbot J) ([1983] 2 All ER 448, [1983] 2 WLR 768) dismissed his appeal in a reserved judgment given on 8 March 1983 by Lord Lane CJ.

Burnside was convicted at Manchester Magistrates' Court on 27 January 1982 on a single charge of theft contrary to s 1(1) of the 1968 Act. He appealed by way of case stated. On 5 November 1982, the Divisional Court (Ackner LJ and Webster J) dismissed the appeal.
c
Both the Court of Appeal, Criminal Division and the Divisional Court granted certificates. The former certificate read thus:

d
'If a person has substituted on an item of goods displayed in a self-service store a price label showing a lesser price for one showing a greater price, with the intention of paying the lesser price and then pays the lesser price at the till and takes the goods, is there at any stage a "dishonest appropriation" for the purposes of section 1 of the Theft Act 1968, and if so, at what point does such appropriation take place?'

The certificate in the latter case reads:

e
'If a person has substituted on an item of goods displayed in a self-service store a price label showing a lesser price for one showing a greater price, with the intention of paying the lesser price, and then pays the lesser price at the till and takes the goods, is there at any stage a "dishonest appropriation" for the purposes of Section 1 of the Theft Act 1968.'

f
The two certificates though clearly intended to raise the same point of law are somewhat differently worded and, with respect, as both counsel ultimately accepted during the debate before your Lordships, do not precisely raise the real issue for decision, at least in the terms in which it falls to be decided.

g
My Lords, in his submissions for the appellants, which were conspicuous both for their clarity and their brevity, counsel for the appellants urged that on these simple facts neither appellant was guilty of theft. He accepted that Morris would have had no defence to a charge under s 15(1) of obtaining property by deception for he dishonestly paid the lesser prices and passed through the check-point having done so before he was arrested. But Morris, he said, was not guilty of theft because there was no appropriation by him before payment at the check-point sufficient to support a charge of theft, however dishonest his actions may have been in previously switching the labels.

h
Counsel for the appellants pointed out that if, as he accepted, an offence was committed against s 15(1) and if the prosecution case were right, Morris would be liable to be convicted of obtaining property by deception which he had already stolen, a situation which counsel suggested was somewhat anomalous.

As regards Burnside, counsel for the appellants submitted that for the same reason there was no appropriation before his arrest sufficient to support a charge of theft. He also submitted that Burnside's actions however dishonest would not support a charge of attempting to obtain property by deception contrary to s 15(1) since his dishonest act was
j
no more than an act preparatory to obtaining property by deception and was not sufficiently proximate to an attempt to obtain property by deception.

My Lords, if these submissions be well founded it is clear that however dishonest their actions, each appellant was wrongly convicted of theft. The question is whether they are well founded. The answer must depend on the true construction of the relevant sections of the 1968 Act and it is to these that I now turn. For ease of reference I set them out:

'**1.**—(1) A person is guilty of theft if he dishonestly appropriates property belonging to another with the intention of permanently depriving the other of it; and "thief" and "steal" shall be construed accordingly.

(2) It is immaterial whether the appropriation is made with a view to gain, or is made for the thief's own benefit.

(3) The five following sections of this Act shall have effect as regards the interpretation and operation of this section (and, except as otherwise provided by this Act, shall apply only for the purposes of this section).

2.—(1) A person's appropriation of property belonging to another is not to be regarded as dishonest—(a) if he appropriates the property in the belief that he has in law the right to deprive the other of it, on behalf of himself or of a third person; or (b) if he appropriates the property in the belief that he would have the other's consent if the other knew of the appropriation and the circumstances of it; or (c) (except where the property came to him as trustee or personal representative) if he appropriates the property in the belief that the person to whom the property belongs cannot be discovered by taking reasonable steps.

(2) A person's appropriation of property belonging to another may be dishonest notwithstanding that he is willing to pay for the property.

3.—(1) Any assumption by a person of the rights of an owner amounts to an appropriation, and this includes, where he has come by the property (innocently or not) without stealing it, any later assumption of a right to it by keeping or dealing with it as owner.

(2) Where property or a right or interest in property is or purports to be transferred for value to a person acting in good faith, no later assumption by him of rights which he believed himself to be acquiring shall, by reason of any defect in the transferor's title amount to theft of the property.

4.—(1) "Property" includes money and all other property, real or personal, including things in action and other intangible property . . .'

It is to be observed that the definition of 'appropriation' in s 3(1) is not exhaustive. But ss 1(1) and 3(1) show clearly that there can be no conviction for theft contrary to s 1(1) even if all the other ingredients of the offence are proved unless 'appropriation' is also proved.

The starting point of any consideration of the submissions of counsel for the appellants must, I think, be the decision of this House in *Lawrence v Comr of Police for the Metropolis* [1971] 2 All ER 1253, [1972] AC 626; *affg* [1970] 3 All ER 933, [1971] 1 QB 373. In the leading speech, Viscount Dilhorne expressly accepted the view of the Court of Appeal, Criminal Division in that case that the offence of theft involved four elements: (1) a dishonest (2) appropriation (3) of property belonging to another, (4) with the intention of permanently depriving the owner of it. Viscount Dilhorne also rejected the argument that even if these four elements were all present there could not be theft within the section if the owner of the property in question had consented to the acts which were done by the defendant. That there was in that case a dishonest appropriation was beyond question and the House did not have to consider the precise meaning of that word in s 3(1).

Counsel for the appellants submitted that the phrase in s 3(1) 'Any assumption by a person of *the* rights [my emphasis] of an owner amounts to an appropriation' must mean any assumption of '*all* the rights of an owner'. Since neither appellant had at the time of the removal of the goods from the shelves and of the label-switching assumed *all* the rights of the owner, there was no appropriation and therefore no theft. Counsel for the prosecution, on the other hand, contended that *the* rights in this context only meant *any* of the rights. An owner of goods has many rights: they have been described as 'a bundle or package of rights'. Counsel for the prosecution contended that on a fair reading of the subsection it cannot have been the intention that every one of an owner's rights had to be assumed by the alleged thief before an appropriation was proved and that essential ingredient of the offence of theft established.

a
My Lords, if one reads the words 'the rights' at the opening of s 3(1) literally and in isolation from the rest of the section, the submission of counsel for the appellants undoubtedly has force. But the later words 'any later assumption of a right' in sub-s (1) and the words in sub-s (2) 'no later assumption by him of rights' seem to me to militate strongly against the correctness of the submission. Moreover, the provisions of s 2(1)(a) also seem to point in the same direction. It follows therefore that it is enough for the prosecution if they have proved in these cases the assumption by the defendants of any of
b
the rights of the owner of the goods in question, that is to say, the supermarket concerned, it being common ground in these cases that the other three of the four elements mentioned in Viscount Dilhorne's speech in *Lawrence*'s case had been fully established.

My Lords, counsel for the prosecution sought to argue that any removal from the shelves of the supermarket, even if unaccompanied by label-switching, was without more an appropriation. In one passage in his judgment in *Morris*'s case, Lord Lane CJ
c
appears to have accepted the submission, for he said:

'. . . It seems to us that in taking the article from the shelf the customer is indeed assuming one of the rights of the owner, the right to move the article from its position on the shelf to carry it to the check-out . . .'

With the utmost respect, I cannot accept this statement as correct. If one postulates an
d
honest customer taking goods from a shelf to put in his or her trolley to take to the check-point there to pay the proper price, I am unable to see that any of these actions involves any assumption by the shopper of the rights of the supermarket. In the context of s 3(1), the concept of appropriation in my view involves not an act expressly or impliedly authorised by the owner but an act by way of adverse interference with or usurpation of those rights. When the honest shopper acts as I have just described, he or
e
she is acting with the implied authority of the owner of the supermarket to take the goods from the shelf, put them in the trolley, take them to the check-point and there to pay the correct price, at which moment the property in the goods will pass to the shopper for the first time. It is with the consent of the owners of the supermarket, be that consent express or implied, that the shopper does these acts and thus obtained at least control if not actual possession of the goods preparatory, at a later stage, to obtaining the property
f
in them on payment of the proper amount at the check-point. I do not think that s 3(1) envisages any such act as an 'appropriation', whatever may be the meaning of that word in other fields such as contract or sale of goods law.

If, as I understand all of your Lordships to agree, the concept of appropriation in s 3(1) involves an element of adverse interference with or usurpation of some right of the owner, it is necessary next to consider whether that requirement is satisfied in either of these cases. As I have already said, in my view mere removal from the shelves without
g
more is not an appropriation. Further, if a shopper with some perverted sense of humour, intending only to create confusion and nothing more, both for the supermarket and for other shoppers, switches labels, I do not think that that act of label-switching alone is without more an appropriation, though it is not difficult to envisage some cases of dishonest label-switching which could be. In cases such as the present, it is in truth a combination of these actions, the removal from the shelf and the switching of the labels
h
which evidences adverse interference with or usurpation of the right of the owner. Those acts, therefore, amount to an appropriation and if they are accompanied by proof of the other three elements to which I have referred, the offence of theft is established. Further, if they are accompanied by other acts such as putting the goods so removed and relabelled into a receptacle, whether a trolley or the shopper's own bag or basket, proof of appropriation within s 3(1) becomes overwhelming. It is the doing of one or more acts
j
which individually or collectively amount to such adverse interference with or usurpation of the owner's rights which constitute appropriation under s 3(1) and I do not think it matters where there is more than one such act in which order the successive acts take place, or whether there is any interval of time between them. To suggest that it matters whether the mislabelling precedes or succeeds removal from the shelves is to reduce this branch of the law to an absurdity.

My Lords, it will have been observed that I have endeavoured so far to resolve the question for determination in these appeals without reference to any decided cases except *Lawrence's* case which alone of the many cases cited in argument is a decision of this House. If your Lordships accept as correct the analysis which I have endeavoured to express by reference to the construction of the relevant sections of the 1968 Act, a trail through a forest of decisions, many briefly and indeed inadequately reported, will tend to confuse rather than to enlighten. There are, however, some to which brief reference should perhaps be made.

First, *R v McPherson* [1973] Crim LR 191. Your Lordships have had the benefit of a transcript of the judgment of Lord Widgery CJ. I quote from the transcript:

'Reducing this case to its bare essentials we have this. Mrs McPherson in common design with the others takes two bottles of whisky from the stand, puts them in her shopping bag; at the time she intends to take them out without paying for them, in other words she intends to steal them from the very beginning. She acts dishonestly as the jury found, and the sole question is whether that is an appropriation of the bottles within the meaning of s 1. We have no hesitation whatever in saying that it is such an appropriation and indeed we content ourselves with a judgment of this brevity because we have been unable to accept or to find any argument to the contrary, to suggest that an appropriation is not effective in those simple circumstances.'

That was not, of course, a label-switching case, but it is a plain case of appropriation effected by the combination of the acts of removing the goods from the shelf and of concealing them in the shopping bag. *R v McPherson* is to my mind clearly correctly decided as are all the cases which have followed it. It is wholly consistent with the principles which I have endeavoured to state in this speech.

It has been suggested that *R v Meech* [1973] 3 All ER 939, [1974] QB 549, *R v Skipp* [1975] Crim LR 114 (your Lordships also have a transcript of the judgment in this case), and certain other cases are inconsistent with *R v McPherson*. I do not propose to examine these or other cases in detail. Suffice it to say that I am far from convinced that there is any inconsistency between them and other cases as has been suggested once it is appreciated that facts will vary infinitely. The precise moment when dishonest acts, not of themselves amounting to an appropriation, subsequently, because of some other and later acts combined with those earlier acts, do bring about an appropriation within s 3(1), will necessarily vary according to the particular case in which the question arises.

Of the other cases referred to, I understand all your Lordships to agree that *Anderton v Wish* (1980) 72 Cr App R 23 was rightly decided for the reasons given. I need not therefore refer to it further. *Eddy v Niman* (1981) 73 Cr App R 237 was in my view also correctly decided on its somewhat unusual facts. I think that Webster J, giving the first judgment, asked the right question (at 241), though, with respect, I think that the phrase 'some overt act . . . inconsistent with the true owner's rights' is too narrow. I think that the act need not necessarily be 'overt'.

Dip Kaur v Chief Constable of Hampshire [1981] 2 All ER 430, [1981] 1 WLR 578 is a difficult case. I am disposed to agree with Lord Lane CJ that it was wrongly decided but without going into further detail I respectfully suggest that it is on any view wrong to introduce into this branch of the criminal law questions whether particular contracts are void or voidable on the ground of mistake or fraud or whether any mistake is sufficiently fundamental to vitiate a contract. These difficult questions should so far as possible be confined to those fields of law to which they are immediately relevant and I do not regard them as relevant questions under the 1968 Act.

My Lords, it remains briefly to consider any relationship between s 1 and s 15. If the conclusion I have reached that theft takes place at the moment of appropriation and before any payment is made at the check-point be correct it is wrong to assert, as has been asserted, that the same act of appropriation creates two offences, one against s 1(1) and the other against s 15(1), because the two offences occur at different points of time: the

s 15(1) offence is not committed until payment of the wrong amount is made at the
a check-point while the theft has been committed earlier. It follows that in cases such as
Morris two offences were committed. I do not doubt that it was perfectly proper to add
the third count under s 15(1) in this case. I think the assistant recorder was right to leave
all three counts to the jury. While one may sympathise with his preventing them from
returning a verdict on the third count once they convicted on the theft counts if only in
the interests of simplification, the counts were not alternative as he appears to have
b treated them. They were cumulative and once they were left to the jury verdicts should
have been taken on all of them.

My Lords, these shoplifting cases by switching labels are essentially simple in their
facts and their factual simplicity should not be allowed to be obscured by ingenious legal
arguments on the 1968 Act which for some time have bedevilled this branch of the
criminal law without noticeably contributing to the efficient administration of justice,
c rather the reverse. The law to be applied to simple cases, whether in magistrates' courts
or the Crown Court, should if possible be equally simple. I see no reason in principle
why, when there is clear evidence of both offences being committed, both offences
should not be charged. But where a shoplifter has passed the check-point and quite
clearly has, by deception, obtained goods either without paying or by paying only a lesser
price than he should, those concerned with prosecutions may in future think it preferable
d in the interests of simplicity to charge only an offence against s 15(1). In many cases of
that kind it is difficult to see what possible defence there can be and that course may well
avoid any opportunity for further ingenious legal arguments on the first few sections of
the 1968 Act. Of course when the dishonesty is detected before the defendant has reached
the check-point and he or she is arrested before that point so that no property has been
obtained by deception, then theft is properly charged and if appropriation, within the
e meaning I have attributed to that word in this speech, is proved as well as the other three
ingredients of the offence of theft, the defendant is plainly guilty of that offence.

My Lords, as already explained I have not gone through all the cases cited though I
have mentioned some. Of the rest, those inconsistent with this speech must henceforth
be treated as overruled.

I would answer the certified questions in this way: there is a dishonest appropriation
f for the purposes of the Theft Act 1968 where by the substitution of a price label showing
a lesser price on goods for one showing a greater price, a defendant either by that act
alone or by that act in conjunction with another act or other acts (whether done before
or after the substitution of the labels) adversely interferes with or usurps the right of the
owner to ensure that the goods concerned are sold and paid for at that greater price.

I would dismiss these appeals.

g
LORD BRANDON OF OAKBROOK. My Lords, I have had the advantage of
reading in draft the speech prepared by my noble and learned friend Lord Roskill. I
agree with it, and for the reasons which he gives I would dismiss both appeals.

LORD BRIGHTMAN. My Lords, I would dismiss these appeals for the reasons given
h by my noble and learned friend Lord Roskill.

Appeals dismissed.

Solicitors: *W A G Davidson & Co*, Acton (for the appellants); *Ferris & Evans*, Ealing (for
the prosecution).

Mary Rose Plummer   Barrister.

Nationwide Building Society v Registry of Friendly Societies

CHANCERY DIVISION
PETER GIBSON J
15 JULY 1983

Building society – Advances – Repayment of advance – Advance on terms that principal amount secured by charge to be index-linked to real value of sum advanced to take account of inflation – Whether advances made on such terms are within building societies' powers – Building Societies Act 1962, s 1(1).

A building society may, under s 1(1)ᵃ of the Building Societies Act 1962, make advances to its members on terms that the amount of the principal sum advanced which is to be repaid to the society and secured by legal charge shall be index-linked to the real value of the money advanced to take account of inflation, provided that the amount repayable to the society is not less than the amount initially advanced by it (see p 298 c d, p 299 c d and g to p 300 b, post).

Multiservice Bookbinding Ltd v Marden [1978] 2 All ER 489 applied.

Notes
For the purpose for which building societies are established, see 4 Halsbury's Laws (4th edn) para 1501, and for cases on building society advances, see 7 Digest (Reissue) 489–491, 2776–2787.

For the Building Societies Act 1962, s 1, see 3 Halsbury's Statutes (3rd edn) 315.

Cases referred to in judgment
Halifax Building Society v Registry of Friendly Societies [1978] 3 All ER 403, [1978] 1 WLR 1544.
Multiservice Bookbinding Ltd v Marden [1978] 2 All ER 489, [1979] Ch 84, [1978] 2 WLR 535.

Originating summons
By a summons dated 24 May 1983 the Nationwide Building Society sought as against the Registry of Friendly Societies a declaration that it was lawful for the society to make advances to its members on the terms set out in, and to be secured by, a legal charge in the form of a draft intended to be exhibited to an affidavit to be sworn on behalf of the society. The facts are set out in the judgment.

John Mills QC and *Timothy Lloyd* for the society.
John Mummery for the registry.

PETER GIBSON J. By this originating summons the Nationwide Building Society seeks a declaration as against the Registry of Friendly Societies that it is lawful for the society to make advances to its members on the terms set out in, and to be secured by, a legal charge in a particular form. That form provides that the amount of principal, as distinct from interest, to be paid by the borrower under the legal charge should be index-linked. The society is one that is registered under the Building Societies Act 1962. It is the third largest building society in the United Kingdom. Its business is the raising of funds for the purpose of making advances to members on the security of freehold or leasehold estate in accordance with s 1(1) of the 1962 Act. The major part of the society's

---

a   Section 1(1) is set out at p 298 g, post

lending is, and always has been, made to facilitate the purchase of freehold and leasehold
property. For some years the society has been looking at ways of making its services
available to a wider cross-section of the public, whilst keeping within the traditional
confines of finance for housing. This particular application is concerned with one such
method, and the society intends to carry out that method if it may lawfully do so.

The essence of what is proposed is that the society should be able to make advances on
terms designed to ensure that what it calls the real value of the advance is repaid to it by
adjustments made to take account of inflation, but under which the rate of interest
charged would be substantially lower than the rates ordinarily charged by the society.
The advantage of such an advance is that the monthly payments which are customarily
required to be paid under building society mortgages would be significantly lower in the
early years of the loan because of the low rate of interest. This, it is expected, would make
the scheme available to some borrowers who could not afford to borrow on the usual
terms of mortgage under which a higher rate of interest would be charged without any
adjustment of principal to take account of inflation. It is expected that an index-linked
mortgage might be seen to be desirable not only to individuals but also to institutions
such as housing associations.

The possibility of making such index-linked mortgages is a subject which has
undergone discussion from time to time for some years in the building societies, but
there have been fears expressed that such index-linking was not permissible under the
general law relating to mortgages or under the 1962 Act. In the leading textbook,
Wurtzburg and Mills *Building Society Law* (14th edn, 1976), doubts as to that legality were
expressed by the authors. However, since then there have been two developments. One
is that the government has increasingly used index-linking in connection with borrowing
money by way of issue of Treasury stock. The other and more significant happening has
been the decision of Browne-Wilkinson J in 1977 in *Multiservice Bookbinding Ltd v Marden*
[1978] 2 All ER 489, [1979] Ch 84. In that case the question that arose for decision was
whether a mortgage was valid the terms of which provided for the increase in the capital
as well as interest to be paid by reference to the value of the Swiss franc against the
pound. The judge held that an index-linked money obligation was not contrary to public
policy, and accordingly that the relevant provisions of the mortgage whereby payments
of capital and interest were linked to the value of the Swiss franc were valid. In reaching
that conclusion Browne-Wilkinson J said ([1978] 2 All ER 489 at 497, [1979] Ch 84 at
104):

> 'In any economy where there is inflation there are few inducements to make
> long-term loans expressed in a currency the value of which is being eroded. It is at
> least possible that, unless lenders can ensure that they are repaid the real value of the
> money they advanced (and not merely a sum of the same nominal amount but in
> devalued currency) the availability of loan capital will be much diminished. This
> would surely not be in the public interest.'

The judge also held that the mortgage in question was not unfair or unconscionable,
and in so holding he had regard to the particular terms of the mortgage. He said ([1978]
2 All ER 489 at 502, [1979] Ch 84 at 111):

> '... I do not think it is right to treat the Swiss franc uplift element in the capital
> repayments as being in any sense a premium or collateral advantage. In my
> judgment a lender of money is entitled to ensure that he is repaid the real value of
> his loan, and if he introduces a term which so provides, he is not stipulating for
> anything beyond the repayment of principal.'

Thus the judge reached the conclusion under the general law that there was no objection
to an index-linked mortgage.

The society prepared the draft legal charge, the legality of which I am asked to
pronounce on, with the words of Browne-Wilkinson J very much in mind. In cl 2, which
deals with provisions for payment, there are the following provisions, so far as material:

'(a) The Charge is intended to provide for repayment of capital and payment of interest primarily by combined payments at monthly intervals. (b) The Borrower will in accordance and consistently with the terms of the Charge (including these Provisions) (i) repay to the Society the real value of the Principal Sum the Capital Indebtedness being adjusted for this purpose by reference to changes in the Index in accordance with Provision 3.'

Those provisions refer to a number of defined terms the meaning of most of which is I think manifest on their face, but the capital indebtedness, I should explain, means the amount from time to time outstanding from the borrower to the society in respect of the principal sum which is the amount advanced, and the reference to the index and provision 3 is a reference to the United Kingdom general index of retail prices or any substitute index. As originally drafted the amount of capital that the borrower would be required to pay would vary according to movements in the index, whether up or down. In circumstances which I shall mention in a moment the society has agreed to include a provision which will limit the downward movement of the amount of the capital to be repaid so that the society should receive back by way of capital not less than what it has advanced.

The defendant is the authorised government department for the purpose of s 17 of the Crown Proceedings Act 1947, and as such the appropriate party in proceedings concerning the Chief Registrar of Friendly Societies. It is the chief registrar's responsibility to oversee building societies. In an earlier case, *Halifax Building Society v Registry of Friendly Societies* [1978] 3 All ER 403, [1978] 1 WLR 1544, the registry was similarly joined where a question as to the validity of what was proposed by certain societies was debated, the registrar then being joined to present arguments in opposition to the plaintiff society. So in front of me today the chief registrar, concerned, as he very properly is, that what is now proposed by the society should not be ultra vires or otherwise offend any provision of the Building Societies Act 1962, has been joined to present argument against what the society proposes. I have been greatly assisted by the presence of counsel appearing for the registry.

Counsel for the registry accepts that what is proposed is not contrary to public policy, but he submits that, having regard to the fact that the society is a statutory corporation and can only do what it is authorised expressly or impliedly by statute to do, and having regard to the provisions of the 1962 Act, it would be ultra vires the society to grant such an index-linked mortgage.

Counsel relies on two provisions of the Act. First, s 1(1):

'The purpose for which a society may be established under this Act is that of raising, by the subscriptions of the members, a stock or fund for making advances to members out of the funds of the society upon security by way of mortgage of freehold or leasehold estate.'

He submits that the society is limited by those words in this way, that the advances which are made must be repaid and in the interim must be secured by way of mortgage. That which must be repaid and must be secured is the initial sum lent. To provide for repayment of, as well as security for, not what is advanced but the real value of the sum advanced is conceptually very different from what is expressly authorised by the statute, and accordingly, he says, the society cannot properly carry out what is proposed. He submits that s 4(1)(g) is entirely consistent with that submission. This provides that the rules of every building society shall set out the manner in which advances are to be made and repaid, the deductions, if any, for premiums and the conditions on which a borrower can redeem the amount due from him before the end of the period for which the advance was made with tables where in the opinion of the central office they are applicable showing the amount due from the borrower after each stipulated payment. The reference to the central office is to the registry, and I am told that no tables have been required in respect of the society. Counsel for the registry points in particular to the reference to the

making and repaying of advances. Rule 31 of the society's rules, he says, is also consistent
a   therewith. This provides, so far as material:

> 'Advances shall be made to members by way of mortgage on freehold and
> leasehold property in such manner and upon such conditions and upon such terms
> as to payment of interest and to repayment of principal whether by monthly or
> other instalments or otherwise as the directors shall determine.'

b   And again he points to the reference to repayment of principal.
        Leading counsel for the society, wearing his advocate's wig rather than his author's
hat, and his junior submit that there is nothing in s 1(1) or in s 4(1)(g) of the 1962 Act
that prevents the society from doing what it proposes to do. Their first submission was
that, following what Browne-Wilkinson J said in the *Multiservice* case, one can treat the
advance and the repayment of the advance as effectively referring to the real value of
c   what is advanced, and there is no inconsistency in the fact that there may be a greater or
lesser sum payable by the borrower.
        Counsel for the registry points out that Browne-Wilkinson J was not concerned in any
way with statutory language but was merely stating his view of the general law. I confess
that at first blush references to repayment seem to me more naturally to be construed as
references to payment back of the sum that has been lent. Under the scheme as originally
d   drafted it was, of course, possible that the principal sum to be paid by the borrower
    would be less in amount than the amount that had been advanced; but, as I have
indicated, the society now undertakes to amend the scheme so as to meet that point.
        If one treats the statutory language literally in the way that I have indicated is my
inclination, the result of the amendment is that the society will be repaid and will have
secured by way of mortgage before it is repaid at least that which it has advanced.
e   If one looks then at s 1(1) on that footing, there is nothing in the wording of that
section that prohibits the society from doing what it proposes to do. The question, I
think, turns on whether the fact that there probably will be additional principal sums
secured by way of mortgage makes the proposed scheme one outside the scope of the
section. The mere fact that there is security for other sums to be paid does not, I think,
mean that the section is not being complied with, nor is it inconsistent with the concept
f   of a mortgage. It is commonplace to provide that interest, for example, will be part of
the security by way of mortgage.
        When I consider the scheme as a whole and I bear in mind what I can only describe as
the very sensible proposals contained therein, I would be loath to find that the scheme
was outside the section. The section refers to security by way of mortgage, thereby
introducing into the section general concepts of the law relating to mortgages. It would
g   be surprising if the society was prevented from doing that which is permissible under
the general law, and, as I have already indicated, the *Multiservice* decision establishes that
there is no objection in principle to the index-linking of mortgages.
        For my part, I cannot see that the additional security and the additional sum probably
to be paid by way of principal under the proposed scheme make the proposed mortgage
so different a creature as to fall outside what the Act contemplates. Section 4(1)(g) merely
h   sets out what it is that rules of building societies must contain. It does not prohibit other
provisions in the rules not inconsistent therewith. For the like reasons to those I have
given in relation to s 1(1), I can see nothing in that provision which prevents a society
from carrying out an index-linked scheme such as is now proposed.
        All this is on the basis that one should be construing the references to advances and
repayments in what might be called a literal manner. I leave, because it is unnecessary in
i   view of the conclusion that I have reached, the question whether those references should
be construed more broadly, consistently with the approach of Browne-Wilkinson J, so
that a reference to the repayment of the advance would include the repayment of the
sums originally advanced but kept to their real value.
        In short, despite the helpful submissions of counsel for the registry, I can see no
objection on the grounds of vires to the legal charge put before me as amended in the

manner that I have indicated. This case cannot, of course, decide anything in relation to other grounds on which a legal charge in this form might be attacked, whether on grounds of unconscionability or otherwise. That must depend on the particular circumstances of a particular case that happens to arise.

I am therefore prepared to grant a declaration on the lines that I have indicated, and I shall discuss with counsel the exact form of that declaration.

Declaration accordingly.

Solicitors: *Church Adams Tatham & Co* (for the society); *Treasury Solicitor.*

Vivian Horvath   Barrister.

Law v National Greyhound Racing Club Ltd

COURT OF APPEAL, CIVIL DIVISION
LAWTON, FOX AND SLADE LJJ
18, 19, 29 JULY 1983

Judicial review – Availability of remedy – Declaration or injunction – Relief sought in action begun by originating summons for declaration or injunction – Suspension of greyhound trainer by stewards controlling greyhound racing – Disciplinary procedure derived from contract between trainer and domestic body controlling greyhound racing – Whether relief by way of judicial review of trainer's suspension available – Supreme Court Act 1981, s 31(1)(2) – RSC Ord 53.

The defendants, a company limited by guarantee, acted as the judicial body for the discipline and conduct of greyhound racing in Great Britain. It licensed greyhound racecourses, racecourse executives, trainers and owners. In order to achieve an orderly and reliable method of conducting racing it promulgated rules of racing and appointed stewards to enforce the rules. All participants in greyhound racing stadiums licensed by the defendants were deemed under those rules to have submitted to the rules and to the defendants' jurisdiction. Following an inquiry the stewards suspended the plaintiff's trainer's licence for six months because he had in his charge a greyhound which had been doped in breach of the rules. The plaintiff issued an originating summons seeking, inter alia, declarations that the stewards' decision was void and ultra vires, in that it was a breach of an implied term of the agreement between the plaintiff and the defendants that all actions taken by the stewards which could deprive the plaintiff of his licence would be reasonable and fair and made on reasonable grounds, and was in restraint of trade and contrary to public policy. The defendants applied to have the claim struck out for want of jurisdiction, contending that it should have been made by way of an application for judicial review under RSC Ord 53[a] and not by way of an originating summons. The judge refused to strike out the claim. The defendants appealed, contending that a complainant who alleged that a domestic tribunal, acting in abuse of its powers, had made a decision adversely affecting a member of the public or the public generally was required by s 31[b] of the Supreme Court Act 1981 to apply for judicial

---

a   Order 53 provides, in r 1(2): 'An application for a declaration or an injunction . . . may be made by way of an application for judicial review, and on such an application the Court may grant the declaration or injunction claimed if it considers that, having regard to—(a) the nature of the matters in respect of which relief may be granted by way of an order of mandamus, prohibition or certiorari, (b) the nature of the persons and bodies against whom relief may be granted by way of such an order, and (c) all the circumstances of the case, it would be just and convenient for the declaration or injunction to be granted on an application for judicial review.'

b   Section 31, so far as material, is set out at p 304 *d e* and p 309 *c*, post

a   review and could not proceed by an action or an originating summons for a declaration
or an injunction.

Held – The jurisdiction which the court had under RSC Ord 53 to grant an injunction
or declaration on an application for judicial review was confined to the review of activities
of a public nature as opposed to those of a purely private or domestic nature and s 31 of
the 1981 Act had not extended that jurisdiction. Although s 31(2) did not explicitly limit
b   the ambit of the grant of an injunction or declaration on an application for judicial
review but merely required the court to issue such relief where it was 'just and
convenient' to do so, s 31 had to be read in the light of s 29(1)^c of that Act, which
restricted the grant of prerogative orders to those cases in which prerogative orders might
have been granted before the 1981 Act, which cases did not include the decisions of
private or domestic tribunals. Since the stewards' authority to suspend the plaintiff's
c   licence derived solely from a contract between him and the defendants there was no
public element in their jurisdiction as such (although the public might be affected) and
therefore their decision was not reviewable by prerogative order. It followed that it was
not open to the plaintiff to seek relief by way of judicial review and, conversely, that it
was open to him to seek a declaration in the ordinary way. The appeal would therefore
be dismissed (see p 303 f to h, p 304 g to p 305 j, p 306 e to p 307 b and h to p 308 a and
d   h j and p 309 a b and h to p 310 e, post).
    R v BBC, ex p Lavelle [1983] 1 All ER 241 approved.

Notes
For judicial remedies in general and for certiorari, injunctions and declaratory judgments
in particular, see 1 Halsbury's Laws (4th edn) paras 80–84, 147–149, 159, 168, 185–186.
e   For the Supreme Court Act 1981, ss 29, 31, see 51 Halsbury's Statutes (3rd edn) 624,
625.

Cases referred to in judgments
Cocks v Thanet DC [1982] 3 All ER 1135, [1983] 2 AC 286, [1982] 2 WLR 1121, HL.
Fisher v National Greyhound Racing Club Ltd [1981] CA Bound Transcript 420.
f   *Herring v Templeman* [1973] 3 All ER 569, CA.
    IRC v National Federation of Self-Employed and Small Businesses Ltd [1981] 2 All ER 93,
        [1982] AC 617, [1981] 2 WLR 722, HL.
    Lee v Showmen's Guild of Great Britain [1952] 1 All ER 1175, [1952] 2 QB 329, CA.
    Nakkuda Ali v M F De S Jayaratne [1951] AC 66, PC.
    O'Reilly v Mackman [1982] 3 All ER 1124, [1983] 2 AC 237, [1982] 3 WLR 1096, HL; *affg*
g   [1982] 3 All ER 680, [1983] AC 237, [1982] 3 WLR 604, CA.
    R v BBC, ex p Lavelle [1983] 1 All ER 241, [1983] 1 WLR 23.
    R v Criminal Injuries Compensation Board, ex p Lain [1967] 2 All ER 770, [1967] 2 QB 864,
        [1967] 3 WLR 348, DC.
    R v Lincoln's Inn Benchers (1825) 4 B & C 855, 107 ER 1277.
    R v Post Office, ex p Byrne [1975] ICR 221, DC.
h   *R v Senate of the University of Aston, ex p Roffey* [1969] 2 All ER 964, [1969] 2 QB 538,
        [1969] 2 WLR 1418, DC.
    Ridge v Baldwin [1963] 2 All ER 66, [1964] AC 40, [1963] 2 WLR 935, HL.

Cases also cited
Currie v Chief Constable of Surrey [1982] 1 All ER 89, [1982] 1 WLR 215.
j   *Nagle v Feilden* [1966] 1 All ER 689, [1966] 2 QB 633, CA.
    R v National Joint Council for the Craft of Dental Technicians (Disputes Committee), ex p Neate
        [1953] 1 All ER 327, [1953] 1 QB 704, DC.
    Russell v Duke of Norfolk [1949] 1 All ER 109, CA.

---

c   Section 29(1) is set out at p 306 f g, post

Interlocutory appeal
The defendants, the National Greyhound Racing Club Ltd, a company limited by   *a*
guarantee, appealed with leave of Robert Goff LJ given on 23 June 1983 against the
judgment of Walton J given on 10 May 1983 whereby he refused to strike out for want
of jurisdiction under the inherent jurisdiction of the court the action of the plaintiff,
Cecil Law, commenced by originating summons dated 11 February 1983, seeking
declarations and other consequential relief arising out of the suspension by the stewards
of his trainer's licence. The facts are set out in the judgment of Lawton LJ.   *b*

Roger Henderson QC and *Adrian Brunner* for the defendants.
Anthony Scrivener QC and *Ian Croxford* for the plaintiff.

Cur adv vult

c

29 July. The following judgments were delivered.

LAWTON LJ. This is an appeal by the defendants, the National Greyhound Racing
Club Ltd, a company limited by guarantee, from the judgment of Walton J given on 10
May 1983, whereby he refused to strike out the plaintiff's claim for want of jurisdiction.
    By an originating summons issued on 11 February 1983 the plaintiff, who trains   *d*
racing greyhounds, asked the court to grant him relief as follows:

> '1. A declaration that the decision made by the Stewards of the Defendants on
> the 9th December 1982 in so far as they purported to suspend the Plaintiff's trainer's
> licence, was void and ultra vires the Stewards' powers, in that the said action
> amounted to a breach of the implied term of the agreement between the Plaintiff   *e*
> and the Defendants, that all actions taken by the Stewards which could deprive the
> Plaintiff of his licence, would be reasonable and fair and made on reasonable
> grounds.
> 2. Further, or in the alternative, a Declaration in the same terms as set out in
> paragraph 1 above, on the grounds that the Stewards' said action was ultra vires and
> void in that it was in unreasonable restraint of trade and contrary to public policy.   *f*
> 3. A Declaration that Rule 174(a)(ii) of the "Rules of Racing" is invalid and of no
> effect, and/or limited by the implied term that it would not be invoked to suspend
> or disqualify a licence-holder without proof of culpability and/or blameworthiness
> on the part of the licence-holder.
> 4. An Order that the suspension of the Plaintiff's licence imposed on the 9th
> December 1982 shall not take effect.   *g*
> 5. Further, and/or in the alternative, if the suspension referred to above shall take
> effect damages in respect thereof for breach of contract and/or interference or
> restraint of trade.
> 6. Further or other relief as may be just.'

    The defendants tried to persuade Walton J that the plaintiff's claim was misconceived
because if he had any valid complaint about the way the stewards had treated him, he   *h*
should have applied for judicial review. They failed. They have tried to persuade this
court that, on the correct construction of s 31 of the Supreme Court Act 1981, when a
domestic tribunal is alleged to have made, in abuse of its powers, a decision which affects
a member of the public or the public generally, the complainant must apply for judicial
review and cannot proceed by way of an action or an originating summons for either a
declaration or an injunction.   *j*
    In a judgment of this court given on 16 October 1981 in a restrictive practices case
unsuccessfully brought against the defendants (see *Fisher v National Greyhound Racing Club
Ltd* [1981] CA Bound Transcript 420), Waller LJ referred to them as follows:

> 'The NGRC [that is the defendants] is a limited company whose objects include

a acting as the judicial body for the discipline and conduct of greyhound racing in England, Wales and Scotland. Also, after consultation with the British Greyhound Racing Board, to frame and amend a code of rules for greyhound racing. Further, to license greyhound race courses, trainers, kennel hands and officials. Also to improve the care and welfare of greyhounds generally. There are 107 greyhound racing stadia in Great Britain, of which 48 are licensed by the NGRC. The remainder are unapproved by the NGRC. A principal objective of the rules of the NGRC is to b achieve an orderly and reliable method of conducting greyhound racing in England, Wales and Scotland. The NGRC licenses, among others, race courses, race course executives, trainers and owners.'

In order to achieve these objects the defendants have issued 'Rules of Racing' and have appointed stewards who have no financial interest in greyhound racing, to enforce them. All who wish to take part in greyhound racing in stadiums licensed by the defendants c are deemed under r 2 to have read the rules and to have submitted themselves to such rules and to the defendants' jurisdiction. Trainers of greyhounds racing at licensed stadiums themselves have to be licensed and if their licences are suspended they cannot act as trainers during the period of suspension.

One of the malpractices with which the stewards have to deal is the doping of greyhounds. The stewards try to stop it. The rules give them wide powers to do so. d Proving that someone has doped a greyhound is difficult. No doubt because of this, the rules empower the stewards to impose penalties, including the suspension of licence, on any licensed trainer who, under r 174(a)(ii):

e 'Has in his charge a greyhound which on examination . . . shows presence in its tissues or body fluids or excreta any quantities of any substance which by its nature could affect the performance of a greyhound or shows evidence in any way of administration for any improper use of such substance the origin of which cannot be traced to normal and ordinary feeding.'

On 9 December 1982 the stewards held an inquiry which the plaintiff attended and decided that he had had in his charge a greyhound which on examination showed presence in its tissues of substances which would affect its performance. They suspended f his trainer's licence for six months. It is this decision which the plaintiff has challenged in his originating summons.

In my judgment, such powers as the stewards had to suspend the plaintiff's licence were derived from a contract between him and the defendants. This was so for all who took part in greyhound racing in stadiums licensed by the defendants. A stewards' inquiry under the defendants' rules of racing concerned only those who voluntarily g submitted themselves to the stewards' jurisdiction. There was no public element in the jurisdiction itself. Its exercise, however, could have consequences from which the public benefited, as for example by the stamping out of malpractices, and from which individuals might have their rights restricted by, for example, being prevented from employing a trainer whose licence had been suspended. Consequences affecting the h public generally can flow from the decisions of many domestic tribunals. In the past the courts have always refused to use the orders of certiorari to review the decisions of domestic tribunals. In R v Criminal Injuries Compensation Board, ex p Lain [1967] 2 All ER 770 at 778, [1967] 2 QB 864 at 882 Lord Parker CJ said:

j 'Private or domestic tribunals have always been outside the scope of certiorari since their authority is derived solely from contract, that is from the agreement of the parties concerned.'

Before the passing of the Supreme Court Act 1981, as I think counsel for the defendants accepted, anyone aggrieved by a decision of a domestic tribunal could only proceed by way of a claim for damages or for relief by way of a declaration or an injunction. The old case of R v Lincoln's Inn Benchers (1825) 4 B & C 855, 107 ER 1277 is no authority to the contrary effect, nor is *R v Senate of the University of Aston, ex p Roffey* [1969] 2 All ER 964, [1969] 2 QB 538, which on the issue of jurisdiction was probably wrongly decided: see *a* *Herring v Templeman* [1973] 3 All ER 569 at 585.

Counsel for the defendants, however, submitted that s 31 of the Supreme Court Act 1981 has given the court jurisdiction to entertain judicial review of the proceedings of a domestic tribunal if, as in this case, those proceedings were likely to have consequences affecting the public generally. It was desirable, he said, that the quick remedy of judicial review should be available. He gave this case as an example. The plaintiff has challenged *b* the right of the stewards to apply r 174(a)(ii). If the plaintiff is allowed to continue with his originating summons, other cases may occur in which the stewards would feel it right to apply r 174(a)(ii) but until judgment in this case is given there will be uncertainty as to their power to do so.

This submission was based on the use of the word 'shall' in s 31(1) and the terms of sub-s (2). Subsection (1) provides that if an application is made to the High Court for a *c* declaration or injunction under sub-s (2) it shall be made in accordance with rules of court by a procedure to be known as an application for judicial review. Subsection (2) provides:

> 'A declaration may be made or an injunction granted under this subsection in any case where an application for judicial review, seeking that relief, has been made and the High Court considers that, having regard to—(a) the nature of the matters in *d* respect of which relief may be granted by orders of mandamus, prohibition or certiorari; (b) the nature of the persons and bodies against whom relief may be granted by such orders; and (c) all the circumstances of the case, it would be just and convenient for the declaration to be made or the injunction to be granted, as the case may be.'

e

The nature of the matters with which the plaintiff's originating summons deals is the alleged abuse of power by the stewards. Abuse of power, submitted counsel for the defendants, was a matter with which prerogative orders dealt. The circumstances of the case involved the public interest because of the need to stamp out malpractices in greyhound racing. Although prerogative orders had not in the past been made against domestic tribunals, in this case 'it would be just and convenient' for the declarations *f* asked for by the plaintiff to be made or refused. Counsel for the defendants saw no difficulty in the fact that when the court had regard to 'the nature of the persons and bodies against whom relief may be granted by orders of mandamus, prohibition or certiorari', it would find that domestic tribunals were not amongst them. All the subsection required the court to do was to have regard to this factor. If, despite its absence, the court was of the opinion that it was just and convenient to make the *g* declaration it could do so.

I cannot accept this submission. The purpose of s 31 is to regulate procedure in relation to judicial reviews, not to extend the jurisdiction of the court. It puts into statutory language, with modifications, what is in RSC Ord 53. That order 'introduced a most beneficent reform in the practice and procedure relating to administrative law': see *The Supreme Court Practice 1982* vol 1, p 865, para 58/1–14/1. It did not purport to enlarge *h* the jurisdiction of the court so as to enable it to review the decisions of domestic tribunals. In *R v BBC, ex p Lavelle* [1983] 1 All ER 241 at 248, [1983] 1 WLR 23 at 30, which was a case in which an employee of the British Broadcasting Corp applied for judicial review and for an order of certiorari under Ord 53, in respect of a decision to dismiss her, Woolf J said:

> 'Rule 1 [of RSC Ord 53] has since received statutory confirmation in almost *j* identical terms in s 31 of the Supreme Court Act 1981. There is nothing in r 1 or s 31 which expressly extends the circumstances in which the prerogative remedies of mandamus, prohibition or certiorari are available. These remedies were not previously available to enforce private rights but were, what could be described as,

public law remedies. They were not appropriate, and in my view remain
inappropriate remedies, for enforcing performance of ordinary obligations owed by
a master to his servant. An application for judicial review has not and should not be
extended to a pure employment situation. Nor does it, in my view, make any
difference that what is sought to be attacked is a decision of a domestic tribunal such
as the series of disciplinary tribunals provided for by the BBC.'

He then referred to what Denning LJ had said in *Lee v Showmen's Guild of Great Britain*
[1952] 1 All ER 1175 at 1183, [1952] 2 QB 329 at 346 and to Lord Parker CJ's judgment
in *R v Criminal Injuries Compensation Board, ex p Lain*. He continued ([1983] 1 All ER 241
at 249, [1983] 1 WLR 23 at 30–31):

'Notwithstanding the present wording of Ord 53, r 1 and s 31 of the 1981 Act,
the position remains the same and, if this application had been confined to an
application for an order of certiorari, in my view there would have been no
jurisdiction to make the order sought. However, in seeking a stay, the applicant is
seeking, in effect, an injunction. The matter was argued before me on the basis that
relief by way of an injunction was being sought on the application for judicial
review. Paragraph (2) of r 1 of Ord 53 does not strictly confine applications for
judicial review to cases where an order for mandamus, prohibition or certiorari
could be granted. It merely requires that the court should have regard to the nature
of the matter in respect of which such relief may be granted. However, although
applications for judicial review are not confined to those cases where relief could be
granted by way of prerogative order, I regard the wording of Ord 53, r 1(2) and sub-
s (2) of s 31 of the 1981 Act as making it clear that the application for judicial review
is confined to reviewing activities of a public nature as opposed to those of a purely
private or domestic character. The disciplinary appeal procedure set up by the BBC
depends purely on the contract of employment between the applicant and the BBC,
and therefore it is a procedure of a purely private or domestic character.'

I agree with Woolf J. Support for what he said is implicit in two decisions of the House
of Lords, namely *O'Reilly v Mackman* [1982] 3 All ER 1124, [1983] 2 AC 237 and *Cocks v
Thanet DC* [1982] 3 All ER 1135, [1983] 2 AC 286.
I would dismiss the appeal.

FOX LJ. Under r 2 of the Rules of Racing established by the National Greyhound Racing
Club Ltd it is provided, inter alia, that—

'every person who is an Owner, Authorised Agent, holder of a Licence or the
holder of a temporary appointment under Rule 104, or who is a subject of Rule
83(v) shall be deemed to have read the Rules of Racing ... and to submit himself/
herself to such Rules and to the jurisdiction of the NGRC ...'

Accordingly, in my view, the authority of the stewards to suspend the licence of the
plaintiff derives wholly from a contract between him and the defendants. I see nothing
to suggest that the defendants have rights or duties relating to members of the public as
such. What the defendants do in relation to the control of greyhound racing may affect
the public, or a section of it, but the defendants' powers in relation to the matters with
which this case is concerned are contractual.
Apart from the alteration of the Rules of the Supreme Court in 1978 and the provisions
of the Supreme Court Act 1981 the prerogative orders would not, in my view, lie to a
tribunal set up by the defendants because the powers of such a tribunal derive from
contract only. I do not think that the authorities leave scope for any real doubt as to that.
In *R v Criminal Injuries Compensation Board, ex p Lain* [1967] 2 QB 864 at 882; cf [1967] 2
All ER 770 at 778 Lord Parker CJ said:

'The only constant limits throughout were that it was performing a public duty.
Private or domestic tribunals have always been outside the scope of certiorari since

their authority is derived solely from contract, that is, from the agreement of the parties concerned.'

In *R v Post Office, ex p Byrne* [1975] ICR 221, where that statement was followed, it was held that certiorari did not lie in respect of a Post Office disciplinary decision as regards an employee because—

'the only legal authority which any Post Office employee superior in rank to the present applicant exercises, or can exercise, in relation to the applicant is an authority which derives exclusively from the contract which the applicant has made with the Post Office, namely, his contract of employment.'

We were referred to *R v Lincoln's Inn Benchers* (1825) 4 B & C 855, 107 ER 1277. If there is anything in that case which is contrary to the rule as recognised in the other authorities to which I have referred it is obiter only.

I come then to the effect produced by the amendments to the rules of court and by the Supreme Court Act 1981.

I take the effect of the present Ord 53 to be as stated by Lord Diplock in *IRC v National Federation of Self-Employed and Small Businesses Ltd* [1981] 2 All ER 93 at 103, [1982] AC 617 at 639:

'In contrast to this, judicial review is a remedy that lies exclusively in public law. In my view the language of r 1(2) and (3) of the new Ord 53 shows an intention that on an application for judicial review the court should have jurisdiction to grant a declaration or an injunction as an alternative to making one of the prerogative orders, whenever in its discretion it thinks that it is just and convenient to do so, and that this jurisdiction should be exercisable in any case in which the applicant would previously have had locus standi to apply for any of the prerogative orders.'

Accordingly, it seems to me that the power under Ord 53 to grant an injunction or to make a declaration is only exercisable in cases where, previously to the change in the rules, the applicant could have obtained a prerogative order, and the opening words of the passage which I have quoted make it clear that the remedy is in the realm of public law only.

I see nothing in the Supreme Court Act 1981 which suggests any parliamentary intention to extend the scope of the prerogative orders. Section 29(1) states:

'The High Court shall have jurisdiction to make orders of mandamus, prohibition and certiorari in those classes of cases in which it had power to do so immediately before the commencement of this Act.'

The jurisdiction, therefore, remains unaltered with the result that certiorari would not lie against the defendants in respect of the stewards' decisions.

It is said, however, on behalf of the plaintiff that s 31(1) of the 1981 Act (which uses the word 'shall') makes it obligatory to apply for judicial review in any case falling within s 31(2) where an injunction or declaration is sought. It is said the public interest in greyhound racing is such that the stewards' decisions have a public impact, that the stewards' authority is quasi-judicial in nature, that if the defendants were, for example, established by royal charter the prerogative orders would lie and that it would be just and convenient to deal with the matter by way of judicial review (bearing in mind, in particular, the need to protect the stewards from unreasonable claims and for speedy decisions). It is, therefore, said that the case comes within s 31(2).

Section 31(2) is not in terms limited to cases where the prerogative orders would, in fact, lie. But Parliament having chosen in s 29(1) to enact that the jurisdiction of the High Court to grant the orders is unaltered, I find it impossible, when one comes to s 31, to suppose that the section was intended to require that applications for injunction or declarations in cases coming within s 31(2) should be made in respect of the review of purely private law matters. It seems to me that it would be a very curious result if the court, being required to have regard to 'the nature of the matters in respect of which

a relief may be granted by orders of mandamus, prohibition or certiorari' should make orders on an application for judicial review in cases where the prerogative orders would not apply at all. I agree with the observations of Woolf J in *R v BBC, ex p Lavelle* [1983] 1 All ER 241, [1983] 1 WLR 23 which are cited by Lawton LJ in his judgment.
I agree that the appeal should be dismissed.

SLADE LJ. I agree that this appeal should be dismissed. The National Greyhound
b Racing Club Ltd (the NGRC) is a company limited by guarantee, incorporated under the Companies Acts 1948–1976. Its objects are set out in its memorandum of association. The first three stated objects reflect a number of its primary activities. It is to act as a 'judicial body' for the discipline and conduct of greyhound racing in England, Wales and Scotland. After consultation and agreement with the British Greyhound Racing Board Ltd (the BGRB), it is to frame, amend and administer a code of rules. It is to license,
c among others, greyhound racecourses, trainers and officials, and, after consultation with the BGRB, to fix and collect fees relating to such licences.
In exercise of these powers the NGRC has promulgated rules of racing, which are intended to apply to holders of its licences, among other persons. The rules are such as to prohibit those persons who train or race under licence from the NGRC from being associated with an unapproved racecourse. We were, I think, told that, while the NGRC
d enjoys no monopoly north of Bedford, all the greyhound racecourses in the south of England hold licences from the NGRC and that every year several millions of persons visit racecourses licensed by it. The senior steward of the NGRC, Major-General J H S Majury, who has acted in this capacity at the inquiries which have led to the plaintiff's suspension as a trainer, has stated in an affidavit that towards the end of 1981 and during the early months of 1982 the incidence of administration of drugs to greyhounds
e increased. He states that this increase was of major concern to him and his fellow stewards as guardians of the integrity of the sport and the interests of the racegoing public.
I do not doubt the genuineness of this concern or the importance to the general public of the activities which the NGRC performs, not least its disciplinary functions. Furthermore, it is easy to understand why the NGRC would prefer that any person who seeks to challenge the exercise of its disciplinary functions should be compelled to do so,
f if at all, by way of an application for judicial review. In this manner the NGRC would enjoy the benefit of what Lord Diplock in *O'Reilly v Mackman* [1982] 3 All ER 1124 at 1131, [1983] 2 AC 237 at 282 described as 'the safeguards imposed in the public interest against groundless, unmeritorious or tardy attacks on the validity of decisions made by public authorities in the field of public law'. Notwithstanding recent procedural changes, these safeguards are still real and substantial. Leave is required to bring proceedings.
g Terms may be imposed as to costs and the giving of security. There is a time-bar of three months, though the court has power for sufficient reason to extend this. The court retains firm control over discovery and cross-examination (see generally *O'Reilly v Mackman* [1982] 3 All ER 680 at 698–699, [1983] 2 AC 237 at 263 per Ackner LJ).
The difficulty, to my mind insuperable, which has faced counsel for the defendants in contending that the process of judicial review is a procedure, and indeed the only
h procedure, available to the plaintiff in the present case is that, as he frankly accepted, the rules of racing of the NGRC and its decision to suspend the plaintiff in purported compliance with those rules have not been made in the field of public law. Furthermore, its authority to perform judicial or quasi-judicial functions in respect of persons holding licences from it is not derived from statute or statutory instrument or from the Crown. It is derived solely from contract. Rule 2 of the NGRC's rules of racing provides that
j every person who is the holder of a licence shall be deemed to have read the rules and to submit himself to them and to the jurisdiction of the NGRC. The relief, by way of declaration and injunction, sought by the plaintiff in his originating summons is correspondingly based primarily and explicitly on alleged breach of contract.
Thus, this is a claim against a body of persons whose status is essentially that of a domestic, as opposed to a public, tribunal, albeit one whose decisions may be of public

concern. Counsel for the defendants has not been able to refer us to any case in which relief, by way of any of the prerogative orders, has ever been granted against any such domestic tribunal. The high-water mark of the authority relied on in support of the proposition that such relief would have been available even before the passing of the Supreme Court Act 1981 was a passage from the judgment of the Privy Council in *Nakkuda Ali v M F De S Jayaratne* [1951] AC 66 at 75 when Lord Radcliffe said:

'In truth, the only relevant criterion by English law is not the general status of the person or body of persons by whom the impugned decision is made but the nature of the process by which he or they are empowered to arrive at their decision. When it is a judicial process or a process analogous to the judicial, certiorari can be granted.'

But those dicta were obiter and were made in the context of a judgment which attempted to draw a distinction (later shown to be erroneous by the decision of the House of Lords in *Ridge v Baldwin* [1963] 2 All ER 66, [1964] AC 40) between decisions that were quasi-judicial and those that were administrative only. They are, I think, of no assistance to the NGRC for present purposes.

The relevant law, as it stood in 1975, is to be found reflected in the decision in *R v Post Office, ex p Byrne* [1975] ICR 221. In that case a Post Office official, acting under the disciplinary procedure of the Post Office, found that a Post Office telephonist had committed an offence against a supervising officer and placed him on a suspended dismissal. The applicant applied for an order of certiorari to quash the decision on the grounds, among others, that the procedure had contravened the Post Office disciplinary rules. The Divisional Court dismissed the application on the grounds that the only legal authority which any Post Office employee superior in rank to the applicant could exercise in relation to him derived exclusively from the contract of employment made by the applicant with the Post Office, and that such authority affected the applicant's rights not qua subject but qua Post Office employee (at 227). Bridge J (at 225), with whose judgment Lord Widgery CJ and Ashworth J agreed, quoted with approval a passage from the judgment of Lord Parker CJ in *R v Criminal Injuries Compensation Board, ex p Lain* [1967] 2 QB 864; cf [1967] 2 All ER 770 at 778 in which, after referring to certain extensions to the ambit of the remedy of certiorari which had occurred over the years, Lord Parker CJ said:

'The only constant limits throughout were that it was performing a public duty. Private or domestic tribunals have always been outside the scope of certiorari since their authority is derived solely from contract, that is, from the agreement of the parties concerned.'

Such, I think, remained the state of the law in January 1978 when the amendments to RSC Ord 53, already referred to by Lawton LJ, came into effect. Lord Diplock described the scope of the amended rule in *IRC v National Federation of Self-Employed and Small Businesses Ltd* [1981] 2 All ER 93 at 103, [1982] AC 617 at 639 in a passage which has already been quoted by Fox LJ. Two points are implicit in this passage. First, on the wording of the new Ord 53, the new jurisdiction to grant a declaration or an injunction on an application for judicial review, as an alternative to making one of the prerogative orders, is exercisable only in a case 'in which the applicant would previously have had locus standi to apply for any of the prerogative orders'. Second, this new jurisdiction is a remedy that still lies exclusively in public law.

Accordingly, in my opinion, it is plain that, apart from any changes in law or procedure which may have been affected by s 31 of the Supreme Court Act 1981, the present is not a case where the process of judicial review would have been open to the plaintiff.

Counsel for the defendants, however, has submitted, as the main feature of his argument, that s 31 makes it not only possible, but obligatory, for the plaintiff to use the process of judicial review for the purpose of seeking the declarations and injunctions which he seeks by his originating summons.

Section 29(1) of the 1981 Act provides:

a
'The High Court shall have jurisdiction to make orders of mandamus, prohibition and certiorari in those classes of cases in which it had power to do so immediately before the commencement of this Act.'

The wording of this subsection, in my opinion, shows that the Act was not intended to extend the jurisdiction of the court to make orders of mandamus, prohibition and certiorari, and I did not understand counsel for the defendants to contend otherwise. I

b
therefore think it clear that the court would not have jurisdiction to make orders of this nature at the suit of the plaintiff in the present case.

Counsel for the defendants, however, pointed out that, omitting immaterial words, s 31(1) of the 1981 Act provides:

c
'An application to the High Court for . . . (b) a declaration or injunction under subsection (2) . . . shall be made in accordance with rules of court by a procedure to be known as an application for judicial review.'

The mandatory word 'shall', which does not appear in the new RSC Ord 53, in his submission, renders it obligatory to apply to the court by way of an application for judicial review in any case where the relief sought is a declaration or injunction falling within sub-s (2). The provisions of sub-s (2) are set out in the judgment of Lawton LJ.

d
In relation to para (a) of that subsection counsel for the defendants submitted that the nature of the matters in respect of which relief might be granted by the three traditional prerogative orders included, inter alia, excess of jurisdiction, abuse of power, misconstruction of a relevant power-giving rule, denial of natural justice and bias. He referred us to certain rules of the NGRC (for example, rr 160(e) and 163) which, he submitted, indicated that their stewards' inquiries had all the hallmarks of a quasi-

e
judicial inquiry. The nature of the plaintiff's complaint, he submitted, is such that proceedings for judicial review would undoubtedly be the appropriate procedure if the NGRC were a body created by statute, or statutory instrument or royal charter. It is important in the public interest that any questioning of the powers of the stewards of the NGRC, or the exercise of such powers, should take place promptly. In all the circumstances of the case, he submitted, justice and convenience requires that the stewards should have

f
the benefit of the protections available to persons and bodies against whom relief is sought by way of judicial review. In his submission such protections ought to be available, provided that the nature of the matter is such that relief might be granted by one of the traditional prerogative orders and all the circumstances render it just and convenient for the declaration sought to be made or the injunction sought to be granted. If this is so, it matters not that the respondent to the application is a person or body against whom relief could not be granted by such traditional orders. Though the court

g
must 'have regard to' the matters mentioned in s 31(2)(b), so it is said, the paragraph does not absolutely preclude the court from granting relief by way of declaration or injunction on an application for judicial review, in an appropriate case, against such a respondent.

I accept that the wording of s 31(2) does not explicitly confine applications for injunctions or declarations by way of judicial review to cases where, on the particular

h
facts, orders for mandamus, prohibition or certiorari could appropriately be granted. Nevertheless, paras (a) and (b) of s 31(2) must, in my opinion, be read together with s 29(1) of the 1981 Act, which restricts the court, in making orders of mandamus, prohibition and certiorari, to 'those classes of cases in which it had power to do so immediately before the commencement of this Act'. It is thus, in my opinion, clear that even since the passing of the Act, on an application for judicial review, the court would

j
have no jurisdiction to make an order in any of these three traditional forms in respect of a private law dispute arising out of a contractual relationship between the NGRC and one of its licence-holders, whether or not the court would have otherwise thought it just and convenient to grant such relief. In these circumstances it would be anomalous in the extreme if the effect of the Act was to confer on the court a new jurisdiction on an application for judicial review to grant an injunction or declaration in respect of a private

law dispute of this nature. I do not think that s 31 compels, or indeed permits, such an interpretation. If the court in such a case were to grant relief by way of declaration or injunction in purported exercise of its powers under s 31(2), it would be acting not so much 'having regard to' the factors mentioned in paras (a) and (b) as in flagrant disregard of such factors.

RSC Ord 53, r 1(2), which uses the permissive word 'may', on the face of it gives (or gave) a litigant the option to seek a declaration or injunction by a process other than an application for judicial review, even in a case which demonstrably falls within the sub-rule. The force of the word 'shall' in s 31(1), in my opinion, is merely to render obligatory the use of the judicial review procedure, in accordance with the rules of court, in any case where relief is sought by way of an order for mandamus, prohibition or certiorari or where a declaration or injunction may *appropriately* be sought under sub-s (2). However, the word 'shall', on which counsel for the defendants relied so strongly in his argument, does not, in my opinion, operate so as to extend the jurisdiction of the court to grant a declaration or injunction by way of judicial review beyond the jurisdiction already enjoyed by it under the new rule. It may, or may not, be desirable that this jurisdiction should be extended so as to cover the quasi-judicial activities of certain domestic tribunals such as the stewards of the NGRC, particularly when a large section of the public are interested in those activities. However, in his very persuasive argument, counsel for the defendants has not persuaded me that this was either the effect or intention of the 1981 Act.

Accordingly, in the present case there is, in my opinion, nothing in RSC Ord 53 or in s 31 to oblige or entitle the plaintiff to proceed against the NGRC by way of application for judicial review. Correspondingly, there is no procedural objection to his seeking the declaration which he seeks under RSC Ord 15, r 16 in the ordinary way. I therefore think that Walton J was right to refuse to strike out his proceedings and I too would dismiss this appeal.

Appeal dismissed. Leave to appeal to House of Lords refused.

Solicitors: *Bristows Cooke & Carpmael* (for the defendants); *Mitchell Williams*, Southend-on-Sea (for the plaintiff).

Mary Rose Plummer   Barrister.

Re Wynn (deceased)
Landolt v Wynn

CHANCERY DIVISION
WARNER J
4, 5, 6, 7, 8 JULY 1983

Will – Construction – Intention of testator – Holograph will providing only for exclusion of testatrix's husband from sharing in estate – Whether husband validly excluded from taking under will and also on resulting intestacy – Whether exclusion of husband operating as gift by implication of husband's share to persons entitled to the estate on the intestacy.

On 9 January 1981 the testatrix, while staying in France, validly executed a holograph will in accordance with French law. In the will the testratrix revoked all previous wills and then made provision to the effect only that she did not wish the defendant, her husband, to share in her estate. The testatrix died soon afterwards leaving property in England, Switzerland and California. The husband was entitled under Californian law to one-third of the property there irrespective of the will and it was also possible that Swiss law would govern the distribution of the remainder of the estate, in which case he would *a* be similarly entitled to a fixed proportion of it. The plaintiffs, who were the testatrix's children by an earlier marriage and were also entitled on intestacy, issued a summons to determine whether, so far as English law was concerned, the will validly precluded the husband from taking an interest in the testatrix's estate. The husband contended that his exclusion under the will was ineffective because there was no indication in the will of a positive intention by the testatrix to benefit her children or alternatively that if he was precluded from taking under the will he was not precluded from taking on the resulting

b intestacy.

Held – On its true construction the will excluded the husband from taking under the will or on the intestacy. Furthermore, the exclusion was valid (subject to the operation of the law of California and of Switzerland so far as each was relevant) and operated as a gift by implication of the husband's share to the other persons interested on the intestacy (see p 314 *j* to p 315 *a*, post).

c Dictum of Stuart V-C in *Lett v Randall* (1855) 3 Sm & G at 89 and *Bund v Green* (1879) 12 Ch D 819 applied.

Per curiam. A direction in a will that one of the testator's next of kin shall not benefit from his estate at all operates as an implied gift to the other next of kin unless there is something in the will to indicate a contrary intention (see p 314 *f g*, post).

d ### Notes

For wills generally, see 17 Halsbury's Laws (4th edn) paras 701–1591.

For intestate succession when named next of kin are excluded, see ibid para 1397, and for cases on the subject, see 24 Digest (Reissue) 758, 766, 8059–8063, 8160.

e ### Cases referred to in judgment

Bund v Green (1879) 12 Ch D 819.
Henchman v A-G (1834) 3 My & K 485, 40 ER 185, LC.
Holmes, Re, Holmes v Holmes (1890) 62 LT 383.
Johnson v Johnson (1841) 4 Beav 318, 49 ER 361.
Lett v Randall (1855) 3 Sm & G 83, 65 ER 572; *on appeal* (1860) 2 De GF & J 388, 45 ER 671, LC.

f *Pickering v Lord Stamford* (1797) 3 Ves 492, 30 ER 1121, LC.
Ramsay v Shelmerdine (1865) LR 1 Eq 129.
Sykes v Sykes (1868) LR 4 Eq 200; *affd* LR 3 Ch App 301, LC.

Action

By a writ dated 31 July 1981 and subsequently amended pursuant to the fiat of Master

g Chamberlain dated 15 July 1982 the plaintiffs, Max Egon Alexis Landolt, Carlo Phillippe Andre Landolt and Christine May Eliane Reuse-Landolt, being the three surviving adult children of the testatrix, Olga Emilie Berthe Wynn deceased, sought as against the first defendant, Thomas George Anthony Wynn, being the testatrix's surviving husband, and the second to fourth defendants, Anne Brown, Stephane Reuse, a minor, and Pascal Arnaud, a minor, being the testatrix's surviving grandchildren, that the court pronounce

h for the force and validity of the testatrix's last will dated 9 January 1981 in solemn form of law. The facts are set out in the judgment.

John L Knox QC and *Paul Teverson* for the plaintiffs.
Edward Evans-Lombe QC and *Edward Davidson* for Mr Wynn.
The second, third and fourth defendants did not appear.

j **WARNER J.** This is a probate action relating to the estate of the late Olga Emilie Berthe Wynn, who died on 21 January 1981 and whom I shall call 'the testatrix'. On the pleadings as they stood when the trial of the action began the issues between the parties were complex. As a result, however, of amendments to the pleadings made during the trial, the issues were narrowed down to two, and those two were such that, if I decided in favour of the plaintiffs on the first, the second would not arise.

Shortly stated, the first issue was whether the effect of the last will of the testatrix was
(so far, at all events, as English law is concerned) to preclude the first defendant, who was   *a*
her third husband, from taking any interest in her estate. The second issue was whether,
if not, he was, in the circumstances, estopped from claiming such an interest. At the end
of the argument on the first issue I was satisfied that I should decide that issue in favour
of the plaintiffs, so that it was unnecessary for me to hear argument on the second issue.

The facts that are or may be relevant on the first issue are not in dispute. The testatrix
was born in Brussels in 1906. Her father, whose surname was Ditmar, was German. So   *b*
the testatrix was born with German nationality as well as Belgian. Her father, however,
died when she was very young. During the 1914–18 war her mother and she fled from
Belgium to England, with the result that the testatrix was largely educated in England
and spoke and wrote both English and French, though neither of them very well.

The testatrix was married three times. She married first, in 1927, one Max Landolt,
who was Swiss. By him she had four children, one of whom died aged three in her   *c*
lifetime. The three who have survived are the plaintiffs in this action. Two of them have
themselves had children, who were the second, third and fourth defendants. As a result,
however, of the amendments to the pleadings, they have gone out of the case and I need
say no more about them. The testatrix's first marriage ended in divorce in 1951. In the
same year (she was then about 45) she married one Jacob Ernst Ringger. I have not been
told his nationality, but he was a rich man. He died in 1970 leaving a substantial fortune   *d*
to the testatrix. There was no child of that marriage. Lastly, on 25 November 1979, the
testatrix married the first defendant, Mr Thomas George Anthony Wynn. He was 48 at
the time. She, of course, was 73 or thereabouts.

I have been supplied with an agreed statement of facts as to the events that followed
the testatrix's marriage to Mr Wynn. On the view that I take of the case, I need not recite
those facts in detail. Suffice it to say that allegations were made against Mr Wynn to the   *e*
effect that he was a confidence trickster who had married the testatrix only in order to
obtain her money for himself, and had in fact set about obtaining it. Those allegations
resulted in criminal proceedings being instituted against Mr Wynn in Switzerland. The
proceedings were dropped after the testatrix's death. I have been shown the Swiss court's
order reciting the reasons why they were dropped.

The testatrix made her last will on 9 January 1981 at a hotel in Lyon, where she and   *f*
Mr Wynn were staying on their way back to England after a short visit to Switzerland. It
is a holograph will, executed in accordance with the law of France. That law provides
that a holograph will is valid if entirely written, dated and signed by the hand of the
testator. No other formality is required. The text of the will, which is very short, is as
follows:

> 'I, Olga Wynn, revoke all previous wills today 9th Jan. 1981. I hereby wish that   *g*
> all I possess is not given to my husband Anthony Wynn.'

It is signed 'Olga Wynn'.

It is common ground that that will was executed by the testatrix in response to an oral
request that Mr Wynn himself made to her at the hotel in Lyon that 'it should be shown
that he would not benefit from her money'. It is also common ground that the will is   *h*
effective to revoke all previous wills of the testatrix and that by the words 'I hereby wish
that all I possess is not given to my husband Anthony Wynn' the testatrix meant 'I hereby
wish that nothing I possess is given to my husband Anthony Wynn'. The dispute is as to
the effect of those words.

It was not in fact open to the testatrix to deprive Mr Wynn of all interest in her estate.
Her estate includes a leasehold flat in Long Beach, California, worth about $US185,000,   *j*
property in England worth about £93,000 and property in Switzerland worth about
£7,000. Under the law of California, Mr Wynn is entitled to a one-third share in the flat
regardless of the provisions of the testatrix's will. There is moreover a doubt whether she
died domiciled in England or in Switzerland. If and to the extent that Swiss law applies
to the devolution of her estate, Mr Wynn is entitled to a life interest in half the estate or,
at his option, to an absolute interest in a quarter of it.

The only other facts that I need mention are that at about the time of her marriage to
a Mr Wynn the testatrix transferred property worth about SF600,000 to a Swiss bank on
terms that she should receive the income of it during her life and that, on her death, the
capital should be divided between the plaintiffs in equal shares. During 1980 she
indicated in a number of wills and other documents that she considered that she had
thereby made adequate provision for the plaintiffs. Counsel for Mr Wynn submitted
that that made it improbable that, when she executed her last will, she intended to
b benefit the plaintiffs.

Counsel for the plaintiffs relies on authorities showing that, where a testator directs
that one or more, but not all, of the persons entitled on his intestacy shall take nothing
under his will or on his intestacy, the direction prima facie constitutes an implied gift to
the other person or persons entitled on intestacy. In *Lett v Randall* (1855) 3 Sm & G 83 at
89, 65 ER 572 at 575–576, Stuart V-C said:

c   'It was asked during the argument in *Pickering* v. *Stamford* ((1797) 3 Ves 492, 30
      ER 1121) whether, supposing the testator annexed a clause of exclusion from any
      further part of his estate to the legacy he gave to each of the next of kin, would that
      have excluded everyone to whom the Statute of Distribution gave the property in
      case of intestacy? The answer must be certainly not if the clause of exclusion extends
      to all the next of kin, for then there could be no one in whose favour the exclusion
d   could operate, and therefore the attempt to exclude being made universal becomes
      nugatory and fails. It would be as nugatory as an universal exclusion of all mankind.
      But although by making the declaration of exclusion from any further share too
      extensive it becomes inoperative; nevertheless, where it has a limited operation, so
      as to give a benefit to other persons, it may unquestionably be valid. There is little
      difference between a declaration by a testator that neither his heir at law nor next of
e   kin shall take any part of his real or personal estate, and a declaration that no human
      being shall ever take or enjoy any part of his real or personal estate. Both are equally
      nugatory and both equally in defiance of the law, because a declaration that none of
      his next of kin shall take any part of his personal estate, nor his heir at law any part
      of his real estate, can never operate by implication so as to give the Crown a right to
      the real or personal estate. For it has been decided, *Attorney-General* v. *Henchman* (3
f   My & K 485, 40 ER 185) that the Crown can never claim by escheat where there is
      an heir at law capable of inheriting, or as to personal estate where there are any next
      of kin. But the exclusion by declaration of one or some only of the next of kin, if it
      be valid, must enure to the benefit of the rest, and has the same effect as a gift by
      implication to them of the share of those who are excluded.'

g That principle was applied by Hall V-C in *Bund v Green* (1879) 12 Ch D 819 and
referred to by Kay J in *Re Holmes* (1890) 62 LT 383. That kind of case is, counsel for the
plaintiffs pointed out, to be distinguished from cases such as *Ramsay v Shelmerdine* (1865)
LR 1 Eq 129, *Sykes v Sykes* (1868) LR 4 Eq 200; *affd* LR 3 Ch App 301, and *Re Holmes*
itself, where the direction is so worded as to preclude the named next of kin from taking
under the will of the testator but not from taking on his intestacy.

h Counsel for Mr Wynn's primary submission was that the present case fell into the
latter category. He stressed the testatrix's use of the word 'given'. That word was
appropriate, he said, in relation to a testamentary disposition but not in relation to a
benefit taken on intestacy. Counsel submitted that *Bund v Green* was distinguishable
because in that case the testator had expressly referred to intestacy. I cannot accept that
submission. The testatrix in this case, by her will, did two things and two things only.
j She revoked all previous wills and she expressed the wish that nothing she possessed
should be given to her husband. The very fact that she revoked all previous wills without
making any fresh disposition of her property entailed that it would devolve as on
intestacy. The exclusion of her husband can only therefore have been meant as an
exclusion from taking on her intestacy. I cannot, in the context, attach to the word
'given' the force that counsel for Mr Wynn claims for it.

Counsel's second submission was that, if his primary submission was wrong, the

testatrix's attempt to exclude Mr Wynn must fail because there was no indication in the
will of a positive intention on her part to benefit the other persons entitled on intestacy, *a*
ie the plaintiffs. There again counsel distinguished *Bund v Green* on the ground that there
the testator had expressly referred to intestacy. In support of this submission counsel
cited *Johnson v Johnson* (1841) 4 Beav 318, 49 ER 361, a decision of Shadwell V-C.
Counsel submitted that in the light of that decision, which was cited in *Lett v Randall*, the dicta of
Stuart V-C in the latter case could only have been intended to distinguish between a case
where a testator sought to exclude all his next of kin from benefit and a case where he *b*
excluded only one or some of them, and could not have been intended to go further and
state as a principle that the exclusion of one or some by itself operated as a gift to the
others. *Johnson v Johnson* is not, however, a satisfactory authority. Only the facts and the
terms of the decree are reported, not the argument nor even the judgment. So one does
not know what the reasons were that led Shadwell V-C to make that decree. The case was
cited in *Bund v Green*, but not referred to by Hall V-C in his judgment. A footnote in *c*
Jarman on Wills (8th edn, 1951) vol 2, p 684 suggests that *Johnson v Johnson*, if it decided
the present point, is not good law. I agree and I think that the law is correctly stated in
the passage on the same page in *Jarman* which reads:

'If a testator declares that his heir-at-law shall not take any part of his real estate,
or that none of his next-of-kin shall take any part of his personal estate, this is
nugatory and void, and cannot operate by implication so as to give the Crown a *d*
right to the real or personal estate. But a declaration excluding one or some only of
the next-of-kin if made in clear and appropriate language, is valid, and operates as a
gift by implication to the rest of the share of those who are excluded.'

On the other hand, I do not think that the effect of the authorities is accurately
reflected in the passage in *Theobald on Wills* (14th edn, 1982) p 784, which reads: *e*

'A direction that one of the testator's next-of-kin shall take no share in his property
will not prevent him from taking his share on an intestacy. But a clause excluding
some of the next-of-kin may be so framed as to amount to a gift by implication to
the others.'

The first sentence there fails to distinguish between a direction that one of the testator's *f*
next of kin shall not take under his will and a direction that that next of kin shall not
benefit from the testator's estate at all, whilst the second sentence suggests, as did counsel
for Mr Wynn's argument, that something more than a direction of the latter kind is
needed for a gift to the other next of kin to be implied. In my view such a direction will
operate as such an implied gift unless there is something in the will to indicate a contrary
intention. I accordingly reject counsel's second submission.

In support of his submissions counsel stressed that, if the effect of the testatrix's will is *g*
as I think it is, she purported to do that which, having regard to the law of California and
possibly also to the law of Switzerland, she could not do; and he invited me to lean in
favour of a construction of her will according to which she thereby did no more than
that which she undoubtedly could do, which was to exclude Mr Wynn from any benefit
under the will itself. One can imagine circumstances in which such an argument would *h*
be attractive. It seems to me, however, that it cannot be a sound argument in the present
case where the will itself makes no disposition whatever of the testatrix's property other
than that which is implied by virtue of the provision excluding Mr Wynn from benefit.

Lastly I should mention that counsel urged me to disregard, in construing the will, the
fact that it was made in response to Mr Wynn's own request in the hotel in Lyon. That,
counsel says, amounted to direct evidence of the testatrix's intention. I have disregarded *j*
that fact, not for the reason suggested by counsel, but because I think that it merely
explains why the testatrix made the will at that hotel in the terms she did, and that it has
no bearing on the question of the effect of the will. Had the fact of Mr Wynn's request
been withheld from me, I would have been left to conjecture as to the testatrix's reasons
for making the will, but it would have made no difference to the result.

I hold therefore that (subject to the operation of the law of California and of the law of
Switzerland so far as each is relevant) the testatrix's will is effective to dispose of the whole

of her estate in favour of the persons other than Mr Wynn entitled thereto on intestacy,
namely, in the events that have occurred, the plaintiffs. I will hear counsel as to the
consequences of that.

[Following submissions by both counsel on costs, Warner J continued:]

The general rule, and I do not think there is any question about that, is that in a
probate action, as in most other cases, costs follow the event. Counsel for Mr Wynn
suggests that I should in this case make an exception in favour of Mr Wynn on the
footing that the litigation was caused by the poor draftsmanship of the testatrix's will. If
that will had been properly drafted, he says, the litigation would never have happened. I
am not sure that that is right having regard to some of the allegations that were made in
the pleadings at earlier stages, but at all events there is this special and even peculiar
feature about the present case, that the will was executed by the testatrix at Mr Wynn's
request in order to bring about the result which I have held it does bring about. In those
circumstances it is difficult to understand why Mr Wynn thought it necessary to have
this litigation at all. I will not speculate as to his reasons. I will simply say that in those
circumstances I do not see why I should make any exception in his favour from the
general rule that costs follow the event.

It follows that I order Mr Wynn to pay the plaintiffs' costs, to indemnify the estate
against the grandchildren's costs and to pay the plaintiffs' costs reserved at interlocutory
stages.

[Following submissions by both counsel on the legal aid position, Warner J continued:]

I am now called on to exercise the discretion which the court has under s 8(1)(e) of the
Legal Aid Act 1974. That means that I must assess 'the amount (if any) which is a
reasonable one' for Mr Wynn to pay 'having regard to all the circumstances, including
the means of all the parties and their conduct in connection with the dispute'. Counsel
for the plaintiffs points out that the interest in the Californian property which Mr Wynn
was given by Californian law as a result of his marriage is in reality part of the testatrix's
estate, which has been put to expense amounting to something between £40,000 and
£50,000 by Mr Wynn's action in contesting these proceedings. Counsel says, not
unreasonably, that every bit of the estate ought to be available towards those costs.

On the other hand counsel for Mr Wynn submits, and I think he is right, that one of
the purposes of the legal aid legislation is to protect poor litigants from the risk of
bankruptcy or penury, and that, on the figures that I have been given, if I strip Mr Wynn
of the entirety of his interest in the Californian property, he will be bankrupt.

The right approach to this, I think, though it is a difficult matter, is to treat Mr Wynn's
assets other than his interest in the Californian property and his liabilities other than his
liabilities to the estate as not to be taken into account for present purposes. It looks as
though his one asset is a Jaguar car worth about £3,000 and his liabilities apart from his
liabilities to the estate amount to £2,870. I am told that he lives on social security, so it
would be reasonable to expect him to sell the Jaguar and pay his other liabilities out of
the proceeds of that.

That leaves the estate's claim against Mr Wynn for £1,800 in respect of the flat in
Torquay, and the question whether I should accede to counsel's submission that I should
do what the Department of Health and Social Security would do, which is to leave Mr
Wynn with something between £2,500 and £4,000. Perhaps I am being over-generous
to Mr Wynn, but, bearing in mind those figures of disposable assets which the DHSS
works on, I propose to say that he may retain the first £3,000 of his share of the proceeds
of the American property, that the next £1,800, or whatever is required, is to be available
to meet the estate's claim in respect of the flat in Torquay, and that over and above that
the proceeds will be available to meet the costs of this action.

Order accordingly.

Solicitors: *Lewis W Taylor & Co* (for the plaintiffs); *Robbins Olivey & Blake Lapthorn* (for Mr
Wynn).

Vivian Horvath   Barrister.

R v Kimber

a

COURT OF APPEAL, CRIMINAL DIVISION
LAWTON LJ, MICHAEL DAVIES AND SHELDON JJ
26 APRIL, 26 MAY 1983

Criminal law – Indecent assault – Consent – Belief of accused – Belief in victim's consent – No
reasonable grounds for belief – Whether belief must be both honest and reasonable – Sexual
Offences Act 1956, s 14(1).

b

The appellant sexually interfered with a woman who was a patient in a mental hospital.
He was charged with indecent assault, contrary to s 14(1)ᵃ of the Sexual Offences Act
1956. His defence at his trial was that he had believed that the woman had consented to
his actions. The evidence did not establish any reasonable grounds for that belief. The
judge directed the jury that the only question in issue was whether in fact the woman
had consented to the appellant's actions and further directed them that the appellant's
belief that she was consenting was not a defence. The appellant was convicted. He
appealed, contending that the issue for the jury was whether he had honestly believed
that the woman had consented to what he did. The Crown conceded that the judge's
direction was wrong but contended that the issue was whether the appellant had
reasonable grounds for believing that the woman had consented.

c

d

Held – Since the prohibited act in an indecent assault on a woman was the use of personal
violence against the woman without her consent, the mens rea of the offence was the
intent to use violence against her without her consent. It followed that the prosecution
had to prove such intent and, conversely, that it was a good defence for the defendant to
show that he had honestly believed that the victim had consented to his actions. On the
facts, the trial judge's direction had been wrong but, since the appellant had had no
reasonable grounds for believing that the woman had consented, a reasonable jury
properly instructed would still have found that the appellant had not honestly believed
that the woman had consented. The appeal would therefore be dismissed (see p 318 g to
j, p 319 a to f and p 320 e to g, post).

e

DPP v Morgan [1975] 2 All ER 347 applied.
Dicta of Hodgson J in *Albert v Lavin* [1981] 1 All ER at 639 and of Hollings J in *R v*
Phekoo [1981] 3 All ER at 93 doubted.

f

Notes
For the offence of indecent assault, see 11 Halsbury's Laws (4th edn) para 1241.
For the Sexual Offences Act 1956, s 14, see 8 Halsbury's Statutes (3rd edn) 425.

g

Cases referred to in judgment
Albert v Lavin [1981] 1 All ER 628, [1982] AC 546, [1981] 2 WLR 1070, DC; *affd on other*
    grounds [1981] 3 All ER 879, [1982] AC 546, [1981] 3 WLR 955, HL.
DPP v Morgan [1975] 2 All ER 347, [1976] AC 182, [1975] 2 WLR 913, HL.
R v Donovan [1934] 2 KB 498, [1934] All ER Rep 207, CCA.
R v May [1912] 3 KB 572, CCA.
R v Phekoo [1981] 3 All ER 84, [1981] 1 WLR 1117, CA.
R v Tolson (1889) 23 QBD 168, [1886–90] All ER Rep 26, CCR.
R v Venna [1975] 3 All ER 788, [1976] QB 421, [1975] 3 WLR 737, CA.

h

Appeal
On 7 April 1982 in the Crown Court at Devizes before Mr Recorder Smyth QC and a

j

---

a Section 14(1), so far as material, provides: 'It is an offence . . . for a person to make an indecent
    assault on a woman.'

jury the appellant, David Kimber, was convicted of indecent assault contrary to s 14 of
the Sexual Offences Act 1956. He was sentenced to six months' imprisonment suspended
for two years and fined £100. With the leave of the single judge he appealed against the
conviction. The grounds of the appeal were that the recorder erred in law (1) in directing
the jury that in a case of indecent assault all that the Crown had to prove was that the
assault was carried out without the complainant's consent and the defendant's view of
whether or not she was consenting, and therefore his honest belief that she was
consenting, were irrelevant and the only question for the jury to decide was whether in
fact the complainant had consented to the assault; and (2) in failing to direct the jury
that, as in rape, account should be taken of the defendant's state of mind, knowledge and
intention when committing the acts complained of and that the Crown was required to
prove an intention by the defendant knowingly to commit the indecent assault without
the complainant's consent and/or in spite of or regardless of the absence of her consent.
The facts are set out in the judgment.

John Isherwood for the appellant.
Nigel Pascoe for the Crown.

Cur adv vult

26 May. The following judgment of the court was delivered.

LAWTON LJ. On 7 April 1982 in the Crown Court at Devizes the appellant was
convicted of an indecent assault on a woman and sentenced to six months' imprisonment
suspended for two years and fined £100. He appeals against his conviction by leave of
the single judge.

The appeal raises these points. First, can a defendant charged with an indecent assault
on a woman raise the defence that he believed she had consented to what he did? The
trial judge, Mr Recorder Smyth QC, ruled that he could not. Second, if he could, did the
jury have to consider merely whether his belief was honestly held or, if it was, did they
have to go on to consider whether it was based on reasonable grounds? Another way of
putting these points is to ask whether the principles on which the House of Lords decided
DPP v Morgan [1975] 2 All ER 347, [1976] AC 182 should be applied to a charge of
indecent assault on a woman.

The victim was a female patient in a mental hospital. Her mental disorder had been
diagnosed as schizophrenia. She was aged 56. We will refer to her as Betty. Although she
was not a defective within the meaning of ss 7 and 45 of the Sexual Offences Act 1956 (as
amended by the Mental Health Act 1959, s 127) she was suffering from a severe degree
of mental disorder. She had been a patient in the mental hospital since 1957. Her
movements and appearance were odd: she made strange movements with her face and
mouth. She tended to give one word answers to questions. She was usually quiet and
withdrawn but could become manic and aggressive without provocation. Most days she
had to be helped to eat and dress. It must have been obvious to anyone of sound mind
meeting her that she was suffering from a severe degree of mental disorder. She had
never been known to take any erotic interest in men or to respond to sexual stimuli. The
hospital doctor in charge of her said that it was highly unlikely that she would be capable
of giving comprehending consent to sexual advances, but she might agree without
understanding the full implications of what she was agreeing to. Her condition was such
that the prosecution did not call her as a witness.

On 1 August 1981 she was walking by herself in the hospital gardens near the cricket
ground when she was approached by the appellant. He had come to the hospital to visit
a relative who was a patient. A ward sister said in evidence that she saw the appellant
talking to Betty. He had his hands cupped. There were coins in them and he went
through the motions of counting them out. The appellant then nodded in the direction
of a lane and walked down it. Betty followed a pace or so behind. Ten minutes later the

ward sister saw her again. She was naked from the waist down, her dress having been
rolled up to her waist. She was screaming loudly and was so distressed that she had to be   *a*
given a tranquilliser injection and put to bed. Her knickers were found later in the lane.
A hospital porter who had been alerted by the ward sister that something untoward
might have happened saw the appellant in the grounds. He stopped him and asked him
if he had been near the cricket ground with a woman. He said he had not. This he
admitted at his trial was a lie. Later the same day he was interviewed by the police. At
first he denied that he had been involved in any incident. Later, according to the police   *b*
witnesses, he admitted trying to have sexual intercourse with Betty but said he had not
succeeded. He told them that she had followed him and 'chucked' her knickers on the
ground and that he had interfered with her in a way which clearly amounted to an
indecent assault if it had been done without her consent. He admitted to them that he
knew she was a patient. He was asked whether she had said anything. He replied: 'No,
she did not. She just started mumbling. I couldn't understand that. She was mumbling   *c*
all the time, really stupid.' Then came these questions and answers:

'Q. You accept that this woman was mentally subnormal? A. Well I should think
so, the way she was mumbling and that.
Q. Did you ask her to have intercourse with you? A. No, I did not.
Q. Why? A. Silly thing to do isn't it, ask a woman for intercourse.'
                                                                                          d
The appellant gave evidence and the substance of what he said was this. When he was
near the cricket ground Betty started to follow him. She had some knickers in her hand
which she threw down. She lay on the ground. She was mumbling. According to the
recorder's note of his evidence he said:

'I was going to have sexual intercourse, but it was too tight so I decided not. I did   *e*
not think about what was in her mind. I knelt between her legs playing with her.
There was no response. She was just lying there mumbling all the time. I never
scratched her . . . I thought she was an unstable woman because she kept mumbling.
As far as I was aware, she knew what was going on. When she lay down, I thought
she was giving consent to have sexual intercourse and so she lay down with her legs
open . . . I do not agree when I heard her mumbling it was clear to me I was trying   *f*
to make love to a sick woman. I was not really interested in Betty's feelings at all.'

At the close of the prosecution's case the recorder ruled that the sole issue for the jury
was whether Betty had given her real and genuine consent. He directed the jury to this
effect. He said:

'It is no defence that the defendant thought or believed Betty was consenting.   *g*
The question is: was she consenting? It does not matter what he thought or
believed.'

Before this court it was accepted by counsel for the Crown that his direction was
wrong. The recorder had not had his attention drawn to *R v Tolson* (1889) 23 QBD 168,
[1886–90] All ER Rep 26. Before us counsel for the Crown submitted that the jury
should have been directed that the appellant had a defence if he had believed that Betty   *h*
was consenting and he had had reasonable grounds for thinking so. On the facts the
appellant could not have had any such grounds with the result that, despite the recorder's
misdirection, there had been no miscarriage of justice. We agree that on the evidence the
appellant had no reasonable grounds for thinking that Betty was consenting and no jury
other than a perverse one could have thought he had. Counsel for the appellant argued,
relying on the decision in *DPP v Morgan*, that the sole issue was whether the appellant   *j*
had honestly believed that Betty was consenting. Unless the jury were sure that he had
not so believed, he was entitled to be acquitted. The grounds for his belief was irrelevant
save in so far as they might have assisted the jury to decide whether he did believe what
he said he did. As this issue was never left to the jury, this court should not apply the
proviso to s 2 of the Criminal Appeal Act 1968.

The offence of indecent assault is now statutory: see s 14 of the Sexual Offences Act
1956. The Crown had to prove that the appellant made an indecent assault on Betty. As
there are no words in the section to indicate that Parliament intended to exclude mens
rea as an element in this offence, it follows that the Crown had to prove that the appellant
intended to commit it. This could not be done without first proving that the appellant
intended to assault Betty. In this context assault clearly includes battery. An assault is an
act by which the defendant intentionally or recklessly causes the complainant to
apprehend immediate, or to sustain, unlawful personal violence: see *R v Venna* [1975] 3
All ER 788 at 793, [1976] QB 421 at 428–429. In this case the appellant by his own
admissions did intentionally lay his hands on Betty. That would not, however, have been
enough to prove the charge. There had to be evidence that the appellant had intended to
do what he did unlawfully. When there is a charge of indecent assault on a woman, the
unlawfulness can be proved, as was sought to be done in *R v Donovan* [1934] 2 KB 498,
[1934] All ER Rep 207, by evidence that the defendant intended to cause bodily harm.
In most cases, however, the prosecution tries to prove that the complainant did not
consent to what was done. The burden of proving lack of consent rests on the prosecution:
see *R v May* [1912] 3 KB 572 at 575 per Lord Alverstone CJ. The consequence is that the
prosecution has to prove that the defendant intended to lay hands on his victim without
her consent. If he did not intend to do this, he is entitled to be found not guilty; and if
he did not so intend because he believed she was consenting, the prosecution will have
failed to prove the charge. It is the defendant's belief, not the grounds on which it was
based, which goes to negative the intent.

In analysing the issue in this way we have followed what was said by the majority in
DPP v Morgan [1975] 2 All ER 347 at 361–362, 382, [1976] AC 182 at 214, 237 per Lord
Hailsham and Lord Fraser. If, as we adjudge, the prohibited act in indecent assault is the
use of personal violence to a woman without her consent, then the guilty state of mind is
the intent to do it without her consent. Then, as in rape at common law, the inexorable
logic, to which Lord Hailsham referred in *Morgan*, takes over and there is no room either
for a 'defence' of honest belief or mistake, or of a 'defence' of honest and reasonable belief
or mistake (see [1975] 2 All ER 347 at 361–362, [1976] AC 182 at 214).

The decision in *Morgan*, probably because of its sordid facts and the improbability of
the defence raised, caused unease amongst lawyers and some members of the public.
Parliament reacted by passing the Sexual Offences (Amendment) Act 1976. The courts
from time to time have shown a propensity to distinguish other offences from the
common law concept of rape so as to avoid having to follow the reasoning in *Morgan*.
This has been described by one academic writer as 'The Retreat from Morgan' (see David
Cowley ([1982] Crim LR 198)). Since each case must be decided after a careful analysis as
to what constituted the prohibited act and what is the nature of the mens rea, if any,
which has to be proved, a detailed consideration of these cases would be obiter for the
purposes of this judgment. In these circumstances we do not intend to adjudge whether
these cases were correctly decided or to attempt to distinguish them from this case. The
application of the *Morgan* principle to offences other than indecent assault on a woman
will have to be considered when such offences come before the courts. We do, however,
think it necessary to consider two of them because of what was said in the judgments.
The first is a decision of the Divisional Court in *Albert v Lavin* [1981] 1 All ER 628, [1982]
AC 546. The offence charged was assaulting a police officer in the execution of his duty,
contrary to s 51 of the Police Act 1964. The defendant, in his defence, contended, inter
alia, that he had not believed the police officer to be such and in consequence had resisted
arrest. His counsel analysed the offence in the same way as we have done and referred to
the reasoning in *Morgan*. Hodgson J, delivering the leading judgment, rejected this
argument and in doing so said ([1981] 1 All ER 628 at 639, [1982] AC 546 at 561–562):

> 'In my judgment counsel's ingenious argument for the appellant fails at an earlier
> stage. It does not seem to me that the element of unlawfulness can properly be
> regarded as part of the definitional element of the offence. In defining a criminal
> offence the word "unlawful" is surely tautologous and can add nothing to its essential

ingredients ... And, no matter how strange it may seem that a defendant charged
with assault can escape conviction if he shows that he mistakenly but unreasonably   *a*
thought his victim was consenting but not if he was in the same state of mind
whether his victim had a right to detain him, that in my judgment is the law.'

We have found difficulty in agreeing with this reasoning, even though the judge
seems to be accepting that belief in consent does entitle a defendant to an acquittal on a
charge of assault. We cannot accept that the word 'unlawful' when used in a definition of
an offence is to be regarded as 'tautologous'. In our judgment the word 'unlawful' does   *b*
import an essential element into the offence. If it were not there, social life would be
unbearable, because every touching would amount to a battery unless there was an
evidential basis for a defence. This case was considered by the House of Lords (see [1981]
3 All ER 879, [1982] AC 546). The appeal was dismissed, but their Lordships declined to
deal with the issue of belief.

In *R v Phekoo* [1981] 3 All ER 84, [1981] 1 WLR 1117 the defendant was charged with   *c*
doing acts calculated to interfere with the peace and comfort of a residential occupier of
premises with intent to cause such person to give up occupation of the premises, contrary
to s 1(3)(*a*) of the Protection from Eviction Act 1977. At his trial the defendant said that
he believed he was evicting squatters. This court adjudged that the offence was not one
of strict liability and that once the issue of belief in the presence of squatters had been
raised the prosecution had to disprove that belief in order to obtain a conviction. That   *d*
would have been enough to dispose of the appeal, but Hollings J giving the judgment of
the court went on, after referring to *DPP v Morgan*, to say, clearly obiter ([1981] 3 All ER
84 at 93, [1981] 1 WLR 1117 at 1127): '... it seems to us clear that this decision was
confined and intended to be confined to the offence of rape.' We do not accept that this
was the intention of their Lordships in *Morgan's* case. Lord Hailsham started his speech
by saying that the issue as to belief was a question of great academic importance in the   *e*
theory of English criminal law.

In our judgment the recorder should have directed the jury that the Crown had to
make them sure that the appellant never had believed that Betty was consenting. As he
did not do so, the jury never considered an important aspect of his defence. But, if he
had directed them as he should have done, could a jury have found him not guilty? We   *f*
have already set out in this judgment the admissions which he is alleged to have made to
the police and relevant parts of his own evidence. In our judgment a reasonable jury
would inevitably have decided that he had no honest belief that Betty was consenting.
His own evidence showed that his attitude to her was one of indifference to her feelings
and wishes. This state of mind is aptly described in the colloquial expression, 'Couldn't
care less.' In law this is recklessness. Had the jury been directed on recklessness we are
sure they would have found that he had acted recklessly. That would have been enough   *g*
to support a conviction of the offence charged. There has been no miscarriage of justice
in this case. The appeal is dismissed.

Appeal dismissed.

Solicitors: *A Hodge & Co*, Devizes (for the appellant); *Goughs*, Calne (for the Crown).

April Weiss   Barrister.

a R v Secretary of State for the Environment,
ex parte Brent London Borough Council
and others

QUEEN'S BENCH DIVISION

b ACKNER LJ AND PHILLIPS J

14, 15, 16, 17, 20, 21, 22, 23, 24, 27, 30 JULY, 21 OCTOBER 1981

Rates – Rate support grant – Reduction – Statutory discretion of Secretary of State to reduce grant – Exercise of discretion – Secretary of State hearing representations from rating authorities before receiving statutory power to reduce their grants – Secretary of State refusing to hear
c *further representations from authorities after receiving power and before exercising his discretion – Secretary of State applying formula contained in order to determine amount of reduction – Whether order valid – Whether decision of Secretary of State valid – Local Government, Planning and Land Act 1980, ss 48, 49, 50 – Rate Support Grant (Principles for Multipliers) Order 1980, art 3, Sch.*

d In 1974 the government introduced, in the Local Government Act 1974, a system for the payment by the Secretary of State of annual rate support grants to local authorities in England and Wales to aid their general expenditure. In 1979 a different government decided to alter the system for the distribution of rate support grants prescribed by the 1974 Act because it was incompatible with its desire to achieve substantial reductions in public expenditure. Pending the introduction of amending legislation, the government
e decided that it would encourage local authorities to economise by laying down a two-year target for expenditure for local authorities and asking them to reduce their expenditure accordingly for the financial years 1979–80 and 1980–81. It informed the authorities that it proposed to introduce a Bill (the Local Government, Planning and Land Bill) which would in 1981–82 substitute a new system for the distribution of rate support grants, namely a single block grant in place of the existing system. The
f government also told the authorities that the Bill would make 'transitional arrangements' for 1980–81, which would foreshadow the principles of the new block grant system as far as possible within the framework of the old system. Under the proposed transitional arrangements the Secretary of State would be given power to reduce the rate support grant payable to an authority under the 1974 Act where the authority's expenditure in that year exceeded a specified level. The Bill was presented to the House of Commons in
g January 1980 and in the ensuing months the government's proposals received wide coverage and were extensively discussed in the press, Parliament and elsewhere. When local authorities submitted budgets for 1980–81 to the Secretary of State he decided that some of them had not reduced their expenditure in accordance with the government's targets. He therefore asked those authorities to submit revised budgets, some of which he still found to be unsatisfactory. After considering further representations from various
h local authorities, he announced on 18 September 1980 that when the transitional arrangements in the Bill were in force he would implement them against those authorities who had blatantly disregarded the government's targets for reduced expenditure unless they could show by then that they had made exceptional efforts to hold down their expenditure in 1980–81 or that they had achieved their two-year target. Some authorities failed to comply with those conditions by the time the Local Government, Planning and
j Land Act 1980 received the royal assent on 13 November 1980. Sections 48 to 50[a] of the 1980 Act, which contained the transitional arrangements, came into operation immediately but the Secretary of State could not exercise his power to reduce the amount of the rate support grant payable to an authority for 1980–81 until the House of Commons approved a 'multipliers order' made by the Secretary of State specifying, in accordance with ss 49(4) and 50(2), the principles for determining the multipliers to be

---

a　Sections 48 to 50, so far as material, are set out at p 330 *e* to p 331 *g*, post

used for calculating the amount of the reduction of the rate support grant. On 16 December a rate support grant increase order, specifying the notional uniform rate for 1980–81, and the Rate Support Grant (Principles for Multipliers) Order 1980 were laid before the House of Commons. Article 3*b* of and the schedule*c* to the multipliers order purported to specify, by means of a formula, the principles on which the multipliers for 1980–81 were to be determined pursuant to ss 49(4) and 50(2). On 18 December those local authorities who were in danger of being subject to a grant reduction were informed that the last day on which they could secure exemption from the application of the transitional arrangements was the day the multipliers order was approved, which would probably be 15 January 1981. On 19 December 1980 the local authorities' association wrote to the Secretary of State asking him to meet the authorities' representatives to discuss the matter. The Secretary of State replied on 9 January 1981 saying that in the short time available before the multipliers order was debated he did not believe that a meeting would have any practical effect. On 15 January the multipliers order and the rate support grant increase order were approved. On 26 January the Secretary of State decided to exercise his discretion under ss 48 to 50 of the 1980 Act to reduce the amount of the rate support grant payable to the applicants, six authorities who had not complied with his conditions for waiving the application of the transitional provisions. The applicants applied for an order of certiorari to quash the Secretary of State's decision on the grounds (i) that the multipliers order was ultra vires and of no effect because it did not specify 'the principles on which the multipliers were to be determined' in accordance with ss 49(4) and 50(2) but merely prescribed how the multipliers were ascertained, and it was unreasonable and capricious in its effect, (ii) that the Secretary of State had misdirected himself as to his obligations under ss 48 to 50 of the 1980 Act because he had considered that he was legally bound to exercise his powers under those sections in accordance with the new block grant system, (iii) that the Secretary of State's decision of 26 January to reduce the amount of the grants payable to the applicants was a decision which no reasonable Secretary of State could have reached, and (iv) that the Secretary of State had not lawfully exercised the discretion conferred on him by ss 48 to 50 because he had refused to hear representations from the applicants after the 1980 Act had been passed and before he exercised his discretion and had instead acted on the basis of a policy formulated prior to the enactment of the Act, with the result that he had fettered his discretion and was in breach of the rules of natural justice by not acting fairly.

Held – (1) The multipliers order was valid and effective from 15 January 1981 because the formula set out in the order disclosed the principles on which the Secretary of State had determined the multipliers to be applied in reducing the amount of the rate support grant payable to those authorities who had not curtailed their expenditure and accordingly the order complied with the requirements of ss 49(4) and 50(2) of the 1980 Act. Furthermore, the applicants had not established that the order was unreasonable and capricious in its effect, nor had the Secretary of State misdirected himself as to his powers under ss 48 to 50, and the policy which the Secretary of State had adopted in the exercise of his powers under ss 48 to 50 was not of itself unreasonable (see p 345 *e* to *j*, p 347 *a* and p 357 *e f*, post).

(2) However, the Secretary of State's decision on 26 January 1981 to reduce the rate support grant payable to the applicants was not a valid exercise of his discretion under ss 48 to 50 of the 1980 Act because having acquired his powers under those sections he had a duty not to fetter his discretion and a duty to act fairly towards authorities likely to be affected before exercising his discretion and he was in breach of those duties by refusing to meet the applicants' representatives and to see whether they had any new suggestions to make about the policy which he had formulated before he made his decision. Accordingly the Secretary of State's decision would be quashed (see p 355 *h* to p 356 *b* and *f g* and p 357 *f*, post); *British Oxygen Co Ltd v Minister of Technology* [1970] 3 All ER 165, *McInnes v Onslow Fane* [1978] 3 All ER 211 and dictum of Templeman LJ in

---

b   Article 3 is set out at p 344 *a b*, post
c   The schedule is set out at p 344 *b* to p 345 *d*, post

a A-G ex rel Tilley v Wandsworth London BC [1981] 1 All ER at 1170–1171 applied; Sagnata
Investments Ltd v Norwich Corp [1971] 2 All ER 1441 considered.

Notes
For rate support grants, see 28 Halsbury's Laws (4th edn) paras 1262–1271.
   For the Local Government, Planning and Land Act 1980, ss 48, 49, 50, see 50(2)
Halsbury's Statutes (3rd edn) 1345, 1346.

b
Cases referred to in judgment
A-G ex rel Tilley v Wandsworth London BC [1981] 1 All ER 1162, [1981] 1 WLR 854, CA.
A-G for Canada v Hallett & Carey Ltd [1952] AC 427, PC.
Associated Provincial Picture Houses Ltd v Wednesbury Corp [1947] 2 All ER 680, [1948] 1
   KB 223, CA.
c British Oxygen Co Ltd v Minister of Technology [1970] 3 All ER 165, [1971] AC 610, [1970]
   3 WLR 488, HL.
Carltona Ltd v Comr of Works [1943] 2 All ER 560.
General Medical Council v Spackman [1943] 2 All ER 337, [1943] AC 627, HL.
John v Rees [1969] 2 All ER 274, [1970] Ch 345, [1969] 2 WLR 1294.
McEldowney v Forde [1969] 2 All ER 1039, [1971] AC 632, [1969] 3 WLR 179, HL.
d McInnes v Onslow Fane [1978] 3 All ER 211, [1978] 1 WLR 1520.
R v Gaming Board for Great Britain, ex p Benaim [1970] 2 All ER 528, [1970] 2 QB 417,
   [1970] 2 WLR 1009, CA.
R v Port of London Authority, ex p Kynoch Ltd [1919] 1 KB 176, CA.
Ridge v Baldwin [1963] 2 All ER 66, [1964] AC 40, [1963] 2 WLR 935, HL.
Sagnata Investments Ltd v Norwich Corp [1971] 2 All ER 1441, [1971] 2 QB 614, [1971] 3
   WLR 133, CA.
e Smith v Inner London Education Authority [1978] 1 All ER 411, CA.
W (an infant), Re [1971] 2 All ER 49, [1971] AC 682, [1971] 2 WLR 1011, HL.

Cases also cited
A-G v Ryan [1980] AC 718, PC.
f Anisminic Ltd v Foreign Compensation Commission [1969] 1 All ER 208, [1969] 2 AC 147,
   HL.
Annamunthodo v Oilfield Workers' Trade Union [1961] 3 All ER 621, [1961] AC 945, PC.
Essex CC v Ministry of Housing and Local Government (1967) 66 LGR 23.
Franklin v Minister of Town and Country Planning [1947] 1 All ER 612, [1948] AC 87, CA.
George v Secretary of State for the Environment (1979) 38 P & CR 609, CA.
g Glynn v Keele University [1971] 2 All ER 89, [1971] 1 WLR 487.
Hoffman-La Roche (F) & Co AG v Secretary of State for Trade and Industry [1974] 2 All ER
   1128, [1975] AC 295, HL.
Inglis v Robertson [1898] AC 616, HL.
Johnson (B) & Co (Builders) Ltd v Minister of Health [1947] 2 All ER 395, CA.
K (H) (an infant), Re [1967] 1 All ER 226, [1967] 2 QB 617, DC.
h Kruse v Johnson [1898] 2 QB 91, DC.
Liverpool Taxi Owners' Association, Re [1972] 2 All ER 589, [1972] 2 QB 299, CA.
M'Creagh v Frearson [1922] WN 37, DC.
Milford Haven Conservancy Board v IRC [1976] 3 All ER 263, [1976] 1 WLR 817, CA.
Padfield v Minister of Agriculture, Fisheries and Food [1968] 1 All ER 694, [1968] AC 997,
   HL.
j R v Barnsley Metropolitan BC, ex p Hook [1976] 3 All ER 452, [1976] 1 WLR 1052, CA.
R v Secretary of State for the Environment, ex p Stewart (1979) 39 P & CR 534.
R v Stafford Justices, ex p Stafford Corp [1940] 2 KB 33, CA.
Secretary of State for Education and Science v Tameside Metropolitan BC [1976] 3 All ER 665,
   [1977] AC 1014, HL.
Steeples v Derbyshire CC (10 February 1981, unreported), QBD.
Stringer v Minister of Housing and Local Government [1971] 1 All ER 65, [1970] 1 WLR
   1281.

Application for judicial review
The London boroughs of Brent, Camden, Hackney, Hounslow, Tower Hamlets and
Walton Forest, applied, with the leave of Forbes J granted on 17 February 1981, for (i) an
order of certiorari to quash a decision of the respondent, the Secretary of State for the
Environment, dated 26 January 1981, to reduce the amount of the rate support grant
payable to each of them for the year 1980–81, (ii) alternatively, if the decision of the
Secretary of State was invalid, a declaration that the Rate Support Grant (Principles of
Multipliers) Order 1980, SI 1980/2047 (the multipliers order) did not constitute a decision
to reduce and/or vary the amount of the rate support grant, (iii) a declaration that the
multipliers order was ultra vires and of no effect, (iv) a declaration of the rights of the
parties in lieu of an injunction restraining the Secretary of State from causing the amount
of the rate support grant otherwise payable to each of the applicants to be reduced or
varied otherwise than pursuant to a decision according to law and in any event not before
any order under ss 49(4) and 50(2) of the Local Government, Planning and Land Act
1980 had effect. The facts are set out in the judgment of the court.

Roger Henderson QC, Charles George and *Jeffrey Jowell* for the applicants.
Robert Alexander QC, Simon D Brown and *Paul Walker* for the Secretary of State.

Cur adv vult

21 October. The following judgment of the court was delivered.

ACKNER LJ.

Nature of the application
    The applicants, who are six London boroughs, the London boroughs of Brent, Camden,
Hackney, Hounslow, Tower Hamlets and Waltham Forest, apply for orders of certiorari
to quash the decisions made in January 1981 by the Secretary of State for the Environment
reducing the amount of rate support grant payable to those six boroughs for the year
1980–81.
    The grounds on which the relief is sought are set out extensively in the applicants'
amended grounds and, although they overlap to a large extent, they can be conveniently
summarised under four headings. (1) The Rate Support Grant (Principles for Multipliers)
Order 1980, SI 1980/2047 (the multipliers order), which provided the formula for
reducing the rate support grant was ultra vires. (2) The Secretary of State misdirected
himself in law as to his obligations under ss 48 to 50 of the Local Government, Planning
and Land Act 1980. (3) The decisions of the Secretary of State were decisions to which no
reasonable Secretary of State could have come. (4) Prior to the enactment of the 1980 Act
on 13 November, which gave the discretionary power to reduce the rate support grant,
the Secretary of State had already formulated a policy to reduce the amounts of rates
support grant by the application of a fixed formula, subject to a power of waiver if certain
conditions were satisfied, and following the enactment and prior to the exercise of his
discretion he refused to listen to representations which the applicants wished to make,
thereby fettering his discretion and acting in breach of the rules of natural justice.

Rate support grants
    The rate support grant system is a complex one and a simple account is not possible.
While anxious to avoid a thesis on this subject, there is no escape from a somewhat
lengthy exposition on a subject which few will find riveting.
    There are two types of government grants paid to local authorities. Firstly, there are
specific and supplementary grants, which are paid in support of specific services such as
police and transport. Secondly, there are rate support grants which are paid to local
authorities in aid of their expenditure generally and are not earmarked for any particular
service. Until 1958 a much higher proportion of grants was paid in the form of specific

grants. This gave central government considerable influence over the amount of revenue
a resources which local authorities allocated to the individual services they provided. In
1958 there was a marked shift towards the general rate support grants which local
authorities may allocate between services at their own discretion. Approximately 15%
only of government grants is now accounted for by specific and supplementary grants
and 85% by rate support grants. There thus has been coined the somewhat emotionally
toned phrase 'the sanctity of local authority independence'. This is a misleading phrase,
b since although central government is not able to dictate how much or in what manner
local authorities spend, local authorities are heavily dependent on central government
for over 50% of their funds. Thus, indirectly, central government can and does exert
control to some extent over the total of local authority expenditure through the medium
of limiting rate support grants.

It has not been challenged that expenditure by local authorities is a very significant
c part of the national economy. In total, their estimated current and capital expenditure in
1980–81 amounted to about 25% of all public expenditure. In 1980–81 estimated central
government expenditure amounted to over £58,000m, the largest components of which
were £20,000m on social security payments, nearly £10,000m on defence and nearly
£8,000m on health services. Thus the total of planned local authority expenditure in the
United Kingdom in 1980–81 was approaching £20,000m, more than the defence and
d health budgets put together. After taking account of income from fees and charges for
services provided, about 60% of local government revenue expenditure has in recent
years been met by government grants, the most important being the rate support grant.
The remainder is met by rates.

The system
e With the reorganisation of local government in 1974, the Local Government Act 1974
introduced the system of rate support grants, which the Secretary of State is required
each year to make towards the relevant expenditure of local authorities in England and
Wales. For the purpose of fixing the estimated aggregate amount of the rate support
grant for any year, the Secretary of State determines the aggregate amount of exchequer
grants available for payment to local authorities in respect of their relevant expenditure
for the year, that is virtually all expenditure chargeable against the rate levy. From these
f total exchequer grants the Secretary of State must deduct the portions to be applied in
transport, supplementary grant and national parks supplementary grant, both of which
are prescribed in the rate support grant order which the Secretary of State must make
each year. He must also deduct the estimated total of the specific grants in aid of revenue
expenditure of certain services for which such specific grants are payable. The resulting
balance of exchequer grants is the estimated aggregate of the rate support grants.
g Before determining the amount available for grants, and the portions of that amount
to be allocated to supplementary and specific grants, the Secretary of State must consult
with such associations of local authorities as appear to him to be concerned and with any
local authority with which consultation appears to him to be desirable and must take
into account certain matters, such as the latest information available to him as to the rate
h of relevant expenditure, fluctuations in the demand for services, the need for developing
those services, current prices, costs and remuneration.

The Secretary of State must divide the aggregate amount of the rate support grant into
three elements, namely:

1. *The needs element*
j This is the portion of the total rate support grant as is prescribed by the order and
which equates to the Secretary of State's assessment of the needs of a local authority. The
assessment of the expenditure needs is based on the statistical technique known as
'multiple regression analysis' involving the computer-based comparison of the incidence
of a series of social and economic indicators and their cash effect on authorities'
expenditure.

The factors are chosen by the Secretary of State in the annual rate support grant order, together with a multiplier which determines for each authority the amount it is entitled *a* to receive for each factor which applies to that authority. In order to ensure common and uniform methods of calculation for each authority the incidence, in relation to that authority, of the prescribed factors of need, the Secretary of State makes regulations defining the method of calculation. The aim of the needs element formula is to reduce the cost of providing a standard level of service in each local authority to a standard amount per head. To define by objective factors an authority's need to incur expenditure *b* is a difficult task. Past expenditure has been taken as the best indicator of need. This formula approach to expenditure need assessment through the multiple regression analysis will have to be further referred to in more detail later. It is an important factor in the Secretary of State's case that he acted reasonably.

In effect the needs element was distributed in such a way as to compensate local authorities fully for differences in their assessed spending needs, expressed in terms of *c* pounds per head of population. Thus each authority with assessed spending needs above that of the authority with the lowest spending need per head of population (the minimum need authority), received a sufficient grant to bring its assessed expenditure need per head down to the level of the minimum need authority. Distribution on this basis exhausted about half the needs element; the rest was distributed amongst the authorities pro rata to their population, which further reduced by an equal amount per *d* head that which the local authorities had to raise from rate income and other sources to finance their expenditure.

In London a separate formula based on the same principles was used to calculate needs assessment, because of its special structure of local government. Needs element was paid to non-metropolitan counties (with some reallocation to their constituent districts in recent years), metropolitan districts and London boroughs.

e

2. *The resources element*

This represents that element of grant which is paid to an authority whose rateable value per head of the population is less than the 'national standard rateable' value per head of population. The government, in effect, comes in as an additional notional ratepayer to each rating authority paying the rate levied on the deficiency in its actual *f* rateable value below the national standard. This national standard is prescribed annually by the Secretary of State.

3. *The domestic element*

This is the prescribed amount by which the rate poundage in respect of residential property is reduced and compensated for by grant.

g

The Secretary of State has power to make *increase orders* if it appears to him, after the time when the amount available for grants was determined for any year, that the relevant expenditure for local authorities for that year has been or is likely to be substantially increased by reason of an increase which has taken place in the level of prices, costs or remuneration, or the coming into operation of a provision of an enactment passed after the 1974 Act.

h

The national standard rateable value (see resources element above) is prescribed by the Secretary of State at such level as it is estimated will exhaust the total resources element provision in the rate support grants. In 1980–81 the prescribed figure was £178 per head of population. Since rateable values in London, particularly in central inner London, are high, all the applicants, with the exception of Waltham Forest, received the resources element. In 1980–81 37 out of 403 rating authorities in England and Wales had rateable *j* values per head above the national standard.

Rate support grants orders and regulations

In the course of referring to the system, mention has been made of orders and regulations. The estimated annual aggregate of the rate support grants and other matters

to be prescribed are required to be fixed and prescribed by an order, called a 'rate support
a grant order', made by the Secretary of State with Treasury consent, as a separate support
grant order in each year. Together with such order there must be laid before the House
of Commons a report of the considerations leading to the determination of the amount
available for grants and the portions to be deducted in arriving at the rate support grant
aggregate. The Secretary of State is empowered to make regulations to carry into effect
the provisions for rate support grants. He may, in particular, make provision for
b determining the manner in which the calculations or estimates are to be made. Before
making such regulations the Secretary of State must consult with such associations of
local authorities as appear to him to be concerned, and with any local authority with
which consultation appears to him to be desirable. His power to make such regulations
must be exercised by statutory instrument which is subject to annulment in pursuance
of a resolution of either House of Parliament.

c
Defects in the rate support grant system 1974–1980
   Apart from its cumbersome and complex nature there were two matters in particular
which motivated the Secretary of State to produce a new system. These were as follows.
(i) The formula used to assess authorities' expenditure needs was derived from an analysis
of actual *past* expenditure. This was seen as importing an element of self-fulfilling
d prophecy into the assessments. Authorities with similar characteristics and similar high
spending could, if they all decided to maintain or increase their levels, influence the
needs assessments and thereby receive more grant. (ii) The resources element, by
underwriting a given level of rateable value (the national standard) for any level of
spending provided a constant rate of grant support for *all* levels of spending. Since the
total amount of resources element was fixed, the extra grant attracted at the constant rate
e by high-spending authorities was at the direct expense of other authorities who restrained
their expenditure (see the first affidavit of Mr Heiser, then Deputy Secretary, Department
of the Environment, para 35 and para 29 of the statement made by the Secretary of State
on 16 November 1979).
   The present government regarded a grant distribution system with these features as
intrinsically inequitable and in particular as incompatible with its commitment to
f achieving substantial and sustained reductions in public expenditure. Whilst the rate
support grant mechanism enabled central government to influence total local expenditure,
it only did so in a non-selective, across-the-board way. Therefore, shortly after taking
office in 1979 it began to consider changes to the rate support grant system arrangements
in order to remove what it regarded as an incentive to spending, and instead sought to
provide authorities with an incentive for economy. The action it took will be considered
g in detail later. It is accepted that, although the needs assessment deficiency could have
been resolved within the existing grant framework, the defects in the distribution of the
resources element and concern about the inadequacies and complexity of the grant
system generally pointed towards changes in the structure of the grant system as a whole.
   The combined effect of the needs and resources element was that, if *all* authorities
spent in line with their spending needs, as assessed on the formula basis described above,
h they were meeting the same amount of expenditure per head from the same rateable
value per head (apart from those above the national standard) and could thus levy the
same rate in the pound (leaving aside any rating effect for changes in reserves) throughout
England and Wales. The rate poundage for spending at this level was termed the 'notional
uniform rate'. It is and was the Secretary of State's view that this principle was always
implicit in the rates support grant system under the 1974 Act and, as the concept of the
'notional uniform rate' formed an important part in the arrangements which he desired
j to operate before the new system came into force, the term was defined in s 48(2) of the
1980 Act.
   An essential element in the calculation of the notional uniform rate was the concept of
the national standard rateable value, referred to above, and which ensured that the rate
poundage cost of a given increment of expenditure was the same for all authorities

eligible for resources element. In 1980–81 the national standard of £178 per head meant that the additional cost on the rate of each £1 per head of expenditure for all authorities entitled to resources element was 56p (ie £1 or 100p divided by £178) at all levels of expenditure. This meant that authorities spending at comparable levels (in terms of pound per head of population) in relation to their assessed spending needs would need, other things being equal, to levy at the same rate in the pound. The relevance of this in regard to the interim arrangements prior to the implementation of the new block grant system will shortly become apparent.

New block grant system

It was the government's intention to bring this system into operation for the year 1981–82. The steps it took to announce that intention and to consider objections will be considered in detail later. However, in order to provide flexibility, should this be necessary, the 1980 Act provided for the new system to come into force for the 'commencing year' and each subsequent year. The 'commencing year' was defined as such year as the Secretary of State may by order made by statutory instrument appoint (see s 53(9)). The new system was in no way designed to interfere with the local authorities' autonomy to determine the pattern and level of their own expenditure. It was only in the area of *grant distribution* that the Secretary of State sought changes to the rate support grant system. To meet the two criticisms referred to above, the two elements, the needs element and the resources element, were to be replaced by a single grant, the block grant. Thus there were to be only two components of rates support grant, the domestic rate relief grant (equivalent to the former domestic element) and the block grant.

The block grant has two separate objectives. These are:

1. *An equalisation objective*

This is to enable all authorities to levy similar rate poundages (the amount in pence by which the rateable value of a property is multiplied to produce the amount of rates payable by a ratepayer) for similar standards of service. This was broadly the combined effect of the needs and resources element achieved through the assessment of spending need for each area and the setting of a national standard rateable value to which all authorities' rateable resources were raised.

2. *The discouragement of high spending*

This is to be achieved by tapering or reducing gradually grant supports for those authorities whose expenditure exceeds a predetermined level which is different for each authority. This represents an innovation and was the government's main reason for the changes in the grant system associated with block grant. The national total of rates support grant is calculated as before. A total of relevant expenditure is determined annually and the total of exchequer assistance derived as a percentage of this sum. Out of this total of grant there is allocated, first, specific and supplementary grants and then domestic rate relief grant, so that the residual amount will be available for distribution as a block grant. The block grant is subject to a cash limit. This method of calculating the block grant is no different from the derivation of the total available needs and resources elements under the previous grant system. However, the *individual* authority's block grant entitlement is calculated as the difference between the authority's total expenditure and the amount which it is deemed to be able to raise from rates to finance that level of spending. Each authority has a centrally determined assessment of its costs in providing normal average standards of service after taking account of its own particular circumstances. This grant-related expenditure (GRE) level is a figure unique to each authority. Although it is intended to reflect the cost of comparable levels of service, it is not intended to be a prescribed level of spending since authorities are free to determine expenditure appropriate to their own view of local conditions in the light of national economic circumstances. For grant purposes, the importance of the central assessment of a GRE is twofold for each authority. It allows government to determine a point beyond which the rate grant is tapered, that is reduced, and it provides the link to grant-related poundage schedules.

The tapering mechanism
As stated above, the major innovation with block grant is the tapering of grant support for additional expenditure above a predetermined level. This may mean that grant b entitlement increases at a *lower rate* for additional expenditure, or that total grant falls as expenditure increases. It was, however, considered that in practice, centrally assessed expenditure levels could not be regarded as a perfect measure of comparable service standards and for that reason alone the grant taper could not reasonably be introduced immediately expenditure exceeded GRE. Therefore, a *threshold* is set at a level of expenditure above GRE, beyond which the grant-related poundage increases at a faster c rate. This has the effect of increasing the amount of the deemed income from rates in the grant calculation and thus reducing the block grant entitlement from what it would have been without the grant taper. It is this part of the block grant system which is designed to achieve the second objective of providing a disincentive to high spending, since it requires a higher contribution from the local ratepayer to increased expenditure above the threshold.

d
The modification of the rates support grants system under the 1974 Act
The new system of rate support grants, the block grant system, is provided for by ss 53 ff, and was to be brought into effect as soon as the Secretary of State appointed 'the commencing year', which it was his manifest intention to do for the year 1981–82. To provide for the interim, amendments to the existing system of rate support grants were e made by ss 48 to 52 inclusive. These have been referred to as 'transitional arrangements'. Counsel for the applicants has criticised this description of these sections, largely because they are not thus entitled. As we state in more detail hereafter when considering whether the Secretary of State misdirected himself as to his obligations under those sections, we cannot accept this criticism. There clearly was to be an interim period, be it for the year 1980 81 or longer, depending on whether the Secretary of State's intentions were carried f into effect in accordance with the programme which he intended to follow. The 1980 Act therefore contemplated a period of transition before the new system became operative. Moreover, it is plain that Parliament intended the power to be available to be used in respect of a period which was partly completed. The Secretary of State, as a matter of policy, decided that the modification to the 1974 Act should foreshadow as closely as possible the new block grant system. To achieve this he decided that the transitional g arrangements should enable him to reduce the grant paid to authorities whose expenditure exceeded their assessed expenditure needs and that the reduction in grant should, where possible, take the form of a reduction in the rate of resources element support, since entitlement to this part of the grant was related to expenditure.
The notional uniform rate represented the rate which could be levied, taking grant payments into account, if authorities spent in line with their assessed expenditure needs. h The national standard rateable value meant that the rate poundage cost of equal levels of expenditure in relation to assessed expenditure need was, other things being equal, the same for all authorities eligible for resources element. Thus, a comparison between an authority's *actual* uniform rate, the average rate levy required to be raised to meet a particular authority's *notional* rate-borne expenditure and the uniform rate, would indicate the relationship between actual expenditure and assessed expenditure need for j authorities in that area. A uniform rate above the notional uniform rate would mean expenditure in excess of assessed expenditure need and vice versa. However, as Mr Heiser points out in his first affidavit, the comparison between actual uniform rates and the notional uniform rate as a proxy for a comparison between expenditure and assessed expenditure needs, could not be made in the first instance for *London authorities* with rateable values above the national standard. This was principally because they retained a

substantial proportion of their rateable value excess over the national standard and thus, for a comparable level of expenditure, could levy a lower rate in the pound than authorities whose expenditure was enhanced only to the level of the national standard rateable value. In order to obtain a true comparison with the notional uniform rate for such authorities, it was necessary to recalculate their uniform rates as if their rateable value was equivalent only to the level of the national standard. Thus, their actual uniform rate was required to be an *adjusted rate*.

In order to make the abatement of grant calculated under the transitional arrangements consistent with the block grant system it was thus provided that equal degrees of expenditure in excess of authorities' assessed expenditure needs, as measured by the amount by which authorities' uniform rates exceeded the notional uniform rate, should incur equal reductions in grant, expressed in terms of a rate poundage equivalent, ie a grant reduction corresponding to the amount which would be raised in each authority concerned by a given penny rate. This corresponded with the way in which the block grant system would work, whereby the rate of grant support for high-spending authorities was to be reduced in a way which would increase the cost of their spending by equal rate poundage amounts.

A further consideration regarding London authorities with rateable values above the national standard rateable value was that they were not entitled to receive resources element and could not therefore be subject to an abatement of that part of the grant. For this reason the modification to the 1974 Act included a comparable power to abate the *needs* element of London authorities with rateable values above the national standard.

Thus, the transitional arrangements represented a foreshadowing of the mechanical principles of block grant as far as could be achieved *within the framework of the old rate support grant system*, of which the then prevailing needs assessment was an integral part.

It is now convenient to set out in extenso ss 48 to 50 of the 1980 Act:

'PART VI
RATE SUPPORT GRANT
Amendments relating to existing system of rate support grants

'**48.**—(1) The Secretary of State may reduce the amount of rate support grant payable to a local authority for the year 1980–81 and any subsequent year before the commencing year if the uniform rate for that authority's area in that year exceeds the notional uniform rate.

(2) In this section—"notional uniform rate" means the rate which, having regard to payments of the needs element of rate support grant and the prescribed national standard rateable value per head of population, the Secretary of State considers that each rating authority in England and Wales would need to levy in order to finance the spending needs of the authority and of all authorities with power to issue precepts to the authority; and "uniform rate"—(a) in relation to authorities outside Greater London, has the meaning assigned to it for the purposes of sub-paragraph (1) of paragraph 10 of Schedule 2 to the Local Government Act 1974 by sub-paragraph (3) of that paragraph; and (b) in relation to authorities in Greater London, has that meaning subject to any adjustment of the amount made by the Secretary of State.

(3) A report under section 3(3) of the Local Government Act 1974 (reports on rate support grant orders) shall specify the amount of the notional uniform rate.

(4) The notional uniform rate for the year 1980–81 shall be of such an amount as is specified in the report for that year under section 3(3) of the Local Government Act 1974.

(5) A report under section 4(2) of that Act (reports on redetermination) shall specify the principles on which the Secretary of State has made any adjustment of the uniform rates of authorities in Greater London.

(6) Where the Secretary of State makes any such adjustment, he shall apply the same principles in making it to all authorities in Greater London.

a

(7) Any expression used in this section or in section 49 or 50 below and to which a meaning is assigned by the Local Government Act 1974 has that meaning for the purposes of those sections.

49.—(1) In any case where the Secretary of State makes an order under section 4 of the Local Government Act 1974 (orders varying rate support grant orders) he may make a fresh determination of the amount of the resources element of rate support grant payable to a local authority for the year to which the order relates as provided in this section.

b

(2) A determination under this section shall be made by multiplying the uniform rate for the area of a local authority by a multiplier of an amount less than unity.

(3) Different multipliers may be determined under this section for different authorities.

c

(4) The principles on which multipliers are determined under this section shall be specified in an order made by statutory instrument by the Secretary of State.

(5) The same principles shall be applied to every determination under this section of a multiplier for any year.

(6) An order under this section shall be laid before the House of Commons and shall not have effect until approved by a resolution of that House; and no determination shall be made under this section until the order has effect.

d

50.—(1) The Secretary of State may vary the amount of the needs element of rate support grant payable to the council of a London borough or the Common Council of the City of London for any year, in the manner provided in this section, if the rateable value per head of the population of their area, as determined under paragraph 9 of Schedule 2 to the Local Government Act 1974, exceeds the national standard rateable value per head of population, as defined by paragraph 8 of that Schedule.

e

(2) The Secretary of State shall carry out the variation mentioned in subsection (1) above, in relation to any authority, by multiplying the additional amount of needs element payable by virtue of the additional factors prescribed in relation to them under paragraph 1(b) of Schedule 2 to the Local Government Act 1974 by a multiplier determined on principles specified in an order made by statutory instrument by the Secretary of State.

f

(3) Different multipliers may be determined under this section for different authorities.

(4) The same principles shall be applied to every determination under this section for any year.

(5) An order under this section shall be laid before the House of Commons and shall not have effect until approved by a resolution of that House; and no variation shall be made under this section until the order has effect.'

g

Certain important decisions and events

Although we provide hereafter a detailed historical survey under the heading 'Background of Events', it is convenient to refer now briefly and in summary form to certain important decisions and events.

h

The notional uniform rate for the year 1980–81 was fixed at 119p. Advance notice was given of the transitional machinery and how, in general terms, it would work if the Secretary of State decided to invoke it. It was stated that the arrangements would only be used if it became evident that some authorities were not following government expenditure guidelines and had deliberately not reduced the volume of their expenditure.

j

It was further stated that the precise basis on which grant abatement would be applied could not be determined until after the grant year had started and information on authorities' budget plans for 1980–81 was available. It was envisaged that there would be a threshold above the level of the notional uniform rate before any question of grant abatement would arise, and there would be a set of multipliers which would enable the amount of abatement to be calculated and which could help to smooth the transition to the new system. The Secretary of State further stated that he would be prepared to consider a 'waiver' based on general principles which would reduce or eliminate the abatement of grant if authorities with historically high levels of expenditure, too high to be reduced below any threshold in one year, had nevertheless made exceptional reductions in that expenditure.

The royal assent was given to the 1980 Act on 13 November 1980 when ss 48 to 50 came into operation. On 16 December 1980 the Rate Support Grant (Principles for Multipliers) Order 1980, SI 1980/2047 (the multipliers order) was laid before the House of Commons. It was debated and approved on 14 January 1981.

The order will be dealt with in more detail later when it will be seen that the threshold was fixed at 155p, some 30% above the notional uniform rate of 119p. The order discloses how the multiplier applicable to any authority is identified, the calculation of grant abatement under the transitional arrangements being expressed in terms of the product of a given penny rate and calculated as a minimum of one penny for an authority whose uniform or adjusted uniform rate exceeded 155p plus a further one-twentieth of a penny up to a maximum of 5p for an authority with a uniform or adjusted uniform rate of 235p or more. The amount of grant abatement is thus obtained by applying the penny rate, obtained as described, to the sum of the effective rateable value of the authority (a term which is precisely defined in the Rate Support Grant Regulations 1979, SI 1979/1514) and the local deficiency in rateable value which is defined in Sch 2 to the 1974 Act. We set out below a table showing how the abatement of grants was calculated in respect, inter alia, of each of the six boroughs.

Authority	Adjusted uniform rate minus urban programme abatement	Column 2 minus 155p	Rate poundage equivalent of grant abatement	Effective rateable value plus LDRV*	Amount of grant abatement
	(p)	(p)	(p)	(£m)	(£m)
Brent	161·36	6·36	1·32	50·20	0·661
Camden	263·73	108·73	5·00 (max)	102·25	5·112
Hackney	185·74	30·74	2·54	36·64	0·929
Hounslow	156·40	1·40	1·07	47·53	0·509
Lambeth	222·08	67·08	4·35	57·30	2·495
Lewisham	177·45	22·45	2·12	42·74	0·907
Tower Hamlets	201·07	46·07	3·30	40·90	1·351
Waltham Forest	160·62	5·62	1·28	39·07	0·501

*LDRV = local deficiency in rateable value

It is perhaps convenient to take the first two of the applicants, since they are in marked contrast. Brent's adjusted uniform rate, after deducting the urban programme abatement, was 161·36p and was therefore 6·36p above the threshold of 155p. This resulted in a rate poundage equivalent of grant abatement of 1·32p. The effective rateable value plus the local deficiency in rateable value was £50,200,000 and the amount of grant abatement was thus worked out to £661,000. Camden's adjusted uniform rate was the highest at £263·73 ie an excess of £108·73 over the threshold. This involved the application of the maximum rate poundage equivalent of grant abatement of 5p. Since its effective rateable value plus LDRV was £102,250,000 the amount of its grant abatement amounted to £5,112,000.

BACKGROUND OF EVENTS

a   The complaints made by the applicants of the decision of the Secretary of State to reduce their share of the rate support grant for 1980–81 must be seen in the light of the circumstances and events leading up to the formal decision on 26 January 1981. The detail contained in the evidence filed is very considerable and it is desirable to make a summary so as to be able to see the picture of events in outline.

b   *The government's policy in relation to local authority expenditure*
    After the general election in 1979, the new administration announced a policy of curtailing all public expenditure, including that by local authorities. In May 1979 the government announced its intention to reduce by 3% the planned level of local authority expenditure for 1979–80 (fixed by the previous government). On 31 July 1979, a meeting was held between ministers and local authority associations. The Secretary of
c   State for the Environment had tabled a statement which contained the following observations:

d   'Within the overall need for spending reductions, the Government thinks it right to give local authorities the maximum freedom to decide on the allocation of funds in accordance with their own local spending priorities. For its part, the Government intends to seek certain legislative changes to give them more latitude in achieving the total. But the Government considers that local authorities should plan on the basis of a reduction of 5% on the plans for current expenditure in Circular 15/79 for 1980–81 which amounted in total to £12,163m. This would be a reduction of 1% on the levels I have asked local authorities to achieve in 1979–80.'

    The Association of Metropolitan Authorities stated, inter alia, that the reductions could
e   be achieved, but the government was asked if it had reached decisions on the 1979–80 cash limit, rate support grant for 1980–81 or on the level of capital expenditure. These were important factors in local authority budgeting. The government said that it recognised that early notices of a government expenditure target were necessary to enable local authorities to plan their current expenditure for 1980–81 within that framework. Decisions had not yet been taken, inter alia, for the rate support grant for 1980–81. These
f   would as usual be announced towards the end of the year (1979). The legislative changes promised would be laid before Parliament in November, but how soon they took effect would depend on the passage of the legislation through Parliament.
    These proposals were confirmed in the White Paper *The Government's Expenditure Plans 1980–81* (Cmnd 7746) (1979), and were discussed at the meeting of the Consultative Council on Local Government Finance on 16 November 1979. At this meeting the
g   details of the rate support grant settlement for 1980–81 were announced. Two further proposals were also announced, namely, first, for the introduction of legislation which, if enacted, would enable the new block grant system to be introduced for 1981–82 in place of the existing system of rate support grants, and, second, for transitional arrangements for 1980–81 designed to reduce the entitlement to an increase in rate support grant of those local authorities who overspent substantially in 1980–81.
h   Part of the statement of the Secretary of State reads as follows:

        '29. I now want to come to one of the most debated aspects of the present RSG system. In essence, the present rate support grant arrangements are based on the assumption that need is demonstrated by authorities' expenditure. Resources element provides the same marginal rate of grant support to a local authority's expenditure regardless of how extravagant that expenditure might be. Furthermore,
j   high spending authorities can actually attract to themselves a larger share of the resources grant at the expense of other more prudent authorities. Needs element is distributed on the basis of an analysis of past expenditure patterns. The consequence of this is that if authorities with high levels of expenditure all decided to maintain or increase their levels, they could create a feed-back that enhanced their measured needs.

30. Within such a system it is very difficult to convince authorities that it is in their interest to economise, for to do so might, over a period, reduce their eligibility *a* for central government support . . .

31. The Government therefore proposes to make provision in the forthcoming Local Government, Planning and Land Bill for a new block grant system to come into operation in 1981–82. The system will replace the present needs and resources element with a single grant payable to all authorities . . .

32. Authorities spending in line with standard expenditure—leaving an *b* allowance for inevitable variations in local circumstances—will get the full rate of government support. Expenditure in excess of "standard expenditure" will also attract grant—as under the present resources element arrangements—but if it is significantly in excess of "standard expenditure" the rate of grant will be reduced and reduced progressively as expenditure increases still further.

33. This system will still leave authorities free as now to decide how much they *c* wish to spend, and how much income they wish to raise by way of rates. But the Government's contribution through grant will be limited. There will be full consultation with the local authority associations on detailed mechanics of the new block grant, including the definition of standard expenditure and standard rate poundage . . .

35. The new block grant cannot be brought into effect until the 1981–82 grant *d* year. We have therefore decided to provide in the legislation for transitional arrangements for 1980–81 which will make it possible to apply as far as practicable the principles of block grant through adjustment of grant entitlements under existing legislation at Increase Order stage.

36. The transitional arrangements will apply primarily through the resources element, but they will also be capable of operating in respect of London authorities *e* that do not receive resources element through the needs element. These arrangements will involve a reduction in entitlements at the stage of the Increase Order for 1980–81 which will be made next November if there are local authorities who overspend substantially. The measure of overspending will be any large difference between an authority's actual rate, with certain adjustments in London, and the "notional uniform rate", implicit in the present grant system, which *f* authorities would have to charge, after taking account of entitlements to the needs and resources elements, to fund expenditure in line with assessed expenditure needs. Any such reduction in grant will be distributed among all authorities.

37. The "notional uniform rate" will be published in the Report on this year's RSG Order. I recognise that there is a measure of rough justice in using the "notional uniform rate" to distinguish between substantial overspenders and others for grant *g* purposes, because it means that we must consider the spending behaviour of each county and its districts as a single entity. But this is unavoidable under the present system of RSG which does not have separate spending assessments for each local authority, and has different grant arrangements for the different tiers of local government. And the justice is less rough than it would be if we allowed the present system to continue unmodified for 1980–81. *h*

38. Nothing would give me greater pleasure than to have to make no use of the transitional arrangements. The traditional practice has been for local government—of whatever political colour—to comply with central government guidelines on expenditure. This has reinforced the basis of common trust that has made it possible for local and national government to work together. But I do not see how I can expect the majority of local authorities to curtail their expenditure plans if they see *j* a handful of authorities conspicuously disregarding the national interest by pushing up their expenditure, and actually getting a larger share of the available grant as a result. I threaten nobody. But it would be irresponsible to leave the government powerless in the face of such behaviour should it arise in 1980–81.'

At this meeting the Secretary of State further observed that this statement made it
a clear that the government was concerned to deal with a small number of potential
overspending authorities. He said that there would be substantial safeguards to prevent
the new system leading to dramatic changes because it was envisaged that there would
be a *threshold* above the level of standard expenditure before any question of grant
abatement would arise, and there would be a set of *multipliers* which would help to
smooth the transition to the new system. There would in any case be full consultation
b with the associations on the mechanics of the new system. He assured the associations
that he envisaged the transitional arrangements, if used at all, would apply only to a
small minority of authorities and that there would be a significant threshold above the
notional uniform rate before any question of grant abatement would arise.

Reaction of the local authorities
c On 6 December 1979 a letter was sent by the Association of Metropolitan Authorities
to Mr Heiser on the subject of the transitional arrangements for 1980–81 with particular
regard to the safeguards for the operation of these arrangements, assuming that
Parliament granted the necessary powers. A general approach was suggested, namely by
looking at the relationship of a period of years between the notional uniform rate and
the actual uniform rate for individual authorities and a comparison between these and
d the actual and uniform rates for 1980–81.

On 11 December 1979 the London Boroughs Association wrote to Mr Heiser enclosing
a report as an indication of their concern about the block grant and more particularly the
transitional arrangements for 1980–81, stressing their view that the existing needs
assessments were an adequate yardstick of alleged overspending. They drew particular
attention to para 10 of the report which suggested an additional cl 48(1) of the Bill
e suggesting a form of waiver on a general basis.

On 19 December there was a meeting chaired by Mr Heiser attended, inter alios, by
the Association of Metropolitan Authorities and the London Boroughs Association.
Amongst other matters which were considered was the 'safety net', as a form of safeguard,
for which it was stated the ministers had sympathy, but it was pointed out that it was not
possible to specify either the threshold beyond which grant abatements would apply, or
f a safety net based on cuts in budgeted expenditure until after authorities had fixed their
rates. Any 'safety net' would be based on general principles.

On 20 December Mr Heiser wrote to the London Boroughs Association on the subject
of the 'safety net' limitation, giving his reasons why this was considered unsatisfactory.
He ended his letter by saying that the only solution seemed to be to offer, in general
terms, the possibility of a partial or total exemption related to changes in expenditure.
g He gave advance warning of a letter shortly to be received explaining the operation of
the transitional arrangements, including a reference to possible exemptions. He sent
copies of his letter to secretaries of other associations.

Further details of the transitional arrangements
On 21 December 1979 the Department of the Environment wrote to the local
h authorities giving further details of the proposals for the reduction of rate support grant.
We must refer to certain paragraphs of this letter:

'4. The transitional arrangements (which will apply in 1980/81 only) seek to
follow as far as possible the principle of the new block grant system. But the scope
for this is limited by the fact that under the present grant arrangements, expenditure
j needs (the equivalent within the present arrangements of the standard expenditure
to be used under block grant) are assessed for all tiers of authorities in a particular
area, and not for individual authorities considered separately. The comparison
between planned expenditure and expenditure needs therefore has to be on a basis
that embraces all the spending authorities in an area.

5. The most convenient way of making this comparison is by looking at rate levels. The uniform rate fixed by a district or London borough reflects expenditure *a* both by the rating authority itself, and by other authorities—normally the county— precepting upon it. It is therefore a reasonable indication of the expenditure of both tiers taken together. This can be compared with a notional uniform rate which can be calculated under the present rate support grant arrangements as the rate poundage that all local authorities would have to levy, after equalisation of expenditure needs and resources by needs and resources element, if their expenditure is in line with *b* their assessed expenditure needs. This year the notional uniform rate is 119p.

6. The comparison of an authority's actual uniform rate . . . with the notional uniform rate is thus a convenient device for establishing whether the planned expenditure of the different tiers of authorities in an area is in line with the assessed expenditure needs of those authorities. If the uniform rate is above the notional uniform rate, then expenditure in that area is above the area's assessed expenditure *c* needs. The Secretary of State recognises, however, that generalised formula assessments of expenditure need cannot give an accurate picture of the requirements of each individual authority, though he considers it reasonable to use such a yardstick for determining the basis of grant distribution which must also operate in accordance with general principles and cannot have regard to special circumstances in particular areas. *d*

7. Because of the special resources position of London, certain adjustments must be made to the uniform rates of London authorities before they can be compared, on a consistent basis with those of non-London authorities, with notional uniform rate . . . Because of the City's unique characteristics—financially and demographi- cally—its "needs and assessment" is constructed on an ad hoc basis not comparable with that of other authorities. Moreover the London rate equalisation scheme means *e* that the City in practice receives no grant—it is a net contributor. It will therefore not be affected by the transitional arrangements.

8. I must emphasise that the notional uniform rate is *not* a prescriptive rate poundage which all authorities would be expected to charge. Individual circumstances vary, and authorities remain free to set their rates at the level they consider appropriate to their circumstances. The notional uniform rate is intended *f* to be used solely as a yardstick so as to establish whether expenditure is significantly in excess of assessed expenditure need.

9. The legislation on the transitional arrangements will provide for abatement of entitlements to resources element, or in the case of some London authorities needs element, in accordance with a schedule to be prescribed by the Secretary of State, where authorities' uniform rates are *substantially* in excess of the notional uniform *g* rate of 119p. The precise basis on which grant abatement would be applied cannot be determined until after the grant year has started and information on authorities' budget plans for 1980/81 is available.

10. The Secretary of State has made it clear, however, that he would intend to use the transitional arrangements only if it became evident that some authorities were *h* not following government expenditure guidelines and had deliberately not reduced the volume of their expenditure. He has said that—he hopes that it will be unnecessary for him to make use of the transitional arrangement;—if the arrangements are used, no abatement of grant would be contemplated unless planned expenditure was very substantially in excess of assessed expenditure need (the Secretary of State does not expect that more than 10—and almost certainly not *j* more than 20—authorities would be affected by the arrangements);—he would be prepared to consider a "waiver", based on general principles, which would reduce or eliminate the abatement of grant if authorities with historically high levels of expenditure—too high to be reduced below any threshold in one year—had nevertheless made reductions in that expenditure.'

Mr Heiser, in his affidavit, states that the willingness to consider a waiver referred to
a in his letter of 21 December was a direct result of the representations from the local
authority associations to which we have made brief reference. Further, that it was in
recognition of the concern about the adequacy of the expenditure needs assessments, that
the threshold above which grant abatement was to apply was eventually set at 155p, 30%
above the notional uniform rate, and also that a limit (5p) was set on the amount of grant
abatement. No representations were made following this letter and prior to the Secretary
b of State acquiring the powers which he sought, that a formula-based approach to grant
abatement was wrong and that individual treatment of each and every authority should
be available. Nor was any suggestion made for a system of partial waivers.

Counsel for the applicants expressly disavows any allegation against the Secretary of
State of political bias. However, the point has been made in the applicants' affidavits that
the Secretary of State had decided to select the applicants for abatement of grant by the
c very choice of a fixed formula. To this Mr Heiser answers, and in our view correctly
answers, by making the point that the statement that the Secretary of State did not expect
more than 10 authorities to be affected etc, was made *before* any authorities set their rates
for the year in question, 1980–81. Secondly, only 15 out of the 23 authorities above the
threshold of 155p specified before 1980–81 were among the 23 authorities with the
highest rates in 1979–80. Of the eight authorities finally affected under the arrangements,
d only five were among the top 23 authorities in 1979–80; of the remaining three (Brent,
Hounslow and Waltham Forest) only Brent was among the 50 authorities (at no 46) with
the highest uniform rate. At that stage it was impossible to state what would be regarded
as constituting either the highest levels of spending or exceptional reductions in
expenditure in advance of the 'norm' established by the generality of authorities'
spending and rating decisions. Moreover, more than half of the authorities ultimately
e liable for grant abatement under the terms of the transitional arrangements secured
exemption by qualifying for a waiver.

Subsequent parliamentary statements
On 16 January 1980 the report on the Rate Support Grant Order 1979, which had been
laid before Parliament on 28 November 1979, was debated and approved by the House
f of Commons. In the course of the debate, the Rt Hon Tom King MP, Minister of State at
the Department of the Environment, stated that any abatement of grant under the
transitional arrangements would not involve the recoupment of grant already paid out
to the authorities concerned, but a reduction in the extra grant they would otherwise
receive under the terms of the first order for 1980–81 in the following November. On
24 January 1980 the Local Government, Planning and Land (No 2) Bill was introduced
g into the House of Commons, the previous Bill having been withdrawn. On 5 February
1980, when it was given its second reading in the House of Commons, the Secretary of
State stressed that authorities were being put on warning about the possible
implementation of the arrangements well before the start of the grant year.

In March 1980 Standing Committee D of the House of Commons, which was
considering the Bill, dealt with the clauses relating to transitional arrangements. Mr
h King on 18 March made the following points: (a) that there would be a substantial
threshold above which authorities would be liable for grant abatement; (b) that any grant
abatement would be applied on a formula basis to all authorities above the threshold;
that the government had in mind that equal degrees of overspending, measured by the
amount by which the uniform rate exceeded the threshold, would lead to equal
reductions in grant expressed in terms of rate poundage equivalent, that is the loss of
j grant equal to the product in that authority of a particular penny rate; (c) that increases
in authorities' expenditure as a result of such emergencies as flood and snow damage
would be excluded from the calculation of any grant abatement under the transitional
arrangements; (d) that the principles on which the multipliers for abating the grant
would be determined would be the subject of a *separate* order which would have to be
approved by affirmative resolution of the House of Commons.

Thus, to sum up, by the end of 1979 all local authorities were aware of the government's policy to reduce public expenditure including local government expenditure, of its *a* intention to introduce legislation to introduce a block grant system for the year 1981–82 to reduce the entitlement to rate support grant of those authorities whose expenditure was substantially excessive and by transitional arrangements to cover the year 1980–81. The government's proposals were extensively discussed in 1980, in the press, in meetings between the department and the local authorities' associations and in Parliament in debates and in committee, on the Rates Support Grant Order 1979 and on the Bill.   *b*

Response of local authorities to the government's policy
As already stated, the power of the government to restrict expenditure by a local authority is not great, and not direct: primarily, it is exhortatory. Not all local authorities were sympathetic to the government's policies, and some made their opposition clear. Those opposed varied in their behaviour. Some co-operated, albeit grudgingly; some *c* made token concessions to the government's wishes. Some, far from reducing their level of expenditure, increased it. Naturally, those local authorities opposed to the government's policies, and in favour of a high level of local authority expenditure, were those of a different political colour from that of the government, with the result that those local authorities made the subject of a reduction in rate support grant are mostly politically opposed to the government. But, as previously stated, it is not submitted on behalf of the *d* applicants that the Secretary of State acted out of political bias.
By the time when they had to determine their budgets for 1980–81, the local authorities were thus well aware of the government's policies and intentions for the future. There is no doubt that the government's proposals to reduce the rate support grant in the case of local authorities whose expenditure was substantially excessive was intended to bring pressure on the more determinedly opposed local authorities, and to *e* underpin the government's otherwise mainly exhortatory endeavours.
When the local authorities' budgets were received in May 1980 they showed a budgeted expenditure of £740,000,000 (5·6%) in excess of the expenditure volume targets set by the government for 1980–81. It was estimated that if local government expenditure were to come back into line with the government plans for 1980–81 all authorities would need to reduce their planned volume of current expenditure for that *f* year to a point 2% below their actual volume of current expenditure in 1978–79. The original budgets of the applicants for 1980–81 showed planned expenditure in real terms in excess of what they spent in 1978–79. The revised budgets for five of the six applicants showed no reductions on their original budgets for 1980–81. The one exception was the London Borough of Hounslow, which showed a reduction of £223,000 from £52,824,000 to £52,601,000 at 1979 prices. In July revised budgets were therefore called for by *g* 1 August. Meanwhile, in July 1980 in the House of Commons, it was explained that the final terms of the 'waiver', ie the exemption from the transitional arrangements, could not be settled. The response was varied, but in the aggregate the government's plans were not fully achieved. The excess was reduced from 5·6% to 2·6%.

The press statement of 18 September 1980   *h*
Being dissatisfied with the result of the revised budgeting the Secretary of State proposed to withhold £200m of the rate support grant, to withhold in part urban programme grant, and to implement the plans for a reduction of the rate support grant by withholding increases, if given the necessary powers. A statement dealing with these matters was made by him on 18 September 1980. It reads, in part, as follows:

'7. Clearly, such an overspend would be unacceptable. Public expenditure targets *j* are too important to disregard any overspending. I have therefore concluded that I must take action on two levels. First, I propose to take action against those authorities who have blatantly disregarded the Government's exhortations to reduce their expenditure. I shall, therefore, subject to Parliamentary approval, implement the transitional arrangements so as to reduce grant to those authorities with rates above a threshold level of 155p unless at the time when the transitional arrangements

a
Order is presented to Parliament they can be shown to have made exceptional efforts to hold down their rateborne expenditure in the current year or to have achieved their two-year volume target as requested in the call for revised budgets. I attach a list of these authorities and the effect on each of the announcement I am making (Annex 1): this is subject of course, to any further relevant changes in their finances before the Order is presented.'

b
We set out below part of the terms of Annex 1:

'THE RSG TRANSITIONAL ARRANGEMENTS
1. The application of the transitional arrangements is subject to the enactment of the relevant provisions of the Local Government, Planning and Land Bill, and Parliamentary approval of the appropriate Order. The legislation provides for reductions in grant to be applied to authorities whose uniform rates (adjusted in the
c
case of London authorities to discount the resource advantage left with London in recent RSG settlements so as to help keep rate bills down) in 1980/81 are above the 119p "notional uniform rate" that would apply in areas where authorities were spending in line with their expenditure need assessments.
2. The Secretary of State has discretion to limit the application of the arrangements and has previously indicated that relatively few—almost certainly not more than
d
20—authorities would suffer grant reductions under the scheme. The *limitation on the scope of the scheme* will apply as follows: (a) authorities will be liable for grant reductions only if their uniform/adjusted uniform rate is above 155p (ie more than 30% higher than the notional uniform rate); (b) authorities within this category will nevertheless be exempted if *either* they have contained their expenditure in the current year (by providing for a cash increase at least three percentage points below
e
the average for their class) *or* met their two-year public expenditure volume targets; (c) in addition the City of London, whose exceptionally high adjusted uniform rate arises from the fact that its services are provided predominantly for a non-resident population (its night-time population is less than one-sixtieth of its day-time population) will be excluded.
3. The scale of grant abatement will be an amount equivalent to a penny rate for
f
the authority concerned *plus* an amount equivalent to one-twentieth of a penny rate for each penny by which the authority's uniform/adjusted uniform rate exceeds the threshold level of 155p. There will be a maximum abatement equivalent to a 5p rate. The calculation of grant abatement will be subject to amendment where on application by the authorities affected it is shown that uniform rates have been increased by (a) expenditure on emergencies; (b) loss of rate income arising from
g
steelworks closures; (c) rate fund contributions to urban programme expenditure.
4. Subject to any such amendments, or to any further relevant changes in authorities' finances before the transitional arrangements Order is presented to Parliament, the Order will provide for grant reductions as set out in the table attached.'

h
The three categories of exempted expenditure in calculating grant abatement were proposed in response to representations which had previously been made to the Secretary of State. Only the third category requires some further explanation. Certain authorities with the highest uniform rates were receiving special assistance under the government's urban programme. Their rates and spending were high, both because of serious problems of urban deprivation and because they had been encouraged by successive governments to spend money on dealing with their problems. It was therefore argued, and argued
j
successfully, that this fact should be recognised by some sort of concession if the transitional arrangements were to be applied.

Of the 23 authorities with uniform or adjusted uniform rates of above 155p listed in the annex to the Secretary of State's statement of 18 September, the City of London was to be exempted for the reasons to which reference has already been made (see para 2(c) of Annex 1 referred to above). Of the other authorities with uniform or adjusted uniform rates above 155p, three already qualified for the first of the two waivers which became

known as the 'rate and RSG-borne expenditure' and six for the second waiver known as
the 'volume target' waiver; one qualified for both. This left 14 authorities potentially
liable for grant abatement under the proposed transitional arrangements, as and when
the Secretary of State obtained his power to make the abatements.

Events subsequent to the 18 September 1980 statement
The 1980 Act received the royal assent on 13 November 1980, and ss 48, 49 and 50
came into operation.
After the details of the proposed transitional arrangements had been announced on 18
September, only one applicant, namely the London Borough of Brent, sought individual
consideration. It made representations why it considered that it needed to spend at a level
above the government's target. It also made a new point in its second letter of the same
date about the need in its area for spending on the education of Commonwealth
immigrants under s 11 of the Local Government Act 1966. These representations were
considered by the department. It was decided not to make a special allowance for the s 11
expenditure and as to the criteria for waiver on 17 November 1980 the department wrote
saying that the criteria for waiver and for amendment to grant abatement had been
clearly laid down and that in all fairness to the other authorities listed in the 18 September
list, different rules could not be applied to Brent.
On 25 November 1980, that is after the 1980 Act was in force, the London Borough of
Camden asked for an 'off the record' meeting with officers of the department. They
raised the possibility of securing a partial reduction in the amount of grant abatement in
return for partial compliance with one or other of the waivers. By that date five
authorities above the threshold, namely the London boroughs of Islington, of
Hammersmith and Fulham, Newcastle upon Tyne and Sheffield Metropolitan District
Councils, and the Borough of Afan, had reduced their budgetary expenditure so as to
comply with the terms of a waiver. The department considered that partial compliance
with the waivers would have justifiably laid the government open to charges of
inconsistency and partiality in the application of its policy, and refused.
On 16 December 1980 the multipliers order was laid before the House of Commons.
Until it was approved the Secretary of State could not make the determinations and
variations which he planned under s 49 or s 50 of the Act to reduce the rate support
grant. The order was due to be debated on 14 January 1981. On 5 December and 18
December, the potentially vulnerable nine local authorities were informed that the last
day on which they could secure exemption was the day on which the order was approved
(which was 15 January) so that any budget revision must be made by the date. The
London Borough of Greenwich succeeded in doing so.
On the same day as the multipliers order was laid before the House of Commons, so
also was there laid the Rate Support Grant (Increase) (No 2) Order 1980, SI 1980/2049,
and the report. The report explained the distribution of the needs element in these
terms:

'14. The needs element is distributed by reference to population and to other
objective factors prescribed in The Rate Support Grant Order 1979. The weightings
for each factor, that is the amount to be paid per head of population, per education
unit, and so on, which were prescribed in that Order now require revision to
distribute the increased amounts of the needs element. To achieve this a factor of
1·17839 will be applied to each of the weightings prescribed in that Order. For those
authorities affected by the transitional arrangements a multiplier will be applied to
the additional amount of needs element payable by virtue of the additional factors
so prescribed to give effect to The Rate Support Grant (Principle for Multipliers)
Order 1980.'

Of course the same process was to be applied to the resources element (see s 49). The
report dealt in detail with the transitional arrangements consistent with the Secretary of
State's statement of 18 September, explaining in detail the exemptions from liability

a   from abatement and the two waivers. It also explained that the principle on which the Secretary of State has adjusted uniform rates in Greater London was that rateable values in excess of rateable value at national standard would be disregarded in calculating adjusted uniform rates, so that the expenditure of authorities in Greater London was compared on an equivalent base to that used for authorities outside London qualifying for resources element.

b   On 19 December 1980 a letter was sent by Councillor Jack Smart, chairman of the Association of Metropolitan Authorities, to the Secretary of State on behalf of all the authorities who were at risk of being penalised. He wrote personally to the Secretary of State and we quote from his second paragraph:

c
> 'So that there can be no possibility of any misunderstanding, I should be grateful if you would agree to meet a delegation of representatives of those Authorities [authorities which are to be penalised this year under the transitional arrangements] to discuss not only what appears, from our point of view, to be a combination of unfairness and illogicality, but also exactly what it will mean financially for those Authorities to comply with the Government's terms.'

d   On 9 January 1981, that is some five days before the multipliers order was due to be debated and six days before it came into operation, the Secretary of State replied. He agreed with the importance of avoiding misunderstanding, but stated that in the short time available before the order giving effect to the transitional arrangements was debated in Parliament, he did not believe that a meeting would have any practical effect. He said:

> 'I think it would achieve more for my officials to talk direct to the authorities concerned about how they might still qualify for one of the two waivers.'

e   He went on to say that it might be helpful if he was to set out exactly where the authorities concerned at present stood. We quote his next two paragraphs:

> 'First, I have to say that the Government has no intention of suspending generally the operation of the transitional arrangements. We have made it clear on many occasions since November 1979 that the arrangements would be applied to a small number of the highest rating and spending authorities unless they could show that they had made some real effort in 1980/81 to moderate the volume of their spending. In the event we have provided two ways rather than one way in which they could demonstrate this. So far, the authorities still liable for grant abatement have not made such reductions.
>
> As to procedure, we have made it clear to the authorities concerned that the deadline for qualification for exemption would be the date of the RSG debate, now fixed for 14 January, when Parliament will be asked to approve the Order giving effect to the arrangements. This is nearly 4 months after the announcement of the transitional arrangement list on 18 September (enclosed) . . .'

He then went on to state what it would mean financially for those authorities to qualify for exemption. He set out the terms of the two waivers and provided a table summarising the total required in each case to meet each waiver.

h   On 16 January a letter was sent by the chief executive of the borough of Camden to the Secretary of State in these terms:

> *'Re: Rate Support Grant—Transitional Arrangements*
> Camden has been led to believe by your officers that whatever representations we might make to you, if they constitute less than the savings you have indicated you require, that is, £8·161m or £4·746m respectively, you will inevitably reduce our Rate Support Grant. Accordingly, there was no point in our submitting proposals for lesser savings to you. We also clearly understand you to have said that the time has now passed for us to make representations to you. Two points arise: 1. Are we correct in our understanding on the first matter? 2. Are you prepared to consider any representations from Camden now that the 14th January has passed?'

The private secretary to the Secretary of State replied on the same day as follows:

'I have been asked to reply to your teleprinter message of today's date to the a
Secretary of State in which you asked two questions. First, you were correctly
informed by the DOE officials that it was not possible for an authority to secure a
partial waiver. At that time you told the Department that your Council could not
qualify under either waiver. Second, it is not legally possible for the Secretary of
State to change the grant abatement under the transitional provisions to which your
Council is now subject . . .'   b

Also on 16 January 1981 Mr Osborn, an assistant secretary in the Department of the
Environment, wrote a memorandum headed: 'Rate Support Grant 1980–81 Transitional
Arrangements'. It read:

'You will be aware that the Secretary of State has discretion not to implement the
powers to reduce rate support grant payments under the so-called transitional   c
arrangements and that he has expressed his intention to exercise his discretion not
to implement those powers in the case of 15 authorities (including Greenwich).
Before I put in motion steps to actually reduce their grant I would be grateful if the
Secretary of State would now finally and formally confirm that the powers under
sections 49 and 50 of the Local Government, Planning and Land Act 1980 are indeed
to be applied to reduce the grant of the following eight London Borough Councils: d
Camden, Tower Hamlets, Lambeth, Hackney, Brent, Waltham Forest, Hounslow,
Lewisham, in accordance with the Rate Support Grant (Principles for Multipliers)
Order 1980. I attach a table showing the adjustments to be made though these are
still subject to final checking, particularly in the case of Lambeth, where the full
implications of the supplementary rate have yet to be confirmed. I should also be
grateful for confirmation that Greenwich is to be exempted from these   e
arrangements.'

The memorandum went to Mr McDonald, who noted on the memorandum the
position of Greenwich. It then was submitted up through the various officials until it
reached the Secretary of State who wrote thereon, 'I confirm that the eight remaining
authorities should be subject to the powers listed.'
On 26 January 1981 Mr Edmonds, principal private secretary to the Secretary of State,   f
wrote a memorandum to Mr Osborn in these terms:

'Rate Support Grant 1980–81: Transitional Arrangements. The Secretary of State
was grateful for your Minute of the 16th January 1981. He confirms that the eight
remaining authorities should be subject to the powers listed.'
          g
The table showing the amount of grant reduction, which was subject to final checking,
does not in fact show the final figures but they were not very far out. They ranged in
round terms, so far as the six applicants are concerned, from a little over £500,000 in the
case of Waltham Forest up to £5¼m in the case of Camden.
On 30 January 1981 each applicant was informed by the department that on 14
January 1981 the multipliers order was approved, and that the department's letter of 18   h
December had stated that 14 January was the latest date by which the authority would
need to have confirmed its intention to make reductions in its 1980–81 budget in order
to qualify for exemption from application of the transitional provisions. Since no such
confirmation was received by that date, the Secretary of State had decided to exercise his
discretion to reduce the amount of rate support grant payable in respect of 1980–81 and
that details of the grant adjustments to be made to give effect to this decision would   j
shortly be notified.

Summary
Thus the detail of the events leading up to the exercise by the Secretary of State of his
discretion under the 1980 Act is extensive and complicated, but the outline is simple

a enough. The newly elected government in 1979 wished to promote a policy of
   retrenchment, and was anxious to encourage local authorities to follow suit. At an early
   stage it informed the local authorities of its wishes in this respect, and of its intention to
   introduce legislation conferring on it discretionary powers to reduce the rate support
   grant payable to local authorities. Prior to the enactment of that legislation, many
   discussions took place between the Department of the Environment and the local
   authorities about how these powers, if conferred, should be exercised. In due course the
b Secretary of State announced the policy which he intended to follow, including the
   principles which he intended to apply in deciding whether to exercise his power to
   reduce, when granted, in the case of those local authorities found to be liable to reduction
   ('the waivers'). In arriving at this policy the Secretary of State took into account some of
   the suggestions made by the local authorities and also their response to his earlier
   exhortations to economise. This policy was, for all practical purposes, settled and
c announced before November 1980, when the 1980 Act was enacted, and was applied by
   the Secretary of State unchanged, after full debate in Parliament. It is this circumstance,
   ie that the negotiations with those potentially affected preceded and did not follow the
   grant of the discretionary powers, which distinguishes this case from other decided cases.
        We now turn to the submissions of the applicants.

d

   I. *Rate Support Grant (Principles for Multipliers) Order 1980 (the multipliers order)*
        The submission is that the multipliers order is ultra vires and of no effect.
        The multipliers order purports to be made by the Secretary of State in the exercise of
   powers conferred on him by ss 49 and 50 of the 1980 Act. The determination by the
e Secretary of State reducing the amount of the applicant local authorities' entitlement to
   rate support grant involved the application of multipliers determined in accordance with
   the multipliers order and without them could not have been effectively or lawfully made
   under s 49 or s 50 of the 1980 Act. Accordingly, if the multipliers order is ultra vires and
   of no effect, it must follow that the determination of the Secretary of State is of no effect,
   because he did not enjoy the powers that he purported to exercise. This submission is
f different in kind from the applicants' other submissions, which concede the existence of
   the powers but claim that the Secretary of State in effect abused them. It is convenient to
   set out ss 49 and 50 of the 1980 Act in part again:

g '**49.** *Reduction of resources element* . . . (2) A determination under this section shall
   be made by multiplying the uniform rate for the area of a local authority by a
   multiplier of an amount less than unity.
        (3) Different multipliers may be determined under this section for different
   authorities.
        (4) The principles on which multipliers are determined under this section shall
   be specified in an order made by statutory instrument by the Secretary of State.
h   (5) The same principles shall be applied to every determination under this section
   of a multiplier for any year.

   50. *Reduction of needs element for authorities in Greater London* . . . (2) The Secretary
   of State shall carry out the variation mentioned in subsection (1) above, in relation
   to any authority, by multiplying the additional amount of needs element payable
j by virtue of the additional factors prescribed in relation to them under paragraph
   1(b) of Schedule 2 to the Local Government Act 1974 by a multiplier determined on
   principles specified in an order made by statutory instrument by the Secretary of
   State.
        (3) Different multipliers may be determined under this section for different
   authorities.

(4) The same principles shall be applied to every determination under this section for any year.'

Article 3 of the order provides:

'The principles set out in the Schedule to this order are hereby specified as the principles on which multipliers are determined for the purpose of section 49 or 50 of the Act.'

The schedule reads as follows:

'PRINCIPLES.

1. A multiplier for the purpose of section 49 of the Act shall be such that it will, when applied to the amount of the resources element of rate support grant payable to an authority in relation to which the uniform rate for the year exceeds £1·55p produce a reduction in the amount of that element for the year of the lesser of the following amounts, namely, (a) the aggregate of—(i) one hundredth part of the sum of the effective rateable values of all the hereditaments in the area of the authority and the local deficiency in rateable value in relation to the authority for the year; and (ii) one twentieth of one hundredth part of that sum in respect of each penny poundage by which the uniform rate for the year in relation to the authority exceeds £1·55p; (b) five hundredth parts of the sum mentioned in sub-paragraph (i) above.

2. A multiplier for the purpose of section 50 of the Act, shall be such that it will, when applied to the additional amount of the needs element of rate support grant payable by virtue of the additional factors prescribed under paragraph 1(b) of Schedule 2 to the Local Government Act 1974 in relation to an authority in relation to which the uniform rate for the year exceeds £1·55p, produce a variation in the amount of that element for the year equivalent to a reduction therein of the lesser of the following amounts, namely, (a) the aggregate of—(i) one hundredth part of the sum of the effective rateable values of all the hereditaments in the area of the authority and the local deficiency in rateable value in relation to the authority for the year; and (ii) one twentieth of one hundredth part of that sum in respect of each penny poundage by which the uniform rate for the year in relation to the authority exceeds £1·55p; (b) five hundredths parts of the sum mentioned in sub-paragraph (i) above.

3.—(1) In determining for the purpose of sub-paragraph (a) of paragraph 1 or 2 above the amount of the rate poundage by which the uniform rate of an authority exceeds £1·55p no account shall be taken of—(a) the net expenditure by the authority in respect of which grant is payable under the Local Government Grants (Social Need) Act 1969, after deducting the amount of grant so paid; or (b) in relation to the council of a district, of such part of a precept payable by the council to the council of the county of which the district forms part as is equivalent to the relevant proportion of such net expenditure by the county council; or (c) in relation to the council of a London borough or the Common Council of the City of London, of such part of a precept payable by the council to the Greater London Council as is equivalent to the relevant proportion of such net expenditure by that council; (d) expenditure incurred in taking action, and grants and loans made pursuant to and in the circumstances described in, section 138 of the Local Government Act 1972 (powers of principal councils with respect to emergencies or disasters) insofar as such expenditure would not have been incurred if the circumstances had not arisen, except expenditure on repair or replacement of property belonging to the authority as respects which the risk which occurred was an insurable one.

(2) In sub-paragraph (1) above the relevant proportion—(a) in relation to expenditure by a county council, means the proportion which the penny rate product for the area of the district bears to the aggregate of such products for the areas of all the districts in the county of which the district forms part; (b) in relation to expenditure by the Greater London Council—(i) for general London purposes, means the proportion which the penny rate product for the area of the relevant

a   London borough or the City of London as the case may be bears to the aggregate of
such products for all the rating areas in Greater London; and (ii) for Inner London
Education Authority purposes, means the proportion which the penny rate product
for the area of the relevant London borough or the City of London as the case may
be bears to the aggregate of such products for all the rating areas in the Inner London
Education Area.

        4. In paragraphs 1 and 2 above—(a) references to a reduction in the amount of
b   an element are references to a reduction in the amount of that element which would
have been payable to the authority if no multiplier for the purpose of section 48 or
49 of the Act had been applied to the amount payable in respect of that element to
the authority or to any other authority; and (b) reference to the hereditaments in the
area of an authority include references to any hereditaments which, by virtue of any
enactment, any body is to be treated as occupying in that area.

c   5. In this Schedule—"effective rateable value", in relation to a hereditament, has
the meaning assigned to it by paragraph 9(2) of Schedule 2 to the Local Government
Act 1974; "local deficiency in rateable value" has the meaning assigned to it by
paragraph 10(2) of that Schedule; "penny rate product" means the product of a rate
of one penny in the pound for the area of an authority in the year as estimated for
the purpose of section 12(4) of the General Rate Act 1967; "uniform rate" has the
d   meaning assigned to it by section 48 of the Act; "the year" means the year 1980–81.'

        The applicants make two different submissions. We will deal with them separately.

(i) *The order does not specify 'the principles on which multipliers are determined' as required by
ss 49(4) and 50(2) of the 1980 Act*
        The applicants' contention is that to comply with the requirements of the above
e   subsections the order must disclose the philosophy or the rationale or justification for the
multiplier; it does not do so: it merely prescribes how the multipliers are to be
ascertained. In our judgment, however, this overlooks that the basic principle is to be
found in s 48, namely that the Secretary of State may reduce the amount of rate support
grant payable to a local authority for the year 1980–81 and any subsequent year before
the commencing year if the uniform rate for that authority's area in that year exceeds
f   the notional uniform rate. The multipliers order provides the secondary principles: how
that reduction is to be effected.

        Counsel for the applicants concedes that a formula can expose the principles behind it.
In our judgment, the order does just that, and in the following manner: (a) the Secretary
of State sets the limit or threshold (155p) substantially above the uniform rate (119p); (b)
a minimum abatement is provided for, immediately the local authority exceeds that
g   threshold: 1p rate; (c) the order provides for a further 1/20th of a penny for each penny
by which the authority's uniform or adjusted uniform rate exceeds the threshold; (d) it
imposes a ceiling to the abatement by providing a maximum of 5p thus seeking no
further abatement for an authority with a uniform or adjusted uniform rate in excess of
235p; (e) the formula is to be applied both to the needs and resources element; (f) certain
expenditure is put into a special category and is therefore not to be taken into account.
h   Thus the multipliers order does a good deal more than merely specify, uno flatu, the
multipliers (which might well be insufficient for an order required to determine
principles) and states how they are to be determined, and in such detail that the instructed
reader can discern the underlying principles. Furthermore, they are prescribed in terms
of general application to all local authorities. We reject this submission.

j   (ii) *The order was unreasonable and capricious in its effect*
        Mr Marlow, on behalf of Camden, in his second affidavit sets out a table which shows
the extent to which the various applicants exceeded the government targets and the
amount of the penalties.· He demonstrates that the amount of the penalties bears no
relationship to the extent of the failure to reach the volume targets set by the government.
But the short answer to this point is that Parliament decided, as it was entitled to, to
relate abatement, not to the extent to which a local authority failed to reach volume

targets but to the excess of its uniform or adjusted uniform rate over the notional uniform rate (see s 48).

We take the law to be conveniently expressed in the following statement by Lord Guest in *McEldowney v Forde* [1969] 2 All ER 1039 at 1061, [1971] AC 632 at 649, where he said:

'The Court will only interfere if the Minister is shown to have gone outside the four corners of the Act or has acted in bad faith (see LORD GREENE M.R., in *Carltona, Ltd. v. Comrs of Works* ([1943] 2 All ER 560)). LORD RADCLIFFE in *A.-G. for Canada v. Hallet & Carey, Ltd.* ([1952] AC 427 at 450) said that the executive Act to be valid must be "capable of being related to one of the prescribed purposes" of the empowering Act.'

Here the order clearly relates to its prescribed purposes: to act against those who over-budget or overspend. At that stage it is not to encourage them to make reductions. The year 1980–81 in respect of which the Secretary of State is given power to reduce the amount of rate support grant payable commences in April 1980 and the Act came into force in November 1980. At the time when the power was given, January 1981, it was then far too late for the overspenders to take any decisive action. It is common knowledge that it is not possible to take action at short notice which makes any substantial reduction in the expenditure budgeted for the immediate or near future, especially so in the case of local government. That was the reason for the earlier warning or exhortations in 1979 and the advance notice by the Secretary of State of the nature of the powers which he would seek and how he would exercise them. The purpose of s 48 is, to our mind, quite clear. It is to give power to take action against those whose uniform rate, or adjusted uniform rate, exceed their notional uniform rate. This must have been patently obvious to Parliament when the Bill was debated and to the House of Commons when the multipliers order was laid, and subsequently considered and approved on 14 January.

It was entirely a matter for the Secretary of State's discretion to decide to treat the City of London as a special case and to grant an exemption and to conclude that no special treatment be accorded to Camden because of its ratio of daytime to resident population (the City's ratio being 30 times greater than the ratio for Camden). Again, it was entirely a matter for the Secretary of State's discretion as to how he dealt with inner city programme expenditure.

Inner city programme expenditure is financed by a combination of government grant (75%) and contributions from the rates (25%). The local authority contribution is included in the rate support grant calculations. The calculation of the rate and RSG-borne expenditure waiver therefore included an authority's 25% contribution from the rates. However, the government decided that where an authority became liable to abatement of grant, calculation of that abatement would be effected in such a way as to ensure that the authority did not lose grant in respect of its 25% contribution. However, the volume targets which had been set for individual local authorities included all current expenditure because they had been constructed on the basis of a fixed percentage reduction of the total of local authority net current expenditure. Of necessity, this definition included expenditure on inner city programmes. It seems to us equally to have been a matter for the discretion of the Secretary of State to decide to exclude from consideration the effect of local authority expenditure pursuant to s 11 of the Local Government Act 1966, which relates to certain expenditure due to immigrant population.

Complaint is made that the threshold of 155p did not provide for the applicants as much as a 30% margin over the notional uniform rate of 119p. That may very well be so, but the threshold nevertheless provided a significant tolerance above 119p for each applicant, so this attack fails.

Finally, it is said that the system of abatement failed to provide for partial abatement for partial compliance with the government's budgetary targets. Maybe a case can be made for the desirability of greater flexibility which such a provision would have provided, but this does not make the scheme capricious and unreasonable. Not every reasonable exercise of judgment is right and not every mistaken exercise of judgment is

unreasonable (per Lord Hailsham LC in *Re W (an infant)* [1971] 2 All ER 49 at 56, [1971]
a AC 682 at 700).
We reject this submission also. In our judgment the multipliers order was not ultra
vires and is effective.

II. *The Secretary of State misdirected himself as to his obligations under ss 48 to 50 of the Act*
The contention is that the Secretary of State regarded his power under these sections as
b transitional and considered himself legally obliged to exercise them in accordance with
the operational principles of the new block grant system, as provided for in ss 53 to 60.
We accept that the Secretary of State did regard and rightly regarded his powers as
transitional in the sense that they were designed to deal with the interim period before
the new block grant system came into effect. Although s 48(3) recognised the possibility
(which did not turn out to be the fact) that the block grant system might not be brought
c into effect for the year 1981–82, it is quite unrealistic to infer from the existence of this
subsection that Parliament had in mind that the block grant system would never come
into effect.
As to the contention that the Secretary of State considered himself legally bound so to
exercise these transitional powers in the manner in which he did, this arose by late
amendment and is based on the following observations in Mr Heiser's first affidavit, paras
d 40 and 41, the material parts of which read:

'40. As I have said above, the Government decided not only to introduce block
grant from 1981/82 onwards but also to modify the 1974 Act rate support grant
system for 1980/81. Clearly this modification needed to foreshadow as closely as
possible the block grant system. Consequently, the Government decided that these
transitional arrangements should enable it to reduce the grant paid to authorities
e whose expenditure exceeded their assessed expenditure need and that the reduction
in grant should, where possible, take the form of a reduction in the rate of resources
element support, since entitlement to this part of the grant was related to
expenditure . . .
41. The way in which any abatement of grant was to be calculated under the
transitional arrangements also needed to be consistent with the block grant system.
f Accordingly the eventual arrangements provided that equal degrees of expenditure
in excess of authorities' assessed expenditure needs, as measured by the amount by
which authorities' uniform rates exceeded the notional uniform rate, should incur
equal reductions in grant, expressed in terms of a rate poundage equivalent, ie a
grant reduction corresponding to the amount which would be raised in each
authority concerned by a given penny rate. This corresponded exactly to the way in
g which the block grant system would operate, whereby the rate of grant support for
high-spending authorities was to be reduced in a way which would increase the cost
of their spending by equal rate poundage amounts. The scale of grant abatements
under the transitional arrangements was therefore to be systemically consistent with
the rate poundage equalisation objective, with relatively higher rate poundage costs
for higher levels of expenditure, to be effected by the block grant system.'
h
Counsel for the applicants interprets the word 'needed', found in both paras 40 and 41
quoted above, as being synonymous with legal obligation rather than practicability or
sound policy. We do not consider that he was justified in so doing. We accept that the
word related to the government policy intention, in response to the defects of the old
rate support grant system, to introduce the new block grant system in 1981–82, and, as
j an interim measure, to modify the 1974 Act system in 1980–81 in a manner which
foreshadowed the principles of the block grant system, adopting certain of its
characteristics. It did not do so slavishly, for instance it provided the two waivers referred
to above and an upper limit of 5p. This policy intention was made clear by the Secretary
of State in his statement of 16 November 1979 on the rate support grant settlement
1980–81 when he said at para 35:
'The new block grant cannot be brought into effect until the 1981–82 grant year.

We have therefore decided to provide in the legislation for transitional arrangements
for 1980–81 which will make it possible to apply as far as practicable the principles   *a*
of block grant through adjustments of grant entitlement under existing legislation
at Increase Order stage.'

It was just over a year later (9 December 1980) that the Local Government, Planning
and Land Act 1980 (Commencement No 2) Order 1980, SI 1980/1893, was made by the
Secretary of State under s 53(9) of the Act appointing the year 1 April 1981–82 as the
'commencing year'.   *b*

III. No reasonable Secretary of State could have exercised his discretion by reducing the applicants'
rate support grant
    It is convenient to set out the oft-quoted words of Lord Greene MR in *Associated*
Provincial Picture Houses Ltd v Wednesbury Corp [1948] 1 KB 223 at 228–229; cf [1947] 2
All ER 680 at 682–683:   *c*

    'What, then, is the power of the courts? They can only interfere with an act of
    executive authority if it be shown that the authority has contravened the law...
    When an executive discretion is entrusted by Parliament to a body ... what appears
    to be an exercise of that discretion can only be challenged in the courts in a strictly
    limited class of case. As I have said; it must always be remembered that the court is   *d*
    not a court of appeal. When discretion of this kind is granted the law recognizes
    certain principles upon which that discretion must be exercised, but within the four
    corners of those principles the discretion, in my opinion, is an absolute one and
    cannot be questioned in any court of law. What then are those principles? They are
    well understood. They are principles which the court looks to in considering any
    question of discretion of this kind. The exercise of such a discretion must be a real   *e*
    exercise of the discretion . . . . It is true the discretion must be exercised reasonably.
    Now what does that mean? Lawyers familiar with the phraseology commonly used
    in relation to exercise of statutory discretions often use the word "unreasonable" in
    rather a comprehensive sense. It has frequently been used and is frequently used as
    a general description of the things that must not be done. For instance, a person
    entrusted with a discretion must, so to speak, direct himself properly in law. He   *f*
    must call his own attention to the matters which he is bound to consider. He must
    exclude from his consideration matters which are irrelevant to what he has to
    consider. If he does not obey those rules, he may truly be said, and often is said, to
    be acting "unreasonably". Similarly, there may be something so absurd that no
    sensible person could ever dream that it lay within the powers of the authority.'

    We have already dealt with certain specific matters relied on by the applicants to show   *g*
that in effect the Secretary of State's decision was so unreasonable as to be perverse, when
considering the contention that the multipliers order was unreasonable and capricious.
We will, of course, not repeat our decision on those matters. Although the applicants'
submissions on this particular aspect of the case were somewhat diffuse, we think we can
do them justice under the following headings:
       h
(a) *Irrelevant considerations*
    The applicants contend that the Secretary of State took into account irrelevant
considerations and in particular: (i) the disregard by the applicants of the government's
exhortations; (ii) non-compliance by the applicants with the waiver conditions; (iii)
compliance with the waiver conditions by certain local authorities before the enactment
of the 1980 Act; (iv) that the Secretary of State had given 'advance warning' prior to the   *j*
enactment of the Act as to the scheme under which he would exercise his discretion.
    This is in substance an attack on the Secretary of State's waivers.

Waivers
    The nature of the waivers, and the way in which they came about, has already been
outlined in the 'Background of Events' (see p 338ff, ante). It needs to be stressed that the

waivers were no more than declarations by the Secretary of State of the policy which he
a proposed to adopt in deciding whether to exempt local authorities from abatement in
cases where they would be liable to it. It was, in effect, reward for 'exceptional efforts',
but which had not succeeded in getting the local authority below the threshold.

It should also be remembered that once the multipliers order was approved it was no
longer possible for the Secretary of State to grant partial exemption; he could then only
decide to abate or not to abate.

b The applicants complain that as from the date when the Act came into force, November
1980, the waivers were not attainable by them. Counsel for the Secretary of State is
prepared to accept that this may be; counsel for the applicants does not suggest, nor is
there any evidence to support such a suggestion, that the applicants would have been
unable to comply with either of the waivers if they had made strenuous efforts so to do
from the moment in the autumn of 1979 when the Secretary of State exhorted local
c authorities to reduce their volume expenditure. It is common ground that there was no
obligation to provide any waivers, it being no part of the statutory scheme. As previously
stated, the Secretary of State recognised that certain high spenders might start from a
situation which made it very difficult for them to get down to the threshold which he
was setting, with the result that if he provided no special escape route, they would
inevitably qualify for grant abatement under the transitional arrangements because this
d depended on the amount by which their budget expenditure, as represented by the
uniform or adjusted uniform rate, exceeded their assessed expenditure needs, as
represented by the notional uniform rate.

For grant abatement this is the relevant measure of 'over-spend'. He therefore decided
to give waivers to those who met certain targets but could not get down to the threshold.

The two waivers are fully described in paras 18 and 19 of the report on the Rate
e Support Grant (Increase) (No 2) Order 1980. Briefly, the 'rate and RSG-borne expenditure'
waiver was to be based on a cash definition of expenditure. It would apply if the increase
between 1979–80 and 1980–81 in the budgeted rate fund revenue expenditure of an
authority was at least three percentage points less than the weighted average increase in
such expenditure for all authorities in the authority's class. This was judged to meet the
requirement for 'exceptional' reductions referred to in Mr Heiser's letter of 21 December
f 1979. The 'volume target' waiver would apply if the authority achieved the expenditure
target notified in June 1980.

In formulating the policy of waivers, the Secretary of State was entitled to take the
view that waivers should be measured by targets reflecting local authorities' attempts to
comply with government policy from the time the policy was announced. We accept
the submission of counsel for the Secretary of State that the Secretary of State was entitled
g in the exercise of his discretion to conclude that it would not be reasonable to set waivers
which were so generous that they were attainable by those who had not complied with
government policy, and only sought to do so after the Act came into force, by which
time it was too late. He was entitled to conclude that this would be unfair to those who
had successfully made the efforts which he had exhorted them to make.

It has to be borne in mind that both before and after the Act, the Secretary had no
h power to require reductions in spending. After the Act he had power to abate the rate
support grant in accordance with the order to be subsequently laid. It was a matter for
his judgment as to what exemptions, if any, to make in a context in which he was not
obliged to make any exemptions at all. It was open to him to reach the conclusion that to
grant, after November 1980, exemptions which could then be attained by efforts only
made after that date would substantially neutralise the very power that he had sought
j and which Parliament had given to him under s 48.

We cannot accept that the applicants have established any abuse by the Secretary of
State of his powers, either in the terms of the two waivers which he provided or in his
refusal to grant partial waivers. We do not infer from his private secretary's letter of 16
January 1981, referred to above, that he at any time laboured under the illusion that he
had not the power to grant a partial waiver. He had in fact, as the previous history
indicated, considered partial waivers and decided against them. We of course accept that

he had no power to change the basis of grant abatement once the multipliers order was in force. His power then was either to abate or not to abate. There was no middle course, *a* and a partial waiver had become impossible.

Complaint is made of the terms of Mr Osborn's memorandum referred to above and of the other departmental memoranda. The suggestion is made that the Secretary of State and his advisers wrongly thought that once the multipliers order was approved, the Secretary of State was obliged to exercise his discretion in favour of abatement or, at the least, that abatement would automatically occur unless he decided not to implement his *b* power of reduction. The language is not entirely happy and there is a hint of a 'reversed onus', but we do not believe that the Secretary of State, or his advisers, misdirected themselves. The truth is that the decision to abate had, for all practical purposes, been taken before the enactment of the 1980 Act, or the approval of the multipliers order; say by, or early in, November 1980. The language of the memoranda is merely a reflection of this situation. The Secretary of State was not misdirected and did not consider himself *c* obliged to do what he did; rather he did it because by November it had become his settled policy to do so.

(b) *The Secretary of State paid no regard to the individual circumstances of the applicants or to their need to spend at their chosen level*

The Secretary of State had, prior to obtaining his powers to abate grants, fully disclosed *d* to the public and Parliament the basis on which he proposed to exercise those powers. His basis was a formula approach, and did not contemplate any individual consideration of any rating authority save in so far as their individual circumstances had been reflected in the formula. Attempts had in fact been made in Parliament to achieve a different approach.

On 9 October 1980 a clause in the Bill, dealing with the transitional arrangements, *e* was debated by the House of Lords in committee. Replying to an opposition amendment to the transitional arrangements that would have obliged the Secretary of State to 'demonstrate that those authorities whose grant is to be reduced have acted unreasonably', Lord Bellwin, the Parliamentary Under-Secretary of State to the department, said that for the government to look at a particular authority's accounts and to make judgments on particular aspects of expenditure would be bitterly resented and it would neither *f* practicable nor desirable for the government to do so. Criteria had been set on an arithmetic basis. The amendment was, by leave, withdrawn.

On 27 October 1980 the clauses on the transitional arrangements in the Bill were considered at report stage by the House of Lords. The Opposition retabled an earlier amendment to require the Secretary of State to consult each authority concerned before reducing its grant under the transitional arrangement. Another retabled amendment *g* would have obliged the Secretary of State to demonstrate that an authority had acted unreasonably. Lord Bellwin reiterated the government's view that it was not the job of central government to tell authorities how they should order the priority of expenditure on their individual services. These amendments were also, by leave, withdrawn.

The formula approach was not a new approach. It was a fundamental feature of both the old and the new systems. Since 1966, central government had based its distribution *h* of the rate support grant on principles of general application to authorities. As a matter of principle it had not involved itself in the detailed financial affairs of individual authorities. As Mr Heiser points out in his affidavit, it had been accepted by successive administrations, with the agreement of local government, that in the context of the rate support grant system, central government is not in a position to form a judgment about the circumstances of individual authorities in order to say how much it considers an *j* authority should spend in order to meet its contractual obligations and carry out its statutory functions. Of necessity it had to operate an across-the-board formula based policy, both in the assessment of the authority's expenditure needs for the purpose of distributing rate support grant and in issuing the expenditure reduction targets requested of authorities in 1980–81.

As to the practical considerations the number of local authorities in England and Wales
is 457 (412 in England and 45 in Wales). They vary considerably in their size and
circumstances, in the services they provide, the population they serve and the money
they spend. The number and diversity of local authorities would have presented a major
obstacle to any attempt by government to measure on an individual as opposed to a
formula basis.

The government's inability to undertake examination of individual authorities'
circumstances on a case-by-case basis, looking at the books and the situation on the
ground and building up a tailor-made assessment of what that particular authority
needed to spend on its services does not mean that the circumstances of individual
authorities were not taken into account in the formula assessment of expenditure needs
in the grant distribution. Each authority's needs assessment was calculated as the product
of the weightings of the various factors in the formula, and the data for each factor
relating to that authority (ie the factor weightings for schoolchildren, elderly persons
living alone, overcrowded households etc *times* the number of schoolchildren, elderly
persons living alone, overcrowded households etc in each authority). Thus, within the
constraints of the formula and its factors, an authority's own circumstances were reflected
in the calculation of its needs assessment and its share of the equalising needs element
(which, together with resources element, enabled it to spend at the level of its assessed
expenditure need, whatever that might be, for a common rate in the pound, namely the
notional uniform rate).

It is convenient here to deal in more detail with the multiple regression analysis
approach to expenditure needs assessment. This rested on the assumption that, while
there were inevitably exceptions, there was generally a consistent pattern across the
country between what authorities actually spent and what they needed to spend. Rather
than accept individual authorities' actual expenditure as direct evidence of need for grant
distribution purposes, however (since this would have been a straightforward inducement
to authorities to spend more and more) the principle of multiple regression analysis
approach was to establish what constituted a comparable standard of service by reference
to the way the pattern of variation in expenditure in each area related to the pattern of
variation in the characteristics of each area. The aim was to identify the average 'equation'
of the incidence of such characteristics with expenditure, taking all areas in the country
from which a formula could be derived and applied to all authorities.

Although the analysis was a lengthy and complex operation its essential principles
were straightforward. In order to identify the 'average equation' the computer compared
data relating to each authority in the country in respect of a series of pre-selected factors
(such as numbers of school pupils, single parent families, elderly people living alone,
overcrowded households, etc per head of population) with actual post expenditure figures
for each authority in the country (expressed as a single pound per head amount for each
authority, covering all its services in total).

Broadly speaking, the analysis identified those indicators whose incidence was most
strongly correlated with the past pattern of authorities' expenditure per head of
population and weighted them according to the extent to which it accounted for
variations in expenditure. Subject to certain technical procedures, the factors thus selected
and weighted become the needs assessment formula for application to individual
authorities. Thus the analysis chose the selection of a series of factors and by means of
weightings identified their relative importance in accounting for variations in local
authority expenditure. Thus any one factor in the formula could not be modified in
recognition of the special circumstances of an individual authority without affecting all
other authorities subject to the formula, some advantageously and some disadvanta-
geously.

The necessity for operating within a formula is further exemplified by Mr Heiser in
para 4 of his third affidavit when dealing with certain specific examples of expenditure
provided by some of the applicants.

The Secretary of State was, in our judgment, fully entitled to adopt a formula approach.

(c) *The Secretary of State failed to consider the figures for 'assumed need' (GREs) to be used under the block grant system as a cross-check in considering whether and by how much to reduce the applicants' rate support grants.*
There is clearly room for a difference of opinion as to the value of this cross-check. But the existence of potentially competing views does not establish that the Secretary of State's approach was so wrong that no reasonable Secretary of State would sensibly have taken his view.

We are conscious that we have not dealt with what we respectfully consider are a few quite minor and trivial points which were relied on under this main heading. To detail them all would make this judgment even longer than unfortunately it is already. Counsel for the applicants was, we understand, prepared to accept that, if he failed to establish 'unreasonableness' in relation to the main points with which we have dealt under this heading and under the second submission relative to the multipliers order, he would be unable to establish that the Secretary of State's decision was so unreasonable that no reasonable Secretary of State could ever have come to it.

We are thus satisfied that the policy of the Secretary of State was not 'unreasonable' and accordingly we reject this submission.

IV. *The Secretary of State failed validly to exercise his discretion under ss 48 to 50 of the 1980 Act*
The question whether the Secretary of State validly exercised the discretion given to him under the 1980 Act to abate the rate support grants payable to the applicants is the main issue in this case. It was contended in a variety of ways that he failed to do so. In the end it came down basically to one proposition. There can be no real or genuine exercise of the discretion unless, after having obtained that discretionary power, the Secretary of State was prepared to listen to any new representations made to him. It is important to have well in mind the limited nature of this submission.

It was ultimately accepted on behalf of the applicants: (1) the Secretary of State is entitled to remain consistent with his policy announced before obtaining his powers, so long as he remains open to persuasion; (2) after the 1980 Act came into force there was no duty on the Secretary of State to consult, ie to make positive moves to hear any representations; (3) the Secretary of State is under no obligation to listen again to representations made to him when he was in process of formulating that policy, hence the reference to 'new representations'; (4) there is no need for any oral hearing of any new representations; (5) in the light of time spent on past consultations and representations, the Secretary of State is entitled to fix a reasonable time limit for the presentation of new representations.

It was submitted by the applicants that an unwillingness to listen to new representations sought to be made after obtaining the statutory power and before its exercise, because of a policy laid down in advance of obtaining those statutory powers, results in a failure lawfully to exercise that discretion. Such an unwillingness, it is contended, amounts to an unlawful fetter being imposed on the discretionary power, and to a denial of the principles of natural justice to act fairly.

Counsel for the Secretary of State contended that where the discretionary power is given by the legislature to pursue a policy on a general basis for the public benefit generally, so that the Secretary of State has a choice solely of whether or not to exercise the power, he is entitled to implement the policy of which Parliament has approved without listening to any representations.

The law
(a) *Fettering of discretion*
Counsel for the applicants adopts the following statement from H W R Wade *Administrative Law* (4th edn, 1977) p 317:

'It is a fundamental rule for the exercise of discretionary power that discretion must be brought to bear on every case: each one must be considered on its own merits and decided as the public interest requires at the time.'

The authority on which the applicants mainly rely is *British Oxygen Co Ltd v Minister of*
a *Technology* [1970] 3 All ER 165 esp at 170–171, [1971] AC 610 esp at 625 per Lord Reid:

'The general rule is that anyone who has to exercise a statutory discretion must
not "shut [his] ears to an application". . . . I do not think there is any great difference
between a policy and a rule. There may be cases where an officer or authority ought
to listen to a substantial argument reasonably presented urging a change of policy.
What the authority must not do is to refuse to listen at all. But a Ministry or large
b authority may have had to deal already with a multitude of similar applications and
then they will almost certainly have evolved a policy so precise that it could well be
called a rule. There can be no objection to that, provided the authority is always
willing to listen to anyone with something new to say—of course I do not mean to
say that there need be an oral hearing.'

c
Counsel for the Secretary of State contended that these observations must be read in
their proper context and this involved the extent to which a passage in the judgment of
Bankes LJ in *R v Port of London Authority, ex p Kynoch Ltd* [1919] 1 KB 176 at 184 was of
general application. He was considering, counsel for the Secretary of State contended, the
usual run of case where the discretionary power conferred is of a general nature, to be
d exercised on more than one occasion and in relation to applications for the grant of some
right which the person holding the power can confer, such as a permission or licence. He
referred to an earlier part of Lord Reid's speech, which reads ([1970] 3 All ER 165 at 170,
[1971] AC 610 at 624):

'If the Minister who now administers the Act, acting on behalf of the government,
should decide not to give grants in respect of certain kinds of expenditure, I can find
e nothing to prevent him. There are two general grounds on which the exercise of an
unqualified discretion can be attacked. It must not be exercised in bad faith, and it
must not be so unreasonably exercised as to show that there cannot have been any
real or genuine exercise of the discretion. But, apart from that, if the Minister thinks
that policy or good administration requires the operation of some limiting rule, I
f find nothing to stop him.'

The Act to which Lord Reid was referring was the Industrial Development Act 1966,
which provided for the making of grants out of moneys provided by Parliament towards
expenditure on the provision of new business assets.
In support of his proposition that a distinction has to be drawn when the statute
g contemplates a singular rather than a regular exercise of discretion, counsel for the
Secretary of State relied on *Sagnata Investments Ltd v Norwich Corp* [1971] 2 All ER 1441
esp at 1447–1448, [1971] 2 QB 614 esp at 626–627 per Lord Denning MR:

'I take it to be perfectly clear now that an administrative body, including a
licensing body, which may have to consider numerous applications of a similar
h kind, is entitled to lay down a general policy which it proposes to follow in coming
to its individual decisions, provided always that it is a reasonable policy which it is
fair and just to apply. Once laid down, the administrative body is entitled to apply
the policy in the individual cases which may come before it. The only qualification
is that the administrative body must not apply the policy so rigidly as to reject an
applicant without hearing what he has to say. It must not "shut its ears to an
j application" (see per Lord Reid in *British Oxygen Co Ltd v Minister of Technology* [1970]
3 All ER 165 at 170, [1971] AC 610 at 625, quoting Barkes LJ in *R v Port of London
Authority, ex p Kynoch Ltd* [1971] 1 KB 176 at 183). The applicant is entitled to put
forward reasons urging that the policy should be changed, or saying that in any case
that it should not be applied to him. But, so long as the administrative body is ready
to hear him and consider what he has to say, it is entitled to apply its general policy
to him as to others.'

However, *de Smith's Judicial Review of Administrative Action* (4th edn, 1980) pp 313–314
makes clear that the 'fettering' principle does not apply only to cases concerned with the   a
discretionary grant of licences and permits and gives examples of such other cases.
Moreover, in *Smith v Inner London Education Authority* [1978] 1 All ER 411 at 418 Lord
Denning MR, applying the *British Oxygen* case, said:

> 'I cannot see that there is anything ultra vires in an education authority having a
> policy by which they aim at the comprehensive principle throughout their area.
> Nor do I see anything unlawful to their applying that policy in the case of any   b
> individual school, provided that they listen to all the objections and consider
> whether or no the policy should be applied.'

Further support for the applicants' contention is to be found in the judgment of
Templeman LJ in *A-G ex rel Tilley v Wandsworth London BC* [1981] 1 All ER 1162 at 1170–
1171, [1981] 1 WLR 854 at 858, where he said: c

> 'On well-recognised principles public authorities are not entitled to fetter the
> exercise of a discretion or to fetter the manner in which they are empowered to
> discharge the many duties that are thrust on them. They must at all times, in every
> particular case, consider how to exercise their discretion and how to perform their
> duties.'

   d

We are not prepared to accept counsel for the Secretary of State's broad and far-reaching
proposition, devoid as it is of any clear authority and running counter to the general
principles referred to above.

(b) *Natural justice*

It is not possible to lay down rigid rules as to when principles of natural justice are   e
to apply, nor as to their scope and extent. Everything depends on the subject matter
(see *R v Gaming Board for Great Britain, ex p Benaim* [1970] 2 All ER 528 at 533, [1970]
2 QB 417 at 430 per Lord Denning MR). It is clear that different classes of cases were
recognised in *Ridge v Baldwin* [1963] 2 All ER 66 at 74, [1964] AC 40 at 72 per Lord Reid.

The scope of 'fairness' was carefully examined by Sir Robert Megarry V-C in *McInnes v
Onslow Fane* [1978] 3 All ER 211, [1978] 1 WLR 1520. In that case a fair hearing was   f
denied to an applicant for a boxing manager's licence. The Vice-Chancellor, while not
suggesting that there was any clear or exhaustive classification, thought that at least three
categories of decision could be identified. In the first there is a decision which takes away
some existing right or position, as when a member is expelled or a licence is revoked.
The second, at the other extreme, are what may be called the application cases. These are
cases where the decision merely refuses to grant the applicant the right or position that   g
he seeks, such as membership of the organisation, or a licence to do certain acts. Third,
there is an intermediate category, which may be called the expectation cases, which differ
from the application cases only in that the applicant has some legitimate expectation
from what has already happened that his application will be granted. This heading
includes cases where an existing licence holder applies for a renewal of his licence, or a
person already elected or appointed to some position seeks confirmation from some   h
confirming authority. In the first category of case where there is a threat to take
something away the Vice-Chancellor held that the right to be heard was plainly apt.

Does the Secretary of State's decision in this case involve taking away some existing
right? The answer to this seems plain. On 15 January 1981 the Rate Support Grant
(Increase)(No 2) Order 1980 came into operation. Thus on that date all the applicants
were entitled to receive the rate support grant provided by the Rate Support Grant Order   j
1979 as thus increased. Although the multipliers order came into effect on 15 January
thus enabling the Secretary of State effectively to exercise the power given to him under
s 48 of the Act to reduce the rate support grants, he was not *obliged* to make a
redetermination under s 49 thereby reducing Waltham Forest's resources element of the
rate support grant or a variation under s 50 thereby reducing the needs element of the

rate support grant of the other applicants. He had a discretion as to whether or not to
a make such a redetermination or variation.

   Thus the decision (made on 26 January 1981) to reduce the applicants' rate support
grants adversely affected not merely an expectation but a right to substantial sums of
money. The applicants do not assert that the Secretary of State was under a duty to act as
though his was a judicial decision requiring the process of a lis to be applied. This is not
a surprising admission in view of the degree of consultation and discussion which had
b preceded the 1980 Act. As Lord Reid observed in *Ridge v Baldwin* [1963] 2 All ER 66 at
81, [1964] AC 40 at 80:

   'The body with the power to decide cannot lawfully proceed to make a decision
   until it has afforded the person affected a proper opportunity to state his case.'

   The applicants are content to limit the duty, in the context of this case, to the obligation
c to receive any new representations which the applicants wish to make. Moreover, they
do not claim that the Secretary of State in listening to any such representation is not
entitled to have well in his mind his policy. To this extent the reference to keeping an
open mind does not mean an empty mind. His mind must be kept 'ajar'. We accept the
validity of this submission.

d
   (c) *Facts*
   It is common ground that before the 1980 Act received the royal assent on 13
November 1980 the Secretary of State had already formulated a policy how he might
exercise his statutory discretion if and when Parliament gave him the powers he sought.
This, counsel for applicants accepted, he was clearly entitled to do. Further we are satisfied
e that the Secretary of State in formulating his policy (i) did not act unreasonably, (ii) was
entitled to adopt a broad policy, not paying attention to the detailed circumstances of
individual authorities, (iii) did act in a way consistent with the purpose of the 1980 Act
when eventually enacted, (iv) did not create a retrospective effect beyond that
contemplated by the 1980 Act, (v) acted properly in terms of discussions, negotiations
and openness to representations until 1980.
f   In short, had the Secretary of State enjoyed and exercised his discretionary powers in
1979 or early in 1980, we would say that there was no ground on which to criticise his
exercise of them. Counsel for the applicants' attack is based on his policy, once formulated,
being fixed and immutable. The press notice of 18 September 1980 identified that policy.
   After 13 November, when the Act received the royal assent, it is clear that the Secretary
of State refused to listen to any suggestion from the applicants which in any way sought
g to cause him to alter or amend or reconsider his announced scheme. His attitude between
November 1980 and the exercise of his discretion towards the end of January 1981 was
in effect that the policy was settled, and that the only topic open for discussion was
whether a local authority might still be able to qualify for waiver, as some had done at a
later stage (see 'Background of Events' and in particular the Secretary of State's reply dated
9 January 1981 to Councillor Smart's letter of 19 December asking the Secretary of State
h to meet a delegation of the authorities to be penalised under the transitional arrangements
and the letter of 16 January 1981 from the Secretary of State's personal secretary
purporting to answer the two questions raised on that day by Camden). The very terms
of the opening paragraph of Mr Osborn's memorandum of 16 January, to which we have
already referred, incorrectly expressing the discretion in negative terms, assumes that the
reduction of the support grant was a foregone conclusion. The Secretary of State, although
j he had from 13 November 1981 a discretion whether or not to implement his power to
reduce the rate support grant in respect of each of the applicants, until 26 January when
he made his decision, clearly decided to turn a deaf ear to any and all representations to
change the policy formulated by him before he obtained his statutory powers.
   Was he entitled to adopt this attitude? He had announced in general terms what he
intended to do if given the power to do it, he had listened to representations and had

formulated his policy in the light of them. We do not feel that this is an adequate answer. In our judgment the Secretary of State was obliged to be ready to listen to any objector who showed that he might have something new to say; putting it negatively, he was obliged not to declare his unwillingness to listen or to be unwilling, in advance of any representations. We accept that to be entitled to be heard it was for the objector to show that he had, or might have, something new to say. If the Secretary of State then refused to listen or indicated in advance that he would not listen to any representations of whatever kind, he would be in the wrong. He would be unlawfully fettering his discretion. Moreover, having regard to the applicants' accrued right to the support grant, he would not be properly discharging his duty of fairness.

How does the Secretary of State stand in relation to this statement of his duty?

The main event relied on by the applicants as constituting representations by them, or as a further and final effort by them to be heard, is the letter of 19 December 1980 from Councillor Smart to the Secretary of State on behalf of the vulnerable local authorities and the reply of the Secretary of State dated 9 January 1981, summarised in the 'Background of Events' (see p 341, ante). By this time the political battle had been strongly joined, there had been debates in Parliament and there was to be another on the multipliers order in a few days' time. The pros and cons of the argument had been widely debated and canvassed; no doubt the Secretary of State thought that he knew the views of the local authorities as well as they did, and vice versa. The letter from Councillor Smart and the later telex have something of the air of a legal manoeuvre.

None the less, we see no reason to doubt that the local authorities genuinely felt themselves to be aggrieved. The exhortations of the Secretary of State were originally made, and continued to be urged, at a time when he had no power, legal or practical, to insist on what he wanted to be done and were backed up by threats of action, the so-called 'penalties', which he did not then have power to impose. The local authorities perhaps did not fully understand the apparent lack of relationship between the degree of their overspending and the size of the penalty. He, for his part, no doubt felt that he would hear nothing new and that any tales of hardship of which he might be told had their origin in the refusal of the local authorities to listen to his exhortations in the autumn of 1979 or early in 1980.

Weighing it all up we conclude, applying the test stated above, that the Secretary of State ought not to have rejected this approach out of hand and ought to have been prepared to receive the deputation proposed by Councillor Smart, or otherwise have listened to what he desired to say on behalf of the vulnerable local authorities. However, by this time it was clear that the Secretary of State regarded his policy as settled, the only room for further consideration being as to the application of the waivers. In short, he should have been, but was not, ready to *hear anything new which might be said.*

Should the applicants be granted the relief they claim?

Counsel for the Secretary of State contended that, if the Secretary of State was obliged before he exercised his discretion to consider new representations made to him, then we should be satisfied that the Secretary of State after fairly listening to these representations would inevitably have adhered to his declared policy. Accordingly it would be a pointless operation to quash the Secretary of State's decision and require him to consider the representations which the applicants wish to advance.

Having spent many days reading the voluminous affidavits and exhibits and hearing the contentions urged by counsel for the Secretary of State, it would of course be unrealistic not to accept that it is certainly probable that, if the representations had been listened to by the Secretary of State, he would nevertheless have adhered to his policy. However, we are not satisfied that such a result must inevitably have followed. To take but one argument advanced by the applicants, other than Waltham Forest, there is material to support the proposition that the Secretary of State might have been under some misapprehension as to the working of the rate support grant system under the 1974 Act, in that he *may* have assumed that all authorities, whether in receipt of the

needs element or resources element, could attract extra grants as a *direct* consequence of
their expenditure, whereas this only applied to those in receipt of resources element (see
in particular the Secretary of State's speech on 14 January 1981 when seeking approval
for the rate support grant report together with the 1980 order and multipliers order). It
would in our view be wrong for this court to speculate how the Secretary of State would
have exercised his discretion if he had heard the representations. We respectfully adopt
the words of Megarry J in *John v Rees* [1969] 2 All ER 274 at 309, [1970] Ch 345 at 402,
when he said:

'As everybody who has anything to do with the law well knows, the path of the
law is strewn with examples of open and shut cases which, somehow, were not; of
unanswerable charges which, in the event, were completely answered; of inexplicable
conduct which was fully explained; of fixed and unalterable determinations that,
by discussion, suffered a change.'

As H W R Wade, *Administrative Law* (4th edn, 1977) p 455, n 3 points out, the report
of *Ridge v Baldwin* [1964] AC 40 at 47 records that the hearing later given to the chief
constable's solicitor at least induced three members of the watch committee to change
their mind. Thus, even if the ultimate outcome of our decision were to be that the
Secretary of State, having fairly considered the applicants' representations, nevertheless
decides to abate their rate support grants, we are not prepared to hold that it would have
been a useless formality for the Secretary of State to have listened to the representations.
The importance of the principles to which we have referred to above far transcend the
significance of this case. If our decision is inconvenient, it cannot be helped. Convenience
and justice are often not on speaking terms (per Lord Atkin in *General Medical Council v
Spackman* [1943] 2 All ER 337 at 341, [1943] AC 627 at 638).

Conclusions

(1) The multipliers order is valid. (2) The Secretary of State did not misdirect himself
as to his powers under ss 48 to 50 of the 1980 Act. (3) The Secretary of State's decision to
reduce the rate support grants of each of the applicants was a decision which, subject to
(4) below, the Secretary of State was entitled to reach. (4) The Secretary of State did not
validly exercise his discretionary powers because, after obtaining them and before making
his decision to reduce the rate support grants, he refused to listen to any new
representations which the applicants desired to make. (5) The Secretary of State's decision
must be quashed.

It will of course be open to the Secretary of State after considering the applicants'
representations, now fully documented, to reach any decision he considers right, and
which is within the terms of the 1980 Act and the multipliers order.

Finally, we should like to thank counsel for their assistance in this somewhat
complicated case. Having learned a few weeks before the hearing that the affidavit and
exhibits numbered close on 1,000 pages we had a prehearing review. At our request we
were most helpfully provided with a useful glossary of terms, a reading guide, a
chronological statement of events and an outline of the submissions to be made. This
enabled us to save much hearing time by some useful advance reading.

Orders of certiorari granted.

Solicitors: *F Nickson* (for the applicants); *Treasury Solicitor*.

N P Metcalfe Esq   Barrister.

R v Secretary of State for the Environment, ex parte Hackney London Borough Council and another

QUEEN'S BENCH DIVISION

MAY LJ AND McNEILL J

14, 15, 16, 17 DECEMBER 1982, 28 JANUARY 1983

Estoppel – Issue estoppel – Judicial review – Whether doctrine of issue estoppel can be relied on in applications for judicial review.

The doctrine of issue estoppel has no relevance to applications for judicial review under RSC Ord 53, because (a) in proceedings for judicial review there are no formal pleadings and therefore it is often impossible to identify the particular issues which were decided in earlier proceedings between the parties, (b) in Ord 53 proceedings there is no lis between the Crown (in whose name the proceedings are brought) and the respondent, or between the ex parte applicant and the respondent, and (c) a decision in Ord 53 proceedings is not 'final' in the sense necessary for issue estoppel to operate because the relief granted is always discretionary and in many cases leaves the matter in dispute to be reconsidered by the person or body making the original decision (see p 359 *d*, p 366 *d* and p 367 *c d* and *h j*, post).

Dicta of Diplock LJ in *Mills v Cooper* [1967] 2 All ER at 104 and of Viscount Dilhorne and Lord Hailsham in *DPP v Humphrys* [1976] 2 All ER at 505, 516 applied.

Dictum of Coleridge J in *R v Hartington Middle Quarter (Inhabitants)* (1855) 4 E & B at 794 considered.

Quaere. Whether issue estoppel can ever operate against the Crown (see p 359 *d* and p 367 *d*, post).

Notes

For issue estoppel, see 16 Halsbury's Laws (4th edn) paras 1530–1533, and for cases on the subject, see 21 Digest (Reissue) 37–106, 232–727.

For judicial review generally, see 37 Halsbury's Laws (4th edn) paras 567–583.

Cases referred to in judgment

DPP v Humphrys [1976] 2 All ER 497, [1977] AC 1, [1976] 2 WLR 857, HL.

Dunlop v Wollahra Municipal Council [1981] 1 All ER 1202, [1982] AC 158, [1981] 2 WLR 693, PC.

McInnes v Onslow Fane [1978] 3 All ER 211, [1978] 1 WLR 1520.

Mills v Cooper [1967] 2 All ER 100, [1967] 2 QB 459, [1967] 2 WLR 1343, DC.

R v Hartington Middle Quarter (Inhabitants) (1855) 4 E & B 780, 119 ER 288.

R v Secretary of State for the Environment, ex p Brent London BC [1983] 3 All ER 321, [1982] QB 593, [1982] 2 WLR 693, DC.

R v Wye (Inhabitants) (1838) 7 Ad & El 761, 112 ER 656.

Applications for judicial review

Hackney London Borough Council and Camden London Borough Council applied, with the leave of Glidewell J granted on 9 February 1982, for (i) a declaration that the Secretary of State for the Environment misdirected himself in law in reaching the decision or decisions made on a date unknown to the applicants but prior to 26 November 1981 and evidenced by letters dated 9 November 1981 and 26 November 1981 (a) that the duty to cause payments to be made to the applicants and each of them of increased rate support grant for the year 1980–81 did not then exist and could not arise until he had decided whether or not to reduce their rate support grant for that year, (b) that in the premises no interest would be payable to the applicants, (ii) orders of certiorari to quash those

decisions and (iii) a declaration that the applicants and each of them was entitled to
interest on the amounts of rate support grant unlawfully withheld and to damages in
respect of such interest. Camden London Borough Council alone sought (iv) a declaration
that the Secretary of State for the Environment had misdirected himself in law in
reaching the decision made on a date unknown to Camden Borough Council but prior
to 19 February 1982 and evidenced by a letter dated 19 February 1982 from the
Department of the Environment to Camden London Borough Council to withhold and/
or to reduce the amount of rate support grant payable to Camden London Borough
Council in respect of the year 1980–81, (v) an order of certiorari to quash that decision,
(vi) an order of mandamus directing the Secretary of State to cause or permit payment to
be made to Camden London Borough Council of its full entitlement to increased rate
support grant for 1980–81, (vii) as an alternative to (vi), damages for non-payment. The
facts are set out in the judgment of the court.

Roger Henderson QC and *Charles George* for the applicants.
Robert Alexander QC, *Simon D Brown* and *Paul Walker* for the Secretary of State.

Cur adv vult

28 January. The following judgment of the court was delivered.

MAY LJ. McNeill J and I have co-operated in preparing this judgment and he has
authorised me to say that he entirely agrees with it.

In this case counsel moved on behalf of the London boroughs of Hackney and Camden
for certain relief by way of judicial review of decisions of the Secretary of State for the
Environment, of November 1981, relating to the rate support grant for each of the two
boroughs for the year 1980–81. These present applications follow previous similar ones
made by the same two and other London boroughs and the judgment of this court on
them in *R v Secretary of State for the Environment, ex p Brent London BC* [1983] 3 All ER
321. We very gratefully adopt the description of the earlier rate support grant system
under the Local Government Act 1974 and the history of its replacement by the new
block grant system under the Local Government, Planning and Land Act 1980 set out in
the *Brent* case (at 324–332). We similarly adopt the background to and the history of the
relevant events between the general election in 1979 and 30 January 1981 detailed in the
Brent case (at 333–343).

We then record what this court held on the previous applications. First, that the Rate
Support Grant (Principles for Multipliers) Order 1980, SI 1980/2047, was not ultra vires
and is and has been effective since it was approved by the House of Commons on 14
January 1981. Second and third, that neither did the Secretary of State misdirect himself
as to his obligations under ss 48 to 50 of the 1980 Act, in regarding them as transitional
provisions, nor was the policy which he adopted in exercising his powers under those
sections of itself unreasonable. But fourth, that the Secretary of State's decision of 26
January 1981 to abate the rate support grants payable to the applicants then before the
court, which of course included those making the instant applications, was an invalid
exercise of his discretion under the relevant sections, because after obtaining the powers
enabling him so to act he refused to listen to any new representations which any of the
London boroughs involved desired to make to him. That decision of the Secretary of
State was therefore quashed. The present applications are concerned with the respective
positions in law of the Secretary of State on the one hand and the relevant London
boroughs on the other, in so far as any rate support grant was concerned, after the original
decision of the Secretary of State had been quashed and in the light of subsequent events.

The relevant statutory provisions and those of the related statutory instruments are as
follows. Section 1(1) of the Local Government Act 1974 is in these terms:

'Subject to the provisions of this Part of this Act, the Secretary of State shall, for
the year 1974–75 and each subsequent year, make grants to local authorities in

England and Wales in accordance with this section; and any grants made in pursuance of this subsection shall be known as "rate support grants".'

The remainder of s 1 and s 2 set out how the amounts of rate support grants are to be calculated; of these provisions only s 2(2) requires quoting in full for present purposes:

'Subject to the following provisions of this section, payments in respect of the elements of rate support grant shall be made to a local authority at such times as the Secretary of State may with the consent of the Treasury determine, and shall be made in aid of the revenues of the authority generally; and the provisions of Schedule 2 to this Act shall have effect with respect to the determination of the amounts payable to any local authority in respect of those elements for any year.'

Once the appropriate estimates and calculations have been made, s 3 requires the Secretary of State to make what is described as a rate support grant order. The section is in these terms:

'Rate support grant orders.—(1) The estimated aggregate amount of the rate support grants fixed in accordance with section 1(2) above for any year and the matters which under this Part of this Act are to be prescribed shall be fixed and prescribed by an order (in this Part of this Act referred to as a "rate support grant order") made by the Secretary of State with the consent of the Treasury and after consultation with such associations of local authorities as appear to the Secretary of State to be concerned and with any local authority with whom consultation appears to him to be desirable.

(2) Every rate support grant order shall be laid before the Commons House of Parliament and shall not have effect until approved by a resolution of that House.

(3) Together with any rate support grant order laid before the Commons House of Parliament there shall be laid a report of the considerations leading to the provisions of the order, including the considerations leading to the determination of the amount available for grants and the portions mentioned in paragraphs (a) to (c) of section 1(2) above.

(4) A separate rate support grant order shall be made in advance for each year.'

Section 4 enables the Secretary of State to increase rate support grants in any year to take account, for instance, of the effects of inflation and to that end to make the appropriate statutory instrument in the same way as rate support grant orders. We understand that in recent years the Secretary of State has found it necessary to make at least one, and sometimes more rate support grant (increase) orders for a given year.

In addition to the statutory instruments made under ss 3 and 4 of the 1974 Act, s 10 gives the Secretary of State power to make general regulations for operating and bringing the rate support grant system into effect. We are concerned with the Rate Support Grant Regulations 1979, SI 1979/1514, made thereunder and in particular with reg 5, which is in these terms:

'(1) The Secretary of State shall, upon the best information available to him, estimate and notify to each local authority the amounts of the constituent elements of rate support grant which will become payable to the authority for the year; and he may make and notify to the authority such further estimates of the said amounts, taking into account information not previously available, as he may think fit.

(2) As soon as practicable after he has received what appears to him to be sufficient information for the purpose, the Secretary of State shall make a conclusive calculation of the said amounts and notify the result thereof to each local authority.

(3) The amount of any element of rate support grant payable to a local authority shall be calculated to the nearest pound.

(4) Where it appears to the Secretary of State from any estimate or calculation made under this regulation that a sum in excess of the amount of the estimate or calculation has already been paid to a local authority in respect of rate support grants for the year, he may recover that sum by deduction from any amounts due to that

a authority in respect of rate support grants, whether for the year or for any subsequent year, or by payment to him by the authority after a demand therefor or partly by such deduction and partly by such a payment, as he thinks fit.'

In the 1980 Act, as this court held in the first judgment, ss 48 to 50 inclusive contain the transitional provisions enabling the Secretary of State to reduce the rate support grant payable to a local authority for the year 1980–81 pending the changeover to the new block grant system of rate support grants provided for by ss 53 to 68 of the same Act.

b The transitional provisions were in the event only applicable to 1980–81 because the year beginning with 1 April 1981 was appointed as 'the commencing year' for the purposes of Pt VI (ss 48–68) of the 1980 Act by the relevant commencement order (SI 1980/1893).

We now set out certain events and refer to various documents which were not referred to in the earlier judgment of this court either because they were irrelevant to the applications then before it or because they occurred or came into existence after it was

c delivered.

On 9 January 1980 the Department of the Environment wrote a letter to the chief financial officers of both the Camden and Hackney councils, and no doubt of all other local authorities entitled to rate support grants, relating to those grants for the three years 1978–79, 1979–80 and 1980–81. In so far as the first two years were concerned, the letter recorded that two increase orders had been laid before the House of Commons and went

d into various details of the grant increases which the councils might expect. It would not be possible for the increase orders to be debated by Parliament for a little time and consequently the department proposed to bring forward some of the remaining payments under the main order for 1979–80. As will be seen, the usual procedure was to pay the main rate support grant in each year by stipulated proportions on stated dates at approximately weekly intervals.

e The letters then went on to deal with the grant for 1980–81. They explained how the various elements would be calculated. Paragraph 18 of the letters was then in these terms:

'The grants for 1980/81 will be paid on the following basis: a. One forty-eighth part of each authority's calculated entitlement will be paid on Thursday, 3 April.

f b. The remainder of the grant will be divided by twelve. One quarter of each twelfth will be paid on about the 8th of each month; one quarter on about the 15th of each month; and one half on about the 23rd of each month. A list showing the precise dates of payment throughout the year is at Annex H.'

Annex H listed 37 specific dates between 3 April 1980 and 23 March 1981 for the payment of the main grant for 1980–81, including in particular six dates between 26

g January 1981 and the end of that fiscal year. It will be remembered that 26 January 1981 was ultimately the date of the Secretary of State's purported decision to reduce the grant to some London boroughs, including Hackney and Camden, under his transitional powers in ss 48 to 50 of the 1980 Act, which this court quashed in the *Brent* case.

The Rate Support Grant Order 1979 (ie the main order for the year 1980–81) came into force on 17 January 1980.

h Our adoption of the statement of facts in the earlier judgment then enables us to move quickly through 1980 and most of 1981. We merely record that the Rate Support Grant (Increase) (No 2) Order 1980, SI 1980/2049, came into operation on the 15 January 1981, as did the multipliers order, and we now refer to material events which occurred after the first judgment.

On 23 October 1981 the chief executive of the London Borough of Camden wrote to

j the Secretary of State contending, first, that as the decision of the Secretary of State to withhold payments of the grant under the Rate Support Grant (Increase) (No 2) Order for 1980–81 had been set aside, the borough was entitled to payment of the amount withheld. Second, the borough argued that the Secretary of State should not exercise a discretion to continue to withhold the sums which should have been deemed to have been paid, particularly as by that time the budgets for 1980–81 had been 'spent'. Third, the borough told the Secretary of State that, should he nevertheless be reconsidering whether to abate its grant for 1980–81, there were further representations of substance which it would wish to put before him.

The department's reply was dated 9 November 1981. It argued that this court had held in its earlier judgment that it was open to the Secretary of State to reconsider the matter afresh, after considering any further representations which the councils affected might wish to make. It disputed that the amounts of grant for 1980–81 still withheld became payable forthwith once the Secretary of State's first decision had been quashed. Finally, it expressed the Secretary of State's view that any question of any additional grant should be held over until any appeal against the court's earlier decision had been decided, or until all parties had agreed not to appeal and he had taken a new decision in the matter.

Neither side did appeal and there was further correspondence between the councils and the Secretary of State reiterating each side's contentions. In addition both the present applicants made further representations to the Secretary of State seeking to persuade him not to continue to withhold any of their grant for 1980–81, even on a reconsideration of the whole question in the light of this court's decision. Further, in the course of the exchange of correspondence over this period, the councils first made a claim to interest on the outstanding amounts of the rate support grant which they contended that the department should have paid to them.

On 10 February 1982 the present applications were issued. We refer to them in their now amended form in more detail hereafter.

By letters dated 19 February 1982 to the chief executives of both the present applicants, the department informed them of what we will call the second decision of the Secretary of State, namely whether and the extent to which he proposed to exercise the discretion which the department contended he still had to abate the applicants' rate support grant for 1980–81 under ss 48 to 50 of the 1980 Act. In brief the Secretary of State decided to abate these grants to the same extent as he had when he made his first decision, provided that the relevant council failed to comply with either of the 'waivers' which are referred to and explained in the previous judgment of this court, but subject to this modification, that the relevant expenditure would be calculated on actual out-turn figures instead of budgeted figures as they had originally been prescribed.

Of the two present applicants Camden borough was unable to comply with either of the two waivers and as a result of the second decision of the Secretary of State he has withheld rate support grant for 1980–81 from it of a total amount of £5,112,289. Hackney borough on the other hand, was able to show that on out-turn figures it qualified for the 'rate and RSG-borne expenditure' waiver and consequently on 9 August 1982 it was paid £929,416, being the amount by which its rate support grant for 1980–81 had been reduced.

In these circumstances the first submission made by counsel on behalf of the applicants was that the Secretary of State's second decision in February 1982 to exercise his discretion to reduce local authorities' rate support grants for 1980–81 in certain instances was also unlawful. He based this submission on the precise wording of s 48 of the 1980 Act, stressing that this formed part of the transitional provisions in so far as the introduction of the block grant system was concerned. By February 1982 the latter had been in force for nearly a year. In these circumstances counsel for the applicants contended that on its proper construction the Secretary of State was only entitled to act under s 48(1) during the 1980–81 year. Having regard to the factual context in which the 1980 Act was passed and the multiplier order approved, he submitted that Parliament cannot have contemplated nor intended that the Secretary of State would or could seek to exercise his discretion under s 48(1) after March 1981.

Alternatively, if the Secretary of State did have power to act under s 48(1) as late as February 1982, nevertheless he was only entitled to withhold any part of the grant for 1980–81 which was properly outstanding at that time. Counsel for the applicants developed this alternative submission in this way. The word 'payable' in s 48(1) could in any event only be construed in some such sense as 'still liable to be paid'; it could not entitle the Secretary of State to withhold any part of a grant which he ought already to have paid. If this were correct, then s 2(2) of the 1974 Act provided that payments in

respect of a grant should be made to a local authority at such times as the Secretary of
a State might, with the consent of the Treasury, determine. In this case, in respect of the
grant payments for 1980–81, the Secretary of State had determined that the various
payments should be made to the applicants on the dates set out in annex H to his letter
of 9 January 1980. All such payments had been made on the specified dates until the
Secretary of State's first decision of 26 January 1981. They were then stopped as a result
of that decision. Once the latter had been quashed by the earlier judgment of this court
b then the instalments due to be paid between 26 January and the end of March 1981
should in law have been paid at once and could not be said to have remained 'payable'
until the Secretary of State took his second decision in February 1982. When the first
decision was quashed, the Secretary of State had no power to defer payment of those
amounts of the rate support grants which he had previously determined should be paid.
If one goes back to the 1974 Act, Sch 2 in particular gives the Secretary of State power to
c adjust the amounts of the various elements in a grant pursuant to regulations which he
has power to make, but gives him no power to defer payment of that which is already
due. It may very well be that adjustments will have to be made to the amounts of grant
paid, even up to two years after the end of the relevant fiscal year, as more precise or
further information becomes available, but these are adjustments contemplated and
provided for either by the Act or the regulations made thereunder. The regulations were
d made pursuant to the power to make them in s 10 of the 1974 Act. No power to defer
payments which it has already been determined should be made is given by them;
indeed it would be surprising if any such power was claimed, because s 10 does not itself
contemplate that any regulations made thereunder should be able to give such a power
(see, for instance, s 10(3)(c) of the 1974 Act). In any event at no time did the Secretary of
State contend that he was deferring the payments listed in annex H to the letter of 9
e January 1980 pursuant to any power given to him by Act or regulations; he merely
contended that he was entitled to take time to reconsider his decision under ss 48 to 50
of the 1980 Act, the first decision having been quashed, and was withholding further
payments until he had done so.

In answer to these contentions counsel for the Secretary of State submitted that on the
previous applications to this court all that was decided was that the Secretary of State had
f failed to hear last minute representations and that it was for this and this reason only that
the court had quashed the first decision. The court did not hold that the Secretary of State
could not lawfully make a decision to reduce a grant under ss 48 to 50 of the 1980 Act,
merely that the first decision to do so had been taken unlawfully. Indeed counsel for the
Secretary of State drew our attention to the passage in the judgment of this court on the
previous occasion (see [1983] 3 All ER 321 at 357) that notwithstanding their decision it
g would of course be open to the Secretary of State, after hearing full representations, to
reach any decision which he thought right, provided that it was within the terms of the
1980 Act and the multipliers order. We incline to the view that strictly this dictum was
obiter on the previous occasion and that the point may not have been argued as fully as
it has been before us. Nevertheless we respectfully agree with the conclusion.

Counsel for the Secretary of State submitted and we agree that, on its proper
h construction, the phrase 'payable to a local authority for the year 1980–81' in s 48(1) of
the 1980 Act is descriptive and not as strictly temporal as counsel for the applicants
suggested. In our opinion the word 'for' in this phrase in the subsection is to be construed
as 'in respect of'. Further, we think that the provisions of s 2(2) of the 1974 Act are to be
construed in this permissive sense, namely that although a local authority is entitled to
receive rate support grants calculated in accordance with the statutory provisions and the
regulations made thereunder for any given fiscal year, they are only entitled to receive
j these as and when the Secretary of State, with the consent of the Treasury, may decide.

We agree that so far as is practicable local authorities should know when and how
much they will be receiving by way of instalments of grants during a fiscal year, in order
properly to be able to do their own budgeting, and to be at no general disadvantage in
the money market. Nevertheless we think that in general s 2(2) of the 1974 Act gives the
Secretary of State and the Treasury the final say, subject to general legal principles, about

when and in what amounts instalments of grants are paid. We do not think that the word 'determine' in s 2(2) connotes the type of formal decision for which counsel for the applicants contended. We have no doubt that if the Secretary of State refused or delayed making rate support grants to local authorities under what is now s 53(8) of the 1980 Act for no good reason, so as to frustrate the purpose of this part of the legislation, then this court could intervene by way of judicial review and grant whatever relief was required. However, we do not think that any 'determination' of when and in what instalments a grant is to be paid is immutable.

In normal circumstances, having received the letters of 9 January 1980, the present two applicants could have expected at least the instalments of their grants specified in those letters on the dates listed in annex H and indeed any additional sums to which they might become entitled under any increase orders that might be made for 1980–81. However, it is quite clear from the background history set out in the judgment of this court on the first occasion, and from the additional facts to which we have referred, that in so far as rate support grants were concerned, circumstances were not normal. Prior to the first application to this court everyone involved knew that the Secretary of State was considering using his transitional powers under ss 48 to 50 of the 1980 Act. After this court's first decision, despite the somewhat forensic exchange of correspondence that followed it, all concerned knew that the Secretary of State was reconsidering whether and in what circumstances to use the same powers. Consequently, provided that the Secretary of State was doing so bona fide, and no one suggests that he was not, we do not think that there was any reason in law why he should not continue to defer paying the balance of the rate support grants to which these applicants would otherwise have been entitled, until he had decided whether to use his transitional powers after hearing any further representations which these applicants might wish to make. For these reasons we cannot accept the construction of the relevant statutory provisions and regulations for which counsel for the applicants contended.

Counsel's principal alternative submission was that, whatever might be the correct construction of the relevant statutory provisions and statutory instruments, nevertheless the content and terms of parts of the first judgment raised an issue estoppel between the parties which entitled him to relief. He based this submission on three particular passages in that judgment. In brief, these were as follows ([1983] 3 All ER 321 at 354–355):

'Thus on that date [15 January 1981 when the Rate Support Grant (Increase) (No 2) Order 1980 came into operation] all the applicants were entitled to receive the rate support grant provided by the Rate Support Grant Order 1979 as thus increased ... Thus the decision (made on 26 January 1981) to reduce the applicants' rate support grants adversely affected not merely an expectation but a right to substantial sums of money ... Moreover, having regard to the applicants' accrued right to the support grant ...'

Basing himself on what he submitted were quite clearly findings by this court on the earlier occasion that the nature of the local authorities' entitlement to the remainder of the rate support grants provided by the original and first increase orders for 1980–81, as well as the further grant provided for by the second increase order, was or were an accrued legal right or rights, then, whatever may be the proper legal construction of the relevant statutory provisions and statutory instruments, on the hearing of these present applications the Secretary of State is now estopped from contending that such entitlement was anything other than an accrued legal right. Consequently, the submission proceeded, once the first decision to withhold part of the grants had been quashed, the local authorities were entitled to enforce that accrued legal right; even though this court, after full argument, may consider, as we do and have so said, that a construction of the relevant provisions which gives rise to the creation or existence of an accrued legal right is incorrect, nevertheless we must decide these applications on the basis that there was an accrued right and give relief to the London boroughs accordingly.

For a statement of the nature and extent of the doctrine of issue estoppel counsel for

the applicants referred us to a passage from the judgment of Diplock LJ in *Mills v Cooper*
a [1967] 2 All ER 100 at 104, [1967] 2 QB 459 at 468–469. The facts of that case are
immaterial for present purposes but in a passage approved subsequently by the House of
Lords in *DPP v Humphrys* [1976] 2 All ER 497, [1977] AC 1, Diplock LJ said:

'This doctrine [namely of issue estoppel], so far as it affects civil proceedings, may
be stated thus: a party to civil proceedings is not entitled to make, as against the
b   other party, an assertion, whether of fact or of the legal consequences of facts, the
correctness of which is an essential element in his cause of action or defence, if the
same assertion was an essential element in his previous cause of action or defence in
previous civil proceedings between the same parties or their predecessors in title and
was found by a court of competent jurisdiction in such previous civil proceedings to
be incorrect, unless further material which is relevant to the correctness or
c   incorrectness of the assertion and could not by reasonable diligence have been
adduced by that party in the previous proceedings has since become available to
him.'

Counsel for the applicants submitted that the doctrine applied even though it was
apparent, or the court on the second occasion held, that the decision on the first occasion,
d said to give rise to the estoppel, had been come to on a mistaken appreciation of the
underlying facts, or indeed on an incorrect view of the underlying law. In support of this
proposition he referred to *R v Hartington Middle Quarter (Inhabitants)* (1855) 4 E & B 780
at 794, 119 ER 288 at 293, and to the following passage in the judgment of Coleridge J,
delivering the judgment of the court:

'The question then is, whether the judgment concludes, not merely as to the
e   point actually decided, but as to a matter which it was necessary to decide, and
which was actually decided, as the groundwork of the decision itself, though not
then directly the point at issue. And we think it does conclude to that extent. It is
unnecessary now to rely on the judgment having been in rem; for it was a judgment
between the same parties: the matters which are cardinal in the present litigation
cannot now be disputed, without asserting that the decision upon them in the
f   former case was erroneous. But this they cannot do directly; they have passed their
time, and neglected the lawful mode; they cannot now shew by adducing new
evidence that the Court was misled as to the facts, nor by new argument or authority
that it drew a wrong conclusion in law. In the case of *Regina v. Wye* ((1838) 7
Ad & El 761, 112 ER 656), a case sometimes misunderstood, this principle was very
clearly affirmed, in accordance with prior decisions. If, then, the former decision
g   cannot be impeached, and these facts are so cardinal to it that without them it
cannot stand, on principle, when these facts are again in question between the same
parties, they must be considered as having been conclusively determined.'

We respectfully think that this statement correctly sets out the principles of law
comprising the doctrine of issue estoppel at least in so far as it applies to the usual type of
h civil proceedings inter partes.
In the present case, however, we think that there are two answers to the powerful
submissions on this point made by counsel for the applicants. First, although on their
face the passages from the first judgment which we have quoted do appear to contain a
finding in favour of the present applicants on the particular issue, in our opinion a careful
reading of the context in which the passages occur makes it quite clear that the court on
j the first occasion was not purporting to make the finding for which counsel for the
applicants contends. In the first place the circumstances in which and the times at which
the Secretary of State was liable under the statutes to make payments of rate support
grants were not in issue on the earlier applications. They were concerned with the
validity of the minister's underlying policy and the multipliers order, and with the
lawfulness of the first decision to withhold part of the grants by virtue of that order.

In relation to this last question the court on the first occasion had to consider the extent
to which natural justice required the Secretary of State to hear further representations on   *a*
behalf of the London boroughs concerned after he had acquired the transitional powers
in ss 48 to 50 of the 1980 Act, but before he took the decision to use them. In doing so
the court referred to the decision of Sir Robert Megarry V-C in *McInnes v Onslow Fane*
[1978] 3 All ER 211, [1978] 1 WLR 1520, in which the Vice-Chancellor discussed when
the considerations of natural justice required a complainant to be given the opportunity
of being heard on his own behalf. He did so by identifying on the authorities three   *b*
possible categories by reference to which a court could be assisted in deciding whether
and the extent to which natural justice required a person to be given the opportunity of
being heard, while not suggesting that there was any clear or exhaustive classification.
    Reading the first judgment as a whole, we have no doubt that in the passages relied on
by counsel for the applicants, and which we have quoted, the court on the previous
occasion was merely considering into which of the possible categories identified by the   *c*
Vice-Chancellor the decision of the Secretary of State to withhold part of the rate support
grant ought to be put. We think that at the material point the court was setting out part
of the reasoning by which it reached the decision that the Secretary of State ought to have
heard further representations rather than purporting to make any definite findings,
whether of fact or law or both.
    If we are wrong in this analysis of those parts of the first judgment, we think that the   *d*
second answer to the arguments of counsel for the applicants based on the doctrine of
issue estoppel is that in law that doctrine cannot be relied on in applications for judicial
review under RSC Ord 53. That issue estoppel has no application in criminal cases is clear
from the decision of the House of Lords in *DPP v Humphrys* [1976] 2 All ER 497, [1977]
AC 1. Viscount Dilhorne quoted with approval a further passage from the judgment of
Diplock LJ in *Mills v Cooper* [1967] 2 All ER 100 at 105, [1967] 2 QB 459 at 469 (see   *e*
[1976] 2 All ER 497 at 505, [1977] AC 1 at 20):

   'Issue estoppel is a particular application of the general rule of public policy that
   there should be finality in litigation. That general rule applies also to criminal
   proceedings, but in a form modified by the distinctive character of criminal as
   compared with civil litigation. Here it takes the form of the rule against double
   jeopardy . . . I think with great respect that the use of that expression [issue estoppel]   *f*
   in criminal and civil proceedings alike may lead to confusion, for there are obvious
   differences—lack of mutuality is but one—between the application of the rule
   against double jeopardy in criminal cases, and the rule that there should be finality
   in civil litigation.'

    As we read his speech, and particularly that part of it which follows on the passage   *g*
quoted above, the reasons which led Viscount Dilhorne to the conclusion that issue
estoppel has no place in criminal proceedings were, first, the difficulty that there must
be in identifying a particular issue which ex hypothesi must be taken to have been
decided between the parties merely from a jury's verdict of guilty or not guilty; and,
second, that if issue estoppel were to apply in criminal proceedings, there would have to
be a mutuality, which it is difficult to contemplate.   *h*
    Lord Hailsham reverted to the same point in his speech where he said ([1976] 2 All ER
497 at 516, [1977] AC 1 at 32–33):

   'The fallacy of the whole argument appears to me to reside in the supposition that
   the Crown and the accused are, in criminal proceedings, in the same analogous
   position as any two litigants in civil proceedings. I agree with Diplock LJ in *Mills v
   Cooper* [1967] 2 All ER 100 at 104–105, [1967] 2 QB 459 at 468–469, in the passage *j*
   I have already quoted, that this is by no means the case. In civil proceedings the
   litigants are on an equal footing, and the rules of public policy applying to each are
   the same in principle. In criminal proceedings this is not the case. The subject
   requires to be protected against oppression by the executive, and in particular by the
   maxim, nemo debet bis vexari pro una et eadem causa. As Diplock LJ points out,

and as I shall shortly be showing, the cases in which issue estoppel has been sought
a   to be applied in criminal cases really spring from this rule of public policy, the
prohibition of double jeopardy, which is intrinsically unavailable to the Crown. By
contrast, the rule of issue estoppel in civil cases springs from quite a different rule of
public policy, viz the need for finality in litigation summarised in the maxim, ut
finis sit litium, which is intrinsically applicable to both parties. By contrast again, in
criminal proceedings the Crown is charged with the duty of protecting the innocent
b   citizens against crime, and vindicating public justice as such. It therefore has
interests and duties which are not simply those of a civil litigant. The application of
artificial rules, like those of estoppel, to the criminal process must be seen in the
light of these considerations which both as regards defence and prosecution are not
applicable to civil proceedings. For these reasons I wholly reject the doctrine that
issue estoppel is available to the Crown . . .'

c   We respectfully think that similar considerations apply to proceedings for judicial
review. In such proceedings, there are no formal pleadings and it will frequently be
difficult if not impossible to identify a particular issue which the 'first' application will
have decided. Moreover, we do not think that there is in proceedings brought under RSC
Ord 53 any true lis between the Crown, in whose name the proceedings are brought (and
we venture a reservation about whether or not issue estoppel *could* operate against the
d   Crown), and the respondent or between the ex parte applicant and the respondent.
Further, we doubt whether a decision in such proceedings, in the sense necessary for
issue estoppel to operate, is a *final* decision: the nature of the relief, in many cases, leaves
open reconsideration by the statutory or other tribunal of the matter in dispute.
We respectfully adopt a passage from H W R Wade *Administrative Law* (5th edn, 1982)
e   p 246:

'. . . in these procedures the court "is not finally determining the validity of the
tribunal's order as between the parties themselves" but "is merely deciding whether
there has been a plain excess of jurisdiction or not". They are a special class of
remedies designed to maintain due order in the legal system, nominally at the suit
of the Crown, and they may well fall outside the ambit of the ordinary doctrine of
f   res judicata. But the court may refuse to entertain questions which were or could
have been litigated in earlier proceedings, when this would be an abuse of legal
process; and in the case of habeas corpus there is a statutory bar against repeated
applications made on the same grounds.'

We also quote a short passage from de Smith's *Judicial Review of Administrative Action*
(4th edn, 1980) p 108:
g
'It is difficult not to conclude that the concept of res judicata in administrative
law is so nebulous as to occlude rather than clarify practical issues, and that it should
be used as little as possible.'

The principle that relief under RSC Ord 53 is granted in discretion only, as well as the
obligation to obtain leave from the court before an application for relief can be made,
h   seems to us to be contrary to the concept of a final determination of an issue between
parties which is at the root of issue estoppel. The court, under this jurisdiction, is fully
able to give effect to the rule of public policy that there should be finality in litigation,
which underlies the doctrines of issue estoppel in civil litigation and the prohibition
against double jeopardy in criminal prosecution, by the use of its powers to refuse to
entertain applications and to refuse to grant relief in the process of judicial review of
j   administrative acts or omissions; this is particularly but not exclusively so when the
application may be oppressive, vexatious or an abuse of the process of the court.
Counsel for the applicants also sought to argue that at least the London Borough of
Camden was entitled to recover the amount of the grant withheld for 1980–81 as
damages for breach by the Secretary of State of his statutory duty under the provisions to
which we have referred to pay rate support grant in accordance with them. However, as

we have held that on their proper construction the relevant statutory provisions imposed no such duty, clearly there can be no liability to pay a similar or any sum by way of damages. We deal with the question of lost interest, particularly in so far as the London Borough of Hackney is concerned in a moment. On the question of damages, however, we do not think that even if there were at any time a statutory duty on the Secretary of State to pay the amounts of grant withheld, his failure to do so could give rise to a claim for damages. In the circumstances of this case such a claim could only be made good if the borough could at least show malice or knowledge by the Secretary of State of the invalidity of one or other or both of his decisions: see *Dunlop v Woollahra Municipal Council* [1981] 1 All ER 1202, [1982] AC 158.

Finally, we turn to the question of interest on the amount of grant withheld. Counsel for the applicants submitted that on the facts of the present case the applicants were entitled to interest, either by way of damages or by virtue of s 3 of the Law Reform (Miscellaneous Provisions) Act 1934. At least until the Secretary of State made a valid decision to withhold rate support grants for 1980–81 under the powers given him by the 1980 Act, the applicants had been kept out of their money and this should entitle them to recover interest for the relevant periods. In so far as the London borough of Hackney was concerned, it was clear from the fact of the ultimate payment to it on 9 August 1982 of the sums withheld that there had throughout been an obligation on the Secretary of State to pay the full amount of the grant and that it should be compensated by an award of interest on the sum ultimately paid for the period at least between the date of the Secretary of State's first invalid decision and August 1982.

In so far as the claim to interest is founded on an alleged entitlement to damages for breach of statutory duty, this must fail for the reason we have just given. In so far as the 1934 Act is concerned, on the construction of the relevant provisions of the 1974 and 1980 Acts which we have held to be the correct one, at no time was the Secretary of State indebted to either of the applicants. There is no material before us to suggest that there was any unreasonable delay on his part between the date when he made his second valid decision and his payment to the London Borough of Hackney in August 1982 when he was satisfied that they had complied with one of the waivers. There can be no valid claim to interest, therefore, under the 1934 Act.

In the result and for the reasons we have given, these applications fail.

Applications dismissed.

Solicitors: *R A Benge* (for the applicants); *Treasury Solicitor.*

N P Metcalfe Esq   Barrister.

Conry v Simpson and others

COURT OF APPEAL, CIVIL DIVISION
STEPHENSON, O'CONNOR LJJ AND DAME ELIZABETH LANE
25 FEBRUARY 1982

Limitation of action – Court's power to override time limit in personal injury or fatal accident claim – Exercise of discretion – Appeal against exercise of discretion – When Court of Appeal will interfere with judge's exercise of his discretion – Limitation Act 1980, ss 11, 33.

The Limitation Act 1980, s 33[a] confers on a judge of the High Court an unfettered discretion to disapply the primary limitation period of three years imposed by s 11[b] of that Act on actions for damages for personal injuries, and the Court of Appeal will not interfere with the exercise of his discretion unless he goes very wrong and fails to follow the directions in s 33 which require him to have regard to (a) the degree to which the imposition of the primary limitation period prejudices the plaintiff, (b) the degree to which his decision would prejudice the defendant and (c) all the circumstances of the case and, in particular, those circumstances specified in s 33(3) (see p 370 e f, p 374 e to h and p 375 a b, post).

Firman v Ellis [1978] 2 All ER 851 and *Thompson v Brown Construction (Ebbw Vale) Ltd* [1981] 2 All ER 296 followed.

Notes

For the court's power to override the limitation period in personal injury actions, see 28 Halsbury's Laws (4th edn) para 694.

For the Limitation Act 1980, ss 11, 33, see 50(1) Halsbury's Statutes (3rd edn) 1262, 1286.

---

a   Section 33, so far as material, provides:
  '(1) If it appears to the court that it would be equitable to allow an action to proceed having regard to the degree to which— (a) the provisions of section 11 . . . of this Act prejudice the plaintiff or any person whom he represents; and (b) any decision of the court under this subsection would prejudice the defendant or any person whom he represents; the court may direct that those provisions shall not apply to the action, or shall not apply to any specified cause of action to which the action relates . . .
  (3) In acting under this section the court shall have regard to all the circumstances of the case and in particular to—(a) the length of, and the reasons for, the delay on the part of the plaintiff; (b) the extent to which, having regard to the delay, the evidence adduced or likely to be adduced by the plaintiff or the defendant is or is likely to be less cogent than if the action had been brought within the time allowed by section 11 . . . (c) the conduct of the defendant after the cause of action arose, including the extent (if any) to which he responded to requests reasonably made by the plaintiff for information or inspection for the purpose of ascertaining facts which were or might be relevant to the plaintiff's cause of action against the defendant; (d) the duration of any disability of the plaintiff arising after the date of the accrual of the cause of action; (e) the extent to which the plaintiff acted promptly and reasonably once he knew whether or not the act or omission of the defendant, to which the injury was attributable, might be capable at that time of giving rise to an action for damages; (f) the steps, if any, taken by the plaintiff to obtain medical, legal or other expert advice and the nature of any such advice he may have received . . .'
b   Section 11, so far as material, provides:
  '(1) This section applies to any action for damages for negligence, nuisance or breach of duty . . . where the damages claimed by the plaintiff for the negligence, nuisance or breach of duty consist of or include damages in respect of personal injuries to the plaintiff or any other person . . .
  (4) . . . the [limitation] period applicable is three years from—(a) the date on which the cause of action accrued; or (b) the date of knowledge (if later) of the person injured . . .'

Cases referred to in judgments

Firman v Ellis [1978] 2 All ER 851, [1978] QB 886, [1978] 3 WLR 1, CA.

Thompson v Brown Construction (Ebbw Vale) Ltd [1981] 2 All ER 296, [1981] 1 WLR 744, HL.

Interlocutory appeal

The first defendant, Brian Ernest Simpson, appealed, with the leave of the Court of Appeal, against an order of Skinner J in the Queen's Bench Division at Sheffield, dated 27 July 1981, whereby he exercised his discretionary power under s 33 of the Limitation Act 1980 to disapply the primary period of three years' limitation imposed on actions for damages for personal injuries by s 11 of that Act and allowed the plaintiff, Roy Kevan Conry, to proceed with an action against the first defendant in which he claimed damages for the personal injuries which he sustained on 12 January 1973 in a road accident at Aldham House Lane, Wombwell, South Yorkshire. The facts are set out in the judgment of Stephenson LJ.

Christopher Rose QC and *R J Scholes* for the first defendant.
L D Lawton QC and *John Hoggett* for the plaintiff.

STEPHENSON LJ. This is a defendant's appeal from an order made by Skinner J on 27 July 1981 by which he exercised his discretionary power under s 33 of the Limitation Act 1980 to disapply the primary period of three years' limitation imposed on actions for personal injuries by s 11 of that Act. As is now well known since the decision in *Firman v Ellis* [1978] 2 All ER 851, [1978] QB 886, approved by the House of Lords in *Thompson v Brown Construction (Ebbw Vale) Ltd* [1981] 2 All ER 296, [1981] 1 WLR 744, that provision, like the provision of the 1975 Limitation Act which it repeated, confers on judges of the High Court an unfettered discretion, and provided a judge of the High Court follows the directions in that section and has regard to the degree to which the imposition of the primary period of limitation prejudices the plaintiff and his decision would prejudice the defendant, and provided he has regard to all the circumstances of the case and in particular those six circumstances specified in s 33(3), this court will not interfere with the exercise of his discretion.

This appeal comes by leave of this court. It has some rather special features, which no doubt explain why that leave was granted. But the case has been the subject of a meticulously careful consideration by Skinner J in a judgment which he gave after a two-day hearing and after having had the weekend to consider the matter, and counsel for the appellant first defendant has therefore had an uphill task in seeking to discharge the burden of persuading the appellate court that the judge came to a decision that it would be equitable to allow the plaintiff's action against the first defendant to proceed in a way which was so wrong that this court can interfere with it.

The first defendant is one of what were three defendants to an action brought by the plaintiff, a young steel erector. He was a passenger in the second defendant's van, a van that belonged to the third defendant and which may or may not have been driven by the second defendant in the course of his employment. The plaintiff got out of the van being driven by the second defendant when it had pulled up on its offside of a wide road in order, apparently, to open the passenger door; and while, according to contemporary statements which have been preserved, he was standing by the nearside of that van, according to one statement, with his hand still on the passenger door, he was struck by a car coming in the opposite direction and driven by the first defendant. That misfortune befell him as long ago as 12 January 1973; no writ was issued against the first defendant or the driver or owners of the van in which the plaintiff had been travelling until 22 November 1979. There has therefore, on the face of it, been inordinate and inexcusable delay and a reasonable certainty of some prejudice to the defendant, to say nothing of any prejudice to the plaintiff.

Matters started well. The plaintiff consulted a solicitor, who took all the right early steps, but there came a time when that solicitor thought that he was not able to give

adequate attention to the plaintiff's case, and he wrote a letter to the plaintiff informing
a him of that fact. Unfortunately, by the time the plaintiff had gone to see him and had
discussed the position with him he had, by a matter of a few days, allowed the three-year
period of limitation to expire, and he told the plaintiff frankly that his action in respect
of the injury which he had received in the road accident in 1973 was gone.

The injury which the plaintiff received in that accident was an injury to his left knee.
There were other minor injuries, concussion and so on, but in fact he was left after the
b accident with an unstable left knee, so unstable that it was put in plaster of Paris for a
couple of months, and that left him with a certain residual disability whose extent and
duration are a matter of dispute.

The circumstance which makes the case rather unusual is that after that first accident
but before the period of limitation had expired, the plaintiff met with a second accident
at work in which he injured his left hand. Difficult questions of fact may arise as to the
c contributions made by the injury to his knee and the injury to his hand to his ability to
work as a steel erector at heights or anywhere above ground. That second accident took
place on 18 May 1974.

By 21 February 1975, as found by the judge, a stage had been reached when the first
defendant's insurers asked the solicitors acting for the plaintiff to quantify his claim.
They did not deny liability; they never have denied liability, although they have alleged
d contributory negligence on the part of the plaintiff, and no doubt have alleged that the
other two defendants had made their contribution by their negligence, the third
defendant as vicariously responsible for the negligence of the second defendant in
parking where he did, on the wrong side of the road. In 1975 that claim was valued at
£1,500 by the plaintiff's then solicitor.

I need not go in detail into the subsequent course of events, but they may be
e summarised in this way. Various doctors and surgeons saw the plaintiff both on behalf
of himself and of the first defendant. No notification of any claim was given to the
second and third defendants until much later. The plaintiff put the matter into the hands
of a second firm of solicitors, who are still acting for him; those solicitors issued a writ on
his behalf against the first solicitor in 1977 for professional negligence. As I have said,
they did not issue the writ in this action until November 1979, but at the time when
f they were pursuing the plaintiff's first solicitor a different view was taken generally of
the court's power to disapply the period of primary limitation under the predecessor of
s 33 of the 1980 Act, and it was not until the decision of *Firman v Ellis* [1978] 2 All ER
851, [1978] QB 886 was first reported in February 1978 that it was appreciated how
unfettered that power was, and the plaintiff's solicitors switched, as it were, from
pursuing the plaintiff's former solicitor for negligence to a possible claim against the
g original tortfeasors, the first defendant and the second and third defendants.

In his order the judge disapplied the provisions of s 11 to allow the plaintiff's action to
go on against the first defendant, but he dismissed the second and third defendants from
the action, refusing to disapply the provisions in the action as against them on the ground
that the plaintiff would hardly be prejudiced at all if the direction were refused in their
cases, whereas they would be prejudiced by having to defend a not very strong case
h without having had the opportunity to investigate it at the time it arose; so he thought
that it would be inequitable to allow the case to proceed against them, but equitable to
allow the case to proceed against the first defendant.

The view that he took, and expressed in an extremely clear and careful judgment, was
that the plaintiff had a strong case in negligence against the first defendant, an arguable
case only against the second and third defendants and a strong case in that the damage to
j his knee had caused him permanent disability and loss of earning capacity. He also
thought that the plaintiff had a strong but by no means a cast-iron or watertight case
against his first solicitor.

Counsel for the first defendant, who has said everything that could be said on his
behalf, says that the judge's exercise of his discretion was wrong in that he failed to give
proper weight to seven matters which, in combination, clearly demonstrated prejudice

to the first defendant and lack of prejudice to the plaintiff; or, I suppose, to put it in another way, such prejudice to the first defendant as outweighed the prejudice to the plaintiff.

The first matter was that the writ was issued no less than six years and ten months after the accident. The second point is that by that time the first defendant's insurers had in 1977, as the judge found quite reasonable because of shortage of storage, destroyed their file relating to the plaintiff's case. That file included a medical report obtained in April 1974 from a Mr Redwood and may have included, no one can be certain about that, witness statements as well. Thirdly, he said that the claim of the plaintiff in this action raised factual issues relating both to contributory negligence and negligence; fourthly, that it raised very substantial medical issues, not only in relation to the effect of the road accident but also as to the effect of the accident to the plaintiff's hand in May 1974. I should say that proceedings were brought against his employers by the plaintiff in respect of that accident and settled for the sum of £3,000, a fact which the judge was undoubtedly mistaken about in the judgment, because he said that no proceedings had been brought; that is an immaterial mistake in his judgment on that point. The fifth matter which counsel for the first defendant said the judge should have taken into account and given great weight to was that here was a case in which there was not just a possibility of action being taken against the plaintiff's first solicitor, but an action was actually pending, and after it had been going on from July 1977 to June 1978, as he put it, it ground to a halt after an offer of £750 had been rejected by the plaintiff. Sixthly he says that between July 1976, when the first defendant's insurers told the plaintiff's present solicitors that they did intend to plead the Limitation Act if they were sued, and November 1978 when they wrote the letter before action to the plaintiff's first solicitor, they were guilty of further prejudicial delay. Finally, counsel for the first defendant's seventh point is that the second and third defendants being dismissed from the action, the first defendant will have to pay all the damages which presumably, on his admission of liability, he would have to pay to the plaintiff subject to anything he can knock off for the plaintiff's contributory negligence, and will be unable to recover any part of those damages from the second or the third defendant.

That sounds a formidable catalogue, but in my judgment the judge considered every one of those points and dealt with them in a way which does not vitiate the conclusion he reached. I think counsel for the first defendant really conceded that the only factual issue on liability was contributory negligence, and he argued that there was no clear evidence now of where the plaintiff was standing, or how long he had been standing where he was, when he was struck by the first defendant's motor vehicle.

Without going into the details of that matter, it seems to me that the first defendant is in no worse position for dealing with any questions of that kind than he would have been if the action had been started in time.

As to the last matter, as has been pointed out, there is nothing to stop the first defendant from bringing third party proceedings against the second and third defendants if so advised; and as to the fifth and sixth points, it seems to me that the judge was completely justified, bearing in mind the decision in *Firman v Ellis* [1978] 2 All ER 851, [1978] QB 886 and the timing of it, in finding as he did that the length of the delay between the time when the plaintiff's present solicitors were instructed in March 1976, and February 1978 when *Firman v Ellis* was decided, was perfectly excusable and thereafter all reasonable steps were taken. The delay that he refers to is a delay of six years and ten months. It is pointed out by counsel for the first defendant that in accordance with what Lord Diplock said in *Thompson v Brown Construction (Ebbw Vale) Ltd* [1981] 2 All ER 296 at 302, [1981] 1 WLR 744 at 751, the delay which he should have been considering was a delay of 2½ years from the expiry of the primary period of limitation in January 1976; but that is an extension of the delay which is favourable to the defendant's case and it seems to me that there is nothing in that point; nor is there any room for criticising the plaintiff's solicitors for switching from pressing the plaintiff's claim against his former solicitor to reactivating the claim against the first defendant; nor is there anything in what he called 'the years of silence', which really were brim-full a of suitable and reasonable activity as one can see when one looks at the chronological note supplied to us. There is no ground for criticising the judge's findings as to that period.

That leaves the real criticism of the judge's judgment, on which I think the first defendant has to stake his case; that is as to the disappearance of Mr Redwood's report, of which no copy has been retained, and the medical position generally as it affects the issue of damages.

b We have been taken, quite rightly, through no fewer than eight medical reports, some obtained for the plaintiff and some obtained for the first defendant. I do not propose to go through them in detail. It is to be regretted that the first defendant's insurers' file has gone, and with it Mr Redwood's full report; but we have, in the second report of a Dr Price, who examined and reported on the plaintiff on four occasions, his statement that he had read that report and his comments on it, and we have a letter giving the gist of Mr Redwood's report, both of which documents indicate that Mr Redwood was c attributing more of the plaintiff's condition after the road accident to loss of confidence, or functional overlay, than Dr Price was prepared to attribute to it, and less to the actual physical instability of the knee resulting, apparently, from some tearing of the ligaments and the possible stretching of another ligament.

Great importance was attached by counsel for the first defendant to a report of Mr Porter, obtained for the first defendant on 21 September 1976, in which, in the course of d examining the condition of the plaintiff's hand, he recorded that the plaintiff had made a full recovery from the knee injury (something which he must have obtained from the defendant). The reports which we have seen in fact ended with a third report from a Dr Sharrard, who examined the plaintiff at the request of the plaintiff's solicitors.

But before that, in connection with his hand injury, there was a report from a Mr Nichol, in which he attempted to balance all the previous reports which had been put e before him, and to decide what the effect of them was both as regards the hand injury and the knee injury. Again I find it unnecessary to go through that report, or to say more than that it seems to me that at any time after the May 1974 accident to the plaintiff's hand the problem which faced the defendants and their medical advisers, and which faces the plaintiff and his medical advisers, has not materially changed; and I find it difficult to see how they can have been deprived, by not examining the plaintiff's knee f during the years 1975 and 1976, of the opportunity of testing, and it may be successfully testing, the plaintiff's claim that as it stands at the moment his knee injury is solely responsible, without assistance from the hand injury, for in effect his present unemployment. For after being brought down to ground level by the knee injury and, as it appears, kept there by the hand injury, with the assistance, or it may be without the assistance, of the knee injury (that is a matter which will have to be resolved if the trial g ever comes on) he went to other employment and then gave up one job after some form of row, and left another because he did not want to travel, and he is now unemployed.

I appreciate the difficulty in which the first defendant finds himself, his insurers having thought that they might be meeting a claim for £1,500 and, if the judge's order stands now, finding themselves meeting a claim which may run into as many thousands. But in my judgment it would be doing the judge a great injustice to suppose that he did h not read the medical reports which we have read, or weigh the arguments on them which he had submitted to him, and that he was wrong in thinking that the loss of the file and the later course of events, the delay, had not seriously prejudiced the defendants in contesting the quantum of damages which may now be claimed in medical evidence, bearing in mind, as the judge pointed out, that the plaintiff still has his knee and his hand. The judge summed the matter up by saying:

j   'So far as Mr Redwood's report goes, the real answer is that the plaintiff still has his knee available for examination by the first defendant, and the prognosis will now be clearer. In my judgment, the prejudice to the plaintiff would be substantial if I refused this application, whereas the prejudice to the first defendant would be small.'

I should mention one other matter. The judge did say of the plaintiff's claim against his former solicitor that—

> 'he would have a strong claim against the former solicitor but who no one is sure *a*
> will be able to satisfy any judgment against him.'

That appeared to be a misunderstanding of what counsel, not counsel representing that
solicitor, had said to the judge, he having told the judge that there was a letter from the
solicitor saying that he had resources to meet a judgment against him and that therefore
a remedy did exist in regard to any damage suffered by the plaintiff. Further on, that   *b*
same counsel had said:

> 'In my submission those prejudices are not present in this case. It is true that there
> is some doubt about (the solicitor's) ability to meet the claim, but nevertheless the
> signs are encouraging.'

We are told by counsel for the plaintiff that, at any rate at the material date, the Law   *c*
Society's compensation fund would not be available to meet any damages awarded against
the plaintiff's former solicitor. We have had read to us by counsel for the first defendant
a letter from that solicitor of recent date, saying that he would be able to meet any
liability up to £20,000; but in my judgment the judge was justified in putting the
matter as he did: 'No one can be sure.' I see no reason to suppose that he disregarded Lord
Diplock's opinion in *Thompson v Brown Construction (Ebbw Vale) Ltd* [1981] 2 All ER 296   *d*
at 303, [1981] 1 WLR 744 at 752, concurred in by the other Law Lords, that the existence
of a good claim in negligence against a solicitor was a highly relevant consideration when
the judge has regard to all the circumstances of the case. But, rightly, in the judge's view
it was not a cast-iron case; it is very seldom that a remedy against a solicitor can be as
satisfactory as a remedy against the original tortfeasor, and I cannot see that the judge
was wrong in taking the view which he did of this claim against the solicitor, although it   *e*
had already started, and in not deciding that that circumstance, in conjunction with all
the other circumstances, would make it inequitable for him to do what he did. When is
it equitable or inequitable to allow a claim which is barred by the statute to go ahead? It
is a very vague term; the statute confers an unfettered discretion, and I repeat what has
been said in this court and in the House of Lords, that it is not for an appellate court to
reverse the discretion of the judge, to whom Parliament has committed it, unless he has   *f*
gone very wrong. I cannot see that the judge exercised his discretion wrongly in this
case. I think I should have exercised it as he did, but that is not the question; even if I
would not have exercised it as he did, I cannot possibly say that it was wrong for him to
exercise it as he did.

For these reasons I would dismiss this appeal.

O'CONNOR LJ. I agree. Like Stephenson LJ, I can find no grounds for saying that the   *g*
judge, in exercising his discretion as he did, has fallen into error.

DAME ELIZABETH LANE. I also agree, but it is right that I should say that I only
do so with some hesitation in the light particularly of two of the grounds relied on by
counsel for the first defendant.   *h*

The first is the stage actually reached in the action against the plaintiff's first solicitor.
There was an action, properly constituted with an open offer being made and on its way
to trial, with no need to seek discretionary leave. Although at first I was concerned that
the judge had made a real error with regard to the availability of funds to satisfy any
judgment in that action, I think that counsel for the plaintiff has assuaged my fears on
that score.

The second matter is that as a result of proceedings being brought against the solicitor,   *j*
the first defendant's solicitors in 1977 reasonably, and quite properly, destroyed their file,
and with it the early medical report from Mr Redwood, to which the first defendant
attached, and still does attach, considerable importance because it was made so early and
before the second accident happened to the plaintiff. This is also of importance because

a
whereas the first solicitor was actively pursuing the plaintiff's claim, a sum of £1,500 was mentioned as being an appropriate award of damages, now, with the lapse of time, we are told that a figure of something like £20,000 may be in the air.

Nevertheless, these are matters to which the judge gave due consideration, and I respectfully agree that his discretion should be decisive and, in the absence of real error on his part, I am not prepared to dissent and accordingly I agree that this appeal should be dismissed.

b
Appeal dismissed.

Solicitors: *Stevensons*, agents for *Geoffrey Warhurst & Co*, Manchester (for the first defendant); *Irwin Mitchell & Co*, Sheffield (for the plaintiff).

c
Sophie Craven   Barrister.

British Airways Board
v Laker Airways Ltd and others
and other proceedings

QUEEN'S BENCH DIVISION

PARKER J

22, 23, 24, 25, 28, 29 MARCH, 5, 6, 20 MAY 1983

e

COURT OF APPEAL, CIVIL DIVISION

SIR JOHN DONALDSON MR, OLIVER AND WATKINS LJJ

4, 5, 6, 7, 8, 11, 13, 19, 20, 26 JULY 1983

f
Trade – Protection of trading interests – Damage to United Kingdom trading interests – Conflict of laws – Foreign measures which threaten to damage United Kingdom trading interests – Conditions under which Secretary of State may make order or direction prohibiting compliance with foreign measures – Measures – What constitutes foreign 'measures' which threaten to damage United Kingdom trading interests – Protection of Trading Interests Act 1980, ss 1, 2(1) – Protection of Trading Interests (US Antitrust Measures) Order 1983.

g
Treaty – Treaty relevant to dispute between private persons – Relevance of government's attitude to treaty – Whether government's attitude should be taken into consideration by court when deciding dispute.

h
Conflict of laws – Foreign proceedings – Restraint of foreign proceedings – Circumstances in which court will restrain foreign proceedings – No alternative forum in England or elsewhere – Critical equation of advantage to defendant and disadvantage to plaintiff if foreign proceedings restrained – Whether injunction should be granted restraining plaintiff from continuing foreign proceedings.

j
International air carriage between the United Kingdom and the United States was regulated by a treaty signed in 1977 under which each country was entitled to designate airlines of its own nationality to fly particular routes across the Atlantic. The plaintiffs and, from 1977 until 1982, the defendant were designated United Kingdom airlines and were licensed on terms that their fares were approved by the aviation authorities of both countries. The defendant started a low-fare scheduled service across the Atlantic which considerably undercut the fares charged by the plaintiffs and other international airlines.

In 1982 the defendant went into liquidation and shortly afterwards brought an action in
the United States district court against a number of international airline companies,
including the plaintiffs, alleging a combination by the airline companies against the   *a*
defendant and conspiracy in restraint of trade and conspiracy to monopolise the airline
trade in violation of the Sherman Antitrust Act of the United States. The defendant
claimed in the United States action that, between 1977 and 1982 when it went into
liquidation, the international airline companies conspired to eliminate the defendant as
a competitor by fixing air fare tariffs so low that the defendant was forced out of business.
The defendant further alleged 'intentional tort', and in respect of both claims it sought   *b*
triple damages under the Clayton Act of the United States and punitive damages in excess
of $US2 billion. In the course of the United States proceedings the defendant sought
extensive discovery of documents and answers to far-reaching interrogatories. Following
the commencement of the defendant's action the United States Department of Justice
initiated an investigation into the alleged breaches of the Sherman Act and a grand jury   *c*
was empanelled for the purpose of the investigation. The United Kingdom government's
policy was against the application of the anti-trust legislation contained in the Sherman
and Clayton Acts to international air transport and, in particular, to the activities of
British designated airlines as being a breach of the 1977 treaty by the United States.

In January 1983 the plaintiffs applied to the High Court for injunctions restraining
the defendant from pursuing its action in the United States against them, on the grounds,   *d*
inter alia, that (i) to allow the action to continue would be contrary to English public
policy and in breach of the 1977 treaty and (ii) that compliance with the discovery and
interrogatory requirements in the United States action would impose on the plaintiffs a
burden which would be unjust in the circumstances. The defendant contended, inter
alia, (i) that its action was not inconsistent with United Kingdom policy since that policy
emphasised that parties within the jurisdiction of the United States should comply with   *e*
the laws of that country and had principally expressed concern over anti-trust proceedings
where the 'effects doctrine' operated, ie where extra-territorial acts were relied on to
substantiate claims, (ii) that the English court had no jurisdiction to restrain the defendant
because there was no alternative forum either in England or elsewhere in which its claim
could be brought. The judge refused to grant the relief sought. The plaintiffs appealed.

In June 1983, before the hearing of the appeal, the Secretary of State for Trade and   *f*
Industry, in the exercise of his powers under ss 1*a* and 2(1)*b* of the Protection of Trading
Interests Act 1980, issued (i) the Protection of Trading Interests (US Antitrust Measures)
Order 1983*c*, (ii) a general direction under s 1(3) of the 1980 Act prohibiting United
Kingdom designated airlines from complying with any requirement or prohibition
imposed on them under the Sherman and Clayton Acts as a result of a judgment in the
defendant's United States action, and (iii) a general direction under s 2 of the 1980 Act   *g*
prohibiting United Kingdom designated airlines from complying with any requirement
for the production of documents or commercial information in the United States action.
Section 1 of the 1980 Act empowered the Secretary of State to issue such orders or
directions if it appeared to him that 'measures' had been or were proposed to be taken in
a foreign country which threatened to damage the trading interests of the United
Kingdom. The defendant applied for leave to apply for judicial review of the order and   *h*
the directions, claiming (i) that the 1983 order was ultra vires the Secretary of State
because the Sherman and Clayton Acts to which the 1983 order was stated to apply were
not 'measures' taken by a foreign country 'for regulating or controlling' international

---

a   Section 1, so far as material, is set out at p 405 *e*, post
b   Section 2(1), so far as material, provides: 'If it appears to the Secretary of State—(*a*) that a
      requirement has been or may be imposed on a person or persons in the United Kingdom to   *j*
      produce to any court . . . of an overseas country any commercial document which is not within
      the territorial jurisdiction of that country or to furnish any commercial information to any such
      court . . . the Secretary of State may, if it appears to him that the requirement is inadmissible by
      virtue of subsection (2) or (3) below, give directions for prohibiting compliance with the
      requirement.'
c   The 1983 order is set out at p 404 *j* to p 405 *d*, post

trade, within s 1, since the Sherman and Clayton Acts were intended to free international
trade from the constrictions of anti-competitive cartels rather than to regulate or control

a international trade, and in any event the Sherman and Clayton Acts were the authority
under which measures might be taken and were not the measures themselves, (ii) that
the direction under s 1(3) was invalid because the Secretary of State had no power to
make a direction under s 1(3) prohibiting a person from complying with requirements
made under the anti-trust laws unless he had first issued an order under s 1(2) that he be

b notified of such requirements and no such order had been made under s 1(2), and (iii)
that the Secretary of State could only prohibit compliance with a requirement for the
production of documents to an overseas court by making a direction under s 2 of the
1980 Act that the requirement was 'inadmissible' and in making his direction under s 2
the Secretary of State had failed to specify the grounds on which he regarded the
requirements imposed on the plaintiffs by the United States district court to be

c 'inadmissible' within the meaning of s 2(2) and (3) of the 1980 Act. The judge refused
leave. The defendant appealed to the Court of Appeal.
    Both appeals were heard together.

Held – (1) The defendant's appeal against the refusal of leave to apply for judicial review
would be dismissed for the following reasons—

d (a) On its true construction 'measures' in s 1 of the 1980 Act was a very wide generic
term which could include statutory provisions, and the fact that the measures referred to
in s 1 were 'measures . . . taken . . . by . . . the law of any overseas country' showed that
the term included foreign statutory provisions. Furthermore, a foreign statute was none
the less controlling or regulatory even though it sought to prevent international trade
being conducted on the basis of co-operative agreements designed to minimise or

e eliminate competition. It followed that the anti-trust provisions in the Sherman and
Clayton Acts were 'measures . . . for regulating and controlling trade', for the purposes of
s 1, and that the 1983 order was not ultra vires by referring to those Acts (see p 405 g to j,
post).
    (b) The Secretary of State was not required to make an order under s 1(2) that he be
notified of any requirement for the production of documents to a foreign court before

f he gave a direction under s 1(3) prohibiting compliance with any such requirement,
because sub-ss (2) and (3) were independent of each other and therefore, in addition to
having power under s 1(2) to obtain information about such requirements, the Secretary
of State's prohibitory powers under s 1(3) encompassed particular categories of
requirements and prohibitions regardless of whether he had knowledge of them or not
(see p 406 d e, post).

g (c) Although the Secretary of State was not required to specify in the s 2 direction why
it appeared to him that the requirement for the production of documents to the United
States district court was 'inadmissible', the s 2 direction itself showed that the Secretary
of State had grounds for believing that the United States Department of Justice's
requirements were inadmissible and, furthermore, there was evidence that the United
States Department of Justice was seeking to use the defendant's liquidator to obtain

h discovery from the plaintiffs in the defendant's action for the purposes of the grand jury
investigation, and that abundantly justified the Secretary of State's view that inadmissible
requirements might be made (see p 406 f g and p 407 b to h, post); *Secretary of State for
Employment v Associated Society of Locomotive Engineers and Firemen (No 2)* [1972] 2 All ER
949 applied.
    (2) On the plaintiffs' application for injunctions restraining the defendant from
pursuing its United States action, the plaintiffs' appeal would be allowed for the following

j reasons—
    (a) Since foreign policy was distinct from domestic policy, in that it was not subject to
direct parliamentary action but rather consisted of acts of state done by the executive as
the government of the United Kingdom, and since treaties were not part of the domestic
laws of the United Kingdom and gave rise to no private rights or obligations under
English law, the court had no jurisdiction to determine the meaning or effect of any

treaty to which the United Kingdom was a party. However, while it was of constitutional importance that the courts were independent of the executive, they needed to be *a* informed, where necessary, of the views of the government concerning any treaty which was relevant to a dispute between private parties, and therefore the government's attitude to the 1977 treaty was a relevant factor to be taken into account when considering the plaintiffs' claim for relief, and the plaintiffs were entitled to rely on the assistance which such public policy considerations afforded them (see p 401 *h*, p 402 *h j*, p 403 *d* to *f* and p 409 *c* to *e*, post); dicta of Lord Wilberforce and Lord Fraser in *Rio Tinto Zinc Corp v* *b* *Westinghouse Electric Corp* [1978] 1 All ER at 448, 475 considered.

(b) The court had jurisdiction to grant the plaintiffs the relief sought, even though there was no alternative forum in England or elsewhere in which the defendant might bring its action, if it was nevertheless appropriate to grant the relief in the circumstances in order to avoid injustice or a greater injustice. However, the absence of an alternative forum was a very important factor to be taken into account and required the jurisdiction *c* to be exercised with extreme caution. In the critical equation of the advantages to the defendants and disadvantages to the plaintiffs if relief was not granted, the effect of the 1983 order and the directions issued under the 1980 Act were decisive since the order and directions meant that the plaintiffs were unable to comply with the requirement for the production of documents to the United States district court and would thereby be unable to defend themselves in that action if they needed to rely on such documents to *d* do so. The order and directions had in effect rendered the issues raised by the defendant in the district court action wholly untriable as between the parties and in those circumstances to allow the defendant to proceed with its United States claim against them would amount to a total denial of justice to the plaintiffs (see p 398 *a b f g*, p 399 *f g* and p 409 *j* to p 410 *c* and *f* to *h*, post); dictum of Lord Scarman in *Castanho v Brown &* *e* *Root (UK) Ltd* [1981] 1 All ER at 150–151 applied; *Siskina (cargo owners) v Distos Compania* *Naviera SA, The Siskina* [1977] 3 All ER 803 distinguished.

Notes
For the general principles governing the stay of foreign proceedings, see 8 Halsbury's Laws (4th edn) paras 787–788, and for cases on the subject, see 11 Digest (Reissue) 637– *f* 641, 1720–1746.

For the Protection of Trading Interests Act 1980, ss 1, 2, see 50(1) Halsbury's Statutes (3rd edn) 259–262.

Cases referred to in judgments
Adams v Adams (A-G intervening) [1970] 3 All ER 572, [1971] P 188, [1970] 3 WLR 934. *g*
Arantzazu Mendi, The [1939] 1 All ER 719, [1939] AC 256, HL.
Atlantic Star, The, Atlantic Star (owners) v Bona Spes (owners) [1973] 2 All ER 175, [1974] AC 436, [1973] 2 WLR 795, HL; *rvsg* [1972] 3 All ER 705, [1973] QB 364, [1972] 3 WLR 746, CA.
Castanho v Brown & Root (UK) Ltd [1981] 1 All ER 143, [1981] AC 557, [1980] 3 WLR 991, HL; *varying* [1980] 3 All ER 72, [1980] 1 WLR 833, CA. *h*
Laker Airways Ltd v Dept of Trade [1977] 2 All ER 182, [1977] QB 643, [1977] 2 WLR 234, CA.
MacShannon v Rockware Glass Ltd, Fyfe v Redpath Dorman Long Ltd [1978] 1 All ER 625, [1978] AC 795, [1978] 2 WLR 362, HL; *rvsg* [1977] 2 All ER 449, [1977] 1 WLR 376, CA.
Rio Tinto Zinc Corp v Westinghouse Electric Corp, R T Z Services Ltd v Westinghouse Electric *j* *Corp* [1978] 1 All ER 434, [1978] AC 547, [1978] 2 WLR 81, HL.
St Pierre v South American Stores (Gath & Chaves) Ltd [1936] 1 KB 382, [1935] All ER Rep 408, CA.
Secretary of State for Employment v Associated Society of Locomotive Engineers and Firemen (No 2) [1972] 2 All ER 949, [1972] 1 QB 455, [1972] 2 WLR 1370, CA.

Siskina (cargo owners) v Distos Compania Naviera SA, The Siskina [1977] 3 All ER 803, [1979]
a   AC 210, [1977] 3 WLR 818, HL.
Smith Kline & French Laboratories Ltd v Bloch [1983] 2 All ER 72, [1983] 1 WLR 730, CA.

Cases also cited
*Bremer Vulkan Schiffau und Maschinenfabrik v South India Shipping Corp, Gregg v Raytheon
Ltd* [1981] 2 All ER 289, [1981] AC 909, HL.
b   *British Nylon Spinners Ltd v ICI Ltd* [1952] 2 All ER 780, [1953] Ch 19, CA.
Chief Constable of Kent v V [1982] 3 All ER 36, [1983] QB 34, CA.
Fender v Mildmay [1937] 3 All ER 402, [1938] AC 1, HL.
Gorthon Investment AB v Ford Motor Co Ltd, The Maria Gorthon [1976] 2 Lloyd's Rep 720.
Gouriet v Union of Post Office Workers [1977] 3 All ER 70, [1978] AC 435, HL.
Hoani Te Heuheu Tukino v Aotea District Maori Land Board [1941] 2 All ER 93, [1941] AC
c   308, PC.
Midland Bank plc v Laker Airways Ltd (4th February 1983, unreported), QBD.
McEldowney v Forde [1969] 2 All ER 1039, [1971] AC 632, HL.
Padfield v Minister of Agriculture, Fisheries and Food [1968] 1 All ER 694, [1968] AC 997,
HL.
Pan American World Airways Inc v Dept of Trade [1976] 1 Lloyd's Rep 257, CA.
d   *R v Industrial Injuries Comr, ex p Amalgamated Engineering Union (No 2)* [1966] 1 All ER 97,
[1966] 2 QB 21, CA.
Secretary of State for Education and Science v Tameside Metropolitan Borough [1976] 3 All ER
665, [1977] AC 1014, HL.
Texas Industries Inc v Radcliff Materials Inc (1981) 451 US 630, US SC.
Walker v Baird [1892] AC 491, PC.

e
Actions
By a writ issued on 21 January 1983 the plaintiffs, British Airways Board, sought as
against the defendants, Laker Airways Ltd, Nigel James Hamilton, Christopher Morris,
Laker Air Services Ltd and Laker Airways (International) Ltd (collectively referred to as
Laker), declarations that the plaintiffs had not engaged in any unlawful combination or
f   conspiracy unreasonably to restrain or monopolise trade and commerce in air
transportation between the United States and the United Kingdom and that they had not
intentionally or unlawfully caused injury to Laker Airways Ltd, and an order that Laker
be restrained, inter alia, from causing or permitting to be continued against the plaintiffs
civil action no 82–3362 in the United States District Court, District of Columbia, between
Laker Airways Ltd and Pan American World Airways Inc and others. By a writ issued on
g   24 January 1983 the plaintiffs, British Caledonian Airways Ltd, sought a similar
declaration and injunction against the defendants excluding Nigel James Hamilton.
During the course of the hearing Parker J invited the Attorney General to be represented
to present the views of the executive on the issues before the court. The facts are set out
in the judgment of Parker J.

h   *Richard Scott QC* and *Jonathan Sumption* for British Airways.
Colin Ross-Munro QC and *David Donaldson* for British Caledonian.
David Johnson QC, Michael Crystal and *Richard Hacker* for Laker.
Peter Scott QC and *Nicolas Bratza* for the Attorney General.

Cur adv vult

j
20 May. The following judgment was delivered.

PARKER J. There are before the court for decision applications by the plaintiffs and
cross-applications by the defendants in two actions commenced respectively by British
Airways Board (British Airways) on 21 January 1983 and by British Caledonian Airways

Ltd (British Caledonian) on 24 January 1983. In both actions the first and real defendant is Laker Airways Ltd (Laker), a Jersey company now in liquidation, but formerly the *a* operator of the well-known transatlantic Skytrain service, whose principal place of business was at all material times in London. The other defendants need no separate mention. They are added for the purpose only of ensuring that if the plaintiffs are granted the relief which they seek against Laker that relief may be fully effective.

Both actions are the direct result of the fact that on 24 November 1982 Laker commenced proceedings (the American action) in the United States District Court for *b* the District of Columbia against eight defendants, of which two are the present applicants, British Airways and British Caledonian, and the other six are two American airlines (Pan Am and TWA), two European airlines (Lufthansa and Swissair), the American aircraft manufacturers, McDonnell Douglas Corp and, finally, the last-mentioned corporation's subsidiary, McDonnell Douglas Finance Corp. In that action Laker claims against the eight defendants that its collapse in February 1982 was brought about by a conspiracy *c* between the eight defendants and others or by intentional and unlawful injury caused by the eight defendants jointly and severally. Under both heads the damages claimed exceed $US1 billion, albeit the damage allegedly suffered by Laker is, in both cases, presently estimated at some $US350m.

The conspiracy claim, to which I shall refer as 'the anti-trust claim', alleges a conspiracy unreasonably to restrain and to monopolise United States foreign trade and commerce in *d* air transportation between the United States and the United Kingdom and other European countries in violation of ss 1 and 2 of the Sherman Antitrust Act of the United States (15 USC §§1–7), with the object of eliminating Laker as an independent competitive force in trade and commerce between the United States and foreign nations. If the claim is established, Laker is, under s 4 of the Clayton Act of the United States (15 USC §§ 12–27), entitled to triple damages. Hence the difference between the damage allegedly *e* suffered and the damages claimed in the action. Under the alternative head that difference is accounted for by a claim for punitive damages in the amount of $US700m.

By their writs British Airways and British Caledonian claim declarations that they are under no liability to Laker, and injunctions to restrain it from continuing the American action as against them. Each of them, at the time of commencement of their respective actions, applied for and obtained ex parte interlocutory injunctions restraining Laker, *f* pending the determination of a summons for wider relief or further order, from seeking in the American action injunctions or any order which would prevent them from proceeding further with the actions which they had respectively launched in this court, while leaving Laker otherwise free to pursue that action without restraint. On 2 March 1983, however, both of them applied for and obtained further ex parte interlocutory relief for the like period preventing Laker from taking any steps as against them in the *g* American action save as to any applications already in being at the date of notification of the order granting such additional relief.

At that time the hearing of the summonses for further relief was fixed for 21 March, some 19 days ahead. The duration of the restraint on Laker in its conduct, as against the present plaintiffs, of the American action was therefore of short duration and affected no applications then already pending. Furthermore, the order granting the relief specifically *h* included, as is usual, liberty to Laker to apply on short notice at any time to discharge or vary the order granting the relief. No such application was made. I mention these matters for it is important that they should be fully understood by the judge seised of the American proceedings. As in America, so here it is and always has been regarded as of great importance that a conflict, or even an apparent conflict, between the courts of one country and another should be avoided if at all possible. However, the courts both in *j* America and here recognise that there may be occasions when it will be necessary for them, by orders in personam, to restrain the pursuit of proceedings in another country. Given that such occasions may exist our procedure enables temporary relief to be granted to hold the position pending full argument and evidence, in order that, if the plaintiff in the end establishes that it is such an occasion, he may not, in the meantime, have suffered

irreparable damage. The granting of such relief, when fully understood, involves neither
a actual nor apparent conflict.

The plaintiffs' applications for the wider relief of an injunction restraining Laker from
pursuing the American action at all and the defendants' cross-applications, which are to
dismiss the actions here, were, save as to two matters, argued and a mass of evidence was
tendered on 22, 23, 24, 25, 28 and 29 March 1983. On the conclusion of the argument
there was no dispute but that the original ex parte injunction should continue until after
b judgment. The plaintiffs submitted that the wider relief afforded by the orders of 2
March should also be continued for a like period, but such continuation was resisted by
Laker. Being then not satisfied that there was good ground for continuation of such
wider relief no matter what might be the decision on the plaintiffs' applications, I
discharged such orders but granted a short stay in order to enable the plaintiffs to seek
from the Court of Appeal a reversal of the order of discharge or, possibly, a longer stay to
c enable the appeal to be fully argued.

On 30 March Sir John Donaldson MR, sitting alone, restored the order of 2 March
pending the hearing of the appeal from its discharge, reserving to Laker, as had been
done when the injunction was originally granted, liberty to apply in the mean time for
discharge or variation of the order.

The two matters which, on 29 March, remained outstanding were any submissions
d which the parties might wish to make as a result of, first, a reserved judgment of Judge
Harold H Greene on an application in the American action, for which I considered it
desirable if possible to wait before giving judgment myself and, second, a statement on
behalf of the Attorney General as to executive policy which, in the light of the
submissions made on these applications and what had been said in the House of Lords in
Rio Tinto Zinc Corp v Westinghouse Electric Corp [1978] 1 All ER 434, [1978] AC 547, it
e appeared to me proper to invite. Such statement was made on behalf of the Attorney
General by counsel on 6 May. Submissions with regard to this and Judge Greene's
judgment, which was by then available, were made on the same day.

Before considering the background to the issues which arise I should mention certain
additional matters. First, British Caledonian, but not British Airways, amended their
summons to include an application for a mandatory order against Laker to discontinue
f its American action as against them. Second, although the applications by both plaintiffs
were originally for injunctions restraining pursuit of the American proceedings until
trial or further order it was common ground between the parties that I should determine
the plaintiffs' entitlement to such relief finally.

The crux of the dispute between the parties is Laker's anti-trust claim in the American
action. It is a claim which can only be pursued in a district court in America. Accordingly,
g if prevented from pursuing it there Laker cannot pursue it in this country or, indeed,
anywhere else. The relief claimed by the plaintiffs is not, therefore, sought on the usual
basis that the opposing party can equally well litigate here. Furthermore, since the
plaintiffs have places of business in the United States and conduct part of their operations
in, and in the airspace of, the United States it is not suggested that the plaintiffs were not
properly served in the United States or that the district court lacks jurisdiction to try their
h claim. The applications are, therefore, at least unusual. Indeed, they are probably unique.

Both British Airways and British Caledonian submit, however, that they are entitled
to or should be granted the relief which they seek on the grounds, first, that it would be
an injustice to them to allow the American action to proceed against them and, second,
that it would be contrary to public policy to allow it to do so. British Caledonian advance
a further ground, namely that the claim against them is frivolous and vexatious.

j With that preliminary I can now turn to consider the background to the plaintiffs'
claim for relief. From 1977 the plaintiffs, Laker and the two American airline defendants
in the American action all derived their right to operate scheduled transatlantic air
services between the United States and this country from the fact that they were
designated respectively by the governments of this country and the United States under
an agreement between those governments made or done in Bermuda on 23 July 1977,

which I shall hereafter refer to as 'Bermuda 2' (Cmnd 7016 (1977)). That agreement replaces an earlier agreement made in 1946 but although Laker's conspiracy allegations in its anti-trust claim go back beyond 1977 it is unnecessary for present purposes to make further reference to such earlier agreement.

By art 2(2) of Bermuda 2 each government grants to the other the rights specified in the agreement for the purpose of operating scheduled international air services on routes specified therein. By art 3(1)(a) each government has the right to designate an airline or airlines for the purpose of operating the agreed services on each of the specified routes, and by art 3(6) it is provided that on receipt of such a designation and on receipt of an application from the designated airline for operating authorisations and technical permissions the other government shall grant the appropriate authorisations and permissions provided certain conditions are satisfied. Once so designated and authorised it is provided that an airline shall be entitled to operate the relevant agreed services on the specified routes provided it complies with the applicable provisions of the agreement.

These are the basic conditions on which each government permits an airline of the other to fly in its airspace and land on its territory. An airline will, however, have also to obtain from the appropriate authorities of its own country whatever licences or authorisations the law of that country requires.

Article 11 of Bermuda 2 provides for the designated airline or airlines of one country to have a fair and equal opportunity to compete with the designated airline or airlines of the other, but makes no provision as to competition between the airlines of one country inter se, a matter which is internal to each country. Some reliance was placed on this article by the plaintiffs.

In the American action Laker contends, at any rate by implication, that Pan Am and TWA did not afford Laker a fair opportunity to compete but this takes the matter no further. It may give the government of this country cause for complaint. It may even, if proved, justify the government of this country in withdrawing authorisations for Pan Am and TWA to fly into its airspace and land on its territory, but it does not appear to me to affect the matters which presently fall for decision.

The article principally relied on by the plaintiffs is, however, art 12, which provides for the fixing of the tariffs of the designated airlines. Its importance lies in the fact that one of Laker's principal allegations in the anti-trust claim is that the airlines combined to charge predatory fares, i e fares which were deliberately and uneconomically low in order to damage Laker and cause its collapse.

Article 12(1) provides that the tariffs shall be established in accordance with the procedures set out in the article, and art 12(2) provides that such tariffs shall be established at the lowest level consistent with a high standard of safety and an adequate return to efficient airlines operating on the agreed routes.

Article 12(2) further provides that each tariff shall, to the extent feasible, be based on the cost of providing the service in question assuming reasonable load factors and that amongst other factors to be taken into account will be the need for an airline to meet competition from scheduled or charter air services, taking into account differences in cost and quality of service and the prevention of unjust discrimination and undue preferences or advantages. Finally, art 12(2) provides that individual airlines should be encouraged to initiate innovative cost-based tariffs.

There are in the article two basic procedures with regard to the establishment of tariffs. First, by art 12(4) any tariff agreement concluded as a result of inter-carrier discussions, including those held under the traffic conference procedures of the International Air Transport Association (IATA) and involving the airlines of the contracting parties, is to be subject to the approval of the aeronautical authorities of both the contracting parties and may be disapproved at any time.

It is provided that such agreements shall be submitted for approval to both aeronautical authorities at least 105 days before the proposed date of effectiveness (unless shorter notice is permitted) accompanied by such justification as each contracting party may require of its own designated airlines. The submission of such an agreement for approval is, however, not the filing of a tariff under art 12(5), which provides the second procedure

for the establishment of tariffs. Under it any designated airline may file a tariff with the
a aeronautical authority of the other contracting party at least 75 days before the proposed
effective date (again unless shorter notice is permitted). It will then become effective
unless action is taken to continue the existing tariff in force under art 12(7). Since the
designated airlines of both countries require tariff approval from their own authority it
follows that all charges in fact made must have received express or tacit approval from
the aeronautical authorities of both countries before they are put into effect. Hence all
b the fares of which Laker complains had to be, and it is common ground they were, in
receipt of such approval before they were put into effect, such approval being given in
America by the Civil Aeronautics Board (the CAB), and in this country by the Civil
Aviation Authority (the CAA). Furthermore, before such fares were approved Laker was
given by the respective authorities the opportunity, of which it took advantage, to object
to the introduction of such fares.
c   Article 12 ends with two provisions of some importance. First, the aeronautical
authority of each government are to use their best endeavours to ensure that the
designated airlines conform to the agreed tariffs filed with the aeronautical authorities of
the two governments and that no airline rebates any portion of such tariffs by any means,
directly or indirectly. Second, art 12(9) provides that in order to avoid tariff disputes as
far as possible (i) a 'tariff working group' shall be established in accordance with Annex 3,
d (ii) the aeronautical authorities of the two countries shall keep each other informed of
such guidance as they may give to their own airlines in advance of or during IATA
conferences, (iii) during the time when the civil aeronautical authority of either
government have under consideration agreements pursuant to art 12(4), the two
governments may exchange views and recommendations which shall, if requested by
either government, be presented to the aeronautical authority of the other who will take
e them into account in reaching its decision.
       It is thus clear that both governments were to be closely involved in the fixing of tariffs
and that it was contemplated that all tariff agreements would be placed before the
aeronautical authorities of both countries, which authorities would take into account
government views before reaching a decision.
       So much for Bermuda 2. It is now necessary to refer shortly to the Sherman Antitrust
f Act 1890, the Clayton Act 1914, and the Federal Aviation Act 1958 of the United States.
       By § 1 of the Sherman Act 'Every contract, combination in the form of trust or
otherwise, or conspiracy, in restraint of trade or commerce among the several States, or
with foreign nations, is . . . declared to be illegal' and any person who makes any such
contract, combination or conspiracy is guilty of a criminal offence. By § 2 every person
who monopolises or attempts to monopolise or combines or conspires with any other
g person or persons to monopolise any part of such trade or commerce is also guilty of a
criminal offence.
       Section 4 of the Clayton Act provides:

> 'That any person who shall be injured in his business or property by reason of
> anything forbidden in the antitrust laws [which include the Sherman Act] may sue
> therefor in any district court of the United States in the district in which the
h > defendant resides or is found or has an agent, without respect to the amount in
> controversy, and shall recover threefold the damages by him sustained, and the cost
> of suit, including a reasonable attorney's fee.'

       These three sections are the foundation of Laker's anti-trust claim. The breaches of
§§ 1 and 2 of the Sherman Act alleged go back many years, but for present purposes I
j need mention only events occurring shortly before Laker's final collapse. By the late
summer of 1981 Laker was, and was known to be, in grave financial trouble, and if it
was to survive it required massive financial assistance. The substance of what is alleged
by Laker is that the plaintiffs and other defendants in the American action, in pursuit of
a combination between them to drive it out of business, then did two things. First when
Laker, in order to improve failing business on its Skytrain service, or at least to stop
further deterioration in its position, had introduced a fare known as a 'Regency fare'

(offering better facilities than the normal Skytrain fare, but lesser facilities than those offered by the plaintiffs and other airline defendants), Pan Am, TWA and British Airways dropped their fares for better facilities to match Laker's fares although it was wholly uneconomic so to do, and thus further damaged Laker's business and increased its financial difficulties. Next, having done this, British Caledonian and others, in pursuit of the combination, exerted pressure on McDonnell Douglas to prevent them from putting into effect an essential part of a financial rescue operation then being negotiated, with the result that it did not reach fruition and Laker could no longer continue in business.

I shall return to these matters hereafter.

I now consider two sections of the Federal Aviation Act 1958. Under § 412 as it stood up to 1978 every United States air carrier was obliged to file with the CAB a true copy or, if oral, a true and complete memorandum of every contract or agreement affecting air transport between it and any other air carrier, foreign air carrier or other carrier, inter alia, relating to the establishment of fares or controlling, regulating, preventing or otherwise eliminating destructive, oppressive or wasteful competition. The CAB was then obliged by order to disapprove any such contract or agreement that it found to be adverse to the public interest and to approve any such contract or agreement that it did not find to be adverse to the public interest or in violation of the Act. Under § 414 any person affected by an order made under § 412 was exempted from the operation of the anti-trust laws in so far as might be necessary to enable him to do anything approved by such order.

In 1978 § 412 was amended, inter alia, so as to make the filing of any such agreement optional and to make it possible to apply for authority to discuss possible cooperative working arrangements, and in 1980 it was further amended so as to enable not only a United States air carrier but also a foreign air carrier to file an agreement or request for authority to discuss and thus obtain anti-trust exemption.

In summary form the position with regard to exemption may therefore be stated as follows. (1) At the time of Bermuda 2 an American airline was obliged to file any tariff agreement whether with another American airline or a foreign airline, but a foreign airline was under no such obligation. Hence there was no provision under which a British airline, making an agreement only with another British airline, could of its own motion or otherwise obtain anti-trust exemption. If, however, an American airline was a party to such an agreement anti-trust exemption could be obtained provided that the American airline complied with its obligations under § 412. (2) From 1978 to 1980 the position changed in that a British airline could only obtain exemption if an American airline was a party, and that airline exercised the *option* to file the agreement. (3) From 1980 onwards a British airline could also obtain exemption by obtaining of its own motion an order of the CAB under § 412.

It was in this state of affairs that, at the end of 1980, the matter of anti-trust legislation was raised between the two governments in connection with, and at the same time as, an annex (Annex 5) to Bermuda 2 providing for air cargo operations was entered into between them. The government of this country was concerned to obtain protection from anti-trust laws for agreements between United Kingdom cargo airlines. By a letter dated 4 December, the same day on which Annex 5 was added, the United States government gave no assurances as to exemption but pointed out that under § 412, as recently amended, exemption could be obtained. An Under-secretary of the Department of Trade, in reply, stated:

'. . . As you know my Government does not accept the jurisdiction which the U.S. claims in respect of these laws, nor their appropriateness in some circumstances to international air service operations. It is only fair to advise you that if, after consultation, H.M.G. indicates that it sees no objection to the arrangements proposed but nevertheless anti-trust action is brought against the U.K. airlines concerned, then we might consider such action as a reason for seeking modification and if necessary termination, of the cargo agreement as provided for in part 5 of [the annex].'

a It is to be noted that the specific matters under consideration at the time were agreements (i) between UK airlines only, (ii) agreements to which the government of this country saw no objection, and (iii) agreements to enable small UK cargo airlines better to compete with the larger and more experienced American cargo airlines.

No anti-trust question with regard to scheduled passenger services was raised or mentioned either in Bermuda 2 itself or in exchanges between the governments at the time it was entered into or thereafter.

b To complete the background to the anti-trust claim so far as is required for present purposes, it is necessary only to mention that both British Airways and British Caledonian are United Kingdom companies, the former being statutory and having statutory functions to fulfil, that both have their principal places of business here, that like Laker they also have, and at all material times had, places of business in the United States from which they conduct and conducted the United States end of the transatlantic air services *c* which they were and are designated under Bermuda 2 to operate, and that Laker, although a Jersey company, not only had, as already mentioned, its principal place of business in London but was also owned and controlled by a United Kingdom company.

I now turn to those features of the anti-trust action itself which are of importance. First, it is an action in which triple damages are awarded as of right. Second, Laker, although in liquidation, can institute and pursue it without affording any defendant any *d* security for costs should it in the end fail. Third, if in the end Laker does fail a successful defendant will not, save in exceptional circumstances, be entitled to recover any costs against it. Fourth, Laker will have the advantage of pre-trial procedures for depositions, interrogatories and discovery of documents of a very wide ranging nature which are far more extensive and costly than any procedures known in this country and which would be regarded as onerous or oppressive in this country. Fifth, save possibly as against British *e* Airways, Laker will be entitled to trial by jury. Sixth and last, but of great importance, there is no right of contribution as between defendants, so that Laker would be entitled, if successful, to enforce any judgment against, for example, British Airways alone, who would then be unable to recover from any other defendant also held liable.

So much for the background to the plaintiffs' claim. It is next necessary to consider the law applicable where a party seeks an order restraining an opposite party from taking or *f* pursuing proceedings in another country.

The principal authorities on this matter are *The Atlantic Star, Atlantic Star (owners) v Bona Spes (owners)* [1973] 2 All ER 175, [1974] AC 436, *MacShannon v Rockware Glass Ltd* [1978] 1 All ER 625, [1978] AC 795, *Castanho v Brown & Root (UK) Ltd* [1981] 1 All ER 143, [1981] AC 557 and *Smith Kline & French Laboratories Ltd v Bloch* [1983] 2 All ER 72, [1983] 1 WLR 730.

g *The Atlantic Star* was a case in which Dutch owners of a barge had initiated actions both in this country and in Belgium against the Dutch owners of the Atlantic Star in respect of a collision in the River Schelde. The owners of the Atlantic Star applied for a stay of the English proceedings. This was refused both at first instance and in the Court of Appeal, but was granted by the House of Lords by a majority. The case is of importance in that the earlier authorities were examined, an attempt to introduce the forum non *h* conveniens principle was rejected and there was a broadening of, albeit adherence to, the long-established principle enunciated by Scott LJ in *St Pierre v South American Stores (Gath & Chaves) Ltd* [1936] 1 KB 382, [1935] All ER Rep 408, to which I shall later revert. For present purposes, however, its principal importance lies in two observations, one by Lord Reid and one by Lord Simon.

Lord Reid said ([1973] 2 All ER 175 at 181, [1974] AC 436 at 453):

j 'It is a function of this House to try, so far as possible, to keep the development of the common law in line with the policy of Parliament and the movement of public opinion.'

And Lord Simon said ([1973] 2 All ER 175 at 197, [1974] AC 436 at 471):

'English courts are normally confined to examining the statutes giving effect to a treaty or international convention, and precluded from scrutinising the treaty itself. But where public policy and international comity are invoked (as they were here by the appellants, in their endeavour to persuade your Lordships to depart from the rule of English law heretobefore established and accepted), it is permissible (indeed, incumbent) to examine our formal international obligations. As Lord Atkin said in *The Arantzazu Mendi* [1939] 1 All ER 719 at 722, [1939] AC 256 at 264: "Our state cannot speak with two voices ... the judiciary saying one thing, the executive another." (Though Lord Atkin was speaking of recognition of foreign sovereignty, his observations must be of general application with a unitary state in cases such as the instant: see *Adams v Adams (Attorney-General intervening* [1970] 3 All ER 572 at 577, [1971] P 188 at 189).'

Similar observations are to be found in the *Westinghouse* case [1978] 1 All ER 434, [1978] AC 547.

MacShannon v Rockware Glass was also a case where what was sought was a stay of English proceedings, but in that case no other proceedings were pending. Four Scotsmen, living and working in Scotland, brought actions against English companies in respect of industrial accidents in Scotland. In two of the actions Robert Goff J refused the defendants' application for a stay of the English actions and his decision was affirmed by the Court of Appeal. In the other two cases, which fell for consideration after the decision of the Court of Appeal, Griffiths J, considering himself bound by that decision, also refused a stay. On appeal to the House of Lords (in the latter two cases in pursuance of the 'leap frog' procedure) a stay was granted, and the plaintiffs were left to pursue their remedy in Scotland.

The case is of great importance to a decision in the instant case and it is necessary to quote certain passages. In referring to *The Atlantic Star* Lord Diplock said ([1978] 1 All ER 625 at 630, [1978] AC 795 at 811):

'... the gist of the three speeches of Lord Reid, Lord Wilberforce and Lord Kilbrandon, in my opinion, enables the second part of it [ie Scott LJ's statement in the *St Pierre* case] to be restated thus: "In order to justify a stay two conditions must be satisfied, one positive and the other negative: (a) the defendant must satisfy the court that there is another forum to whose jurisdiction he is amenable in which justice can be done between the parties at substantially less inconvenience or expense, and (b) the stay must not deprive the plaintiff of a legitimate personal or juridical advantage which would be available to him if he invoked the jurisdiction of the English court" ...'

The above formulation removed the requirement originally contained that the defendant must show that the continuance of the action would work an injustice to him 'because it would be oppressive or vexatious to him or would be an abuse of the process of the court in some other way'. Both Lord Salmon and Lord Fraser also expressly negatived any such requirement: (see [1978] 1 All ER 625 at 636, 639, [1978] AC 795 at 819, 822–823). Lord Salmon expressed the matter on a very broad basis as follows ([1978] 1 All ER 625 at 636, [1978] AC 795 at 819):

'... the question as to whether it should be stayed depends on whether the defendants can establish that to refuse a stay would produce injustice. ... To my mind, the real test of stay depends on what the court in its discretion considers that justice demands.'

This approach was also adopted by Lord Russell and Lord Keith.

Before leaving this case it is necessary to mention that counsel for Laker relied on certain passages which were said to indicate that the question of public policy must be considered irrelevant in applications such as were then and are here under consideration. These passages appear in the speeches of Lord Salmon, Lord Fraser, Lord Russell and Lord Keith (see [1978] 1 All ER 625 at 639, 640, 648, [1978] AC 795 at 822, 823, 833). In my judgment the 'public policy' which was there canvassed was of a very different a nature to that which is advanced here. What was argued was that the courts should, as a matter of policy, discourage the bringing of proceedings in England in respect of industrial accidents in Scotland. This argument was rejected, the House expressing the clear view that the question to be determined was in each individual case whether, as between an individual defendant and an individual plaintiff, justice demanded a stay.

Both the foregoing cases involved the question of a stay of English proceedings, but in *Castanho v Brown & Root (UK) Ltd* [1981] 1 All ER 143, [1981] AC 557 the question of a
b stay of foreign proceedings was considered. The opinion of the House is to be found in the speech of Lord Scarman, with which the four other members of the House concurred. When considering that case it is important to bear in mind that the plaintiff had instituted an action in this country and also in the United States. He desired to discontinue here and pursue his action in the United States. The defendant sought to obtain an injunction to restrain him from proceeding further in the United States. There was thus no question
c of the plaintiff being deprived of a remedy if the injunction was granted. He could obtain justice here. The stay was, however, refused.

Having affirmed the existence of the jurisdiction to restrain foreign proceedings, albeit the necessity to exercise that jurisdiction with caution, Lord Scarman referred to a submission that the jurisdiction had only been exercised in two classes of case, namely (1) to prevent harassment by two actions, and (2) where there is a right justiciable in
d England which the court seeks to protect. He then said ([1981] 1 All ER 143 at 149, [1981] AC 557 at 573):

> 'No doubt, in practice, most cases fall within one or other of these two classes. But the width and flexibility of equity are not to be undermined by categorisation. Caution in the exercise of the jurisdiction is certainly needed; but the way in which the judges have expressed themselves from 1821 onwards amply supports the view
e for which the defendants contend that the injunction can be granted against a party properly before the court, where it is appropriate to avoid injustice.'

By 'properly before the court' Lord Scarman was, it appears, referring to the question whether the party suing abroad had sufficient connection with England to justify the granting of an injunction at all (see [1981] 1 All ER 143 at 150, [1981] AC 557 at 574).
f In the instant case there is no question about this. As a designated airline under Bermuda 2 with a principal place of business in London, owned and controlled by an English company, in turn owned and controlled by Sir Freddie Laker, Laker clearly had the closest connection with England. Although no longer carrying on business it still has, for its liquidator is an English chartered accountant carrying on his profession in London.

Next Lord Scarman considered the criteria which should govern the exercise of the
g discretion (see [1981] 1 All ER 143 at 150, [1981] AC 557 at 574): 'The principle is the same whether the remedy sought is a stay of English proceedings or a restraint on foreign proceedings.' He then referred to Lord Diplock's formulation of the principle in the *Rockware Glass* case and said ([1981] 1 All ER 143 at 151, [1981] AC 557 at 575):

> 'Transposed into the context of the present case, this formulation means that to justify the grant of an injunction the defendants must show (a) that the English
h court is a forum to whose jurisdiction they are amenable in which justice can be done at substantially less inconvenience and expense, *and* (b) that the injunction must not deprive the plaintiff of a legitimate personal or juridical advantage which would be available to him if he invoked the American jurisdiction.' (Lord Scarman's emphasis.)

j This formulation, like that propounded by Lord Diplock in the *MacShannon* case, has, as an element, the existence of another forum in which, as between the plaintiff and the defendant, justice can be done, but this requirement, if regarded as being of universal application, would, it seems to me, undermine the flexibility of equity by categorisation, for it would mean either (a) that justice could *never* demand a stay of foreign proceedings unless the plaintiff in those proceedings could pursue his remedy here or elsewhere or (b) that even if justice clearly did demand a stay in a particular case the courts were prohibited from doing justice. In the light of Lord Scarman's very general statement I cannot accept that the House was intending to lay down either of those two rules.

Suppose, for example, that two United Kingdom companies, neither of which traded in or to America, openly made a price agreement lawful in this country but that the purchasers of their goods in this country exported them to the United States. Suppose further that some time later both United Kingdom companies appointed agents in the United States and thus enabled United States proceedings to be served on them and that a United Kingdom company, with a place of business in the United States who had purchased the goods, launched an anti-trust action. In such circumstances it appears to me that justice might well demand that the plaintiff be prevented from pursuing an action in respect of acts performed wholly in this country and wholly lawful here even though, if so prevented, the plaintiff would be left without a remedy. To allow such an action to proceed at the suit of a United Kingdom company would involve exposing United Kingdom defendants to an action based on what is regarded here as an exorbitant assertion of extra-territoriality.

No doubt, where there is no alternative forum, the jurisdiction to restrain should be exercised with even greater caution than is required when there is such a forum, but I am not prepared, unless compelled by precedent, to hold that the courts of this country are powerless to protect residents of this country from being pursued abroad by other residents of this country in respect of acts which are lawful in this country and wholly committed in this country. Such protection may well be necessary to avoid injustice at least in some circumstances.

The last of the four cases principally relied on by the plaintiffs is *Smith Kline & French Laboratories Ltd v Bloch* [1983] 2 All ER 72, [1983] 1 WLR 730, where an injunction staying proceedings in the United States was granted and the plaintiff in the action there was left to pursue any claim which he might have either by way of counterclaim in the pending English action in which the plaintiffs here were seeking a declaration of non-liability or by way of separate proceedings. That case, in my judgment, takes matters no further. The general principles must be taken to be those culled from the three cases in the House of Lords.

Those principles, so far as immediately relevant, appear to me to be as follows. (1) The jurisdiction to stay proceedings in this country is a general equitable jurisdiction which can be exercised whenever its exercise is necessary to prevent injustice. (2) Although the cases may show specific categories in which the jurisdiction has been exercised in the past and although the formula enunciated by Lord Diplock in the *MacShannon* case will or may cover most cases the flexibility of equity is not to be limited or undermined by either categorisation or formula. (3) In exercising the jurisdiction general considerations as to the desirability or otherwise of the type of proceedings sought to be stayed or restrained are irrelevant, the question in each case being what, as between the two parties, justice requires. (4) Nevertheless, in exercising the discretion, it is legitimate in some cases to take into account specific matters of policy be it judicially recognised public policy as revealed by the cases, or parliamentary as revealed by legislation, or governmental as revealed by treaty or convention to which the government is a party. (5) The same principles apply where it is sought to restrain a party properly before the court from instituting or pursuing proceedings abroad. (6) Both jurisdictions must be exercised with caution, but more caution is required in exercising the jurisdiction to restrain the pursuit of proceedings abroad than to stay proceedings here (see *Castanho v Brown & Root (UK) Ltd* [1980] 3 All ER 74 at 91–92, [1980] 1 WLR 833 at 869 per Brandon LJ in the Court of Appeal) and more caution still where the result of any restraint will leave the party restrained without a remedy.

It appears to me also to follow from *Adams v Adams* [1970] 3 All ER 572, [1971] P 188, *The Atlantic Star* [1973] 2 All ER 175, [1974] AC 436 and *Rio Tinto Zinc Corp v Westinghouse Electric Corp* [1978] 1 All ER 434, [1978] AC 547 that in ascertaining specific governmental policy it may be legitimate for the court in certain cases to receive any statement as to such policy which may be tendered through the Attorney General. The extent, however, to which any such statement should be taken into account in any particular case will be

very limited for it is of the essence of the rule of law that the rights and obligations of
a individuals depend on the law and not on executive policy, which does not and must
never be allowed to override the law for, if it is so allowed, the rule of law will cease to
exist.

In the *Westinghouse* case the Attorney General intervened, whereas in the present case
he did not intervene but was invited by the court to attend for the purpose of stating the
views of the government. In the *Westinghouse* case the question for decision was whether
b certain letters rogatory, issued by the court in Virginia in proceedings in which
Westinghouse were defendants and in which they alleged in their defence that the
contracts for breach of which they were being sued were incapable of performance by
reason of a cartel of uranium producers, including two United Kingdom companies, Rio
Tinto Corp Ltd and RTZ Services Ltd, should be given effect. These companies were also
defendants in anti-trust proceedings in Illinois, in which triple damages were being
c claimed. There was, in addition, in existence a grand jury investigation into possible
violation of anti-trust laws by the alleged cartel. After the letters rogatory had been
issued, indeed after orders implementing them had been made and upheld by the Court
of Appeal, the United States Department of Justice intervened and, in effect, converted
the letters rogatory into a request for evidence for the purpose of the grand jury
investigation. The House of Lords held, inter alia, that this attempt to extend the grand
d jury's investigation internationally was not permissible and constituted an infringement
of United Kingdom sovereignty. The decision of the Court of Appeal was reversed. The
foregoing description of the case constitutes a drastic simplification but is sufficient for
present purposes.

In that case what was held to be an invasion of sovereignty was the attempt by the
United States government to enforce its anti-trust laws in their criminal aspect against
e individuals not subject to United States jurisdiction in respect of acts taking place
exclusively outside the United States on the ground that such acts had had an effect
within the United States (see [1978] 1 All ER 434 at 475, [1978] AC 547 at 650 per Lord
Fraser). This is the 'effects' doctrine asserted by the United States which has been a long
standing source of dispute between the United States and this and other countries, some
attempt to counter which had already been made by legislation in the Shipping Contracts
f and Commercial Documents Act 1944.

Although, in argument, objection was taken to the letters rogatory also on the ground
that the evidence sought would be available in the anti-trust suit in Illinois (in which
RTZ were taking no part on the basis that the court lacked jurisdiction) this formed no
part of the decision of the House and was specifically left open by Lord Dilhorne (see
[1970] 1 All ER 434 at 460, [1978] AC 547 at 632).

g For this reason and also because there has since been further Parliamentary intervention
to counter further invasion of sovereignty the case itself and the content of the Attorney
General's intervention in it are of limited assistance for present purposes. It appears to
me to follow, however, that if, in the present case, it were established that in pursuing its
claim in the United States against the present plaintiffs, Laker were a party to any invasion
of sovereignty it would follow that an injunction should be granted, or at least that the
h position constituted a powerful factor in favour of the grant of an injunction.

The subsequent parliamentary intervention is to be found in the Protection of Trading
Interests Act 1980. This Act gives to the Secretary of State wide powers. Under s 1(1), if
it appears to him that under the law of a foreign country measures have been taken or
are proposed to be taken for regulating or controlling international trade and that those
measures, in so far as they apply or would apply to things done or to be done outside the
j territorial jurisdiction of that country by persons carrying on business in the United
Kingdom, are damaging or threaten to damage the trading interests of the United
Kingdom, he may direct that the section shall apply to those measures. Under s 1(3) he
may then give to any person carrying on business in the United Kingdom directions
forbidding compliance with such measures.

Section 2 further empowers the Secretary of State to prohibit any person in the United
Kingdom from producing pursuant to the requirement of any court, tribunal or

authority of a foreign country any commercial document outside the territorial jurisdiction of that country if the requirement infringes the jurisdiction of the United Kingdom or is otherwise prejudicial to the sovereignty of the United Kingdom.

No relevant directions have been given.

Under s 4 the courts of the United Kingdom are prohibited from making orders under s 2 of the Evidence (Proceedings in Other Jurisdictions) Act 1975 giving effect to requests from a foreign tribunal if it is shown that the request infringes the jurisdiction of the United Kingdom or is otherwise prejudicial to the sovereignty of the United Kingdom, and a certificate signed by or on behalf of the Secretary of State to the effect that it infringes that jurisdiction or is so prejudicial is conclusive evidence to that effect.

Sections 1, 2 and 4 thus give the Secretary of State the power where he sees fit effectively to counter exorbitant assertions of jurisdiction.

Next the Act concerns itself with judgments. By s 5 no foreign judgment is enforceable in this country, inter alia, if it is a judgment for multiple damages. This is aimed directly at judgments in anti-trust actions and goes to the whole of the judgment, not merely the multiple or penal part of it.

The plaintiffs not unnaturally rely on this as showing Parliamentary disapproval of anti-trust actions as a whole. Section 5 however must be considered together with s 6. By sub-s (1) that section applies where a foreign court has given a judgment for multiple damages against a 'qualifying defendant', namely (a) a citizen of the United Kingdom or Colonies, or (b) a United Kingdom company or a company incorporated in a territory for whose international relations Her Majesty's Government in the United Kingdom is responsible, or (c) a person carrying on business in the United Kingdom, and the qualifying defendant has paid an amount on account of damages either to the party in whose favour the judgment was given or to another party who is entitled as against the qualifying defendant to contribution in respect of damage.

The primary substantive provision is contained in sub-s (2). This gives the qualifying defendant the right to recover against the party in whose favour the judgment was given, in effect, that part of any sum paid which represents the excess over compensation. In anti-trust actions therefore a qualifying defendant is entitled to recover against the plaintiff two-thirds of any amount which he may have paid.

The overall disapproval demonstrated by s 5 is thus only taken as far as non-enforcement. If a qualifying defendant has paid the whole amount he cannot recover the whole. He can only recover in the case of triple damages two-thirds. It is thus for the excess over compensation that maximum disapproval is demonstrated.

There follow in sub-ss (3) and (4) of s 6 two important qualifications. The right of recovery given by sub-s (2) does not apply in the case of (a) an individual who was ordinarily resident in the foreign country *at the time when the proceedings in which judgment was given were instituted* or a body corporate which had its principal place of business there *at that time*, or (b) a qualifying defendant who carried on business in the foreign country and where the proceedings in which the judgment was given were concerned with activities exclusively carried on in that country.

In the instant case the right of recovery would be of very limited use to British Airways or British Caledonian for Laker is in liquidation, albeit neither would be deprived of the remedy by sub-s (3) or sub-s (4) since (a) neither had its principal place of business in the United States at any time, and (b) although both carried on business in the United States the anti-trust claim (and indeed the alternative claim) is not concerned exclusively with activities carried on in the United States.

It is in my view clear that s 5 has nothing whatever to do with sovereignty. It would for example prevent one United States corporation enforcing in this country a judgment in an anti-trust suit against another United States corporation which had assets and a place of business here, notwithstanding that the anti-trust infringements took place wholly within the United States. In such a case no question of any invasion of sovereignty could arise.

Section 6 requires closer examination for to give a right of recovery in respect of monies properly paid under the judgment of a foreign court would on the face of it seem

to require for its justification some such strong ground as that the proceedings in which the judgment was given constituted in whole or in part an invasion of sovereignty.
a Subsections (3) and (4) may seem to suggest that this is indeed the basis of the right given, but in my view this is not so.

Under sub-s (3) a qualifying individual defendant will have no right of recovery if at the time the proceedings in question were instituted he was ordinarily resident in the country in which the judgment was given and the same will apply to a corporate defendant with its principal place of business in that country at that time.
b The proceedings may however be concerned exclusively with acts carried out outside the foreign country and lawful where they were so carried out and the defendant or defendants concerned may at the time they were carried out, have neither resided nor had a principal or indeed any place of business there. To seek to make such defendants answerable in the foreign court in such circumstances is the sort of excess of sovereignty which was, at least in the criminal field, held to be unacceptable in *Rio Tinto Zinc Corp v*
c *Westinghouse Electric Corp* [1978] 1 All ER 434, [1978] AC 547, yet the subsection appears to accept that so long as the defendants are fully within the jurisdiction of the foreign court at the time when proceedings are instituted there should be no right of recovery.

Subsection (4) does concern itself with the subject matter of the proceedings but it excludes the right of recovery only where the qualifying defendant was carrying on business in the foreign country and the proceedings are concerned with activities
d *exclusively* carried on in the foreign country. It is therefore taking objection to the triple element of the damages in a positive way, as opposed to the negative refusal to enforce judgments, even where the defendant was carrying on business in the foreign country and even where the proceedings concerned activities which were carried on for the most part in that country. This goes further than the *Westinghouse* case and further than would,
e as it seems to me, be justified by any principle of comity or international law. It is moreover to be considered in the light of the earlier sections of the Act. Under s 1 there is power to prohibit compliance with foreign law in so far as it would apply to things outside the territory of the country in which the law is in force. This is clearly aimed, although not in express words, at invasion of sovereignty and under s 2 there is express reference to prejudice to the sovereignty of the United Kingdom.

f I conclude, therefore, that while s 5 is based in essence on the principle that the courts here will not enforce the penal laws of another country and s 6 extends that principle so as to enable the penal element of any amount paid to be recovered in certain circumstances, they cannot be regarded as a sound foundation for any submission that an anti-trust action based in part, or even substantially, on acts committed outside the United States by English companies carrying on business in the United States in relation to the carrying on of that business constitutes such an invasion of sovereignty that a United Kingdom
g company engaged in a like business should be restrained from pursuing his claim.

In essence the position is that a United Kingdom designated airline with its principal place of business in the United Kingdom, but also carrying on business in the United States as an essential part of the operation of the services which it is designated by the United Kingdom and permitted by the United States to perform, is suing two
h other United Kingdom airlines in like case in respect of actions which could only be effective if the CAB's approval was obtained and thus necessarily involved action being taken in the United States.

Parliament has said that if judgment is recovered in that action it will not be enforced here. Parliament has also said that the defendants, if they pay under any such action, shall be entitled to recover back the penal element from the plaintiff but it has not said that such an action shall not be pursued. If Parliament has not said so then some other
j ground must be shown for preventing Laker from pursuing it.

That the penal nature of an anti-trust suit affords no such ground is in my judgment plain. It has, as I have said, been dealt with by Parliament so far as Parliament has seen fit to deal with it, and counsel for the Attorney General, not surprisingly, did not suggest that there was any policy basis on which the penal element should be given any wider effect than Parliament has seen fit to give it.

It is equally clear that invasion of sovereignty or extra-territoriality afford no ground. They too have been dealt with by Parliament, to some extent directly and to some extent by giving to the Secretary of State wide powers to act in case of need. The direct parliamentary intervention does not avail the plaintiffs. The powers conferred by Parliament have not been exercised and a United Kingdom designated airline carrying on business in the United States by permission of the United States government must prima facie comply with United States law or take the consequences.

This conclusion fully accords with the statement by counsel for the Attorney General:

'Her Majesty's Government has consistently taken the position that British enterprises engaged in transnational business operations should comply with the laws and governmental policies of the countries in which they transact business.'

It is said, however, both by the plaintiffs and on behalf of the government that this prima facie position is vitally affected by the relationship between the anti-trust laws and the provisions of Bermuda 2.

Her Majesty's government regards the government of the United States as being in breach of its obligations under Bermuda 2 in allowing anti-trust laws to be applied directly or indirectly, in respect of damage alleged to have flowed from tariffs approved under Bermuda 2 or scheduling arrangements made under the provisions of Bermuda 2 for, it is said, any such application will undermine Bermuda 2. This position is disputed by the government of the United States and as between the two governments the dispute procedure has been invoked. If the dispute is not resolved by agreement, I was informed that an arbitral decision could be obtained in about a year. It is to be noted that Her Majesty's government's position is all embracing and covers the case not merely where one United Kingdom designated airline seeks to invoke anti-trust laws in respect of damage flowing from the application of approved tariffs against another United Kingdom designated airline but also where any plaintiff claims against any defendant airline on a like basis. No doubt, in so far as defendants were American airlines, Her Majesty's government might not seek to complain but the proposition involves the contention that an American plaintiff should not be permitted to bring such an action against American defendants.

The plaintiffs do not seek to go so far. They limit their proposition to cases where a designated United Kingdom airline is suing other designated United Kingdom airlines for damage alleged to flow from tariffs approved under Bermuda 2. Such cases, it is said, involve an airline, which only operates in right of Her Majesty's government, taking part in a derogation of the rights granted to Her Majesty's government under Bermuda 2 and, as I understand it, passed on to other United Kingdom airlines who also thus operate in right of Her Majesty's government.

Counsel for the Attorney General, developed his contention in some 16 separate points all of which are recorded in the transcript and I will not lengthen this judgment by setting them out here. Counsel for the plaintiffs also presented their arguments in a number of ways all of which are also recorded. For the same reasons I will not rehearse them here. I shall simply set out the reasons which lead me to the conclusion that the relationship between the anti-trust laws and Bermuda 2 afford no ground, in my judgment, on which it would be right to grant an injunction. They are as follows.

1. An injunction would deprive Laker of a cause of action which can only be asserted in proceedings properly brought in America against American defendants and the present plaintiffs.

2. It is possible that under American law Bermuda 2 becomes part of that law without further enactment. If this is right, the American courts will decide whether its effect is to grant anti-trust exemption or not. It may be that the American courts will so hold, in which case the anti-trust claim will fail. If they do not so hold, then, if other conditions are established, it will succeed.

3. Bermuda 2 is not part of English domestic law and to use it to deprive Laker of the right to pursue a claim would at the very least require a very strong case.

4. I cannot accept that Laker's claim involves an undermining of Bermuda 2 or any
a derogation of rights. The essence of Laker's case is that there was a tariff agreement not
submitted for approval under Bermuda 2, which provides for the submission of tariff
agreements. Furthermore, it is conceded by the plaintiffs that if any combination went
as far as to constitute a common law conspiracy, Laker could sue without undermining
or derogating from the rights granted under Bermuda 2. For the Attorney General,
counsel made no such express concession but said that each case would depend on its own
b circumstances. If this be so, it is clear that there is no settled policy or clear international
right or obligation preventing the pursuit of a conspiracy claim. An anti-trust claim need
not establish anything like as much as is required in the case of a common law conspiracy,
although Laker's allegations in the American action amount very nearly, if not quite, to
the assertion of a common law conspiracy. An anti-trust claim, as was stressed by Judge
Greene in his recent judgment, is of a different and special kind. Nevertheless, if there is
c no obstacle to a conspiracy claim and if, by obtaining authority to discuss and laying
before the CAB any agreement reached, anti-trust exemption can be obtained, I see no
reason for saying that the application of anti-trust laws undermines Bermuda 2. What, if
anything, would undermine it, is a secret agreement not disclosed to the CAB followed
by the filing of a tariff presented as an individual tariff when it was in fact filed pursuant
to the secret agreement and possibly accompanied by the advancing of false or misleading
d information as to costs.

5. Finally, it is not to be forgotten that the final alleged blow to Laker was the
frustration of the rescue scheme by pressure on McDonnell Douglas. As to this, counsel
for the Attorney General made no submissions. It has in my judgment nothing to do
with Bermuda 2.

If, then, public or governmental policy, extra-territoriality and the penal nature of the
e remedy do not avail as special factors, one comes back to the essential question: would it
be an injustice to the plaintiffs to allow the action against them in America to proceed?

The claim is for damage to a United Kingdom designated airline in its transatlantic air
transport operations carried on alike in the United States by permission of the United
States government, and in the United Kingdom by permission of Her Majesty's
government. The defendants include both United Kingdom and United States designated
f airlines. Laker alleges that the United States and United Kingdom airlines carrying on
like operations have combined to damage it by means which necessarily involve acts
taking place in the United States and which affect the fares paid by American citizens.
What is unjust in allowing the United Kingdom airlines, if the facts are established, from
answering alike with the American airlines for breach of the laws of the country by
permission of whose government they were operating? I can see no injustice. Suppose,
g for example, that there was in a given case an anti-trust conspiracy. Suppose, further,
that two United Kingdom airlines hatched up a scheme to drive another airline out of
business, and persuaded Pan Am and TWA to join in, making sure that their agreement
to do so was secured on British soil. Suppose, finally, that in order to disguise what was
happening the United Kingdom airlines proposed, and the others agreed that initially
one of them would file with the CAA and the CAB for approval what appeared to be an
h individual tariff and that thereafter, when it had been approved, the others would file
like tariffs on the basis that it was merely to meet competition. In such circumstances,
whether the damaged airline was a United States or a United Kingdom designated airline,
I can see no injustice in allowing the instigators of the scheme to be answerable to the
plaintiffs as well as those whom they had persuaded to join it. Indeed, it would seem a
manifest injustice to allow them to escape, the more particularly when their actions
j would constitute a plain abuse of the hospitality of and permission to operate given by
the United States government.

It is true that an anti-trust claim has the undesirable features which I have already
mentioned but some of these are common to all United States actions, and the others
appear to me to have been dealt with by Parliament, so far as Parliament has deemed it
to be necessary to do so. This court should, in my judgment, go no further.

If then there is a prima facie cause of action in America, I can see no ground for restraining Laker from pursuing it. In the result, British Airways' application must fail. As to British Caledonian, there still remains the argument that the action as against them is frivolous or vexatious. In pursuit of this argument, counsel for British Caledonian took me through the evidence as it presently stands in great detail. If, however, the action, as such, is one which affords no ground for a stay, it is in principle a matter for the American courts to decide whether it should proceed to trial. They might decide that it should not for any one of a number of reasons, eg because as a matter of law anti-trust laws cannot apply to combinations with regard to the establishment of fares approved by the CAB and the CAA under Bermuda 2 or because the allegations against British Caledonian are manifestly without foundation.

I do not say that there can be no case where the plaintiff in a foreign action which sets up a cause of action which can only be pursued in that action cannot be restrained on the ground that it is vexatious or oppressive. If for example the plaintiff's claim was firmly tied to an agreement alleged to have been made at a single meeting and there were incontrovertible evidence that the defendant had not been at the meeting, eg because he had been in some entirely different part of the world at the time, it might well be that it would be held that the plaintiff was pursuing the action for some ulterior purpose and that to avoid injustice to the defendant the plaintiff must be stopped.

But that is not this case. I accept that the evidence as presently before me is not strong but I am quite unable to say that the position is so clear that Laker must be prevented from pursuing the action at all. Speaking of late events, counsel for British Caledonian stressed that when in the winter of 1981 Pan Am, TWA and British Airways dropped their fares British Caledonian had not done so. He also stressed that although British Caledonian had objected strongly to McDonnell Douglas becoming a major shareholder in Laker, which was its main contribution to the rescue scheme, this was, on the evidence, merely because McDonnell Douglas was its aircraft supplier, and it did not wish to have such a supplier as a shareholder in a competitor. This is so, but there is certainly some evidence that McDonnell Douglas was influenced by pressure coming, inter alia, from British Caledonian, and its evidence as to the reason for it might in the end be rejected. If it was, then, taken with all other matters, including cross-examination of British Caledonian's witnesses, an inference might be drawn that the pressure was exerted pursuant to a combined scheme. Laker was at the time seeking to get into Europe and it was in the interests of British Caledonian and others that it should not do so.

Again, with regard to the fact that British Caledonian did not lower its fares this is of little significance. It was not flying on any routes then being operated by Laker and for it to lower its fares would have therefore had much less impact than a lowering of fares by the other three. It is possible that it was nevertheless a party to an agreement that fares would be lowered by those flying competing routes.

These matters must, in my judgment, be left for the United States court to determine.

I have considered the matters now before me at considerable length in deference to the arguments advanced but, in my judgment, the applications by British Airways and British Caledonian could be shortly disposed of on the following grounds.

(1) There is nothing in Bermuda 2 to justify a court in saying it would be unjust to allow the action to proceed. It is conceded that, notwithstanding Bermuda 2, a common law action for conspiracy could properly be brought. Hence, it cannot be alleged that Bermuda 2 provides a complete code, provided its provisions are complied with. Furthermore, even if it could, it is inherent in the allegations that the provisions of Bermuda 2 have not been complied with. If there was an agreement then it should under article 12 have been submitted for approval. It was not.

(2) Since, if there was a fares agreement, anti-trust exemption could have been sought and since both British Airways and British Caledonian (a) carried on business in the United States at the material time, (b) while so doing are alleged to have combined with American airlines in breach of the anti-trust laws, (c) had necessarily, in order to put the alleged combination into effect to put fares before the CAB for approval and (d) also

concealed from the CAB the existence of the alleged agreement, I can see nothing unjust
a in allowing Laker to proceed.

(3) The submission that if the anti-trust laws continue to operate it would be a
derogation from the grant by the United States of rights under Bermuda 2 is wholly
unsustainable unless Bermuda 2 can be construed as granting to the United Kingdom a
blanket exemption from anti-trust actions against its designated airlines by others of its
designated airlines. I can see no basis on which it can be so construed.

b   (4) I am unable to accept that there is any invasion of sovereignty involved in applying
anti-trust laws to companies carrying on business in the United States under Bermuda 2
in respect of their operation of such business even if part or even the very much greater
part of what is complained of took place outside the United States and in this country. I
would regard it as being inherent in the grant of permission to operate in the United
States that the designated airlines comply with United States law. If at any time the
c Secretary of State were to consider that the application of anti-trust laws damaged the
essential trading interests of this country he could take action under s 1 of the 1980 Act
in respect of acts taking place outside the United States. If and when such action is taken
it might well be that an action by one United Kingdom company against another could
not be allowed to proceed, for such an action might constitute an attempt to obtain
damages for doing that which was expressly authorised under English law.

d   (5) Accordingly, the attempt to prevent Laker from proceeding fails and the airlines
anti-trust action must be allowed to proceed. This being so, I need not deal separately
with the alternative claim. It is common ground that it too must be allowed to proceed.

As to the counter-applications, it is common ground that if Laker is allowed to pursue
the American action the plaintiffs' actions should be stayed or dismissed. They would
serve no useful purpose and would merely involve both sides in unnecessary expense.

e   Accordingly, the applications by British Airways and British Caledonian will be
dismissed. On Laker's counter-applications, the appropriate order appears to me to be
that the British Airways and British Caledonian actions be stayed, rather than dismissed,
if only to ensure that no confusion can arise. If the actions were dismissed, my experience
of this litigation leads me to believe that someone might seek to raise some res judicata
argument. This would of course be quite wrong. I wish to make it clear that nothing
f which I have said must be taken to indicate that I consider, much less that I find, that
British Airways, British Caledonian or anyone else has acted in any way in breach of the
Sherman Act or caused damage to Laker otherwise than by that lawful competition
which the Sherman Act is designed to secure and which Bermuda 2 expressly encourages.
I am concerned only with the question whether Laker should be prevented from seeking
to establish in the sole forum available to it that there have been breaches of the Sherman
g Act and that damage to Laker has been thereby caused. I conclude only that it should not
be so prevented.

There remains the question of the injunctions presently in force. In the light of the
decision of Sir John Donaldson MR in relation to the injunction of 2 March, it would
seem clear that the appropriate order will be that the injunctions will be continued for a
fixed period and if, within that time, notice of appeal is given, they be continued
h thereafter until the determination of such appeal or further order.

Plaintiffs' applications dismissed; plaintiffs' actions stayed.

Appeals

British Airways Board v Laker Airways Ltd and others
and another appeal
j
The plaintiffs, British Airways Board and British Caledonian Airways Ltd, appealed
against the judgment of Parker J dated 20 May 1983.

R v Secretary of State for Trade and Industry, ex parte Laker Airways Ltd and another
Laker Airways Ltd and Christopher Morris, the liquidator of Laker Airways Ltd,

(collectively referred to as 'Laker'), applied on 13 July 1983 to Woolf J for leave to apply for judicial review of the Protection of Trading Interests (US Antitrust Measures) Order **a** 1983, SI 1983/900, and two directions dated 23 June and 1 July 1983 made by the Secretary of State for Trade and Industry under ss 1 and 2 respectively of the Protection of Trading Interests Act 1980. Woolf J refused leave stating that the matter should be heard by the Court of Appeal. On 13 July 1983 the Court of Appeal granted the leave sought. The facts are set out in the judgment of Sir John Donaldson MR.

Richard Scott QC and *Jonathan Sumption* for British Airways.   **b**
Colin Ross-Munro QC and *David Donaldson* for British Caledonian.
David Johnson QC, Michael Crystal and *Richard Hacker* for Laker.
Peter Scott QC and *Christopher S C S Clarke* for the Attorney General.
Peter Scott QC, Simon D Brown and *Timothy Walker* for the Secretary of State.

19 July. The court announced that it would refuse Laker's application that the 1983 order **c** and the general directions were ultra vires, null and void for reasons to be given later.

20 July. The court reserved its decision on the plaintiffs' appeal.

26 July. The following judgment of the court was delivered.

d

SIR JOHN DONALDSON MR.

Introduction
    In these appeals the plaintiffs, British Airways Board and British Caledonian Airways Ltd, seek to reverse decisions of Parker J given on 20 May 1983. Although he was concerned with two separate actions brought by the respective plaintiffs, there was a **e** large measure of common ground and the two actions were heard together and were the subject matter of a single judgment.
    In hearing the appeals, we have adopted a similar approach, save that we have not heard counsel for British Caledonian in so far as he wished to contend that there were special features depending on the evidence or lack of evidence in their case which, in his submission, entitle them to succeed in their appeal, even if the appeal of British Airways **f** is dismissed.
    In each of the actions the respective plaintiffs sought injunctions restraining the defendants (whom we will refer to collectively simply as 'Laker') from causing or permitting the continuance against the plaintiffs of a civil action, no 82–3362, which Laker had instituted in the United States District Court, District of Columbia. Although the matter came before the judge at an early stage in the life of the actions and would **g** normally have been considered solely on the basis of what relief, if any, should be granted pending their trial, all concerned were agreed that in the general interest Parker J should decide the matter on the materials then available as if he were concerned with claims for final relief. On this basis the judge refused the relief sought by the plaintiffs and, on the application of Laker, stayed the actions.
    Since Parker J gave judgment, the Secretary of State for Trade and Industry has made **h** the Protection of Trading Interests (US Antitrust Measures) Order 1983, SI 1983/900, under the Protection of Trading Interests Act 1980, and has given directions under that order. We do not have to decide whether or not Parker J was correct in the decision which he reached in the circumstances as they then existed, having regard to the effects of this legislative and executive intervention of which we have had to take account and which, on any view, produces a wholly different situation.   **j**
    During the hearing of the appeals, Laker indicated that it wished to challenge the validity both of the order and the directions by judicial review. For this purpose it applied to Woolf J for leave to apply for judicial review. Woolf J rightly took the view that the interests of justice would best be served if the issues which would be raised by such an application were able to be considered by this court concurrently with the instant appeals. This result could be and was achieved by his refusal of leave to apply for judicial

review followed, as he intended, by a renewal of that application to this court. We
a granted leave and directed that the application be served on the Secretary of State and on
the plaintiffs and that notice of it be given to any other bodies, such as other airlines,
which might have a sufficient interest in the matter to justify their applying to be joined
if they so wished (see RSC Ord 53, r 3(7)). In the Practice Direction of 2 November 1982
([1982] 3 All ER 800, [1982] 1 WLR 1375) it was stated that where the Court of Appeal
grants leave to apply for judicial review the substantive application should be made to
b the Divisional Court unless the Court of Appeal otherwise orders. In the exceptional
circumstances, we ordered that the substantive application be heard before us and it has
been heard accordingly.

It follows that in determining these appeals not only have we had to take account of
the legislative order and executive directions made thereunder, but we have also had to
determine the validity of that order and of those directions.

c

Jurisdiction

The jurisdiction of the High Court, and of this court on appeal from it, to grant the
relief sought has been challenged by Laker. In addition, Judge Harold H Greene of the
United States District Court which is seised of United States civil action 82–3362 has
expressed strong views on the propriety of the English courts granting the relief sought.
d We refer in particular to the judge's opinion dated 9 March 1983 on a motion by Laker
for a preliminary injunction.

Whatever the ultimate conclusion in this litigation, and it seems likely that the
unsuccessful party or parties will wish to take the matter to the House of Lords, we and
all other English judges would deeply regret any misunderstanding on the part of our
brethren in the United States of what exactly we are doing and why we are doing it. I
e personally sought to avoid any such misunderstanding in relation to the interim order
which I made on 30 March 1983 in my judgment of that date and we wish now to
extend that effort in relation to the present decision of this court. Accordingly, we
propose to consider the issue of jurisdiction in greater detail than might otherwise have
been necessary.

First let it be said, and said loud and clear, that no one has ever suggested that the
f United States District Court is without jurisdiction to try Laker's complaint against the
plaintiffs both under the Sherman Antitrust Act (15 USC §§ 1–7) and the Clayton Act (15
USC §§ 12–27) of the United States and in respect of the commission of an intentional
tort. Both plaintiffs carry on business in the United States of America sufficiently to make
them amenable to the jurisdiction of its courts. If any such submission had been made,
it would have been rejected out of hand.

g Second, let it be said at no less volume and with no less clarity that no submission has
been made to this court that the civil procedures of the United States courts and, in
particular, the system of pre-trial discovery by the taking of depositions, the administration
of interrogatories and the disclosure of documents, the limited circumstances in which a
successful defendant would be awarded costs, and the conduct of litigation on the basis
of contingency fees are in any way to be criticised. They are different from English civil
h procedures, but the days are long past when English courts and judges thought that there
was only one way of administering justice and that that was the English way. Each
nation must decide for itself which way is appropriate to its needs and there is nothing
strange in two nations which enjoy a common legal heritage and which could be
described as 'cousins-in-law' rightly deciding that different procedures suited them best.

Third, let it be said no less loudly and clearly that neither English courts nor English
j judges entertain any feelings of hostility towards the American anti-trust laws or would
ever wish to denigrate that or any other American law. Judicial comity is shorthand for
good neighbourliness, common courtesy and mutual respect between those who labour
in adjoining judicial vineyards. In the context of the United Kingdom and the United
States, this comes naturally and, so far as we are concerned, effortlessly.

We learn from Judge Greene's opinion that a United States court 'has power to enjoin
a party over whom it has personal jurisdiction from pursuing litigation before a foreign

tribunal', but that it is a jurisdiction which is only exercised in 'unusual [and] very
narrow circumstances'. We also learn that an examination of the reported circumstances   a
in which it has been used shows that the circumstances were there quite different from
those obtaining in the present case.

Precisely the same situation obtains under English law in relation to English courts.
The jurisdiction exists, but it is to be exercised with extreme caution. Furthermore, the
reported authorities do not disclose any case in which consideration has ever been given
to restraining the prosecution of proceedings in a foreign court when, as here, there is no   b
alternative English forum before which the same, or substantially the same, right could
be asserted.

All this counsel for Laker accepts. But he goes a little further and submits that there is
an obvious reason why the reports do not reveal any case in which the prosecution of
proceedings in a foreign court has been restrained in the absence of an alternative English
forum. It is that an injunction can only issue in support of a legal or equitable right or   c
interest justiciable in the English courts: see Siskina (cargo owners) v Distos Compania
Naviera SA, The Siskina [1977] 3 All ER 803, [1979] AC 210.

In The Siskina the plaintiffs, who were cargo owners, were in dispute with shipowners
and were seeking a Mareva injunction freezing insurance moneys owing to the
shipowners. They had no legal or equitable right or interest over or in respect of those
insurance moneys and, although they may well have had such a right or interest   d
enforceable against the shipowners, the shipowners were outside the jurisdiction of the
English courts. By contrast there is no territorial limitation on the court's jurisdiction in
the present case, all concerned being admittedly subject to that jurisdiction. Accordingly
the sole question is whether the plaintiffs are seeking to enforce a justiciable legal or
equitable right against Laker. Many years ago it might have been debatable whether a
plaintiff could have a legal or equitable right not to be a defendant in litigation before a   e
foreign tribunal. But that debate is long since over. The sole question now open concerns
the circumstances in which the jurisdiction is to be exercised. Accordingly we conclude
that, properly analysed, the submission of counsel for Laker is not that this court has no
jurisdiction to grant the relief sought by the plaintiffs, but that, regardless of any other
circumstance, it should not exercise that jurisdiction unless there is an alternative English
forum available to Laker. This submission, if accepted, would dispose of the appeal and   f
we therefore examine it before any other consideration of the issues in dispute.

Fortunately we have the benefit of a very recent decision of the House of Lords,
Castanho v Brown & Root (UK) Ltd [1981] 1 All ER 143, [1981] AC 557, which, in our
judgment, is decisive in establishing that the absence of an alternative English forum is
not, of itself, fatal to the plaintiffs' claims to relief, although the absence of such a forum
is without doubt a major obstacle which powerfully reinforces the caution which, as a   g
matter of English law, English judges are bidden to display and do display when
considering the exercise of this jurisdiction.

Equally fortunately Lord Wilberforce, Lord Diplock, Lord Keith and Lord Bridge
agreed with the speech of Lord Scarman and accordingly we are not faced with the
problem of interpreting different shades of judicial opinion.

Lord Scarman, in considering the criteria which should govern the exercise of the   h
court's discretion either to impose a stay in English proceedings or to grant an injunction
restraining a person who is subject to the jurisdiction of the English courts from
prosecuting a claim in a foreign court, said that whichever remedy was sought the
principle was the same (see [1981] 1 All ER 143 at 150, [1981] AC 557 at 574). In
determining and defining that principle, it was no longer necessary to examine the older
case law since the modern statement of the law was to be found in the majority speeches   j
in The Atlantic Star, Atlantic Star (owners) v Bona Spes (owners) [1973] 2 All ER 175, [1974]
AC 476. Lord Scarman continued ([1981] 1 All ER 143 at 150–151, [1981] AC 557 at
575):

'In MacShannon v Rockware Glass Ltd [1978] 1 All ER 625 at 630, [1978] AC 795 at
812 Lord Diplock interpreted the majority speeches in The Atlantic Star as an

a invitation to drop the use of the words "vexatious" and "oppressive" (an invitation which I gladly accept) and formulated his distillation of principle in words which are now very familiar: "In order to justify a stay two conditions must be satisfied, one positive and the other negative: (a) the defendant must satisfy the court that there is another forum to whose jurisdiction he is amenable in which justice can be done between the parties at substantially less inconvenience or expense, and (b) the stay must not deprive the plaintiff of a legitimate personal or juridical advantage

b which would be available to him if he invoked the jurisdiction of the English court." Transposed into the context of the present case, this formulation means that to justify the grant of an injunction the defendants must show (a) that the English court is a forum to whose jurisdiction they are amenable in which justice can be done at substantially less inconvenience and expense, and (b) that the injunction must not deprive the plaintiff of a legitimate personal or juridical advantage which

c would be available to him if he invoked the American jurisdiction. The formula is not, however, to be construed as a statute. No time should be spent in speculating what is meant by "legitimate". It, like the whole of the context, is but a guide to solving in the particular circumstances of the case the "critical equation" between advantage to the plaintiff and disadvantage to the defendants.'

d The submission of counsel for Laker that the critical equation presupposes an alternative forum to whose jurisdiction the parties are amenable and that, in its absence, the jurisdiction can never be exercised is, as it seems to us, a mere variant of the submission by Mr Castanho's counsel that the jurisdiction is to be found to have been exercised only in two classes of case: (1) lis alibi pendens, where the object is to prevent harassment, and (2) where there is a right justiciable in England, which the court seeks to protect. Commenting on this submission, Lord Scarman said ([1981] 1 All ER 143 at

e 149, [1981] AC 557 at 573):

'No doubt, in practice, most cases fall within one or other of these two classes. But the width and flexibility of equity are not to be undermined by categorisation. Caution in the exercise of the jurisdiction is certainly needed; but the way in which the judges have expressed themselves from 1821 onwards amply supports the view

f for which the defendants contend that the injunction can be granted against a party properly before the court, where it is appropriate to avoid injustice.'

In our judgment that passage confirms the existence of the jurisdiction which we are asked to exercise and poses the question which we have to ask ourselves, namely: in all the circumstances, is it appropriate to grant the relief sought in order to avoid injustice? In the context of this case, the avoidance of injustice to all parties may not be possible,

g but, failing that, we have to ask ourselves whether the grant or the refusal of the relief sought will create the lesser injustice. We have, in Lord Scarman's words, to resolve that 'critical equation'. That involves taking account of a number of circumstances to which we now turn.

h *The Laker story*
The story of the rise and fall of Laker Airways is well known. Suffice it to say that Sir Freddie Laker conceived the idea of creating an airline which would provide low-cost scheduled air services across the Atlantic and elsewhere. He founded Laker Airways in 1966 and entered the air charter business. In 1971, at a time when Laker Airways was already undertaking transatlantic charter flights, he applied for permission to operate a

j 'Skytrain' scheduled service between London and New York. The basic distinction between the proposed service and existing services was that, in the case of Skytrain, passengers would buy tickets at the airport on the day of travel on a 'first come, first served' basis and that the ticket would not entitle the passenger to a free meal service. There were other distinctions, such as the inability to purchase through-tickets for travel by Laker Airways and other airlines, and the whole concept could be summed up by saying that it was intended to be a 'no frills, low cost' operation.

Transatlantic scheduled air services between the United Kingdom and the United
States are controlled by an inter-governmental licensing system and it was not until 1977   *a*
that Laker Airways obtained permission to operate the Skytrain scheduled service. The
reasons for this delay are recorded in *Laker Airways Ltd v Dept of Trade* [1977] 2 All ER
182, [1977] 1 QB 643. Its first route was London–New York, but the service was extended
to London–Los Angeles in September 1978, London–Miami in May 1980 and London–
Tampa in April 1981. Laker Airways hoped to continue this expansionary process and,
with that end in view, obtained licences from the United Kingdom government for a   *b*
trans-Pacific route from Los Angeles and San Francisco to Hong Kong via Honolulu and
Tokyo, a London–Hong Kong route via the Middle East and European routes between
London and Berlin and London and Zurich.

Unfortunately, in the second half of 1981 Laker Airways encountered financial
difficulties engendered, in part at least, by a drop in the dollar value of the pound sterling
and was unable to service the large loans which it had obtained. Despite considerable   *c*
efforts to rescue it, Laker Airways was forced to cease trading in early February 1982.

The United States proceedings

On 24 November 1982 Laker instituted civil action no 82–3362 in the United States
District Court, District of Columbia, by a complaint indorsed 'jury trial demanded'. Lest
any summary do less than justice to Laker, we append a copy (see pp 411–416, post). By   *d*
the consolidation of a further action, two other airlines, KLM and Sabena, have been
added as defendants. As will be seen, it alleges a combination and conspiracy in restraint
of trade and to monopolise in violation of the United States Sherman Antitrust Act 1890
(15 USC §§ 1–7) causing damage to Laker in excess of $US350m. It also repeats the same
narrative as a basis for an allegation of a further cause of action, namely 'intentional tort'.
The relief claimed is $US350m compensatory damages in respect of both causes of action   *e*
and $US700m as punitive damages in respect of the cause of action under the Sherman
Act, together with interest, costs and attorneys' fees.

The complaint itself was accompanied by a very extensive request for the production
of documents and another request for answers to interrogatories of a far-reaching nature.
The requests were respectively made pursuant to rr 34 and 33 of the Federal Rules of
Civil Procedure, and we have no reason to believe that they were not proper requests in   *f*
accordance with those rules.

It is or may be material that they appear to be requests which were made in
circumstances in which a requirement to the same effect could be imposed pursuant to
r 37 (see s 2(5) of the Protection of Trading Interests Act 1980). These were followed a
month later by a second request for the production of documents and a second request
for answers to interrogatories to which similar considerations appear to apply. These   *g*
requests too are appended to this judgment[1].

We should perhaps explain that the word 'predatory', which is frequently referred to
in the pleadings, is defined in and for the purpose of the United States Federal Aviation
Act 1958 as 'any practice which would constitute a violation of the Antitrust Laws as set
forth in the first section of the Clayton Act (15 U.S.C. § 12)'. In the context of the dispute
between Laker and the other airline defendants, it is usually used adjectivally in   *h*
conjunction with the word 'fares' as meaning a loss-making level of fares having no
commercial justification and intended solely to eliminate Laker Airways as a competitor.

The plaintiffs responded in the United States action to such extent as was necessary to
avoid being in contempt of the district court or having a default judgment signed, but
no more, and in January 1983 they began the present actions seeking to restrain Laker
from further prosecuting the United States action against them.   *j*

Since then Laker has been restrained from proceeding further with that action as
against the plaintiffs by a series of interim injunctions. These have been granted solely
on the basis that justice requires that the status quo be preserved whilst the plaintiffs'

---

1   Editor's note. The requests have been omitted from this report.

claims to relief were being considered by Parker J and, after he had refused that relief, by
a this court on appeal from his decision.

Section 1 of the Sherman Act, which was enacted in 1890, subject to immaterial
exceptions renders every contract, combination in the form of trust or otherwise, or
conspiracy in restrain of trade or commerce among the several states or with foreign
nations illegal and provides, as amended, that every person who makes any contract or
engages in any combination or conspiracy thereby declared to be illegal shall be guilty of
b a felony and on conviction shall, if a corporation, be punishable by a fine not exceeding
$1m and, if any other person, by a fine not exceeding $100,000 or by imprisonment not
exceeding three years or both in the discretion of the court.

Section 2 of the Sherman Act provides that every person who shall monopolise, or
attempt to monopolise, or combine or conspire with any other person or persons to
monopolise any part of the trade or commerce among the several states or with foreign
c nations shall also be guilty of a felony and subject to similar penalties.

Section 4 of the Clayton Act (15 USC §§ 12–27), enacted in 1914, provides that any
person who shall be injured in his business or property by reason of anything forbidden
in the anti-trust laws (which is defined to include the Sherman Antitrust Act) may sue
therefor in any district court of the United States in the district in which the defendant
resides or is found or has an agent, without respect to the amount in controversy, and
d shall recover threefold the damages by him sustained, and the cost of suit, including a
reasonable attorney's fee.

Section 4A provides a similar right of recovery for the United States, limited to actual
damages sustained and the cost of the suit.

There is a four-year limitation period on suits under §§ 4 and 4A.

e *The Bermuda 2 treaty*

Since the 1939–45 war United Kingdom airlines, including both the plaintiffs and
Laker, together with their aircraft, have been subject to control by the United Kingdom
Civil Aviation Authority (the CAA). The corresponding body for United States airlines
and aircraft is the United States Civil Aviation Board (the CAB). The CAA regulates, inter
alia, the fares chargeable by British airlines.

f A similar regulatory function is performed by the CAB. Neither body can, of course,
authorise a flight into foreign territory, although they can no doubt forbid it.

In the absence of a treaty between the United States and the United Kingdom, United
Kingdom airlines could only fly to the United States on such terms as the United States
government in its absolute discretion saw fit to impose. Furthermore, that government
could alter those terms at any time and from time to time. Equally United States airlines
g seeking to fly to the United Kingdom would have been at the mercy of the United
Kingdom government. Faced with this impossible situation, the two nations concluded
bilateral treaties: first 'Bermuda 1' in 1946 (Cmd 6747) and then 'Bermuda 2' in 1977
(Cmnd 7016). The essence of both treaties was equality of opportunity for the airlines of
each country.

It is important to bear in mind that, as a matter of English law, treaties are not part of
h the domestic laws of the United Kingdom and give rise to no private rights under English
law. They are agreements between states and they can only be honoured or breached by
states. If and in so far as they involve an obligation to ensure that domestic laws conform
with the treaty, this is a matter for the states concerned. There have been indications that
the position may be different under United States law and that the provisions of treaties
to which the United States is a party may themselves vary or limit the scope of pre-
j existing United States laws. We express no view on whether or not that is the case and do
not think it material for present purposes. We mention the status of a treaty in English
law solely because there are passages in the judgment of Parker J which might be taken
to suggest that he thought that if Laker's complaints were proved it would follow that
the plaintiffs were in breach of art 12 of the treaty which deals with tariffs. This article
cannot bind either Laker or the plaintiffs and they cannot be in breach of it.

For present purposes, the essence of the treaty was that each country had the right to designate airlines of its own nationality to fly particular routes and enter through specified 'gateways'. But each country had the right to refuse to accept the other's *a* designation of an airline and each national civil aviation authority had the right to refuse to accept tariffs and other licensing matters approved by the other authority. In practice, as one would expect, the two national authorities were at one on issues such as safety. Where they differed was on the acceptability of particular fare structures and similar commercial considerations in terms of their respective national interests which, inevitably, were liable to differ. *b*

This is amply demonstrated on the evidence, but it is important to note that both the CAA and the CAB when asked to approve tariffs gave every opportunity to all who might be affected to make representations. Both Laker and the plaintiffs as United Kingdom airlines were licensed on terms that they charged fares approved by the CAA and were only authorised to fly into the territory and airspace of the United States if those fares were also approved by the CAB. Thus Laker had the opportunity of objecting to the fares *c* now characterised as 'predatory' both before the CAA and the CAB and availed itself of that opportunity.

It is also clear, as one would expect, that the CAB applied the same criteria as those prescribed by the Sherman Act, which has been described by Judge Greene as 'the charter of economic freedom', comparing its role to that which the Bill of Rights (1688) plays with respect to personal freedoms. The interrelationship between the Sherman Act and *d* the CAB's duties under the United States Federal Aviation Act 1958 is underlined by the fact that under § 414 of that Act the CAB is empowered to grant exemption from the operations of the 'antitrust laws' set forth in § 1(a) of the Clayton Act. The exercise of this exemptive power is referred to by the rather quaint term of 'immunization', which, by inference, we feel does less than justice to the United States Economic Bill of Rights. Furthermore, if the CAB approves a tariff agreement, it is required to 'immunize' the *e* parties to such extent as is necessary to enable them to proceed with the transactions specifically approved by the CAB. Curiously, if the CAB refuses to approve such an agreement, but its decision is overriden by the President of the United States, the President appears to have neither the power nor the duty to grant 'immunization' and it would be necessary to ask the CAB for relief which it might or might not grant in the exercise of its discretion. *f*

It is reasonably clear on the evidence that throughout the currency of Bermuda 1 and Bermuda 2 the application of United States anti-trust laws to United Kingdom designated airlines was a potential source of disagreement between the two governments. However, all concerned avoided anything in the nature of a confrontation until Laker sought to avail itself of the Sherman and Clayton Acts in a suit against the plaintiffs and Pan American and Trans World airlines in 1974 which was speedily settled and in the present *g* United States litigation. As the latter action has not been settled and indeed has led directly or indirectly to a grand jury investigation, this sensible 'agreement to differ' has been impossible to sustain any longer.

As we have said, as a matter of English law, a treaty is an agreement between sovereign states which does not of itself give rise to either rights or obligations in private individuals. Consistently with this approach this court has no jurisdiction to determine the meaning *h* or effect of any treaty to which the government of the United Kingdom is a party and indeed is not equipped to do so, that being a matter of public international law. This court is, however, concerned to be informed of the views of Her Majesty's government concerning any treaty which forms part of the background to a dispute between private persons. In the present appeals we have been so informed in the usual way, namely by a statement in open court by or on behalf of Her Majesty's Attorney General. Counsel for *j* the Attorney General has stated that Her Majesty's government regard the government of the United States as being in breach of its obligations under Bermuda 2 in applying or permitting the application of United States anti-trust laws to international commerce and, in particular, to operations carried out under or pursuant to Bermuda 2.

The treaty itself provides the mechanism for the resolution of inter-governmental disputes. First there must be formal consultations under art 16 and then, if this does not

resolve the dispute, either side may invoke the compulsory arbitral procedure provided
a under art 17. In March 1983 Her Majesty's government requested formal consultations
under art 16 on the question of whether it is consistent with the rights and obligations of
the contracting parties for the provisions of the United States anti-trust laws to apply to
the activities of the designated airlines. Although the United States government claims
that the application of these laws is wholly outside the scope of Bermuda 2 and, therefore,
not a matter for consultation under art 16, it agreed to take part in such consultations
b and they have taken place. We were told that Her Majesty's government hopes to resolve
the dispute by negotiation, but that deep differences remain between the two
governments over the question of whether and to what extent the United States anti-
trust laws are incompatible with the arrangements contained in Bermuda 2 and what
steps are called for to remedy the situation. At present neither government has begun
arbitration proceedings against the other, but Her Majesty's government has fully
c reserved its right to do so.

Public policy
    It is a matter of considerable constitutional importance that the courts should be
wholly independent of the executive, and they are. Thus, while the judges, as private
citizens, will be aware of the 'policy' of the government of the day, in the sense of its
d political purpose, aspirations and programme, these are not matters which are in any
way relevant to the courts' decisions and are wholly ignored. In matters of home policy,
the courts have regard only to the will of Parliament as expressed in the statutes, in
subordinate legislation and in executive acts authorised by Parliament.
    The position is different in relation to foreign affairs. Relations between the United
Kingdom and foreign states are not the subject of direct parliamentary action, but are a
e matter for Her Majesty acting on the advice of her government. The foreign policy
which is adopted is referred to as that of the United Kingdom government, but this is
misleading since in reality it is that of the nation. Accordingly, it would be strange if in
this field the courts and the executive spoke with different voices and they should not do
so: see *Rio Tinto Zinc Corp v Westinghouse Electric Corp* [1978] 1 All ER 434 at 448, 475,
[1978] AC 547 at 617, 650–651 per Lord Wilberforce and Lord Fraser.
f   We have already recorded the attitude and contentions of the United Kingdom
government in relation to Bermuda 2. Its policy externally and that of Parliament
internally is also indicated by the terms of the Protection of Trading Interests Act 1980
and the Protection of Trading Interests (US Antitrust Measures) Order 1983. However,
we have also been assisted by fuller information on the United Kingdom government's
foreign policy which has been provided by counsel on the instructions of the Attorney
g General, and to this we must now turn.
    It was contended by counsel for Laker in the course of argument that the concern of
the United Kingdom government over the United States anti-trust laws was confined to
the extra-territorial operation claimed for them under the 'effects doctrine'. This was
coupled with a repeated contention that the United Kingdom government accepted
unreservedly the obligation of all those who carried on business within the United States
h to comply with the laws of that country. Counsel for the Attorney General made it clear
that both contentions are over-simplified.
    The plaintiffs carry on business in a large number of different countries, including the
United States. This is inherent in the business of an international airline. The United
Kingdom government accepts that it follows that each of these countries will have an in
personam jurisdiction over the plaintiffs in accordance with international law. However,
j counsel for the Attorney General told us that the United Kingdom government takes the
view that there is another sense in which jurisdiction has to be considered, namely in
relation to its subject matter, and that it is here that it parts company with the
government of the United States. He put the matter this way:

    'In general, substantive jurisdiction in anti-trust matters, in the view of the British
    government, should only be taken on the basis either of the territorial principle or

the nationality principle. There is nothing in the nature of anti-trust proceedings as such which justifies a wider application of these principles, that is to say a wider *a* application than is generally accepted in other matters. On the contrary, there is much in the nature of anti-trust which is the reflection of the public economic law of the state which calls for a narrower application of these principles. As your Lordships will appreciate, in inherently international activity, like aviation or shipping, it may be difficult to apply these principles with precision, but the activities can take place in both of the states concerned. In those cases, Her Majesty's *b* government would expect a state enforcing its regulatory laws to do so with restraint and only after paying due attention and due regard to the interests of the other state concerned, and to its own treaty obligations. The matter is complicated, of course: I say "complicated", I perhaps should say "enforced" [reinforced] by the peculiar nature of the Sherman Act and Clayton Act procedures, with the penal nature of the judgments sought, the breadth of discovery, the cost and the other elements which *c* are relied on by [the plaintiffs]. These are all matters which, in a sense, only make a fortiori the submission that one would make even if it was an ordinary claim for compensation.'

Earlier in his address to the court, counsel for the Attorney General had referred to remarks made by him before Parker J, and said:
d
'What I was attempting to do was to lay the foundation for the submissions which I wish to make in the particular circumstances of this case and certainly not to make some broad statement that in all and any circumstances Her Majesty's government would expect nationals of this country to obey domestic laws in the course of trans-national business operations. In the ordinary way, of course, Her Majesty's government would not wish to intervene between the laws of other countries and *e* people who find themselves for one reason or another in those other countries, but there most certainly are cases where it would wish to do so.'

He then went on to refer to the recent dispute concerning British companies who carried on business in the United States and had contracted outside the United States to deliver goods which were also outside the United States to contractors working on the *f* Russia to Western Europe gas pipeline. On the basis of the undoubted United States in personam jurisdiction over these companies, the United States government had claimed the right to issue executive orders requiring the companies not to deliver. This right was disputed by the United Kingdom government, which took action to prevent the companies complying with the United States executive order.
g
The Protection of Trading Interests (US Antitrust Measures) Order 1983 and general directions dated 23 June and 1 July 1983
The making of this order and the giving of these directions have, on any view, fundamentally altered the 'critical equation' if they are valid. However, their validity is challenged by way of judicial review.

The order, which came into operation on 27 June 1983, over a month after Parker J *h* gave judgment, is in the following terms, omitting footnotes:

'Whereas it appears to the Secretary of State that the measures to which this Order relates have been taken by or under the law of the United States of America ("the United States") for regulating or controlling international trade and that those measures, in so far as they apply to things done or to be done outside the territorial *j* jurisdiction of the United States by persons carrying on business in the United Kingdom, are damaging or threaten to damage the trading interests of the United Kingdom: Now therefore the Secretary of State, in exercise of his powers under section 1(1) of the Protection of Trading Interests Act 1980 ("the 1980 Act") and of all other powers enabling him in that behalf, hereby makes the following Order—

a   **1.**—(1) This Order may be cited as the Protection of Trading Interests (US Anti-trust Measures) Order 1983 and shall come into operation on 27th June 1983.

(2) In this Order— "the Bermuda 2 Agreement" means the Agreement between the Government of the United Kingdom of Great Britain and Northern Ireland and the Government of the United States signed at Bermuda on 23rd July 1977, concerning air services; "air service" and "tariff" shall be construed in accordance with the Bermuda 2 Agreement; "UK designated airline" means a British airline
b   (within the meaning of section 4(2) of the Civil Aviation Act 1982) designated by the Government of the United Kingdom under the Bermuda 2 Agreement.

2.—(1) The Secretary of State hereby directs that section 1 of the 1980 Act shall apply to sections 1 and 2 of the United States' Sherman Act and sections 4 and 4A of the United States' Clayton Act in their application to the cases described in the following paragraph.

c   (2) The cases mentioned in paragraph (1) of this Article are: (i) an agreement or arrangement (whether legally enforceable or not) to which a UK designated airline is a party, (ii) a discussion or communication to which a UK designated airline is a party, (iii) any act done by a UK designated airline, which, in respect of each case, concerns the tariffs charged or to be charged by any such airline or otherwise relates to the operation by it of an air service authorised pursuant to the Bermuda 2
d   Agreement.'

The power to make such an order is derived from s 1(1) of the Protection of Trading Interests Act 1980, which is in the following terms:

'If it appears to the Secretary of State—(a) that measures have been or are proposed to be taken by or under the law of any overseas country for regulating or controlling
e   international trade; and (b) that those measures, in so far as they apply or would apply to things done or to be done outside the territorial jurisdiction of that country by persons carrying on business in the United Kingdom, are damaging or threaten to damage the trading interests of the United Kingdom, the Secretary of State may by order direct that this section shall apply to those measures either generally or in their application to such cases as may be specified in the order.'

f   Counsel for Laker submits that the order is ultra vires the power for two reasons.

The first reason is that 'measures' in the 1980 Act can only refer to things done under the authority of the statute or executive power and cannot refer to the authority itself. In the submission of counsel for Laker this is supported by the references to requests, requirements and prohibitions in sub-ss (2) and (3) of s 1 and in ss 2, 3 and 4. Accordingly,
g   whilst the order could apply s 1 of the 1980 Act to measures taken under the Sherman and Clayton Acts, it could not apply the section to the Acts themselves or any specified sections of those Acts. We do not accept this submission. 'Measures' is a very wide term of generic description, which could well include statutes and, far from limiting the prima facie width of the meaning of the term, s 1(1)(a) by referring to 'measures . . . taken . . . by . . . the law of any overseas country' confirms that 'measures' is intended to include
h   foreign statutory provisions.

Second, it is submitted that in any event the measures to which s 1 can be applied must be restrictive or regulatory of international trade, whereas the Sherman and Clayton Acts are intended to free international trade from the constructions of anti-competitive cartels. This submission seems to us to be disingenuous and we reject it. A statute is none the less controlling or regulatory because it seeks to prevent international trade being
j   conducted on the basis of co-operative agreements designed to minimise or eliminate competition.

There is a further objection to the order, but as it also applies to the directions we will defer consideration of it until after we have considered the specific objections to the directions.

There are two directions to be considered. The first is dated 23 June 1983 and was made under s 1 of the 1980 Act. The second is dated 1 July 1983 (in replacement of another direction dated 23 June) and was made under s 2 of that Act.

The specific objection to the s 1 direction is that, as counsel for Laker submits, there is no power to make a direction under s 1(3) unless a direction has first been made under s 1(2) and no such direction has been made. Subsections (2) and (3) of s 1 are in the following terms:

'(2) The Secretary of State may by order make provision for requiring, or enabling the Secretary of State to require, a person in the United Kingdom who carries on business there to give notice to the Secretary of State of any requirement or prohibition imposed or threatened to be imposed on that person pursuant to any measures in so far as this section applies to them by virtue of an order under subsection (1) above.

(3) The Secretary of State may give to any person in the United Kingdom who carries on business there such directions for prohibiting compliance with any such requirement or prohibition as aforesaid as he considers appropriate for avoiding damage to the trading interests of the United Kingdom.'

The issue here is one of construction. Does 'any such requirement or prohibition as aforesaid' mean a prohibition or requirement of which notice is required to be given pursuant to a direction under s 1(2) or does it mean a 'requirement or prohibition imposed or threatened to be imposed on that person pursuant to any measures in so far as this section applies to them by virtue of an order under subsection (1) above'? We can see no reason why Parliament should have intended to limit the powers of the Secretary of State to prohibiting compliance with requirements or prohibitions which have been notified to him. The clear intention is that his prohibitory power shall extend to a category of requirements and prohibitions, whether he knows of them or not, and that, in addition, he can, if he wishes, obtain information as to what requirements or prohibitions are being made. In other words the two subsections are quite independent of one another.

The specific objection to the s 2 direction is that it does not specify the ground or grounds on which the requirements to which it relates appear to the Secretary of State to be 'inadmissible' within the meaning of s 2 of the 1980 Act. It is well settled that in using this form of enabling power a Secretary of State need only state that it appears to him that the specified preconditions exist. It is then for an objector to challenge his good faith, which has not been done in this case, or to show that the Secretary of State has misdirected himself in law. The Secretary of State does not have to explain why it appears to him that the preconditions exist. If authority be required for this proposition, it is to be found in *Secretary of State for Employment v Associated Society of Locomotive Engineers and Firemen (No 2)* [1972] 2 All ER 949, [1972] 2 QB 455.

The s 2 direction recites that—

'. . . it appears to the Secretary of State: (a) that the United States' Department of Justice has begun an investigation into alleged price fixing and other allegations relating to the air transport of passengers over the North Atlantic for possible violations of sections 1 and 2 of the "Sherman" Act; and that for this purpose a grand jury ("the grand jury") has been empanelled in the District of Columbia in the United States of America; (b) that a requirement may be imposed on a person or persons in the United Kingdom to produce to the United States' Department of Justice or the grand jury commercial documents which are not within the territorial jurisdiction of the United States or to furnish to the United States' Department of Justice or the grand jury commercial information; (c) that civil antitrust proceedings of a penal nature are now pending in the United States' District Court for the District of Columbia ("the District Court") relating to similar matters to those which are the subject of the United States' Department of Justice investigation and that commercial documents and commercial information which are produced in the civil antitrust proceedings may be utilised in the Department of Justice investigation or before the a   grand jury; (d) that a requirement may be imposed on a person or persons in the United Kingdom to produce to the District Court commercial documents which are not within the territorial jurisdiction of the United States or to furnish to the District Court commercial information; (e) that any such requirement would be inadmissible within the meaning of section 2(2) and (3) of the Protection of Trading Interests Act 1980 (the "1980 Act").'

b   If there were nothing more, there would be no reason to doubt the Secretary of State's assertion, since he might very well consider that requirements by the United States Department of Justice would infringe the jurisdiction of the United Kingdom or otherwise be prejudicial to its sovereignty (see s 2(2)(a)) and/or compliance with such requirements would be prejudicial to the relations of the government of the United Kingdom with the government of another country (see s 2(2)(b)). He might also very well consider that a requirement in the context of a grand jury investigation would be one 'made otherwise than for the purposes of civil or criminal proceedings which have been instituted in the overseas country' (see s 2(3)(a)) and that a requirement in the context of the district court proceedings satisfied s 2(3)(b) as requiring 'a person to state what documents relevant to any such proceedings are or have been in his possession, custody or power or to produce for the purposes of any such proceedings any documents other than the particular documents specified in the requirement'.

d   However, there is more. Mr Andrew Turek, a legal assistant in the office of the Treasury Solicitor, has deposed that the substance of correspondence between the liquidator of Laker Airways Ltd and the CAA and between the CAA and the Department of Trade and Industry, which he exhibited, was brought to the attention of the Secretary of State before he made the directions. This correspondence clearly shows the link between the district court proceedings and the grand jury investigation and that the United States Department of Justice was seeking to use the liquidator as its agent to obtain discovery from the plaintiffs for the purposes of the grand jury investigation. This abundantly justifies the Secretary of State's view that 'inadmissible requirements' might be made.

Lastly, Laker objects to the order and to both directions on the grounds that—

f   'The terms of the Order and of the two general directions are (a) so wide as to exceed the sections under which they purport to be made and (b) so general as insufficiently to indicate what is and what is not sought to be prohibited.'

We accept the possibility that circumstances may arise in which it may be debatable whether or not the order or directions apply, but we do so not because of any excessive width or generality in the words but because any order or direction which is not all-embracing (and this order and the directions are not) is capable of giving rise to problems on the periphery of its ambit. Certainly, in our judgment, the Secretary of State has in no way exceeded his jurisdiction.

It was for these reasons that we dismissed the application for judicial review.

The critical equation
h   We now come back to the 'critical equation' and ask ourselves the question: in all the circumstances, is it appropriate in the interest of avoiding injustice to enjoin Laker from pursuing its claim against the plaintiffs in the United States courts?

If we are to grant the plaintiffs the relief which they seek, it will, so far as is known, be the first occasion on which an English court has exercised its jurisdiction to prevent the further prosecution of proceedings before a foreign court or tribunal when there is no alternative forum in England or elsewhere to which the defendant can have resort. It follows that the plaintiffs have a very heavy burden to discharge.

The starting point must be what Laker will lose. The plaintiffs are only two of ten defendants against whom Laker is making the same or substantially the same claim. If it were to be wholly successful, it could levy execution against any or all, and the defendants who satisfied the judgment would have no right of contribution inter se or from other defendants. Accordingly, it might appear that the disappearance of the plaintiffs as defendants in the United States action would leave both Laker and the other defendants *a* in exactly the same position as if Laker had succeeded against all, but only levied execution on the other defendants. There is no suggestion that the other defendants could not satisfy such a judgment and it may be asked whether Laker really stands to lose anything at all.

This in our judgment is too simple a view of the position. First, it is possible that other actions might be brought by the other defendants seeking similar relief. We express no *b* view on whether they would succeed, because different considerations might apply in their cases. By way of illustration, we would mention that only the two United States airlines would appear to have been flying under the auspices of Bermuda 2, and they have the benefit of a consent from the Secretary of State disapplying the general direction under s 1 of the 1980 Act. The other airlines presumably fly under the auspices of other bilateral treaties. And there will probably, if not inevitably, be other distinctions. *c* Furthermore it was suggested in argument, and may be correct, that the burden of fighting an anti-trust claim is so heavy in terms of time, expense and disruption to the carrying on of a business that defendants are often willing to settle with the plaintiff. On this assumption, the more defendants there are, the greater the chances of achieving settlements which, in the aggregate, will be as satisfactory as a judgment. Yet again the elimination of two defendants will mean that fewer parties are available to give discovery *d* which may assist in proving the claim against all, although account must be taken of the inhibitions on the plaintiffs giving Laker assistance in this respect in the light of the Secretary of State's order and directions.

Accordingly we assume, for the purposes of the critical equation, that the grant of the relief sought by the plaintiffs might well have far-reaching adverse effects on what would otherwise be Laker's prospects of success in the United States litigation and might indeed *e* eliminate them. Logically this must lead on to a consideration of what is the value of those prospects if no relief is granted to the plaintiffs. In this connection it is tempting to speculate whether and, if so, how, Laker will overcome the argument that its real loss flows from the fact that the plaintiffs and the other airlines adopted fares and schedules which were authorised and largely 'immunized' for anti-trust purposes. However, it is a temptation which must be resolutely resisted, because it would involve this court in *f* virtually trying a United States anti-trust action, which we are wholly incompetent to do.

This may be a convenient moment to notice the argument that this court should not in any event restrain Laker from pursuing its claim against British Caledonian in so far as it is alleged that British Caledonian interfered with the Laker financial rescue operation by bringing pressure to bear on McDonnell Douglas, since this activity, unlike the charging of 'predatory' fares, was outside the scope of Bermuda 2. Again it is said that *g* this court should not in any event restrain Laker from pursuing its claim based on 'intentional tort', as contrasted with that based on the Sherman and Clayton Acts and that similar considerations would apply if Laker was minded to start an action claiming damages in the United States for common law conspiracy under United States law.

We are at the moment only concerned with a claim for relief in respect of the proceedings in the United States District Court for the District of Columbia and no claims *h* have been made in that court on the basis of common law conspiracy. However, the claims which have been made seem to us not to be capable of severance. The allegation of 'intentional tort' is in terms based on exactly the same material as that which forms the basis of the anti-trust claim and, save that penal damages cannot be claimed for 'intentional tort', the two causes of action seem to us to be indistinguishable. So far as the financing allegation is concerned, it is clear that this is but one aspect of the overall anti- *j* trust conspiracy which is alleged and could not stand by itself. We therefore conclude that it is a case of 'all or nothing'. Either we must wholly restrain the further prosecution of the district court proceedings by Laker against the plaintiffs or we must refuse the plaintiffs any relief.

So much for Laker's side of the equation. We now turn to the plaintiffs' side. They have no right to submit, and do not submit, that the United States civil procedures create

any injustice whatsoever. But they are entitled to rely on the fact that these procedures
a impose a great burden on defendants in terms of time, expense and disruption to their
business and that in no circumstances will this be made good by Laker. Similarly, a
United States company would have no right to submit that United Kingdom civil
procedures create any injustice. But they would be entitled to rely on the fact that our
rules as to costs, which involve an unsuccessful claimant in paying the costs of the
defendant and may involve him in giving security for those costs, together with the
b refusal by the legal professions to permit legal assistance to be provided on a contingency
basis can impose a very heavy burden in terms of actual and potential expense. These
burdens are facts which have to be faced, and facing them involves no criticism of the
legal system concerned. There can be no doubt that in anti-trust suits this burden is of
formidable proportions.

Next, contrary to the views of Parker J, we think that the plaintiffs are entitled to rely
c indirectly on Bermuda 2, in the sense that account must be taken of the United Kingdom's
view of the effect of Bermuda 2 on the United States. The acceptance of that view by the
United States would render Laker's claim unsustainable. This is a public policy
consideration. Both Laker and the plaintiffs were designated as United Kingdom carriers
under that treaty. The United Kingdom government is of the opinion that the United
States government is in breach of its obligations under the treaty in permitting the
d bringing of a claim such as that which Laker is advancing in the district court and is
threatening to invade its sovereign rights by instituting grand jury proceedings and
seeking to use material obtained in the civil proceedings for that purpose. Laker Airways
is a United Kingdom corporation which is entitled to look, and would in appropriate
circumstances look, to the protection of the United Kingdom and its government if it
was being unfairly treated abroad. This benefit seems to us to carry with it some degree
e of obligation and to cast some doubt on the legitimacy of the juridical advantage which
it seeks to preserve in the United States.

Added to this is the fact that Laker is seeking triple damages under foreign penal
legislation and, which is a separate point, that under the 1980 Act the plaintiffs would be
entitled to reclaim the excess over compensatory damages. In fact, of course, this right of
recovery may not be as valuable as it would seem at first in the light of Laker's insolvency.
f It was suggested in argument that this consideration works in Laker's favour in that
Parliament has expressed a clear intention not to intervene in so far as the damages are
compensatory. This is fallacious. The 1980 Act is concerned with a situation in which
the claimants may well be of foreign nationality and perhaps not subject to the
jurisdiction of the English courts. Different considerations can well apply where the
claimant is not only subject to the jurisdiction of these courts but is also a United
g Kingdom company.

Regard must also be had to the extent to which Laker's claim depends on action taken
outside the territory of the United States. In English proceedings this would be easier to
evaluate, because Laker would have first to allege the conspiracy, including any overt acts
relied on, with some degree of particularity and only then would obtain discovery. In
United States proceedings it is permissible to make a largely unparticularised allegation,
h as Laker has done, and then see what turns on discovery. However, it appears at present
that only two overt acts within the United States are relied on. The first is a meeting in
September 1974 in Washington DC with respect to capacity levels to be operated in the
1974–75 winter season, which we would have expected to be irrelevant as having
occurred more than four years before the proceedings were begun in the district court.
The second is a meeting which took place on the occasion of the IATA conference at
j Hollywood, Florida, in January 1982. The conference machinery itself was 'immunized',
but it is said that this was a secret and collateral meeting. To this can perhaps be added
the sending by British Caledonian from England of a threatening telex message to
McDonnell Douglas in the USA, but there is obviously room for debate whether this was
an act done inside or outside the United States.

Finally the plaintiffs can and do rely on the new situation which has been created by
the making of the Protection of Trading Interests (US Antitrust Measures) Order 1983

and the giving of directions under ss 1 and 2 of the 1980 Act. The direction under s 1
prevents the plaintiffs complying with any judgment of the district court, in so far as it   *a*
is given pursuant to the Sherman and Clayton Acts. The plaintiffs would thus be forced
into a situation in which execution was levied on their aircraft. The direction under s 2
creates a more immediate problem and a wholly impossible situation for both Laker and
the plaintiffs. Due to the very wide scope of the requests for discovery and interrogatories
administered by Laker, which, by s 2(5) of the 1980 Act, constitute 'requirements' of the
district court, the plaintiffs are unable to furnish Laker or the district court with any of   *b*
the relevant documentation which is in the United Kingdom or with any relevant
information, wherever situate, in so far as they have been required to give it by the terms
of the interrogatories. Laker seems to think that this damages it more than the plaintiffs,
but this is based on an assumption that there was an anti-trust conspiracy. If there was
not, it is the plaintiffs who will be the sufferers, since they will be unable to defend
themselves before the district court. The likelihood is, of course, that both will be   *c*
seriously affected, but that the main effect will be on the plaintiffs, since Laker may be
able to obtain discovery from other parties. The evidence so disclosed may point the
finger at the plaintiffs, who will be prevented from explaining their conduct.

In this context, we have an affidavit from Mr Simon Chamberlain, one of the British
Airways solicitors, which confirms what we would in any event have assumed to be the
case, namely that 'British Airways has an enormous volume of documentation located   *d*
exclusively within the United Kingdom and falling within the very wide scope of the
request for document discovery made by Laker in the United States proceedings'. Mr
Chamberlain continues:

> 'British Airways has not nearly completed its investigation of these documents. It
> is, however, apparent, on the basis of work already carried out, that they include a
> substantial number of documents on which British Airways would wish to rely for   *e*
> the purpose of defending itself against the allegations made by Laker in the United
> States proceedings.'

Counsel for British Caledonian wished to file a similar affidavit in relation to his
clients' position, but we did not think that this was necessary at this stage.

Whatever weight may or may not be given to the other factors in the critical equation,   *f*
in our judgment the effect of the order and directions is decisive. They have rendered
the issues raised by Laker in the district court action wholly untriable as between Laker
and the plaintiffs. To allow Laker to proceed with its claim in these circumstances would
amount to a total denial of justice to the plaintiffs. In our judgment this cannot be
allowed to occur, and, in principle, we consider that relief of the nature sought by the
plaintiffs should be granted. The details of what order is appropriate can be discussed at
a later date, when the parties have had time to consider the court's judgment.   *g*

Accordingly, the appeals will be allowed. In principle, for the reasons stated, we
consider that relief of the nature sought by the appellants should be granted, but the
exact wording of the injunction may require discussion.

Plaintiffs' appeals allowed. Leave to apply for judicial review refused. Leave to appeal to the   *h*
House of Lords refused.

Solicitors: *Richards Butler & Co* (for British Airways); *Herbert Smith & Co* (for British
Caledonian); *Durrant Piesse* (for Laker); *Treasury Solicitor.*

Diana Procter   Barrister.   *j*

APPENDIX

IN THE UNITED STATES DISTRICT COURT FOR THE DISTRICT OF COLUMBIA

Civil Action No 82–3362

LAKER AIRWAYS LTD (a foreign corporation in liquidation)
Hill House
1 Little New Street
London EC4A 3TR
England

Plaintiff

against

PAN AMERICAN WORLD AIRWAYS INC (a domestic corporation)
Pan Am Building, 200 Park Avenue   Serve: 1600 K Street NW
New York, New York 10166   Washington DC 20006

TRANS WORLD AIRLINES INC (a domestic corporation)
605 Third Avenue   Serve: Suite 704, Solar Building
New York, New York 10158   1000 Sixteenth Street NW
                                     Washington DC 20036

BRITISH AIRWAYS BOARD (a foreign corporation)
Speedbird House, PO Box 10   Serve: 1850 K Street NW
Heathrow Airport–London   Washington DC 20006
Hounslow, Middlesex TW6 2JA
England

LUFTHANSA GERMAN AIRLINES (Deutsche Lufthansa Aktiengesellschaft) (a foreign corporation)
Von-Gablenz-Strasse 2–6   Serve: 1101 Sixteenth Street NW
Cologne 21   Washington DC 20036
Federal Republic of German D–5000

SWISSAIR, SWISS AIR TRANSPORT CO LTD (a foreign corporation)
Balsberg Building   Serve: Suite 1100
Balz-Zimmermann-Strasse   1717 K Street NW
Zurich Airport   Washington DC 20006
Zurich
Switzerland CH-8058

BRITISH CALEDONIAN AIRWAYS LTD (a foreign corporation)
Caledonian House   Serve: Leonard Bebchick, agent
Crawley, West Surrey RH10 2XA   Suite 1102
England   1701 Pennsylvania Avenue NW
                                     Washington DC 20006

McDONNELL DOUGLAS CORP (a domestic corporation)
Box 516   Serve: Suite 500
St Louis, Missouri 63166   1150 Seventeenth Street NW
                                     Washington DC 20036

McDONNELL DOUGLAS FINANCE CORP (a domestic corporation)
100 Oceangate   Serve: Suite 500
Long Beach, California 90801   1150 Seventeenth Street NW
                                     Washington DC 20036

Defendants

COMPLAINT

Anti-trust Violation

Laker Airways Ltd (Laker), acting through its attorneys, brings this civil action against the defendants named above and complains and alleges as follows:

Jurisdiction and venue

1. This complaint is filed and this action is instituted under § 4 of the Clayton Act (15 USC § 15), to secure damages for the defendants' violations, as alleged in this complaint, of §§ 1 and 2 of the Sherman Act (15 USC §§ 1 and 2), and for other relief, as set forth below. Jurisdiction is conferred on this court by 15 USC § 15, by 28 USC § 1337 and

under the doctrine of pendant jurisdiction. Venue is properly laid in this district pursuant
to §§ 4 and 12 of the Clayton Act (15 USC §§ 15 and 22) and 28 USC §1391.   *a*

2. Each of the defendants transacts and does business, can be found or has an agent
within the District of Columbia and is otherwise amenable to the personal jurisdiction
of this court.

The parties

3. Plaintiff Laker Airways Ltd (Laker) is a foreign corporation registered under the   *b*
laws of Jersey, Channel Islands. Laker maintains its principal office in London, England.
Laker is a subsidiary of Laker Airways (International) Ltd, which is in turn controlled by
Sir Freddie Laker. Prior to 5 February 1982 Laker was the largest individually controlled
scheduled air carrier in the world and provided 42 widebodied jet aircraft flights per
week in scheduled airline service between various points in the United Kingdom and the
United States. Laker also provided extensive charter services between the United States   *c*
and the United Kingdom, and to numerous other countries. On 5 February 1982 Laker
ceased trading and, pursuant to the laws of Jersey, liquidators were subsequently
appointed.

4. Defendant Pan American World Airways Inc (Pan Am) is a New York corporation
with its headquarters in New York, New York. Pan Am provides scheduled and charter
air transportation between various states in the United States and between the United   *d*
States and the United Kingdom and other countries. Pan Am transacts and does business
within the District of Columbia at 1600 K Street NW, Washington DC 20006.

5. Defendant Trans World Airlines Inc (TWA) is a Delaware corporation with its
corporate headquarters in New York, New York. TWA provides scheduled and charter
air transportation between various states in the United States and between the United
States and the United Kingdom and other countries. TWA transacts and does business   *e*
within the District of Columbia at 1000 16th Street NW, Washington DC 20036.

6. Defendant British Airways Board (British Airways) is a foreign corporation with its
headquarters in Hounslow, Middlesex, England. British Airways provides scheduled and
charter air transportation between the United Kingdom and the United States, including
Washington DC. British Airways transacts and does business within the District of
Columbia at 1850 K Street NW, Washington DC 20006.   *f*

7. Defendant Lufthansa German Airlines (Deutsche Lufthansa Aktiengesellschaft)
(Lufthansa) is a foreign corporation with its headquarters in Cologne, Federal Republic
of Germany. Lufthansa provides scheduled and charter air transportation between the
Federal Republic of Germany and several points in the United States. Lufthansa transacts
and does business within the District of Columbia at 1101 Sixteenth Street NW,
Washington DC 20036.   *g*

8. Defendant Swissair, Swiss Air Transport Co Ltd (Swissair), is a foreign corporation
with its headquarters in Zurich, Switzerland. Swissair provides scheduled and charter air
transportation between Switzerland and several points in the United States. Swissair
transacts and does business within the District of Columbia at 1717 K Street NW,
Washington DC 20006.

9. Defendant British Caledonian Airways Ltd (British Caledonian) is a foreign   *h*
corporation with its headquarters in Crawley, West Surrey, England. British Caledonian
provides scheduled and charter air transportation between the United Kingdom and
several points in the United States. British Caledonian transacts and does business within
the District of Columbia through various agents. Its registered agent for service of process
is Leonard Bebchick, Suite 1102, 1701 Pennsylvania Avenue NW, Washington DC
20006.   *j*

10. Defendant McDonnell Douglas Corp (MDC) is a Maryland corporation with its
headquarters in St Louis, Missouri. MDC is a manufacturer of aircraft and aerospace
equipment and sells its products in interstate and foreign commerce. MDC transacts and
does business within the District of Columbia at Suite 500, 1150 Seventeenth Street NW,
Washington DC 20036.

a   11. Defendant McDonnell Douglas Finance Corp (MDFC) is a Delaware corporation with its headquarters in Long Beach, California. MDFC is a wholly-owned subsidiary of MDC and finances sales of aircraft and other equipment sold in interstate and foreign commerce by MDC. MDFC transacts and does business within the District of Columbia at Suite 500, 1150 Seventeenth Street NW, Washington DC 20036.

    12. Defendants Pan Am, TWA, British Airways, Lufthansa, Swissair and British Caledonian will be referred to below as the 'airline defendants'. Defendants MDC and
b   MDFC will be referred to below as the 'lender defendants'.

Trade and commerce
    13. Since 1946 the fares for scheduled air transportation on North Atlantic airline routes have been set, with very few exceptions, by government approved agreements among the airline members of the International Air Transport Association (IATA). IATA
c   agreements set fares at a higher level than would prevail in a competititve market.
    14. The IATA airlines sell several types of tickets for their scheduled services which include a number of privileges such as the ability to make and change a reservation, to get a refund without charge, to buy a ticket at any one of the thousands of travel agency offices throughout the world, or from a different airline than the one that provided the transportation, to make connections with other airlines on the same ticket and have
d   baggage automatically transferred, to travel on routings that are not the most direct route, to make stopovers, to be served meals and refreshments, to have hotel and car reservations made by the airline and many other extra services. These extra services are included in the price of the ticket whether the passenger wants them or not. Before 1977 many charter (non-scheduled) air charters operated over the North Atlantic, attracting large numbers of passengers primarily because charter prices were lower than fares
e   offered by the IATA carriers on their scheduled flights. Charter flights, however, were and are subject to a number of foreign government restrictions such as requirement that the passenger pay for the ticket far in advance and minimum stay requirements. Also, charter programs typically offer only a limited number of flights and destinations from which to choose.
    15. Laker Airways Ltd was founded in 1966 and rapidly grew into a major operator
f   of charter air transportation. Laker began charter flight operations between the United Kingdom and North America in 1970 and continued as a North Atlantic charter operator until 5 February 1982. Despite the success of Laker's charter business, Laker recognized in 1971 that the types of international airline service then in existence did not meet the needs of passengers who were not willing or able to plan far in advance and conform to the many restrictions on charter air transportation, or who could not afford or were not
g   willing to pay the high prices charged by the IATA airlines.
    16. Laker proposed a novel 'Skytrain' service which was designed to provide a new type of low-cost air transportation that would meet the needs of these passengers on simple terms at the lowerst possible price. Skytrain service passengers would arrive at the airport on the day chosen for travel and purchase a ticket there on a first-come first-served basis. Passengers could bring their own food or purchase meal service at an additional
h   price from Laker. If a passenger wished to travel beyond Laker's routes, he could buy another ticket separately from another airline or a travel agent.
    17. Commencing on 15 June 1971 Laker sought authority from the British government and then the US government to operate Skytrain service between New York and London. The airline defendants resisted Laker's efforts to the limits of their ability in the United States and the United Kingdom. The resistance of the airline defendants
j   delayed implementation of Laker's Skytrain service until 1977.
    18. Before the advent of Laker's Skytrain service, the IATA-fixed economy fare from New York to London was $313 for a one-way ticket. Laker offered New York–London service for $115. The IATA members, including the airline defendants, saw Laker's Skytrain service as a threat to the entire IATA system of maintaining high prices by airline agreement. The airline defendants agreed to a predatory scheme to destroy

transatlantic charters and Laker's scheduled Skytrain service by offering, among other
things, high-cost service at prices below the costs of those services. The IATA members *a*
agreed which of them would offer below-cost services on the New York–London route.
The airline defendants expected to experience short-term financial losses in carrying out
this scheme, but intended to recoup these losses by raising prices after they had eliminated
the competition of charter services and Laker's scheduled Skytrain service.

19. When their concerted predatory action failed to destroy or deter Laker, the airline
defendants expanded the scope of their predatory scheme as described below. Laker *b*
nevertheless survived, expanded its scheduled operations, and showed profits until 1981,
although its profits were lower than they would have been in a market free of predatory
activity.

20. Despite the joint efforts by its competitors, Laker increased the number of routes
on which it offered scheduled airline service between the United States and the United
Kingdom. Even while Laker was applying for government permission to provide *c*
schedule service between Los Angeles and London, Pan Am, TWA and British Airways
instituted below-cost fares on that route, seeking to prevent Laker's entry. After Laker
began providing Los Angeles–London Skytrain service in 1978, Pan Am, TWA and
British Airways coordinated their fares, services and schedules so as to take as many
passengers from Laker as possible. When Laker provided Skytrain service between
Miami and London, Pan Am and British Airways agreed to offer below-cost services on *d*
that route. Pan Am, TWA and British Airways acted in concert to target their below-cost
services on Laker's routes.

21. By 1981 Laker was operating nine scheduled non-stop US–UK routes: New York–
London, New York–Manchester, Los Angeles–London, Los Angeles–Manchester, Los
Angeles–Prestwick (Scotland), Miami–London, Miami–Manchester, Miami–Prestwick
and Tampa–London. In 1981 Laker carried one out of every seven air passengers between *e*
the United States and the United Kingdom, and Laker's total North Atlantic passenger
traffic ranked sixth out of the 43 airlines operating scheduled air services between North
America and Europe.

22. Many passengers going to or from continental European countries such as
Germany and Switzerland arranged to travel via London in order to use Laker's Skytrain
service across the Atlantic. European IATA members, including defendants Lufthansa *f*
and Swissair, found that Laker was attracting many passengers travelling between
continental Europe and the United States, thereby competing with those airlines and
putting downward pressure on their fares.

23. In addition to its North Atlantic routes, by 1981 Laker held licences from the UK
government for a transpacific route from Los Angeles and San Francisco to Hong Kong
via Honolulu and Tokyo, a London–Hong Kong route via Sharjah, United Arab Emirates, *g*
and European routes between London and Berlin and between London and Zurich.
Laker was actively pursuing authority from the other governments involved and
planning the commencement of worldwide low-fare service. Laker also had instituted
legal proceedings to declare unlawful under the Treaty of Rome the denial of Laker's
application to provide low-fare Skytrain services throughout Europe. Laker's successful
low-fare operations and its efforts to expand the scope and availability of those operations *h*
were a unique competitive threat to the airline defendants.

24. In 1981 the precipitous drop in the US dollar value of the pound sterling affected
Laker's ability to pay its dollar debts. Already weakened by the airline defendants'
concerted predatory attacks, Laker realized in May of 1981 that it might be unable to
meet its aircraft loan repayment requirements in January 1982 and explained the
situation to its lenders. Laker made clear that it was prepared, if necessary, to terminate *j*
its business in an orderly manner so that no passengers would be inconvenienced, but
sought refinancing of its obligations in order to continue in business.

25. At approximately the same time as Laker's financial problems became publicly
known in the summer of 1981, Pan Am raised approximately $800m from the sale of
assets. Without these large sales of assets, the company would have been in default of its
own loan agreements. Although these extraordinary sales of assets temporarily provided

Pan Am with a large amount of cash, it continued to suffer massive losses on its airline
a operations.

26. British Airways also suffered massive losses in 1980 and 1981, which were financed
by the British government. British Airways' auditors said later, in October 1982, that the
company could be considered a 'going concern' only because the British government
guaranteed $1·7 billion of its debt. British Airways also sold significant assets to raise cash
in 1980 and 1981. TWA was also losing large sums on its US–UK operations in 1981. All
b the airline defendants stated in public that they needed to increase their fares, particularly
their lowest fares.

27. The airline defendants realized that Laker's financial condition presented them
with an opportunity finally to eliminate Laker's price competition and to recoup their
losses by raising their fares in 1982 through an IATA agreement. In the fall of 1981, Pan
Am, TWA and British Airways threatened to drop the prices for their higher-cost, more
c attractive services to the same level as Laker's Skytrain service fares, thereby causing
Laker enormous losses, unless Laker abandoned its policy of price competition. Laker
refused, and insisted that its less valuable services required lower fares in order for Laker
to compete. In October 1981 Pan Am, TWA and British Airways agreed to and did carry
out their threat to offer their more attractive, higher-cost services at Laker's prices on all
of Laker's routes served by those defendants.

d 28. As part of their predatory scheme, Pan Am, TWA and British Airways agreed to
pay extraordinarily high secret commissions to travel agents, at great loss, to divert
potential Laker passengers. These defendants also pressured large Laker clients to switch
their business from Laker, and spread false rumors that Laker was going bankrupt.

29. The aforesaid predatory conduct was successful and prevented Laker from offering
the public a price differential. To the detriment of Laker and the public, Laker was
e forced to charge the prices that its IATA competitors agreed among themselves to charge.

30. In the mean time, Laker had reached an agreement with its lenders for financial
support which assured Laker's survival notwithstanding the losses Laker suffered due to
the predatory conduct of its IATA competitors. By Christmas Eve 1981 Laker was advised
that all of the lenders had agreed to provide the necessary finance. The lender defendants
authorized a public announcement to this effect and authorized Laker to state publicly
f that Laker's long-term financial future had been assured.

31. When they learned of the financing agreement, defendants Lufthansa, Swissair
and British Caledonian, knowing of the predatory scheme described above, pressured
Laker's lenders to further the objectives of the scheme by denying Laker the necessary
finance and forcing Laker out of business. As late as 3 February 1982 the lender
defendants continued to mislead Laker into believing that the financing was being
g provided as agreed, even though the lender defendants had joined with the airline
defendants to withhold such financing and thereby destroy Laker.

32. Laker relied on the lender defendants' misrepresentations that its financing was
assured and therefore did not seek other sources of finance which were available to it. On
4–5 February 1982 the lender defendants, without warning, forced Laker to cease
trading.

h

OFFENSES

Count 1: combination and conspiracy in restraint of trade and to monopolize

33. Plaintiff repeats and realleges paras 1 through 32 of this complaint.

34. This count is instituted against all defendants named in this complaint. Beginning
j at a time presently unknown to plaintiff, but at least as early as 1974 and continuing
thereafter at least until 5 February 1982, defendants and co-conspirators have engaged in
an unlawful combination and conspiracy unreasonably to restrain and to monopolize
United States foreign trade and commerce in air transportation between the United States
and the United Kingdom and other European countries in violation of §§1 and 2 of the
Sherman Act (15 USC §§ 1 and 2).

35. The unlawful conduct of the defendants and their co-conspirators had direct,

substantial and foreseeable effects on United States foreign trade and commerce, and on trade and commerce which is not trade or commerce with foreign nations, on import trade or import commerce with foreign nations, and on export trade and export commerce with foreign nations of persons engaged in such trade or commerce in the United States.

36. Pursuant to this unlawful combination and conspiracy each defendant has taken a number of actions, including the actions set forth in this complaint, with the intent to further the purpose and objective of the combination and conspiracy, which was to eliminate Laker as an independent competitive force in trade and commerce between the United States and foreign nations.

37. Various other persons, firms and corporations have participated as co-conspirators with the defendants in the offenses charged in this count and have performed acts in furtherance of those offenses. These co-conspirators include: C Edward Acker, Chairman and Chief Executive Officer of defendant Pan Am; Herbert Culmann, Director and former Chairman of defendant Lufthansa; Gerald C Draper, Director and former Commercial Director of defendant British Airways; Sanford N McDonnell, Chairman and Chief Executive Officer of defendant MDC; James T McMillan, President of defendant MDFC; David E Sedgewick, Senior Vice President (Planning) of defendant MDFC; Robert Staubli, President of defendant Swissair; and William Waltrip, formerly President and Chief Operating Officer of defendant Pan Am, now President, Purolator Courier Corp.

38. By the actions alleged in this complaint, and by other actions, each and every defendant named herein, acting in concert with some or all of the other defendants and co-conspirators and others, directly or indirectly violated or participated in the violation of, or aided and abetted the violation of, §§ 1 and 2 of the Sherman Act (15 USC §§ 1 and 2).

39. As a direct result of the defendants' unlawful conduct, Laker had suffered substantial injury to its business and property.

Count 2: intentional tort

40. Plaintiff repeats and realleges paras 1 through 32 of this complaint.

41. This count is instituted against all defendants named in this complaint. Without justification, the defendants have intentionally and unlawfully caused injury to Laker.

42. As a direct result of defendants' unlawful and tortious acts, Laker has suffered substantial injury to its business and property.

PRAYER FOR RELIEF

43. Because of defendants' unlawful conduct as alleged in this complaint, plaintiff Laker Airways demands judgment on each count and prays:

a. under count 1, for judgment against the defendants, jointly and severally, for the injury to Laker's business and property, in such amount as shall be determined after trial, now estimated to be in excess of $350 million, to be trebled as provided by law;

b. under count 2, for compensatory damages from the defendants, jointly and severally, in an amount in excess of $350 million, plus punitive damages of $700m;

c. under both causes of action, for interest, costs and attorneys' fees as provided by law; and

d. for such other and further relief as the court decides is just and proper.

44. Plaintiff demands a jury trial.

[Signed by attorneys for the plaintiff.]

24 November 1982

Governors of the Peabody Donation Fund v Sir Lindsay Parkinson & Co Ltd and others

COURT OF APPEAL, CIVIL DIVISION
LAWTON, FOX AND SLADE LJJ
11, 12, 13, 29 JULY 1983

Negligence – Duty to take care – Statutory powers – Compliance with statutory requirements – Building operations – Duty of care owed to building owner – Building owner not adhering to approved plans for drainage system – Local authority aware of building owner's non-compliance with its requirements but taking no action to enforce compliance – Drainage system proving defective – Building owner suffering loss by having to replace drains – Whether local authority owing duty of care to building owner to force him to comply with its requirements – London Building Act 1963, Sch 9, Pt III, paras 13, 15.

Negligence – Duty to take care – Statutory powers – Compliance with statutory requirements – Non-compliance with statutory requirements – Whether duty to prevent person acting unlawfully to his own detriment.

In 1972 the plaintiffs decided to build 245 houses on a hillside site in inner London. Under para 13 of Pt III of Sch 9 to the London Government Act 1963 the plaintiffs were required to install for the development, to the satisfaction of the local authority, a suitable drainage system which conformed to the requirements of para 13 as supplemented by drainage byelaws. Paragraph 15(2) of Pt III of Sch 9 provided for fines or demolition of the property and the relaying of the drains in the event of non-compliance with the drainage requirements specified by the authority. The plaintiffs' architects designed a suitable drainage system consisting of flexible pipes to allow for movement of the clay subsoil. The plans were deposited with the local authority and approved by it shortly afterwards. Before the drainage work began a drainage inspector who was employed by the local authority but who was acting without authority agreed with an employee of the plaintiffs' architects that a different and unsatisfactory system of rigid drains should be installed and thereafter the architects instructed the contractors to construct the drainage system in that way. Shortly after the drainage work began the inspector was replaced on the site by another inspector, who asked the contractors' site agent for information about the drains and their construction. On 4 May 1973 the site agent wrote a letter to the inspector giving the information sought, which indicated that a flexible system was not being installed. The inspector did not inform his superiors of its contents and did nothing to stop the contractors from departing from the approved design. During 1975 and early 1976, before the development had been completed, testing of the drains revealed that a substantial number of them had failed, with the result that the drainage system had to be reconstructed and the development was delayed by three years. The plaintiffs sought to recover the cost of reconstruction and also damages from the local authority, alleging that it was in breach of duties owed to them under Sch 9 to the 1963 Act first to ensure that the drainage system being installed complied with the plans approved by the authority and second to exercise its powers under para 15 of Pt III of Sch 9 to require the defective system to be remedied. The plaintiffs contended (i) that when the second inspector received the letter of 4 May 1973 the authority, through him, was to be deemed to have acquired knowledge that the plaintiffs' contractors were installing a drainage system which did not conform to the approved plans, (ii) that the authority thereupon came under a duty, which it owed to the plaintiffs, to require the plaintiffs to comply with the statutory requirements, and (iii) that it had been in breach of that duty because it had failed to take steps to enforce such compliance. The judge held that the local authority was liable to the plaintiffs for breach of duty. The local authority appealed.

Held – A local authority owed no duty of care to a person to compel that person to comply with the authority's requirements and thereby prevent that person acting unlawfully to his own detriment. On the facts, the local authority was under a public duty under paras 13 and 15 of Pt III of Sch 9 to the 1963 Act to ensure that the plaintiffs' proposed housing development had a satisfactory drainage system, but it had discharged that duty by requiring the plaintiffs to deposit plans which provided for a satisfactory drainage system and by properly considering those plans. The duty to construct the drains to the authority's satisfaction and in the manner specified by para 13 and the byelaws rested on the plaintiffs, who had not discharged that duty. Accordingly, although the local authority had had power to require the defective system to be remedied after it had received the letter of 4 May 1973, it had owed no duty of care to the plaintiffs to exercise that power of enforcement and to prevent the plaintiffs from acting unlawfully to their own detriment, since that particular power of enforcement existed for the protection of persons other than the person in default. It followed therefore that the local authority had not been in breach of any relevant duty of care to the plaintiffs and that the appeal would be allowed (see p 421 j, p 422 d to g and j to p 423 a, p 424 b to j, p 426 d and f to j and p 427 c to h, post).

Anns v Merton London Borough [1977] 2 All ER 492 and Acrecrest Ltd v W S Hattrell & Partners (a firm) [1983] 1 All ER 17 distinguished.

Semble. A London borough council may owe a duty of care, arising out of its duties under paras 13 and 15 of Pt III of Sch 9 to the 1963 Act, to an occupier of a house who suffers injury to health because the council has failed, through inaction, to require the builder of the house to comply with approved building plans (see p 422 f g, p 423 j and p 426 e f, post).

Notes

For negligence in relation to statutory functions and the duty to take care, see 34 Halsbury's Laws (4th edn) paras 4–7, and for cases on the subject, see 36(1) Digest (Reissue) 17–55, 34–177.

For the London Government Act 1963, Sch 9, Pt III, paras 13, 15, see 20 Halsbury's Statutes (3rd edn) 583, 585.

Cases referred to in judgments

Acrecrest Ltd v W S Hattrell & Partners (a firm) [1983] 1 All ER 17, [1983] QB 260, [1982] 3 WLR 1076, CA.

Anns v Merton London Borough [1977] 2 All ER 492, [1978] AC 728, [1977] 2 WLR 1024, HL.

Dutton v Bognor Regis United Building Co Ltd [1972] 1 All ER 462, [1972] 1 QB 373, [1972] 2 WLR 299, CA.

Cases also cited

Crump v Torfaen UDC (1981) 261 EG 678.

Junior Books Ltd v Veichi Co Ltd [1982] 3 All ER 201, [1983] AC 520, HL.

McLoughlin v O'Brian [1982] 2 All ER 298, [1983] AC 410, HL.

Appeal

Lambeth London Borough Council, the third defendant in an action brought by the plaintiffs, the governors of the Peabody Donation Fund (Peabody), against (1) the first defendants, Sir Lindsay Parkinson & Co Ltd, building contractors, (2) the second defendants, Austin Vernon & Partners, a firm of architects, and (3) Lambeth, which was consolidated with an action brought by the first defendants against Peabody with the second defendants and Lambeth as third parties, appealed against part of a judgment given by his Honour Judge Oddie, sitting as an official referee on 24 January 1983, whereby he declared that Peabody were entitled to the payment of damages from Lambeth representing such part of the sums for which Peabody were liable to the first defendants in respect of the failure of a rigid drainage system installed on Peabody's building development on the ground that Lambeth was in breach of its statutory duty to Peabody under Sch 9 to the London Government Act 1963. The facts are set out in the judgment of Lawton LJ.

John Owen QC and Richard Fernyhough for Lambeth.
John Dyson QC and Stephen Furst for Peabody.

Cur adv vult

29 July. The following judgments were delivered.

a   **LAWTON LJ.** This is an appeal by the third defendant, the London Borough of Lambeth, from part of a judgment given by his Honour Judge Oddie, sitting as an official referee, on 24 January 1983 whereby he adjudged that Lambeth were liable to pay the plaintiffs (Peabody) damages to be assessed for breach of its statutory duty to Peabody under Sch 9 to the London Government Act 1963. The damages may be very large. One

b   estimate, which is not accepted by either Peabody or Lambeth, is that they will be about £1m. The principal issue in the appeal is this: if an inner London borough (and Lambeth is one) approves the design of a drainage system for a building development and through one of its inspectors, whom it has appointed to inspect the construction of that system, fails to notice that the developer's architect, acting as an independent contractor, without its approval, alters the design and instructs the developer's contractor to build one which,

c   before the completion of the development, is found to be unsatisfactory, can the developer recover from the borough the cost of redoing the drainage work plus any other reasonably forseeable damages?

In or about 1972 Peabody decided to build 245 houses on a hillside site known as Knight's Hill, Lambeth. The site was a difficult one on which to build. It had to be terraced and any drainage scheme for it had to take into account the fact that the subsoil

d   was London clay which tends to expand and contract with the changes of the seasons. Peabody engaged the well-known contractors, Sir Lindsay Parkinson & Co, to do the building work and Messrs Austin Vernon & Partners as the architects. It was their function to design a drainage system for the site and that of the contractors to construct drains in accordance with the architects' instructions.

By about 1972 architects and civil engineers had come to appreciate that the traditional

e   drainage system, consisting of rigid pipes, was unsuitable for a housing development of this size and kind on a difficult subsoil like London clay. Movement in the subsoil was likely to cause breaks in the pipes. The architects knew this. They designed a flexible system which would allow for subsoil movements. Pursuant to drainage byelaws made by the Greater London Council under various statutory powers and applicable in Lambeth, on 6 April 1972 the architects applied, on behalf of Peabody, for leave to

f   construct a flexible system on the site. They deposited plans. The application form which they completed stated that the drainage system would be constructed to the satisfaction of Lambeth and in accordance with statutory requirements and 'By-laws, Regulations and other statutory requirements'. The byelaws contained detailed provisions for the construction of drains. Lambeth would have been unable to decide whether most of these provisions had been complied with once the drains had been covered. By testing it

g   could find out whether when completed the drains were effective as such but not how they had been constructed. No doubt because of this problem, para 15(1)(*b*) of Pt III of Sch 9 to the 1963 Act provided that 'no person shall . . . (*b*) begin to make any drain . . . unless, at least seven days previously, he has given to the borough council notice of his intention so to do . . .' Soon after the plans had been deposited Lambeth's civil engineering department, the senior members of which had professional qualifications, intimated that

h   the suggested drainage design seemed to be satisfactory but formal approval in writing was not given until 14 February 1973: it was stated to be 'in principle'.

By the beginning of 1973 the contractors were ready to start constructing the drainage system. The architects had on site, supervising for them, a trainee architect named Mitchell. The contractors had a site engineer. The drainage inspector appointed by Lambeth to inspect the drainage work on site was a man named Marlow. He had no

j   professional qualifications but he had had long experience in the building trade. On 2 February 1973 Mitchell and Marlow met and made an agreement. That agreement is going to cost either Peabody or Lambeth a lot of money. This appeal will decide who is going to pay. The reason is this: these two professionally unqualified men decided that the drains should be constructed in the traditional way and not in the way set out in the design plans deposited with Lambeth and which were to receive formal approval by Lambeth a few days later. In the words of counsel for Lambeth this change of design was doomed to failure. The evidence about this meeting was confused. The trial judge was

not satisfied that Marlow had required Mitchell to make the change; but that an
agreement to which Marlow had been a party had been made was clear beyond any   *a*
doubt. The terms of it were set out in a letter written by the architects to the contractors'
site engineer dated 7 February 1973. The judge found that Marlow had no authority
from Lambeth to be a party to this agreement. Thereafter the contractors were instructed
by the architects to construct the drainage system in the traditional, unsuitable way. This
they did. Shortly after the work on the drainage system began, Marlow was succeeded as
Lambeth's drainage inspector for the site by a man named Toogood. Like Marlow he too   *b*
had no professional qualifications. He had only been a drainage inspector for a short time
before carrying out inspections on this site. His previous occupation had been that of a
plumber. Between the time when he started working on this site and 4 May 1973, he
carried out 20 inspections. There was no evidence as to what he did or what he saw. On
3 May 1973 he asked the contractors' site agent for some information about the drains
and what was being used for their construction. He was given the information in a letter   *c*
dated 4 May 1973. Peabody have based their case against Lambeth on this letter. It was
admitted by Lambeth at the trial that Toogood on reading this letter should have
appreciated that the contractors were constructing a drainage system which was different
from the approved design set out in the plans to which he had access. Toogood did not
show this letter to his superiors. He let the contractors go on constructing the drainage
system in a way which was doomed to failure. His inaction, submit Peabody, amounted   *d*
to a breach of duty which caused them great loss.
    Although he did nothing to stop the contractors from departing from the approved
design, he went on inspecting their work. Peabody have not suggested that he made his
inspections negligently.
    During 1975 and the early part of 1976 and before the development had been
completed, testing of the drains revealed that a substantial number of them had failed.   *e*
    As a result of the failures the drainage system had to be reconstructed by the contractors
at a cost which they estimate to have been £118,139. The development was delayed for
about three years. Peabody lost rents which they would have received if the delay had
not occurred. The contractors have claimed that under their contract with Peabody they
are entitled to be paid substantial additional sums because of the delay. Peabody started
proceedings against the contractors, the architects and Lambeth claiming to be   *f*
reimbursed by one or other or all of them for the losses they had sustained. The
contractors issued a writ against Peabody for the sums they alleged were due to them
under their contract. The two actions were consolidated. There was a lengthy trial on
preliminary issues, first whether the cause of the replacement of the original drains was
the unsuitability of the architects' design or the contractors' defective workmanship, and
second whether the contractors were entitled to extra payments under their contract   *g*
with Peabody. The judge found that the cause of the failure of the drains was their
unsuitable design and not the contractors' workmanship and that the contractors were
entitled to be paid various sums, to be assessed, under their contract with Peabody. His
finding against Lambeth is set out in the order as follows: that Peabody were entitled to
payment of damages from Lambeth representing such part of the sums for which
Peabody were liable to the contractors arising out of the failure of the rigid drainage   *h*
system as would not have been incurred had Lambeth, following the receipt of the letter
from the contractors dated 4 May 1973 taken steps to ensure that the system of drainage
then being installed complied with the original drainage scheme approved by Lambeth.
The judge made no finding against the architects because, before judgment, Peabody's
claim against them had been settled. It is to be inferred from what the judge said in his
judgment that he would have found the architects negligent had Peabody's claim against   *j*
them not been settled. He assessed Lambeth's proportion of liability at 15%. This could
only have been relevant to a claim for contribution which Lambeth had made against
the architects. In the event they had none because of the terms of compromise which
Lambeth itself had made with the architects.
    If this judgment is right in so far as it affects Lambeth, that local authority has become
liable to indemnify Peabody against a substantial part of a huge claim made against them

by the contractors. This has come about because an inexperienced drainage inspector had
a taken no action following receipt of one letter from the experienced contractors who had
done what the architects had told them to do. He may not have appreciated the
significance of this letter; but if he did not, he should have done, as was admitted. Since
the drainage inspector was acting in the course of his employment, Lambeth is vicariously
responsible for any breach of duty he may have committed, however disastrous the
consequences of the breach may have been, to anyone to whom the duty was owed, if
b they were reasonably foreseeable. The first question is whether he was in breach of duty
to Peabody. If he was not, Peabody cannot recover their loss from Lambeth.

Peabody alleged that Lambeth owed them a duty under Sch 9 to the London
Government Act 1963. That schedule reproduced with modifications Pt II of the Public
Health (London) Act 1936. Its wording in matters relating to drainage was different
from the drainage provisions of the Public Health Act 1936 which were more explicit as
c to what drainage authorities had to do. Both Acts empowered specified local authorities
to control drainage works. The object was to safeguard the health of those occupying
houses or other buildings whether as owners, tenants, employees or visitors. We were
told by counsel that drainage byelaws made by the Greater London Council in December
1961 and applicable to Lambeth supplemented the specific provisions of paras 13 to 16
of Pt III of Sch 9 to the 1963 Act. Paragraph 2(1) of these byelaws provides that—

d
'... all drainage works and all materials, appliances and fittings used in the
execution of any drainage work shall be—(a) of a suitable nature and quality for the
purpose for which they are used ...'

This byelaw, together with paras 13 and 15 of Pt III of Sch 9, imposed a duty on Peabody
to ensure that the drainage works which they were proposing to construct and which
e their contractors did construct were suitable for draining the houses to be erected. For
the reasons found by the judge they were not. Byelaw 14(1) requires 'Every person about
to construct, reconstruct or alter any drainage work' to deposit plans with—

'such detailed description and particulars of the proposed construction,
reconstruction or alteration as may be necessary for the purpose of enabling such
f authority to ascertain whether such construction, reconstruction or alteration will
be in accordance with the statutory provisions relative thereto and with these by
laws ...'

Sub-paragraph (2) requires notice in writing to be given of the day and time at which any
drainage work is to be started. This is an echo of what is enacted in para 15(1)(a) of Pt III
of Sch 9. Further, by para 13(1) of Pt III of Sch 9:

g
'It shall not be lawful in an inner London borough—(a) to erect any house or
other building ... unless there are provided to the satisfaction of the borough
council drains conforming with the requirements of this paragraph and all such
drains and all works and apparatus in connection therewith are constructed to the
satisfaction of the council and, in particular, are constructed of such materials and
size, at such level and with such fall, as are approved by the council and are provided
h with a water supply.'

Since a house or building cannot be erected unless the drainage authority is satisfied that
provision has been made for suitable drains constructed in the specified way and with
the specified materials and it is an offence punishable by fine (para 15(1)) to start drainage
works without giving the authority an opportunity to inspect them, in my judgment
j the statute does impose a duty on the authority to ensure first that the plans of houses
and buildings intended to be erected provide for satisfactory drains and, second, that
suitable drains are constructed in accordance with those plans. If houses or buildings are
erected without suitable drains there will be a potential danger to the health not only of
any occupiers but also of the immediate neighbourhood. Local authorities in urban areas
have been empowered since at least 1875 to ensure the proper drainage of houses: see the
Public Health Act 1875, ss 23 to 25. In 1875 the health hazards likely to arise from faulty

drains would not have been overlooked having regard to the fact that the Prince Consort's death in 1865 had been attributed to this cause. Paragraph 13(7) of Pt III to Sch 9 envisages that the authority can give orders, directions, requirements or other decisions. The wording of this sub-paragraph is not clear. The only reference to a requirement is in sub-para (6). An expression of dissatisfaction could be a decision given under the sub-para (1). There is no specific reference to an order or direction. The byelaws, however, are replete with directions as to how drains are to be constructed. I would construe sub-para (7) as enabling the authority to do more than merely express satisfaction or dissatisfaction with proposed drainage work or with works in the course of construction. For these reasons I have been unable to accept counsel's submission on behalf of Lambeth that its only duty was to express satisfaction or dissatisfaction and that it had no power to direct the contractors to revert to the flexible design of the drawing of the drainage works which it had approved, when on 4 May 1973, through Toogood, it must be deemed to have learned that the design had been changed. Still less have I been able to accept his submission that Lambeth could express its satisfaction or dissatisfaction at any time before the completion of the development. The provisions of para 15(1) of Pt III of Sch 9 when read with para 13 go to show that drainage authorities should inspect drainage works as they progress.

It follows, in my judgment, that Lambeth had a public duty to ensure that Peabody's proposed housing development had a satisfactory drainage system. It had discharged its duty in part at least by requiring Peabody to deposit plans and it had given proper consideration to those plans which on their face provided for a satisfactory drainage system. The drains, however, had not only to be properly designed, they had to be constructed by Peabody as the building owners to Lambeth's satisfaction and in the manner specified in the statute and in the byelaws. The duty to comply with these statutory requirements rested on Peabody. They did not discharge their duty in this respect because of their architects' departure from the drainage scheme set out in the deposited plans which Lambeth had approved.

The only relevant allegation of breach of duty against Lambeth in the reamended statement of claim was that it had failed, through Toogood, to require Peabody to comply with the statutory requirements. In all other respects, as was admitted, Lambeth had performed its statutory duties. This being so, can Peabody rightly claim, as they have done, that Lambeth owed them a duty to require them to do that which they ought to have done anyway? The answer to this question is clearly No. It may be that, if the drainage system had not been put right, an occupier of the houses when completed who suffered injury to health through Toogood's inaction could have sued Lambeth for breach of duty in failing to require Peabody to comply with the deposited plans.

I would allow the appeal.

FOX LJ. Paragraph 13(1) of Pt III of Sch 9 to the London Government Act 1963 provides:

> 'It shall not be lawful in an inner London borough—(a) to erect any house or other building ... unless there are provided to the satisfaction of the borough council drains conforming with the requirements of this paragraph and all such drains and all works and apparatus in connection therewith are constructed to the satisfaction of the council and, in particular, are constructed of such materials and size, at such level and with such fall, as are approved by the council ...'

And para 13(3) of Pt III of the schedule provides:

> 'In order to conform with the requirements of this paragraph a drain must provide for the drainage of the house or building in connection with which it is required—(a) into such sewer ... as the borough council may direct; or (b) if no sewer is or will be available ... into such covered cesspool ... as the council may direct; and the drains must secure efficient drainage by gravitation at all times and under all conditions of all parts of the house or building.'

The result of these provisions, in my view, is that there was an obligation on Peabody

to install, to the satisfaction of the borough council (Lambeth), drains which secured
efficient drainage at all times and under all conditions to all parts of the houses. The
a drains as installed did not do that. They were fundamentally defective. The circumstances
in which that occurred were, briefly, these. A perfectly satisfactory drainage system, with
flexible pipes, was devised by Peabody's advisers and submitted to Lambeth. The
proposed system was formally approved by Lambeth on 14 February 1973; the approval
was stated to be 'in principle' but it has not been suggested that anything turns on that.
b On 2 February 1973 Young (the builders' site agent), Mitchell (a trainee architect
employed by Peabody's architects) and Marlow (Lambeth's drainage inspector) met on
the site and agreed a quite different, and unsatisfactory, system of rigid drains. Marlow
had, the judge found, no authority ostensible or otherwise to bind Lambeth. Shortly
after the drainage works began Marlow left the district and was succeeded by Toogood.
On 3 May 1973 Toogood asked the builders' site agent for some information about the
c drains. On 4 May 1973 the site agent wrote to the Public Health Department of Lambeth
('for the attention of Mr. Toogood') giving the information which indicated that a flexible
system was not being installed. Toogood did not act on that letter and Peabody's builders
continued to construct rigid drains.

The allegations of negligence made against Lambeth as particularised in the statement
of claim are as follows: '(7) The plaintiffs refer to and repeat (6) above.' Paragraph (6) was
d as follows (it related to the claim against the second defendants):

'Instructing the first defendants to change the drainage specification when they
knew or ought to have known that the ground comprised shrinkable clay which
was subject to seasonal movement, so that it was necessary to provide for such
movement in the design of the drains.'

e Lambeth did not instruct the first defendants, the builders, to change the drainage
system. Marlow's actions on 2 February 1973 were made without authority and did not
bind Lambeth (even if they purported to be directions at all).

'(8) Knowing that rigid drains were being installed between the vertical stacks in
the buildings and the manholes following receipt of the said letter of the 4th May
1973, thereafter failing to require flexibly jointed drains wherever rigid drains had
f been or were to be installed.'

The allegation, in effect, therefore, is of failure by Lambeth to require the position to
be remedied after 4 May 1973. There is no allegation that Lambeth, by anything done
or omitted after the letter of 4 May, impliedly expressed its satisfaction with or approval
of the altered drainage system. I would accept that Lambeth had power, under para
15(2) of Pt III of Sch 9, to require the defective system to be remedied. And I accept that
g Lambeth did not do so. The question is whether Lambeth was in breach of a duty to
Peabody in not doing so. Following *Anns v Merton London Borough* [1977] 2 All ER 492 at
498, [1978] AC 728 at 751 the matter has to be approached in two stages. First, as
between Peabody and Lambeth, was there a sufficient relationship of proximity such
that in the reasonable contemplation of Lambeth carelessness by it would be likely to
h cause damage to Peabody, in which case a prima facie duty of care exists? Second, if the
first question is answered affirmatively, it is necessary to consider whether there are any
considerations which ought to negative or to reduce or limit the scope of the duty or the
class of persons to whom it is owed.

Now I can see that, in circumstances such as the present, there may be persons to
whom Lambeth, prima facie, owes a duty of care in relation to the exercise of its powers
j to require compliance with the statute; and that there would be no reason to reduce or
limit the scope of such duty. Thus if Lambeth, knowing that a defective drainage system
has been installed, took no steps to direct that it be remedied and houses with defective
drainage are then sold to members of the public who suffer damage in consequence, it
may be that those purchasers would have a cause of action against Lambeth. The purpose
of the statute is the protection of the health and safety of the public and the powers are
given to the local authorities for that purpose.

The present case, however, raises different problems. The statute requires the building owners to provide a drainage system, to the satisfaction of the borough council, conforming with the requirements of para 13 of Pt III of Sch 9. Suppose that an owner builder, without seeking the approval of the council, starts to put in a defective system. And suppose that the council became aware of that from some other source. I do not think that, in those circumstances, the council would be liable to the owner if it failed to exercise its power to require the drainage system to be altered. There may be a sufficiently proximate relationship to establish that the council could reasonably foresee damage to the owner. But it seems to me that considerations of policy negative the duty. It is not the purpose of the statute to protect owners who act negligently or irresponsibly and so cause themselves harm. That seems to be recognised in *Anns v Merton London Borough* [1977] 2 All ER 492 at 504, [1978] AC 728 at 758.

In the present case Peabody devised a satisfactory drainage system and obtained Lambeth's approval to it. But Peabody then proceeded to put in a quite different, and unsatisfactory, system for which they never sought approval at all. They have not established, and indeed do not seek to establish, that what they did was 'to the satisfaction of the borough council'. Marlow may have approved it but we can disregard that because of the absence of authority.

In installing the system Peabody were therefore in breach of the provisions of Sch 9. They now say to Lambeth, 'You knew what we were doing; you should have required us to stop.' Let it be accepted for present purposes that Lambeth could reasonably foresee damage to Peabody if it did not intervene. It seems to me, nevertheless, that the circumstances negative any prima facie duty of care by Lambeth to Peabody to ensure that a faulty system was not installed. Lambeth had, by normal and formal processes, approved a satisfactory system. I think that the courts should view with caution the suggestion that the owner can, without seeking new approval from the council, throw that system to the winds in favour of a defective system, and then visit the consequences on the council for not stopping him, even if some junior official of the council knew or ought to have known what was happening. Since Peabody had specifically sought and obtained approval for a satisfactory system it seems to me foolhardy to jettison that without precise and formal notice to Lambeth. Peabody themselves may not have been negligent, but I do not think that is a sufficient answer in a case such as the present. Knight's Hill was a very substantial development of some 245 houses. An application to alter the approved drainage was an important matter which would obviously have been considered at a level in the Lambeth administration where the defects of the new proposal would have been likely to be apparent. It seems to me in those circumstances to be placing an unreasonable burden on a local authority which has actually approved a proper drainage system and which was never given the opportunity, at an appropriate level, of considering anything else, to impose on it a duty to an owner to prevent him from acting unlawfully and contrary to that approval merely because notice of the owner's actions or intentions has come to the attention of an official of the authority. The owner, it seems to me, should give the authority the fullest opportunity, on formal application, of reconsidering the position since very large amounts of money may be involved. I do not say that the mere fact that the owner is acting in breach of the statute will, by itself, necessarily be conclusive against him. But, where the local authority has actually approved a satisfactory system and the owner, albeit on the advice of independent contractors, then abandons that system and unlawfully installs an unsatisfactory one, I think it is material when considering whether a duty of care to that owner is negatived, to have regard to the fact that the owner has acted unlawfully.

We were referred to the decision in *Acrecrest Ltd v W S Hattrell & Partners (a firm)* [1983] 1 All ER 17, [1983] QB 260. In my view that was a very different case. The site was such that there should have been uniform foundations 5 feet deep. The local authority's building inspector, however, gave directions that in part of the site the foundations should be 5 ft deep and in the remainder of the site 3 ft 6 in deep. Thus the position was that the local authority gave a specific direction for the laying of inadequate foundations. I think that is far removed from this case.

I agree that the appeal should be allowed.

SLADE LJ. I have had the advantage of reading in draft the judgment of Lawton LJ. I
gratefully adopt his statement of the facts and, as to them, wish to highlight only a few
points.

(1) On 2 February 1973 Marlow, the drainage inspector appointed by Lambeth to
inspect the drainage work on site, agreed with Mitchell, the employee of Peabody's
architects, that the drainage might be constructed by the traditional manner of rigid
construction. The judge, however, found that Marlow had no express authority to agree
to such departure from the plans which had been deposited by Peabody, that Lambeth
had not held him out as having any ostensible authority of this nature, and that his action
was never ratified by any person with knowledge or authority to do so. On this appeal,
these findings of fact have not been challenged, so that it is not open to Peabody to rely
in any way on this conversation of 2 February 1973 for the purposes of establishing
liability against Lambeth; and they do not now seek to do so. It is thus clear that neither
Mitchell nor his employers nor Peabody were entitled to rely on anything that had been
said by Marlow as constituting permission by Lambeth to adopt a system of rigid
construction.

(2) On 14 February 1973 the senior assistant director of Lambeth's civil engineering
department wrote to the architects, stating that the drainage application and
accompanying drawings, which had been deposited by them with Lambeth, were
approved in principle. The application and drawings provided for a system of flexible
construction. On this appeal it has not been suggested that the writer of this letter did
not have the requisite authority from Lambeth to write it, or that the architects would
not have been entitled to act on it (subject to supplying any further particulars which
Lambeth might from time to time require) or that the system thus approved would not
have satisfactorily performed its function. It is not claimed that Lambeth, in approving
the application and plans, acted negligently or otherwise in breach of duty to anyone.

(3) Regrettably, however, the architects, instead of acting on the letter of 14 February
1973, on which they were entitled to rely, instructed the contractors to construct the
drainage system by the traditional manner of rigid construction. During the weeks
which followed the start of this work, Toogood, who had by then replaced Marlow as
Lambeth's inspector for the site, inspected it on some 20 occasions before 4 May 1973.
There are, however, no findings as to what he saw or did and it is not claimed that he was
negligent in any way in carrying out these inspections. On this appeal it has not been
suggested that, before receipt of the contractors' letter of 4 May 1973, Lambeth either
knew or ought to have known of the contractors' departure from the plans which had
been approved by it on 14 February 1973 or that, before such receipt, Lambeth was
guilty of any breach of any duty owed to Peabody or anyone else.

(4) But then, on 4 May 1973, in response to a request for clarification as to the type of
drain which the contractors were using, their site agent wrote to Toogood a letter which,
it is common ground, should have put him on notice that they were installing a drainage
system of rigid construction, rather than the already approved system of flexible
construction. On receipt of this letter, Toogood did nothing. His employer, who,
according to the judge's findings, was not informed by him of the contents of this letter,
likewise did nothing.

(5) Toogood continued to inspect the site from time to time after receipt of the letter
of 4 May 1973. It has not been suggested on behalf of Peabody that he carried out these
inspections negligently or that Lambeth during this period effected fewer inspections
than it should have done. On the other hand, until the drains began to fail, neither
Toogood nor anyone else on Lambeth's behalf informed Peabody or the contractors that
the method which had been adopted for the construction of the drains was unsatisfactory.

In all the circumstances, I could have understood a submission on behalf of Peabody
that Lambeth by its conduct had implicitly approved a departure from the deposited
plans by the installation of a system of rigid drains. If, on the evidence, it had been
established that such implicit approval had been given, and given negligently, it is
possible that Peabody could have successfully relied on the decisions in *Anns v Merton
London Borough* [1977] 2 All ER 492, [1978] AC 728 and *Acrecrest Ltd v W S Hattrell &*

Partners (a firm) [1983] 1 All ER 17, [1983] QB 260 to establish the breach of a duty owed
to them by Lambeth. The latter case illustrates that a local authority, which does not take
reasonable care in the approval of building works, may, on appropriate facts, be held
liable in negligence at the suit of the building owner, who has contracted the building
work to an independent contractor and has not himself been negligent.

This, however, is not the way in which Peabody have pleaded or argued their case.
Their claim rests on the propositions that (a) on receipt by Toogood of the letter of 4 May
1973, Lambeth, through him, must be deemed to have acquired knowledge that the
contractors employed by Peabody were proceeding with the construction of the drainage
system otherwise than in compliance with the plans which had been approved by
Lambeth, (b) Lambeth, on acquiring such knowledge, was under a duty *owed to Peabody*
to require flexibly jointed drains to be installed on the site in the place of rigid drains, (c)
Lambeth has been in breach of this duty, because it took no steps to enforce such
compliance.

The striking feature of this claim is that it is made by plaintiffs who, on the facts as
found by the judge, carried out the building development on the site in a manner quite
contrary to the requirements of Lambeth (of which architects, duly authorised to act on
their behalf, had been duly notified in Lambeth's letter of 14 February 1973) and thus in
breach of para 13(1) of Pt III of Sch 9 to the London Government Act 1963. In general
terms I accept the submission of counsel for the plaintiffs that it is the duty of a local
authority, in carrying out its functions under para 13, to make known to the building
owner its requirements in relation to drainage from time to time. The letter of 14
February 1973, however, had, in my opinion, constituted a notification of this nature.

Paragraph 15(2) of Pt III of Sch 9 confers on a borough council a sanction designed to
enable it to enforce compliance with its requirements in relation to drainage, against the
owner of the relevant site. I accept that Lambeth could have availed itself of this sanction
against Peabody after 4 May 1973. Though it is not necessary to decide the point, I also
accept that certain persons other than Peabody (falling within a class of persons to whom
damage might reasonably have been foreseen) might have had a good cause of action
against Lambeth if, with knowledge of the relevant breaches of its requirements,
Lambeth had failed, within a reasonable time, to exercise its powers under para 15(2) to
secure compliance by Peabody with its requirements, and those other persons had
thereby suffered damage. I cannot accept the submission of counsel for Lambeth that no
relevant duty is owed by Lambeth to anyone until the building is ready for occupation.

However, as sufficiently appears from Lord Wilberforce's speech in *Anns v Merton
London Borough* [1977] 2 All ER 492 at 498, [1978] AC 728 at 751–752, the mere fact that
Lambeth might reasonably have foreseen the likelihood of damage being suffered by
Peabody, among other persons, in the event of Lambeth's failure to enforce compliance
with its requirements, would not by itself suffice to establish the existence of a relevant
duty of care owed by Lambeth to Peabody; it would still be 'necessary to consider
whether there are any considerations which ought to negative, or to reduce or limit the
scope of the duty or the class of person to whom it is owed or the damages to which a
breach of it may give rise'.

In the present case I think that the ultimate question for decision is: to whom is the
relevant duty owed? Does a local authority, which discovers that an owner of a site is
acting in breach of specific requirements duly made by it under para 13 of Pt III of Sch 9,
owe a duty to *that owner* to exercise its powers to enforce compliance with such
requirements *by the offending owner*? The answer to this question must, in my judgment,
be No. I think that none of the authorities which have been cited to us cover the point.
The House of Lords in *Anns v Merton London Borough* [1977] 2 All ER 492 at 504, 1978
AC 728 at 758 per Lord Wilberforce affirmed in general terms the duty of a local
authority to enforce compliance with its byelaws in regard to the foundations of a
building, and held that this duty was owed to owners or occupiers of the building other
than a 'negligent building owner, the source of his own loss'. The Court of Appeal
followed this decision in *Acrecrest* and in addition held that a building owner, who has

a contracted the building work to an independent contractor and has not himself been negligent, is included in the class of persons to whom a local authority owes a duty to take reasonable care in the inspection and approval of building works.

The *Acrecrest* decision may provide grounds for saying that Peabody are not a 'negligent building owner', within Lord Wilberforce's phraseology. Nevertheless, the facts of the present case are, in my opinion, far removed from those of *Anns* and *Acrecrest* in at least two material respects. First, as counsel for Peabody made clear at the start of his address, *b* Peabody are not relying on any alleged breach of byelaws or building regulations; the relevant obligations of Peabody are to be found simply in paras 13 and 15(1) of Pt III of Sch 9. Second, on the facts in *Acrecrest* it was clear that the foundations were laid *in accordance with* the requirements of the building inspector and because of his requirements (see [1983] 1 All ER 17 at 33, [1983] QB 260 at 283 per Sir David Cairns). It seems that in *Anns* also the council's specified requirements were duly complied with. In neither of *c* these two cases was the court considering the situation, such as that in the present case, where the plaintiff has been acting in disobedience to the specific and proper requirements of the local authority, made in accordance with the functions imposed on it by para 13. Neither these two decisions, nor any other case which has been cited to us, oblige or entitle us to conclude that a local authority owes a duty *to such a person* to compel compliance with its requirements.

d The question whether the alleged duty is owed to Peabody thus has to be considered in the absence of direct authority. Lord Wilberforce, in analysing the nature of the duty to enforce compliance with the byelaws, which was under consideration in *Anns*, said that it must be related closely to the purpose for which the relevant powers of inspection had been granted (see [1977] 2 All ER 492 at 504, [1978] AC 728 at 758). Similarly, in *Dutton v Bognor Regis United Building Co Ltd* [1972] 1 All ER 462 at 484, [1972] 1 QB 373 *e* at 408, Sachs LJ, in considering the measure of damages, asked himself the question: 'What range of damage is the proper exercise of the relevant power designed to prevent?'

Can it have been the intention of the legislature, in conferring on a borough council power to enforce against a defaulting site-owner requirements made by it in accordance with para 13 of Pt III of Sch 9, to protect such owner against damage which he himself might suffer through his own failure to comply with such requirements? In my opinion, *f* this question can only be answered in the negative. This particular power exists for the protection of other persons, not for that of the person in default. I say nothing about the case where a local authority has failed to make known its requirements or where it has made requirements of an inadequate or defective nature. However, I can see no justification for extending the law of negligence by imposing on a local authority, over and above its public law powers and duties under paras 13 and 15, a duty to exercise its *g* powers of enforcement under para 15(2), owed in private law towards a site-owner, who, whether with or without personal negligence, disregards the proper requirements of the local authority, duly made under para 13 and duly communicated to him or persons authorised to receive them on his behalf. The practical implications of giving the defaulting owner a right to sue the local authority for damages in such circumstances need consideration, but no elaboration.

h For these reasons, I conclude that Peabody have not established the breach of any relevant duty of care owed to them by Lambeth. Accordingly, I too would allow this appeal.

Appeal allowed; all actions dismissed. Leave to appeal to House of Lords refused.

Solicitors: *Barlow Lyde & Gilbert* (for Lambeth); *Bridges Sawtell & Adams* (for Peabody).

Mary Rose Plummer   Barrister.

Bank Mellat v Helliniki Techniki SA

COURT OF APPEAL, CIVIL DIVISION
WALLER, KERR AND ROBERT GOFF LJJ
8, 9, 28 JUNE 1983

Arbitration – Costs – Security for costs – Claimant ordinarily resident out of the jurisdiction – International arbitration in accordance with rules of International Chamber of Commerce – Arbitration commenced in England – Parties' sole connection with England that they had agreed that arbitration should take place there – Application by respondent for security for costs – Claimant's ability to pay respondent's costs uncertain – Whether order for security for costs would be inconsistent with ICC rules – Whether court should make the order – Arbitration Act 1950, s 12(6)(a).

The claimant, a Greek company, and the respondent, an Iranian bank, entered into a contract regarding the development of certain land in Iran. Neither party carried on business in or had any other connection with England. The contract, which was governed by Iranian law, stated that any dispute arising between the parties in connection with it should be settled in London in accordance with the Rules on Conciliation and Arbitration of the International Chamber of Commerce in Paris (the ICC rules). A dispute in connection with the contract having arisen, the claimant commenced arbitration proceedings in London against the respondent. After the terms of the reference had been settled and both parties had paid deposits in accordance with the ICC rules, the respondent applied to the High Court for an order for security for costs under s 12(6)(a)[a] of the Arbitration Act 1950 on the grounds (i) that the claimant was resident out of the jurisdiction and (ii) that there was reason to believe that the claimant would be unable to pay the respondent's costs if the respondent succeeded in the arbitration proceedings. The claimant contended that such an order would be inconsistent with the provisions of the ICC rules and inappropriate in an international arbitration which took place in London between parties neither of whom had any other connection with England. The judge refused to make the order. The respondent appealed to the Court of Appeal.

Held – (1) As a general rule in international arbitrations, the English courts would decline to exercise their jurisdiction under s 12(6)(a) of the 1950 Act to order security for costs unless there was a more specific connection with England than the mere fact that the parties had agreed that any arbitration was to take place there (see p 437 *b c*, p 438 *a b*, p 441 *d*, p 442 *e* and *h* and p 444 *a b*, post).

(2) No special circumstances having been shown, it was not an appropriate case in which to make an order for security for costs, and the appeal would accordingly be dismissed, for the following reasons—

(a) (Robert Goff LJ dissenting) such an order would be inconsistent with the spirit and scheme of the ICC rules (see p 434 *j*, p 435 *d* to *g*, p 437 *d e*, p 438 *a b* and p 444 *b*, post);

(b) the fact that the claimant was ordinarily resident outside the jurisdiction was, in principle, not a special circumstance which would justify the court in ordering security for costs (see p 438 *a b*, p 442 *a* to *c* and p 444 *a b*, post);

(c) (per Waller and Kerr LJJ) it was wrong in principle to order security for costs on the ground that the claimant might be unable to pay the respondent's costs if the award required it to do so or (per Robert Goff LJ) the evidence was not sufficient to establish the basis for such an order on that ground (see p 438 *a b* and p 444 *a b*, post).

Notes

For the interlocutory powers of the court to order security for costs in arbitration

---

a Section 12(6), so far as material, is set out at p 432 *a b*, post

proceedings, see 2 Halsbury's Laws (4th edn) para 595, and for cases on the subject, see 3
a Digest (Reissue) 335–336, 2310–2313.
For the Arbitration Act 1950, s 12, see 2 Halsbury's Statutes (3rd edn) 444.

Cases referred to in judgments
Hudson Strumpffabrik GmbH v Bentley Engineering Co Ltd [1962] 3 All ER 460, [1962] 2 QB
587, [1962] 3 WLR 758.
b *Mavani v Ralli Bros Ltd* [1973] 1 All ER 555, [1973] 1 WLR 468.
Miller (James) & Partners Ltd v Whitworth Street Estates (Manchester) Ltd [1970] 1 All ER
796, [1970] AC 583, [1970] 2 WLR 728, HL.
Parkinson (Sir Lindsay) & Co Ltd v Triplan Ltd [1973] 2 All ER 273, [1973] QB 609, [1973]
2 WLR 632, CA.

c #### Cases also cited
Aeronave SpA v Westland Charters Ltd [1971] 3 All ER 531, [1971] 1 WLR 1445, CA.
Bremer Vulkan Schiffbau Und Maschinenfabrik v South India Shipping Corp [1981] 1 All ER
289, [1981] AC 909, HL.

Interlocutory appeal
d Bank Mellat, the respondent in arbitration proceedings arising out of a contract dated 29
September 1972, appealed against an order of Bingham J, dated 25 March 1983, whereby
he dismissed its application for an order under s 12(6)(a) of the Arbitration Act 1950 that
Helleniki Techniki SA (HT), the claimant in the arbitration proceedings, give security
for the bank's costs. The facts are set out in the judgment of Kerr LJ.

e *Mark Littman QC* and *Nicholas Chambers* for Bank Mellat.
Ian Glick for HT.

Cur adv vult

f 28th June. The following judgments were delivered.

KERR LJ (giving the first judgment at the invitation of Waller LJ). This is an appeal
from a judgment of Bingham J, given on 25 March 1983 which raises an important
question on orders for security for costs in relation to international arbitrations held in
this country. In the present case this question arises in the context of the Rules of
Conciliation and Arbitration of the International Chamber of Commerce in Paris, to
g which I will refer generally as 'the ICC rules'.

The facts
   The arbitration arises out of a contract in the form of a tripartite 'Participation-
Agreement' concluded on 29 September 1974 between Bank Omram of Teheran,
Helleniki Techniki SA (HT) of Athens and a Danish company, Larsen & Nielsen. The
h contract concerned a joint venture for the development of certain land near Teheran.
The land was to be provided by Bank Omran, and HT and the Danish company were to
provide the necessary design and construction services for its development. The contract
stated that it was to be governed by the laws of Iran and contained an arbitration clause
of which the following terms are material:

j   'Any dispute arising between the parties hereto in any way related to or connected
   with the interpretation or implementation of this agreement shall be finally settled
   by arbitration, by an arbitral Tribunal composed of 3 arbitrators, in accordance with
   the Rules of Conciliation and Arbitration of The International Chamber of
   Commerce, Paris ... The venue shall be the City of London, and the arbitration
   proceedings shall be conducted in the English language.'

None of the parties carried on business in England or had any other connection with this country. Subsequently HT took over all rights and liabilities of the Danish company, which disappears from the scene for present purposes. In June 1979 Bank Omran was merged, together with other banks, into Bank Mellat, which took over all the rights and liabilities of Bank Omran under the contract. Bank Mellat is registered here under Pt X of the Companies Act 1948 and holds a full licence under the Banking Act 1979 to carry on banking business in this country, but its place of incorporation is Iran.

By 1980 serious disputes had arisen between Bank Mellat and HT under the contract. On 26 July 1980 HT served a notice of default and commenced the present arbitration proceedings against Bank Mellat by a request addressed to the ICC dated 20 November 1980. Three arbitrators were thereupon appointed: an English barrister by HT, an Iranian lawyer by Bank Mellat and a Swedish lawyer appointed by the Swedish National Committe of the ICC. I shall have to deal with the ICC rules in some detail hereafter, but meanwhile it is convenient to refer to certain payments made by both parties to the ICC under the ICC rules at the request of the Court of Arbitration in Paris. Initially each party paid $US500 by way of an advance towards the ICC's administrative expenses. Thereafter each party paid a further sum of $US95,000 following a request from the ICC dated 28 July 1981 in the following terms:

'The deposit to cover the administrative expenses and the arbitrators' fees has been fixed at US$190,000. In accordance with the spirit of arbitration and the customs of the Court, each party is therefore requested to forward to us within 30 days one half of this sum, i.e. US$95,000 in the manner set out in the enclosed circular. (in deducting the sum of US$500 when already paid to the Court).'

The matter was then referred to the three arbitrators, who drew up the necessary terms of reference pursuant to the ICC rules on 6 October 1982 in agreement with the parties. These defined the issues in dispute. HT claims damages in the sum of $6,753,200 and reimbursement of a further sum alleged to be in excess of $1,000,000, and Bank Mellat counterclaims damages of about $30,000,000. As regards the conduct of the arbitration, the terms of reference merely recite the provisions of the contract concerning the application of the ICC rules, as set out above, and that the contract is governed by the law of Iran.

Having considered the terms of reference and the amounts in dispute, the ICC increased the deposit by a letter of 22 October 1982, requiring each of the parties to pay a further sum of $50,000 within 30 days. Since the letter also stated that 'failure to effectuate the payment in a timely manner may result in the halting of the instruction of this case', it appears that these payments have also been made, but since the increase was largely attributable to Bank Mellat's counterclaim, nothing turns on this further deposit for present purposes.

The arbitration is at present listed to commence on 5 September 1983 and the hearing is estimated to take about four weeks. Meanwhile, however, Bank Mellat issued a summons on 18 February 1983 for an order that HT should provide security for Bank Mellat's costs in a total sum of $118,850. By far the largest item of this amount is the deposit of $95,000 paid by Bank Mellat to the ICC; the remainder relate to legal fees and other costs which have so far been incurred. For present purposes it is unnecessary to consider these in detail, although some of them have also been challenged by HT on particular grounds, save to say that they appear to be reasonable, and indeed modest, since each of these items other than the deposit of $95,000 has been reduced to take account of the counterclaim. There is no cross-application by HT for security for costs in relation to the counterclaim which we understand to raise substantially the same issues as HT's claim. The grounds of the bank's application are that HT is ordinarily resident outside the jurisdiction, and also that there is reason to believe that it will be unable to pay the costs of Bank Mellat if the latter is successful in the arbitration. The submission of HT is that any order for security would be inappropriate under the ICC rules and generally in relation to an arbitration of this kind. Bingham J declined to make any

order, and Bank Mellat is now appealing against this decision. I will deal first with the
a ground that HT is resident outside the jurisdiction, the ICC rules and the problems
concerning international arbitrations generally, which appear to me to raise questions of
principle, and then at the end with the additional factor of HT's financial position.

The applicable law
It is convenient to begin by summarising the general law which provides the
b background to the issues, even though there is substantially no controversy about it
between the parties. Before the Arbitration Act 1934 the power to order security for costs
in favour of a defendant (or a plaintiff as defendant to a counterclaim) only existed in
relation to actions in the courts, but since 1934 this power has been extended to
arbitrations, as explained below. Although always discretionary, such orders have been
the norm if a defendant to an action is resident here and the plaintiff is a non-resident
c with no assets within the jurisdiction. The reason, obviously, is that in the event of the
English defendant winning the action and being awarded his costs, he should not be
exposed to the difficulties, expense and delay of seeking to enforce the order for costs
against the plaintiff somewhere abroad. The fact that the grant or refusal of an order for
security for costs against non-resident plaintiffs is discretionary has been made explicit
by a change in the wording of the present RSC Ord 23 in comparison with the former
d Ord 65. Order 23, r 1(1) provides expressly that the court may make an order for security
for costs against, inter alios, plaintiffs who are ordinarily resident outside the jurisdiction
'if, having regard to all the circumstances of the case, the Court thinks it just to do so'.
But the recent decisions do not suggest that there has been any change in the normal
practice of making such orders in favour of English defendants against foreign plaintiffs
who are outside the jurisdiction and have no assets in this country.
e This is the position in relation to actions in the courts. However, the problem in the
present case (if one has regard to the position of the original contracting party, Bank
Omram, which had no connection with, or assets in, this country) is unlikely to arise in
litigation. Defendants in this position are unlikely to be sued here in practice, even
though leave to serve them out of the jurisdiction may be given pursuant to RSC Ord 11.
However, such situations frequently arise in relation to arbitrations, since foreign parties
f frequently contract on the basis that any disputes arising out of their contracts should be
resolved by arbitration in this country, as in the present case. Such agreements may take
different forms, to which I turn in a moment. First, it is necessary to summarise the
position concerning the procedural law applicable to arbitrations held in this country.
The fundamental principle in this connection is that under our rules of private
international law, in the absence of any contractual provision to the contrary, the
g procedural (or curial) law governing arbitrations is that of the forum of the arbitration,
whether this be England, Scotland or some foreign country, since this is the system of
law with which the agreement to arbitrate in the particular forum will have its closest
connections: see *James Miller & Partners Ltd v Whitworth Street Estates (Manchester) Ltd*
[1970] 1 All ER 796, [1970] AC 583. Despite suggestions to the contrary by some learned
writers under other systems, our jurisprudence does not recognise the concept of arbitral
h procedures floating in the transnational firmament, unconnected with any municipal
system of law: see, eg, F A Mann 'Lex Facit Arbitrum' (Liber Amicorum for M Domke
(Sanders ed) Martinus Nijhoff, The Hague, 1967) pp 167ff. A particular feature of English
law, however, is the relationship between the courts and arbitrations, which is well
known to be considerably closer than in most civil law jurisdictions, as well as in the
United States. This involves a measure of control or supervision by the courts over
j arbitrations, as well as various means whereby the courts assist references to arbitration
and the conduct of arbitrations. Thus, our courts exercise a measure of control over the
awards of arbitrators on questions of law, although this aspect has been deliberately and
significantly curtailed by the Arbitration Act 1979 and we are not concerned with it here.
The relevant aspect of the relationship between the courts and arbitral tribunals,
proceeding on parallel lines, is that the courts are empowered by statute to lend their

assistance to arbitrations in different ways. For present purposes the relevant powers are
those listed in s 12(6) of the Arbitration Act 1950. This provides that in respect of certain
matters, as referred to below—   *a*

> 'The High Court shall have, for the purpose of and in relation to a reference [to
> arbitration], the same power of making orders . . . as it has for the purpose of and in
> relation to an action or matter in the High Court: Provided that nothing in this
> subsection shall be taken to prejudice any power which may be vested in an
> arbitrator or umpire of making orders with respect to any of the matters aforesaid.'   *b*

For present purposes the only such relevant power is in para (a), which simply contains
the words 'security for costs', re-enacting a provision of the Arbitration Act 1934.
However, the other powers in this connection should also briefly be noted. Paragraph
(*f*) of sub-s (6) relates to 'securing the amount in dispute in the reference', and para (*h*)
provides for 'interim injunctions or the appointment of a receiver'; indeed it is now
settled law that Mareva injunctions may issue in aid of arbitrations. The other powers, in *c*
summary form, concern orders for discovery of documents and interrogatories, the
giving of evidence by affidavit, the examination of witnesses in England or before an
examiner abroad, and the preservation or sale of any goods, or the detention, preservation
or inspection of any property, and other measures concerning the subject matter of the
dispute.

Most of the reported cases on the exercise of these powers by the courts have arisen, as *d*
here, in connection with applications for security for costs. However, before dealing with
the main situations which fall to be considered in this regard, it is convenient to state or
restate certain general propositions in the context of s 12(6) of the 1950 Act.

First, as already mentioned, by agreeing to arbitrate in England the parties will, in the
absence of any express or implied agreement to the contrary, be deemed to have subjected
themselves to the English rules of procedure as those of the forum which they have   *e*
selected, including the jurisdictions conferred on the English courts by s 12(6). Second,
while some of the powers mentioned in s 12(6) can clearly only be exercised by the
courts, such as the summoning of witnesses or the grant of injunctions, others may also
be conferred on the arbitral tribunal by agreement between the parties. These include
the power to make orders for security for costs: see Mustill and Boyd *Commercial*   *f*
Arbitration (1982) p 296. Third, however, and of overriding importance, it must be borne
in mind that all the powers of the courts under s 12(6) are wholly discretionary, and that
their grant or refusal will take account of the applicable contractual provisions and of the
requirements of justice in the circumstances of each particular case. Thus, although the
parties to an English arbitration cannot exclude the statutory jurisdiction of the court,
they may agree in advance that neither will apply for an order for security for costs
against the other. In such cases no security will be ordered, because it would clearly be   *g*
unjust to do so: see *Mavani v Ralli Bros Ltd* [1973] 1 All ER 555, [1973] 1 WLR 468. For
present purposes it is unnecessary to go further by considering whether the same
conclusion would necessarily also apply to other powers of the court under s 12(6), for
instance to make orders for discovery when the parties have agreed to a procedure which
does not provide for this, if the court is nevertheless convinced that such orders have
become necessary to do justice between the parties. All that needs to be said in this   *h*
connection for present purposes is that the decision whether or not to make one of the
various discretionary orders will always take account of the terms of the parties' contract,
since the basis of arbitration rests on consensus.

The exercise of the discretion concerning orders for security for costs
    Leaving aside cases of express or clearly implied agreement between the parties that   *j*
neither should apply for security, the grant or refusal of an order for security in
international arbitrations must depend on all the circumstances of each case. However,
particular regard would, I think, be given to the degree of connection which the parties
or the arbitration have with this country and its legal system. Thus, if the respondent is

English and the claimant is foreign, and there is no agreement that any particular rules
a are to apply, then an order for security is likely to be the norm, in the same way as in
actions: cf. *Hudson Strumpffabrik GmbH v Bentley Engineering Co Ltd* [1962] 3 All ER 460,
[1962] 2 QB 587. On the other hand, if the parties have agreed that a particular set of
rules is to apply, then the choice of rules may well be relevant in deciding how the court's
discretion is to be exercised. Thus, an agreement to arbitrate here under some English
arbitral rules, such as those of an English trade association, or under the terms of an
b English standard form of contract, with the consequence that the substantive law will
also be English, may well carry weight in favour of the exercise of the discretion, even if
both parties are foreign and the contract has no other connection with this country. This
was the position in *Mavani v Ralli Bros Ltd*. Per contra, if foreign parties have agreed to
arbitrate in this country under some foreign or international set of rules, such as those of
the ICC, the case for the exercise of a purely English discretionary jurisdiction must
c inevitably be weakened.

All such situations involve questions of degree, depending on the circumstances of
each case, which will be relevant to the exercise of the discretion. The particular
combination of circumstances in the present case is that the contract provided that the
arbitration should take place in the City of London, albeit that the substantive law was to
be foreign, that the original contracting parties and the subject matter of the contract
d had no connection with this country, and that the arbitration was to be conducted under
the ICC rules. It is the latter factor, the parties' agreement to subject themselves to the
ICC rules, which is in my view ultimately the most important one in considering the
exercise of the court's discretion in this combination of circumstances, and I therefore
now turn to these rules.

e *The ICC rules*

Counsel for HT submitted that the ICC rules are an exhaustive code covering every
aspect of arbitrations conducted under their terms, and that, on their true construction,
the rules expressly or by necessary implication exclude all applications to the local courts
other than 'for interim or conservatory measures', as explained below. For the reasons
discussed later I cannot accept these submissions, and I do not think that they were
f accepted by the judge. A less extreme submission, however, which was, I think, accepted
by the judge, is that the rules provide a code which is intended to be self-sufficient, in the
sense that it is capable of covering all aspects of arbitrations conducted under the rules,
without the need for any recourse to any municipal system of law or any application to
the courts of the forum. On this basis counsel for HT submitted that the scheme of the
rules, broadly speaking, is inconsistent with the application for security for costs made
g by Bank Mellat against HT in the present case and with the exercise of the court's
discretion in favour of the order which is sought. It is this submission which in my view
requires careful examination.

I think that it is true that the rules provide a code which is intended to be self-sufficient
in the sense explained above. The detailed provisions of the rules are designed to cover
every step in an arbitration conducted under their terms, from the inception of the
h arbitration to the issue of a final award which is designed to be enforceable against the
unsuccessful party. If one traces these steps through the rules, they proceed (though not
always in numerical order) from the original request for arbitration and the answer to
the request to the appointment of the tribunal, then to the pleadings, including
counterclaims, then to the conduct of the proceedings and the procedural rules to be
applied, and finally to all aspects of the award. They also deal with the costs of the
j arbitration in two distinct respects. First, there is that part of the costs which is payable
to the ICC. In the terminology current in relation to English arbitrations, these costs can
broadly be described as 'the costs of the award', ie those which are secured to the ICC,
and through the ICC to the arbitral tribunal and its experts, by advance deposit. Second,
there are the respective legal costs of the parties arising out of the arbitration apart from
the costs of the award. In relation to the latter there is no provision for the giving of any

security in advance, and this is clearly significant. However, it is also significant that, in the same way as under s 18 of the Arbitration Act 1950, the arbitrators are expressly *a* required by the rules to deal with these costs in their final award; and I return to this aspect later.

This is the general picture. However, in order to analyse the scheme of the rules in the context of the courts' discretion to make orders for security for costs pursuant to s 12(6)(a) of the 1950 Act, it is necessary to set out a number of their provisions and to discuss these in some detail. Article 8 provides: *b*

'*Effect of the agreement to arbitrate.* 1 Where the parties have agreed to submit to arbitration by the International Chamber of Commerce, they shall be deemed thereby to have submitted ipso facto to the present Rules. [This requires no further comment.]...

5 Before the file is transmitted to the arbitrator, and in exceptional circumstances even thereafter, the parties shall be at liberty to apply to any competent judicial *c* authority for interim or conservatory measures, and they shall not by so doing be held to infringe the agreement to arbitrate or to affect the relevant powers reserved to the arbitrator. Any such application and any measures taken by the judicial authority must be notified without delay to the Secretariat of the Court of Arbitration. The Secretariat shall inform the arbitrator thereof.'

d
This is the provision on which counsel for HT mainly relies for the submission that the present application for security for costs is excluded under the ICC rules, either expressly or by necessary implication. He submits that an application for security for costs is not one 'for interim or conservatory measures'. Alternatively, if such an application is covered by these words, then he submits that there were no 'exceptional circumstances' in the present case which justified such an application as late as February *e* 1983, since the file had been transmitted to the tribunal many months previously and the terms of reference had been settled and agreed in October 1982. As regards the financial position of HT, to which I refer later in this judgment, he submitted in this connection, and the judge rightly accepted, that there had been no relevant change, and therefore no exceptional circumstances, to justify the lateness of the application.

Counsel for Bank Mellat was inclined to agree that an application for security for costs *f* is not one 'for interim or conservatory measures'. Similar words appear in ss 25 and 27 of the Civil Jurisdiction and Judgments Act 1982, and in particular in art 24 of the EEC convention on jurisdiction and the enforcement of judgments in civil and commercial matters which is scheduled to it. I share both parties' doubts whether the peculiarly English procedure of providing for security for costs is intended to be covered by these words, which stem from the context of other systems of law. However, I find it *g* unnecessary to express any concluded view on this point, since I agree with the submission of counsel for Bank Mellat that art 8(5) of the ICC rules cannot in any event be construed as excluding such applications by necessary implication; and it clearly does not exclude any such application expressly. Thus, depending on the law of the forum, there are no doubt various kinds of application, which may be made by one of the parties to the courts of the forum in connection with an arbitration, which would go beyond *h* applications for 'interim or conservatory measures'. In England, for instance, applications may be made to remove an arbitrator for misconduct by virtue of s 23 of the 1950 Act, and similar, though perhaps less far-reaching, powers of intervention no doubt exist in other systems. These can hardly have been intended to be excluded by art 8(5) as a matter of necessary implication.

Nevertheless, since art 8(5) is the only provision in the rules which expressly refers to *j* applications to the courts of the forum, and since the present application does not fall within its scope for one or other of the reasons put forward by counsel for HT, it seems to me that this provision must on balance weigh against the exercise of the court's discretion in the present case.

There then follows art 9 of the rules, the first of the provisions dealing with costs, which is in the following terms:

'*Deposit to cover costs of arbitration.* 1 The Court [ie the ICC Court of Arbitration] shall fix the amount of the deposit in a sum likely to cover the costs of arbitration of the claims which have been referred to it. Where, apart from the principal claim, one or more counterclaims are submitted, the Court may fix separate deposits for the principal claim and the counter-claim or counter-claims.

2 As a general rule, the deposits shall be paid in equal shares by the Claimant or Claimants and the Defendant or Defendants. However, any one party shall be free to pay the whole deposit in respect of the claim or the counter-claim should the other party fail to pay a share.

3 The Secretariat may make the transmission of the file to the arbitrator conditional upon the payment by the parties or one of them of the whole or part of the deposit to the International Chamber of Commerce.

4 ... The Terms of Reference shall only become operative and the arbitrator shall only proceed in respect of those claims for which the deposit has been duly paid to the International Chamber of Commerce.'

These provisions of course only deal with those aspects of the costs to which I have referred compendiously as the costs of the award. They do not deal with the ordinary legal costs of the parties. Nevertheless, I think that these provisions weigh against the exercise of the court's discretion to make an order for security for costs for at least two reasons.

First, art 9 envisages that the costs of the award will in the first place be borne equally between the parties, even though (as appears later on in the rules) the ultimate award of costs in favour of one of the parties should include the amount deposited by it. In the present case, however, the main item claimed by Bank Mellat by way of advance security is the deposit of $US95,000 which it has paid to the ICC pursuant to art 9. This, as it seems to me, is clearly inconsistent with the even-handed scheme which the rules envisage in this regard. An order for security for costs against HT would have the effect of compelling it to make a double deposit of this sum: first to the ICC and second by way of security in favour of the bank.

Second, though perhaps of lesser significance, there is the fact that art 9 makes provision for the giving of security in advance in relation to one part of the costs, albeit only the costs of the award, in favour of the ICC and the arbitral tribunal. It makes no provision for any security in favour of either of the parties. This express provision for a prepayment of part of the costs of the arbitration by way of security appears to me to militate against any intention, in the scheme of the rules, for the provision of security in relation to any party's own legal costs, even though these may ultimately turn out to be considerably greater.

The next relevant provision is art 11:

'*Rules governing the proceedings.* The rules governing the proceedings before the arbitrator shall be those resulting from these Rules and, where these Rules are silent, any rules which the parties (or, failing them, the arbitrator) may settle, and whether or not reference is thereby made to any municipal procedural law to be applied to the arbitration.'

Since this provision refers expressly to the possibility of the proceedings being governed by some municipal system of law, and primarily no doubt that of the forum, and since English law, the lex fori in the present case, provides for application to the court under s 12(6) of the 1950 Act, it appears to me that for present purposes this provision is neutral in its effect. It is also neutral because, in the present case, the arbitrators and parties have not gone further in the terms of reference than to recite the relevant provision of the contract as already set out, which in its turn merely takes one back to the ICC rules. However, I think that art 11 is of some significance in showing that the rules were intended to be, if not exhaustive, at any rate self-sufficient in the sense indicated above, viz in the same sense that they do not envisage the necessity for any recourse to any municipal system of law, or to the courts of the forum, in order to enable all aspects of an arbitration conducted under the ICC rules to be dealt with under the terms of the rules themselves.

Article 12, headed 'Place of arbitration', provides that the place of arbitration 'shall be fixed by the Court, unless agreed upon by the parties'. The only comment which I would make on this is that, where England has been selected by the parties as the contractual forum in advance, as in the present case, there would no doubt be a substantially stronger case for exercising the statutory discretion to make an order for security for costs than if this selection had been made subsequently by the ICC.

Next, art 20 deals with costs generally and is of considerable importance:

'*Decision as to costs of arbitration.* 1   The arbitrator's award shall, in addition to dealing with the merits of the case, fix the costs of the arbitration and decide which of the parties shall bear the costs or in what proportions the costs shall be borne by the parties.

2   The costs of the arbitration shall include the arbitrator's fees and the administrative costs fixed by the Court in accordance with the scale annexed to the present Rules, the expenses, if any, of the arbitrator, the fees and expenses of any experts, and the normal legal costs incurred by the parties . . .'

Appendix III to the rules contains a schedule of costs, but it is unnecessary to refer to it further for present purposes. The importance of art 20 is, as already mentioned, that it expressly requires the arbitral tribunal to deal with both aspects of the costs of the arbitration in its awards, viz the costs to which I have referred as the costs of the award, which will have been secured by way of deposit to the ICC, as well as with the parties' other legal costs.

Lastly, it is perhaps appropriate to quote art 26, the final provision:

'*General rule.* In all matters not expressly provided for in these Rules, the Court of Arbitration and the arbitrator shall act in the spirit of these Rules and shall make every effort to make sure that the award is enforceable at law.'

The significance of arts 20 and 26 for present purposes, in addition to the matters already mentioned when art 20 is read in the context of art 9, is that these provisions require all costs to be dealt with by the arbitral tribunal in their award, and that they expressly envisage that the award should, so far as possible, be made enforceable at law in favour of the successful party. I think that this is significant, not only in the context of the ICC rules, but also in the context of international arbitrations generally, where questions of enforcement are always a primary preoccupation of all the participants. Most of the important trading nations are now parties to the New York Convention on the Recognition and Enforcement of Foreign Arbitral Awards (10 June 1958, TS 20 (1976); Cmnd 6419), and many of those which are not remain parties to the Convention on the Execution of Foreign Arbitral Awards concluded at Geneva on 26 September 1927 (TS 28 (1930); Cmd 3655). It is to this international network of enforceability of arbitral awards that parties mainly have regard when they enter into arbitration under international contracts. I do not think that they differentiate in this respect between the enforceability of the substantive award and of the award as to costs. The parties hope that, if an arbitration should ensue, they will be successful, and that the ultimate award, dealing both with the claim or counterclaim and the legal costs, will prove to be enforceable. However, I do not think that they envisage any advance provision being made by way of security, whether for or against them, in relation to any of the matters to be dealt with in the award, unless they agree to arbitrate under rules which make express provision in this regard or possibly under rules governed by some municipal system of law which expressly provides for such security.

In this connection there is the additional factor that the power of the English courts under s 12(6)(*a*) of the 1950 Act is a somewhat exceptional procedure in comparison with most systems of law. There was evidence on the present appeal that no similar power exists either in Iran or in Greece, and also indirect evidence that in the experience of a a well-known Swiss international lawyer 'such a security is not given by the court in any western European jurisdiction or in the United States'. Counsel for Bank Mellat understandably challenged this statement as being too generalised to constitute any reliable evidence. It may well be too wide, particularly in relation to other common law jurisdictions. However, I do not think that there can be any doubt that, broadly speaking, the power of our courts under s 12(6)(a) of the 1950 Act is exceptional on the international arbitral scene.

b

Conclusion in principle

As it seems to me, the English courts should be slow in applying the jurisdiction to order security for costs in international arbitration unless, in the particular circumstances of each case, there is some more specific connection with this country, as discussed earlier in this judgment, than the mere fact that the parties have agreed that any arbitration is c to take place in England. In the present case we are concerned with such an arbitration under the ICC rules. The judge's conclusion in this connection is mainly contained in the following passages of his judgment;

> 'But what is quite clear is that the detailed provisions of the rules with respect to the giving of deposits, the payment of costs and the question of applications to local courts contain no express permission for the parties to make such application and d probably by implication envisage that applications of that kind will not be made.'

This language may not be very precise, but I am wholly in agreement with the thought which underlies it. As I see it, the application for security for costs in the present case is one which is inconsistent with the scheme and spirit of the ICC rules, not literally inconsistent, either expressly or even by necessary implication, but sufficiently e inconsistent, for the reasons explained above, to make it inappropriate in principle for the court to exercise its statutory discretion in favour of the order sought in this case.

The financial position of HT

The final question which remains is whether the evidence as to HT's financial position should affect the foregoing conclusion. Bank Mellat alleges, as one of its grounds for the f application, that there is reason to believe that HT will be unable to pay the bank's costs if the bank is successful in its defence of the arbitration. By virtue of s 447 of the Companies Act 1948 this is a ground for ordering an English limited company to give security for costs. The court's jurisdiction under this section is discretionary, in the same way as under RSC Ord 23, and its exercise will depend on all the circumstances of the particular case: see *Sir Lindsay Parkinson & Co Ltd v Triplan Ltd* [1973] 2 All ER 273, g [1973] QB 609. However, since the bank is a foreign company, it is common ground that it cannot rely on this provision directly but only by way of analogy. In effect the bank's reliance on this ground can only constitute a makeweight to the exercise of the court's discretionary power which is derived from HT being resident outside the jurisdiction.

The evidence before Bingham J indicated that HT appeared to be in a parlous financial h position and that it might well be insolvent. He considered that this evidence was relevant to the exercise of the discretion, but he nevertheless declined to make the order. On this appeal a good deal of further evidence was adduced on behalf of HT by way of riposte and admitted by consent. This strongly denies that HT is insolvent and shows that it is engaged on a number of important contracts in the Middle East. It also claims that part of HT's past financial difficulties were due to the bank's alleged repudiation of j the present contract. On the other hand, the evidence before the judge also indicated that, in effect, HT may be in the hands of the National Bank of Greece, to which it is heavily indebted, and this picture has not been changed by the evidence admitted on appeal to this court.

I agree with the judge that in considering whether or not to make an order for security for costs, in circumstances where, as here, the court has jurisdiction to do so, it is relevant to take account of the financial position of the party against whom the order is sought. But I equally agree with him that in the present case this is not a sufficient factor to outweigh the considerations which led him to the conclusion that no such order should be made. Indeed, I would go further. Since I consider that in an arbitration under the ICC rules, which has no connection with this country other than that it had been agreed between foreign parties that any such arbitration was to take place here, it would be inappropriate in principle to make an order for security for costs on the ground that the claimant is ordinarily resident abroad, I would also regard it as wrong in principle to make any such order on the ground that the claimant may be unable to pay the other party's costs if the award requires him to do so.

For all these reasons I would dismiss this appeal.

ROBERT GOFF LJ. In this case the appellant, Bank Mellat, is appealing against a decision of Bingham J by which, in the exercise of his discretion, he refused to make an order under s 12(6)(a) of the Arbitration Act 1950 that the respondent, Helleniki Techniki SA (HT), furnish security for costs in an arbitration pending between the parties in London. The application for security was made on two grounds: (1) that HT, which is the claimant in the arbitration, is a company resident outside the jurisdiction (in Greece) and has no assets within the jurisdiction, and (2) that there is reason to believe that HT, whose solvency is said to be in question, will be unable to pay the bank's costs if it is successful in its defence in the arbitration.

The background of the matter has been set out in detail in the judgment of Kerr LJ, and I am therefore relieved of the burden of setting it out myself. As regards the applicable principles, there is a considerable amount of common ground between the parties. First, the curial law of the arbitration is English: see *James Miller & Partners Ltd v Whitworth Street Estates (Manchester) Ltd* [1970] 1 All ER 796, [1970] AC 583. Second, the court has, by virtue of s 12(6)(a) of the 1950 Act, the same power to make an order in respect of security for costs in the arbitration as it has for the purpose of and in relation to an action or matter in the High Court. Third, having regard to the provisions of RSC Ord 23, r 1 and to *Sir Lindsay Parkinson & Co Ltd v Triplan Ltd* [1973] 2 All ER 273, [1973] QB 609, the power to make an order for security for costs is discretionary. Fourth, the court's discretion to exercise that power cannot (having regard to the provisions of s 12 of the 1950 Act) be ousted by agreement; but any agreement between the parties not to apply for security for costs will be a matter which can properly be taken into account by the court in exercising its discretion whether to make an order for security, and indeed will constitute a powerful argument against the making of any such order since in such circumstances it may be unjust to do so: see *Mavani v Ralli Bros Ltd* [1973] 1 All ER 555, [1973] 1 WLR 468.

Before the judge, the bank's application for security was based, as I have stated, on two very common grounds, the first being founded on r 1(1)(a) of Ord 23, and the second on s 447 of the Companies Act 1948, not directly, because HT is not an English company, but by analogy. I shall refer later in this judgment to the evidence relating to the alleged insolvency of HT. The submission of HT was that, since the parties had by their contract agreed to arbitration in accordance with the Rules of Conciliation and Arbitration of the International Chamber of Commerce (the ICC rules) they had thereby agreed, expressly or impliedly, that there should be no order for security for costs. The express agreement was said to be derived from art 8(5) of the ICC rules, and the implied agreement from the ICC rules as a whole, though primarily from art 9 and also, I understand, from art 20. The judge accepted the latter submission. He said:

'... what is quite clear is that the detailed provisions of the rules with respect to the giving of deposits, the payment of costs and the question of applications to local courts contain no express permission for the parties to make such application and probably by implication envisage that applications of that kind will not be made. That being so, there seems to me to be in such a case very great force in the

submission made by [counsel for HT], both in reliance on the express terms of the
rules and of the implications to be drawn from them, that the court should be very
slow to exercise its discretion in favour of making an order for security ... The
question is, I think, one of balancing the argument based by [HT] on the language
of the rules against the grounds advanced by [counsel for the bank] both on the
grounds of foreign residence and insolvency, but I find that on weighing these
matters up as best I can the balance comes down in favour of what I take to have
been the intention of the parties as expressed in their express subjection to or choice
of the rules of the ICC. Accordingly, and despite the arguments advanced by
[counsel for the bank], I think that the proper course in this case is not to make the
order for security which is sought.'

In his argument before this court, counsel for HT (in my judgment rightly) abandoned
the argument that the parties had, by virtue of art 8(5) of the ICC rules, expressly agreed
that no order should be made. He however maintained his submission that it was
implicit in the ICC rules that no such order should be made; alternatively, as he put it
before this court, it was inconsistent with the rules that any such order should be made.
His argument ran as follows. The ICC rules provide a complete code of conduct for the
arbitration. In the ICC rules, there is to be found in art 9 provision for a deposit in a sum
likely to cover the costs of the arbitration, and for a separate deposit where there is a
counterclaim, such deposit to be paid as a general rule by both parties in equal shares.
From para 2 of App III to the ICC rules it appears that the costs of the arbitration in this
context comprise what may broadly be called the costs of the award, viz the arbitrator's
fees, administrative expenses, the arbitrator's personal expenses and costs of 'expertise' (ie
costs of experts appointed by the arbitrators). Furthermore, although by art 20 the
arbitrators' award shall fix the costs of the arbitration (which in this context includes not
only the matters in respect of which the deposit has been made but also the normal legal
costs incurred by the parties) and decide which of the parties shall bear such costs, and in
what proportion, nevertheless there is no provision in the rules for ordering either party
to furnish security for the other party's costs. It is therefore, submitted counsel for HT, a
clear implication that neither party's costs are to be secured.

In support of this submission, counsel for HT also relied on art 8(5) of the ICC rules,
which provides:

'Before the file is transmitted to the arbitrator, and in exceptional circumstances
even thereafter, the parties shall be at liberty to apply to any competent judicial
authority for interim or conservatory measures, and they shall not by so doing be
held to infringe the agreement to arbitrate or to affect the relevant powers reserved
to the arbitrator ...'

It was on this provision that counsel for HT had founded his argument before the
judge that the parties had expressly agreed that neither should make an application for
security for costs. The argument had been to the effect that (1) an application for security
for costs was an application for an interim measure, (2) such an application was only
authorised under art 8(5) before the file had been transmitted to the arbitrator, or in
exceptional circumstances thereafter, (3) HT's application was made after the file had
been transmitted to the arbitrator and there were no exceptional circumstances justifying
the application, therefore (4) the application was contrary to the provisions of art 8(5).
This argument was abandoned, it being accepted that an application for security for costs
was not an application for an interim measure within the meaning of those words in art
8(5). Nevertheless, submitted counsel for HT, art 8(5) at least indicated the circumstances
in which an application to the court was contemplated by the rules; and these did not
include an application for security for costs.

Unlike the judge, I find myself unable to accept this submission. It is of course true
that the ICC rules, while providing for deposits to be made in equal shares covering the
costs of the award, are silent on the question of either party providing security for the

other party's legal costs. I cannot infer from that, or indeed from the ICC rules as a whole, any implicit agreement that neither party should be free to take advantage of any provision of the curial law of the arbitration under which security for costs may be applied for. In truth, the silence of the ICC rules on that matter in all probability reflects no more than that the experience of those who drew up the rules was of systems of law under which security of that kind is not ordered. The fact that the ICC rules provide for deposits to cover the costs of the award reflects only the intention that those persons for whom the ICC is responsible shall have their remuneration and expenses secured; and, since the outcome of the arbitration is unknown, it is obviously sensible and just that such deposits should in general be furnished by both parties in equal shares. But the fact that security in the form of deposits for costs of that kind is required by the rules is, in my judgment, in no way inconsistent with either party taking advantage of a provision of the curial law under which security for a party's legal costs may be ordered. Indeed, the readiness of the ICC, as envisaged in its own rules, to extract from the parties security (in the onerous form of a deposit) for their own costs, can arguably be regarded as entirely consistent with a party taking advantage of an opportunity available to him under the curial law to obtain, where appropriate, an order for security for his own legal costs. I was equally unimpressed by a submission by counsel for HT that an award for security of costs embracing the bank's deposit to the ICC was inconsistent with the 'even-handed' approach to such deposits demonstrated in the ICC rules. Obviously, the rules are 'even-handed' in relation to such deposits: it is only right that security given by the parties to the ICC for the costs of the award should prima facie be borne by them in equal shares. But I can see no inconsistency between that requirement and the possibility that, if under the curial law one party is ordered to provide security for the other's legal costs (which obviously, in relation to those different costs, may very well not be an 'evenhanded' order), such security should include security for the other party's deposit with the ICC. There is of course no question of the party who furnishes such security having to duplicate his security: he simply makes his own deposit to the ICC, and secures the other party's costs including the amount of that party's deposit. Nor can I see any force in the argument founded on art 8(5). The mere fact that reference is made in that article to a particular form of application to the court (which is in fact a form of application well known under continental systems of law) cannot impliedly exclude other forms of application available under the curial law; indeed, if that argument were right, it could likewise be argued that an application under s 12(6)(b) of the 1950 Act for an order for discovery of documents should be inhibited by reason of the implied agreement of the parties not to make any such application.

I do not consider that the argument can be made any more persuasive by advancing it not on the basis of an implication, but on the basis of 'inconsistency with the rules'. Indeed there is a certain imprecision in this submission which demands that the submission itself should be analysed and defined. As I see it, the submission can only mean one of two things. It can mean first that an application for security for costs is inconsistent with the rules in the sense that it would be inconsistent with the agreement of the parties, as contained in the rules as incorporated in their contract, to make any such application; but that is no more than saying that the parties have, by incorporating the rules in their contract, expressly or impliedly agreed not to make any such application, which is precisely the same as the argument which I have already considered and rejected. Alternatively, it can mean that the rules, being silent on the matter, do not envisage any such application being made. That however cannot of itself inhibit any application for security for costs. As I have already indicated, the reason for this silence is in all likelihood to be found in the simple historical fact that those who framed the ICC rules were familiar only with systems of law under which such security is not ordered. At the most, this silence in the ICC rules may be regarded as a factor (though, in my judgment, taken by itself a very minor factor) to be taken into account when the court considers whether to exercise its discretion to make an order for security for costs. It is important however that the court should not be tempted to elide the two separate meanings which may be

attributed to this submission, with the effect that the one derives, illegitimately, colour
from the other. Either the parties have, by incorporating the ICC rules in their contract,
expressly or impliedly agreed not to apply for security for costs or they have not. In my
judgment, plainly they have not.

It follows that, in my view, the judge erred in the exercise of his discretion, since he
proceeded on the basis of a construction of the ICC rules, as incorporated in the contract
between the parties, which I am unable to accept. I therefore proceed to consider how, in
my judgment, the discretion should be exercised. I shall consider first the application for
security on the basis that HT (the claimant in the arbitration) is resident outside the
jurisdiction and has no assets within the jurisdiction.

Now I wish to say at once that I do not consider it right that nowadays a court, in
considering such an application, should always approach the matter in the same way as it
approaches an application by a defendant in an action in the High Court. Historically,
the basis of an application by such a defendant has been that, if he were not provided
with security for his costs by a plaintiff resident outside the jurisdiction who had no assets
here, he might if successful in his defence be unable to recover his costs from the
plaintiff; the order for security for costs is intended to prevent the occurrence of any such
injustice, and so put him in at least as strong a position in that respect as if he had been
sued by a party who was resident within the jurisdiction. But it by no means follows that
the same practice should invariably be followed in international arbitrations which,
because held in England, are subject to English law as the curial law. I appreciate that, in
the case of many arbitrations held in this country, the practice is at present to award
security for costs; but these are in general commercial arbitrations of a type which are
regularly held in London under standard English forms of contract generally governed
by English law, and so have a very close connection with the English jurisdiction. Since
the 1939–45 war, however, we have seen the development of a different type of
commercial arbitration. A typical example is an arbitration arising out of a substantial
construction or civil engineering contract, under which the contractor undertakes to
carry out works in a foreign country. Such contracts commonly contain an arbitration
clause providing for arbitration in a neutral forum (ie in a country other than the country
of either contracting party), and for a neutral arbitrator or chairman of the arbitral
tribunal. Such contracts may incorporate arbitration rules of a body such as the ICC to
govern the conduct of the arbitration. If the contract is silent on the forum, that body
may itself select a neutral forum where the arbitration will be held.

Side by side with the growth of this type of international arbitration, there have been
developments in the provisions made for enforceability of awards in international
arbitrations. Before the war, there was the Geneva convention of 1927. Now there is the
New York convention of 1958. The latter convention provides, in art III, that each
contracting state shall recognise arbitral awards as binding and enforce them in
accordance with the rules of procedure of the territory where the award is relied on,
under the conditions laid down in the convention. Many important states are now parties
to the New York convention; and in this country the Arbitration Act 1975 was enacted
to give effect to the convention, to which this country is a party. Parties to international
arbitrations must nowadays frequently rely on the convention for the purpose of
enforcing awards; and when the award contains (as it will, for example, where the
arbitration is conducted in accordance with the ICC rules) an order for costs, the
enforcement of the award will include enforcement of an order for costs comprised in
the award.

Parties to such an arbitration may well choose London as a convenient neutral forum.
There are now excellent and rapidly developing services available in London for the
conduct of such arbitrations. The English language is frequently a language familiar to
both parties, and often too the language of the contract; for that reason, too, London may
be a suitable forum. The services of very experienced solicitors, counsel, experts and
arbitrators are readily available here. So London may be chosen as a convenient neutral
forum; or it may be nominated as such by a body such as the ICC.

The holding of such an arbitration in London appears to me to be a far cry from litigation where a foreign litigant comes to this country to sue an English resident in the English courts. Even in such litigation, the case for the exercise of the discretionary power to award security for costs is perhaps weakening, as judgments and orders become more readily enforceable overseas. But if parties simply choose to arbitrate here as a matter of convenience, in the circumstances I have described, the policy which historically underlies an order for security for costs by a foreign litigant appears to me to be, in most cases, inapplicable. It is of course true that English law will, as the curial law, apply to the conduct of the arbitration; and the parties will, by holding their arbitration here, subject themselves for that purpose to English law, which confers on them the right to invoke the discretionary power of the court to award security for costs. But it does not follow that, in such cases as I have described, it would be right for the court to exercise its discretion to award security in any particular case. It is not only that the choice of England as a forum is a mutual, not a unilateral, choice. In addition, the parties will in most cases both be resident outside the jurisdiction; England will generally have been chosen as a neutral forum on pure grounds of convenience; in some cases it may be pure accident which party is claimant and which respondent; and it may very readily be inferred in most cases that the parties will be proceeding in reliance on the ordinary procedure for enforcement of awards (including awards as to costs), often under the provisions of the New York convention. The force of these points must be even greater where it is not the parties who have selected England as a forum, but a body such as the ICC acting on the parties' behalf.

Of course, in considering whether to exercise its discretion to make an order for the provision of security for costs by a foreign claimant in an international arbitration, the court must consider all the circumstances of the particular case. But in the case of international arbitrations of the kind I have described the court should, in my judgment, as a general rule decline to make an order for security for costs against a foreign claimant unless there are special circumstances which warrant it, because the policy underlying an order for the provision of security for costs by a foreign claimant is not generally applicable in such cases.

In reaching this conclusion, I wish to state first that I should not be understood to be expressing any view about awards of security for costs in the case of ordinary commercial arbitrations of the type which have for many years been regularly held in this country, in particular arbitrations on maritime disputes and in the commodity trades. I mention in parenthesis that a comparable distinction has been drawn between different types of arbitration, for the purposes of appeals to the court, in the Arbitration Act 1979. Nor should I be understood as suggesting that there is any special barrier against parties in international arbitrations taking advantage of other provisions of English law as the curial law relating, for example, to the conduct of the arbitration (including discovery of documents) or to interim measures and orders. My observations should be understood as concerned only with the exercise of the court's discretion to award security for costs.

It follows from what I have said that, in my judgment, this being a typical international arbitration of the kind I have described, prima facie no order for security for costs should be made against HT as foreign claimant unless there are special circumstances justifying such an order. I add in parenthesis that, since Greece is a party to the New York convention, there seems to be no reason why an award in the arbitration in favour of the bank, including any award as to costs, should not be enforceable by it against HT in Greece under the provisions of that convention. I also add that, in reaching this conclusion, I do not attach any particular weight to the fact that the parties have agreed to arbitration in accordance with the ICC rules, save that that fact serves to emphasise the character of the international arbitration with which we are here concerned. A similar conclusion could well have been reached in this case if the parties had agreed to incorporate some other set of rules, or indeed no rules at all. The solution to the present problem must, I consider, lie in a realistic appreciation of the character of the relevant arbitration and the circumstances in which England comes to be chosen as the forum, *a* rather than in squeezing indications, often with great difficulty, out of rules the draftsman of which in all probability never even addressed his mind to the question of security for costs. Indeed, it is theoretically possible that there could be arbitrations under the ICC rules which are not of the character which I have described, in which it might be proper to make an award for security. But in practical terms, having regard to the character of arbitrations conducted under the ICC rules, I cannot myself conceive of any such case.

b   For the bank, however, it is submitted that there are in the present case special circumstances arising from the suspected insolvency of HT. In my judgment, if a claimant in an internatioanl arbitration held in this country is an English or foreign company as to which it appears by credible testimony that there is reason to believe that it will be unable to pay the costs of the respondent if successful in his defence, then it would be proper for the court, in an appropriate case, by virtue of s 447 of the Companies
c Act 1948 or by analogy with that section, to exercise its discretion to order the claimant to furnish security for the respondent's costs. The policy underlying an order for security in such a case is untouched by the considerations which I have mentioned, which in my judgment negative the policy of ordering security for costs on the ground only that the claimant is resident outside the jurisdiction. It follows that I am unable to accept the view expressed by the judge that the insolvency of a claimant company (if such be the
d case) is a matter to be weighed in the balance with the effect of incorporation of the ICC rules. Such matters are not, I consider, comparable. It is necessary to decide, as a matter of policy, whether in an international arbitration of the kind I have described it may be proper for the court to exercise its discretion to order an insolvent claimant company to furnish security. In my judgment, it may be proper to do so. It must however be borne in mind that the making of an order for security for costs under s 447, directly or by
e analogy, is discretionary and that security will not be ordered as a matter of course: see *Sir Lindsay Parkinson & Co Ltd v Triplan Ltd* [1973] 2 All ER 273 at 285, [1973] QB 609 at 626, where various matters which may be taken into consideration are listed by Lord Denning MR.

     I turn then to consider the evidence about the financial state of HT. The bank relied on a business report by Dun & Bradstreet which referred (on the basis of reports by
f informants) to many protested bills, payment orders and seizures, and some bankruptcy petitions, in the years 1978–82, and to information that 'due to the political situation in Iran (the construction work there has ceased) and delay in payment from the Greek Government for public works', HT has experienced severe difficulties; and further stated that HT is now under the management of the National Bank of Greece, due to debts owed to the bank reported to amount to approximately 2·5 billion drachmas. In answer
g to this evidence, HT submitted evidence before the judge (1) identifying petitions for bankruptcy which had been made, and stating that all had been settled, (2) stating that 'it is usual and standard practice for lawyers in Greece to file petitions for bankruptcy against debtors even for very small and insignificant amounts', and that 'the same procedure is also adopted for short time delays of payment which may arise from temporary cash flow difficulties', the procedure being adopted by Greek lawyers in order to exercise maximum
h pressure on debtors to settle debts immediately as a declaration of bankruptcy involves serious consequences, (3) further stating that the Dun & Bradstreet report was wrong in referring to HT as being under the management of the National Bank of Greece, though the shares of HT had been pledged to the bank; we were told, to secure a debt of 3·5 billion drachmas owed by HT to the bank. The evidence also showed HT to be involved in a number of substantial construction projects in Greece and Iraq, which were
j progressing towards completion; and stated that the net worth of HT in 1981 was about 2·25 billion drachmas, excluding the value of HT's claim against the bank. This evidence was supplemented by further evidence before this court, including financial statements relating to the affairs of HT. The overall picture to be derived from this evidence is of a substantial construction company which has indeed experienced financial difficulties, primarily in relation to its work in Iran under its contract with the bank, no doubt due

to the political difficulties in that country; but which is very much a going concern, apparently with financial support from the National Bank of Greece. This evidence, in my judgment, falls short of evidence necessary to establish the basis for an order for security for costs under s 447 of the Companies Act 1948, directly or by analogy.

In all the circumstances, therefore, I do not consider this to be an appropriate case for the court to exercise its discretion to order security for costs. For these reasons, I would dismiss the appeal.

WALLER LJ. I would dismiss this appeal for the reasons given by Kerr LJ.

Appeal dismissed. Leave to appeal to the House of Lords refused.

Solicitors: *Stephenson Harwood* (for Bank Mellat); *Denton Hall & Burgin* (for HT).

Sophie Craven   Barrister.

R v Greensmith

COURT OF APPEAL, CRIMINAL DIVISION
LAWTON LJ, CROOM-JOHNSON AND STOCKER JJ
13, 27 MAY 1983

Drugs – Controlled drugs – Unlawful possession – Cocaine – Proof that substance cocaine – Crown adducing expert evidence that substance was cocaine but not adducing evidence as to specific form of cocaine comprised in substance – Whether Crown required to prove specific form of cocaine – Whether the substance 'cocaine' including natural cocaine and other cocaine substances which can result from chemical transformation of natural cocaine – Whether proof that substance was 'cocaine' sufficient to establish offence – Misuse of Drugs Act 1971, s 5(3), Sch 2, Pt I, para 1.

On its true construction, the word 'cocaine' in para 1 of Pt I of Sch 2 to the Misuse of Drugs Act 1971 in the list of controlled drugs is a generic word which includes within its ambit both the direct extracts of the coca leaf (being the natural form of cocaine) and also any products resulting from the application of a chemical process to the natural form (which products are also set out in paras 2 to 4 of Pt I of Sch 2 as controlled drugs). It follows therefore that an indictment charging, in respect of cocaine, the offence of possession of a controlled drug with intent to supply it to another, contrary to s 5(3)[a] of the 1971 Act, need only allege, and the Crown need only prove at the trial, that the accused was in possession of 'cocaine'; the indictment need not state, nor need the Crown establish, whether the substance found in the accused's possession was cocaine in its natural form or a product resulting from the application of a chemical process to the natural form (see p 446 *f g* and p 447 *a* to *d* and *f*, post).

Notes

For controlled drugs generally, see 30 Halsbury's Laws (4th edn) paras 737, 738.

For the Misuse of Drugs Act 1971, s 5, Sch 2, see 41 Halsbury's Statutes (3rd edn) 884, 913.

Cases referred to in judgment

R v Leaman (17 May 1978, unreported), Crown Court at Maidstone.
R v Steeper (27 September 1979, unreported), Crown Court at Inner London Sessions.

---

a   Section 5(3), so far as material, provides: '. . . it is an offence for a person to have a controlled drug in his possession, whether lawfully or not, with intent to supply it to another . . .'

Case also cited

a   *DPP v Goodchild* [1978] 2 All ER 161, [1978] 1 WLR 578, HL.

Application for leave to appeal against conviction and sentence.
On 30 September 1982 in the Crown Court at Mold before his Honour Judge Morgan Hughes and a jury the appellant, Tony Greensmith, pleaded guilty to possessing a controlled drug, cannabis resin, contrary to s 5(2) of the Misuse of Drugs Act 1971 (count

b   1 of the indictment) and on 1 October 1982 was convicted of possessing a controlled drug, cocaine, with intent to supply it to another, contrary to s 5(3) of the 1971 Act (count 2). The jury was discharged from returning a verdict on a charge of possessing cocaine contrary to s 5(2) of the 1971 Act (count 3). He was sentenced to concurrent terms of one month's imprisonment on count 1 and 12 months' imprisonment on count 2. He applied to the full court for an extension of time to apply for leave to appeal against

c   his conviction and sentence. The court granted that application and went on to grant leave to appeal against conviction and sentence and then treated the hearing of the application as the hearing of the appeal. The appeal against conviction was on the ground that the trial judge had erred in rejecting the defence submission that since the Crown had failed to establish whether the controlled drug forming the subject matter of count 2 was cocaine, or a stereoisomeric form or salt thereof, the appellant ought not to have

d   been convicted. The facts are set out in the judgment of the court.

Maurice Kay for the appellant.
Elgan Edwards for the Crown.

At the conclusion of the argument the court announced that it would allow the appeal against sentence and order the appellant's immediate release, but it reserved its decision

e   on the appeal against conviction.

27 May. The following judgment of the court was delivered.

LAWTON LJ. On 30 September 1982 the appellant pleaded guilty to possessing a controlled drug (cannabis resin) and the next day he was convicted of possessing a

f   controlled drug (cocaine) with intent to supply. He was sentenced to concurrent terms of one month's imprisonment in respect of the cannabis resin and 12 months' imprisonment in respect of the cocaine.
He applied for an extension of time in which to apply for leave to appeal against his conviction and sentence. This we granted. The appeal against conviction, on one view of the case, raised a point of law in respect of which he was entitled to appeal as of right. On

g   another view it raised a question of mixed fact and law. In so far as it raised a question of mixed fact and law, we granted leave and treated the hearing of the application as the hearing of the appeal. We also granted him leave to appeal against his sentence.
The point of law turns on the construction of ss 2 and 5(3) of the Misuse of Drugs Act 1971, and Pt I of Sch 2 to that Act. More particularly, the problem is whether the word 'cocaine' when used in para 1 of that part of the schedule is used in a generic sense so as

h   to include the specific forms, derivatives or preparations of it which come within the wording of paras 2 to 5 of Pt I. If what is referred to in these paragraphs are different substances or products from 'cocaine' as that word is used in para 1, important analytical and legal consequences follow. The analysis of a substance suspected to be 'cocaine' will have to be more elaborate than it has commonly been in the past and informations and indictments will have to specify whether the controlled drug is 'cocaine' within the

j   meaning of para 1 or a form, derivative or preparation of it within one of the paras 2 to 5. We have found this problem of construction difficult, as have judges in the Crown Court who have arrived at conflicting conclusions.
On 11 February 1982 two police officers searched the appellant's house at Saltney, Clwyd, for drugs. They found a small amount of cannabis resin and a bag containing 11 silver foil wraps in each of which was a white powder. The total weight of the powder

was 9·04 g. The appellant was arrested and after caution made a written statement which
began as follows:

> 'With reference to the charlie or coke the police found at my house earlier tonight
> I bought it three weeks ago. I did not buy it in North Wales. I paid £500 for it. It is
> for my own personal use and very close friends.'

The powder was sent for analysis to Mr Michael Lewis, a forensic scientist employed at
the Home Office Forensic Science Laboratory at Chorley. Unfortunately, we have not
had before us a transcript of his evidence at the trial. Counsel have accepted, save as to
one matter, that what he said is summarised in the transcript which we have before us.
The judge set out his evidence as follows:

> 'This substance which I analysed contains 40% cocaine, was made up as to 40% of
> the volume of the substance of cocaine; I did not break down or carry out tests to
> determine, I do not consider it necessary, whether it was a particular stereoisomeric
> form of cocaine or whether it was a salt of cocaine . . . Whether it is a particular
> stereoisomeric form of cocaine or whether it is a salt, it is still cocaine in one or other
> of those forms.'

He had a shrewd idea which it was; he said:

> 'I did one test but that is not quite certain because I did not do sufficient, I have a
> fair idea, but whatever it is it still is cocaine.'

Mr Lewis also said, according to the recollection of counsel, that sometimes it is not
possible to carry out an analysis beyond the stage of discovering that the substance is
cocaine.

On this evidence counsel for the appellant submitted that his client had no case to
answer because the Crown had to prove that the cocaine in the white powder belonged
to one particular type of that substance and the evidence left open whether it was a
stereoisomeric form or a salt form. He quoted in support a short ruling of his Honour
Judge Kee in the Crown Court at Maidstone in *R v Leaman* (17 May 1978, unreported)
and a carefully reasoned ruling of his Honour Judge Rubin given in the Crown Court at
Inner London Sessions in *R v Steeper* (27 September 1979, unreported). The trial judge,
his Honour Judge Morgan Hughes, declined to follow these judgments and ruled that
the indictment was properly drawn, that there was no need for the Crown to prove that
the substance submitted to the laboratory was cocaine in either the stereoisomeric form
or a mixture form or a salt form and that in the absence of any other evidence which
might be led they had proved their case. The appellant did not give evidence. No
scientific evidence was called on his behalf. The judge directed the jury in accordance
with his ruling. They convicted the appellant.

On the evidence in this case the Crown could have said that as the forensic scientist
stuck to his assertion that the white powder contained cocaine and the appellant had
admitted in his written statement that he had been in possession of 'charlie or coke',
colloquial terms for cocaine, the jury were bound to convict. Counsel for the Crown did
not put the Crown's case in that way before us. We have decided not to deal with it on
the evidence alone. The problem of construction has got to be solved at some time. We
were told that already some forensic experts are making tests which may be unnecessary
if Judge Morgan Hughes's ruling was right.

The particulars of the offence for which the appellant was convicted were that on 11
February 1982, he 'unlawfully had in his possession 9·04g of powder containing 40%
cocaine, a class A controlled drug with intent to supply it to another'. A controlled drug
is defined by s 2(1) of the Misuse of Drugs Act 1971 as follows:

> 'In this Act—(a) the expression "controlled drug" means any substance or product
> for the time being specified in Part I, II, or III of Schedule 2 to this Act; and (b) the
> expressions "Class A drug", "Class B drug" and "Class C drug" mean any of the
> substances and products for the time being specified respectively in Part I, Part II

a
and Part III of that Schedule; and the provisions of Part IV of that Schedule shall have effect with respect to the meanings of expressions used in that Schedule.'

We attach importance to the words 'any substance or product'. The word 'substance' has a wider meaning than 'product'. Any kind of matter comes within 'substance' whereas 'product' envisages the result of some kind of process. It is an offence to have possession of a controlled drug with intent to supply to another: see s 5(3). Part I of Sch 2 to the Act is headed 'Class A Drugs' and para 1 identifies 'The following substances and
b
products' as such drugs. Amongst a long list comes 'Coca leaf' and 'Cocaine'. Part IV of this schedule, to which s 2 specifically refers for 'the meanings of expressions', contains this definition: '"coca leaf" means the leaf of any plant of the genus *Erythroxylon* from whose leaves cocaine can be extracted either directly or by chemical transformation.'

It follows that 'cocaine' can be a natural substance or a substance resulting from a chemical transformation; but both substances are cocaine. In our judgment the word
c
'cocaine' as used in para 1 is a generic word which includes within its ambit both the direct extracts of the coca leaf, the natural form, and whatever results from a chemical transformation. Paragraphs 2 to 5 of Pt I of the schedule, in our judgment, deal with the various kinds of substance which can result from chemical transformations. It is significant that in each of these paragraphs what is referred to is a chemical form 'of the substance specified'. What ss 2 and 5(3) are dealing with are 'substances or products'. This
d
case is concerned with the substance 'cocaine' which may have a number of forms but they are still cocaine.

Judge Rubin was much influenced in his construction of paras 1 to 5 by the presence of para 6 in Pt I. This provides as follows:

e
'Any preparation designed for administration by injection which includes a substance or product for the time being specified in any of paragraphs 1 to 3 of Part II of this Schedule.'

This paragraph is not dealing with the same kind of subject matter as paras 2 to 5. It is concerned to convert a class B drug into a class A one in the circumstances set out, that is to say if it is a preparation designed for administration by injection. Its juxtaposition in
f
Pt I to forms of cocaine derived by chemical transformations from the coca leaf is, in our judgment, no guide to the construction of the preceding paragraphs.

In our judgment, Judge Morgan Hughes came to the right conclusion. *R v Leaman* and *R v Steeper* should not be followed. The appeal against conviction is dismissed.

By the time the appellant's appeal against sentence came on for hearing in this court he would have served all but a few days of his sentence having regard to the remission
g
which he had earned. There seemed to be no point in ordering his return to prison so we quashed his sentence and substituted one which allowed for his immediate release.

Appeal against conviction dismissed. Appeal against sentence allowed.

The court refused leave to appeal to the House of Lords but certified, under s 33(2) of the Criminal
h
Appeal Act 1968, that the following point of law of general public importance was involved in the decision: whether, on the correct construction of Sch 2 to the Misuse of Drugs Act 1971, paras 2 to 5 of Pt I of that schedule referred to forms of the substances or products mentioned in para 1 or whether they were different substances or products which had to be specifically identified in informations and indictments and if a prosecution was to succeed had to be proved to be as they were alleged to be.
j

Solicitors: *Thomas Andrews Humphrys & Co*, Wrexham (for the appellant); *Clement Jones & Co*, Holywell (for the Crown).

Raina Levy   Barrister.

R v Wilson (Clarence)
R v Jenkins (Edward John) and another

HOUSE OF LORDS

LORD FRASER OF TULLYBELTON, LORD ELWYN-JONES, LORD EDMUND-DAVIES, LORD ROSKILL AND LORD BRIGHTMAN

13, 14, 18 JULY, 13 OCTOBER 1983

Indictment – Conviction of another offence – Inflicting grievous bodily harm – No allegation of how grievous bodily harm caused – Whether open to jury to convict of assault occasioning actual bodily harm – Offences against the Person Act 1861, ss 20, 47 – Criminal Law Act 1967, s 6(3).

Indictment – Conviction of another offence – Inflicting grievous bodily harm – Charge of burglary by having entered a building as a trespasser and inflicting grievous bodily harm – Whether open to jury to convict of assault occasioning actual bodily harm – Criminal Law Act 1967, s 6(3) – Theft Act 1968, s 9(1)(b).

In determining for the purposes of s 6(3)[a] of the Criminal Law Act 1967 whether the allegations in an indictment 'amount to or include (expressly or by implication) an allegation of another offence' the words 'amount to or include' are to be read disjunctively, so that s 6(3) envisages that the allegations in the indictment expressly amount to, or expressly include, or impliedly amount to, or impliedly include, an allegation of another offence. Accordingly an accused may be acquitted of the offence charged in the indictment but still be found guilty of the other offence in any of those four situations (see p 450 b to d, p 453 e to j and p 456 d, post).

On the true construction of s 6(3) of the 1967 Act an accused can be convicted of an offence other than that specifically charged if the allegations in the indictment are capable of including, either expressly or impliedly, an allegation of the other offence; the allegations in the particular indictment need not necessarily involve a specific allegation of the other offence, it is enough that they are capable of including such an allegation. Accordingly, where an accused is charged on indictment with inflicting grievous bodily harm contrary to s 20[b] of the Offences against the Person Act 1861 or with burglary contrary to s 9(1)(b)[c] of the Theft Act 1968 and the particulars in either case allege that the accused inflicted grievous bodily harm on a person, the accused may be found not guilty as charged but, under s 6(3) of the 1967 Act, guilty of assault occasioning actual bodily harm contrary to s 47[d] of the 1861 Act since the inflicting of grievous bodily harm will often (though not necessarily always) involve an assault and grievous bodily harm will necessarily include the less serious injuries involved in actual bodily harm (see p 450 b to d, p 454 a to d, p 455 f to h and p 456 b to d, post); R v Lillis [1972] 2 All ER 1209 approved; R v Salisbury [1976] VR 452 considered; R v Springfield (1969) 53 Cr App R 608 overruled.

A trial judge should always ensure, before deciding to leave the possibility of conviction of another offence to a jury under s 6(3) of the 1967 Act, that that course will involve no risk of injustice to the accused and that he has had the opportunity of fully meeting the alternative charge in the course of his defence (see p 450 b to d and p 456 a b d, post).

Decisions of the Court of Appeal, Criminal Division in R v Wilson (Clarence) [1983] 1 All ER 993 and R v Jenkins (Edward John) [1983] 1 All ER 100 reversed.

Notes

For the power to convict of an offence other than that charged, see 11 Halsbury's Laws (4th edn) para 311, and for cases on the subject see 14(1) Digest (Reissue) 416–422, 3522–3609.

a   Section 6(3) is set out at p 451 h j, post
b   Section 20, so far as material, is set out at p 452 a b, post
c   Section 9(1), so far as material, is set out at p 452 c, post
d   Section 47, so far as material, is set out at p 452 b c, post

a For grievous bodily harm, see 11 Halsbury's Laws (4th edn) para 1199, and for cases on the subject, see 15 Digest (Reissue) 1180–1181, 10068–10076.
   For the Offences against the Person Act 1861, ss 20, 47, see 8 Halsbury's Statutes (3rd edn) 154, 165.
   For the Criminal Law Act 1967, s 6, see ibid 557.
   For the Theft Act 1968, s 9, see ibid 788.

b **Cases referred to in opinions**
   R v Clarence (1888) 22 QBD 23, [1886–90] All ER Rep 133, CCR.
   R v Halliday (1889) 61 LT 701, [1886–90] All ER Rep 1028, CCR.
   R v Hodgson [1973] 2 All ER 552, [1973] 1 QB 565, [1973] 2 WLR 570, CA.
   R v Hollingberry (1825) 4 B & C 329, 107 ER 1081.
c R v Lillis [1972] 2 All ER 1209, [1972] 2 QB 236, [1972] 2 WLR 1409, CA.
   R v Martin (1881) 8 QBD 54, [1881–5] All ER Rep 699, CCR.
   R v O'Brien (1911) 104 LT 113, CCA.
   R v Salisbury [1976] VR 452, Vic Full Ct.
   R v Springfield (1969) 53 Cr App R 608, CA.
   R v Taylor (1869) LR 1 CCR 194.

d **Consolidated appeals**
                          R v Wilson (Clarence)
   The Crown appealed with leave of the Appeal Committee of the House of Lords granted on 17 March 1983 against the decision of the Court of Appeal, Criminal Division (Watkins LJ, Cantley and Hirst JJ) ([1983] 1 All ER 993, [1983] 1 WLR 356) on 28
e January 1983 allowing an appeal by the respondent, Clarence George Wilson, against his conviction on 4 November 1981 in the Crown Court at Kingston-upon-Thames before his Honour Judge Rubin and a jury of the offence of assault occasioning actual bodily harm on an indictment containing a single count of inflicting grievous bodily harm contrary to s 20 of the Offences against the Person Act 1861 by maliciously inflicting grievous bodily harm on a Maxim James Latham. He was sentenced to one month's
f imprisonment suspended for two years. Although the Court of Appeal refused leave to the Crown to appeal to the House of Lords it certified, under s 33(2) of the Criminal Appeal Act 1968, that a question of law of general public importance (set out at p 451 b, post) was involved in its decision. The facts are set out in the opinion of Lord Roskill.

                     R v Jenkins (Edward John) and another
g The Crown appealed with leave of the Appeal Committee of the House of Lords granted on 28 March 1983 against the decision of the Court of Appeal, Criminal Division (Purchas LJ, Talbot and Staughton JJ) ([1983] 1 All ER 1000) on 8 February 1983 allowing appeals by the respondents, Edward John Jenkins and Ronald Patrick Jenkins, against their conviction on 4 December 1981 in the Crown Court at Canterbury before Mr Recorder Michael Lewis QC and a jury of the offence of assault occasioning actual bodily harm on
h an indictment charging burglary contrary to s 9(1)(b) of the Theft Act 1968 by, having entered a building as trespassers, inflicting grievous bodily harm on a Jeffrey Brian Wilson therein. Edward John Jenkins was sentenced to 7 days' imprisonment and Ronald Patrick Jenkins was sentenced to 21 days' imprisonment. Although the Court of Appeal refused leave to the Crown to appeal to the House of Lords it certified, under s 33(2) of the Criminal Appeal Act 1968, that a question of law of general public importance (set
j out at p 451 c, post) was involved in its decision. The facts are set out in the opinion of Lord Roskill.

   The appeals were consolidated by order of the House dated 7 June 1983.

   Michael Hill QC and *Derek Zeitlin* for the Crown in the first appeal.
   Michael Hill QC and *Anthony Webb* for the Crown in the second appeal.

Anthony Scrivener QC and *David Guy* for the respondent Wilson.
David Guy and *Gregory Stone* for the respondents E J and R P Jenkins.

Their Lordships took time for consideration.

13 October. The following opinions were delivered.

LORD FRASER OF TULLYBELTON. My Lords, I have had the advantage of reading in draft the speech prepared by my noble and learned friend Lord Roskill.
For the reasons given by him I would allow both appeals and answer both certified questions in the affirmative.

LORD ELWYN-JONES. My Lords, I have had the benefit of reading in draft the speech to be delivered by my noble and learned friend Lord Roskill. I agree with it and for the reasons he gives I would allow both appeals.

LORD EDMUND-DAVIES. My Lords, I am grateful for the opportunity of reading during the long vacation the speech prepared by my noble and learned friend Lord Roskill. I am in respectful agreement with the views he has expressed and the conclusions at which he has arrived.

LORD ROSKILL. My Lords, these two consolidated appeals by the prosecution are brought by leave of your Lordships' House and necessitate the House considering the true construction of s 6(3) of the Criminal Law Act 1967 for the first time since its enactment some sixteen years ago. The Court of Appeal, Criminal Division, granted certificates in each case. Wilson, the respondent in the first appeal, was indicted at the Crown Court at Kingston-upon-Thames on a single count that he 'maliciously inflicted grievous bodily harm' on a man named Latham. Wilson was acquitted on that count but the trial judge, his Honour Judge Rubin, directed the jury that, if they were not satisfied that Latham's injuries were sufficiently serious to justify conviction, they might on that single count convict Wilson of assault occasioning actual bodily harm. The jury did so. That direction was given after the judge had heard argument. I shall refer to this case as *Wilson*.

The two respondents Edward and Ronald Jenkins were father and son. They faced a single count of burglary at the Crown Court at Canterbury before Mr Recorder Michael Lewis QC and a jury. That charge was laid under s 9(1)(b) of the Theft Act 1968, the particulars being that they had entered a building at Westgate 'as trespassers' and there 'inflicted grievous bodily harm' on a man named Wilson. If one omits the references to entering the building 'as trespassers' the particulars, apart from the omission of the word 'maliciously', were identical with those in *Wilson*. I shall refer to this case as *Jenkins*. The recorder, after lengthy legal arguments (he himself had first raised the question), gave the same direction to the jury as had been given in *Wilson* regarding the possibility, in the event of acquittal on the burglary count, of convicting these respondents of assault occasioning actual bodily harm.

These rulings and directions were founded on s 6(3) of the 1967 Act. All the respondents, on their respective convictions, appealed. *Wilson* was heard by the Court of Appeal, Criminal Division (Watkins LJ, Cantley and Hirst JJ) ([1983] 1 All ER 993, [1983] 1 WLR 356), judgment being given on 28 January 1983 by Cantley J *Jenkins* was heard by a differently constituted Court of Appeal, Criminal Division (Purchas LJ, Talbot and Staughton JJ) ([1983] 1 All ER 1000), judgment being given on 18 February 1983 by Purchas LJ. The convictions in both cases were quashed. The reasons were substantially the same, with the additional reason in *Jenkins* that that court was bound by the earlier decision in *Wilson*. Stated briefly, the reason was that the decision of the Court of Appeal, Criminal Division, in *R v Springfield* (1969) 53 Cr App R 608 made it impossible to justify a conviction for assault occasioning actual bodily harm, contrary to s 47 of the Offences *a* against the Person Act 1861, by virtue of s 6(3) of the 1967 Act, since the offence charged of *'inflicting* grievous bodily harm' did not, on the authorities, *necessarily* include the offence of *assault* occasioning actual bodily harm (the emphasis added to these three words is mine).

Both courts granted certificates but refused leave to appeal. That leave was, as already stated, granted by this House. The certificate in *Wilson* was in the following terms:

b   'Whether on a charge of inflicting grievous bodily harm contrary to s. 20 of the Offences Against the Person Act 1861 it is open to a jury to return a verdict of not guilty as charged but guilty of assault occasioning actual bodily harm.'

The certificate in *Jenkins* was in slightly different terms. It read thus:

c   'Whether on a charge of burglary contrary to s. 9(1)(b) of the Theft Act 1968, the particulars of the offence being that the accused having entered a building as trespassers inflicted grievous bodily harm upon a person therein, it is open to a jury to return a verdict of not guilty as charged but guilty of assault occasioning actual bodily harm.'

In substance both certificates raised the same point of law.

d My Lords, it is a regrettable fact that, at least in *Wilson*, the question raised in the courts below and now in your Lordships' House need never have arisen had the prosecution's case at the time of committal for trial been properly prepared in the magistrates' court. Wilson was committed only on the s 20 charge. Two applications were made to the trial judge when the present issue arose, one to add a count under s 47 of the 1861 Act, and the other to overcome the point on which both appeals ultimately succeeded, by adding to the particulars of the offence charged under s 20 the words 'by assaulting'.

e The judge rejected the first application, on the ground that he had no power to add the count under s 47, since the witness statement from Latham did not even identify Wilson as his assailant. This reasoning was unassailable. Your Lordships were shown a copy of the statement. It is a matter for severe criticism of those who had charge of the prosecution's case at the time of committal that it should have been so slovenly prepared.

f For this reason the judge declined, to quote his own words, 'to help the prosecution' by amending the count since the problem was entirely of the prosecution's own making.

It was in these circumstances that the judge came to leave the s 47 charge to the jury in the exercise of what he believed to be his power under s 6(3) of the 1967 Act. Thus it was as regards *Wilson* that this matter has reached this House. This need never have happened. In *Jenkins* the recorder himself raised the question but, after an argument the transcript of which occupied some 40 pages, decided against any other course than that

g he would leave the alternative s 47 charge to the jury in accordance with his view of s 6(3).

My Lords, it would be convenient to preface discussion of the problems to which s 6(3) of the 1967 Act gives rise by first setting out the several statutory provisions which fall for consideration in this appeal.

h Section 6(3) itself reads:

'Where, on a person's trial on indictment for any offence except treason or murder, the jury find him not guilty of the offence specifically charged in the indictment, but the allegations in the indictment amount to or include (expressly or by implication) an allegation of another offence falling within the jurisdiction of the court of trial, the jury may find him guilty of that other offence or of an offence *j* of which he could be found guilty on an indictment specifically charging that other offence.'

The words 'falling within the jurisdiction of the court of trial' can now be ignored since the creation of the Crown Court.

Section 18 of the 1861 Act so far as presently relevant reads:

'Whosoever shall unlawfully and maliciously by any means whatsoever wound
or cause any grievous bodily harm to any person with intent to do some grievous   *a*
bodily harm to any person . . . shall be guilty of [an offence]. . .'

Section 20 of the 1861 Act reads:

'Whosoever shall unlawfully and maliciously wound or inflict any grievous bodily
harm upon any other person . . . shall be guilty of [an offence]. . .'

I draw attention to the fact that the word 'assault' nowhere appears in this section.   *b*
Section 47 of the 1861 Act reads:

'Whosoever shall be convicted upon an indictment of any assault occasioning
actual bodily harm shall be liable [to imprisonment]. . .'

Section 9(1)(b) of the 1968 Act reads:
                                                                                       c
'A person is guilty of burglary if . . . (b) having entered any building or part of a
building as a trespasser he . . . inflicts or attempts to inflict on any person therein
any grievous bodily harm.'

My Lords, there can be no doubt that before 1967 the view was widely held that at
common law on a charge under s 20 a defendant might be convicted of at least common
assault: *d*

'Upon an indictment for assaulting and unlawfully wounding and ill-treating the
prosecutor, and thereby occasioning him actual bodily harm, the prisoner may be
convicted of a common assault . . . The prisoner may also be convicted of a common
assault upon either count of an indictment charging him in the first count with
unlawfully and maliciously wounding, and in the second count with unlawfully   *e*
and maliciously inflicting grievous bodily harm, although the word "assault" is not
used in the indictment. R v. Taylor ((1869) LR 1 CCR 194).'

(See *Archbold's Pleading, Evidence and Practice in Criminal Cases* (36th edn, 1966) para 575.)
It will be within the recollection of those of your Lordships who have in the past sat,
either as recorders or chairmen of quarter sessions, that this statement in *Archbold*
accurately stated the practice, at least before 1967. If this be right, it is not easy to see   *f*
why in principle such a defendant should not equally, at common law, be liable to
conviction under s 47. The current edition of *Archbold* (41st edn, 1982) para 20.145 states
that on an indictment under s 20 either for unlawful wounding or for inflicting grievous
bodily harm the defendant may be convicted of common assault. Thus, long after 1967,
the same view was expressed as I have already quoted from the 36th edition, published
in 1966. These two passages justify the statement by counsel for the Crown, in opening   *g*
these appeals, that both before and after 1967 the view was widely held that assault,
whether common assault or assault occasioning actual bodily harm, was available at
common law as an alternative charge to inflicting grievous bodily harm contrary to s 20
in the event of an acquittal on that latter charge.

My Lords, in *R v Lillis* [1972] 2 All ER 1209 at 1212, [1972] 2 QB 236 at 240 a five-
judge Court of Appeal, Criminal Division, which included Edmund Davies LJ, in a   *h*
judgment delivered by Lawton LJ, described the purposes and effect of s 6(3) as follows:

'Before the passing of the Criminal Law Act 1967 the law applicable to the kind
of problem which presented itself to the trial judge in this case was partly to be
found in the common law and partly in a number of statutes. At common law on
an indictment charging felony the accused could be convicted of a less aggravated   *j*
felony of which the ingredients were included in the felony charged and similarly
as regards misdemeanours; but except under statute a conviction for a misdemeanour
was not allowed on a charge of felony. The object of s 6(3) of the Criminal Law Act
1967 was to provide a general rule continuing and combining the rules of common
law and the provisions of most of the statutes which enabled alternative verdicts to
be returned in specific cases or types of cases.'

I would respectfully accept that statement as correct. In *R v Lillis* the court, as in effect it
a was bound to do, accepted that *R v Springfield* ((1969) 53 Cr App R 608) had been correctly
decided. Indeed, the contrary does not appear to have been argued. Applying *R v
Springfield*, the court held that the indictment, which had charged burglary, *expressly*
(my emphasis) included an allegation of theft, and that burglary not having been proved,
but theft having been proved, a conviction for theft could be sustained under s 6(3). My
Lords, I entertain no doubt that *R v Lillis* was correctly decided. But that leaves open the
b question whether *R v Springfield* was also correctly decided. The statements in *R v Lillis* to
the effect that *R v Sprinfield* was correctly decided are, in the circumstances, plainly obiter.
The crucial passage in the judgment of Sachs LJ in *R v Springfield* (at 610–611) reads:

'The question accordingly arises as follows. Where an indictment thus charges a
major offence without setting out any particulars of the matters relied upon, what
is the correct test for ascertaining whether it contains allegations which expressly or
c impliedly include an allegation of a lesser offence? The test is to see whether it is a
necessary step towards establishing the major offence to prove the commission of
the lesser offence: in other words, is the lesser offence an essential ingredient of the
major one?'

Two comments may be made on this passage. First, the words 'major offence' and
d 'lesser offence' nowhere appear in the subsection. Second, the subsection says nothing
about it being 'a necessary step' towards establishing the 'major offence' to prove the
commission of the lesser offence, so that the so-called lesser offence has to be an 'essential
ingredient' of the major offence. Neither the adjective 'necessary' nor the adverb
'necessarily' appear anywhere in the subsection.
My Lords, the right approach to the solution of the present problem must first be to
e determine the true construction of s 6(3), bearing in mind the observations of Lawton LJ
in *R v Lillis* as to its purpose and as to the position before its enactment. Ignoring the
reference to murder or treason, there seem to me to be four possibilities envisaged by the
subsection. First, the allegation in the indictment expressly amounts to an allegation of
another offence. Second, the allegation in the indictment impliedly amounts to an
allegation of another offence. Third, the allegation in the indictment expressly includes
f an allegation of another offence. Fourth, the allegation in the indictment impliedly
includes an allegation of another offence.
If any one of these four requirements is fulfilled, then the accused may be found guilty
of that other offence. My Lords, if that approach to the construction of the subsection be
correct, it avoids any consideration of 'necessary steps' or of 'major' or 'lesser' offences,
and further avoids reading into the subsection words which were never used by the
g draftsman. I am unable to find that this approach to the construction of the subsection
was ever advanced in *R v Springfield*. If it were, there is no reflection of such an argument
in the judgment. I would add the observation that, although s 6(3) is often spoken of as
permitting conviction for a less serious offence on a count charging a more serious
offence, the maximum penalties for offences against both s 20 and s 47 are the same: five
years' imprisonment.
h There is, in my view, a clear antithesis in the subsection between 'amount to' and
'include'; the word 'or' which joins those two words is clearly disjunctive and must not
be ignored. If either limb of the phrase is satisfied, then the stated consequences can
follow. Thus, in *R v Lillis* the allegation of burglary plainly *expressly included* (my
emphasis) the allegation of theft. *R v O'Brien* (1911) 104 LT 113 is another example of
one charge being expressly included in another. The charge was of riot but that charge
j included an allegation of assault. The appellant was acquitted of riot but convicted of
common assault and the conviction was upheld. *R v Hollingberry* (1825) 4 B & C 329, 107
ER 1081, which was followed in *R v O'Brien*, is another and much earlier example of the
application of the same principle. These are examples of the so-called 'red pencil' rule.
The rule was that all the facts charged in the indictment need not be proved, provided
those facts proved constituted an offence of which by law the offender might be convicted
on the indictment. These cases today would plainly fall within that particular limb of s

6(3). In the present case, the issue to my mind is not whether the allegations in the s 20 charge, expressly or impliedly, *amount to* an allegation of a s 47 charge, for they plainly do not. The issue is whether they either expressly or impliedly *include* such an allegation. The answer to that question must depend on what is expressly or impliedly *included* in a charge of 'inflicting any grievous bodily harm'.

I can, for present purposes, ignore the first limb of s 20, which is concerned only with unlawful wounding. As regards the second, if A includes B, it must be because A is sufficiently comprehensive to include B. Thus A may include B, but B will not necessarily include A, though of course B may do so. If this reasoning be right, I do not think it is relevant, in order to determine whether A includes B, to ask whether proof of B is a 'necessary step' to proof of A. This seems to me to state the problem the wrong way round and, with all respect to Sachs LJ in *R v Springfield*, after he asked the right question he applied the wrong test in order to answer it.

What, then, are the allegations expressly or impliedly included in a charge of 'inflicting grievous bodily harm'. Plainly that allegation must, so far as physical injuries are concerned, at least impliedly if not indeed expressly, include the infliction of 'actual bodily harm' because infliction of the more serious injuries must include the infliction of the less serious injuries. But does the allegation of 'inflicting' include an allegation of 'assault'? The problem arises by reason of the fact that the relevant English case law has proceeded along two different paths. In one group it has, as has already been pointed out, been held that a verdict of assault was a possible alternative verdict on a charge of inflicting grievous bodily harm contrary to s 20. In the other group grievous bodily harm was said to have been inflicted without any assault having taken place, unless of course the offence of assault were to be given a much wider significance than is usually attached to it. This problem has been the subject of recent detailed analysis in the Supreme Court of Victoria in *R v Salisbury* [1976] VR 452. In a most valuable judgment (I most gratefully acknowledge the assistance I have derived from that judgment in preparing this speech) the full court drew attention, in relation to comparable legislation in Victoria, to the problems which arose from this divergence in the mainstream of English authority. The problem with which your Lordships' House is now faced arose in *R v Salisbury* in a different way from the present appeals. There, the appellant was convicted of an offence against the Victorian equivalent of s 20. He appealed on the ground that the trial judge had refused to leave to the jury the possibility of convicting him on that single charge of assault occasioning actual bodily harm or of common assault. The full court dismissed the appeal on the ground that at common law these latter offences were not 'necessarily included' in the offence of 'inflicting grievous bodily harm'. The reasoning leading to this conclusion is plain ([1976] VR 452 at 461):

> 'It may be that the somewhat different wording of s. 20 of the English Act has played a part in bringing about the existence of the two lines of authority in England, but, be that as it may, we have come to the conclusion that, although the word "inflicts" . . . does not have as wide a meaning as the word "causes" . . . the word "inflicts" does have a wider meaning than it would have if it were construed so that inflicting grievous bodily harm always involved assaulting the victim. In our opinion, grievous bodily harm may be inflicted . . . either where the accused has directly and violently "inflicted" it by assaulting the victim, or where the accused has "inflicted" it by doing something, intentionally, which, though it is not itself a direct application of force to the body of the victim, does directly result in force being applied violently to the body of the victim, so that he suffers grievous bodily harm. Hence, the lesser misdemeanours of assault occasioning actual bodily harm and common assault . . . are not necessarily included in the misdemeanour of inflicting grievous bodily harm . . .'

This conclusion was reached after careful consideration of English authorities such as *R v Taylor* (1869) LR 1 CCR 194, *R v Martin* (1881) 8 QBD 54, [1881–5] All ER Rep 699, *R v Clarence* (1888) 22 QBD 23, [1886–90] All ER Rep 133, *R v Halliday* (1889) 61 LT

701, [1886–90] All ER Rep 1028. My Lords, it would be idle to pretend that these cases
a are wholly consistent with each other, or even that, as in *R v Clarence*, though there was a
majority in favour of quashing the conviction then in question, the judgments of those
judges among the thirteen present who formed the majority are consistent with each
other. Some of these cases were not argued on both sides. Others are very inadequately
reported and different reports vary. Thus Stephen J, who was in the majority in *R v
Clarence* 22 QBD 23 at 41, [1886–90] All ER Rep 133 at 143, described the infliction of
b grievous bodily harm in these words:

> 'The words appear to me to mean the direct causing of some grievous injury to
> the body itself with a weapon, as by a cut with a knife, or without a weapon, as by a
> blow with the fist, or by pushing a person down. Indeed, though the word "assault"
> is not used in the section, I think the words imply an assault and battery of which a
c > wound or grievous bodily harm is the manifest immediate and obvious result. This
> is supported by *Reg. v. Taylor* . . .'

But Wills J, also in the majority, was clearly of the view that grievous bodily harm could
be inflicted without an assault, as for example, by creating panic. On the other hand, in
R v Taylor, where the accused was charged on two counts, one under each limb of s 20,
d the jury convicted him of common assault. Kelly CB said that each count was for an
offence which necessarily included an assault, and a verdict of guilty of common assault
was upheld. *R v Taylor* is not easy to reconcile with the later cases unless it is to be
supported on the basis of the wounding count in the indictment. In *R v Martin*, on the
other hand, there was no reference to the issue whether the accused's conduct in creating
panic among a theatre audience constituted assault. He did an unlawful act calculated to
e cause injury and injury was thereby caused. He was thus guilty of an offence against s 20.
   My Lords, I doubt whether any useful purpose would be served by further detailed
analysis of these and other cases, since to do so would only be to repeat less felicitously
what has already been done by the full court of Victoria in *R v Salisbury*. I am content to
accept, as did the full court, that there can be an infliction of grievous bodily harm
contrary to s 20 without an assault being committed. The critical question is, therefore,
f whether it being accepted that a charge of inflicting grievous bodily harm contrary to
s 20 may not necessarily involve an allegation of assault, but may none the less do so, and
in very many cases will involve such an allegation, the allegations in a s 20 charge 'include
(expressly or by implication)' allegations of assault occasioning actual bodily harm. If
'inflicting' can, as the cases show, include 'inflicting by assault', then, even though such a
charge may not necessarily do so, I do not for myself see why on a fair reading of s 6(3)
g these allegations do not at least impliedly *include* 'inflicting by assault'. That is sufficient
for present purposes, though I also regard it as also a possible view that those former
allegations *expressly* include the other allegations.
   The courts below were bound by *R v Springfield*. On the basis that *Springfield* was
correctly decided, those decisions were without doubt correct. But once the reasoning in
R v Springfield is rejected, and the reasoning I have endeavoured to set out in this speech
h is accepted, it follows that both the judge and the recorder were correct in leaving the
possibility of conviction of the s 47 offences to the jury in these cases. It also follows that
by the law of this country, as I conceive it to be, *R v Salisbury* would have been differently
decided.
   Counsel for the respondent Wilson urged your Lordships to leave *R v Springfield*
undisturbed on the ground that it had not given rise to difficulties. With respect, I cannot
j accept that that is so. Not only does it produce a result inconsistent with that previously
widely accepted as correct and still accepted in the 41st edition of *Archbold*, but the
difficulties to which it has given rise are demonstrated by cases such as *R v Hodgson* [1973]
2 All ER 552 at 555, [1973] 1 QB 565 at 570 and a number of more recent cases to which
your Lordships' attention was drawn in argument but to which I do not find it necessary
to refer in detail. I hope that in the future some of those difficulties at least will disappear

and technical arguments of the type which have arisen in the present cases avoided for
the future.

If it be said that this conclusion exposes the defendant to the risk of conviction on a
charge which would not have been fully investigated at the trial on the count in the
indictment, the answer is that a trial judge must always ensure, before deciding to leave
the possibility of conviction of another offence to the jury under s 6(3), that that course
will involve no risk of injustice to the defendant and that he has had the opportunity of
fully meeting that alternative in the course of his defence.

I would, therefore, allow both appeals and answer both certified questions in the
affirmative. It follows that the convictions for offences against s 47 of the 1861 Act
should be restored in both appeals.

My Lords, at the close of the argument a request was made that your Lordships should
allow three counsel on either side in this case. My Lords, in my view it would be
improper so to do. Two counsel on either side are adequate. I suggest that the appellants'
costs should be borne out of central funds but that only two counsel should be allowed
on taxation. The respondents' costs, limited to two counsel, will be taxed in accordance
with the appropriate legal aid provisions.

LORD BRIGHTMAN. My Lords, I would allow both appeals for the reasons given by
my noble and learned friend Lord Roskill.

Appeals allowed.

Solicitors: *D M O'Shea* (for the Crown in the first appeal); *Sharpe Pritchard & Co*, agents
for *R A Crabb*, Maidstone (for the Crown in the second appeal); *H C L Hanne & Co*,
Battersea (for the respondent Wilson); *Boxall & Boxall*, agents for *Godfrey Davis & Waitt*,
Ramsgate (for the respondents E J and R P Jenkins).

Mary Rose Plummer   Barrister.

O'Kelly and others v Trusthouse Forte plc

COURT OF APPEAL, CIVIL DIVISION
SIR JOHN DONALDSON MR, ACKNER AND FOX LJJ
20, 21 JUNE, 20 JULY 1983

*Master and servant – Contract of service – Distinction between contract of service and contract
for services – Whether issue of law or mixed fact and law – Jurisdiction of Employment Appeal
Tribunal – Employment Protection (Consolidation) Act 1978, ss 136(1), 153(1).*

The employers carried on a banqueting business at their hotel. Only a few of the
banqueting staff were employed permanently under contracts of employment, the rest
of the banqueting staff being casual workers engaged for each function, that being the
usual practice in the catering industry. However a large number of the casual staff were
so-called 'regular casuals', ie they were engaged on a regular basis by the employers to
such an extent that some of them had no other regular work. Regular casuals were given
priority of engagement over other casual workers. The applicants, who were three
regular casuals, sought, through their union, recognition by the employers that regular
casuals were permanent employees working under contracts of employment because of
the length and continuity of their service and the manner in which they were paid.
Thereupon the employers dismissed the applicants, who then complained to an industrial
tribunal, pursuant to the Employment Protection (Consolidation) Act 1978, that they
had been unfairly dismissed for taking part in trade union activities. On the question
whether the applicants were working under a contract of employment within s 153(1)[a]

a   Section 153(1), so far as material, is set out at p 460 g, post

of the 1978 Act and were thus entitled to complain of wrongful dismissal, the industrial
a tribunal concluded that there was no overall contract between the parties and that the
applicants were in business on their own account as independent contractors supplying
services. The applicants appealed to the Employment Appeal Tribunal, which held that
the question whether a contract was a contract of employment or a contract for services
was a question of law and therefore under s 136(1)[b] of the 1978 Act the appeal tribunal
had jurisdiction to hear the appeal. The appeal tribunal held, as had the industrial
b tribunal, that there was no overall contract of employment between the parties but
further held that each separate contract entered into on the occasion of each engagement
was a contract of employment. The employers appealed, contending (i) that whether a
contract was a contract of employment or a contract for services was a question of fact
and therefore the appeal tribunal had had no jurisdiction to hear the appeal, and (ii) that
instead of itself considering whether there were separate contracts of employment the
c appeal tribunal should have remitted that issue to the industrial tribunal.

Held – (1) (Per Sir John Donaldson MR and Fox LJ) Where an appellate tribunal was
limited to hearing an appeal on a point of law it had no jurisdiction to consider a question
of mixed law and fact until it had distilled or extracted a question of pure law, since it
was not entitled to intervene unless it was satisfied that the tribunal below had misdirected
itself in law, and, if the tribunal below did not make any express direction as to the law,
d the appellate tribunal could only be so satisfied if it was satisfied that no reasonable
tribunal, properly directing itself on the relevant questions of law, could have come to
the conclusion under appeal (see p 476 e and p 477 f to j, post); *Edwards (Inspector of
Taxes) v Bairstow* [1955] 3 All ER 48 applied.
   (2) (Per Sir John Donaldson MR and Fox LJ) Although the formulation of the test of
whether a contract was a contract of employment or a contract for services was a pure
e question of law, the application of the test so formulated to the relevant facts depended
so much on the finding and assessment of the relevant facts and the precise quality to be
attributed to them that the primary question was one of fact and degree. Accordingly,
the appeal tribunal had been wrong to assume jurisdiction on the basis that the issue was
a question of law. Furthermore, it was impossible to say that no reasonable tribunal,
properly directed, could have reached the conclusion the industrial tribunal had come to
f and therefore on that basis also the appeal tribunal could not have assumed jurisdiction.
It followed (Ackner LJ concurring on the facts) that the industrial tribunal's decision that
there was no overall contract of employment between the employers and the applicants
was not open to appeal (see p 473 d e, p 476 b c f to j, p 478 d to j, p 479 j to p 480 a c d,
post); *Simmons v Heath Laundry Co* [1910] 1 KB 543 followed; *Currie v IRC* [1921] 2 KB
332 applied; dictum of Stephenson LJ in *Young & Woods Ltd v West* [1980] IRLR at 205
g considered.
   (3) Furthermore (Ackner LJ dissenting), it was apparent on the facts that the industrial
tribunal had considered the question whether there were separate contracts of
employment between the employers and the applicants, and since there had been no
misdirection by the industrial tribunal and its conclusion had not been unreasonable on
the facts the applicants had no right of appeal on that issue. Accordingly, the employers'
h appeal would be allowed and the industrial tribunal's decision would be restored (see
p 477 a to d, p 479 e to j and p 480 h j, post).

Notes
For the nature of a contract of employment and the characteristics of the relationship of
employer and employee, see 16 Halsbury's Laws (4th edn), paras 501, 520, and for cases
j on the subject, see 20 Digest (Reissue) 238–255, 2302–2407.
   For the jurisdiction of the Employment Appeal Tribunal, see 16 Halsbury's Laws (4th
Edn) para 1044.
   For the Employment Protection (Consolidation) Act 1978, ss 136, 153, see 48 Halsbury's
Statutes (3rd edn) 593, 610.

---

b   Section 136(1), so far as material, is set out at p 465 j, post

Cases referred to in judgments

Addison v London Philharmonic Orchestra Ltd [1981] ICR 261, EAT.
Ahmet v Trusthouse Forte Catering Ltd (13 January 1983, unreported), EAT.
Airfix Footwear Ltd v Cope [1978] ICR 1210, EAT.
Construction Industry Training Board v Labour Force [1970] 3 All ER 220, DC.
Currie v IRC, Durant v IRC [1921] 2 KB 332, CA.
Edwards (Inspector of Taxes) v Bairstow [1955] 3 All ER 48, [1956] AC 14, [1955] 3 WLR 410, HL.
Ferguson v John Dawson & Partners (Contractors) Ltd [1976] 3 All ER 817, [1976] 1 WLR 1213, CA.
Global Plant Ltd v Secretary of State for Health and Social Security [1971] 3 All ER 385, [1972] 1 QB 139, [1971] 3 WLR 269.
Massey v Crown Life Insurance Co [1978] 2 All ER 576, [1978] 1 WLR 676, CA.
Melon v Hector Powe Ltd [1981] 1 All ER 313, HL.
Morren v Swinton and Pendlebury BC [1965] 2 All ER 349, [1965] 1 WLR 576, DC.
Nethermere (St Neots) Ltd v Gardiner [1983] ICR 319, EAT.
Pioneer Shipping Ltd v BTP Tioxide Ltd, The Nema [1981] 2 All ER 1030, [1982] AC 724, [1981] 2 WLR 292, HL.
Ready Mixed Concrete (South East) Ltd v Minister of Pensions and National Insurance [1968] 1 All ER 433, [1968] 2 QB 497, [1968] 2 WLR 775.
Simmons v Heath Laundry Co [1910] 1 KB 543, CA.
Union of Construction, Allied Trades and Technicians v Brain [1981] ICR 542, CA.
Wiltshire CC v National Association of Teachers in Further and Higher Education [1980] ICR 455, CA.
Woods v WM Car Services (Peterborough) Ltd [1982] ICR 693, EAT.
Young & Woods Ltd v West [1980] IRLR 201, CA.

Cases also cited

Challiner v Taylor [1972] ICR 129, NIRC.
Coates v Modern Methods & Materials Ltd [1982] 3 All ER 946, [1983] QB 192, CA.
Devonald v Rosser & Sons [1906] 2 KB 728, [1904–7] All ER Rep 988, CA.
Heathcote v Haunchwood Collieries Ltd (1917) 117 LT 677, HL.
Market Investigations Ltd v Minister of Social Security [1968] 3 All ER 732, [1969] 2 QB 173.
Martin v Glynwed Distribution Ltd [1983] ICR 511, CA.
National Coal Board v Galley [1958] 1 All ER 91, [1958] 1 WLR 16, CA.
Pedersen v Camden London Borough [1981] ICR 674, CA.
Puttick v John Wright & Sons (Blackwall) Ltd [1972] ICR 457, NIRC.
Reardon Smith Line v Hansen-Tangen, Hansen-Tangen v Sanko Steamship Co [1976] 3 All ER 570, [1976] 1 WLR 989, HL.
Retarded Children's Aid Society v Day [1978] 1 WLR 763, CA.

Appeal and cross-appeal

The applicants, Harry O'Kelly, Thomas M Pearman and Philip Florent (the respondents), who were regular casual workers in the banqueting business carried on by the appellants, Trusthouse Forte plc (the employers), at the Grosvenor House Hotel, applied to an industrial tribunal complaining that the employers unfairly dismissed them from their employment for taking part in trade union activities and applied for interim relief under s 77 of the Employment Protection (Consolidation) Act 1978. An industrial tribunal (chairman Mr G E Heggs) sitting at London Central directed the hearing of a preliminary point, namely whether the respondents were employees who worked under a contract of employment within s 153(1) of the 1978 Act (and thus were entitled to complain of wrongful dismissal and to claim interim relief). By a decision made on 31 March and 11 April 1983 the tribunal decided that the respondents were not employees who worked under a contract of employment within the 1978 Act because they were in business on their own account as independent contractors supplying services, and accordingly the tribunal decided that they were not qualified to claim interim relief under s 77 of the a 1978 Act. The respondents appealed to the Employment Appeal Tribunal (Browne-Wilkinson J and Mr T D Anderson and Mrs M L Boyle) which by a judgment given on 11 May 1983 allowed the appeal holding that even though the industrial tribunal were correct in deciding that there was no overall contract regulating the position between the respondents and the employers, nevertheless on each occasion that the respondents worked for the employers they entered into separate contract of service with the employers and accordingly the respondents were employees under contracts of

b employment within the 1978 Act and were qualified to claim interim relief under s 77. The employers appealed to the Court of Appeal. The grounds of the appeal were (1) that the appeal tribunal wrongly decided to consider for themselves whether the respondents were engaged under separate contracts rather than under an overall contract and ought in the circumstances to have remitted the separate contracts issue to the industrial tribunal. Alternatively, if it was proper for the appeal tribunal to consider the separate

c contracts issue they wrongly concluded that the separate contracts entered into were contracts of service, rather than for services, and were thus contracts of employment within the 1978 Act. (2) The appeal tribunal was wrong in holding that there was no evidence before the industrial tribunal to justify its findings that it was both parties' view that the relationship between them was not that of employer and employee, and that it was a recognised custom and practice of the catering industry that casual workers were

d engaged to work under contracts for services. By a respondents' notice the respondents gave notice that on the hearing of the appeal they would contend that the contracts of service found by the appeal tribunal to exist were continuous and not intermittent contracts. They also cross-appealed for an order that there was a continuing contractual obligation on the employers' part to offer them work as and when it was available and on the respondents' part to make themselves available for such work. The grounds of the

e cross-appeal were that the appeal tribunal wrongly held that on the facts found by the industrial tribunal there was no continuing mutuality of obligation between the parties and ought to have held (a) that economic forces did not negative but supported mutuality of obligation and/or (b) that the relationship of the parties was only or was best explicable as one of continuing mutual obligation. The facts are set out in the judgment of Ackner LJ.

f *Alexander Irvine QC* and *Timothy Charlton* for the employers.
Stephen Sedley QC for the respondents.

Cur adv vult

g 20 July. The following judgments were delivered.

ACKNER LJ (giving the first judgment at the invitation of Sir John Donaldson MR). At the Grosvenor House Hotel the appellants (the employers) carry on two distinct operations. They operate an hotel and a restaurant business which is open to the public, and by reason of the regular and continuous nature of that business the staff engaged are

h all employees working under contracts of employment. The employers also carry on the business of hiring out rooms for private functions for which they provide the catering and other services. This part of the business is undertaken by the banqueting department. Because of the fluctuating and seasonal nature of this trade there are only 34 permanent staff, including the banqueting staff manager, Mr Hourigan, the bar manager, Mr Mardel, and the managerial and supervisory staff and the head waiters. All the other staff

j in the department are known as casual staff and they are paid at a set rate for the work actually performed.

Because of the large number of casual staff required during the busy season and the difficulty of finding staff in sufficient numbers during the slack season Mr Hourigan maintains a list of some 44 wine butlers and 60 food service waiters and waitresses. They are known as 'regulars' and are rostered in preference to other casual staff, numbering between 200 and 300, who work less regularly and are employed for fewer functions.

The 'regulars' are members of staff who can be relied on by the employers to offer their
services regularly and, in return, have the assurance of preference in the allocation of an *a*
available work. They receive exactly the same rate of remuneration as other casuals, but
have the ability to earn more money by being offered more frequent engagements, and
there is more regularity in their earnings. 'Regulars' are offered any available engagement
during the slack season. Because of the extent of the work they are offered they may
work longer hours than the permanent staff working a regular 40-hour week. Because of
the extent to which they make their services available to the employers some 'regulars', *b*
including the respondents, have no other regular employment.

The employers' practice of staffing banquets and other functions with workers
designated as casual staff is widespread throughout the hotel and catering industry in
London, although there may be individual variations in rates and conditions. The staff
are considered by the employers to be casual workers and not employees engaged under
a contract of employment. The separate position of casual workers is recognised by the *c*
Wages Council and in App 2 to the current Wages (Licensed Residential Establishment
and Licensed Restaurant) Order 1982 (Order LR(65)) a 'casual worker' is defined as
meaning—

> 'a worker who undertakes engagements on either an hourly or day to day basis
> and has the right to choose, without penalty, whether or not to come to work.'

d

The respondents are members and stewards of the Hotel and Catering Workers' Union.
They have made an application to the industrial tribunal for interim relief under s 77 of
the Employment Protection (Consolidation) Act 1978, as amended by the Employment
Act 1982. By their letter of 26 February 1983 they complain that the employers unfairly
dismissed them from their employment at the Grosvenor House Hotel, London, and
that their dismissal is to be regarded as unfair by virtue of s 58 of the 1978 Act, as *e*
substituted by the 1982 Act, that is to say, they were dismissed for an inadmissible reason,
the alleged reason for the dismissal being that they were members of a trade union and
had taken part in its activities. The industrial tribunal directed the hearing of a
preliminary issue, namely whether or not the respondents were 'employees' who worked
under a contract of employment within the meaning of s 153(1) of the 1978 Act, or
whether they were independent contractors who worked under a contract for services. If *f*
the respondents were not 'employees' of the employers it followed that their complaint
of unfair dismissal and their application for interim relief must necessarily fail. After a
hearing which lasted some two days the industrial tribunal held that the respondents
were not 'employees'. The respondents appealed to the Employment Appeal Tribunal,
and after a hearing which lasted some three days it allowed the appeal, but gave leave to
appeal to this court.

Section 153(1) of the 1978 Act define 'employment' as being 'employment under a *g*
contract of employment'. It defines 'employee' as meaning 'an individual who has entered
into or works under or (where the employment has ceased, worked under) a contract of
employment'. It defines 'contract of employment' as meaning 'a contract of service or
apprenticeship, whether express or implied, and (if it is express) whether it is oral or in
writing'.

This appeal therefore raises the familiar problem: were the respondents working under *h*
a contract *of service* or under a contract *for services*?

As the Employment Appeal Tribunal pointed out, just because a person is an 'employee'
within the meaning of the 1978 Act, he does not automatically enjoy all the rights and
protection accorded by the Act. For most purposes an 'employee' does not enjoy such
protection unless he has a period of qualifying continuous employment with the *j*
employer against whom he brings his case, the most common example of which is the
requirement that an employee shall have 52 weeks of continuous employment with that
employer before becoming entitled to bring a claim for unfair dismissal. The period of
continuous employment is calculated in accordance with the provisions of Sch 13 to the
1978 Act which, amongst other things, normally requires the minimum number of
hours employment in each week in order for that week to be counted. However, there is

a one exception to the requirement for a qualifying period of employment: where the claim is based on dismissal for an inadmissible reason there is no minimum period before an employee may bring a claim for unfair dismissal (see s 64(3) of the 1978 Act); dismissal because of taking part in trade union activities is an inadmissible reason (see s 58(1) and (5)).

b So far as the respondents are concerned, Mr O'Kelly and Mr Pearman were wine butlers and Mr Florent was a dispense barman. They were 'regular' casuals in regard to whom the evidence established that in practice they worked virtually every week for hours varying in number from as little as three in some weeks up to as much as 57 in others. In the last year they each had only two weeks in which they did not work. Over this period of 52 weeks two had worked an average of 31 hours per week and one 42 hours per week.

c I join in the tribute which the Employment Appeal Tribunal paid to the industrial tribunal for the most careful way in which they investigated the facts and for the detailed grounds which it gave for its decision. They found that—

> 'The principles on which a casual worker is employed are simple. There is no obligation for the worker to offer his services and there is no obligation for the employer to provide work.'

d The accuracy of this proposition, in so far as it related to 'regulars', was strongly contested before us. They continued:

> 'If an engagement is undertaken the worker is paid at the appropriate hourly or sessional rate for the work performed. During the function the casual worker works under the direction and control of the employer as part of his organisation and the relationship ends automatically at the end of the function without the need of notice on either side. Many casual workers have other regular employment.'

e

The industrial tribunal conveniently set out a number of headings under which they considered the facts of the case, and it would be convenient if I now referred to these in summary form.

Engagement. Mr Hourigan has the responsibility of engaging casual staff for functions.
f He receives a list of functions for the following month and this is updated weekly on Thursday mornings. He prepares a list of wine service staff and a separate list of food service staff required for the following days. The lists are posted on Thursday evenings showing the names of the casual staff rostered for each function. Thus, the casual staff know what work, if any, is available for them for the week commencing on a Friday. During the slack period the lists are posted fortnightly. A similar roster of bar staff is
g prepared by Mr Mardel.

Tax treatment and payment. The Inland Revenue requires the employers to deduct from the remuneration they pay to casual workers income tax under PAYE and social security contributions and to account to the Inland revenue for the money deducted. As a matter of necessary convenience the employers ensure that any casual staff working regularly at the hotel are entered on the computer payroll and they are paid weekly, in arrear, on
h Thursdays like any weekly paid employees. The industrial tribunal accepted that the tax and social security contributions are deducted as a requirement imposed on the employers by the Inland Revenue and that this is not, of itself, indicative of the legal basis of the relationship between the employers and the casual staff, for employment protection purposes.

Holiday pay. Although casual workers were not assured of any regular work and
j received no sick pay and did not participate in the employers' pension scheme or enjoy any of the other fringe benefits accorded to their permanent staff, and they were not included in the annual pay review, casual workers had a holiday pay entitlement based on the number of full weeks worked during the preceding year. However, unlike the holiday pay entitlement of permanent staff, the payment was not made when they took their holiday but during the last two years it was paid to them at the commencement of the new banqueting season in September. The industrial tribunal accepted that it was in

reality a discretionary incentive payment to workers who were prepared to continue
offering their services during the new season.   *a*
   Disciplinary and grievance procedures. The employers adapted their existing disciplinary
and appeal procedure and recognised a formal grievance procedure for their casual staff.
The industrial tribunal did not find that this was tantamount to recognising that the
casual worker was an employee. They were merely using a fair procedure appropriate to
a reasonable management and it said nothing about the underlying nature of the
relationship.   *b*
   Incorporation in the organisation. Casual workers in the banqueting department were
supplied with jackets, as is the practice for permanent employees, and they worked under
the direction and control of the head waiters. As a dispense barman, Mr Florent worked
under the direction of Mr Mardel and the permanent dispense barman. As so much of
the work in the department was performed by casual staff, the 'regulars' were introduced
into the consultation process. Towards the end of 1982 the employers put forward the   *c*
draft of a handbook for casual staff, in order to aquaint casual workers with general
arrangements at the hotel and give information about conditions of engagement and
procedures. The industrial tribunal were satisfied that the handbook, taken as a whole,
referred only to casual workers and its provisions were consistent only with the casual
worker status.
   Enforcing attendance. This part of the findings of the industrial tribunal is of crucial   *d*
importance and it is worth setting verbatim paras 10 and 11 of their reasons:

'10. It is an essential feature of casual work that the worker has the right to
   choose, without penalty, whether or not to come to work. It is, however, necessary
   to the running of the banqueting business that the employer should be assured that
   a casual worker who has accepted an engagement does not withdraw at the last
   minute. As the employer has no obligation to offer future engagements he has the   *e*
   opportunity of exercising extremely effective control over attendance. The balance
   in the relationship exclusively favours the employer because a casual worker can be
   denied future engagements without reason given and without any form of inquiry
   or the right to be heard.
      11. For a banqueting business operated on the scale of Grosvenor House it would *f*
   clearly be impracticable to recruit casual workers on a daily basis. The publication
   of weekly rosters was not merely of convenience to the casual workers but it was of
   importance to Mr Hourigan to be assured in advance that all necessary staff were
   available and booked for each function. While the rostering of staff might be
   considered as an offer of engagement for each of the functions, which a worker
   could decline by asking that his name be removed from the roster prior to the
   function, it is only a short step for the employer to exercise his dominant position   *g*
   to require a casual worker to accept an engagement he would prefer to decline. It
   was the uncontested evidence on behalf of the applicants [the respondents] that
   difficulty was experienced in securing variations to the published roster, that Mr
   Hourigan would raise objection to medical appointments, and that he was
   unsympathetic towards certified sickness. While the [employers] could have declined
   to offer any future engagements, the penalty imposed on "regulars" for non-   *h*
   attendance or other infractions was to "suspend" the worker from a limited number
   of future engagements, even if those engagements had been rostered and therefore
   impliedly accepted by the worker. We did not have the benefit of Mr Hourigan's
   evidence, and the fact that he may have exceeded his authority does not in itself
   alter the contractual nature of the relationship, but we refer to the system as   *j*
   indicative of the fact that the freedom to choose whether or not to come to work, if
   Mr Hourigan wanted the individual to work, was more apparent than real if that
   individual wished to continue working at the hotel. A "regular" had to conform
   with the requirements of Mr Hourigan both in respect of rostered engagements and
   future engagements or he would risk losing his assured livelihood. In the context of

casual work for these or any other employees the expression "without penalty" has little practical meaning when the consequences of failure to attend can so nearly imply an obligation to attend.'

Acts exemplifying the understanding of the parties. The industrial tribunal, though accepting that the understanding of the parties was only one of the relevant factors since they may well be mistaken and the relationship may alter as a result of developments, made the following findings. From the commencement of their engagement the respondents were treated by the employers as casual staff on terms and conditions entirely distinct from those accorded to the wine butlers and dispense barmen who were permanent employees and issued with written contracts of employment. The respondents were aware of the distinction and did not challenge it.

It was not until October 1982 that Mr O'Kelly and Mr Pearman first raised the question of contracts of employment with Mr Green, one of the employers' senior managers. They asked that the casual wine butlers should be classified as full-time staff 'because of the hours we done'. Mr O'Kelly said that he was seeking recognition as 'permanent employees', but Mr Green said, 'No, we were casual'. After that Mr O'Kelly raised the matter with the union, it being his wish to obtain recognition of a change in the status of the employment in order to obtain the benefits accorded to permanent employees. The industrial tribunal referred to the correspondence from Miss T A Gudgin, the union's recruitment officer for London hotel and catering establishments, and concluded that Miss Gudgin was seeking an alteration in the prevailing legal status of casual workers involving them being issued with contracts of employment to which they would not otherwise be entitled.

In March 1983 Mrs Gill, legal officer for the union, wrote to the employers' solicitors setting out four grounds on which the respondents based their claim that they were employees:

'1. They are regularly called upon to serve at banquets according to rota arrangements which are posted a week in advance. 2. They normally work over 16 hours a week. 3. They are paid weekly and tax and national insurance is deducted by your clients. 4. They receive holiday pay.'

It was thus, said the industrial tribunal, a claim based on length and continuity of service and the manner of payment. It noted that despite discussing the basis of a claim for some two months it was not the respondents' assertion that there was a mutual obligation to provide and perform work. I observe that no alternative was then raised of employment by successive individual contracts of service.

Before the industrial tribunal the submission was made on behalf of the respondents that the 'regulars' were employees because they were provided with regular and frequent work on the basis of weekly engagements, with a build-up of holiday entitlement over the year. The contention was that there was no freedom to refuse work and accordingly there was an implied obligation on the part of the employers to provide work. The industrial tribunal did not accept that it was necessary to imply an obligation to provide work in order to give business efficacy to the contract. They stated:

'The rights and obligations of casual workers and employers are well established by the custom and practice of the trade. In return for making their services available, the "regulars" were assured of preferential treatment in the allocation of work. There was mutual advantage to the parties of which both were well aware, and it is not necessary to imply any terms, even if they could be expressed with precision, to give business sense to the arrangement . . . It would be impossible in an objective sense to draw a line between the time when an individual ceases being a casual worker disentitled to protection and a "regular" who is to be considered an employee.'

It is common ground that the industrial tribunal's approach was not open to criticism.

It was in these terms:

'The tribunal should consider all aspects of the relationship, no single feature *a* being in itself decisive and each of which may vary in weight and direction, and having given such balance to the factors as seems appropriate to determine whether the person was carrying on business on his own account.'

In making their assessment, the industrial tribunal took into account the following factors which they considered consistent with a contract of employment: (a) The *b* respondents provided their services in return for remuneration for work actually performed. They did not invest their own capital or stand to gain or lose from the commercial success of the functions organised by the banqueting department. (b) They performed their work under the direction and control of the employers. (c) When the casual workers attended at functions they were part of the employers' organisation and for the purpose of ensuring the smooth running of the business they were represented in *c* the staff consultation process. (d) When working they were carrying on the business of the employers. (e) Clothing and equipment were provided by the employers. (f) The respondents were paid weekly in arrear and were paid under deduction of income tax and social security contributions. (g) Their work was organised on the basis of a weekly rota and they required permission to take time off from rostered duties. (h) There was a disciplinary and grievance procedure. (i) There was holiday pay or an incentive bonus *d* calculated by reference to past service.

The following additional factors in the relationship the industrial tribunal considered were *not inconsistent* with the contract of employment: (j) The respondents were paid for work actually performed and did not receive a regular wage or retainer. The method of calculating entitlement to remuneration is not an essential aspect of the employment relationship. (k) Casual workers were not remunerated on the same basis as permanent *e* employees and did not receive sick pay and were not included in the employers' staff pension scheme and did not receive the fringe benefits accorded to established employees. There is, however, no objection to employers adopting different terms and conditions of employment for different categories of employee (eg, different terms for manual and managerial staff). (l) There were no regular or assured working hours. It is not a requirement of employment that there should be 'normal working hours' (see Sch 3 to *f* the 1978 Act). (m) Casual workers were not provided with written particulars of employment. If it is established that casual workers are employees there is a statutory obligation to furnish written particulars.

The following factors were considered by the industrial tribunal to be *inconsistent* with a contract of employment: (n) The engagement was terminable without notice on either side. (o) The respondents had the right to decide whether or not to accept work, although *g* whether or not it would be in their interest to exercise the right to refuse work is another matter. (p) The employers had no obligation to provide any work. (q) During the subsistence of the relationship it was the parties' view that casual workers were independent contractors engaged under successive contracts for services. (r) It is the recognised custom and practice of the industry that casual workers are engaged under a contract for services.

I shall return later to deal in some little detail with the third category, because this has *h* given rise to a substantial degree of controversy.

The majority decision of the industrial tribunal was in these terms:

'It is freely recognised that the relationship of the [respondents] to the employers had many of the characteristics of a contract of service. In our view the one important ingredient which was missing was mutuality of obligation. The *j* [respondents] entered into their relationship with the employers in the expectation that they would be provided with any work which was currently available. It was a purely commercial transaction for the supply and purchase of services for specific events, because there was no obligation for the [employers] to provide further work and no obligation for the [respondents] to offer their further services. By making themselves available on a regular basis the [respondents] had the prospect of enhanced profit for themselves. If they could obtain more regular and profitable work elsewhere they were free to take it. The [respondents] were in no different position than any independent contractor who offers his services for a particular purpose or event (e g, a jobbing gardener or a day labourer) and it was by their choice that they made their services available to a single customer. Where the commodity offered is the simple supply of semi-skilled labour for a specific occasion, or series of occasions, it is not to be expected that there would be a financial investment or participation in the profits or losses of the business. We are, of course, aware that lack of mutuality of obligation is not, in itself, a decisive factor and that outworkers can, in appropriate circumstances, be employees working under a contract of employment, even though there is no obligation to provide work or perform it: see *Airfix Footwear Ltd v Cope* [1978] ICR 1210 and *Nethermere (St Neots) Ltd v Gardiner* [1983] ICR 319. Nevertheless, this was a factor on which we placed very considerable weight in making our assessment. What is required of us in these proceedings is to determine the nature of the contractual relationship between the parties. This is not the description which the parties give to their relationship but the nature of the engagement resulting from the terms (whether express or implied) of their mutual agreement. No detailed terms were discussed at the time of engagement because there was no need to discuss them. All parties were fully aware of the custom and practice of the industry that casual workers were not considered to be employees working under a contract of employment. They entered into and continued the relationship on that understanding until Mr O'Kelly and the union attempted to negotiate an alteration in the fundamental basis of the relationship. As Lord Denning MR said in *Massey v Crown Life Insurance Co* [1978] 2 All ER 576 at 580, [1978] 1 WLR 676 at 680: "It seems to me on the authorities that, when it is a situation which is in doubt or which is ambiguous, so that it can be brought under one relationship or the other, it is open to the parties by agreement to stipulate what the legal situation shall be. That was said in *Ready Mixed Concrete (South East) Ltd v Minister of Pensions and National Insurance* [1968] 1 All ER 433, [1968] 2 QB 497 in 1968 by MacKenna J. He said ([1968] 2 QB 497 at 513) 'If it were doubtful what rights and duties the parties wished to provide for, a declaration of this kind might help in resolving the doubt and fixing them in the sense required to give effect to that intention.' So the way in which they draw up their agreement and express it may be a very important factor in defining what the true relation was between them. If they declare that he is self-employed, that may be decisive." We conclude that when the parties embarked on their engagement pursuant to the known custom and practice of the industry, it was indicative of their intention not to create an employment relationship.'

The majority decision concluded by stating that custom and practice is not, in itself, decisive because each case must be determined on its individual facts and the evidence may indicate that other developments occurred to alter the status of the relationship. However, they considered that it would be irresponsible lightly to disregard the clear evidence of the intentions of the parties derived from an engagement under custom and practice, because this could have widespread and damaging repercussions throughout the whole industry. In the industrial tribunal's judgment the respondents were in business on their own account as independent contractors supplying services and were not qualified for interim relief because they were not employees who worked under a contract of employment.

JURISDICTION

Under the provisions of s 136(1) of the 1978 Act an appeal lies to the Employment Appeal Tribunal only on a 'question of law'. The proceedings before the Employment

Appeal Tribunal are thus by way of appeal and not by way of rehearing. If the Employment Appeal Tribunal is to allow the appeal it can only do so on the basis that *a* the industrial tribunal was wrong in law.

The employers contend that the appeal tribunal can only interfere with the decision of the industrial tribunal if it is shown that they have applied the wrong legal principles or that they have reached a conclusion on the facts which no reasonable tribunal applying the law could have reached. In the submission of counsel for the employers the limited question which the Employment Appeal Tribunal was entitled to ask itself was: on the *b* facts found by the industrial tribunal, have they arrived at a conclusion which could be reasonably entertained? In his submission, the appeal tribunal are not entitled to ask themselves whether, on the facts found, the industrial tribunal have reached the correct conclusion.

The issue before the industrial tribunal was whether the respondents worked for the employers pursuant to a contract or contracts of service or a contract or contracts for *c* services. Before dealing with the substance of the appeal the appeal tribunal dealt with the extent of their jurisdiction in the following terms:

'As is well known, an appeal lies here on a question of law only. There is a pronounced difference of judicial view whether the question, "Is a contract a contract of employment or a contract for services?" is a mixed question of fact and law or a question of law. The older view was that it was at best a mixed question of fact and *d* law. As a result, an appellate court with jurisdiction to correct errors of law only could not intervene in the decision of the lower court unless it was shown that the lower court, in deciding whether or not there was a contract of employment, had on the face of its reasons for its decision indicated that it had misdirected itself in law, or had reached a conclusion that was in a legal sense "perverse". This was the approach of the Court of Appeal in *Simmons v Heath Laundry Co* [1910] 1 KB 543, *e* and of the Queen's Bench Divisional Court in *Construction Industry Training Board v Labour Force Ltd* [1970] 3 All ER 220 and *Global Plant Ltd v Secretary of State for Health and Social Security* [1971] 3 All ER 385, [1972] 1 QB 139. It was also the approach of Browne LJ in the Court of Appeal in *Ferguson v John Dawson & Partners* [1976] 3 All ER 817 at 832, [1976] 1 WLR 1213 at 1230, a case in which the appeal to the Court of Appeal lay on questions of fact as well as law. On the other side, in *Young & Woods* *f* *Ltd v West* [1980] IRLR 201 at 205 Stephenson LJ following the view which he understood Megaw LJ to have expressed in *Ferguson's* case, held that the question was one of pure law so that the appellate court can, and indeed must, reach its own view whether or not, on the findings of fact made by the lower court, the true legal analysis is that there was a contract of employment. Ackner LJ, whilst agreeing with the conclusion reached by Stephenson LJ, did not specifically deal with this point. *g* Since the *Young & Woods* case this appeal tribunal has often been confronted with a choice between these two conflicting views but in general has felt bound to follow the views of Stephenson LJ in *Young & Woods*: see, e g, *Addison v London Philharmonic Orchestra* [1981] ICR 261 at 270, *Ahmet v Trusthouse Forte Catering Ltd* (13 January 1983, unreported), *Nethermere (St Neots) Ltd v Gardiner* [1983] ICR 319. We do not propose to increase the learning on this matter. Very many cases come before this *h* appeal tribunal on the point and it is in the highest degree desirable that the matter should be settled by the Court of Appeal one way or another at an early date. In the meantime it seems to us important to maintain a consistency of approach by this appeal tribunal. For that reason we, too, will approach the case on the basis laid down by Stephenson LJ, ie, that the question is a question of law on which we must make up our own minds on the basis of the facts found by the industrial tribunal *j* whether the relationship between the parties is or is not a contract of employment.'

I think it may be helpful to go straight to *Young & Woods Ltd v West*. Mr West was a skilled sheet metal worker and when he joined Young & Woods Ltd he was offered alternative methods of payment: either he could become an employee in the ordinary way or he could be treated as a self-employed person. Mr West chose to be treated as self-

employed. No deductions were made from his pay for tax, he was responsible for his
a own national insurance contributions, he did not receive any holiday pay or sickness
benefit from the company. This agreement was entered into with the knowledge of the
Inland Revenue, who treated Mr West for tax purposes as self-employed. When Mr
West's work was terminated he complained that he had been unfairly dismissed. Young
& Woods Ltd contended that he was not an employee under a contract of service, but he
was self-employed under a contract for services. The industrial tribunal held that Mr
b West was an employee as defined by the statute and not self-employed as he and the
company had agreed that he was. The Employment Appeal Tribunal, by a majority,
dismissed the company's appeal. They held that the parties cannot, by a mere label, alter
realities and that the realities were that Mr West was no more than a skilled sheet metal
worker working under a contract of service, just as other employees who were admittedly
working under a contract of service. The minority view was that a deliberate choice had
c been made by Mr West to be treated as self-employed in order that he might reap fiscal
advantages. The reality was that he deliberately chose to be in the position of a self-
employed person. On behalf of Young & Woods Ltd it was argued in the Court of
Appeal, inter alia, that the presumption created by Mr West deliberately and openly
choosing the relationship of self-employed, although rebuttable, was not easily rebutted
and had not been rebutted by him. The complaint was made that the appeal tribunal did
d not pay any, or any adequate, regard to those facts which pointed away from a contract
of service to a contract for services.

In the course of his judgment Stephenson LJ commented on the observation made by
Browne LJ at the conclusion of his judgment in *Ferguson v Dawson & Partners (Contractors)*
Ltd [1976] 3 All ER 817 at 832, [1976] 1 WLR 1213 at 1230, which were in these terms:

e 'When the right tests have been applied, the conclusion to be drawn is in my view
a question of fact: see *Global Plant Ltd v Secretary of State for Health and Social Security*
[1971] 3 All ER 385 at 391–393, [1972] 1 QB 139 at 152–155.'

The *Global Plant* case was a decision of the Divisional Court.

The *Ferguson* decision was a case in which the majority of the Court of Appeal held
that notwithstanding the label which the parties had put on their relationship to the
f effect that the plaintiff was to be, or was deemed to be 'a self-employed labour only
subcontractor', in reality the relationship was that of employer and employee.

Stephenson LJ cited the following excerpt from the judgment of MacKenna J in the
well-known case of *Ready Mixed Concrete (South East) Ltd v Minister of Pensions and National
Insurance* [1968] 2 QB 497 at 512–513, which Megaw LJ had clearly cited with approval
in the *Ferguson* case:

g 'It may be stated here that whether the relation between the parties to the contract
is that of master and servant or otherwise is a conclusion of law dependent upon the
rights conferred and the duties imposed by the contract. If these are such that the
relation is that of master and servant, it is irrelevant that the parties have declared it
to be something else. I do not say that a declaration of this kind is always necessarily
ineffective. If it were doubtful what rights and duties the parties wished to provide
h for, a declaration of this kind might help in resolving the doubt and fixing them in
the sense required to give effect to that intention.'

That part of Stephenson LJ's judgment which the appeal tribunal rely on in *Young &
Woods Ltd v West* [1980] IRLR 201 at 205 is as follows:

j '... but I must respectfully express my dissent from what [Browne LJ] said at the
very conclusion of his judgment, that the conclusion to be drawn from the facts as
to the true legal relationship between the parties after the right tests have been
applied is a question of fact. If by that he meant that it was a question on which this
court cannot interfere, I prefer the view of Lord Justice Megaw that it is a question
of law, in those cases of service or services as in the case of lease or licence, whether
the true inference from the facts, the true construction or interpretation of a written

agreement or of an agreement partly oral and partly written or of a wholly oral agreement, is a matter of law on which there is a right and a wrong view, and if an Industrial Tribunal comes to what in the view of this court is a wrong view of the true nature of the agreement, it can and should find an error in law on the part of the Industrial Tribunal and reverse its decision. It cannot say that two views are possible of the true construction of this particular agreement on the facts which the Industrial Tribunal has found, and we cannot say that no reasonable tribunal could have come to the interpretation which the Industrial Tribunal has put upon the facts. It must make up its mind what the true interpretation of the facts and the true legal relationship created by the contract between the parties is.'

Stephenson LJ rejected the submission that the appeal tribunal had ignored or undervalued those facts which pointed away from a contract of service to a contract for services. He took the view that the pointers in the other direction were strong enough to satisfy the burden which no doubt rested on Mr West to show that the label was a false label and that, though the mutual intention of the parties was undoubtedly to call the work which Mr West was going to do for them services under a contract for services, nevertheless it was in reality service rendered under a contract of service. There was no such ambiguity in the relationship between Mr West and the company as could make their declared intention as to what it should be decisive of it.

The extent of the appeal tribunal's jurisdiction was not called into question, as I recall the appeal, and in my judgment I did not deal with that subject in express terms. I did, however, at the outset of my judgment, express my agreement with the judgment of Stephenson LJ, and this was certainly intended to cover all that he said.

Sir David Cairns began his judgment in these terms (at 208–209):

'I found this a difficult case. I was much impressed by [counsel for the respondent's] contention that the right conclusion from the facts found in paragraph 3 of the decision of the Industrial Tribunal was that there was in reality, and not merely as a matter of label, a contract for services rather than a contract of service. An alternative argument of [counsel] which also seemed to me to have much force was that, taking account of the facts in paragraph 3 together with those in paragraph 5 of the decision indicating that Mr West's working conditions were indistinguishable from those of the company's employees, the case was one of ambiguity where the label might be decisive.'

It seems to me clear that Sir David Cairns was approaching the case not on the basis that the appeal court had merely to be satisfied that the industrial tribunal reached a decision which was reasonably open to them when properly applying the law to the facts. The appellate tribunal, be it the Employment Appeal Tribunal or the Court of Appeal, had to be satisfied that the industrial tribunal had reached the correct decision.

Towards the end of his judgment he said (at 209):

'. . . on balance, the matters pointing to its being a contract of service do outweigh the matters pointing in the other direction . . .'

It is clear that the approach of the Court of Appeal in the Young & Woods Ltd v West case was that an error of law could be established if: (a) the industrial tribunal took into account the wrong criteria in concluding that a contract was a contract of service or a contract for services and/or (b) if the tribunal, although applying the proper criteria, gave the wrong weight to one or more of the relevant factors.

Counsel for the employers, while accepting that it is a question of law whether or not the right criteria had been applied in answering the question 'Contract of service or contract for services?', contends that it is entirely a matter of fact as to the weight given to the relevant criteria. I am bound to say that I find this submission difficult to accept. For example, it is well established that the power to direct and control the work of the employee is an important factor, but only one of the factors to be considered. If an

industrial tribunal decided that so much weight should be given to the control exercised
a or exercisable by the employer that it concluded the issue, I would have thought that an
appeal tribunal would clearly be entitled itself to make the proper evaluation of that
particular factor and reverse the decision.

The one case in the Court of Appeal on which counsel for the employers relies is
Simmons v Heath Laundry Co [1910] 1 KB 543. The facts are quite simple. A laundry girl
had her hand injured by an accident arising out of and in the course of her employment.
b She earned 7s a week at the laundry, but she also gave piano lessons to a man's children
at his house at 3s a week. She applied under the Workmen's Compensation Act 1906 that
the latter sum might be taken into account under para 2(*b*) of Sch 1 to that Act in assessing
her compensation. This paragraph provided that where a workman had entered into
concurrent contracts of service with two or more employers under which he worked at
one time for one such employer and at another time for another such employer his
c average weekly earnings should be computed as if his earnings under all such contracts
were earnings in the employment of the employer for whom he was working at the time
of the accident. 'Workman' in s 13 of the 1906 Act meant—

> 'any person who has entered into or works under a contract of service or
> apprenticeship with an employer, whether by way of manual labour, clerical work,
> or otherwise, and whether the contract is expressed or implied, is oral or in
d > writing . . .'

Liability was admitted on the footing of the wages of 7s per week paid by the
respondents, but they denied that the case fell within para 2(*b*) of Sch 1, contending
successfully before the county court judge that the appellant had not entered into
concurrent contracts of service. The issue which had to be decided was whether the
e girl, as a teacher of music, came within the definition of 'workman' in the Act. In his
judgment, Cozens-Hardy MR said (at 548):

> 'In any particular case it will be for the arbitrator, after considering all the
> circumstances, to decide whether the injured professional person is or is not a
> "workman". This is not a question of law, but a question of fact, and, unless the
> arbitrator has misdirected himself, this court ought not to interefere.'
f
Fletcher Moulton LJ said (at 549):

> 'These facts, although very simple, raise a question of law of considerable
> importance and difficulty. It turns substantially on the scope which is to be given to
> the phrase "contract of service" in the [Workmen's Compensation] Act.'

g Towards the end of his judgment he said (at 550):

> 'The learned county court judge has decided that it was not a contract of service,
> and that therefore the earnings under it cannot be counted in assessing the
> compensation to be paid to the injured girl. This is a question of fact as to which we
> cannot interfere with his decision.'

h Buckley LJ began his judgment in these words (at 550):

> 'This appeal involves a decision trifling in pecuniary amount, but of the largest
> consequence in its possible application to other cases. The question in substance is as
> to the true meaning of the words "contract of service" in the definition of a workman
> contained in s. 13 of the Act.'

j Buckley LJ dealt in some little detail with examples of contracts under which services
are rendered but which could not be described as contracts of service. He then said (at
553):

> 'The question to be answered is, Was he employed as a workman or was he
> employed as a skilled adviser? I do not know whether it is possible to approach more
> closely to an answer to the question as to what is a contract of service under this Act

than to say that in each case the question to be asked is what was the man employed
to do; was he employed upon the terms that he should within the scope of his
employment obey his master's orders, or was he employed to exercise his skill and
achieve an indicated result in such a manner as in his judgment was most likely to
ensure success? Was his contract a contract of service within the meaning which an
ordinary person would give to the words? Was it a contract under which he would
be appropriately described as the servant of the employer? If the question which the
county court judge puts to himself is that question, and his answer is given in view
of those principles, then I think his finding is a finding of fact.'

I must confess that I was surprised at the terms of this decision, emanating, as it does,
from so strong a Court of Appeal. I am relieved to find that my diffident conclusion that
the decision was wrong seems to me to be amply borne out by the two main speeches in
the well-known case of *Edwards (Inspector of Taxes) v Bairstow* [1955] 3 All ER 48, [1956]
AC 14. The facts of the case are simple enough. In 1946 Mr Bairstow and Mr Harrison
embarked on a joint venture involving the purchase of a complete spinning plant,
agreeing between themselves not to hold it but to make a quick resale. After much
negotiation and not until 1948 the plant was sold in several lots at a substantial profit.
Expenses had been incurred, inter alia, for commission for help in effecting the sales, for
insurance, renovation of the plant, etc. The General Commissioners found that there was
not an adventure in the nature of trade to justify an assessment to income tax under Case
1 of Sch D to the Income Tax Act 1918. Viscount Simonds said ([1955] 3 All ER 48 at 54,
[1956] AC 14 at 30–31):

'To say that a transaction is, or is not, an adventure in the nature of trade is to say
that it has or has not the characteristics which distinguish such an adventure. But it
is a question of law, not of fact, what are those characteristics, or, in other words,
what the statutory language means. It follows that the inference can only be
regarded as an inference of fact if it is assumed that the tribunal which makes it is
rightly directed in law what the characteristics are and that, I think, is the assumption
that is made. It is a question of law what is murder; a jury finding as a fact that
murder has been committed has been directed on the law and acts under that
direction. The commissioners making an inference of fact that a transaction is, or is
not, an adventure in the nature of trade are assumed to be similarly directed, and
their finding thus becomes an inference of fact.'

Lord Radcliffe said ([1955] 3 All ER 48 at 55, [1956] AC 14 at 33):

'My Lords, I think that it is a question of law what meaning is to be given to the
words of the Income Tax Act "trade, manufacture, adventure or concern in the
nature of trade" and for that matter what constitutes "profits or gains" arising from
it. Here we have a statutory phrase involving a charge of tax, and it is for the courts
to interpret its meaning, having regard to the context in which it occurs, and to the
principles which they bring to bear on the meaning of income.'

He then went on to observe that the law did not supply a precise definition of the word
'trade', much less did it prescribe a detailed or exhaustive set of rules for application to
any particular set of circumstances. He said ([1955] 3 All ER 48 at 55–56, [1956] AC 14
at 33):

'In effect, it lays down the limits within which it would be permissible to say that
a "trade" as interpreted by s. 237 of the Act does or does not exist. The field so
marked out is a wide one and there are many combinations of circumstances in
which it could not be said to be wrong to arrive at a conclusion one way or the other.
If the facts of any particular case are fairly capable of being so described, it seems to
me that it necessarily follows that the determination of the commissioners, special
or general, to the effect that a trade does or does not exist is not "erroneous in point
of law"; and, if a determination cannot be shown to be erroneous in point of law,
the statute does not admit of its being upset by the court on appeal. I except the

a
occasions when the commissioners, although dealing with a set of facts which would
warrant a decision either way, show by some reason they give or statement they
make in the body of the Case that they have misunderstood the law in some relevant
particular. All these cases in which the facts warrant a determination either way can
be described as questions of degree and therefore as questions of fact.'

It seems to me clear that in the *Heath Laundry* case it was a question of law what
meaning had to be given to para 2(b) of Sch 1 to the Workmen's Compensation Act 1906.
b
Further, it must be axiomatic that whether or not A has entered into a contract with B,
whether such contract be in writing or partly in writing and partly oral, or wholly oral,
is a question of law involving the true interpretation of a document and/or the conduct
of the parties. The facts cannot warrant a determination either way. It is not a question
of degree, as in the case of the meaning of reasonableness (see *Union of Construction, Allied
Trades and Technicians v Brain* [1981] ICR 542) or whether a breach amounted to a
c
repudiatory breach (see *Woods v WM Car Services (Peterborough) Ltd* [1982] ICR 693). If
then it is a question of law, whether on the correct interpretation of a document or
whether on the true inference from the facts, parties have entered into a contract, then
in my judgment it must be equally a question of law what on the facts found is the true
nature or quality of that legal relationship? Given that A has entered into a contract with
B to allow him to use his, A's, premises, I would have thought it axiomatic that whether
d
such an agreement amounts to a lease or a licence is a question of law depending on
either a proper construction of the relevant document(s) and/or on the true interpretation
of the facts. If this be correct, then having established as a matter of law that there was a
contract of employment between A and B, the quality or nature of that contract must
equally be a question of law: Was it a contract of service or a contract for services, did B
enter A's employment as an ordinary employee or was he employed by A as an
e
independent contractor?

I do not think that it is profitable to consider all the other cases of a lesser status than
that of the *Heath Laundry* case. I should perhaps refer to *Morren v Swinton and Pendlebury
BC* [1965] 2 All ER 349, [1965] 1 WLR 576, which involved a case stated by the Minister
of Housing and Local Government under s 35 of the Local Government Superannuation
Act 1937 for the opinion of the High Court on 'any question of law . . .' The dispute was
f
between a local authority and a resident engineer whom they had appointed, and the
issue was whether or not he came within the definition of 'employee' in s 40(1) of the
Local Government Superannuation Act 1937. Lord Parker CJ, with whose judgment
Marshall and Widgery JJ agreed, said ([1965] 2 All ER 349 at 352, [1965] 1 WLR 576 at
583):

g
          'Counsel for the respondents has pressed on the court that the question of what is
     the legal quality of the contract is a question of fact, and that, being a question of
     fact, it is for the Minister and not for this court to determine, provided that there is
     any evidence which would justify the Minister in arriving at this conclusion. For
     my part, I am quite unable to accept that. The terms of the contract of course are
     fact, and to that extent the determination depends on fact, but it seems to me
h
     perfectly clear that, once the primary facts are found, then it is a pure question of
     law what is the reasonable inference based on the legal interpretation of the contract.'

In *Global Plant Ltd v Secretary of State for Health and Social Security* [1971] 3 All ER 385,
[1972] 1 QB 139, Lord Widgery CJ declined to follow the view expressed by Lord Parker
CJ, distinguishing it on the ground that in that case the issue of contract of service or no
j
had to be determined substantially from a written contract. I cannot accept the validity
of this distinction.

It was objected by counsel for the employers that if the Employment Appeal Tribunal
and the Court of Appeal were entitled to intervene where in their opinion the industrial
tribunal had reached the wrong, although an arguable decision, this would lead to a
multiplicity of litigation. In my judgment the contrary would be the case. Without the
Employment Appeal Tribunal being entitled to intervene where in its view the industrial

tribunal has wrongly evaluated the weight of a relevant consideration(s) then it will be open to industrial tribunals to reach differing conclusions, so long as they are reasonably maintainable, on essentially the same facts. This is clearly highly undesirable, particularly where a substantial number of statutory provisions impose duties on an employer in relation to his employees, or confer benefits on employees, where they work under a contract of service, but not under a contract for services. Quite apart from the 1978 Act, there are the Transfer of Undertakings (Protection of Employment) Regulations 1981, SI 1981/1794 dealing with rights and obligations relating to employers and employees on certain transfers or mergers of undertakings, business or parts of business, the Social Security Act 1975, which makes the employer responsible for contributions in respect of an employed 'earner', and the Factories Acts. To permit conflicting decisions on the basis that a broad band exists where a tribunal or a court might be said reasonably entitled to decide the issue either way would seem most unsatisfactory.

At the appeal tribunal two attacks were mounted on the decision of the industrial tribunal and I will seek to deal with these separately.

1. *The finding that there is no contractual obligation either on the employers, Trusthouse Forte, to offer work or on the respondents to do work once rostered*

It was submitted that the industrial tribunal, having found that in practice 'regular' casuals on the list had priority in the offer of available work and a reciprocal practical requirement to do the work once rostered (because failure to do the work could lead to possible suspension and subsequent removal from the list) the right conclusion to draw was that there was a contractual obligation on the employers to offer work to 'regulars' in priority and on 'regulars' to do the work when offered. It was therefore contended that factors (o) and (p) in para 23 of the industrial tribunal's reasons should not have been placed in the balance against there being a contract of employment. On the contrary, 'the one important ingredient' (namely mutuality of obligation) which the industrial tribunal found to be missing was indeed present.

The appeal tribunal rejected this submission. It was, as found by the industrial tribunal, the commanding economic power of the employers and the financial advantages to the respondents of conforming with the employers' requirements which enabled the employers to be able to rely on the 'regulars' accepting the work when it was rostered, and the 'regulars', for their part, being able to rely on receiving the priority to which I have referred. The same attack has been repeated before us. Counsel for the respondents complained that the industrial tribunal had begged the question in factors (o) and (p). I do not think this is right. The 'assurance of preference in the allocation of any available work' which the 'regulars' enjoyed was no more than a firm expectation in practice. It was not a contractual promise. The employers, of course, expected the respondents to accept engagements rostered, but to suggest that a failure to accept amounted to a breach of contract is going too far. They were entitled to choose whether or not to attend, and however irritating it might have been to the employers if faced with a refusal, it would have been quite unreal to conclude that either party would have thought it was a breach of contract.

2. *The industrial tribunal erred in law in weighing in the balance factors (q) and (r)*

Factor (q) was that during the subsistence of the relationship it was the parties' view that the casual workers were independent contractors engaged under successive contracts for services. Factor (r) was that it is the recognised custom and practice of the industry that casual workers are engaged under a contract for services.

The Employment Appeal Tribunal accepted this submission, concluding that the evidence fell far short of showing that the parties had any view of the nature of the existing contractual relationship between them, let alone a shared intentional desire to produce a particular legal relationship. Having accepted the finding by the industrial tribunal that there was no overall contractual obligation to roster any 'regular' casuals and accordingly unless and until in each week a 'regular' casual was rostered for a job there could be no contractual bond of any kind between the employers and the employee, the respondents' success on this subsidiary issue was, however, considered to be irrelevant.

a   Since I agree that the Employment Appeal Tribunal were right to conclude that the respondents' success on the subsidiary point was of no practical consequence, there is no need to inquire into the correctness or otherwise of their accepting the respondents' submissions with regard to paras (q) and (r). I add, however, these short observations since they may have some relevance to the next main heading. I accept counsel for the employers' submission that there was ample evidence that the respondents and the

b   employers were aware of the factual distinctions between 'regular' casuals and the employees of the employers, but since there was no ambiguity as to the relationship it seems to me to be irrelevant to consider what was the legal result the parties intended to produce. Clearly the 'custom and practice' found in factor (r) did not amount to a legal custom properly so described. However, the respondents' evidence was initially that the employers were out of step with the industry. They said that they were the only

c   employers who did not issue contracts of employment. This was subsequently withdrawn as a result of the employers, during an adjournment, calling evidence to establish that the practice which they adopted, referred to earlier in this judgment, was indeed the practice adopted generally throughout the trade. This was a factor, although not a particularly important factor, which the industrial tribunal were entitled to take into account as part of the background against which the parties regulated their relationship.

d   The industrial tribunal were entitled to find as they did that from the commencement of their engagement the respondents were treated by the employers as casual staff, on terms and conditions entirely distinct from those accorded to the wine butlers and dispense barmen who were permanent employees and issued with written contracts of employment. The respondents were aware of the distinction and did not challenge it.

Separate contracts. It seems quite clear that at the hearing before the industrial tribunal

e   the essence of the respondents' case was that there was one overall or continuous contract in relation to the 'regulars'. The chairman's notes show that it was in his mind that certainly one alleged feature, the casual nature of the contract, might affect 'whether we conclude a continuing or successive contract'. The tribunal note of counsel for the employers' closing speech again makes it clear that he was dealing with a case in which it had been maintained throughout that the nature of the relationship was not short-term

f   but a continuous contract of service, which had been terminated by the employers' letter of 26 February. The reply by Mrs Gill, on behalf of the respondents, again made it clear that the employment was 'continuous'. However, it was accepted before the appeal tribunal, before whom Mr Irvine did not appear for the employers, that the point had been made that each hiring was a separate contract and the nature of that contract was a contract of service. The point was not dealt with by the industrial tribunal, but the appeal

g   tribunal felt at liberty to decide it. They took the view that the factors relied on as indicating the existence of a contract of employment enumerated by the industrial tribunal was as much applicable to each individual contract as to an overall contract. They left out of account factors (j) to (m) which the industrial tribunal, rightly in the view of the appeal tribunal, regarded as neutral. When they came to the factors which in relation to the overall contract were treated as being inconsistent with a contract of

h   employment, the lack of mutuality factors (o) and (p) did not apply to the individual contracts, since once a 'regular' had turned up for the function then it was accepted there was a contractual obligation to allow the work to be done. They repeated their views in relation to factors (q) and (r), namely that there was no evidence justifying a finding of any specific intention by the parties as to the nature of the legal relationship that they were creating. They therefore concluded that all those elements pointing against a

j   contract of employment had disappeared, leaving in existence factors all of which point to there being a contract of employment. The appeal tribunal said:

'We find it difficult to see on what grounds it can be urged that each individual contract is a contract for services, given the degree of control, the nature of payment, the holiday pay, the background of recurrence, the de facto requirement to work for one person only.'

However, the nature of payment, the holiday pay, the background of recurrence and the de facto requirement to work for one person only are not relevant to status when working pursuant to an individual contract: they are only relevant to the issue, 'Was there an overall contract?', as to which the appeal tribunal have agreed with the decision of the industrial tribunal. The appeal tribunal concluded that each individual contract was a contract of employment and not a contract for services. Counsel for the employers, of course, accepts that there were individual contracts with the 'regulars', as, indeed, with all casuals. He contends that they were not contracts of employment and that this issue was never properly before the industrial tribunal. He takes the further point that in each single contract the engagement was for a particular task and when that task was performed that engagement was discharged by performance. In such circumstances there was no dismissal and therefore no entitlement to invoke the Act: see *Wiltshire County Council v National Association of Teachers in Further and Higher Education* [1980] ICR 455, a decision of this court. There is, in fact, indeed a finding in this regard in para 6 of the industrial tribunal's reasons for its decision:

'If an engagement is undertaken the worker is paid at the appropriate hourly or sessional rate for the work performed. During the function the casual worker works under the direction and control of the employer as part of his organisation and the relationship ends automatically at the end of the function without the need of notice on either side.'

It appears to have been accepted before the industrial tribunal that it cannot be determined in advance precisely how long each function will last, therefore how long the casual will be employed in relation to that function. He will, of course, stay until he has completed all the work for which he was engaged.

The point whether the expiry of each such individual contract at the conclusion of each session constitutes a 'dismissal' within the meaning of s 55 of the 1978 Act was not considered by the appeal tribunal and, indeed, was not investigated by the industrial tribunal. In my judgment the appeal tribunal, having allowed the individual contract point to be raised, should have remitted it to the industrial tribunal in order to consider not only whether such individual contracts were contracts of service or for services, but also whether, since counsel for the respondents wishes to contest the point, each such contract was discharged by performance at the conclusion of the work involved in the session and whether, in such circumstances, where was a 'dismissal' within the meaning of s 55 of the 1978 Act.

I would accordingly have allowed this appeal to the limited extent of ordering the remission to the industrial tribunal of what can be called, conveniently, 'the single or successive contract issue', and dismissed the cross-appeal.

FOX LJ. The preliminary issue with which we are concerned is whether the applicants, the respondents in this court, were 'employees' under a 'contract of employment' within s 153(1) of the Employment Protection (Consolidation) Act 1978 or whether they were independent contractors working under a contract for services.

Under s 136(1) of the Act an appeal lies to the Employment Appeal Tribunal 'on a question of law' arising from a decision of the industrial tribunal. The first question which we have to determine is the extent of the jurisdiction of the Employment Appeal Tribunal to interfere with the decision of the industrial tribunal. It is said, by the applicants, that the question whether a contract is a contract of service or a contract for services is a question of law, that s 136(1) permits an appeal on a question of law, and that accordingly the Employment Appeal Tribunal were free to make up their own minds on that question of law on the basis of the facts found by the industrial tribunal.

I accept that the question whether a contract is a contract of service can, in a general sense, be called one of law. But I doubt if that is useful in relation to the present problem. It gives too general an answer to a more complex matter. Thus it is evident from the authorities that a question can, in a general sense, be characterised as one of law without excluding the possibility that, in the end, it resolves itself into a question of fact in

individual cases. In *Currie v IRC* [1921] 2 KB 332 the question was whether a person was
a carrying on a 'profession' within the meaning of exception (*c*) of s 39 of the Finance (No
2) Act 1915. Lord Sterndale MR said (at 335–336):

> 'Is the question whether a man is carrying on a profession or not a matter of law
> or a matter of fact? I do not know that it is possible to give a positive answer to that
> question; it must depend upon the circumstances with which the Court is dealing.
> There may be circumstances in which nobody could arrive at any other conclusion
b > than that what the man was doing was carrying on a profession; and therefore,
> looking at the matter from the point of view of the judge directing a jury, the judge
> would be bound to direct them that on the facts they could only find that he was
> carrying on a profession. That reduces it to a question of law. On the other hand,
> there may be facts on which the direction would have to be given the other way.
> But between those two extremes there is a very large tract of country in which the
c > matter becomes a question of degree; and where that is the case the question is
> undoubtedly, in my opinion, one of fact . . .'

In *Edwards (Inspector of Taxes) v Bairstow* [1955] 3 All ER 48, [1956] AC 14 the question
was whether a transaction was 'an adventure or concern in the nature of trade' and so
taxable under Case I of Sch D to the Income Tax Act 1918. Lord Radcliffe said that was a
d question of law: see [1955] 3 All ER 48 at 55, [1956] AC 14 at 33. But he also said that
the law provided no precise definition of the word 'trade' and that there were many
combinations of circumstances in which it could not be said to be wrong to arrive at a
conclusion one way or the other. All such cases could be described 'as questions of degree
and, therefore, as questions of fact'.

Simmons v Heath Laundry Co [1910] 1 KB 543 is a much earlier example of the principle
e stated in *Currie v IRC* and *Edwards v Bairstow*. The case turned on the meaning of the
term 'contract of service' in the Workmen's Compensation Act 1906; the problem related
to part-time earnings of the applicant from giving piano lessons and giving
accompaniments on the piano. The arbitrator decided that the earnings did not arise
under contracts of service. That was held to be a question of fact for the arbitrator, and
accordingly the Court of Appeal refused to interfere. Fletcher Moulton LJ said (at 549):

f > 'Some cases present no difficulty. For example, where the proprietor of a private
> boarding school engages ushers to teach the boys and to maintain discipline, it does
> not, in my opinion, admit of reasonable doubt that the contracts into which those
> ushers enter are "contracts of service" within the Act. On the other hand it is in my
> mind equally clear that where a person goes to a music or singing master to take
> lessons it would be absurd to hold that the person giving the lessons is the servant of
g > the person taking them in any sense of the word. The contract between them is a
> contract for services, but it is not a contract of service. Between these two extreme
> cases lie an infinite number of intermediate cases where the special circumstances
> point with greater or less force towards the one conclusion or the other, and in my
> opinion it is impossible to lay down any rule of law distinguishing the one from the
> other. It is a question of fact to be decided by all the circumstances of the case.'

h
Woods v WM Car Services (Peterborough) Ltd [1982] ICR 693, which was concerned with
the question whether the employer had repudiated the contract of service, seems to me
to follow the same principles as those stated by Lord Sterndale MR, Fletcher Moulton LJ
and Lord Radcliffe.

In *Woods* (at 698) Lord Denning MR said:

j > 'In each case it depends on whether the misconduct amounted to a repudiatory
> breach . . . The circumstances are so infinitely various there can be, and is, no rule
> of law saying what circumstances justify and what do not. It is a question of fact for
> the tribunal of fact—in this case the industrial tribunal.'

Now what is said on behalf of the respondents in the present case is this. It is accepted
that in *Woods v WM Car Services*, for example, the nature of the issue before the court

was such that there was a grey area, or a band of uncertainty, where one could not say
that it would be wrong for the tribunal to decide the case one way or the other. The
confines of the law were imprecise and, within the grey area, it was a matter of degree in
individual cases whether the case was within the statutory provision or not. That,
however, is not, so it is said, the position here. There can only be one correct answer to
the question whether a contract of service exists. Reliance is placed on the decision of this
court in *Young & Woods Ltd v West* [1980] IRLR 201 and, in particular, the observations
of Stephenson LJ (at 205).

I do not feel able to accept that argument. The issue seems to me to be no more
susceptible of the analysis that there is a right and a wrong answer to be determined as a
matter of pure law than was the issue in *Heath Laundry* or *Currie v IRC* or *Woods v WM
Car Services*. The precise quality to be attributed to various individual facts is so much a
matter of degree that is is unrealistic to regard the issue as attracting a clear 'legal' answer.

I do not think that *Heath Laundry* was wrongly decided. It seems to me to be consistent
with the principles applied by the Court of Appeal in *Currie v IRC* and the House of
Lords in *Edwards v Bairstow*, and if there be any conflict between it and *Young & Woods v
West* (in which, in fact, the Court of Appeal was of opinion that the decision of the
industrial tribunal was right and did not have to interfere with it), I would follow the
Heath Laundry case.

I should add that I do not detect in the more recent authorities any tendency to depart
from the *Edwards v Bairstow* principles. In *Melon v Hector Powe Ltd* [1981] 1 All ER 313
they were applied by the House of Lords in an appeal from an industrial tribunal under
the Redundancy Payments Act 1965: see the speech of Lord Fraser (at 316). And in
Pioneer Shipping Ltd v BTP Tioxide Ltd, The Nema [1981] 2 All ER 1030 at 1047, [1982] AC
724 at 752 Lord Roskill said that in *Edwards v Bairstow* the House of Lords made it clear
that the court should only interfere with the conclusion of special commissioners if it
were shown either that they had erred in law or had reached a conclusion which no
reasonable tribunal, properly instructed, could have reached. And he went on to deprecate
the suggestion that since the question whether a contract was frustrated was one of law
the court was free to decide the matter itself and contrary to the decision of the arbitrators.

In the present case the industrial tribunal in their full and careful reasons list nine
circumstances which are consistent with the existence of a contract of employment, four
which are not inconsistent with it and five which are inconsistent with it. It seems to me
that the case was indeed one where the answer, in the end, was a matter of degree and,
therefore, of fact. For example there may, I think, be a narrow line between the
conclusion that the employers were undertaking to offer work to the regular casuals in
return for the regular casuals undertaking to accept the work which was offered (ie a
contract of employment) and the conclusion that there was no contract to employ and
that the arrangement was simply the consequence of market forces (in effect, the
dominant economic position of the employers). It was essentially a matter of fact for the
industrial tribunal to decide which was correct after considering the evidence.

The result, in my view, is that the Employment Appeal Tribunal was not entitled to
interfere with the decision of the industrial tribunal unless that tribunal misdirected
itself in law or its decision was one which no tribunal, properly instructed, could have
reached on the facts. Neither of those exceptions can be demonstrated here in relation to
the overall contract question. I cannot see any misdirection and I find it quite impossible
to say that no reasonable tribunal, properly instructed, could have reached the conclusion
that the industrial tribunal did. They had evidence on which to do so. I agree, therefore,
with the conclusion of the appeal tribunal that the industrial tribunal's decision that
there was no overall contract of employment must stand.

There remains the question whether there was a series of individual contracts of
employment of the 'regular' casuals. The appeal tribunal were of the opinion that the
industrial tribunal had not dealt with the point at all. Mrs Gill, who appeared for the
respondents before the industrial tribunal, is, we are informed, in no doubt that she put
the point. In the light of its careful reasons, I should be surprised if this tribunal
overlooked it.

a If the point was not dealt with by the industrial tribunal I do not think that the appeal tribunal was justified in dealing with the point itself. The appeal tribunal should, in the circumstances of this case, have remitted the matter. In fact, however, what the industrial tribunal decided was this:

'The majority decision of the tribunal is that the applicants [the respondents] are not qualified for interim relief because they are not employees who worked under a contract of employment.'

b That was the question the industrial tribunal were required to decide.

Now the industrial tribunal, no doubt, decided that there was no overall contract of employment. But they decided more than that. In the final paragraph of their reasons they state:

c 'It is our decision that the applicants [the respondents] were in business on their own account as independent contractors supplying services and are not qualified for interim relief because they were not employees who worked under a contract of employment.'

That seems to me to be inconsistent with the 'separate contracts' contention. Since it does not appear to me that there was any misdirection by the industrial tribunal and the d conclusion was not unreasonable on the facts, I would therefore regard the point as concluded.

I would allow the appeal and dismiss the cross-appeal.

SIR JOHN DONALDSON MR. The judgment of the Employment Appeal Tribunal in this case suggests that there is a difference of judicial view whether the question 'Is a contract a contract of employment or a contract for services?' is a mixed question of fact e and law or a question of law, but I do rather doubt whether the triple categorisation of issues as 'fact', 'law' and 'mixed fact and law' is very helpful in the context of the jurisdiction of the Employment Appeal Tribunal.

The Employment Appeal Tribunal is a court with a statutory jurisdiction. So far as is material, that jurisdiction is limited to hearing appeals on questions of law arising from f any decision of, or arising in any proceedings before, an industrial tribunal: see s 136(1) of the Employment Protection (Consolidation) Act 1978. If it is to vary or reverse a decision of an industrial tribunal it has to be satisfied that the tribunal has erred on a question of law.

Whilst it may be convenient for some purposes to refer to questions of 'pure' law as contrasted with 'mixed' questions of fact and law, the fact is that the Employment Appeal g Tribunal has no jurisdiction to consider any question of mixed fact and law until it has purified or distilled the mixture and extracted a question of pure law.

The purification methods are well known. In the last analysis all courts have to direct themselves as to the law and then apply those directions in finding the facts (in relation to admissibility and relevance) and to the facts as so found. When reviewing such a decision, the only problem is to divine the direction on law which the lower court gave h to itself. Sometimes it will have been expressed in its reasons, but more often it has to be inferred. This is the point of temptation for the appellate court. It may well have a shrewd suspicion, or gut reaction, that it would have reached a different decision, but it must never forget that this may be because it thinks that it would have found or weighed the facts differently. Unpalatable though it may be on occasion, it must loyally accept the conclusions of fact with which it is presented and, accepting those conclusions, it must j be satisfied that there *must* have been a misdirection on a question of law before it can intervene. Unless the direction on law has been expressed it can only be so satisfied if, in its opinion, no reasonable tribunal, properly directing itself on the relevant questions of law, could have reached the conclusion under appeal. This is a heavy burden on an appellant. I would have thought that all this was trite law, but if it is not, it is set out with the greatest possible clarity in *Edwards (Inspector of Taxes) v Bairstow* [1955] 3 All ER 48, [1956] AC 14.

Why, then, is there a problem in relation to an issue whether an applicant to an industrial tribunal is or is not employed under a contract of employment? The answer lies in the interpretation which the Employment Appeal Tribunal has placed on a passage in a judgment of Stephenson LJ in *Young & Woods Ltd v West* [1980] IRLR 201 at para 15, which, in the appeal tribunal's judgment, Browne-Wilkinson J interpreted as authority for the proposition that—

> 'the question is one of pure law, so that the appellate court can, and indeed must, reach its own view on whether or not, on the findings of fact made by the lower court, the true analysis is that there was a contract of employment.'

If this is the true interpretation of Stephenson LJ's judgment, it represents a sudden and unexplained departure from what has been understood to be the law for over 70 years, for it was as long ago as that that this court went so far, in *Simmons v Heath Laundry Co* [1910] 1 KB 543, as to described the issue as one of fact with which an appellate court could not interfere in the absence of reason to believe that the arbitrator had misdirected himself. For my part I do not think that Stephenson LJ can be taken as having intended to make such a departure.

There is no doubt that there are pure questions of law which throw a court back to questions of fact. The most obvious example is what length of notice is required to terminate a contract which does not expressly make provision for termination. This is a pure question of law and the answer is: such time as is reasonable in all the circumstances. Applying that direction to facts whose nature, quality and degree are known with complete precision will no doubt always produce the same answer. But this is not real life. In reality every tribunal of fact will find and assess the factual circumstances in ways which differ to a greater or lesser extent and so can give rise to different conclusions, each of which is unassailable on appeal. In this sense, but in this sense alone, their conclusions are conclusions of fact. More accurately they are conclusions of law which are wholly dependent on conclusions of fact.

The test to be applied in identifying whether a contract is one of employment or for services is a pure question of law and so is its application to the facts. But it is for the tribunal of fact not only to find those facts but to assess them qualitatively and within limits, which are indefinable in the abstract, those findings and that assessment will dictate the correct legal answer. In the familiar phrase, it is all a question of fact and degree.

It is only if the weight given to a particular factor shows a self-misdirection in law that an appellate court with a limited jurisdiction can interfere. It is difficult to demonstrate such a misdirection and, to the extent that it is not done, the issue is one of fact. This, I think, is what this court meant in *Simmons v Heath Laundry Co* which, so construed, is consistent with *Edwards v Bairstow*.

In the instant appeal the industrial tribunal directed itself to—

> 'consider all aspects of the relationship, no single factor being in itself decisive and each of which may vary in weight and direction, and having given such balance to the factors as seems appropriate, to determine whether the person was carrying on business on his own account.'

This is wholly correct as a matter of law and it is not for this court or for the Employment Appeal Tribunal to reweigh the facts.

The industrial tribunal then concluded that there was no contract of employment extending over a series of engagements. This conclusion was based on an evaluation of the large number of factors set out in their reasons, but it is clear that the majority attached great importance to the fact that, as they saw it, there was no mutuality of obligation and that in the industry casual workers were not regarded as working under any overall contract of employment.

The Employment Appeal Tribunal refused to interfere with this conclusion and in my judgment they were right to do so. So far as mutuality is concerned, the 'arrangement', to use a neutral term, could have been that the employers promised to offer work to the regular casuals and, in exchange, the regular casuals undertook to accept and perform

such work as was offered. This would have constituted a contract. But what happened in
a fact could equally well be attributed to market forces. Which represented the true view
could only be determined by the tribunal which heard the witnesses and evaluated the
facts. Against, although how the industry and its casual workers regarded their status is
not directly material, any generally accepted view would be part of the contractual
matrix and so indirectly material, although in no way decisive. This again was a matter
for the industrial tribunal.

b   Although I, like the Employment Appeal Tribunal, am content to accept the industrial
tribunal's conclusion that there was no overall or umbrella contract, I think that there is
a shorter answer. It is that, giving the respondents' evidence its fullest possible weight,
all that could emerge was an umbrella or master contract *for*, not *of*, employment. It
would be a contract to offer and accept individual contracts of employment and, as such,
outside the scope of the unfair dismissal provisions.

c   This leaves the question of whether the respondents entered into individual contracts
of employment on each occasion when they worked for the employers and it is here that
the Employment Appeal Tribunal and the industrial tribunal parted company. The
Employment Appeal Tribunal dealt with this aspect of the matter by saying:

d   'For whatever reason, the industrial tribunal have not dealt with the point, nor
have they weighed the factors bearing on the question, "Was each contract a contract
for services?" in the same careful way in which they weighed those factors when
looking at the nature of an overall contract of employment. In our judgment, the
mere assertion by the industrial tribunal that it was a succession of contracts for
services entered into by independent contractors cannot stand as good in law in the
absence of any reason for that conclusion. We must therefore consider the point and
reach our own decision on it.'

e   This, in my judgment, does less than justice to the decision of the industrial tribunal.
It had weighed the relevant factors governing the relationship between the parties with
great care in the course of determining whether any umbrella contract was one of
employment or for the provision of services. It had rejected the umbrella contract on the
grounds that there was no contract at all, but it had also concluded that—

f   'the applicants [the respondents] were in business on their own account as
independent contractors supplying services and are not qualified for interim relief
because they were not employees who worked under a contract of employment'.

This, unless erroneous in law, was a wholly sufficient reason for holding that the
individual contracts, which clearly existed, were contracts for the provision of services. If
g and in so far as the Employment Appeal Tribunal was criticising the industrial tribunal
for failing to say so, it should be pointed out that there was only one question which it
had to decide, namely whether the respondents were employees who worked under a
contract of employment. It answered this question in the negative as a matter for decision
under the heading 'Decision'. The purpose of what followed under the heading 'Reasons'
was to explain this decision. Those reasons, by explaining that there was no umbrella
h contract and that the respondents were independent contractors, disposed in different
ways of the two different forms of contract of employment which had been suggested in
argument. The fact that the argument was primarily about the umbrella contract does
not persuade me that the status of the individual contracts was not carefully considered,
particularly as Mrs Gill, who appeared for the respondents, says that she argued in the
alternative for a succession of individual contracts of employment. Furthermore, in the
j light of the industrial tribunal's finding of lack of mutuality in relation to the umbrella
contract the only point of considering 'service v services' was in relation to the individual
contracts.

Even if the Employment Appeal Tribunal had been correct in holding that the
industrial tribunal's reasons were not sufficiently clear, this would not have entitled it to
arrogate to itself the full functions of an industrial tribunal and so reach its own decision.
The Employment Appeal Tribunal can correct errors of law and substitute its own
decision in so far as the industrial tribunal must, but for the error of law, have reached

such a decision. But if it is an open question how the industrial tribunal would have decided the matter if it had directed itself correctly, the Employment Appeal Tribunal can only remit the case for further consideration.

In the course of argument it was suggested that the course adopted by the Employment Appeal Tribunal could be justified by para 21(1) of Sch 11 to the Employment Protection (Consolidation) Act 1978, which provides:

'For the purpose of disposing of an appeal the Appeal Tribunal may exercise any powers of the body or officer from whom the appeal was brought or may remit the case to that body or officer.'

However, I do not read that paragraph as doing more than authorising the Employment Appeal Tribunal to record a decision which, on the facts found, it could have directed the industrial tribunal to record.

In pursuance of this declared intention to reach its own decision, the Employment Appeal Tribunal reviewed and re-evaluated the various factors, concluding that there was a series of ad hoc contracts of employment. In so doing, in my judgment it quite clearly usurped the function of the industrial tribunal. This was not a case in which no reasonable tribunal could have reached the conclusion reached by the industrial tribunal and no reasonable tribunal could have failed to reach that reached by the Employment Appeal Tribunal. The industrial tribunal's decision may have been surprising, but it was certainly not 'perverse' in the legal or any other sense.

The Employment Appeal Tribunal justified its own conclusion by saying:

'Standing back and looking at the matter in the round, what we have to ask is whether these applicants [the respondents] can be said to have been carrying on business on their own account. We can well understand that casuals who have their services to sell, and sell them in the market to whoever needs them for the time being, can be said to be in business on their own account in the marketing or selling of their services; but we find it difficult to reach that conclusion in a situation where the services are, in fact, being offered to one person only against a background arrangement (albeit not contractual) which requires the services to be offered to one person only and which involves a repetition of those contracts (albeit under no obligation to do so) as is shown by the weekly pay packet, the holiday pay and other matters of that kind. In our judgment, each of these individual contracts is a contract of employment, not a contract for services.'

This must involve a misdirection on a question of law or every independent contractor who is content or able only to attract one client would be held to work under a contract of employment. Indeed, I could as well point out that what distinguishes the respondents' contracts from those of waiters who admittedly work under contracts of employment is that the respondents were employed to wait at a given function and were not available to the employers for general deployment as waiters during their hours of work. But if I did so, I too should be usurping the functions of the industrial tribunal.

I can detect no error of law on the part of the industrial tribunal and I would therefore allow the appeal and dismiss the cross-appeal, thereby restoring the decision of the industrial tribunal.

For the reasons which are set out in the judgments which have already been given to counsel, and shown, no doubt, to their clients, the appeal is allowed, although there is a small difference between Ackner LJ, on the one hand, and Fox LJ and myself on the other hand, as to the consequential orders which should be made. Ackner LJ would have remitted the successive individual contracts point to the industrial tribunal for further consideration. The cross-appeal is unanimously dismissed.

Appeal allowed. Cross-appeal dismissed. Leave to appeal to the House of Lords refused.

Solicitors: *Linklaters & Paines* (for the employers); *Tess Gill*, Claygate (for the respondents).

Frances Rustin   Barrister.

a # Inland Revenue Commissioners v Trustees of Sir John Aird's Settlement

COURT OF APPEAL, CIVIL DIVISION
WALLER, OLIVER AND ROBERT GOFF LJJ
22, 23 JUNE, 25 JULY 1983

b

Capital transfer tax – Exemption – Survivorship – Person surviving another person for specified period – Appointment made contingent on appointee surviving 'designated person' for specified period – Designated person ascertained by reference to newspaper announcement – Whether 'another person' referred to any person – Whether contingency truly one of surviving another person for a specified period – Finance Act 1975, Sch 5, para 6(2)(7).

c

Settlement – Contingent interest – Contingent interest distinguished from interest dependent on event bound to happen – Interest subject to condition that beneficiary survive designated person – Designated person described by reference to newspaper announcement of his death – Whether interest dependent on designated person's death or on survival for specified period.

d By a deed of appointment dated 28 November 1975 the trustees of a settlement comprising a fund held on discretionary trust for, inter alios, the settlor's son irrevocably appointed capital and income of part of the fund in favour of the settlor's son absolutely free from the trusts and from all further exercise of the powers contained in the settlement, contingently on his surviving a designated person for one day. The designated person was described in the deed of appointment as the person whose death occurred on *e* Saturday, 29 November 1975 and who was the first in alphabetical order of the persons dying on that date to be named in the 'deaths' column of the earliest edition of The Times newspaper published in London on Monday, 1 December 1975 (or if there was no edition published on that date then of the earliest edition published after that date) and if no person answered that description the designated person was to be the person who would satisfy that description if references to the Daily Telegraph were substituted for references *f* to The Times. The death of a Major B who died on 29 November 1975 was announced in The Times on 1 December 1975 and the settlor's son survived beyond midnight on 30 November 1975. The Revenue served on the trustees notices of determination to the effect that by virtue of the appointment the settlor's son had become absolutely entitled to the specified property in the funds and that under para 6(2)[a] of Sch 5 to the Finance Act 1975 a capital distribution was to be treated as having been made out of the property *g* comprised in the fund. The trustees appealed to the Special Commissioners, contending that, by virtue of para 6(7)[b] of that schedule, no such capital distribution was to be treated as having been made because the settlor's son had only become entitled to an interest in possession 'on surviving another person for a specified period'. The Crown contended that there was no real possibility that the death of a person on 29 November 1975 might not appear in the 'deaths' columns of either The Times or the Daily Telegraph in its next *h* published edition, that accordingly there was no genuine contingency that the settlor's son should survive another person for a specified period, that survival until midnight on 30 November 1975 was the only condition which the settlor's son had to satisfy for the appointment to take effect and that consequently para 6(7) had no application. The Special Commissioners found in favour of the trustees and the Crown appealed. The judge held that there had been a real possibility that there would be no person satisfying *j* the description of the 'designated person' and that the interest of the settlor's son was in reality and substance contingent on his surviving another person and was therefore

---

a Paragraph 6(2) is set out at p 485 *b*, post
b Paragraph 6(7) is set out at p 485 *e*, post

within the exemption. The judge found it unnecessary to decide what, as a matter of construction, was the precise time to which the settlor's son was required to survive because, as the condition was one of surviving a given person by a specified period, it made no difference to the contingent nature of the interest whether the limit of the period was known in advance. The Crown appealed, contending (i) that since para 6(7) exempted only cases where the propositus became entitled to an interest in possession 'on' surviving another person, the survival, looked at at the time when the instrument creating the interest came into effect, had to be the only condition standing between the beneficiary and the interest or alternatively (ii) that para 6(7) applied only where survival of another person by the requisite period was genuinely the contingency on which vesting of the interest depended. The Crown further contended that the words 'another person' in para 6(7) did not refer to any person in the world but only to a particular person or one on whose death there was a transfer of value which included the value of the settled property in question, and that, in the circumstances, the exemption in para 6(7) did not apply to the appointments. It was common ground (i) that until the settlor's son's interest vested the settlement was one in which no interest in possession subsisted and (ii) that there was no requirement in para 6(7) that the designated person should be identifiable in his lifetime.

Held – (1) There was no basis for treating the word 'person' in para 6(7) of Sch 5 to the 1975 Act as though it were qualified by adjectives such as 'particular', 'named' or 'identified' or by a more complex expression which would exclude every person selected or identified by a random process. Nor was there anything in the 1975 Act which required the phrase 'another person' in the paragraph to be construed as referring only to one whose death gave rise to a transfer of value which included the value of settled property in question (see p 490 *h* to p 491 *c* and p 494 *c* and *h*, post).

(2) The words 'on surviving' in para 6(7) did not have a purely temporal connotation, but referred to a contingency expressed in the trusts under which the interest in question arose. Although the contingency which, under the paragraph, gave rise to the interest was the survival of the relevant person by the requisite period, there was nothing in the paragraph which required that event to be the only condition under the trusts which had to be complied with (see p 491 *d* to *g* and p 494 *h*, post).

(3) There was a prima facie presumption that surviving another person by one day involved surviving for 24 hours from the end of the day on which the death occurred, and, in the circumstances, there were no grounds for departing from that construction but there were considerations of convenience and certainty which strongly favoured following it. It followed therefore that, under the appointment, one of the requirements for the interest to vest was that the settlor's son should survive until midnight on 30 November 1975, and the fact that when he so survived he also survived Major B by the specified period of one day did not lead to the conclusion that it was his having survived Major B that caused his interest to vest. Rather, what determined whether his interest vested or failed, following his survival for the requisite period, was the publication of The Times newspaper carrying the requisite announcement. It followed therefore that under the appointment, the settlor's son did not become entitled to an interest in possession 'on surviving another person for a specified period' within para 6(7). The appeal would accordingly be allowed (see p 491 *h j*, p 492 *e f h j* and p 493 *d* to p 494 *a* and *e* to *h*, post); dictum of Grant MR in *Lester v Garland* [1803–13] All ER Rep at 439 applied.

Decision of Nourse J [1982] 2 All ER 929 reversed.

Notes

For survivorship clauses for the purpose of gift and estate taxation, see 19 Halsbury's Laws (4th edn) para 634.

For the Finance Act 1975, Sch 5, para 6, see 45 Halsbury's Statutes (3rd edn) 1889.

Paragraph 6 of Sch 5 to the 1975 Act was repealed by the Finance Act 1982, s 157, Sch 22, Pt VII in relation to events after 8 March 1982 (subject to certain transitional *a* provisions). Sections 101 to 127 of the 1982 Act made fresh provision with respect to the charge to capital transfer tax in connection with settlements without interests in possession.

Cases referred to in judgments

Cornfoot v Royal Exchange Assurance Corp [1904] 1 KB 40, CA.

Cox v Hakes (1890) 15 App Cas 506, HL.

b *Dreyfus (Camille & Henry) Foundation Inc v IRC* [1955] 3 All ER 97, [1956] AC 39, [1955] 3 WLR 451, HL; *affg* [1954] 2 All ER 466, [1954] Ch 672, [1954] 3 WLR 167, CA.

Federal Steam Navigation Co Ltd v Dept of Trade and Industry [1974] 2 All ER 97, [1974] 1 WLR 505, HL.

Hawkins v Gathercole (1855) 6 De GM & G 1, 43 ER 1129, LJJ.

IRC v Duke of Westminster [1936] AC 1, [1935] All ER Rep 259, HL.

IRC v Hinchy [1960] 1 All ER 505, [1960] AC 748, [1960] 2 WLR 448, HL.

c *IRC v Plummer* [1979] 3 All ER 775, [1980] AC 896, [1979] 3 WLR 689, HL.

Jones v Wrotham Park Settled Estates [1979] 1 All ER 286, [1980] AC 74, [1979] 2 WLR 132, HL.

Kammins Ballrooms Co Ltd v Zenith Investments (Torquay) Ltd [1970] 2 All ER 871, [1971] AC 850, [1970] 3 WLR 287, HL.

d *Lester v Garland* (1808) 15 Ves 248, [1803–13] All ER Rep 436, 33 ER 748.

Luke v IRC [1963] 1 All ER 655, [1963] AC 557, [1963] 2 WLR 559, HL.

Lumsden v IRC [1914] AC 877, HL.

Stenhouse Holdings Ltd v IRC (1970) 46 TC 670, HL.

Stradling v Morgan (1560) 1 Plowd 199, 75 ER 305.

Cases also cited

e *Cadell v Palmer* (1833) 1 Cl & Fin 372, 6 ER 956, HL.

Cape Brandy Syndicate v IRC [1921] 2 KB 403, CA.

Cartwright v MacCormack (Trafalgar Insurance Co Ltd, third parties) [1963] 1 All ER 11, [1963] 1 WLR 18, CA.

Figgis (decd), Re, Roberts v MacLaren [1968] 1 All ER 999, [1969] 1 Ch 123.

f *Imperial Chemical Industries Ltd v Caro (Inspector of Taxes)* [1961] 1 All ER 658, [1961] 1 WLR 529, CA.

Inglewood (Lord) v IRC [1983] 1 WLR 366, CA.

Legh's Resettlement Trusts, Re, Public Trustee v Legh [1937] 3 All ER 823, [1938] Ch 39, CA.

Mangin v IRC [1971] 1 All ER 179, [1971] AC 739, PC.

Micklethwait, Re (1855) 11 Exch 452, 156 ER 908.

Pearson v IRC [1980] 2 All ER 479, [1981] AC 753, HL.

g *Public Trustee v IRC* [1964] 3 All ER 780, [1965] Ch 286, CA; *affd* [1966] 1 All ER 76, [1966] AC 520, HL.

Railway Sleepers Supply Co, Re (1885) 29 Ch D 204.

Ramsay (W T) Ltd v IRC, Eilbeck (Inspector of Taxes) v Rawling [1981] 1 All ER 865, [1982] AC 300, HL.

h ## Appeal

The Crown appealed against the decision of Nourse J ([1982] 2 All ER 929, [1982] 1 WLR 270) dated 16 December 1981 dismissing an appeal by the Crown by way of case stated (set out at [1982] 2 All ER 930–936) against the decision of the Commissioners for the Special Purposes of the Income Tax Acts whereby the commissioners quashed the determination by the Revenue that capital transfer tax was payable on the vesting of two *j* interests in two trust funds on 1 December 1975 where there had previously been no interests in possession subsisting. The facts are set out in the judgment of Oliver LJ.

John L Knox QC and *Michael Hart* for the Crown.
Edward Nugee QC and *Robert Walker QC* for the taxpayers.

Cur adv vult

25 July. The following judgments were delivered.

OLIVER LJ (giving the first judgment at the invitation of Waller LJ). This is an appeal *a*
by the Crown against an order of Nourse J ([1982] 2 All ER 929, [1982] 1 WLR 270),
made on 16 December 1981 dismissing the Crown's appeal and affirming a decision of
the Special Commissioners whereby they quashed a determination issued by the Board
of Inland Revenue under para 6 of Sch 4 to the Finance Act 1975 on 4 August 1977.

The question is whether two appointments made by the trustees of a setttlement *b*
referred to as 'Sir John Aird's Settlement' in favour respectively of Sir John Aird and Susan
Aird (being respectively a son and daughter of the original settlor) attracted a charge to
capital transfer tax, and it involves the determination of whether what has become
known as 'the newspaper–Franco Scheme' is effective to produce the fiscal result for
which it was devised.

It is necessary to say a little of the legislative background to explain the context in *c*
which the problem arises, but I can do so quite briefly since it is admirably summarised
in the judgment of the judge. Capital transfer tax was first introduced by the Finance
Act 1975 and it introduced an entirely novel system. As might be expected the 1975 Act
deals separately with property which is in absolute ownership on the one hand and settled
property on the other, but the latter itself divides into two categories, that is to say
settlements under which there is an interest vesting in possession, the typical example *d*
being the life tenant with a present interest (who is treated, in substance, as if he were
the owner of the settled property) and settlements where there is no interest in possession
for the time being (eg discretionary settlements and accumulation trusts). As regards the
latter category, it was appreciated after the Bill was published that the charging provisions
(which imposed not only a periodic charge on the funds subject to the trusts of such a
settlement but also a charge when the settled funds or part of them passed out of the *e*
settlement or passed, for instance on the appointment of an interest in possession taking
effect, from the discretionary regime to that of an 'interest in possession' settlement) bore
hardly on discretionary settlements already in existence.

As a result transitional provisions were inserted enabling such settlements to be
converted by taking them out of the discretionary regime at a sliding scale of reduced
charges. Those provisions do not matter for present purposes, because it was discovered *f*
that the charging provisions relating to settled property were framed in such a way as, on
the face of them, to permit (until they were amended in 1976) the transfer from the
discretionary regime to the 'interest in possession' regime without any charge at all by
employing the simple device of appointing the settled funds in a particular way. That
arose because, as I surmise, it was decided for very good reasons that an exemption from
charge ought to be provided to meet a fairly common situation which would otherwise *g*
have brought about a chargeable transfer in circumstances which, in effect, would have
involved a double taxation of the same property as a result of the same disposition.
Fortunately or unfortunately, according to one's point of view, the legislature, in leaving,
deliberately, a loophole for the obvious case of hardship, contrived, so it is claimed, to
open a gateway wide enough to accommodate the proverbial coach and horses.

The provisions relating to settled property are to be found in Sch 5 to the 1975 Act. It *h*
is necessary to refer in detail only to the charging provisions, but the definition of
settlement should perhaps be noted so far as is material. Paragraph 1(2) provides:

'"Settlement" means any disposition or dispositions of property, whether effected
by instrument, by parol or by operation of law, or partly in one way and partly in
another, whereby the property is for the time being—(a) held in trust for persons in
succession or for any person subject to a contingency; or (b) held by trustees on trust *j*
to accumulate the whole or part of any income of the property or with power to
make payments out of that income at the discretion of the trustees or some other
person, with or without power to accumulate surplus income . . .'

Charges on capital distributions of settled property are dealt with in para 6. Paragraph
6(1) provides that where a distribution payment is made out of property comprised in a

settlement at a time when no interest in possession subsists it is referred to as a 'capital
a distribution', and a wide definition of distribution payments is contained in para 11. The
only materiality of this in the context of the present appeal is that para 6(2) defines
circumstances in which a capital distribution is treated as being made. It provides as
follows:

b 'Where a person becomes entitled to an interest in possession in the whole or any
part of the property comprised in a settlement at a time when no such interest
subsists in the property or that part, a capital distribution shall be treated as being
made out of the property or that part of the property; and the amount of the
distribution shall be taken to be equal to the value at that time of the property or, if
the interest is in part only of that property, of that part.'

Thus to bring this paragraph into operation in relation to any given property, three
c conditions must coexist: (i) the property must be settled property as defined above in
para 1(2); (ii) there must immediately prior to (iii) below be no subsisting interest in
possession; and (iii) a person must become entitled to an interest in possession. If they do
coexist at any given time, then a charge to tax results.

The provision which gives rise to the problem with which this appeal is concerned is
para 6(7), which clearly relieves and was intended to relieve settled property from the
d charge imposed by para 6(2) in certain defined circumstances. The difficulty is in
determining the ambit of the provision, for it really is impossible to believe that the
legislature can have intended it to be as far-reaching as, on the face of it, it appears to be,
for, if it is, there can only be ascribed to Parliament an intention to furnish taxpayers,
without discrimination, with the means of avoiding the charge which it had just
imposed. Paragraph 6(7) provides:

e 'Sub-paragraph (2) above shall not be taken to apply in the case of a person who,
on surviving another person for a specified period, becomes entitled to an interest
in possession as from the other person's death.'

Thus, on the face of it, all that you have to do if you want to avoid the liability which
will otherwise arise under para 6(2) (and that will normally arise on an appointment by
f trustees of a discretionary trust) is so to appoint your fund that the vesting (a) is made
conditional on surviving for a short period some person conveniently selected as
moribund and (b) is, on becoming unconditional, dated back to that person's death.
Taxes are not normally contemplated as being optional and unless there is to be ascribed
to the legislature a wholly irrational and unusual benevolence towards beneficiaries of
settled property it must be assumed that, in framing this exemption, it had some more
limited object in mind.
g There is nothing in the 1975 Act, or, at least, there is no provision which has been
drawn to the court's attention in the course of an extensive argument, which points to
what that more limited object might be. It is, therefore, and this may be important,
deducible only by searching for some rational explanation outside the Act. It is common
ground that, if para 6(2) is to be construed, as the taxpayers say it is to be construed, in a
h way which places no restriction at all on the identity or relevance of the person from
whose death the specified period is to run, it produces the absurd result that, despite the
most elaborate transitional provisions enabling a transfer out of the discretionary regime
to take place at reduced rates of charge, those provisions are rendered substantially otiose
by the provision of an alternative and universally available means of transfer without
incurring any charge at all. It is also common ground that the only rational explanation
j for what appears, on the face of it, to be a glaring anomaly is that Parliament had in mind
a particular hardship which it was trying to meet and that that hardship was the double
taxation which would otherwise arise under para 6(2) in the relatively common case of a
testator providing in his will against the contingency of a beneficiary dying at substantially
the same time as the testator, for instance in a common accident, and either surviving
him by a very short period or being deemed to have survived him by reason of the
presumption that the elder of two commorientes is the first to die. Under the pre-existing

statutory provision relating to estate duty this might have had undesirable fiscal
consequences and it also, of course, results in the testator's estate devolving under the   a
provisions of the beneficiary's will or on his intestacy. Accordingly it was, and is,
commonplace for draftsmen of wills to insert what is known as a 'commorientes clause'
providing that the benefit conferred by the will shall be contingent on the beneficiary
surviving the testator for a given period, say one month or three months. If the
beneficiary survives, the provision in his favour takes effect as from the testator's death.
Had no relieving provision been inserted in the 1975 Act this would have resulted in a   b
double charge on the estate, since in the intervening period between the death of the
testator and the survival period the property would be settled property within the
definition in para 1(2) (the beneficiary's interest being contingent) but settled property in
which there was no interest in possession, with the result that, there having been already
a transfer of value on the testator's death, there would be a further deemed transfer in
relation to the same property on the beneficiary's interest vesting.   c
    It has, however, to be accepted that no such limitation is apparent on the face of the
provision, and it is, perhaps, not altogether surprising that the tax-avoidance industry
was not slow to avail itself of the opportunity apparently presented to it. It was, for
instance, widely reported in the latter part of 1975 that General Franco was dying and in
a number of cases appointments were made conditional on the appointee surviving him
by a short period. Other equally convenient decedents were chosen, but this type of   d
operation became known as 'the General Franco scheme'. It suffered, however, from the
minor inconvenience that the instinct for survival is strong and that in cases where the
decedent proved more tenacious of life than had been expected the vesting of the interest
created by the appointment was delayed rather longer than was originally anticipated.
We have not been told of any case in which the appointment was frustrated by a
remarkable and unhoped for recovery, but there was always the danger that the decedent   e
might emulate Charles II and, indeed, General Franco himself did not in fact die until 20
November 1975. Tax advisers, however, are nothing if not ingenious and they devised a
variant of the General Franco scheme, of which the instant case is an example and which
avoids the inconvenient obstinacy of a decedent by selecting the date for his death in
advance. In the instant case, the settlement concerned was one executed by Sir John
Renton Aird in 1947. It was a discretionary settlement under which appointments, some   f
revocable and some irrevocable, had been made from time to time. It is unnecessary to
recite the trusts or indeed to say more than that the settled funds were, for administrative
purposes, divided into two, fund A and fund B and that the appointment in favour of Sir
George John Aird with which this appeal is concerned relates to fund B and that in favour
of Susan Aird relates to fund A.
    Both appointments are for material purposes in exactly the same form, both are dated   g
28 November 1975 (a Friday) and it is common ground that until the interest of the
appointee vested the trusts affecting the appointed funds were such that no interest in
possession subsisted. Since, therefore, exactly the same considerations apply to both
appointments, it is necessary to refer only to that in favour of Sir George John Aird
(referred to in the appointment as 'Sir John').
    The appointment was made by the trustees of the settlement under powers contained   h
in it and the material provisions are as follows. Recital (A) defines the appointed property
and the appointee and continues thus:

    '(iii) "the Designated Person" means the person whose death shall occur on
    Saturday the 29th day of November 1975 and who shall be the first (in alphabetical
    order) of the persons dying on that date to be named in the "Deaths" Column on the
    back page of the earliest edition of the newspaper called "The Times" published in   j
    London on Monday the 1st day of December 1975 (or if there shall be no edition of
    "The Times" published on that date then of the earliest edition of that newspaper
    which is next published in London after that date) and if there shall be no person
    who shall answer the foregoing description then "the Designated Person" shall mean
    the person who would satisfy that description if the words "The Daily Telegraph"

a were substituted for the words "The Times" wherever the same appear. (iv) "the Specified Period" means the period of one day.'

The operative part provides that the appointors irrevocably appoint that subject to any capital gains tax which may be incurred but free from all liability for capital transfer tax (if any) the appointed property and the income thereof shall be held on the following trusts:

b '1. IF Sir John shall survive the Designated Person for the Specified Period the Appointed Property and the income thereof as from the death of the Designated Person shall be held upon trust for Sir John absolutely freed and discharged from the trusts and from all further exercise of the powers declared and contained in the Principal Instruments.'

c There follows a provision, which does not matter for present purposes, to deal with the case of the appointment failing to take effect and a further provision excluding s 31 of the Trustee Act 1925 until Sir John's interest becomes vested in possession.

It comes as no surprise to learn that both Sir John and Susan Aird did survive until 1 December 1975 (they are indeed, happily, still living), that The Times was published on that day, and that the earliest edition did, on its back page, contain a deaths column in which there appeared (inter alios) the names of some persons who had died on the previous Saturday, the first in alphabetical order being a Major Bisgood. The Special Commissioners found that it has in fact been known to occur that the deaths column in Monday's edition of The Times has not contained a report of the death of anyone identified as having died on the previous Saturday, so that it could not be said to be inevitable that there would be a designated person for the purposes of the appointment.

e The principal argument of the Crown both before the Special Commissioners and before the judge was that para 6(7) by necessary implication imports a genuine contingency of surviving another person for a specified period and that in the case of these appointments there was no such genuine contingency either because it was, for practical purposes, inevitable that somebody, somewhere would die on the Saturday and that his or her death would be announced in The Times on the following Monday, or because in reality, when analysed, the appointment was contingent on survival to a particular time which was, in truth, unrelated to anybody's death. The former, which was rejected by the judge, really depends on the court being satisfied that the chances of the event not occurring were so remote that they could, in effect, be rejected as de minimis and the event treated as a certainty. The commissioners' finding of fact and, indeed, subsequent events which have shown that it is far from impossible that The Times and, possibly, the Daily Telegraph would not appear at all render that argument unsustainable and it has not been pursued in this court. Counsel for the Crown instead puts his case in a rather different way. He argues that, since the paragraph exempts only cases where the propositus becomes entitled to an interest in possession 'on' surviving another person, that imports, as a matter of construction, that the survival is, looked at at the time when the instrument creating the interest comes into effect, to be the only condition standing between the beneficiary and the interest. As an alternative to that, he submits that it has to be demonstrated that survival is genuinely the contingency on which the interest depends and that, on analysis, that is not satisfied here. I shall have to return to these arguments later in this judgment, but I must first consider two further arguments which were introduced by an amended notice of appeal (to which counsel for the taxpayers raised no objection), which were not raised before the judge, and which, if accepted, clearly dispose of the case in the Crown's favour without the necessity for any analysis of the operation and legal effect of the appointment. The primary argument (although it is put last in the amended notice of appeal) is that as a matter of construction the words 'another person' in para 6(7) do not and cannot mean any person in the world but must be regarded restrictively as referring only to a person on whose death a transfer of value takes or is deemed to take place which includes the value of the settled property in which the interest in possession subsists.

On the face of it that sounds as if it involves the addition to the paragraph of a formidably complicated qualification but counsel for the Crown has submitted forcefully *a* that the authorities, and in particular recent authorities to the construction of statutes, justify and, indeed, might even be said to compel such an addition. Reference has been made to a number of cases in which the courts have felt able to construe apparently general and unlimited words in a restricted sense. Thus, for instance, in *Stradling v Morgan* (1560) 1 Plowd 199, 75 ER 305, a statute of Edward VI referred to 'any Treasurer, Receiver, or Minister Accountant'. This was construed restrictively as referring only to *b* treasurers etc for the Crown. In *Hawkins v Gathercole* (1855) 6 De GM & G 1, 43 ER 1129 the word 'rectory' was construed as confined to a lay rectory and as excluding a rectory held by a beneficed clergyman. Similarly, in *Cox v Hakes* (1890) 15 App Case 506 s 19 of the Supreme Court of Judicature Act 1873, which provided that the Court of Appeal should have jurisdiction to hear and determine 'Appeals from any judgment or order . . . of Her Majesty's High Court of Justice', was construed as excluding an order for the *c* discharge of a person in custody pursuant to a writ of habeas corpus.

In all these cases, however, there was some context in the statute under consideration from which the more limited intention could be inferred. In *Stradling v Morgan* the Act was entitled 'An Acte for the true aunsweringe of the Kinges Majesties Revenues' and other clauses in it spoke of the king's ministers. In *Hawkins v Gathercole* the Act was one which enlarged the scope of execution on a judgment and, quite apart from the fact that *d* the literal construction, which would include an ecclesiastical rectory, would have led to an execution on property which always had been and still remained legally inalienable by the debtor, there were at least two indications in the Act itself that the expression 'rectories' could not have been intended to bear this signification. One was the absence of any reference in the Act to any other benefices of an exclusively ecclesiastical nature, the other a context from which it was tolerably clear that what was intended was merely an *e* increase in the extent of the pre-existing power of execution from 50% to 100% of the property over which execution could be levied, property which had never previously included ecclesiastical property. The context in *Cox v Hakes* was, perhaps, less obvious, the restrictive construction being drawn from the previously well-established law, which itself rested on statute, the absence of any reference in the schedule of repeals to statutory provisions which would require to be repealed or modified if the literal construction *f* were adopted, and the absence of any machinery which would have been necessary if an appeal of the type embraced in a literal construction of the statutory words was to have any effect.

There is, however, nothing in the context of the 1975 Act itself in the instant case which either suggests or requires that any limitation be put on the expression used. A taxing statute is to some extent arbitrary in any event and the limitation here sought has *g* to be implied from the supposition that the legislature must have had some rational purpose in mind, a more or less intelligent speculation what that purpose was likely to be, and an inference that what was intended was a verbal formula limited appropriately to the achievement of that purpose. It is one thing to say that the legislature could not have had a particular species in mind when it used a generic expression and quite another to say that when the legislature used, apparently deliberately, a generic expression it had *h* in mind only one particular species. *Stradling v Morgan* is probably the nearest parallel for such a construction, but there, as mentioned above, there was a pretty clear textual foundation for the restricted and specific construction adopted. Here the concept which, as a matter of surmise, the legislature intended to express can be reached only by a radical and extensive rewriting of the paragraph, and I am bound to say that I see force in the submission of counsel for the taxpayers that what the court is being asked to do crosses *j* the boundary of construction and trespasses on the area of legislation, for what we are urged to do is not to interpret what Parliament did say, in clear and unmistakable terms, but to substitute for what it did say what we think Parliament would have said if our surmise as to the purpose of the paragraph is right and if we were now drafting a provision to give effect to that assumed purpose.

The question is whether so drastic a process is justified by any so-far accepted canon of
a construction. Certainly recent authority indicates a broader approach than was previously
regarded as permissible. In *Stenhouse Holdings Ltd v IRC* (1970) 46 TC 670 at 682 Lord
Reid observed that whereas formerly more importance had been attached to a meticulous
examination of the language used—

> 'more recently courts have tended to give at least equal weight to more general
> considerations, because a strict literal interpretation has been found often to lead to
> *b* a result which cannot really have been intended, and the object of statutory
> construction must be to find what was the intention of the Legislature.'

Nevertheless there are limits within which it is permissible to reframe the express
words which the legislature has chosen to use. Where it is clear that a literal reading
produces a wholly unreasonable or administratively impossible result and there is a
c context for adopting a more restricted reading, there is no particular difficulty. *Camille
& Henry Dreyfus Foundation Inc v IRC* [1955] 3 All ER 97, [1956] AC 39 and *IRC v
Plummer* [1979] 3 All ER 775, [1980] AC 896 were both cases in which a more limited
construction was deducible from other provisions of the statute which pointed to the
legislature's intention. Nor is there any particular difficulty where (as, for instance, in
Federal Steam Navigation Co Ltd v Dept of Trade and Industry [1974] 2 All ER 97, [1974] 1
d · WLR 505) it is impossible, on a literal construction, to give any intelligible meaning at
all to the particular provision. But this case does not fall under either of these heads.
Construed literally the paragraph is perfectly intelligible and perfectly capable of
operation. The problem is simply that the consequences go a great deal further than the
legislature can rationally have been supposed to have foreseen. That, no doubt, points to
a more limited meaning having been intended, but one must, I think, start from the
e position that the intention has to be deduced from the words which Parliament has
chosen to use and that they must be fairly capable of the more limited construction
sought to be put on them. If not, they must be applied as they stand, however strongly it
may be suspected that this was not the real intention of Parliament (see *IRC v Hinchy*
[1960] 1 All ER 505 at 512, [1960] AC 748 at 767 per Lord Reid). Counsel for the Crown
has drawn attention, by way of analogy to the instant case, to *Luke v IRC* [1963] 1 All ER
f 655, [1963] AC 557, where the majority in the House of Lords found themselves able to
construe the words 'production of an asset' as capable of including the repair of an asset.
That was, however, a case where, to quote Lord Reid (see [1963] 1 All ER 655 at 667,
[1963] AC 557 at 581), the result was 'so absurd and capricious that even the Inland
Revenue shy at enforcing it' and where the purpose of the provision was obvious on the
face of it. Counsel for the Crown relies heavily on the following passage from the speech
g of Lord Reid as establishing the general principle of construction which should guide the
court in this case ([1963] 1 All ER 655 at 664, [1963] AC 557 at 577):

> 'To apply the words literally is to defeat the obvious intention of the legislation
> and to produce a wholly unreasonable result. To achieve the obvious intention and
> produce a reasonable result we must do some violence to the words. This is not a
> new problem, though our standard of drafting is such that it rarely emerges. The
> *h* general principle is well settled. It is only where the words are absolutely incapable
> of a construction which will accord with the apparent intention of the provision and
> will avoid a wholly unreasonable result, that the words of the enactment must
> prevail.'

The difficulty that I feel in this case, however, is in saying that the legislature had any
j 'obvious' intention. As Viscount Haldane LC observed in *Lumsden v IRC* [1914] AC 877
at 892:

> '... it is no doubt true that there are cases of construction where the natural
> meaning of the words of a statute is rejected, and another meaning not expressed by
> the words taken in their ordinary sense is read in. That occurs where the context
> and scheme of the statute requires that this should be done in order that the

language of the statute as a whole may be read as consistent. But a mere conjecture
that Parliament entertained a purpose which, however natural, has not been   *a*
embodied in the words it has used if they be literally interpreted is no sufficient
reason for departing from literal interpretation.'

The same theme emerges from the speech of Lord Diplock in *Jones v Wrotham Park
Settled Estates* [1979] 1 All ER 286 at 289, [1980] AC 74, at 105, another case in which the
literal interpretation of the words used produced consequences which could hardly have
been foreseen. Lord Diplock observed: *b*

'. . . I am not reluctant to adopt a purposive construction where to apply the literal
meaning of the legislative language used would lead to results which would clearly
defeat the purpose of the Act. But in doing so the task on which a court of justice is
engaged remains one of construction, even where this involves reading into the Act
words which are not expressly included in it. *Kammins Ballrooms Co Ltd v Zenith*   *c*
Investments (Torquay) Ltd [1970] 2 All ER 871, [1971] AC 850 provides an instance
of this; but in that case the three conditions that must be fulfilled in order to justify
this course were satisfied. First, it was possible to determine from a consideration of
the provisions of the Act read as a whole precisely what the mischief was that it was
the purpose of the Act to remedy; secondly, it was apparent that the draftsman and
Parliament had by inadvertence overlooked, and so omitted to deal with, an   *d*
eventuality that required to be dealt with if the purpose of the Act was to be
achieved; and thirdly, it was possible to state with certainty what were the additional
words that would have been inserted by the draftsman and approved by Parliament
had their attention been drawn to the omission before the Bill passed into law.
Unless this third condition is fulfilled any attempt by a court of justice to repair the
omission in the Act cannot be justified as an exercise of its jurisdiction to determine   *e*
what is the meaning of a written law which Parliament has passed. Such an attempt
crosses the boundary between construction and legislation.'

Counsel for the Crown has ventured to criticise this last requirement, and indeed I
doubt whether Lord Diplock can have intended to signify that the court must be able to
express with total confidence the precise verbal formula that the draftsman would have   *f*
used, for different draftsmen may use different formulae for expressing exactly the same
meaning. Nevertheless, I do not understand counsel for the Crown to quarrel with the
proposition that at least the concept must be certain and that its limitation equally must
be certain, although there may be more than one way of expressing it.

Here, as it seems to me, neither the first nor the third of the conditions stated by Lord
Diplock can be said with confidence to be satisfied. The purpose can be conjectured with   *g*
a fair degree of probability, but there is nothing in the 1975 Act itself to support it and it
remains conjecture based on a reasonable assessment of what Parliament is likely to have
intended. As to the limits which would have been imposed if Parliament had foreseen
the consequences of what it had actually said, there is a further area of uncertainty. If it
was the intention of Parliament to limit 'another person' to a person of a particular type,
what is the type? Counsel for the Crown's first suggestion was 'a person whose death   *h*
gives rise to a transfer of value which includes the value of the settled property', but, as
was pointed out in argument, that would leave uncovered the case of a surviving spouse
who was a beneficiary under the will of a testator who died prior to 13 November 1974
and whose case is transitionally dealt with in s 22(4) of the 1975 Act. Thus one would
have to add to the suggested formula 'or would, but for the provisions of s 22(4) of this
Act, have given rise to such a transfer'. Speaking for myself, I cannot, as a matter of   *j*
construction, read so drastic an alteration into the paragraph. It really amounts, in my
judgment, to rewriting it entirely in order to give effect to what is, at best, a conjectural
intention and without any other context in the Act to support it. That is, in my view, to
legislate rather than to construe. It has been said on many occasions that the subject is
not to be taxed except by clear words and although, as counsel for the Crown has pointed
out, this is a relieving rather than a taxing provision, it is nevertheless part of a code

published by Parliament and on which people were expected and entitled to regulate
a their affairs. For my part I am unable to find any justification as a matter of construction
for departing from the literal meaning of the words.

I accordingly am unable to accept the second of the Crown's additional grounds and I
find at least equal difficulty in accepting the first, which is that 'another person' must as
a matter of construction mean a particular person or one whose identity falls to be
established by something other than a process of random or arbitrary selection. There is
b no context for qualifying 'person' with some such adjective as 'particular' or 'named' or
'identified' or for adding some more complicated qualification which would include
every person other than one selected or identified by a random process. Nor is there any
rational justification for it, for such a qualification would not, by itself, confine the
paragraph within its conjectured purpose. I turn therefore to the question of the
construction of the appointments themselves. Counsel for the taxpayers has pointed out
c that the paragraph nowhere refers expressly to a contingency: on the face of it, he
submits, it is merely looking at an event, the survival for a specified period. If the event
occurs, then para 6(2) has no application. Nevertheless it is common ground that it can
only be related to an interest arising under trusts which, whether they are created orally
or by a document, look to a genuine contingency of surviving another person. The
paragraph refers to a 'person who, on surviving another person for a specified period,
d becomes' and the reference to the entitlement taking effect as from the death of the
person survived demonstrates that 'on surviving' cannot have a purely temporal
connotation but refers to a contingency expressed in the trusts under which the interest
arises.

Counsel for the Crown submits first that, as a matter of construction, the paragraph
applies only where, under the relevant trusts, the contingency of surviving another
e person for the requisite period is the sole contingency on which the interest is made to
depend. Thus, he submits, you have to look at the trusts at the moment when they come
into operation and ascertain whether, at that date, the interest under consideration
depends on anything other than survival. It is, he suggests, demonstrable that viewed in
this way the interest of Sir John depended not simply on survival of another person but
on other conditions being fulfilled, the appearance of the newspaper carrying a deaths
f column containing the necessary particulars. Accordingly, he submits, the appointments
with which this appeal is concerned do not satisfy the paragraph, whatever may be said
about an appointment which adopts the less complicated General Franco scheme. I am,
for my part, unable to accept this view of the matter. Certainly in my judgment it has to
be demonstrated that the survival of the relevant person by the requisite period is what,
in the event, causes the interest to vest, but I can see nothing in the paragraph which
g requires that event to be, under the trusts, the only condition which has to be complied
with. Suppose, for instance, the relevant trusts were 'to my son X if he shall marry a
Roman Catholic and shall survive my wife by one month'. If X survives the wife and
then, a year later, marries a Roman Catholic, the paragraph would not, as I see it apply,
because the interest would then have vested not 'on' his surviving but 'on' his marrying.
On the other hand, if X married during the wife's lifetime and survived, I can see no
h reason why, either as a matter of logic or of construction, the paragraph should not apply,
for it will then have been his survival of the wife which brought about the vesting of the
interest.

Counsel for the Crown's alternative argument is, I think, a more formidable one. The
paragraph cannot, he submits, apply to any case save one where survival of another
person for the requisite period is genuinely the contingency on which in the event the
j interest depends. It is, in other words, no use dressing up your trusts so as to make it
appear that the contingency on which the interest depends is survival of another person
when in fact it is something else. That must, I think, clearly be right. For example, if the
interest is conditioned to vest on the propositus surviving by a particular period a person
who died a week before the execution of the instrument creating the trusts, there is no
genuine contingency of survival at all but merely a requirement that the beneficiary shall
live to a particular date. Indeed, counsel for the taxpayers does not dispute that the

paragraph is necessarily contemplating that the person to be survived must be someone who dies after the instrument creating the trusts comes into effect.

The contentious points are the next two stages of counsel for the Crown's argument. He submits first of all that as a matter of construction the appointment requires that Sir John survive not to some uncertain point of time calculated by reference to the time of death of the decedent but to a time which could be predicated at the date of the appointment, namely midnight on Sunday, 30 November 1975. From that he proceeds to the submission that, as a matter of analysis of the appointment, the contingency on which the interest actually depends is something quite other than surviving the death of another person, and that therefore it cannot be said that Sir John became entitled 'on' surviving another person for a specified period.

The judge found it unnecessary to decide what, as a matter of construction, was the precise time to which Sir John was required to survive, because, as he said ([1982] 2 All ER 929 at 941, [1982] 1 WLR 270 at 278), if the condition was one of surviving a given person by a specified period, it made no difference to the contingent nature of the interest whether or not the limit of the period was known in advance. That must, I think, be right, but on the argument which the Crown has advanced in this court it does, I think, need to be determined for it has an important bearing on his principal contention that there was here no genuine contingency of surviving another person.

There is no uncertainty about what 'the period of one day' means. It means and can only mean 24 hours and the only uncertainty is the point at which it starts. Does surviving another person by one day involve surviving for 24 hours precisely calculated from the time of the event (the 'punctum temporis' construction) or does it involve surviving for 24 hours from the end of the day on which the event occurs (the 'day excluded' construction)? We have been referred to a substantial number of authorities which reflect various circumstances in which one or other of these two constructions has been adopted, starting with the judgment of Grant MR in *Lester v Garland* (1808) 15 Ves 248, [1803–13] All ER Rep 436. The prima facie presumption appears undoubtedly to be in favour of the 'day excluded' construction as appears from the following passage from his judgment in that case (15 Ves 248 at 257, [1803–13] All ER Rep 436 at 439):

'It is not necessary to lay down any general rule upon this subject: but upon technical reasoning I rather think, it would be more easy to maintain, that the day of an act done, or an event happening, ought in all cases to be excluded, than that it should in all cases be included. Our law rejects fractions of a day more generally than the civil law does . . . The effect is to render the day a sort of indivisible point; so that any act, done in the compass of it, is no more referable to any one, than to any other, portion of it; but the act and the day are co-extensive; and therefore the act cannot properly be said to be passed, until the day is passed.'

That it is not difficult to displace this presumption when appropriate circumstances exist appears from, for instance, *Cornfoot v Royal Exchange Assurance Corp* [1904] 1 KB 40 and it has been said that it is easier to adopt the punctum temporis construction where the period concerned is a short one. There is certainly no context here which assists one way or the other, but I can, for my part, see no grounds for departing from the prima facie presumption that the 'day excluded' construction is to be preferred. Indeed, considerations of convenience and certainty strongly favour this approach. In the first place, it is frequently not possible to establish the precise moment of death, and, as was pointed out in argument, that difficulty is greatly increased where the decedent is selected by a random process such as that adopted here, for the decedent's relatives are hardly likely to take kindly to impertinent inquiries from complete strangers. One has to approach the document on the footing that it might become material to inquire whether or not the contingency expressed had occurred and it seems to me therefore that everything points to the likelihood that those who framed the appointment would intend a meaning which was ascertainable with complete certainty and without the necessity of making any embarrassing outside inquiry. In my judgment, therefore, counsel for the Crown is right when he submits that what the appointment requires is that Sir John shall survive until midnight on 30 November 1975.

I pass on, therefore, to the second limb of his argument. Undoubtedly, when Sir John
a survived to that point of time, he did in fact survive Major Bisgood by the specified
period of one day, but can it genuinely be said that it was his having survived Major
Bisgood that caused his interest to vest? Did the interest vest, in other words, 'on surviving
another person' in anything but a purely temporal sense? Counsel for the Crown submits
that the answer is No because, on analysis, he says, it will be found that the vesting
depended on something quite other than the death of Major Bisgood.

b   It was beyond doubt certain that someone, somewhere would die on Saturday, 29
November 1975, so that looking at the matter on the previous Friday, when the
appointment was executed, there were the following uncertainties. (1) Sir John might
fail to survive until Monday morning, in which event the interest would fail. (2) Sir
John might survive and Monday's Times might carry no announcement of a death on
Saturday. In that event the interest would fail. (One can ignore for the purpose of analysis
c the fall-back position of the Daily Telegraph, where exactly the same considerations
apply.) (3) Sir John might survive but there might be no Times on Monday, in which
event it would not be known whether the interest would vest or fail until the next
edition was published and it could be seen whether it contained the name of a person
who died on Saturday. (4) Sir John might survive and Monday's Times might be
published and carry the announcement of the death of a person who died on the previous
d Saturday. In this event the interest would vest.

Now in each case, of course, the vesting of the interest is contingent on Sir John
surviving to Sunday night, but the event in each case which actually causes the interest
to vest or to fail is not the death of another person on Saturday plus survival to Monday
morning but the publication of The Times, whenever that takes place. It is accepted,
although there was no evidence on the point and no finding of the commissioners (since
e it had not been material for them to inquire) that Monday's Times may well be published
(in the sense of distribution having commenced) before midnight on Sunday, but this
does not, in my judgment affect counsel for the Crown's point. However one looks at it,
what determines whether the interest vests or fails is, in the ultimate analysis, the
publication of The Times newspaper carrying the requisite announcement, and in my
judgment counsel for the Crown is right when he says that Sir John became entitled to
f the interest not 'on' surviving another person by a specified period, except in the purely
temporal sense that in one event (that of the appropriate Times being published before
midnight on Sunday) that is the moment of vesting, but 'on' (ie by reason of) The Times
being or having been published and containing a particular announcement.

Counsel for the taxpayers has submitted that so to conclude infringes the principle so
forcefully laid down by Lord Tomlin in IRC v Duke of Westminster [1936] AC 1, [1935]
g All ER Rep 259, because it substitutes for the form in which the appointment is made a
'substance' of a different kind. I am unable to accept that submission. The Westminster
principle no doubt precludes the court from ignoring the legal effect which follows from
the form which the document takes and substituting some quite different legal
transaction with different legal effects, but it does not, as I read it, at all inhibit the court
from analysing what the document as drawn actually does for the purpose of testing
h whether what it actually does conforms with the statutory requirements.

In my judgment, the true effect of the appointment with which this appeal is
concerned is that Sir John became entitled to an interest in possession not 'on' surviving
Major Bisgood by one day (although he did in fact do so, as, indeed, he survived by one
day every other person who died on Saturday, 29 November 1975) but 'on' a quite
different contingency. The critical thing which caused the interest to vest was not the
j previous death of a person, which in itself was as relevant as a horse race or a boxing
match, but the event of the relatives of some person who died on Saturday causing a
notice of his death to be notified in time for inclusion in Monday's Times and the
subsequent publication of that newspaper. What caused the interest to vest was, in my
judgment, either Sir John's surviving that insertion and publication until midnight on
Sunday or (if the publication took place after midnight) the publication itself.

This, as it seems to me, is the reality of the position and in my judgment that is not 'on
surviving another person for a specified period' unless 'on' is used (as I do not think that

it can be) in the purely temporal sense of denoting the termination of the specified period. I am prepared to accept that there was a genuine contingency of surviving until Monday morning but, speaking for myself, I am not satisfied that there was any genuine contingency of surviving another person until Monday morning within the terms of the paragraph. Accordingly I would allow the appeal.

WALLER LJ. Before I had the privilege of reading in draft the judgment of Oliver LJ I was disposed to take a different view of the Crown's argument which had not been delivered to the trial judge. I was disposed to take the view that having regard to the main purpose of this statute, namely to collect capital transfer tax in proper cases, and since it was common ground that the object of para 6(7) of Sch 5 to the Finance Act 1975 was to protect against double taxation where there was a commorientes clause my provisional view was that there must be a limited construction of the phrase 'another person' which would achieve its purpose without providing also an apparently wide opportunity to use this clause to avoid liability to capital transfer tax. Having read the judgment of Oliver LJ, I am satisfied that it is not open to this court to give the restricted meaning contended for.

On the questions which were argued before the judge I briefly express my view. Firstly it is necessary to decide what the meaning is of the phrase 'the specified period of one day'. Is it 24 hours from the moment of death or is it 24 hours from midnight on the day on which the person died? The authorities to which Oliver LJ has referred do indicate that, while the ultimate decision depends on the construction of the individual case and on the facts of the case, a period measured in days rather than hours is more usually construed to exclude the day of the event from which the period is to be calculated. In the present case, although concerned with a period of only one day the difficulties of adopting a construction of 24 hours from the point of time of death would be almost insuperable. It would be necessary to make all sorts of inquiries to find out the time of death from those concerned with the deceased, inquiries which would appear to have no relevance to such people. Furthermore, at the time of death the identity of the person would not be known nor would that person's identity have been decided. This would not be determined until the publication of The Times on Sunday night. The obvious and only practicable construction is that 'day' means midnight, ie ignoring the day of the determining event. Sir John had to survive to Sunday midnight.

Secondly, for the exemption in para 6(7) to apply the contingency was expressed to require 'surviving another person' for one day. In this case the contingency was not somebody's death coupled with survival for one day. There was no way of ascertaining the identity of the person either on Saturday or until late on Sunday night. The real contingency was the publication of a death in The Times. In my opinion there is no difference between starting with a person who is chosen because he dies on Saturday and starting with Saturday. In my opinion the date to which Sir John had to survive was Sunday midnight and the only other contingency was whether a death on Saturday would be reported in Monday's Times. In my judgment that is not 'on surviving another person' for a specified period. I have briefly stated my view on this question because we are differing from the judge. The reasoning is more fully and clearly expressed in the judgment of Oliver LJ, with which I wholly agree.

ROBERT GOFF LJ. I agree.

Appeal allowed. Leave to appeal to the House of Lords refused.

Solicitors: *Solicitor of Inland Revenue ; Travers Smith Braithwaite & Co* (for the taxpayers)

Clare Mainprice   Barrister.

a

Bailey v Bailey and another

COURT OF APPEAL, CIVIL DIVISION
DUNN AND PURCHAS LJJ
26 MAY 1983

b *Action – Dismissal – Abuse of process of court – Second action raising same cause of action as earlier action – Second action commenced within limitation period for cause of action – Earlier action dismissed for want of prosecution because of plaintiff's failure to comply with rules of court – Whether second action an abuse of court's process – Whether difference in principle between action dismissed for want of prosecution and action dismissed for disobedience of peremptory order of court.*

c

In September 1973 the plaintiff was injured while travelling in a car driven by her husband. The accident was caused by the husband's negligence. The plaintiff negotiated direct with her husband's insurers and accepted a relatively small sum in settlement of any claim against her husband. The plaintiff then instructed solicitors, who discovered that the insurers had misrepresented the contents of a medical report on her injuries.
d The plaintiff then issued a writ, within the limitation period, against the husband claiming damages for negligence. The claim was subsequently amended to allege that the plaintiff had been induced to settle her claim as a result of the insurers' fraudulent misrepresentation. In April 1980 the husband, at the instigation of the insurers, applied to strike out the action for want of prosecution. In July the plaintiff commenced a second action, within the limitation period, against both the husband and the insurers claiming
e damages for fraudulent misrepresentation. The husband's application to strike out the first action was heard in August, when the registrar dismissed the first action because of the plaintiff's inordinate and inexcusable delay. In December 1981 the defendants applied to strike out the second action as an abuse of the process of the court because it raised the same claim of fraudulent misrepresentation contained in the first action, which had been dismissed. The registrar struck out the second action. The plaintiff appealed to
f the judge, who upheld the registrar's decision. The plaintiff appealed to the Court of Appeal.

Held – There was a fundamental distinction between the case where a plaintiff disobeyed a peremptory order of the court regarding the prosecution of an action and then commenced fresh proceedings within the limitation period raising the same cause of
g action, and the case where the plaintiff's action had been struck out for want of prosecution and he subsequently commenced fresh proceedings within the limitation period raising the same cause of action, since in the first case the plaintiff was in contempt and commencing the fresh proceedings constituted contumelious conduct which entitled the court to strike out the fresh proceedings, whereas in the second case the mere failure of the plaintiff to comply with the procedural rules of court in the first action did not
h prevent him commencing the fresh proceedings. Since the plaintiff's first action had been struck out for mere failure to observe the rules as to time and the second action had been commenced within the limitation period, the plaintiff was entitled to proceed with the second action. The appeal would therefore be allowed (see p 498 e f, p 499 b to f and p 500 g h, post).

    Birkett v James [1977] 2 All ER 801 and *Tolley v Morris* [1979] 2 All ER 561 applied.
j *Janov v Morris* [1981] 3 All ER 780 distinguished.

Notes
For dismissal of proceedings for want of prosecution under the court's inherent jurisdiction see 37 Halsbury's Laws (4th edn) para 448, and for cases on the subject, see 37(3) Digest (Reissue) 67–76, 3295–3333.

Cases referred to in judgments

Allen v Sir Alfred McAlpine & Sons Ltd [1968] 1 All ER 543, [1968] 2 QB 229, [1968] 2 *a*
WLR 366, CA.
Birkett v James [1977] 2 All ER 801, [1978] AC 297, [1977] 3 WLR 38, HL.
Janov v Morris [1981] 3 All ER 780, [1981] 1 WLR 1389, CA.
Tolley v Morris [1979] 2 All ER 561, [1979] 1 WLR 592, HL.

Appeal

The plaintiff, Patricia Bailey, appealed from the judgment of Park J in the Queen's Bench *b*
Division at Newcastle-upon-Tyne given on 30 April 1982 dismissing her appeal from an
order of Mr District Registrar Ward, dated 22 February 1982, striking out as an abuse of
process an action (the second action) commenced by writ issued on 23 July 1980, brought
by the plaintiff against the first defendant, David Bailey, and the second defendant,
Provincial Insurance Co Ltd, the first defendant's insurers, claiming damages for
fraudulent or negligent misrepresentations contained in letters dated 5, 14 and 26 March *c*
1974 written by the second defendant to the plaintiff whereby the plaintiff was induced
to settle her claim for personal injuries against the first defendant arising out of an
accident on 28 September 1973 for £325 when that sum was substantially below the
true value of her claim. The principle ground of the appeal was that the judge erred in
law and fact in holding that, as the plaintiff had commenced the second action after she
had decided not to proceed with an appeal against an order striking out for want of *d*
prosecution an earlier action she had brought against the first defendant for damages for
negligence and fraudulent misrepresentation by his insurers in inducing her to settle her
claim against the first defendant for the sum of £325, the commencement of the second
action constituted contumelious conduct. The facts are set out in the judgment of Dunn
LJ.

e

Franz J Muller QC and *David Bryson* for the plaintiff.
Robert Moore for the defendants.

DUNN LJ. This is an appeal from an order of Park J in the High Court at Newcastle-
upon-Tyne on 30 April 1982 when he dismissed an appeal from an order of the district *f*
registrar who had ordered that the action be struck out under the relevant rule as being
an abuse of the process of the court.

The case has a long history, and to make it comprehensible it is necessary that I should
shortly recite the various events which led up to the order being made. The plaintiff, Mrs
Bailey, was a passenger, together with other relations, in a motor car driven by her
husband which was involved in an accident on 28 September 1973. The husband, Mr
Bailey, drove the motor car into a wall and there was no possible defence to a claim for *g*
negligence. The plaintiff, Mrs Bailey, instead of instructing solicitors, elected to negotiate
direct with the insurance company, who are the second defendants to this present action.
As the result of correspondence between them on 4 April 1974 she accepted a cheque for
the sum of £325 in full and final settlement of her claim. The judge held that even at
that date (because damages in those days were very much lower than they are now) if she
had been advised by competent counsel and solicitors she would not have settled for *h*
anything like as low a sum as that and, indeed, would probably have been advised not to
settle below the figure of £1,000 having regard to the injuries which she sustained.

After receiving the cheque Mrs Bailey did instruct solicitors, who had some
correspondence with the insurance company, who, on 24 July 1974, disclosed a medical
report from an orthopaedic surgeon, a Mr Davison. The medical report in certain respects
was inconsistent with some of the things which the insurers had said to Mrs Bailey in *j*
the letters which they wrote to her and which had induced her to settle. The reports
showed that the prognosis for recovery from her injuries was not as favourable as the
insurers had led her to believe.

On 24 September 1976, four days before the limitation period expired, she issued a
writ against her husband for damages for personal injuries caused by his negligent

driving. Of course, the effective defendants to the writ were the insurers, who were
a subrogated to the assured. The writ was not served until May 1977, the statement of
claim was served on 24 June 1977, and the defence on 31 July; and, apart from the
normal formal pleading in such a defence, the defendant pleaded an accord and
satisfaction arising out of the acceptance by Mrs Bailey of the sum of £325 in full
settlement.

Following that the statement of claim was amended to allege that the acceptance by
b Mrs Bailey of the £325 was induced by the false and fraudulent misrepresentations of
the insurers contained in some letters which they wrote to her before she accepted the
money. The amendment went on to claim that the settlement should, in effect, be set
aside so that her claim for damages remained at large.

The defence was duly amended in February 1978; there was a counterclaim; and then
nothing further happened, apart from the delivery of some further and better particulars
c of the amended statement of claim in December 1979, until 25 April 1980, when Mr
Bailey, in that action, because he was the only defendant, issued a summons for the action
to be dismissed for want of prosecution. The matter came before the district registrar on
1 July, and he adjourned it until 12 August. In the mean time, on 23 July 1980, this
present action was started by writ against Mr Bailey, the first defendant, and the insurance
company as second defendants, claiming damages for fraudulent misrepresentation
d arising out of the same letters as were relied on in the first action. That writ was issued
the day before the six-year limitation period for fraud expired. On 12 August 1980 the
registrar dismissed the original action for want of prosecution, an appeal was lodged but
withdrawn on 10 October 1980, and on 17 July 1981 the writ in the present action was
served. The defendants duly entered an appearance, a statement of claim was served on 2
October 1981, the defence on 7 December, and then on 21 December a summons was
e issued to strike out the action as an abuse of the process of the court under the appropriate
rule. The registrar made the order striking out the action on 22 February on the basis
that substantially the same claim had been struck out on 12 August when the original
action was dismissed.

The judge relied, at the end of his judgment, on part of the judgment of Watkins LJ
in *Janov v Morris* [1981] 3 All ER 780 at 785, [1981] 1 WLR 1389 at 1395. The passage
f on which he relied is as follows:

> 'In the event of his action being ordered to be struck out for failure to obey a
> peremptory order, he may appeal against that order seeking, if necessary, an
> extension of time within which to do so. The outcome of such an appeal will to
> some extent depend on the excuse for failure preferably set forth in affidavit form
> provided for the court's consideration. If a litigant neglects to avail himself of that
g > procedure and brings a fresh but precisely similar action to that ordered to be struck
> out, without any explanation then or at any later time for a failure to obey the
> peremptory order, he should not be surprised that the commencement of the second
> action is found to be an abuse of the process of the court and for that reason it, too,
> is struck out. To behave in such a way is in my judgment to treat the court with
> intolerable contumely.'

h
Park J decided that those words, 'to treat the court with intolerable contumely', were
apt to cover the situation which existed here, and he relied in particular on two matters:
first, the plaintiff's decision to abandon the appeal against the district registrar's order to
strike out the 1976 action and the institution of the fresh proceedings; and, second, that
there had been inordinate and inexcusable delay at every stage in both actions without a
word of explanation for any part of the delay being put forward by the plaintiff, and that
j it was wrong that any defendant should be required to endure a charge such as this, as
the judge put it, to hang over his head year in and year out without knowing whether or
not the plaintiff seriously intended to proceed with it.

Janov v Morris was a case in which, in the first action, there had been a peremptory
order of the court against the plaintiff which the plaintiff had failed to comply with, and
accordingly had been guilty of what has been described in the authorities as contumelious

conduct. It was on that ground that the first action in *Janov v Morris* was struck out. That has always hitherto been regarded as a different situation from the situation here, where the first action was dismissed for want of prosecution on the ground that there had been inexcusable delay in circumstances in which the conduct of the plaintiff could not be described as contumelious.

But counsel for the defendants, in seeking to uphold the order of the judge, submits that on principle there is no difference between the conduct of a plaintiff who deliberately disregards an order of the court, as was the position in *Janov v Morris*, and the conduct of a plaintiff who disregards the rules of court and takes no action within the rules, and who, in his submission is in the same position as somebody who deliberately disobeys an order of the court. He seeks to justify that submission by reference to a passage in my own judgment in *Janov v Morris* [1981] 3 All ER 780 at 784, [1981] 1 WLR 1389 at 1394, when I said:

'As was said in the course of argument in this court, one can well understand Lord Edmund-Davies's opinion that the conclusion which he preferred would be a highly unfortunate one, because it was conceded by counsel for the plaintiff that if it were right, a litigant could disobey and disregard orders of the court, have his action struck out, and provided he was within the limitation period, he could immediately start another action; and even if another peremptory order was made in the second action and that action dismissed, then if the logic is taken to its ultimate, he could start a third or any number of actions provided they were within the limitation period and none would be regarded as an abuse of the process of the court.'

Counsel for the defendants says that as a matter of principle it matters not whether the plaintiff disobeys and disregards orders of the court or whether he disregards the rules of the court: in either case if his action were struck out it would be a highly unfortunate position, to apply the words which I used in *Janov v Morris*, that he should be able to bring further actions and have them struck out and so on.

The difficulty about that submission is that, as I have said, there has always hitherto been a distinction between the situation where actions are struck out for disobedience of peremptory orders and where actions are dismissed for want of prosecution. The most recent and authoritative expression of the difference appears in *Tolley v Morris* [1979] 2 All ER 561 at 563, [1979] 1 WLR 592 at 594, where Lord Wilberforce, who dissented in the result, said in relation to the well-known decision of *Birkett v James* [1977] 2 All ER 801, [1978] AC 297:

'The basis of that decision was that an action would not normally be dismissed for want of prosecution while the relevant period of limitation was running, because the plaintiff could, without abuse of the process of the court, issue a fresh writ within that period.'

If I may pause to say so, if counsel for the defendants is right the principal basis for the decision in *Birkett v James* would go, because the logic behind the decision in *Birkett v James* is that an action should not be struck out or dismissed for want of prosecution during the limitation period because the plaintiff would be able to issue a writ the following day in accordance with the law, and no complaint could possibly be made.

Lord Diplock said ([1979] 2 All ER 561 at 571, [1979] 1 WLR 592 at 603):

'In my opinion s 22 of the Limitation Act 1939 would entitle the infant respondent in the instant case to issue a fresh writ tomorrow for the same cause of action as that for which the existing action has been brought. It follows that the Court of Appeal was right in holding that no useful purpose would be served by dismissing the existing action for want of prosecution.'

Then his Lordship drew the distinction between that situation and the situation where a peremptory order is obtained, and went on to say:

'Disobedience to a peremptory order would generally amount to such "contumelious" conduct as is referred to in *Birkett v James* and would justify striking out a fresh action for the same cause of action, as an abuse of the process of the court.'

Counsel for the defendants submitted that those observations were obiter. I do not think that strictly they were; but whether they were or not they are of very persuasive authority so far as we are concerned. Indeed, with great respect, it seems to me that there is a distinction in principle between a situation in which an action has been struck out for disobedience of the order of the court and where the action has been dismissed for want of prosecution because the plaintiff, although he may have failed to obey the rules of court, has issued his second writ quite lawfully within the limitation period and in circumstances in which, it seems to me, it is difficult, if not impossible, to say that his action constitutes an abuse of the process of the court. As we held in *Janov v Morris*, where an action is struck out for failure to obey a peremptory order then if a second action is started against the same party, raising the same cause of action, that second action will normally be regarded as an abuse of the process of the court unless there is some explanation of the failure to obey the order in the first action. As I pointed out in *Janov v Morris* [1981] 3 All ER 780 at 785, [1981] 1 WLR 1389 at 1395, there was no explanation why the plaintiff failed to comply with the order nisi which had been made against him; and, indeed, at the time that he started the second action he was in contempt of court. This present plaintiff is not in contempt of court, and with great respect to a very experienced judge I think that he fell into error in following *Janov v Morris* in circumstances which are not covered by that decision.

Accordingly, I would allow this appeal, with the consequence that the second action will proceed.

PURCHAS LJ. I agree. I add a few sentences because we are differing from the experienced judge, and out of respect for the able arguments of counsel for the defendants.

The history recounted by Dunn LJ demonstrates an immense delay over the prosecution of the action. Indeed, as counsel for the defendants was able to say, the accident out of which the original claim arose occurred some nine years ago. At numerous stages, as can be seen from the chronology with which we have been provided, each party was in breach of time limits for procedural steps provided by the Rules of the Supreme Court. Before *Allen v Sir Alfred McAlpine & Sons Ltd* [1968] 1 All ER 543, [1968] 2 QB 229 the practice was for the opposing party to apply for a peremptory order requiring compliance with the rules, failure to comply with which amounted to contumelious conduct as referred to in *Birkett v James* [1977] 2 All ER 801, [1978] AC 297, which would justify striking out a fresh action for the same cause of action as an abuse of the process of the court: see per Lord Diplock in *Tolley v Morris* [1979] 2 All ER 561 at 571, [1979] 1 WLR 592 at 603.

I wish only to refer to a short extract from Lord Diplock's speech shortly following that part ([1979] 2 All ER 561 at 571, [1979] 1 WLR 592 at 604):

'Where in *Allen v Sir Alfred McAlpine & Sons Ltd* the Court of Appeal broke new ground was in sanctioning the dismissal of an action for want of prosecution in cases where the plaintiff's delay had been inordinate and inexcusable, notwithstanding that the defendant had not taken any steps himself to put an end to the delay. In the last 12 years, dismissal of actions for want of prosecution in accordance with the principles laid down in [*Allen's* case] has largely supplanted the previous procedure by means of peremptory orders requiring the plaintiff to take the appropriate steps under the rules of court to bring his action on for trial. But that previous procedure still exists. It could have been invoked by the respondent, as defendant in the instant case, at any time since May 1968 when the time which the rules prescribe for service of the statement of claim expired.'

It appears to me that Lord Diplock had in mind the very distinction to which Dunn
LJ has been referring in his judgment to point that fact. Glancing at the chronology, the *a*
initiation of the action by the plaintiff was in its two stages at the eleventh hour.
Thereafter matters proceeded with some expedition. There was one month between the
statement of claim and defence, which one must say is acceptable in practice, although
not in accordance with the rules, and then 3½ months later, when the misrepresentation
had been discovered, the statement of claim was amended. Then the defendants took
three months to deliver their defence and a counterclaim. Then there was a period of 22 *b*
months before a request for further and better particulars was answered which had been
made when the defence was delivered. During that period it was open to the defendants,
had they wished so to do, to apply to the court for a peremptory order for the provision
of those further and better particulars, but they appear to have been content to let
sleeping dogs lie. They let the matter rest again for another five months and then issued
the summons to dismiss for want of prosecution, which really was the point of ignition *c*
of the present spurt of activity.

The issue of the second writ (which, it has been pointed out to us by counsel for the
defendants, was during the progress of the application to dismiss for want of prosecution
and therefore would, at first sight, appear to contravene the procedure that was going on
in the first action) is easily explicable. The original return date for the application to
dismiss for want of prosecution was 1 July 1980, but it was adjourned by the registrar to *d*
12 August 1980, so that during the period of that adjournment it must have become
apparent to the plaintiff's advisers that the six-year limitation for fraud or misrepresentation expired on 24 July 1980 and therefore before the application to dismiss could be
determined. That, as I see it, is a reasonable explanation for the fact that that writ had to
be issued to protect the plaintiff's position, albeit yet again at the eleventh hour, during
the hearing of the application to strike out before the registrar. Thereafter matters again *e*
proceeded, and again somehow or other another nearly two years' delay occurred, not all
due to the parties.

So that in my judgment the distinction here, which was clear from the report of *Janov
v Morris* [1981] 3 All ER 780 at 781, [1981] 1 WLR 1389 at 1390, to which counsel for
the defendants referred at some length, and very properly so, is that the ratio decidendi
there was that in that case the court was dealing with action that had been taken, as it *f*
were, under the pre-*Allen v McAlpine* procedures and where there has been a peremptory
order for compliance with an order of the court. One only has to recall the extracts to
which we were referred, and to which Dunn LJ has referred, where the court there
emphasised that the plaintiff had been and, indeed, continued to be in contempt of court
at the time of the application. It is because of the fundamental distinction between
failure to comply with a peremptory order and failure to comply with the ordinary rules *g*
of procedure under the Rules of the Supreme Court, remedy for which lies in the hands
of the opposite party to take steps to enforce proper compliance, that this case is clearly
distinguishable from *Janov v Morris*.

I agree with all that has fallen from Dunn LJ. For these reasons, and for the reasons in
his judgment, I agree that this appeal should be allowed.

h

Appeal allowed.

Solicitors: *P Welsh & Co*, Chester-le-Street (for the plaintiff); *Sinton & Co*, Newcastle-upon-
Tyne (for the defendants).

Diana Procter   Barrister.

Stockler v Fourways Estates Ltd

QUEEN'S BENCH DIVISION
KILNER BROWN J
24, 27 MAY 1983

Land charge – Vacation of entry in register – Writs and orders affecting land – Mareva injunction – Mareva injunction registered in land register – Whether injunction an order made for 'purpose of enforcing a judgment' – Land Charges Act 1972, s 6(1)(a).

Injunction – Interlocutory – Danger that defendant may transfer assets out of jurisdiction – Injunction made in action affecting land – Whether injunction an order made for 'purpose of enforcing a judgment' - Whether injunction may be registered in land register – Land Charges Act 1972, s 6(1)(a).

Section 6(1)(a)[a] of the Land Charges Act 1972, which provides for registering in the register of writs and orders affecting land any order affecting land made or issued by the court 'for the purpose of enforcing a judgment', on its true construction does not permit the registration of a Mareva injunction in the register, since such an injunction is interlocutory in character and continues only until judgment in the action is given (see p 502 g to j, post).

Heywood v BDC Properties Ltd (No 2) [1964] 2 All ER 702 and dictum of Lord Diplock in *Siskina (cargo owners) v Distos Compania Naviera SA, The Siskina* [1977] 3 All ER at 822 applied.

Notes

For what may be registered in the land register, see 26 Halsbury's Laws (4th edn) para 754.

For the Land Charges Act 1972, s 6, see 42 Halsbury's Statutes (3rd edn) 1606.

Cases referred to in judgment

Heywood v BDC Properties Ltd (No 2) [1964] 2 All ER 702, [1964] 1 WLR 971, CA.
Siskina (cargo owners) v Distos Compania Naviera SA, The Siskina [1977] 3 All ER 803, [1979] AC 210, [1977] 3 WLR 818, HL.

Application

By a writ issued on 1 February 1983 the plaintiff, William Thomas Stockler, brought an action against the defendants, Fourways Estates Ltd, claiming damages for breach of a contract whereby the defendants agreed to sell to the plaintiff a property in Dudley in the West Midlands for the sum of £252,000. On 1 March 1983 Tudor Evans J in chambers granted the plaintiff a Mareva injunction restraining the defendants by themselves, their servants or agents or otherwise from removing from the jurisdiction, disposing of, charging or otherwise dealing with any of their assets within the jurisdiction save to the extent as there remained within the jurisdiction such free and unencumbered assets to a total value of £164,000 or in the event that the defendants completed the sale of certain land in Dudley to the plaintiff for the sum of £15,000. The plaintiff secured the registration of the injunction in the register of pending land actions in the Land Registry. By summons dated 17 May 1983 the defendants applied to the judge in chambers for an order that the registration be vacated pursuant to s 5(10) of the Land Charges Act 1972. The application was heard in chambers but the judgment was given by Kilner Brown J in open court. The facts are set out in the judgment.

R J Powell-Jones for the defendants.
Richard Slowe for the plaintiff.

Cur adv vult

---

a   Section 6(1), so far as material, is set out at p 502 e, post

27 May. The following judgment was delivered.

KILNER BROWN J. The Mareva sails again; this time on uncharted seas. As the result of an application under the Land Charges Act 1972 for registration of a writ or order in which the nature of the writ or order was stated to be a Mareva undertaking in proceedings in the Supreme Court of Judicature certain property of the defendant company was registered as subject to charge. The defendants now apply by summons for the charge to be vacated. These proceedings are said to be pursuant to s 5(10) and to involve s 6 of the Land Charges Act 1972. However, s 5 refers to the register of pending actions which may be either a pending land action or a petition in bankruptcy. Subsection (10) enables the court to order the vacating of a registration during the pendency of the proceedings. The first question is whether or not there is a pending land action. Undoubtedly the proceedings before me arise out of a pending land action. It is submitted on behalf of the plaintiff that the summons purporting to be based on s 5(10) is misconceived and that there is no jurisdiction in that, as the notes in 42 Halsbury's Statutes (3rd edn) 1606 indicate, no order to vacate may be made by judge in chambers. It seems to me that the technical difficulty can be overcome by adjourning the matter, as I have done, to open court. However, even if this does not confer jurisdiction, there is clear authority that, in the case of a registration improperly procured, the court has power to make an order for vacation under its inherent jurisdiction (see *Heywood v BDC Properties Ltd (No 2)* [1964] 2 All ER 702, [1964] 1 WLR 971 in the Court of Appeal). This jurisdiction was exercised under the general provision now in s 1(6) of the 1972 Act.

This leads logically and naturally to the real point of substance: was the registration a valid one? Section 6(1) of the Act reads:

'There may be registered in the register of writs and orders affecting land—(a) any writ or order affecting land issued or made by any court for the purpose of enforcing a judgment or recognisance . . .'

The plaintiff submits that the registration is within the terms of the subsection. Reliance is placed on part of the opinion in Lord Diplock's speech in *Siskina (cargo owners) v Distos Compania Naviera SA, The Siskina* [1977] 3 All ER 803 at 822, [1979] AC 210 at 253. True, Lord Diplock, with whom others of their Lordships concurred, recognised that the granting of the injunction was an order of the court and as he put it 'on the face of it the claim for an injunction is part of the substantive relief claimed in the action . . .' However, he went on to say that it was—

'an injunction that is interlocutory in character and will continue only until judgment in the action and payment of any damages that may be awarded to them by such judgment.'

So it is to the next part of the wording in the subsection to which consideration must be given. Is this an order made 'for the purpose of enforcing a judgment'? I suppose it could be said to be an order for the purpose of enforcing a judgment if a judgment with damages was inevitable in due course. But how can this be? The crucial words used by Lord Diplock are 'any damages that may be awarded'. It is plainly a conclusion that is undetermined at the time of the making of the order by way of injunction. In loosely phrased terms it is a freezing or holding order, and not part of a final judgment in which damages are ordered. In my opinion a Mareva injunction is not a form of order contemplated by the 1972 Act and the registration was improper. Accordingly I order that the registration be vacated. Furthermore, I do not consider this to be a question of discretion. It was an error of law.

I am asked to grant a stay of my order for seven days. This I do. The defendants are entitled to the costs of this application as there is no substantial merit in the plaintiff's objection on jurisdiction. It is basically technical, and I have surmounted these objections one way or the other.

a
The order of the court, therefore, is: order for vacation of registered charge no 4851/ 83 with costs.

Order accordingly.

Solicitors: *Tarlo Lyons*, agents for *David W Roberts*, St Helier, Jersey (for the defendants); *William T Stockler* (for the plaintiff).

b
K Mydeen Esq   Barrister.

Roake and others v Chadha and another

c
CHANCERY DIVISION
HIS HONOUR JUDGE PAUL BAKER QC SITTING AS A JUDGE OF THE HIGH COURT
26, 27 APRIL, 9 MAY 1983

d
Restrictive covenant affecting land – Annexation of benefit – Annexation by statute – Covenant not to enure for benefit of covenantee's successors in title unless expressly assigned – Covenant not expressly assigned on transfer of land – Covenant not to build more than one house on plot – Covenantor's successor in title proposing to build additional house on plot – Action by covenantee's successors in title to enforce covenant – Whether benefit of covenant annexed by statute – Whether covenant a 'right appertaining or reputed to appertain to the land' – Law of Property Act 1925, ss 62(1), 78.

e
W Ltd laid out some land which they owned in plots and then proceeded to sell them, using in each case a standard form of transfer, which reserved certain easements to them 'and their assigns'. L bought one such plot. Under the transfer he covenanted with W Ltd, 'so as to bind (so far as practicable) the land hereby transferred into whosesoever hands the same may come . . . but so that this covenant shall not enure for the benefit of any owner or subsequent purchaser of [W Ltd's land] unless the benefit of this covenant shall be expressly assigned', that he and his successors in title would observe all the stipulations set out in the schedule to the transfer. Stipulation 5 in the schedule stated that no building should at any time be erected on any plot other than one private dwelling house. W Ltd subsequently transferred to X a plot adjoining L's plot but they did not expressly assign to him the benefit of L's covenant. Some time later X transferred the plot to the plaintiffs. They discovered that, contrary to stipulation 5 in the schedule to the standard form of transfer, the defendant, L's successor in title, was proposing to erect an additional house on his plot. They brought an action against him seeking a declaration that their plot was entitled to the benefit of the covenant given to W Ltd by his predecessor in title and an injunction restraining the defendant from erecting the additional house. The defendant contended that, as the benefit of the covenant had never been expressly assigned, the plaintiffs were not entitled to the relief sought. The plaintiffs maintained that they were so entitled because the benefit of the covenant had been annexed to their plot by s 78[a] of the Law of Property Act 1925 and the operation of that section could not be excluded by the expression of a contrary intention in the covenant, or alternatively because, even if the benefit of the covenant had not been annexed to the land, it had passed to them by virtue of s 62(1)[b] of the 1925 Act as 'a right appertaining or reputed to appertain to the land'.

j
Held – The plaintiffs were not entitled to the relief sought for the following reasons—
     (1) It did not follow, merely because s 78 of the 1925 Act provided that a covenant relating to land of the covenantee was deemed to be made with the covenantee and his

a   Section 78, so far as material, is set out at p 506 *d*, post
b   Section 62(1) is set out at p 508 *j* to p 509 *a*, post

successors in title, that the benefit of the covenant ran with the land. The covenant still
had to be construed as a whole to see whether the benefit of it was annexed. Where the
covenant was not qualified in any way annexation could readily be inferred; but where
the covenant expressly precluded the benefit from passing unless it was expressly assigned
due weight had to be given to those words. It followed that, in view of the express terms
of the covenant given by L, the benefit of it was not annexed to the plaintiffs' land (see
p 508 *c d* and *g* to *j* and p 509 *g*, post); *Federated Homes Ltd v Mill Lodge Properties Ltd*
[1980] 1 All ER 371 considered.

(2) Since the covenant in terms precluded the benefit from passing unless it was
expressly assigned, it could not be described as 'a right appertaining or reputed to
appertain to the land' within s 62 of the 1925 Act (see p 509 *f g*, post); *Rogers v Hosegood*
[1900–3] All ER Rep 915 considered.

Notes

For right to benefit of covenants running with land, see 42 Halsbury's Laws (4th edn)
paras 344–348, and for cases on the subject of burden and benefit of covenants, see 40
Digest (Repl) 339–343, 2764–3783.

For annexation of covenants to retained land, see 16 Halsbury's Laws (4th edn) para
1353.

For the Law of Property Act 1925, ss 62, 78, see 27 Halsbury's Statutes (3rd edn) 438,
462.

Cases referred to in judgment

Federated Homes Ltd v Mill Lodge Properties Ltd [1980] 1 All ER 371, [1980] 1 WLR 594,
CA.
Jeffs's Transfer, Re, Rogers v Astley (No 2) [1966] 1 All ER 937, [1966] 1 WLR 841.
Rogers v Hosegood [1900] 2 Ch 388, [1900–3] All ER Rep 915, CA.
Tophams Ltd v Earl of Sefton [1966] 1 All ER 1039, [1967] 1 AC 50, [1966] 2 WLR 814,
HL.
Zetland (Marquess) v Driver [1938] 2 All ER 158, [1939] Ch 1, CA.

Cases also cited

Drake v Gray [1936] 1 All ER 363, [1936] Ch 451, CA.
Renals v Cowlishaw (1879) 11 Ch D 886, [1874–80] All ER Rep 359, CA.
Russell v Archdale [1962] 2 All ER 305, [1964] Ch 38.
Stephenson (Robert) & Co Ltd, Re [1915] 1 Ch 802, [1914–15] All ER Rep 1107.
Stilwell v Blackman [1967] 3 All ER 514, [1968] Ch 508.

Summons

The first and second plaintiffs, Dorothy Roake and Margaret Roake, the owners of 104
Abbots Drive, Wembley, Middlesex, and the third and fourth plaintiffs, Arthur George
Taylor and Phyllis Lillian Mary Taylor, the owners of 1 Audrey Gardens, Wembley,
Middlesex, brought an action against the defendants, Manmohan Singh Chadha and
Derek William Way, the owners of 4 Audrey Gardens, Wembley, Middlesex, seeking (i)
a declaration that 104 Abbots Drive and 1 Audrey Gardens were each entitled to the
benefit of a restrictive covenant over 4 Audrey Gardens created by a conveyance dated 4
April 1934 and (ii) an injunction restraining the defendants from erecting any additional
building on 4 Audrey Gardens. By a summons dated 26 February 1983 the plaintiffs
applied under RSC Ord 14 for summary judgment. The facts are set out in the judgment.

Philip Walter for the plaintiffs.
Jonathan Henty for the defendants.

Cur adv vult

9 May. The following judgment was delivered.

a

HIS HONOUR JUDGE PAUL BAKER QC. On 5 March 1930 a section of what was then known as the Sudbury Court Estate in North Wembley was conveyed to Wembley (C & W) Land Co Ltd. That company proceeded to lay out the purchased land in lots and sell them off using a standard form of transfer. On 4 April 1934, 4 Audrey Gardens, one of the plots in the estate and the property now owned by the defendants, **b** was sold off and transferred to William Lambert. In the transfer certain easements are reserved to the vendors (that is the company that I have mentioned) 'and their assigns', and then follows a covenant in the following form:

'AND the Purchaser to the intent and so as to bind (so far as practicable) the land hereby transferred into whosesoever hands the same may come but not so as to render the Purchaser personally liable in damages for any breach of any restrictive **c** covenant after he shall have parted with all interest in the said premises in respect of which such breach shall occur hereby covenants with the Vendors but so that this covenant shall not enure for the benefit of any owner or subsequent purchaser of any part of the Vendors' Sudbury Court Estate at Wembley unless the benefit of this covenant shall be expressly assigned that he the Purchaser and his successors in title will observe and perform all and every the provisions conditions and stipulations set **d** out in the Schedule hereto so far as they relate to or affect the premises hereby transferred or any part thereof.'

The transfer concludes with a further restriction in favour of 'the Vendors or their assigns'.

In the schedule, which is headed 'SPECIAL STIPULATIONS subject to which all Plots are **e** sold', we find the following. There is a list of restrictions and stipulation 5 reads this way:

'No building or other erection of any kind except fences in accordance with Stipulation No. 2 shall at any time be erected on any plot other than one private dwellinghouse with usual out-offices at a cost for each dwellinghouse of not less than £500 and not more than one house with or without a private garage shall be erected on any plot. Such value shall be exclusive of a private garage or other **f** outbuildings. The cost in every case to be the net cost of materials and labour of construction only estimated at the lowest current prices. No building or other erection shall be erected on any such plot unless the exact position of the site of the proposed building or other erection and the plans drawings and elevations shall have been previously submitted to and approved of in writing by the Vendors.'

g

I think I should also read stipulation 10:

'The Vendors reserve the right to sell any part of the said Estate which may be at any time unsold free from the foregoing restrictions and stipulations or any of them in such lot or lots and subject to such restrictions and stipulations if any as they may think fit and also the right with the written consent of the Purchaser of any plot or plots already sold to vary or release the restrictions and stipulations affecting the **h** property purchased by him or her and also at the Vendors' own discretion to vary or abandon the scheme of roads building lines rights of way and other matters as shown on the plan of the said Estate.'

These proceedings have been prompted by a threat to build an additional house on 4 Audrey Gardens. It is admitted that this will amount to a breach of stipulation 5, which **j** I have just read. The sole issue before me is whether the plaintiffs are entitled to the benefit of the covenant which I have read out. The first and second plaintiffs are the owners of 104 Abbots Drive, Wembley; and the third and fourth plaintiffs are the owners of 1 Audrey Gardens.

The transfers from the respective predecessors in title of the plaintiffs are in identical form though later in date to that of 4 Audrey Gardens. The transfer of 1 Audrey Gardens is dated 28 May 1934 and that of 104 Abbots Drive 22 March 1935. Neither transfer

contains any express assignment of the benefit of the covenant contained in the transfer
of 4 Audrey Gardens, nor has it been expressly assigned by any other instrument.
1 Audrey Gardens is almost opposite no 4. 104 Abbots Drive fronts on a street running
at right angles to Audrey Gardens. 4 Audrey Gardens and 104 Abbots Drive have a short
common boundary at the rear of the respective plots. From these facts, which are not in
dispute, the plaintiffs contend that the benefit of the covenant of no 4 has become
annexed to each of the plots respectively owned by them. Alternatively, it is contended
that the benefit has passed under the general words of the Law of Property Act 1925,
s 62.

As to annexation, counsel for the plaintiffs conceded that the express terms of the
covenant appeared to exclude annexation, and there was no suggestion that the case fell
within the category known as building schemes. Counsel for the plaintiffs, however, in
an interesting argument submitted that annexation had come about through the
operation of s 78 of the 1925 Act, as interpreted in *Federated Homes Ltd v Mill Lodge
Properties Ltd* [1980] 1 All ER 371, [1980] 1 WLR 594, a decision of the Court of Appeal.
I can summarise his argument by the following four points. (1) The covenant was a
covenant relating to the land of the covenantee. (2) Section 78(1) of the 1925 Act
provides, as regards such covenants relating to land, that they are deemed—

> 'to be made with the covenantee and his successors in title and the persons
> deriving title under him or them, and shall have effect as if such successors and
> other persons were expressed. For the purposes of this subsection in connexion with
> covenants restrictive of the user of land "successors in title" shall be deemed to
> include the owners and occupiers for the time being of the land of the covenantee
> intended to be benefited.'

(3) In the *Federated Homes* case it was held that by virtue of that section the benefit of a
covenant relating to land retained by the covenantee ran with that land and was annexed
to it and to every part of it. (4) The provisions of s 78, unlike those of s 79 relating to the
burden of the covenant, cannot be excluded by the expression of a contrary intention.
Section 79 reads:

> '(1) A covenant relating to any land of a covenantor or capable of being bound by
> him, shall, unless a contrary intention is expressed, be deemed to be made by the
> covenantor on behalf of himself his successors in title and the persons deriving title
> under him or them, and, subject as aforesaid, shall have effect as if such successors
> and other persons were expressed. This subsection extends to a covenant to do some
> act relating to the land, notwithstanding that the subject-matter may not be in
> existence when the covenant is made.
> (2) For the purposes of this section in connexion with covenants restrictive of the
> user of land "successors in title" shall be deemed to include the owners and occupiers
> for the time being of such land . . .'

Unlike s 78, which had a counterpart in s 58 of the Conveyancing Act 1881, s 79 was a
new section in 1925. The important point to which attention is called is 'unless a contrary
intention is expressed', and that appears in s 79. There is no corresponding expression in
s 78. Those are the main points of the argument.

I have no difficulty in accepting that the covenant in the standard form of transfer
which I have read is a covenant relating to the retained land of the covenantee, that is to
say Wembley (C & W) Land Co Ltd, and that therefore s 78 comes into play. It is the
third and fourth points which have given rise to the argument in this case. I must begin,
therefore, by examining the *Federated Homes* case.

The case concerned a large development site divided into four areas of approximately
equal size of some 30 to 40 acres each. These were known respectively as the red, green,
pink and blue land. The site had the benefit of a planning permission allowing for
approximately 1,250 private dwellings and other development. At the beginning of
1971 the whole site was owned by Mackenzie Hill Ltd. In February of that year the blue
land was sold and conveyed to the defendant company, and the pink land to another

company. The former conveyance (that is the one to the defendant company) contained
a a covenant expressed simply by the purchaser (the defendant) with the vendor (Mackenzie
Hill) that in carrying out the development on the blue land, the purchaser would—

> 'not build at a greater density than a total of 300 dwellings so as not to reduce the
> number of units which the Vendor might eventually erect on the retained land
> under the existing Planning Consent.'

b   The pink land having simultaneously been sold off, the retained land was taken to be
the red and green land. At the time of the action both parcels had come into the hands
of the plaintiff but, whereas in the case of the green land there was an unbroken chain of
assignments of the benefit of the covenant, in the case of the red land the chain had been
broken.

The relief being sought was an injunction to restrain the defendant from building to a
c greater density than that agreed, that is greater than the 300 dwellings. It was argued,
and this is not a point with which I am directly concerned, that the covenant was personal
to Mackenzie Hill and was not assignable. That point having been decided against the
defendant, the plaintiff became clearly entitled to the relief sought in right of the green
land.

Counsel for the defendants in the present case has argued that accordingly the Court
d of Appeal's judgments in relation to the red land were obiter. I am unable to accept this
view of the effect of the judgments. As it seems to me, the status of the covenant in
relation to both pieces of land, the red and the green, was in issue in the case. If the
defendant in subsequent proceedings had sought to challenge the validity of the covenant
in relation to the red land, he could, as I would see it, be met by a plea of issue estoppel
and consequently the principle underlying the court's conclusion cannot be regarded as
e obiter. That principle I take from the following passage in the judgment of Brightman
LJ in the *Federated Homes* case [1980] 1 All ER 371 at 379, [1980] 1 WLR 594 at 605:

> 'If, as the language of s 78 implies, a covenant relating to land which is restrictive
> of the user thereof is enforceable at the suit of (1) a successor in title of the
> covenantee, (2) a person deriving title under the covenantee or under his successors
> in title, and (3) the owner or occupier of the land intended to be benefited by the
f > covenant, it must, in my view, follow that the covenant runs with the land, because
> ex hypothesi every successor in title to the land, every derivative proprietor of the
> land and every other owner and occupier has a right by statute to the covenant. In
> other words, if the condition precedent of s 78 is satisfied, that is to say, there exists
> a covenant which touches and concerns the land of the covenantee, that covenant
> runs with the land for the benefit of his successors in title, persons deriving title
g > under him or them and other owners and occupiers.'

That seems to be the essential point of the decision.

Counsel for the defendants made a frontal attack on this use of s 78, which he
reinforced by reference to an article by G H Newsom QC 'Universal Annexation?' (1981)
97 LQR 32 which is critical of the decision. The main lines of attack are: (1) the
h conclusion overlooks the legislative history of s 78 which it is said shows that it has a
narrower purpose than is claimed and does not in itself bring about annexation; (2) this
narrower purpose has been accepted in relation to the corresponding s 79 (relating to
burden), which I have already read, by Lord Upjohn and Lord Wilberforce in *Tophams
Ltd v Earl of Sefton* [1966] 1 All ER 1039 at 1048, 1053, [1967] 1 AC 50 at 73, 81. Further,
it is said by way of argument sub silentio that in a number of cases, notably *Marquess of
j Zetland v Driver* [1938] 2 All ER 158, [1939] Ch 1 and *Re Jeffs's Transfer, Rogers v Astley
(No 2)* [1966] 1 All ER 937, [1966] 1 WLR 841, the argument could have been used to
good effect but was not deployed.

Now, all this is very interesting, and the views of Mr Newsom are entitled to very
great respect seeing that until his recent retirement he was a practitioner of long
experience who had made a special study of this branch of the law. He has written a
valuable monograph on it. All the same, despite counsel for the defendants'

blandishments, I am not going to succumb to the temptation of joining in any such discussion. Sitting here as a judge of the Chancery Division, I do not consider it to be my place either to criticise or to defend the decisions of the Court of Appeal. I conceive it my clear duty to accept the decision of the Court of Appeal as binding on me and apply it as best I can to the facts I find here.

Counsel for the plaintiffs' method of applying it is simplicity itself. The *Federated Homes* case shows that s 78 brings about annexation, and that the operation of the section cannot be excluded by a contrary intention. As I have indicated, he supports this last point by reference to s 79, which is expressed to operate 'unless a contrary intention is expressed', a qualification which, as we have already noticed, is absent from s 78. Counsel for the plaintiffs could not suggest any reason of policy why s 78 should be mandatory, unlike, for example, s 146 of the 1925 Act, which deals with restrictions on the right to forfeiture of leases and which, by an express provision, 'has effect notwithstanding any stipulation to the contrary'.

I am thus far from satisfied that s 78 has the mandatory operation which counsel for the plaintiffs claimed for it. But, even if one accepts that it is not subject to a contrary intention, I do not consider that it has the effect of annexing the benefit of the covenant in each and every case irrespective of the other express terms of the covenant. I notice that Brightman LJ did not go so far as that, for he said in the *Federated Homes* case [1980] 1 All ER 371 at 381, [1980] 1 WLR 594 at 606:

> 'I find the idea of the annexation of a covenant to the whole of the land but not to a part of it a difficult conception fully to grasp. I can understand that a covenantee may expressly or by necessary implication retain the benefit of a covenant wholly under his own control, so that the benefit will not pass unless the covenantee chooses to assign; but I would have thought, if the benefit of a covenant is, on a proper construction of a document, annexed to the land, prima facie it is annexed to every part thereof, unless the contrary clearly appears.'

So at least in some circumstances Brightman LJ is considering that despite s 78 the benefit may be retained and not pass or be annexed to and run with land. In this connection, I was also referred by counsel for the defendants to Sir Lancelot Elphinstone's *Covenants Affecting Land* (1946) p 17, where the author says, with reference to this point (and I quote from a footnote on that page):

> '. . . but it is thought that, as a covenant must be construed as a whole, the court would give due effect to words excluding or modifying the operation of the section.'

The true position as I see it is that, even where a covenant is deemed to be made with successors in title as s 78 requires, one still has to construe the covenant as a whole to see whether the benefit of the covenant is annexed. Where one finds, as in the *Federated Homes* case, the covenant is not qualified in any way, annexation may be readily inferred; but, where, as in the present case, it is expressly provided that 'this covenant shall not enure for the benefit of any owner or subsequent purchaser of any part of the Vendor's Sudbury Court Estate at Wembley unless the benefit of this covenant shall be expressly assigned', one cannot just ignore these words. One may not be able to exclude the operation of the section in extending the range of covenantees, but one has to consider the covenant as a whole to determine its true effect. When one does that, then it seems to me that the answer is plain and in my judgment the benefit was not annexed. That is giving full weight to both the statute in force and also what is already there in a covenant.

I must now turn to the alternative argument of the plaintiffs based on s 62 of the 1925 Act. This argument is directed to the conveyances or transfers conveying the alleged benefited land to the predecessors of the plaintiffs, and ultimately to the respective plaintiffs themselves. In each of these transfers, so I am prepared to assume, there is to be implied the general words of s 62:

> '(1) A conveyance of land shall be deemed to include and shall by virtue of this Act operate to convey, with the land, all buildings, erections, fixtures, commons,

a
hedges, ditches, fences, ways, waters, watercourses, liberties, privileges, easements, rights, and advantages whatsoever, appertaining or reputed to appertain to the land, or any part thereof, or, at the time of conveyance, demised, occupied, or enjoyed with or reputed or known as part or parcel of or appurtenant to the land or any part thereof . . .'

Then in sub-s (2) it deals with the conveyance of land having houses and buildings and various corresponding rights in relation to buildings. I do not think I need read that

b subsection.

The argument is that the benefit of the covenant contained in the original transfer to the predecessors of the defendants (that is to say William Lambert) was carried by the words 'rights, and advantages whatsoever, appertaining or reputed to appertain to the land, or any part thereof'.

It seems an argument on these lines was accepted by John Mills QC, the deputy judge

c who gave the decision at first instance in the *Federated Homes* case, but I have not seen it, and so cannot comment on it. The proposition now contended for is not a new one. In *Rogers v Hosegood* [1900] 2 Ch 388, [1900–3] All ER Rep 915 it was similarly put forward as an alternative argument to an argument based on annexation. In that case however it was decided that the benefit of the covenant was annexed so that the point on the Conveyancing Act 1881, s 6, the forerunner of s 62 of the 1925 Act, did not have to be

d decided. Nevertheless, Farwell J, sitting in the Chancery Division, said ([1900] 2 Ch 388 at 398):

'It is not necessary for me to determine whether the benefit of the covenants would pass under the general words to which I have referred above, if such covenants did not run with the land. If they are not in fact annexed to the land, it may well be

e that the right to sue thereon cannot be said to belong, or be reputed to belong, thereto; but I express no final opinion on this point.'

In the Court of Appeal the point was canvassed in argument but not referred to in the judgment of the court, which was given by Collins LJ.

In the present case, the covenant in terms precludes the benefit passing unless it is expressly assigned. That being so, as it seems to me, it is not a right appertaining or

f reputed to appertain to land within the meaning of s 62 of the 1925 Act. On whether the benefit of a covenant not annexed can ever pass under s 62, I share the doubts of Farwell J. Counsel for the defendants suggested, and there may well be something in this, that the rights referred to in s 62 are confined to legal rights rather than equitable rights which the benefit of restrictive covenants is. But again I place it on construction. It cannot be described as a right appertaining or reputed to appertain to land when the

g terms of the covenant itself would seem to indicate the opposite.

I thus conclude overall that the plaintiffs have failed to show that they are entitled to the benefit of the covenant in relation to their respective properties. The matter comes before me on a summons for summary judgment under RSC Ord 14. Strictly the only orders I can make on that are to dismiss the summons or to give unconditional leave to defend. Neither seem very satisfactory. Dismissing the summons is a course that one has

h recourse to when there is something defective about it or the application is wholly inappropriate and misconceived. Of course, unconditional leave to defend leaves the action to go on, although the main point here seems to be the determination of a preliminary point of law. But I will invite counsel to address me as to what now should be done. But at the moment formally the only order I can make is to give unconditional leave to defend.

j
Unconditional leave to defend. Leave to appeal refused.

Solicitors: *Hart Fortgang & Co*, Wembley (for the plaintiff); *Church Adams Tatham & Co*, agents for *Matthew Arnold & Baldwin*, Watford (for the defendants).

Hazel Hartman   Barrister.

Damon Cia Naviera SA v Hapag-Lloyd International SA

The Blankenstein, The Bartenstein, The Birkenstein

QUEEN'S BENCH DIVISION (COMMERCIAL COURT)
LEGGATT J
24, 25, 26 MAY 1983

Contract – Offer and acceptance – Acceptance by purchaser with reservation of right to nominate subsequent purchaser – Terms agreed by exchange of telexes – Parties agreeing to execute memorandum of agreement – Purchaser's nominee failing to execute memorandum of agreement – Whether contract validly concluded by exchange of telexes – Whether purchaser bound personally by contract until nomination of subsequent purchaser.

Contract – Damages for breach – Deposit – Sale of ships – Purchaser agreeing to pay deposit as security – Purchaser failing to pay deposit and to complete purchase – Vendor reselling ships for less than contract price – Vendor's actual loss less than amount of unpaid deposit – Whether vendor entitled to recover amount of deposit – Whether vendor limited to recovering actual loss as damages.

In 1977 negotiations for the sale of three ships took place between the sellers and the intending buyers, whose identity was not disclosed to the sellers. Instead the buyers were represented in the negotiations by two brothers, who indicated their intention to nominate a company as a subsequent purchaser. By 8 July 1977 the principal terms of the sale had been agreed by exchanges of telexes between brokers acting for the parties except that the name of the purchasing company had not been disclosed. By the terms of the sale the purchase price was to be $US2,365,000 and a deposit of 10% was to be paid by the buyers. The sellers' broker forwarded a memorandum of agreement dated 8 July 1977, incorporating the agreed terms, to the buyers' broker for execution by the brothers for and on behalf of companies to be nominated later. Clause 2 of the memorandum provided for payment of a deposit of 10% on the execution of the contract and cl 13 provided that in the event of the buyers failing to pay the purchase price the sellers could cancel the contract and retain the deposit. On 1 August by telex to the sellers' broker the buyers' broker nominated a Panamanian company as the purchaser and requested that a new memorandum of agreement be prepared on that basis. A few hours later the brothers acquired shares in the nominated company and were made directors; one brother was appointed chairman and the other treasurer of the company. Under Panamanian law a chairman had power to negotiate, conclude, ratify and affirm contracts made in the company's name. A further memorandum of agreement was sent to the buyers' broker immediately and on 3 and 5 August the buyers' broker sent telexes which indicated the chairman's intention to continue with the purchase. On 9 August the sellers by telex gave the buyers until 12 August to sign the agreement and pay the deposit, failing which the contract would be rescinded. On 15 August, after a final telex to the buyers, the sellers sold the ships to another purchaser for $US2,295,000. The sellers claimed to be entitled to receive the deposit from the company, but it refused to pay. The dispute was referred to arbitration. The arbitrator held that the parties had concluded an enforceable agreement on 8 July 1977 which anticipated the later nomination of the company as purchaser and further held that, although the company's failure to execute the memorandum and pay the deposit was a repudiatory breach which entitled the sellers to withdraw from the sale, the fact that payment of the deposit was conditional on the signing of the memorandum meant that the company was only liable to pay the damage suffered by the sellers, which he assessed at $US60,000. At the request of the company

a the arbitrator stated a special case for the court to determine whether there was a binding
contract concluded between the sellers and the company and whether the sellers were
entitled to recover the amount of the deposit from the company.

Held – (1) The exchange of telex messages between the brokers had resulted in a binding
contract between the sellers and the two brothers or their nominees, since the indication
by the brothers of their intention to nominate different buyers did not mean that they
b were not contractually bound pending such nomination. Furthermore, having regard to
Panamanian law, by appointing one of the brothers to be the chairman the board of the
company had made a representation that the chairman had authority to commit the
company to contracts and to ratify or affirm contracts made in the company's name. In
all the circumstances the chairman had ratified the novation purportedly made on behalf
of the company on 1 August 1977 and accordingly the company was bound by the
c contract (see p 517 e to g, p 518 e to j and p 522 f g, post); *Millichamp v Jones* [1983] 1 All
ER 267 applied.
(2) The sellers were entitled to make time of the essence and to treat the company's
failure to sign the memorandum of agreement and pay the deposit by 12 August 1977 as
a repudiation which entitled them to terminate the contract. Acceptance of the
repudiation by the sellers released the company from liability for future obligations but
d not for obligations already incurred under the contract. Since the deposit was payable by
way of security under the sale contract reached by exchange of telexes, the right to receive
it had accrued before the company's repudiation had been accepted and the sellers were
therefore entitled to recover the amount of the deposit as damages for breach of the
obligation to pay the deposit. The sellers were also entitled to claim damages for the
repudiation but, since the amount recoverable in respect of the deposit was greater than
e their actual loss, only nominal damages could be recovered in addition to the amount of
the deposit (see p 521 a to f and h j and p 522 a to g, post); *Dewar v Mintoft* [1912] 2 KB
373, dicta of Dixon J in *McDonald v Dennys Lascelles Ltd* (1933) 48 CLR at 476–477, of
Lord Wilberforce in *Johnson v Agnew* [1979] 1 All ER at 889 and *Millichamp v Jones* [1983]
1 All ER 267 applied.

f **Notes**
For novation of contractual rights, see 9 Halsbury's Laws (4th edn) paras 580–584, and
for cases on the subject, see 12 Digest (Reissue) 735–745, 5301–5370.

Cases referred to in judgment
Dewar v Mintoft [1912] 2 KB 373.
g *Freeman & Lockyer (a firm) v Buckhurst Park Properties (Mangal) Ltd* [1964] 1 All ER 630,
    [1964] 2 QB 480, [1964] 2 WLR 618, CA.
Heyman v Darwins Ltd [1942] 1 All ER 337, [1942] AC 356, HL.
Johnson v Agnew [1979] 1 All ER 883, [1980] AC 367, [1979] 2 WLR 487, HL.
Lowe v Hope [1969] 3 All ER 605, [1970] Ch 94, [1969] 3 WLR 582.
McDonald v Dennys Lascelles Ltd (1933) 48 CLR 457, Aust HC.
h *Millichamp v Jones* [1983] 1 All ER 267, [1982] 1 WLR 1422.
Myton Ltd v Schwab-Morris [1974] 1 All ER 326, [1974] 1 WLR 331.
Pollway Ltd v Abdullah [1974] 2 All ER 381, [1974] 1 WLR 493, CA.
Rugg Ltd v Street [1962] 1 Lloyd's Rep 364.

Special case stated
j The applicants, Damon Cia Naviera SA (Damon), and the respondents, Hapag-Lloyd
International SA (the sellers), by consent appointed Robert William Reed as sole arbitrator
to determine a dispute between the parties whereby the sellers claimed against Damon
$US236,500, being 10% of the purchase price for the motor vessels Blankenstein,
Bartenstein and Birkenstein which Damon failed to pay as a deposit pursuant to cl 2 of a
memorandum of agreement dated 8 July 1977 which was not executed by Damon, or
alternatively damages in the sum of $US67,500 representing the loss suffered by the

sellers on the resale of the vessels. The arbitrator held that Damon had been in breach of
the sale contract and that the sellers were entitled to damages of $US60,000 representing   a
the loss suffered by them on the resale of the vessels. At the request of Damon the
arbitrator stated a special case for the decision of the High Court pursuant to s 21(1) of
the Arbitration Act 1950 to determine (1)(a) whether there was a binding contract
concluded between the sellers and Damon for the sale of the motor vessels, (b) whether
Damon were estopped from denying that such a contract was concluded, (2) whether the
sellers were entitled to damages from Damon and if so in what amount, and (3) whether   b
the sellers were entitled to recover from Damon the amount of the deposit provided for
in cl 2 of the memorandum of agreement. The facts are set out in the judgment.

Bernard Eder for Damon.
Martin Moore-Bick for the sellers.

                                                                                c
                                                              Cur adv vult

26 May. The following judgment was delivered.

LEGGATT J. This matter comes before me as a special case stated by an arbitrator
pursuant to s 21(1) of the Arbitration Act 1950. The sole arbitrator was Mr Robert Reed.   d
He gave his award on 17 December 1982. The applicants in these proceedings were
respondent buyers in the arbitration. They are called Damon Compania Naviera SA, and
I shall refer to them as 'Damon'. The respondents in these proceedings were claimant
sellers in the arbitration. They are called Hapag-Lloyd International SA, another
Panamanian company, and I shall refer to them as 'the sellers'.
    Damon challenge the award on the ground that the contract relied on by the sellers for   e
the sale of three ships was not a concluded contract. Further they argue that if by
purported novation Damon became buyers, that novation was ineffectual because it was
made without their authority and was never ratified. The sellers, on the other hand, not
content with an award of damages of $US60,000, representing their actual loss in this
transaction, claim to recover instead $US236,500 as a deposit which Damon failed to pay.
    The three ships, the subject of the intended sale, were called Blankenstein, Bartenstein   f
and Birkenstein. The task of selling them on behalf of the sellers was entrusted to their
broker, Mr Nebelsiek. The broker who dealt on behalf of the intending buyers was a
Greek broker called Mr Panas. Following negotiations between brokers, and indeed an
inspection of two of the ships by one of the intending buyers, Mr George Raftopoulos, a
telex from Mr Panas to Mr Nebelsiek was sent on 4 July 1977 containing what was
described as an official firm offer for all three vessels at a price of $US2,250,000. The offer   g
was made for and on behalf of Messrs Raftopoulos, of Athens, and/or for company or
companies to be nominated by them in due course. The two Messrs Raftopoulos referred
to in the telex message were Mr George Raftopoulos and his brother, Mr Menelaos
Raftopoulos.
    The award records that, as is common practice in relation to the sale of second-hand
ships, the Raftopoulos brothers did not intend to buy the vessels personally but would   h
eventually nominate one or more companies in their control whose name or names
would be inserted into the contract as the real purchaser.
    Following that telex and further telex messages exchanged between the brokers, there
was reached on 8 July 1977 a concluded contract in which all the terms and conditions of
the sale, and in particular the price of $US2,365,000, were agreed, save for the name of
the purchasing company or companies which had yet to be disclosed. On that day Mr   j
Nebelsiek sent to Mr Panas a telex message in which he reconfirmed the deal and said
that he was drawing up an MOA, meaning a memorandum of agreement, on the
following Monday. The award records that at that stage both these experienced brokers
were convinced that they had concluded a valid sale contract between their respective
principals. The award goes forward to state that all that remained was the performance
by the sellers and the respondents of their respective obligations. This reference to the

respondents can at that date only have been to the brothers Raftopoulos, and it is fair to
a remark, as both counsel acknowledge, that the term 'respondents' is used throughout the
award to refer either to the brothers Raftopoulos or to Damon indifferently. This is no
doubt accounted for by the fact that the attention of the arbitrator was focused on the
reality of the matter, namely that Damon, a company subsequently acquired by the
Raftopoulos brothers, was at all material times after its acquisition their creature.

After the contract had been in this manner concluded between the brokers there
b followed an exchange of telexes between them over a period of several days. In particular
on 12 July 1977 Mr Panas suggested to Mr Nebelsiek that—

> 'IN ORDER SAVE TIME AND EXPEDITE SIGNATURES AND DEPOSIT OF 10% SHOULD SUGGEST
> YOU ISSUE M.O.A. IN THE NAME OF MESSRS. MENELAOS RAFTOPOULOS AND GEORGE
> RAFTOPOULOS . . .'

c and he suggested that a note be made of the buyers' right to nominate a purchasing
company. On the same day Mr Panas sent another telex message, in which he referred to
a phone conversation with Mr Menelaos Raftopoulos, whom he described as the senior
one. He said that Mr Menelaos Raftopoulos—

> 'CONFIRMED THAT FORMATION OF THE PANAMANIAN COMPANIES WHO WILL OFFICIALLY
> APPEAR AS BUYERS PER EACH SHIP IS IN COURSE . . .'

d
Mr Panas added, however, that he maintained the view expressed in his previous telex
proposing only one alteration, that one name be inserted only, that of Mr Menelaos
Raftopoulos. Still on 12 July 1977, Mr Nebelsiek acknowledged these telex messages,
saying that he had prepared an MOA and inserted as buyers—

> 'MESSRS. MENELAOS RAFTOPOULOS AND GEORGE RAFTOPOULOS . . . FOR AND ON BEHALF
> e OF COMPANIES STILL TO BE NOMINATED.'

A copy of a memorandum of agreement so drawn up was sent by Mr Nebelsiek to Mr
Panas on 13 July 1977. The document bore the date 8 July 1977, being the date on which
the brokers regarded themselves as having concluded the contract, and recited that the
sellers were Hapag-Lloyd International SA of Panama and the buyers Messrs Menelaos
f Raftopoulos and George Raftopoulos for and on behalf of companies still to be nominated.
Clause 2 of the memorandum of agreement, which was in Norwegian Shipbrokers'
Association's Sale Form, recited:

> 'As a security for the correct fulfilment of this contract, the Buyers shall pay a
> deposit of 10% . . . of the Purchase Money on signing this contract. This amount
> shall be deposited with [a bank in Bremen].'

g
The only other clause which I should mention is cl 13, which provided:

> 'Should the Purchase Money not be paid as per cl 16, the Sellers have the right to
> cancel this contract, in which case the amount deposited shall be forfeited to the
> Sellers. If the deposit does not cover the Sellers' loss, they shall be entitled to claim
> further compensation for any loss and for all expenses together with interest at the
> h rate of 5% . . .'

Clause 16 is not material for these purposes, since all it did was to apportion the purchase
price between the three vessels concerned.

Notwithstanding their receipt of the memorandum of agreement, it was not signed
either by the brothers Raftopoulos or by any company or other person nominated by
j them. So it was that Mr Panas sent a telex message to Mr Nebelsiek on 27 July recording
what he termed 'the official statement of the Buyers'. In that statement the buyers
expressed regret for inconvenience and anxiety they might cause to the sellers and
officially declared that they fully maintained the 'DEAL ALREADY STIPULATED DURING
NEGOTIATIONS CONFIRMED ON 8TH INST' and assured sellers 'THERE HAS NEVER BEEN ANY
INTENTION OF STEPPING OUT OF SAME'. They promised that the sale would be confirmed by
Tuesday, 2 August, when they asserted that they would proceed without any other delays

in complete fulfilment of all their contractual obligations towards sellers. They asked the
sellers to be kind enough to wait and to postpone the drydocking of one of the vessels for
a later date.

There followed on 1 August 1977 another telex message from Mr Panas to Mr
Nebelsiek, which began: 'BUYERS HEREBY NOMINATE AS PURCHASING COMPANY MESSRS. "DAMON
COMPANIA NAVIERA S.A., PANAMA".' It continued:

'THEY FURTHER REQUEST SELLERS TO ISSUE AND URGE FORWARD HERE A NEW M.O.A.
(DATED OF COURSE 8TH JULY) BUT IN WHICH DAMON COMPANIA NAVIERA S.A. WILL APPEAR
AS PURCHASING COMPANY, AGAIN WITH OPTION OF NOMINATION OF FURTHER COMPANIES
PRIOR TO DELIVERY OF 2ND AND 3RD UNIT.'

Mr Panas expressed a lack of enthusiasm to keep passing on requests for further delay
on his clients' behalf, but he said that he had been told that on receipt of an amended
form of memorandum of agreement his clients would 'telex remit deposit'. Much of the
difficulty that has arisen in this case would have been avoided if, at the time when that
telex message was sent, Damon, or the shares in Damon, had been acquired by the
Raftopoulos brothers. But the award recites that although the company was incorporated
in Panama on 25 May 1977 and registered there on 1 June 1977, having been created as
an off-the-shelf company, it was not until a few hours after the company had purportedly
been nominated to the sellers as buyers under the contract on 1 August 1977 that the
Raftopoulos brothers acquired the shares in the company from the original subscribers.
Having become shareholders, both of them were made directors of the company, Mr
Menelaos Raftopoulos being appointed chairman and his brother treasurer. The award
recounts, and it is not the subject of dispute, that—

'The Chairman of a Panamanian company holds a position equivalent to that of
the Managing Director of an English company. It is within his usual authority to
negotiate and conclude contracts on the company's behalf or to ratify or affirm
contracts made in the company's name.'

Also on 1 August 1977 two other persons, both named Moschonas, became the only
other two members of the board of Damon. Both were Greek nationals and the arbitrator
found that—

'It is more probable than not that they knew of Messrs. Raftopoulos' intention to
nominate the Respondents (that is Damon) as purchaser of the Claimants' vessels
and that they approved of this course.'

In compliance with Mr Panas's request, Mr Nebelsiek sent to him by express post on
1 August 1977 a fresh front page of the memorandum of agreement, recording Damon
as buyers. Two days later, on 3 August, from the office of the Raftopoulos brothers Mr
Panas sent a telex message in confirmation of an earlier telephone conversation, repeating
that 'MR RAFTOPOULOS HAD TWO WAYS THROUGH WHICH HAS ARRANGED THE FINANCING OF
THE PRESENT DEAL' and containing a further reference to the intentions of Mr Raftopoulos.
Bearing in mind the earlier telex message to which I have referred, in which Mr Menelaos
Raftopoulos was referred to as the person dealing with the formation of the Panamanian
company and suggested as the sole person whose name should be inserted as buyer,
coupled with the fact that it was he who was made chairman of Damon, I am, as I
adjudge, entitled to infer that the Mr Raftopoulos referred to in the telex message of 3
August was Mr Menelaos Raftopoulos who by then, as I have indicated, had become the
chairman of Damon.

On 5 August 1977 Mr Panas sent a further telex message to Mr Nebelsiek in which he
said 'RAFTOPOULOS JUST PHONED ME THAT THE BANK GUARANTEE IN HIS FAVOUR . . . IS READY . . .'
Nothing further was heard from Mr Panas or from any client of his by 9 August 1977,
when accordingly Mr Nebelsiek sent a telex message containing what he called 'an official
statement' for the sellers. It referred to the fact of an agreement having been reached
with Menelaos Raftopoulos and George Raftopoulos. It recorded that a 10% deposit of
the purchase money was to be lodged on signing of the memorandum of agreement, and

although this limit was extended to 3 August there had been a failure to comply with
a those requirements; and it included the phrase:

> 'REQUEST YOU TO LET US KNOW BY FRIDAY, 12TH AUGUST, 1977—5 P.M. GERMAN TIME,
> THAT YOU SIGN THE MEMORANDUM OF AGREEMENT WITH HAPAG-LLOYD INTERNATIONAL
> S.A. AND LODGE THE 10% DEPOSIT.'

It informed the Raftopoulos brothers that if they would not act accordingly within the
b time limit given, the sellers would rescind the contract and reserve all their rights for
compensation of losses caused. The memorandum of agreement was not signed, nor was
any deposit paid within the time allowed or at all, and on 15 August Mr Nebelsiek sent a
final telex message to Mr Panas in which, in default of the lodging of the deposit, he
declared that the sellers were withdrawing from the contract and reserving all their
rights. On the same day the sellers sold all three ships for a price of $US2,295,000 on
c terms not much different from those which had been incorporated in the memorandum
of agreement of 8 July 1977.

Against this background the arbitrator found that—

> 'Following the exchange of offers between the parties, the clean acceptance by the
> Sellers of the purchase offer of 15.10 hours 8th July, made without any "subjects"
d > would be regarded in the Shipping Market as a binding contract of sale not requiring
> a signed Memorandum of Agreement to validate it.'

He found also that—

> 'It was made clear prior to the sale and subsequent thereto, that a company or
> companies would be nominated by the Raftopoulos Brothers to be the Buyers which
e > was later verified when they declared Damon Compania Naviera S.A. on 1st August,
> 1977.'

Subsequent findings should also be recorded, and they are these. First:

> 'Although Mr. Panas began to express his personal doubts of the Respondents to
> Mr. Nebelsiek from about 20th July, he continued to receive and put forward
> instructions received from the Raftopoulos Brothers up to and after 1st August,
f > which gave the impression that the Respondents themselves still expected to
> perform the contract.'

Second:

> 'In failing to sign the Memorandum of Agreement and pay the deposit
> concurrently by 17.00 hours Friday, 12th August, 1977, the Respondents were in
g > repudiatory breach of the sale contract and the Sellers were entitled to withdraw on
> 15th August, when they did.'

Third:

> 'The payment of the deposit was conditional upon the Respondents signing the
> Memorandum of Agreement and since they failed to do so, they became liable only
h > for damages suffered by the Sellers.'

The arbitrator then went forward to assess the damage suffered by the sellers in the sum
of $US60,000.

In these circumstances the principal questions of law which he formulates are (1)
whether there was a binding contract concluded between the sellers and respondents for
i the sale of the ships and (2) whether the sellers are entitled to recover from the respondents
the amount of the deposit provided for in cl 2 of the memorandum of agreement.

In reviewing the facts counsel for Damon invites the conclusions that at 8 July 1977
there was and could be no binding contract with Damon or anyone else, that the identity
of the buyers remained unknown and unspecified until the telex message of 1 August
1977, that despite various proposals to short-cut the procedure these had no legal
significance at all, and that both before and after 1 August 1977 both parties were

insisting that the proper buyers would have to sign the memorandum of agreement and lodge the deposit. He adds that the absence of those two requirements shows that until they were fulfilled there was no binding contract with Damon. In aid of the submission *a* implicit in these conclusions counsel cites *Myton Ltd v Schwab-Morris* [1974] 1 All ER 326, [1974] 1 WLR 331, a case decided by Goulding J, which concerned an agreement for an underlease in which there was a failure to pay the agreed deposit followed by purported rescission by the lessor. A caution having been registered by the intended lessee, the question was whether payment of the deposit constituted a condition precedent of the *b* contract and whether there was an enforceable contract. Counsel for Damon relies on the provision in that case for a deposit, which he says is comparable with cl 2 in the memorandum of agreement in the present case. He asserts that that case was a stronger one than this since there was a contract signed and a cheque given, albeit one which was subsequently dishonoured. But in particular does he rely on the case for its conclusion, that the payment of the deposit was to be regarded as a condition precedent, in default of *c* which there was no binding contract. This conclusion was expressed by Goulding J in these terms ([1974] 1 All ER 326 at 330, [1974] 1 WLR 331 at 336):

> 'Speaking in quite general terms for the moment of contracts to sell land or grant a lease of land at a premium, without reference to the particular language of this document, it is well-established that a deposit is demanded and paid on the signing of the contract as an earnest of the purchaser's ability and intention to complete the *d* purchase in due course. The vendor, in the normal case, never intends to be bound by the contract without having the deposit in his own or his stakeholder's possession as a protection against possible loss from default by the purchaser.'

Counsel for Damon contends that there is no justification for drawing any distinction between a sale of land and the sale of a ship, and he seeks to distinguish the later case of *e* *Millichamp v Jones* [1983] 1 All ER 267, [1982] 1 WLR 1422. That was a case decided by Warner J in 1982. It concerned specific performance of a contract for the sale of land, an option to purchase having been given and the agreement providing for payment of a deposit on exercise of the option. The option was in fact exercised without the deposit being paid, and the question was whether payment of the deposit was indeed to be regarded as a condition precedent, or alternatively a fundamental term. The case was one *f* in which the purchaser's failure to pay the deposit was due to oversight. The judge considered in particular, as he was bound to do, the decision of Goulding J to which I have referred, and he did so in the context of *Lowe v Hope* [1969] 3 All ER 605, [1970] Ch 94, which was apparently not cited to Goulding J, and also in the context of a subsequent decision of the Court of Appeal in *Pollway Ltd v Abdullah* [1974] 2 All ER 381, [1974] 1 WLR 493 and of the House of Lords in *Johnson v Agnew* [1979] 1 All ER 883, [1980] AC *g* 367. The conclusion reached by Warner J after reviewing the authorities was enunciated thus ([1983] 1 All ER 267 at 274, [1982] 1 WLR 1422 at 1430):

> '. . . the weight of authority is in favour of the view that a requirement in a contract for the sale of land that a deposit should be paid by the purchaser does not constitute a condition precedent, failure to fulfil which prevents the contract from *h* coming into existence, but is in general to be taken as a fundamental term of the contract, breach of which entitles the vendor, if he so elects, to treat the contract as at an end and to sue for damages including the amount of the unpaid deposit.'

Counsel for the sellers contends that there was a binding contract reached on 8 July with the Raftopoulos brothers with a right on their part to nominate others as buyers, *j* but that the contract was not subject to any condition precedent. On that issue he remarks with cogency that if in general the payment of a deposit were to be regarded as a condition precedent, it would follow that in any such case the purchaser could keep the deposit in hand in order to avoid the contract and with that effect.

Counsel for Damon, in response to this, remarks that in all the cases which fell to be

considered by Warner J there was either a signed contract or a sale concluded by the fall
of the auctioneer's hammer at auction, whereas none of them was a case as here where
the offending party had refused both to sign and to pay the required deposit. In support
of his conclusion in *Millichamp v Jones* Warner J declared that he had drawn comfort from
reference to other authorities. According to the contention of counsel for Damon, he was
not entitled to do so, and there is indeed no weight of authority fatal to counsel's
arguments. He contends that the only cases of direct relevance in the present context are
Myton Ltd v Schwab-Morris and *Millichamp v Jones*. Since the conclusion in *Millichamp* is,
according to his contention, misguided, it is the earlier case which is to be preferred.

Not without justification, I am sure, counsel for Damon adjures me not to pay too
much regard to contracts for the sale of land but to confine myself rather to the sale
of ships. In so far, however, as I am obliged to choose, as affecting the approach which
should be adopted to cases of this general character, between the last two authorities
which I have mentioned, I choose the later authority, that is to say the decision of
Warner J, and I choose it for the reasons which he gives. But it is counsel's alternative
contention, and it may be his primary one, that what the court in these circumstances is
required to do with particular reference to the facts of the case before it is to decide on a
proper construction of the documents and on the general surrounding circumstances
whether the negotiations or dealings between the parties were or were not intended to
have contractual force until a particular document was signed. This is a test which he
derives from *Rugg Ltd v Street* [1962] 1 Lloyd's Rep 364 at 369, a case to which I need not
otherwise refer.

Adopting that approach and considering the question aside from authority, I see
nothing in the construction of the contract before me or the surrounding circumstances
in which it was entered into to suggest that the parties did not intend to be legally bound
until the memorandum of agreement had been signed or the deposit paid. Analogies are
dangerous, but it appears to me that the same effect was produced by the exchange of
telex messages between the brokers as would be by the signing of a slip by an insurer as a
prelude to the execution of a formal contract of insurance. In the context of this case
itself, and bearing in mind also the reference of the arbitrator to the fact that the exchange
of offers made between the sellers and the Raftopoulos brothers in the present case, made
as it was without any 'subjects', would be regarded in the shipping market as a binding
contract of sale not requiring a signed memorandum of agreement to validate it, I
therefore hold that the exchange of telex messages between the brokers resulted in a
binding contract between the sellers and the Raftopoulos brothers or their nominees.
The mere fact that they indicated an intention to nominate different buyers does not
mean that they were not bound themselves in the mean while.

By way of alternative or as a further argument under this head counsel for Damon
contends that, even if there was a binding contract to which Damon was party on account
of the nomination purportedly made on 1 August 1977, neither Mr Panas nor the
Raftopoulos brothers had any authority to declare Damon as buyers. He remarks that
the company could not be bound unless it was by agents acting with authority. He draws
the distinction between actual and ostensible authority and remarks that on 8 July 1977
no one had any authority of any description to bind Damon. He says that the position
remained the same thereafter, and for the purpose of seeking to show that neither Mr
Panas nor either of the Raftopoulos brothers subsequently had or purported to exercise
authority to bind Damon, he refers to *Bowstead on Agency* (14th edn, 1976) p 244 for its
convenient quotation of a passage from the judgment of Diplock LJ in *Freeman & Lockyer
(a firm) v Buckhurst Park Properties (Mangal) Ltd* [1964] 1 All ER 630 at 646, [1964] 2 QB
480 at 506. Counsel argues that there was no representation as to authority made by
anyone except in the telex message of 1 August 1977, that at that time when the telex
message was sent not only did Mr Panas not have authority but neither of the Raftopoulos
brothers had authority either. He therefore contends that nothing was said at any stage
such as to bind Damon and that there is moreover no evidence that the sellers were in
any way induced by any representation made to them.

Counsel for the sellers responds that there was undoubtedly a purported novation of the contract on 1 August 1977. He remarks by reference to a finding of the arbitrator *a* that all the directors knew what was intended to be done and approved of it. But recognising that it may be said that no authority can be derived from that source since at the stage when the telex message was sent none of those appointed director immediately afterwards had yet been appointed, he contends that soon after the Raftopoulos brothers had acquired authority they, or at any rate Mr Menelaos Raftopoulos, novated the contract on behalf of Damon. He refers for convenience to uncontroversial propositions *b* from Bowstead on Agency to the effect that if an act is ratified it is valid even if done by a person who, when he purported to do it, had no authority because then the agent is deemed to have been the principal's agent duly authorised to sign. Only a person in whose name an act is done may subsequently ratify it. Ratification will be implied when the conduct of the principal shows that he adopts the act, with the result that directors may ratify an act done for the company of which they are directors if they themselves *c* have power to do the act. Counsel for the sellers relies on the representations made on behalf of the company to the effect that the contract would be performed. In particular he refers of course to the telex messages sent by Mr Panas after 1 August 1977. It is convenient to mention at this point that counsel reserves the right to argue, which before me he did not, that there was operative here what he calls 'an estoppel by convention', such as would preclude Damon from denying that there was a concluded contract of sale *d* under which they were the buyers.

On the subject of ratification counsel for Damon contends that the references in the award on which counsel for the sellers might seek to rely are very weak and there is no express finding of ratification. He argues that nothing in the telex messages would amount to ratification on the part of Damon, there being nothing to suggest that Mr Menelaos Raftopoulos did any particular act. At the least, says counsel for Damon, the *e* position is ambiguous as to whether Mr Menelaos Raftopoulos was acting at all and if so in his capacity as chairman of Damon, but he acknowledges, as he must in face of the express finding of the arbitrator, that it would have been within the authority of Mr Menelaos Raftopoulos as chairman to ratify the contract. It appears to me that, where two persons, as here, acquire a Panamanian off-the-shelf company for the purpose of fulfilling an agreement which they have purported to make on its behalf, it requires but *f* the minimum of acknowledgment or adoption of the agreement on behalf of the company after they have become officers for the company to be bound. If directors of a company, after procuring the company to be substituted for themselves as buyers under a contract of sale, continue to promise performance of it, they must be taken to do so in their capacity as directors. I can see an argument that actual authority of Mr Menelaos Raftopoulos as chairman is to be implied from the finding of fact of the arbitrator that *g* all the members of the board approved of the Raftopoulos brothers nominating the company as buyers, but I doubt whether that particular finding is sufficiently unequivocal for the sellers' purposes. More importantly, the board of Damon in effect made a representation creating an apparent authority by their conduct in permitting the Raftopoulos brothers to act as chairman and treasurer in the management of Damon's business. The representation thereby made was that Mr Menelaos Raftopoulos had *h* authority to commit the company to contracts of a kind which a chairman usually enters into in the ordinary course of the company's business. In this context it is of prime importance that, as the arbitrator found, it is within the usual authority of the chairman of a Panamanian company to ratify or affirm contracts made in the company's name.

For these reasons it appears to me that there was sufficient ratification by Mr Menelaos Raftopoulos in what must be taken to have been his capacity as chairman of Damon for *j* Damon to become bound by that novation purportedly made on their behalf which occurred on 1 August 1977. That suffices to conclude the challenge which Damon seek to make to the special case.

I must turn now to consider the claim which the sellers make to be entitled to the amount of the unpaid deposit. Counsel for the sellers contends that the deposit was not

conditional on signing but the payment of the deposit and the signing of the
a memorandum of agreement were concurrent obligations. In aid of the sellers' claim to
be entitled to the amount of the deposit he relies on what is in effect the same sequence
of cases as fell in the earlier context to be considered by Warner J in the *Millichamp* case.
The first to which brief reference is necessary is *Dewar v Mintoft* [1912] 2 KB 373. That
was a case before Horridge J in which the main issue was whether there was a sufficient
memorandum in writing for the purposes of s 4 of the Statute of Frauds (1677) for the
b contract in question to be enforceable. That issue was determined in favour of the
plaintiff on the ground that the jury having found a verbal contract the letters and other
documents in question did constitute a sufficient memorandum. It was a case in which
no deposit having been paid in accordance with the contract, the amount of damage
actually suffered by the seller was a little over £80, whereas the amount of the unpaid
deposit was more than double that sum. The conditions of sale had contained a provision
c for forfeiture of the deposit money in the event of default by the purchaser. Horridge J
said (at 387–388):

> 'At the trial it was contended before me that [the provision to which I have
> referred] did not apply inasmuch as the deposit had not been paid, and that the only
> damages which could be recovered were the actual loss and the expenses on resale. I
> ruled that the defendant could not put himself in a better position by refusing to
d > pay the deposit than if the deposit had in fact been paid, in which case it could be
> retained by the seller . . .'

He accordingly directed the jury that the damages should be such as were computed by
reference to the unpaid deposit.

    That case was considered by Pennycuick J in *Lowe v Hope* [1969] 3 All ER 605 at 608–
e 609, [1970] Ch 94 at 98–99. It was a case in which the purchaser, perhaps unfortunately,
appeared in person. The judge considered *Dewar v Mintoft* after stating the applicable
principle in this way:

> 'Applying those principles in relation to a deposit payable under the contract of
> sale but not in fact paid by the purchaser, it seems to me that the vendor having
> elected to bring the contract to an end by rescission is not entitled to insist on the
f > performance of the contract in relation to the deposit. This is admittedly so, insofar
> as the deposit bears the character of part of the unpaid purchase price. It seems to
> me that it must equally be so, insofar as the deposit bears the character of a pledge;
> for once the vendor has rescinded the contract there are no outstanding obligations
> on the purchaser in respect of which the vendor can be entitled to be protected by a
> pledge.'
g

After citing from *Dewar v Mintoft* the passage from the judgment of Horridge J which I
have read, Pennycuick J said:

> 'The learned judge had been referred to certain authorities which lay down
> principles as to the rights and obligations of the parties on rescission. The ground
> for his decision appears to be contained in the sentence ([1912] 2 KB 373 at 387):
h > ". . . the defendant could not put himself in a better position by refusing to pay the
> deposit than if the deposit had in fact been paid." That, I think, is stated as some
> general rule either of justice or equity, but, with all respect to the learned judge, I
> do not think there is any place for a rule of this kind in the present context. I have,
> with much diffidence, reached the conclusion that the decision in *Dewar v. Mintoft*
j > is contrary to the principles applicable in this connection and that I ought not to
> follow it.'

    Counsel for the sellers argues that a different complexion has, however, been put on
this matter by the decision of the House of Lords in *Johnson v Agnew* [1979] 1 All ER 883,
[1980] AC 367, and in particular by the speech of Lord Wilberforce. In the course of it

Lord Wilberforce stated what he termed some uncontroversial propositions of law (see [1979] 1 All ER 883 at 889, [1980] AC 367 at 392), the first of which was:

'. . . in a contract for the sale of land, after time has been made, or has become, of the essence of the contract, if the purchaser fails to complete, the vendor can *either* treat the purchaser as having repudiated the contract, accept the repudiation, and proceed to claim damages for breach of the contract, both parties being discharged from further performance of the contract; *or* he may seek from the court an order for specific performance with damages for any loss arising from delay in performance. (Similar remedies are of course available to purchasers against vendors). This is simply the ordinary law of contract applied to contracts capable of specific performance.'

The third uncontroversial proposition of law was:

'. . . if the vendor treats the purchaser as having repudiated the contract and accepts the repudiation, he cannot thereafter seek specific performance. This follows from the fact that, the purchaser having repudiated the contract and his repudiation having been accepted, both parties are discharged from further performance.'

Lord Wilberforce went forward to examine the authorities which over a long period proceeded on an assumption that a claim for damages could not be made for breach of an agreement at the same time as applying for rescission. Lord Wilberforce explained that this doctrine, of which he disapproved, was based on a misunderstanding of a dictum of Jessel MR to the effect that these two remedies could not be obtained at the same time, the emphasis being on the phrase 'at the same time', which had a procedural significance at the date when the words were spoken which they have since lost. Lord Wilberforce then quoted with approval from the judgment of Dixon J in *McDonald v Dennys Lascelles Ltd* (1933) 48 CLR 457 at 476–477 where he said:

'When a party to a simple contract, upon a breach by the other contracting party of a condition of the contract, elects to treat the contract as no longer binding upon him, the contract is not rescinded as from the beginning. Both parties are discharged from the further performance of the contract, but rights are not divested or discharged which have already been unconditionally acquired. Rights and obligations which arise from the partial execution of the contract and causes of action which have accrued from its breach alike continue unaffected. When a contract is rescinded because of matters which affect its formation, as in the case of fraud, the parties are to be rehabilitated and restored, so far as may be, to the position they occupied before the contract was made. But when a contract, which is not void or voidable at law, or liable to be set aside in equity, is dissolved at the election of one party because the other has not observed an essential condition or has committed a breach going to its root, the contract is determined so far as it is executory only and the party in default is liable for damages for its breach.'

In conclusion of this sequence of cases counsel for the sellers refers again to *Millichamp v Jones* [1983] 1 All ER 267, [1982] 1 WLR 1422. He contends that if time for payment of the deposit has passed there is an accrued right to recover, which is not lost by subsequent repudiation. According to his contention, after the telex messages had been exchanged, which had the effect of making Damon party to the contract by novation, the buyers enjoyed a reasonable time within which to do what was demanded of them by the contract, namely sign the memorandum of agreement and pay the deposit. He contends that a reasonable time would be a few days and that time having been made of the essence by the telex message of 9 August when three days' grace was given, the obligation to make the payment of the deposit as well as sign the memorandum of agreement concurrently arose on 12 August. Not having been performed, that constituted a repudiation which the sellers were entitled to accept, as they did on 15 August. In the result the right to recover the deposit constituted an accrued right vested in the sellers.

a Counsel for Damon says that the court should lean against a conclusion which gives the innocent party more than the amount of his actual loss. To that, counsel for the sellers retorts that the other side of the coin is that the court should feel no predilection for giving to the guilty party relief from the consequences of his wrongdoing. Where, as here, the guilty party has repudiated the contract by failing to sign the memorandum and pay the deposit, I cannot see why he should be better off than if he had paid the deposit. Having promised to provide security for the due performance of the contract,

b he should not be better off if he defaults in the fulfilment of that promise than if he does not.

In relation to cl 13 of the memorandum of agreement counsel for Damon argues that the contract should only be enforced to the extent to which the sellers can bring themselves within the wording of the clause. The answer to that must be that the language of the clause presupposes that the obligation to provide the deposit has in fact been performed. What has here occurred is breach of the very obligation which requires

c the payment of the deposit. It is for breach of that obligation that the sellers are entitled to damages. The fact that the clause refers to the amount deposited does not involve that the parties intended the sellers not to be entitled to claim or retain the deposit unless they had received it. If counsel for Damon were right, the buyers could indeed avoid liability under the contract by the simple expedient of not paying the deposit. On a true analysis

d of what occurred between the parties it appears to me that either because the parties contracted by reference to the Norwegian Sale Form memorandum of agreement, the terms of which were thereby incorporated into the initial contract made, or by force of the terms of the telex messages themselves, Damon were obliged within a reasonable time of 3 August or possibly 5 August 1977 to sign the memorandum of agreement and pay the deposit. Especially in view of the imminence of the date for drydocking of one

e of the ships, a reasonable time would in the circumstances have been only a matter of days. Eventually the sellers did as they were entitled to do and on 9 August 1977 made time for compliance of the essence of the contract. Damon, having failed to comply by 12 August 1977, as counsel for the sellers submits, on 15 August 1977, the sellers were entitled to accept the repudiation and terminate the contract. Although they used the word 'withdraw', I can attach no significance to that.

f Counsel for Damon invokes the criticisms of the case of *Dewar v Mintoft* to be found in *Lowe v Hope*. First there is the reference in the passage to which I have referred to the role of a deposit as constituting a pledge (see [1969] 3 All ER 605 at 608, [1970] Ch 94 at 98). Although in view of the buyers' default it may be said that the deposit no longer bore the character of a pledge, it is for the loss sustained by the buyers' failure to provide it that the seller is entitled to be compensated in damages. Even though the sellers here

g may not be able to show that the failure to provide security has caused them to lose the benefit of the contract as a whole, yet they can show that they have lost the benefit or the value of the security itself. As for the criticism by Pennycuick J in *Lowe v Hope* [1969] 3 All ER 605 at 609, [1970] Ch 94 at 99, it seems to me that what Horridge J said was said only by way of explanation of the loss which the seller in his case had suffered, rather than as a statement of a general rule of justice or equity. In my judgment *Dewar v Mintoft*

h proceeds on the principle, which is axiomatic to the sale of goods lawyer, that acceptance of repudiation releases the offending party from liability only for future obligations, not for obligations already incurred. That is the basis, for example, of *Heyman v Darwins Ltd* [1942] 1 All ER 337, [1942] AC 356, cited by Lord Wilberforce in *Johnson v Agnew* [1979] 1 All ER 883 at 889, [1980] AC 367 at 393 in a speech from which it does not appear that contracts for the sale of land are in this respect to be regarded as on any different footing

j from contracts for the sale of goods. The position is helpfully summarised by Dixon J in the passage which I have cited. His was a case concerning the sale of land but he expressed himself generally. Next counsel for Damon argued that the memorandum of agreement provides for payment of the deposit only on signing the contract and because the contract was not signed the obligation to pay the deposit never arose. The answer to this is that in failing to sign the memorandum of agreement and pay the deposit concurrently the

buyers were, as the arbitrator has held, in repudiatory breach of the sale contract, reached
by exchange of telex messages. The obligations were, in my judgment, indeed concurrent.
Because Damon were in default in not signing the contract they were in default also in
failing to pay the deposit. Counsel says that the obligation to pay the deposit was not and
never has been an accrued obligation. It seems to me that what had accrued before the
contract was determined by acceptance of the buyers' repudiation was the sellers' right to
claim the deposit or damages in the like amount for breach of contract in failing to pay
it. It is fallacious to argue, as counsel for Damon does, that the purpose and by implication
the sole purpose of the claim in damages is to compensate the claimant as if the whole
contract had been performed. Here the sellers are entitled to claim the deposit, or
damages for failure to pay it, and to make that claim separately from their claim for
damages for repudiation. Finally, counsel for Damon argues that following rescission the
sellers are not entitled to claim specific performance, and that if they are it should not be
ordered because damages are an adequate remedy. This analysis of the claim is in my
judgment wrong because it suggests that the obligation to pay the deposit is only
enforceable by an order of specific performance. On the contrary, the obligation is
enforceable as a money judgment. When in *Johnson v Agnew* Lord Wilberforce said what
he did in the passage I have cited, he was speaking, I do not doubt, of specific performance
strictly so called. He was referring, as counsel for the sellers submitted, to the obligation
to take a conveyance. It is not by chance that Lord Wilberforce speaks of the purchaser
having been relieved, following repudiation, of further performance.

I accept the submission of counsel for the sellers that the present case is analogous with
Dewar v Mintoft. In my judgment the deposit was payable by way of security. Because
the right to receive it and therefore to recover it had accrued before Damon's repudiation
was accepted, it can be recovered now, if not as such, then by way of damages for breach
of the obligation to pay it. The sellers are also entitled to claim damages for repudiation
of the contract, but because the sum to which they are entitled in respect of the deposit is
greater than their actual loss it will follow that they can recover no sum or no more than
nominal damages under this head in addition to the amount of the deposit. I am fortified
in this conclusion by the view of Warner J in *Millichamp v Jones* [1983] 1 All ER 267 at
274, [1982] 1 WLR 1422 at 1430 that in such circumstances the vendor is entitled to sue
for damages including the amount of the unpaid deposit.

I accordingly answer the questions of law posed by the arbitrator as follows. (1)(a)
There was a binding contract concluded between the sellers and Damon for the sale of
the ships. (1)(b) Does not arise. (2) The sellers are entitled to damages from Damon in an
amount which does not arise since it is admittedly less than the amount of the deposit.
(3) The sellers are entitled to recover from Damon the amount of the deposit provided
for in cl 2 of the memorandum of agreement. Since no provision is made by the award
for these answers to the questions of law, the award must be remitted to the arbitrator so
that he may make an award consonant with this judgment.

Order accordingly.

Solicitors: *Lloyd Denby Neal* (for Damon); *Richards Butler & Co* (for the sellers).

K Mydeen Esq   Barrister.

a   # R v Epsom Justices, ex parte Gibbons

QUEEN'S BENCH DIVISION
WATKINS LJ AND TAYLOR J
24 JUNE, 27 JULY 1983

b
Magistrates – Information – Hearing two or more together – Summons and cross-summons arising out of informations founded on same incident and same facts – Whether magistrates having jurisdiction to hear summons and cross-summons together.

Where a summons and a cross-summons arise out of informations founded on the same incident and the same set of facts, a magistrates' court cannot, under any circumstances, order that they be tried together (see p 526 *a* to *c*, post).
c   *Clayton v Chief Constable of Norfolk* [1983] 1 All ER 984 distinguished.

Notes
For the scope of informations, see 29 Halsbury's Laws (4th edn) para 318, and for cases on the subject, see 33 Digest (Reissue) 165, *1281–1285*.

d   **Cases referred to in judgments**
Aldus v Watson [1973] 2 All ER 1018, [1973] QB 902, [1973] 2 WLR 1007, DC.
Brangwynne v Evans [1962] 1 All ER 446, [1962] 1 WLR 267, DC.
Clayton v Chief Constable of Norfolk [1983] 1 All ER 984, [1983] 2 WLR 555, HL.

Application for judicial review
e   Susan Patricia Gibbons applied, with the leave of a Divisional Court of the Queen's Bench Division granted on 7 June 1983, for (i) an order of certiorari to bring up and quash a decision of the Epsom justices, dated 7 April 1983, regarding the dates of trial of an information laid against her by Pc Douglas Corrie of the Metropolitan Police and of an information laid by her against Pc Douglas Corrie, (ii) an order of prohibition directed to the Epsom justices to prevent them from proceeding on 10 June 1983 with the trial of
f   the information laid against her by Pc Douglas Corrie, and (iii) an order of mandamus directed to the Epsom justices requiring them to hear and determine according to law the application which she had made to them for an order that the information laid against her by Pc Douglas Corrie and the information laid by her against him should be tried together. The facts are set out in the judgment of Watkins LJ.

g   *Alexander Cranbrook* for the applicant.
Simon Pratt for the police.

At the conclusion of the argument Watkins LJ announced that the application would be dismissed for reasons to be given later.

h   27 July. The following judgments were delivered.

WATKINS LJ. This is an application by Susan Patricia Gibbons made, pursuant to leave granted on 7 June 1983, for judicial review of a decision of the Epsom justices, on 7 April 1983.
They had before them, on that day, two summonses arising out of informations laid.
j   The first of them, on 13 March 1983, was by Pc Douglas Corrie of the Metropolitan Police, against the applicant alleging that she had on 13 March 1983, at Long Grove Hospital, Horton Lane, Epsom, assaulted him in the execution of his duty, contrary to s 51(1) of the Police Act 1964. The second, laid by the applicant on 23 March 1983, against the constable, alleged that, on the same day and place already mentioned, he did assault and beat her, contrary to s 42 of the Offences against the Person Act 1861.

It was submitted to the justices, by counsel for the prosecution, that the informations should be tried separately. The constable, he said, relying on *Aldus v Watson* [1973] 2 All ER 1018, [1973] QB 902, had an absolute right to a separate trial and, seeing that his information was laid earlier than the applicant's, the charge against her should be heard first. Mr Dirks, the applicant's solicitor, contended that, since the two informations were founded on the same incident and much of the evidence in respect of them was identical, separate trials would serve no good purpose. It would merely produce a waste of time and what was more important, he said, it would prejudice the applicant and deny her natural justice.

The justices, having considered these submissions, decided that the informations should be heard separately, that of the constable first. They adjourned the hearing of the charge against the applicant until 10 June 1983, and that against the constable to a date to be fixed thereafter.

The applicant asks this court (1) to quash the decision of the justices, (2) to order that they do not hear the charge against the applicant on 10 June and (3) to direct them to hear afresh, according to the proper law, the application that the informations be heard together.

The grounds on which this relief is sought are that the justices were wrong to regard themselves as being bound by the decision in *Aldus v Watson*, wrong to order separate trials, seeing that the informations arose out of the same incident and involved the same facts, and failed to have regard to matters explained in *Clayton v Chief Constable of Norfolk* [1983] 1 All ER 984, [1983] 2 WLR 555. It must be said at this point, I think, that the justices were not referred to that case. Thus it is, of course, impossible to criticise the justices for not taking account of it. What effect it has, if any, on this court is an altogether different matter.

That the justices were guided by *Aldus v Watson* in reaching their decision is confirmed by the contents of a letter written by their clerk to the Crown Office of which the following is an extract:

'As explained, when speaking to you on the telephone yesterday afternoon, I am satisfied that the justices concerned with this proceeding would not wish to quarrel with the facts as broadly set out in the applicant's affidavit supporting her application for leave to apply for judicial review, as their decision was clearly based on the authority contained in the case of *Aldus and another v Watson* to which they had been referred. The recent decision of the House of Lords in *Clayton v Chief Constable of Norfolk* ... which seemingly the applicant relies upon, was not brought to the justices' notice and therefore was not considered by them in their deliberations. It would therefore seem unnecessary, in the circumstances of this particular case, for an affidavit to be filed on behalf of the justices. I would, of course, be pleased to hear from you should you consider otherwise.'

The justices have not been called on to provide an affidavit by this court, which feels able, on the available information, to deal fully with the issues involved here.

The question posed to this court in *Aldus v Watson* was, having regard to the fact that each of four defendants was charged separately with an identical offence arising out of the same set of facts and that it was the joint action of the defendants which caused the offences, were the justices right to refuse them separate trials? This court's answer to that was, applying *Brangwynne v Evans* [1962] 1 All ER 446, [1962] 1 WLR 267, that where separate informations are preferred against two or more defendants a magistrates' court has no power to try the informations together without the defendants' consent, even though each defendant is charged with an identical offence arising out of the same set of facts. In *Brangwynne v Evans* [1962] 1 All ER 446 it was held:

'It has always been a principle of law that a defendant in a magistrates' court can only be called on to answer one charge at a time unless he consents, either expressly or impliedly, to informations being heard together; accordingly, a magistrate's court *a*   should never proceed to hear two or more informations at the same time without expressly asking the defendant whether he consents to that course.'

The absence of consent in the present case by the constable, the prosecutor, to a joint hearing of the two informations in the light of these authorities, obviously induced the decision of the justices complained of. They regarded the absence of consent as depriving them entirely of a discretion to decide the procedural point in issue, according to notions of what would have been a just and reasonable manner of proceeding.

b   However, the House of Lords in *Clayton v Chief Constable of Norfolk*, in reviewing *Brangwynne v Evans*, *Aldus v Watson* and a number of other cases bearing on practice and procedure in magistrates' courts, ruled that lack of consent by a defendant or a number of defendants, although an important consideration, does not deprive justices of a discretion to proceed in their court in a manner which, in the circumstances, appears to them to be just. In the only speech, Lord Roskill stated in clear terms how this discretion

c   should be exercised (see [1983] 1 All ER 984 at 991–992, [1983] 2 WLR 555 at 564–566). Justices would, in my view, be well advised to follow carefully the guidance there provided. I do not enlarge this judgment by quoting the relevant passages, solely and simply because the circumstances to which that decision can be applied differ from those which obtain in the present case. In *Clayton's* case, and in all those cases reviewed in it, the facts involved either the trial of one defendant on more than one information, or the

d   trial of more than one defendant on separate informations. Here, what is contemplated is the trial of two informations together on one of which the prosecutor is the constable and on the other that same constable is the defendant. Therefore, counsel who has appeared before us, instructed by the Metropolitan Police, argues that the present case is vitally distinguishable from *Clayton*.

There are many reasons, he has submitted, why it would be wholly impractical for

e   informations such as are usually referred to as summons and cross-summons to be heard together even if the prosecution and defence agreed to such a course being taken. The following seem to be the most impressive of these reasons, some of which were easily forseeable, I think, before argument on them was developed.

It is a basic right of every defendant to decline to cross-examine prosecution witnesses, to make a submission of no case to answer at the close of the prosecution, to decline to

f   give evidence and to make any kind of address to the court. When that person is both defendant and prosecutor, in the same proceeding, how is he to decide in advance how he would conduct himself in these respects when he may, according to the procedure decided on, either have to prosecute or defend at short notice? Problems may well arise about the order in which witnesses will be called on one side or the other. Who really will have the right to go first and who to make the final address? Suppose one or other of

g   the persons involved has previous convictions, how is the question to be resolved whether to allow those to be referred to, if such an issue properly arises? The calling of the wife of one of these persons could give rise to difficulties.

Justices should not, it is said, be subjected to a proceeding which could give rise to these and many other complications of evidence and procedure which might well defy the ability of the most experienced of judges to resolve.

h   Furthermore, we are invited to have regard to the sinister purpose with which some cross-summonses are served and which would probably encourage an exacerbation of the tendency to use the cross-summons merely as an unjustifiable weapon of defence if a joint hearing of summons and cross-summons is permitted.

Counsel for the applicant endeavoured valiantly to minimise the force of these arguments by contending that the present and *Clayton's* case are not distinguishable.

j   Justices, he said, should be masters of their procedure, subject only to a proper and just exercise of their discretion. Accordingly, the Epsom justices should be called on to exercise their discretion in accordance with the guidance provided in *Clayton*.

I do not agree with him. No argument was addressed to the House of Lords on the matter of joint trial of summons and cross-summons and I see no reason, therefore, to suppose that they could have had that in their contemplation when reaching their conclusions on very different circumstances.

The kind of trial which concerns us cannot, I think, be sensibly compared for procedural purposes with any of the kinds of trials referred to in *Clayton*. It produces unique considerations and I believe that these must lead to the conclusion, accepting as I do the submissions of counsel for the police, that summons and cross-summons can in no circumstances be tried together. There is no authority to the contrary and I am persuaded that justices do not have the power to permit a proceeding of that kind to take place no matter who condescends to consent to it.

Accordingly, although they did so for a reason which I think was irrelevant, I am of the view that the justices reached the right decision and should, as they intend, hold separate trials.

I would dismiss this appeal.

TAYLOR J. I agree.

Application dismissed.

Solicitors: *Spencer Gibson & Son*, Sutton (for the applicant); *D M O'Shea* (for the police).

Raina Levy Barrister.

Mohammed-Holgate v Duke

COURT OF APPEAL, CIVIL DIVISION
SIR JOHN ARNOLD P AND LATEY J
12, 13 JULY 1983

Arrest – Arrest without warrant – Reasonable cause – Exercise of power of arrest – Constable arresting suspect in belief that confession more likely if suspect subjected to stress and pressure of arrest – Whether proper exercise of power of arrest – Whether constable required to make all practicable inquiries before exercising power of arrest – Whether period of detention may be used to establish whether suspicion justified and to seek further material evidence – Criminal Law Act 1967, s 2(4).

The plaintiff and another woman lived in the same house. In December 1979 some jewellery was stolen from the other woman's room and some months later it was found in a jeweller's shop. The jeweller gave a police constable a description of the person who had sold the jewellery to him. The plaintiff fitted that description and, knowing that she had been living in the house at the time of the theft and that she had been in financial difficulties, the constable felt that he had reasonable cause for suspecting that she had stolen the jewellery. Without making any further inquiries, he exercised, in good faith, his power under s 2(4)[a] of the Criminal Law Act 1967 to arrest the plaintiff without a warrant. She was then taken to a police station and interrogated. No evidence was obtained linking her with the crime, and she was released about six hours later. The plaintiff brought an action against the chief constable claiming damages for false imprisonment. The judge found that the arresting officer had had reasonable cause at the time of the arrest to suspect the plaintiff of the theft and that the period of detention had not been excessive, but he awarded the plaintiff £1,000 damages on the ground that the arresting officer had not been justified in exercising the power of arrest under s 2(4) because his sole reason for arresting the plaintiff rather than interviewing her under caution was that he thought she would be more likely to confess if she was subjected to

---

a   Section 2(4) is set out at p 528 f, post

a the greater stress and pressure involved in an arrest and deprivation of liberty. The chief constable appealed.

Held – Where a constable had reasonable cause for suspecting that a person had committed an arrestable offence, he could exercise the power of arrest under s 2(4) of the 1967 Act and use the period of detention to establish whether his suspicions were justified and also to seek further material evidence. The constable was not required to make all *b* practicable inquiries before exercising the power of arrest. In the circumstances the arresting officer had had reasonable cause to suspect the plaintiff of the theft and his decision to arrest her had been within the range of reasonable choices available to him. It followed that, because the arresting officer had not acted improperly, the appeal would be allowed and the award of damages would be set aside (see p 530 *f* to *h*, p 532 *f* to *j*, p 533 *c* to *g*, p 534 *e* to *j* and p 536 *e f*, post).

c   *Dumbell v Roberts* [1944] 1 All ER 326 and *Shaaban Bin Hussien v Chong Fook Kam* [1969] 3 All ER 1626 considered.

Notes

For the exercise by a constable of the power to arrest without warrant, see 11 Halsbury's Laws (4th edn) para 111.

d   For the Criminal Law Act 1967, s 2, see 8 Halsbury's Statutes (3rd edn) 553.

Cases referred to in judgments

Dallison v Caffery [1964] 2 All ER 610, [1965] 1 QB 348, [1964] 3 WLR 385, CA.
Dumbell v Roberts [1944] 1 All ER 326, CA.
Shaaban Bin Hussien v Chong Fook Kam [1969] 3 All ER 1626, [1970] AC 942, [1970] 2
e   WLR 441, PC.

Appeal

The defendant, John Duke, the Chief Constable of Hampshire, appealed against the decision of his Honour Judge Inskip QC in the Portsmouth County Court on 20 December 1982 in an action brought by the plaintiff, Mariam Mohammed-Holgate, *f* against the defendant claiming damages for false imprisonment, whereby, although the judge found (i) that the arresting officer, Det Con Offin, had had reasonable grounds to suspect that the plaintiff had committed an arrestable offence, (ii) that the period of detention in custody had not been excessive and (iii) that the arresting officer had regarded his action in arresting the plaintiff as a proper exercise of the power of arrest conferred on him by s 2(4) of the Criminal Law Act 1967, the judge awarded the plaintiff *g* £1,000 damages on the ground that it had been an unnecessary and wrongful exercise of the power of arrest merely to exercise it for the purpose of conducting an interview with the plaintiff at a police station. By a respondent's notice under RSC Ord 59, r 6(2) the plaintiff gave notice that she would contend that the judgment should be affirmed on the further grounds that the judge should have found (i) that the arresting officer had had no reasonable grounds to suspect that the plaintiff had committed an arrestable *h* offence and (ii) that the period of detention in custody had been excessive. The plaintiff gave further notice that if she succeeded in respect of those contentions she would contend that the judgment should be varied by setting aside the award of £1,000 damages and by substituting therefor such higher figure as the Court of Appeal thought just. The facts are set out in the judgment of Sir John Arnold P.

j   *Robert Beecroft* for the defendant.
Robin W Belben for the plaintiff.

SIR JOHN ARNOLD P. This is a point which arises in the course of an appeal. The appeal is an appeal from the judgment of his Honour Judge Inskip QC which he gave on 20 December 1982 in an action before him for wrongful arrest. The plaintiff is a lady who was resident in a house in which a theft took place. She was apparently in the premises at the time, or might have been. The nature of the theft was that a jewellery *a* box containing some jewellery, which had been placed in a certain part of the house occupied by Mrs Stainer, had been removed therefrom in circumstances which were equally susceptible of the removal having taken place at the hands of a person who was already legitimately in the house or a person who came in from outside and performed the act. All this happened in December 1979, and in December 1979 certain matters were known to the police then involved. They knew of the plaintiff's association with *b* the premises. They knew, or had been told, that there was some indication of impecuniosity on the part of the plaintiff.

There the matter rested. There was some police interrogation of the plaintiff, but it came to nothing, until in the following April part of the stolen property was discovered at a jewellers called Constads in the town in which all this took place, Portsmouth, and that reopened the inquiry. So the police, this time in the person of Det Con Offin, in *c* company with Mrs Stainer, the woman who had been the victim of the theft, went along, I think with another officer (a sergeant), to the shop in which the jewellery had been discovered. The jewellery which was coincident with the discovery and with the theft in fact consisted of three rings. The jeweller, or the managing director of the jewellery company, gave a description of the person who had sold the rings to them. To quote from the judge's judgment, which contains the essential part of the description, '35–45 *d* years, short dark hair, approximately 5 feet, medium build of a nervous disposition'. That, except for the fact that the plaintiff was a lady with auburn hair rather than dark hair, was a reasonable description of the plaintiff, although certainly, as is pointed out on her behalf, it could be a reasonable description of a large number of other people. The victim of the theft observed that that was a pretty good description of the plaintiff. Armed with that, together with the other indicia of the plaintiff's possible involvement *e* to which I have already referred, Det Con Offin arrested the plaintiff.

For that to be a justifiable arrest it is necessary that the provisions of s 2(4) of the Criminal Law Act 1967 should be complied with. That subsection is in these terms:

'Where a constable, with reasonable cause, suspects that an arrestable offence has been committed, he may arrest without warrant anyone whom he, with reasonable *f* cause, suspects to be guilty of the offence.'

There is no doubt that theft is an arrestable offence. There is no doubt that the constable suspected that that offence had been committed; indeed it is common ground that it had. But did he, with reasonable cause, suspect the plaintiff to be guilty of the offence? The judge concluded that he did. He then went on to say, and this is the point in the appeal, that, although the prescriptions of the subsection were satisfied, nevertheless *g* there was an abuse of the power of arrest thus created because the power was exercised unreasonably. To that part of the argument we have not yet come.

The reason why the matter with which I am now dealing arises is that there is a respondent's notice, and the respondent's notice complains that the judge wrongly came to the conclusion that Det Con Offin did, with reasonable cause, suspect that the plaintiff was guilty of the offence. That is the point with which we are at this stage concerned. *h*

The judge in the course of his judgment said, having described the description given by the jeweller to which I have already referred:

'Det Con Offin told me that because of that description and its similarity to the plaintiff (and similarity there certainly was) and other reasons he had reasonable cause for suspecting that the plaintiff had stolen the jewellery. The reasons he gave *j* me for suspecting the plaintiff were first that she was a lodger in the house at the material time and would appear to have been the only person at the house when the property was stolen. There was no evidence before me in this respect to justify the conclusion that the plaintiff was the only person at the house when the property was stolen. The second reason was that she could have had access to the room where the

a
jewellery was. The third reason was that she was possibly one or two weeks in arrear with her rent. The fourth reason was that she had a few money problems at the time. And the fifth reason and the most important was the similarity in the descriptions. There was no doubt Mr Constadt's [that is the jeweller's] description of the lady who had sold him the jewellery in Mrs Stainer's view fitted that of the plaintiff.'

b
Then he set out the material which was relevant to the decision, and he later on made a finding that Det Con Offin had reasonable cause to suspect not only that an arrestable offence had been committed but also that the plaintiff was guilty of that offence.

We have been very properly reminded by counsel for the defendant that in an appellate court the burden to show that the judge was wrong on a matter like this, which is a conclusion to be derived from the primary facts, rests squarely on those who say that he was wrong, and just looking for the moment at no more than the materials which I have

c
listed from the judge as being the materials available to Det Con Offin for the purpose of forming a reasonable view, as he had to do, it seems to me to be quite impossible to show that the judge was wrong in concluding that from those materials the constable with reasonable cause suspected the plaintiff. There was no dispute that the detective constable in fact suspected the plaintiff, and the issue therefore was that of reasonable cause.

d
But is is said that that is not enough, because it is said that there is a requirement of the law that no reasonable suspicion can arise unless inquiries have been made to the extent that they can conveniently be made, the necessity of which is thrown up by the surrounding circumstances. It is suggested that that is a proposition which is to be derived from what was said by Scott LJ in *Dumbell v Roberts* [1944] 1 All ER 326. This is what the judge says about that case and the relevant passage. He is dealing at this stage of

e
his judgment with the proposition which is phrased in these terms: 'If the plaintiff can satisfy me that it was unreasonable for Det Con Offin to have exercised the statutory power of arrest then she succeeds in this action.' That was a proposition which was not in contest, according to the judge. That was a proposition which fell to be advanced after the judge had concluded that there was a justifiable power of arrest within the ambit of the subsection, and it was in relation to that that the judge said that further guidance was

f
to be obtained from the judgment of Scott LJ. He went on:

'Scott LJ's observations were primarily directed to whether there was reasonable cause for suspicion. [That of course was a matter he had already decided.] However Scott LJ said ([1944] 1 All ER 326 at 329) [and then there is a lengthy quotation from Scott LJ's judgment which it is not necessary to reproduce in its entirety at this stage of the hearing of this appeal. I will cite only a relatively short part of it]: ". . .

g
the British principle of personal freedom, that every man should be presumed innocent until he is proved guilty, applies also to the police function of arrest—in a very modified degree, it is true, but at least to the extent of requiring them to be observant, receptive and open-minded and to notice any relevant circumstances which points either way, either to innocence or to guilt. They may have to act on the spur of the moment and have no time to reflect and be bound, therefore, to

h
arrest to prevent escape; but where there is no danger of the person who has *ex hypothesi* aroused their suspicion, that he probable is an 'offender' attempting to escape, they should make all presently practicable enquiries from persons present or immediately accessible who are likely to be able to answer their enquiries forthwith."'

j
There are three matters which are put forward on behalf of the plaintiff as being matters on which the detective constable failed to make that sort of inquiry. The first one was whether the jeweller could have identified the person who sold him the rings if the plaintiff had been put up in a line at an identity parade. The detective constable had already formed the view that the jeweller could not, and, right or wrongly, that view having been formed, it is not, in my view, a practicable inquiry, as the phrase is used by

Scott LJ, to ask the identifier the problem, because the only answer he could possibly have given is, 'I do not know.' But apart from that, even if this is a live point, the only *a* person who could form a view about the potential identification powers of the jeweller, at any rate as between the judge at first instance and ourselves, is the judge at first instance who saw him.

The second point is that no search of the plaintiff's premises before the arrest took place. That might have been useful of course in that some of the other part of the jewellery, not that sold to the jeweller, might have been discovered or perhaps the box *b* might have been discovered or something might have been discovered at the premises to resolve any issue of doubt remaining on that score. Whether that is to be assimilated with a presently practicable inquiry from persons present or immediately accessible is no doubt a matter which is fit for argument but not, as will emerge in a moment, on this part of the case.

The third class of problem subsumes what are called conveniently for this purpose *c* forensic points. The woman who sold the rings to the jeweller had signed a name (as it turned out a false name) on the back of a cheque. So there was material fit for comparison with the plaintiff's handwriting, and a failure to obtain a handwriting sample from the plaintiff before the arrest is put forward under this head. Comparably there was no examination for fingerprints at the scene of the crime or on the cheque, which had been handled, it would seem, by the guilty party at the jeweller's shop. But it is quite plain *d* that no immediate answer to any initiative of that sort could have been forthcoming until there had been a forensic examination. So it instantly follows as far as those avenues of inquiry are concerned that they are not to be assimilated in any way with those instanced by Scott LJ.

Then it is said, although there was no cross-examination to this effect, that Det Con Offin ought to have asked a senior and more expert officer whether it was worth pursuing *e* these lines of inquiry before the arrest. But, as that was never presented to the court, it does not seem to me that that is a matter of much assistance.

The real reason why this line of argument fails is simply that the whole of what Scott LJ says is plainly directed in the context in which it was said not to the question of whether the police arrested with reasonable cause a person whom they suspected of having committed the crime, but whether it was reasonable to carry out the arrest even *f* if the power were available, in other words the very point which was decided by the judge against the police and on which the main appeal is founded. In my judgment there is no colour in authority or principle for the proposition that if there be in the mind of the arrester for reasonable cause a suspicion to the relevant effect there is any need to make further inquiries for the purpose of complying with the section, and accordingly I would not uphold this paragraph in the respondent's notice. *g*

LATEY J. I agree. I also reject the proposition of counsel for the plaintiff as being not only far too wide, but, as I think, quite untenable. Reasonable cause for suspicion can arise at any stage of a police inquiry, and it is reasonable cause for suspicion which at this stage of this appeal we are considering.

h

13 July. **SIR JOHN ARNOLD P** continued delivering his judgment. This appeal arises out of an arrest of the plaintiff in May 1980. The arrest was carried out by Det Con Offin for reasons which date back to an incident which occurred in December 1979. On 8 December a Mrs Stainer had had stolen from her accommodation a jewellery box containing some jewellery, and part of the jewellery which had then been stolen was subsequently sold at a jeweller's shop and as a result of that sale the investigation, which *j* had died away in the mean time, was reopened.

For various reasons, including the reason that the plaintiff had been present at the premises at the date of the theft and that her description was somewhat similar to that which had been given by the manager of the jeweller's shop, a state of things had been reached by the time of the arrest, as the judge in the county court found and as we have

a in a previous judgment in this case concurred, that the conditions of s 2(4) of the Criminal Law Act 1967 were satisfied, that is to say the detective constable, with reasonable cause, suspected that an arrestable offence had been committed and that he, with reasonable cause, suspected the plaintiff to be guilty of the offence. But the arrest is complained of as being unlawful because, as is alleged by the plaintiff and as is not disputed by the defendant, it is not enough that the terms of the subsection should be complied with. In addition to that it must be reasonable to exercise the power thus made
b available. That is not a matter which has been argued before us. It has been disposed of by assertion and acceptance.

The question that we have to decide, as was the question which the judge in the court below had to decide, was: was it reasonable to exercise the power in this case? The judge found that it was not for a perfectly plain and clearly stated reason, which he expressed in these terms:

c
> 'If, as I find here, the power of arrest was only exercised for the purpose of putting someone under greater pressure to confess than if interviewed under caution without being arrested, it is an unreasonable exercise of the power of arrest given by the statute.'

That was the reason and that was the sole reason advanced by the judge for his
d conclusion.

The matter of the motive or purpose had earlier been dealt with in slightly expanded terms, where the judge said:

> 'I am driven to the conclusion by the evidence of what happened or what failed to happen that the only reason why Det Con Offin decided to arrest the plaintiff rather than pursue his investigations which he could have done in the case of a
e woman of good character without arresting her and then interview her under caution was to subject her to the greater stress and pressure involved in arrest and deprivation of liberty in the belief that if she was going to confess she was more likely to do so in a state of arrest.'

Those then are the two passages, and the only two passages, in the judgment of the
f judge which deal with the purpose of the arrest of this plaintiff and the judge's reason for holding that arrest wrongful.

The practice of interrogating persons under arrest for the purpose of obtaining a statement while they are in custody is of course wholly familiar. It is something which is recognised as happening under the Judges' Rules (see Practice Note [1964] 1 All ER 237, [1964] 1 WLR 152), to which we have been referred, and there is no doubt that it is
g perfectly common practice. But what the plaintiff says is that, although that is common practice and, if properly conducted, entirely permissible practice once the person has been arrested, it is not by itself a legitimate cause of arrest or purpose of the exercise of the power of arrest otherwise available.

This proposition is advanced on two bases. One is that there must be present in the mind of the person who effects the arrest, if it is to be reasonably effected, a fear that the
h process of interrogation will be vitiated by the presence of one or other of the following circumstances: the destruction of evidence, interference with other potential witnesses, the warning of an accomplice, a repetition of the offence or the escape of the suspect. The other is that, if there are other steps which the arresting constable could take for the furtherance of the investigation, then the constable should take those other steps first, unless it is demonstrated to be necessary or at least desirable that the other steps should
j not be taken first.

As to each of those matters, there is no authority at all to which we have been referred to sustain them. In a Privy Council case, *Shaaban Bin Hussien v Chong Fook Kam* [1969] 3 All ER 1626 at 1630, [1970] AC 942 at 948, Lord Devlin, giving the judgment of the committee, said:

> 'To give power to arrest on reasonable suspicion does not mean that it is always or

even ordinarily to be exercised. It means that there is an executive discretion. In the
exercise of it many factors have to be considered besides the strength of the case. *a*
The possibility of escape, the prevention of further crime and the obstruction of
police inquiries are examples of those factors with which all judges who have had to
grant or refuse bail are familiar.'

Then he went on to point out that there was no danger in a large measure of executive
discretion because of other safeguards which were available in the form of granting bail
and the necessity of deciding quickly whether to bring proceedings or to release. That by   *b*
no possible canon of construction can be regarded as a concatenation intended to be
exhaustive of, as Lord Devlin calls them, the many factors which have to be considered
or of those factors which alone could justify the exercise of the power of arrest.

The other matter to which we have been referred as bearing on this aspect of the case
are some observations which were made by the Royal Commission on Criminal Procedure
in the report which it produced in January 1981 (Cmnd 8092), from which paras 3.65   *c*
and 3.66 have been read to us, read, I may say, by both sides without any debates as to
their admissibility. They are describing at this point the existing powers of arrest:

> '3.65 . . . the ultimate purpose of arrest is to bring before a court for trial a person
> who commits a criminal offence or is reasonably suspected of so doing. But because
> arrest deprives the citizen of his liberty its use is to be restricted generally to offences   *d*
> that carry the penalty of imprisonment [that is to say, of course, arrestable offences]
> . . . and to persons against whom the summons procedure will not be effective . . .
> 3.66. The period of detention upon arrest may be used for certain purposes, and
> the power of arrest is also related to these. Indeed the purposes for which the existing
> powers of arrest are used in practice can be put in the following terms. It may be
> used to prevent the suspect destroying evidence or interfering with witnesses or   *e*
> warning accomplices who have not yet been arrested. Where there is good reason to
> suspect a repetition of the offence, especially but not exclusively offences of violence,
> it may be used to stop an occurrence. Finally, the criterion of having reasonable
> grounds for suspicion sufficient to justify arrest is not necessarily sufficient to justify
> a charge; hearsay evidence, for example, may be sufficient grounds for reasonable
> suspicion, but it is not sufficient for a person to be charged, since it will not be   *f*
> admissible as evidence at trial. Accordingly, the period of detention may be used to
> dispel or confirm that reasonable suspicion by questioning the suspect or seeking
> further material evidence with his assistance . . .'

In my judgment that passage, where it lists the purposes for which the existing powers
of arrest are used in practice, in the final two sentences which I have read is deliberately   *g*
designed to include among those purposes the purpose of dispelling or confirming the
reasonable suspicion which must antecede the arrest by questioning the suspect or
seeking further material evidence. The penultimate sentence is used to introduce and to
illustrate the necessity for that last conclusion. In my judgment para 3.66 entirely
assimilates to the purposes for which the period of detention may be used those purposes
for which the existing powers of arrest are used, and that, in my judgment, negatives the   *h*
proposition that there is a distinction between those purposes which are legitimately
furthered during the period or arrest and those which may be used for the purpose of
justifying the exercise of the powers of arrest. Moreover, it is plain, in my judgment,
from that paragraph that the concatenation of circumstances put forward by the plaintiff
as being necessary for the exercise of the power of arrest is not exhaustive, and at any rate
the purpose of questioning the suspect for the purpose of confirming or otherwise   *j*
developing the available evidence is to be included in those purposes, and, in my
judgment, that purpose is one which if in truth the purpose in the mind of the arresting
constable, and genuinely in the mind of the arresting constable, will, if the circumstances
of the subsection are fulfilled, justify the arrest.

But it is suggested here that there were other circumstances which ought to have

negatived that state of things. It is absolutely correct to say that the constable thought
a that without a confession he would never have a charge which he could place before
examining magistrates or a jury and that it was necessary if he was to prefer such a charge
that he should obtain a confession. It is also absolutely true that he thought that the
greater stress and pressure (and I quote from the judgment) involved in the arrest and
deprivation of liberty made it more likely that the suspect would confess. Those are the
two circumstances which are advanced as casting a doubt on whether there was in the
b mind of the arresting constable a pure and proper and justifiable motive for this arrest.

It would follow, if the purpose of the constable had been to subject the suspect to
improper questioning or improper pressure during the contemplated period which
would follow the arrest which would be occupied by the questioning, that that would be
an impure motive which could not be relied on, but that is tantamount, in my judgment,
to saying that the officer was not acting bona fide, and there is no suggestion of that. It
c would also, I think, be right that, if the obtaining of a statment by the arresting constable
in accordance with the intention that he had formed at the time of arrest would render,
because of the manner of its obtaining as then contemplated, that statement inadmissible
before a jury, it would again cast doubts sufficiently strong on the bona fides of the officer
to preclude him from relying on that purpose as a proper purpose for the arrest. But in
this case there is nothing of that sort at all, and in my judgment, again using the judge's
d language, the obtaining of a statement by means of the greater stress and pressure
involved in arrest and deprivation of liberty would in no way by itself make that
statement a statement which was improperly obtained or a statement which would be
rejected at a criminal trial. In my judgment the purpose for which the officer exercised
the power of arrest was a proper purpose.

As to the proposition that there were other things which he might have done, no
e doubt there were other things which he might have done first. He might have obtained
a statement from her otherwise than under arrest to see how far he could get. He might
have obtained a specimen of her handwriting and sent that off for forensic examination
against a specimen of the writing of the person who had obtained the money by selling
the stolen jewellery, which happened to exist in the case. All those things he might have
done. He might have carried out fingerprint investigations if he had first obtained a
f print from the plaintiff. But the fact that there were other things which he might have
done does not, in my judgment, make that which he did do into an unreasonable exercise
of the power of arrest if what he did so, namely to arrest, was within the range of
reasonable choices available to him. In my judgment it was, and in my judgment this
appeal ought to be allowed.

g **LATEY J.** I agree. Counsel have said, and rightly so, that this part of the appeal raises a
question of some general importance, and in deference to their research and careful
arguments I add some sentences.

Under s 2(4) of the Criminal Law Act 1967 the exercise of the power of arrest is
discretionary: the constable 'may arrest without warrant'. Was it a reasonable exercise of
the discretionary power in this case for the purpose found by the judge in the passages of
h his judgment which Sir John Arnold P has read out and which I need not repeat? It is
surprisingly, and indeed perhaps significantly, bare of direct authority. The judge had to
reach his decision without the help of direct authority, as do we. It seems that he did not
have the benefit of having the 1981 report of the Royal Commission on Criminal
Procedure (Cmnd 8092) brought to his attention. This records that once the prerequisites
exist to bring into being the power of arrest it is a long-established and widespread
j practice to use it for the purpose of questioning the suspect under detention. Indeed, the
last two sentences of para 3.66, which have already been read out by Sir John Arnold P,
say:

> 'Accordingly, the period of detention may be used to dispel or confirm that
> reasonable suspicion by questioning the suspect or seeking further material evidence

with his assistance. This has not always been the law or practice but now seems to
be well established as one of the primary purposes of detention upon arrest.'

Counsel for the defendant in his address paid tribute to the way the judge heard this
case and to the succinctness and clarity of his judgment and has criticised only his
conclusion on this central question. For my part, I take the opportunity of echoing that
tribute. Whether or not the judge would have reached the conclusion he did had his
attention been drawn to the Royal Commission report recording this well-established
practice we cannot know. Parliament from time to time enacts laws concerning the role
and powers of the police, but leaves a wide area often where it is for the courts to give
such guidance as they can or think it proper to give. Where in the language of the statute
Parliament has invested the police with an apparently unfettered discretion, as it has in
s 2(4) of the 1967 Act, it behoves the courts, in my opinion, to be chary of imposing
fetters where Parliament has not, bearing in mind that Parliament has laid down certain
prerequisites which must exist before the power can be exercised, and those prerequisites
are themselves substantial safeguards against improper or capricious use of the power. It
is the fact of course that an exercise of a discretionary power of arrest deprives the person
arrested of his or her liberty. It also results in indignity and distress. Parliament of course
was well aware of that when it enacted the statute. The other side of the coin, which no
doubt was the reason and purpose of the enactment, was that it provided the police with
an important, indeed necessary, resource or means or weapon for upholding law and
order and bringing criminals to justice. So there are two public interests to be balanced:
the interest that the subject should not be deprived of his liberty and the interest that law
and order should be upheld so that the persons and property of law-abiding citizens are
protected.

Speaking for myself, I do not doubt that Parliament has left it to the courts to give
guidance and, if it thinks right, to impose fetters on this particular power and its exercise,
and therefore that is within the proper jurisdiction of the court to do so. But, where the
power is exercised for a particular purpose, as that recorded in the Royal Commission's
report, and has for a long period been so exercised without apparently any question or
challenge until the instant case, I do not myself think that it would be right for the
courts, at any rate below the level of the House of Lords, to say that it is being wrongly
exercised and by inference has always been wrongly exercised.

The matter does not stop there. In the first place, it would be unreal and wrong for the
courts to lose touch with contemporary circumstances. From time to time Parliament
and the courts have deprived the police, no doubt rightly, of weapons which might
otherwise be in their armoury, but this is surely a time when further deprivation should
only be made for cogent reasons, if, that is to say, the interest of the law-abiding citizen
(the victim or the potential victim) is to be given at least as much consideration as the
liberty of the reasonably suspected person.

In the second place, as counsel for the defendant submitted, the exercise of the power
may well enure to the benefit of the suspect. It may well bring to an immediate or at any
rate speedier end the investigation and the cloud of suspicion hanging over the suspect's
head, as indeed it did in this case.

There is nothing, in my view, in Lord Devlin's speech in *Shaaban Bin Hussien v Chong
Fook Kam* [1969] 3 All ER 1626, [1970] AC 942 or the dicta of Scott LJ in *Dumbell v Roberts*
[1944] 1 All ER 326 to vitiate the views I have ventured to express.

Accordingly, for those reasons and for those which Sir John Arnold P has expressed,
with all of which I wholly agree, the discretion to exercise this power was not wrongly
exercised in this case, in my judgment, and I too would allow the appeal on this part of
the case.

The court then heard further argument from counsel.

SIR JOHN ARNOLD P. There remains one aspect of this case with which we have

not yet dealt, and it is this. A lawful arrest followed by a period of detention which before
a release takes place is unjustifiably long itself provides a cause of action of wrongful
imprisonment during the excess period after the release should have taken place. This
point was specifically raised and argued in the court below and figures in the respondent's
notice. The facts are simple so far as they are known.

The plaintiff was arrested at 9.45 in the morning. She was released at 3.30 in the
afternoon. The course that matters took after the arrest was that between just before
b 10.30 am and 10.50 am she was under interrogation. At the conclusion of that
interrogation mention was made, inaccurately as it turned out, of the circumstance, and
I quote from the police notes of the interview:

'Q. The lady that sold the ring in Constads was paid by cheque, do you have an
account? A. Yes, you're welcome to check anything of mine at home.'

c   In fact it was quite wrong to say that she was paid by cheque. She was in fact paid by
cash obtained by means of a cheque which had been drawn by the jeweller and indorsed
by her. So it would not be a cheque which would figure in the account, if she had one,
but perhaps part or the whole of the resultant cash would. But that does not make any
difference. It was plain that that question and answer introduced into the relevant ambit
of the inquiry any banking account that she might have. The detective constable then
d said to her: 'It would help clarify matters if we returned to your flat.' Then he added,
because this was another reason for going to the flat: 'I would like to satisfy myself that
none of the property stolen from Mrs Stainer's is there.' The plaintiff replied: 'I can assure
you it's not, but you're welcome to search.' That happened at about 10.50 am.

They then went off to the flat, where a search of some sort took place. Nothing relevant
was found and they returned to the police station, and this was at 12.35 pm. The
e following conversation ensued. The plaintiff asked: 'What is happening now?' and the
detective constable said: 'I have a couple of other inquiries to make. As soon as these are
complete, I will return to see you.' Later on he said: 'I can assure you as soon as I have
completed my inquiries I will be back to see you.' That was in answer to a question:
'When will I be released?'

Then the plaintiff very sensibly sent for her solicitor. The solicitor arrived at about
f 1.00 pm, and, according to the recollection of the detective constable, which was
unchallenged in cross-examination having been stated in chief, he saw the solicitor at
about 1.00 pm. The solicitor made no complaint. 'He asked, I think, when she would be
released and I said, "Round about 4 or 5 pm."'

What happened, as appears by what seems to me to be an irresistible inference, is that
soon after that conversation, which took place at about 12.30 pm, the detective constable
g or somebody acting on his behalf set about obtaining the cheque. Various things would
be necessary. The first thing of course would be to obtain the customer's authority, the
customer being the jeweller. The next thing would be to ask the bank to do whatever
searching was required to find the paid cheque. The third thing would be to collect the
paid cheque when it was isolated and discovered. That is what, as it seems to me, is the
proper inference that the detective constable did, starting at some time soon after
h 12.30 pm. The result of that was that at 2.30 pm the cheque arrived and very soon after
that the questioning was resumed at 3.18 pm, and the questioning, so far as is relevant,
was to the effect whether she had written the signature on the cheque, which was the
signature of a made-up name apparently, at all events not one which was able to be
traced, and she said she had not. Although there were further inquiries to be made, as
the officer pointed out to her, that was the end of her detention, and at 3.30 pm she was
j released.

It is, as it seems to me, plain on the law that one of the matters which is relevant to the
question of whether there was an undue, improper prolongation of the detention was
whether that came about from a reasonable cause. But another matter, which emerges
from what was said in this court by Lord Denning MR in *Dallison v Caffery* [1964] 2 All
ER 610 at 617, [1965] QB 348 at 367, was the extent to which what happened as regards

the lapse of time was something which was the product of a consensus between the plaintiff, or inevitably the plaintiff's agent, and the defendant, the detainer. The third element in the law is that, the judge in this case having specifically held that if the power of arrest was reasonably exercised the period during which the plaintiff was detained was not unreasonable, the onus rests on the plaintiff to sustain the burden of reversing that conclusion.

The main point which is relied on (and it is a point not without attraction) by the plaintiff for the purpose of that exercise is this. The detective constable ought reasonably to have known (and it all rests on reasonableness) at the stage at least at which he took the decision to arrest, minutes before 9.45 am, I suppose, that the interrogation which was the very purpose of the arrest would necessarily, or at any rate overwhelmingly probably, involve the confrontation of the plaintiff with the cheque and that he ought therefore to have set in motion at that stage whatever process of dealing was required to procure that document for the purpose of that confrontation. Events later in the day showed that the time which it would have taken to get the cheque did not at least exceed two hours, so that if he had started the process at, say, 10 am, as, so it is said, he ought reasonably to have done, the document would have been available at noon and that part of the affair which took place at about 3.18 pm could have taken place in practical terms at 12.25 pm when they returned to the police station.

There is much to be said for that. Against that stands the circumstance that the solicitor had been involved from 1 pm onwards and had been told at that time that the plaintiff would be released round about 4 or 5 pm and that the plaintiff had been advised by him, as she said, that she was to complain to him if she thought that her detention was being unduly prolonged.

At the end of all the question is whether the prolongation of the detention was unreasonable enough and is sufficiently demonstrated to be unreasonable enough to warrant a reversal by this court of the judge's conclusion to the contrary. The matter is well balanced, but on balance I do not find the onus discharged and I would not therefore allow this part of the appeal on the respondent's notice.

LATEY J. I agree.

Appeal allowed. No order for costs save for legal aid taxation. Leave to appeal to the House of Lords refused.

Solicitors: *Theodore Goddard & Co*, agents for *R A Leyland*, Winchester (for the defendant); *Lovell Son & Pitfield*, agents for *H F E Mathews*, Portsmouth (for the plaintiff).

Bebe Chua   Barrister.

Brazil v Chief Constable of Surrey

a

QUEEN'S BENCH DIVISION
ROBERT GOFF LJ AND McNEILL J
29 MARCH 1983

Police – Right of search – Arrested person – Extent of right of search – Whether general right of
b *search – Whether reason for search required to be given – Police Act 1964, s 51(1).*

The appellant, a female, was arrested for acting in a manner likely to cause a breach of
the peace and was taken to a police station, where she was told by a policewoman that
everyone brought into the station had to be searched for their own safety. Before any
attempt had been made to search her, she struck the policewoman (the first assault) and
c had to be restrained. As she still refused to co-operate with the search, she was seen by
the officer in charge of the police station, who suspected that she was in possession of
prohibited drugs and ordered her to be searched by another policewoman. The appellant
was not informed of the officer's suspicions or the new reason why she was to be searched.
While the search was being forcibly carried out, the appellant struck the second
policewoman (the second assault). She was convicted by magistrates on separate charges
d of assaulting both policewomen in the execution of their duty, contrary to s 51(1)[a] of the
Police Act 1964. She appealed against both convictions, contending that in neither case
could she be guilty of an offence under s 51(1), because (i) at the time of the first assault
the policewoman was acting outside the scope of her duty because she had no right to
require the appellant to be searched simply on the basis of a general rule that everyone
brought into the police station had to be searched, and (ii) at the time of the second
e assault the second policewoman was acting outside the scope of her duty because she had
no right to search the appellant without first informing her of the reason for the search,
namely that she was suspected of being in possession of prohibited drugs.

Held – The appeal would be allowed for the following reasons—
(1) A police constable could not justify a search simply on the basis of a general rule;
f instead, the constable had to consider in each case whether in the particular circumstances
a search was necessary. Since there was no evidence in respect of the first assault that the
policewoman had considered whether a search was necessary she could not be said to
have been acting in the execution of her duty when she was assaulted (see p 540 j, p 541
b and p 543 e to j, post); *Lindley v Rutter* [1981] QB 128 followed.
(2) Because a search involved an affront to the dignity of a person a police constable
g was not normally entitled to carry out a search without first telling the victim of the
search why it was necessary in the particular case. The magistrates not having made any
finding that there had been special grounds for exempting the second policewoman from
the need to tell the appellant why the officer in charge had ordered her to search the
appellant, it followed that she also could not be said to have been acting in the execution
of her duty when she was assaulted while searching the appellant without first telling
h her of the reason for the search (see p 542 g to j and p 543 b to j, post); dicta of Viscount
Simon and Lord Simonds in *Christie v Leachinsky* [1947] 1 All ER at 572–573, 574–575
followed.

Notes
For the power of police officers to search persons in police custody, see 36 Halsbury's
j Laws (4th edn) para 324, and for police powers of search generally, see ibid para 323.
For the Police Act 1964, s 51, see 25 Halsbury's Statutes (3rd edn) 364.

---

a Section 51(1), so far as material, provides: 'Any person who assaults a constable in the execution of
his duty . . . shall be guilty of an offence . . .'

Cases referred to in judgments
Christie v Leachinsky [1947] 1 All ER 567, [1947] AC 573, HL.
Lindley v Rutter [1981] QB 128, [1980] 3 WLR 660, DC.

Case also cited
R v Green [1982] Crim LR 604, CA.

Case stated
Karen Frances Brazil appealed by way of case stated by the justices for the county of
Surrey acting in and for the petty sessional division of Guildford in respect of their
adjudication as a magistrates' court, sitting at Guildford on 12 March 1982, whereby they
convicted her (i) of assaulting, on 1 January 1982, Carole Young, a constable of the Surrey
Constabulary, in the execution of her duty, contrary to s 51(1) of the Police Act 1964, (ii)
of assaulting, on 1 January 1982, Rosemary Shields, a constable of the Surrey Constabulary,
in the execution of her duty, contrary to s 51(1) of the 1964 Act, and fined the appellant
£50 in respect of each offence. The respondent was the Chief Constable of Surrey. The
question for the opinion of the High Court was whether the police officers were acting
in the execution of their duty in requiring the appellant to be searched when arrested for
causing a breach of the peace and whether the appellant was guilty of assault for resisting
a forcible search in such circumstances. The facts are set out in the judgment of Robert
Goff LJ.

Gayle Hallon for the appellant.
Inigo Bing for the respondent.

ROBERT GOFF LJ. There is before the court a case stated by the justices for the
county of Surrey, sitting at Guildford. It raises a question with regard to the power of
police officers to search persons who are in custody at a police station.

The case in question is concerned with two assaults which the appellant, Karen Frances
Brazil, was found to have carried out on two police officers, Wpc Carole Young and Wpc
Rosemary Shields. She was charged with assaulting both those police officers in the
execution of their duty, contrary to s 51(1) of the Police Act 1964. The magistrates came
to the conclusion that the appellant was guilty of both these charges and, having reached
that conclusion, they convicted her and imposed a fine of £50 in respect of each charge
and ordered her to pay a contribution towards her legal aid and towards the cost of the
prosecution.

The question which they have stated for the opinion of this court is—

'whether the Police Officers were acting in the execution of their duty in requiring
the appellant to be searched in this way when arrested for causing a breach of the
peace and whether the appellant is guilty of assault for resisting a forcible search in
such circumstances.'

That question of course reveals the fact that it was in the context of a proposed search of
the appellant that in each case the police officers were assaulted.

The magistrates found the following facts:

'(a) Police Officers were called to a public house in Guildford at the instance of
the licensee in order to eject the appellant from the premises. (b) The appellant
became abusive and was requested to leave on several occasions by the Police
Officers. The appellant refused to leave and was arrested for conducting herself in a
manner likely to cause a breach of the peace. (c) The appellant was conveyed
peaceably to Guildford Police Station and placed in the chargeroom. (d) The
appellant was interviewed in the chargeroom and initially gave a false name and
address. (e) The appellant was requested to empty her handbag and pockets which
request was complied with. (f) Woman Police Constable Young entered the

a chargeroom and informed the appellant that everyone brought into the Police Station had to be searched for their own safety. (g) Woman Police Constable Young did not suspect the appellant to be in possession of prohibited drugs. (h) The appellant replied abusively to the statement concerning the search, took hold of her own handbag and struck the Constable across the face. This action was the assault referred to in the first charge. At this stage, no attempt had been made to search the appellant nor did we find any other ground for apprehension on the part of the

b appellant of imminent battery. (i) Woman Police Constable Young did not inform the appellant that she would need to strip to be searched. (j) Following this assault the appellant was restrained and Woman Police Constable Shields attended in the chargeroom and explained to the appellant that it was necessary for her to be searched. (k) Woman Police Constable Shields gave no reason why the search was necessary nor did she suspect the appellant to be in possession of prohibited drugs.

c (l) The appellant refused to co-operate with the search. (m) Accordingly, the Officer in charge of the Police Station, Acting Inspector Martin, attended the chargeroom. He suspected the appellant of being in possession of prohibited drugs which suspicion we found to be based on reasonable grounds, namely:—(i) The physical appearance of the appellant in that her eyes were glazed although there was no indication of drunkenness. (ii) The appellant's bizarre behaviour in the Police

d Station. (iii) Local knowledge of the reputation with regard to drugs of the premises at which the appellant had been arrested. Acting Inspector Martin informed the appellant that she had to be searched. No reference was made to the suspicion that had been formed. (n) The appellant declined to be searched. (o) Acting Inspector Martin gave orders for the appellant to be searched. (p) The appellant was forcibly searched. She was held down by the officers, her boots removed, her jeans taken

e down to her thighs and her jumper raised to allow a visual check on her brassiere. At this point the assault occurred which is the subject of the second charge.'

The contention of the appellant before the magistrates was that the police officers had no right to force or request her to submit to a search and were, therefore, acting outside the scope of their duty and that any reasonable cause to suspect possession of drugs must be based on grounds personal to the person being searched and not by association with

f premises or districts.

The respondent contended, with regard to the first assault, that no attempt had been made physically to search the appellant and that the mere request to search her did not take the officers outside the scope of their duty. With regard to the second assault, the respondent contended that this did not take place until an attempt was made forcibly to search the appellant and that the officers were acting on the direct orders of acting

g Inspector Martin, who had reasonable cause to believe that the appellant might be in possession of prohibited drugs. Therefore, the officers were acting in the execution of their duty because s 23(2) of the Misuse of Drugs Act 1971 gives a statutory power of search. The respondent then cited *Lindley v Rutter* [1981] QB 128, to which I shall refer in a moment. It is plain that the magistrates accepted the submissions of the respondent. In those circumstances, they convicted the appellant.

h Before dealing with the submissions made to this court, it is necessary to refer to *Lindley v Rutter*, which was drawn to the attention of the magistrates and was also relied on before us. This was a decision of the Divisional Court. It was concerned with the question of the circumstances in which police officers may carry out a search. The offence charged in that case (as in the present) raised the question whether or not the police officer was acting in the course of her duty. Donaldson LJ said ([1981] QB 128 at 134–

j 135):

'It is the duty of the courts to be ever zealous to protect the personal freedom, privacy and dignity of all who live in these islands. Any claim to be entitled to take action which infringes these rights is to be examined with very great care. But such rights are not absolute. They have to be weighed against the rights and duties of police officers, acting on behalf of society as a whole. It is the duty of any constable who lawfully has a prisoner in his charge to take all reasonable measures to ensure *a* that the prisoner does not escape or assist others to do so, does not injure himself or others, does not destroy or dispose of evidence and does not commit further crime such as, for example, malicious damage to property. This list is not exhaustive, but it is sufficient for present purposes. What measures are reasonable in the discharge of this duty will depend upon the likelihood that the particular prisoner will do any of these things unless prevented. That in turn will involve the constable in *b* considering the known or apparent disposition and sobriety of the prisoner. What can never be justified is the adoption of any particular measures without regard to all the circumstances of the particular case. This is not to say that there can be no standing instructions. Although there may always be special features in any individual case, the circumstances in which people are taken into custody are capable of being categorised and experience may show that certain measures, including *c* searches, are prima facie reasonable and necessary in a particular category of case. The fruits of this experience may be passed on to officers in the form of standing instructions. But the officer having custody of the prisoner must always consider, and be allowed and encouraged to consider, whether the special circumstances of the particular case justify or demand a departure from the standard procedure either by omitting what would otherwise be done or by taking additional measures. So far *d* as searches are concerned, he should appreciate that they involve an affront to the dignity and privacy of the individual. Furthermore, there are degrees of affront involved in such a search. Clearly going through someone's pockets or handbag is less of an affront than a body search. In every case a police officer ordering a search or depriving a prisoner of property should have a very good reason for doing so.'

These were the principles laid down in *Lindley v Rutter*, and these are the principles that *e* we have to apply in the present case.

In the light of that authority, I turn to the first assault. The findings of fact, which I have already read, indicate that the appellant was interviewed in the chargeroom, when she first of all gave a false name and address. She was asked to empty her handbag and her pockets and she did so. Then Wpc Young entered the chargeroom and, on the findings of fact, informed the appellant that 'everyone brought into the Police Station *f* had to be searched for their own safety'. As a response to that proposal, there was an abusive reply from the appellant, who took hold of her own handbag and struck the police constable across the face.

The submissions of counsel for the appellant in relation to those particular facts were as follows. She accepted that, in those circumstances, there plainly was a common assault. That is obviously right. But, she submitted, this could not be a case of an assault on a *g* police officer in the execution of her duty because the justification for the search, as given in the findings of fact, viz 'everyone brought into the Police Station had to be searched for their own safety', was not a proper justification. In this connection, she relied on a passage in the judgment of Donaldson LJ, which I have already cited and which reads: 'What can never be justified is the adoption of any particular measure without regard to all the circumstances of the particular case.'   *h*

No doubt there are circumstances where a person is brought into a police station, where it would be proper to carry out a personal search, for example where the view is formed that it would be desirable to make certain that that person is not in possession of any article with which he might injure himself. But, in my judgment, on the findings of fact in this case, counsel for the appellant is justified in her submission that the police cannot proceed to carry out a personal search simply on the basis that 'everyone brought *j* into the Police Station has to be searched for their own safety'. Such a blanket rule cannot be upheld in the face of the decision of this court in *Lindley v Rutter*. There must be cases of persons brought into police stations where it would not be justifiable to carry out such a search. Here the difficulty on the findings of fact is that there is no finding that the police officer concerned addressed her mind to the question whether in the circumstances of this particular case a personal search of the appellant was called for.

There have been placed before us the actual notes of evidence, which were brought up
a by order of this court on the occasion of a previous hearing. It is plain from those notes
of evidence that the witnesses did not speak with a united voice as to what precisely Wpc
Young said to the appellant in the chargeroom. In the circumstance of this case, I do not
think that it would be right for us to go behind the finding of fact of the magistrates
with regard to what the police constable said on this particular occasion; they formed
their own view of the evidence and they made their own finding on it. I, for my part,
b would proceed simply on the basis of considering the conviction of this assault on the
facts as found. On those findings of fact, I accept counsel for the appellant's submission
that this police officer was not acting in the execution of her duty when she proceeded to
carry out a personal search of the appellant simply on the basis that 'everyone brought
into the Police Station had to be searched for their own safety'.

I turn then to the second assault. The second assault, as appears from the findings of
c fact which I have already read out, occurred after Wpc Shields had attended and explained
to the appellant that it was necessary for her to be searched. It is difficult to believe that
this was not simply because she had resisted the first search. The appellant refused to co-
operate with the search, and so acting Inspector Martin came into the chargeroom. The
finding of the magistrates was that he formed the suspicion that she was in possession of
a prohibited drug. The magistrates formed the view, on the basis of certain matters set
d out in para (m) of their findings, that he did so on reasonable grounds. They also made a
finding of fact that no reference was made to the appellant that such a suspicion had been
formed.

Counsel for the appellant's submission with regard to this matter was twofold. First of
all she submitted that, on the basis of the notes of evidence (which are before the court),
there was no foundation for at least some of the findings of the magistrates leading to
e their conclusion that there were reasonable grounds on which the acting inspector could
have suspected the appellant to be in possession of prohibited drugs. In particular, counsel
for the appellant attacked the words 'although there was no indication of drunkenness',
having regard to the evidence, first of all, that the acting inspector had spoken to the
police officer who had arrested the appellant in the public house, in circumstances where
the police officer considered that the appellant had been drinking and, secondly, that the
f acting inspector himself said in his evidence: 'I heard from officers she had been drinking.'

The second of counsel for the appellant's submissions was a more fundamental one.
She submitted that, if a search is to be carried out by a police officer, that search
constitutes, as was stated in Lindley v Rutter [1981] QB 128 at 135, an affront to the dignity
of a human being. She said that in those circumstances the proper course is for the police
officer to inform the person concerned, no doubt in ordinary language, of the reason
g why that search is to be carried out. If persons do not know why they are being searched,
they have no basis on which to form a view whether or not that search is justified in the
circumstances.

In the second, more fundamental, of those two submissions, counsel for the appellant
relied on certain passages from the speeches in the House of Lords in Christie v Leachinsky
[1947] 1 All ER 567, [1947] AC 573. That case was concerned with the circumstances
h when an arrest may be made without a warrant. I need not set out the facts of the case,
but I wish to cite two passages, the first from the speech of Viscount Simon, and the
second from the speech of Lord Simonds. Viscount Simon referred to certain matters
and said that they seemed to him to establish these propositions ([1947] 1 All ER 567 at
572–573, [1947] AC 573 at 587–588):

j   '1. If a policeman arrests without warrant on reasonable suspicion of felony, or of
     other crime of a sort which does not require a warrant, he must in ordinary
     circumstances inform the person arrested of the true ground of arrest. He is not
     entitled to keep the reason to himself or to give a reason which is not the true reason.
     In other words, a citizen is entitled to know on what charge or on suspicion of what
     crime he is seized. 2. If the citizen is not so informed but is nevertheless seized, the
     policeman, apart from certain exceptions, is liable for false imprisonment. 3. The
     requirement that the person arrested should be informed of the reason why he is

seized naturally does not exist if the circumstances are such that he must know the general nature of the alleged offence for which he is detained. 4. The requirement that he should be so informed does not mean that technical or precise language need be used. The matter is a matter of substance, and turns on the elementary proposition that in this country a person is, *prima facie*, entitled to his freedom and is only required to submit to restraint on his freedom if he knows in substance the reason why it is claimed that this restraint should be imposed. 5. The person arrested cannot complain that he has not been supplied with the above information as and when he should be, if he himself produces the situation which makes it practically impossible to inform him, *e.g.*, by immediate counter-attack or by running away. There may well be other exceptions to the general rule in addition to those I have indicated, and the above propositions are not intended to constitute a formal or complete code, but to indicate the general principles of our law on a very important matter.'

Lord Simonds said ([1947] 1 All ER 567 at 574–575, [1947] AC 573 at 591):

'First, I would say that it is the right of every citizen to be free from arrest unless there is in some other citizen, whether a constable or not, the right to arrest him. I would say next that it is the corollary of the right of every citizen to be thus free from arrest that he should be entitled to resist arrest unless that arrest is lawful. How can these rights be reconciled with the proposition that he may be arrested without knowing why he is arrested?'

Counsel for the appellant submitted that, although there was no direct authority in support of the proposition that she had advanced, nevertheless in *Christie v Leachinsky*, and in particular in the passages which I have read, there was guidance which should persuade this court to adopt a similar approach, in the matter of searches, to that adopted by the House of Lords in the matter of arrests without warrant.

I, for myself, accept that proposition. I refer, in particular, to the passage in Viscount Simon's judgment, where he said:

'The matter is a matter of substance, and turns on the elementary proposition that in this country a person is, *prima facie*, entitled to his freedom and is only required to submit to restraint on his freedom if he knows in substance the reason why it is claimed that this restraint should be imposed.'

In my judgment, to require a person to submit to a personal search is to impose on that person a restraint on their freedom. Generally speaking, a person should not be required to submit to that restraint unless they know in substance the reason why that restraint is being imposed.

It was submitted by counsel for the respondent, that this would create great difficulties for the police. Speaking for myself, I am much concerned that nothing I say in this judgment should in fact create difficulties for the police. But, having regard to what was said by Donaldson LJ in *Lindley v Rutter* [1981] QB 128 at 134–135, it is plain that when the question arises whether a search should be carried out at a police station, the officer has to consider whether or not, in the circumstances of that case, the search is really necessary. True it is that there may well be standing orders, but the officer still has to consider whether or not to apply those standing orders in the circumstances of the particular case. If that is so, it follows that if the officer has to address his or her mind to that question, the officer has to consider not merely whether or not to carry out the search, but why it should be necessary. If an officer considers that question and then forms the view that a search should be carried out, he should have formed a view as to the reason why it is necessary; for example, that it is necessary for the safety of the person concerned, or for any of the other reasons listed in the judgment of Donaldson LJ. That being so, I can see no difficulty in general terms in the officer explaining to the person, no doubt in the simplest and most ordinary language, why the search is proposed. In my judgment, generally speaking, that ought to be done.

Consistent with the speech of Viscount Simon in *Christie v Leachinsky* [1947] 1 All ER
567 at 572–573, [1947] AC 573 at 587–588, there may well be circumstances where the
giving of such reasons would not be necessary. To give an example, the circumstances
may be such that it is perfectly obvious why a search is necessary. If so, it would be otiose
for the officer concerned to give an explanation. Again, the circumstances may be such
that the person concerned is, as Viscount Simon puts it, creating a situation where it is
practically impossible to inform him. If the person is making a scene of some kind,
communication may be impossible. Also, there may be circumstances where for example,
a person is so drunk that communication is impracticable. I am not trying, any more
than Viscount Simon did in *Christie v Leachinsky*, to make an exhaustive list of the
circumstances where such communication would not be necessary, but merely to indicate
that such circumstances may exist. In general terms, the citizens of this country should
not have their freedom interfered with unless it would be lawful to do so and, in my
judgment, an explanation should generally be given to persons why a personal search is
to be carried out.

That being so, I turn to the facts of the second assault, as found by the justices in the
case. First of all, it was found that acting Inspector Martin formed the suspicion that the
appellant was in possession of prohibited drugs, but made no reference to the suspicion
that he had formed. Indeed, on the facts as found in the case by the magistrates, the only
reason which had been given to the appellant for the search was the reason originally
given by Wpc Young, viz 'everyone brought into the Police Station had to be searched
for their own safety'.

In those circumstances, it seems to me that the second conviction of the assault on a
police officer in the execution of her duty cannot stand, for the reason that the officer
failed to communicate to the appellant the ground for the search being carried out. It
may be that, if the magistrates had addressed their minds to the question, they might
have concluded (I do not know) that there was no point in trying to communicate with
the appellant in the condition that she was in. But, the magistrates did not address their
minds to that question at all. In those circumstances, I have formed the view that the
convictions on both the first and second assaults cannot stand.

That being so, there is no necessity for me to go further and consider counsel for the
appellant's first submission, which was based on the notes of evidence. In that submission,
she attacked the reasonableness of the grounds on which acting Inspector Martin formed
the view that the appellant may be in possession of prohibited drugs. I accept, for what
it is worth, counsel for the appellant's submission that there was no basis for the finding
of fact that there was no indication of drunkenness, but there appears at least to have
been a basis for the other matters which were found as facts as constituting the grounds
for Inspector Martin's view. However, in the circumstances of the case and having regard
to the view which I have formed about counsel for the appellant's second submission, it
is not necessary for me to consider her first submission.

Accordingly, I, for my part, would answer the question whether the police officers
were acting in the execution of their duty in requiring the appellant to be searched in
this way when arrested for causing a breach of the peace and whether the appellant is
guilty of assault for resisting a forcible search in such circumstances in the negative.

In my judgment, therefore, the appeal on both charges of assaulting a police officer in
the execution of her duty should be allowed, and those convictions quashed.

McNEILL J. I agree.

Appeal allowed.

Solicitors: *Day Whately & Co*, Godalming (for the appellant); *Wontner & Sons* (for the
respondent).

April Weiss   Barrister.

Practice Note

COURT OF APPEAL, CIVIL DIVISION
SIR JOHN DONALDSON MR, MAY AND DILLON LJJ
28 OCTOBER 1983

Court of Appeal – Appeal – Estimate of length of hearing – Civil Division – Importance of estimates for listing appeals – Registrar to be informed of any revision of original estimate.

SIR JOHN DONALDSON MR made the following statement at the sitting of the court. In listing appeals before the Civil Division of the Court of Appeal, the registrar and his staff rightly place considerable reliance on estimates given by counsel and solicitors of the time likely to be occupied by the hearing. Recently there have been a significant number of cases in which the estimates have overstated the time required, in one case by a factor of five. This has had adverse effects on the listing.

Counsel and solicitors may like to be reminded that the members of the court will almost always have read the notice of appeal, the judgment under appeal and any skeleton arguments before the appeal is called on. This produces a considerable saving in time, which should be reflected in the estimates.

It not infrequently happens that, in the course of preparing for the hearing of an appeal, counsel decides that the argument can be confined to a more limited number of issues than at first seemed likely. When this happens or if, for any other reason, the original estimate requires revision, the registrar should be informed immediately.

Frances Rustin   Barrister.

Practice Direction

CHANCERY DIVISION

Practice – Chancery Division – Interlocutory applications – Causes or matters outside London.

1. Where a Chancery cause or matter is proceeding in a district registry, any interlocutory application to a judge should normally be made or adjourned to the judge exercising Chancery jurisdiction in the area of that registry. This includes appeals from the district registrar, and to these RSC Ord 58, r 4 applies. Any such application issues out of the district registry. This procedure was established in 1972 for Chancery cases in the northern area (see paras 3 to 5 of the Practice Direction of 10 December 1971 ([1972] 1 All ER 103, [1972] 1 WLR 1), and it applies equally to Chancery cases in the Birmingham, Bristol and Cardiff district registries.

2. If it is impracticable or inexpedient to follow this procedure, and the court so directs, or if the parties so agree, the application may instead be made to a Chancery judge in London. In these exceptional cases the application is issued out of room 157 at the Royal Courts of Justice.

By direction of the Vice-Chancellor.

EDMUND HEWARD
13 October 1983   Chief Master.

a **Re a debtor (No 75N of 1982, Warrington),
ex parte the debtor v National Westminster
Bank plc**

and another appeal
b
CHANCERY DIVISION

SIR ROBERT MEGARRY V-C AND WARNER J

6, 9, 10, 11, 12, 18 MAY 1983

*Bankruptcy – Bankruptcy notice – Withdrawal – Effectiveness – Creditor serving bankruptcy
notice on debtor – Debtor offering to secure or compound for debt – Creditor withdrawing notice*
c *before court could adjudicate on merits of debtor's offer – Creditor serving second bankruptcy
notice on debtor – Whether first bankruptcy notice could be withdrawn without debtor's consent.*

*Bankruptcy – Bankruptcy notice – Service – Substituted service – Ex parte application for order
for substituted service – Whether application can be made ex parte – Bankruptcy Rules 1952,
rr 31, 32, 141, 154.*
d
*Practice – Ex parte application – Duty of applicant – Duty to be candid with court – Extent of
duty.*

*Bankruptcy – Bankruptcy notice – Setting aside – Cross-demand – What judgment debtor must
show before bankruptcy notice can be set aside – Whether cross-demand must be for liquidated*
e *sum – Whether judgment creditor can set up in opposition to cross-demand another claim of his
own against judgment debtor in addition to judgment debt – Bankruptcy Act 1914, s 1(1)(g) –
Bankruptcy Rules 1952, rr 137, 138.*

*Bankruptcy – Bankruptcy notice – Form – Need for statutory forms to be redrafted – Bankruptcy
Rules 1952, App I, Forms 6, 7.*

f   On 30 September 1982 a bank obtained judgment against a debtor. The debtor failed to
pay the bank the amount due, and on 10 November the bank served a bankruptcy notice
on him requiring him, within 10 days, to pay the amount which it said was due, or to
secure or compound for that sum, or to satisfy the court that he had a counterclaim, set-
off or cross-demand against the bank which equalled or exceeded the sum claimed by it
and which could not have been set up in the proceedings in which the judgment was
g   obtained. In reply to the notice, the debtor filed an affidavit in which he challenged the
validity of the notice and put forward proposals to compound or secure the amount due.
The bank discovered that it had overstated in the notice the amount due to it. It then
withdrew the notice and, at its request, the registrar issued, on 30 November, a fresh
bankruptcy notice in place of the first. The bank's attempts to serve the new notice on
h   the debtor being unsuccessful, it applied ex parte, by motion, to the registrar for an order
for substituted service. On 1 February 1983 the registrar made the order sought under
rr 141[a] and 154[b] of the Bankruptcy Rules 1952, and service of the notice was deemed to
be effected on 11 February. The debtor applied to have the order set aside. His application
was dismissed on 17 February. He appealed against the decision, contending (i) that the
registrar had had no jurisdiction to allow the second bankruptcy notice to be issued, or to
j   order substituted service of it, because the first bankruptcy notice, in response to which
he had made an offer to secure the debt, still subsisted as it could not, in view of that
offer, be withdrawn without his consent, (ii) that the application for the order for
substituted service should not have been made ex parte because r 31[c] of the 1952 rules

---

a   Rule 141 is set out at p 552 c d, post

b   Rule 154 is set out at p 552 e, post

c   Rule 31 is set out at p 551 h, post

required every application to the court to be made by motion, supported by affidavit, and r 32^d of those rules provided that, where a person other than the applicant was affected by the motion, no order could be made except with that person's consent or on proof that the notice of motion and a copy of the affidavit had been duly served on him, and (iii) that in any event, by failing to disclose certain material facts to the registrar at the hearing of its application for the order, the bank had been in breach of the requirement that an applicant for an ex parte order be candid with the court. Pending the hearing of the appeal, the judgment debtor filed an affidavit under rr 137 and 138 of the 1952 rules, putting forward a number of cross-demands which he claimed equalled or exceeded the amount of the judgment debt, with the result that, by virtue of s 1(1)(g)^e of the Bankruptcy Act 1914, he avoided committing an act of bankruptcy. After considering the affidavit, the registrar set aside the second bankruptcy notice on 20 April. The bank appealed against the registrar's decision.

Held – (1) The debtor's appeal would be dismissed for the following reasons—

(a) The bank was entitled to withdraw the first bankruptcy notice without the debtor's consent because the purpose of a bankruptcy notice was merely to inform the debtor of what he had to do if he was to avoid committing an act of bankruptcy. Once the bank had exercised its right to withdraw the notice, any right which the debtor might have had to have the merits of his offer to secure or compound the debt adjudicated on by the court lapsed. It followed that the first bankruptcy notice did not affect the registrar's jurisdiction to issue the second bankruptcy notice and order substituted service (see p 550 e to g, p 552 b c and p 558 e, post).

(b) On the true construction of the 1952 rules, the provisions of rr 141 and 154 prevailed over those of rr 31 and 32, and, in consequence, rr 31 and 32 applied to an application for an order for substituted service only to the extent that the application had to be by motion and that any party affected by an order made ex parte as a result of the motion could apply to have it set aside. Accordingly, as a motion could be ex parte, the bank had been entitled to apply ex parte for the order for substituted service (see p 552 f g and p 558 e, post).

(c) The bank had not been in breach of the requirement of candour because the facts which the debtor maintained the bank had not disclosed to the registrar only went to reinforce its case, and the duty of an ex parte applicant was to inform the court of any facts in favour of the absent person (see p 551 d e and p 558 e, post); R v Kensington Income Tax Comrs, ex p Princess de Polignac [1917] 1 KB 486 explained.

(2) The bank's appeal would be allowed and the bankruptcy notice restored because, in order to come within s 1(1)(g) of the 1914 Act, a debtor had to show in an affidavit under rr 137 and 138 of the 1952 rules (a) that he had a cross-demand against the creditor which was genuine and gave rise to a triable issue, (b) that the cross-demand could not have been set up in the action in which the judgment relied on by the creditor had been obtained, and (c) that the cross-demand equalled or exceeded the amount of the judgment debt, and on the face of it the debtor's affidavit did not fulfil all three requirements (see p 553 c to f, p 554 g to j, p 555 b, p 556 f and p 558 c to e, post).

Per curiam. (1) The statutory forms of bankruptcy notice set out as Forms 6 and 7 in App I to the 1952 rules seem calculated to puzzle, perplex or mislead the debtor and ought to be redrafted to achieve greater clarity, accuracy and helpfulness (see p 558 f g and p 560 a e h j, post).

---

d   Rule 32 is set out at p 551 j, post

e   Section 1(1), so far as material, provides: 'A debtor commits an act of bankruptcy ... (g) If a creditor has obtained a final judgment ... against him for any amount, and, execution thereon not having been stayed, has served on him ... a bankruptcy notice under this Act, and he does not, within ten days after service of the notice ... either comply with the requirements of the notice or satisfy the court that he has a counter-claim set off or cross demand which equals or exceeds the amount of the judgment debt ... and which he could not set up in the action in which the judgment was obtained ...'

a
(2) On the true construction of s 1(1)(*g*) of the 1914 Act, a judgment creditor who is confronted with a counterclaim, set-off or cross-demand by the judgment debtor may himself set up, in opposition thereto, another claim of his own against the judgment debtor which, when added to the judgment debt, overtops the debtor's counterclaim, set-off or cross-demand (see p 558 *b* to *e*, post).

b
(3) A counterclaim, set-off or cross demand under s 1(1)(*g*) of the 1914 Act need not be for a liquidated sum or even for a sum of money at all, but it must be capable of being quantified in terms of money, and the affidavit or affidavits must quantify it (see p 553 *e* *f* and p 558 *e*, post).

Notes

For the issue of a second bankruptcy notice, see 3 Halsbury's Laws (4th edn) para 265.

c
For counterclaim, set-off or cross-demand and setting aside a bankruptcy notice, see ibid paras 271–273, and for cases on the subject, see 4 Digest (Reissue) 111–115, 976, 984–985, 990–998.

For the form of a bankruptcy notice, see 3 Halsbury's Laws (4th edn) para 267.

For the Bankruptcy Act 1914, s 1, see 3 Halsbury's Statutes (3rd edn) 38.

For the Bankruptcy Rules 1952, rr 31, 32, 137, 138, 141, 154, see 3 Halsbury's Statutory Instruments (4th reissue) 223, 246, 247, 250.

d
Cases referred to in judgments

Debtor, Re a, Bankruptcy Notice (No 619 of 1947) [1947] LJR 1413, CA.

Debtor (No 523 of 1934), Re a [1935] Ch 347, CA.

Debtor (No 80 of 1957), Re a, ex p the debtor v Wiseburgh [1957] 2 All ER 551, [1958] Ch 81, [1957] 3 WLR 184, CA.

e
Debtor (No 991 of 1962) Re a, ex p the debtor v Tossoun [1963] 1 All ER 85, [1963] 1 WLR 51, CA.

Debtor (No 6864 of 1980, High Court), Re a, the debtor v Slater Walker Ltd [1981] 2 All ER 987, [1981] 1 WLR 1205, CA.

Feast, Re, ex p Feast (1887) 4 Morr 37, CA.

Judgment debtor (No 530 of 1908), Re a [1908] 2 KB 474, [1908–10] All ER Rep 368, CA.

f
Lawrence, Re, Evennett v Lawrence (1876) 4 Ch D 139, CA.

R v Kensington Income Tax Comrs, ex p Princess de Polignac [1917] 1 KB 486, CA.

Vanbergen (a bankrupt), Re, ex p the trustee of the property of the bankrupt v Vanbergen (married woman) [1955] 1 All ER 40, [1955] 1 WLR 20, CA.

Appeals

g
Re a debtor (No 75N of 1982), ex p the debtor v National Westminster Bank plc

Charles Richard Buckley, the judgment debtor appealed against an order made by Mr Registrar Metcalfe in Warrington County Court on 17 February 1983 whereby he refused to set aside an order which had been made on 1 February by another registrar of the same court on an ex parte application by the judgment creditor, National Westminster Bank plc, for substituted service of a bankruptcy notice dated 30 November 1982. The facts *h* are set out in the judgment of Warner J.

Re a debtor (No 75N of 1982), ex p National Westminster Bank plc v the debtor

The judgment creditors, National Westminster Bank plc, appealed against an order made by Mr Registrar Metcalfe in Warrington County Court on 20 April 1983 whereby he set aside a bankruptcy notice dated 30 November 1982. The facts are set out in the judgment *j* of Warner J.

Mr Buckley appeared in person in his appeal.
Edward Evans-Lombe QC and *M J Brindle* for the bank in both appeals.
David Graham QC and *Ian McCulloch* for Mr Buckley in the bank's appeal.

Cur adv vult

18 May. The following judgments were delivered.

a

WARNER J (giving the first judgment at the invitation of Sir Robert Megarry V-C).
We have before us in this case two appeals against orders made by Mr Registrar Metcalfe
in the Warrington County Court. Both orders relate to a bankruptcy notice dated 30
November 1982, served by the National Westminster Bank plc on Mr Charles Richard
Buckley. Mr Buckley is a solicitor. The first appeal is an appeal by Mr Buckley against an   *b*
order made by the registrar on 17 February 1983, whereby he refused to set aside an
order, which had been made on 1 February 1983 by another registrar of the same court,
for substituted service of that bankruptcy notice on Mr Buckley. The second appeal is an
appeal by the bank against an order made by Mr Registrar Metcalfe on 20 April 1983
setting the bankruptcy notice aside.

The bankruptcy notice was based on a judgment for £20,927·61 obtained by the bank   *c*
against Mr Buckley in the Queen's Bench Division of this court on 30 September 1982.
The circumstances in which that judgment was obtained were these. On 27 May 1981
the bank started two actions in the Queen's Bench Division against Mr Buckley for
payment of sums that were due to the bank by Mr Buckley personally. I say 'personally'
because there are also in existence proceedings, to which I will have to refer later, in
which the bank seeks to enforce claims that it has against Mr Buckley and two former   *d*
partners of his in a firm of solicitors called Hall Brydon. On 10 November 1981
summonses under RSC Ord 14 in the two actions against Mr Buckley personally came
before the master. In one the master gave summary judgment for the bank; in the other
he gave Mr Buckley leave to defend. The master's orders were appealed against and the
appeals were compromised on terms that were set out in an order made by the judge in
chambers on 18 February 1982. By that order the actions were consolidated. The order   *e*
was otherwise in Tomlin form (see Practice Note [1927] WN 290). By the terms set out in
it Mr Buckley acknowledged that his total indebtedness to the bank was then £69,290·76
and he agreed to pay that sum (and interest on it) by instalments. He also agreed to pay
the bank's costs. It was provided that, if Mr Buckley should default in respect of any of
his obligations under those terms, the bank should be at liberty forthwith to sign
judgment in the consolidated action for the full amount of Mr Buckley's debts then   *f*
outstanding. Subsequently Mr Buckley did fall behind with the instalments and the
bank exercised its right to sign judgment for the amount remaining due from him,
which was £20,927·61.

The bankruptcy notice to which these appeals relate was not the first to have been
issued by the bank on the basis of that judgment. The first was a bankruptcy notice dated
13 October 1982, which was, by arrangement, served on Mr Buckley at the offices of the   *g*
bank's solicitors on 10 November 1982. Mr Buckley's response to that bankruptcy notice
was to swear, on 15 November 1982, an affidavit in which he challenged the validity of
the notice on a number of grounds and also put forward what he called 'a proposal to
compound and secure' the amount due to the bank, which proposal he invited the court
to make the bank accept 'in default of agreement'. That was, of course, an allusion to the
sentence in the bankruptcy notice by which he, as the debtor, was given the option of   *h*
securing or compounding for the debt to the satisfaction of the bank or of its agent, or to
the satisfaction of the court. Mr Buckley's proposal was in fact that he should give the
bank a charge on the proceeds of certain claims which he said he had against a number
of third parties, including his former accountants, his former partners, Barclays Bank Ltd
and the Law Society.

The bank's solicitors, however, discovered, or it was pointed out to them, that that first   *j*
bankruptcy notice had a defect, in that the amounts of the judgment debt and of the
interest due thereon for the period since the date of the judgment had been wrongly
added up, so that the total amount claimed in the notice was excessive. Those solicitors,
accordingly, on 24 November 1982, wrote two letters referring to the defect and
intimating that, in view of it, a fresh bankruptcy notice would be issued. Of those letters,

one was addressed to the registrar of the Warrington County Court. The other was
a   addressed to Betesh & Co, a firm of solicitors to which, so I understand, Mr Buckley has
never belonged, but who were by this time, and who indeed still are, acting for him,
under the legal aid scheme, in these bankruptcy proceedings. So it came about that the
bankruptcy notice now in question was issued on 30 November 1982.

Mr Buckley was advised not to co-operate with the bank's solicitors by voluntarily
accepting service of that bankruptcy notice, as he had done in the case of the first
b   bankruptcy notice. The reason for that, or at least a reason for it, was this. On 17 August
1982 the Law Society, in exercise of its powers under para 6 of Sch 1 to the Solicitors Act
1974, had appointed what Mr Buckley conveniently, if not quite accurately, called a
'receiver' of all sums of money held by him or on his behalf in connection with his
practice as a solicitor. On 3 September 1982 Mr Buckley had issued a writ in the Queen's
Bench Division against the bank, claiming that the agreement embodied in the Tomlin
c   order of 18 February 1982 had thereby been frustrated. Mr Buckley was advised that, if
the bankruptcy notice was served on him while that action was pending, the purpose of
the action would be defeated. In fact, as the evidence that was placed before the registrar
of the county court on 1 February 1983 amply showed, Mr Buckley took care to avoid
being served with the bankruptcy notice. At that date, the position in Mr Buckley's
action against the bank was that, by an order of the master made on 19 January 1983, Mr
d   Buckley's claim had been struck out as disclosing no cause of action. An appeal by Mr
Buckley to the judge in chambers against that order was pending, as was a summons by
Mr Buckley for an injunction restraining the bank from proceeding further under the
Tomlin order or the judgment of 30 September 1982. It so happens that Mr Buckley's
appeal to the judge in chambers was dismissed on 2 February 1983. An application by
him to the Court of Appeal for leave to appeal against that dismissal was dismissed on 16
e   February 1983.

The bank's application for the order for substituted service was, I need hardly say,
made ex parte. The registrar's order was that the sending of a sealed copy of the
bankruptcy notice together with a sealed copy of that order by first class prepaid ordinary
post to Mr Buckley c/o Mr Bloom, who was the partner in Betesh & Co dealing with his
affairs, at Betesh & Co's address, should be good and sufficient service of the bankruptcy
f   notice on Mr Buckley on the seventh day after such posting. Such posting was in fact
effected on 4 February 1983, so that the bankruptcy notice was deemed to be served on
Mr Buckley on 11 February 1983. As I have already mentioned, Mr Buckley's application
to set aside the order for substituted service was dismissed by Mr Registrar Metcalfe on
17 February 1983.

Mr Buckley, having been refused legal aid for his appeal to this court, conducted it in
g   person, and I should like to pay tribute to the moderation and courtesy with which he
conducted it. He was not the draftsman of his notice of appeal and he accepted that, in a
number of respects, it was unsatisfactory. In the end he put forward four contentions in
support of his appeal.

The first was that the county court had no jurisdiction to issue the second bankruptcy
notice, or at all events no jurisdiction to order substituted service of it, because on
h   1 February 1983 the first bankruptcy notice, in response to which he had made an offer
to secure the debt, still subsisted. Mr Buckley's contention was that, when a creditor
serves a bankruptcy notice in response to which the debtor offers to secure or compound
for the debt, the debtor acquires a vested right, which is a right to apply to the court to
compel the creditor, if the court thinks fit, to accept the offer. It followed, Mr Buckley
said, that, in such a case, the creditor cannot withdraw the bankruptcy notice without
j   the debtor's consent; and he had not consented to the withdrawal of the first bankruptcy
notice. Mr Buckley distinguished *Re Feast, ex p Feast* (1887) 4 Morr 37 on the ground
that in that case the first bankruptcy notice had been withdrawn by agreement. Mr
Buckely accepted that there was no authority to support his contention. It was, he said, a
novel point.

One difficulty in Mr Buckley's way is that, at the hearing before him on 20 April 1983,

Mr Registrar Metcalfe dealt with the question whether the first bankruptcy notice had been effectively withdrawn. He held that it had been withdrawn 'as at' 24 November 1982, and there is no appeal from that part of his order. The view is accordingly tenable that, as between Mr Buckley and the bank, the question is res judicata. I do not, however, for my part feel disposed to reject Mr Buckley's contention on that ground. The view is equally tenable that the registrar could not, by an order made in April, retrospectively validate an order made without jurisdiction in February.

I am prepared to assume in Mr Buckley's favour that, if a debtor, in response to a bankruptcy notice, makes an offer to secure or compound for the debt, he is entitled to have it decided by the court whether or not that offer should be accepted by the creditor. On a literal construction of the statutory form of bankruptcy notice, the requirement is that the debtor should, within the ten-day period, actually secure or compound for the debt to the satisfaction of the creditor, or of his agent, or of the court. Likewise, however, on a literal construction of the statutory form, if the debtor chooses the third option that it gives him, he must within ten days satisfy the court that he has a counterclaim, set-off or cross-demand which equals or exceeds the debt and which he could not set up in the action in which the judgment was obtained. But, if the debtor files an affidavit under rr 137 and 138 of the Bankruptcy Rules 1952, SI 1952/2113, within the seven days there specified, the registrar is, by virtue of r 139(2), under an obligation, if the application cannot be heard within the ten days (which must be in virtually every case), to extend the ten-day period, and no act of bankruptcy is to be deemed to have been committed under the notice until the application has been heard and determined. There seems to be no parallel provision in the rules for the case where the debtor elects to offer to secure or compound for the debt, but I should have thought that, in such a situation, s 109(4) of the Bankruptcy Act 1914 afforded the means of securing the like result, though probably, having regard to the reasoning of the Court of Appeal in *Re a debtor (No 6864 of 1980, High Court), the debtor v Slater Walker Ltd* [1981] 2 All ER 987, [1981] 1 WLR 1205, only if the section is invoked within the ten days.

Be that as it may, I think it impossible to hold that the existence of the right thus (I have assumed) conferred on the debtor makes it impossible for the creditor to withdraw the bankruptcy notice without the consent of the debtor. So to hold would be to hold that a creditor, in serving a bankruptcy notice, inevitably took the risk of having an unwanted security or an unwanted composition foisted on him. I do not think that that is the purpose of a bankruptcy notice. Its purpose is to tell the debtor what he must do if he is to avoid committing an act of bankruptcy. It is not to put in the debtor's hands a stick with which to beat the creditor. The creditor is, in my opinion, free to withdraw the bankruptcy notice if he chooses. If he does so, the debtor's right (if any) to have the merits of his offer adjudicated on by the court simply lapses, because the object of it has gone. For that reason I think that Mr Buckley's first contention fails. That being so, I need not pursue the other points relevant to it that were canvassed in argument, such as whether, having regard to the defect in it, the first bankruptcy notice was in truth no bankruptcy notice at all.

Mr Buckley's second contention was that the registrar had no jurisdiction to make the order for substituted service because the second bankruptcy notice was itself defective in that the name of the bank had not been inserted in the note on the back of it. That, however, was a formal defect capable of being cured, and which was in fact cured, under s 147 of the 1914 Act. By his order of 20 April 1983 Mr Registrar Metcalfe gave the bank leave to amend the bankruptcy notice by inserting its name on the back, and that was done before the case came before us. No doubt, if the registrar on 1 February 1983 had noticed the defect, he might, in the exercise of his discretion, have declined to order substituted service until the defect had been cured. But his failure to do so did not, in my judgment, vitiate his order.

Mr Buckley's third contention was that when the bank's solicitors applied for the order for substituted service they failed to disclose certain material facts to the registrar. They were thus, he said, in breach of the rule that an applicant for an ex parte order must be

candid with the court, so that, in accordance with the principle laid down by the Court
a of Appeal in *R v Kensington Income Tax Comrs, ex p Princess de Polignac* [1917] 1 KB 486,
the order for substituted service should have been set aside without any examination of
the merits of the case. There were three things that Mr Buckley said should have been
disclosed and were not disclosed to the registrar. The first was the existence of the first
bankruptcy notice, coupled with the fact that Mr Buckley had, in response to it, offered
security for the debt. If I am right, however, in the view that I take on Mr Buckley's first
b contention, the first bankruptcy notice had been effectively withdrawn long before
1 February 1983 and the facts relating to it were of no possible relevance to what the
registrar had to decide.

Second, Mr Buckley suggested that the bank's solicitors should have disclosed to the
registrar some correspondence exchanged in January 1983 between themselves and the
solicitors acting for Mr Buckley in his action against the bank for a declaration that the
c Tomlin order had been frustrated. That correspondence has been put before us. No
doubt the registrar would have gathered from it why it was that Mr Buckley was avoiding
service of the bankruptcy notice. Having regard, however, to the terms of r 154 of the
Bankruptcy Rules 1952, the question for the registrar was whether Mr Buckley was
'keeping out of the way to avoid service' so that 'prompt personal service' could not be
effected, not *why* he was keeping out of the way. In truth, the only effect of that
d correspondence, if it had been placed before the registrar, would have been to reinforce
the bank's case for an order for substituted service. The rule in *Ex p Princess de Polignac*
exists because, by definition, on an ex parte application the person against whom the
order is sought is absent. It is accordingly the duty of the applicant to inform the court
of any facts which he knows which might tell in that person's favour. But the applicant
is under no obligation to place before the court every fact that might reinforce his own
e case.

Third, Mr Buckley said, though he did not press this, that the bank's solicitors should
have disclosed a letter dated 17 January 1983 written by Mr Bloom to the inquiry agent
instructed by the bank to effect personal service of the bankruptcy notice on Mr Buckley.
That letter was written in response to a letter from the inquiry agent to Mr Buckley,
dated 13 January 1983, by which the inquiry agent, having failed to find Mr Buckley on
f previous occasions, gave him notice that he would call again at his home (though Mr
Buckley says that it was no longer his home) to serve him with the bankruptcy notice on
20 January 1983 between 10 and 10.15 am, 'or', the inquiry agent added, 'any reasonable
time and place that you may in the meantime let me know will be more convenient to
you'. Mr Bloom's letter of 17 January 1983 informed the inquiry agent that Mr Buckley
would be in Ireland on 20 January and that it would be impossible for him to keep an
g appointment on that day. It might, I think, have been better if that letter had been placed
before the registrar, but I hardly think that it told in Mr Buckley's favour, because it
conspicuously omitted to suggest a more convenient time and place for Mr Buckley to
be served.

Mr Buckley's fourth contention was that the application for an order for substituted
service ought not to have been made ex parte. Mr Buckley drew our attention to rr 31
h and 32 of the Bankruptcy Rules 1952. These provide as follows:

'**31.** Except where these Rules otherwise provide, every application to the court
shall, unless the court otherwise directs, be made by motion supported by affidavit.
32.—(1) Where any party other than the applicant is affected by the motion, no
order shall be made except with the consent of that party, or upon proof that notice
j of the motion and a copy of the affidavits in support thereof have been duly served
upon him: Provided that where the court is satisfied that serious mischief may result
from delay caused by proceeding in the ordinary way, it may make an order *ex parte*
upon such terms as to costs and otherwise, and subject to such undertaking, if any,
as the court thinks just.
(2) Any party affected by an order made *ex parte* may move to set it aside.'

Mr Buckley pointed out to us that a notice of motion, unlike a bankruptcy notice, did
not have to be served personally and that he had solicitors on the record who could have   *a*
been served under r 84. In this case, he said, there should have been an inter partes
hearing because a vested right of his was at stake. He referred us, in that connection, to
Re Lawrence, Evennett v Lawrence (1876) 4 Ch D 139 and Re Vanbergen (a bankrupt), ex p
the trustee of the property of the bankrupt v Vanbergen (married woman) [1955] 1 All ER 40,
[1955] 1 WLR 20. The vested right to which Mr Buckley referred was, however, so I
understood, the right that he claimed to be entitled to rely on the first bankruptcy notice   *b*
and his response to it, with the consequent right not to have the second bankruptcy
notice served on him. There again, however, if I am right in the view that I take on his
first contention, he had no such right. The bank was entitled to withdraw the first
bankruptcy notice and to serve the second. I am moreover satisfied that rr 31 and 32 of
the 1952 rules apply only to a limited extent to an application for an order for substituted
service of a bankruptcy notice. Rule 31 begins with the words 'Except where these Rules   *c*
otherwise provide', and r 141 provides:

> 'Rules 153 to 156 shall apply to the service of a bankruptcy notice as they apply to
> the service of a creditor's petition.'

Rules 153 and 154 provide:
d
> '**153.** Subject to the provisions of Rule 154, service of a creditor's petition shall be
> effected by an officer of the court, or by the creditor or his solicitor, or a person in
> their employment, delivering a sealed copy of the petition to the debtor.
> **154.**—(1) If the court is satisfied by affidavit or other evidence on oath that
> prompt personal service cannot be effected because the debtor is keeping out of the
> way to avoid service of the petition or any other legal process, or for any other cause,   *e*
> it may order substituted service to be effected in such manner as it thinks fit.
> (2) Where any such order has been carried out, the petition shall be deemed to
> have been duly served on the debtor.'

To the extent, therefore, that r 154 is incompatible with rr 31 and 32, r 154 prevails.
The result appears to me to be that, of the provisions of r 31, only the words 'every   *f*
application to the court shall . . . be made by motion' can apply, bearing in mind that a
motion can be ex parte; and that, of r 32, only para (2), entitling a party affected by an
order made ex parte to move to set it aside, can apply.

In the result, Mr Buckley's appeal, in my judgment, fails.

I turn to the bank's appeal. On that, Mr Buckley was granted legal aid, and we had the
benefit of hearing submissions on his behalf from counsel.
g
In response to the second bankruptcy notice, Mr Buckley filed an affidavit in which he
repeated his offer to secure the debt but also availed himself of the third option given
him by the bankruptcy notice by putting forward four counterclaims, set-offs or cross-
demands. For the sake of brevity I will refer to them as cross-demands.

At the hearing before Mr Registrar Metcalfe on 20 April 1983, at which Mr Buckley
was represented by Mr Bloom, the matter of his offer to secure the debt was not pursued   *h*
save in relation to the first bankruptcy notice. In support of his case that the second
bankruptcy notice should be set aside, Mr Bloom relied on three of the cross-demands
put forward in Mr Buckley's affidavit. We have a note of that hearing prepared by the
bank's solicitors and approved by the registrar. In that note what the registrar said in
giving his decision is recorded in these terms:

> 'The Registrar said that having heard all the evidence, he found himself in some   *j*
> difficulty. He said, however, that, although it ought not to affect his decision, he
> knew that, whatever his decision, there would be an appeal to the Divisional Court.
> The Registrar said of Mr. Buckley that "it may well be that he has an action which
> he can set up and I will therefore set aside the Bankruptcy Notice.'

Before us, counsel for Mr Buckley relied on only two of Mr Buckley's cross-demands.
a They were conveniently labelled during the course of the argument 'the Stansfield claim'
and 'the Harrison claim'. Unfortunately, neither of them has been formulated in any
pleading. We invited counsel to formulate them for us, but he confined himself to
referring us to the evidence. That is somewhat diffuse and repetitive, being scattered
among a number of affidavits sworn by Mr Buckley on a variety of occasions.

Before I turn to the evidence, I propose to advert briefly to the relevant law. Counsel
b for the bank referred us to a number of cases in which the effect of s 1(1)(g) of the
Bankruptcy Act 1914 and of rr 137, 138 and 139 of the Bankruptcy Rules 1952 (or their
predecessors) was considered. Those cases were all in the Court of Appeal and all entitled
Re a debtor with a number (see [1935] Ch 347; [1947] LJR 1413; [1957] 2 All ER 551,
[1958] Ch 81; [1963] 1 All ER 85, [1963] 1 WLR 51; and [1981] 2 All ER 987, [1981] 1
WLR 1205). Counsel for the bank also referred us to passages in *Williams and Muir Hunter*
c *on Bankruptcy* (19th edn, 1979) pp 37–38, 583 and in 3 Halsbury's Laws (4th edn) paras
271–272. So far as relevant for present purposes, what emerges from those authorities
may be summarised as follows. It behoves a debtor who wishes to avail himself of the
third option in a bankruptcy notice to file an affidavit, or affidavits, under rr 137 and 138
of the 1952 rules showing three things on the face of it or of them, with adequate
particularity, the burden of proof being on the debtor. First, the affidavit or affidavits
d must show that he has a cross-demand against the creditor which is genuine. To satisfy
that requirement, the cross-demand must be put forward in good faith and must have a
reasonable probability of success, or, as it has also been expressed, must give rise to a
triable issue. In the latter respect, there is no hard and fast rule as to the degree of proof
required. It depends in each case on the particular facts and circumstances of that case.
Second, the affidavit or affidavits must show that the cross-demand could not have been
e set up in the action in which the judgment relied on by the creditor was obtained. Third,
the affidavit or affidavits must show that the cross-demand equals or exceeds the amount
of the judgment debt. For that purpose the cross-demand need not be for a liquidated
sum or even for a sum of money at all. But it must be capable of being quantified in
terms of money and the affidavit or affidavits must quantify it.

With those principles in mind, I turn to the evidence, first about the Stansfield claim.
f The facts about that claim, as deposed to by Mr Buckley and as evinced by an exhibit
to one of his affidavits, are these. At some date which his evidence does not precisely
establish, but which must have been soon after 15 January 1982, Mr Buckley was
introduced to a Mr Stansfield, a solicitor who practised in Warrington under the firm
name of Longland Stansfield & Keeble and who wished to sell his practice and also the
freehold premises in which it was carried on. The introduction was effected by a company
g called Simlodge Ltd, which describes its activities as those of 'corporate strategy and
business development advisors'. Mr Stansfield's practice was a small, quiet family practice,
which had been established in about 1900. Mr Stansfield's pre-tax profits from it for the
year to May 1981 had been about £10,000, with no rent having been charged for the
freehold premises. Those premises were built as a double-fronted dwelling house which
had ten rooms on two floors, plus a cellar. Mr Buckley describes it as 'a fine corner
h building offering a considerable development potential'. Mr Buckley negotiated for the
acquisition of a 50% interest in the practice and an option to purchase one-half of the
freehold at its current value at the time of the exercise of the option. After the broad
terms of the deal had been agreed, and after Mr Buckley had told Mr Stansfield that, to
quote Mr Buckley's own words, 'I was involved in litigation with the bank over personal
matters which I expected to be resolved' (that was a reference to the negotiations for the
j Tomlin order), Mr Stansfield spoke to a friend of his, Mr Stanley Morris, who was the
area director of the bank for Warrington. Mr Buckley does not know the precise date of
the conversation, but he does say that it took place shortly after the death of his own
father, which occurred on 16 January 1982. According to Mr Buckley, Mr Stansfield told
him that Mr Morris had told him that Mr Buckley owed the bank £400,000 and that he
(Mr Stansfield) could 'draw his own conclusions' about doing business with Mr Buckley.

Mr Buckley expresses what he says the outcome was in these terms:

> 'The deal which I believe would otherwise have proceeded was killed as a direct *a*
> result and Mr Stansfield withdrew following his holiday in Israel in April 1982.'

Mr Buckley sets out his computation of his consequent loss in these terms:

> 'I assess the loss of bargain here in terms of income losses at £5,000 per annum ×
> 4 a loss of perquisites and expenses of £2,000 per annum × 4 all of which would be
> tax free to me for the fiscal years 1981/2, 1982/3. To the loss of capital being the *b*
> value of my share in the goodwill of Longland Stansfield & Keeble and to the loss of
> capital profit in relation to the proposed development of Mr Stansfield's building I
> put figures of £10,000 and £30,000 respectively after allowances for tax and
> provision for refurbishment. A round total of £60,000.'

We were told by counsel for Mr Buckley that the multiplier of four, in two places there, *c*
connoted four years' purchase and that Mr Buckley's freedom from income tax for two
years would be due to earlier tax losses.

Mr Buckley claims that sum of £60,000 from the bank as damages for its breach of
confidence in telling Mr Stansfield of his (Mr Buckley's) indebtedness to the bank. In
January 1982 Mr Buckley's total indebtedness to the bank (including his indebtedness as
a former partner in Hall Brydon) was in fact about £310,000. When it was put to counsel *d*
for Mr Buckley during the argument that Mr Buckley would anyway, before entering
into partnership with Mr Stansfield, have had to inform him frankly of the extent of his
indebtedness to the bank, counsel agreed but said that it was for Mr Buckley to decide on
the timing and manner of that disclosure.

In fairness to the bank I should mention that its evidence is to the effect that a figure
of £400,000 was never mentioned by Mr Morris. *e*

The question is whether what Mr Buckley has put before the court about the Stansfield
claim, in his affidavits, satisfies the requirements that I summarised a moment ago.

Counsel for the bank, after some hesitation, conceded, sensibly in my view, that it
satisfied the second requirement, that the claim could not have been set up in the action
in which the judgment relied on by the bank was obtained. He accepted that, to have
failed to satisfy that requirement, the claim would have had to arise, at the latest, before *f*
the Tomlin order was made, which was on 18 February 1982, whereas, on Mr Buckley's
formulation (if I may call it that) of the claim, it arose in April 1982, when Mr Stansfield
broke off the negotiations.

Counsel for the bank, however, made two submissions that I found convincing.

One, which went to the first requirement, was that Mr Buckley's affidavits left
unexplained the delay between January 1982, when the conversation between Mr Morris *g*
and Mr Stansfield took place, and April 1982, when Mr Stansfield broke off the
negotiations. If the latter event was caused by the former, the gap of three months
between them is puzzling; and, of course, in order to succeed, Mr Buckley has to prove
that the latter event was caused by the former. It seems to me that, in that respect, Mr
Buckley's evidence lacks the particularity, in other words the precision of detail, that is
required.   The other submission made by counsel for the bank that I found convincing *h*
was that Mr Buckley's evidence did not satisfy the third requirement, in that it did not
show with sufficient particularity how the figure of £60,000 put forward by Mr Buckley
as the amount of his claim was computed. I have quoted a passage in Mr Buckley's
evidence where he sought to fulfil that requirement. The figure of £5,000 per annum
for loss of income is intelligible, as is perhaps, on a generous view, the figure of £2,000
per annum for loss of perquisites. But the multiplier of four is unsupported by any *j*
evidence. Worse, there is no evidence as to the price that Mr Buckley was to pay for his
share in the goodwill and other assets of Mr Stansfield's practice, no evidence as to the
value of the freehold property, no evidence as to the nature of the proposed development
of it, no evidence as to the probable cost of that development, no evidence whether
planning permission would be required and, if so, was likely to be obtained, and no
evidence how the profit on the development was intended to be realised. I do not

a   overlook that counsel for Mr Buckley told us, on instructions, that Mr Buckley was to pay nothing for his share of the assets of the practice and that the consideration flowing from him for that was to be the work that he was to contribute to the practice. An allegation such as that needs, however, in my view, to be substantiated by credible sworn testimony.

For those reasons I do not think that, in relation to the Stansfield claim, Mr Buckley has fulfilled the requirements that it is incumbent on a debtor to fulfil, by his affidavit or
b   affidavits, in order, in the words of s 1(1)(g) of the 1914 Act, to 'satisfy the court that he has a counter-claim set off or cross demand which equals or exceeds the amount of the judgment debt'.

I turn to the Harrison claim. The facts as to that are these. In 1978 a firm of solicitors called Charles Buckley & Co, in which Mr Buckley was the senior partner, was acting for a Mr Harrison, a customer of the bank against whom a receiving order in bankruptcy
c   had been made on the bank's petition. That firm prepared, for the benefit of Mr Harrison and of a relative of his who was financially supporting his case, a report about his affairs, which contained some confidential information and also set out the terms of a proposed scheme of arrangement which had been filed with the Official Receiver. On 8 May 1978 Mr Buckley, on his own initiative, sent a copy of that report to the bank, in the hope, so I understand, that the bank would favourably consider the scheme of arrangement. On 12
d   May 1978 the bank wrote to Mr Buckley a letter that we have not seen, but which, presumably, acknowledged receipt of the report. On 15 May 1978 Mr Buckley wrote to the bank, asking that the report 'should be regarded as being sent under the cloak of banking privilege', and adding:

e   'I say this because I wanted you, the Bank, to form a fair view, with the benefit (if it is of any benefit), of our researches. I would therefore request that the Report be for your file only. I didn't mention this in my original letter, but time was somewhat short.'

On 16 May 1978 the bank replied confirming, and I quote, 'that this report will be treated by ourselves as confidential and for our own internal use'.

Some four years later, in the early part of 1982, the bank put the report in evidence in
f   proceedings in which Mr Harrison was seeking to have set aside a judgment in default of defence obtained against him by the bank on 6 December 1977. Those proceedings came in the first instance before a district registrar, who refused to look at the report and who did set aside the judgment. On an appeal from the district registrar's decision, Hirst J looked at the report and decided that the judgment should be restored.

There is a factual mistake in Mr Buckley's affidavit evidence as to what Hirst J said in
g   his judgment. Mr Buckley states that, but for the report, Hirst J would have upheld the district registrar's decision, and that he said so. We have a transcript of Hirst J's judgment and it is clear that that is incorrect. I do not think it necessary for me to burden the present, already lengthy, judgment, with an analysis of Hirst J's judgment. Suffice it to say that I have read the whole of it and that I am quite sure that Hirst J would have decided the case before him in the same way even without the report.

h   At all events, on those facts, Mr Buckley claims damages against the bank under two heads. First, he claims to be entitled to be indemnified by the bank against any claim that may be made against him by Mr Harrison for having sent the report to the bank without Mr Harrison's authority. Second, he claims to be entitled to damages from the bank for alleged harm done to his (Mr Buckley's) reputation by the disclosure by the bank, in the proceedings before Hirst J, of the fact that he (Mr Buckley) had sent the
j   report to the bank without that authority.

Mr Buckley quantifies the total damages to which he is entitled from the bank in respect of this claim at £21,000, of which he attributes £10,000 to his own claim for loss of reputation. He gives no indication at all of the way in which he has computed or estimated those figures.

In his affidavits Mr Buckley states his cause of action against the bank to be breach of a banker's duty of confidence. The difficulty about that is, of course, that, in the

circumstances, the bank's duty of confidence was owed to Mr Harrison, not to Mr
Buckley. Faced with that, counsel for Mr Buckley relied on a contract which he submitted   *a*
had been brought into existence between Mr Buckley and the bank by the letters that
they exchanged in May 1978. The difficulty about *that* is that Mr Buckley, when he sent
the report to the bank on 8 May 1978, attached no limit to the use that the bank might
make of it. It was not until 15 May 1978, after the bank had received the report, that he
wrote asking that it should be 'regarded as being sent under the cloak of banking
privilege'. There was therefore no consideration to support the bank's subsequent   *b*
promise to accede to that request, and so no consideration to support any such contract as
counsel relied on.

The difficulties in the way of this claim do not end there.

In the latest of his affidavits Mr Buckley stated that it had been 'indicated' to him that
he would be 'subjected to' a claim for damages by Mr Harrison. On the last day of the
hearing of these appeals before us, however, it became common ground that no claim   *c*
had been made by Mr Harrison against Mr Buckley, and Mr Buckley informed us that
he had recently been told by Mr Harrison that he had no intention of making any claim
against Mr Buckley. However, said Mr Buckley, Mr Harrison is a person who could
change his mind. Be that as it may, it does not seem to me that Mr Buckley could have a
quantifiable claim against the bank for present purposes until Mr Harrison had, in some
way, made a successful claim against him that was itself quantified or quantifiable.   *d*

As to the claim for damage to Mr Buckley's reputation, the fact is that he produces not
a shred of evidence in support of it. There is but the bare assertion on his part that his
reputation has been damaged. We are left to speculate *with whom* and *how* his reputation
has been damaged. He says that he sent the report to the bank in what he conceived to
be the best interests of his client. Right-thinking people might think that, none the less,
it was misguided of him to do so. But which right-thinking people know that he did so,   *e*
or mind? The proceedings before Hirst J were in chambers. We do not know who was
present, apart from the judge and counsel and solicitors on both sides, the solicitor for
Mr Harrison being Mr Buckley himself. As to Mr Harrison himself, he is, as is evinced
by Hirst J's judgment, not only a bankrupt but also a person who was sentenced to three
years' imprisonment. So his opinion of Mr Buckley is unlikely to be of any great moment.

In the result I take the view that Mr Buckley's Harrison claim is quite hopeless.   *f*

If that were all, I would conclude that the bank's appeal should be allowed. Counsel
for the bank contended, however, that that conclusion was reinforced if one took into
account the situation in the proceedings that I mentioned earlier in which the bank seeks
to enforce claims that it has against Mr Buckley as a former partner in Hall Brydon. In
view of the possibility that I may be wrong in my assessment of Mr Buckley's Stansfield
claim, I think it right to consider that contention.   *g*

The facts as to those proceedings are essentially these. On 9 September 1982 the bank
issued a writ in the Queen's Bench Division against Mr Buckley and his two former
partners, namely Mr Haworth and Mr Lea, claiming against Mr Buckley and Mr Haworth
a sum of £250,094·45 and interest thereon, and against Mr Lea a lesser sum, on the
footing that Mr Lea did not become a partner in Hall Brydon until the major part of the
debt had been incurred. The debt was alleged to arise from overdrawn banking accounts   *h*
kept by the firm with the bank. We were told that Mr Lea denies ever having been a
partner in the firm, but nothing turns on that in the present case.

The bank has issued in those proceedings a summons under RSC Ord 14 for summary
judgment. That summons, together with a cross-summons by Mr Buckley, is due to be
heard on the day after tomorrow.

Among the affidavits sworn by Mr Buckley that we have before us is his affidavit in   *j*
opposition to that Ord 14 summons. Mr Buckley does not, in that affidavit, dispute his
prima facie liability to the bank for the £250,094·45. He puts forward, however, a
number of reasons why he should have unconditional leave to defend. In the light of his
counsel's submissions, I need mention only four of those reasons. The first two are the
existence of counterclaims by Mr Buckley in respect of the Stansfield claim and of the
Harrison claim. The third is that, according to Mr Buckley, there may have been an

agreement in March 1981 under which, in consideration of his resigning as a partner in
a Hall Brydon, which he did on 9 March 1981, the bank agreed to reduce its claim against
that firm by £150,000. The fourth is that, again according to Mr Buckley, an agreement
was reached, at a meeting on 25 March 1982, under which he was to discharge his
liability to the bank in respect of Hall Brydon's debt by instalments. Mr Buckley relies,
as evidencing that agreement, on a letter that he wrote to the bank on 4 May 1982, which
is in these terms:

b
'Re: Hall Brydon
   I refer to the meeting of the 25th March, 1982. Because of events which have
occurred since then I have been unable to write to you earlier. I have explained the
reasons for this in a separate letter marked "Private and Confidential" which please
treat as Private and Confidential. The meeting followed requests that I had made
previously to discuss the Hall Brydon borrowing on a Banker to Customer basis as
c long ago as last December, and again in late February. At the meeting I proposed
that repayment of outstandings should take place half yearly with a £25,000 down
payment on the 1st June, 1982 and thereafter at six monthly intervals. You proposed
that interest would be put to the back end and repaid similarly. I accepted your
proposals over interest and you accepted my proposals to pay the principal and
interest on my undertaking to deposit a life policy of £250,000 with you and to pay
d the premiums thereon as part of the settlement. Your acceptance was further on the
basis that following the initial down payment of £25,000 you would like to have
the instalments on a monthly basis and I agreed to this.
                                                              Yours sincerely,
                                                              Charles Buckley.'

e To that Mr Buckley added a manuscript postscript, which reads: 'As mentioned I shall be
pleased to discuss any fine tuning.'
   The bank denies that any such agreement as is alleged by Mr Buckley, or any agreement
at all, was reached at the meeting on 25 March 1982, and it has put in evidence its own
minutes of that meeting, and some subsequent correspondence, to bolster its denial. The
bank also denies that there was any earlier agreement under which it was to reduce its
f claim against Hall Brydon by £150,000.
   The contention of counsel for the bank was this. Assuming in Mr Buckley's favour,
despite the bank's denials, that the bank did, in 1981, agree to reduce its claim against
Hall Brydon by £150,000 and that it did, at the meeting on 25 March 1982, agree to
accept payment of the balance from Mr Buckley by instalments on the terms set out in
his letter of 4 May 1982, the fact remains that its residual claim against Mr Buckley in its
g action against the partners in Hall Brydon, when added to its claim against Mr Buckley
under the judgment of 30 September 1982, exceeds the aggregate of Mr Buckley's cross-
demands in respect of the Stansfield claim and of the Harrison claim.
   That, so it seems to me, must, as a matter of fact, be right. If the bank did agree in
1981 to reduce its claim against Hall Brydon by £150,000, the amount of that claim in
March 1982 was about £100,000. If the agreement alleged by Mr Buckley was made on
h 25 March 1982, it was repudiated by the bank and, as counsel for Mr Buckley conceded,
its repudiation was accepted by Mr Buckley because he never made any payment
thereunder and never produced a policy on his life for £250,000 or any other sum. That
left Mr Buckley owing the bank £100,000 plus the amount of the judgment of 30
September 1982, a total of about £121,000, which easily exceeds the aggregate of Mr
Buckley's own estimates of what is due to him from the bank in respect of the Stansfield
j claim and the Harrison claim, let alone what may be due to him, on any reasonable
estimate, in respect of the Stansfield claim alone. No doubt, one should, on that
hypothesis, add to Mr Buckley's claims against the bank a claim for damages for breach
of the agreement of 25 March 1982, but (as again counsel conceded) such damages could
only be minimal, bearing in mind that Mr Buckley was saved from having to pay the
premiums on a policy on his life for £250,000 and saved from paying monthly
instalments of £25,000 to the bank, beginning on 1 June 1982.

Counsel for Mr Buckley suggested that a possible alternative view of the facts was that, whether or not there was an agreement in 1981 for the reduction of Hall Brydon's debt by £150,000, the agreement made on 25 March 1982 was for the repayment of the whole £250,000-odd by instalments. If so, however, it would mean only that, instead of four instalments being due from Mr Buckley under the latter agreement, ten were due. It would make no substantial difference to the result.

We are thus left with a question of law, which both counsel told us was a novel one, on which there was no authority. That question is whether, on a true construction of s 1(1)(g) of the Bankruptcy Act 1914, a judgment creditor who is confronted with a cross-demand by the judgment debtor may himself set up, in opposition to that cross-demand, another claim of his own against the judgment debtor which, when added to the judgment debt, overtops the debtor's cross-demand. Counsel for Mr Buckley argued for a negative answer to that question, saying that the court was not permitted, under the section, to look beyond the judgment debt and the amount of the judgment debtor's cross-demand. I, for my part, however, agree with the submissions of counsel for the bank to the contrary. It seems to me that, when the section refers to the judgment debtor having 'a counter-claim set off or cross demand which equals or exceeds the amount of the judgment debt', it cannot mean a counterclaim, set-off or cross-demand which, if set up in an independent action, would itself be defeated by a counterclaim by the creditor. It must, in accordance with the authorities that I referred to earlier, mean a cross-demand having at least some chance of success.

For those reasons, I think that the bank's appeal should be allowed and that the bankruptcy notice should be restored.

SIR ROBERT MEGARRY V-C. I entirely agree. I have nothing to add, save on certain questions relating to the statutory forms of bankruptcy notice which arose during the argument. Nothing has to be decided on this subject, but as it is a matter of some concern I propose to say something about it. Over the years, the courts have evolved a doctrine which requires bankruptcy notices to be construed strictly, because of the penal consequences that flow from non-compliance, and so it is well settled that such notices must be in a form which is not calculated to puzzle, perplex or mislead the debtor: see, for example, *Re a judgment debtor* (No 530 of 1908) [1908] 2 KB 474 at 478, 481, [1908–10] All ER Rep 368 at 370, 372. The cases all relate to the way in which the blanks in the statutory forms have been completed by the creditor; but what concerns me is that the statutory forms themselves seem to me to be forms which could be said to be calculated to puzzle, perplex or mislead the debtor. I therefore turn to these forms.

The statutory forms of bankruptcy notice are those set out as Forms 6 and 7 in App I to the Bankruptcy Rules 1952, SI 1952/2113, made under the Bankruptcy Act 1914, s 132(1); and r 7(1) requires these forms to be used with such variations as circumstances may require. Form 6 is a bankruptcy notice based on a judgment or order of the High Court, and Form 7 is a closely similar form for a judgment or order of a county court. The main difference is that Form 6 requires payment to be made to the creditor or his agent, whereas Form 7 requires payment to be made to the registrar of a specified county court. For simplicity, I shall, unless otherwise indicated, refer only to Form 6. I take the forms as set out in *Williams and Muir Hunter on Bankruptcy* (19th edn, 1979) pp 653–654; and for intelligibility I shall fill in certain of the blanks in accordance with the marginal notes in the statutory form, and ignore bankrupcty notices which are to be served outside England.

The notice begins with the words: 'TAKE NOTICE that within [ten] days after service of this notice on you excluding the day of such service . . .' One then looks to see what it is that has to be done within this time, and one finds three separate requirements, each beginning with the phrase 'you must'. The first is that 'you must pay to' the person specified the sum due on a specified judgment or order of the High Court. The second is—

'or you must secure or compound for the said sum to [his *or* their] satisfaction [*or* the satisfaction of his (*or* their) said agent] or to the satisfaction of this Court . . .'

The third is—

a

'or you must satisfy this Court that you have a counterclaim, set-off, or cross-demand against [him or them] which equals or exceeds the sum claimed by [him or them] and which you could not set up in the action or other proceedings in which the judgment or order was obtained.'

Apart from a curiosity of punctuation which I shall mention later, it seems clear that
b the debtor is being told that, although he may choose which of those three requirements he will comply with, in each case he must comply with it within the ten days. Yet the three are very different. The first is entirely within the debtor's control: it is simply to pay the sum within the ten days. The second, that of securing or compounding for the sum, requires him to satisfy the creditor or his agent or the court as to the security or compounding. The third, that of a sufficient cross-demand, requires the debtor to satisfy
c the court as to that cross-demand. The debtor, reading the notice, may well be puzzled about how to achieve the satisfaction under the second and third heads within the time limit.

So far as the third head is concerned, the statutory form provides an indorsement which must be set out in the notice. This informs the debtor that where he has a counterclaim, set-off or cross-demand which he could not set up in the action or other
d proceedings in which the judgment or order was obtained he must within seven days apply to the court to set aside the notice by filing an affidavit to the above effect. (The seven days comes from r 138, as amended.) The bankruptcy notice thus appears to tell the debtor that if he relies on the third head he must both satisfy the court within the ten days and file his affidavit within the seven days. What it does not tell him is that if he files his affidavit within the seven days, then unless it fails to disclose a sufficient cross-
e demand the registrar is bound, by r 139, to give at least three clear days' notice of a hearing and to extend the time for compliance with the bankruptcy notice; and the filing of the affidavit operates per se as an application to set aside the bankruptcy notice. In short, the real requirement under the third head is not one of achieving the virtual impossibility of actually satisfying the court within the ten days that a sufficient cross-demand exists, as well as filing the affidavit within the seven days, but instead is one of
f simply filing the affidavit within the seven days, and then satisfying the court within the extended time that the registrar must fix.

As for the second head, I need say nothing about securing or compounding for the sum to the satisfaction of the creditor or his agent: if the debtor chooses this path, he must achieve the result within the ten days by taking whatever steps he thinks appropriate. But to secure or compound for the sum to the satisfaction of the court
g within the ten days requires the matter to be brought before the court, and here neither the statutory form nor the rules provide any counterpart to the application by affidavit which is provided for the third head. Naturally I accept that even so important a document as a bankruptcy notice cannot be expected to set out all the relevant rules of procedure; yet the information given by the bankruptcy notice as to the affidavit for the third head (incomplete though it is) forms a striking contrast with the absence of any
h information at all about the second head. With so short a time limit as ten days, a debtor who has spent a few days in attempting to secure or compound for the sum to the creditor's satisfaction, only to be met with what he regards as an unreasonable refusal, may well think that it is hopeless to seek to secure or compound for the sum to the satisfaction of the court in what little is left of the ten days. As Warner J has pointed out in his judgment, under s 109(4) of the 1914 Act, as read with *Re a debtor (No 6864 of*
j *1980, High Court), the debtor v Slater Walker Ltd* [1981] 2 All ER 987, [1981] 1 WLR 1205, the court appears to have power to extend the debtor's time, but only if he applies within the ten days. The fact that for the third head the indorsement sets out both the mode of proceeding and the relevant time limit throws into contrast the silence about both for the second head. The debtor is simply left to fend for himself, with no warning that the little time that remains is slipping away; and he may well be misled about the operation of the time limit.

Despite the assistance given to me by counsel for the bank during argument (and he, of course, is very experienced in these matters), it still seems to me that the statutory *a* form is one which may well puzzle, perplex or mislead debtors. I feel no hesitation in saying that it certainly has perplexed me. That perplexity has not been lessened by a point about punctuation. In Form 6, as set out in *Williams and Muir Hunter* p 653, a comma separates the first head from the second, and the second from the third. In both the bankruptcy notices which are before us, it is a semicolon and not a comma which separates the second head from the third; and as the Queens's Printer's copy of Form 6 *b* also has a semicolon there it appears that the bankruptcy notices are correct and *Williams and Muir Hunter* wrong. This punctuation led to a suggestion during argument that the ten days applied to the first and second heads but not to the third, which, unlike the second head, was screened from the ten days by the semicolon. On this footing, the requirement of the notice is that within ten days you must do A or B; or you must do C. The curiosity of this reading, which leaves the third head with no time limit apart from *c* any that may be imported from the indorsement, is enhanced by the fact that, unlike Form 6, Form 7 has a comma in place of the semicolon; and it is inconceivable that two such similar documents should have such different meanings. Nor can I imagine that a draftsman who had any intention on the point would entrust that intention to so frail a carrier as a semicolon in place of a comma. That semicolon must, I think, be a slip in the drafting or printing. Nevertheless, the debtor on whom an accurate notice in Form 6 is *d* served sees only that notice with its semicolon, and not a copy of Form 7; and it is he whom the notice ought not to puzzle, perplex or mislead.

I do not, of course, suggest that a bankruptcy notice which correctly follows the prescribed form will be held bad merely because the form may be said to be calculated to puzzle, perplex or mislead. What I do say is that the language of the statutory forms ought to be revised so as to bring the forms up to the standard which the courts require *e* to be observed by those who have to complete the forms. I am sure that modern methods of drafting could produce forms of greater clarity, accuracy and helpfulness than the present forms attain. Thus if each of the three requirements were to be set out in numbered paragraphs it would obviate some of the uncertainties and also throw into relief the difference in treatment between the second and third heads. It should also be possible to evolve a form with fewer blanks requiring completion, and thus fewer sources *f* of those arguments on the wording of bankruptcy notices which, despite s 147 of the 1914 Act, take up so much of the time of the courts to such little profit.

I would only add that I make no apology for having dealt at length with a matter that does not arise for decision. Bankruptcy notices are of such importance to their recipients, who almost by definition are likely to be in a state of anxiety and financial stress, that it seems to me to be essential that the statutory forms of notice should not fall below the *g* standards which the courts have for long been requiring in filling up the blanks in the forms. It may be that other judges will regard the statutory forms as being clear and free from what I regard as being blemishes. Yet even if this is so, what matters is what the forms will convey to a debtor, not to a judge. Even if only one judge has been puzzled by the forms (as I have been), no debtor can very well be blamed for saying that he too was puzzled. In the result, I simply say that in my opinion the statutory forms of *h* bankruptcy notice ought to be redrafted.

WARNER J. I entirely agree. I am certainly not one who thinks that these statutory forms are clear, and I share the view of Sir Robert Megarry V-C that they are in fact highly unsatisfactory.

j

Mr Buckley's appeal dismissed. Bank's appeal allowed.

Solicitors: *Wilde Sapte* (for the bank); *Betesh & Co*, Manchester (for the Mr Buckley).

Vivian Horvath   Barrister.

a
Harris v Empress Motors Ltd
Cole v Crown Poultry Packers Ltd

COURT OF APPEAL, CIVIL DIVISION
STEPHENSON, O'CONNOR AND ROBERT GOFF LJJ
9, 10, 11 MAY, 14 JULY 1983

b

Fatal accident – Damages – Loss of future earnings – Survival of claim for benefit of estate – Measure of damages – Principles of assessment – Deductions to be made from estimated net future earnings in arriving at earnings on which award to be based – Living expenses – Method of calculating deductible living expenses not the same as method of calculation under Fatal Accidents Act – Only that proportion of deceased's net earnings that he would have spent exclusively on c *himself deductible – Proportion of net earnings which would have been expended on household expenses for joint benefit of deceased's family to be treated as exclusively attributable to deceased's living expenses and deductible from estimated net future earnings – Proportion to be deducted dependent on number of dependants – Amount of living expenses to be deducted if deceased a young unmarried man – Law Reform (Miscellaneous Provisions) Act 1934, s 1(1).*

d In assessing the damages recoverable by a deceased's estate under s 1(1)[a] of the Law Reform (Miscellaneous Provisions) Act 1934 for the deceased's loss of earnings in the 'lost years', ie the years in which he would have been earning had he lived, the following principles are to be applied in calculating the living expenses to be deducted from his net earnings in the lost years in order to reach the amount of recoverable damages: (i) the ingredients that go to make up 'living expenses' are the same whether the deceased was e young or old, single or married, or with or without dependants; (ii) the sum to be deducted as living expenses is the proportion of the deceased's net earnings that he would have spent exclusively on himself to maintain himself at the standard of life appropriate to his situation; (iii) accordingly, any sums that he would have expended exclusively to maintain or benefit others will not form part of his living expenses and will not be deductible from his net earnings for the purposes of the 1934 Act. However, where the f deceased expended the whole or part of his net earnings on living expenses (such as rent, mortgage interest, rates, heating, electricity, gas, telephone etc and the cost of running a car) for the joint benefit of himself and his dependants, a proportion of that expenditure (the exact proportion being dependent on the number of dependants) should be treated as expenditure exclusively attributable to his living expenses and thus deductible from his net earnings in making the assessment under the 1934 Act; for example, where the g only dependant is the deceased's wife one half of the expenditure for their joint benefit should be deducted from his net earnings, but where there is a wife and two dependent children one-quarter of the expenditure for the family's benefit should be deducted from his net earnings. It follows that the calculation of the deceased's deductible living expenses for the purpose of assessing damages is different under the 1934 Act on the one hand and the Fatal Accidents Act 1976 on the other, because any part of the estimated h expenditure for the joint benefit of the deceased and his dependants is excluded from the calculation of his living expenses under the 1976 Act. It also follows that the amount of living expenses deductible from the deceased's net earnings for the purposes of the 1934 Act will generally be greater than the amount of the living expenses deductible under the 1976 Act, because under the latter Act the amount of his living expenses is conventionally assessed at no more than one-third of his net earnings (see p 565 f g, j p 575 c to p 576 b and p 577 e and g h, post).

Skelton v Collins (1966) 115 CLR 94, *Pickett v British Rail Engineering Ltd* [1979] 1 All ER

---

a   Section 1(1), so far as material, provides: 'Subject to the provisions of this section, on the death of any person after the commencement of this Act all causes of action . . . vested in him shall survive . . . for the benefit of, his estate . . .'

774, *Gammell v Wilson* [1981] 1 All ER 578 and *White v London Transport Executive* [1982] 1 All ER 410 considered.   *a*

The deduction for living expenses to be made in the case of a young unmarried man for the purpose of assessing the recoverable damages for his loss of earnings in the lost years is likely to be higher than in the case of an older married man because it is more easy to estimate the amount which should not be deducted from net earnings in the case of an older married man than in the case of a young unmarried man whose future is speculative (see p 577 *b* to *d*, post).   *b*

Gammell v Wilson [1981] 1 All ER 578 and *White v London Transport Executive* [1982] 1 All ER 410 considered.

Decision of McCowan J in *Harris v Empress Motors Ltd* [1982] 3 All ER 306 varied.

Notes

For damages for loss of earnings, see 12 Halsbury's Laws (4th edn) para 1154.   *c*

For the Law Reform (Miscellaneous Provisions) Act 1934, s 1, see 13 Halsbury's Statutes (3rd edn) 115.

For the Fatal Accidents Act 1976, see 46 ibid 1115.

The Administration of Justice Act 1982, s 4(2) substituted s 1(2)(*a*) of the 1934 Act, with the result that damages recoverable under s 1(1) of the 1934 Act for the benefit of the estate of a person who died on or after 1 January 1983 shall not include any damages   *d* for loss of income in respect of any period after that person's death.

Cases referred to in judgments
Benham v Gambling [1941] 1 All ER 7, [1941] AC 157, HL.
Chaplin v Hicks [1911] 2 KB 786, [1911–13] All ER Rep 224, CA.
Flint v Lovell [1935] 1 KB 354, [1934] All ER Rep 200, CA.   *e*
Gammell v Wilson, Furness v B & S Massey Ltd [1981] 1 All ER 578, [1982] AC 27, [1981] 2
        WLR 248, HL: *affg* [1980] 2 All ER 557, [1982] AC 27, [1980] 3 WLR 591, CA.
Griffiths v Kerkemeyer (1977) 15 ALR 387, (1977) 51 ALJR 792, Aust HC.
Harris v Brights Asphalt Contractors Ltd [1953] 1 All ER 395, [1953] 1 QB 617, [1953] 1
        WLR 341.
Mallett v McMonagle [1969] 2 All ER 178, [1970] AC 166, [1969] 2 WLR 767, HL.   *f*
McCann v Sheppard [1973] 2 All ER 881, [1978] 1 WLR 540, CA.
Murray v Shuter [1975] 3 All ER 375, [1976] QB 972, [1975] 3 WLR 597, CA.
Oliver v Ashman [1961] 3 All ER 323, [1962] 2 QB 210, [1961] 3 WLR 669, CA.
Pickett v British Rail Engineering Ltd [1979] 1 All ER 774, [1980] AC 136, [1978] 3 WLR
        955, HL.
Pope v D Murphy & Son Ltd [1960] 2 All ER 873, [1961] 1 QB 222, [1960] 2 WLR 861.   *g*
Rose v Ford [1937] 3 All ER 359, [1937] AC 826, HL.
Skelton v Collins (1966) 115 CLR 94, Aust HC.
Sullivan v West Yorkshire Passenger Transport Executive (17 December 1980, unreported),
        QBD.
White v London Transport Executive [1982] 1 All ER 410, [1982] QB 489 [1982] 2 WLR
        791.   *h*
Young v Percival [1974] 3 All ER 677, [1975] 1 WLR 17, CA.

Appeals

Harris v Empress Motors Ltd

The defendants, Empress Motors Ltd, appealed from so much of the judgment of *j*
McCowan J given on 21 January 1982 ([1982] 3 All ER 306, [1983] 1 WLR 65) whereby it was adjudged that the defendants should pay the plaintiff, Susan Harris, the administratrix of the estate of Peter Harris deceased, her husband, damages in respect of his death in the sum of £90,601·98 made up of £82,325 damages under the Law Reform (Miscellaneous Provisions) Act 1934 and £8,276·88 damages under the Fatal Accidents Act 1976. The defendants sought an order that judgment should be entered for the

a
plaintiff in such lesser sum as might seem just to the court having regard to the
defendants' grounds of appeal. Those grounds were that the damages awarded under the
1934 Act and under 1976 Act were excessive in the circumstances; that the trial judge
failed to deduct from the 'lost years' earnings of the deceased awarded under the 1934
Act a proper or sufficient sum for the deceased's living expenses; that the award of a
purchase of 16 years from the deceased's death in respect of the dependency and the lost
years award was excessive in all the circumstances; that the apportionment of the

b
damages awarded under the 1976 Act in favour of the deceased's children was insufficient
in all the circumstances; and that the award of damages resulted in the plaintiff recovering
more than £5,000 in excess of her damages under the 1976 Act. The facts are set out in
the judgment of O'Connor LJ.

Cole and another v Crown Poultry Packers Ltd

c
The defendants, Crown Poultry Packers Ltd, appealed against the judgment of Forbes J
given on 2 February 1983 whereby it was adjudged that the plaintiffs, John Albert Cole
and Albert Edward Cole, suing as administrators of the estate of William Malcolm Cole
deceased, should recover damages of £65,894·89 under the Law Reform (Miscellaneous
Provisions) Act 1934 in respect of the deceased's death, for his loss of earnings in the 'lost
years'. The defendants sought an order that judgment for a reduced sum be entered for

d
the plaintiff on the ground that the trial judge misdirected himself in the amount he
deducted for the deceased's living expenses in making the award. The facts are set out in
the judgment of O'Connor LJ.

Charles Whitby QC and *Julien Hooper* for the defendants in the Harris case.
Patrick Bennett QC and *Jonathan Acton-Bond* for the plaintiff in the Harris case.

e
Michael Ogden QC and *John Stevenson* for the defendants in the Cole case.
Christopher Sumner for the plaintiffs in the Cole case.

Cur adv vult

f
14 July. The following judgments were delivered.

O'CONNOR LJ (giving the first judgment at the invitation of Stephenson LJ). These
two cases raise questions on the assessment of damages where the court has to value the
earning capacity of the injured person whose expectation of life has been shortened. In
both cases the injured man had died as a result of injuries received in an accident caused

g
by the negligence of the defendants. In *Harris v Empress Motors Ltd* the action was
brought under the Fatal Accidents Act 1976 for the benefit of the dependent widow and
children and under the Law Reform (Miscellaneous Provisions) Act 1934 for the benefit
of the estate. In the Cole case, as the parents had never married and the children were
nearly grown up, the claim was in effect under the Law Reform (Miscellaneous Provisions)
Act 1934 alone. I will set out the relevant facts in each case.

h
The Harris case
     The deceased died on 10 February 1978 from injuries received on 3 February 1978.
The deceased and his widow were both aged 29; they had married in 1969. There were
two children, Nicholas born on 11 August 1974 and Timothy born on 22 April 1978.
The trial was at the end of January 1982. The judge approached the calculation of the

j
damages under the Fatal Accidents Act 1976 in the conventional way and no criticism is
made of the result, save as to the multiplier of 16 used by him. The judge found that the
deceased would have earned £23,500 net during the four years to the date of trial. For
the future he assessed a multiplicand of £7,000 per annum net, and gave 12 years'
purchase, making a total of £84,000. The dependency of the widow and two children
was agreed at 75%. To the resulting figure of £80,625 there was added the funeral
expenses and interest on the pre-trial assessment at an agreed rate, producing a total

assessment under this head of £85,276·88. The judge apportioned that sum: Nicholas
£7,500; Timothy £12,500; widow £65,276·88.

The judge then assessed the Law Reform Act damages. The loss of expectation of life
plus two small matters of special damage produced a total of £1,700; this is not
challenged. That left the 'lost years' calculation. The loss of net earnings were necessarily
the same as under the previous calculation; he used the same multiplier to produce a
total £107,500. From that sum there was to be deducted a sum to represent what I will
for the moment call the deceased's living expenses. The correct assessment of this
deduction is the real issue in these appeals. The judge came to the conclusion that the
deduction should be the same as that made to produce the dependency under the Fatal
Accidents Act, namely 25%. In the result the total assessment under this head was
£82,325.

The deceased died intestate; there was no estate except the Law Reform Act damages.
The division of the estate under the intestacy produces the following result: the widow
benefits in the sum of £57,000 (the first £25,000 plus 4 years' statutory interest, £7,000,
plus value of life interest in half the residue, £25,000). Nicholas and Timothy each
benefit in the sum of £12,581·50 (one quarter of the residue each). It remains to set these
sums against the Fatal Accidents Act assessments; those of Nicholas and Timothy are
extinguished; that of the widow is reduced to £8,276·88. The result is that judgment
was entered against the defendants for £82,325 under the Law Reform Act and £8,276·88
under the Fatal Accidents Act making a total of £90,601·88. There has been a duplication
of damage in the sum of £5,325, the difference between the judgment and the Fatal
Accidents Act assessment. The amount of this duplication can be varied up or down in a
number of ways without any alteration in the assessment for loss of earnings at £23,500
and £7,000 per annum. A deduction of 50% for living expenses produces a total
judgment for only £225 more than the Fatal Accidents Act assessment. An increase in
the apportionment of the Fatal Accidents Act award to the children will reduce the
duplication. A reduction in the Fatal Accidents Act multiplier will have the same effect.

The Cole case

The deceased died on 24 July 1979 from injuries received on 23 July; he was 38 years
old. There were two daughters, born in 1964 and 1965; they were the only Fatal
Accidents Act dependents as the parents had never married, and it was accepted that the
Fatal Accidents Act claim was bound to be extinguished by the Law Reform Act award.
The parties agreed that if the parents had been married the dependency under the Fatal
Accidents Act would have been 75% and the multiplier 13½. They agreed a figure for loss
of earnings in the lost years at £84,000 in round figures, and the only matter for the
judge was the amount of the deduction to be made for the deceased's living expenses.
The judge decided 25% and that is the only issue in the appeal.

Before I consider the main issue common to the appeals I will deal with two subsidiary
submissions made by counsel for the defendants in the *Harris* case. The first submission
was that the judge did not apportion a sufficient sum to the two children. The basis of
this submission is a little evidence given by the widow in cross-examination that she
might even consider private education for the boys as the husband had been anxious to
do his best for the children. In my judgment the judge directed himself correctly in
Harris v Empress Motors Ltd [1982] 3 All ER 306 at 311–312, [1983] 1 WLR 65 at 71–72
that he should make an estimate of the genuine dependency of the children. He accepted
a submission from counsel for the widow (the plaintiff) that he should ignore the
damages for the four years to the date of trial because the widow had kept the children at
her own expense. I think that he was wrong to accept that submission because the
children would have been dependent on the earnings of their father had he lived. The
judge then assessed a multiplicand of £1,250 for each child and applied a multiplier of
six for the 7½ year old and ten for the 4 year old. When it is remembered that the total
available multiplicand was £5,250, this was a generous apportionment. In my judgment
£20,000 between the two boys was an adequate apportionment even if the four years to

trial are taken into account. I would not have made so great a distinction between the
a two boys but it is a minor matter in the judge's discretion and we are not asked to vary it
by the plaintiff.

The second submission was that the multiplier of 16 was excessive. Counsel for the
defendants relied on the speech of Lord Diplock in *Mallett v McMonagle* [1969] 2 All ER
178 at 191, [1970] AC 166 at 177, where he said:

b
    'In cases such as the present where the deceased was aged 25 and the appellant, his
    widow, about the same age, courts have not infrequently awarded 16 years' purchase
    of the dependency. It is seldom that this number of years' purchase is exceeded.'

In *Young v Percival* [1974] 3 All ER 677, [1975] 1 WLR 17 the Court of Appeal altered
a multiplier of 12 to one of 14 where the deceased and the widow were 29 years old.
Megaw LJ said ([1974] 3 All ER 677 at 681, [1975] 1 WLR 17 at 22):

c
    '... the multiplier of 16 contended for on behalf of the plaintiff ... is too high
    ... We think that the right multiplier is 14. We reach this conclusion taking into
    account all the factors here, including the ages of the deceased and of the plaintiff
    both of whom were approaching 30, the fact that the deceased had not been long
    established in his employment after a series of other employments, and that it was
    employment in a trade (if that be the right word) where, on the evidence, the
d   general prospects of continuing profitability were uncertain'.

In the present case the deceased was a skilled electrician not a coach-tour salesman, and
his earning capacity was not in doubt. I think that a multiplier of 16 was at the top for
this case, but I cannot say that it was too high.

I come now to the main problem in these cases: how should the deduction which has
e to be made from the net loss of earnings for the lost years be calculated?

In the course of time the courts have worked out a simple solution to the similar
problem of calculating the net dependency under the Fatal Accidents Acts in cases where
the dependents are wife and children. In times past the calculation called for a tedious
inquiry into how much housekeeping money was paid to the wife, who paid how much
for the children's shoes etc. This has all been swept away and the modern practice is to
f deduct a percentage from the net income figure to represent what the deceased would
have spent exclusively on himself. The percentages have become conventional in the
sense that they are used unless there is striking evidence to make the conventional figure
inappropriate because there is no departure from the principle that each case must be
decided on its own facts. Where the family unit was husband and wife the conventional
figure is 33% and the rationale of this is that broadly speaking the net income was spent
g as to one-third for the benefit of each and one-third for their joint benefit. Clothing is an
example of several benefit, rent an example of joint benefit. No deduction is made in
respect of the joint portion because one cannot buy or drive half a motor car. Part of the
net income may be spent for the benefit of neither husband nor wife. If the facts be, for
example, that out of a net income of £8,000 per annum the deceased was paying £2,000
to a charity the percentage would be applied to £6,000 and not £8,000. Where there are
h children the deduction falls to 25%, as was the agreed figure in the *Harris* case.

One solution to the problem, at least in cases where there is a collateral claim by the
dependent widow or widow and children, is to make the same deduction as is made
when assessing the Fatal Accidents Acts dependency. This was the solution adopted by
both McCowan J and Forbes J in the present cases and it is a solution favoured by other
judges at first instance.

j Two other solutions have emerged at first instance. At the other extreme to the Fatal
Accidents Act solution is what may be called 'the savings only' solution. This solution
was reached by Mustill J in *Sullivan v West Yorkshire Passenger Transport Executive* (17
December 1980, unreported). Here 'living expenses' is given a very wide meaning,
namely all expenditure except savings; but savings are to include expenditure generating
wealth such as mortgage repayments. On the facts in *Sullivan's* case Mustill J assessed the

proportion of the deceased's savings which went to build up wealth at 15% of the net earnings and so deducted 85%.

The other solution may properly be called the 'available surplus' solution, as expounded by Webster J in *White v London Transport Executive* [1982] 1 All ER 410, [1982] 1 QB 489. I shall return to this case later in this judgment, but for the moment it is sufficient to say that the available surplus is what remains after deducting from the net earnings the cost of maintaining the deceased in his station in life. Webster J said ([1982] 1 All ER 410 at 418, [1982] QB 489 at 499):

'. . . in the cost of maintaining himself I include the cost of his housing, heating, food, clothing, necessary travelling and insurances and things of that kind . . .'

On the facts the available surplus was assessed at 33⅓% for the first five years of the 15 years' purchase and 25% for the balance.

Oliver v Ashman [1961] 3 All ER 323, [1962] 2 QB 210 was decided in this court in July 1961. Before that date the problem of the lost years had been considered in two cases at first instance. In *Harris v Brights Asphalt Contractors Ltd* [1953] 1 All ER 395, [1953] 1 QB 617, Slade J held that no sum was recoverable in respect of the lost years. In *Pope v D Murphy & Son Ltd* [1960] 2 All ER 873, [1961] 1 QB 222 Streatfeild J held that damages were recoverable in respect of them. In neither case was there any hint that the damages recoverable for the lost years should be assessed on any different basis from that on which damages are normally assessed for loss of earnings. In *Oliver v Ashman* the infant plaintiff was aged 20 months when he received a serious brain injury which reduced him to an epileptic dumb cabbage with a shortened expectation of life; it would be difficult to think of a case more unsuitable for consideration of the lost years problem. The trial judge, Lord Parker CJ, made a single award of £11,000 by way of damages and said that he accepted the reasoning of Streatfeild J in *Pope's* case and had ignored the shortened expectation of life. The Court of Appeal considered the problem in depth, and held on the authority of *Rose v Ford* [1937] 3 All ER 359, [1937] AC 826 and *Benham v Gambling* [1941] 1 All ER 7, [1941] AC 157 in the House of Lords that no claim could be made in respect of the lost years. It made no difference to the amount of the award because the court held that it must have been a minimal consideration. Once again there is no hint in the judgments that if the claim was available it should be treated in any different way from that in which an ordinary claim for loss of earnings or loss of earning capacity is treated.

The concept that the assessment of damages for loss of earnings during the lost years should be on a different basis from the normal first appears, as far as I have been able to discover, in the judgment of Taylor J in *Skelton v Collins* (1966) 115 CLR 94, in the High Court of Australia. This was a 'sleeping beauty' case, the plaintiff at the age of 17 having been rendered irreversibly unconscious as a result of brain damage. At the date of trial in March 1965 he was just 19 with an expectation of life of six months. The trial judge assessed damages under four heads: (i) £4,673 special damage to date of trial including hospital expenses and some £782 loss of wages; (ii) £1,201 cost of future maintainance in hospital; (iii) £346 future loss of earnings for six months (following *Oliver v Ashman* [1961] 3 All ER 323, [1962] 2 QB 210); (iv) £1,500 general damages. Having set out these heads Taylor J commented obiter (115 CLR 94 at 105–106):

'. . . before dealing with the points which were raised on behalf of the appellant I pause to observe that the inclusion in the award of practically the whole of the total amount that the appellant would probably have received for wages up to the date of trial, if he had not been injured, and for six months thereafter, operated unduly to inflate the assessment in the circumstances of the case. In the ordinary run of cases it is no doubt proper to assess damages substantially by reference to the amount of wages actually lost up to the date of trial and by reference to the present value of any probable future loss of that character. But where, as here, there is nothing to suggest that, if the appellant had not been injured, his wages would have been more than a   sufficient to provide for his own maintenance during his shortened life, it was erroneous to award a sum for loss of wages in addition to a larger sum calculated to provide for his complete maintenance and care during that period. The respondent, however, has made no complaint on this score but it is a material matter to be borne in mind when we come to consider whether the total amount awarded was or was not inadequate.'

b   Here was the origin of the concept and it was to provide a ready-made answer to one of the difficulties which Taylor J foresaw as a consequence of not following *Oliver v Ashman* [1961] 3 All ER 323, [1962] 2 QB 210. Unfortunately Taylor J has himself fallen into error; he had quite correctly pointed out the double recovery, but he picked the wrong head of damage to adjust. The deduction should have been made from the cost of maintenance in hospital in so far as that payment relieved him from making payments that he otherwise would have made, in practice what he would have spent on food. Such a deduction is common form where for example an en pension convalescent holiday is claimed. I can find no justification for reducing the claim for loss of earnings, the very fund which provides the money for buying the food. I am not concerned whether on the facts in *Skelton v Collins* a sum equivalent to the whole loss of wages ought to have been deducted as was in fact done by the High Court.

c

d   Taylor J in *Skelton v Collins* demonstrated that the passages in *Rose v Ford* [1937] 3 All ER 359, [1937] AC 826, *Flint v Lovell* [1935] 1 KB 354, [1934] All ER Rep 200 and *Benham v Gambling* [1941] 1 All ER 7, [1941] AC 157, on which this court had relied in *Oliver v Ashman* [1961] 3 All ER 323, [1962] 2 QB 210, on analysis did not support the conclusion. The crucial passage in his judgment on double recovery is where he said (115 CLR 94 at 114):

e   'It was pointed out in *Oliver v Ashman* . . . that "Where the estate was left to the dependants the claims under the *Fatal Accidents Act* and the *Law Reform Act* could be set off. But if the beneficiary of the estate was some person other than his dependants, there might be a double claim in respect of part of the benefit of the lost earnings" ([1961] 3 All ER 323 at 329, [1962] 2 QB 210 at 227). How far this possibility—if it be a possibility—influenced the decision in *Oliver v. Ashman* . . . does not clearly

f   appear but, in my view, it has no bearing upon the question of what damages should be awarded for an injured person's destroyed earning capacity whether the action be brought by the injured person himself or, upon his death, by his legal personal representative. Indeed, this, I think, is implicit in the observations of Lord Atkin and Lord Wright in *Rose v. Ford* ([1937] 3 All ER 359 at 363, 374–375, [1937] AC 826 at 835, 852). As to the possibility of the duplication of damages I observe that if

g   an injured person has, himself, recovered damages no further action will lie for the benefit of his dependants in the event of his subsequent death whilst in the case where an action is brought, not by the injured person himself but, upon his death, by his legal personal representative for the benefit of his estate, the damages would be assessed having regard to the gain, if any, which would have accrued to the deceased from his future probable earnings after taking into account the expenditure

h   which he would have incurred, if he had survived, in maintaining himself and his dependants, if any. Damages in any action for the benefit of the deceased's dependants would, of course, be assessed having regard to the magnitude of their loss as dependants so that the possibility of the duplication of damages would, to say the least, be remote.'

j   That passage is clear authority for the 'savings only' solution. I must quote two further passages from Taylor J's judgment (115 CLR 94 at 121–122):

'Accordingly in my view damages in the present case should have been assessed under the head having regard to the plaintiff's pre-accident expectancy and not only to the expectancy of life remaining to him after the receipt of his injuries. Any assessment should, of course, take into account the vicissitudes and uncertainties of

life and also the fact that if the plaintiff had survived for the full period it would
have been necessary for him to maintain himself out of his earnings and, no doubt, *a*
his expenditure on his own maintenance would have increased as his earnings
increased . . . So far as his economic loss is concerned the material before us indicates
that the plaintiff at the time of the injury was earning approximately £13 a week,
that at the age of twenty-one he would probably have earned something in excess of
£20 a week and that by the time he attained the age of thirty his salary would have
been, had it not been for the accident, some £2,000 or £2,500 per annum. In those *b*
circumstances it seems to me that on a balance of what his future income and
expenditure on maintenance would have been the economic loss resulting from his
destroyed earning capacity should not be rated highly. Particularly is this so when
account is taken of the uncertainties and vicissitudes of life. Under this head of
damages I would assess the sum of £2,000 as reasonable compensation. In the result
the damages assessed by his Honour should be increased by the difference between *c*
the last-mentioned sum and the amount of approximately £1,100 which was
wrongly included and to which I have previously referred.'

The calculation in this last passage shows beyond doubt that Taylor J adopted the 'savings
only' solution. All other members of the court in *Skelton v Collins* agreed with the
judgment of Taylor J on this aspect of the case.

In *Griffiths v Kerkemeyer* (1977) 15 ALR 387 the trial judge had assessed future loss of *d*
earnings for a 25-year-old quadraplegic on the basis of his shortened expectation of life,
30 years from the date of trial; the High Court said that this was wrong, but as the court
decided not to increase the award for other reasons no help is to be had from the
judgments on the topic of deduction for living expenses. I only mention this case because
it was cited by Lord Wilberforce in *Pickett v British Rail Engineering Ltd* [1979] 1 All ER
774, [1980] AC 136, where *Oliver v Ashman* [1961] 3 All ER 323, [1962] 2 QB 210 was *e*
overruled and to which I now turn.

The facts in *Pickett v British Rail Engineering Ltd* were that the deceased had been
employed by British Rail for 25 years when in 1974 he developed lung trouble from
exposure to asbestos dust; he issued a writ in 1975 and the case was tried in October 1976
when the trial judge awarded damages for loss of earnings down to the date of trial and *f*
for a further 12 months because the evidence was that his expectation of life was one
year. This proved to be accurate for before the matter came to the Court of Appeal in
November 1977 the deceased had died. The fact that he had brought a claim, and that
judgment had been given in his favour barred any claim under the Fatal Accidents Act
and it was obvious that the rule in *Oliver v Ashman* operated to the detriment of his
dependants as he was only 51 years of age at the date of his death.

The House of Lords overruled the Court of Appeal in *Oliver v Ashman*, declared that a *g*
plaintiff could claim for loss of earnings in respect of the lost years, gave guidance on
how the damages were to be assessed and sent the case back to the Queen's Bench Division
for assessment. In that part of his speech where he was considering the validity of the
decision in *Oliver v Ashman* Lord Wilberforce said ([1979] 1 All ER 774 at 780–781,
[1980] AC 136 at 149–150): *h*

'But is the main line of reasoning acceptable? Does it not ignore the fact that a
particular man, in good health, and sound earning, has in these two things an asset
of present value quite separate and distinct from the expectation of life which every
man possesses? Compare him with a man in poor health and out of a job. Is he not,
and not only in the immediate present, a richer man? Is he not entitled to say, at
one moment I am a man with existing capability to earn well for 14 years, the next *j*
moment I can only earn less well for one year? And why should he be compensated
only for the immediate reduction in his earnings and not for the loss of the whole
period for which he has been deprived of his ability to earn them? To the argument
that "they are of no value because you will not be there to enjoy them" can he not
reply, "Yes they are; what is of value to me is not only my opportunity to spend
them enjoyably, but to use such part of them as I do not need for my dependants, or

a for other persons or causes which I wish to support. If I cannot do this, I have been deprived of something on which a value, a present value, can be placed"? I do not think that the problem can be solved by describing what has been lost as an "opportunity" or a "prospect" or an "expectation". Indeed these words are invoked both ways, by the Lords Justices as denying a right to recover (on grounds of remoteness, intangibility or speculation), by those supporting the appellant's argument as demonstrating the loss of some real asset of true value. The fact is that

b the law sometimes allows damages to be given for the loss of things so described (eg *Chaplin v Hicks* [1911] 2 KB 786, [1911–13] All ER Rep 224), sometimes it does not. It always has to answer a question which in the end can hardly be more accurately framed than as: "Is the loss of this something for which the claimant should and reasonably can be compensated?" The defendant, in an impressive argument, urged on us that the real loss in such cases as the present was to the victim's dependants

c and that the right way in which to compensate them was to change the law (by statute; judicially it would be impossible) so as to enable the dependants to recover their loss independently of any action by the victim. There is much force in this, and no doubt the law could be changed in this way. But I think that the argument fails because it does not take account, as in an action for damages account must be taken, of the interest of the victim. Future earnings are of value to him in order that

d he may satisfy legitimate desires, but these may not correspond with the allocation which the law makes of money recovered by dependants on account of his loss. He may wish to benefit some dependants more than, or to the exclusion of, others; this (subject to family inheritance legislation) he is entitled to do. He may not have dependants, but he may have others, or causes, whom he would wish to benefit, for whom he might even regard himself as working. One cannot make a distinction,

e for the purposes of assessing damages, between men in different family situations.'

The principle which emerges from this part of the speech is found in the last sentence of the passage which I have quoted. So far there is no hint that the assessment should be any different for the lost years from that for the live years. Lord Wilberforce then turned to the assessment of damages and said ([1979] 1 All ER 774 at 781–782, [1980] AC 136 at

f 150–151):

'My Lords, in the case of the adult wage earner with or without dependants who sues for damages during his lifetime, I am convinced that a rule which enables the "lost years" to be taken account of comes closer to the ordinary man's expectations than one which limits his interest to his shortened span of life. The interest which such a man has in the earnings he might hope to make over a normal life, if not

g saleable in a market, has a value which can be assessed. A man who receives that assessed value would surely consider himself and be considered compensated; a man denied it would not. And I do not think that to act in this way creates insoluble problems of assessment in other cases. In that of a young child (cf *Benham v Gambling* [1941] 1 All ER 7, [1941] AC 157) neither present nor future earnings could enter into the matter; in the more difficult case of adolescents just embarking on the

h process of earning (cf *Skelton v Collins* (1966) 115 CLR 94) the value of "lost" earnings might be real but would probably be assessable as small.

There will remain some difficulties. In cases, probably the normal, where a man's actual dependants coincide with those for whom he provides out of the damages he receives, whatever they obtain by inheritance will simply be set off against their own claim. If on the other hand this coincidence is lacking, there might be

j duplication of recovery. To that extent injustice may be caused to the wrongdoer. But if there is a choice between taking a view of the law which mitigates a clear and recognised injustice in cases of normal occurrence, at the cost of the possibility in fewer cases of excess payments being made, or leaving the law as it is, I think that our duty is clear. We should carry the judicial process of seeking a just principle as far as we can, confident that a wise legislator will correct resultant anomalies.

My Lords, I have reached the conclusion which I would recommend so far

without reference to *Skelton v Collins* 115 CLR 94 in which the High Court of
Australia, refusing to follow *Oliver v Ashman* [1961] 3 All ER 323, [1962] 2 QB 210, *a*
achieved the same result. The value of this authority is twofold: first in
recommending by reference to authority (per Taylor J) and in principle (per
Windeyer J) the preferable solution, and, secondly, in demonstrating that this can
properly be reached by judicial process. The judgments, further, bring out an
important ingredient, which I would accept, namely that the amount to be recovered
in respect of earnings in the "lost" years should be that amount after deduction of an *b*
estimated sum to represent the victim's probable living expenses during those years.
I think that this is right because the basis, in principle, for recovery lies in the
interest which he has in making provision for dependants and others, and this he
would do out of his surplus. There is the additional merit of bringing awards under
this head into line with what could be recovered under the Fatal Accidents Acts.
Skelton v Collins has been followed and applied recently by the High Court of *c*
Australia in *Griffiths v Kerkemeyer* (1977) 15 ALR 387.

　　I would allow the appeal on this point and remit the action to the Queen's Bench
Division for damages to be assessed accordingly. We are not called on in this appeal
to lay down any rules as to the manner in which such damages should be calculated;
this must be left to the courts to work out in conformity with established principles.'

In the first paragraph of this passage Lord Wilberforce is doing no more than pointing *d*
out that the amounts recovered will depend on the facts of each case. In the second
paragraph he recognises that in certain circumstances there may be duplication of
recovery where the claim is made after the death of the deceased. In the third paragraph
he expressly approves the deduction principle formulated in *Skelton v Collins*. This
justification for the deduction of 'the victim's probable living expenses' creates two
difficulties; first he appears to be saying that damages for loss of earnings in the lost years *e*
are not compensation to the victim for his economic loss in the ordinary sense but
compensation for depriving him of the chance of making provision for others, be they
dependants, charities or others. When this passage is coupled with the earlier passage that
no distinction is to be drawn between men in different family situations, and with the
approval of *Skelton v Collins*, this is quite clearly the 'savings only' solution. The second *f*
difficulty is created by the assertion that the deduction has 'the additional merit of
bringing awards under this head into line with what could be recovered under the Fatal
Accidents Acts'. This cannot be reconciled with the 'savings only' solution.

　　Lord Salmon in his speech said ([1979] 1 All ER 774 at 783–784, [1980] AC 136 at
153–154:

　　'The clear intention of Parliament in passing those Acts appears to have been to *g*
deal with the all too frequent cases in which, as a result of someone else's negligence,
a man suffered injuries which incapacitated him from earning and caused his death
before he could obtain any damages from the tortfeasor to compensate him for the
loss of the money he would have earned but for the tort. The policy of the Act was,
in my opinion, clearly to put that man's dependants, as far as possible, in the same
financial position as they would have been in if the breadwinner had lived long *h*
enough to obtain judgment against the tortfeasor. In my opinion, Parliament
correctly assumed that, had the deceased lived, he would have recovered judgment
for a lump sum by way of damages as compensation for the money he would have
earned but for the tortfeasor's negligence, and that these damages would have
included the money which the deceased would have earned during "the lost years".
Otherwise, Parliament would, surely, have made it plain that no judgment in favour *j*
of the deceased or settlement of his claim could bar a claim by his dependants under
the Fatal Accidents Acts; I certainly do not think that Parliament would have used
the language which it did use in s 1 of those Acts. The common law does not award
a plaintiff annual payments in respect of the money he would have earned during
the rest of his life had it not been for the defendant's negligence. It awards him a

lump sum by way of damages to compensate him for all the money he has probably
been prevented from earning because of the defendant's negligence. The common
law takes many factors into account in assessing those damages, eg that the lump
sum awarded will yield interest in the future, that the plaintiff might have lost his
job in any event, that he might have been incapacitated or killed in some other way,
so that the defendant's negligence may not necessarily have been the cause of his
loss of earnings. One of the factors which, however, the common law does not, in
my view, take into account for the purpose of reducing damages is that some of the
earnings, lost as a result of the defendant's negligence, would have been earned in
the "lost years". Damages for the loss of earnings during the "lost years" should be
assessed justly and with moderation. There can be no question of these damages
being fixed at any conventional figure because damages for pecuniary loss, unlike
damages for pain and suffering can be naturally measured in money. The amount
awarded will depend on the facts of each particular case. They may vary greatly
from case to case. At one end of the scale, the claim may be made on behalf of a
young child or his estate. In such a case, the lost earnings are so unpredictable and
speculative that only a minimal sum could properly be awarded. At the other end
of the scale, the claim may be made by a man in the prime of life or, if he dies, on
behalf of his estate; if he has been in good employment for years with every prospect
of continuing to earn a good living until he reaches the age of retirement, after all
the relevant factors have been taken into account, the damages recoverable from the
defendant are likely to be substantial. The amount will, of course, vary, sometimes
greatly, according to the particular facts of the case under consideration. I recognise
that there is a comparatively small minority of cases in which a man whose life, and
therefore his capacity to earn, is cut short, dies intestate with no dependants or has
made a will excluding dependants, leaving all his money to others or to charity.
Subject to the family inheritance legislation, a man may do what he likes with his
own. Certainly, the law can make no distinction between the plaintiff who looks
after dependants and the plaintiff who does not, in assessing the damages recoverable
to compensate the plaintiff for the money he would have earned during the "lost
years" but for the defendant's negligence. On his death those damages will pass to
whomsoever benefits under his will or on an intestacy. I think that in assessing
those damages there should be deducted the plaintiff's own living expenses which
he would have expended during the "lost years" because these clearly can never
constitute any part of his estate. The assessment of these living expenses may, no
doubt, sometimes present difficulties, but certainly no difficulties which would be
insuperable for the courts to resolve, as they always have done in assessing
dependency under the Fatal Accidents Acts.'

The justification of the deduction on the ground that the living expenses could never
form part of the estate is support for the 'savings only' solution, but again is quite
irreconcilable with what Lord Salmon has said earlier in the passage I have quoted.

Lord Edmund-Davies said ([1979] 1 All ER 774 at 791, [1980] AC 136 at 162):

'I prefer not to complicate the problem by considering the impact on dependants
of an award to a living plaintiff whose life has been shortened, as to which see s 1(1)
of the Fatal Accidents Act 1976, Murray v Shuter [1975] 3 All ER 375, [1976] QB
972 and McCann v Sheppard [1973] 2 All ER 881, [1973] 1 WLR 540, for our present
consideration relates solely to the personal entitlement of an injured party to recover
damages for the "lost years", regardless both of whether he has dependants and of
whether or not he would (if he has any) make provision for them out of any
compensation awarded to him or his estate. With respect, it appears to me simply
not right to say that when a man's working life and his natural life are each
shortened by the wrongful act of another, he must be regarded as having lost
nothing by the deprivation of the prospect of future earnings for some period
extending beyond the anticipated date of his premature death.'

Later in his speech he said ([1979] 1 All ER 774 at 792, [1980] AC 136 at 163):

'This House lacks the material to enable it to estimate what would be proper   *a*
compensation for the "lost years", and the task will have to be remitted to the
Queen's Bench Division for determination. It is likely to prove a task of some
difficulty, though (contrary to the view expressed by Willmer LJ in *Oliver v Ashman*
[1961] 3 All ER 323 at 338, [1962] 2 QB 210 at 240) the lost earnings are not "far
too speculative to be capable of assessment by any court of law". The only guidance   *b*
I can proffer is that, in reaching their final figure, the court should make what it
regards as a suitable deduction for the total sum which Mr Pickett would have been
likely to expend on himself during the "lost years". This calculation, too, is by no
means free from difficulty, but a similar task has to be performed regularly in cases
brought under the Fatal Accidents Act. And in Scotland the court is required, in
such cases as the present, to "have regard to any diminution . . . by virtue of expenses
which in the opinion of the court the pursuer . . . would reasonably have incurred   *c*
. . . by way of living expenses" (see the Damages (Scotland) Act 1976, s 9(2)(c)). For,
macabre though it be to say so, it does not seem right that, in respect of those years
when ex hypothesi the injured plaintiff's personal expenses will be nil, he should
recover more than that which would have remained at his disposal after such
expenses had been discharged.'
                                                                                        d

In this last passage I understand Lord Edmund-Davies to assume that the deduction will
be different from that made in a Fatal Accidents Act case, but although the assessment
may be a difficult task it is similar to that performed in Fatal Accidents Act cases. Lord
Russell, dissenting, said ([1979] 1 All ER 774 at 794, [1980] AC 136 at 166):

'It has, my Lords, correctly been remarked that though in the instant case the   *e*
plaintiff has dependants who (it was assumed) were barred from a Fatal Accidents
Act claim by the judgment, the question of the lost years must be answered in the
same way in a case of a plaintiff without dependants. But the solution proposed,
involving as it does deduction from lost years' earnings of the plaintiff's living
expenses, appears to me to attempt to splice two quite separate types of claim: a
claim by dependants for dependency and a claim by the plaintiff himself. If a   *f*
plaintiff is to be entitled to claim in respect of lost years' earnings, why should his
claim be reduced by what, no doubt enjoyably, he would have spent on himself?
Why should he be limited to that which he would have given away either inter
vivos or by will or intestacy? The answer is I suppose that being dead he has no
living expenses. But this, in the current phrase, is where we came in. I find it
difficult in point of principle to accept as part of compensatory damages a sum based   *g*
on that for which, had he lived longer, he would ex hypothesi have had no use save
to give it away. The comment that the law is not concerned with what a plaintiff
does with the damages to which he is entitled is of course sound, but it assumes
entitlement to the damages, which is the very question. My Lords, these problems
have been debated by the Law Commission. An attempt to solve them has been
made for Scotland by the Damages (Scotland) Act 1976. My own opinion is that the   *h*
solution is a matter whose complications are more suited for legislation than judicial
decision by this House in the manner proposed. Your Lordships being unanimously
of opinion on this problem to the contrary, I have not felt it necessary to argue the
point in great detail.'

Two things emerge from this speech. Firstly, that Lord Russell, like the other members   *j*
of the House, was satisfied that the question of the lost years must be answered in the
same way in a case of a plaintiff without dependants, as for a plaintiff with dependants.
Secondly he understood that the deduction for living expenses was being made on the
'savings only' solution.

    Lord Scarman, noting the existence of the problem of double recovery, said of it that
it—

a
'appears to me unavoidable, though further argument and analysis in a case in which the point arose for decision might lead to a judicial solution which was satisfactory. But I suspect that the point will need legislation. However, if one must choose between a law which in some cases will deprive dependants of their dependency through the chances of life and litigation and a law which, in avoiding such a deprival, will entail in some cases both the estate and the dependants recovering damages in respect of the lost years, I find the latter to be the lesser evil.

b
I conclude, therefore, that damages for loss of future earnings (and future expectations) during the lost years are recoverable, where the facts are such that the loss is not too remote to be measurable. But I think, for the reasons given by Lord Wilberforce, Lord Salmon and Lord Edmund Davies, that a plaintiff (or his estate) should not recover more than that which would have remained at his disposal after meeting his own living expenses.'

c
(See [1979] 1 All ER 774 at 798, [1980] AC 136 at 170–171.)

The House of Lords returned to this problem in *Gammell v Wilson, Furness v B & S Massey Ltd* [1981] 1 All ER 578, [1982] AC 27. There the main issue was whether s 1(2)(c) of the Law Reform (Miscellaneous Provisions) Act 1934 operated to prevent recovery by the estate of any sum in respect of earnings in the lost years. The House also had to

d
consider the assessment of damages. Two cases were before the House. In *Gammell's* case the deceased was a 15-year-old gipsy and the claim was brought under the Fatal Accidents Act 1976 on behalf of his parents, and under the Law Reform Act on behalf of the estate. The young man was single, living at home, doing a bit of fruit picking and suchlike jobs, and earning some £20 a week. Mr Hytner QC, who tried the case, came to the conclusion that after deducting living expenses the young man on an average might be expected to

e
have over some £8 per week. This figure gave him a multiplicand, he applied a multiplier of 16 and the damages came out at £6,656. The Fatal Accidents Act damages were assessed at £2,000 and extinguished by the Law Reform Act award.

In the other case, *Furness v B & S Massey Ltd*, the deceased was 22 years old, single and living at home; the claim was brought by the parents on behalf of themselves under the Fatal Accidents Acts 1846 to 1959 and on behalf of the estate under the Law Reform Act.

f
The case was tried by Tudor Evans J who on the evidence before him found that the deceased was earning about £4,000 a year and he concluded that his living expenses would amount to two-thirds of his net income while living at home, but that in a few years he would move out from his home and then his living expenses would account for three-quarters of his net income. On a 16-year purchase he applied the one-third multiplicand for five years and the one-quarter multiplicand for 11 years and assessed the

g
Law Reform Act damages at £17,275. Once again this assessment extinguished the damages under the Fatal Accidents Acts, which were assessed at £2,000.

In *Gammell's* case Mr Hytner QC said that in the case of a young man of 15 he thought it right to disregard the joint expenses which are not deducted in the ordinary Fatal Accidents Act claim and deduct the whole of what he called the deceased's 'true living expenses', and it was on that basis that he reached a multiplicand of £8 per week. In the

h
Furness case Tudor Evans J said:

'. . . on the authority of *Pickett* I think that I must take into account what I estimate the deceased would have spent both in maintaining himself and on enjoying his life.'

He defined what he meant by the later in his judgment where he said:

j
'. . . in all these circumstances whilst recognising the speculative nature of the calculations I value his savings out of his surplus at one-third for as long as he was at home and one-quarter thereafter.'

The Court of Appeal in *Gammell's* case [1980] 2 All ER 557, [1982] AC 27 and the House of Lords in both cases could find no error of principle in the trial judges' approaches to the problem, though they regarded the awards as very high.

After summarising the facts in *Pickett's* case, Lord Diplock said ([1981] 1 All ER 578 at 583, [1982] AC 27 at 65):

'Here was an obvious injustice which this House remedied by overruling *Oliver v Ashman* [1961] 3 All ER 323, [1962] 2 QB 210 and holding that a living plaintiff could recover damages for loss of earnings during the lost years, but that in assessing the measure of such damages there should be deducted from the total earnings the amount that he would have spent out of those earnings on his own living expenses and pleasures since these would represent an expense that would be saved in consequence of his death. In the case of a married man of middle age and of a settled pattern of life, which was the case of Mr Pickett, the effect of this deduction is to leave a net figure which represents the amount which he would have spent on providing for his wife and any other dependants, together with any savings that he might set aside out of his income. If one ignores the savings element, which in most cases would be likely to be small, this net figure is substantially the same as the damages that would have been recoverable by the widow under the Fatal Accidents Act; it represents the dependency. So, in the particular case of Mr Pickett's widow the result was to do substantial justice. My Lords, if the only victims of fatal accidents were middle-aged married men in steady employment living their lives according to a well-settled pattern that would have been unlikely to change if they had lived on uninjured, the assessment of damages for loss of earnings during the lost years may not involve what can only be matters of purest speculation. But, as the instant appeals demonstrate and so do other unreported cases which have been drawn to the attention of this House, in cases where there is no such settled pattern (and this must be so in a high proportion of cases of fatal injuries) the judge is faced with a task that is so purely one of guesswork that it is not susceptible of solution by the judicial process. Guesses by different judges are likely to differ widely, yet no one can say that one is right and another wrong.'

Lord Edmund-Davies said of the award in *Furness's* case ([1981] 1 All ER 578 at 588, [1982] AC 27 at 71):

'... I see no error in principle, and, while counselling moderation in assessing such claims so as to reflect the high degree of speculation inevitably involved, I am not prepared to hold that the award calls for adjustment.'

Lord Fraser said ([1981] 1 All ER 578 at 588, [1982] AC 27 at 71–72):

'... it is, I think, quite impossible to take the further step of making a reasonable estimate of the free balance that would have been available above the cost of maintaining himself throughout the "lost years", and the amount of that free balance is the relevant figure for calculating damages.'

Lord Scarman said ([1981] 1 All ER 578 at 593, [1982] AC 27 at 78–79):

'The problem in these cases, which has troubled the judges since the decision in *Pickett's* case has been the calculation of the annual loss before applying the multiplier (ie the estimated number of lost working years accepted as reasonable in the case). My Lords, the principle has been settled by the speeches in this House in *Pickett's* case. The loss to the estate is what the deceased would have been likely to have available to save, spend, or distribute after meeting the cost of his living at a standard which his job and career prospects at time of death would suggest he was reasonably likely to achieve. Subtle mathematical calculations, based as they must be on events or contingencies of a life which he will not live, are out of place; the judge must make the best estimate based on the known facts and his prospects at time of death. The principle was stated by Lord Wilberforce in *Pickett's* case [1979] 1 All ER 774 at 781–782, [1980] AC 136 at 150–151 ...'

I digress for a moment to point out that in *Gammell* the House of Lords invited

Parliament to legislate in order to overcome the difficulties created in those two cases and
a as a result by s 4(2) of the Administration of Justice Act 1982, s 1(2)(*a*) of the Law Reform
Act has been amended to read:

'(*a*) shall not include—(i) any exemplary damages; (ii) any damages for loss of
income in respect of any period after that person's death.'

This has been the law in respect of deaths occurring after the commencement of the
b 1982 Act on 1 January 1983. So that the problem which has arisen in the present cases
will not arise again except in those cases where death has occurred before 1 January 1983,
and to a much more limited extent remains in cases where a live plaintiff is claiming in
respect of loss of earnings during a period of time that his working life has been shortened
by the tort of the defendant.

I return to the two decisions in the House of Lords, *Pickett v British Rail Engineering Ltd*
c [1979] 1 All ER 774, [1980] AC 136 and *Gammell v Wilson, Furness v B & S Massey Ltd*
[1981] 1 All ER 578, [1982] AC 27. In my judgment three principles emerge.

(1) The ingredients that go to make up 'living expenses' are the same whether the
victim be young or old, single or married, with or without dependants.

(2) The sum to be deducted as living expenses is the proportion of the victims's net
earnings that he spends to maintain himself at the standard of life appropriate to his case.

d (3) Any sums expended to maintain or benefit others do not form part of the victim's
living expenses and are not to be deducted from the net earnings.

The second and third principles, apparently straightforward enough, in fact contain a
hidden difficulty. The difficulty is well exemplified by the example given by counsel for
the defendants in the Cole case in argument. A bachelor is living in a flat which is costing
him £2,000 per annum for rent, rates, light and heat. This expenditure undoubtedly
e forms part of his living expenses. He marries a wife who moves in to live in the flat, and,
for this example, is not herself earning or providing money to the family fund. Her
presence makes no difference whatsoever to the cost of the flat. I find it quite impossible
to say that this expenditure has suddenly ceased to be part of the husband's living
expenses, yet the Fatal Accidents Act solution would lead inexorably to that result, for if
one is considering the wife's dependency she is dependent to the value of the whole cost
f of the flat. In contrast I can see the attraction of asserting that the full cost of the flat
remains part of the husband's living expenses, but I do not think that that result is
compatible with the third principle.

The cost of the flat which had been expenditure solely for the benefit of the husband
has now become expenditure for the joint benefit of husband and wife; this presents a
simple compromise, namely that half the cost should be looked on as referable to each of
g them. I recognise that it may be argued that it is no more logical to assert that this head
of living expense has been halved by marriage, rather than altogether extinguished, but
I do not think that this is right because to consider it extinguished involves a change in
principle, namely that the cost of housing does not form part of a person's living expenses,
whereas to consider it halved does not involve such a change but only an alteration in the
amount of money allocated to it. It also confirms the old adage that 'two can live cheaper
h than one'.

The items of living expenses which are shared in practice will be found to be limited
to the cost of housing, that is to say rent or mortgage interest, rates, heating, electricity
and gas, the cost of running a motor car, the telephone and I suppose the television
licence. Further, it seems to me that as the numbers of persons provided for out of the
victim's net earnings increase, so must the amount to be allocated as being his share of
j those items fall. Therefore, in the present case, where the households consisted of four
persons, one-quarter of the cost of the joint items should be deducted. In practice this
may result in the total deduction not being very much greater than that made for the
purposes of the Fatal Accidents Act.

I think one can say in relation to a man's net earnings that any proportion thereof that
he saves or spends exclusively for the maintenance or benefit of others does not form part

of his living expenses. Any proportion that he spends exclusively on himself does. In cases where there is a proportion of the earnings expended on what may conveniently be *a* called shared living expenses, a pro rata part of that proportion should be allocated for deduction. In rejecting the straight Fatal Accidents Act solution I realise that I am differing from a considerable body of judicial opinion in the Queen's Bench Division, including the two judges in the present cases. I also reject the 'savings only' solution because I do not think it possible to say that money spent on others should be reckoned as part of a man's living expenses in the sense required by the House of Lords.   *b*

This leaves the 'surplus funds' solution propounded by Webster J in *White v London Transport Executive* [1982] 1 All ER 410, [1982] QB 489. In that case the deceased was a single man aged 25 living with his mother. He was killed in the course of his employment in December 1976, and the trial was in July 1981. It was agreed that for 4½ years to the date of trial net earnings lost were £21,800 and that the continuing loss was at the rate of £6,000 pa. Webster J said ([1982] 1 All ER 410 at 418, [1982] QB 489 at 499):   *c*

> '. . . it seems to me that the thing, the loss of which has to be measured, is the amenity of earning more than is needed to live a reasonably satisfying and potentially enjoyable life, taking into account in each case the particular circumstances of life of the particular deceased person. Thus, for example, in this day and age the ordinary working man's life would not be regarded by him as reasonably satisfactory and *d* potentially enjoyable if he could not afford a short holiday, a modest amount of entertainment and social activity and, depending on his particular circumstances, a car. And it seems to me, therefore, that the amenity which he is deemed to have lost is the difference between what would be the cost of maintaining himself and providing those facilities, and his prospective net earnings; and in the cost of maintaining himself I include the cost of his housing, heating, food, clothing, *e* necessary travelling and insurances and things of that kind, if relevant. Although it seems to me in some ways artificial to do so, for reasons I have already given it appears that he is to be treated for this purpose as an eternally single man, on the principle, I suppose, that the money he in fact spends on his family, if he has one, or if it is likely that he will have one, is money which would be available after making provision for all the matters I have referred to, to be spent in other ways if he so *f* desired, that is to say, if he were to prefer to spend it in other ways rather than to have a family. If he is to be treated in this way it must follow that, although the House of Lords, as I have mentioned, said that the award of damages should be moderate, his notional surplus must be large enough to cover at least a not insubstantial part of the cost of maintaining a family, for although in the case of a man in the deceased's circumstances it can be regarded as probable in normal *g* circumstances that his wife, if he were to marry, would do some paid work from time to time, it cannot be supposed that she alone would pay for the housing and maintenance of the children.'

Later in his judgment Webster J said ([1982] 1 All ER 410 at 418–419, [1982] QB 489 at 500):   *h*

> 'If I am to make an award which covers the whole period I must, therefore, do so in some other way, and in particular in some way which involves the drawing and application of reasonable inferences, including inferences as to what would be likely or most likely to have happened to the deceased if any of the relevant circumstances existing at his death were unlikely to remain constant. The first inference which needs to be drawn, as it seems to me, if my definition of the loss in question is *j* correct, is whether, and, if so, broadly to what extent, the deceased's prospective earnings matched the circumstances into which he had been born and was living. Because if a man born and brought up in very comfortable circumstances is a relatively low earner his earnings might not even be sufficient to meet his reasonable needs, let alone to exceed them, while, on the other hand, a man with relatively

modest demands, earning relatively a lot of money compared with that earned by most men in his circumstances, would be likely to have a large surplus. Applying that test first therefore to the present case, I find on the available evidence that the deceased's earnings were reasonably appropriate for a man in his circumstances, giving him neither more nor less than an average surplus expressed as a percentage of his net earnings.'

The judge then inferred that the available surplus would be one-third of the net income for five years until he left home and one-quarter for the remaining ten years' purchase, much as Tudor Evans J had done in the *Furness* case. Save that I do not agree that the deceased is to be treated as an eternally single man and bearing in mind what I have said about joint expenditure and that the resulting awards were thought in *Gammell's* case to be very high, this seems to me an acceptable way of arriving at the deduction to be made in cases of young persons. The reason for supporting this high rate of deduction in cases such as *White*, *Gammell* and *Furness*, is that the future is speculative and allowance has to be made for the fact that a man may never marry, may never save a farthing, may never support anybody; but when one is faced with the position in *Pickett* or in the present two cases, the position is entirely different. That which was speculative in *Gammell* to a very high degree is not speculative at all; that which is not to be deducted can be seen with reasonable clarity and, as one would expect, a very much smaller part of the net earnings will fall to be deducted.

We were asked by counsel for the defendants in the *Cole* case and counsel for the defendants in the *Harris* case to give guidance, if we could, as to what proportion of the net earnings in the lost years should be deducted for the purpose of the Law Reform Act claim. Regretfully, I find it impossible to do this because so much depends on the amount of the joint expenditure and the number of persons among whom it is to be divided; but in general, according to the circumstances, it seems to me that the proportion will be greater than the percentage used for calculating the dependency under the Fatal Accidents Act.

What is to be done in the present two cases? As I am clear that the judges have made the Law Reform Act assessment on an erroneous principle, the appeals must be allowed. We have no material on which we can make the assessment ourselves; therefore the cases will have to go back for reassessment unless, as I hope, the parties can agree what the figures should be in these two cases. As I have said earlier in this judgment, it may well be that the result will not have any drastic effect on the double recovery that has occurred in the *Harris* case, and nor will there be any great reduction in the amount of the award in the *Cole* case.

ROBERT GOFF LJ. I agree.

STEPHENSON LJ. I agree. The judgment of O'Connor LJ, with which Robert Goff LJ and I agree, has been handed down; the appeals will be allowed and the order will be made as proposed by O'Connor LJ.

Appeals allowed. Leave to appeal to the House of Lords refused.

Solicitors: *Edward Lewis & Co* (for the defendants in the Harris case); *Romain Coleman & Co*, Walthamstow (for the plaintiff in the Harris case); *Hill & Perks*, Norwich (for the defendants in the Cole case); *Daynes Chittock & Back*, Norwich (for the plaintiffs in the Cole case).

Diana Brahams   Barrister.

R v Marlow Justices, ex parte O'Sullivan

QUEEN'S BENCH DIVISION
ROBERT GOFF LJ AND WEBSTER J
19, 29 JULY 1983

Magistrates – Binding over – Forfeiture of recognisance – Standard of proof – Recognisance to keep peace or be of good behaviour – No conviction when recognisance entered into – Forfeiture of recognisance only liability on breach of recognisance – Application to forfeit recognisance for breach – Whether breach of recognisance to be proved according to civil or criminal standard – Magistrates' Courts Act 1980, s 120.

When a summons by the complainant against the applicant alleging various offences came on for hearing before the magistrates the applicant agreed to enter into a recognisance in the sum of £1,000 to keep the peace and be of good behaviour towards the complainant, with the result that the summons was not heard and the applicant was not convicted of any offence. The complainant subsequently applied to the magistrates to have the recognisance forfeited on the ground that the applicant had breached the condition to be of good behaviour towards the complainant. On the hearing of that application the magistrates heard evidence regarding the alleged breaches of the condition and, applying the civil standard of proof, found on the balance of probabilities that the complainant's allegations were proved. The magistrates, acting pursuant to their powers under s 120[a] of the Magistrates' Courts Act 1980, ordered the applicant to forfeit his recognisance and bound him over in the sum of £1,500 for 12 months. The applicant applied for certiorari to quash the order on the ground that in determining whether breach of the recognisance was proved the magistrates ought to have applied the criminal standard of proof, namely proof beyond reasonable doubt.

Held – Where a person entered into a recognisance to keep the peace or be of good behaviour and the only liability which he was under if a breach of the recognisance was proved was forfeiture of his recognisance, rather than being sentenced for an offence, an application to forfeit or estreat the recognisance was, both substantively and procedurally, a civil proceeding and accordingly, in determining the application, the civil standard of proof was to be applied. It followed that the magistrates had applied the correct standard of proof and that the application would therefore be refused (see p 580 j to p 581 b g h and p 582 b to d, post).

R v Southampton Justices, ex p Green [1975] 2 All ER 1073 applied.

R v Smith [1925] 1 KB 603 and *R v McGarry* (1945) 173 LT 72 distinguished.

Notes

For magistrates' jurisdiction to order a person to enter into a recognisance to keep the peace or be of good behaviour, see 29 Halsbury's Laws (4th edn) paras 402–405.

For breach of condition of a recognisance, see 11 ibid para 523.

For the Magistrates' Courts Act 1980, s 120, see 50(2) Halsbury's Statutes (3rd edn) 1546.

Cases referred to in judgment

Amand v Secretary of State for Home Affairs [1942] 2 All ER 381, [1943] AC 147, HL.

R v McGarry (1945) 173 LT 72, CCA.

R v Smith [1925] 1 KB 603, CCA.

R v Southampton Justices, ex p Green [1975] 2 All ER 1073, [1976] QB 11, [1975] 3 WLR 277, CA.

---

a   Section 120, so far as material, is set out at p 579 j to p 580 a, post

Application for judicial review

a The applicant, Dennis John O'Sullivan, applied for an order of certiorari to quash an order of the Marlow justices, sitting at the High Wycombe Magistrates' Court, made on 28 October 1983 that (1) the applicant should forfeit the sum of £1,000 for breach of a condition of a recognisance he entered into on 15 July 1982, to keep the peace and be of good behaviour and (2) that he should be bound over in the sum of £1,500 for 12 months. The ground on which the relief was sought was that the justices applied the
b wrong standard of proof in reaching their finding that the applicant was in breach of the condition of his recognisance to be of good behaviour because they applied the civil standard of proof, namely the balance of probabilities, whereas they should have applied the standard of proof in criminal cases, namely proof beyond reasonable doubt. The facts are set out in the judgment of the court.

c *Brendan Finucane* for the applicant.
The justices were not represented.

Cur adv vult

29 July. The following judgment of the court was delivered.

d **WEBSTER J.** This is an application for judicial review to quash an order of the Marlow justices whereby on 28 October 1982 they declared to be forfeited recognisances in the sum of £1,000 entered into by the applicant, and ordered him to be bound over in the sum of £1,500 for a period of 12 months.

The application comes before this court in the following circumstances. On 7 June 1982 the complainant, Mr Higgins, issued a summons against the applicant in the
e Marlow Magistrates' Court, alleging various matters of complaint against him. When the summons came on for hearing before the Marlow justices, sitting at the High Wycombe Magistrates' Court, on 15 July, the applicant agreed to enter into a recognisance, without sureties, to keep the peace or to be of good behaviour towards the complainant, in the sum of £1,000, for a period of 12 months, under s 115(1) of the Magistrates' Courts Act 1980. In those circumstances, the complainant's summons was not heard.

f On 3 September 1982 the complainant issued a summons alleging that the applicant had not been of good behaviour towards him in that on 30 August he had damaged the complainant's home and the complainant's car, and summonsed the applicant to appear to show cause why the recognisance in the sum of £1,000 should not be forfeited. The summons of 3 September was heard on 28 October when the applicant denied the allegations. Evidence was given and the justices, having retired, returned to court, stated
g that they found the allegations to have been proved on a balance of probabilities and ordered the applicant to forfeit the sum of £1,000 and to be bound over in the sum of £1,500 for a period of 12 months.

The short point that arises on this application is whether the justices rightly applied the civil burden of proof in determining those allegations or whether, as counsel for the applicant contends, they ought to have applied the criminal standard of proof.

h The justices' order of 28 October was, or purported to be, made pursuant to their powers under s 120(1) and (2) of the Magistrates' Courts Act 1980. Those subsections provide as follows:

'(1) Where a recognizance to keep the peace or to be of good behaviour has been entered into before a magistrates' court or any recognizance is conditioned for the
j appearance of a person before a magistrates' court or for his doing any other thing connected with a proceeding before a magistrates' court, and the recognizance appears to the court to be forfeited, the court may, subject to subsection (2) below, declare the recognizance to be forfeited and adjudge the persons bound thereby, whether as principal or sureties, or any of them, to pay the sum in which they are respectively bound.

(2) Where a recognizance is conditioned to keep the peace or to be of good behaviour, the court shall not declare it forfeited except by order made on complaint.'

The authorities relied on by the applicant in support of the contention that the justices ought to have applied the criminal standard of proof were *R v Smith* [1925] 1 KB 603 and *R v McGarry* (1945) 173 LT 72.

In *R v Smith* the appellant, having been convicted on his own confession of stealing a motor car, was discharged conditionally on his entering into a recognisance of £50 to be of good behaviour for two years. According to the statement of facts contained in that report, the appellant was conditionally discharged under the Probation of Offenders Act 1907 (presumably under s 1(2) of that Act), which empowered the court, on his conviction, in lieu of imposing a sentence of imprisonment on him, to discharge him conditionally on his entering into a recognisance, with or without sureties, to be of good behaviour and to appear for sentence when called on at any time during such period, not exceeding three years, as might be specified in the order. No reference to that Act was made, however, in the judgment of the court delivered by Salter J; and it seems to us that the same order could have been made under the common law to bind over, which is preserved for the Crown Court by the Courts Act 1971, s 6(4)(*b*), in which the power is described as—

'the release, after respite of judgment, of a convicted person on recognizance to come up for judgment if called on, but meanwhile to be of good behaviour . . .'

In *R v Smith* the appellant, having been conditionally bound over, was later brought up for sentence on an allegation that he had broken his recognisance; and on the footing that he had done so, he was sentenced to 18 months' imprisonment with hard labour. He appealed to the Court of Criminal Appeal against that sentence on the ground that it was not proved that he had broken his recognisance.

The first question that arose was whether such an appeal lay to the court. The court held that it did. Salter J said (at 605):

'Where the defendant appeals against his sentence on the ground that he has not broken his recognisance, he is entitled to appeal to this Court, by leave of this Court, against the whole of his sentence.'

The second question was whether it had been properly proved that he had broken his recognisance. As to that question, Salter J said (at 606):

'Where a defendant is brought up on an allegation that he has broken his recognisance, he cannot properly be sentenced unless that allegation of fact is proved, and it must be proved as any other allegation of fact is proved in a criminal court.'

R v McGarry is to the same effect as to that second question. Humphreys J, delivering the judgment of the Court of Criminal Appeal, said (173 LT 72 at 73):

'. . . we would suggest to chairmen of quarter sessions, and to others who may have to deal with such matters, that they should see that, when a man or woman is, brought up for sentence upon a charge many months or years old, those facts are proved just as they would be proved if the allegation were the commission of a crime; because it is the justification, and the only justification, for passing a serious sentence, as was done in this case, of 12 months' imprisonment upon one of His Majesty's subjects.'

These two decisions are clear authority for the proposition that the criminal standard of proof must be applied in determining whether a person is liable to be sentenced for an offence on conviction of which he entered into a recognisance to be of good behaviour, on the ground that he has breached that recognisance.

But in our view those decisions do not apply to this case. In each of those cases, the
a breach of the recognisance rendered the appellant liable to be sentenced for the offence
for which he had been convicted when he entered into that recognisance; whereas, in
this case, the only liability of the applicant, if the breach of the recognisance was proved,
was the forfeiture of his recognisance. In our view, the proceedings which put in issue
that liability are, for two reasons, to be regarded as civil, not criminal, proceedings, to
which the civil, not criminal, standard of proof applies.

b The first of those two reasons is that, in our view, proceedings for the forfeiture or
estreatment of a recognisance are to be regarded as civil, not criminal, proceedings.

The Court of Appeal so decided in R v Southampton Justices, ex p Green [1975] 2 All ER
1073, [1976] QB 11, in which case the applicant's husband was charged with offences
relating to the importation of cannabis. He was released on bail on terms that he should
himself enter into recognisance of £500 and provide two sureties in the sum of £3,000
c and £1,000, and the applicant was accepted as the surety in the sum of £3,000. When he
was due to come before the justices for committal for trial, the applicant's husband did
not surrender to his bail. The Customs authorities issued a summons against the applicant
and the other surety for forfeiture of their recognisances under s 96(1) of the Magistrates'
Courts Act 1952, which was in precisely the same terms as s 120(1) of the 1980 Act. The
Divisional Court refused the applicant leave to apply for an order of certiorari and, on
d her motion for leave in the Court of Appeal, a preliminary point was raised on behalf of
the prosecuting authority whether the forfeiture summons arose out of a 'criminal cause
or matter' so that, if it did, any appeal from the Divisional Court should have been to the
House of Lords and not to the Court of Appeal. The Court of Appeal held that a
recognisance was in the nature of a bond, a failure to fulfil which gave rise to a civil debt,
differing only in the method of enforcement. Accordingly, an appeal from the justices'
e decision to estreat a recognisance was not an appeal in a criminal cause or matter.

Lord Denning MR said ([1975] 2 All ER 1073 at 1076, [1976] QB 11 at 15–16):

'The words "criminal cause or matter" were considered by the House of Lords in
Amand v Secretary of State for Home Affairs [1942] 2 All ER 381 at 385, [1943] AC 147
at 156. Viscount Simon LC said: "If the matter is one the direct outcome of which
may be trial of the applicant and his possible punishment for an alleged offence by a
f court claiming jurisdiction to do so, the matter is criminal." Apply that test to an
application to estreat a recognisance. The outcome is not a "trial" of the surety.
There is no "possible punishment" of the surety for an "offence". A recognisance is
in the nature of a bond. A failure to fulfil it gives rise to a civil debt. It is different
from the ordinary kind of civil debt, because the enforcement is different. It is
enforceable like a fine . . . But that method of enforcement does not alter the nature
g of the debt. It is simply a civil debt on a bond and as such it is not a criminal cause
or matter.'

With that judgment Browne LJ and Brightman J agreed.

In our view, precisely the same considerations apply to an application to estreat the
recognisance of a person bound over to keep the peace or to be of good behaviour as to an
h application to estreat the recognisance of a surety. And, in our view, the application
before the justices in this case was no more a criminal cause or matter than was the
application to the Southampton justices.

Our second reason for concluding that the proceedings are civil, not criminal, goes not
to the substance of those proceedings, as does our first reason, but to their form.

We have already cited the provisions of s 120(2) of the 1980 Act, which provides that
j a recognisance conditioned to keep the peace or be of good behaviour shall not be
declared forfeited 'except by order made on complaint'. As we understand it, although
the words 'complaint and information' are often used interchangeably, as if they were
synonymous, a complaint is ordinarily the form which originates a civil process, so that
proceedings begun by complaint are, prima facie, civil not criminal proceedings. Section
50 of the Magistrates' Courts Act 1980 reinforces our understanding of the meaning of

those words and, at the same time, provides for the fact that they are, none the less, sometimes used as if they were synonymous. That section provides:

> 'In any enactment conferring power on a magistrates' court to deal with an offence, or to issue a summons or warrant against a person suspected of an offence, on the complaint of any person, for references to a complaint there shall be substituted references to an information.'

We conclude, therefore, that an application to forfeit or estreat a recognisance constitutes, both substantively and procedurely, a civil proceeding in which the appropriate standard of proof is the civil, not the criminal, standard.

We note that, if this conclusion is correct, there is if not an error then at least a misleading elision in 11 Halsbury's Laws (4th edn) para 523 where, in reliance on *R v Smith* and *R v McGarry*, it is said that a breach of recognisance must be proved as any other allegation of fact is proved in a criminal court, without distinguishing, as we have done, between a breach of recognisance which renders a person liable to a sentence of imprisonment for an offence of which he was convicted when he entered into the recognisance and a breach of recognisance which renders him liable only to forfeiture of the recognisance.

For all these reasons, we dismiss this application.

Certiorari refused.

Solicitors: *Ferris & Evans*, Ealing (for the applicant).

N P Metcalfe Esq   Barrister.

Whittaker and another v Campbell

QUEEN'S BENCH DIVISION
ROBERT GOFF LJ AND GLIDEWELL J
3, 20 MAY 1983

Road traffic – Taking vehicle without authority – Consent – Taking and driving away without owner's consent – Consent obtained by fraudulent misrepresentation – Whether consent vitiated – Theft Act 1968, s 12(1).

The appellant, who did not have a driving licence of his own, found one belonging to another person. In order to hire a van, he showed the licence to R, a director of a vehicle hire firm, and represented to him that he was the person named in the licence. R, believing that he was that person, agreed to hire the van to him. The appellant paid the hire charge and drove the van away. The van was later stopped by the police, who discovered the appellant's true identity. He was charged with, and subsequently convicted by the justices of, taking a conveyance for his own use without the consent of the owner or other lawful authority, contrary to s 12(1)[a] of the Theft Act 1968. He appealed against conviction, contending that he could not be guilty of the offence because R had consented to hire the van to him. The Crown Court dismissed the appeal on the ground that, as the evidence showed that R would not have parted with possession of the van if he had known the true position, the appellant's fraudulent misrepresentation had vitiated R's consent to the hire transaction. The appellant appealed to the High Court.

---

a   Section 12(1), so far as material, provides: '. . . a person shall be guilty of an offence if, without having the consent of the owner or other lawful authority, he takes any conveyance for his own or another's use . . .'

a
Held – On the true construction of s 12(1) of the 1968 Act the consent of the owner of a motor vehicle to its use by another was not vitiated where that consent was obtained by fraud. It followed that the appellant's fraudulent misrepresentation did not have the effect of vitiating R's consent. Since no offence under s 12(1) had been committed, the appeal would be allowed and the conviction quashed (see p 587 *d e* and p 588 *e* to *h*, post).

R v Peart [1970] 2 All ER 823 considered.

b
Notes
For the taking of motor vehicles without consent or lawful authority, see 33 Halsbury's Laws (3rd edn) 631, para 1065, and for cases on the subject, see 45 Digest (Repl) 103–104, *331–340*.

For the Theft Act 1968, s 12, see 8 Halsbury's Statutes (3rd edn) 790.

c
Cases referred to in judgment
Centrovincial Estates plc v Merchant Investors Assurance Co Ltd (1983) Times, 8 March, [1983] CA Bound Transcript 103.
Ingram v Little [1960] 3 All ER 332, [1961] 1 QB 31, [1960] 3 WLR 504, CA.
Lewis v Averay [1971] 3 All ER 907, [1972] 1 QB 198, [1971] 3 WLR 603, CA.
R v Peart [1970] 2 All ER 823, [1970] 2 QB 672, [1970] 3 WLR 63, CA.

d
R v Tolson (1889) 23 QBD 168, [1886–90] All ER Rep 26, CCR.

Cases also cited
McNight v Davies [1974] RTR 4, DC.
Phillips v Brooks Ltd [1919] 2 KB 243.
R v Hogdon [1962] Crim LR 563, CCA.

e
R v Phipps (1970) 54 Cr App R 300, CA.

Case stated
On 4 March 1982 the appellants, Wilson Coglan Whittaker and Stewart Whittaker, were convicted by the justices for the petty sessional division of Teesdale and Wear Valley, sitting as a magistrates' court at Bishop Auckland, of a joint offence committed on 16

f
October 1981 of taking a conveyance for their own use without the consent of the owner or other lawful authority, contrary to s 12(1) of the Theft Act 1968. They appealed to the Crown Court at Durham against conviction. His Honour Judge Hewitt and justices dismissed the appeal on 24 May 1982 but, at the request of the appellants, stated a case for the opinion of the High Court. The questions for the opinion of the High Court were: (1) whether in law the de facto consent to take a conveyance, namely a motor

g
vehicle, given by the vehicle owner to a person hiring that vehicle was vitiated by reason of its being induced by the false representations of the person hiring the vehicle as to his identity and the holding of a full driving licence, so that the person taking the vehicle under the contract of hire was guilty of taking a conveyance without the owner's consent or other lawful authority, contrary to s 12(1) of the Theft Act 1968; (2) whether, on the facts found by the judge and having regard to the cases cited, the Crown Court was

h
wrong in law in rejecting the appeals of the appellants. The facts are set out in the judgment of the court.

John Bassett for the appellants.
Eric Elliott for the respondent.

Cur adv vult

j
20 May. The following judgment of the court was delivered.

ROBERT GOFF LJ. There is before the court a case stated by the Crown Court at Durham, when sitting on appeal from Durham justices of the petty sessional division of Teesdale and Wear Valley. The case raises for decision a point of construction of s 12(1) of the Theft Act 1968, relating to the meaning of the words 'without having the consent of the owner' in the offence which is committed under that subsection if a person, without having the consent of the owner or other lawful authority, takes any conveyance for his own or another's use. The appellants were also charged with a number of other offences arising out of the same facts, to which they pleaded guilty.

The justices convicted the two appellants of such an offence, committed on 16 October 1981. Appeals against these convictions were heard by the Crown Court at Durham on 24 May 1982. The facts were not in dispute, and the appeals proceeded on a question of law only. The following agreed facts are taken from the case:

'(1) In about June 1981 the Appellants, who are brothers aged 27 and 25 years, and who live in St. Helens Auckland, County Durham, had an opportunity to obtain some coal at an advantageous price from a private colliery quite lawfully. (2) In order to remove the said coal the Appellants required their own means of transport. At all material times, the Appellant Wilson Coglan Whittaker had no driving licence whatsoever and the Appellant Stewart Whittaker had a provisional licence only and neither Appellant had a vehicle of his own. (3) In about June 1981 the Appellants came into possession of a full driving licence belonging to one Derek Dunn. The Appellant Wilson Coglan Whittaker said that he had found it near Mr Dunn's place of work. The Appellants decided to use the licence to hire a van to remove the coal (4) On the 24th June 1981 the Appellants went to a local vehicle hire firm called Stangarths Limited in Leazes Lane, St Helens Auckland and there hired from a director, one Duncan Stuart Robson, aged 23 years, a Ford Transit van for a day. The Appellant Wilson Coglan Whittaker represented himself as being Derek Dunn of the address shown on the driving licence which he produced to Mr Robson. The same Appellant also signed the name "D Dunn" on the hire agreement form No. 0309 . . . The appropriate hire charge was paid by the Appellants and the Appellant Wilson Coglan Whittaker drove away the Ford Transit van. (5) On five subsequent occasions the Appellants did the same thing—on the 2nd July 1981, 16th July 1981, 22nd July 1981, 8th October and the 15th October 1981, on each occasion the Appellant Wilson Coglan Whittaker signing the hire agreement [form] "D Dunn" . . . On the later occasions the driving licence was not produced to Mr Robson who acted in reliance of what had happened on earlier occasions. On each occasion the Appellants paid the appropriate hire charge. (6) On the 16th October 1981, the Appellant Stewart Whittaker was driving the hire van when it was stopped and checked by Police Officers. The van was found to have an incorrect excise licence displayed. The Appellants were questioned and their true identities were established (7) According to Mr Robson, the hire company's director, on the occasion of each hire, he was deceived by the Appellants into believing that the Appellant Wilson Coglan Whittaker was Derek Dunn and that he was the holder of a full driving licence, and had he known that that was not the case the Appellant Wilson Coglan Whittaker would not have been allowed to hire any of his (Robson's) vehicles or drive any of his vehicles (8) By summonses dated the 21st January 1982 it was alleged that the Appellants jointly on the 16th October 1981 without the consent of the owner or other lawful authority took a certain conveyance, namely a motor van for their own use, contrary to Section 12(1) of the Theft Act 1968. The offence alleged referred to the last occasion of hire. They were convicted by the Justices of the said offence following a submission that there was no case to answer in law. The Appellants pleaded guilty to various related road traffic offences, including driving with no licence, no insurance, no "L" plates and fraudulent use of a driving licence. The appeals related solely to the offence of taking a conveyance without the owners consent.'

Before the Crown Court it was contended by the appellants that they had the consent of the owner to take the conveyance, that consent having been given by Mr Robson to the persons with whom he was dealing, namely the appellants, and that consent not having been vitiated by the misrepresentation of Wilson Coglan Whittaker that he was in fact Derek Dunn and the holder of a full driving licence. The misrepresentations as to

identity and the holding of a full driving licence were not fundamental so as to vitiate
the consent given, but were merely misrepresentations as to the representor's attributes,
such as to render a contract voidable and not void ab initio. The mere fact that Mr
Robson would not have consented to parting with possession of the vehicle if he had
known of the true position was not conclusive against the appellants; nor was the fact
that the appellants would not be insured to drive the vehicle.

The respondent, on the other hand, contended that the appellants were guilty of the
offence because in law and in fact they did not have the consent of the vehicle owner or
other lawful authority to take the vehicle in question. Although the vehicle owner gave
his de facto consent to the appellants taking the vehicle, that consent was not a true
consent or a consent at all in law or in fact because it was vitiated by the fraudulent
misrepresentations as to identity and the holding of a full driving licence made by the
appellants which induced the owner to part with possession of his vehicle. These
misrepresentations were fundamental to the transaction in that the owner would not
have parted with possession had he known of the true position because the hirer would
not have been insured to drive the vehicle.

These arguments were repeated and developed in the submissions made by counsel
before this court. We, like the Crown Court, were referred to certain authorities, some
of which we shall consider later in this judgment. The conclusion of the Crown Court
was that the appellants' misrepresentations were fundamental in that the vehicle owner
would not have contemplated handing over the vehicle had he known the true position,
and that his consent was therefore vitiated by the fraudulent misrepresentation of the
appellants. We quote from the case:

> 'The question in the present appeals was whether the vehicle owner gave his
> consent to the Appellants taking the vehicle. In my opinion he did not. He consented
> to someone called Derek Dunn with a full driving licence taking the vehicle. I
> accordingly held that in law the Appellants were guilty of the offence under Section
> 12(1) of the Theft Act 1968.'

The following questions were stated for the opinion of the court:

> '(1) Whether in law the de facto consent to take a conveyance namely a motor
> vehicle given by the vehicle owner to a person hiring that vehicle is vitiated by
> reason of its being induced by the false representations of the person hiring the
> vehicle as to his identity and the holding of a full driving licence, so that the person
> taking the vehicle under the contract of hire is guilty of taking a conveyance without
> the owners consent or other lawful authority contrary to Section 12(1) of the Theft
> Act 1968. (2) Whether, on the facts found by me and having regard to the cases
> cited, the Crown Court was wrong in law in rejecting the appeals of the Appellants.'

We are concerned in the present case with the construction of certain words, viz
'without having the consent of the owner', in their context in a particular subsection of a
criminal statute. However, the concept of consent is relevant in many branches of the
law, including not only certain crimes but also the law of contract and the law of
property. There is, we believe, danger in assuming that the law adopts a uniform
definition of the word 'consent' in all its branches.

Furthermore there is, in our opinion, no general principle of law that fraud vitiates
consent. Let us consider this proposition first with reference to the law of contract. In
English law every valid contract presupposes an offer by one party which has been
accepted by the offeree. Plainly there can be no such acceptance unless offer and
acceptance correspond, so the offer can only be accepted by the offeree, the acceptance
must relate to the same subject matter as the offer and must also be, in all material
respects, in the same terms as the offer. But the test whether there has been correspondence
between offer and acceptance is not subjective but objective. If there is objective
agreement, there may be a binding contract, even if in his mind one party or another has
not consented to it, a principle recently affirmed by the Court of Appeal in *Centrovincial
Estates plc v Merchant Investors Assurance Co Ltd* (1983) Times, 8 March. Furthermore,

putting on one side such matters as the ancient doctrine of non est factum and relief from mistake in equity, there is no principle of English law that any contract may be 'avoided', ie not come into existence, by reason simply of a mistake, whether a mistake of one or both parties. The question is simply whether objective agreement has been reached and, if so, on what terms. If objective agreement has been reached, in the sense we have described, then the parties will be bound, unless on a true construction the agreement was subject to a condition precedent, express or implied, failure of which has in the event prevented a contract from coming into existence.

What is the effect of fraud? Fraud is, in relation to a contract, a fraudulent misrepresentation by one party which induces the other to enter into a contract or apparent contract with the representor. Apart from the innocent party's right to recover damages for the tort of deceit, the effect of the fraud is simply to give the innocent party the right, subject to certain limits, to rescind the contract. These rights are similar to (though not identical with) the rights of a party who has been induced to enter into a contract by an innocent, as opposed to a fraudulent, misrepresentation, though there the right to recover damages derives from statute, and the limits to rescission are somewhat more severe. It is plain, however, that in this context fraud does not 'vitiate consent', any more than an innocent misrepresentation 'vitiates consent'. Looked at realistically, a misrepresentation, whether fraudulent or innocent, induces a party to enter into a contract in circumstances where it may be unjust that the representor should be permitted to retain the benefit (the chose in action) so acquired by him. The remedy of rescission, by which the unjust enrichment of the representor is prevented, though for historical and practical reasons treated in books on the law of contract, is a straightforward remedy in restitution subject to limits which are characteristic of that branch of the law.

The effect of rescission of a contract induced by a misrepresentation is that property in goods transferred under it may be revested in the transferor (the misrepresentee). But this may not be possible if the goods have been transferred to a third party, for the intervention of third party rights may preclude rescission. In such a case, especially if the misrepresentor has disappeared from the scene or is a man of straw so that damages are an ineffective remedy, the misrepresentee's only practical course may be to seek to establish that there never was any contract (ie that the supposed contract was 'void'), so that he never parted with the property in the goods and he can claim the goods or their value from the third party. To succeed in such a claim, he has generally to show that there was no objective agreement between him and the representor. For that purpose, however, the misrepresentation (fraudulent or innocent) is simply the origin of a set of circumstances in which it may be shown that there was no objective agreement, e g that the offer was, objectively speaking, made to one person and (perhaps as a result of fraud), objectively speaking, accepted by another. Again, it cannot be said that fraud 'vitiates consent'; fraud was merely the occasion for an apparent contract which was, in law, no contract at all.

Similar criteria to those applied in order to ascertain whether property in goods had passed in circumstances such as these were at one time of particular relevance in criminal law. This was because, under the old law of larceny, the crime of larceny as the result of a mistake was only committed if the mistake was sufficient to prevent the property from passing to the accused; and the crime of larceny by a trick was only committed if the accused, having the relevant mens rea, induced the owner to transfer possession of the goods to him, though the owner did not intend to convey the property to the accused. If the owner was induced to convey the property to the accused, the latter could not be guilty of larceny but could be guilty of obtaining by false pretences. The nature of the mistake in cases of larceny as the result of a mistake and the distinction between larceny by a trick and obtaining by false pretences were, not surprisingly, fruitful sources of dispute and of nice distinctions. But one purpose of the Theft Act 1968 was to avoid, as far as possible, problems of this kind. And even under the old law of larceny it could not be said that fraud 'vitiated consent', for the existence of the crime of larceny as the result of a mistake demonstrates that the 'vitiating' of the consent of the owner to part with the property in the goods was not dependent on fraud on the part of the accused.

It is against this background that we turn to the problem in the instant case. There

a being no general principle that fraud vitiates consent, we see the problem simply as this: can a person be said to have taken a conveyance for his own or another's use 'without having the consent of the owner or other lawful authority' within those words as used in s 12(1) of the Theft Act 1968 if he induces the owner to part with possession of the conveyance by a fraudulent misrepresentation of the kind employed by the appellants in the present case?

b Now there is no doubt about the mischief towards which this provision (like its predecessors, ss 28(1) and 217(1) of the Road Traffic Acts 1930 and 1960, respectively) is directed. It is directed against persons simply taking other persons' vehicles for their own purposes, for example, for use in the commission of a crime, or for a joyride, or just to get home, without troubling to obtain the consent of the owner but without having the animus furandi necessary for theft. In the vast majority of circumstances, no approach is

c made to the owner at all: the vehicle is just taken. But is the crime committed when the owner is approached, and when he is compelled to part with his possession by force, or when he is induced to part with his possession by fraud?

Now it may be that, if the owner is induced by force to part with possession of his vehicle, the offence is committed, because a sensible distinction may be drawn between consent on the one hand and submission to force on the other. This is a point which,

d however, we do not have to decide, though we comment that, in the generality of such cases, the accused is likely to have committed one or more other offences with which he could perhaps be more appropriately charged.

But where the owner is induced by fraud to part with the possession of his vehicle, no such sensible distinction can be drawn. In commonsense terms, he has consented to part with the possession of his vehicle, but his consent has been obtained by the fraud. In such

e a case no offence under this subsection will have been committed unless, on a true construction, a different meaning is to be placed on the word 'consent' in the subsection. We do not however consider that any such construction is required.

It is to be observed, in the first instance, that the presence or absence of consent would be as much affected by innocent as by fraudulent misrepresentation. We do not however regard this point as persuasive, for the answer may lie in the fact that, where the

f misrepresentation is innocent, the accused would lack the mens rea which, on the principle in *R v Tolson* (1889) 23 QBD 168, [1886–90] All ER Rep 26, may well be required as a matter of implication (a point which, once again, we do not have to decide). It is also to be observed that the owner's consent may, to the knowledge of the accused, have been self-induced, without any misrepresentation, fraudulent or innocent, on the part of the accused. More compelling, however, is the fact that it does not appear sensible

g to us that, in cases of fraud, the commission of the offence should depend not on the simple question whether possession of the vehicle had been obtained by fraud but on the intricate question whether the effect of the fraud had been such that it precluded the existence of objective agreement to part with possession of the car, as might for example be the case where the owner was only willing to part with possession to a third party and the accused fraudently induced him to do so by impersonating that third party.

h We find it very difficult to accept that the commission of an offence under this subsection should depend on the drawing of such a line, which, having regard to the mischief to which this subsection is directed, appears to us to be irrelevant. The judge in the Crown Court felt it necessary to inquire, on the appeal before him, whether this line had been crossed before he could hold that the appellants had committed the offence. An inquiry of this kind is by no means an easy one, as is demonstrated by, for example, the

j disagreement on a similar point among the members of the Court of Appeal in *Ingram v Little* [1960] 3 All ER 332, [1961] 1 QB 31, and by the subsequent preference by the Court of Appeal in *Lewis v Averay* [1971] 3 All ER 907, [1972] 1 QB 198, for the dissenting judgment of Devlin LJ in the earlier case. Indeed, we would (had we thought it necessary to do so) have reached a different conclusion on the point from that reached by the judge in the Crown Court in the present case, considering that the effect of the appellants' fraud was not that the owner parted with possession of his vehicle to a different person from the one to whom he intended to give possession but that the owner believed that the person to whom he gave possession had the attribute, albeit a very important attribute, of holding a driving licence. However, on our view of the subsection, the point does not arise.

In circumstances such as those of the present case, the criminality (if any) of the act would appear to rest rather in the fact of the deception, inducing the person to part with the possession of his vehicle, rather than in the fact (if it be the case) that the fraud has the effect of inducing a mistake as to, for example, 'identity' rather than 'attributes' of the deceiver. It would be very strange if fraudulent conduct of this kind has only to be punished if it happened to induce a fundamental mistake; and it would be even more strange if such fraudulent conduct has only to be punished where the chattel in question happened to be a vehicle. If such fraudulent conduct is to be the subject of prosecution, the crime should surely be classified as one of obtaining by deception, rather than an offence under s 12(1) of the 1968 Act, which appears to us to be directed to the prohibition and punishment of a different form of activity. It was suggested to us in argument that, in the present case, the appellants could have been accused of dishonestly obtaining services by deception contrary to s 1(1) of the Theft Act 1978; the submission was that, having regard to the broad definition of 'services' inherent in s 1(2) of the 1978 Act, the hiring of a vehicle could, untypically, be regarded as a form of services. Since we did not hear full argument on the point, we express no opinion on it, commenting only that, in a comprehensive law of theft and related offences, a decision of policy has to be made whether a fraudulent obtaining of temporary possession of a vehicle or other goods should be punishable, irrespective of any of the nice distinctions which the Crown Court felt required to consider in the present case.

We are fortified in our conclusion by the opinion expressed by Sachs LJ in R v Peart [1970] 2 All ER 823, [1970] 2 QB 672. In that case, on comparable facts, the Court of Appeal held that no offence had been committed under s 12(1) of the 1968 Act, because the fraudulent misrepresentation did not relate to a fact which was sufficiently fundamental. But Sachs LJ, in delivering the judgment of the court, expressly reserved the question whether, in any case where consent had been induced by fraud, an offence would be committed under the subsection; and it is plain from his comments that he had serious misgivings whether any such offence would be committed in those circumstances ([1970] 2 All ER 823 at 825, [1970] 2 QB 672 at 676). These misgivings we share in full measure, and it is our conclusion that the subsection on its true construction contemplates no such offence.

We wish to add that our judgment is confined to the construction of s 12(1) of the Theft Act 1978. We are not to be understood to be expressing any opinion on the meaning to be attached to the word 'consent' in other parts of the criminal law, where the word must be construed in its own particular context.

It follows that we answer the first question posed for our decision in the negative and the second question in the affirmative, and that the convictions of the appellants under s 12(1) of the Theft Act 1968 will be quashed.

Appeal allowed. Convictions quashed. Leave to appeal to the House of Lords refused.

23 June. The court certified, under s 1(2) of the Administration of Justice Act 1960, that the following point of law of general public importance was involved in the decision: whether, on a true construction of s 12(1) of the Theft Act 1968, the consent of the owner of a motor car to its use by another could be vitiated if such consent was obtained by a fraudulent misrepresentation by that other.

Solicitors: *Hextall Erskine & Co*, agents for *Llewellyn Vickers & Chisman*, Stockton-on-Tees (for the appellants); *D I Morgan*, Durham (for the respondent).

April Weiss　Barrister.

Freeman v Home Office

QUEEN'S BENCH DIVISION
McCOWAN J
3–6, 9–13, 16–19 MAY 1983

Medical practitioner – Trespass to the person – Consent to medical treatment – Prison – Prison medical officer administering drug to prisoner – Prisoner contending that drug administered by force without his consent – Whether medical officer acting as disciplinarian and not in capacity as doctor – Whether prisoner's consent required to be informed consent – Whether sufficient that prisoner consenting in broad terms.

Prison – Medical officer – Whether prison officers including medical officer – Prison Act 1952, s 7(1).

In 1973, while serving a term of life imprisonment, the plaintiff had administered to him certain drugs. In 1979 the plaintiff brought an action against the Home Office claiming damages for trespass to the person, on the grounds that a medical officer employed by the prison authorities, together with other prison officers, had administered the drugs to him by force against his consent. He contended (i) that the drugs prescribed by the medical officer were not for the relief of any recognisable mental illness or disorder but were purely to control him, and that a prisoner could not, in law, give consent to treatment by a prison medical officer where the medical officer was not acting in his capacity as a doctor but as a disciplinarian, and (ii) that for a patient's consent to be operative in law it had to be informed, ie the patient had to be told (a) what he was suffering from, (b) what was the precise nature of the treatment being proposed, and (c) what, if any, were the adverse effects and risks involved in the treatment.

Held – The action would be dismissed for the following reasons—

(1) On the facts, it could not be inferred that the drugs were given for other than a medical purpose and furthermore the drugs had not been administered by force. It followed that the medical officer was acting in his capacity as a doctor and not as a disciplinarian (see p 592 *a b* and p 597 *h*, post).

(2) The doctrine of informed consent, which was part of the law of negligence, had no bearing on the law of battery. For consent to be a defence to an allegation of battery it was sufficient that the plaintiff knew in broad terms what he was consenting to, not because of any special doctrine but because otherwise his consent would not be real. The reality of such consent could be vitiated by fraud or misdescription, but on the facts the plaintiff's consent was real and not vitiated. If, however, the consent had to be informed consent before it could be raised as a defence, the burden of proving absence of consent was on the plaintiff, and he had failed to prove the absence of such consent (see p 593 *c* to *f*, p 595 *b c* and p 597 *h*, post); *Bowater v Rowley Regis BC* [1944] 1 All ER 465 and *Reibl v Hughes* (1980) 114 DLR (3d) 1 considered.

(3) Although by virtue of s 7(1)[a] of the Prison Act 1952 a medical officer was a 'prison officer' that did not mean that because the plaintiff was in the custody of a 'prison officer' when receiving treatment from the medical officer he was incapable of consenting to the treatment. Nevertheless, where, in a prison setting, a doctor had the power to influence a prisoner's situation and prospects, the court had to be alive to the risk that what might on the face of it appear to be real consent was not in fact so. However, the matter was one of fact and, on the facts, the plaintiff had not proved that he was incapable of giving his consent to the treatment in question or that he had not done so (see p 595 *h j* and p 597 *g h*, post).

---

a Section 7(1) is set out at p 595 *e f*, post

Notes

For trespass to the person, see 38 Halsbury's Laws (3rd edn) 760, para 1251, and for cases **a** on the subject, see 46 Digest (Repl) 415–429, 581–740.

For prison officers, see 37 Halsbury's Laws (4th edn) para 1116.

For the Prison Act 1952, s 7, see 25 Halsbury's Statutes (3rd edn) 832.

Cases referred to in judgment

Bowater v Rowley Regis BC [1944] 1 All ER 465, [1944] KB 476, CA.   **b**

Chatterton v Gerson [1981] 1 All ER 257, [1981] QB 432, [1980] 3 WLR 1003.

Kaimowitz v Michigan Dept of Mental Health (1973) 42 USLW 101, 2063, Cir Ct, Wayne Cty, Mich.

Reibl v Hughes (1980) 114 DLR (3d) 1, Can SC.

Action   **c**

By a writ issued on 15 October 1979 the plaintiff, David Freeman, claimed against the defendants, the Home Office, damages for assault and/or battery and/or trespass to the person by the administration to him of certain drugs by or under the direction of Dr Cedric Melville Xavier, the servant or agent of the defendants and/or certain prison officers at HM Prison Wakefield being also servants or agents of the defendants, between September 1972 and December 1972 against the plaintiff's will and/or without his **d** consent. The facts are set out in the judgment.

Louis Blom-Cooper QC and *Judith Beale* for the plaintiff.
John Laws and *Robert Jay* for the defendants.

McCOWAN J. This is a claim for damages, including exemplary damages, for trespass **e** to the person, brought by a life sentence prisoner against the Home Office, alleging that one of their servants, a medical officer called Xavier, prescribed certain drugs, namely Stelazin, Serenace and Modecate, to be administered to the plaintiff when an inmate in prison and that those drugs were there administered to the plaintiff by Dr Xavier and/or prison officers under his direction, the plaintiff not consenting but on the contrary actively resisting, but being overcome forcibly by Dr Xavier and/or the prison officers. **f** The Home Office admits the prescription and the administration of the drugs to the plaintiff but denies the use of force and says that the plaintiff expressly consented to their administration. The period of prescription and administration is September to December 1972.

The writ was issued on 15 October 1979 and served on 17 October 1979. It included, in addition to the claim in trespass to the person, an alternative claim that Dr Xavier was **g** negligent in prescribing and/or administering and/or causing to be administered to the plaintiff those same drugs.

The defence denied negligence as well as trespass to the person but, in addition, pleaded that the plaintiff's claim was statute-barred pursuant to s 2 of the Limitation Act 1939, as amended.

The defendants then made application for an order that the plaintiff's claim be **h** dismissed or stayed on the grounds that it was statute-barred and/or that it would be inequitable to permit the action to proceed. The point was taken that the cause of action arose, according to the statement of claim, between September and December 1972 and hence that it became statute-barred not later than January 1976, and further, in consequence, that the writ was almost four years out of time. They further argued that they were hopelessly prejudiced in the conduct of the action by reason of the plaintiff's **j** delay, Dr Xavier, who is alleged to have prescribed the drugs and who would have been their principal witness, having died on 1 October 1977. The plaintiff countered that application by invoking the power conferred on the court under s 2D of the 1939 Act to direct that the provisions of s 2A should not apply to some or all of the causes of action specified in the writ.

On 23 January 1981 Taylor J rejected the defendants' application, but on appeal to the
a Court of Appeal that court allowed the defendants' appeal and held that, having regard
to the death of Dr Xavier, it would not be equitable to allow the plaintiff to pursue his
claim in negligence but that it would be equitable to permit him to pursue his claim in
respect of trespass to the person, since it appeared from the plaintiff's affidavit that he
was not alleging that Dr Xavier was present when the prison officers forcibly injected
him and since, in addition, there was no suggestion that those officers were not alive and
b capable of giving evidence.

In opening the case to me, counsel for the plaintiff, who was not before the Court of
Appeal, continued to rely on the allegation of trespass to the person by reason of prison
officers coming into the room where the plaintiff was and by force injecting the drug in
question into his buttocks, despite his struggles, which were overcome by superior force.
But counsel put up an alternative case. He said that even if there is no word of truth in
c that, he is still entitled to succeed, because, first, the drugs were prescribed by Dr Xavier
not for relief of some recognisable mental illness or disorder but purely in order to
control the prisoner (that is to say, the plaintiff) and that a prisoner can never, in the eyes
of the law, give such consent to treatment if the doctor prescribing it is not acting as a
medical man but in truth as a disciplinarian; and, second, for consent to be operative in
law it must be informed, that is to say, the plaintiff must have been told (a) what he was
d suffering from, (b) what was the precise nature of the treatment being proposed and (c)
what, if any, were the adverse effects and risks involved in the treatment. Counsel for the
defendants objected to counsel for the plaintiff pursuing either of those points.

I was asked to rule on this as a preliminary point, and I did so. I held that the additional
ways in which the case was now being put were not covered by the pleadings, no
application having been made by counsel for the plaintiff to amend them. I further held
e that in any event these points had not been canvassed before the Court of Appeal and
that, had they been, the Court of Appeal would have held that the defendants would
have been at least as gravely prejudiced in respect of them by reason of Dr Xavier's death
as they were in relation to the claim founded on his alleged negligence. Accordingly I
held that the action could only proceed in respect of the claim that he was forcibly
subjected to the treatment in question.

f After I had so ruled, counsel for the plaintiff asked to be allowed to call his evidence on
what I have called his additional ways of putting the case and that I should make findings
on them, the object being that, should my preliminary ruling be held by a higher court
to have been wrong, the necessity for a new trial would be avoided. I permitted him to
call this evidence and, it followed of course, the defendants to call any evidence to counter
it so far as they were able. But I indicated that I would only make the findings sought if I
g felt able to on the material available.

Counsel for the plaintiff then applied to reamend the statement of claim by adding a
para 4A to allege that the plaintiff was incapable of consenting in law to the treatment
complained of by reason of the fact that he was at all material times a prisoner in the
custody of the defendants. Counsel for the defendants did not feel able to object to this
reamendment despite the late stage at which it was sought because it was not in any way
h dependent on evidence.

Accordingly I gave leave to the plaintiff to make that reamendment and that point has
been fully argued before me.

[His Lordship then considered the evidence in detail and concluded that the plaintiff
had consented to the administration of the drugs by Dr Xavier and that they had not
been administered by force. His Lordship went on to consider the alternative case
j advanced by counsel for the plaintiff:]

The first point was that the drugs were prescribed by Dr Xavier not for relief of some
recognisable mental illness or disorder but purely in order to control the prisoner, that is
to say, the plaintiff, and that a prisoner can never, in the eyes of the law, give consent to
treatment if the doctor prescribing it is not acting as a medical man but in truth as a
disciplinarian. On this matter Dr MacKeith (the psychiatrist called by the plaintiff) said:

'It is certainly impossible to say what his mental state was at the relevant time. I would not infer from the documents that the drugs were given for other than a *a* medical purpose. There is no material on which I could form such a view.'

Thereafter, that point did not figure much, if at all, in the submissions of counsel for the plaintiff. In any event, I agree with Dr MacKeith. Any such claim is quite without substance on the evidence and, if it were before the court, would not in my judgment have got off the ground.

The second point was that for consent to be operative in law it must be informed, *b* namely the plaintiff must have been told (a) what he was suffering from, (b) what was the precise nature of the treatment being proposed and (c) what, if any, were the adverse effects and risks involved in the treatment. Counsel for the plaintiff says that if the plaintiff was never told of those things, he never possessed the requisite information on which he could make his choice either to consent to or to refuse treatment, and in those circumstances any consent given was not real. He relies on a passage in the judgment of *c* Scott LJ in the case of *Bowater v Rowley Regis BC* [1944] 1 All ER 465 at 465, [1944] KB 476 at 479. This was a case in which the plaintiff sued in negligence and the defence pleaded volenti non fit injuria. Dealing with the latter point Scott LJ said:

'For the purpose of the rule, if it be a rule, a man cannot be said to be truly "willing", unless he is in a position to choose freely; and freedom of choice predicates, *d* not only full knowledge of the circumstances upon which the exercise of choice is conditioned, in order that he may be able to choose wisely, but the absence from his mind of any feeling of constraint, in order that nothing shall interfere with the freedom of his will.'

Counsel for the plaintiff relies further on passages in the judgment in *Kaimowitz v Michigan Dept of Mental Health* (1973) 42 USLW 101, 2063, which is reprinted in Brooks *e* *Law, Psychiatry and the Mental Health System* (1974) p 902. I shall return to this case later, as counsel relies on it in another context, but these phrases from it will suffice for present purposes. These words are to be found (at p 910): 'An operation performed upon a patient without his informed consent is the tort of battery.' And (at p 912): 'To be legally adequate, a subject's informed consent must be competent, knowing and voluntary.' These, I make clear, are passages from the judgment given in the case. *f*

Counsel for the defendants ripostes with a Canadian case called *Reibl v Hughes* (1980) 114 DLR (3d) 1. He refers to the following passages in the judgment of Laskin CJ, the first under the heading 'Liability for battery' (at 8):

'In my opinion, these findings do not justify the imposition of liability for battery. The popularization of the term "informed consent" for what is, in essence, a duty of *g* disclosure of certain risks of surgery or therapy appears to have had some influence in the retention of battery as a ground of liability, even in cases where there was express consent to such treatment and the surgeon or therapist did not go beyond that to which consent was given. It would be better to abandon the term when it tends to confuse battery and negligence.'

Then counsel for the defendants relies on two passages (at 10), the first reading: *h*

'In my opinion, actions of battery in respect of surgical or other medical treatment should be confined to cases where surgery or treatment has been performed or given to which there has been no consent at all or where, emergency situations aside, surgery or treatment has been performed or given beyond that to which there was consent.' *j*

The second passage reads:

'In situations where the allegation is that attendant risks which should have been disclosed were not communicated to the patient and yet the surgery or other medical treatment carried out was that to which the plaintiff consented (there being no

a   negligence basis of liability for the recommended surgery or treatment to deal with
    the patient's condition), I do not understand how it can be said that the consent was
    vitiated by the failure of disclosure so as to make the surgery or other treatment an
    unprivileged, unconsented to and intentional invasion of the patient's bodily
    integrity. I can appreciate the temptation to say that the genuineness of consent to
    medical treatment depends on proper disclosure of the risk which it entails, but in
    my view, unless there has been misrepresentation or fraud to secure consent to the
b   treatment, a failure to disclose the attendant risks, however serious, should go to
    negligence rather than to battery. Although such a failure relates to an informed
    choice of submitting to or refusing recommended and appropriate treatment, it
    arises as the breach of an anterior duty of due care, comparable in legal obligation to
    the duty of due care in carrying out the particular treatment to which the plaintiff
    has consented. It is not a test of the validity of the consent.'

c   In my judgment the doctrine of informed consent has no place in the law of battery.
    Properly understood, it is part of the law of negligence. If a doctor gives treatment
    without explaining to the patient what the patient is suffering from, what the doctor is
    proposing to do for it and the likely or possible side effects from it, he may be liable in
    negligence. That would not be properly constituted as a claim in battery at all. What the
    patient would be saying was that the doctor was guilty of a breach of the duty of care,
d   and the court would then in that context have to consider whether there was any need in
    the circumstances for the doctor to have given an explanation and, if so, to what extent.
    I do not think such matters figure appropriately in the tort of battery. For consent in
    battery, it is sufficient if the plaintiff knew in broad terms what he was consenting to,
    not because of any special doctrine but because otherwise his consent would not be real.
    The reality of such consent would of course be vitiated by fraud or misdescription. In
e   this case I am satisfied that the plaintiff's consent was real and not so vitiated.
       If I am wrong and the consent has to be informed before it can amount to a defence to
    battery, the next problem that arises is on whom the burden of proof lies. The pleader of
    the plaintiff's case appeared to assume that the burden was on the plaintiff to disprove
    consent in that he pleaded, at para 4 of the statement of claim: 'The Plaintiff did not
    consent to the administration of the said drugs.' That stands unamended, but counsel for
f   the plaintiff says it is an unnecessary averment. The defendants in their defence denied
    para 4 of the statement of claim and went on to allege:

        'At all material times the plaintiff expressly consented to the administration of
        each of the said drugs and no drug was administered without his said consent.'

       On the submission of counsel for the plaintiff as to where the burden lies one could
g   conceivably get the following situation. A statement of claim would need only to assert
    that the defendant, a doctor of medicine, had injected the plaintiff. If the defence
    admitted the injection but pleaded consent, as it would have to do, and the defendant
    then died before the hearing of the action so that the defence were unable to call him,
    the plaintiff would be entitled to judgment without calling any evidence at all.
       This is not a point on which there is clear authority. In the Canadian case of *Reibl v*
h   *Hughes* (at 9) already referred to, the Chief Justice of Canada, dealing with the tort of
    battery, said:

        'The tort is an intentional one, consisting of an unprivileged and unconsented to
        invasion of one's bodily security. True enough, it has some advantages for a plaintiff
        over an action of negligence since it does not require proof of causation and it casts
j   upon the defendant the burden of proving consent to what was done.'

    Both counsel before me have agreed that, while the first sentence I have read appears to
    put the burden of disproving consent on the plaintiff, the second sentence clearly puts
    the burden of proving consent on the defendants.
       In a recent decision of Bristow J in *Chatterton v Gerson* [1981] 1 All ER 257, [1981] QB

432, a claim by a patient against a doctor, the headnote suggests that Bristow J decided the point. It reads ([1981] QB 432):

'*Held*, giving judgment for the defendants, (1) that in order to establish trespass to the person a patient had to show that she did not consent to the operation . . .'

However, when one looks at his actual words, it is not so clear. He said ([1981] 1 All ER 257 at 265, [1981] QB 432 at 442):

'When the claim is based on negligence the plaintiff must prove not only the breach of duty to inform but that had the duty not been broken she would not have chosen to have the operation. Where the claim is based on trespass to the person, once it is shown that the consent is unreal, then what the plaintiff would have decided if she had been given the information which would have prevented vitiation of the reality of her consent is irrelevant.'

None the less, I would read this as indicating that Bristow J took the view that it was for the plaintiff to show the absence of real consent.

Turning to the textbook writers *Salmond and Heuston on the Law of Torts* (18th edn, 1981) p 466 says: 'No act is actionable as a tort at the suit of any person who has expressly or impliedly assented to it: *Volenti non fit injuria*.' It says (at p 467):

'So the maxim affords a defence to a physician or surgeon for an act done in the proper course of medical or surgical treatment, which is within the scope of the patient's real consent, whether express or implied. The defendant must establish that the plaintiff's consent was fully and freely given.'

Winfield and Jolowicz on Tort (11th edn, 1979) p 656, under the heading 'Consent. Volenti non fit injuria', says:

'There are many occasions on which harm—sometimes grievous harm—may be inflicted on a person for which he has no remedy in tort, because he consented, or at least assented, to the doing of the act which caused his harm. Simple examples are the injuries received in the course of a lawful game or sport, or in a lawful surgical operation. The effect of such consent or assent is commonly expressed in the maxim "Volenti non fit injuria", which is certainly of respectable antiquity.'

I read two further passages (at p 657). The first says:

'The maxim is of general application but no question of *volens* arises until it is established that the defendant has committed a tort, at least a presumptive one, against the plaintiff. It is only then that the defendant need defend himself by proving that the plaintiff was *volens*.'

The second passage reads:

'For the defence of consent to succeed it is necessary for the Defendant to establish not simply that the plaintiff consented to the *physical* risk, *i.e.* the risk of actual damage, but to the *legal* risk, *i.e.* the risk of actual damage for which there will be no redress at law.'

Finally, it says (at p 661), under the heading 'The consent must be freely given':

'The main point to notice here is that "a man cannot be said to be truly 'willing' unless he is in a position to choose freely, and freedom of choice predicates, not only full knowledge of the circumstances on which the exercise of choice is conditional, so that he may be able to choose wisely, but the absence of any feeling of constraint so that nothing shall interfere with the freedom of his will".'

It is to be noted that in those passages the writers are dealing with volenti. Counsel for the defendants submits that volenti is consent to the risk of injury and is accordingly a defence most apt to a claim in negligence. What a plaintiff consents to in a case of alleged

battery is not risk but a specific intrusion on his body. Therefore, consent to a surgical
a operation is not properly an example of volenti. The action fails not because of volenti
but because there is no tort. Volenti, he submits, does not arise at all unless the tort of
battery, which he defines as 'the unconsented to intrusion of another's bodily integrity' is
made out. That definition, he says, meets the vice at which the tort is aimed. I accept the
submission of counsel for the defendants and rule that the burden of proving absence of
consent is on the plaintiff.

b   If informed consent were an issue before me and if I am right that the burden of
proving the absence of such consent is on the plaintiff, I would have no hesitation in
saying that he has failed to discharge it, since I find myself unable to rely in any way on
his account of what passed between him and Dr Xavier. If, on the other hand, I am
wrong and the burden of proving absence of informed consent rests on the defence, then
in my judgment the prejudice arising to the defendants from the death of Dr Xavier
c would be greater than if the plaintiff had been allowed to continue his action in
negligence. Much the same issues would be being litigated, the difference being that the
burden would rest on the defendants. In the absence of Dr Xavier, I find myself unable
to conclude positively whether he told the plaintiff all the things that counsel for the
plaintiff says are necessary for informed consent, notably what was the precise nature of
the treatment being proposed. I am not, therefore, prepared to make any findings on
d that matter.

     I turn finally to deal with the point which was added by way of amendment of the
statement of claim during the course of counsel for the plaintiff's opening, that is, para
4A of the reamended statement of claim, namely that the plaintiff was incapable of
consenting in law to the said treatment complained of by reason of the fact that he was
at all material times a prisoner in the custody of the defendants. If this is right, the
e plaintiff is entitled to judgment whatever my view of the facts. Indeed, counsel for the
plaintiff agreed that there would have been no need for him to call any evidence at all.

     The first question that arises is whether a prison medical officer such as Dr Xavier is a
prison officer. The answer to that question is to be found in s 7(1) of the Prison Act 1952,
which provides: 'Every prison shall have a governor, a chaplain and a medical officer and
such other officers as may be necessary.' Counsel for the plaintiff says there is no
f ambiguity in those words and that if there is he can pray in aid the heading 'Prison
officers', which is to be found in the Queen's Printer's copy. He has also been able to
point out most helpfully to me that the history of legislative enactments dealing with
this subject matter indicates that prison medical officers have always been numbered
among the prison officers. This is so, for example, in the last Act before the 1952 one,
namely the Prison Act 1898. There, s 14(2) reads:

g   'For the purposes of the Prison Acts, 1865 to 1893, all officers of a prison shall be
          deemed to be subordinate officers, except the governor, the chaplain, the medical
          officer, the matron, and any minister appointed under the Prison Ministers Act,
          1863.'

Counsel for the plaintiff says that the 1952 Act was simply repeating in modern language
h what had been the statutory position since 1816. Counsel for the defendants argues that
s 7(1) of the 1952 Act does not clearly say that medical officers are prison officers and
that, if regard is had to the Prison Rules, many of them are inapt for medical officers. In
my judgment counsel for the plaintiff is right. Section 7(1) clearly includes medical
officers among prison officers.

     Counsel for the plaintiff therefore starts his submission on this aspect of the case from
j the established proposition that the medical officer is a prison officer and exercises all the
authority of any other officer within the prison. He goes on to argue that it is not
possible, except in emergency situations, for a prisoner to give a consent in law so as to
amount to a defence in battery to an injection prescribed by a full-time member of the
prison service. This is because an injection involves a physical touching, a violation of the
body constituting a trespass to the person. Treatment which does not involve touching
would not be affected, nor would touching by a doctor who was not a full-time member

of the prison service. The consequences of this would be somewhat startling, since it
would mean that no prison medical officer could risk touching a prisoner even with his   *a*
full informed consent given to him in writing.

Counsel for the plaintiff says that his subsidiary submission would be that his
proposition should apply at least if there was no such signed written consent, but his
main contention, and, he agrees, the logic of his argument, is that it would apply even if
there was such a signed written consent. He says the simple answer for a prison medical
officer who is contemplating touching a prisoner is to call in a doctor from outside the   *b*
prison service either to do the touching or at least to accept the consent of the prisoner.
He adds that if the facts showed full informed consent on the part of a prisoner who
voluntarily approached the prison medical officer, the damages would be small. I doubt
if he is necessarily right about that. The consequences might be very serious, and since
the damages to be awarded for battery resulting in physical injury are, he says and I
accept, to be calculated as in any other action for personal injury, the damages might be   *c*
very large. In addition, counsel for the plaintiff argues that exemplary damages would
be awardable because the action of the medical officer would have been oppressive,
arbitrary and unconstitutional.

As I say, the consequences would be startling, and they were found so by the plaintiff's
own witness, Dr MacKeith, who had been at one time a prison medical officer. He said
in evidence: *d*

'I have many times given an injection to a prisoner. [He was referring of course
to the times when he was in the capacity of a prison medical officer.] I have
conducted many examinations which involved touching the prisoner when I was a
full-time medical officer, and I did so believing I could because the prisoner had
given his consent. I have been aware of the difficulty of getting real consent, for
example if the patient is grossly disturbed or if the patient has a misplaced concern   *e*
to conform with my wishes. I would be troubled to think that every injection I had
given to a prisoner or in a hospital was without consent in law and laid me open to
an action for damages.'

Counsel for the plaintiff justifies his proposition on the ground that a prison medical
officer is 'part medical man and part turnkey'. The prisoner, he says, cannot choose his   *f*
doctor. The medical officer can order a prisoner to be brought before him. By r 77(2) of
the Prison Rules 1964, 'An officer shall inform the governor promptly of any abuse or
impropriety which comes to his knowledge.' So, says counsel for the plaintiff, there is no
confidentiality in the relationship. He can put the prisoner on report for disobeying any
lawful order, pursuant to r 47(18); he can say whether the prisoner is fit for work or for
cellular confinement; he can by the tenor of his reports affect the prisoner's categorisation   *g*
and his prospects for release on parole. A prisoner, counsel for the plaintiff submits, is
bound, therefore, to fear a disadvantage if he does not fall in with the medical officer's
wishes on treatment. Hence, the prisoner's consent cannot be voluntary.

Counsel for the plaintiff relies here too on the American case of *Kaimowitz*, to which I
have already referred. There the patient had been committed to a state hospital as a
criminal sexual psychopath. It was proposed to subject him to experimental brain surgery   *h*
and he signed a written informed consent. The court held that informed consent cannot
be given by an involuntarily detained mental patient for experimental psychosurgery. It
appears from the book in which this judgment is contained that the following words
were used in the judgment (see Brooks *Law, Psychiatry and the Mental Health System* (1974)
p 914):

'An involuntarily confined mental patient clearly has diminished capacity for   *j*
making a decision about irreversible experimental psychosurgery . . . It is impossible
for an involuntarily detained mental patient to be free of ulterior forms of restraint
or coercion when his very release from the institution may depend upon his co-
operating with the institution authorities and giving consent to experimental
surgery.'

It appears that these words were used in the judgment (at p 915):

> 'Involuntarily confined mental patients live in an inherently coercive institutional environment. Indirect and subtle psychological coercion has profound effect upon the patient population. Involuntarily confined patients cannot reason as equals with the doctors and administrators over whether they should undergo psychosurgery. They are not able to voluntarily give informed consent because of the inherent inequality in their position.'

Counsel for the defendants says that that case is to be distinguished because it was dealing with experimental psychosurgery. Counsel for the plaintiff says it establishes a much broader principle. I note, however, the words which were used in the judgment, namely (at p 911):

> 'We do not agree that a truly informed consent cannot be given for a regular surgical procedure by a patient, institutionalized or not. The law has long recognised that such valid consent can be given. But we do hold that informed consent cannot be given by an involuntarily detained mental patient for experimental psychosurgery for the reasons set forth below.'

To my mind, those words appear to be against the proposition for which counsel for the plaintiff argues in this case.

The defendants say that their position is accurately set out in para 177 of the *Report on the work of the Prison Department 1979* (Cmnd 7965), which has been extracted and put before me. I read the relevant passage:

> 'It is worth re-stating here the important principle that medical officers have complete clinical freedom and the same ethical standards as their colleagues practising outside prisons; a medicine is prescribed only when, in the clinical judgement of the doctor concerned, it is necessary for the restoration of health or the relief of symptoms. Unlike doctors caring for patients compulsorily detained in psychiatric hospitals under the provisions of the Mental Health Act 1959, doctors working in prisons have no statutory authority to administer treatment against the wishes of their patients. It follows that the administration of a medicine against the wishes of a prisoner would only be defensible if, without it, his life would be endangered, serious harm to the prisoner or others would be likely, or there would be an irreversible deterioration in his condition . . .'

Counsel for the defendants submits that it is a question of fact in each case. He uses the analogy of a police officer taking a statement from an arrested man who is in a position to influence that man's position with regard to bail. Yet it is not the law that no voluntary statement can ever be made to a police officer. Similarly, questions of duress and relative strength of bargaining power are always questions of fact.

The right approach, in my judgment, is to say that where, in a prison setting, a doctor has the power to influence a prisoner's situation and prospects a court must be alive to the risk that what may appear, on the face of it, to be a real consent is not in fact so. I have borne that in mind throughout the case. Essentially, however, the matter is one of fact. Accordingly, I rule against the submission of counsel for the plaintiff that he is entitled to judgment because the plaintiff was incapable in law of giving his consent to the treatment by Dr Xavier which is in question. It follows that I hold for the defendants on all the grounds of claim before me, and the action must be dismissed.

Action dismissed.

Solicitors: *Bindman & Partners* (for the plaintiff); *Treasury Solicitor.*

K Mydeen Esq   Barrister.

Rocco Giuseppe & Figli v Tradax Export SA   *a*

QUEEN'S BENCH DIVISION (COMMERCIAL COURT)
PARKER J
16 MAY 1983

Arbitration – Award – Interest from date of award – Rate – Rate of interest varied after date of   *b*
award – Whether rate of interest effective at date of award only rate recoverable – Whether
court empowered to award interest at different rate.

Unless an arbitrator directs that his award is to carry no interest, the award carries interest
at the rate applicable to a judgment debt, namely the rate specified by the statutory
instrument made under s 44^a of the Administration of Justice Act 1970 which is in force
at the date of the award. The court has no inherent power to award interest at a different   *c*
rate (see p 600 *e*, p 601 *f* to *j* and p 602 *a*, post).

    Timber Shipping Co SA v London and Overseas Freighters Ltd [1971] 2 All ER 599
considered.

Notes   *d*
For interest on judgment debts, see 37 Halsbury's Laws (4th edn) para 551.
    For the Administration of Justice Act 1970, s 44, see 40 Halsbury's Statutes (3rd edn)
976.

Cases referred to in judgment
Churcher v Stringer (1831) 2 B & Ad 777, 109 ER 1334.
Johnson v Durant (1830) 4 C & P 327, 172 ER 725, NP.   *e*
Pinhorn v Tuckington (1813) 3 Camp 468, 170 ER 1448, NP.
Timber Shipping Co SA v London and Overseas Freighters Ltd [1971] 2 All ER 599, [1972] AC
    1, [1972] 2 WLR 1360, HL.

Originating summons   *f*
By an originating summons dated 5 May 1982 the plaintiffs, Rocco Giuseppe & Figli,
sought a declaration (a) that they were entitled to interest on two arbitration awards,
made on 11 April 1978 by the Board of Appeal of the Grain and Feed Trade Association
Ltd, by which the defendants, Tradax Export SA, were directed to pay the plaintiffs
$US21,535·58 and $US98,487·48 (including interest) respectively, (b) that interest on the
sums specified in the awards was payable at the following rates: 10% from 11 April 1978 -
to 2 December 1979; 12% from 3 December 1979 to 8 June 1980; 15% from 9 June 1980   *g*
onwards (subject to (c) below), and (c) that if the rate of interest payable on judgment
debts pursuant to s 17 of the Judgments Act 1838 was decreased or increased by an order
made by statutory instrument, the interest payable on the two arbitration awards should
be at the rate stipulated in the order, as from the date on which the order came into force.
Alternatively, the plaintiffs sought a declaration that they were entitled to a sum by way   *h*
of interest on the sums awarded in the two arbitration awards and payable from the date
of the awards until payment thereof, at such rate as seemed just and equitable to the
court. The facts are set out in the judgment.

Richard Aikens for the plaintiffs.
Nicholas Merriman for the defendants.
                                                    j

PARKER J. This originating summons raises a point which has hitherto apparently
not arisen. The short facts are that the Board of Appeal of GAFTA made two awards on
11 April 1978. Those awards provided for payment of interest to the date of the award

---

a Section 44 is set out at p 600 *e f*, post

but, of course, made no provision for payment of interest thereafter. There was a special
a case determined on 27 March 1980 when the awards of the Board of Appeal were upheld.
An appeal was then instituted but was abandoned on 11 November 1981. The principal
and interest to the date of the award were paid on 2 February 1982. On 9 April 1982
there was a further payment made consisting of interest from the date of the award until
27 January 1982, at the rate prevailing under the statutory instrument in force as at the
date of the award. That statutory instrument (the Judgment Debts (Rate of Interest)
b Order 1977, SI 1977/141) provided for the rate of interest on judgment debts to be 10%.
As a result of s 20 of the Arbitration Act 1950 that rate would, prima facie, be applicable
to the awards. Between 11 April 1978 and payment of the principal and interest awarded
by the board there were, however, successively, further statutory instruments providing
for interest rates on judgments, increasing the rate, first to 12½% and then to 15%. By
reason of the time lapse, the changes in interest rates, and the amount of principal
c involved, the difference between applying the rate in force at the time of the award and
applying instead the rates under the successive statutory instruments is considerable.

That is how and why the present dispute arises. It is contended for the plaintiff that
the rate applicable under the successive orders should be applied. That is done by one of
three routes. First, it is said that if this had been a judgment instead of an award and it
had been given on 11 April 1978, then on the true construction of the Judgments Act
d 1838, s 44 of the Administration of Justice Act 1970 and the successive orders made
thereunder, the result follows. Second, it is said that even if that be not the case in respect
of the judgment, then under s 20 of the Arbitration Act 1950 (properly construed) the
same result would follow on awards, albeit it is not available in the case of judgments.
Third and as a final fallback position, it is submitted that if all that is wrong the court has
an inherent power to award interest at other than the judgment rate, and that,
e notwithstanding that s 20 of the Arbitration Act 1950 expressly fixes the rate of judgment
interest on awards to the rate of interest on judgment debts, the court may award some
different rate.

I have been referred to the history of the matter and to a number of cases, but I find it
unnecessary to deal with more than a fraction of the material before me for the purpose
of actual decision. The matter starts with the Judgments Act 1838, s 17 of which
f originally provided:

> '. . . every Judgment Debt shall carry Interest at the Rate of Four Pounds *per
> Centum per Annum* from the Time of entering up the Judgment, or from the Time
> of the Commencement of this Act in Cases of Judgments then entered up and not
> carrying Interest, until the same shall be satisfied, and such Interest may be levied
> under a Writ of Execution on such Judgment.'

g
At that time (1838), therefore, Parliament was expressly dealing with judgments entered
up after the date of commencement of the Act, and with judgments entered up prior to
commencement of the Act which were not then carrying interest. And it was applying
the new statutory right to interest to the old judgments from such time as the Act itself
commenced. It was, therefore, awarding or enabling the judgment creditor to get interest
h as from the date of the judgment, albeit on a judgment previously entered up and not at
that time carrying interest.

The reference to previously entered up judgments was removed from s 17 of the 1838
Act by repeal pursuant to s 2 of and Pt 1 of the schedule to the Civil Procedure Acts
Repeal Act 1879. No particular submission with regard to that repeal was made. I assume
the repeal was made simply because it was realised that by 1879 it was unlikely that there
j would be still extant a judgment which had been given before 1838 and was still
unsatisfied, or (if it was unsatisfied) that the time when it could be regarded as being of
the slightest value had long since passed.

Prior to the Arbitration Act 1934 the position with regard to awards had been that, if
an action were brought on the award, the court would award interest on the amount of
the award on the basis that there was an implied promise by the parties to the arbitration

to pay the amount of the award, and accordingly, there being a contractual promise to
pay the sum of money, the court could and would award interest: see *Pinhorn v Tuckington*　*a*
(1813) 3 Camp 468, 170 ER 1448, *Johnson v Durant* (1830) 4 C & P 327, 172 ER 725 and
Churcher v Stringer (1831) 2 B & Ad 777, 109 ER 1334. The proposition that this was a
power in the courts in an action on an award is not challenged.

An alternative theory advanced by counsel for the plaintiffs was that it was by reason
of treating interest as special damage for non-payment of the award that this right arose.
It matters not what it is, or why, because it is plain that there was a power in the common　*b*
law courts at that stage, and without the aid of statute, to award interest where there was
an action on an award. There was, however, apparently no such power where, instead of
bringing an action on the award, the successful claimant in the arbitration proceeded to
try and enforce the award by way of motion for attachment. Then in 1934 there appeared
in the Arbitration Act of that year (in s 11) the selfsame section which was re-enacted in
the same words in s 20 of the 1950 Act. That section read as follows:　*c*

> 'A sum directed to be paid by an award shall, unless the award otherwise directs,
> carry interest as from the date of the award and at the same rate as a judgment debt.'

That appears on its plain language to be mandatory as to the rate at which interest shall
run. But for the fact that it was the subject later of very great debate, I would have
thought that there was little room for argument about it.　*d*

The matter was laid to rest, albeit only by a majority, in the House of Lords in *Timber
Shipping Co SA v London and Overseas Freighters Ltd* [1971] 2 All ER 599, [1972] AC 1.
That case decided that arbitrators have no power to award any rate of interest, as from
date of the award, other than the judgment rate. In other words, that they can do no
more than specify that the award shall not carry interest. They cannot say that it will
bear interest other than at the same rate as the judgment debt.　*e*

Section 44 of the Administration of Justice Act 1970 provides:

> '(1) The Lord Chancellor may by order made with the concurrence of the Treasury
> direct that section 17 of the Judgments Act 1838 (as that enactment has effect for
> the time being whether by virtue of this subsection or otherwise) shall be amended
> so as to substitute for the rate specified in that section as the rate at which judgment
> debts shall carry interest such rate as may be specified in the order.　*f*
> (2) An order under this section shall be made by statutory instrument which shall
> be laid before Parliament after being made.'

At that time s 17 of the Judgments Act 1838 specified one rate, and specified it as being
the rate at which judgment debts should carry interest from the time of entry up of the
judgment. Pursuant to that provision six orders in all have been made, the first of them　*g*
being made in 1971 (the Judgment Debts (Rate of Interest) Order 1971, SI 1971/491).
Each order is in common form, no one repeals its predecessor or predecessors. Each order
provides by art 2 as follows:

> 'In relation to any judgment entered up after the coming into operation of this
> Order, section 17 of the Judgments Act 1838 shall be amended so as to substitute for
> the rate specified in that section as to the rate at which judgment debts shall carry　*h*
> interest, the rate of [and then the new rate is set out].'

On the plain wording of art 2, the rate when it applied did so only to judgments entered
after the date of the order. So read there is a logical reason for the way in which the
matter has been dealt with, because each order stands on its own and neither incorporates
into itself any judgments, or deals with any judgments, which have been dealt with by　*j*
previous orders, nor repeals those previous orders. It recognises that they will continue
to be dealt with by the previous order, and specifies what is to happen to what I may call
'new judgments' entered up after the coming into force of the order. The words appear
to me to be beyond all argument, albeit I see the force of the submission of counsel for
the plaintiffs' that a purpose behind the enactment of s 44 of the 1970 Act may have been
to provide for current interest rates to be applicable.

a There is also counsel's submission that it would be very odd and perhaps unfair that somebody against whom judgment is given on the Thursday before the coming into force of an order raising the interest rate should have to pay (or be able to pay) at the lower rate. And if the order came into force on the following day another unfortunate defendant would find himself saddled (owing to the fact that the judge has taken overnight to consider his judgment) with a higher rate of interest.

b Those arguments are, undoubtedly, arguments for saying that Parliament should have dealt with the matter differently. They go some way to support an argument that, if the language will fairly bear it, the court should at any rate consider carefully applying the wording of the various statutory instruments so as to enable judgments to bear interest at the rates for the time being in force. But I am quite unable to reach that result. Nor does it appear to me that there is any material on which I can conclude that that result can have been intended.

c These orders have followed each other over a period from 1971. They have taken in each case the same form. The notes in *The Supreme Court Practice 1982* vol 1, paras 42/1/8–42/1/13, pp 714–716 and in the textbooks make no suggestion that fluctuating rates were intended. Such observations as appear in the cases do not indicate that the courts have ever supposed that fluctuating rates were intended. The prescribed form for a writ of fieri facias in *The Supreme Court Practice 1982*, vol 2, p 22, para 53 presupposes *d* that there will be one judgment rate entered, and that that will be the rate at the date of entry up. The sheriffs must have executed many judgments which have been outstanding, partly during the currency of one order and partly during the currency of that order *and* its successor. I stress 'and' for the reason that both would have continued to operate. There has hitherto been, so far as I know, no suggestion from anybody that the words could mean anything other than what they mean on their face. When the judgment is *e* given the judgment debtor is then faced with a rate. Subsequent changes may, if applicable, be either to his benefit or against him. But, if the Lord Chancellor and Parliament (since parliamentary procedure involves the laying before Parliament of these orders) choose to proceed in that way rather than by imposing or providing for fluctuating rates, there is no compelling reason or no such obvious total injustice as would cause me to try to put a strained construction on the words. Even if I were to try, *f* I am bound to say I should find myself unable to do so. There is, in my judgment, no way in which the statutes can be so construed.

I accordingly come to the conclusion that, so far as a judgment is concerned, the rate applicable is the rate under the order in force under the Judgments Act 1838 at the time that the judgment is entered up.

Counsel for the plaintiffs' alternative route proceeds by way of s 20 of the Arbitration *g* Act. He says it is perfectly true that that provides for awards to carry interest as from the date of the award, and also at the same rate as a judgment debt. But, he says, it is silent as to time. Therefore, if one were to look over a period, it could be found that an award could be said to carry interest at the same rate as a judgment debt, if one applied the rate for the time being in force under the various orders. That, again, is an argument which I find myself totally unable to accept. The plain intention was that an award should be *h* treated exactly like a judgment, and on that basis (where an award is made) all one has to do is to say, 'If this were a judgment, at what rate would it bear interest?' The answer would be, for a judgment, 'The rate specified in the order in operation when judgment was entered,' and the answer must, in my view, be the same with regard to an award.

Finally, counsel for the plaintiffs submitted that the court had (or had at the date of the enactment of the Arbitration Act 1934, s 11) an inherent power to award interest, *j* that parties in whose favour arbitration awards had been made had then a right of entitlement to be awarded interest, and that that right could not be taken away save by express words, it being a fundamental principle that the rights of the public are not to be taken away by legislation, save by express words or necessary implication.

I accept that there was such a power before the Act. I also accept that there are no express words saying 'And the heretofor existing power in the court to award different rates of interest shall cease to exist'. But when one finds that s 11 and its successor (s 20 of the 1950 Act) provide in mandatory terms for the interest on an award to be at the same rate as the interest on a judgment debt, I find it impossible to say that any power the *a* court had to award a different rate of interest has survived. There is, in my judgment, the clearest possible necessary implication that any such power can no longer be exercised.

Accordingly, the relief asked for must in all cases be denied, and I think that the appropriate order is the simple one that the motion be dismissed.

Summons dismissed.   *b*

Solicitors: *Middleton Potts & Co* (for the plaintiffs); *William A Crump & Son* (for the defendants).

K Mydeen Esq   Barrister.

c

Jedranska Slobodna Plovidba v Oleagine SA   *d*
The Luka Botic

COURT OF APPEAL, CIVIL DIVISION
ACKNER AND O'CONNOR LJJ
15, 30 SEPTEMBER 1983   *e*

Arbitration – Commencement – Extension of time – Charterparty incorporating Centrocon arbitration clause – Arbitration clause providing that any claim to be made in writing and claimants' arbitrator appointed within three months of discharge – No claim in writing made within time specified – Whether claim in writing 'some other step to commence arbitration proceedings' – Whether court having jurisdiction to extend time for making claim in writing –   f Arbitration Act 1950, s 27.

In 1980 the shipowners chartered their vessel to the charterers for a voyage from the United States to West Africa. The charterparty incorporated the Centrocon arbitration clause, which provided for all disputes to be referred to arbitration and further provided that 'Any claim must be made in writing and Claimants' Arbitrator appointed within   *g* three months of final discharge and where this provision is not complied with the claim shall be deemed to be waived and barred'. The vessel arrived at the Lagos/Cotonou anchorage off Nigeria on 1 May 1980 and waited for discharge until 7 September 1980. Discharge was finally completed on 15 November 1980. The shipowners wished to make a claim against the charterers arising out of the delay in discharging at Lagos but failed to make any such claim in writing or appoint an arbitrator by 15 February 1981 when,   *h* according to the arbitration clause, the time for commencing arbitration expired. In July 1982 the owners applied to the court under s 27[a] of the Arbitration Act 1950 for an extension of the time for commencing arbitration. Under s 27 the court was empowered to extend the time for giving notice to appoint an arbitrator or for appointing an arbitrator or for taking 'some other step to commence arbitration proceedings'. The judge granted the extension. The charterers appealed, contending that the arbitration   *j* clause contained separate time limits for making a claim in writing and appointing an arbitrator (although the time limit in each case was the same, namely three months), that making a claim in writing could not properly be described as 'some other step to

---

a   Section 27 is set out at p 604 *j* to p 605 *b*, post

a commence arbitration proceedings' within s 27, and that, in relation to the arbitration clause, the court therefore had jurisdiction under s 27 only to extend the time limit for appointing an arbitrator and had no jurisdiction to extend the time limit for making a claim in writing.

Held – A claim in writing could be a 'step to commence arbitration proceedings' within s 27 of the 1950 Act if the parties agreed that it was to be such a step. The terms of the *b* Centrocon arbitration clause clearly indicated that making the claim in writing and appointing an arbitrator went hand in hand and were so inextricably bound up together that they were to be regarded as part of the same process of commencing arbitration proceedings. Accordingly, making a claim in writing was 'some other step to commence arbitration proceedings' within s 27 and the court had jurisdiction to extend the time for making the claim. The charterers' appeal would therefore be dismissed (see p 607 *f* to *h*, post).

c
Dictum of Lloyd J in *Tradax Export SA v Italcarbo Societa di Navigazione SpA, The Sandalion* [1983] 1 Lloyd's Rep 514 approved.

Babanaft International Co SA v Avant Petroleum Inc, The Oltenia [1982] 3 All ER 244 and *Nestlé Co Ltd v E Biggins & Co Ltd* [1958] 1 Lloyd's Rep 398 distinguished.

Notes
d For the extension of time limits contained in arbitration agreements, see 2 Halsbury's Laws (4th edn) para 544, and for cases on the subject, see 3 Digest (Reissue) 7–9, 40–43, 7–15, 195–205.

For the Arbitration Act 1950, s 27, see 2 Halsbury's Statutes (3rd edn) 457.

Cases referred to in judgment
e *Alma Shipping Corp v Union of India, The Astraea* [1971] 2 Lloyd's Rep 494.
A/S Det Dansk-Franske Dampskibsselskab v Compagnie Financière d'Investissements Transatlantiques SA (Compafina), The Himmerland [1965] 2 Lloyd's Rep 353.
Astro Venturoso Compania Naviera SA v Oleagine SA, The Mariannina (26 May 1982, unreported), QBD.
Atlantic Shipping and Trading Co Ltd v Louis Dreyfus & Co [1922] 2 AC 250, [1922] All ER
f Rep 559, HL.
Babanaft International Co SA v Avant Petroleum Inc, The Oltenia [1982] 3 All ER 244, [1982] 1 WLR 871, CA; *affg* [1982] 1 Lloyd's Rep 448.
Ford (H) & Co Ltd v Compagnie Furness (France) [1922] 2 KB 797.
Nestlé Co Ltd v E Biggins & Co Ltd [1958] 1 Lloyd's Rep 398, DC.
Pinnock Bros v Lewis & Peat Ltd [1923] 1 KB 690.
g *Rolimpex (Ch E) Ltd v Avra Shipping Co Ltd, The Angeliki* [1973] 2 Lloyd's Rep 226.
Tradax Export SA v Italcarbo Societa di Navigazione SpA, The Sandalion [1983] 1 Lloyd's Rep 514.
Williams & Mordey v W H Muller & Co (London) Ltd (1924) 18 Ll L Rep 50.

Cases also cited
h *Aaby's (E B) Rederi A/S v Union of India, The Evje* [1972] 2 Lloyd's Rep 129; *on appeal* [1973] 1 Lloyd's Rep 509, CA; [1974] 2 All ER 874, [1975] AC 797, HL.
Annefield, The [1971] 1 All ER 394, [1971] P 168, CA.
A/S Rendal v Arcos Ltd [1937] 3 All ER 577, HL.
Bulgaris v La Plata Cereal Co SA (1947) 80 Ll L Rep 445.
F E Hookway & Co Ltd v H W Hooper & Co [1950] 2 All ER 842n, CA.
j *Metalimex Foreign Trade Corp v Eugenie Maritime Co Ltd* [1962] 1 Lloyd's Rep 378.
Sigalas (G) & Sons v Man Mohan Singh & Co [1958] 2 Lloyd's Rep 298, DC.
Smeaton Hanscomb & Co Ltd v Sasson I Setty, Son & Co (No 2) [1953] 2 All ER 1588, [1953] 1 WLR 1468.
Tradax SA v Volkswagenwerk AG [1969] 2 All ER 144, [1969] 2 QB 599; *affd* [1970] 1 All ER 420, [1970] 1 QB 537, CA.

Interlocutory appeal

The defendants, Oleagine SA of Geneva, Switzerland (the charterers), the intended   *a*
respondents in an arbitration, appealed against the judgment of Hobhouse J given in
chambers on 10 December 1982 granting the application made by way of originating
summons dated 21 July 1982 by the plaintiffs, Jedranska Slobodna Plovidba (a company
incorporated under the laws of Yugoslavia) (the shipowners), the intended claimants in
the arbitration, that time for the commencement of arbitration proceedings under a
charterparty dated 29 February 1980, made between the plaintiffs and the defendants,   *b*
whereby the defendants chartered their vessel the mv Luka Botic to the plaintiffs for a
voyage from the US Gulf to the Dakar–Douala range with a cargo of 10,000 tonnes of
bagged rice, should be extended by 18 months so that the plaintiffs' appointment of their
arbitrator in the said arbitration be rendered and declared valid and their claims be
declared to be neither waived nor absolutely barred. The shipowners' defended claim
was for $US198,385 arising out of the charterers' alleged breach of a 'safe berth always   *c*
accessible' clause in the charterparty, the cost of drydocking and cleaning resulting from
the vessel's hull fouling while waiting to discharge at Lagos, and the cost of fumigating
the holds when the charterers failed to do so. The facts are set out in the judgment of the
court.

Jeffrey Gruder for the charterers.   *d*
Timothy Young for the shipowners.

Cur adv vult

30 September. The following judgment of the court was delivered.   *e*

ACKNER LJ. The respondents (the shipowners) are the registered owners of the mv
Luka Botic. They chartered her to the appellants (the charterers) for a voyage from the
US Gulf to Dakar–Douala range. The relevant charterparty was in substantially the
Gencon form with additional clauses, the relevant one being the Centrocon arbitration
clause, which reads as follows: *f*

'All disputes from time to time arising out of this contract shall, unless the parties
agree forthwith on a single Arbitrator, be referred to the final arbitrament of two
Arbitrators carrying on business in London who shall be Members of the Baltic and
engaged in the Shipping and/or Grain trades, one to be appointed by each of the
parties, with power to such Arbitrators to appoint an Umpire. Any claim must be
made in writing and Claimants' Arbitrator appointed within three months of final   *g*
discharge and where this provision is not complied with the claim shall be deemed
to be waived and absolutely barred. No award shall be questioned or invalidated on
the ground that any of the arbitrators is not qualified as above, unless objection to
his acting be taken before the award is made.'

The vessel arrived at the Lagos/Cotonou anchorage on 1 May 1980 and waited for   *h*
discharge until 7 September 1980. Discharge was finally completed on 15 November
1980, and accordingly the time for the commencement of arbitration expired on 15
February 1981.

No claim in writing having been made, nor the shipowners' arbitrator appointed
within that period, the question arose whether the court had jurisdiction under s 27 of
the Arbitration Act 1950 to extend the time, and if it had jurisdiction whether it should   *j*
extend time. This section reads:

'*Power of court to extend time for commencing arbitration proceedings.* Where the
terms of an agreement to refer future disputes to arbitration provide that any claims
to which the agreement applies shall be barred unless notice to appoint an arbitrator
is given or an arbitrator is appointed or some other step to commence arbitration

proceedings is taken within a time fixed by the agreement, and a dispute arises to which the agreement applies, the High Court, if it is of opinion that in the circumstances of the case undue hardship would otherwise be caused, and notwithstanding that the time so fixed has expired, may, on such terms, if any, as the justice of the case may require, but without prejudice to the provisions of any enactment limiting the time for the commencement of arbitration proceedings, extend the time for such period as it thinks proper.'

On 10 December 1982 Hobhouse J was satisfied that he had jurisdiction to extend time and that it was a proper case in which to grant the required extension. The course taken before Hobhouse J was somewhat unusual because the actual hearing was devoted to whether or not the judge should exercise his discretion. Counsel for the charterers did however take the point that the court had no power under s 27 of the Arbitration Act 1950 to extend the time for the shipowners to make a claim in writing in view of the decision of this court in *Babanaft International Co SA v Avant Petroleum Inc, The Oltenia* [1982] 3 All ER 244, [1982] 1 WLR 871. That was not a decision on the wording of the Centrocon arbitration clause, but on quite a different clause, and it had been distinguished by Lloyd J in *Tradax Export SA v Italcarbo Societa di Navigazione SpA, The Sandalion* [1983] 1 Lloyd's Rep 514, a decision on the selfsame Centrocon arbitration clause. A similiar such decision had been made a few months earlier by Staughton J in *Astro Venturoso Compania Naviera SA v Oleagine SA, The Mariannina* (26 May 1982, unreported), but an agreed note by counsel of his judgment had been put before us. Hobhouse J had, a week before the application, decided the point in the same way as Lloyd J, although that decision is unreported. Counsel for the charterers therefore reserved the point and Hobhouse J gave them leave to appeal specifically on the question whether on the true construction of the contract and of s 27 of the Arbitration Act 1950 he had jurisdiction to make his order.

There is no dispute as to the history of this section which is succinctly set out by Kerr J in *Ch E Rolimpex Ltd v Avra Shipping Co Ltd, The Angeliki* [1973] 2 Lloyd's Rep 226 at 229:

'The section was first enacted as sect. 16 of the Arbitration Act, 1934. It is clear that it owes its origin either to the Centrocon arbitration clause or to clauses of this type, which provide that all claims are to be barred unless an arbitrator is appointed or notice of arbitration is given within a certain time from the discharge or delivery of the goods: see in particular *Atlantic Shipping and Trading Co. Ltd. v. Louis Dreyfus & Company* ([1922] 2 AC 250, [1922] All ER Rep 559); *H. Ford & Co Ltd v. Compagnie Furness (France)* ([1922] 2 KB 797), and *Williams & Mordey v. W. H. Muller & Co. (London) Ltd.* ((1924) 18 Ll L Rep 50). The hardship caused by such clauses, together with a reference to these cases, was discussed in paras 33 to 35 of the Report of the Committee on the Law of Arbitration in 1927 (Cmnd 2817) under the chairmanship of Mr. Justice MacKinnon (as he then was). This report recommended the enactment of what later became sect. 16 of the Act of 1934.'

The point of counsel for the charterers, and that of his colleagues in the recent cases to which we have referred, can be expressed quite simply. The Centrocon arbitration clause contains two different requirements which have to be fulfilled by the claimants within three months of final discharge, namely (i) the making of a claim in writing and (ii) the appointment of an arbitrator. Section 27 clearly gives the court power to extend time if the appointment of an arbitrator is not made in time, since this is one of the matters specifically referred to in the section. However, the claim in writing cannot be properly described as 'some other step to commence arbitration proceedings', and there is accordingly no jurisdiction to grant an extension of time for making the claim.

A similar such submission in *The Mariannina* provoked Staughton J to observe that—

'To anyone familiar with the Centrocon arbitration clause this would have been an astonishing submission until a few months ago because extensions of time were frequently given over the years in cases in which this clause has applied.'

The judge in particular drew attention to two cases. The first was *A/S Det Dansk-Franske Dampskibsselskab v Compagnie Financière d'Investissements Transatlantiques SA (Compafina)*, **a** *The Himmerland* [1965] 2 Lloyd's Rep 353. In that case, Mocatta J dismissed an application under s 27 in the exercise of his discretion, but both he and counsel, then Mr Robert Goff, appear to have assumed that jurisdiction existed. The other case was *Alma Shipping Corp v Union of India, The Astraea* [1971] 2 Lloyd's Rep 494. In that case no claim was made for two years and a s 27 application was made which was not contested as a matter of jurisdiction but was dismissed as a matter of discretion. If the point of counsel for the **b** charterers is a good one it was missed both by counsel, then Mr Hobhouse, and by the judge then Roskill J. In each of the above cases, if counsel for the charterers is right, there was no need to spend time on whether or not discretion should have been exercised in favour of granting an extension of time. The short answer was that since there was no claim in writing in time, the court had no jurisdiction to grant an extension.

We come now to *The Oltenia*, a case in which both Bingham J (see [1982] 1 Lloyd's Rep **c** 448) and the Court of Appeal (see [1982] 3 All ER 244, [1982] 1 WLR 871) reluctantly concluded that there was a serious gap in the clause which prevented them from granting relief from the time-bar. That case was not a decision on the Centrocon arbitration clause. Had it been, the gap would have been significantly more serious. In that case the charterparty contained an arbitration clause, cl 24, which provided for any and all differences and disputes of whatsoever nature arising out of the charterparty to be put to **d** arbitration in the City of London. It contained no time-limit for commencing arbitration proceedings.

Quite separate and distinct and in no way connected with cl 24 was a typed special provision of the charterparty namely, cl M2 which read as follows:

'Charterers shall be discharged and released from all liability in respect of any **e** claims Owners may have under this Charter Party ... unless a claim has been presented to Charterers in writing with all available supporting documents, within 90 (ninety) days from completion of discharge of the cargo concerned under this Charter Party.'

It was submitted in that case that by reading the contract as a whole it was possible to reach the conclusion that the parties had agreed that the owner's claims should be barred **f** if some step to commence arbitration proceedings is not taken within a fixed period. Donaldson LJ observed that this involved linking the M2 time-limit to the arbitration clause and in giving a very wide construction to the concept of taking a step to commence arbitration proceedings. As to the linking, he had earlier observed that cl M2 had no apparent connection with the commencement of arbitration proceedings within 90 days or any other time. It appeared to relate solely to making a claim in a particular form **g** within a fixed period. He continued ([1982] 3 All ER 244 at 255, [1982] 1 WLR 871 at 884–885):

'I doubt whether the argument could have been advanced with the faintest air of plausibility but for the discovery since the hearing below of the decision of the Divisional Court in *Nestlé Co Ltd v E Biggins & Co Ltd* [1958] 1 Lloyd's Rep 398. **h** There a contract for the sale of coffee provided that, failing amicable agreement, any dispute should be referred to arbitration in London according to the rules of the Coffee Trade Federation of London. Those rules required all arbitrations to be "claimed within 14 days following final day of weighing and/or warehousing of the contract goods at port of final destination". The contract then provided that "any claim on quality or condition of the goods must be made not later than 14 days **j** from final day of weighing and/or discharge of goods at port of final destination". Lord Goddard CJ, sitting with Hilbery and Donovan LJJ, in giving the judgment of the Court said (at 400): "It seems to me that the Court has clear jurisdiction under [s 27] to extend the time in which a claim is to be made because the claim is the first step towards arbitration. If the claim is not made within 14 days and if the parties a go before the arbitrator, the objection will at once be taken that the arbitrator cannot make an award in favour of the buyer here in question because the claim was not made within 14 days. Therefore, it seems to me that, taking the provision in the contract that the making of an claim on quality must be made not later than 14 days from a particular date, the making of such a claim is a step to commence proceedings; and, therefore, the Court had got jurisdiction to enlarge the time. In fact, I think it is just this sort of provision in a contract with which this section is intended to deal".

b The concept of "claiming arbitration" is well known in the commodity trades. Telex messages fly to and fro and at some stage one party or the other says, "We claim arbitration". The arbitration rules of the trade concerned then provide the steps to be taken by each party. I would therefore accept that in such cases "claiming arbitration" may be regarded as a step to commence arbitration proceedings within the meaning of s 27. I would also accept that under that particular contract, the

c claim for quality or condition had to precede or accompany the claim for arbitration, since arbitration cannot be claimed in vaccuo: it has to be linked to a specific dispute. Where I have much more difficulty is in seeing why the making of a claim for quality or condition is a step to commence arbitration proceedings. It is a condition precedent to such proceedings, but it does not of itself commence the proceedings or necessarily lead to their being commenced. The claim may be conceded or settled

d amicably. In my judgment, the decision of the Divisional Court was wrong and should be overruled. In essence s 27 empowers the court to extend the time fixed for giving notice to appoint an arbitrator, appointing an arbitrator or taking some other step to commence arbitration proceedings if doing so will prevent a claim becoming time-barred. It does not empower the court to extend any other time limits. In parenthesis I would add that it does not empower the court to extend a

e time limit for commencing arbitration if, in the absence of such an extension, the claim would remain alive and could be litigated as was the case, for example, in *Pinnock Bros v Lewis & Peat Ltd* [1923] 1 KB 690.'

We agree with Lloyd J in *The Sandalion* [1983] 1 Lloyd's Rep 514 at 519 that nothing in *The Oltenia* decides that a claim in writing *cannot* be a step to commence arbitration

f proceedings within the meaning of s 27, if the parties so agree. The whole of the clause with which we are concerned relates to arbitration. The first sentence requires claims to be referred to arbitration; the second sentence deals with the requirement that the claim is to be in writing and the arbitrator appointed in the limited period and the consequences if this does not occur. The third sentence deals with the invalidation of awards. Moreover, the use of the singular 'where this provision is not complied with' is a clear indication that the notice requirement is 'a step to commence arbitration proceedings'. As previously

g stated, in *The Oltenia* the arbitration clause and the M2 clause were separate, distinct and unrelated. In *Nestlé Co Ltd v E Biggins & Co Ltd* the time-limit for making claims for quality or condition was a separate and distinct provision in the same clause. We agree with Lloyd J that the appointment of the arbitrator and the making of the claim in writing in the arbitration clause go hand in hand, and that both provisions are so

h inextricably bound together that they should be regarded as part of the same process of commencing arbitration proceedings within the meaning of s 27.

We accordingly dismiss this appeal.

Appeal dismissed. Leave to appeal to House of Lords granted.

Solicitors: *Thomas Cooper & Stibbard* (for the charterers); *Richards Butler & Co* (for the shipowners).

Mary Rose Plummer   Barrister.

Practice Note

COURT OF APPEAL, CRIMINAL DIVISION
LORD LANE CJ, MUSTILL AND LEONARD JJ
10 NOVEMBER 1983

Crown Court – Bail – Applications – Bail pending appeal to Court of Appeal – Procedure – Fitness for appeal – Grant of bail by judge – Matters to be considered – Length of time before hearing of appeal – Urgent cases – Criminal Appeal Act 1968, ss 1(2), 11(1A) – Supreme Court Act 1981, s 81(1B).

LORD LANE CJ made the following statement at the sitting of the court. The procedure for granting bail by a judge of the Crown Court pending an appeal to the Court of Appeal, Criminal Division (see the Criminal Appeal Act 1968, ss 1(2) and 11(1A) and the Supreme Court Act 1981, s 81(1B)) is described in *A Guide to Proceedings in the Court of Appeal Criminal Division*. This is available at Crown Courts and is to be found at (1983) 77 Cr App R 138 and [1983] Crim LR 145.

The procedure is also set out in outline on Criminal Appeal Office Form C (Crown Court judge's certificate of fitness for appeal) and Form BC (Crown Court judge's order granting bail), copies of which are held by the Crown Court. The court clerk will ensure that these forms are always available when a judge hears an application under these provisions.

The judge may well think it right (a) to hear the application in chambers with a shorthand writer present, (b) to invite the defendant's counsel to submit before the hearing of the application a draft of the grounds which he will ask the judge to certify on Form C. Counsel for the Crown will be better able to assist the judge at the hearing if the draft ground is sent beforehand to him also.

The first question is whether there exists a particular and cogent ground of appeal. If there is no such ground there can be no certificate, and if there is no certificate there can be no bail. A judge should not grant a certificate with regard to sentence merely in the light of mitigation to which he has, in his opinion, given due weight, or in regard to conviction on a ground where he considers the chance of a successful appeal is not substantial. The judge should bear in mind that, where a certificate is refused, application may be made to the Court of Appeal for leave to appeal and for bail.

The length of the period which might elapse before the hearing of the appeal is *not* a ground of appeal appropriate to the judge's certificate.

That period, if there is otherwise good ground for a certificate, may be one factor in the decision whether or not to grant bail; but a judge who is minded to take this factor into account may find it advisable to have the court clerk contact the Criminal Appeal Office listing co-ordinator in order that he may have an accurate and up-to-date assessment of the likely waiting time. The co-ordinator will require a general account of the weight and urgency of the case.

Where the defendant's representative considers that bail should be applied for as a matter of urgency, the application should normally be made, in the first instance, to the trial judge, and the Court of Appeal may decline to treat such an application as urgent if there is no good reason why it has not been made to the trial judge.

N P Metcalfe Esq   Barrister.

K Shoe Shops Ltd v Hardy (Valuation Officer) and others

and other appeals

HOUSE OF LORDS
LORD FRASER OF TULLYBELTON, LORD KEITH OF KINKEL, LORD SCARMAN, LORD BRIDGE OF
HARWICH AND LORD TEMPLEMAN
4, 5 OCTOBER, 3 NOVEMBER 1983

Rates – Valuation list – Date of valuation – Common valuation date – Assessment of rateable value of shop premises – Valuation officer estimating rent payable on 1 April 1973 when valuation list came into force – Estimate made in 1972 from information supplied to valuation officer in 1971 – Whether 1 April 1973 common valuation date – General Rate Act 1967, s 68(1).

The appellants were ratepayers who occupied shop premises which were included in the 1973 valuation list as having rateable values based on the estimated rent at which the premises might reasonably be expected to let on 1 April 1973, being the date when, by virtue of s 68(1)[d] of the General Rate Act 1967, the 1973 valuation list came into force. The rateable values in the valuation list had, however, been prepared by the valuation officer in 1972 from information supplied to him by the public in 1971 in response to requests for such information made by him in 1970. The ratepayers proposed that their rateable values should be reduced to those prevailing in 1970, on the basis that the rateable values of certain other properties in the same area corresponded with their 1970 values. A local valuation court reduced the assessment and both the ratepayers and the valuation officer appealed. The ratepayers conceded that on values current at 1 April 1973 the valuation officer's estimates were not excessive, but they contended that the valuation officer when valuing for a new list was not required to value as at a particular date but merely to value all the hereditaments in the area by reference to the same date, and that by valuing other properties in the area according to their value as at late 1970 he had determined that that date should be the common valuation date for the area. The Lands Tribunal held that the rateable values were to be determined as at the date after which no further evidence as to rental values had been collected, which it determined to be the end of 1971, and it held that accordingly the appropriate values were the values obtaining at the end of 1971 projected forward to April 1973. An appeal by the valuation officer was upheld by the Court of Appeal, which held that the common valuation date, as determined by s 68(1), was 1 April 1973 and that the valuation officer's assessment corresponded to rental values prevalent on that date. The ratepayers appealed.

Held – Although the 1967 Act contained no express requirement that for the purposes of a valuation list hereditaments were to be valued as at the date when the valuation list came into force, it was necessary to make an implication to that effect because (a) the working of the Act required there to be a common valuation date, (b) s 68(1) pointed to the date when the valuation list came into force as being the common valuation date, and (c) there was no provision for the determination or ascertainment of any other valuation date. It followed that since the valuation officer's estimates reflected the rental values of the ratepayers' premises on the common valuation date of 1 April 1973 the ratepayers' appeals would be dismissed (see p 610 f to h, p 612 a to c and g, p 613 a to e and p 614 h j, post).

Notes

For the date of valuation for rating purposes, see 39 Halsbury's Laws (4th edn) para 113.

---

a   Section 68(1) is set out at p 611 d, post

For the General Rate Act 1967, ss 20, 68, see 27 Halsbury's Statutes (3rd edn) 98, 159.

As from 13 November 1980 s 20 of the 1967 Act was amended by s 30 of the Local Government, Planning and Land Act 1980 and s 68(1) of the 1967 Act was substituted by s 28 of the 1980 Act.

Case referred to in opinions

R v Paddington Valuation Officer, ex p Peachey Property Corp Ltd [1965] 2 All ER 836, [1966] 1 QB 380, [1965] 3 WLR 426, CA.

Consolidated appeals

K Shoe Shops Ltd and Saxone Shoe Co Ltd (the ratepayers) appealed with leave of the Court of Appeal against the decision of the Court of Appeal (Stephenson, Kerr LJJ and Sir Patrick Browne) on 9 December 1982 allowing an appeal by the first respondent, Brian David Hardy (the valuation officer), and the second respondents, Westminster City Council (the rating authority), by way of case stated, and dismissing the ratepayers' cross-appeal from the decision of the Lands Tribunal dated 13 October 1980 on appeals by the ratepayers and the valuation officer and rating authority from decisions of the Greater London Central Valuation Court given on 29 November 1976 reducing the assessments on certain shop premises in Regent Street, London W1 of which the ratepayers were the occupiers. The appeals were consolidated by order of the registrar of the Lands Tribunal. The facts are set out in the opinion of Lord Templeman.

David Widdicombe QC and Guy Roots for the ratepayers.
William Glover QC and Alan Fletcher for the valuation officer.
Richard Tucker QC and Richard Hone for the rating authority.

Their Lordships took time for consideration.

3 November. The following opinions were delivered.

LORD FRASER OF TULLYBELTON. My Lords, I have had the advantage of reading in draft the speech prepared by my noble and learned friend Lord Templeman, and I agree with it. For the reasons given by him I would dismiss these appeals.

LORD KEITH OF KINKEL. My Lords, I agree that for the reasons set out in the speech to be delivered by my noble and learned friend Lord Templeman these appeals should be dismissed.

LORD SCARMAN. My Lords, I have had the advantage of reading in draft the speech to be delivered by my noble and learned friend Lord Templeman. I agree with it and for the reasons he gives I would dismiss the appeals. I also concur in the order my noble and learned friend proposes in respect of costs.

LORD BRIDGE OF HARWICH. My Lords, for the reasons given by my noble and learned friend Lord Templeman I too would dismiss these appeals.

LORD TEMPLEMAN. My Lords, these appeals call for the determination of a question of construction which arises under the General Rate Act 1967. The appellants are ratepayers of shop premises at Regent Street in Westminster. The first respondent is the valuation officer and the second respondents are the rating authority for Westminster. The question is whether the appellants' premises should be valued as at late 1970 as the appellants contend or whether they should be valued as at 1 April 1973 as the respondents maintain and as the Court of Appeal held for the purposes of the rating valuation list which came into force on 1 April 1973.

The General Rate Act 1967 received the royal assent on 22 March 1967 and has since
been amended, but the amendments are not relevant to the present question. Section
1(1) of the Act establishes rating areas and rating authorities corresponding to borough
and district areas and authorities. By s 1(2)—

> 'Every rating authority shall have power in accordance with this Act to make and
> levy rates on the basis of an assessment in respect of the yearly value of property in
> their rating area . . .'

By s 2(4)—

> 'the general rate for any rating area . . . (b) shall be made and levied in accordance
> with the valuation list in force for the time being . . .'

Sections 12 to 15 enable county councils and the Greater London Council and certain
other authorities to issue precepts requiring the rating authorities within their jurisdiction
to levy rates for the purposes of the precepting authorities.

By s 19(3) the rateable value of a hereditament shall be based on 'the rent at which it is
estimated the hereditament might reasonably be expected to let from year to year' on
certain specified assumptions as to the burden of the usual covenants entered into
between landlord and tenant.

Section 68(1) provides:

> 'In the case of each rating area, new valuation lists shall be prepared and made by
> the valuation officer so as to come into force on 1st April in 1973 and each fifth year
> thereafter.'

A valuation officer as defined by s 115(1) means any officer of the Commissioners of
Inland Revenue appointed by the commissioners in relation to each valuation list.

Section 68(2) requires that the valuation officer—

> 'shall, not later than the end of the month of December preceding the date on
> which the list is to come into force (or if in any particular case the Minister, either
> before or after the end of that month, allows an extended period, then not later than
> the end of that period) sign the list and transmit it . . . to the rating authority . . .'

The 1967 Act thus provides for a quinquennial valuation which will bring all rateable
values up to date when each new list comes into force and which will last for the next
five years. The Act does not require the valuation officer to begin to make his estimates
of rateable value on any particular date. The date fixed for the completion of his task, 31
December, may be extended by the minister. But the task of every valuation officer is
the same and every valuation list must come into force on the same day. Consistently
with the principles of uniformity and fairness which are applicable to rating valuations,
each valuation officer must value each property by reference to the same date. It is not
conceivable that Parliament intended that, for example, the valuation officer of
Westminster should value some premises in his area on the assumption of an annual
tenancy granted and commencing at the end of 1970 but should value other premises in
his area on the assumption of an annual tenancy granted and commencing on 31
December 1972 or 1 April 1973. Nor is it conceivable that Parliament intended that
premises in different rating areas in the same or different precept areas could be valued
by reference to different dates. The only fixed and immutable date provided by the 1967
Act is the relevant quinquennial 1 April, in the present case 1 April 1973, and the Act
directs that each valuation officer shall prepare and make a new list 'so as to come into
force on 1st April in 1973'. In the words of Sir Patrick Browne delivering the judgment
of the Court of Appeal in the instant case:

> 'Uniformity and fairness as between all rating areas can only be achieved if all
> rating areas are valued by reference to the same date, and the only possible common
> date is . . . the date when the valuation list comes into force, in this case 1 April
> 1973.'

Similar views were expressed, albeit by obiter dicta, by Lord Denning MR in *R v Paddington Valuation Officer, ex p Peachey Property Corp Ltd* [1965] 2 All ER 836 at 843, *a* [1966] 1 QB 380 at 405 where, dealing with the statutory predecessor of the 1967 Act, Lord Denning MR said that the valuation was 'to be based on current values so as to reflect, so far as possible, the values prevailing at the time when the list was to take effect'. In my opinion the 1967 Act requires the rateable value of each of the appellants' hereditaments, as entered in the 1973 valuation list, to be based on an estimate of the rent which the landlord of that hereditament could reasonably expect to negotiate on 1 *b* April 1973 for an annual tenancy commencing on that date.

The appellants deny that the Act requires that the valuation list which came into force on 1 April 1973 should reflect rental values current at that date. They rely on the fact that the 1967 Act does not contain an express requirement that hereditaments should be valued as at 1 April 1973. But such a requirement must be implied because a common valuation date is necessary, the language of s 68 points to 1 April 1973 as that common *c* valuation date and there is no provision in the Act for the determination or ascertainment of any other common valuation date.

The appellants assert that the valuation officer could not make in advance correct estimates of rents payable on 1 April 1973. The Westminster valuation list was based on information sought from the public in 1970 and supplied to the valuation officer in 1971 and the estimate was prepared during 1972. But it does not seem to me that the *d* Westminster valuation officer or any other trained valuer would have any great difficulty in estimating the rents obtainable on 1 April 1973. The valuation officer could, down to the date when he finalised his estimates, take account of any information which became available. He would take into consideration rents negotiated for each hereditament and for comparable premises down to the date when he finally completed his estimate. He would consider the state and history of the hereditament and of the neighbourhood, the *e* pattern of past rents and such other information as, in his professional opinion, assisted him to estimate the rent which the landlord could reasonably expect to obtain on the common valuation date 1 April 1973. If the valuation officer's estimate was not accepted after the publication of the list on 31 December 1972, the ratepayer and the rating authority could, as envisaged by the Act, propose an alteration to the valuation list to the valuation officer and if he demurred then to the local valuation court and could appeal *f* from that court to the Lands Tribunal. Both the local valuation court and the Lands Tribunal would inevitably not be able to consider the validity of the estimate until after 1 April 1973 and all parties could then check the valuation officer's estimate with lettings made up to 1 April 1973. Thus the correctness of the valuation officer's estimate can be checked after the valuation list has come into force and the common valuation date has passed. In the present case a comparison of the valuation officer's estimate of rents *g* reasonably obtainable for the appellants' premises with the rents proved to be obtained or obtainable in the first quarter of 1973 for comparable premises showed that the valuation officer's estimate was accurate. So much is now conceded.

On behalf of the appellants it was submitted that the provisions of ss 20 and 68(4) of the 1967 Act are inconsistent with any implication that the Act created a common valuation date which was 1 April 1973. *h*

Section 20 does not deal with the making of the valuation list but with the alteration of a list after it has come into force on 1 April 1973. Such an alteration to a valuation list must not result in the value of the hereditament exceeding—

> 'the value which would have been ascribed thereto in that list if the hereditament had been subsisting throughout the year before that in which the valuation list came into force, on the assumptions that at the time by reference to which that *j* value would have been ascertained . . .'

the hereditament was in the same state and the locality in which the hereditament is situated was in the same state as at the date of the proposal for alteration of the valuation list (see sub-s (1)). In the present case this section merely prevents an alteration to the list reflecting increases in rent value for any period after 1 April 1973. The appellants

a contend that if the original valuation list was intended to reflect values as at 1 April 1973, that being the common valuation date, the draftsman of s 20 would not have used the cumbersome expression 'time by reference to which that value would have been ascertained' but would have referred to the common valuation date or the date when the valuation list came into force. I do not accept this inference; s 20 is appropriately worded to fulfil its purpose, it does not contradict s 68(1) or suggest any common valuation date

b for the purposes of the valuation list other than 1 April 1973.

The appellants also suggested that s 68(3) and (4) was inconsistent with any inference that there was a common valuation date of 1 April 1973. Section 68(3) and (4) does not deal with the preparation of a valuation list but enables a valuation officer to revise a list between 31 December 1972 after it has been completed and 1 April 1973 when it comes into force. Section 68(3) enables a valuation officer to revise the list in the light of any

c material change of circumstances defined by s 68(4) which occurs after 'the time by reference to which the valuation officer prepared so much of the list as is affected by that change of circumstances'. Section 68(4) sheds no light on the common valuation date, the date when each hereditament must be deemed to be let for the purposes of preparing the list. Section 68(3) and (4) deals only with a hereditament which suffers a change of circumstances occurring after the date when the valuation officer ascertained the relevant

d facts on which his estimate was based.

In the result I can find nothing in the Act inconsistent with the inference that s 68(1) established 1 April 1973 as the common valuation date by reference to which each valuation officer must estimate the rental value of each hereditament. The appellants admitted that nothing in the Act indicated any common valuation date save 1 April 1973. They accepted that the principles of rating valuation required that all valuation

e officers should accept the same common valuation date. The appellants' counsel was quite unable to provide any convincing answer to the questions posed by my noble and learned friend Lord Bridge how the common valuation date, if not 1 April 1983, was to be ascertained and by whom it was to be determined. The appellants asserted, by reference to a graph which their surveyor dignified by the name of a tonogram and by deductions from that graph by a process which their surveyor exalted to the science or

f art of 'tonometry', that in relation to premises in Oxford Street and Bond Street and elsewhere consisting of 182 hereditaments out of 135,000 hereditaments comprised in the Westminster rating area it was possible to show that on average the rent estimates made by the valuation officer corresponded more closely to rents current in late 1970 than they corresponded to rents payable subsequently. Therefore, according to the argument of the appellants, the valuation officer had intentionally or accidentally

g determined that the common valuation date for the Westminister rating area should be late 1970. The rental value for the appellants' premises estimated by the valuation officer was £250 per square metre of zone A floor space (a rent for the basic unit from which, it is common ground, the rent of the whole shop can be calculated) corresponding to rents prevailing on 1 April 1973; the zone A rent should be reduced uniformly to £175 equivalent to average rents prevailing in late 1970. It must be assumed that a common

h valuation date of late 1970 had been co-ordinated by the Commissioners of Inland Revenue with all valuation officers. This assumption was flatly contradicted by the actual instructions of the Commissioners of Inland Revenue, which plainly indicated to valuation officers that they ought to estimate rents payable on a common valuation date of 1 April 1973.

The evolution of the thoroughly fallacious reasoning of the appellants followed a

j tortuous path. The valuation officer for Westminster duly signed the valuation list by 31 December 1972. On 2 August 1973 the appellants, unhelpfully, but in accordance with recognised practice, proposed a reduction in the rateable values of their Regent Street premises to the nominal sum of £1. In December 1975, January 1976 and April 1976 the appellants' surveyor, acting on behalf of certain other ratepayers in Oxford Street and Bond Street, secured the agreement of the valuation officer to a reduction of the rateable values of his clients' premises. The reductions were not uniform but varied in terms of zone A rent from £25 to £95. No such agreement was reached with regard to the *a* appellants' premises in Regent Street. The appellants pursued their proposals for alteration of the valuation list pursuant to s 76(5) of the 1967 Act to the local valuation court, which is required to—

    'give such directions with respect to the manner in which the hereditament in *b* question is to be treated in the valuation list as appear to them to be necessary to give effect to the contention of the appellant if and so far as that contention appears to the court to be well founded . . .'

The court gave its decision on 29 November 1976. The respondents appealed to the *c* Lands Tribunal on quantum. The appellants appealed to the Lands Tribunal on the grounds that their hereditaments ought to be valued by reference to rents 'equivalent to 1969 rental levels'. By s 77 of the 1967 Act the Lands Tribunal 'may give any directions which the local valuation court might have given'. The Lands Tribunal rejected the jargon of tonometry which provided the argument in favour of a common valuation date of late 1970. The Lands Tribunal, however, fell victim to alternative jargon which *d* involved the determination of a 'stop date' by means of which it was argued, and accepted by the Lands Tribunal, that the appellants' premises should be valued as though they had been let at the end of 1971.

    The appellants, pursuant to s 3(4) of the Lands Tribunal Act 1949, required the Lands Tribunal to state a case for the decision of the Court of Appeal on the grounds that the decision of the Lands Tribunal was 'erroneous in point of law'. All three parties appealed *e* to the Court of Appeal. On 9 December 1982 the Court of Appeal, in an impeccable judgment of the court delivered by Sir Patrick Browne, ignored the tonogram and the stop date, construed the General Rate Act 1967 according to its terms and intentions and upheld the valuation officer's estimate of the rental values of the appellants' premises because those estimates corresponded to rental values prevailing on the common valuation date 1 April 1973 pointed out by the Act. The Court of Appeal granted the *f* appellants leave to appeal to your Lordships' House.

    While I acknowledge the ingenuity, sincerity and experience of the surveyor who was responsible for the 'tonogram', I reject this method of approach entirely. It is always open to a ratepayer to urge that his rateable value should be decreased because other comparable properties have been assessed at lower figures. Disputed questions of fact and fairness lie within the province of the local valuation court and the Lands Tribunal. But a ratepayer *g* cannot as a matter of law require his assessment to be reduced to the lowest plausible common denominator said to be deducible from a comparison of rents and estimates of other hereditaments on a time basis. In the case of each hereditament it is for the valuation officer, the local valuation court and the Lands Tribunal to determine the rental value appropriate to that hereditament in the light of all the circumstances and available information. If as in the present case the estimate of the valuation officer reflects *h* the rental value of the hereditament on the common valuation date, 1 April 1973, the ratepayer has no cause for complaint. Estimates for other premises which are too high can be reduced at the behest of the ratepayer. Estimates which are too low can be increased on the initiative of the valuation officer or the rating authority.

    The appeals must be dismissed and the appellants must pay the costs of the first respondent valuation officer of the appeal to your Lordships' House. The second *j* respondents, the rating authority, were financially interested in the results of these appeals but their interests were identical with those of the valuation officer. Moreover, it was in my opinion the task of the valuation officer rather than the task of the rating authority to ascertain whether as a matter of law all the estimates of all valuation officers should be based on a common valuation date which was the quinquennial first day of *a* April. The rating authority were entitled to appear before your Lordships but must pay their own costs of exercising that privilege.

Appeals dismissed.

Solicitors: *Titmuss Sainer & Webb* (for the ratepayers); *Solicitor of Inland Revenue*; *Terence F Neville* (for the rating authority).

b   Mary Rose Plummer   Barrister.

Ebrahim v Ali (otherwise Ebrahim) (Queen's Proctor intervening)

c
FAMILY DIVISION
SIR JOHN ARNOLD P
12 APRIL 1983

d
Divorce – Intervention – Queen's Proctor showing cause why decree nisi and absolute should be declared void – Husband not serving petition on wife – Whether proceedings 'in progress' – Whether Queen's Proctor entitled to intervene – Matrimonial Causes Act 1973, s 8(1).

For the purposes of s 8(1)(b)[a] of the Matrimonial Causes Act 1973, proceedings are 'in progress' after the filing of a valid petition for divorce until such steps have been taken to dispose of the petition either by withdrawal, discontinuance or dismissal or by an order made on it, and until then the Queen's Proctor is entitled to intervene on any matter
e material to the decision of the case. Furthermore, where a valid divorce petition has been filed but not served on the respondent (and no order has been made dispensing with service or making alternative provision for services on the respondent), a decree absolute granted to the petitioner is void rather than merely voidable, and therefore, notwithstanding the granting of the decree, the Queen's Proctor may make application to the court for relief pursuant to s 8(1)(b) since the void order cannot dispose of the
f proceedings (see p 616 *e* and p 617 *d e*, post).

Craig v Kanseen [1943] 1 All ER 108 applied.

Notes
For service of petition for divorce, see 13 Halsbury's Laws (4th edn) para 739, and for cases on the subject, see 27(2) Digest (Reissue) 624 626, 4608–4626.
g   For the Matrimonial Causes Act 1973, s 8, see 43 Halsbury's Statutes (3rd edn) 550.

Cases referred to in judgment
Clutterbuck v Clutterbuck and Reynolds (1961) 105 SJ 1012.
Craig v Kanseen [1943] 1 All ER 108, [1943] 1 KB 256, CA.
Purse v Purse [1981] 2 All ER 465, [1981] Fam 143, [1981] 2 WLR 759, CA.
h *Woolfenden (orse Clegg) v Woolfenden (orse Clegg)* [1947] 2 All ER 653, [1948] P 27.

Cases also cited
Dryden v Dryden [1973] 3 All ER 526, [1973] Fam 217.
Everitt v Everitt [1948] 2 All ER 545, CA.
F (infants) (adoption order: validity), Re [1977] 2 All ER 777, [1977] Fam 165, CA.
Wiseman v Wiseman [1953] 1 All ER 601, [1953] P 79, CA.
j

Application
The Queen's Proctor applied by plea under s 8(1)(b) of the Matrimonial Causes Act 1973 seeking that the order of decree nisi granted on 18 July 1979 in favour of the petitioner,

---

a   Section 8(1), so far as material, is set out, at p 617 *b*, post

Mohammed Ali Ebrahim (the husband), and the decree absolute made on 23 October 1979 be declared void on the ground that there had been no service of the petition on the respondent, Shirley Ann Ali (otherwise Ebrahim) (the wife) and (ii) that the petition filed by the husband on 11 June 1979 be dimissed on the ground that the particulars of unreasonable behaviour of the wife relied on in the petition were untrue. The facts are set out in the judgment of Sir John Arnold P.

The Solicitor General (Sir Ian Percival QC) and *E James Holman* for the Queen's Proctor. The husband and the wife did not appear.

SIR JOHN ARNOLD P. This is a claim by the Queen's Proctor, asking for the decree nisi, which was pronounced on 18 July 1979, purporting to begin the process of the dissolution of the marriage of Mohamed Said Mohamed Ali Ebrahim and Shirley Ann Ali (otherwise Ebrahim), his wife, void and equally to declare the decree absolute purporting to be made on the basis of that decree nisi on 23 October 1979 void and also to have dismissed the petition on the basis of which those decrees were purportedly made.

Mr and Mrs Ali, as I shall call them, were married on 10 December 1975, and on 11 June 1979 a petition was presented to the court by the husband for the dissolution of that marriage. That, on the face of it, was a wholly valid petition, and there is no fact known to me which suggests otherwise. But the petition was never served on the wife, the respondent, nor was any order dispensing with service or ordering any other form of service ever made or indeed purported to be made. Those facts are stated in the plea and, on the authority of *Clutterbuck v Clutterbuck and Reynolds* (1961) 105 SJ 1012, the facts stated in a plea in the circumstances of this case, that is to say circumstances in which no answer denying the allegations has been filed, are to be taken as proved.

It is, in my judgment, quite plain that where there has been no service of process any order made in the litigation in which process should have been served must necessarily be void, unless service has been in some way validly dispensed with. This is a case in which orders were made: first the decree nisi, subsequently the making absolute of that decree, on the basis of a supposed service of a process which had never been served at all. I take that fundamental proposition as regards the law in general from *Craig v Kanseen* [1943] 1 All ER 108 at 113, [1943] KB 256 at 262–263, a decision of the Court of Appeal, in which such lack of service was described by Lord Greene MR as rendering the subsequent orders void because of that, as he said, fundamental vice.

In the case of a void order, once it is established by the facts and relevant law that it is void, it follows that it will be declared to be so by the court on the application of a party; so much is clear. It is also perfectly clear that that declaration may be made by the court of first instance. It may also be made in the Court of Appeal, and that matter was fully considered, debated and decided in *Purse v Purse* [1981] 2 All ER 465, [1981] Fam 143. There is ample precedent for that declaration being made in this division in, among other cases, *Woolfenden (orse Clegg) v Woolfenden (orse Clegg)* [1947] 2 All ER 653, [1948] P 27. It is not necessary to refer except tangentially to an altogether different class of case, cases in which the orders concerned were not void but voidable, in which case those orders are and are to be treated as valid until they are avoided, there being, of course, in such cases a discretion whether to avoid or not to avoid. But that has nothing to do with this case, in which the court proceeds on the basis of a void order, an order, that is to say, which is aptly described as null and void, it being quite simply a nullity.

Thus, it is plain that there is ample jurisdiction in this court to declare such an order void at the suit of a party. But this is not a case in which it is sought to have that relief at the suit of a party. It is sought to have that relief on the application by plea of the Queen's Proctor.

It must be right, indeed it must be a fundamental truth, that in a matter in which the Queen's Proctor is entitled to intervene, and in which if a party were seeking the order the order would be made, the Queen's Proctor, if properly entitled to intervene must be

entitled to the same relief. It is, therefore, relevant to examine the question whether the
a Queen's Proctor is entitled to intervene.

There might be all sorts of reasons why the Queen's Proctor is entitled to intervene,
but that on which the Solicitor General representing the Queen's Proctor has relied, and
the only matter which has been opened to me, is the provision in that behalf in s 8(1)(b)
of the Matrimonial Causes Act 1973, which says that—

b
> 'In the case of a petition for divorce . . . (b) any person may at any time during the
> progress of the proceedings or before the decree nisi is made absolute give
> information to the Queen's Proctor on any matter material to the due decision of
> the case, and the Queen's Proctor may thereupon take such steps as the Attorney-
> General considers necessary or expedient.'

So far as the last part of that provision is concerned, the Queen's Proctor has throughout
c this plea and in the whole of his intervention in the matter acted on the direction of the
Attorney General, so that no problem arises in relation to that. Nor is it difficult to
establish that a person did give information to the Queen's Proctor. Indeed, it was the
court on my direction which so did. The only matter fit for debate is whether the
information was given at any time during the progress of the proceedings.

I mentioned earlier that the petition in this case was a wholly valid petition, lacking
d effect only because it was not served. It must follow, in my judgment, that the
proceedings after the filing of a valid petition are in progress until that petition is disposed
of either by a process of withdrawal or discontinuance, or by its dismissal, or by an order
being made on it. It is established, as indeed is the whole basis of this application, that no
order ever has been made on it. Nothing has purported to be done, save that which, in
my judgment, is altogether a nullity. Accordingly, in my view, the Queen's Proctor is
e validly before the court, has validly made his plea and is, as I have mentioned, in those
circumstances, entitled to any relief to which a party would be entitled, and a party
would be entitled ex debito justitiae, these orders having been shown to be void, to have
them so declared, and I so declare them.

I now proceed to the second part of the relief which is asked for by the Queen's Proctor.
That is that the petition may be dismissed. At this point it is necessary to refer to the
f contents of the petition.

The petition alleges that the marriage has broken down irretrievably but, of course,
that is not a finding to which the court is entitled to arrive, unless one of the relevant five
facts are proved, and the relevant one which is selected in this petition (and the only one)
is that the respondent, that is to say the wife, has behaved in such a way that the petitioner
husband cannot reasonably be expected to live with her. That matter is particularised
g and particularised only in relation to a period of time beginning in 1977 and going
through until shortly before the date of the petition.

In the Queen's Proctor's plea it is stated that the husband and the wife parted on 10
December 1975, immediately after the marriage and, indeed, the marriage took place on
that very day. For the reasons which I have already indicated, on this intervention, there
being no answer to the plea filed, the court is bound to accept that fact as true. Because
h that fact is true, it must necessarily follow that the whole of the particulars relied on as,
in effect, evidence of the irretrievable breakdown of the marriage are false, so that that
plea is not made out. Accordingly, I dismiss the petition.

Petition dismissed.

Solicitors: *Queen's Proctor.*

Bebe Chua   Barrister.

Batchelor v Batchelor

a

FAMILY DIVISION
SIR JOHN ARNOLD P
8 JULY 1983

Divorce – Decree absolute – Irregularity – Application by spouse for decree nisi pronounced
against him to be made absolute – Failure to serve on other spouse summons by which application   *b*
made – Husband remarrying after decree made absolute – Whether decree void or voidable –
Whether irregularity a mere technicality – Whether decree should be avoided if merely voidable –
Matrimonial Causes Rules 1977, r 66(2).

In 1982 a decree nisi was pronounced against the husband on the wife's answer to his
divorce petition. The wife's application for ancillary relief was settled by the wife   *c*
receiving and accepting an offer of generous financial provision from the husband. In
April 1983 the husband applied to have the decree made absolute but, on advice received
from the divorce registry, did not do so by summons as envisaged by r 66(2)[a] of the
Matrimonial Causes Rules 1977, which applied where a spouse against whom a decree
nisi had been pronounced applied for the decree to be made absolute. The husband did   *d*
not therefore comply with the requirement in r 66(2) that 'the summons by which the
application is made . . . shall be served on the other spouse'. On 14 April the court made
the decree absolute and in May the husband remarried. In June the wife applied to set
aside the decree absolute on the ground that it was void for non-compliance with the
requirement as to service of the summons contained in r 66(2).

Held – The wife's application would be refused for the following reasons—   *e*
   (1) The failure to comply with the requirement in r 66(2) of the 1977 rules that the
summons applying for a decree nisi to be made absolute was to be served on the other
spouse was a mere technicality which rendered the resulting decree absolute merely
voidable rather than void (see p 620 g to j, post); F v F [1970] 1 All ER 200, P v P and J
[1971] 1 All ER 616 and *Bernstein v Jackson* [1982] 2 All ER 806 considered.
   (2) The court would not, in all the circumstances, avoid the decree absolute but would   *f*
confirm it because of the husband's subsequent remarriage and because of the fact that
the husband had made proper and generous provision for the wife, who would therefore
not be disadvantaged if the decree absolute were confirmed (see p 620 j to p 621 b, post).

Notes

g

For application for a decree absolute by the spouse against whom the decree nisi was
pronounced, see 13 Halsbury's Laws (4th edn) para 980.
   For the Matrimonial Causes Rules 1977, r 66, see 10 Halsbury's Statutory Instruments
(4th reissue) 262.

Cases referred to in judgment

h

Bernstein v Jackson [1982] 2 All ER 806, [1982] 1 WLR 1082, CA.
F v F [1970] 1 All ER 200, [1971] P 1, [1970] 2 WLR 346.
P v P and J [1971] 1 All ER 616, [1971] P 217, [1971] 2 WLR 510, CA.

Application

Patricia Rae Batchelor (the wife) applied for an order that the decree absolute of divorce   *j*
made on 14 April 1983 in proceedings between her, as the respondent, and the petitioner,
William Hazzard Batchelor (the husband), be set aside by reason of non-compliance with

---

a   Rule 66, so far as material, is set out at p 619 *c*, post

r 66(2) of the Matrimonial Causes Rules 1977, SI 1977/344. The facts are set out in the
a judgment.

J C J Tatham for the wife.
Paul Norris for the husband.

SIR JOHN ARNOLD P. This is a case in which a decree absolute of divorce was made
b on 14 April 1983 in a suit, *Batchelor v Batchelor*, in which a decree nisi had previously
been pronounced. But some doubt attends the question of the validity of that decree
absolute because, although para (2) of r 66 of the Matrimonial Causes Rules 1977,
SI 1977/344, envisages the existence of a summons for the purpose because the decree
was made absolute by the petitioner (the husband) and not by the respondent (the wife),
to whom the decree nisi had been granted, there was no summons. Rule 66(2) says:

c   'An application by a spouse for a decree nisi pronounced against him to be made
        absolute may be made to a judge or the registrar, and the summons by which the
        application is made . . . shall be served on the other spouse . . .'

Then there is a direction as to when it should be served.
    That language is apparently mandatory and there was no summons in this case.
d   It may be possible to argue that on the construction of that rule the apparently
mandatory direction for service of the summons is not really mandatory at all and
contains no more than a prescription as to service of any summons that there might be,
but that has not been argued and the case has been treated on both sides as if that is in
fact a mandatory requirement, and I deal with the case on that basis.
    The question which is left is whether the decree absolute is void, in which case there is
e nothing that I can do about the matter, or whether it is voidable, which would give rise
to the further question whether in the circumstances of this case the court should avoid
it or not. There is not any direct authority so far as diligent researches of counsel have
revealed on this question where it arises through a failure to issue a summons under para
(2) of r 66. There is authority in the cognate matter of the effect of a decree absolute
pronounced or purported to be pronounced where there has not been a certificate of
f satisfaction as to the children of the family under what is now s 41 of the Matrimonial
Causes Act 1973. That was at a time when the Matrimonial Causes Act 1965 was in
operation, which did not, just as r 66 does not, say anything one way or the other about
the consequences of the default. There are two cases, both decided in 1971. The first is
F v F [1970] 1 All ER 200, [1971] P 1. It is noticeable that in that case the Solicitor
General, Sir Arthur Irvine QC, appeared for the Queen's Proctor as amicus curiae to give
g his advice to Simon P on that matter as it arose in the circumstances that I have described,
the relevant section in those days being s 33 of the Matrimonial Causes Act 1965.
Act 1965.
    One matter which emerges from the observations of the Solicitor General, which were
adopted in effect by the court, demonstrates a bias in the court to hold voidable rather
than void an order which has been obtained with a degree of irregularity. He said ([1971]
h P 1 at 4):

        'The court's attention is drawn to a line of authority which broadly is to the effect
        that a decree or order which is in some way irregular should be held voidable rather
        than void if that would involve injustice.'

    One could expand without bending the meaning of that the word 'would' to the word
j 'might', because the force of what the Solicitor General says must be the same. So it was
that in *F v F* [1971] P 1 at 2 Simon P was able to come to the conclusion (to quote from
the headnote) that 'the failure to comply with section 33 of the Matrimonial Causes Act,
1965, rendered the decree absolute voidable . . .'
    In a later case, *P v P and J* [1971] 1 All ER 616, [1971] P 217, precisely the same point
came before the Court of Appeal, which adopted and approved Simon P's decision in

F v F. It is interesting to observe that in the course of the judgment of Phillimore LJ it was pointed out that the language of s 17 of the Matrimonial Proceedings and Property Act 1970 (which is the direct and immediate predecessor of s 41 of the Matrimonial Causes Act 1973) had changed, and it prescribed that a failure to comply with the first subsection of that section did render the decree absolute void, which is a pointer to the possibility that Parliament at least considered whether it was doubtful that such a result would follow in the absence of such prescription (see [1971] 1 All ER 616 at 622, [1971] P 217 at 225).

It is of course true that what I have to consider in this case is the making absolute of a decree with an irregularity, and to that extent this case is comparable to *F v F* and *P v P*, but it does not necessarily follow that the result will be the same. Whether that follows must, as it seems to me, depend on the application of the general principle as to voidness or voidability to the facts of this case and more particularly the legal matters which have to be dealt with in this case, and in relation to that matter I find great assistance from *Bernstein v Jackson* [1982] 2 All ER 806, [1982] 1 WLR 1082 (which was helpfully cited by counsel for the husband) in which Dunn LJ, delivering the leading judgment in the Court of Appeal, recited at very considerable length the submissions which ultimately prevailed which had been made in support of the appeal. In effect those were adopted by the Court of Appeal. One of them was quoted in these terms ([1982] 2 All ER 806 at 810–811, [1982] 1 WLR 1082 at 1087):

'Counsel for the first defendant submitted that what had happened here was not a mere technicality or slip or mistaken step in the litigation because the renewal of the writ was a fundamental step in the proceedings . . .'

It is instructive, I think, if that is, as I believe it is, the determinant factor, to examine the matter in relation to what was omitted in this case.

Rule 3 of the Matrimonial Causes Rules 1977 provides that subject to the provisions of the rules and any enactment the Rules of the Supreme Court are to apply to the practice and procedure in matrimonial proceedings. So one can derive from the application of those rules to the matter which arose in *Bernstein v Jackson* some help. What had happened in *Bernstein v Jackson* was that a writ had run out at the end of 12 months and had not been renewed. There was then purported service and the issue which arose related to the consequence of that. One has to consider, I think, on applying the standard which was applied in *Bernstein v Jackson* on the basis of the submission by counsel in that case to which I have referred how the matter stands in the present case. In that case temporarily at least until it was renewed the writ had lost its essential validity. What was served therefore was an unhallowed piece of paper. Perhaps that is a somewhat exaggerated way of describing it but it very nearly comes to that. What had happened in this case was that there was undoubtedly jurisdiction to make this decree absolute; there is no question about that. The only thing which was lacking was the summons. In fact no summons was filed or served because the registry thought it was not necessary. That may add to the merits of the case but it cannot found a new jurisdiction. But undoubtedly the registrar when the application was made could have done what judicial officers often do in such circumstances and say: 'If you undertake to issue a summons I will make the order.' The absence of the summons is, as it seems to me, the most technical defect that one could really imagine, and if one has to decide whether it falls on the side of, to requote counsel in the *Bernstein* case through the mouth of Dunn LJ 'a mere technicality or slip or mistaken step in the litigation', or whether it was a fundamental mistake in the proceedings not to issue a summons, it seems to me impossible to come to the conclusion that it was other than of the first character. My conclusion therefore is that this was a technicality which resulted in an imperfection in the resultant decree absolute, but an imperfection of voidability and not voidness.

I turn therefore to consider whether the court should or should not avoid the decree absolute. It is at this point that the circumstances of this particular case become of compelling importance. In the first place this husband has remarried. Plainly that would *a* be a strong factor against avoiding the voidable decree absolute which purportedly terminated his previous marriage. Second, a proper and generous provision for the wife in this case has been proposed and accepted, which has the effect of removing from the wife any disadvantage which the making of this decree absolute might have created for her. So justice is secured by the provision which has been accepted by the wife's advisers and by the wife as being a sufficient and proper provision. It seems to me that I should have no hesitation whatever in saying that in my judgment this decree should not be *b* avoided, voidable as it is, but should be confirmed and should operate according to its tenor.

Application refused.

Solicitors: *Watkins Pulleyn & Ellison* (for the wife); *Barlow Lyde & Gilbert* (for the husband).

c
Bebe Chua   Barrister.

d

Mitchell v Mitchell

COURT OF APPEAL, CIVIL DIVISION
e CUMMING-BRUCE AND MAY LJJ
29, 30 JUNE, 15 JULY 1983

Divorce – Practice – Undefended causes – Special procedure – Failure to file answer within time limit – Application to file answer out of time after registrar has certified that petitioner entitled to decree – Principles applicable to determination of application to file answer out of time – Whether *f* *judge having jurisdiction to hear appeal from registrar's refusal of application – Matrimonial Causes Rules 1977, rr 48(1)(a), 124(1)*

The wife applied ex parte for an order to oust the husband from the matrimonial home and also filed a petition for divorce alleging that the marriage had irretrievably broken down because of the husband's unreasonable behaviour. The husband's solicitors took *g* steps to contest the ouster proceedings, but they wrongly assumed that the husband did not wish to defend the divorce proceedings and therefore failed to return the acknowledgment of service of the petition or to file an answer to it within the prescribed time, with the result that the cause was entered in the special procedure list for undefended divorces. In accordance with the special procedure the registrar certified, under r 48(1)(a)[a] of the Matrimonial Causes Rules 1977, that the wife had sufficiently *h* proved her petition and was entitled to a decree on the ground of the husband's unreasonable behaviour. When he received notice of the date fixed for pronouncement of a decree nisi, the husband, who desired a reconciliation, applied for postponement of the pronouncement of the decree, for the registrar's certificate to be set aside and for leave to file an answer to the petition out of time. He also filed a proposed answer in which he denied the wife's allegations of unreasonable behaviour. Pronouncement of the *j* decree was adjourned until the husband's application was heard by a registrar. The

---

a   Rule 48(1), so far as material, provides: '(1) As soon as practicable after a cause has been entered in the special procedure list, the registrar shall consider the evidence filed by the petitioner and—(a) if he is satisfied that the petitioner has sufficiently proved the contents of the petition and is entitled to a decree, the registrar shall make and file a certificate to that effect . . .'

registrar dismissed the application. The husband appealed to the judge, who decided, on the basis of the husband's reasons for failing to file an answer in time but without considering the merits of his case generally, that the appeal should be allowed, that the husband should have leave to file an answer within seven days and that if he did the registrar's certificate should be set aside. The wife appealed to the Court of Appeal, contending (i) that the judge had no jurisdiction to hear the appeal because matters relating to the special procedure for undefended divorces were within the exclusive jurisdiction of the registrar, and (ii) that if the judge did have jurisdiction he had been wrong to restrict the hearing to a consideration of the husband's reasons for failing to file his answer in time without also considering the merits of the case generally.

Held – The wife's appeal would be dismissed for the following reasons—

(1) The judge had had jurisdiction to hear the husband's appeal, because the husband's application to the registrar for leave to file an answer out of time was not a step in the special procedure for undefended divorces but an interlocutory application for the purposes of r 124(1)^b of the 1977 rules, which provided for a right of appeal from the registrar's decision to the judge. The appeal to the judge was by way of a rehearing, at which the judge could exercise his own discretion in determining the application (see p 632 *a* to *d* and p 636 *g h*, post); G (*formerly P*) v P [1978] 1 All ER 1099 applied; *Day v Day* [1979] 2 All ER 187 explained.

(2) Where a respondent to a divorce petition failed, because of ignorance or lack of proper legal advice, to file an answer to the petition in time the court ought to exercise its discretion by giving the respondent leave to file his answer out of time if it was satisfied that if the respondent were allowed to defend the petition the result might well be different, and in such circumstances ought to give leave even when the registrar had already issued a certificate under r 48(1)(*a*) of the 1977 rules; and, in determining whether to give leave, the court should neither accept the respondent's affidavit evidence at face value nor embark on the sort of investigation appropriate at the hearing of the contested suit. The judge had erred in law in failing to consider the merits of the case generally when giving leave and therefore his decision was open to review, but, on the facts, his decision had been right since the husband's answer might well have led to the wife's petition being rejected and the husband had therefore been rightly given leave to file his answer out of time (see p 633 *j* to p 634 *h* and p 635 *j* to p 636 *a* and *e* to *h*, post); *Nash v Nash* [1967] 1 All ER 535 approved; *Day v Day* [1979] 2 All ER 187 distinguished.

Notes

For the entry of undefended divorces in the special procedure list and the disposal of undefended divorces in the special procedure list see 13 Halsbury's Laws (4th edn) paras 847–848.

For filing an answer to a petition, see ibid para 753.

For the Matrimonial Causes Act 1973, s 1, see 43 Halsbury's Statutes (3rd edn) 541.

For the Matrimonial Causes Rules 1977, rr 48, 124, see 10 Halsbury's Statutory Instruments (4th reissue) 255, 289.

Cases referred to in judgment

Collins v Collins [1972] 2 All ER 658, [1972] 1 WLR 689, CA.
Day v Day [1979] 2 All ER 187, [1980] Fam 29, [1979] 2 WLR 681, CA.
Evans v Bartlam [1937] 2 All ER 646, [1937] AC 473, HL.
G (formerly P) v P (ancillary relief: appeal) [1978] 1 All ER 1099, [1977] 1 WLR 1376, CA.

---

b Rule 124(1), so far as material, provides: '. . . any party may appeal from . . . an order or decision [made or given by the registrar in matrimonial proceedings pending in a divorce county court] to a judge on notice filed within five days after the order or decision was made or given and served not less than two clear days before the day fixed for hearing of the appeal, which shall be heard in chambers unless the judge otherwise orders.' See now CCR 1981 Ord 13, r 1(10).

Nash v Nash [1967] 1 All ER 535, [1968] P 597, [1967] 2 WLR 1009, DC.
Owen v Owen [1964] 2 All ER 58, [1964] P 277, [1964] 2 WLR 654, DC.
Rogers v Rogers [1974] 2 All ER 361, [1974] 1 WLR 709, CA.
Stevens v Stevens [1965] 1 All ER 1003, [1965] P 147, [1965] 2 WLR 736, CA.
Tucker v Tucker [1949] P 105.
Walker v Walker [1978] 3 All ER 141, [1978] 1 WLR 533, CA.
Winter v Winter [1942] 2 All ER 390, [1942] P 151.

Interlocutory appeal

On 14 December 1982 the respondent husband, Leo Victor Mitchell, applied in Uxbridge County Court for an order (1) that pronouncement of a decree nisi on the undefended petition of his wife, Ann Rosemary Mitchell, in accordance with a certificate dated 8 November 1982 given by Mr Registrar Smee in Uxbridge County Court that the petitioner had sufficiently proved the contents of her petition and was entitled to a divorce decree on the ground alleged in the petition of the respondent's unreasonable behaviour, should be postponed; (2) that the registrar's certificate be set aside; (3) that the respondent be given leave to file an answer to the petition out of time and (4) that on filing an answer the cause should be transferred to the High Court. On 17 December 1982 his Honour Judge Main sitting in Uxbridge County Court postponed pronouncement of the decree nisi for 28 days and for so long thereafter as the respondent's application remained undetermined, and adjourned the hearing of the application to Mr Registrar Smee. On 17 January 1983 the registrar dismissed the respondent's application. The respondent appealed and on 24 March 1983 his Honour Judge Barr sitting at Uxbridge County Court allowed the appeal and ordered that the respondent be at liberty to file an answer to the petition within seven days and that on filing an answer the registrar's certificate dated 8 November 1982 should be set aside and the cause should be transferred to the High Court. Judge Barr refused the petitioner leave to appeal from his order. She applied to the Court of Appeal for leave to appeal and also gave notice of appeal from the judge's order. The grounds of her appeal were that the judge erred in law, and/or misdirected himself, and/or wrongly exercised his discretion in that, inter alia, he failed properly or at all to inquire into the merits of the respondent's appeal, failed to apply the law that the burden of proof was on the respondent who had to make out a positive case to succeed in his appeal, and failed to hear evidence on the merits of appeal. The facts are set out in the judgment of the court.

Philip Turl for the petitioner.
Paul Norris for the respondent.

Cur adv vult

15 July. The following judgment of the court was delivered.

CUMMING-BRUCE LJ. On 11 June 1982 Mrs Ann Rosemary Mitchell (the petitioner) made an application ex parte to the Uxbridge County Court supported by an affidavit sworn the same day. She exhibited a copy of a proposed petition for dissolution of marriage with a prayer for custody of four children of the family under 16, and a copy of her proposed statement of arrangements for the children. She alleged that, as a result of the behaviour of her husband (the respondent) as particularised in para 11 of her proposed petition and generally, she feared for the safety of herself and of the children of the family and property. She sought injunctions ordering her husband to vacate the matrimonial home and restraining him from entering or approaching it, and restraining him from threatening, molesting, assaulting, communicating with or interfering with her or the children and damaging or interfering with the matrimonial home and the contents. She asked for an order granting her the custody, care and control of the children. She swore that she was in fear of what the respondent would do when served with the papers. Her application was not founded on the Domestic Violence and Matrimonial Proceedings Act 1976 or on the Matrimonial Homes Act 1967.

The proposed petition pleaded that the marriage was in June 1960, that there were four children, all boys under 16, born respectively in 1967, 1970, 1974 and 1975, and that she and the respondent were still living together in a council house in Hayes, Middlesex. She alleged that the marriage had broken down irretrievably and that he had behaved in such a way that it was not reasonable for her to live with him. In para 11 the particulars of that behaviour were pleaded as follows:

'PARTICULARS

(a) The Respondent domineers the Petitioner and times how long she is out of the house doing shopping or otherwise.

(b) The Respondent is excessively jealous of the Petitioner and objects to her going out with her sister or to see friends.

(c) The Respondent has from time to time assaulted the Petitioner. On an occasion about four years ago, he caused quite some bruising.

(d) In about mid-May 1982, the Respondent attacked the Petitioner and punched her and hit her with the open hand and caused her to be in fear for her safety and caused her pain. This was during a row when he was screaming at her and swearing.

(e) On about Saturday, 5th June, 1982 the Respondent had left the matrimonial home for a week but returned and said that "I'm back now and you can keep me for ever". At about that time, he again hit her in the manner aforesaid.

(f) On Thursday, 10th June 1982 the Respondent again hit the Petitioner during a row and on this as on other recent occasions, he threatened to kill her if she left him.

(g) The Respondent has often threatened the Petitioner by holding his fist up to her and he screams and swears at her. He now gives her no money and he has on occasion insisted on intercourse by nagging her and if she refused he would say that he was married to her and she would have to comply.

(h) On occasion, the Respondent has told the Petitioner to get out of the house and locked her out once in early 1982.

(i) The Petitioner has, as a result of the Respondent's behaviour as particularised herein and generally, become in an extremely nervous state and is in fear for her health (particularly as fairly recently she has had two major operations and cannot stand the atmosphere in the house any further).

(j) The Respondent has, on occasion, ignored the Petitioner for long periods and has also belittled her in front of her sister.'

By the prayer of the proposed petition she sought dissolution of the marriage, custody of the four boys, financial provision, a property adjustment order and an order that the council tenancy be transferred to her sole name under the Housing Act 1980.

The ex parte application came before his Honour Judge Main QC the same day, 11 June 1982. He gave leave to file the petition without filing a marriage certificate on her undertaking to lodge it before applying for directions for trial. On her undertaking to file the petition by noon on 16 June, he granted injunctions restraining the respondent from assaulting or molesting the petitioner or their children and from interfering with the contents of the home, to continue until 28 June when the court would consider further continuance and the other matters contained in her application. The judge granted her interim custody of the children.

This petition was filed, but never served. The reason appears from a letter dated 25 August 1982 from the petitioner's solicitors to Messrs Woodbridge & Sons, the respondent's second solicitors. This reason was that after their initial instructions which

were hastily given, presumably in order to make the ex parte application for injunction
a and interim custody on 11 June, the petitioner's solicitors learnt that the parties had
changed their surnames and the names of the children from Pulhover to Mitchell, and
that their client had omitted to tell them of the existence of the eldest son, Stephen, born
on 2 June 1960 and therefore over 18.

On 28 June 1982 the petitioner's applications for injunctions came on before Mr D C
Humphreys, sitting as assistant recorder at Uxbridge County Court. The order recites
b that he heard 'the solicitor for the Petitioner and the Respondent in person'. On the
undertaking of the respondent not to assault, threaten, molest, communicate with or
otherwise interfere with the petitioner or the four youngest children, and not to damage
or interfere with the matrimonial home, or its contents, and to hand his marriage
certificate to his solicitors within 48 hours, the petitioner's application dated 11 June was
adjourned until 22 July and a court welfare report was ordered.

c So on 22 July 1982 the application of 11 June came on for hearing inter partes before
Mr Curtis-Bennett sitting as assistant recorder at Uxbridge County Court. The petitioner
was represented by her solicitors. The respondent was in person. The respondent applied
for an adjournment. The assistant recorder refused an adjournment. He stated his reasons
in his judgment: after considering the situation in the home and the failure of the
respondent to keep appointments with his solicitor it was desirable to hear the case
d urgently. After hearing the evidence of the petitioner and the respondent, he held that
in spite of the respondent's moving plea for a reconciliation, this was a pipe dream and
the welfare of the parties and the children required that they should go their separate
ways. He held that the respondent's and the petitioner's accounts of the matrimonial
history might be true, but he did not accept the respondent's evidence that if the parties
were left to themselves they would settle down. To say the least, they got on each other's
e nerves. He proceeded on the broad test stated by Geoffrey Lane LJ in *Walker v Walker*
[1978] 3 All ER 141, [1978] 1 WLR 533 and concluded that the right thing was to
separate respondent and petitioner and free each from the presence of the other, giving
the three younger children into the custody of the petitioner and Leslie, aged 15, to the
respondent. This led him to decide that the petitioner should stay in the matrimonial
home with the three younger children and the respondent should seek accommodation
f for himself and Leslie from the local authority. His orders were: (1) a non molestation
injunction against the respondent, power of arrest to attach until 22 October; (2) the
respondent to leave the matrimonial home in 14 days, ie by 5 August; (3) interim
custody care and control of Leslie to his father; (4) a supervision order over all the
children.

On or about 2 August 1982 the respondent instructed his present solicitors. On 5
g August the respondent applied ex parte for a variation of the order of 22 July supported
by an affidavit sworn on the same day. He complained that he had not then been
represented and the true facts of the relationship between himself and the petitioner had
been distorted. He alleged that the petitioner did not look after the children properly
and neglected them when she went out in the evening to enjoy herself. He alleged that
he could look after the children in spite of his high blood pressure. He alleged that the
h petitioner was suffering from cancer, had had two serious operations in December 1980
and December 1981 and, if there were a recurrence, he could look after all the children
provided he was allowed to live in the matrimonial home. The whole trouble was, in his
belief, simply that he had ordered his sister-in-law, Christine, out of the matrimonial
home. Judge Main, on hearing the solicitors for the respondent and reading the
respondent's affidavit, varied the order of 22 July by substituting 12 August for 5 August
j as the date for the ouster to take effect. The ground for the variation appears probably to
have been the difficulty facing the local authority in offering at short notice any
accommodation except on a bed and breakfast basis. In a letter dated 6 August 1982 the
petitioner's solicitors told Messrs Woodbridge & Sons, the respondent's second solicitors,
that it had not initially been possible to serve the respondent with the papers but that he
had known about them and had made appointments with his first solicitors on 24 or 25

June but had failed to attend. Mr Shine of Messrs Brecher & Co, the petitioner's solicitors, had personally served 'the papers' on the respondent on 2 July. He had had an *a* appointment to see his solicitors about 'the papers' on 7 July, but had not turned up. The petitioner's solicitors gave this information, together with a summary of the hearing before the assistant recorder and the reason for his judgment on 22 July, by way of explanation for their view that if Messrs Woodbridge & Sons had known the earlier history they would never have made an ex parte application for variation.

On 12 August 1982 the respondent left the matrimonial home with Leslie and was *b* given accommodation by the council. On the same day the petitioner filed her amended petition. The amendments were formal. The allegations against the respondent were unchanged. By a letter dated 25 August addressed to Messrs Woodbridge & Sons, the petitioner's solicitors complained of breaches of the injunctions, explained why they had never served the original divorce petition and asked them to obtain instructions to accept service. Thus, it is clear that, when the petitioner's solicitors had in their letter of 6 *c* August 1982 described service of 'the papers' on the respondent on 2 July, they meant that they had served on him the petitioner's application for injunctions, with her affidavit exhibiting her proposed divorce petition which alone, by the particulars in para 11, stated her allegations of misbehaviour on the part of the respondent.

On 16 September 1982 a process server served personally on the respondent the amended petition and an application for committal, supported by an affidavit alleging *d* breaches of the injunctions made on 22 July.

On 24 September 1982 his Honour Judge Wakley had before him the petitioner's application for committal. On reading letters from both solicitors for both parties he adjourned the application generally.

After service of the amended petition the respondent under the Matrimonial Causes Rules 1977, SI 1977/344, had eight days within which to return the acknowledgment of *e* service and a further 21 days within which to file an answer. The acknowledgment of service was not returned. No answer was filed within the time limited by the rules. The solicitors for the petitioner then proceeded in accordance with the rules. An appointment was made for application for the registrar's certificate under r 48(1). On 8 November Mr Registrar Smee gave his certificate that the petitioner had sufficiently proved the contents of her petition, and was entitled to a decree of divorce on the grounds that the respondent *f* had so behaved that the petitioner could not reasonably be expected to live with him. The evidence before him was an affidavit of the petitioner swearing that the contents of her petition were true.

On 9 November 1982 the county court gave notice to the petitioner's solicitors (and the respondent's solicitors) that the welfare officer's report had been filed, enclosed a copy and asked the petitioner whether she wished her applications for custody and certificate *g* for satisfaction to be listed for hearing.

Notice under r 48(2) was given to the respondent's solicitors of the date fixed for pronouncement by the judge of the decree nisi on 17 December. On 14 December 1982 the respondent gave notice of his applications to the judge on that day for (1) postponement of the decree nisi, (2) that the registrar's certificate be set aside, (3) that the respondent have leave to file an answer out of time, and (4) that on such filing the cause *h* be transferred to the High Court.

On 17 December, on hearing counsel for the respondent and the petitioner not attending, Judge Main ordered that (1) the date fixed for the pronouncement of the decree in accordance with the registrar's certificate be postponed for 28 days and for so long thereafter as the respondent's application dated 14 December 1982 remained undetermined; (2) the hearing of the respondent's application be adjourned to be heard *j* before the registrar in chambers at 2.30 p m on 17 January 1983.

On 20 December 1982 the respondent gave notice of two further applications. One was for an order discharging the injunction made on 22 July so far as it restrained him from returning to the matrimonial home, to be heard on 14 January 1983. This appears to have been supported by an affidavit sworn on 10 January 1983. In this affidavit (a) he

described his formidable accommodation problems, (b) he described the satisfactory
a relationship between Leslie and himself, the petitioner's inability to control him, and the
fact that Leslie was missing his brothers, (c) he described friendly relations between the
petitioner and himself, and continuing frequent sexual intercourse between them at his
flat, (d) he described and complained of the facts that the petitioner's sister, Christine,
and her boyfriend, a man aged 30 were living at the matrimonial home, and that at
weekends the petitioner's sister, Elaine, and her boyfriend, Paul, also slept there while
b the boys were in the house, (e) he described how he had seen his sister-in-law Christine as
threatening his marriage and family stability, how he consulted the citizens' advice
bureau and the court welfare office because of his concern before any proceedings were
commenced, and as a result he evicted his sister-in-law and the next day his wife applied
for an injunction. He said that if he was permitted to return he would raise no objection
to the petitioner's sister being present in the house and that he would not interfere with
c them going out together. He would be prepared to occupy a separate room and live
separately from his wife and to undertake not to assault or interfere with his wife.

The other notice dated 20 December related to his application to be heard by the
registrar on 17 January 1983 for an order that the certificate of the registrar dated
8 November 1982 be set aside and that he be given leave to file an answer out of time.
This was supported by an affidavit which we are told was sworn on 17 December 1982,
d exhibiting his proposed answer.

In para 2 he swore that the petition dated 11 June was duly served on him to the best
of his knowledge about Sunday 4 July, when a bundle of documents were thrown at his
feet by a strange man who came into his home at the invitation of the petitioner. He
understood that he was being served primarily with notice of injunction proceedings
and undertakings which the petitioner had been granted earlier that week. Evidently he
e was confused in thinking that the petition dated 11 June had been duly served, as the
papers served related only to the injunction proceedings, though they included a copy of
the proposed petition as an exhibit to the applicant's affidavit. He said that he looked at
the documents and when he realised that they were legal documents he took them
straight to his solicitors, who were then Messrs Hart Fortgang & Co. He did not
understand the nature of the documents given to him.

f In para 3 he swore that, due to sickness through hypertension, he was unable to see
anyone from his solicitors before the return date of the adjourned application for an
injunction on 22 July, and he therefore appeared at court unrepresented and without any
real knowledge of the papers which had been served on him. After the injunction had
been ordered on 22 July he changed his solicitors. When he first consulted Messrs
Woodbridge & Sons his immediate concern was to get the injunction discharged. He
g succeeded only in postponing the date of ouster to 12 August. He continually asked Mr
Baldwin of that firm to 'get him in front of a judge', being under the impression that the
injunction and divorce proceedings were one and the same thing, and that by contesting
the injunction he was contesting the divorce. He did not appreciate that there were two
different proceedings pending and therefore gave no separate instructions to his solicitors
in relation to the divorce. In para 6 he stated his position in relation to his wife's petition
h for dissolution:

'I have never intended that the Divorce should go through undefended because I
love the Petitioner and feel that our relationship has been prejudiced only by the
presence of the Petitioner's sister in the Matrimonial Home and that when she lives
with her new boyfriend the Petitioner will lose the influence which has driven her
to bring the matter thus far. I refer to my draft answer for further details of our
j matrimonial dispute.'

And in para 10:

'I strenuously wish to keep my marriage together not least for the sake of the
children. The Petitioner has terminal cancer further details of which are set out in

paragraph 11 of my draft answer and I fear that the children may be split up in later
years if I cannot keep the family together now.'   *a*

So he wished to defend, and submitted that in the interests of justice he should be given
leave to file an answer. He exhibited his draft answer. Therein he denied that the
marriage had broken down irretrievably or at all. He denied every allegation in paras 10
and 11 of the petition and in ten paragraphs pleaded specifically to all the sub-paragraphs
of para 11 of the petition.   *b*

The application to set aside the registrar's certificate was also supported by an affidavit
of Mr Baldwin, the solicitor's clerk in the firm of Messrs Woodbridge & Sons, the
respondent's second solicitors, who had been personally dealing with the respondent's
case in or about September 1982. The papers on the firm's file indicated that the solicitors
had regarded themselves as concerned only with the ouster proceedings and in particular
with pressing for a welfare report. Divorce had not been discussed and the file contained   *c*
no notes referring to it. The first time that Mr Baldwin discussed divorce with the
respondent was on 16 September when he told the client that he saw no point in
defending the divorce proceedings. He did not, however, specifically discuss the divorce
proceedings with the respondent until 26 November when he attended to discuss the
welfare report. The last three paragraphs of his attendance note of 26 November gave a
summary of the advice given by Mr Baldwin but also the insistence of his client that he   *d*
wished to defend. A meeting on 30 November confirmed to Mr Baldwin that the
respondent had never understood that, by taking no action relating to the petition, his
marriage would be dissolved. On 13 December the respondent attended a conference
with counsel. It there was apparent that not only had he failed to understand the advice
given to him, but he was unaware that a petition for divorce had been filed but thought
that the petition would simply result in a separation, not dissolution of the marriage. Mr   *e*
Baldwin swore that although he had considered, shortly after taking over the respondent's
affairs, the question of divorce, he took no steps to complete and return the
acknowledgment of service. He mistakenly believed that the respondent would not
defend and knew that the petitioner could set down the matter as undefended. He gave
no thought to the acknowledgment of service form or its absence from the file, though
he later found it in a separate bundle of papers. He accepted responsibility for failing to   *f*
return it but it was his view that it was by no means certain that it would have disclosed
an intention to defend. Nevertheless he submitted that the respondent not only had a
strong answer to the allegations pleaded against him but believed on reasonable grounds
that his marriage had not irretrievably broken down, so that it would be contrary to the
interests of justice to deny him an opportunity of defending the suit. Apparently he
never thought of filing an answer, or took instructions about it, before time expired.   *g*

By an affidavit dated 12 January 1983 the petitioner gave her grounds for opposing
the respondent's applications for setting aside the registrar's certificate and for leave to
file an answer out of time. She swore that the marriage was definitely at an end and that
there was no prospect of reconciliation. In her view the respondent had had ample
opportunity to deal with the papers served on him and to attend his solicitors. He did
not want the marriage to end and was using every possible ploy to delay its end. She   *h*
denied nearly all his allegations and gave explanations which put a quite different
construction on many of the matters he relied on, including the circumstances of their
continued sexual intercourse after her original divorce petition had been filed. She
submitted that it would be contrary to the interests of herself, her health, the children,
or the legal aid fund to permit the petitioner to defend the suit.

Her opposition was also supported by the affirmation of Mr Shine, her solicitor. He   *j*
described his advice to her on the prospects of reconciliation, and that she had been
increasingly adamant that she did not wish to live with the respondent and did not wish
to see him. She had often told him that she had been frightened or confused and had
frequently let him into the house if he called there, though she did not wish him to call
even for access. She told him that, if the ouster injunction was lifted, she did not see how

she could live with him in any circumstances. In view of that position he suggested that
a whatever the views of the respondent, it would be a complete waste of public funds if
the divorce went to a contested hearing as even if he succeeded she would still refuse to
live with him, and he had admitted some acts of physical violence both at the hearing on
22 July and in his proposed answer. The petitioner had confirmed to him the truth of
the contents of the petition both in the presence of the respondent on 2 July and on other
occasions. He said that the respondent had tried to wear the petitioner down to a position
b where she is deemed to want to continue her relationship with him. He submitted that
the respondent's application should be dismissed on the ground that all the court rules
had been properly complied with and prior opportunity had been given to defend, as
well as on the grounds of the respondent's behaviour and the petitioner's stated attitude
and the waste of two sets of substantial legal aid costs that would be involved if the
application was granted.

c   He exhibited a letter from Dr Wright dated 3 September 1982, who had had the
petitioner under his care since she was admitted to Hillingdon Hospital as an emergency
on 14 December 1980. He described the history of adencarcinoma and its treatment by
surgery and chemistry. There was no evidence of any spread of the tumour outside the
pelvis. She had been left with deposits of malignant growth in her pelvis but the growth
of the tumour was obviously slow and it was impossible to give any accurate long-term
d prognosis for her.

On 12 January 1983 the petitioner swore a second affidavit in opposition to the
respondent's application to discharge the ouster injunction. She contradicted the evidence
given in his affidavit in support of discharge of the ouster injunction and dealt in detail
with his allegation that the whole trouble had been that her sister, Christine, had been
living in the matrimonial home. She swore that she could never live with him again and
e that she would have to leave with the children if the injunction was discharged. She
explained the problems that she and the younger children had with Leslie. She ended as
follows:

'Despite the fact that he has not threatened me of late, he is on medication and
suffers from hypertension and his character and nature is such that, together with
the behaviour which I have suffered from him to date, I just could not possibly
f   stand living in the same house as he. The house is too small to split up in the way
that he is now suggesting.'

On 14 January Judge Main heard the respondent's application to discharge the
injunction. He heard counsel for the respondent and the solicitor for the petitioner and
presumably, though the order is silent about it, read the evidence filed by both sides in
g the application. There was no oral evidence. The respondent's application to discharge
the injunction was dismissed.

On 17 January 1983 Mr Registrar Smee heard the respondent's applications to set aside
the registrar's certificate granted on 8 November 1982 and for leave to file an answer out
of time, pursuant to the notice dated 14 December 1982. We have the note made by Mr
Shine, the petitioner's solicitor, of those proceedings. Counsel opened, and said that the
h respondent had considered that the petition was one for separation, not divorce, as
described in the welfare officer's report. The registrar read the affidavits and draft answer.
The respondent (the applicant) gave evidence and was cross-examined. Mr Baldwin gave
evidence and described his conduct of the cases in which he was instructed. When the
respondent first had come to see him the only outstanding proceeding had been the
ouster injunction. He saw the divorce petition and put it to the respondent that it was
j not necessary to defend the divorce because no stigma attached. The respondent insisted
in that interview, 'Get me before a judge.' With hindsight he felt that the respondent
had not understood anything about divorce. He was the most difficult client he had ever
had concerning understanding matters. The respondent, at interview in about November
1982, wanted to preserve his marriage at all costs. The respondent still had little
understanding of the proceedings. When asked why the respondent had insisted on

26 November that he must defend the divorce, Mr Baldwin replied that it was because he did not think that the marriage had broken down, she had left him many times before, but he also believed that the allegations in the petition were false and that he would not be able to raise some of the allegations in the cross-petition. (No proposed-cross petition has yet been exhibited.) The registrar said it was not necessary for Mr Shine to call Mrs Mitchell. Mr Shine addressed the registrar and relied on the affidavits in support of the petitioner's opposition to the application. The respondent's counsel addressed the registrar. The registrar gave judgment, dismissing the applications. He found: (1) that the marriage had broken down as alleged in the petition; the respondent was innocently deceiving himself; (2) that at an early enough stage the respondent knew that the petition was for divorce: he later persuaded himself that he did not know that; (3) that he, the registrar himself, was on the horns of a dilemma: 'I was satisfied that the marriage had broken down because of the husband's unreasonable behaviour.' (This may be a reference to the registrar's previous finding when he granted his certificate in November 1982.) He did not think that the husband would be prejudiced in the custody proceedings; (4) that late in the day, or at least at the end of November 1982, the husband decided that he wanted to defend; (5) that he, the registrar, had already reached his conclusion and the contents of the wife's petition being true, that injustice would be done if he were to allow the application; (6) that the decree should stand. He extended time for filing a notice of appeal against his order for 14 days.

Notice was given on 10 February 1983 that 24 February had been fixed for pronouncement of the decree nisi and consideration of the arrangements for the children. On that day his Honour Judge Paynter Reece gave leave to the respondent to appeal against the order of 17 January within seven days and adjourned pronouncement of the decree nisi until 18 March. On 1 March the respondent in person, in a notice addressed to the registrar of Uxbridge County Court, said that he desired to appeal against the order of Mr Registrar Smee of 17 January and said that his application would be heard by a registrar on 11 March.

On 8 March 1983 a welfare report supplementary to the report of 5 November 1982 was filed in the county court. The main developments were that Lee, aged 12½, had been living with his father since 24 January because he preferred to do so. This upset the petitioner but she accepted that, in the past, she had not exercised firm parental control over him and would not insist on his return to her against his wish. The welfare officer reported:

'Mr. and Mrs. Mitchell have on occasions in the period since the last report seen a good deal of each other, but in the long term these visits appear to have upset rather than healed Mr. and Mrs. Mitchell's feelings towards each other. It has sometimes been difficult to understand the interactions between this couple. I have the impression that Mr. Mitchell, deep down does still love his wife; is finding it very difficult to let her go and is very bitter about the whole divorce experience. Mrs. Mitchell is clear that she would like the marriage ended but on occasions—she would claim—"out of kindness of her heart"—she does collude with Mr. Mitchell's approach. At the present time Mrs. Mitchell states that she liked to have minimal contact with Mr. Mitchell and Mr. Mitchell is stating that he now only wants custody of all his four children and wants very little to do with Mrs. Mitchell. There is also a good deal of accusation regarding each party's ability to care for the children—particularly by Mr. Mitchell against Mrs. Mitchell. In this welter of accusation it is difficult to establish where the truth lies.'

She considered that custody care and control should be settled as soon as possible, in view of the continuing bitterness between the adults and the welter of accusation being made.

She recommended a joint custody order in respect of all four children, care and control of the two oldest to the father and of the two youngest to the mother, with a supervision order. This was the background of the hearing on 24 March when Judge Barr heard the

respondent's appeal against the order of Mr Registrar Smee made on 17 January. The
a judge allowed the appeal, gave leave to the respondent to file an answer in seven days and
directed that, on the filing of it, the registrar's certificate of 8 November 1982 be set aside
and the cause transferred to the High Court. The next day Judge Barr refused the
petitioner leave to appeal. On 22 April in this court the single Lord Justice adjourned the
petitioner's application for leave to appeal to a court of two judges and gave directions
about the notice of appeal and the application for leave to appeal. On 27 April the
b petitioner filed an amended notice of appeal including an application for leave to appeal.
On 29 June and 30 June this court heard argument on both the application for leave to
appeal and the appeal itself.

Judge Barr himself took no note of the proceedings before him. By a mistake in the
petitioner's solicitors' office the judge was sent for approval a note which included
comments by Mr Shine, which the judge rightly refused to sign. We have the note made
c by Mr Shine which should have been sent for approval. Counsel for the respondent
agrees that we should admit it as an accurate record of the hearing before the judge. In
the circumstances we admit it although the judge was not asked to approve it. The
respondent was in person. The petitioner was represented by her solicitor, Mr Shine. Mr
Baldwin, the respondent's solicitor, was present and ready to give any assistance or
information required but the respondent had no legal aid certificate for the appeal.

d The judge asked the respondent why he had not defended before. He replied that it
had been a mistake. Mr Baldwin explained that there was an answer exhibited to an
affidavit. The judge said that he had read the papers. He was directed to the respondent's
affidavit of 17 December 1982, to the draft answer exhibited to it, and to the affidavit of
the petitioner in reply dated 12 January 1983. Mr Shine told him that there was on the
file a typed note that he had made of the hearing before the registrar, but the judge said
e that he was not interested in 'the merits'. The judge read the draft answer and the
respondent's affidavit of 17 December. Mr Shine referred the judge to his affirmation of
13 January. The judge then said to the respondent that he saw no reason why he should
not defend. He asked Mr Shine to make his observations, and Mr Shine pointed out that
the court has power to allow or refuse a respondent to file an answer out of time. The
judge warned the respondent that if he lost the case he would have a heavy bill to pay
f and asked Mr Shine to address him:

> 'I pointed out the main salient points, firstly that the Respondent would
> undoubtedly file his Answer and an increasingly huge legal aid bill would be payable
> and the marriage is at an end, as I asked my client, sometimes more than once a
> week. I also mentioned that she had been ill with cancer and although this is under
> control, nevertheless she merely wanted to live a quiet life away from the
g > Respondent. As to the "financial peril" in which the Judge said the Respondent
> would find himself, I pointed out that he was unemployed and likely to be so and it
> is unlikely that any Order for costs would, in fact, be made against him. I said that
> the rest of my argument was already contained in my Affidavit and that of my
> client and notes of the application on 17th January 1983 and the Judge nodded his
h > agreement that there was no point in my repeating it. I also pointed out that there
> was an Affidavit from the Petitioner in reply to that of the Respondent on the
> question of his application to set aside the Registrar's Certificate and that this dealt
> with the Answer but the Judge again said that he was not concerned with the merits.
> He gave an order that the Respondent file an Answer within seven days in which
> case the Registrar's Certificate would be set aside and the matter proceed. If the
> Respondent did not do this, then the Decree Nisi would be listed. Legal Aid Taxation
i > of my costs was ordered. I had put in the cases of Collins v. Collins ([1972] 2 All ER
> 658, [1972] 1 WLR 689) and Rogers v. Rogers ([1974] 2 All ER 361, [1974] 1 WLR
> 709). The Judge said he had looked at these and they just show that each case
> depends on its own facts. I said that this was exactly what I had wanted to show and
> that I had merely put in Collins v. Collins because a Counsel of Mr. Mitchell's had
> sought to rely on Rogers v. Rogers.'

The first point taken before us on behalf of the appellant, the petitioner, was that the judge had no jurisdiction to hear the respondent's appeal from the refusal of the registrar *a* to give leave to file an answer out of time because, for the reasons explained in *Day v Day* [1979] 2 All ER 187, [1980] Fam 29, by the so-called 'special procedure', in the absence of an answer, it is the registrar who is empowered to grant his certificate under the Matrimonial Causes Rules 1977, r 48(1)(*a*) and thus adjudication has been transferred from the judge to the registrar. This is a misunderstanding of the judgment of Ormrod LJ in the cited case. The applications made to Mr Registrar Smee were interlocutory *b* applications to which r 124 of the 1977 rules applied. The hearing before the judge was an appeal under that rule. Such an appeal is a rehearing and the only procedural difference from the hearing before the registrar is that the party appealing opens the case before the judge. The procedure and the approach to be taken by the judge to the registrar's order are specifically explained in the judgment of Ormrod LJ in *G (formerly P) v P (ancillary relief: appeal)* [1978] 1 All ER 1099 at 1100–1103, [1977] 1 WLR 1376 at 1378–1382. *c* The discretion to be exercised was that of the judge, and the appellate duty of this court is limited to review of the exercise of that discretion as explained in *Evans v Bartlam* [1937] 2 All ER 646, [1937] AC 473 and the cases in *Rayden on Divorce* (14th edn, 1983) vol 1, pp 644–645, note 7.

The first substantial ground of appeal was that the judge on his own showing failed or refused to consider the merits of the case other than to satisfy himself that the reason *d* why an answer was not filed in time was a mistake of the respondent's second solicitors, or at least confusion between an unsophisticated client and a solicitor who failed until much too late to take explicit instructions on whether the respondent (the husband) wanted to defend. In order to determine this ground of appeal it is necessary to consider the principles which the judge should apply. They were explained in *Day v Day* [1979] 2 All ER 187 at 191, [1980] Fam 29 at 34: *e*

'The second question concerns the principles to be applied when considering whether or not to grant leave to file an answer out of time. It follows from what we have already said that it is difficult not to regard the registrar's certificate in the special procedure under r 48 as tantamount to a decree nisi under the former procedure. Consequently, an application by a respondent after the registrar's *f* certificate has been made should, logically, be dealt with on the same lines as an application for a rehearing after decree nisi under the former procedure. If this is right, the present application falls to be dealt with in accordance with the principles laid down by a strong Divisional Court consisting of Sir Jocelyn Simon P and Scarman J in *Owen v Owen* [1964] 2 All ER 58, [1964] P 277, that is to say the application should have been refused unless there were "substantial grounds for the *g* belief" that the decree would have been obtained "contrary to the justice of the case". The analogy, however, is not wholly accurate because in some respects a respondent is less favourably placed under the special procedure than he was under the ordinary procedure in force in 1964 and too rigid an approach to these matters may cause injustice, particularly now that many people will have to act in person in these matters. Under the special procedure rules the filing of an answer is the crucial *h* step since it alone will stop the progress from petition to registrar's certificate under r 48 and the almost inevitable pronouncement of a decree. But respondents must find the rules difficult to follow. For example, rr 15(1) and (2) and 18(1), and forms 5 and 6 which accompany the petition at the time of service, are quite clear. Notice of intention to defend must be given within eight days and an answer filed within 21 days thereafter, making 29 days in all. But rr 15(3) and 18(2) seem to contradict *i* this simple scheme because they respectively provide that a notice of intention to defend or an answer may properly be given or filed "at any time before directions have been given for the trial of the cause". But a respondent does not know, and is not told, when directions for trial are going to be applied for under r 33(1) or given. Under the ordinary procedure he *does* receive notice that directions have been given

and is informed of the date and place of trial (see rule 33(2)). Under the special
procedure the registrar enters the cause in the special procedure list, but does not
notify the respondent that he is about to consider the evidence with a view to
making his certificate that the petitioner has proved his or her case. The first that
the respondent knows of what is happening, is the receipt of a notice of the date and
place for the pronouncement of the decree, by which time the process of adjudication
is over. Thus, if he allows the original 29 days to elapse without filing an answer, he
is in the dark until he is told the date for the pronouncement of the decree, whether
or not he has given notice of intention to defend. Unless he studies the rules he is
also unaware of his rights under rr 15(3) and 18(2) and is necessarily unaware of the
deadline, ie the date when directions for trial have been, or are about to be, given.
These handicaps must be borne in mind in considering whether to grant an
application by a respondent to enable him or her to defend the suit after the initial
29 days have elapsed. They may have an important bearing on whether the justice
of the case requires that he be given, in effect, leave to defend.'

Counsel for the respondent submitted that the test declared in *Owen v Owen* that 'the
application should have been refused unless there were "substantial grounds for the
belief" that the decree would have been obtained "contrary to the justice of the case"'
imposed too heavy a burden on the applicant. This submission derives from the
judgments of the Divisional Court in *Nash v Nash* [1967] 1 All ER 535 at 537–538, [1968]
P 597 at 601–602 where Simon P and Cairns J examined the principles stated by Davies
LJ in *Stevens v Stevens* [1965] 1 All ER 1003, [1965] P 147 and decided that there was a
class of cases additional to the two classes of case there considered in *Stevens v Stevens*.
Davies LJ had said ([1965] 1 All ER 1003 at 1010, [1965] P 147 at 162–163):

'As it seems to me, these applications in the Divisional Court fall into at least two
classes. There is the class where the applicant comes along and says, "I was not
served: I knew nothing about it", or, "I was deceived: all the proceedings took place
behind my back". In that sort of case the applicant gets a re-hearing almost
automatically. The other class of case is the *Winter* ([1942] 2 All ER 390, [1942]
P 151) class of case, the *Tucker* ([1949] P 105) class of case, and this class of case,
where an applicant may come along and say "I knew all about this: I chose not to
defend; but it was all wrong: let me defend now and grant me a re-hearing". In a
case of that latter kind, speaking for myself, I think that for an applicant to succeed
he has to convince the Divisional Court, or this court if it comes before this court,
that on the evidence before the court on the application as a whole it is more
probable that the decree was obtained contrary to the justice of the case.'

The third class is that described by Cairns J in *Nash v Nash* [1967] 1 All ER 535 at 538,
[1968] P 597 at 603:

'I think that there is probably at least one more class. That is the type of case
where the respondent in divorce proceedings is aware that the proceedings are in
progress and is anxious to defend and, although no sort of deception has occurred,
nevertheless, through ignorance or lack of full advice, he is unaware of the necessity
of taking procedural steps in order to preserve his position and has no knowledge of
the actual hearing until after it has taken place. In such circumstances, I am of
opinion that this court should not automatically, or almost automatically, grant a
re-hearing, but on the other hand should not require to be satisfied that, if there
were a re-hearing, a different result would be more probable than not. I think it is
necessary and sufficient that the applicant should satisfy the court that he has a case
which he wishes to put forward and which, if accepted, might well lead to a different
result. The court is not bound to accept the applicant's affidavit at its face value, but
on the other hand should not attempt to make any such investigation of its truth as
would be more appropriate at the hearing of the suit . . . I take the view that [the
husband's] affidavit is sufficient to show that [he] has a case which he wants to put

before the court and which, if accepted might well lead to a result different from
the result of the first hearing.'

Simon P expressly concurred with the way that Cairns J had put it in his judgment.

The appeal to this court in *Day v Day* [1979] 2 All ER 187, [1980] Fam 29 arose in the
context of facts which came within the second class of case described by Davies LJ in
Stevens v Stevens [1965] 1 All ER 1003 at 1010, [1965] P 147 at 162–163, as were the facts
on which the Divisional Court had decided *Owen v Owen* [1964] 2 All ER 58, [1964]
P 277. The instant appeal, however, arose on facts which came within the category of the
third class of case described by the Divisional Court in *Nash v Nash* [1967] 1 All ER 535
at 538, [1968] P 597 at 603. It follows that the test approved by this court in *Day v Day*,
ie the application should have been granted if there were substantial grounds for the
belief that the decree would have been obtained contrary to the justice of the case, is not
binding on us. We have to decide whether the test stated in *Nash v Nash* in respect of the
third class of case is correct and should be applied in the instant case. We so hold. On the
facts of the respondent's (the husband's) application to set aside the registrar's certificate,
it is necessary and sufficient that he should satisfy the court that he has a case which he
wishes to put forward and which, if accepted, might well lead to a different result. And
we also indorse the words of Cairns J:

'The court is not bound to accept the applicant's affidavit at its face value, but on
the other hand should not attempt to make any such investigation of its truth as
would be more appropriate at the hearing of the suit.'

Consideration of Mr Shine's note of the proceedings before Judge Barr compels us to
hold that when the judge stated that he was 'not interested' in 'the merits' he must have
meant that he was satisfied that the failure to file an answer within time was due to
genuine mistake for which the respondent was not personally responsible and that he
was not concerned to consider critically whether, if the respondent was allowed to defend,
this might well lead to a different result. This may be unfair to the judge because when
Mr Shine made his final address he relied on the petitioner's cancer, her wish to lead a
quiet life and to the costs of a defended suit which the legal aid fund would have to bear,
all which considerations were irrelevant. The judge indicated that he had read both Mr
Shine's affidavit and the petitioner's affidavit in reply to the respondent's application to
set aside the certificate. But when Mr Shine again referred to the petitioner's affidavit,
the judge said once more that he was not concerned with the merits. *Day v Day* [1979] 2
All ER 187, [1980] Fam 29 was apparently referred to in the proceedings, though not
discussed. There are in our view sufficient grounds for holding that the judge did not
address his mind sufficiently to the question whether, if the respondent was allowed to
defend, the result might well be different.

In these circumstances we are entitled to hold that the judge misdirected himself in
law, and we are entitled, on a review of the relevant material, to decide whether he came
to the right result. In effect, this court should itself decide how the discretion should be
exercised on application of the correct legal criteria and thus decide whether to grant or
refuse the applications.

The primary material for consideration is the respondent's affidavits dated 17 December
1982 and 10 January 1983 and the proposed answer exhibited to the earlier affidavit. By
the terms of that answer he seeks to put in issue the truth of the allegations in the petition
(1) that the marriage had irretrievably broken down and (2) that he had so behaved that
the petitioner could not reasonably be expected to live with him on the grounds
particularised in para 11 of the petition. There do seem to us to be arguable grounds for
believing, as he pleads, that the marriage had not irretrievably broken down. We are not
moved by the grant of the ouster injunction on 22 July 1982 nor its continuance, because
the ground of the ouster was not the respondent's behaviour to the petitioner but the
broad ground, now known to be wrong in law, that the children's interests were
paramount and that it would be better for the children if the parents lived apart, although

the respondent's account of the trouble might be true. It must also be material that

a sexual intercourse has continued after the separation of the spouses and the filing of the divorce petition. More formidable is the history of the matrimonial proceedings. It does look as if the petition for dissolution after 25 years of marriage was instigated by the decision of the petitioner to apply for an ouster injunction. To provide jurisdiction for this she filed a divorce petition which was not served for several months. The ouster proceedings and the proceedings for dissolution have been so closely interlinked that we

b have thought it right to set out at the beginning of this judgment a summary of the history of both sets of proceedings, because that is necessary for an understanding of the respondent's contention that the marriage had not irretrievably broken down. Our conclusion, after considering also the petitioner's affidavit dated 12 January 1983, is that we cannot hold that if the respondent is allowed to defend he may well show that the parties are likely to live together again, though that may be due to the petitioner's

c personal wishes to live independently as she resents the respondent's objection to her way of life. That probably means that the marriage has irretrievably broken down.

That, however, is not the end of the matter. The petitioner is not entitled to a decree merely on proof that she is unlikely to live with the respondent again. By s 1(2) of the Matrimonial Causes Act 1973:

d 'The court hearing a petition for divorce shall not hold the marriage to have broken down irretrievably unless the petitioner satisfies the court of one or more of the following facts, that is to say . . . (b) that the respondent has behaved in such a way that the petitioner cannot reasonably be expected to live with the respondent . . .'

And by s 1(3):

e 'On a petition for divorce it shall be the duty of the court to inquire, so far as it reasonably can, into the facts alleged by the petitioner and into any facts alleged by the respondent.'

In the draft answer exhibited to his affidavit of 17 December 1982 in support of his application to set aside the certificate and for leave to file an answer out of time, the

f respondent has pleaded a detailed response to all the allegations in para 11 of the petition. In some paragraphs he pleads a straight denial, in others he pleads affirmatively by way of explanation, confession and avoidance, facts which, if proved, would make it most unlikely that a decree would be granted on the ground that the petitioner had proved para 10 of the petition, or that any of the matters pleaded in sub-paras (a) to (j) of para 11 were facts that together or in isolation proved that the respondent had behaved in such a

g way that the petitioner could not reasonably be expected to live with him. His draft answer is confirmed by the terms of his affidavit and also by the affidavit of Mr Baldwin dated 17 December 1982.

The affidavit of the petitioner dated 12 January 1983 gives a totally different account of the respondent's behaviour from that given by the respondent in his affidavit and answer.

h She further submits that it would be contrary to the interests of herself, her health, the children and the legal aid fund to permit the respondent to defend the suit. The affirmation of Mr Shine dated 13 January 1983 gives his grounds for thinking that the petitioner would not live with the respondent again. He goes on to say that whatever the respondent's views are about the matter, it would be a complete waste of public funds in this matter in which both parties are legally aided, if the divorce were to proceed to trial

j on a defended basis as, if he succeeded, she would still refuse to live with him. This contention is manifestly irrelevant to the question whether if he defended he might well succeed. The interest which lies at the root of jurisdiction to set aside a decree nisi on the ground that the respondent through ignorance or his solicitor's failure failed to file an answer in time is the public interest. That interest is to ensure that decrees of dissolution of marriage shall not be allowed to stand if a respondent has a case which may well succeed and, if heard and successful, will have a result different from the result obtained in undefended proceedings. This is made clear enough in the judgment of Simon P in *Nash v Nash* [1967] 1 All ER 535, [1968] P 597 and his approval of the passage which he quotes (see [1967] 1 All ER 535 at 537, [1968] P 597 at 601) from the judgment of Scarman J in *Owen v Owen* [1964] 2 All ER 58 at 64, [1964] P 277 at 284. It would be a strange thing if the court's decision on the justice of the case depended on a decision of the legal aid committee not to grant a legal aid certificate to a respondent who wanted to defend, if that decision was based on some policy decision that public funds should not be used irrespective of the merits of the respondent's pleaded case.

The petitioner relies on her health. But she protests that she is quite well and has evidently been strong enough to persist in late nights at her disco club. She has a history of serious chronic disease, and the doctor's letter cannot give a prognosis. She obtained her registrar's certificate on 8 November 1982 and has been waiting for a decree nisi ever since. It is contended that it is not humane to prolong her anxiety and that it would be better to allow her to reach early finality in her proceedings for dissolution. There is not sufficient force in these considerations to make it just to allow the certificate to stand if the respondent has a case which he has always wanted to present which may well succeed. The failure to file an answer within time was shown to be a mistake of the respondent's solicitor who had not taken specific instructions about defending the case until the time for filing an answer had already expired. That appears from Mr Baldwin's affidavit of 17 December. If the petitioner had not then opposed the application to set aside the certificate, the answer would probably have been filed in January. The time programme of the contested proceedings would have been postponed for three months longer than if an answer had been filed in mid-October within the time limited by the rules. It is this period of three months which is the relevant delay due to failure to file an answer within time, not the difference between the programme in an undefended suit and that in a defended one.

Approaching the material before the court in the way proposed by Cairns J in *Nash v Nash* [1967] 1 All ER 535 at 538, [1968] P 597 at 603, we would therefore hold that the respondent's case may well lead to a rejection of the wife's petition for dissolution. We exercise the discretion to set aside the registrar's certificate in the respondent's favour, and give him leave to file an answer out of time. Our reasons may not be the same as the judge's reasons, though as he gave no judgment we do not precisely know what his reasons were. On our understanding of the note of the hearing before the registrar on 17 January, the horn of the dilemma on which he regarded himself as impaled was that, although on that day he again held that the marriage had irretrievably broken down, he nevertheless could not still find that the respondent had so behaved that the petitioner could not reasonably be required to live with him, although he had so certified in November. This greatly reduces the weight to be given to the registrar's decision of 17 January.

We therefore arrive at the same result as the judge and dismiss the appeal.

Appeal dismissed. Leave to appeal to the House of Lords refused.

Solicitors: *Brecher & Co*, Hayes (for the petitioner); *Turberville & Woodbridge*, Uxbridge (for the respondent).

Bebe Chua   Barrister.

R v Chard

HOUSE OF LORDS

LORD DIPLOCK, LORD SCARMAN, LORD ROSKILL, LORD BRANDON OF OAKBROOK AND LORD TEMPLEMAN

17 OCTOBER, 10 NOVEMBER 1983

Criminal law – Reference by Secretary of State – Reference of 'the whole case' – Court of Appeal confining itself to grounds set out in Secretary of State's reference – Whether appellant entitled to raise matters not referred to in Secretary of State's reference – Criminal Appeal Act 1968, s 17(1)(a).

When the Secretary of State decides that the case of a convicted person or a person who has been found insane or to be under a disability should be reconsidered (eg as the result of fresh evidence) and accordingly exercises his discretion under s 17(1)(a)[a] of the Criminal Appeal Act 1968 to refer 'the whole case' relating to that person to the Court of Appeal, the court is under a duty to treat the case so referred as being for all purposes an appeal to the court by that person, and accordingly the person is entitled to bring up and argue before the court matters unconnected with the reasons for the Secretary of State's reference (see p 639 g, p 641 c to f, p 642 j to p 643 b j and p 644 d to f, post).

R v Caborn-Waterfield [1956] 2 All ER 636, *R v Stones (No 2)* (1968) 52 Cr App R 624 and *R v Bardoe* [1969] 1 All ER 948 overruled.

Observations on the effect of judicial construction of particular words and phrases used in previous statutes when the same words in subsequent statutes in pari materia require to be construed (see p 641 h j, p 643 j to p 644 f, post); *Barras v Aberdeen Steam Trawling and Fishing Co Ltd* [1933] All ER Rep 52 criticised.

Notes

For references to the Court of Appeal, Criminal Division by the Secretary of State, see 11 Halsbury Laws (4th edn) para 619.

For the Criminal Appeal Act 1968, s 17, see 8 Halsbury's Statutes (3rd edn) 703.

Cases referred to in opinions

Barras v Aberdeen Steam Trawling and Fishing Co Ltd [1933] AC 402, [1933] All ER Rep 52, HL.

DPP v Humphrys [1976] 2 All ER 497, [1977] AC 1, [1976] 2 WLR 857, HL.

R v Bardoe [1969] 1 All ER 948, [1969] 1 WLR 398, CA.

R v Caborn-Waterfield [1956] 2 All ER 636, [1956] 2 QB 379, [1956] 3 WLR 277, CA.

R v Stones (No 2) (1968) 52 Cr App R 624, CA.

Appeal

On 7 November 1975 at the Central Criminal Court before Nield J and a jury the appellant, Alan John Chard, was convicted on three counts alleging conspiracy to rob and on 21 November 1975 he was sentenced to 15 years' imprisonment on each count, the sentences to run concurrently. On 8 March 1977 the Court of Appeal, Criminal Division (Lawton, Bridge LJJ and MacKenna J) dismissed his application for leave to appeal against conviction but reduced his sentences to 12 years on each count. On 2 April 1981 the Secretary of State for the Home Department, by letter, referred 'the whole case of Alan John Chard' to the Court of Appeal under s 17(1)(a) of the Criminal Appeal Act 1968 in respect of all three convictions. On 21 December 1982 the Court of Appeal, Criminal Division (O'Connor LJ, Peter Pain and Stuart-Smith JJ) dismissed the appeal. On 10 February 1983 the Court of Appeal refused the appellant leave to appeal to the House of Lords but certified, under s 33(2) of the Criminal Appeal Act 1968, that points of law of

---

a   Section 17 is set out at p 639 e f, post

general public importance (set out at p 641 *a*, post) were involved in its decision. On 23 June 1983 the Appeal Committee of the House of Lords granted Chard leave to appeal. *a* The facts are set out in the opinion of Lord Diplock.

Patrick O'Connor for Chard.
Brian Leary QC and *Timothy Cassel* for the Crown.

Their Lordships took time for consideration. *b*

10 November. The following opinions were delivered.

LORD DIPLOCK. My Lords, after a trial that had lasted nine weeks before Nield J and a jury at the Old Bailey, the appellant Chard was convicted on 7 November 1975 on three counts of conspiracies to commit robbery. On 21 November he was sentenced to 15 *c* years' imprisonment on each count to run concurrently. The first count against him (count 6 in the indictment) was a general count of conspiracy in June and July 1974, which did not specify any particular places where robberies which were the subject of the conspiracy were to be committed; the other two counts (14 and 15) referred to robberies at two identified places, Chigwell in Essex and a bank at Park Royal, London, respectively. *d*

At the arraignment Chard was charged with nine other defendants, alleged to be fellow members with him of a gang engaged in armed robberies for which Chard's principal function was to provide the firearms used by other members of the gang in carrying out the robberies. His role as armourer to the gang was the subject of the general conspiracy count, count 6. Count 14, relating to Chigwell, was based on his allegedly proposing and providing detailed information for carrying out a robbery of a bank there *e* which, in the event, did not take place owing to the arrest of some of the leading members of the gang. Count 15 was based on his having participated in 'casing the joint' before the robbery of the bank at Park Royal, which, in the event, was carried out successfully. Of those nine members of the gang arraigned with Chard, five pleaded guilty, four on arraignment, and a fifth at the close of the prosecution's case. Thereafter the trial proceeded against Chard and the other three remaining defendants. These gave *f* evidence in their own defence. Chard chose not to go into the witness box, nor did he, as was then permitted, make any unsworn statement from the dock.

The principal evidence for the prosecution was that of three other members of the gang who had been charged, had pleaded guilty and had been sentenced before the trial in which Chard was a defendant began. These accomplices were 'Billy' Williams, James Trusty and Peter Wilding, of whom Billy Williams was probably the first criminal to *g* earn the now familiar sobriquet of 'supergrass'.

The only evidence against Chard on each of the three counts of which he was convicted was that of these accomplices, all three of them on count 6, the general count of conspiracy to commit robberies (although Wilding does not appear to have referred to Chard's role as armourer); Billy Williams and James Trusty implicated him on count 14 relating specifically to Chigwell, and Billy Williams and Peter Wilding did so on count *h* 15 relating to the Park Royal bank.

Chard and two other of the four defendants who had been found guilty by verdict of the jury applied for leave to appeal against their convictions and sentences. Their applications (the 1977 appeal) were heard by a Court of Appeal, consisting of Lawton and Bridge LJJ and McKenna J. Lawton LJ delivered the judgment of that court on 8 March 1977. Leave to appeal against conviction was refused to all three applicants, but leave to *j* appeal against sentence was granted to Chard (and another appellant). Chard's sentence was reduced to 12 years' imprisonment concurrent on each count.

All three appellants were represented separately on the 1977 appeal by counsel of great experience in criminal cases; as appears from the transcript of the judgment of the Court of Appeal, none of these counsel had criticised the summing up by the trial judge which a had extended over two days and was described by the Court of Appeal as 'a model of clarity and conciseness'. The judgement also records that counsel on behalf of Chard had made detailed submissions that there were inconsistencies in the prosecution's evidence of such a character as to make the verdicts against his client unsafe; and the latter part of the judgment in the 1977 appeal deals with and rejects those submissions.

Peter Wilding was released on parole early in 1981, and gave an interview to a journalist on the Guardian newspaper in which he retracted evidence that he had given
b at the trial and, in particular, his positive identification of Chard as being one of the persons who had 'cased the joint' before the raid on the bank at Park Royal. In consequence of this article the Home Secretary had caused Wilding to be interviewed by a detective chief superintendent to whom Wilding repeated, albeit not entirely unequivocally, that his positive identification of Chard's presence on that occasion was untrue.

c By letter of 2 April 1981 the Home Secretary, in exercise of his powers under s 17(1)(a) of the Criminal Appeal Act 1968, referred to the Court of Appeal, Criminal Division, 'the whole of the case of Alan John Chard for determination in respect of his conviction on 7th November 1975 of three offences of conspiracy to rob'. In the previous paragraph of his letter he had referred to the article in the Guardian newspaper and also to Wilding's statement to the detective chief superintendent. A copy of the record of this statement
d was enclosed.

Section 17 of the Criminal Appeal Act 1968 is in the following terms:

'(1) Where a person has been convicted on indictment, or been tried on indictment and found not guilty by reason of insanity, or been found by a jury to be under disability, the Secretary of State may, if he thinks fit, at any time either—
e (a) refer the whole case to the Court of Appeal and the case shall then be treated for all purposes as an appeal to the Court by that person; or (b) if he desires the assistance of the Court on any point arising in the case, refer that point to the Court for their opinion thereon, and the Court shall consider the point so referred and furnish the Secretary of State with their opinion thereon accordingly.
(2) A reference by the Secretary of State under this section may be made by him either on an application by the person referred to in subsection (1), or without any
f such application.'

In my view, which I understand is shared by all your Lordships, the words of sub-s (1)(a) in their natural and ordinary meaning are free from any trace of ambiguity: the person whose case which resulted in his conviction is the subject matter of the reference is to be treated for all purposes as if he were a person on whom there is conferred by s 1
g of the Criminal Appeal Act 1968 a general right of appeal to the Court of Appeal on any ground which he wishes to rely (whether it be of law or fact or mixed law and fact), without need to obtain the prior leave of that court.

The Court of Appeal by whom there was heard the whole case of Chard that had been referred to it by the Home Secretary (the second appeal) was composed of O'Connor LJ, Peter Pain and Stuart-Smith JJ, none of whom had sat on the 1977 appeal. Application
h was made on Chard's behalf to adduce at the hearing of the second appeal fresh evidence in the form of the statement made by Wilding to the detective chief superintendent of which a copy had been enclosed with the Home Secretary's letter; and a perfected notice of grounds of appeal in the following terms was lodged:

'1. The Appellant's convictions upon all three counts of conspiracy to rob
j (originally Counts 10, 20 and 21; later renumbered Counts 6, 14 and 15) are unsafe and unsatisfactory and should be quashed for the following reasons:— (a) fresh evidence is now available to the effect that the prosecution witness, Peter Wilding has admitted committing perjury in relation to his evidence against the Appellant on Counts 6 and 15. (b) although the said Peter Wilding gave no evidence against the Appellant on Count 14, his own admissions of perjury implicate the main

prosecution witness on that Count, "Billy" Williams, in instigating and blackmailing
him into giving his perjured evidence. (c) all three convictions depended on the
uncorroborated evidence of accomplices as to Count 6:—"Billy" Williams, James
Trusty and Peter Wilding. as to *Count 14* "Billy" Williams and James Trusty. as to
Count 15 "Billy" Williams and Peter Wilding. (d) The said uncorroborated accomplice
evidence was subject to particular contradictions and weaknesses on each count
against this Appellant.'

It is to be observed that although paras (a) and (b) rely on the fresh evidence of Peter
Wilding, paras (c) and (d) seek to impugn the verdicts against Chard as unsafe or
unsatisfactory on wider grounds that are not alluded to in the Home Secretary's letter of
reference of 2 April 1981. The ground relied on para (c) that the convictions were
based on the uncorroborated evidence of accomplices would open the door to criticism
(expressly disclaimed by Chard's counsel at the 1977 appeal) of the adequacy of the trial
judge's warning to the jury of the danger of convicting on such evidence; while the
ground relied on in para (d) (ie that even if such warning had been adequate the
accomplice evidence against Chard was itself subject to contradictions and weaknesses
that made a verdict of guilty based on it unsafe or unsatisfactory) was a complaint that
had been advanced by Chard's counsel in the 1977 appeal and is dealt with in some detail
in the judgment of the court on that occasion when it was rejected as insufficient ground
for granting Chard leave to appeal against conviction.

Wilding himself gave oral evidence to the Court of Appeal at the hearing of the second
appeal. He confirmed that the evidence that he had given at the trial in 1975 which
inculpated Chard was true; this confirmation and his explanation that he had said what
he did to the journalist and the detective chief superintendent in order to escape
harassment of himself and his family by members of the underworld (with whom
'grasses' are understandably unpopular) were accepted by the Court of Appeal as being
true; and no complaint against this part of the judgment in the second appeal has been
advanced before this House.

What is complained of on behalf of Chard is the Court of Appeal's ruling that on a
reference by the Home Secretary under s 17(1)(a) of the Criminal Appeal Act 1968 the
court, in its consideration of the appeal, must confine itself to the grounds set out in the
Home Secretary's letter as his reasons for making the reference; the court may not
consider other grounds for allowing the appeal on which the convicted person whose
case has been referred might wish to rely. Pursuant to this ruling the Court of Appeal
refused to allow Chard's counsel to argue the grounds sought to be relied on in paras (c)
and (d) of Chard's perfected notice of appeal.

In so ruling the Court of Appeal relied on two previous authorities. The first in date
was a judgment of the Court of Criminal Appeal delivered by Lord Goddard CJ in *R v
Caborn-Waterfield* [1956] 2 All ER 636, [1956] 2 QB 379, a case that was decided on a
reference under s 19(a) of the Criminal Appeal Act 1907, before that section had been
amended by s 19 of Sch 3 to the Administration of Justice Act 1960, so as to adopt the
wording later reproduced in s 17(1)(a) of the (consolidating) Criminal Appeal Act 1968.
The second authority was *R v Stones (No 2)* (1968) 52 Cr App R 624, decided by the
Criminal Division of the Court of Appeal also on a reference under s 19(a) of the Criminal
Appeal Act 1907 but after the 1960 amendment to it. The judgment of the court,
delivered by Sachs LJ, treated the case as governed by *R v Caborn-Waterfield*. There are
other reported cases subsequent to *R v Stones (No 2)* that proceed on the same basis, and
the Court of Appeal in the instant case was, in my opinion, constrained by authority to
make the restrictive ruling that it did as to the matters open to be argued in the second
appeal.

In view of what would seem to be the plain and unambiguous wording of s 17(1)(a) of
the Criminal Appeal Act 1968, this ruling raises a point of law that is of general public
importance. The terms in which the Court of Appeal certified the questions of law
involved were:

a '1. Where as a result of fresh evidence placed before him the Secretary of State has referred "the whole of the case" to the Court of Appeal Criminal Division under Section 17(1)(a) of the Criminal Appeal Act, 1968, is the Appellant entitled to argue matters unconnected with the reasons for the reference in the Secretary of State's letter referring the case? 2. If the answer to Question 1 is "No", has the Court of Appeal Criminal Division a discretion to permit the Appellant to argue such matters?'

b Leave to appeal was granted by this House; and in the printed case for the appellant your Lordships were invited in the event of either of the certified questions being answered in favour of Chard to dispose of the second appeal finally by yourselves hearing argument on and dealing with the matters that are referred to in paras (c) and (d) of the perfected grounds of appeal which counsel for Chard had been debarred from raising in the Court of Appeal.

c My Lords, the point of law raised by the certified questions is purely one of statutory construction; and, as I have already indicated, the language of s 17(1)(a) in my opinion capable of bearing one meaning only. If the Home Secretary decides to act under para (a), rather than para (b), in the case of a particular convicted person, it is the whole case and nothing less than the whole case of that person that the Home Secretary is empowered by the section to refer to the Court of Appeal. On receipt of such a reference it then

d becomes the duty of the Court of Appeal to treat the case so referred *for all purposes* as an appeal to the court by *that* person.

Since it is the 'whole case' that is referred, this must include all questions of fact and law involved in it; and the requirement that it shall be treated as an appeal by the convicted person 'for all purposes' must include its being so treated for the purposes of the Criminal Appeal Rules 1968, SI 1968/1262 as they apply to appellants who, under s 1

e of the Criminal Appeal Act 1968, have a right of appeal to the Court of Appeal without the leave of that court on all questions of law or fact or mixed law and fact involved in the trial that resulted in their conviction. Those rules entitle, and indeed require, such persons to give notice of any grounds, whether of law or fact or mixed law and fact, on which they propose to rely on the hearing of the appeal. No limitation is imposed by the rules on the grounds that such appellants may rely on.

f Counsel for the Crown did not seek to argue that if one gave to the words of s 17(1)(a), to which I have drawn particular attention, their natural and ordinary meaning, it is possible to extract from the words themselves any restriction on the grounds on which the person who is to be treated as if he were appellant may rely. Nevertheless counsel submitted that the restrictive effect that had been attributed to s 19(a) of the Criminal Appeal Act 1907 by judicial decisions of appellate courts from 1956 onwards must be

g understood as expressing the intention of Parliament when the same words were re-enacted by it in s 17(1)(a) of the Criminal Appeal Act 1968.

My Lords, the role that judicial construction of particular words and phrases used in previous statutes may play in the interpretation of the same words in subsequent statutes in pari materia was the subject of discussion in four of the speeches in this House in *Barras v Aberdeen Steam Trawling and Fishing Co Ltd* [1933] AC 402, [1933] All ER Rep 52.

h The divergence between the different speeches makes it in my view a thoroughly unsatisfactory authority for any rule of statutory construction of general application or one that could assist the Crown in the instant case. It is certainly no authority for either of the propositions: (a) that mere failure by Parliament to take an opportunity of passing amending legislation to substitute other words for those which have been construed by a court that is not one of final resort as having borne a meaning which this House

j subsequently holds to have been incorrect can throw any retrospective light on the intention of a differently constituted Parliament at the time that the Act to be construed as passed; or (b) that re-enactment of ipsissima verba of an existing statute in an Act that is passed for the purposes of consolidation only (which is subject to a special parliamentary procedure precluding debate on the merits of any of the individual clauses) is capable of having any effect on the construction of those words.

Moreover, the legislative history of s 19(a) of the Criminal Appeal Act 1907 from the
date of the decision of *R v Caborn-Waterfield* in 1956 and its incorporation in a pure
consolidation Act as s 17(1)(a) of the Criminal Appeal Act 1968 itself puts paid to any
submission on the lines counsel for the Crown sought to advance. At the time of *R v
Caborn-Waterfield* the relevant words in 19(a) were:

'the case shall then be heard and determined by the Court of Criminal Appeal as
in the case of an appeal by a person convicted.'

These words are less emphatic than those of s 17(1)(a) of the Criminal Appeal Act 1968
which it falls to your Lordships to construe. The reference to the case being treated *for all
purposes* as an appeal is missing and the person by whom the appeal is to be treated as
having been brought is not specifically identified by the demonstrative adjective 'that',
ie the person whose whole case has been referred to the court by the Home Secretary,
but is described by the indefinitive article 'x'.

R v Caborn-Waterfield was a case which had been referred by the Home Secretary on
the grounds of fresh evidence having become available. At the hearing of the reference
counsel for Caborn-Waterfield refused to call any of such fresh evidence but sought to
rely exclusively on grounds which had been relied on some eighteen months previously
in an application by Caborn-Waterfield for leave to appeal. As would appear from his
reported interlocutory interventions this tactic excited the wrath of Lord Goddard CJ and
in a characteristically robust passage at the conclusion of his judgment, which it is
unnecessary to quote in full, he said ([1956] 2 All ER 636 at 638, [1956] 2 QB 379 at 385):

'This court desires to say quite definitely that on a reference by the Home Secretary
under s. 19(a) the court will go through the grounds on which the Home Secretary
has referred the case and confine itself to those grounds. The court cannot go into
all sorts of different grounds, otherwise if it did, there might be no end to it.'

It is not wholly clear from the full passage whether Lord Goddard CJ was saying the
court had no jurisdiction to consider any grounds of appeal other than those on which
the Home Secretary had referred the case, or that as a matter of practice the court would
refuse to do so. If it meant the former, and it has been uniformly treated as having done
so, it was in my respectful view wrong, even on the language of s 19(a) of the Criminal
Appeal Act 1907, as it stood in 1956. By the Administration of Justice Act 1960, however,
Parliament itself stepped in and by Sch 3 amended s 19(a) of the 1907 Act and, among
other changes, took the occasion to substitute the more emphatic words that still remain
in force as s 17(1)(a) of the Criminal Justice Act 1968, with the immaterial difference that
the words 'that person' in the 1968 consolidating Act were 'the person' in the 1960
amendment. It is difficult to think of any other explanation for this part of the 1960
amendment than a parliamentary intention to overrule the effect of the judgment of
Lord Goddard CJ in *R v Caborn-Waterfield*.

R v Stones (No 2), in which the attention of the court does not appear to have been
drawn to the change of wording of s 19(a) since *R v Caborn-Waterfield*, was not decided
until after there had been passed the Criminal Appeal Act 1966 and the Criminal Justice
Act 1967, the Acts incorporating, inter alia, amendments to the Criminal Appeal Act
1907 which paved the way for the consolidation effected by the Criminal Appeal
Act 1968 and one month after the consolidation Act itself was passed. So there is simply
no foundation for the suggestion that on the two occasions when Parliament had the
opportunity of making further amendments to the wording of s 19(a) of the 1907 Act, it
had any reason to suppose that judicial construction would subsequently ascribe to the
altered wording that it had enacted in 1960 the same meaning as had been ascribed in *R
v Caborn-Waterfield* to the wording that it had so recently been at pains to repeal and
replace.

So I see no reason that could justify your Lordships giving to the words of s 17(1)(a) of
the Criminal Appeal Act 1968 any meaning other than their natural and ordinary

meaning which I find to be plain and free from any ambiguity. I would accordingly
a answer the first certified question Yes.

It follows that *R v Stones (No 2)* and all subsequent decisions in which *R v Caborn-Waterfield* has been applied to references under s 17(1)(a) of the Criminal Appeal Act 1968, including among them *R v Bardoe* [1969] 1 All ER 948, [1969] 1 WLR 398, should be treated as overruled.

As has been demonstrated by the briefness of the additional time that it has taken to
b hear the instant appeal in consequence of your Lordship's acceptance of the appellant's invitation to dispose of the reference finally by hearing argument on the grounds relied on in paras (c) and (d) of his perfected grounds of appeal, this does not mean that the time taken up in hearing references under s 17(1)(a) is likely to be significantly increased. Where, on such a reference, an appellant seeks to argue grounds of appeal which not only are unconnected with the reasons in the Home Secretary's letter referring the case, but
c also have been unsuccessfully relied on in a previous appeal or application for leave to appeal against conviction in the case that has been referred, the court which hears the reference will have had before it and have read, as your Lordships have done in the instant case, the judgment of the Court of Appeal in the previous appeal or application for leave to appeal. While it is true that the doctrine of issue estoppel plays no part in criminal law (see *DPP v Humphrys* [1976] 2 All ER 497, [1977] AC 1), the court that hears
d the reference will give weight to that previous judgment, from which it will be very slow to differ, unless it is persuaded that some cogent argument that had not been advanced at the previous hearing would, if it had been properly developed at such hearing, have resulted in the appeal against conviction being allowed.

In the instant case counsel, who appeared on behalf of Chard in your Lordships' house but had not represented him on any earlier occasion, sought to criticise Nield J's summing
e up at the original trial on the ground that, although he gave an impeccable instruction on the danger of convicting on the uncorroborated evidence of accomplices, he weakened its effect by inviting the jury to consider whether there was any reason why particular accomplices should want to give false evidence incriminating particular defendants. No such criticism had been advanced by counsel appearing for Chard in the 1977 appeal. In my opinion there is nothing in it. It is a question, dictated by simple common sense,
f which the members of the jury would probably have asked for themselves in the course of their deliberations even if the judge had not mentioned it. I have read for myself the whole of the judge's summing up and I understand that each of your Lordships has done likewise. For my part I think it a model of clarity, accuracy and fairness in a case of considerable complexity.

Counsel for Chard also drew your Lordships' attention to what he suggested were
g inconsistencies and weaknesses in the accomplice evidence that notwithstanding an impeccable summing up were in themselves sufficient to render the jury's verdict unsafe or unsatisfactory. For the most part these were the same as those that had been relied on for the same purpose by counsel who appeared as counsel for Chard in the 1977 appeal. They are dealt with in the Court of Appeal's judgment dismissing Chard's application for leave to appeal against conviction. For my part I remain wholly unconvinced that such
h inconsistencies and weaknesses as counsel for Chard has drawn to your Lordships' attention have the cumulative effect of rendering unsafe or unsatisfactory the jury's verdict against Chard on any of the three counts on which he was found guilty.

I would dismiss the appeal.

LORD SCARMAN. My Lords, I agree with the speech delivered by my noble and
i learned friend Lord Diplock, and for the reasons which he gives I would dismiss the appeal.

I respectfully agree with my noble and learned friend that it would be wrong to extract from the speeches of their Lordships in *Barras v Aberdeen Steam Trawling and Fishing Co Ltd* [1933] AC 402, [1933] All ER Rep 52 an inflexible rule of construction to the effect that where once certain words in an Act of Parliament have received a judicial construction in one of the superior courts and the legislature has repeated them without alteration in a subsequent statute, the legislature must be taken to have used them *a* according to the meaning which a court of competent jurisdiction has given to them. Viscount Buckmaster clearly thought that such a rule existed and that it was a salutary and necessary (see [1933] AC 402 at 412, [1933] All ER Rep 52 at 55); but others of their Lordships took a different view, notably Lord Blanesburgh and Lord Macmillan (see [1933] AC 402 at 414, 446–447, [1933] All ER Rep 52 at 56, 72). Lord Macmillan, for, as I respectfully think, compelling reasons, treated the rule not 'as a canon of construction *b* of absolute obligation' but as a presumption in circumstances where the judicial interpretation was well settled and well recognised; and even then his Lordship thought the rule must yield to the fundamental rule that in construing statutes the grammatical and ordinary sense of the words is to be adhered to, unless it leads to some absurdity, repugnance, or inconsistency. This view accords with modern principles of statutory interpretation and should, in my opinion, be preferred to that adopted by Viscount *c* Buckmaster.

LORD ROSKILL. My Lords, I have had the advantage of reading in draft the speech delivered by my noble and learned friend Lord Diplock. For the reasons he gives I too would answer the first certified question in the affirmative but also for the reasons he gives I would dismiss this appeal. I would also respectfully indorse what both he and my *d* noble and learned friend Lord Scarman have said regarding the unsatisfactory decision of the House in *Barras v Aberdeen Steam Trawling and Fishing Co Ltd* [1933] AC 402, [1933] All ER Rep 52 and especially Lord Scarman's expression of preference for the reasoning in the speech of Lord Macmillan in that case.

LORD BRANDON OF OAKBROOK. My Lords, I agree entirely with the speech *e* delivered by my noble and learned friend Lord Diplock, and would accordingly dispose of the appeal in the manner proposed by him.

LORD TEMPLEMAN. My Lords, for the reasons given by my noble and learned friend Lord Diplock I too would dismiss this appeal. I agree with the observations of Lord Scarman. *f*

Appeal dismissed.

Solicitors: *B M Birnberg & Co* (for Chard); *Director of Public Prosecutions.*

Mary Rose Plummer   Barrister.

a

Skips A/S Nordheim and others v Syrian Petroleum Co Ltd and another
The Varenna

COURT OF APPEAL, CIVIL DIVISION

b

SIR JOHN DONALDSON MR, OLIVER AND WATKINS LJJ

27, 28, 29 JULY, 5 OCTOBER 1983

Shipping – Bill of lading – Incorporation of terms of charterparty – Arbitration clause – Bill of lading providing that 'all conditions and exceptions of [the] charterparty' deemed to be incorporated in bill of lading – Charterparty providing for bill of lading to incorporate 'all terms and conditions of [the] charter including . . . the arbitration clause' – Whether arbitration clause a

c

'condition' incorporated in bill of lading – Whether arbitration clause incorporated in bill of lading by charterparty or bill of lading.

The shipowners chartered their vessel to the charterers for the shipment of a cargo of crude oil on behalf of the shippers for delivery to the consignees under a bill of lading which stated that 'all conditions and exceptions of [the] Charter party' were deemed to be incorporated in the bill of lading. The charterparty provided, inter alia, that disputes

d

under the charter were to be settled by arbitration in London and that all bills of lading issued pursuant to the charter were to 'incorporate by reference all terms and conditions of [the] charter including the terms of the Arbitration clause . . .' The bill of lading did not specifically provide for the arbitration of disputes. When the charterers defaulted in payment of demurrage the shipowners brought an action against the shippers and the consignees claiming the amount of the demurrage. The consignees applied for the

e

shipowners' action to be stayed, contending that the arbitration clause in the charterparty had been incorporated into the bill of lading and that therefore any dispute between the shipowners and the consignees arising out of the bill of lading was to be settled by arbitration. The judge held that the arbitration clause in the charterparty was not incorporated into the bill of lading by the incorporation clause in the bill of lading nor was it incorporated by the terms of the charterparty itself and accordingly he dismissed

f

the consignees' application. The consignees appealed.

Held – (1) Whether a bill of lading incorporated terms, conditions or other provisions from a charterparty depended primarily on the construction of the bill of lading rather than the charterparty, since the bill of lading was the only contract to which the shipowners and the consignees were parties and the operative words of incorporation had

g

accordingly to be found in the bill of lading (see p 647 j to 648 c, p 650 c to g and p 653 e f and h j, post).

(2) Conditions contained in a charterparty which were to be referentially incorporated into a bill of lading were limited to conditions under which the goods were to be carried and delivered and did not extend to a collateral term such as an arbitration clause, even if that clause was expressed in terms which were capable, without modification, of referring

h

to the bill of lading contract. It followed that the incorporation clause in the bill of lading was not sufficient to incorporate the arbitration clause contained in the charterparty into the bill of lading. The appeal would accordingly be dismissed (see p 649 f to h, p 651 d to g and p 653 b c f and h j, post); *Serraino & Sons v Campbell* [1891] 1 QB 283, *T W Thomas & Co Ltd v Portsea Steamship Co Ltd* [1912] AC 1 and *Hogarth Shipping Co Ltd v Blyth Greene Jourdain & Co Ltd* [1917] 2 KB 534 applied; *Astro Valiente Compania Naviera SA v Pakistan*

j

Ministry of Food and Agriculture (No 2), The Emmanuel Colocotronis (No 2) [1982] 1 All ER 823 disapproved.

Per Sir John Donaldson MR and Oliver LJ. Where documents commonly used contain particular phrases and expressions which have a clear and well-established meaning among commercial lawyers, it is important that those expressions should be construed consistently with that meaning, unless there are compulsive surrounding circumstances or a context strongly suggestive of some other meaning (see p 648 f and p 651 d to g, post); dictum of Staughton J in *Astro Valiente Compania Naviera SA v Pakistan Ministry of*

Food and Agriculture (No. 2), The Emmanuel Coloctronis (No. 2) [1982] 1 All ER at 825
disapproved.

Decision of Hobhouse J [1983] 2 All ER 375 affirmed.   *a*

Notes

For the incorporation of an arbitration clause from a charterparty into a bill of lading, see
2 Halsbury's Laws (4th edn) para 522, and for cases on the subject, see 3 Digest (Reissue)
31–34, 160–172.

Cases referred to in judgments   *b*

Annefield, The, Annefield (owners) v Annefield (cargo owners) [1971] 1 All ER 394, [1971] P
    168, [1971] 2 WLR 320, CA.
*Astro Valiente Compania Naviera SA v Pakistan Ministry of Food and Agriculture (No 2), The
    Emmanuel Colocotronis (No 2)* [1982] 1 All ER 823, [1982] 1 WLR 1096.
Fort Shipping Co Ltd v Pederson & Co (1924) 19 Ll L Rep 26.
Gray v Carr (1871) LR 6 QB 522.   *c*
Hogarth Shipping Co Ltd v Blyth Greene Jourdain & Co Ltd [1917] 2 KB 534, CA.
Manchester Trust v Furness Withy & Co [1895] 2 QB 539, CA.
Merak, The, T B & S Batchelor & Co Ltd v SS Merak (owners) [1965] 1 All ER 230, [1965]
    P 223, [1965] 2 WLR 250, CA.
Njegos, The [1936] P 90, [1935] All ER Rep 863.
Northumbria, The [1906] P 292, DC.   *d*
Serraino & Sons v Campbell [1891] 1 QB 283, CA.
Thomas (T W) & Co Ltd v Portsea Steamship Co Ltd [1912] AC 1, HL.
Wickman Machine Tool Sales Ltd v L Schuler AG [1973] 2 All ER 39, [1974] AC 235, [1973]
    2 WLR 683, HL.

Cases also cited   *e*

Atlas Levante-Linie Akt v Gesellschaft Fuer Getreidehandel AG & Becher, The Phönizien [1966]
    1 Lloyd's Rep 150.
East Yorkshire Steamship Co Ltd v Hancock (1900) 5 Com Cas 266.
European Grain and Shipping Ltd v Johnston [1982] 1 Lloyd's Rep 414.
Gardner & Sons v Trechmann (1884) 15 QBD 154, CA.
Hamilton & Co v Mackie & Sons (1889) 5 TLR 677, CA.   *f*
Rena K, The [1979] 1 All ER 397, [1979] QB 377.

Interlocutory appeal

By a writ issued on 1 March 1982 pursuant to an order of Parker J, the plaintiffs, Skips
A/S Nordheim, A/S Vestheim, Skips A/S Vaarheim, and Marit Ditlev Simonsen, Halfdan
Ditlev-Simonsen and Guttorm Fossen (all trading as Sameiet Varenna), claimed against
the defendants, Syrian Petroleum Co Ltd and Petrofina SA, damages amounting to   *g*
$US104,527·04 and/or damages and interest. The seond defendants applied by summons
for a stay of the action under s 1 of the Arbitration Act 1975 claiming that a bill of lading
dated 17 March 1976 issued and signed by the master of the vessel Varenna owned by
the plaintiffs contained a contract between the parties for the arbitration of disputes
between them. On 26 November 1982 Hobhouse J ([1983] 2 All ER 375) dismissed the
summons to stay the action and the second defendants appealed. The facts are set out in   *h*
the judgment of Sir John Donaldson MR.

A H M Evans QC and *Jeffrey Gruder* for the second defendants.
David *Johnson* QC and *Timothy Young* for the plaintiffs.
The first defendants were not represented.

Cur adv vult   *j*

5 October. The following judgments were delivered.

SIR JOHN DONALDSON MR. In this appeal there appear to be four parties in two
groups. First there are the appellants and the respondents. The appellants, the second

defendants in the action, were holders of a bill of lading relating to a quantity of crude
_a_ oil of which they took delivery in West Germany. The respondents, the plaintiffs in the
action, were owners of the vessel Varenna in which the oil was carried. The plaintiffs by
their writ claimed demurrage alleged to be due under the terms of the bill of lading
contract. The second defendants sought a stay of the action on the grounds that the bill
of lading contract contained an arbitration clause by incorporation from the charterparty.

The dispute is not entirely, or even mainly, about who shall resolve the disputed claim
_b_ for demurrage. The commercial point, with which we are not concerned, is somewhat
different. The second defendants say that they put the charterers in funds to pay the
demurrage in question and that the charterers went into liquidation before paying the
plaintiffs. They can avoid paying twice if the plaintiffs are obliged to arbitrate, because
they can then pray in aid a time bar.

The second pair of parties to this appeal appear to be Staughton and Hobhouse JJ. At
_c_ all events, the appeal has been presented on the basis that the decision of Hobhouse J
([1983] 2 All ER 375) in the present case cannot stand with that of Staughton J in _Astro
Valiente Compania Naviera SA v Ministry of Food and Agriculture (No 2), The Emmanuel
Colocotronis (No 2)_ [1982] 1 All ER 823, 1 WLR 1096 and Hobhouse J in terms declined
to follow it.

The issue, in a nutshell, is whether the wording of the bill of lading is apt to introduce
_d_ the provisions of the charterparty arbitration clause (cl 46) and apply it to the bill of
lading contract.

The terms of the bill of lading, so far as is material, are as follows:

'SHIPPED in apparent good order and condition [a quantity of crude oil in bulk] to
be delivered (subject to the undermentioned conditions and exception) in like good
order and condition at the port of WILHELMSHAVEN – W. GERMANY or as near thereto
_e_   as she may safely get (always afloat) unto Order PETROFINA S.A. or to their assigns
upon payment of freight as per Charter party, all conditions and exceptions of which
Charter party including the negligence clause, are deemed to be incorporated in Bill
of Lading . . .'

Any summary of Hobhouse J's detailed review of the authorities would do it less than
_f_ justice, but his conclusion is contained in two sentences ([1983] 2 All ER 375 at 381):

'The correct construction of the present bill of lading therefore is that when it
refers to conditions it refers only to conditions properly so called to be performed
by the consignee on the arrival of the vessel. On no view is an arbitration clause
such a condition.'

_g_   The contrary view, urged by the second defendants, is that 'conditions' in the context
is a term which is wide enough to incorporate all the provisions of the charterparty,
albeit some will thereafter have to be rejected as inappropriate. The second defendants
then submit that although the arbitration clause is itself inappropriate, since it refers to
'disputes arising under this charter' and to the 'owners and charterers' each appointing an
arbitrator, cl 44 justifies all necessary modifications to make it appropriate, since that
_h_ clause requires that all bills of lading issued pursuant to the charterparty—

'shall incorporate by reference all terms and conditions of this charter including
the terms of the Arbitration clause and shall contain the following Paramount clause
. . .'

The plaintiffs retort that under cl 33 it is expressly provided that 'Bills of Lading are to be
_i_ signed as Charterers direct' without prejudice to this charter and that the charterers must
be deemed to have exercised this power and directed the master to sign bills of lading
which excluded the arbitration clause.

The starting point for the resolution of this dispute must be the contract contained in,
or evidenced by, the bill of lading, for this is the only contract to which the plaintiff
shipowners and the defendant receivers are both parties. What the plaintiffs agreed with

the charterers, whether in the charterparty or otherwise, is wholly irrelevant, save in so
far as the whole or part of any such agreement has become part of the bill of lading   *a*
contract. Such an incorporation cannot be achieved by agreement between the owners
and the charterers. It can only be achieved by the agreement of the parties to the bill of
lading contract and thus the operative words of incorporation must be found in the bill
of lading itself.

Operative words of incorporation may be precise or general, narrow or wide. Where
they are general, and in particular where they are general and wide, they may have the   *b*
effect of incorporating more than can make any sense in the context of an agreement
governing the rights and liabilities of the shipowner and of the bill of lading holder. In
such circumstances, what one might describe as 'surplus', 'insensible' or 'inconsistent'
provisions fall to be 'disincorporated', 'rejected' or ignored as 'surplusage'. But the starting
point must always be the provisions of the bill of lading contract producing the initial
incorporation. And what must be sought is *incorporation*, not *notice* of the existence or   *c*
terms of another contract which is not incorporated (see *Manchester Trust v Furness Withy
& Co* [1895] 2 QB 539).

In the *Astro Valiente* case [1982] 1 All ER 823 at 825, [1982] 1 WLR 1096 at 1098
Staughton J referred to the variety of incorporating words which have been judicially
considered over the past 90 years or more and said:

> 'If one looks at the cases, it appears to depend on whether the words of   *d*
> incorporation used are "conditions", "terms", "clauses" or "exceptions", or any
> combination of the four; and perhaps on whether such words are used in conjunction
> with the participial phrase "he or they paying freight as per charterparty". Such nice
> distinctions are in my judgment not wholly appropriate to a commercial relationship,
> and should if possible be avoided. So too should the interpretation of an ordinary
> English word, "conditions", in a sense different from that which it naturally bears,   *e*
> particularly in a document which may well not be prepared by a lawyer, or at any
> rate by an English lawyer.'

In principle I have considerable sympathy with this view, but this is a corner of the
law where the commercial customers, shipowners, shippers and receivers, attach supreme
importance to certainty, and where particular phrases have established meanings and   *f*
effects it is not the policy of the law to seek to change them even if, in the absence of
precedent, there would be a case for so doing.

The second defendants submit that the phrase 'all conditions and exceptions ...
including the negligence clause' are very wide words of incorporation and indeed are all-
embracing. Accordingly, they entitle the court to incorporate the whole charterparty
into the bill of lading contract and then to proceed to eliminate inconsistent or insensible   *g*
provisions. They are however faced with two obstacles. The first is that an arbitration
clause is not an 'exception'. They must therefore rely on the words 'all conditions' as
words of incorporation. The second is that 'conditions' in the context of incorporating
charterparty provisions into a bill of lading contract has been the subject of considerable
judicial consideration and the conclusions reached, unless distinguishable, fully support
the decision of Hobhouse J.   *h*

In *T W Thomas & Co Ltd v Portsea Steamship Co Ltd* [1912] AC 1 there were two separate
paragraphs relied on as incorporating an arbitration clause. The first was '[the consignee]
paying freight for the said goods, with other conditions as per charterparty with average
accustomed'. The second was 'Deck load at shippers' risk, and all other terms and
conditions and exceptions of charter to be as per charterparty, including negligence
clause'. Earlier authorities had established that a reference to 'other conditions' coupled   *j*
with the obligation to pay freight only incorporated such of the charterparty conditions
as were to be performed by the consignee (see *Gray v Carr* (1871) LR 6 QB 522 and
Serraino & Sons v Campbell [1891] 1 QB 283). In this situation Leslie Scott KC, later Scott
LJ, who was a specialist in this branch of the law, did not argue that these decisions were
wrong, but that they were distinguishable. The suggested ground of distinction was that

a   the deckload paragraph was divorced from the provisions referring to the payment of freight. From this it followed, as he submitted, that the ejusdem generis considerations which restricted the ambit of 'conditions' in the context of payment of freight and taking delivery did not apply and the word should have a wider meaning. He also relied on the presence of a cesser clause as having the effect that the charterparty contract was spent and likely to be transferred to and incorporated in the bill of lading contract. This feature is not present in the charterparty which we have had to consider.

b   This submission was rejected. Lord Loreburn LC, with the concurrence of Lord Atkinson, held that all that was incorporated were provisions which governed shipment or carriage or delievery or the terms on which delivery was to be made or taken (see [1912] AC 1 at 6). Lord Gorrell (at 8) held that 'terms and conditions' only incorporated 'matters which have to be dealt with both by the shippers and the consignees in relation to the carriage, discharge and delivery of the cargo'. Lord Robson (at 10) dealt with the

c   matter on the basis of inconsistency. I can find no trace in the judgments of Lord Loreburn LC, Lord Atkinson or Lord Gorrell of their decision being dependent on 'conditions' having to be construed ejusdem generis with freight in the second paragraph, because of the presence of that word in the first paragraph or on the conjunction of the word 'other' in the second paragraph. Accordingly, I regard the decision as clear authority for the true construction of the word 'conditions' simpliciter. Of the later cases, all that

d   need be said is that in *Hogarth Shipping Co Ltd v Blyth Greene Jourdain & Co Ltd* [1917] 2 KB 534 the incorporating words were 'freight and all other conditions and exceptions as per charterparty', whose meaning had been established long before *Thomas v Portsea* and that, apart from the *Astro Valiente* case, all the other cases contained wider words of incorporation than are present in the instant case. I can find no trace of *Thomas v Portsea* ever having been doubted or modified and that decision is in my judgment fatal to the

e   appeal.

    Counsel for the second defendants referred to *Wickman Machine Tools Sales Ltd v L Schuler AG* [1973] 2 All ER 39, [1974] AC 235 as authority for the proposition that the word 'conditions' has no precise legal meaning, but that was in the context of an agency contract for the sale of panel presses which is wholly different. Staughton J wished the word to receive its ordinary interpretation, but 'conditions' is a chameleon-like word

f   which takes its meaning from its surroundings. In the context of incorporating into a bill of lading contract provisions which found their birth in a charterparty, I would have thought that the ordinary English meaning of the word was 'the conditions under which the goods are loaded, stowed, kept, cared for, carried and discharged'. An arbitration clause is not in this category.

    As, in my judgment, the arbitration clause was never incorporated, it is unnecessary to

g   consider whether, if it was, it has to be rejected as being insensible in view of its references to 'this charter', 'under this charter' and the appointment of arbitrators by 'owners and charterers'. Clearly the clause would have required 'manipulation' to use the colourful phrase of Lord Denning MR in *The Annefield* [1971] 1 All ER 394 at 406, [1971] P 168 at 184. Whether such manipulation could be justified having regard to cll 33 and 44 of the charterparty is an interesting point but not one which, in my judgment, arises for

h   decision on this appeal.

    I would dismiss the appeal.

OLIVER LJ. The question raised by this appeal is one which, to the tyro, appears deceptively simple. It is whether an arbitration clause contained in a charterparty and which was clearly intended by the parties to that contract to be incorporated referentially

j   in any bill of lading issued thereunder was in fact effectively incorporated by the terms of such a bill of lading. On the face of it that is a comparatively simple question of the true construction of the bill of lading in question and it is discouraging to one whose unfamiliarity with this field is unrivalled to find what appears to be a simple construction point overlaid by a great weight of authority which, it is claimed, compulsively restricts the inquiry to predestinate grooves. In the recent case of *Astro Valiente Compania Naviera*

SA v Pakistan Ministry of Food and Agriculture (No 2), The Emmanuel Colocotronis (No 2)
[1982] 1 All ER 823, [1982] 1 WLR 1096 Staughton J, in construing a bill of lading   *a*
containing somewhat similar wording to that with which the instant appeal is concerned,
considered himself freed from the inhibitions which might be thought to have been
imposed by the earlier cases. In the instant case, however, Hobhouse J ([1983] 2 All ER
375) felt himself unable to follow Staughton J in so adventurous an excursion from what
clearly has become, to commercial lawyers, a familiar route.

The question squarely raised by this appeal is: which of them was right?   *b*

Coming as I do entirely fresh to the field, it seems to me that the primary consideration
which must govern any approach to the problem is that the document which falls to be
construed is the bill of lading, and not the charterparty. It may well be that, once having
arrived at a conclusion that, as a matter of construction of the bill of lading, there fall to
be incorporated referentially clauses of a particular type or description in the charterparty,
it will then become necessary to construe the charterparty in order to see whether   *c*
particular terms do or do not fall within that type or description. But the initial task
must be to look at the bill of lading and at that document alone to see what its terms are
and then, so far as it purports to include the terms of some other document by reference,
to ascertain what are the terms so included.

One point can be disposed of at the outset of the inquiry. It clearly cannot be sufficient
to assert that the bill of lading refers generally to the charterparty and that that reference   *d*
therefore, as it were, incorporates all the provisions of the charterparty because the holder
of the bill of lading has notice (either actual or constructive) of the charterparty. No
doubt every holder of a bill of lading knows that there is a charterparty in the background
whether referred to or not but such knowledge cannot of itself furnish any reason why,
in the construction of his contract, he should be in any way concerned with the terms
which have been negotiated altogether separately between the charterer and the   *e*
shipowner. So elementary a proposition may seem self-evident, but I mention it only
because there seemed to be lurking in the second defendants' argument a suggestion that
because the bill of lading in the instant case compels reference to the charterparty to
ascertain the contents of some of its clauses, it follows that the whole charterparty must
be referred to to ascertain the meaning which the parties to that contract attached to
those clauses. That seems to me to be an impermissible approach. The purpose of   *f*
referential incorporation is not, or at least is not generally, to incorporate the intentions
of the parties to the contract whose clauses are incorporated but to incorporate the clauses
themselves in order to avoid the necessity of writing them out verbatim. The meaning
and effect of the incorporated clause has to be determined as a matter of construction of
the contract into which it is incorporated having regard to all the terms of that contract.

There are in fact, as Staughton J pointed out in the *Astro Valiente* case, likely to be two   *g*
stages in the inquiry, for it inevitably happens that an incorporation in very wide general
terms is appropriate to incorporate into the bill of lading terms not strictly appropriate
for such a contract. One then has to see whether the terms are so clearly inconsistent
with the contract constituted by the bill of lading that they have to be rejected or whether
the intention to incorporate a particular clause is so clearly expressed as to require, by
necessary implication, some modification of the language of the incorporated clause so as   *h*
to adapt it to the new contract into which it is incorporated. The question of consistency
is, however, a quite separate question.

The primary contest between the parties to the instant appeal is on the ambit of the
provision in the bill of lading that 'all conditions and exceptions of which Charter party
including the negligence clause, are deemed to be incorporated in Bill of Lading'. The
plaintiffs say that, as a result of a long line of authorities over the past century and beyond,   *j*
the words 'all conditions and exceptions' in the context of a bill of lading have a well-
established and well-recognised commercial meaning. They mean such conditions and
exceptions as are appropriate to the carriage and delivery of goods and do not, as a matter
of ordinary construction, extend to a collateral term such as an arbitration clause even if
that clause is expressed (which they submit this one is not) in terms which are capable,
without modification, of referring to the bill of lading contract.

The general proposition contended for by the plaintiffs is clearly established by a line
a of cases which were extensively reviwed by Hobhouse J in the instant case, the most
striking of which are, perhaps, *Serraino & Sons v Campbell* [1891] 1 QB 283, *T W Thomas
& Co Ltd v Portsea Steamship Co Ltd* [1912] AC 1 and *Hogarth Shipping Co Ltd v Blyth Greene
Jourdain & Co Ltd* [1917] 2 KB 534.

The argument has been restricted in fact to the meaning of the word 'conditions', for
it is unnecessary in the context of the instant case to consider the more extensive formula
b sometimes found of 'terms and conditions'. Bailhache J in *Fort Shipping Co Ltd v Pederson
& Co* (1924) 19 Ll L Rep 26 held that the word 'terms' was wider than 'conditions' and
that accordingly in a case in which the incorporation was of 'all terms and conditions' the
restricted interpretation established by the cases above referred to did not prevent him
from treating as incorporated a clause not strictly germane to the carriage and delivery of
the goods; but in fact it seems to have been the view of both Lord Atkinson and Lord
c Gorell in *T W Thomas & Co Ltd v Portsea Steamship Co Ltd* that the addition of 'terms', at
any rate when conjoined with the word 'other', made no difference to the construction, a
view apparently shared by Merriman P in *The Njegos* [1936] P 90, [1935] All ER Rep 863
and, I rather think, by Cairns LJ in *The Annefield* [1971] 1 All ER 394, [1971] P 168.
Whether or not this is so, it is unnecessary to decide for present purposes although
speaking for myself I find it difficult to see any logical distinction between 'all terms and
d conditions' and 'all conditions'. What is, I think, tolerably clear is that, certainly standing
alone, an incorporation of the 'conditions' of the charterparty does not suffice, as a matter
of authority, to incorporate an arbitration clause in the charterparty.

The defendants, however, support the view favoured by Staughton J in the *Astro
Valiente* case [1982] 1 All ER 823, [1982] 1 WLR 1096, by reference to the judgment of
Kay LJ in *Serraino & Sons v Campbell* [1891] 1 QB 283 and in particular a passage of the
e report of that case where Kay LJ appears to reject any rigid or accepted construction
applicable to all cases and to favour a flexible approach dependant on the surrounding
circumstances in each case (at 301).

They also point to the observations of Lord Reid in *Wickman Machine Tools Sales Ltd v L
Schuler AG* [1973] 2 All ER 39 at 44, [1974] AC 235 at 250–251 that the word 'condition'
has many meanings and that its use cannot be more than an indication, albeit perhaps a
f strong indication, of intention. Speaking for myself, I do not find that these references
help very much in the context of the instant case. The authorities clearly show that the
use of general incorporating words, whether 'terms' or 'conditions', in a bill of lading are
and have for years been normally construed in the restrictive way for which the plaintiffs
contend, but no one has argued that there may not be a context or surrounding
circumstances from which some wider connotation may be culled, and that, as it seems
g to me, was all that Kay LJ was saying, for in fact he concurred in the result in the *Serraino*
case.

What does seem to me important is that documents so commonly in use and
containing familiar expressions which have a well-established meaning among
commercial lawyers should be consistently construed and that a well-established meaning,
particularly as regards something like an arbitration clause where clarity and certainty
h are important to both parties, should not be departed from in the absence of compulsive
surrounding circumstances or a context which is strongly suggestive of some other
meaning.

It has been submitted that the decision of the Divisional Court in *The Northumbria*
[1906] P 292 in some way justifies the attribution to the word 'conditions' of some wider
meaning, that word being conjoined in that case (as it is in the present case) with the
j words 'including negligence clause'. Again, I do not see how that case helps in the present
context. The question there was not what was meant by the word 'conditions' but what
was brought in by the words 'including negligence clause', the fact being that the clause
referred to as the 'negligence clause' not only excluded liability for accidents occasioned
by negligence but also an exception of the warranty of seaworthiness. Thus the question
was not what was the ambit of the general words but what was the ambit of an express
reference to a particular clause.

I would have considerable sympathy with Staughton J's approach in the *Astro Valiente* case were the matter res integra, although even then I am impressed by the argument of counsel for the plaintiffs with regard to the importance of clarity in seeking to incorporate an arbitration clause. But the matter is not res integra and in the light of the authorities to which we have been referred I am, for my part, compelled to the conclusion that Hobhouse J was right in his approach to the construction of the general words of incorporation in this case.

It is argued, however, that there is another route by which, even though the words of incorporation are, standing by themselves, insufficient to bring in the arbitration clause, that clause can be incorporated. It is said that if you have general words of incorporation in the bill of lading and you find that those general words are coupled with express words in a clause in the charterparty which show that that clause was intended to be or was suitable for incorporation in the bill of lading without adaptation then, even though the clause is not one which is germane to the contract constituted by the bill of lading on an application of the ordinary rule of construction referred to above, the clause will nevertheless be treated as incorporated. That proposition is supported by reference to two more recent cases: *The Annefield* [1971] 1 All ER 394, [1971] P 168, and *The Merak, T B & S Batchelor & Co Ltd v SS Merak (owners)* [1965] 1 All ER 230, [1965] P 223. In the former case Brandon J formulated the result of the authorities in a series of propositions, the fourth of which was that—

> 'where the arbitration clause by its terms applies both to disputes under the charterparty and to disputes under the bill of lading, general words of incorporation will bring the clause into the bill of lading so as to make it applicable to disputes under that document.'

(See [1971] 1 All ER 394 at 399, [1971] P 168 at 173.)

That was echoed in this court by Lord Denning MR when he said ([1971] 1 All ER 394 at 406, [1971] P 168 at 184):

> 'But if the clause is one which is not thus directly germane, it should not be incorporated into the bill of lading contract unless it is done explicitly in clear words either in the bill of lading or in the *charterparty*.' (My emphasis.)

On analysis, however, it appears that that view of the matter derives entirely from *The Merak*, where the words of the arbitration clause were such as to make it clear that it was intended to apply, in terms, both to disputes under the charterparty and to disputes under any bill of lading issued under it.

With the greatest deference I am bound to say that I doubt whether that proposition does in fact clearly emerge from *The Merak*. The incorporating words in that case were, it is true, general words but they were as wide as they could possibly be. They purported to incorporate into the bill of lading 'All the terms, conditions, clauses and exceptions . . . contained in the charterparty', and the court held that they were of such strength and width that they could not, in the absence of some strong indication to the contrary, be cut down or restricted. Thus there was, as I read the decision, strictly no need to consider whether the incorporation was limited only to those clauses germane to the contract of carriage. All the clauses of the charterparty were to be applied, subject only to the test of consistency, a test clearly passed by the arbitration clause in that case. Davies LJ, dealing with a submission that *T W Thomas & Co Ltd v Portsea Steamship Co Ltd* established the general proposition that general words could only incorporate those terms germane to the shipment, carriage and delivery of the goods, observed ([1965] 1 All ER 230 at 236, [1965] P 230 at 254):

> 'It is difficult, however, to see that the *Thomas* case, when considered on its facts, does establish such a proposition or that parties to a bill of lading, if *they use wide enough words of incorporation*, cannot, if they are so minded, agree to incorporate into the bill an arbitration clause which expressly applies to disputes arising out of the bill, that is to say, disputes arising out of the shipment, carriage or delivery of the goods.' (My emphasis.)

An alternative way of putting it is, I suppose, to say that, where the arbitration clause
is so expressed as to make it clear that it is not merely apt to apply but is intended to
apply to disputes arising under bills of lading, it is to be treated in the same way as clauses
which are germane to the shipment, carriage or delivery of goods. It is not, however,
clear from the case how far this can result in incorporation in the absence of sufficiently
wide words of incorporation in the bill of lading, although it appears to have been the
view of Russell LJ that even the words in *T W Thomas & Co v Portsea Steamship Co Ltd*
would have been sufficient in the case of an arbitration clause in the charterparty
expressed in the terms of the clause in *The Merak* (see [1965] 1 All ER 230 at 239, [1965]
P 223 at 260).

It is this proposition which lies at the core of the second defendants' argument in the
instant case, but they have to face the fact that the clause on which they have to rely is
not, in fact, a *Merak* type of clause. It refers expressly only to disputes 'under this charter'
so that it can only be incorporated on its face, not as a clause which, by its terms, has to
be treated as germane to the shipment, carriage and delivery of goods, but as a clause
which requires verbal manipulation to adapt it to the bill of lading.

The second defendants seek to escape from this dilemma by reference to cl 44 of the
charterparty, which provides that bills of lading issued under the charterparty shall
incorporate by reference, inter alia, the arbitration clause. Now it can scarcely be argued
that this clause itself is one which can be incorporated in the bill of lading but what is
said is that if you take the charterparty and construe it as a whole you will then deduce
an intention that the words 'this charter' in the arbitration clause have to be read as
including a reference, by adaptation or manipulation, to a bill of lading. Thus, it is
argued, the clause so construed becomes a clause of the same purport if not in the same
terms as the clause in *The Merak*.

For the reasons mentioned above, this seems to me not to be a permissible approach.
It is, in fact, the same argument as was adduced in *The Merak* for reading the erroneous
reference in that case to cl 30 as a reference to cl 32 (the arbitration clause) and it was
decisively rejected by Russell LJ. Although Hobhouse J appears to have entertained some
reservations about this, I, for my part, find Russell LJ's reasoning persuasive. I do not see
how it can be permissible to ascertain what the parties to a particular contract intended
to be incorporated by reference to an entirely different document.

I respectfully concur in the conclusion at which Hobhouse J arrived and I agree that
the appeal should be dismissed.

WATKINS LJ. When parties to a contract are in dispute about the manner of its
performance it is obviously of the utmost importance that any agreement they have
made in that contract as to the forum where such a dispute should be resolved be given
effect to. Here we have a charterparty which contains a clear provision for reference of
disputes to arbitration and a bill of lading to which it is related, the terms of which would
appear, on a robust commonsense construction of them in the absence of authority, so it
seems to me, to incorporate the charterparty arbitration clause in that bill. Hence I have
striven in considering the large accumulation of authority to which we were referred to
ascertain whether the view taken of them by Staughton J in *Astro Valiente Compania
Naviera SA v Pakistan Ministry of Food and Agriculture (No 2), The Emmanuel Colocotronis
(No 2)* [1982] 1 All ER 823, [1982] 1 WLR 1096, which continues to have an attraction
for me, can be supported. Alas! with no enthusiasm I am obliged to say that I have
reached the conclusion that the weight of authority is opposed to that view.

So I, too, agree that Hobhouse J in law correctly construed the bill of lading and,
therefore, would dismiss this appeal.

Appeal dismissed. Leave to appeal to the House of Lords refused.

Solicitors: *Ince & Co* (for the second defendants); *Sinclair Roche & Temperley* (for the
plaintiffs).

Frances Rustin   Barrister.

Customs and Excise Commissioners
v A E Hamlin & Co (a firm)

a

CHANCERY DIVISION
FALCONER J
30 JUNE, 1 JULY 1983

b

Practice – Inspection of property – Property subject matter of action or in respect of which question arising – Undertaking by plaintiff's solicitors – Extent of undertaking – Customs and Excise Commissioners seeking access to documents and articles held by solicitors under Anton Piller order – Commissioners acting in exercise of power to require furnishing of information or production of documents in connection with supplies of goods or services – Whether commissioners or plaintiff's solicitors requiring leave of court before commissioners to be allowed access to documents or articles – Finance Act 1972, s 35(2).

c

Value added tax – Information – Commissioners' power to require information relating to supply of goods or services – Goods and documents seized under authority of Anton Piller orders – Solicitors undertaking to retain custody of seized goods and documents until further order – Commissioners' application to inspect seized goods and documents – Whether solicitors entitled to make goods and documents available to commissioners without court order – Finance Act 1972, s 35(2).

d

Immediately before bringing an action for alleged infringement of the plaintiffs' copyright in certain films, the plaintiffs' solicitors obtained, ex parte, Anton Piller orders requiring the defendants to allow them to enter their premises and take all documents and equipment relevant to the action. Embodied in the order was an undertaking by the solicitors that all records, tapes, equipment, documents or other articles obtained as a result of the orders would be retained in their safe custody or to their order 'until further order'. The Anton Piller orders were executed and certain goods and documents relevant to the action were taken into custody by the solicitors. The Commissioners of Customs and Excise, who had been investigating the defendants' business affairs and had formed the view that the defendants might have been concerned with the fraudulent evasion of value added tax, wished to inspect and copy such documents or articles in the solicitors' custody pursuant to the Anton Piller orders as were relevant to their inquiries. One of the defendants granted the solicitors permission to allow inspection by the commissioners. The commissioners then applied to the court for an order that the solicitors permit them to inspect all relevant materials in their custody in respect of which they had no authority from the defendants, contending that they were entitled, by virtue of s 35(2)[a] of the Finance Act 1972, to inspect material which might be relevant to their inquiries and that it was not necessary for a solicitor holding material under an Anton Piller order to obtain the leave of the court before allowing the commissioners access, if the commissioners would have been entitled to exercise their power to inspect such material were it in the custody of the person liable to tax.

e

f

g

h

Held – The express undertaking which the plaintiffs' solicitors had been required to give in order to take the defendants' goods and documents into their custody under the Anton Piller orders precluded them from giving access to those goods or documents to anyone other than the defendants and the defendants' solicitors in the action without the defendants' authority or the order of the court. Furthermore, documents and goods held under an Anton Piller order were subject to the same implied undertaking which covered documents disclosed on discovery, and accordingly a solicitor having the custody of goods and documents under such an order was not entitled to allow the use of them for

j

---

a Section 35(2), so far as material, is set out at p 658 *j* to p 659 *a*, post a   any collateral or ulterior purpose of his own, his client or anyone else without the leave of the court. It followed, therefore, that in order for the commissioners to exercise their right to inspect and copy the documents in question they or the plaintiffs' solicitors required the leave of the court or the authority of the defendants themselves. In the circumstances it was appropriate that the commissioners should have that leave and the court would accordingly make the order sought by the commissioners (see p p 661 c to p 662 c, post).

b   Dictum of Lord Diplock in *Home Office v Harman* [1982] 1 All ER at 538 applied.

Notes

For Anton Piller orders, see 37 Halsbury's Laws (4th edn) para 372, and for cases on the subject, see 37(2) Digest (Reissue) 480–483, 2978–2990.

c   For the duty to furnish information and produce documents in connection with supplies of goods or services, see 12 Halsbury's Laws (4th edn) para 944.

For the Finance Act 1972, s 35, see 42 Halsbury's Statutes (3rd edn) 193.

As from 26 October 1983, s 35 of the 1972 Act was replaced by para 8 of Sch 7 to the Value Added Tax Act 1983.

Cases referred to in judgment

d   *Anton Piller KG v Manufacturing Processes Ltd* [1976] 1 All ER 779, [1976] Ch 55, [1976] 2 WLR 162, CA.

EMI Ltd v Pandit [1975] 1 All ER 418, [1975] 1 WLR 302.

Home Office v Harman [1982] 1 All ER 532, [1983] 1 AC 280, [1982] 2 WLR 338, HL.

Universal City Studios Inc v Hubbard [1983] 2 All ER 596, [1983] Ch 241, [1983] 2 WLR 882.

e   *Universal City Studios Inc v Mukhtar & Sons* [1976] 2 All ER 330, [1976] 1 WLR 568.

Case also cited

CBS UK Ltd v Lambert [1982] 3 All ER 237, [1983] Ch 37, CA.

Motion

f   By a notice of motion dated 13 June 1983 the Commissioners of Customs and Excise applied for an order under the inherent jurisdiction of the court that A E Hamlin & Co (a firm) permit the commissioners to inspect and copy all documents or articles in their possession or control relating to the trading activities of Peter George Phillip Hubbard and Neil Richard William Rivers, which Hamlin & Co had obtained following the execution of Anton Piller orders dated 29 and 30 September 1982. The facts are set out g   in the judgment.

John Mummery for the commissioners.
John P Baldwin for Hamlin & Co

Cur adv vult

h   1 July. The following judgment was delivered.

FALCONER J. I have before me a motion in a proceeding commenced by originating summons, the proceedings being of a somewhat unusual nature. The defendants are Messrs A E Hamlin & Co, a well-known and eminent firm of solicitors (whom I shall refer to as Hamlin & Co hereafter), who act for the plaintiffs in an action 1982 U No j   1096, in which the plaintiffs were Universal City Studios Inc and 13 other plaintiffs engaged in the making and marketing of cinematograph films, if I may put it that way. The defendants were four in number, of which two were a Peter Hubbard and a Neil Richard William Rivers, whom I shall refer to respectively as Mr Hubbard and Mr Rivers hereafter. In that action the plaintiffs sued the defendants for infringement of copyright and passing off and for alleged production of and dealing in video cassettes which were counterfeit, or alleged to be counterfeit, infringing copies of films in which the plaintiffs claimed to have rights of copyright.

On 29 September 1982, immediately before the action commenced, Hamlin & Co, on behalf of the intended plaintiffs in the intended action (as it was then), obtained an Anton Piller order against Mr Hubbard in what is, I think, the usual form of such orders. The following day, on 30 September, they obtained a similar Anton Piller order against Mr Rivers. In the order against Mr Hubbard it was ordered, inter alia, that the defendants should permit the person serving the order together with such persons as might be authorised by Hamlin & Co to enter forthwith each of the premises known as, and there were a number of them—

'36 Pield Heath Road Uxbridge Middlesex, 14b Seymour Road Chiswick W4, 67 Tolworth Road Tolworth Surbiton Surrey and Second floor flat above 8 and 8A York Parade Great West Road Brentford Middlesex and First and Second floor flat above 7 and 7A York Parade aforesaid . . .

The defendants were required to disclose to the person serving the order (in other words the representatives of Hamlin & Co) for the purpose of inspecting, photographing, looking for and removing, any illicit goods (those were defined earlier on in the order and in effect they were copies of films made by any of the plaintiffs, being films less than 50 years old), any labels or sleeves or plates intended for making such copies, and also, in addition to such goods, including the sleeves and plates as well as the illicit copies, 'all or any documents relating in any way to any of the aforesaid items', that is to say such goods. I particularly draw attention to the premises featured in that order.

Before leaving the order I should also, I think, draw attention to the express undertaking in an earlier part of the order, again in the usual form in an Anton Piller order, by which Hamlin & Co gave an express undertaking, firstly, that they would inform the defendants of their right to seek and obtain legal advice before complying with the order and, secondly, and this is the important express undertaking, 'that all records tapes equipment documents or other articles obtained as a result of this Order will be retained in their safe custody or to their order until further order'.

The Anton Piller order made the following day against Mr Rivers was in exactly the same form except for the particular premises in which it was ordered Hamlin & Co were to be able to enter and take away documents and those kinds of goods. There the premises mentioned were simply 'premises known as 7A York Parade Great West Road Brentford Middlesex', which is, it will be noted, one of the premises stated in the order against Mr Hubbard.

Now, the Anton Piller orders were executed and documents and materials, such as copies of films, were taken into the custody of Hamlin & Co as the plaintiffs' solicitors and, as the evidence of Mr Cumberland, a member of the firm of Hamlin & Co, explains in a short affidavit: 'Those documents are separated into bundles according to the premises from whence they were taken.' In fact, Mr Hubbard subsequently applied to the court to have the documents and the goods, the various tapes, taken into custody returned to him on the ground that he would find it difficult to explain in evidence documents taken into the possession of Hamlin & Co without running the risk of incrimination. I put that rather shortly but that is in essence what the ground was. That application was refused. It is reported in *Universal City Studios Inc v Hubbard* [1983] 2 All ER 596, [1983] Ch 241, and I understand that in fact it is the subject of appeal.

There have been a number of other interlocutory proceedings in the action but I do not need to go into them for present purposes.

Now, it appears that the activities of Mr Hubbard and Mr Rivers, amongst others, were and are being investigated by the Commissioners of Customs and Excise in relation to alleged unpaid value added tax. Their investigations, so the commissioners say, are hampered in that Mr Hubbard's and Mr Rivers's business books, records and documents are now in the custody of Hamlin & Co pursuant to the execution of those two Anton Piller orders. The commissioners or their officers have been able to see some of Mr

Hubbard's documents and material because of an authority given by Mr Hubbard
himself, which is exhibited to the second affidavit of Mr Webb, one of the commissioners'
officers, who gave evidence on behalf of the commissioners on this motion. That
authority is in these terms:

> 'I, PETER HUBBARD hereby authorise Messrs. A. E. HAMLIN & CO. to permit inspection
> of all the documents and other items removed from 36 Pieldheath Road and 7A and
> 8A York Parade Great West Road, Brentford, Middlesex, to representatives of H.M.
> Customs & Excise and also to permit the taking of copies of such documents as are
> required by the representatives of H.M. Customs & Excise.'

It will be seen in that authority that the authority to see and take copies of the
documents in the hands of Hamlin & Co is expressed to relate to documents removed
from 7A and 8A York Parade, and it will be remembered that 7A York Parade was the
particular address to which the Anton Piller order against Mr Rivers was directed.

In this second affidavit Mr Webb, who is a higher executive officer in the permanent
employment of the commissioners and is authorised to make both the affidavits before
me on behalf of the commissioners, states in paras 3 and 4, and referring to that authority
of Mr Hubbard, as follows:

> 'I am informed and verily believe that officers of the [commissioners'] Investigation
> division acting on the Hubbard authority went to [Hamlin & Co's] premises on or
> about the 2nd of November and inspected some documents and other items
> belonging to the said Hubbard and, or, to the said Rivers which were in [Hamlin &
> Co's] control pursuant to the Order mentioned in paragraph 5 of my above
> mentioned affidavit. I am also informed, and verily believe, that copies of some
> documents were taken and that these, or some of them, were mentioned and put to
> the said Hubbard in the course of interviews with him by the [commissioners']
> officers at later dates, I being present at an interview when some of those copy
> documents were so put to him. [He refers then to a paragraph in his previous
> affidavit (which I will come to later) and goes on:] I am informed and verily believe
> that [Hamlin & Co] in the light of the Hubbard authority do not object to the
> [commissioners] and their officers inspecting documents and items taken up,
> pursuant to the above mentioned Order, from 36 Pield Heath Road, which address
> is mentioned in the Hubbard authority: but that in respect of the documents and
> items taken up from 7A and 8A York Parade, [Hamlin & Co] are of the view that the
> [commissioners] should apply to this Honourable Court for leave to inspect and take
> copies of the documents and goods taken up from the said York Parade.'

I should mention that Mr Rivers has given authority to the commissioners for Hamlin
& Co to see books and documents taken into custody by the commissioners from Mr
Rivers. That has been acted on but, of course, that has no relevance to anything I am
concerned with today. But there has been no authority from Mr Rivers to Hamlin & Co
corresponding to that given by Mr Hubbard to allow the Rivers documents to be shown
to the commissioners and, if desired, copied by them. Therefore, the position is that
Hamlin & Co, in view of the terms of the Anton Piller orders and, in particular, their
express undertaking therein, and their implied undertaking to the court in respect of
such documents, not unnaturally feel some difficulty about allowing the commissioners
to have a sight of the documents not covered by Mr Hubbard's express authority without
the leave of the court allowing them to do so.

In this application by motion in these proceedings the commissioners seek to have a
sight of all documents and material now in custody of Hamlin & Co under the two
Anton Piller orders. I should read the relief sought on the motion, which is in the
following terms:

> '1. An order under the inherent jurisdiction of the Court that [Hamlin & Co] do
> permit the [commissioners] to inspect and take copies of all documents or articles in

[Hamlin & Co's] possession or control relating to the trading activities of Peter
George Phillip Hubbard of 36 Pield Heath Road, Hillingdon, Uxbridge, Middlesex, *a*
and Neil Richard William Rivers of 167 Station Road West Drayton, Middlesex,
including all the documents and articles of or relating to the said Peter George
Phillip Hubbard and Neil Richard William Rivers obtained by [Hamlin & Co]
pursuant to the execution of orders dated the 29th September 1982 made in the
matter of an intended action and on the 30th September 1982 made in the action
the short title . . . whereof is [and the title is given] . . .'   *b*

Those are the two Anton Piller orders to which I have referred. Then there is a request
for provision for costs of the application and further or other relief.

I should, before coming to the submissions put by counsel for the commissioners, just
add one further piece of procedural history, and that is that on 27 May 1983 judgment
was entered against Mr Rivers in default of service of defence for a liquidated sum of
£4½m; so, as far as Mr Rivers is concerned, in that respect the action appears to be over.   *c*

For the commissioners, counsel's main contention is based on the statutory powers of
the commissioners under the Finance Act 1972 under which value added tax was
introduced, and which statute contains the principal provisions relating to value added
tax, and, in particular, on the relevant powers of the commissioners in respect of value
added tax. I should look at those.

Section 1(1) of the 1972 Act instituted value added tax and sub-s (2) says that tax shall   *d*
be under the care and management of the commissioners. Going to s 34, this section
deals with the duty of persons who are taxable in respect of value added tax to keep
records. Section 34 reads:

'(1) Every taxable person shall keep such records as the Commissioners may
require.   *e*
(2) The Commissioners may require any records kept in pursuance of this section
to be preserved for such period not exceeding three years as they may require.
(3) The duty under this section to preserve records may be discharged by the
preservation of the information contained therein by such means as the
Commissioners may approve . . .
(4) The Commissioners may, as a condition of approving under subsection (3) of   *f*
this section any means of preserving information contained in any records, impose
such reasonable requirements as appear to them necessary for securing that the
information will be as readily available to them as if the records themselves had
been preserved . . .'

Coming on to s 35, this deals with the furnishing of information and the production
of documents, and it contains, for present purposes, the most important powers of the   *g*
commissioners:

'(1) The Commissioners may by regulations make provision for requiring taxable
persons to notify to the Commissioners such particulars of changes in circumstances
relating to those persons or any business carried on by them as appear to the
Commissioners required for the purpose of keeping the register kept under this Part   *h*
of this Act up to date.'

Then sub-s (2) of s 35 deals with goods and, as we shall see, sub-s (3) deals with services:

'(2) Every person who is concerned (in whatever capacity) in the supply of goods
in the course or furtherance of any business or to whom such a supply is made
shall—(a) furnish to the Commissioners, within such time and in such form as they   *j*
may require, such information relating to the goods or to the supply as the
Commissioners may specify; and [here we come to what is really the material power
for present purposes] (b) upon demand made by an authorised person, produce or
cause to be produced any documents relating to the goods or to the supply for
inspection by the authorised person and permit him to take copies of or to make

a
extracts from them or to remove them at a reasonable time and for a reasonable period.'

I interpolate there to point out that, under the 1972 Act, an authorised person (and this is in the interpretation section, s 46(1)) means any person acting under the authority of the commissioners. Going back to s 35, just before I leave sub-s (2)(b) thereof, it is to be observed that the duty to produce the documents and permit copies to be taken is on demand made by the authorised person. Subsection (3) is an exactly similar provision to
b
that of sub-s (2) but in relation to services, and in para (b) there is an exactly similar paragraph to para (b) of sub-s (2), and I need not read that again. Subsection (4) reads:

'For the purposes of this section [that is s 35], the documents relating to the supply of goods, or to the consideration for the supply of services, in the course or furtherance of any business shall be taken to include any profit and loss account and
c
balance sheet relating to that business.'

I should also, I think, draw attention to s 37:

'(1) For the purpose of exercising any powers under this Part of this Act an authorised person may at any reasonable time enter premises used in connection with the carrying on of a business.
d
(2) Where an authorised person has reasonable cause to believe that any premises are used in connection with the supply of goods under taxable supplies and that goods to be so supplied are on those premises, he may at any reasonable time enter and inspect those premises and inspect any goods found on them . . .'

Subsection (3) of s 37, with which we are not really concerned, I think, in the present matter, relates to the obtaining of a warrant from a justice of the peace where there is
e
reasonable ground for suspecting that there has been an offence in connection with value added tax.

The only other provision that I should draw attention to is s 38(7), which provides:

'If any person fails to comply with any requirement imposed under section 34 or 35 of this Act or any regulations or rules made under this Part of this Act, he shall
f
be liable to a penalty of £100, together with a penalty of £10 for each day on which the failure continues.'

I think now, before proceeding further with considering the submissions put by counsel for the commissioners, that I ought to look a little more at the evidence for the commissioners. Going back to Mr Webb's first affidavit, I should read paras 4, 5, 6, 7 and 8. They are short paragraphs and appertain to what comes afterwards:
g
'4. In the course of making certain enquiries into the business affairs of Peter George Phillip Hubbard [and he gives the address] and Neil Richard William Rivers [and he gives the address] it appeared to the [commissioners] that Mr. Hubbard was a person who ought to have been registered for the purposes of VAT and who ought to have been accounting for and paying VAT as required by statute and that both
h
Mr. Hubbard and Mr. Rivers were or might have been concerned in the fraudulent evasion of VAT.
5. The [commissioners'] officers have been unable to assess the VAT payable by Mr. Hubbard by reason of the fact that his business books and records or some of them are believed to be in the possession of [Hamlin & Co] in these proceedings pursuant to an Order [and he refers to the two Anton Piller orders].
j
6. The [commissioners] have been unable to complete their investigation into the said fraudulent evasion of VAT because documents and goods relating to the said business are believed to be in the possession of [Hamlin & Co] pursuant to the said Order.
7. Because the said documents are in the possession of [Hamlin & Co] the [commissioners] are unable to exercise their statutory powers to demand production

thereof or to make full enquiries concerning the amount of tax which may have
been evaded and the extent to which criminal offences may be committed.   *a*

8. I verily believe the said documents and goods belonging to Mr. Hubbard and
Mr. Rivers in the possession of [Hamlin & Co] are material to the questions of how
much VAT may be due from Mr. Hubbard and whether there have been any
criminal offences committed by Mr. Hubbard and Mr. Rivers.'

There is one further paragraph from Mr Webb's second affidavit I would like to refer
to and that is para 6. After referring to paras 4 and 5 of the first affidavit, which I have   *b*
just read, he goes on:

'One of the matters which the [commissioners] and their officers wish to explore
is whether there is sufficient material and evidence for the purpose of the
[commissioners] making an assessment of value added tax to the best of their
judgment (as provided for by Section 31 of the Finance Act 1972 as amended). The   *c*
[commissioners] have evidence that the said Hubbard together, it is alleged, with
the said Rivers and for the purposes of a business, made or arranged the making of
supplies of pre-recorded video cassette tapes during the second part of the year 1981
and during the following year of 1982 until approximately the month of September.
The [commissioners] have evidence indicating that the said Hubbard purchased
during the aforesaid periods video recording machinery and related blank video   *d*
tapes to an amount just in excess of half a million pounds; and that the sellers of the
machinery and tapes provided tax invoices, thereby indicating, I believe, that these
supplies to him were for the purposes of a business in his control. The
[commissioners] I believe do not have any evidence to show that the said Hubbard,
or any other person, has accounted to the [commissioners] for value added tax due
on these alleged supplies.'   *e*

Then he goes on to say that, for the purposes of making an assessment, he believes the
commissioners should inspect the documents and articles in the control of Hamlin & Co
pursuant to the Anton Piller orders.

As I have mentioned already, Mr Hubbard has given Hamlin & Co an authority to
allow the commissioners to see and take copies of documents taken from the address in   *f*
Pield Heath Road and 7A and 8A York Parade. But, as I have already pointed out also,
there is no such authority from Mr Rivers and I understand that Mr Rivers cannot at
present be found. But there is some difficulty whether the documents taken from the
York Parade address are Mr Hubbard's or Mr Rivers's, or are in some way mixed up.

The main contention of counsel for the commissioners is that it is not legally necessary
for Hamlin & Co to have leave of the court to allow the commissioners to inspect and   *g*
take copies of documents which the commissioners, he says, have a statutory duty to see,
and he points out the inconvenience and expense which would be involved if it were
held to be necessary that, in each case where this sort of situation arises, the commissioners
have to come to the court for leave, or the solicitors concerned have to come and ask the
court for leave. He submits that it should not be necessary for the commissioners to have
to seek the authority of the court in circumstances where the facts are such as would   *h*
entitle the commissioners to exercise their statutory powers in relation to documents and
goods of persons liable to tax if the documents and goods were still in the hands of the
person so liable to tax.

In developing this main contention counsel pointed out, and rightly pointed out, that
all that Hamlin & Co have is physical custody of the documents and goods pursuant to
the two Anton Piller orders of the court. Mr Hubbard and Mr Rivers, he submits, retain   *j*
the ownership and the right to their possession subject only to the court's order, and that,
it seems to me, is plainly right. The purpose of giving Hamlin & Co, as solicitors for the
plaintiffs in the action in which the two Anton Piller orders were made, physical custody
of the documents and goods in question was, of course, as that of all Anton Piller orders,
to ensure preservation of the documents and goods from destruction or defacement: see

a   the judgment of Lord Denning MR in *Anton Piller KG v Manufacturing Processes Ltd* [1976] 1 All ER 779 at 783, [1976] Ch 55 at 61; see also the judgment of Templeman J in *Universal City Studios Inc v Mukhtar & Sons* [1976] 2 All ER 330 at 332–333, [1976] 1 WLR 568 at 570–571. Counsel for the commissioners submits the mere change of custody pursuant to the order of the court for purposes of keeping safe the documents or goods in question cannot affect the width of the exercise of the statutory powers of the commissioners and, therefore, it should not be necessary, he submits, for the
b   commissioners to seek, or for Hamlin & Co to have, leave of the court to allow what is sought here in the notice of motion, and that is permission to see the documents and take copies.

The difficulty I see in the way of this contention is in the nature of the express and implied undertakings of Hamlin & Co under the orders. As to the express undertaking, I have already read it, but again the relevant one is 'that all records tapes equipment
c   documents or other articles obtained as a result of this Order will be retained in their safe custody or to their order until further order'. The further order, of course, is the further order of the court.

Now, counsel, in a very interesting submission on behalf of Hamlin & Co, submitted that there is nothing which is sought by the commissioners in the notice of motion in these proceedings that would be in breach of the express undertaking if the permission
d   to take copies were to be given by the solicitors. I do not accept that submission. The sole purpose of Hamlin & Co having the safe custody of the documents and goods is to ensure their preservation, and Hamlin & Co do not have their custody for any other purpose. If there is any doubt as to the ambit of this form of the express undertaking in this regard (and I should add that I do not myself have any doubt) it may be that this form of wording in the Anton Piller orders should be reconsidered to remove any such doubt.
e   But, in my judgment, under the express undertaking Hamlin & Co are not at liberty to allow anyone else access to those documents or goods other than, of course, the defendants and the defendants' solicitors in the action without, that is to say, the leave of the court or, of course, the authority of the defendants themselves.

As to the exercise of the commissioners' statutory powers under the 1972 Act in relation to value added tax, there is no difficulty really. The power in s 35(2)(*b*) and the
f   corresponding para (*b*) under s 35(3) are, as I have pointed out, exercisable on demand. If the defendant in any particular case does not authorise inspection and copying by the commissioners on demand, as there has been no authority in this case from Mr Rivers, the commissioners can, as in this case, apply to the court and, in a proper case, the court will, of course, give the necessary order to the solicitors under the express undertaking.

As to the implied undertaking of the solicitors to the court, it is to be borne in mind
g   that essentially the placing of the defendants' documents in the safe custody of the plaintiffs' solicitors under an Anton Piller order to preserve them from destruction or defacement is really part of the process of discovery: see the observations of Templeman J in *EMI Ltd v Pandit* [1975] 1 All ER 418 at 424, [1975] 1 WLR 302 at 307.

It is common ground on this motion between counsel for the commissioners and for Hamlin & Co, and I agree with them, that Hamlin & Co hold the documents and the
h   goods subject to the same implied undertaking as covers documents disclosed on discovery. As to that implied undertaking it was explained by Lord Diplock in the recent case of *Home Office v Harman* [1982] 1 All ER 532 at 538, [1983] 1 AC 280 at 304–305, in these terms:

j   'This is why an order for production of documents to a solicitor on behalf of a party to civil litigation is made on the implied undertaking given by the solicitor personally to the court (of which he is an officer) that he himself will not use or allow the documents or copies of them to be used for any collateral or ulterior purpose of his own, his client or anyone else; and any breach of that implied undertaking is a contempt of court by the solicitor himself. Save as respects the gravity of the contempt, no distinction is to be drawn between those documents which have and those which have not been admitted in evidence; to make use for some collateral or ulterior purpose of the special advantage obtained by having *a* possession of copies of any of an adverse party's documents obtained on discovery is, in my view, a contempt of court.'

I draw particular attention to the words in the first sentence of that passage where Lord Diplock was stating the implied undertaking as concluding with the words 'or anyone else'. Again, it seems to me that it is for the court to give leave for any departure from the solicitor's obligation under that implied undertaking which, under the inherent *b* jurisdiction of the court, the court could certainly do. The court, no doubt, would normally do so in a case where, as here, the commissioners and/or the solicitors apply for such leave so that the commissioners may exercise their statutory rights of inspection and copying. I think this is a proper case to make the order sought in the notice of motion and I do so. In the circumstances, it is not necessary for me to consider further the rather wider submission which was made by counsel for Hamlin & Co in his very *c* interesting argument, for which I am grateful.

Order accordingly.

Solicitors: *Solicitor for the Customs and Excise; A E Hamlin & Co.*

d

Evelyn M C Budd   Barrister.

Lear and another v Blizzard

e

QUEEN'S BENCH DIVISION
TUDOR EVANS J
10, 13, 14, 15 JUNE, 6 JULY 1983

Landlord and tenant – Rent – Review – Renewal of lease – New rent payable to be rent agreed *f* *between parties or fixed by arbitrator in default of agreement – Whether rent to be fair rent as between parties or market rent – Whether improvements made by tenant's predecessor in title to be taken into account – Whether premium to be added to take account of anticipated inflation.*

In 1961 L's predecessors in title granted C Ltd a 21-year lease of premises at a rent of £350 per annum. By cl 2 of the lease C Ltd covenanted that they would not make any *g* additions to the premises without the landlords' consent and that they would use the premises only for the purpose of a petrol filling station. By cl 3(2) the landlords covenanted that, at the request of the tenant, they would renew the lease for a further term of 21 years from the date of the expiration of the original term 'at a rent to be agreed between the parties . . . or in default of agreement at a rent to be determined by a single arbitrator'. In 1967 C Ltd, in breach of cl 2, improved the premises by building a *h* tune-up bay, a car port and a car wash area, and enlarged their business to include vehicle maintenance work. In 1970 the landlords consented to the improvements and C Ltd agreed to pay an additional rent of £150 per annum in return for the lease being varied to cover not only the petrol filling station business but also the vehicle maintenance work. In 1974 C Ltd assigned the lease, as varied, to E Ltd, and in 1981 E Ltd assigned it to B for £12,500. In 1982 B asked L, in whom the freehold reversion had vested, to *j* renew the lease in accordance with cl 3(2). The parties failed to agree on the new rent, and the matter was referred to a single arbitrator. L submitted (i) that, by virtue of cl 3(2), the new rent should be what the arbitrator determined would be a reasonable rent for the premises, as improved, on the open market, and (ii) that, no provision having been made in the lease for a rent review, the arbitrator should add a percentage or premium to take account of anticipated inflation during the currency of the new term.

a B contended (i) that, in determining the new rent, the arbitrator should apply a subjective test and determine what would be a fair rent as between L and B, (ii) that the 1967 improvements should be disregarded in calculating the amount of the new rent and (iii) that it would be wrong for the arbitrator to add a premium because if he did do so he would in effect be making provision for a rent review. The arbitrator being unable to reconcile their submissions, the matter was referred to the High Court.

b **Held** – (1) Since cl 3(2) of the lease provided for renewal of the lease at a rent 'to be agreed between the parties', it followed that on the true construction of the lease the arbitrator was to determine, subjectively, what would be a fair rent for L and B to agree in all the circumstances, taking into account all the considerations which would have affected the minds of the parties if they had been negotiating the rent themselves (see p 668 *b c j*, p 669 *e f*, p 670 *j* to p 671 *b* and p 672 *e f*, post); *Thomas Bates & Son Ltd v*

c *Wyndham's (Lingerie) Ltd* [1981] 1 All ER 1077 applied; *Foley v Classique Coaches Ltd* [1934] All ER Rep 88 and *Beer v Bowden* [1981] 1 All ER 1070 considered; *Ponsford v HMS Aerosols Ltd* [1978] 2 All ER 837 distinguished.

(2) It was for B to show that by way of assignment he had paid wholly for or contributed towards the 1967 improvements to the premises, and accordingly they were to be disregarded only to the extent that he satisfied the arbitrator that he had contributed

d in money or money's worth to their value (see p 669 *f*, p 670 *f* to *h* and p 672 *f*, post); *Cuff v J & F Stone Property Co Ltd* [1978] 2 All ER 833, *Ponsford v HMS Aerosols Ltd* [1978] 2 All ER 837 and *Thomas Bates & Son Ltd v Wyndham's (Lingerie) Ltd* [1981] 1 All ER 1077 considered.

(3) Since the arbitrator had no power to introduce any variations between the original lease and the new lease, it followed that he had no power to add a premium to take

e account of anticipated inflation during the currency of the new term (see p 672 *c d f*, post); *National Westminster Bank Ltd v BSC Footwear Ltd* (1980) 42 P & CR 90 followed.

Notes

For rent review clauses and their effect, see 27 Halsbury's Laws (4th edn) paras 215, 217.

Cases referred to in judgment

f *Bates (Thomas) & Son Ltd v Wyndham's (Lingerie) Ltd* [1981] 1 All ER 1077, [1981] 1 WLR 505, CA.

Beer v Bowden [1981] 1 All ER 1070, [1981] 1 WLR 522, CA.

Cuff v J & F Stone Property Co Ltd [1978] 2 All ER 833, [1979] AC 87, [1978] 3 WLR 256.

Foley v Classique Coaches Ltd [1934] 2 KB 1, [1934] All ER Rep 88, CA.

National Westminster Bank Ltd v BSC Footwear Ltd (1980) 42 P & CR 90, CA.

g *Ponsford v HMS Aerosols Ltd* [1978] 2 All ER 837, [1979] AC 63, [1978] 3 WLR 241, HL.

Motion

Basil Montagu Lear and Lindsay Ann Smith (the landlords) and Oliver Harry James Blizzard (the tenant) failed to agree on the rent payable under an option clause, cl 3(2), in a lease dated 23 December 1961. In accordance with cl 3(2), the matter was referred to a

h single arbitrator. As he was unable to reconcile the submissions made to him by the parties, the landlords, at his request, applied to the court for the determination of the following questions: (a) whether the rent to be determined by the single arbitrator should be assessed as an open market rent or as a fair rent; (b) if a fair rent was to be assessed, whether that meant that the rent was to be a rent which would be a fair rent for the particular landlord and the particular tenant to have agreed on had they both been

j willing negotiators anxious to reach agreement, and whether, in deciding what the particular landlord and the particular tenant would have agreed, account could be taken of all considerations which might affect the mind of either party to such negotiations; (c) whether the tenant's improvements were to be taken into account or to be disregarded; (d) whether, having regard to the fact that a 21-year lease without further rent reviews during the currency of the term was provided for by cl 3(2) of the lease, a premium to

take into account anticipated inflation during the currency of the term should be built
into the new rent and, if so, whether it should be assessed at the level of the premium
applicable in 1961 which should then be converted into a premium and applied to the
current rental value or whether the percentage should be assessed by reference to the
current market conditions at the date of renewal. The facts are set out in the judgment.

John Grace for the landlords.
Malcolm D Warner for the tenant.

Cur adv vult

6 July. The following judgment was delivered.

TUDOR EVANS J. This is an application under s 2(1) of the Arbitration Act 1979 to
determine questions of law which have arisen during the course of an arbitration between
the applicants and the respondent, who are respectively the landlords and the tenant of a
petrol service station in Gloucester. The parties were unable to agree the rent payable
under an option to renew a lease of the premises. The dispute was referred to arbitration
under cl 3(2) of the lease. At the conclusion of the evidence, the arbitrator was unable to
reconcile the submissions made to him. These proceedings were brought at his
instigation. I am asked to determine the true construction of the rent formula within
cl 3(2) and the basis on which the arbitrator should assess the rent. Four questions have
been drafted by or on behalf of the arbitrator to which I shall refer later.

On 23 December 1961 predecessors in title of the landlords granted a 21-year lease of
the premises to the Cleveland Petroleum Co Ltd (Cleveland) at a rent of £350 a year. I
need refer only to three clauses in the lease. By cl 2(6), the then tenants covenanted not
to erect or permit or suffer to be erected any other building on or alterations or additions
to the demised premises, without previous consent in writing of the landlords, such
consent not to be unreasonably withheld. By cl 2(9) the tenants covenanted not to carry
on or to permit or suffer to be carried on in or on the demised premises any trade or
business other than that of a petrol filling station and the sale of accessories appertaining
to motor vehicles. The option to renew is contained in cl 3(2) of the lease, the material
language of which provides:

'The Landlords hereby covenant with the Tenant . . .
(2) THAT the Landlords will on the written request of the Tenant made six months
before the expiration of the term hereby granted . . . grant to the Tenant a Lease of
the demised premises for the further term of twenty-one years from the expiration
of the said term at a rent to be agreed between the parties hereto or in default of
agreement at a rent to be determined by a single arbitrator . . .'

In 1967, and in breach of covenant, Cleveland carried out improvements to the
premises by building a tune-up bay, a car port and a car wash area and they enlarged the
business by carrying on vehicle maintenance work. On 12 January 1970 the lease was
varied by a deed of variation. Cleveland were thereby released from cl 2(9) of the lease
and the existing use of the premises was extended to cover not only the original business
but the carrying on of vehicle and repair work. The landlords granted a licence and
consent to the improvements. The deed provided for the payment of an additional rent
of £150 a year in consideration of the variations of the lease.

In August 1974 Cleveland assigned the lease to the Esso Petroleum Co Ltd. On 13 July
1981 Esso assigned the lease, as varied, to the respondent tenant at a price of £12,500.
The original term of 21 years expired on 31 July 1982.

I am asked to construe cl 3(2) of the lease. The four questions as drafted by or on behalf
of the arbitrator are these:

'(a) Whether the rent to be determined by the single Arbitrator should be assessed
as an open market rent or whether it should be assessed as a fair rent, and (b) If a fair

a   rent was to be assessed, whether that meant that the rent was to be a rent which would be a fair rent for this particular landlord and this particular tenant to have agreed upon had they both been willing negotiators anxious to reach agreement. In deciding what this particular landlord and this particular tenant would have agreed to, account can be taken of all considerations which might affect the mind of either party to such negotiations.'

b   Counsel for each party agree that the last sentence in (b) is incorrectly drafted and that the question I have to decide is 'whether, in deciding what this particular landlord and this particular tenant would have agreed, account can be taken of all considerations which might affect the mind of either party to such negotiations'. Counsel for the landlords submits that the test to be applied is objective and that the arbitrator has to determine what would be a reasonable rent for the demised premises, together with the improvements, on the open market. Counsel for the tenant contends that the proper

c   test, on a true construction of cl 3(2) of the lease, is subjective and that the rent is to be a fair rent for these particular landlords and this particular tenant.

The third question, as drafted, is:

'(c) As to how the tenant's improvements should be taken into account or disregarded, as the case may be.'

d   Counsel also agree that the question as drafted does not accurately set out the question which has to be answered. The question, correctly stated, is 'whether the tenant's improvements are to be taken into account or to be disregarded'. The improvements are, of course, those carried out by Cleveland in 1967. Counsel have agreed that there are three possible answers to question (c) which they have drafted: (i) that the improvements are to be wholly disregarded by the arbitrator when determining the rent on renewal.

e   Counsel for the tenant submits that, once it has been decided that cl 3(2) is to be construed on a subjective basis, the improvements must be disregarded when determining the rent. He contends that the £12,500 paid by the tenant to Esso in July 1981 covered the cost of the improvements and that it would be wholly unreasonable and unfair to require him to pay for them again in the form of rent for the further 21 years; (ii) alternatively, the improvements are to be either wholly or partly disregarded if the arbitrator is satisfied

f   by the tenant that he has contributed in money or money's worth to the value of the improvements; (iii) that the improvements are to be taken into account in full.

The fourth question, as drafted, is:

'(d) Whether, having regard to the fact that a 21 year lease without further rent reviews during the currency of the term was provided for by clause 3(2) of the lease, a premium to take into account anticipated inflation during the currency of the
g   term should be built into the new rent and, if so, whether it should be assessed at the level of the premium applicable in 1961 which should then be converted into a premium and applied to the current rental value or whether the percentage should be assessed by reference to the current market conditions at the date of renewal.'

h   Counsel for the landlords submits that the word 'reasonable' should be implied into the language of cl 3(2) so that the clause should be construed in an objective sense requiring a reasonable rent to be assessed on an open market basis for the premises as improved. It is submitted that the word 'reasonable' should be implied in order to exclude from the arbitrator's consideration any freak rent which may be offered on the open market. For the implication of the word 'reasonable', counsel for the landlords relies on *Foley v Classique Coaches Ltd* [1934] 2 KB 1, [1934] All ER Rep 88. In that case, by two separate

j   contemporaneous agreements, the plaintiff sold land to the defendants, who carried on a motor business, on terms that the defendants would buy all petrol from the plaintiff. After the petrol agreement had been performed for some time, the defendants repudiated it. The plaintiff sought a declaration that the petrol agreement was binding, an injunction to restrain the defendants from purchasing petrol elsewhere and damages. The defendants contended that the agreement was not binding since there was no agreement as to price.

It was held at first instance and in the Court of Appeal that the parties intended to make
a binding agreement and considered that they had done so and that a term should   *a*
therefore be implied that the petrol would be supplied at a reasonable price in order to
give effect to what the parties intended. Counsel for the landlords submits that the same
principle should be applied in the case of a lease. He relies on the decision of the Court of
Appeal in *Beer v Bowden* [1981] 1 All ER 1070, [1981] 1 WLR 522. A landlord and a
tenant were unable to agree what rent should be paid under a review clause. There was
no provision for arbitration in default of agreement. Applying the principle in *Foley v*   *b*
Classique Coaches Ltd the court implied a term in the lease that, in the absence of
agreement, the rent should be a fair rent.

Provided the clause is to be construed objectively on the basis of an open market rent,
I agree that a term should be implied as counsel for the landlords contends. But the
question is whether cl 3(2) is to be construed on a subjective or objective basis. In support
of the latter construction, counsel for the landlords relies strongly on the decision in the   *c*
House of Lords in *Ponsford v HMS Aerosols Ltd* [1978] 2 All ER 837, [1979] AC 63. In that
case the landlords' predecessors had granted a 21-year lease to tenants at a rent of £9,000
a year for the first seven years. The rent for the second and third period of seven years
was the subject of a review clause expressing the rent to be £9,000 a year 'or such sum
whichever shall be higher as shall be assessed as a reasonable rent for the demised premises
for the appropriate period'. The lease provided that the reasonable rent for the second   *d*
and third periods should be agreed between the parties but that, if they failed to do so, it
should be assessed by an independent surveyor appointed by them. In 1969 the premises
were burnt down. They were rebuilt by the landlords, but the new building incorporated
substantial improvements paid for by the tenants at a cost of £31,780. When the rent
came to be reviewed for the second period of seven years, the tenants contended that the
rent should be a reasonable rent without taking into account the improvements for   *e*
which they had already paid. In proceedings to determine the meaning of the rent
review clause, it was argued that if the tenants' improvements were included they would
in effect be paying twice over. It was contended that the surveyor should assess what was
a reasonable rent for the tenants to pay and not what was a reasonable rent for the
demised premises as they stood. The House of Lords, by a majority, rejected the
argument. It was held that, on a true construction of the relevant clause, the surveyor's   *f*
task was simply to assess what was a reasonable rent for the demised premises on the
open market. Speaking of the surveyor's task, Viscount Dilhorne said ([1978] 2 All ER
837 at 842, [1979] AC 63 at 76–77):

> 'Surely it is to assess what rent the demised premises would command if let on
> the terms of the lease and for the period the assessed rent is to cover at the time the
> assessment falls to be made ... In assessing it, the surveyor will be assessing the   *g*
> reasonable rent that others, not just the sitting tenant, would be prepared to pay for
> the use and occupation of the premises. He will not consider the tenant's position
> separately.'

Lord Fraser said ([1978] 2 All ER 837 at 847, [1979] AC 63 at 83):

> 'It is true that the words "for the demised premises" do not add anything new,   *h*
> because there is no doubt about the identity of the premises for which the rent is
> payable, but in my opinion the words are of importance because they emphasise
> that the assessment is to be made by reference to the premises and not by reference
> to wider considerations or to what would be reasonable between these particular
> landlords and tenants.'

                                                                                                  j
Lord Keith, the third member of the majority, said ([1978] 2 All ER 837 at 849–850,
[1979] AC 63 at 85–86):

> 'At first impression the words "reasonable rent for the demised premises" suggest
> that what has to be ascertained is simply the rent that is reasonable for the premises

as such in their actual state, the situation being viewed entirely objectively. "The demised premises" must mean the demised premises as improved . . . In my opinion the words "a reasonable rent for the demised premises" simply mean "the rent at which the demised premises might reasonably be expected to let".'

It is contended on behalf of the landlords that the words in cl 3(2) 'a lease of the demised premises . . . at a rent to be agreed between the parties hereto' are the same, in effect, as the language in the review clause in that case. But it seems to me that there are material differences between the language of the two clauses. The clause in *Ponsford v HMS Aerosols Ltd* did not contain any reference to an agreement between the parties.

The importance of this distinction was emphasised in *Thomas Bates & Son Ltd v Wyndham's (Lingerie) Ltd* [1981] 1 All ER 1077, [1981] 1 WLR 505, on which the tenant relies. That case contained many points which are not relevant in the present case but the essential facts were these. Landlords let premises to predecessors of the tenants for seven years with an option for a further lease 'of the demised premises . . . at a rent to be agreed between the lessor and lessee'. There was provision for an arbitrator to fix the rent in default of agreement. In 1963 the option was exercised and a further lease was granted with an option in terms identical with the original lease. In 1970, when the tenant exercised the option, the landlords sought to introduce a review clause. A new lease was executed for 14 years with a review at the fifth and tenth years. By a mistake, the lease contained no provision for arbitration in default of agreement of the rent on review. The material language of the clause provided:

'Yielding and Paying therefor during the first Five Years of the said term unto the lessor the rent of Two Thousand Three Hundred and Fifty Pounds and for the next period of five years of the said term and the final period of four years of the said term such rents as shall have been agreed between the Lessor and the Lessee . . .'

In proceedings for rectification, the court ordered that language should be inserted into the clause providing for an arbitrator to determine the rent in default of agreement. On appeal, one of the questions which arose was: on the lease as rectified, by what measure was the arbitrator to fix the rent if the parties failed to agree? Buckley LJ, having referred to the language of the review clause in *Ponsoford v HMS Aerosols Ltd*, said ([1981] 1 All ER 1077 at 1088, [1981] 1 WLR 505 at 518):

'That form of clause, as it seems to me, focuses attention on what is there described as "a reasonable rent for the demised premises" for the appropriate period, and that expression is first used without any reference to agreement between the parties to the lease at all. It then goes on to provide that such assessment (that is to say, the fixing of the amount of the rent to be charged) shall be either agreed or, in default of agreement, arrived at by valuation by an independent surveyor. That form of wording, in my judgment, certainly affected the views of the majority of the House of Lords in that case.'

Buckley LJ then referred to passages in the majority opinions and continued ([1981] 1 All ER 1077 at 1088, [1981] 1 WLR 505 at 518–519):

'But it appears to me that the terms of the clause there under consideration were noticeably different in important respects from the clause which we have, which refers to nothing other than such rent as the parties shall have agreed . . . In my judgment, in default of agreement between the parties, the arbitrator would have to assess what rent it would be reasonable for these landlords and these tenants to have agreed under this lease having regard to all the circumstances relevant to any negotiations between them of a new rent from the review date.'

Eveleigh LJ expressed the same opinion ([1981] 1 All 1077 at 1090, [1981] 1 WLR 505 at 521):

'I should just add that I, too, regard this case as different from *Ponsford v HMS*

Aerosols Ltd. There the reference was specifically to the demised premises and that is
an important difference.'

Counsel for the tenant points out that the option in *Thomas Bates & Son Ltd v Wyndham's
(Lingerie) Ltd*, with immaterial differences, is indistinguishable from the language of the
option clause in the present case. But it was the review clause which fell to be construed
in that case. Even so, I can find no material difference in the language and its effect. The
option clause is radically different from the clause which had to be construed in *Ponsford
v HMS Aerosols Ltd*. It seems to me that in the present case the emphasis in the clause is
on what is to be agreed between the parties, and the arbitrator is required to determine
what it would be reasonable for these landlords and this tenant to agree in all the
circumstances of the case. I think that it was the intention of the parties to the lease that,
in default of agreement between them, the arbitrator should determine a rent which it
would have been reasonable for these landlords and this tenant to agree and to take into
account all the considerations which would affect the minds of the parties. In other
words, the test to be applied is subjective and not objective. Counsel for the landlords
accepted that the decision in *Thomas Bates & Son Ltd v Wyndham's (Lingerie) Ltd* was against
his submission but he contends that the decision was based on a concession by counsel
for the landlords in that case and that the construction put on the clause was in default of
argument to the contrary. That is not accurate. It is true that counsel for the landlords in
that case ultimately conceded, in effect, that a subjective construction was the proper
construction but the Court of Appeal examined whether the concession was well
founded. Buckley LJ said ([1981] 1 All ER 1077 at 1087, [1981] 1 WLR 505 at 517–518):

> 'Counsel for the landlords initially contended that the arbitrator so-called would
> act not as an arbitrator but as a valuer. He based that argument on the use of the
> words "shall have agreed" and the word "fixed" in the review clause. On that basis
> he submitted that the rent should be the market rent for the property, on the
> authority of a decision of the House of Lords in *Ponsford v HMS Aerosols Ltd*.
> Subsequently he conceded that the clause must be read as an agreement to arbitrate
> and not as an agreement to abide by a valuation. On that footing he agreed that, on
> the true construction of the clause, the rent should be such as it would have been
> reasonable for this landlord and this tenant to have agreed under the lease. It would
> consequently be proper for the arbitrator to take into account all considerations
> which would affect the mind of either party in connection with the negotiation of
> such a rent, as, for example, past expenditure by the tenant in improvements. In
> my judgment, counsel for the landlords was right to make that concession and to
> have accepted that the present case falls within the reasoning of the minority of the
> House of Lords in *Ponsford v HMS Aerosols Ltd* and not within the reasoning of the
> majority in that case.'

Buckley LJ then proceeded to give the reasons why he considered the concession to have
been properly made in the passage in his judgment to which I have referred.

Counsel for the landlords here made three further submissions with respect to the
Thomas Bates case. Firstly, he pointed out that the clause in that case provided for 'such
rents as shall have been agreed', which he contends is significantly different from 'a rent
to be agreed', the words used in the present case. The former language is said to lay
greater emphasis, as I understood the argument, on the word 'agreement' and that
therefore the arbitrator was required to fix a rent such as these particular landlords and
tenant would have agreed. But I do not follow why this should be so. Both clauses
emphasise the fact of agreement between the parties. It seems to me that the arbitrator
in the present case is to assess the rent which it would be reasonable for the parties to
agree. Secondly, counsel for the landlords submitted that a clause, similar in language to
the clause in the present case, had been construed in an objective sense in *Beer v Bowden*
[1981] 1 All ER 1070, [1981] 1 WLR 522 and that, since the decision in that case conflicts
with the decision in *Thomas Bates & Son Ltd v Wyndham's (Lingerie) Ltd*, I am free and I

have to choose which to follow. In *Beer v Bowden* the material clause provided, in language
part of which was very similar to that in the present case, for a rent review of—

> 'such rent as shall thereupon be agreed between the Landlords and the Tenant
> but no account shall be taken of any improvement carried out by the Tenant in
> computing the amount of increase, if any . . .'

The parties failed to agree a new rent. On the landlord's originating application, it was
ordered that the tenant was to pay as rent 'what the . . . premises are reasonably worth',
which was taken in the Court of Appeal as meaning a fair rental value for the premises
on the open market. The argument of the tenant before the Court of Appeal, on the basis
that the court had to imply some term as to what the rent should be, was that it could
only be either a fair market rent or the rent originally reserved in the lease (see [1981] 1
All ER 1070 at 1073, [1981] 1 WLR 522 at 525 per Goff LJ). The court implied the
former term. As far as I can see, it was never argued that a subjective test should be
applied in deciding what the rent should be, whereas in the *Thomas Bates* case the point
was central to the whole case. In these circumstances, I do not think that it can be
properly said that there is a conflict between the two cases, but if I am wrong I should
follow the decision in the *Thomas Bates* case where the question whether the clause should
be construed in an objective or subjective sense was directly considered and the relevant
authorities were referred to. Thirdly, counsel for the landlords submitted that the clause
in the present case contains the words 'the demised premises', indicating that the rent is
to be determined in relation to their actual state at the time of assessment by the
arbitrator, whereas those words were absent from the review clause in the *Thomas Bates*
case. It is quite true that the clause in the latter case did not expressly contain the words,
but for what was the new rent to be paid if it was not for the demised premises? I think
that the presence of the words in the clause in the present case are superfluous to the
question of the construction of the meaning of the words 'at a rent to be agreed between
the parties'. It seems to me that they do not add anything to the meaning of the clause.

I therefore construe the option clause in the present case in a subjective sense and I
must now consider the question of the improvements. Since the rent to be assessed by
the arbitrator is to be a rent for these particular landlords and this particular tenant,
taking into account all considerations which would affect the mind of either party, it
must follow that he should consider as one of those considerations the question of past
expenditure on the improvements. This was the approach of Buckley LJ in the *Thomas
Bates* case [1981] 1 All ER 1077 at 1087, [1981] 1 WLR 505 at 517. But they were not
carried out by the present tenant but by a predecessor many years before. Does it make
any difference in principle that the tenant did not himself carry out the improvements
but took the premises by assignment? Counsel for the landlords submits that it does. On
the assumption that the present tenant paid for the improvements, either wholly or in
part, counsel for the landlords contends that such payment is irrelevant: it is res inter
alios acta. But, as counsel for the tenant pointed out, when the tenant took the premises
by assignment, he stepped into the shoes of the previous tenant and is entitled to say, if it
be the fact, that he paid for the improvements then, and to argue either that they should
be wholly disregarded when determining the rent or that the rent should be affected by
a partial payment made for the improvements. Counsel for the landlords relies on the
general law that improvements become part of the demised premises for the benefit of
the landlord and he submits that it must follow that the tenant should pay for them in
the new rent. He contends that if they were to be disregarded it would have been so
stated in the deed of variation. He has referred to passages in the speeches of Viscount
Dilhorne and Lord Fraser in *Ponsford v HMS Aerosols Ltd* [1978] 2 All ER 837 at 841, 848,
[1979] AC 63 at 76, 84. Viscount Dilhorne said:

> 'Landlords and tenants are usually advised by lawyers on the terms of leases. If
> the parties to this lease had agreed that the effect of the improvements was to be
> disregarded in assessing the rent, I expect it would have been.'

Lord Fraser said:

> 'If the parties intended that the general law was to be varied by special provisions *a*
> in favour of the tenants, the time to make such provisions would have been when
> the licence for improvements was granted by the landlords, but that was not done.'

It is quite true that the deed of variation is silent on the effect of the improvements on
the question of rent. All that the deed provides is for a variation of the existing user in
consideration of an additional rent of £150 a year and, by cl 3, it provides a licence by   *b*
the landlords to the development of the land. But cl 3(2) of the lease means that, if a new
rent fell to be assessed, it was to be assessed on the basis of taking into account all
considerations, including any tenant's improvements, that is the new rent was to be
assessed on a subjective basis. If this is the meaning of the clause, as I have held it to be,
I do not see why, when the deed of variation was made in 1970, it was necessary for the
then tenants to make a special provision for what was already provided in the lease. The   *c*
present tenant has taken the benefit of cl 3(2) by assignment.

Counsel for the landlords also submitted that it is in practical terms impossible for the
arbitrator to assess whether and, if so, to what extent the tenant contributed to the value
of the improvements when he paid £12,500 in July 1981. He referred to the decision of
Megarry J in *Cuff v J & F Stone Property Co Ltd* [1978] 2 All ER 833, [1979] AC 87. The   *d*
clause which had to be construed was a rent review clause which provided for a rent of
£2,400 a year 'or such sum as shall be assessed as a reasonable rent for the demised
premises', with provision for assessment by an arbitrator in default of agreement. Counsel
for the tenant in that case conceded that improvements which had been made by the
tenant could not be wholly disregarded but he argued, in effect, that a discount could be
made by the surveyor assessing the rent, inter alia, for the improvements which had been
carried out by the tenant or someone on his behalf. Megarry J envisaged considerable   *e*
practical difficulties for an arbitrator in performing such a task although he thought that
the tenant's hand would have been strengthened if the formula used in the lease had
admitted of a construction which allowed regard to the individual circumstances of the
individual tenant (see [1978] 2 All ER 833 at 836, [1979] AC 87 at 90–91). Here it does.
Moreover, the question of assessing the tenant's contribution was accepted by Buckley LJ
in *Thomas Bates & Son v Wyndham's (Lingerie) Ltd* [1981] 1 All ER 1077, [1981] 1 WLR   *f*
505. Counsel for the landlords told me, and it was not contended otherwise, that there is
no evidence from the tenant to show that he contributed in any way by way of the
assignment towards the cost of the improvements. The arbitrator, not having made his
award, would have power to allow such evidence to be called even though he has heard
or is in the course of hearing submissions. It is, of course, entirely a matter for him
whether he exercises his discretion in this respect.
                                                                                          g
Counsel for the tenant submits that once it is established that the subjective approach
is the correct method of construing cl 3(2) it must follow that the improvements are to
be wholly disregarded when determining the rent. I do not accept that submission. It is
for the tenant to show that by way of assignment he paid wholly or contributed partly
towards the improvements. It is true that in *Ponsford v HMS Aerosols Ltd* [1978] 2 All ER
837 at 840, [1979] AC 63 at 75, Lord Wilberforce, in a minority speech, concluded that   *h*
the tenant's improvements should be wholly disregarded but the amount of the
improvements were precisely known in that case.

Finally, on this aspect of the case, counsel for the tenant submits that I should imply a
term in cl 3(2) that the rent to be determined by the arbitrator is a 'fair' rent as between
the parties. According to the argument, two factors are present in the option clause: the
formula by which the rent is to be calculated and the machinery by which the formula   *j*
is to be applied. According to counsel for the tenant, the formula is the 'fair' rent and the
machinery is as agreed between the parties or determined by the arbitrator. I think that
the correct approach is first to determine whether cl 3(2) is to be construed in an objective
or subjective sense. It may be said that, once it is established that the latter construction
is to prevail, it is not necessary to imply any term since the approach itself provides for

a an assessment of rent which it would be reasonable for these landlords and this tenant to have agreed. But in case I were wrong in this, I should conclude that such a term should be implied. Counsel for the tenant submitted that in any event the arbitrator might take the open market rent as a datum and work up or down from that standard. In these circumstances, he submits that the word 'fair', if implied, will exclude the exceptional tenant when considering the datum of the market rent. If that is how the arbitrator approaches his task, I agree that a word must be implied to exclude a freak offer.

b Finally, before I answer the four specific questions raised by or on behalf of the arbitrator, I must consider the argument of counsel for the landlords on inflation. He submits that the arbitrator should apply what he described as a premium or percentage uplift to take account of the fact that in the new lease for 21 years there is no provision for a rent review. The uplift is said to be necessary to protect the landlords from inflation over the period of the new lease. If, submits counsel for the landlords, the arbitrator c concludes, on the basis of his experience and on looking at the market as it is at the moment, that an uplift is to be taken into account, he is entitled to do so when assessing the rent. He should look at the length of the new lease, allow for the fact of past inflation and, making the assumption that inflation will continue, add a percentage to provide for future inflation. Counsel submits that, even on the subjective construction of cl 3(2), the arbitrator will take the market value as his starting point and it is at this stage that he will d make the necessary provision.

Counsel for the tenant contends that, if I accede to the landlords' argument, I shall in effect be permitting the arbitrator to build in a provision for a rent review into the lease. He submits that the landlords are seeking a guarantee of future inflation of an amount which, in the nature of events, can only be pure speculation. If his point fails, counsel for the tenant advances what is to me the rather surprising argument that the premium or e uplift should be assessed at 1961 levels (the date of the original lease) and not the present level of inflation.

Counsel for the landlords relies on an article published in the journal of the Law Society ((1979) 76 LS Gaz 332). The author states at the beginning of the article that—

f 'The idea of charging premium rentals for properties let on leases with historically long periods between rent reviews has been put into practice by a few brave souls with amenable tenants in the past.'

The author then points out that most new leases make provision for rent reviews every five years or even every three years. But in the case of leases made in the 1950s or 1960s there was usually incorporated a 21-year period of rent reviews. To cope with such a long period without review, the method of adding a premium at the outset of the lease has g been devised in order to protect the landlord against inflation and static rent. One case is referred to in the article which went to arbitration in which the arbitrator awarded a 20% premium over market rents. Two methods of achieving this end are suggested. The first is to use a formula which requires certain assumptions about the rate of growth in market rents over the years, but the author points out that it is almost impossible accurately to predict the extent to which rents will rise. The second method, which does h not involve the use of actuarial methods, is by negotiation, and, failing agreement, arbitration.

The practice described in the article is dealing with the problem (related to that which arises here) of long periods between rent reviews. Counsel for the tenant referred me to the decision in the Court of Appeal in *National Westminster Bank Ltd v BSC Footwear Ltd* (1980) 42 P & CR 90. In that case, by a lease made in 1957, premises were let for 21 years. j There was a provision for a renewal of the lease for a further 21 years 'at the then prevailing market rent' to be determined in default of agreement by a single arbitrator. There was no provision for a rent review. The question which came before the Court of Appeal was whether the arbitrator's power to determine the rent included a power to direct that the rent should be periodically reviewed. The Court of Appeal held that it did not. Templeman LJ said (at 92–93):

'In my judgment, the arbitrator has no power to introduce any variations between the original lease and the renewed lease. The arbitrator must determine the rent, *a* and only the rent, and for this purpose he must determine the prevailing market rent . . . The result of that declaration [by the judge at first instance] is to confer on the arbitrator a discretion to decline to determine the rent payable under the renewed lease for 21 years, but only to determine the rent for a period of three or five years, or some other period which he is free to choose, having heard indeterminate evidence; and then he has power to direct that subsequent rent for *b* subsequent parts of the term of 21 years shall be determined by such persons, at such intervals and by such machinery, as the arbitrator may think fit to draft and award. What is said is that, if the arbitrator fixes the rent at the beginning of 21 years for the whole period, then the landlord is in danger of not getting the fruits of inflation which he might otherwise get if there were rent review clauses. But what the landlords' predecessors in title gave away these landlords cannot now take back.' *c*

These observations of Templeman LJ are in effect precisely the arguments advanced on behalf of the landlords in the present case. They are seeking to introduce the effect of a rent review clause into a lease which makes no such provision. It seems to me that the concluding observations of Templeman LJ about the impossibility of taking back what the predecessors in title have given away are apposite here. Moreover, I think that there *d* is great force in the contention of counsel for the tenant that the whole process of making a calculation and building in a percentage for the effect of inflation on rents is entirely speculative both as to the continuation of inflation and as to the rates which might prevail from time to time.

Because of my conclusion on this issue, I do not find it necessary to consider or to express any view on the alternative argument advanced on behalf of the tenant that, if inflation is to be expressed in the rent, it should be at 1961 levels. *e*

My answers to the four questions are these:

Questions (a) and (b): the rent to be determined by the arbitrator is a fair rent for these particular landlords and this particular tenant, account being taken of all considerations which would affect the mind of either party to such negotiations. Question (c): the improvements are either to be disregarded wholly or partly if the tenant satisfies the *f* arbitrator by evidence that he has contributed in money or money's worth to the value of the improvements. Question (d): a premium is not to be added to take into account anticipated inflation during the currency of the new terms.

Order accordingly.

Solicitors: *Stanleys & Simpson North*, agents for *Treasures & Rivers Wyatt*, Gloucester (for the applicants); *Rowberry Morris*, Gloucester (for the respondent).

K Mydeen Esq   Barrister.

a Grampian Regional Council and others v Secretary of State for Scotland and others and other appeals

b HOUSE OF LORDS
LORD FRASER OF TULLYBELTON, LORD KEITH OF KINKEL, LORD SCARMAN, LORD BRIDGE OF HARWICH AND LORD TEMPLEMAN
10, 11 OCTOBER, 10 NOVEMBER 1983

c *Compulsory purchase – Compensation – Certificate of alternative development – Application for certificate – Matters to be considered – Assumptions to be made by planning authority – Assumption that no part of land in question to be acquired by authority having compulsory purchase powers – Whether planning authority must also assume that land not to be used for public purposes – Whether relevant that alternative sites available to meet public need – Whether application to be considered by reference to date of application for certificate or date of first d proposal to acquire land compulsorily – Land Compensation (Scotland) Act 1963, s 25.*

A Scottish education authority with compulsory purchase powers acquired from the owners two plots of land near Aberdeen for the erection thereon of two schools. The acquisition was made on terms agreed pursuant to two offers in writing made by the education authority on 15 December 1976 and 13 January 1977. The agreements e provided for the owners to receive the same compensation, fixed at the date of the respective offers, as if the land had been acquired compulsorily. On 28 July 1978 the owners applied to the planning authority under s 25[a] of the Land Compensation (Scotland) Act 1963 for certificates of appropriate alternative development for each site, namely development which would be appropriate for the land if it were not proposed to be acquired compulsorily. The planning authority issued certificates under s 25(4)(b) f stating that in its opinion planning permission would not have been granted for any development other than that proposed to be carried out by the education authority. The owners appealed to the Secretary of State, who allowed the appeals, cancelled the certificates issued by the planning authority and issued new certificates under s 25(4)(a) stating that, subject to conditions, planning permission would have been granted for residential development for one of the sites and for residential and commercial g development for the other. The education authority and the planning authority appealed against those decisions to the Court of Session, which affirmed the Secretary of State's decisions, and then to the House of Lords, contending that when an application was made to a planning authority for a certificate under s 25 the planning authority, in determining the application, was required to disregard only the fact that the land was proposed to be acquired by an authority having compulsory purchase powers and that it h had to take into account the underlying purpose of the proposed acquisition and accordingly only if the applicant could show that at the date of his application there were suitable alternative sites available to meet the public need for which the land was proposed to be acquired was he entitled to a certificate under s 25(4)(a) stating that planning permission for development would have been granted. The appellants further contended that a planning authority was required to consider and determine the j application for a certificate by reference to the facts existing at the date when the application was made and not the date when the land was first proposed to be acquired compulsorily.

a   Section 25, so far as material, is set out at p 676 b to f, post

Held – The appeals would be dismissed for the following reasons—

(1) Since the sole purpose of the certification procedure, as part of the overall scheme a of the 1963 Act to secure fair compensation to landowners who were compulsorily expropriated, was to provide a basis for determining the value, if any, to be taken into account in assessing the compensation payable on compulsory acquisition, the planning authority in considering an application for a certificate under s 25 of that Act was required to ignore not only the fact that an authority with compulsory purchase powers wished to acquire the land but also any underlying requirement to use that land for a b public purpose, and the availability of alternative sites to meet the public need for which the land was proposed to be acquired had no relevance in determining the fair basis of compensation which the acquiring authority ought to pay to the owner of the land to be acquired compulsorily (see p 675 b to d, p 676 g h, p 677 f, p 678 b to g and p 680 a c h, post); *Margate Corp v Devotwill Investments Ltd* [1970] 3 All ER 864 distinguished.

(2) The appropriate date by reference to which an application for a certificate under c s 25 was to be decided and on which permission for the certified development, if the certificate did not specify a future time, would be assumed to have been granted under s 23(5)[b] of the 1963 Act was the date of the acquiring authority's offer to purchase, which was also the date for the assessment of compensation, because the purpose of the certificate was solely to aid the assessment of compensation by indicating what planning permission would have been granted at or before the date when compensation fell to be d assessed or at any future time specified in the certificate (see p 675 b to d and p 680 e to g, post).

Notes

For assumed permission in accordance with certificate of appropriate alternative development, see 8 Halsbury's Laws (4th edn) paras 276–284. e

Sections 23 and 25 of the Land Compensation (Scotland) Act 1963 correspond to ss 15 and 17 of the Land Compensation Act 1961. For ss 15 and 17 of the 1961 Act, see 6 Halsbury's Statutes (3rd edn) 254, 257.

Cases referred to in opinions

Bell v Lord Advocate 1968 SC 14. f
Margate Corp v Devotwill Investments Ltd [1970] 3 All ER 864, HL.
Skelmersdale Development Corp v Secretary of State for the Environment [1980] JPL 322.

Consolidated appeals

The appellants, Grampian Regional Council (the education authority) and Gordon District Council (the planning authority), appealed against interlocutors of the Second g Division of the Court of Session (Lord Dunpark and Lord McDonald, Lord Avonside dissenting) dated 28 January 1983 dismissing their appeals against decisions of the first respondent, the Secretary of State for Scotland, dated 18 May 1981 cancelling certificates of appropriate alternative development issued by the planning authority on 27 September 1978 in respect of two areas of land acquired by the education authority from the second respondents, Ashdale Land and Property Co Ltd (the landowners), at Westhill, Skene, h Aberdeenshire, and substituting therefor certificates in different terms. The facts are set out in the opinion of Lord Bridge.

---

b Section 23(5), so far as material, provides: 'Where a certificate [of appropriate alternative development] is issued under ... this Act, it shall be assumed that any planning permission which, j according to the certificate, would have been granted in respect of the relevant land or part thereof if it were not proposed to be acquired by any authority possessing compulsory purchase powers would be so granted, but, where any conditions are, in accordance with those provisions, specified in the certificate, only subject to those conditions and, if any future time is so specified, only at that time.'

J A Cameron QC and *A F Rodger* (both of the Scottish Bar) for the education authority and
the planning authority.
M S R Bruce QC and *A C Henry* (both of the Scottish Bar) for the Secretary of State.
I C Kirkwood QC and *A M Philip* (both of the Scottish bar) for the landowners.

Their Lordships took time for consideration.

10 November. The following opinions were delivered.

LORD FRASER OF TULLYBELTON. My Lords, I have had the advantage of
reading in draft the speech of my noble and learned friend Lord Bridge. I agree with it
and for the reasons stated in it I would dismiss these appeals.

LORD KEITH OF KINKEL. My Lords, I agree that these appeals should be dismissed
for the reasons set out in the speech to be delivered by my noble and learned friend Lord
Bridge.

LORD SCARMAN. My Lords, I have had the advantage of reading in draft the speech
to be delivered by my noble and learned friend Lord Bridge. I agree with it, and for the
reasons he gives I would dismiss the appeals. I also agree with the proposed order as to
costs.

LORD BRIDGE OF HARWICH. My Lords, the first appellants (the education
authority) acquired from the second respondents (the landowners) sites for a primary and
a secondary school in a newly developed suburb of Aberdeen called Westhill on terms
agreed pursuant to offers in writing made by the education authority on 15 December
1976 and 13 January 1977 respectively. The agreements provided for the landowners to
receive the same compensation, fixed as at the date of the respective offers, as if the land
had been acquired compulsorily.

On 28 July 1978 the landowners applied to the second appellants (the planning
authority) pursuant to s 25 of the Land Compensation (Scotland) Act 1963 for certificates
of appropriate alternative development. Parallel applications by the education authority
give rise to no separate issue and can for present purposes be ignored. The planning
authority issued certificates to the landowners stating that, in their opinion, planning
permission would not have been granted for any development other than that proposed
to be carried out by the education authority. The landowners appealed to the first
respondent (the Secretary of State) pursuant to s 26 of the Act who, after receiving the
report of a public inquiry, allowed the appeals, cancelled the certificates issued by the
planning authority, and certified that planning permission would have been granted, in
respect of the primary school site for residential development, and in respect of the
secondary school site for residential or commercial development, in each case subject to
conditions. The education authority and the planning authority applied to the Court of
Session, pursuant to s 29 of the 1963 Act, to quash the decision of the Secretary of State.
By a majority (Lord Dunpark and Lord McDonald, Lord Avonside dissenting) the court
affirmed the decision. The education authority and the planning authority now appeal
to your Lordships' House.

The substantive provisions governing the assessment of compensation for the
compulsory purchase of land on which the questions raised by these consolidated appeals
depend were first enacted in the Town and Country Planning Act 1959 and the Town
and Country Planning (Scotland) Act 1959. They are now embodied in the Land
Compensation Act 1961 (the English Act) and the 1963 Act. Both Acts have been subject
to minor amendments, which do not, in my opinion, affect the questions presently
arising for decision. As one would expect in relation to such a subject matter, the
substance of the law is the same on both sides of the border. I shall not encumber this
opinion with references to the English Act, but merely note here that the sections of the
1963 Act to which I shall be referring have their exact counterparts in the English Act.

Part III of the 1963 Act (ss 12 to 24) is headed: 'Provisions Determining Amount of Compensation'. Part IV (ss 25 to 30) is headed: 'Certification by Planning Authorities of Appropriate Alternative Development'. These two parts are interdependent.

Section 25 of the 1963 Act (as amended by the Community Land Act 1975) provides, so far as relevant, as follows:

'(1) Where an interest in land is proposed to be acquired by an authority possessing compulsory purchase powers, and that land or part thereof does not consist or form part of—(a) an area defined in the development plan as an area of comprehensive development, or (b) an area shown in the development plan as an area allocated primarily for a use which is of a residential, commercial or industrial character, or for a range of two or more uses any of which is of such a character, then, subject to subsection (2) of this section, either of the parties directly concerned may apply to the planning authority for a certificate under this section . . .

(3) An application for a certificate under this section—(a) shall state whether or not there are, in the applicant's opinion, any classes of development which, either immediately or at a future time, would be appropriate for the land in question if it were not proposed to be acquired by any authority possessing compulsory purchase powers and, if so, shall specify the classes of development and the times at which they would be so appropriate . . .

(4) Where an application is made to the planning authority for a certificate under this section in respect of an interest in land, the planning authority shall . . . issue to the applicant a certificate stating that, in the opinion of the planning authority in respect of the land in question, either—(a) planning permission for development of one or more classes specified in the certificate (whether specified in the application or not) would have been granted; or (b) planning permission would not have been granted for any development other than the development (if any) which is proposed to be carried out by the authority by whom the interest is proposed to be acquired.

(5) Where, in the opinion of the planning authority, planning permission would have been granted as mentioned in subsection (4)(a) of this section, but would only have been granted subject to conditions, or at a future time, or both subject to conditions and at a future time, the certificate shall specify those conditions, or that future time, or both, as the case may be, in addition to the other matters required to be contained in the certificate . . .'

It will be convenient to refer to the certificates contemplated by sub-s (4)(a) and (b) as positive and negative certificates respectively. A decision by a planning authority, or by the Secretary of State on appeal, whether a positive or a negative certificate is appropriate, must proceed on the hypothesis predicated by sub-s (3) and determine what planning permission, if any, would have been granted if the land were not proposed to be acquired by any authority possessing compulsory purchase powers. The sole purpose of the certification procedure is to provide a basis for determining the development value, if any, to be taken into account in assessing the compensation payable on compulsory acquisition. If a positive certificate is issued, it is to be assumed that the certified permission would be granted, subject to such conditions and at such future time, if any, as may be specified in the certificate (s 23(5)). If a negative certificate is issued, 'regard is to be had' to the negative opinion certified (s 22(3)). Although this is not conclusive, it is difficult to envisage a situation in practice in which the Lands Tribunal, when assessing compensation, could be persuaded to act on a contrary opinion to that certified by the planning authority or the Secretary of State on appeal.

The general Westhill development was not carried out pursuant to formal provisions of the development plan. It was approved by the Secretary of State as a departure from the plan. To use ordinary language and avoid planning jargon, it has always been envisaged that this substantial new urban community would need to be served by schools provided by the education authority and the two school sites which are the subject of these appeals have from the outset been earmarked to meet that need. The primary *a* school site is surrounded by residential development. The secondary school site has residential development on three sides and either has, or will in due course have, commercial and public buildings on the fourth. The landowners have no doubt profited handsomely from the development of other land in their ownership at Westhill. But it has not been suggested that this has any relevance in deciding what certificates are appropriate for the school sites under s 25(4). The same certificates would be appropriate if these two sites were isolated pockets of land in separate ownership from any other land

b at Westhill.

The cornerstone of the argument for the appellants is s 30(2) of the Act which provides:

'For the purposes of sections 25 and 26 of this Act, an interest in land shall be taken to be an interest proposed to be acquired by an authority possessing compulsory purchase powers in the following (but no other) circumstances, that is to say—(a) where, for the purposes of a compulsory acquisition by that authority of

c land consisting of or including land in which that interest subsists, a notice required to be published or served in connection with that acquisition, either by an Act or by any Standing Order of either House of Parliament relating to petitions for private bills, has been published or served in accordance with that Act or Order; or (b) where a notice requiring the purchase of that interest has been served under any enactment, and in accordance with that enactment that authority are to be deemed to have

d served a notice to treat in respect of that interest; or (c) where an offer in writing has been made by or on behalf of that authority to negotiate for the purchase of that interest.'

It is said that the only circumstance which the planning authority, or the Secretary of State on appeal, is required to ignore in answering the hypothetical question raised by an

e application under s 25 is the immediate event which had resulted in the applicant's interest in land becoming one which is 'proposed to be acquired by an authority possessing compulsory purchase powers' under s 25(1), in this case the education authority's written offers to purchase. Whilst those offers must be ignored, so runs the argument, the underlying requirement to devote these sites to fulfil the needs of public education remains and affords a complete answer to the claims for positive certificates.

f If it were right to confine attention to ss 25(3) and (4) and 30(2) alone, this literalistic argument might have some appeal. If, however, one considers the wider statutory context and the function of certificates of appropriate alternative development in the scheme of the 1963 Act as a whole, it becomes clear that the argument is untenable.

First, the argument flies in the face of s 16 of the 1963 Act which provides:

'No account shall be taken of any depreciation of the value of the relevant interest

g which is attributable to the fact that (whether by way of designation, allocation or other particulars contained in the current development plan, or by any other means) an indication has been given that the relevant land is, or is likely, to be acquired by an authority possessing compulsory purchase powers.'

As Lord Dunpark succinctly put it:

h 'It seems to me to follow from the fact that the value of the land is not to be affected by the prospect of compulsory acquisition, that its value is not to be affected by the development proposed by the acquiring authority. One cannot discount the one without the other.'

Next, I refer to s 25(7) which provides:

j 'In determining, for the purposes of the issue of a certificate under this section, whether planning permission for any particular class of development would have been granted in respect of any land, the planning authority shall not treat development of that class as development for which planning permission would have been refused by reason only that it would have involved development of the land in question (or of that land together with other land) otherwise than in accordance with the provisions of the development plan relating thereto.'

The primary purpose of this provision, in my view, is to obviate the possibility that where, as in the usual case, urban land is allocated in the development plan for a necessary public purpose for which it will in due course need to be acquired, that provision of the plan can be relied on to deny the landowner a positive certificate. If the planning need to use land for a public purpose, which underlies a proposed compulsory acquisition, is not a sufficient ground to withhold a positive certificate where that need is recognised and provided for in the development plan, I do not see how the underlying planning need can ever be such a sufficient ground.

But the overriding consideration which impels me to reject the argument for the appellants is that it would, in my opinion, if accepted, defeat the essential purpose of the procedure for obtaining certificates of appropriate alternative development, as part of the overall scheme of the 1963 Act to secure the payment of fair compensation to landowners who are compulsorily expropriated, or, expressed more specifically, to ensure that, when urban land, otherwise available for some form of urban building development, is acquired for a necessary public purpose, the compensation will reflect its urban development value. Assuming, as I do, that every compulsory purchase of land can be justified by reference to the public purpose for which the land is required, to allow reliance on that public requirement to determine the question raised by an application under s 25 would lead to the issue of a negative certificate in every case. Counsel for the appellants' recognising that this conclusion would be fatal to his argument, sought to avoid it by contending that the applicant for a positive certificate could succeed if, but only if, he could show that, at the date of his application, there were one or more alternative sites available which could equally well or perhaps better be used to meet the public need for which his own land was proposed to be taken. I unhesitatingly reject this contention. An application for a certificate of appropriate alternative development presupposes that the land to which it relates is in fact to be acquired by an authority possessing compulsory purchase powers and a certificate issued will only be of significance if the acquisition proceeds to completion. The availability of alternative sites is very relevant at the stage when a proposed compulsory acquisition is being resisted. But once it has been decided that site A, rather than site B or site C, is to be acquired, the fact that site B or site C might have been chosen instead can have no conceivable relevance in determining the fair basis of compensation which the acquiring authority ought to pay to the owner of site A.

The appellants have sought support for their arguments in three decided cases to which I should briefly refer. In *Bell v Lord Advocate* 1968 SC 14, Glasgow Corporation acquired 40 acres of land as public open space. The land was allocated for that purpose in the development plan. The landowner sought a certificate under s 25 for industrial, commercial or residential development. The certificate issued by the planning authority and affirmed by the Secretary of State on appeal was limited to development 'for a commercial sports stadium, private golf course, private playing fields or for other private open air recreational use'. This was challenged in the Court of Session as a contravention of s 25(7). The court affirmed the decision of the Secretary of State. As I understand the judgments, the court upheld the reasoning of the Secretary of State on the footing that he was not merely relying on the provision of the development plan as a ground for refusing to certify the kind of building development sought by the landowner, but on a planning policy to keep the 40 acres in question as open space substantially free from building development, which could be supported on planning grounds quite independently of any scheme for acquisition of the land as public open space. So understood, I respectfully agree with the decision and can find nothing in it to assist the appellants in this case.

Very similar considerations apply to the decision of Griffith J in *Skelmersdale Development Corp v Secretary of State for the Environment* [1980] JPL 322. A large site of 45 acres was to

be acquired for educational purposes. The certificate of appropriate alternative
development issued by the planning authority and affirmed by the Secretary of State on
appeal was confined to development 'for an institute in large ground or for open
recreational use playing fields'. Here again, the essential ground on which, as I read his
judgment, Griffith J refused an application to set aside the decision of the Secretary of
State was that it was based on a planning policy which justified the preservation of the
site as part of a larger area of substantially open land, independently of any scheme to use
it for educational purposes. I do not think the judgment lends any support to the
proposition that the educational requirement in itself could afford a ground for the issue
of a negative certificate. If it does, I must, to that extent, respectfully disagree with it.

Finally, it was submitted that the decision of this House in *Margate Corp v Devotwill
Investments Ltd* [1970] 3 All ER 864 established the relevance of the availability of
alternative sites. This case arose, not from an application for a certificate of appropriate
alternative development, but from a decision of the Lands Tribunal on disputed
compensation. The land to be acquired was shown in the development plan as allocated
for residential use. Permission for actual residential development was refused on the
ground that part of the land was required for a by-pass road. The owners served a
purchase notice. They were entitled to have the land valued with the benefit of the
assumption derived from s 16(2) and (7) of the English Act that planning permission
would be granted for such residential development as might reasonably have been
expected to be permitted if the land were not proposed to be acquired by any authority
possessing compulsory purchase powers. Access to the site was from a highway suffering
from severe traffic congestion, which the proposed by-pass road was designed to relieve.
The owners contended that it must be assumed in deciding the scope of the notional
residential development of the site that the by-pass road would be built elsewhere and
would relieve the local traffic problem, so that the notional development of the subject
land should not be restricted in any way by reference to the difficulties of access arising
from the existing local traffic congestion. This contention prevailed before the Lands
Tribunal and in the Court of Appeal. This House allowed an appeal by the acquiring
authority and remitted the case to the Lands Tribunal on the ground that the effect on
the development to be assumed under s 16(2) and (7) of a bypass road on an alternative
route was not a matter of assumption but of evidence. In a speech with which all the
other members of the Appellate Committee agreed, Lord Morris said (at 869–870):

> If there was not to be a by-pass on the respondents' land it by no means followed
> that there would inevitably be a by-pass somewhere else. There might be or there
> might not be. It might have been possible to have another route for a by-pass; it
> might have been quite impossible. It would be a question depending on
> topographical and various and many other factors whether there could be a by-pass
> somewhere else. It would be for consideration whether any alternative by-pass was
> or was not possible or probably and further whether its construction was or was not
> likely. These matters could not rest on any assumptions but rather on an examination
> of all the evidence.'

It is to be noted that in the *Margate* case it was never suggested that the underlying
requirement to use part of the claimant's land for the construction of a by-pass road
provided any ground for restricting the extent of the residential development for which
it ought to be assumed that permission would be granted if the land were not to be
acquired. The restriction on the extent of the notional development for which the
acquiring authority contended arose solely from the undoubted problems of access to the
site due to the existing traffic congestion on the main road from which access would
have to be obtained. A by-pass road, if provided elsewhere than on the claimant's land,
would relieve the traffic congestion and substantially diminish the problems of access.
Hence the relevance of considering, in the hypothetical situation predicated by the
statute, the prospect of a by-pass being provided elsewhere than on the claimant's land
was not and could not be disputed. The decision of your Lordships' House that the

strength of that prospect fell to be decided as a matter of evidence and could not be founded on any assumption does not seem to me to be of the least help to the present appellants, or indeed to be relevant to any issue arising in these appeals.

The conclusions I have already expressed are sufficient to dispose of these appeals. The appellants, however, sought to raise a further question as to what is the relevant date by reference to which an application for a certificate under s 25 should be decided and on which permission for the certified development, if the certificate does not specify a future time, will be assumed to have been granted under s 23(5). The submission for the appellants is that the relevant date is the date of the application under s 25. The Secretary of State and the majority of the Court of Session have held that it is the date when the land is first 'proposed to be acquired by an authority possessing compulsory purchase powers' in accordance with the definition of that formula in s 30(2). If that is right, it means that the relevant date in relation to each school site is the date of the education authority's offer to purchase, which is also the date for the assessment of compensation.

Having concluded that the availability of alternative school sites is irrelevant, it seems to me that the point as to date, in the circumstances of this case, is entirely academic, since the appellants are unable to suggest that there was any change in planning policy or other material change of circumstance between the dates of the offers to purchase and the date of the application for certificates. However, since the point was argued, it is right to express an opinion about it.

The words 'either immediately or at a future time' were introduced into s 25(3)(a) of the 1963 Act by the Community Land Act 1975. It seems to have been suggested to the Court of Session that they changed the previous law. Counsel before your Lordships disclaimed this suggestion, but relied on the word 'immediately' as emphasising what he submitted the law had always been. The applicant for a certificate, counsel points out, is, and always has been, required to specify the classes of development which, he claims, 'would be appropriate for the land in question if it were not proposed to be acquired by any authority possessing compulsory purchase powers'. Counsel submits that the words 'would be' can only refer to the present, not to the past. That is the beginning and end of his argument. Here again, consideration of the scheme of the 1963 Act shows the argument to be fallacious. The purpose of the certificate is solely as an aid to the assessment of compensation. Unless it is effective to indicate what planning permission would have been granted at or before the date when compensation falls to be assessed or at some future time specified in the certificate, it will not serve that purpose effectively. In agreement with Lord Dunpark, I consider that the submission for the appellants on this point leads to a nonsensical result.

My Lords, I would accordingly dismiss these appeals. Both respondents were properly represented. The Secretary of State was vitally interested in the principle at issue, the landowners in the effect of the outcome on the compensation they will receive. Joint representation would, for obvious reasons, have been inappropriate. I would propose that the appellants be ordered to pay both respondents' costs of the appeals to your Lordships' House.

LORD TEMPLEMAN. My Lords, for the reasons given by my noble and learned friend Lord Bridge, I too would dismiss these appeals.

Appeals dismissed.

Solicitors: *Martin & Co*, agents for *Shepherd & Wedderburn WS*, Edinburgh (for the education authority and the planning authority); *Treasury Solicitor*, agent for *Solicitor to the Secretary of State for Scotland*; *Simmons & Simmons*, agents for *A C Bennett & Fairweather WS*, Edinburgh, agents for *Storie Cruden & Simpson*, Aberdeen (for the landowners).

Mary Rose Plummer   Barrister.

a

Ditchfield (Inspector of Taxes) v Sharp and others

COURT OF APPEAL, CIVIL DIVISION
WALLER, FOX AND MAY LJJ
4, 5 MAY, 23 JUNE 1983

b

Income tax – Discounts – Bill of exchange or promissory note – Interest-free promissory note purchased by taxpayer for less than face value – Promissory note originally issued as consideration for purchase of shares – Whether profit realised on maturity a 'discount' – Income and Corporation Taxes Act 1970, ss 108, Sch D, para 1(a), 109(2) Case III, para (b).

c On 26 February 1970 the trustees of a settlement, who did not carry on a trade in securities or promissory notes, purchased on behalf of themselves and others for £1,779,631 a promissory note dated 23 May 1969 made by B, an English company, promising to pay to a subsidiary of C, an American company, the sum of £2,399,000 free of interest in February 1973 in part consideration for the sale by C to B of the entire share capital in another of C's subsidiaries. The note was purchased from R (who had
d purchased it from the grantee) with R's guarantee that at maturity the trustees would receive 75% of its face value. On 1 February 1973 the note was duly discharged by payment in full by B and the trustees received £460,065 in excess of the amount they had paid for their share of the note. The trustees were assessed to income tax under Case III of Sch D for the year 1972–73 on that excess on the footing that it constituted an annual profit on the discharge of the promissory note and was a 'discount' within para (b)
e of Case III in s 109(2)[a] of the Income and Corporation Taxes Act 1970. The trustees appealed against the assessment, contending that the profit was of a capital nature and not a discount, since the original transaction whereby the note had been issued was not a discounting transaction but one by which part of the purchase price of the shares (owed by B to C) was left outstanding for the period of the currency of the note. They further contended that para (b) of Case III was subject to para 1(a) of Sch D in s 108[b], and that
f accordingly a discount was taxable under Case III only if it was an annual profit or gain, and a gain arising three years after the acquisition of the promissory note could not be an annual profit or gain within the meaning of para 1(a) of Sch D. The Crown contended, in the absence of evidence surrounding the issue of the note, that since it was interest free the value of the consideration given to B for the note must have been less than its face value and therefore the issue constituted a discounting transaction and accordingly
g the gain to the trustees when the note was honoured was in the nature of income, properly described as an annual profit or gain chargeable to income tax under Case III. The Special Commissioners decided that the difference between the purchase price of the note and its face value represented a capital gain and not an annual profit or gain. They therefore discharged the assessment to income tax and confirmed the assessment to capital gains tax. The judge allowed an appeal by the Crown, holding that the original
h transaction was a discounting transaction and that the profit realised by the trustees was a discount chargeable to tax under Case III. The trustees appealed to the Court of Appeal, contending in the alternative that if there was an income element in the amount which they had received it was in the nature of interest, not discount, and accordingly the wrong amount had been assessed under the wrong head.

j **Held** – The appeal would be dismissed for the following reasons—
    (1) A 'discount' was the deduction made from the amount of a bill of exchange or promissory note by one who gave value for it before it was due. Since the transaction

---

a   Section 109(2), so far as material, is set out at p 683 j, post
b   Section 108, so far as material, is set out at p 683 h, post

which had given rise to the receipt by the trustees of the £460,065 was the purchase of the note by the them from R before maturity at an amount less than its face value, it followed that it was a discounting transaction and accordingly the sum received by the trustees on the maturity of the note was a profit arising from a discount (see p 684 e to g, p 686 d e, p 687 d and p 688 c to e, post); dictum of Lord Atkinson in *Brown (Surveyor of Taxes) v National Provident Institution* [1921] 2 AC at 251–252 followed.

(2) In determining whether a receipt was of an income or capital nature, each case was to be decided on its own facts. In the circumstances, the only conclusion which the commissioners could have come to on the facts was that the profit realised by the trustees had been of an income nature, and, even if there was an interest element in the profit realised by the trustees, that did not prevent the transaction being a discounting transaction. It followed that the sum received by the trustees was a profit on a discount and was an amount of annual profit or gain within para 1(a) of s 108 of the 1970 Act (see p 685 a e h to p 686 a c d, p 687 d e and p 688 c to e, post); dictum of Lord Greene MR in *Lomax (Inspector of Taxes) v Peter Dixon & Co Ltd* [1943] 2 All ER at 262–263 applied.

Notes

For the taxation of discounts, see 23 Halsbury's Laws (4th edn) para 548.

For the Income and Corporation Taxes Act 1970, ss 108, 109, see 33 Halsbury's Statutes (3rd edn) 150, 154.

Cases referred to in judgments

Brown (Surveyor of Taxes) v National Provident Institution, Ogston (Surveyor of Taxes) v Provident Mutual Life Association [1921] 2 AC 222, HL; *affg in part and varying* [1920] 3 KB 35, CA; *affg in part and rvsg in part* [1919] 2 KB 497.

Davies (Inspector of Taxes) v Premier Investment Co Ltd, Hewetson v Carlyle (Inspector of Taxes) [1945] 2 All ER 681.

Edwards (Inspector of Taxes) v Bairstow [1955] 3 All ER 48, [1956] AC 14, [1955] 3 WLR 410, HL.

Lomax (Inspector of Taxes) v Peter Dixon & Co Ltd [1943] 2 All ER 255, [1943] KB 671, CA.

Cases also cited

Haythornthwaite (T) & Sons Ltd v Kelly (Inspector of Taxes) (1927) 11 TC 657, CA.

Jones (Inspector of Taxes) v Leeming [1930] AC 415, [1930] All ER Rep 584, HL.

Ryall (Inspector of Taxes) v Hoare, Ryall (Inspector of Taxes) v Honeywill [1923] 2 KB 447, [1923] All ER Rep 528.

Southport BC v Lancashire CC [1937] 2 All ER 626, [1937] 2 KB 589.

Willingale (Inspector of Taxes) v International Commercial Bank Ltd [1978] 1 All ER 754, [1978] AC 834, HL.

Appeal

David Buckley Sharp and others, as trustees of the Orwell Share Settlement, appealed against an order of Walton J ([1982] STC 124) made on 6 November 1981 allowing an appeal by the Crown by way of case stated (set out at [1982] STC 125–129) by the Commissioners for the Special Purposes of the Income Tax Acts in respect of their decision to discharge an assessment to income tax under Sch D, Case III for the year 1972–73 in respect of the profit realised by the trustees on the maturity of a promissory note which the trustees had purchased at 75% of its face value. The facts are set out in the judgment of Fox LJ.

C N Beattie QC for the trustees.
James Holroyd Pearce QC and *Viscount Dilhorne* for the Crown.

Cur adv vult

23 June. The following judgments were delivered.

a   **FOX LJ** (giving the first judgment at the invitation of Waller LJ). This is an appeal from a decision of Walton J ([1982] STC 124), who determined that a payment received by the taxpayers on the maturity of a promissory note was taxable as a 'discount' under the provisions of ss 108 and 109 of the Income and Corporation Taxes Act 1970.

The taxpayers are the trustees of a settlement made in 1934 by Mr W S Cottingham **b**   whereby certain shares in a Canadian company called Orwell Investments Ltd, together with shares in Lewis Berger & Sons Ltd, and certain other property were settled on trusts which are not material to this case.

In 1939 Orwell Investments Ltd went into liquidation and the trustees, as shareholders, received shares in Lewis Berger & Sons Ltd. Subsequently, Lewis Berger & Sons Ltd merged with another company and became Berger Jensen & Nicholson Ltd (Bergers).

c   In 1969 the Celanese Corp sold to Bergers all the share capital of the British Paints Group in consideration of stock units and loan stocks of Bergers together with a promissory note dated 23 May 1969 whereby Bergers promised to pay to a Dutch company Cel Euro NV (a subsidiary of the Celanese Corp) the sum of £2,399,000 (free of interest) on 1 February 1973.

In 1970 a company called Hoechst UK Ltd made a takeover bid for the ordinary shares **d**   of Bergers. That offer was accepted by the shareholders of Bergers, including the trustees. As a result the trustees had a large cash sum available which, to quote the case stated, 'they were minded to invest in purchasing jointly with others' the promissory note of 23 May 1969. This was, in fact, done. As a condition of purchase, the trustees required Cel Euro NV first to sell the note to Rothschilds, the merchant bankers, who would guarantee payment of 75% of the note on maturity.

e   On 18 February 1970 the trustees wrote to Rothschilds offering to purchase the promissory note for £1,779,631 conditionally, inter alia, on Rothschilds giving the guarantee. That offer was accepted and the purchase was completed on 26 February 1970. The purchase though made by the trustees alone was, in fact, made on behalf of the trustees and other persons in agreed amounts. The amount contributed by the trustees was £1,321,004.

f   On 1 February 1973 the promissory note matured and Bergers paid the trustees £2,399,000 in discharge of the note of which £1,781,969 was received by the trustees as such. Accordingly, the trustees received £460,065 in excess of the amount they had paid for their share of the note.

The Crown contends that the excess was a 'discount' of an income nature constituting an annual profit of the year in which it was received and attracting income tax accordingly. The trustees' primary contention is that the excess is of a capital nature and **g**   not liable to income tax. The Special Commissioners decided in favour of the trustees. That decision was reversed by the judge.

I come to the statutory provisions.

Sections 108 and 109 of the Income and Corporation Taxes Act 1970 provide:

'**108.** The Schedule referred to as Schedule D is as follows:—

h

SCHEDULE D

1. Tax under this Schedule shall be charged in respect of—(*a*) the annual profits or gains arising or accruing—(i) to any person residing in the United Kingdom from any kind of property whatever . . .

109.—(1) Tax under Schedule D shall be charged under the Cases set out in **j**   subsection (2) below . . .

(2) The Cases are . . . Case III—tax in respect of . . . (*b*) all discounts . . .'

The taxation of discounts is of long standing. In the Act 45 Geo 3 c 49 (income tax (1805)) the reference under the Third Case of Sch D was to 'The Profits on all Exchequer Bills . . . and on all Discounts . . .' In the Income Tax Act 1842 the language under the

Third Case was 'Second.—The Profits on all Securities bearing Interest payable out of the public Revenue . . . and on all Discounts . . . shall be charged according to the preceding *a* Rule in this Case'. In the Income Tax Act 1918 the reference under r 1(*b*) of the Case III rules is to 'all discounts', which is the same as in the 1970 Act.

As the judge observed, it is perhaps easier to treat the language of the older statutes as meaning 'profits arising from discounts received on discounting transactions' than it is to give that meaning to the sparser language 'all discounts' (see [1982] STC 124 at 131). But I see no reason to suppose that the ambit of the statutory references to discounts has *b* changed with the years and I think the judge was correct to give that meaning to 'all discounts' since it is, I think, in practical terms the sensible construction.

Accordingly, there are I think two questions to be determined in the present case. First, was the sum of £460,065 a profit arising from a discount received on a discounting transaction? Second, if it was such a profit, was it an 'annual profit or gain' within s 108 of the 1970 Act, which is the charging section. It must be a profit of an income and not a *c* capital nature.

As to the first of these questions I take the following extracts from Murray's *Oxford English Dictionary* (1897) as cited by Lord Atkinson in *Brown (Surveyor of Taxes) v National Provident Institution* [1921] 2 AC 222 at 251–252, as being sufficiently accurate definitions of 'discount' for present purposes:

> '. . . an abatement or deduction from the amount, or from the gross reckoning or *d* value of anything, and, as used in commerce (1.) is defined to mean a deduction (usually at a certain rate per cent.) made for payment before it is due of a bill or account . . . (2.) "the deduction made from the amount of a bill of exchange or promissory note by one who gives value for it before it is due."'

It is the trustees' case, and the judge accepted it, that the relevant transaction was the *e* original issue of the promissory note on 23 May 1969. I differ from the judge as to that. It seems to me that the transaction which gave rise to the receipt by the trustees of the £460,065 was the purchase of the note by the trustees on 20 February 1970, which must, I think, be regarded as a separate transaction. It was in Lord Sumner's words in *Brown's* case at 254–255 the original transaction 'as modified by the introduction of the bona fide holder for value'. It was that second transaction which gave rise to the actual profit which *f* is claimed to be taxable. I see no reason to doubt that such transaction was a 'discount' transaction within the meaning of the word in the dictionary definitions to which I have referred and particularly the definition in relation to commercial usage regarding bills and promissory notes. The trustees acquired the note before maturity at an amount less than its face value. It seems to me to be a plain case of a discount in a strict commercial sense. I see no reason for characterising the note as a premium transaction rather than a *g* discount. The line between discounts and premiums may, in substance, be a slender one. But the fact is that the note in the present case took the form of a discount and the trustees bought it at a discount from its face value. *Davies (Inspector of Taxes) v Premier Investment Co Ltd* [1945] 2 All ER 681, where notes were issued at par and repayable at a premium of 30%, is an example of a premium case.

I proceed then on the basis that this transaction was a discount. Was the profit on the *h* discount an annual profit or gain? Rowlatt J said in *Brown's* case [1919] 2 KB 497 at 506:

> '. . . it is clear that it is not every difference in amount between a sum payable in future and the same sum represented by cash down which is an annual profit or gain by way of discount, even though popularly the word "discount" may be used to describe it. As Sir John Simon [who was leading counsel for one of the taxpayers] pointed out, the difference between the cash and the credit prices of an article *j* bought is commonly described as discount for ready money allowed by the seller, but it is not taxable as income under Case 3.'

In *Brown's* case the profit on the treasury bills (which were substantially in the form of promissory notes), whether arising where the bill was held until maturity or sold prior

to maturity, was held to be taxable under the combined provisions of the Income Tax
a Acts 1842 and 1853 as profits on discounts. In that case, as in this, it was contended by
the taxpayer that the profit was a capital profit (see [1921] 2 AC 222 at 253 per Lord
Atkinson). The House of Lords rejected that. The case has some similarities with the
present but I would accept that in determining whether a receipt is of an income or a
capital nature every case must be decided on its own facts.

At this point I should mention that counsel for the trustees in the court below and in
b opening the appeal in this court expressly accepted that the question whether, on the
facts found, the profit received by the trustees was income or capital was one of law. And
that accordingly, even though the commissioners had found that the receipt was capital,
the matter was at large on the appeal. In the course of his reply in this court, however,
counsel for the trustees, in reliance on the statement of Lord Greene MR in *Lomax
(Inspector of Taxes) v Peter Dixon & Co Ltd* [1943] 2 All ER 255 at 262, [1943] KB 671 at
c 682, submitted that the question was one of fact for the commissioners and that
accordingly the matter was concluded against the Crown by the commissioners' decision.

I do not think that, in the present case, the point is of any consequence. Assuming the
question to be one of fact, the court on appeal from the commissioners can still displace
the decision of the commissioners if there is no evidence to support it or (which really
comes to the same thing) if the only true conclusion which a tribunal, properly instructed
d as to law, could reach on the evidence is contrary to that in fact reached by the
commissioners (see *Edwards (Inspector of Taxes) v Bairstow* [1955] 3 All ER 48, [1956] AC
14). That in my view is the situation in this case.

The basic facts in the present case are simple and are not in dispute. As indicated in
Lomax v Peter Dixon & Co Ltd it was open to the parties when the matter was before the
commissioners to call evidence to indicate the true nature or quality of the sum in
e question. That was not done in this case. We merely have the facts which I have
recounted. The question is: what is the proper conclusion from those facts? In my
opinion the only proper conclusion is that the profit was of an income nature. The onus
was on the trustees to show that the assessment was wrong. But they called no evidence
to demonstrate the basis on which the discounting transaction was entered into. We
know nothing of the genesis of the matter in financial terms. What we do know is that
f no interest was payable as such. It was the unanimous view of the Court of Appeal in
Lomax v Peter Dixon & Co Ltd [1943] 2 All ER 255 at 263, [1943] KB 671 at 683 that
where no interest is payable as such the transaction 'will normally, if not always, be a
discount chargeable under case III, r. 1(b)' (that reference was to the Income Tax Act 1918
but nothing turns on it). I see no reason to doubt the correctness of that opinion. It must,
I think, be a reasonable approach. The holder of the discount must, one assumes, be
g getting a return for his money. It is up to him to demonstrate the capital quality of the
discount if he asserts its existence. As regards the trustees' return on their money, as is
indicated by May LJ in his judgment, the profit which was made by the trustees
represented a return of about $11\frac{1}{2}\%$ per annum on a simple interest basis.

In these circumstances and on the limited facts which we have it seems to me that the
commissioners' conclusion that the profit was of a capital nature is unfounded. The facts
h do not admit of such a conclusion. This was plainly a discount, no interest was payable as
such and there is nothing to indicate that the receipt was other than of an income nature.

Counsel for the trustees, however, presses on us two arguments in support of his case
that this profit is not within the statute. First, as I have mentioned, he contends that the
transaction on which we must concentrate is the original issue of the note. And he says
that that was not a discounting transaction at all; it was, he says, simply part of the
j consideration on a purchase and sale of property. But the fact that the issue of the note
formed part of such consideration seems to me immaterial. I can see no reason why a
discounting transaction should not form part of a larger transaction which is itself a
purchase and sale. Consideration on a purchase and sale can, it seems to me, consist of a
mixture of cash, property in specie, discounts and loans at a commercial rate of interest.
Together they form the consideration. They do not thereby lose their character

individually. I do not, therefore, think it helps the trustees to rely on the original transaction.

Second, reliance is placed on the fact that this was not a short-term note; the note was originally issued in 1969 for a maturity date in 1973. Even after the purchase of the note by the trustees the maturity date was some three years ahead.

As to that, I observe in passing that while in *Brown's* case [1921] 2 AC 222 at 253–254 the bills were short-term bills Lord Atkinson and Lord Simon were evidently of the view that the 'length' of the bills was immaterial. But, in my view, the substantial objection to the point is that, if the trustees wished to assert that the 'length' of the note was material to the question of the profit in terms of capital, they should have brought evidence on the point before the commissioners.

Counsel for the trustees also raises an alternative argument. He says that, if there was an income element in the amount which the trustees received, it was in the nature of interest not discount; the wrong amount was assessed under the wrong head. I do not accept that. If there was an interest element in the transaction that does not prevent it being a discounting transaction. And if it was a discounting transaction the Crown is entitled to succeed unless the profit was of a capital rather than an income nature. In my view the trustees have wholly failed to show that it was. The point I may say was raised for the first time in the Court of Appeal.

In the circumstances, I think the judge reached the right conclusion and I would dismiss the appeal.

MAY LJ. I agree that this appeal should be dismissed. Although we were referred to a number of authorities in the course of the argument, I think that for the purposes of the instant appeal we need only concern ourselves with *Brown (Surveyor of Taxes) v National Provident Institution* [1921] 2 AC 222 on the one hand and *Lomax (Inspector of Taxes) v Peter Dixon & Co Ltd* [1943] 2 All ER 255, [1943] KB 671 on the other.

The tax statute under consideration in *Brown's* case was the Income Tax Act 1842 as revised and applied by the Income Tax Act 1853. The material provision of the 1842 Act so applied was that 'The Profits . . . on all Discounts . . . shall be charged according to the preceding Rule in this Case'. Of the issues which came before the House of Lords for decision in *Brown's* case, the two material ones for the purposes of this present appeal were (1) whether the transactions in Treasury Bills with which that case was concerned were transactions in discounts within the provision of the 1842 Act which I have quoted and (2) whether, when a bill had been sold before maturity, all the profit then made was to be brought into the charge to tax, or whether any part of that profit should properly be regarded as a capital accretion.

All the Law Lords in *Brown's* case were clearly of the opinion that the material Treasury Bill transactions were transactions in discounts within the relevant statutory provision.

In so far as the second issue before them was concerned, however, although it was implicit in most of the speeches, in particular on another point which arose in *Brown's* case but which is not material for the instant appeal, that it is only income as distinct from any capital gain which is taxable under the provisions of the Income Tax Acts, nevertheless in my opinion the ultimate decision on the second issue turned not on this distinction but on the proper construction of the brief phrase from the 1842 Act which I quoted earlier in this judgment. As Viscount Cave said ([1921] 2 AC 222 at 238–239):

'The expression "profit on a discount" is unusual, and . . . is probably elliptical for "profit on . . . (. . . a transaction involving) a discount"; and if one has once embarked on such a transaction, I think that the resulting profit, though enhanced by adventitious circumstances, is all profit on the discount.'

Lord Atkinson said (at 252–253):

'But if the transaction of purchasing and selling such a bill be, as it has been by the Court of Appeal held rightly, I think, to be, a discounting transaction, otherwise a   no part of the difference between the two prices would be profits on a discount, I utterly fail to see how the entire difference between the original price and the enhanced price, which has been obtained, by and through this discount transaction, is not a "profit on discount" within the meaning of [the material statutory provision].'

Lord Sumner put the point even more clearly (at 256):

b   'Similarly I see no warrant for trying to discriminate between the capital used in the transaction and the income obtained from its use. The statute says nothing about it. To discount a bill, even a Treasury Bill, you must have money or money's worth, but whether an accountant would say that it came out of or should be debited to capital or income makes no difference to the fact of discounting. The excess of what is got back to-morrow over what is put in to-day is profit, and it is but rarely that even an economist can tell what is appreciation of capital and what is

c   not. The Acts invite no such curious inquiry as the Court of Appeal directed on this point.'

For my part, therefore, I respectfully do not think that *Brown's* case is of assistance when the real issue in a matter is whether a profit obtained from a discounting transaction is of an income or capital nature, which is the situation in the instant appeal.

d   On the facts of our case I agree, first, that the relevant transaction at which one must look is the purchase of the promissory note by the trustees on 20 February 1970 and, second, that this was clearly a discounting transaction. Further, I think that the question whether the trustees' profit on that discounting transaction was income or a capital gain is a question of fact, not of law. I believe that this will usually be so in cases such as the present, although in some instances, for example where the proper construction of a document is material to the issue, the question may be one of mixed law and fact. On

e   this point I respectfully find substantial assistance from the judgment of Lord Greene MR in *Lomax's* case [1943] 2 All ER 255 at 260, [1943] KB 671 at 677. He said:

'I refer to these problems not for the purpose of attempting to solve them, but in order to show that there can be no general rule that any sum which a lender receives over and above the amount which he lends ought to be treated as income. Each case

f   must, in my opinion, depend on its own facts and evidence *dehors* the contract must always be admissible in order to explain what the contract itself usually disregards, namely, the quality which ought to be attributed to the sum in question.'

I think that in Lord Greene MR's view the question was one of fact. This is apparent from the last paragraph of his judgment, where he said ([1943] 2 All ER 255 at 262–263, [1943] KB 671 at 682–683):

g   'It may be convenient to sum up my conclusions in a few propositions. (i) Where a loan is made at or above such a reasonable commercial rate of interest as is applicable to a reasonably sound security there is no presumption that a "discount" at which the loan is made or a premium at which it is payable is in the nature of interest. (ii) The true nature of the "discount" or the premium (as the case may be)

h   is to be ascertained from all the circumstances of the case and apart from any matter of law which may bear upon the question (such as the interpretation of the contract), will fall to be determined as a matter of fact by the Commissioners. (iii) In deciding the true nature of the "discount" or premium, in so far as it is not conclusively determined by the contract, the following matters together with any other relevant circumstances are important to be considered, viz., the term of the loan, the rate of

j   interest expressly stipulated for, the nature of the capital risk, the extent to which, if at all, the parties expressly took or may reasonably be supposed to have taken the capital risk into account in fixing the terms of the contract. In this summary I have purposely confined myself to a case such as the present where a reasonable commercial rate of interest is charged. Where no interest is payable as such, different considerations will, of course, apply. In such a case, a "discount" will normally, if not always, be a discount chargeable under case III, r. 1(b). Similarly, a "premium" will normally, if not always, be interest. But it is neither necessary nor desirable to do more than to point out the distinction between such cases and the case of a contract similar to that which we are considering. For these reasons I am of opinion that the Special Commissioners came to the right conclusion and that their decision ought to be restored.'

The evidence available to us on this issue, which as I have said I think to be one of fact, is certainly not extensive. Indeed, having regard to the concession made by counsel for the trustees, wrongly as I respectfully think, that the question was one of law, this is not surprising. However we do know that the promissory note carried no interest; as Lord Greene MR said, in such circumstances the 'discount' will normally, if not always, be a discount of an income nature chargeable to tax. Secondly, we know that the trustees made a profit of £460,065 on an outlay of £1,321,004 in a period of three years. This represents a return of about $11\frac{1}{2}\%$ per annum on a simple interest basis, somewhat less if the interest were notionally compounded. In my judgment the decision by the Special Commissioners on the facts of this case that the profit on the material discounting transaction had been of a capital rather than an income nature was plainly wrong, even on the limited evidence before them and us, and was thus one which in law we can reverse, notwithstanding the well-known decision in *Edwards (Inspector of Taxes) v Bairstow* [1955] 3 All ER 48, [1956] AC 14. Alternatively, the onus of showing that the profit was of a capital and not an income nature was on the trustees and this they clearly failed to discharge.

For the reasons which I have sought to outline, which are however in some respects different from those relied on by the judge below, I too would dismiss this appeal.

WALLER LJ. I agree.

Appeal dismissed.

Solicitors: *Stephenson Harwood* (for the trustees); *Solicitor of Inland Revenue*.

Edwina Epstein   Barrister.

a
R v South Tameside Magistrates' Court, ex parte Rowland

QUEEN'S BENCH DIVISION
ROBERT GOFF LJ AND GLIDEWELL J
5 MAY 1983

b
Criminal law – Plea – Withdrawal of plea of guilty – Plea in unequivocal terms – Magistrates concluding defendant seeking to change plea in hope of avoiding custodial sentence – Whether magistrates entitled to refuse to allow withdrawal of plea.

The applicant appeared before magistrates charged with burglary. She was not legally
c represented. The charge was read to her and she indicated that she understood it and consented to being dealt with summarily. The applicant then entered a plea of guilty and asked to have a similar offence taken into consideration. The magistrates, instead of passing sentence immediately, told her that they were considering passing a custodial sentence and asked her if in those circumstances she would like to be legally represented. She said that she would and the magistrates adjourned sentence for a week to enable her
d to obtain representation. She consulted a solicitor who, on the basis of what she was told by the applicant, advised her to withdraw her plea of guilty and enter a plea of not guilty. When the applicant again appeared before the magistrates she sought to change her plea. The magistrates concluded that her original plea had been unequivocal and that a likely reason for her application was a desire to avoid a custodial sentence. They accordingly refused to allow her to change her plea and convicted her. The applicant sought an order
e of certiorari to quash the magistrates' decision to refuse to allow her to change her plea.

Held – The magistrates were entitled to balance the instructions the applicant had given her solicitor after the first hearing against the prospect that the applicant had changed her story because of the possibility that she might receive a custodial sentence, and accordingly they were entitled to exercise their discretion not to allow the applicant to
f withdraw her unequivocal plea of guilty. The application would therefore be dismissed (see p 692 g j to p 693 b, post).

R v Durham Quarter Sessions, ex p Virgo [1952] 1 All ER 466, *S (an infant) v Manchester City Recorder* [1969] 3 All ER 1230 and *P Foster (Haulage) Ltd v Roberts* [1978] 2 All ER 751 distinguished.

g **Notes**
For the court's discretion to allow a change of plea, see 29 Halsbury's Laws (4th edn) para 360, and for cases on the subject, see 14(1) Digest (Reissue) 332–333, 2621–2635.

Cases referred to in judgments
Foster (P) (Haulage) Ltd v Roberts [1978] 2 All ER 751, DC.
h *R v Durham Quarter Sessions, ex p Virgo* [1952] 1 All ER 466, [1952] 2 QB 1, DC.
S (an infant) v Manchester City Recorder [1969] 3 All ER 1230, [1971] AC 481, [1970] 2 WLR 21, HL.

Application for judicial review
Jacquelyn Ann Rowland applied, with the leave of Stephen Brown J granted on 18
j January 1983, for an order of certiorari to quash a decision made by the South Tameside Magistrates' Court on 27 October 1982 refusing to allow the applicant to withdraw her plea of guilty to a charge of burglary entered before the court on 20 October 1982 and enter a plea of not guilty. The facts are set out in the judgment of Glidewell J.

Richard Humphry for the applicant.
Peter Openshaw for the respondent.

GLIDEWELL J (delivering the first judgment at the invitation of Robert Goff LJ). The applicant seeks an order of certiorari to quash a decision made by the South Tameside Magistrates' Court on 27 October 1982 not to allow her to withdraw a plea of guilty to a charge of burglary which she had entered a week previously on 20 October before the same court and to substitute a plea of not guilty.

The circumstances which led to her appearance before the court were these. On 30 September 1982 the applicant, who was then aged just 18 years, together with a younger girl, who was 16, went to the flat of an old lady in Hyde, and they were permitted into the flat by the occupant, because the younger girl had visited her previously and on that occasion had given her what purported to be tickets for a coffee afternoon. The applicant knew about the previous visit of the younger girl; indeed, she had forged these tickets in agreement with the younger girl. They were not tickets for a coffee afternoon; there was no coffee afternoon at all.

On 30 September the two of them went to the flat and told the old lady that the coffee afternoon had been cancelled and she then invited the two girls in. She gave them a cup of coffee. While they were sitting and talking, the younger girl asked if she could go to the toilet, but what she in fact did was to steal the lady's handbag, take it into the lavatory with her and remove £21 from it. The lady then became suspicious. She found that her handbag was missing from where she had put it. She hammered on the lavatory door, but when it was opened the younger girl ran out. The applicant stayed for a short time and then followed her friend. They shared the money and spent some of it.

Later the same day the police arrested both of them at the applicant's flat. The applicant made a statement to the police setting out the facts more or less as I have summarised them, though not saying in terms that she knew that the younger girl was going to steal the money before she did. She did, however, make it clear that the tickets had been made by her and she also made it clear in the statement that when she left she told the old lady that she would get someone to come and see her, which was a lie.

She originally appeared before the magistrates in Tameside on 20 October 1982. She was not then represented. We have an affidavit before us of Mr Rusdale, who was then sitting. He says, and of course we accept, that she was asked if she wanted to be represented by a solicitor and she said that she was not so represented and did not want to be. Mr Rusdale then says: 'The Applicant was asked if she was ready for the case to proceed that morning and she indicated that she was.' The charge was then read to her. The charge was that on Thursday, 30 September 1982 she entered as a trespasser a dwelling in Hyde, and stole therein £21, the moneys of the old lady. It was a perfectly clear charge. The applicant was asked if she understood the charge and she said she did. The solicitor then appearing for the prosecuting authority outlined the facts of the prosecution case briefly and asked the court to deal with the matter summarily. The applicant was asked if she consented to it being dealt with summarily and she said that she did. The court proceeded to treat it as a summary trial. She was then asked how she pleaded and she pleaded guilty. The prosecuting solicitor then outlined the facts in more detail and he read, or certainly gave the substance of, the written statement which was in the applicant's own handwriting. It was not a case where the police officer had written it out for her.

The applicant had already given details of another offence of theft of which she was guilty relating to another even older lady. The prosecution told the magistrates that it was understood that she wished to have this offence taken into consideration, so at the conclusion of the prosecution case she was asked if she did indeed wish to have that taken into consideration and she said that she did. She was then asked by the chairman if she wished to say anything about the offences or her personal circumstances and she said: 'I'm sorry.' The magistrates then retired to consider sentence and they came to the conclusion, having regard not merely to the offences but also to her record which had been put before them, that they ought to consider a custodial sentence. But, instead of coming back in and passing such a sentence immediately, they took the very proper course of returning to court and telling the applicant that they were considering such a a sentence (I think they used the word 'custodial', because it is clear that at first the applicant did not understand what they meant and I suppose they then said 'prison' or 'borstal'). They asked her whether she would now like to be represented by a solicitor and she said that she would. So they adjourned sentence for a week to enable her to be legally represented.

b On 25 October the applicant went to consult a Miss Fitzpatrick, who is a solicitor in Hyde, and during the course of the interview with Miss Fitzpatrick she told her that she had not known that the younger girl had intended to steal anything before the younger girl did so. Miss Fitzpatrick formed the view, correctly of course, that if that was true the applicant was not guilty of the charge to which she had pleaded guilty. She therefore advised the applicant that she should apply to the court for leave to change her plea to one of not guilty, that is to say to withdraw the guilty plea. Miss Fitzpatrick advised both the clerk to the magistrates and the prosecuting solicitors that she was going to make an application to this effect and, when the matter came back before the magistrates on 27 c October, she did indeed make such an application.

It is right to say that the basis of the application which she made, so we are told, was not that the plea had been equivocal in the first place, but that the magistrates had a discretion to allow the plea of guilty to be withdrawn; that on the instructions which she, Miss Fitzpatrick, had received, if correct, the applicant was not guilty and therefore d that it would be a proper exercise of the magistrates' discretion to allow that plea to be withdrawn. The application was opposed by the solicitor then appearing for the prosecution. The magistrates were referred to the two authorities which in our view are the most germane. The leading case of S (an infant) v Manchester City Recorder [1969] 3 All ER 1230, [1971] AC 481 is authority for the proposition that even where a plea is unequivocal the magistrates nevertheless have discretion to allow a plea of guilty to be e withdrawn at any time before sentence in appropriate circumstances. They were also referred to the more recent case of P Foster (Haulage) Ltd v Roberts [1978] 2 All ER 751. That was a case in this court, with Lord Widgery CJ agreeing with the judgment of O'Connor J. During the course of his judgment O'Connor J said (at 754–755):

f 'In my judgment, a clear distinction must be drawn between the duties of a court faced with an equivocal plea at the time it is made and the exercise of the court's jurisdiction to permit a defendant to change an unequivocal plea of guilty at a later stage of the proceedings. A court cannot accept an equivocal plea of guilty: it has no discretion in the matter; faced with an equivocal plea the court must either obtain an unequivocal plea of guilty or enter a plea of not guilty. For a plea to be equivocal the defendant must add to the plea of guilty a qualification which, if true, may show that he is not guilty of the offence charged. An example of this type of qualification g is found where a man charged with handling a stolen motor car pleads "guilty to handling but I didn't know it was stolen". It is not every qualification which makes a plea of guilty equivocal; for example, the burglar charged with stealing spoons, forks and a camera, who pleads "guilty but I did not take the camera" is making an unequivocal plea to burglary. Once an unequivocal plea of guilty has been made, then the position is entirely different. From this stage forward until sentence has h been passed the court has power to permit the plea of guilty to be changed to one of not guilty, but the exercise of this power is entirely a matter of discretion. This is clearly stated by all of their lordships in S (an infant) v Manchester City Recorder. In that case the appellant, aged 16, had pleaded guilty to attempted rape before a juvenile court; the hearing was adjourned for three weeks for reports and on the adjourned hearing the appellant was legally represented and his solicitor applied to j withdraw the plea of guilty on the ground that the youth had made many previous spurious confessions and that his confession of guilt was unsafe. The justices refused the application on the ground that they were functi officio and had no power to grant it. That decision was upheld in the Divisional Court but the House of Lords allowed the appeal.'

Going back to the magistrates on 27 October, the chairman on that day, Miss King, says in her affidavit that having been referred to those authorities they were advised by their clerk in open court 'that to allow a change of plea was a matter for our absolute discretion, and that once an unequivocal plea had been entered the discretionary power should be exercised judicially, very sparingly and only in clear cases'. If I may say so, that advice seems to me to be correct and clear. She goes on: 'There was no doubt in our minds that the original plea was an unequivocal plea of guilty.' She gave reasons for that and one of them was that the applicant admitted one other similar offence, she made clear and total admissions in open court and she apologised, all of which, according to the chairman, indicated an unequivocal plea of guilty.

The chairman then goes on:

> 'Despite this we still considered that we had a discretion to allow a change of plea and we considered whether to exercise this discretion. We took into account that one likely reason for the application was the Applicant's desire to avoid the custodial sentence that had been indicated to her at the conclusion of the first hearing. We declined to exercise our discretion to permit the change of plea.'

Before us, counsel for the applicant, who has argued this case as fully and clearly as could possibly be done on her behalf, has submitted, firstly, that there was material before the magistrates on which they should have concluded that the plea was equivocal and, secondly, if that were so, that they exercised their discretion unjudicially. So far as the first of those matters are concerned he relies on the statement made by the applicant to the police as containing material which he suggests should at least have put the magistrates on inquiry whether the plea of guilty was a proper plea or not. I do not agree. In my view, there is nothing in the statement which would indicate to the magistrates that the applicant was saying that she did not know that the younger girl intended to steal on 30 September. It is perfectly true that the statement does not say that she did know that the younger girl intended to steal. The statement is silent and neutral on that point. But there is material in the statement which indicates guilty intention, at least to this extent: she admitted that she forged the tickets which were the means by which, in the first place, the younger girl on the previous occasion had gained admission to the flat and thus the means by which on 30 September both girls had gained admission to the flat. She also admitted that after the younger girl had left she told the old lady a lie by means of which she herself gained exit from the flat. Accordingly, there was, if anything, some material in the statement to support her plea of guilty. One need not go as far as that. It is sufficient to say that in my view there was not any material on which the magistrates ought to have been put on inquiry whether the plea was equivocal or not. Thus I entirely agree with the magistrates' first conclusion, which was that the plea was an unequivocal plea of guilty.

That being so, I come to counsel's second point: did the magistrates exercise their discretion judicially? It is quite clear that they did exercise their discretion. They gave the matter anxious thought, having received proper advice. There may well be instances where it become entirely apparent from something said by the defendant before the magistrates that he or she had misunderstood the nature of the offence. It seems to me that *R v Durham Quarter Sessions, ex p Virgo* [1952] 1 All ER 466, [1952] 2 QB 1 was probably such a case where, after pleading guilty to receiving stolen goods, a defendant (using O'Connor J's example in *P Foster (Haulage) Ltd v Roberts* [1978] 2 All ER 751 at 755), later says something which indicates quite clearly that he did not know the goods were stolen. Then it may very well be that, albeit it would be within the magistrates' discretion whether to allow the plea to be withdrawn or not, in normal circumstances the discretion would only be exercised one way.

But this present case is not such a case at all. The magistrates, in my view rightly, balanced the instructions which the applicant had given to her solicitor after 20 October against the prospect that she was changing her story because of the possibility that she might be sentenced to a custodial sentence. They were, in my view, perfectly entitled to a come to the conclusion to which they did come and they were thus perfectly entitled to exercise their discretion not to allow the plea of guilty to be withdrawn. With that exercise of discretion, this court therefore cannot interfere. The application in my judgment must fail and it should be dismissed.

ROBERT GOFF LJ. I agree.

b *Application dismissed.*

Solicitors: *Chronnell Fitzpatrick & Jones*, Hyde (for the applicant); *D S Gandy*, Manchester (for the respondent).

N P Metcalfe Esq   Barrister.

c

Goldman v Thai Airways International Ltd

COURT OF APPEAL, CIVIL DIVISION
EVELEIGH, O'CONNOR AND PURCHAS LJJ
d 8–10, 14–17 MARCH, 5 MAY 1983

Carriage by air – Carriage of passengers – International carriage – Limitation of carrier's liability – Aircraft on international flight entering area of severe clear air turbulence – Pilot failing to switch on seat belt sign contrary to flight rules – Plaintiff suffering personal injuries and bringing action for damages against carrier – Whether carrier's liability limited – Whether
e *carrier's liability unlimited by reason of pilot's omission amounting to conduct done 'recklessly and with knowledge that damage would probably result' – Carriage by Air Act 1961, Sch 1, arts 22(1), 25.*

The plaintiff was a passenger on a flight from London to Bangkok aboard an aircraft owned and operated by the defendant airline. Before leaving London the pilot of the
f aircraft was provided with a weather chart forecasting two areas of moderate clear air turbulence on the aircraft's flight path. The defendants' flight operations manual contained instructions for the 'fasten seat belts' sign ordering passengers to fasten their seat belts to be lit during all flying in turbulent air and when turbulence could be expected. During the flight the pilot failed to illuminate the seat belt sign when the aircraft entered an area for which moderate clear air turbulence had been forecast and
g when severe turbulence was encountered in that area the plaintiff, whose seat belt was not fastened, was thrown from his seat and sustained severe injuries. The plaintiff brought an action for damages against the defendants under the Warsaw Convention, as amended at The Hague in 1955 and as set out in Sch 1 to the Carriage by Air Act 1961. Article 22(1)[a] of the convention limited the amount of damages recoverable to approximately £11,800, but art 25[b] provided that the limitation on the amount
h recoverable did not apply if it was shown that 'the damage resulted from an act or omission of the carrier [which was] done with intent to cause damage or recklessly and with knowledge that damage would probably result'. The defendants contended, inter alia, that if damages were recoverable they ought not to exceed the amount specified in art 22(1). The judge found that the pilot should have switched on the seat belt sign ten minutes before entering the area of clear air turbulence and further found that the pilot
j had deliberately disregarded the instructions on the use of seat belts set out in the flight operations manual and that since they were instructions designed for the safety of the

---

a   Article 22(1), so far as material, provides: 'In the carriage of persons the liability of the carrier for each passenger is limited to the sum of [£11,799·00] . . .'
b   Article 25 is set out at p 696 *f*, post

passengers his conduct amounted to recklessness. The judge accordingly held that the plaintiff's claim for damages was not limited under art 22(1), since it came within the provisions of art 25, and he awarded damages of some £41,000. The defendants appealed.

Held – Under art 25 of the Warsaw Convention a plaintiff was not freed from the limitation on the amount of damages imposed by art 22(1) unless he proved (a) that the damage suffered by him resulted from an act or omission of the defendant carrier, (b) that the defendant intended by the act or omission to cause damage or was aware that damage would probably result but nevertheless had acted or failed to act regardless of that probability, and (c) that the damage complained of was of the kind of damage known to be the probable result of the act or omission. In determining whether an act or omission had been done 'recklessly' the court had to consider the nature of the risk involved, and moreover, since the reckless act or omission had to be done 'with knowledge that damage would probably result' from the act or omission if damages were to be at large, the test of recklessness was subjective and the court could not attribute to the defendant knowledge which another person in the same situation might have possessed or which, on an objective basis, he himself ought to have possessed. It followed that, in order for the pilot's omission to amount to recklessness, it had to be shown not only that prudent flying required him to switch on the seat belt sign before entering the area of clear air turbulence but also that he had knowledge that injury would probably result from his failure to do so. On the facts, it had not been shown that the instructions in the flight operations manual would necessarily be interpreted as meaning that the pilot was obliged to switch on the seat belt sign before entering an area of clear air turbulence, and on the evidence there was nothing to show that the pilot knew that damage would probably result from his failure to do so. It followed that the plaintiff had not shown that his claim was within the provisions of art 25 and therefore damages would be limited as provided by art 22(1). The appeal would accordingly be allowed (see p 698 h j, p 699 b to f, p 700 d e and g to j, p 703 d, p 704 a b f h j and p 705 a and e to h, post).

R v Caldwell [1981] 1 All ER 961 and *R v Lawrence (Stephen)* [1981] 1 All ER 974 considered.

Notes

For the liability of international carriers by air, see 2 Halsbury's Laws (4th edn) paras 1376–1396, and for cases on the subject, see 8(2) Digest (Reissue) 604–606, 31–41.

For the Carriage by Air Act 1961, Sch 1, arts 22, 25, see 2 Halsbury's Statutes (3rd edn) 617, 618.

Cases referred to in judgments

Fothergill v Monarch Airlines Ltd [1980] 2 All ER 696, [1981] AC 251, [1980] 3 WLR 209, HL.

R v Caldwell [1981] 1 All ER 961, [1982] AC 341, [1981] 2 WLR 509, HL.

R v Lawrence (Stephen) [1981] 1 All ER 974, [1982] AC 510, [1981] 2 WLR 524, HL.

Cases also cited

British Rlys Board v Herrington [1972] 1 All ER 749, [1972] AC 877, HL.

Bulmer (HP) Ltd v J Bollinger SA [1974] 2 All ER 1226, [1974] Ch 401, CA.

Collins v British Airways Board [1982] 1 All ER 302, [1982] QB 734, CA.

Emery v Sabena (1968) 22 RFDA 184.

EMI Records Ltd v Ian Cameron Wallace Ltd [1982] 2 All ER 980, [1983] Ch 59.

Grove, Re, Vaucher v Treasury Solicitor (1888) 40 Ch D 216, CA.

Horabin v British Overseas Airways Corp [1952] 2 All ER 1016.

Joyce v Yeomans [1981] 2 All ER 21, [1981] 1 WLR 549, CA.

Preston v Preston [1982] 1 All ER 41, [1982] Fam 17.

R v Hyam [1974] 2 All ER 41, [1975] AC 55, HL.

Rustenberg Platinum Mines Ltd v South African Airways [1979] 1 Lloyd's Rep 19, CA.

Appeal

a The defendants, Thai Airways International Ltd, appealed against the judgment of Chapman J dated 31 March 1981 whereby he gave judgment for the plaintiff, Philip Goldman, for the sum of £41,852·42 with interest and costs in the plaintiff's action for damages for personal injuries and special damage arising out of an accident on 1 July 1977 on board an aircraft belonging to the defendants. The facts are set out in the judgment of Eveleigh LJ.

b
Charles Sparrow QC and *Robert Webb* for the defendants.
Robert L Johnson QC and *Hugh Bennett* for the plaintiff.

Cur adv vult

c
5 May. The following judgments were delivered.

EVELEIGH LJ. On 1 July 1977 the plaintiff was on a Thai Airways DC8 which left Heathrow for Bangkok. It had scheduled landings at Amsterdam and Karachi. At 1425 GMT when it was about 80 nautical miles north-west of Istanbul the plaintiff, to d use his words, felt a series of bumps which were sufficient to make him desire to fasten his seat belt. As he was in the act of doing so he was thrown from his seat and struck the ceiling. The aircraft had encountered clear air turbulence (CAT). About 13 passengers and crew members struck the roof. A stewardess was unconscious. One passenger had a broken arm. The plaintiff himself sustained a serious injury to his lower spine in the lumbar region. A Thai doctor who was himself injured gave some assistance to the e plaintiff, but told the steward who informed the pilot, Captain Swang, that he needed medical attention and treatment right away. The nearest practicable landing place was Ankara. The pilot decided to fly on to Karachi. At Karachi the plaintiff was given a pain-killing injection. The plane was given a short visual inspection. It took about 17 minutes. Nothing abnormal was found and the plane continued its journey. The plaintiff agreed to go on to Bangkok. There he was taken to hospital.

f Before leaving Heathrow and again at Amsterdam the captain was provided with a significant weather chart for the journey. The charts forecasted two areas of CAT for the aircraft's flight path. They were delineated on the chart. The first, designated CAT 1, stretched from east of Ankara to Italy with an average width of some 215 nautical miles. The second, designated CAT 3, was shown as a narrow corridor covering Sicily and the foot of Italy and running at a constant width first eastward and then turning north-east g about Mesopotamia over the Caspian Sea and into Siberia. Both areas of CAT were classified as moderate.

The peculiar feature of CAT is that it is not detectable before it is encountered. By way of contrast, thunderstorm turbulence can be seen. However it is possible to warn a pilot that he may encounter CAT in a particular area and consequently that he should be on his guard against it. A forecast of CAT in an area does not mean that an encounter with h turbulence is inevitable. The evidence was to the effect that a plane could pass through the area for a number of journeys in succession without meeting it at all. It was described as turbulent air, swirling and twisting about like a snake which may or may not foul the flight path.

Three degrees of CAT were mentioned: slight, moderate and severe. While it is the practice of the weather charts to give a forecast of moderate or severe CAT, they do not j indicate areas where only light CAT may occur.

The following specifications for turbulence reporting have been defined by the International Civil Aviation Organisation (ICAO).

Moderate turbulence There may be moderate changes in aircraft attitude and/or altitude, but the aircraft remains in positive control at all times; usually small variations in airspeed; changes in accelerometer readings of 0·5 G to 1·0 G at the aircraft's centre of gravity; difficulty in walking; occupants feel strain against seat belts; loose objects move about.

Severe turbulence   Abrupt changes in aircraft attitude and/or altitude; aircraft may be out of control for short periods; usually large variations in airspeed; change in accelerometer readings greater than 1·0 G at the aircraft's centre of gravity; occupants are forced violently against seat belts; loose objects are tossed about.

It is extremely difficult to give other than a general indication of the extent to which a pilot in the course of his flying career would be likely to encounter turbulence of the three different classifications. In cross-examination of Captain Pritchard, counsel for the defendants put to him certain figures which had been produced in a Lufthansa report on the strength of answers given by their pilots in a questionnaire. In about 6% of all flight time some turbulence was experienced. However, this 6% included thunderstorm turbulence, orographic (mountainous) turbulence, as well as CAT. CAT accounted for 45% of the turbulence encountered, thunderstorm for 30% and orographic for 25%. It then appeared that of all turbulence experienced, 79% was light, 20% moderate and 1% severe.

I do not obtain any great assistance from these figures. If figures were to be of any assistance, we would wish to know how often severe turbulence is encountered when only moderate turbulence is forecast. However, the figures do indicate that severe air turbulence is a relatively rare occurrence, and to this extent they tie in with the evidence given in the case. Captain Pritchard, with 30 years of flying experience, had only once encountered severe air turbulence. Captain Price, with 12,000 flying hours, had never experienced it, but he had frequently flown through areas where CAT was forecast.

The plaintiff's claim was governed by the provisions of the Warsaw Convention as amended at The Hague in 1955 which is made applicable to the case by s 1(1) of the Carriage by Air Act 1961. At the trial the defendants sought to avoid all liability by asserting that they were without fault in accordance with art 21. Alternatively, they claimed that they were only liable to pay limited damages under the provisions of art 22. The judge however held that there was no limit applicable to the plaintiff's claim because he had successfully brought his case within the provisions of art 25 which provides:

'The limits of liability specified in Article 22 shall not apply if it is proved that the damage resulted from an act or omission of the carrier, his servants or agents, done with intent to cause damage or recklessly and with knowledge that damage would probably result; provided that, in the case of such act or omission of a servant or agent, it is also proved that he was acting within the scope of his employment.'

The judge found that the pilot should have illuminated the 'fasten seat belts' sign ten minutes before entering the CAT 1 area. He accepted the evidence of the expert witness called for the plaintiff. Moreover, the defendants' flight operations manual contained the following instructions:

'10.3 Use of Seat Belts. The passengers must use their seat belts and the sign "FASTEN SEAT BELTS" should be lit—During taxiing, take-off and landing—During all flying in turbulent air and when turbulence can be expected.'

The judge found that those instructions were disregarded by the pilot and, seeing that they were instructions which were designed for the safety of the passengers, it was reckless for the pilot to disregard them. He quoted the words of Lord Diplock in *R v Caldwell* [1981] 1 All ER 961 at 967, [1982] AC 341 at 354 where he said:

'In my opinion, a person charged with an offence under [s 1(1) of the Criminal Damage Act 1971] is "reckless as to whether or not any property would be destroyed or damaged" if (1) he does an act which in fact creates an obvious risk that property will be destroyed or damaged and (2) when he does the act he either has not given any thought to the possibility of there being any such risk or has recognised that there was some risk involved and has none the less gone on to do it.'

Having quoted those words the judge said: 'That is the definition which I think has now
a to be regarded as of general application and which I apply in the present case.'

He also relied on the words of Lord Hailsham LC in *R v Lawrence (Stephen)* [1981] 1 All
ER 974 at 978, [1982] AC 510 at 520 where he said:

> 'It only surprises me that there should have been any question regarding the
> existence of mens rea in relation to the words "reckless", "recklessly" or "recklessness".
> Unlike most English words it has been in the English language as a word in general
b > use at least since the eighth century AD almost always with the same meaning,
> applied to a person or conduct evincing a state of mind stopping short of deliberate
> intention, and going beyond mere inadvertence, or, in its modern though not its
> etymological and original sense, mere carelessness.'

As to the phrase 'with knowledge that damage would probably result', the judge said
c this:

> 'The probability of the result must be read as qualifying the nature of the act, and
> if the nature of the act is to make the damage probable (I agree it is not "possible",
> but "probable") provided the concurrent circumstances for impact or damage are
> there, then the probability of damage is fulfilled.'

d He said that the accident occurred in an area where CAT existed. Exactly where it was,
was unknown. He then said: 'It seems to me that damage then would probably almost
inevitably result if in fact there is CAT there.' (As I understand it, 'there' means actually
in the flight path.)

As to the nature of the probable damage, he said that the knowledge is fulfilled by
showing that 'any damage' would probably result and not 'the damage'. He went on to
e say:

> 'That is made abundantly plain by the French text, which is paramount in this,
> where the distinction is drawn in terms between what is said in line 2, "le dommage"
> and "un dommage". So knowledge that damage of any sort may result as a
> probability, not necessarily the predominant probability, is sufficient to satisfy the
> section.'
f

He said that, as in moderate turbulence, things may be moved about and there is
difficulty in walking. Then there is the kind of turbulence as a result of which a person
may be lurched into a seat and twist his ankle. He said:

> 'Similarly if they have got a glass of wine sitting on their tray in front of them, if
> the glass falls off because of turbulence, which may easily happen, he may cut his
g > leg. That is damage . . . Any sort of damage, it seems to me, is sufficient to meet the
> requirement . . .'

I think one can summarise the judge's conclusion in this way: the pilot, having been
informed by the weather forecast that CAT was expected, wilfully disregarded the
instructions in the flight operations manual when he knew that they were designed for
h the passengers' safety; he knew that damage of some kind would probably result if the
risk (ie of encountering CAT), which he was taking, materialised; it was immaterial
whether or not the pilot actually knew that injury would probably result from his
omission in the circumstances as he, the pilot, saw them.

The basic findings on which the judge relied were as follows: (1) that when an area of
CAT was forecast across the aircraft's flight path then turbulence was to be expected; (2)
j that the flight operations manual required seat belts to be worn in such an area; (3) that
this precaution was necessary because turbulence and, in particular, moderate turbulence
could develop into something more intense than its basic definition, and without any
adequate warning.

The defendants' contention, based on the evidence of their expert witnesses, was this.
(1) A forecast indicated only a possibility of turbulence. It was indeed accepted on both

sides that there could be many successive flights through a CAT predicted area without
encountering it at all. (2) It was for the pilot to decide whether or not he actually expected
CAT. Severe or moderate CAT would be preceded by light turbulence and the pilot
concentrating on the situation would decide whether he could expect it to build up into
moderate turbulence or die away. In this way it was for him to decide when to switch on
the seat belt sign. In cross-examination the following was put to Captain Pritchard:
'When one enters a zone of clear air turbulence, one usually first encounters a series of
minor shocks that serve as a warning and allow the pilot time to caution his passengers
to be sure to remain seated and have their seat belts fastened.' He answered: 'I wouldn't
quarrel with that.' (3) The pilot had no reason to suppose that he would not be able to
give passengers a timely warning to fasten their seat belts.

The approach of the plaintiff's experts, which the judge accepted, is summarised by
Captain Pritchard who said:

'Clear air turbulence forecast is clear air turbulence. It is undetectable and it's
never detectable in its severity, so clear air turbulence, moderate clear air turbulence,
could well be severe clear air turbulence.'

The judge saw and heard the expert witnesses. He concluded that he preferred the
evidence of the plaintiff's experts. I can find no valid reason for saying that he was wrong
in his preference and I therefore would not disturb the finding that the correct procedure
was for seat belts to be fastened before entering a CAT area. I am also not prepared to
disagree with his interpretation of the words of the flight operations manual, namely
that the phrase 'when turbulence can be expected' is equivalent to saying 'when
turbulence is forecast'. I would not go so far as to say that when something is forecast it
is expected. I think of the verb expect as meaning 'to regard as certain or likely to happen:
to anticipate'. However, we are not construing a legal document and we are concerned
with the words 'can be expected' and not 'is expected'.

I must first consider the judge's interpretation of art 25 of the Warsaw Convention as
amended at The Hague in 1955. His interpretation was influenced, perhaps (as he saw it)
governed, by the two cases which he cited. However, I do not think that much assistance
is to be gained from decided cases where the meaning of statutes containing the words
'recklessly' or 'recklessness' has to be discovered. In construing an English statute, the
first thing to do is to consider the meaning of the words themselves. While decided cases
may be resorted to for assistance in the case of doubt, it must always be remembered that
a word will have a different meaning or shade of meaning depending on its context. It is
therefore dangerous to examine the meaning of a word in isolation and then to adopt an
isolated meaning given to it in a previous case where it has been considered as a step in
the solution of the meaning of some different phrase.

There is another reason in the present case why decisions on English statutes, if resorted
to at all, should be treated with the greatest caution. We are not concerned to construe
an English statute. We have to determine the meaning of a convention which has been
incorporated into English law by a statute, namely the Carriage by Air Act 1961. The
approach to such a construction is set out in *Fothergill v Monarch Airlines Ltd* [1980] 2 All
ER 696, [1981] AC 251.

I say at once that, reading art 25 as a whole for the moment and not pausing to give an
isolated meaning to the word 'recklessly', the article requires the plaintiff to prove the
following: (1) that the damage resulted from an act or omission; (2) that it was done with
intent to cause damage, or (3) that it was done when the doer was aware that damage
would probably result, but he did so regardless of that probability; (4) that the damage
complained of is the kind of damage known to be the probable result. The judge took a
different view. We have been told that the Belgian Cour de Cassation has adopted a
subjective approach to the meaning of the article and required proof of actual knowledge
on the part of the pilot, while the French Cour de Cassation has taken the objective
approach. We have not been shown those decisions. However, in such a situation it is

clearly not enough for me to say that I attribute the above meaning to the words because
that is how I understand them. I am called on to justify my reading.

When conduct is stigmatised as reckless, it is because it engenders the risk of
undesirable consequences. When a person acts recklessly he acts in a manner which
indicates a decision to run the risk or a mental attitude of indifference to its existence.
This is the ordinary meaning of the word as I understand it and, as it seems to me, Lord
Diplock and Lord Hailsham LC understood it in the quotations above referred to. One
cannot therefore decide whether or not an act or omission is done recklessly without
considering the nature of the risk involved. In the present case the omission relied on
was the failure to order seat belts to be fastened. The risk with which we are concerned,
therefore, is the risk of injury to the passenger whose belt should have been fastened. If
the article had stopped at the word 'recklessly' I would have been prepared to say that on
the judge's findings the plaintiff had proved his case. This is because, on those findings,
the pilot had deliberately ignored his instructions which he knew were for the safety of
the passengers, and thus demonstrated a willingness to accept a risk. Also it might he
said that he thought that he knew better than those responsible for the manual and,
while this might mean that he in his own mind saw no risk, he was in fact taking the
risk that his judgment was better than that of other experts. If this is so, I would be
prepared to say, as did the judge, that a deliberate disregard of the rule must be considered
recklessness in the circumstances of the case. I shall consider later whether or not a
deliberate disregard of instructions has been proved. However, the doing of the act or
omission is not only qualified by the adverb 'recklessly', but also by the adverbial phrase
'with knowledge that damage would probably result'. If the pilot did not know that
damage would probably result from his omission, I cannot see that we are entitled to
attribute to him knowledge which another pilot might have possessed or which he
himself should have possessed. I appreciate that when introducing an English version to
coincide with a French text there is naturally an inclination to follow the pattern of that
text and where possible to avoid a free translation. Even so, I cannot believe that lawyers
who intended to convey the meaning of the well-known phrase 'when he knew or ought
to have known' would have adopted 'with knowledge'.

I had thought that I had found support for my reading of art 25 when I looked at the
French text and saw the words 'avec conscience'. I thought that phrase imported the
meaning of awareness. In view of the decision of the French Cour de Cassation I hesitate
to use the French text to support my interpretation of art 25. However, I do see
confirmation in the travaux préparatoires.

At the ICAO international conference at The Hague in 1955–56 a draft of art 25
prepared at Rio de Janiero was considered. This provided for unlimited liability only
where there was proved an intent to cause damage. Widely differing opinions were
expressed, but there seemed to be a general consensus that some further restriction of
liability would be possible if the limits imposed by art 21 were increased. At the same
time it was said that the Rio de Janiero proposal would allow immunity in cases where
there clearly was moral turpitude. The Norwegian delegation submitted a proposal that
after the words 'done with intent to cause damage' there should be added 'or recklessly
by not caring whether or not damage was likely to result'. In discussion reference was
made to the question of whether or not actual knowledge of the risk would be required.
The record reads:

> 'Mr Garnault (France) said . . . The text of the Working Group included the idea
> of "recklessness" as well as the idea of "without caring that damage would probably
> result". For some delegates, the latter words meant that the author of the fault had
> knowledge of the damage which would probably result. Therefore, he suggested
> that the words "without caring", in the text of the Working Group be replaced by
> the words "with knowledge".'

A vote was taken as to which of the following three phrases should be added to the
requirement that an intention should be proved: (a) 'and has acted recklessly'; (b) 'and

has acted recklessly and knew or should have known that damage would probably result'; (c) 'and has acted recklessly and knew that damage would probably result'. It was (c) that received the largest number of votes. If the interpretation adopted by the judge was the one intended, it would be sufficient to stop at the word 'recklessly' as in (a). It seems to me that his interpretation makes unnecessary the reference to knowledge which follows.

I must not be thought to give undue weight to submissions made by the United Kingdom delegation, but it is interesting to read the reference to what Mr Wilberforce (as he then was) said in relation to the Norwegian proposal:

'In the text submitted it was stated "recklessly without caring that damage would probably result", and his delegation understood and hoped that these words had been introduced in order to state that the person concerned did know that the probable consequences of his act would be to produce damage.'

I have looked at these papers, not in order to interpret art 25, but to check on the interpretation which to me it seems to bear. I think that the papers do indeed do that.

The meaning of probable

An act may be reckless when it involves a risk, even though it cannot be said that the danger envisaged is a probable consequence. It is enough that it is a possible consequence, although of course there comes a point where the risk is so remote that it would not be considered reckless to take it. We look for an element of rashness which is perhaps more clearly indicated in the French text 'témérairement'. Article 25 however refers not to possibility, but to the probability of resulting damage. Thus something more than a possibility is required. The word 'probable' is a common enough word. I understand it to mean that something is likely to happen. I think that is what is meant in art 25. In other words, one anticipates damage from the act or omission.

The kind of damage

It is with rather less confidence that I have said that the damage anticipated must be of the same kind of damage as that suffered. I have reached my conclusion because art 25 is designed to cover cases of damage both to the person, in other words, injury, and to property. The article contains no exception from liability in the case of an act done for justifiable cause. There may be occasions when an act can be said to be done recklessly in regard to one possible kind of damage, although morally wholly justified as the price of averting some other more serious hurt. Perhaps one could resolve this matter by saying that recklessness involves an element of moral turpitude. If all that can be anticipated is the spilling of a cup of tea over someone's dress, it does seem wrong that the pilot should be blamed for unexpected personal injuries. Whether or not I am right in this, I am satisfied that the pilot must have knowledge that damage will result from his omission. With respect to the judge, I cannot see that the fact that a wine glass may slip from a tray and cut a passenger's leg should make the carriers liable for unlimited damages in respect of an injury suffered because there was no sealt belt to protect the passenger. The damage, whether it is referred to as 'the damage' or merely 'damage', refers to something which results from the omission. The French text, by the use of the word 'en', clearly establishes this.

For the pilot's omission to amount to recklessness, it is in my opinion necessary to show that he knew that prudent flying required him to illuminate the seat belt sign before entering the CAT area, in other words that it was wrong to wait for warning ripples. Primarily the plaintiff relied on para 10.3 of the flight operations manual to establish this. While I am prepared to accept that the judge's interpretation of that instruction is correct, I am not satisfied that every pilot would understand it in that way. If it was so understood universally, I find it difficult to believe that two distinguished pilots such as Captain Price and Captain Todd would be prepared to say on oath that they adopted some other approach to a CAT forecast. Captain Todd was currently employed by British Airways. I cannot believe that he would openly say that he deliberately disobeyed the orders of the flight operations manual. I bear in mind that the judge considered the defence witnesses to be partisan, but I cannot believe that their support for the defendants' case would go as far as this. I am not satisfied therefore that the pilot, Captain Swang, understood para 10.3 of the flight operations manual as requiring him to put on the seat belt sign before actually entering a CAT area, or indeed before the first indications of CAT were felt. I say this in spite of the criticism properly directed at his voyage report, to which I refer later.

Some indication of the latitude with which the aircraft flight manual may be interpreted is illustrated by the experts' comments on that part of it headed 'Standard Procedures—Cruise'. The Aircraft flight manual vol 2, section 2.4.3, para 05 is headed 'Turbulence and/or Thunderstorm'. It says: '. . . when flight through turbulent air is anticipated and/or unavoidable, the following is recommended . . .' Sub-paragraph 9 reads: 'wear your shoulder harness and switch on the "Fasten Seat Belts" sign.' Thus the provisions of para 10.3 of the flight operations manual is repeated in another form. Paragraph 05(7) reads: 'Hold the elevator control firmly and disconnect the altitude hold mode by selecting PITCH DAMP.' One would think that if it is necessary to switch on the seat belt sign ten minutes before entering a CAT area, so too would it be necessary to select pitch damp before the area was reached. Pitch damp prevents the auto pilot from seeking its predetermined altitude automatically, which is undesirable in turbulence. Yet the experts agreed that there was no objection to wait until the warning ripples were encountered before selecting pitch damp. I can see that if passengers are already belted in, any untoward movement of the aircraft due to pitch damp not being engaged may not be catastrophic and that therefore the selection of pitch damp may be less urgent. However this is not apparent from the aircraft flight manual. Therefore if the plaintiff's experts treat the pitch damp provision as one which permits the pilot an element of discretion, I am unable to see why it is not permissible or at least reasonably possible for a pilot to read and to treat the seat belt instruction as also giving an element of discretion. Therefore I think that two schools of thought can be said to have existed as to the way in which a CAT area should be dealt with. I think that the judge was entitled and indeed justified in saying that the proper approach was to secure seat belts before entering it. It was a counsel of perfection, but in the control of an aircraft nothing but perfection should suffice. This does not mean that the attitude adopted by Captain Price and Captain Todd would necessarily be reckless. However we are concerned with the behaviour of Captain Swang, the pilot, his understanding of the instructions in the manual and his knowledge of the probability of damage.

The plaintiff has relied strongly on Captain Swang's conduct after the incident. The fact that he, as it were, fled for home is capable of many interpretations, but I do not think that it is any evidence that Captain Swang knew that he should have switched on the seat belt sign before entering the CAT area. I can understand that a pilot might wish to reach his base as soon as possible. Moreover, there was a doctor on board and, bearing in mind that the plaintiff was willing to fly on to Bangkok after reaching Karachi, there is some indication that there was not a clamour for the pilot to land at Ankara. However, the plaintiff also relied on Captain Swang's voyage report which contained the following:

> 'At 1425 Z during cruise in clear, sky on top of some few scattered cumuloform clouds approximately 80 NM before Istanbul, we experienced all of a sudden unexpected severe clear air turbulence. The aircraft was hit in a downward big "BANG" for just a second and then returned to a normal smooth phase of flight. According to the attached "PROG CHART" the area of clear air turbulence was located approximately 150 NM south of the active airways.'

As the judge remarked—

> 'Either [Captain Swang] completely forgot about the CAT 1 area altogether and was thinking only in terms of CAT 3, or he was simply covering up that what had happened was in a CAT area.'

In his affidavit sworn on 27 January 1978 at the British Embassy in Bangkok Captain Swang said:

> 'The forecast indicated two possible areas of clear air turbulence located near our flight path. One such zone was located approximately 200 miles southwest of the flight path, and the other area crossed our flight patch just east of Ankara, Turkey . . . After passing over Sofia, which was a Flight Information Region (F.I.R.), there was no indication made to me of any unforecast turbulence on our flight path. At this point, we were heading towards Istanbul. The Air Traffic Controller had our aircraft trailing ten minutes behind an Iran Air jet that was following the same route as our TG-913. Hence, if any disturbance were to be encountered, it would be expected that the Iran Air jet would encounter it first, and a warning would be relayed on to us via the Air Traffic Controller. The Iran Air flight, however, encountered no turbulence on this entire route . . . When one enters a zone of clear air turbulence, one usually first encounters a series of minor shocks that serve as a warning and allow the pilot time to caution his passengers to be sure to remain seated and have their seatbelts fastened. In this particular instance, however, there was no such warning shock.'

There was a disturbing feature in the case. Attached to Captain Swang's report was a copy of the weather chart. It was either the one which he had in the cockpit or a photostat of it. This document was not originally disclosed and it took a great deal of insistence on the part of the defendants' own solicitors before they could obtain it from their clients. On that chart someone had drawn a flight path. It is possible to find a point on that flight path 150 nautical miles from CAT 1. Scratches on the chart were interpreted by the judge as an attempt to indicate that the incident took place somewhere near Belgrade, well outside the CAT area. However, I myself find it very difficult indeed to attach any importance to that flight line, which in evidence was called a phantom line. There is nowhere on that phantom line a point which is 80 nautical miles north of Istanbul. Yet that is where the incident occurred and it is where Captain Swang reported that it had occurred. Furthermore, there is no doubt that that location was well inside CAT 1. Bearing in mind that he gave the same location in his affidavit, I find it very difficult to believe that Captain Swang would trace a flight path which he had not followed, for the purpose of deceiving someone as to where the incident took place or to indicate that it took place outside a CAT area. The plane's flight path had been prescribed and we have seen where it is laid down in the defendants' documents. It was the captain's duty to follow that flight path. I could just understand him plotting a false path which avoided the CAT area at a relevant time, but not when his report stated accurately where the incident occurred and when that location in no way coincides with the phantom flight line. Captain Swang denied drawing the line. It could well have been entered on the chart by someone who misunderstood this case.

The reference to the plane being outside the CAT area when the incident occurred could readily be explained if Captain Swang had forgotten or overlooked the location of the CAT area. A possible alternative explanation is as follows: Captain Swang, like Captain Price and Captain Todd, permitted himself a degree of discretion in determining precisely when to switch on the sign. However, unlike the two expert witnesses, Captain Swang thought that the manual strictly required him to switch on the sign before entering an area where CAT was forecast. He regarded himself as being in breach of his airline's regulations and therefore thought to find an excuse. This is the way the judge regarded it, and concluded that Captain Swang, being knowingly in breach of the regulations, was reckless. As I have said, I think it is possible to say this, but I would not myself draw that inference.

If Captain Swang intended to conceal that he had deliberately refrained from switching on the seat belt sign although he knew that he was entering a CAT area, why does he correctly report the location of the incident which is firmly inside the area? The most likely way to deceive would be to put the location outside a CAT area. I think that the

report and the affidavit are strong indications that Captain Swang had not noticed CAT 1
on his chart or had forgotten it. The chart is not very clear. We ourselves had to have
CAT 1 pointed out to us. There is a 'CAT 1' at the north of the chart over England and
Norway. The other inscription 'CAT 1' is located very close to the corridor labelled 'CAT
3'. This CAT 1 with its numeral in a box could be overlooked. The evidence establishes
that CAT 3 was almost a permanent feature and well known to a pilot regularly flying
this route. I can therefore understand Captain Swang's assertion that, in saying that the
incident occurred 200 miles from CAT, he was referring to CAT 3. He does not confess
in giving evidence that he overlooked CAT 1. On the other hand, there were interruptions
at this point in his evidence and discussions involving the interpreter. The judge found
Captain Swang to be a wholly unsatisfactory witness and drew an inference against him.
He is prepared to say that his practice was to wait for the warning ripples before switching
on the sign. If he knew that this practice was wrong, I find it difficult to see why he so
readily admits to adopting it. I therefore find it easier to draw a different inference
against Captain Swang, namely that he had forgotten CAT 1.

However, I will consider whether the plaintiff has proved his case on my interpretation
of that article, assuming that Captain Swang acted in deliberate breach of para 10.3 of the
flight operations manual.

As I understand art 25, it is not sufficient to show that he deliberately broke a
regulation, even one which is designed for safety, unless it is also shown that he had
knowledge that injury would probably result. While it is not necessary for my decision
in this case, I would go further and say that it is in relation to that knowledge (and not to
the regulations themselves) that his conduct is to be judged in order to determine
whether or not it was reckless.

The evidence in the case on both sides was strongly against the probability of injury.
Indeed it is doubtful whether the evidence went so far as to say that an encounter with
CAT of any kind was probable, let alone CAT of sufficient severity to cause an injury.
There could be no reason for the pilot to omit so trivial a precaution as the seat belt sign
if he thought that injury was probable.

There was another way in which the plaintiff put his case. He said that the flight
recorder trace indicated the beginning of some unusual movement about 50 seconds
before the 'BANG'. This continued and indeed increased, and it is said that the pilot should
have noticed it and switched on the seat belt sign. To this the defendants have said that
the movements shown on the trace would not necessarily be apparent to the pilot, for
the recording box is situated in a different part of the aircraft. It is also said that, although
the plaintiff noticed some unusual movement, this, too, might not be noticeable to the
pilot, for he was at the front and the plaintiff towards the rear. From the trace of the G
load alone, which shows these deviations from normal, I do not think that it can be said
that the pilot must have noticed something unusual in time for him to decide to switch
on the seat belt sign. However, it is suggested that the radio transmission trace indicates
that someone sent out a message some 58 seconds before the 'BANG'. The plaintiff says
that this was probably the pilot, but, if not, it was someone in the cabin and leads to the
inference that the unusual sensations must have been noticed in the cabin so as to cause
someone to transmit and receive a message. As the pilot had made mention of an Iranian
jet flying ahead of him, the theory propounded on behalf of the plaintiff was that, having
noticed some unusual movements, the pilot radioed the Iranian aircraft to ask if it was
experiencing turbulence. It is said that instead of, or as well as, making this inquiry he
should then have switched on the seat belt sign. Captain Swang denies knowing anything
about any such transmission. There can be no doubt that the radio was set to transmit.
The captain was not the only person in the cabin able to use the radio. The defence have
suggested that the control switch was activated inadvertently.

I find it impossible to say that the inference is that Captain Swang radioed ahead to
make inquiries from the Iranian jet and therefore must have noticed the ripples. If,
however, he himself made an inquiry, I do not think that he could be said to be
indifferent whether or not CAT would be encountered to a degree which demanded seat

belts to be worn. A radio transmission would be wholly consistent with the conduct of a
pilot who genuinely believed that there would be no risk of damage before further signs
or information was received in time for him to order seat belts to be worn.

In my opinion it has not been proved that Captain Swang knew that damage would
probably result. I further do not think that it has been proved that he acted recklessly. I
therefore would allow this appeal.

O'CONNOR LJ. I agree that this appeal should be allowed for the reasons given by
Eveleigh LJ and it is only because we are differing from the trial judge that I add a few
sentences of my own.

A passenger injured during a flight governed by the Warsaw Convention as amended
at The Hague in 1955 can recover damages up to a limited sum without proof of fault
(arts 17 and 22). Article 20 allows the airline to avoid even the limited payment in certain
circumstances. Article 25 allows the passenger to escape the limitation of art 22 if he
proves—

> 'that the damage resulted from an act or omission of the carrier, his servants or
> agents, done with intent to cause damage or recklessly and with knowledge that
> damage would probably result . . .'

It must be remembered that art 22 imposes limits not only for personal injury, but
also for loss of or damage to goods, so that 'the damage' referred to in art 25 may be
personal injury or damage to goods. This makes the provisions of an act 'done with intent
to cause damage' more readily intelligible. This provision shows that the limited
recompense is to be the normal liability, and that only exceptional wrongdoing is to
avoid the limit. It is in this context that the provision 'recklessly and with knowledge
that damage would probably result' has to be construed.

In the present case the plaintiff had to prove that his injury resulted from an act or
omission of Captain Swang, done recklessly with knowledge that damage would probably
result.

The judge has found that Captain Swang flew the aircraft into an area where CAT was
forecast without illuminating the seat belt sign in breach of the requirements of the
airline's manual of instructions, and that in so doing he acted recklessly. This finding was
based on the judge's acceptance of the evidence of the plaintiff's expert witnesses, in
preference to those of the defendants, and on his assessment of Captain Swang as a
witness. Having read the whole of the evidence, I would not have come to the same
conclusion, but I am conscious that in this court we must be slow to differ from the
findings of the trial judge which depend on his assessment of the witnesses. There was
evidence that it was good practice to belt up before entering an area where moderate
CAT was forecast. Equally there was evidence that careful pilots exercised a discretion
and waited for tell-tale signs of light turbulence before pinning the passengers to their
seats. There is not, and indeed there could not have been, a finding that that evidence
was deliberately dishonest. It follows that even if I accept the judge's finding that Captain
Swang's omission to light the seat belt sign was reckless, I do not think that there was any
evidence from which the judge could conclude that Captain Swang had knowledge that
damage would result from his omission.

I cannot construe art 25 by such considerations as wine glasses falling off trays. The
damage must be connected with the act or omission, and there was no evidence that
Captain Swang knew that injury to passengers would probably result from this omission.
The judge seems to have thought that any sort of damage was enough. I think he fell
into error in so doing. I do not think that the plaintiff came anywhere near proving that
Captain Swang knew that damage would probably result, and accordingly the plaintiff
cannot invoke the relief given by art 25 of the convention.

PURCHAS LJ. I, too, agree that this appeal should be allowed for the reasons given by
a both Eveleigh and O'Connor LJJ, and for the same reasons as O'Connor LJ I add some
words of my own.

The judge made a careful assessment of the five witnesses on whose evidence the
question of liability turned, that is, Captain Swang and the four professional witnesses
who were pilots of great experience and at least one of whom, Captain Todd, was still in
current employment with British Airways. Although I share the doubts expressed by
b O'Connor LJ as to the judge's assessment of Captain Swang, if this were the only criticism
I would not disturb the judge's findings.

The judge, after careful and anxious consideration, preferred the expert evidence of
Captain Pritchard and Captain Barrow to that of Captain Todd and Captain Price. He
described them, however, as people of vast experience with thousands of hours of flying
experience. He also recognised their high standing and qualifications. Although at a later
c stage in his judgment he criticised Captain Todd as acting as an advocate rather than as a
technical witness and both Captain Todd and Captain Price as 'somewhat doctrinaire', the
judge went on to say: 'They were both, of course, entitled to their opinions.' As I read his
judgment, the judge at no point suggested that either Captain Todd or Captain Price in
giving their evidence were other than entirely genuine.

The judge was therefore faced with a conflict of expert evidence and was entitled to
d prefer one expert opinion in favour of the other on the question whether or not Captain
Swang should have illuminated the seat belt sign ten minutes before entering an area in
which a possibility of CAT had been forecast. A preference of this kind, if the test were
that of ordinary negligence, would be conclusive; however, this is not the test which has
to be satisfied in order for the plaintiff to succeed under art 25 of the Warsaw convention.

I agree that the true interpretation of art 25 when it is read as a whole involves the
e proof of actual knowledge in the mind of the pilot, at the moment at which the omission
occurs, that the omission is taking place and that it does involve probable damage of the
sort contemplated in the article. I also agree that this interpretation is supported by the
travaux préparatoires and in particular with the selections of the particular version which
finally found its way into the article in favour of the alternatives which had been debated.

The inquiry on which the judge should have embarked was not the selection of the
f preferred view as to a course taken by a reasonably prudent pilot, but an examination of
the expert evidence to see whether the course taken by Captain Swang was reasonably
tenable on any accepted professional view. In view of the evidence of Captain Price and
Captain Todd, although not preferred to the evidence of the others, it seems in my
judgment impossible to say that Captain Swang's decision not to illuminate the seat belt
sign fell within the test provided by art 25. In addition, I cannot, with respect, follow the
g judge in his analysis of the significance of the possible radio transmission indicated on
the flight recorder trace during the crucial 90 seconds. In my judgment the judge was
not entitled to draw the inferences which he reached on that evidence, that Captain
Swang had actual knowledge that he was approaching an area of severe clear air
turbulence.

For these reasons and for the reasons given by Eveleigh and O'Connor LJJ I agree this
h appeal must be allowed.

Appeal allowed. Judgment for plaintiff for £11,700. Leave to appeal refused.

Solicitors: *Beaumont & Son* (for the defendants); *Rochman Landau & Co* (for the plaintiff).

Henrietta Steinberg   Barrister.

Castle Insurance Co Ltd and others v Hong Kong Islands Shipping Co Ltd
The Potoi Chau

PRIVY COUNCIL

LORD DIPLOCK, LORD ROSKILL, LORD BRANDON OF OAKBROOK, LORD BRIGHTMAN AND SIR JOHN MEGAW

13, 14, 15 JUNE, 25 JULY 1983

Shipping – General average – Contribution by cargo owners – Accrual of cause of action for contribution – Action by ship managers against consignees of cargo and insurers claiming contribution – Writ issued within six years of first general average act and execution of average bonds in usual Lloyd's form secured by guarantee given by cargo insurers – Application to join shipowners as plaintiffs in action made more than six years after execution of bonds and guarantee – Application made within six years of publication of average adjustment statement – Whether shipowners' claim against consignees and insurers time-barred.

On 25 October 1972 a cargo vessel owned by the shipowners and managed by the ship managers ran aground in a cyclone off the coast of Somalia necessitating the sacrifice of a considerable part of the cargo. On 30 October the services of professional salvors were engaged under a Lloyd's open form of salvage agreement and salvage operations, including the jettisoning of cargo, continued until the vessel and her remaining cargo arrived safely at Aden on 27 November. Between 27 November and 25 December all the cargo, including cargo for onward carriage to other ports except that destined for Bombay, was discharged at Aden. The Aden cargo was released to the respective consignees on their signing average bonds in the usual Lloyd's form secured either by a deposit or by a letter of guarantee from the insurers of the particular consignment of cargo. The bills of lading provided for general average to be 'adjusted, stated and settled' according to the York-Antwerp Rules while the average bonds also provided that the consignees' general average contributions were to be ascertained and adjusted in the usual manner according to the York-Antwerp Rules. After temporary repairs had been effected to the vessel at Aden she proceeded to Bombay where she arrived on 2 January 1973. There the Bombay cargo was discharged and released to the consignees on the signing of average bonds and cargo insurers' letters of guarantee similar to those signed for the release of the Aden cargo. The vessel was then declared a constructive total loss and on 16 January the voyage was abandoned. The cargo left at Aden for onward carriage to other destinations was carried to those destinations by other vessels between 24 January and the end of February 1973. On arrival at the port of destination the cargo was released by the ship managers to the consignees on the signing of similar average bonds and cargo insurers' letter of guarantee. On 9 January 1976 the arbitrator under the Lloyd's open form of salvage agreement made an award to the salvors of salvage in the sum of £120,000 and interest. On 31 August 1977 the average adjustment and statement was delivered to the ship managers. That statement showed a substantial general average contribution due to those concerned in the ship by those concerned in cargo delivered to its destination and released to its consignees. On 25 October 1978 the ship managers brought an action against those consignees and their cargo insurers claiming, as moneys due under the average bonds and letters of guarantee, the consignees' respective contributions to general average as set out in the average statement. On 19 July 1979 the ship managers applied ex parte for leave to join the shipowners as additional plaintiffs in the action. The application was granted by the registrar but his order was set aside in the Supreme Court of Hong Kong on the ground that the shipowners' action against both the insurers and the consignees was time-barred. The ship managers appealed to the *a* Court of Appeal of Hong Kong, which allowed the appeal in part, holding that the shipowners' claims against the consignees were time-barred by the expiry of the six-year limitation period because on the true construction of the York-Antwerp Rules and the bonds a cause of action for general average contribution arose when the general average loss or expenditure was incurred (ie on 25 October 1972), but further holding that their claims against the cargo insurers were not time-barred because the cause of action under the letters of guarantee did not arise until after the average adjustment statement was *b* published. The insurers and the consignees appealed to the Privy Council and the ship managers cross-appealed.

Held – At common law the shipowners' cause of action for general average contribution accrued against the cargo owners at the time when each general average sacrifice or expense was made or incurred, and the clause in the bills of lading providing for adjustment of general average according to the York-Antwerp Rules was intended to *c* regulate and transfer that liability to the consignees of the cargo. Nevertheless, in making the consignees' liability contractual rather than common law based the bills of lading did not postpone the accrual of the shipowners' cause of action for such contribution until publication by the general average adjuster of his general average statement, since an average statement under the York-Antwerp Rules was not binding on cargo owners and therefore its publication was not capable of giving rise to any fresh cause of action or of *d* postponing the accrual of an existing cause of action for an unliquidated sum. However, the Lloyd's form of average bonds subsequently executed by the consignees created fresh contracts under which the consignees, in exchange for the release by the shipowners of their claim to any possessory lien for the general average contribution they might have on the consignment, assumed personal liability (secured by a cash deposit or an insurers' guarantee) to pay such general average contribution which might have been payable at *e* common law by the owner of the consignment at the time of the general average act or by the shipper under a contract of affreightment. Since the consignees' average bonds and insurers' guarantees contemplated that the consignees' obligation to contribute would not arise until their general average contribution had been ascertained on completion of the average adjuster's statement, the publication of that statement was the earliest date at which the shipowners' cause of action could arise against either the *f* consignees or the insurers for payment of general contribution, the cause of action against the insurers being on the basis that their guarantees were an assumption of primary liability to pay the sums due when ascertained. It followed, therefore, that the shipowners' claims against both the consignees and the insurers were not time-barred. The appeal would therefore be dismissed and the cross-appeal allowed (see p 709 *g*, p 710 *e* to *j*, p 712 *c* to *j* and p 714 *b* to p 715 *h*, post).

g *Hain Steamship Co Ltd v Tate & Lyle Ltd* [1936] 2 All ER 597 and *Chandris v Argo Insurance Co Ltd* [1963] 2 Lloyd's Rep 65 approved.

Wavertree Sailing Ship Co Ltd v Love [1897] AC 373 applied.

Dictum of Kerr J in *Schothorst and Schuitema v Franz Dauter GmbH, The Nimrod* [1973] 2 Lloyd's Rep at 97 disapproved.

h **Notes**

For liability to make a general average contribution, see 43 Halsbury's Laws (4th edn) paras 743–758, and for cases on the subject, see 41 Digest (Repl) 506–523, 2789–2974.

Cases referred to in judgment
Chandris v Argo Insurance Co Ltd [1963] 2 Lloyd's Rep 65.
Hain Steamship Co Ltd v Tate & Lyle Ltd [1936] 2 All ER 597, HL; *rvsg* (1934) 49 Ll L Rep
j   123, CA.
Morrison Steamship Co Ltd v SS Greystoke Castle (cargo owners) [1946] 2 All ER 696, [1947] AC 265, HL.
Schothorst and Schuitema v Franz Dauter GmbH, The Nimrod [1973] 2 Lloyd's Rep 91.
Svendsen v Wallace Bros (1884) 10 App Cas 404, HL.
Wavertree Sailing Ship Co Ltd v Love [1897] AC 373, PC.

Interlocutory appeal and cross-appeal

The defendants, Castle Insurance Co Ltd (formerly Pacific and Orient Underwriters (HK) *a*
Ltd), and 84 others (the first 11 defendants being insurance companies and the remaining
74 defendants being consignees of cargo) appealed and the plaintiffs, Hong Kong Islands
Shipping Co Ltd (the managers of the ship Potoi Chau which carried the cargo) cross-
appealed, with final leave of the Court of Appeal of Hong Kong granted on 21 January
1982, against the judgment of the Court of Appeal of Hong Kong (Huggins V-P,
Leonard JA and Silke J) given on 8 July 1981 allowing in part an appeal by the plaintiffs *b*
from the judgment and order of the Supreme Court of Hong Kong (Mr Commissioner
Mayo) given on 15 October 1980 setting aside an ex parte order of Mr Registrar
Barrington-Jones dated 23 July 1979 giving leave to the plaintiffs to add Hong Kong
Atlantic Shipping Co Ltd (the shipowners) as second plaintiffs in a claim for general
average contributions. The Court of Appeal refused to allow the joinder of the shipowners
as plaintiffs in the claim against the cargo owners on the ground that the claim of the *c*
shipowners was time-barred but allowed the joinder of the shipowners as additional
plaintiffs in the claim against the cargo insurers. The facts are set out in the judgment of
the Board.

Ian Hunter QC and *Roderick Cordara* for the insurers and the consignees.
Kenneth Rokison QC and *David Grace* for the ship managers.   *d*

25 July. The following judgment of the Board was delivered.

LORD DIPLOCK. The immediate question in this interlocutory appeal and cross-
appeal from an order of the Court of Appeal of Hong Kong is whether the original
plaintiffs in the action, Hong Kong Islands Shipping Co Ltd (the ship managers), should *e*
be allowed to join Hong Kong Atlantic Shipping Co Ltd (the shipowners) as second
plaintiffs in an action brought by writ issued on 25 October 1978 against 85 defendants,
of whom 74 (the consignees) were consignees of cargo carried on a general ship Potoi
Chau owned by the shipowners and managed by the ship managers and the remaining
11 defendants (the cargo insurers) are insurers of the cargo. The plaintiffs' claims in the
action are for general average contributions to losses consequential on general average *f*
sacrifices made and general average expenditures incurred in the course of a voyage from
ports in the Far East to Jeddah, Hodeidah, Aden and Bombay. The claims against the
consignees are not made against them at common law as owners of the cargo at the time
of the sacrifices and expenditure but are based on the contracts contained in the bills of
lading or, in the preferred alternative, on agreements in one or other of the forms that
are usually, though inaccurately, referred to as Lloyd's average bonds. The claims against *g*
the cargo insurers are based on agreements contained in what are usually, and again
inaccurately, called letters of guarantee.

The Court of Appeal, upholding in this respect the order of Mr Commissioner Mayo
at first instance, refused to allow the joinder of the shipowners as plaintiffs in the claim
against the cargo owners. *This refusal is the subject of the cross-appeal by the plaintiffs.* The
Court of Appeal, however, reversing in this respect the order of the commissioner, *h*
allowed the joinder of the shipowners as additional plaintiffs in the claims against the
cargo insurers. *This is the subject of the appeal.* The grounds of the Court of Appeal's
decision were that as against the cargo owners the shipowners' claims were barred by the
expiry of the six-year limitation period, whereas as against the cargo insurers the
shipowners' claims were not.

Since limitation periods are involved it is necessary to state a few salient dates.   *j*

25 October 1972 The Potoi Chau encountered cyclonic weather in the Indian Ocean
and ran aground off the north-east coast of Somalia.

30 October 1972 The services of professional salvors were engaged under Lloyd's open
form of salvage agreement, and salvage operations, including jettison of considerable
quantities of cargo, continued until 27 November 1972, by which time the ship and her
remaining cargo had arrived at Aden and were in safety.

27 November to 25 December 1972 The Aden cargo and cargo destined for Jeddah and
a Hodeidah were discharged at Aden, the latter for onward carriage to its destination. The
Aden cargo was released to the respective consignees on their signing average bonds in
the usual Lloyd's forms, in the case of uninsured cargo secured by a deposit and in all
other cases by a letter of guarantee from the cargo insurer of the particular consignment.

25 December 1972 The Potoi Chau, to which temporary repairs had been carried out
at Aden, left that port for Bombay with the cargo consigned to Bombay remaining on
b board.

2 January 1973 The Potoi Chau arrived at Bombay and discharged the Bombay cargo.
It was released to its consignees on the terms as respects average bonds and cargo insurers'
letters of guarantee similar to those that had been exacted on the release of the Aden
cargo at that port. Inspection of the vessel after dry-docking at Bombay showed her to be
a constructive total loss and on 16 January 1973 the voyage was abandoned.

c *24 January to end February 1973* The cargo destined for Jeddah and Hodeidah that had
been left at Aden was carried on by other vessels to its port of destination and there
released by the ship managers to the consignees on similar terms as respects average
bonds and cargo insurers' letters of guarantee.

9 January 1976 An award to the salvors of salvage in the sum of £120,000 and
£25,801 interest was made by the arbitrator under the Lloyd's open form of salvage
d agreement.

31 August 1977 The average adjustment and statement was completed and published.
It showed a substantial general average contribution due to those concerned in ship by
those concerned in cargo that had been delivered at its destination and released to its
consignees.

25 October 1978 A specially indorsed writ was issued by the ship managers as sole
e plaintiffs against the consignees and the cargo insurers claiming against them, as moneys
due under the average bonds and letters of guarantee, the consignees' respective
proportions of general average as ascertained and adjusted in the average statement.

19 July 1979 Application by the ship managers to join the shipowners as additional
plaintiffs in the action.

The significance of these dates is that the original writ was issued within six years of
f the first general average act and within six years of the execution of the average bonds by
each of the consignees and of the letters of guarantee by each of the cargo insurers. On
the other hand the application to join the shipowners as plaintiffs in the action was made
more than six years after the last of these events.

Under that branch of English common law into which the lex mercatoria has long ago
become absorbed, the personal liability to pay the general average contribution due in
g respect of any particular consignment of cargo that had been preserved in consequence
of a general average sacrifice or expenditure lies, in legal theory, on the person who was
owner of the consignment at the time when the sacrifice was made or the liability for the
expenditure incurred. In practice, however, the personal liability at common law of
whoever was the owner of the contributing consignment of cargo at the time of the
general average act is hardly ever relied on. There are two reasons for this. The first is
h that the contract of carriage between the shipowner and the owner of the consignment,
whether the contract be contained in a charterparty or a bill of lading, invariably
nowadays (so far as the decided cases show) contains an express clause dealing with
general average and so brings the claim to contribution into the field of contract law.
The second, and this has in practice been the decisive reason, is that there attaches to all
cargo that has been preserved in consequence of a general average sacrifice or expenditure
j a lien in favour of those concerned in ship or cargo who have sustained a general average
loss. The lien attaches to the preserved cargo at the time when the sacrifice is made or the
liability to the expenditure incurred. The lien is a possessory lien and it is the duty of the
master of the vessel to exercise the lien at the time of discharge of the preserved cargo in
such a way as will provide equivalent security for contributions towards general average
sacrifices made or expenditure incurred not only by those concerned in the ship but also
by those concerned in cargo in respect of which a net general average loss has been

sustained. The lien, being a possessory one and not a maritime lien, is exercisable only
against the consignee, but it is exercisable whether or not the consignee was owner of the
consignment at the time of the general average sacrifice or expenditure that gave rise to
the lien, a fact of which the shipowner may well be unaware. At the time of discharge
the sum for which the lien is security (save in the simplest cases, which do not include
that of a general ship) is unquantifiable until after there has been an average adjustment.
Indeed, in the case of some consignees of cargo that has been preserved in part only or
damaged in consequence of a general average loss, so far from being liable to a net general
average contribution they may eventually turn out to be entitled to a net payment in
general average. The disadvantages and legal complications which would result from the
master's actually withholding delivery to its consignee of cargo preserved by general
average acts are conveniently set out in *Lowndes and Rudolf on General Average and York-
Antwerp Rules* (10th edn, 1975) para 453 and need not be repeated here. In practice what
happens is what happened in the instance case: the master, acting on behalf of the
shipowner and of any persons interested in cargo who will be found on the adjustment
to be entitled to a net general average payment, releases the preserved cargo to the
consignees on the execution by each consignee of an average bond in one or other of
Lloyd's standard forms accompanied, in the comparatively rare cases of cargo that is
uninsured or underinsured, by a deposit in a bank in joint names of money as security
or, more usually, by a letter of guarantee from the insurer of the cargo.

Although the instant case is not concerned with the common law liability to general
average contribution of the owner of the cargo at the time of the general average act, the
bills of lading contained an express clause dealing with general average which was in the
following terms:

'28 (General Average) General Average shall be adjusted, stated and settled
according to YORK ANTWERP RULES, 1950.'

This creates a contractual liability on the part of the consignee as indorsee of the bill of
lading to pay general average contribution, if there be any chargeable on the cargo
shipped, whether it was he, the shipper or some intermediate indorsee of the bill of
lading, who happened to be owner of the goods at the time when a general average
sacrifice took place or a liability for a general average expenditure was incurred. Since
this liability arises under a simple contract, the period of limitation is six years from the
accrual of the cause of action; but the clause is intended to regulate, and to transfer to
whoever acquires title to the consignment of cargo under the bill of lading, what would
otherwise be a common law liability of the owner of the cargo at the time of the general
average act; so for the purposes of the instant case a necessary starting point is first to
determine when, at common law, a cause of action for a general average contribution
would have accrued against the owner of cargo, and then to see whether the wording of
the clause is apt to postpone the accrual of a cause of action for such contribution against
a holder of the bill of lading or to create some different cause of action accruing at a later
date than that of the general average act in respect of which contribution was claimed.

The relevant cases as to the time of accrual of a cause of action for a general average
contribution at common law are scanty. They are the subject of close analysis in the
judgments of Huggins V-P and Leonard JA in the Court of Appeal. Scanty though the
cases may be, their Lordships are of opinion that the law is plain and was correctly stated
by Greer LJ in his dissenting judgment in *Tate & Lyle Ltd v Hain Steamship Co Ltd* (1934)
49 Ll L Rep 123 at 135:

'I cannot find that these questions have ever been definitely settled in any of the
decided cases, but the law has been frequently stated by Judges and jurists of
authority in commercial matters in words which lead me to conclude that both the
liability and the lien come into existence as soon as the sacrifice has been made or
the expenses have been incurred, but that the liability and the lien are subject to be
defeated by the non-arrival of the cargo at the port of destination.'

a   This judgment was expressly approved by the House of Lords sub nom *Hain Steamship Co Ltd v Tate & Lyle Ltd* [1936] 2 All ER 597 at 602 on appeal where Lord Atkin said:

> '. . . I think it clear that on principle the contribution falls due from the persons who were owners at the time of the sacrifice . . .'

a statement that is consistent only with the cause of action accruing at the time of the general average act.

b   The passage from Greer LJ's judgment was also expressly approved by the House of Lord in *Morrison Steamship Co Ltd v SS Greystoke Castle (cargo owners)* [1946] 2 All ER 696 at 701–702, [1947] AC 265 at 283 by Lord Roche, and the speech of Lord Uthwatt in the same case is to the like effect.

Finally, and directly on the question of limitation of actions, there is the judgment of Megaw J in *Chandris v Argo Insurance Co Ltd* [1963] 2 Lloyd's Rep 65, a case under a hull policy of marine insurance in which it was held that the limitation period started to run

c   at the date of the general average act in respect of which the contribution was claimed. To this judgment of Megaw J their Lordships will also find it necessary to revert in dealing with the next question: whether the general average clause in the bills of lading has the effect of postponing the accrual of the cause of action or of creating or substituting another cause of action accruing at some later date.

d   Although the claim to general average contribution against the consignees in the instant appeal appears in the points of claim to be based primarily on the average bonds executed by them on discharge of the cargo at its port of destination, a claim based on the general average clause in the bills of lading was permitted to be argued in the Court of Appeal where it is discussed in the judgment of Leonard JA. The Court of Appeal rejected it; but it was renewed, albeit with a justifiable air of diffidence, before this Board.

e   On a claim so framed the judgment in *Chandris v Argo Insurance Co Ltd* is very much in point. That was a single judgment given in six test cases that were heard together and involved, inter alia, claims by assureds against insurers to be indemnified against general average contributions under a hull policy of insurance which incorporated a provision that:

f   > '8. General average and salvage to be adjusted according to the law and practice obtaining at the place where the adventure ends, as if the contract of affreightment contained no special terms upon the subject; but where the contract of affreightment so provides the adjustment shall be according to York-Antwerp Rules 1890 . . . or York-Antwerp Rules 1924.'

The contracts of affreightment did provide that general average should be 'adjusted according to York-Antwerp Rules'.

g   The actions were commenced more than six years after the general average acts in respect of which the liability to general average contributions arose, but less than six years after an average adjustment had been completed by average adjusters and the average statement published. The relevant provision of the Marine Insurance Act 1906 dealing with the assured's right to recover general average contribution from the insurer

h   under the policy is contained in s 66(5), which reads:

> 'Subject to any express provision in the policy, where the assured has paid, or is liable to pay, a general average contribution in respect of the subject insured, he may recover therefor from the insurer.'

So the question for the judge in *Chandris* was: when does a shipowner become liable to

j   pay a general average contribution to a consignee of cargo under a contract of affreightment which provides for adjustment of general average according to York-Antwerp Rules?

The argument for the assured in *Chandris* was that since the contract of affreightment, and hence the policy, contemplated that there would be an adjustment of general average according to York-Antwerp Rules, and since those rules contemplate that the adjustment

will lead to the making by average adjusters of a general average statement, this *a*
statement, the argument goes, will for the first time quantify the net amount of the
general average contribution due from each individual contributor, which up to that
time had been only an unliquidated and unascertained sum, so a fresh cause of action
thereupon arises for recovery of the amount so quantified.

The difficulty in this argument lies in that part of the judgment of the Privy Council
delivered in *Wavertree Sailing Ship Co Ltd v Love* [1897] AC 373 that states what for more
than a century had been the accepted law of general average. *b*

Their Lordships do not refer to this authority for the purpose of relying on the opinion
of the Board that it was *not* an implied term of the contract of affreightment that in the
event of the occurrence of a general average act in the course of the voyage the shipowner
would procure an average adjustment and statement to be prepared by a professional
average adjuster. There is nothing in the instant appeal that makes it necessary for their
Lordships to consider whether changes in mercantile practices which have taken place *c*
since 1897 have made such an implication necessary, at any rate in cases of contracts
contained in bills of lading for carriage in a general ship. In the instant case this question
cannot arise: there was a prolonged and complex average adjustment and statement
made by professional average adjusters. But the Board's other reason for allowing the
appeal in *Wavertree Sailing Ship Co Ltd v Love*, in the view of their Lordships, presents
insuperable difficulties to the consignees' claims so far as they are based on the general *d*
average clause in the bills of lading. It is that an average statement under the York-
Antwerp Rules prepared by average adjusters appointed by shipowners is not binding on
cargo owners either as respects any net general average contribution or any net general
average claim. Cargo owners can not only dispute entire liability on such grounds as that
the vessel was unseaworthy at the beginning of the voyage owing to failure by the
shipowner to exercise due diligence, or that sacrifices or expenses claimed were not made *e*
or incurred to preserve from a common peril the property involved in the adventure and
therefore did not amount to general average acts, but they can also dispute the quantum
of any contribution or claim attributed to their consignment by the average statement.
If there were any such dispute it would fall to be determined by a court of justice of
competent jurisdiction or, if the contract of affreightment contained an arbitration
clause, by arbitration. *f*

So, as a matter of law, in the absence of any agreement to the contrary, the publication
of the average statement settles nothing: it has no other legal effect than as an expression
of opinion by a professional man as to what are the appropriate sums payable to one
another by the various parties interested in ship and cargo. It is just not capable of giving
rise to any fresh cause of action or of postponing the accrual of an existing cause of action
for an unliquidated sum. *g*

Causes of action for unliquidated sums that, in the absence of earlier agreement as to
quantum reached between the parties themselves, will only become quantified by the
judgment of a court or the award of an arbitrator, accrue at the time that the events occur
which give rise to the liability to pay to the plaintiff compensation in an amount to be
subsequently ascertained. They are commonplace in the field of contract as well as in the
field of tort. Unliquidated damages for breach of contract, claims on a quantum merit, *h*
claims for salvage services under Lloyd's open form of salvage agreement are examples
and in their Lordships' view it was rightly decided in *Chandris v Argo Insurance Co Ltd*,
that claims for contributions in general average under contractual provisions which do
no more than require general average to be adjusted according to York-Antwerp Rules
fall within this class and that, accordingly, the cause of action under such a contractual
provision in a bill of lading accrues at the time when each general average sacrifice was *j*
made or general average expense incurred.

It was submitted that a distinction could be drawn between the more common form
of general average clause in bills of lading which refers only to general average being
'adjusted' according to York-Antwerp Rules and the general average clause in bills of
lading in the instant case which refers to general average being 'adjusted, stated and
settled' according to York-Antwerp Rules 1950. In their Lordships' view, however, the
inclusion of the additional words 'stated and settled' makes no difference. The York-

Antwerp Rules do not make the average adjuster's assessments of liability to contribute contained in his general average statement binding on cargo owners nor do the rules impose any legal obligation on cargo owners to settle general average claims by paying the amount so assessed; so in the context the additional words add nothing to what would already be comprehended in 'adjusted according to York-Antwerp Rules'.

The *Chandris* judgment in what were intended to be test cases has stood unchallenged for 20 years. In the interests of business certainty their Lordships would have been very reluctant to overrule it; but, so far as claims in general average between parties to the maritime adventure are concerned, the almost invariable use of average bonds eliminates the need to rely directly on the general average clause in the contract of affreightment.

Their Lordships turn now to the average bonds executed by the consignees on delivery to them of their respective consignments at the port of destination. The Court of Appeal held that the contracts thereby created did not give rise to a fresh cause of action which did not accrue until the amount of the contribution chargeable to the consignment had been ascertained and stated in a general average statement prepared by an average adjuster. It is this decision of the Court of Appeal that is the principal subject of challenge in the ship managers' and the shipowners' appeal.

The average bonds, to give them their common though legally inaccurate description, were in the usual Lloyd's forms which appear to have been in use in substantially the same terms for well over a century: see *Svendsen v Wallace Bros* (1884) 10 App Cas 404 at 410. There are two varieties one of which provides for security in the form of a cash deposit on joint account in a bank, the other does not call for any cash deposit but it is stated on its face that it is 'To be used in conjunction with Underwriters' guarantee'. In both varieties the wording of the preamble and the mutual promises is the same. As respects the bonds providing for cash deposits, of which there were very few in the instant case, it is only necessary for their Lordships to draw attention to the fact that the provisions relating to the cash deposit deal with interim payments on account out of the deposit of sums certified to be proper 'by the Adjuster or Adjusters who may be employed to adjust the said . . . general average'. The implication from this is clear: it was the mutual intention of the parties that there should be an average adjustment undertaken by professional average adjusters.

Since their Lordships differ from the Court of Appeal on the legal effect of these average bonds, it is convenient to set out their terms omitting only those relating to the cash deposit in the bonds which were not accompanied by an insurer's guarantee:

'AN AGREEMENT made this first day of March 1973 BETWEEN Owner of Ship or Vessel called the "POTOI CHAU" of the first part and the several Persons whose names or Firms are set and subscribed hereto being respectively consignees of Cargo on board the said Ship of the second part

WHEREAS the said Ship lately arrived in the Port of   on a voyage from and it is alleged that during such voyage the vessel met with a casualty and sustained damage and loss and that sacrifices were made and expenditure incurred which may form a Charge on the Cargo or some part thereof or be the subject of a salvage and/ or a general average contribution but the same cannot be immediately ascertained and in the meantime it is desirable that the Cargo shall be delivered NOW THEREFORE THESE PRESENTS WITNESS and the said Owner in consideration of the agreement of the parties hereto of the second part hereinafter contained hereby agrees with the respective parties hereto of the second part that he will deliver to them respectively or to their order respectively their respective consignments particulars whereof are contained in the Schedule hereto on payment of the freight payable on delivery if any and the said parties hereto of the second part in consideration of the said Agreement of the said Owner for themselves severally and respectively and not the one for the other of them hereby agree with the said Owner that they will pay to the said Owner of the said Ship the proper and respective proportion of any salvage and/or general average and/or particulars and/or other charges which may be chargeable upon their respective consignments particulars whereof are contained in the Schedule hereto or to which the Shippers or Owners of such consignments may

be liable to contribute in respect of such damage loss sacrifice or expenditure and
the said parties hereto of the second part further promise and agree forthwith to   *a*
furnish to the Owner of the said Ship a correct account and particulars of the value
of the goods delivered to them respectively in order that any such salvage and/or
general average and/or particular and/or other charges may be ascertained and
adjusted in the usual manner.'

This is a fresh agreement which stands on its own independently of the bill of lading   *b*
and is for fresh consideration on either side: the release by the shipowner of his claim to
any possessory lien for a general average contribution (also referred to as a 'charge') he
may have on the consignment, and the assumption by the consignee of a personal
liability, secured by a cash deposit or an insurer's guarantee, to pay such general average
contribution/charge which may have been payable, at common law, by the owner of the
consignment at the time of the general average act or, under the contract of affreightment,   *c*
by the shipper (each of whom, particularly in the case of a general ship, may well be
someone other than the consignee). Their Lordships draw attention to the statement in
the preamble that the general average contribution (if there be one) 'cannot be
immediately ascertained'. The agreement then goes on to deal with what is to be done
by the parties until it is ascertained. First of all the consignment is to be delivered 'on
payment of freight payable on delivery if any', ie against payment to be made   *d*
immediately. This is to be contrasted with the promise by the consignee which
immediately follows expressed in the future tense that he 'will pay' his proper general
average contribution. This is a promise to make a payment of a liquidated sum at some
date in the future which cannot arrive until what is his proper general average
contribution/charge has been ascertained. The contrast between this promise to do
something in the future and a promise to do something immediately is again apparent   *e*
from the succeeding promise by the consignee to furnish particulars of the value of the
consignment 'forthwith' in order that something further may be done in the future that
is needed to enable the liquidated sum that the consignee has promised that he will pay
to be ascertained. What is to be done is in order that the general average contribution/
charge 'may be ascertained and adjusted *in the usual manner*'. The words italicised are
crucial. They direct one to the procedure that is in actual practice followed when general   *f*
average is adjusted according to York-Antwerp Rules even though such practice may
involve the non-insistence by persons interested in the adventure on their strict legal
rights. The usual practice, in the case of a general ship at any rate, is for the shipowner to
employ a professional average adjuster to determine and set out in a general average
statement his determination on the one hand of the sums payable as a contribution from
each party to the adventure who is liable to contribute to general average and on the   *g*
other hand of the sums in respect of general average sacrifices or expenditures which are
recoverable by way of reimbursement by each party to the adventure by whom such
sacrifices were made or expenditures incurred. The usual practice is for actual payment
of contributions/charges to be deferred until completion of the general average statement,
unless, as did not happen in the instant case, the average adjuster has given a certificate
providing for some interim reimbursement to be made to a claimant for a general loss   *h*
without prejudice to ultimate liability.

In their Lordships' view, although, from the point of view of clarity, the draftsmanship
of the Lloyd's forms of average bonds leaves much to be desired, the application of
commercial common sense to the language used makes clear the intention of the parties
to it as respects payments by the consignees. The contractual obligation assumed by the
consignee is to make a payment of a liquidated sum at a future date which will not arrive   *j*
until the general average statement has been completed by an average adjuster appointed
by the shipowners. That in the instant case, where no question of the issue by the adjuster
of certificates for interim reimburements arose, was the earliest date at which the
shipowners' cause of action against the consignees under the average bond for payment
of general average contribution arose. It was not time-barred at the date of the application
of 19 July 1979 to add the shipowners as additional plaintiffs.

a   Since the average bond provided that the consignees' general average contributions should be adjusted in the usual manner, which in the instant case meant according to York-Antwerp Rules, the consignees were not thereby deprived of any defence they might have on the ground that the statement had not been drawn up according to such rules, as for instance that they were excused from liability owing to the unseaworthiness of the Potoi Chau resulting from the failure of the shipowners to exercise due diligence, a defence which it appears from the affidavit evidence they intend to raise.

b   For these reasons their Lordships are of the opinion that the ship managers' cross-appeal should be allowed as against the consignees.

It follows from the foregoing that their Lordships do not accept the correctness of the statement of Kerr J in *Schothorst and Schuitema v Franz Dauter GmbH, The Nimrod* [1973] 2 Lloyd's Rep 91 at 97 that the reasoning of Megaw J in *Chandris* [1963] 2 Lloyd's Rep 65 applies to an average bond in Lloyd's usual form, and that the cause of action on such *c*   bond accrues at the date of the general average act or of the bond if later. This statement by the judge was confessedly obiter; the conclusion expressed was reached without any analysis of the language of the general average bond; it was treated as being the necessary corollary of regarding the reasoning in *Chandris* on a claim under a hull policy of insurance as applying 'equally to a claim for general average contribution made by one party to the adventure against another party to the adventure'. As has already been *d*   indicated their Lordships agree that the reasoning in *Chandris* applies to claims for general average contributions between parties to the adventure where such claims are based on either the liability at common law or contractual liability under a general average clause in the usual terms contained in the contract of affreightment; but the suggestion that the same reasoning leads to the same conclusion in the case of a new and entirely different contract, an average bond, is a non sequitur and in their Lordships' view is wrong.

e   Their Lordships can deal quite briefly with the insurers' and the consignees' appeal against the Court of Appeal's order allowing the joinder of the shipowners as additional plaintiffs in the claims against the insurers, since their Lordships find themselves in agreement with the reasons of the Court of Appeal for making this order.

The letters of guarantee given by the various insurers were not in identical terms. Four different forms are set out in the judgment of Leonard JA in the Court of Appeal, to *f*   which reference can be made; to two of these forms there were also minor variants. Although the expression 'we hereby guarantee' appears in each of the forms the verb 'guarantee' is used loosely, as meaning 'agree' or 'undertake' and not in its strict legal sense of agreeing to answer for the debt, default or miscarriage of another. By each of the forms of letters of guarantee the insurers assume a primary liability to pay a sum of money on the happening of a defined event.

g   The sum agreed to be paid is defined in various terms each of which either expressly or by necessary implication indicates the event on the happening of which it is to become payable. The most explicit language in which the sum and the event are spelt out is: 'The general average contribution that may be properly found to be due upon the completion of the Average Statement by the adjusters'; but their Lordships agree with the Court of Appeal that what is explicit in this form is implicit in each of the others.

h   Their Lordships will accordingly humbly advise Her Majesty that the appeal ought to be dismissed, the cross-appeal allowed and the matter remitted to the Court of Appeal of Hong Kong with a direction that such order be made as is proper to give effect to their Lordships' judgment. The ship managers' costs of this appeal and cross-appeal and of the proceedings before Mr Commissioner Mayo and in the Court of Appeal of Hong Kong must be paid by the insurers and the consignees.

j   *Appeal dismissed; cross-appeal allowed.*

Solicitors: *Clyde & Co* (for the insurers and the consignees); *Norton Rose Botterell & Roche* (for the ship managers).

Mary Rose Plummer   Barrister.

Hills v Potter and others

a

QUEEN'S BENCH DIVISION
HIRST J
3–6, 9, 10, 12, 13, 16, 18 MAY 1983

Medical practitioner – Negligence – Test of liability – Risk of misfortune inherent in treatment proposed by doctor – Doctor's duty to warn of inherent risk of misfortune – Operation to cure b *neck deformity resulting in patient's complete paralysis – Patient electing to have operation – Inherent risk of paralysis following operation – Whether standard of care required of doctor in giving advice before operation the same as that normally required of medical practitioner in course of diagnosis and treatment – Whether higher standard requiring full disclosure to patient before operation of all details and risks.*

c

Medical practitioner – Trespass to the person – Consent to operation – Operation to cure neck deformity resulting in patient's complete paralysis – Patient electing to have operation – Inherent risk of paralysis following operation – Doctor not explaining all aspects of operation to patient before operating – Whether patient's consent to operation vitiated – Whether doctor committing assault and battery by performing operation – Whether claim for assault and battery appropriate.

d

In 1974 the plaintiff, who had suffered from a neck deformity, was left paralysed from the neck down after an operation she had elected to undergo to effect a cure. The operation was performed by the first defendant, a surgeon employed by the second defendants, a health authority. There was an inherent risk that paralysis would result from the operation even if it was performed competently. In 1980 the plaintiff sued the defendants for damages for personal injury, claiming (i) that the first defendant was in e breach of the duty of care he owed to her by failing to provide her with all material information about the operation to enable her to make a truly informed choice whether to undergo it and that had she been properly informed of the risk involved she would not have gone ahead with the operation, and (ii) that in the circumstances her consent had not been real or effective, so that in performing the operation the first defendant had committed an assault and battery on her. The defendants denied negligence and f contended that in any event the plaintiff's action was statute-barred.

Held – (1) On the facts it would have been reasonable for the plaintiff to commence legal proceedings by mid-1974, by which time she knew that her injury was significant and she knew the identity of the potential defendant; and since the writ was not issued until 1980 her action was accordingly statute-barred. In all the circumstances, however, it was g a proper case in which the court would exercise its discretion to disapply the bar (see p 728 *h* to p 729 *a*, post).

(2) The action would, however, be dismissed for the following reasons—
(a) The standard of care required of a doctor when giving information to a patient who had to decide whether to undergo an operation was the same as that normally required of a doctor in the course of his diagnosis and treatment, namely the exercise of h the ordinary skill which a doctor in the defendant's position would be expected to possess. Accordingly, in giving advice prior to an operation a doctor or surgeon did not have to inform the patient of all the details of the proposed treatment or the likely outcome and the risks inherent in it but was merely required to act in accordance with a practice accepted as proper by a responsible body of skilled medical practitioners, and that required the doctor or surgeon to supply the patient with sufficient information to enable j the patient to decide whether to undergo the operation. Applying that test, it was clear that the first defendant had discharged the duty of care which he owed to the plaintiff and was therefore not negligent (see p 720 *f* to *h*, p 727 *e* to p 728 *a* and *d e* and p 729 *a*, post); dictum of the Lord President (Clyde) in *Hunter v Hanley* 1955 SLT at 217, *Bolam v Friern Hospital Management Committee* [1957] 2 All ER 118 and *Chatterton v Gerson* [1981] 1 All ER 257 applied.

a (b) On the facts the plaintiff had given true and effective consent to the operation and accordingly the claim for assault and battery could not succeed (see p 728 *e f* and p 729 *a*, post); *Chatterton v Gerson* [1981] 1 All ER 257 applied.

Per curiam. The tort of assault and battery is an inappropriate cause of action for a claim for personal injuries allegedly resulting from a failure by a defendant doctor adequately to inform a plaintiff of the nature and likely consequences of a proposed operation. Instead such a claim should be pleaded in negligence (see p 728 *f*, post);

b dictum of Bristow J in *Chatterton v Gerson* [1981] 1 All ER at 265 followed.

Notes

For the standard of care required of doctors, see 34 Halsbury's Laws (4th edn) para 12, and for cases on the subject, see 33 Digest (Reissue) 262–288, 2162–2330.

Cases referred to in judgment

c *Bolam v Friern Hospital Management Committee* [1957] 2 All ER 118, [1957] 1 WLR 582, DC.

Canterbury v Spence (1972) 464 F 2d 772, US App, DC; *cert denied* 409 US 1064.

Chatterton v Gerson [1981] 1 All ER 257, [1981] QB 432, [1981] 3 WLR 1003.

Cobbs v Grant (1972) 104 Cal Rep 505, Calif SC.

Hopp v Lepp (1980) 112 DLR (3d) 67, Can SC.

d *Hunter v Hanley* 1955 SLT 213.

Kenny v Lockwood [1932] 1 DLR 507, Ont CA.

Maynard v West Midlands Regional Health Authority (1983) Times, 9 May, HL.

Newton v Cammell Laird & Co (Shipbuilders and Engineers) Ltd [1969] 1 All ER 708, [1969] 1 WLR 415, CA.

Nocton v Lord Ashburton [1914] AC 932, [1914–15] All ER Rep 45, HL.

e *Reibl v Hughes* (1980) 114 DLR (3d) 1, Can SC; *rvsg* (1978) 21 OR (2d) 14, Ont CA.

Sankey v Kensington Chelsea and Westminster Area Health Authority (2 April 1982, unreported), QBD.

Sidaway v Bethlem Royal Hospital (19 February 1982, unreported), QBD.

Whitehouse v Jordan [1981] 1 All ER 267, [1981] 1 WLR 246, HL.

f **Action**

By a writ issued on 12 August 1980 the plaintiff, Sylvia Doreen Hills, claimed against the first defendant, John M Potter, and the second defendants, the Oxfordshire Area Health Authority (Teaching), damages in negligence, and/or for unlawful assault and battery, for personal injuries sustained and losses and expenses incurred as the result of surgery carried out by the first defendants as servant or agent of the second defendants on or

g about 10 January 1974. The facts are set out in the judgment.

Evan Stone QC and *M J Segal* for the plaintiff.
Ian Kennedy QC and *A Whitfield QC* for the defendants.

Cur ad vult

h 18 May. The following judgment was delivered.

HIRST J. In this case the plaintiff, Mrs Sylvia Doreen Hills, claims damages for personal injuries against the first defendant, Mr John M Potter, DM, FRCS, and the second defendants, the Oxfordshire Area Health Authority (Teaching). The first defendant was at the material time a consultant neurosurgeon on the medical staff in the Department

j of Neurological Surgery at the Radcliffe Infirmary, Oxford, which was under the aegis of the second defendants.

On 10 January 1974 the plaintiff underwent an operation at the Radcliffe Infirmary which was performed by the first defendant for the alleviation of a condition called spasmodic torticollis, which is a deformity of the neck.

As a result of the operation the plaintiff was paralysed from the neck downwards. In consequence she is virtually helpless physically, though mercifully her mind is alert. On

any view the operation was a complete and total tragedy for her, and no one who has
seen her as I have during the course of this case can fail to be deeply moved by her   *a*
appalling disabilities and also by the courage with which she faces up to her predicament.

Although, as will appear, her condition was serious at the time of the operation, it is
common ground that this was not an emergency procedure but was 'elective' in character,
so that it was for the plaintiff to choose whether or not to undergo it.

The plaintiff's case, in essence, is that the first defendant was in breach of his duty
towards her by failing to provide her with all appropriate information as to the nature of   *b*
the operation, its prospects and its inherent risks, even when properly performed, and
that in consequence she was never in a position to make an informed choice whether or
not to undergo it. She says that if the risks had been fully and adequately explained to
her she would have decided against having the operation.

The plaintiff further contends that in consequence of the first defendant's failure her
consent to the operation was not real or effective, so that in performing the operation the   *c*
first defendant was guilty of an assault and battery on her.

It is very important to emphasise at this stage that there is no allegation by the plaintiff
that the actual operation was performed otherwise than with due skill and competence.

The defendants deny that the first defendant was in any way in breach of his duty in
relation to the information and warnings he gave to the plaintiff prior to the operation.
They contend that the information and warnings given were in all respects adequate in   *d*
the circumstances. Consequently negligence is denied. They contend that her consent
was a true and effective one, and they therefore deny also that they are guilty of assault
or battery on the plaintiff. In addition, the defendants contend that the plaintiff's cause
of action is statute barred, the operation having been performed in January 1974 and the
writ not having been issued until 2 September 1980.

I should add for completeness at this stage that the present trial has by consent been   *e*
limited to the issues of liability.

[His Lordship considered the medical evidence in detail, including both testimony
from a number of expert medical witnesses and testimony from specialists who treated
the plaintiff, and made the following findings of fact. His Lordship found that the
plaintiff's condition prior to the operation was as follows. The plaintiff first suffered from
symptoms of spasmodic torticollis in 1966. That was a condition of the neck caused by   *f*
malfunction of the neck muscles. Treatment proved to be successful initially but by
1973 the plaintiff's condition had deteriorated again to the point where her neck was
fixed in a permanent spasm caused by involuntary contractions of the neck muscles, and
by the time she was referred to the first defendant with a view to her undergoing surgery
she was near the end of her tether. She suffered considerable pain as part of her illness
and her awkward and ungainly posture was acutely embarrassing to her. His Lordship   *g*
described the operation as involving the cutting of the roots of the cervical anterior
nerves, which provided the motive power for the affected muscle or muscles, together
with the spinal accessory nerve, which also provided motive power. The operation site
was close to though not actually on the spinal cord, since the membrane overlaying the
spinal cord (the dura) had to be cut to get at the nerve roots. There were varying surgical
techniques as to the number of nerves cut. His Lordship found that the prospects and   *h*
risks of the operation were as follows. (1) Even when completely successful, the operation
could at best provide a considerable amelioration, but never a complete cure. The
patient's neck movements would always be handicapped, and the neck somewhat weaker
than normal. A collar would have to be worn for a period after the operation. As a result
there might have been a difference between the surgeon's objective assessment and the
patient's subjective assessment of the outcome of a given operation; the surgeon might   *j*
be quite satisfied, but the patient disappointed because a complete cure had not been
achieved. (2) Taken overall, and allowing for that difference in the standard of assessment,
there had been good results in some 70% to 80% of the cases. (3) Death had occurred in
some 1% to 2% of the cases. In no instance, however, could that be attributed to the
specific risks of the operation. When the individual circumstances of each death were

considered, they could be attributed either to the general risks of neurosurgery where, as
a with the plaintiff, the patient was operated on in a sitting position or alternatively to the
general risks always inherent in major operations of any kind. Taken overall, the risks of
death were no worse than in neurosurgery generally. (4) Prior to 1974 there were no
recorded cases of paralysis as a result of the operation such as the plaintiff underwent.
However, unknown to the first defendant at the time of the operation, a not dissimilar
catastrophe had occurred less than a week before during a performance of a similar
b operation at Hartford, Connecticut. There was also recorded a later disaster which
occurred in Boston, Massachusetts. On the other hand, an operation on the spinal cord
itself was known at the time to carry a small risk of paralysis, or at least consequent
weakness of the arms and legs. (5) A not infrequent complaint after the operation was
difficulty in swallowing (dysphagia). However the problem was negligible if the spinal
accessory nerve was only cut unilaterally, since it was that nerve which controlled the
c trapezius muscle, which enabled a person to position the head for swallowing.
Consequently where, as in the operation on the plaintiff, the spinal accessory nerve was
only cut unilaterally, swallowing was not likely to be a serious problem. The swallowing
difficulties had also been minimised in recent years by advances in physiotherapy. (6) A
very rare complication was a cervical subluxation, where the cutting of the nerves
allowed a vertebra to slip forward, interfering with the spinal cord. This, however, could
d be cured by fusion, and in any event may have been partly attributable to the patient's
preoperational condition. (7) Other minor complications such as neck weakness, the
need for long-term collar support, shoulder weakness and neck pain, though recorded in
the literature, were now much less of a problem in view of improved physiotherapy.

His Lordship then found, in regard to the 'crucial issue' of the conversation at the
consultation between the first defendant and the plaintiff on 12 September 1973 and in
e respect of which there was a conflict of evidence between the parties, that he preferred
the account of that conversation given by the first defendant, which was as follows. The
first defendant in evidence said he would always explain to a patient what the operation
involved, though the detail varied by reference to the particular patient's ability to
understand. He would always ask, 'Do you follow me?' or 'Do you want a further
explanation?' At the minimum, he would explain that, when he made an incision, the
f big muscles in the back of the neck had to be divided and partially cut to get at the site of
the operation, where the spinal cord had to be exposed so that the nerve roots could be
cut. He would never explain merely that he was cutting muscles, still less could he have
said that he must avoid cutting any nerve. He said that he would explain the prospects
of a successful operation by saying that, since the purpose was to stop the affected muscles
moving and going into spasms, the neck would be weak afterwards and it would be
g necessary to wear a collar to support the head for a while, probably weeks rather than
months. But the other muscles which had been left untouched would soon become
strong enough to hold the head steady and almost certainly enable the patient to do
without the collar altogether. There would however be difficulty in moving the head
sideways, but there should be some movement. He said that he would not mention
swallowing difficulties, since he had never encountered any with his patients; that was
h because he only cut the spinal accessory nerve on the affected side (a more radical
procedure was not uncommon in the USA). As to his warnings concerning possible risks
and complications, the first defendant said that he would say that any major operation,
such as the operation on the plaintiff, carried certain risks but that they should not be
exaggerated. There was always a small risk of the patient dying or something going
wrong with the anaesthetics and, where the operation was in the region of the spinal
j cord, a risk of paralysis or at least weakness to the arms and legs, which might only be
temporary or transient. He felt sure he would have said that the operation was
irreversible, in the sense that once the nerves were cut they could never be joined together
again. He saw his duty as one of counselling and advising, but no more: the patient had
to decide. He said he gave the plaintiff every opportunity to do that and that he did not
believe in exercising persuasion on patients to have an operation, unless the consequences

would be very severe if they did not or the patient asked him to decide. His account of the prospects of the operation and the normal side effects would vary according to his assessment of the patient's ability to understand. The same applied to his warning of the complications and risks, but he would routinely make sure that the patient understood them. He agreed that a consultation with a neurosurgeon could be overawing for the patient and said that that was why he approached his warning concerning risks with great circumspection. He evaluated the risk as a small risk of something going badly wrong. Though he could not recall the exact phrase he had used to the plaintiff, he did not think he would have said a 'small' risk as such but would mention death, anaesthetic complications and paralysis. He could not be absolutely sure that he mentioned death or paralysis, but if he had not it would have been for some special reason which he would remember. He agreed that his role was to act as an adviser, not a persuader. He would not have put the advantages higher than the disadvantages, though he would always be anxious not to alarm the patient. He was sure he would have mentioned the spinal cord and probably invited her to ask any questions in that context, since he would not expect her knowledge of anatomy to be sufficient to enable her to understand about the spinal cord. He was sure that he would have discussed the outlook if the plaintiff did not have the operation by saying that she would be likely to get worse and that some people became seriously disabled, others dragged on. He said it was inconceivable that the plaintiff could have thought she could not be worse off after the operation. It was important, however, not to spell out the risks crudely or frighten the patient off. If the plaintiff had decided not to go ahead, he would have thought it was not in her interests, but he would not have worried. He had known patients decline the operation in the first place and then come back later and decide to have it. His Lordship continued:]

It is not necessary for me to make a formal finding as to the cause of the plaintiff's disaster. Indeed, such finding would be injudicious in view of the uncertainties expressed by the surgical experts themselves. Suffice it to say that I think the disaster was caused by some kind of malfunction of a vertebral artery. Unquestionably, whatever the precise cause, it was unforeseeable in 1973–74.

Before I consider the legal standard applicable in this case to the first defendant's conduct, it is convenient to consider as a matter of fact whether it accorded with the standard adopted or approved by responsible practitioners skilled in this field of neurosurgery. All three of the expert neurosurgeons who gave evidence before me, namely Mr Maurice-Williams, Mr Adams and Mr Walsh, were practitioners of the very highest standing in the neuro-surgical field and were in every respect both fair and impressive witnesses. Their evidence shows unanimously and beyond any possible doubt that the explanation of the operation, the account of the prospects if successful and the warning as to possible risks and complications, such as I have found that the first defendant gave, was fully acceptable by their standards. Putting the matter a little more fully, the first defendant's explanation, account and warning were fully in line with the practice advocated by Mr Maurice-Williams; they were a good deal more detailed than the pattern advocated by both Mr Adams and Mr Walsh, but both these witnesses made it perfectly clear that they did not in any way criticise the first defendant for going into greater detail than they would.

I should perhaps add that, even if the first defendant's explanation, account and warning had been confined to no more than the terms described by the plaintiff herself in her evidence, this would also have been consistent with the standards approved by the three surgical experts. It would have substantially accorded with the pattern adopted by Mr Adams and Mr Walsh; and, though less detailed than that advocated by Mr Maurice-Williams, it would not, on his evidence, have merited criticism.

I must now consider as a matter of law the duty owed by the first defendant to the plaintiff and the standard by which that duty is to be judged.

Counsel for the defendants submitted that the duty owed by a surgeon was to use reasonable skill and care in dealing with all his patients, including the giving of information concerning the nature and prospects of the proposed operation and giving warning as to its risks. These three aspects I hereafter refer to compendiously as 'advice'.

a Counsel submitted that the standard to be applied was that accepted as proper by a responsible body of experienced medical men skilled in the relevant art (described hereinafter as 'the medical standard'). He submitted that the duty and standard in this particular context was no more than one application of a general duty of care and of a generally applicable standard by which its fulfilment or otherwise falls to be judged. Counsel for the defendants relied on a number of authorities which I shall refer to in

b more detail below.

Counsel for the plaintiff submitted on the other hand that a special rule applies, or at least ought to be held to apply, in relation to advice. This has become known, at all events in North America, as the 'doctrine of informed consent', and counsel relied on a number of Canadian and United States authorities in support of his proposition. Counsel for the plaintiff submitted that the doctrine of informed consent requires the surgeon to furnish

c to the patient all material details of the proposed treatment, its prospects and the risks inherent in it; and that the criterion by which materiality is to be judged is not by reference to the medical standard, but by reference to what in the judgment of the court the surgeon knows or should know would influence the particular patient in deciding whether or not to undergo the operation. It is, counsel said, for the court and not the doctors to determine the standard.

d Counsel for the defendants submitted that I was precluded by authority from adopting the submission of counsel for the plaintiff, and that in any event importation (as he put it) of the doctrine of informed consent into English law was unwarranted.

I first consider the authorities relied on by counsel for the defendants. In *Bolam v Friern Hospital Management Committee* [1957] 2 All ER 118, [1957] 1 WLR 582 the plaintiff claimed damages against the defendant for the alleged negligence of a consultant who

e had advised the plaintiff to undergo electro-convulsive therapy. One head of negligence alleged was that the consultant had failed to give the plaintiff a warning of the risks involved in the therapy, so that he might have had a chance to decide whether he was going to take these risks or not. The case was tried by McNair J and a jury. In the course of his summing up McNair J directed the jury as follows ([1957] 2 All ER 118 at 121–122, [1957] 1 WLR 582 at 586–587):

f
> '. . . I must explain what in law we mean by "negligence". In the ordinary case which does not involve any special skill, negligence in law means this: Some failure to do some act which a reasonable man in the circumstances would do, or doing some act which a reasonable man in the circumstances would not do; and if that failure or doing of that act results in injury, then there is a cause of action. How do you test whether this act or failure is negligent? In an ordinary case it is generally
> *g* said, that you judge that by the action of the man in the street. He is the ordinary man. In one case it has been said that you judge it by the conduct of the man on the top of a Clapham omnibus. He is the ordinary man. But where you get a situation which involves the use of some special skill or competence, then the test whether there has been negligence or not is not the test of the man on the top of a Clapham
> *h* omnibus, because he has not got this special skill. The test is the standard of the ordinary skilled man exercising and professing to have that special skill. A man need not possess the highest expert skill at the risk of being found negligent. It is well-established law that it is sufficient if he exercises the ordinary skill of an ordinary competent man exercising that particular art.'

j McNair J then went on to cite a passage from the judgment of the Lord President (Clyde) in *Hunter v Hanley* 1955 SLT 213 at 217, a Scottish case:

> '"In the realm of diagnosis and treatment there is ample scope for genuine difference of opinion, and one man clearly is not negligent merely because his conclusion differs from that of other professional men, nor because he has displayed less skill or knowledge than others would have shown. The true test for establishing

negligence in diagnosis or treatment on the part of a doctor is whether he has been proved to be guilty of such failure as no doctor of ordinary skill would be guilty of *a* if acting with ordinary care" . . . A doctor is not guilty of negligence if he has acted in accordance with a practice accepted as proper by a responsible body of medical men skilled in that particular art.'

Bolam's case thus clearly upheld the medical standard as the correct test.

Bolam's case has been frequently cited since and was expressly approved by Lord *b* Edmund-Davies and Lord Fraser in the House of Lords in *Whitehouse v Jordan* [1981] 1 All ER 267 at 276–277, 280, [1981] 1 WLR 246 at 258, 263. The *Whitehouse* case was a medical case, though relating to treatment rather than advice.

In *Chatterton v Gerson* [1981] 1 All ER 257, [1981] QB 432 the plaintiff claimed damages for trespass and negligence against a medical consultant on the ground that she had not consented to an operation and had not been properly informed as to the nature of the operation and its implications. Bristow J found in favour of the defendants. The *c* following passages from his judgment are relevant. First in relation to the claim of trespass he said ([1981] 1 All ER 257 at 264–266, [1981] QB 432 at 442–444):

> 'It is clear law that in any context in which consent of the injured party is a defence to what would otherwise be a crime or a civil wrong, the consent must be real. Where, for example, a woman's consent to sexual intercourse is obtained by *d* fraud, her apparent consent is no defence to a charge of rape. It is not difficult to state the principle or to appreciate its good sense. As so often, the problem lies in its application.'

Bristow J then cited from the Canadian case of *Reibl v Hughes* (1978) 21 OR (2d) 14 at its intermediate stage in the Ontario Court of Appeal. I refer to that case later in this *e* judgment in its final stage when it came before the Supreme Court of Canada. Bristow J then proceeded:

> 'In my judgment what the court has to do in each case is to look at all the circumstances and say, "Was there a real consent?" I think justice requires that in order to vitiate the reality of consent there must be a greater failure of communication between doctor and patient than that involved in a breach of duty if the claim is *f* based on negligence. When the claim is based on negligence the plaintiff must prove not only the breach of duty to inform but that had the duty not been broken she would not have chosen to have the operation. Where the claim is based on trespass to the person, once it is shown that the consent is unreal, then what the plaintiff would have decided if she had been given the information which would have prevented vitiation of the reality of her consent is irrelevant. In my judgment *g* once the patient is informed in broad terms of the nature of the procedure which is intended, and gives her consent, that consent is real, and the cause of the action on which to base a claim for failure to go into risks and implications is negligence, not trespass. Of course, if information is withheld in bad faith, the consent will be vitiated by fraud . . . But in my judgment it would be very much against the interests of justice if actions which are really based on a failure by the doctor to *h* perform his duty adequately to inform were pleaded in trespass.'

Then Bristow J cited the *Bolam case* as specifying the duty in negligence. He then said:

> 'In my judgment there is no obligation on the doctor to canvass with the patient anything other than the inherent implications of the particular operation he intends *j* to carry out. He is certainly under no obligation to say that if he operates incompetently he will do damage. The fundamental assumption is that he knows his job and will do it properly. But he ought to warn of what may happen by misfortune however well the operation is done, if there is a real risk of a misfortune inherent in the procedure . . .'

In *Sidaway v Bethlem Royal Hospital* (19 February 1982, unreported) the plaintiff claimed
damages for negligence by a neuro-surgeon on the grounds of his failure to disclose or to
explain to her the risks inherent in or special to the operative procedures advised. Skinner
J dismissed the claim. In the course of his judgment he said, so far as is relevant:

> 'Before I turn to the question of law this involves, I must first deal with the
> evidence I have heard from four neuro-surgeons about their own practices before an
> operation of this kind and what they conceive to be proper professional practice.
> They all agreed that they would give the patient some warning of the risks involved.
> They differed about the nature and scope of the warning they would give and each
> conceded it might differ from patient to patient and from surgeon to surgeon. All
> agreed that there was a certain minimum of information a neuro-surgeon ought to
> give a patient, viz (a) a description of the general nature of the operation, (b) a
> warning that there was a small risk of untoward results and of an increase in the
> pain the operation was intended to alleviate. The degree to which the surgeon
> should enlarge on this information depended, in the witnesses' opinions, on the
> individual's practice ... The doctor's duty is to warn of the risk of the operation
> going wrong, however much care and skill may have been used, and he can only do
> this by taking, if not an actuarial approach, an approach which takes into account
> the general experience of the profession ... In my judgment it is plain that, in
> disclosing what he did and no more, [the surgeon] was following a practice which,
> in 1974, would have been accepted as proper by a responsible body of skilled and
> experienced neuro-surgeons. It is equally plain that [he] did not make a full
> disclosure to the plaintiff of all the risks involved in the operation she was about to
> undergo so that she was in a position to make a fully informed decision whether to
> agree to it. This raised the question on which I have heard helpful and interesting
> argument from counsel: what is the duty of a doctor in this situation? Did [the
> surgeon], on my findings, fulfil his duty to the plaintiff or ought he to have made a
> full or fuller disclosure of all the risks involved in the operation? [Counsel] for the
> defendants directed my attention to a line of cases which, he submitted, clearly
> demonstrated that there is no duty of full disclosure imposed by English law.'

Skinner J then cited the *Bolam* case, Lord Edmund-Davies in *Whitehouse v Jordan* and
Maynard v West Midlands Regional Health Authority in the Court of Appeal, which I shall
be referring to in the House of Lords. He then cited *Chatterton's* case and proceeded:

> '[Counsel for the plaintiff] accepts that the effect of the English decisions is to
> place a duty on the doctor to act with reasonable care and skill and that the standard
> of care demanded is that submitted by [counsel for the defendants]. However,
> although the plaintiff's case is pleaded on negligence, he says the case cannot be
> treated solely as a case of negligence. He seeks to persuade me that the patient has a
> right to full disclosure of all real risks inherent in any proposed operation. He
> submits that with certain necessary exceptions ... this right is an absolute one and
> that it is for the court to decide the extent of the disclosure demanded, not a
> consensus of medical men. To support his submissions, he relies on a line of
> transatlantic cases ... It is enough for me to say that in [*Canterbury v Spence* (1972)
> 464 F 2d 772, a decision of the United States Court of Appeals, District of Columbia
> Circuit] the court expressly rejected and departed from the English courts' concepts
> of the relationship between doctor and patient and of the standard of care expected
> from the former ...'

Skinner J then cited the Canadian cases to which I shall be referring, and proceeded:

> '[Counsel for the plaintiff] invited me, on the basis of these decisions, to develop
> what he described as "a fast moving branch of the law" further by following [*Reibl v
> Hughes* and other cases] in so far as [they] departed from the English authorities. He
> invited me to do so on two grounds, viz (1) as a matter of principle because the

Canadian decisions flow directly from the decision of the House of Lords in *Nocton
v Lord Ashburton* [1914] AC 932, [1914–15] All ER Rep 45, and (2) as a matter of
policy. As to the former, I need only say that neither the pleadings nor the evidence
would justify me in making a finding that the relationship between the plaintiff
and the surgeon was one to which the doctrines in *Nocton v Lord Ashburton* are
relevant. As to the latter, if policy in this field is a matter for the courts, it is not for
me, in the present clear state of the English authorities, to change it. In my
judgment, there is a clear divergence in principle between the English decisions and
those transatlantic cases relied on by [counsel for the plaintiff], and I am bound to
follow the former. A doctor has a duty to use reasonable care and skill in all his
dealings with his patients and the patients have no more, and no less, than the
concomitant right. The duty is fulfilled if the doctor acts in accordance with a
practice accepted as proper by a body of skilled and experienced medical men.'

In *Sankey v Kensington Chelsea and Westminster Area Health Authority* (2 April 1982,
unreported), a case which was similar on its facts, though in a different medical context,
to *Sidaway's* case, Tudor Evans J followed *Bolam's* case and *Sidaway's* case and reached a
similar conclusion on the law to that reached by Skinner J in *Sidaway's* case, and I do not
think I need read that judgment.

In *Maynard v West Midlands Regional Health Authority* (1983) Times, 9 May the House
of Lords upheld unanimously the decision of the Court of Appeal which had held
(reversing the judgment of Comyn J) that the plaintiff had not made out a claim for
medical negligence based on alleged negligent diagnosis of her complaint. The decision
of the House of Lords was delivered by Lord Scarman, with Lord Fraser, Lord Elwyn-
Jones, Lord Roskill and Lord Templeman all agreeing. In the course of his speech Lord
Scarman set out the relevant principles of law:

'The only other question of law in the appeal is as to the nature of the duty owed
by a doctor to his patient. The most recent authoritative formulation is that by Lord
Edmund-Davies in the *Whitehouse* case. Quoting from the judgment of McNair J in
Bolam v Friern Hospital Management Committee . . . he said [and then Lord Scarman
quoted part of the judgment of McNair J which I have already quoted and
continued:] The present case may be classified as one of clinical judgment. Two
distinguished consultants, a physician and a surgeon experienced in the treatment
of chest diseases, formed a judgment as to what was, in their opinion, in the best
interests of their patient. They recognised that tuberculosis was the most likely
diagnosis. But, in their opinion, there was an unusual factor, viz swollen glands in
the mediastinum unaccompanied by any evidence of lesion in the lungs.'

Lord Scarman then proceeded to discuss the diagnosis in detail. He then went on:

'A case which is based on an allegation that a fully considered decision of two
consultants in the field of their special skill was negligent clearly presents certain
difficulties of proof. It is not enough to show that there is a body of competent
professional opinion which considers that theirs was a wrong decision, if there also
exists a body of professional opinion, equally competent, which supports the
decision as reasonable in the circumstances. It is not enough to show that subsequent
events show that the operation need never have been performed, if at the time the
decision to operate was taken it was reasonable in the sense that a responsible body
of medical opinion would have accepted it as proper.'

Lord Scarman then quoted the passage I have already read from the Lord President
(Clyde) in *Hunter v Hanley* and proceeds:

'I would only add that a doctor who professes to exercise a special skill must
exercise the ordinary skill of his speciality. Differences of opinion and practice exist,
and will always exist, in the medical as in other professions. There is seldom any
one answer exclusive of all others to problems of professional judgment. A court

a   may prefer one body of opinion to the other; but that is no basis for a conclusion of negligence.'

Finally, having reviewed the facts in detail, Lord Scarman concluded at the very end of his judgment:

> 'The judge thought that [a witness] might have had an "idée fixe" about the possibility of Hodgkin's disease. This, with respect, is not a possible view of his
> b   evidence read as a whole especially in the light of the judge's own appraisal of him as a witness. Nor is it consistent with the existence of a strong body of evidence given by distinguished medical men supporting and approving of what he did in the circumstances of this case as they presented themselves to him at the time when he made his decision.'

Here, therefore, in *Maynard's* case the medical standard is declared by the highest
c   authority to be the proper test, at all events in relation to diagnosis and treatment. Counsel for the defendants submitted that *Maynard's* case in effect affirmed the medical standard as applicable to advice also.

Counsel for the plaintiff submitted that in relation to the English cases a distinction should be drawn between diagnosis and treatment on the one hand and advice on the other hand. He accepted that in relation to the former (which he said are matters strictly
d   for medical judgment) the applicable standard was the medical standard, as laid down in *Maynard's* case. The latter, however, in his submission was not strictly a medical matter, but rather one affecting the decision of the lay patient, and was therefore not properly to be judged simply by reference to the opinion of doctors. It should be decided by the court in the light of all the evidence, of which the medical evidence formed only part. *Maynard's* case, he argued, did not relate to advice and was not therefore strictly relevant.

e   On *Bolam's* case counsel for the plaintiff submitted that the direction of McNair J concerning advice had to be read in the context that the plaintiff was mentally ill, and therefore probably incapable of making an informed decision anyway. On *Chatterton's* case counsel for the plaintiff placed reliance on the passages in Bristow J's judgment which emphasise the duty to inform in relation to real risks. He submitted that both *Sidaway's* case and *Sankey's* case were wrongly decided and that, in applying *Bolam's* case,
f   they failed to draw the distinction between diagnosis and treatment on the one hand and advice on the other. Counsel for the plaintiff also made it clear that he did not contend that the surgeon's level of duty was as high as that contended for by counsel for the plaintiff in *Sidaway's* case.

Counsel for the plaintiff prefaced his citation of the North American cases on which he strongly relied by pointing out that the two Canadian cases in particular were very
g   carefully considered decisions of the highest court in Canada applying, as he submitted, common law principles which should prevail in England also. He submitted that they represented an evolution of the common law rather than a revolution.

In *Hopp v Lepp* (1980) 112 DLR (3d) 67 the plaintiff claimed damages for battery and negligence against a surgeon on the ground that the surgeon had not adequately informed the plaintiff as to the risks inherent in the operation and consequently a valid consent
h   had not been given thereto. The judgment of the Supreme Court of Canada was delivered by Laskin CJC and contains the following relevant passages (at 77, 80–81):

> '*Kenny v. Lockwood* ([1932] 1 DLR 507) is important as much for what it portended as for what it actually decided. It indicated that a surgeon who recommends an operation which involves known risks, that is probable risks, or special or unusual
> j   risks, is under an obligation to his patient to disclose those risks and, if he fails to do so, and injury results from one of the undisclosed or not fully disclosed risks, the patient's consent to the operation will be held to be not an informed consent, although the operation itself was competently performed . . . The probable risks would be those that, if he was informed about them, would reasonably be expected to affect the patient's decision to submit or not to submit to a proposed operation or

treatment. I find it difficult, however, to conclude that if there are probable risks (as opposed to mere possibilities such as those inherent in any operation or therapy, e.g., the risk of infection) they would not also be material in the sense of the objective standard that has been proposed in some writings and cases.'

He then quoted from the United States case of *Canterbury v Spence* (1972) 464 F 2d 772 and proceeded:

'No doubt, this invites a finding of fact upon which expert medical evidence of judgment to be exercised would be admissible but not determinative. Indeed, since a particular patient is involved upon whom particular surgery is to be performed or particular therapy administered, and it is a duty of disclosure to him that affects the validity of his consent, evidence of medical experts of custom or general practice as to scope of disclosure cannot be decisive, but at most a factor to be considered. The case law on the question of informed consent or the duty of disclosure has exhibited a variety of classifications of risks involved in proposed surgery or therapy. Probable risks, which must be disclosed, have been contrasted with mere possibilities (as, for example, risks involved in any operation), but this dichotomy cannot be absolute because it ought to take note of whether a risk is or is not quite remote, and here the gravity of the consequences, if a risk should materialise, must be brought into account; for example, the risk of death, even if a mere possibility, as contrasted with some residual stiffness of a member of the body . . . Materiality connotes an objective test, according to what would reasonably be regarded as influencing a patient's consent . . . In summary, the decided cases appear to indicate that, in obtaining the consent of a patient for the performance upon him of a surgical operation, a surgeon, generally, should answer any specific questions posed by the patient as to the risks involved and should, without being questioned, disclose to him the nature of the proposed operation, its gravity, any material risks and any special or unusual risks attendant upon the performance of the operation. However, having said that, it should be added that the scope of the duty of disclosure and whether or not it has been breached are matters which must be decided in relation to the circumstances of each particular case.'

In *Reibl v Hughes* (1980) 114 DLR (3d) 1 there was a similar claim brought by a patient against a surgeon. This case again went to the Supreme Court of Canada and the judgment was again delivered by Laskin CJC. In the course of the judgment the authoritative status of *Hopp v Lepp* was affirmed, and then Laskin CJC said:

'I think the Ontario Court of Appeal went too far, when dealing with the standard of disclosure of risks, in saying . . . that "the manner in which the nature and degree of risk is explained to a particular patient is better left to the judgment of the doctor in dealing with the man before him." Of course, it can be tested by expert medical evidence but that too is not determinative. The patient may have expressed certain concerns to the doctor and the latter is obliged to meet them in a reasonable way. What the doctor knows or should know that the particular patient deems relevant to a decision whether to undergo prescribed treatment goes equally to his duty of disclosure as do the material risks recognised as a matter of required medical knowledge. It is important to examine this issue in greater detail. The Ontario Court of Appeal appears to have adopted a professional medical standard, not only for determining what are the material risks that should be disclosed but also, and concurrently, for determining whether there has been a breach of duty of disclosure. This was also the approach of the trial Judge . . .'

He then discussed in a little more detail what the lower courts had said, and proceeded:

'To allow expert medical evidence to determine what risks are material and, hence, should be disclosed and, correlatively, what risks are not material is to hand over to the medical profession the entire question of the scope of the duty of disclosure, including the question whether there has been a breach of that duty. Expert medical evidence is, of course, relevant to findings as to the risks that reside in or are a result of recommended surgery or other treatment. It will also have a bearing on their materiality but this is not a question that is to be concluded on the basis of the expert medical evidence alone. The issue under consideration is a different issue from that involved where the question is whether the doctor carried out his professional activities by applicable professional standards. What is under consideration here is the patient's right to know what risks are involved in undergoing or foregoing certain surgery or other treatment. The materiality of non-disclosure of certain risks to an informed decision is a matter for the trier of fact, a matter on which there would, in all likelihood, be medical evidence but also other evidence, including evidence from the patient or from members of his family.'

Similar principles have been laid down in some jurisdictions in the United States. In *Canterbury v Spence* (1972) 464 F 2d 772 a claim similar in character to those in the Canadian cases came before the United States Court of Appeals District of Columbia Circuit. Circuit Judge Robinson gave the decision of the court, which to a very substantial extent is in similar vein to the Canadian Supreme Court judgments which I have already read. I am not going to read out passages from *Canterbury v Spence* but those that are principally relevant are at paras 15, 20, 22 and 23 of the judgment (see 464 F 2d 772 at 783, 786–788).

Similar principles were laid down by the Californian Supreme Court in *Cobbs v Grant* (1972) 104 Cal Rep 505. It is however plain from *Canterbury's* case 464 F 2d 772 at 783 itself that this doctrine has not been by any means universally applied throughout the United States.

Before I state my conclusions as to the law, I think it is important to note that the appellation 'doctrine of informed consent', which has come to be used to categorise the principles laid down in these North American cases, may be misleading if it is interpreted as signifying a class of duty dependent on acceptance of these cases. For it is quite clear from the English cases cited above that on any view English law does require the surgeon to supply to the patient information to enable the plaintiff to decide whether or not to undergo the operation. This accords with the practice of all the surgical experts in the case, and also, of course, that of the first defendant himself. The distinctive features of the doctrine as laid down in the Canadian and United States cases relate to the amount of information required and, perhaps more importantly, the standard by which the surgeon's conduct is to be judged.

My conclusions are as follows.

(1) In my judgment McNair J in *Bolam's* case applied the medical standard to advice prior to an operation, as well as to diagnosis and to treatment. This standard is clearly applied without any differentiation to all three aspects of the case which McNair J described as 'the three major points' (see [1957] 2 All ER 118 at 121–122, 124, [1957] 1 WLR 582 at 586–588, 590). The fact that the plaintiff was mentally sick did not affect the legal principle, but might of course affect its application to the facts of the particular case, as McNair J himself said.

(2) Although the House of Lords in *Maynard's* case did not specifically affirm McNair J in relation to advice as such, the general and unqualified approval given to *Bolam's* case in the House of Lords makes it quite impossible for me to depart from McNair J's decision, especially as it has been applied to advice in the other three first instance cases which I have cited. Indeed I respectfully agree with, and would have thought it right to follow, these first instance cases even without the authoritative guidance contained in *Maynard's* case, which they preceded. I for my part doubt whether the distinction in the medical context between advice on the one hand and diagnosis and treatment on the other is really so clear or so stark as counsel for the plaintiff forcefully submitted.

(3) I therefore reject the argument of counsel for the plaintiff that I should apply the standard laid down in the Canadian and cited United States cases, and I hold that the

proper standard is the medical standard, in accordance with *Bolam's* case and the other first instance cases.

(4) This, of course, does not mean that I treat the decisions of the Supreme Court of Canada and the cited United States cases with other than the utmost respect. But in my judgment the principles there laid down could only be incorporated in English law as a result of the decision of an appellate court, which would have to balance the considerations canvassed so cogently in the Canadian and United States judgments against the very formidable problems and potential liabilities which would undoubtedly confront medical men if these principles were applied here. It is common knowledge that the extent of these problems and potential liabilities has caused serious anxiety in the United States, whence the principles laid down in the Canadian decisions are derived (see for example the discussion of this topic in the article by Mr Gerald Robertson, 'Informed Consent to Medical Treatment' (1981) 97 LQR 102 esp at 108). I am bound to say that if the point were free from authority I should be very reluctant indeed to apply the Canadian and United States principles here.

I do not accept the argument of counsel for the plaintiff that, by adopting the *Bolam* principle, the court in effect abdicates its power of decision to the doctors. In every case the court must be satisfied that the standard contended for on their behalf accords with that upheld by a substantial body of medical opinion, and that this body of medical opinion is both respectable and responsible, and experienced in this particular field of medicine.

Applying the medical standard, having regard to the findings I have already made, there can be no question but that the first defendant fulfilled his duty to the plaintiff completely and was not negligent. Indeed, I consider that his conduct would have measured up to the more rigorous Canadian and United States standard, if that had been applicable.

As to the claim for assault and battery, the plaintiff's undoubted consent to the operation which was in fact performed negatives any possibility of liability under this head (see *Chatterton v Gerson* [1981] 1 All ER 257, [1981] QB 432). I should add that I respectfully agree with Bristow J in deploring reliance on these torts in medical cases of this kind; the proper cause of action, if any, is negligence.

For the sake of completeness, I should say that I am not satisfied on the balance of probabilities that even if the plaintiff had received a still fuller explanation (eg by quotation of the figures for percentage of risk) she would have declined to undergo the operation. I wholeheartedly accept that in retrospect she sincerely believes that she would have so declined. But, having regard to the evidence as to the gravity of her condition, I think it is more likely than not that she would have agreed to go ahead with the operation notwithstanding. Equally, if the true test in this context is objective (as *Reibl v Hughes* laid down in Canada), I consider that a reasonable person in the plaintiff's shoes would have been most unlikely to refuse the operation, however strong the warning.

Finally, I must consider the question of limitation. This I can do very briefly. Applying the Limitation Act 1975, the statute in force at the relevant time, s 2A(4) and (6), it is plain that the plaintiff knew by the latest in mid-1974 that her injury was significant, and that she also knew the identity of the potential defendant. I further hold that by that date, or very shortly afterwards, she had constructive knowledge that the injury was or might be attributable to an act or omission of the defendant's, in the sense that by that date it was reasonable for her to take legal advice (see *Newton v Cammell Laird & Co (Shipbuilders and Engineers) Ltd* [1969] 1 All ER 708, [1969] 1 WLR 415). The writ was not issued for a further six years or so.

The action is thus statute-barred, unless in the exercise of my discretion I disapply the bar. Counsel for the defendants dealt with this topic in a very fair and realistic manner. He said that, if the first defendant's evidence was accepted, then he had suffered no prejudice as a result of the delay, and that none of the other factors which might tell against exercising my discretion in the plaintiff's favour applied in this case.

I have accepted the first defendant's evidence. In these circumstances, in the exercise

of my discretion, and particularly having regard to the gravity of the plaintiff's injuries,
a I think it is proper for me to disapply the limitation bar, and I so do.

    But on the case as a whole there will be judgment for the defendants.

Plaintiff's claim dismissed.

Solicitors: *Frimonds*, agents for *R P Huggins & Co*, Reading (for the plaintiff); *Hempsons*
b (for the defendants).

K Mydeen Esq   Barrister.

Salmon v Seafarer Restaurants Ltd (British Gas Corp, third party)

QUEEN'S BENCH DIVISION
WOOLF J
28, 29 JUNE 1982

d

Occupier's liability – Fireman – Duty of care owed to fireman – Nature of duty – Fireman attending premises to put out fire – Fire caused by occupier's negligence – Fire causing explosion injuring fireman – Likelihood of explosion not unusual in type of fire involved – Whether occupier owing common duty of care to fireman – Whether duty of care to fireman limited to protection from special or exceptional risks – Occupiers' Liability Act 1957, s 2.

e

The plaintiff, a fireman, was injured by an explosion on premises occupied by the defendants as a fish and chip shop when a fire in the premises melted a seal on a gas meter thus allowing gas to escape. The fire was caused by an employee of the defendants negligently forgetting to extinguish a gas flame under a chip fryer before leaving the premises for the night, with the result that the oil in the chip fryer continued to heat up
f until it caught fire. The plaintiff brought an action in negligence against the defendants, contending that, because the fire had been started negligently and because he had been injured as a result, he was entitled to recover damages from the defendant. The defendants denied liability, contending that an occupier's duty of care to firemen attending his premises in the course of their work was limited to protecting the firemen from any special or exceptional risks over and above the ordinary risks necessarily
g incidental to a fireman's job, and did not extend to protecting firemen from such ordinary risks which, on the facts, included an explosion of the kind which had taken place on the defendants' premises. At the trial of the action the plaintiff conceded that the defendants could not have foreseen the precise chain of events which led to the explosion.

h **Held** – An occupier of premises owed the same duty of care to a fireman attending his premises to extinguish a fire as he owed to other visitors under s 2[a] of the Occupiers' Liability Act 1957, subject to the fact that in determining whether the occupier was in breach of that duty a fireman was expected to exercise those skills which were ordinarily

---

j   *a*   Section 2, far as material, provides:
      '(1) An occupier of premises owes the same duty, the "common duty of care", to all his visitors, except in so far as he is free to and does extend, restrict, modify or exclude his duty to any visitor or visitors by agreement or otherwise.
      (2) The common duty of care is a duty to take such care as in all the circumstances of the case is reasonable to see that the visitor will be reasonably safe in using the premises for the purposes for which he is invited or permitted by the occupier to be there . . .'

expected to be shown by firemen. Accordingly, the occupier was under the ordinary duty under s 2, namely to take such care as was reasonable in all the circumstances to see that the fireman was reasonably safe in using the premises for the purpose of extinguishing the fire. Since the fire at the defendants' premises was caused by their employee's negligence and since it was reasonably foreseeable that firemen would be required to attend the fire and that an explosion of the kind which occurred might result from the fire, the defendants were liable to the plaintiff (see p 735 *j* to p 736 *g*, post).

Notes

For an occupier's common duty of care to his visitors, see 34 Halsbury's Laws (4th edn) paras 22–24.

For the Occupiers' Liability Act 1957, s 2, see 23 Halsbury's Statutes (3rd edn) 794.

Cases referred to in judgment

Donoghue (or M'Alister) v Stevenson [1932] AC 562, [1932] All ER Rep 1, HL.
Hartley v British Rlys Board (1981) 125 SJ 169, CA.
Merrington v Ironbridge Metal Works Ltd [1952] 2 All ER 1101.
Sibbald or Bermingham v Sher Bros (1980) 124 SJ 117, HL.

Action

By a writ issued on 8 May 1978 the plaintiff, Gary Thomas James Salmon, a fireman employed by the Greater London Council, claimed against the defendants, Seafarer Restaurants Ltd, damages and loss suffered by the plaintiff when as a result of the defendants' negligence a fire occurred at the defendants' premises in the course of which an explosion occurred injuring the plaintiff. On 25 July 1979 the defendants served a third party notice on British Gas Corp claiming indemnity or contribution on the ground of the third party's alleged negligence in installing the gas supply to the defendants' premises. The facts are set out in the judgment.

Benet Hytner QC and *George Pulman* for the plaintiff.
John Loyd QC and *Rupert Jackson* for the defendants.
Veronica Schoeneich for the third party.

WOOLF J. This action raises in acute form the question as to what duty an occupier who causes a fire on premises owes to a fireman who attends at the premises to put out the fire. The facts are largely agreed.

The premises in question were occupied by the defendants and are at Cranbrook Road, Ilford, in the county of Essex. At those premises the defendants have a fish bar which conducts business very much in the same way as a fish-and-chip shop of the traditional sort conducts its business, and, in addition, there is a restaurant which provides meals on the premises. In the fish bar portion of the premises there is a fish fryer and a chip fryer. Those fryers use oil for the purposes of cooking. On 10 March 1977 the premises were left just after midnight and an employee of the defendants failed to extinguish one of the lights under the chip fryer with the consequence that, when the premises were vacated, the oil was continuing to be heated with the result that eventually the oil caught fire and, in turn, the premises themselves caught fire.

In addition to the defendants, the occupiers of the premises, the British Gas Corp is made a third party to the proceedings because there was a gas supply to the fryers to which I have made reference and also a further gas supply to the premises, and there was an allegation made by the defendants that events which I must now recount were the responsibility of the third party.

The fire station is in close proximity to the defendants' premises and, when the alarm was given as a result of the fire, the fire appliances together with the officers were able to attend very promptly at about 3.40am. The actual immediate fire in the vicinity of the fryers was quickly extinguished with the use of foam, or, at least, if it was not completely extinguished, was brought very much under control. It was then observed that there was

a light on the second floor of the premises and, as there was a considerable amount of
a fume caused by the fire, it was decided by the senior fire officers present that access
should be obtained to the second floor by ladder. In order to obtain access in this way to
the second floor use was made of a flat roof to part of the ground floor of the premises
and the ladder was placed on the flat roof so that an officer could climb the ladder and
enter the second floor. It was necessary for another officer to foot that ladder and this job
was given to the plaintiff, Gary Thomas James Salmon. He was standing, footing the
b ladder, on the flat roof when suddenly there was an explosion, as a result of which he was
thrown to the ground and sustained injuries.

Mr Salmon, who is 33 years of age now, had been a fire officer for a number of years,
11 in total, and, because of the injuries he suffered, he eventually had to give up that
employment. He was unemployed for a substantial period but he eventually obtained
employment as a nurse. It is not necessary for me to go into details with regard to his
c injuries, but it is right that I should say that the main injuries were a fracture of the right
os calcis and a laceration of the right middle and ring fingers with the division of a
tendon. The reason why it is not necessary for me to go into the injuries is that it is
agreed by all parties that if the plaintiff succeeds the damages to which he is entitled
amount to £58,500, that sum taking into account his entitlement to interest.

So far as the explosion is concerned, expert evidence was called before me, but, again,
d there really was no issue. I have made reference to the fact that there was a gas supply to
the premises. That gas supply was fed to the premises through two separate gas meters,
the larger of which served the fryers. Those gas meters were sited close to the ceiling on
the ground floor, approximately 40 feet from the fryers. The area of the ground floor
between the position of the meters and the fryers had a false suspended ceiling. What
had happened, in the view of the experts, was that the heat from the fire travelled along
e the suspended ceiling to the larger of the meters; it there melted the seals of the meter,
allowing gas to escape; that gas was able to collect in the void between the false ceiling
and the actual ceiling of the ground floor premises; the gas mingled with the air to form
an explosive mixture and that explosive mixture ignited in some way in consequence of
the fire.

Allegations were made by the plaintiff against the defendants, and by the defendants
f against the third party as to the choice of meters, namely ordinary meters as opposed to
fire-resistant meters, and the positioning of those meters as I have described them.
However, those allegations were not persisted in by the plaintiff, having regard to the
evidence which was given not only by the defendants' expert but by the plaintiff's own
expert, and it was conceded by counsel on behalf of the plaintiff, during the defendants'
submissions to me, that the defendants were not negligent in siting the meters in the
g position in which they were, and also conceded that the defendants could not have
foreseen the precise chain of events which led to the explosion. Having regard to those
concessions, counsel for the defendants did not persist in his claim as against the British
Gas Corp.

However, notwithstanding the concession to which I have made reference, the plaintiff
still contends that he is entitled to recover damages from the defendants. It is his
h contention that this fire was started by negligence, that he was injured as a result and that
he is entitled to damages in respect thereof. The defendants dispute that this is the
position and it is their contention that in relation to firemen the duty of an occupier of
premises is confined to a duty to take reasonable care to protect the firemen against those
risks which he can reasonably foresee could cause injury to firemen, other than those
which are risks or dangers which are the ordinary incident of the job of a fireman. In
j other words, that an occupier in relation to a fireman owes a duty of care to protect the
fireman against some special, exceptional or additional risk, not the ordinary risks which
are a necessary incident of his job. The defendants say, having regard to the concession to
which I have made reference, that there is no evidence here that there was any foreseeable
special, exceptional or additional risk which placed any duty on the defendants to take
care to protect the plaintiff, and that, although there was the explosion, the risk of that
explosion occurring in the way that it did was not foreseeable by the defendants, so that

they are under no liability for not taking steps to prevent injury being caused to the
plaintiff as a result of the explosion.

    The plaintiff disputes that the duty is as limited as the defendants contend. He submits,
first of all, that, where a fire occurs due to the negligence of an individual, then that
individual (or his employers if they are vicariously responsible for the negligence) is
liable to a fireman who attends the fire and is injured, subject to two provisos. First of all,
the negligence must occur in such circumstances that it is reasonably foreseeable that a
fireman, or firemen, will attend the fire which results from the negligence. Secondly,
there must be a continuous chain of causation between the initial negligence that brought
about the fire and the event which resulted in the injury. The chain of causation between
the negligent act and the injury must not be broken. For example, there must not be
some intervening act of negligence by someone else which breaks the link. If the injury
to the fireman is brought about by a gross error on the part of a senior fire officer in
sending a fireman to a particularly hazardous situation, counsel for the plaintiff would
accept that the chain could be broken. But, subject to those two matters, the primary
submission is that, in the case of a fire of this sort, caused by negligence, a fireman is
entitled to succeed.

    The second submission which is made by counsel for the plaintiff, as an alternative to
his first, is to the effect that, if there is need for some special, exceptional or additional
risk, then the existence of that risk is sufficient to create a duty even though it is not
foreseeable by the occupier. Counsel for the plaintiff says there could be three different
situations which resulted in such a risk: firstly, it could be wholly unavoidable; secondly,
it could be avoidable by reasonable care; thirdly (so to speak an intermediate stage
between the first and second situations), the risk could be avoidable, but not avoidable
merely by the exercise of reasonable care. And counsel contended that the second and
third categories of risk are sufficient for a fireman to establish liability.

    I am bound to say I find the greatest difficulty with this last submission by counsel for
the plaintiff. If there is liability owed by an occupier to a person who is injured as a result
of a fire started negligently, then it seems to me that such liability must depend on a
failure to exercise a proper degree of care in circumstances where a duty is owed, and it
seems hard to find any justification for establishing either a failure to exercise proper care
or the existence of a duty where the risk which is said to create the liability is one which
is not avoidable by the exercise of reasonable care and not foreseeable by an occupier
exercising such a standard of care. It seems to me that liability, if there is liability in these
circumstances, must depend on counsel for the plaintiff's first submission, and it is to
that first submission that I now turn.

    The explanation for counsel for the plaintiff feeling that it was necessary to advance an
alternative sumission is to be found in three cases, the first of which is *Merrington v
Ironbridge Metal Works Ltd* [1952] 2 All ER 1101. The judgment in that case was given
by Hallett J and he was dealing with a situation where the defendants carried on a process
which caused the creation of large quantities of dust and this dust was thickly deposited
in numerous parts of the factory. A fire occurred at the factory and the plaintiff, who was
a part-time fireman, attended and was injured when an explosion occurred, that explosion
being due to the dust which had been created by the defendants and allowed to
accumulate on the premises. It seems to me that the situation which Hallett J was
considering was readily distinguishable from the situation that I am considering. First of
all, there was no finding made by Hallett J how the fire originally started. So far as the
fire in this case is concerned there is really no issue that the employee who left the
premises with the fryer still ignited was negligent and the defendants are responsible for
that negligence. However, Hallett J's attention, so far as liability was concerned, was with
the circumstances causing the explosion rather than the circumstances causing the initial
outbreak of fire. It is true that he said this (at 1104):

        'This may be a convenient moment to say emphatically that I do not accept the
    submission of leading counsel for the plaintiff that, if a fireman sustains injury as

a the result of performing his duty at a fire, he ipso facto becomes entitled to recover compensation from any person whose carelessness has caused the fire in question.'

However, when that passage is closely examined, it will be appreciated that what the judge is not accepting is something different from what counsel for the plaintiff in this case contends for in his first submission. The remark of the judge is not subject to the two qualifications which counsel for the plaintiff made to his first submission, as to the circumstances in which liability would arise. Hallett J's ipso facto situation does not

b require that it should be foreseeable that a fireman would attend and might be injured; second, it does not deal with the requirement of the causal link between the initial negligence, or carelessness, and the injury. Later in his judgment Hallett J came to the conclusion that the occupier of that factory owed to the fireman the well-known duty of an invitor. However, he did not base the liability of the defendants in that case on that duty because he saw a difficulty in the plaintiff succeeding on that basis, in that there was

c no evidence to show that the plaintiff would have avoided the danger if he had been warned of it, and, of course, as the law stood at that time in relation to invitors and invitees, if an invitor gave a sufficient warning to an invitee he fulfilled his duty. The way Hallett J approached the matter was to say that he should ask himself certain questions, and the fourth of those questions he answered in these terms, that, if members of the fire service did enter the premises to deal with a fire in the course of their duty,

d they would be exposed to an exceptional and serious risk of being injured by an explosion, they could recover. I draw attention to the reference to an 'exceptional and serious' risk. Hallett J found that there was such an exceptional and serious risk, and, therefore, liability, but I do not regard the judge as laying down that there can be no recovery by a plaintiff fireman without there being exposure to an exceptional and serious risk, at least where the case is based not on what happened subsequent to the fire starting but on the

e negligence in starting the fire. I can well understand that if you are dealing with a situation where it is being alleged that an occupier is liable for injury to a fireman, although he was not shown to be negligent in causing the initial fire, it is necessary in those circumstances that there should be some special additional or unusual hazard (I do not think the adjective is important) to create an obligation to take special precautions for the safety of a fireman who attends the premises. However, it does not follow from

f this that the position is the same where the fire can be shown to have been started by negligence for which the occupier is responsible. Furthermore, it is clear from the judgment that Hallett J was not laying down any general rule. He was invited by counsel to do so but he made it clear that he was dealing with the matter on the facts of the particular case which was before him. He said (at 1106):

g 'I have already pointed out and emphasise again that my judgment depends on the particular facts of this case and will not provide the wide authority for which leading counsel for the plaintiff, in his opening, appeared to be hoping.'

The second of the cases to which I was referred is Sibbald or Bermingham v Sher Bros (1980) 124 SJ 117. That was a decision of the House of Lords of which I have been provided with a transcript. It again concerns a fireman and the tragedy in that case was

h caused when a whole ceiling of a first floor which was made of untreated hardboard suddenly and unexpectedly caught fire and erupted into flames. The decision of their Lordships is to be found in the speech of Lord Fraser, with which all the other members of the House agreed. At the beginning of his speech he again makes it clear that the House of Lords was dealing with the matter other than on the basis of the initial negligence which caused the fire. He sets out the appellant's case and he says:

j 'First she said that the fire had been caused by the dropping of a lighted cigarette or match and that it was attributable to the negligence of the respondents in failing to take reasonable care for the safety of persons, including fireman, liable to be endangered by an outbreak of fire. The Lord Ordinary held that the appellant had not proved her averments of fact in support of this ground, and his view was upheld

by the First Division. Their decision on this part of the case was not challenged in
this House.'

Lord Fraser then deals with what was in issue before the House, in these terms:

'The second ground, which alone was relied on by the appellant before your
Lordships, was that the respondents were said to be liable as occupiers of the
premises in which the fire occurred because they had negligently failed to take
reasonable care to adopt and maintain adequate fire precautions.'

Clearly their Lordships were dealing with the sort of situation where, earlier, I said
that one can understand that there may be a necessity to find some special circumstance
in order to create liability in respect of injury to a fireman. Later in his speech Lord
Fraser refers to the Occupiers' Liability (Scotland) Act 1960 and then goes on to say:

'It would in my opinion impose an impossible burden on an occupier if he had to
take reasonable care to provide firemen with an escape route which will continue to
be adequate during the whole time that they are on his premises fighting a fire.'

And he finally says:

'For all these reasons I am of opinion that the respondents, as occupier of those
premises, owed no duty to fireman, such as the appellant's deceased husband, who
entered the premises for the purpose of fighting a fire there, to provide them with a
means of access and egress which would remain safe during the fire.'

The passages to which I have referred, in my view, make it clear that the decision of
the House of Lords has no direct relevance to the issue which is before me, and is in no
way inconsistent with the primary submission made on behalf of the plaintiff.

The third case to which I have been referred is *Hartley v British Rlys Board* (1981) 125
SJ 169. Again, I have been handed a transcript. It is a decision of the Court of Appeal
given on 28 January 1981. In that case a railway servant had left a railway station
unmanned without giving his superiors notice of that fact, which he should have given.
A fire occurred at the railway station, firemen attended and, because they suspected that
the employee was still in the railway station, the firemen went onto an upper floor and
one of their number was injured. In that case the judge at first instance had rejected the
plaintiff's case on a number of grounds. First of all, he rejected the case that was made
out that the fire had been caused by the negligence of the employee for whose acts the
defendants were responsible. That finding was rejected by Waller LJ, and so this case was
a case where, at least so far as the Court of Appeal was concerned, the initial fire could be
shown to have been caused by negligence. The judge also found that there was no duty
owed by the defendants to the plaintiff, and it was with regard to that (as I understand
from counsel for the plaintiff, who also appeared in that case) that most of the argument
turned. The case was argued before the Court of Appeal and it was accepted by the Court
of Appeal that the particular plaintiff had gone to a part of the premises, namely the
upper floor, which was more hazardous, and in relation to that it was submitted on
behalf of the defendants that a fire officer going to a fire accepts the ordinary risks which
a fireman has to meet, and, according to the report, counsel then went on to submit that
in that particular case, although there was an extra risk in going to this space, nevertheless
it was a risk which firemen have to accept from time to time. It was also argued that, in
the circumstances of the case, the plaintiff would have had to go into the space whether
or not there was somebody on the premises. With regard to that, Waller LJ disagreed.
He came to the conclusion that the prime purpose of a fireman going into this space was
to look for the missing person. He then went on to say:

'So the question is: did the defendants owe a duty to the plaintiff in those
circumstances? If the duty of the defendants was to take reasonable care not to
subject the plaintiff, a visitor to those premises, to unnecessary risk, they were in
breach of that duty.'

Waller LJ then referred to the House of Lords case to which I have just referred, cited
a   *Donoghue v Stevenson* [1932] AC 562, [1932] All ER Rep 1, and went on to say:

> 'In my judgment, it is equally applicable to deal with that situation that the
> occupier owes some duty of care, and the duty of the occupier is to take reasonable
> care not to expose the visitor (the plaintiff) to unnecessary risk. The fact that in
> other circumstances it is a risk which he may have to face from time to time is, in
> my judgment, neither here nor there. In this particular case it was an unnecessary
> **b**   risk; it was a risk which Mr Mcgiveron [the sub-officer in charge of the firemen
> who went to the station] regarded as hazarding the firemen to a greater degree than
> normal and accordingly, in my opinion, there was a breach of that duty.'

He went on to find that the plaintiff was entitled to recover because he was exposed to
that unnecessary risk.
c   While Waller LJ could have considered the position and confined his attention to the
initial start of the fire, and the negligence which caused that, it is quite clear from his
reference to the House of Lords decision (which I have also dealt with) that when he was
considering the question of liability he was primarily looking at the matter in relation to
the responsibilities of occupiers to firemen irrespective of whether they were the initiators
of the fire by negligence, and his remarks, which seem to indicate that the liability was
d   limited to unnecessary risks, must be viewed in that context.
The approach of Cumming-Bruce LJ was similar. The point that caused him concern
was not the nature of the duty which was owed but the question of causation. He makes
this clear where he says:

> 'The point that has given me the greatest difficulty in the case is the question
> whether the plaintiff has proved that the presence of the fireman in an otherwise
> **e**   unnecessarily hazardous position in the roof was caused by the defendants'
> negligence.'

In other words, Cumming-Bruce LJ was worried in case negligence was not the
explanation for the fireman being in the unnecessarily hazardous position, and it is in
regard to that matter that his judgment is directed, though he did go on, again, to deal
f   with unnecessary hazards at the conclusion of his judgment.
The third member of the court was Dame Elizabeth Lane, and, although she refers to
an 'unnecessary hazard', again her approach is reflecting that approach which I referred
to earlier which is to be found in Waller LJ's judgment. I would therefore regard what
was said by the Court of Appeal in that case as being by no means decisive as to the
correctness or otherwise of the primary submission made by counsel on behalf of the
g   plaintiff. Indeed, it would be strange if that case led to any result which was inconsistent
with the plaintiff in this case being entitled to succeed. The reference to unnecessary
hazard being created by the defendants, or by a person for whose acts the defendants are
responsible, could be applied to the circumstances of this case.
The leaving of the fish or chip fryer ignited created the unnecessary hazard in the form
of the fire which occurred. There is a direct link between the fire breaking out and the
h   explosion, and to try and divide one from the other and say that because the precise
explosion was not foreseeable the defendants are not responsible seems to me to be
contrary to the ordinary approach as to causation where the acts of an individual which
are negligent give rise to a series of events all of which are linked one to the other.
Having found nothing in the authorities to which I was referred which is inconsistent
with the ordinary approach to liability in these circumstances, I go on to consider, in the
j   absence of authority, whether there is any basis for limiting the duty which is owed to
firemen. It is true that their very occupation is one where they are specially trained to
deal with the dangers inherent in any outbreak of fire. However, it seems to me that
their consequent special skills should not change the normal approach to the establishing
of liability. It is only a factor to take into account in seeing whether a liability is
established and their calling is not in itself a defence. In deciding whether the negligent

act could foreseeably cause injury to a fireman, it is necessary to take into account the skills that are ordinarily expected to be shown by firemen. To decide whether there has been any breach of the duty, which in my view undoubtedly exists, in certain cases it will be very relevant to consider whether or not the danger to the fireman requires the taking of precautions. Here again it is proper to take into account the special skills of the fireman. Where it can be foreseen that the fire which is negligently started is of the type which could, first of all, require firemen to attend to extinguish that fire, and where, because of the very nature of the fire, when they attend they will be at risk even though they exercise all the skill of their calling, there seems no reason why a fireman should be at any disadvantage when the question of compensation for his injuries arises.

I make the remarks which I have made, with regard to the position of firemen, because it was submitted by counsel on behalf of the defendants, in his very careful and helpful submissions, that in the case of firemen there were good public policy reasons why there should be a restriction on the extent of the duty owed to them, and that they should be treated differently from other 'rescuers' (I here use the expression to identify the category of cases which I have in mind). Notwithstanding the submissions of counsel for the defendants, I find no principle of public policy which requires the ordinary rules to be limited, and it seems to me that the same principles disclosed by the 'rescue' cases should be applied to firemen, though taking into account, of course, in the way I have already indicated, the special skills of firemen.

There may be, and indeed on the authorities there appears to be, an additional basis of liability quite apart from the question as to the responsibility for the initial fire, but that is not the situation with which I am primarily concerned in this case.

Turning to apply the correct approach, as I find it to be, to the facts of this case, it seems to me that there can be no doubt that the defendants are liable to the plaintiff. The fire was caused by negligence of their employee in the course of his employment. As Mr Hunt, the plaintiff's expert, said in the course of his evidence: 'A fire of oil of this nature can give off very considerable heat. That sort of fire often will be readily extinguishable by the use of foam.' However, as again Mr Hunt made clear in his evidence, it is by no means unique or unusual for the sort of sequence of events that occurred in the case of this fire to occur in consequence of that type of fire, and this explosion which was the immediate cause of the injuries to the plaintiff was directly caused by the negligence of the employee, and negligence in those circumstances gives rise to a liability to the plaintiff who, it was readily foreseeable, would be required to attend this fire and be at risk of such injuries.

It follows, therefore, that the plaintiff is entitled to judgment in the sum of £58,500, and that the third party is entitled to be dismissed from the proceedings.

Judgment for the plaintiff for £58,500. Stay of execution for 28 days subject to undertaking to prosecute an appeal with all due expedition.

Solicitors: *Robin Thompson & Partners*, Ilford (for the plaintiff); *Badhams* (for the defendants); *B C Brooks*, Staines (for the third party).

K Mydeen Esq   Barrister.

a
Allied Marine Transport Ltd v Vale do Rio Doce Navegacao SA
The Leonidas D

QUEEN'S BENCH DIVISION (COMMERCIAL COURT)

b   MUSTILL J

22, 23 MARCH, 16, 17, 18 NOVEMBER 1982, 28 MARCH, 13 MAY 1983

Arbitration – Practice – Want of prosecution – Dismissal of claim – Abandonment by accord and satisfaction – Dispute referred to arbitration within limitation period – Claimant taking no further action for next five and a half years – Whether silence and inactivity amounting to offer to give
c *up reference to arbitration – Whether silence and inactivity amounting to offer to give up claim.*

By a time charter dated 24 April 1975 in an expanded New York Produce Exchange form, the owners chartered a vessel to the charterers under a charterparty which provided for arbitration in England. In 1976 a dispute arose between the parties and a notice of arbitration was given by the charterers, following which two arbitrators were appointed,
d   one by each party. Thereafter nothing happened in the arbitration for five and a half years until, in August 1981 the charterers wrote to the owners asking for an admission of liability, in default of which they intended to proceed with the pending arbitration. In November 1981 the charterers served their points of claim. The owners then issued an originating summons seeking, inter alia, a declaration that the arbitration agreement contained in the charterparty was at an end by reason of its having been (a) mutually
e   abandoned and/or (b) repudiated by the charterers and treated as such by the owners. The charterers had in the mean time appointed a new arbitrator in respect of the same dispute to meet the contingency that the existing arbitration would be declared defunct. That appointment was made on the assumption that the appropriate limitation period for claiming under the charterparty was the six-year period applicable to a breach of contract rather than the one-year period prescribed by the Hague Rules. The charterers
f   claimed that, if the relevant time limit was six years rather than one year, then it could not be held that the claim had been abandoned by consent. The questions arose (i) whether the existing reference alone was defunct while the claim and the arbitration agreement remained operative, (ii) whether both the claim and the reference had been abandoned by consent or (iii) whether the charterers' conduct was such that they were estopped from pursuing their claim.

g
Held – (1) Although a claimant in an arbitration concerning a breach of contract had a statutory right to wait until just before the lapse of six years from the date of the breach before commencing his action and delay in commencing an action within the limitation period could not be construed as the abandonment of the claim, once the claimant had commenced his action by appointing an arbitrator the limitation period thereafter
h   became irrelevant in determining whether a claim had been abandoned. Accordingly, a claimant who had commenced his claim could by his conduct be held to have abandoned his claim even though the limitation period had not expired. It followed that even if the relevant time limit in which the charterers could bring their claim was six years the charterers' conduct during that period was capable of being interpreted as being an abandonment of their claim (see p 743 b to d, post).
j   (2) Abandonment of a claim under an arbitration agreement could be brought about either by an estoppel or by an accord and satisfaction. In regard to the latter method, although under the general law of contract inactivity and silence would not usually be regarded as being an offer or an acceptance they could be construed as an offer to abandon a claim under an arbitration agreement or the acceptance of such an offer, so that consensual abandonment of a claim inferred from silence and inactivity could constitute

a valid offer and acceptance for the purposes of an accord and satisfaction. Furthermore the cesser of the respondent's rights under the agreement in return for the cesser of the claimant's rights constituted sufficient consideration for the purposes of an accord and satisfaction (see p 742 *h* to p 743 *b*, post); *André & Cie SA v Marine Transocean Ltd, The Splendid Sun* [1981] 2 All ER 993 and *Paal Wilson & Co A/S v Partenreederei Hannah Blumenthal, The Hannah Blumenthal* [1983] 1 All ER 34 considered.

(3) In order for the court to find that only the reference had been abandoned while the claim remained operative, the court had to be satisfied that the charterers' silence and inactivity amounted to a representation that they wished to give up the arbitration conducted by the nominated arbitrators while reserving the right to pursue their claim before another tribunal. The fact that a claimant had done nothing for a long time could not justify the inference that he merely intended to end the arbitration while reserving his right to pursue the claim. On the facts, there was nothing to show that the parties had consented to abandon the arbitration before the nominated arbitrators while leaving the claim operative or that there was a representation to that effect by the charterers which was relied on by the owners (see p 744 *f* to *h*, post).

(4) In deciding whether both the claim and the reference had been abandoned the court had to consider the conduct of the charterers and the owners as evinced to each other, and (so far as concerned the argument based on an estoppel) also the owners' understanding of the charterers' intention and what, if any, action they had taken in reliance of that understanding. On the facts, the charterers' conduct could properly be interpreted as a tacit representation that they did not intend to pursue either the claim or the reference while the conduct of the owners was sufficient to amount to an acceptance of the tacit offer to abandon both the reference and the claim. The owners' claim to have the arbitration agreement treated as at an end would therefore be granted (see p 744 *h* to p 745 *a* and *h j*, post).

(5) In any event the owners had reacted to the charterers' silence by taking none of the steps in the way of preparing their case which would have been appropriate if the claim was still active and by that omission they had suffered a real detriment sufficient to estop the charterers from pursuing their claim. Accordingly the owners' were also entitled to succeed on the grounds of estoppel (see p 746 *h j*, post).

Per curiam. There is a need for legislation giving either arbitrators or the courts discretionary power to dismiss a claim in an arbitration for want of prosecution (see p 747 *b*, post).

Observations on the principles applicable to the termination of arbitration agreements (see p 741 *d* to p 742 *c*, post).

Notes
For termination of an arbitration agreement, see 2 Halsbury's Laws (4th edn) paras 547–554, and for cases on the subject, see 3 Digest (Reissue) 104–118, 545–646.

Cases referred to in judgment
André & Cie SA v Marine Transocean Ltd, The Splendid Sun [1981] 2 All ER 993, [1981] QB 694, [1981] 3 WLR 43, CA.
Birkett v James [1977] 2 All ER 801, [1978] AC 297, [1977] 3 WLR 38, HL.
Bremer Vulkan Schiffbau Und Maschinenfabrik v South India Shipping Corp [1981] 1 All ER 289, [1981] AC 909, [1981] 2 WLR 141, HL.
Glasgow and South-Western Rly Co v Boyd and Forrest 1918 SC (HL) 14.
Paal Wilson & Co A/S v Partenreederei Hannah Blumenthal, The Hannah Blumenthal [1983] 1 All ER 34, [1983] 1 AC 854, [1982] 3 WLR 1149, HL; *rvsg* [1982] 3 All ER 394, [1983] 1 AC 854, [1982] 3 WLR 49, CA; *affg* [1982] 1 All ER 197, [1983] 1 AC 854, [1981] 3 WLR 823.

Originating summons
By an originating summons issued on 25 January 1982 the plaintiffs, Allied Marine

a Transport Ltd, the owners of the vessel Leonidas D (who were substituted as plaintiffs for Ocean Freighters Corp pursuant to an order dated 15 April 1982 under RSC Ord 20, r 1), sought, inter alia, (i) a declaration that the arbitration agreement contained in a charterparty made between the owners and the defendants, Vale do Rio Doce Navegacao SA (the charterers), dated 24 April 2975 was at an end by reason of its having been (a) mutually abandoned and/or rescinded by the parties and/or (b) frustrated and/or (c) repudiated by the charterers and treated as such by the owners, (ii) an injunction
b restraining the charterers by themselves their servants or agents or otherwise howsoever from taking any further steps in or otherwise attempting to pursue the arbitration commenced by the parties in April 1976 or from commencing or pursuing their claims in that arbitration against the owners in any further or other proceedings whatsoever, and (iii) damages for the charterers' repudiatory breach of the arbitration agreement limited to the owners' costs in the reference. The facts are set out in the judgment.

c
Michael G Collins for the owners.
Richard Aikens for the charterers.

Cur adv vult

d 13 May. The following judgment was delivered.

MUSTILL J. This case has a long and chequered history. It began in April 1975 when Allied Marine Transport Ltd, the plaintiffs (the owners) in the present action, chartered the vessel Leonidas D to Vale do Rio Navegacao SA, the defendants (the charterers) in the action, on an expanded version of the New York Produce Exchange Form, for a period of
e 18 to 24 months. The charterparty incorporated the United States, Canadian and Chamber of Shipping clauses paramount, and a London arbitration clause.

During January 1976 and April 1976 the parties fell into dispute about the cost and time involved in cleaning the holds of the vessel preparatory to loading at two ports. The total sum involved was about $US110,000. Notice of arbitration was given by the charterers, and two arbitrators were appointed, one by each party. Thereafter, nothing at
f all happened in the arbitration for five and a half years, until on 3 August 1981 Richards Butler & Co wrote to Ince & Co, who were the owners' solicitors, stating that they were instructed by the charterers and asking for an admission of liability, in default of which the charterers would proceed with the pending arbitration. Having by 20 November 1981 received no positive response from the owners, Richards Butler served their clients' points of claim. This prompted the owners to issue an originating summons on 25
g January 1982 claiming a declaration that the arbitration agreement contained in the charterparty was at an end by reason of its having been (a) mutually abandoned and/or rescinded by the parties, and/or (b) frustrated, and/or (c) repudiated by the charterers and treated as such by the owners. The originating summons also claimed an injunction restraining the further conduct of the arbitration.

Meanwhile on 4 December 1981 the charterers (who had anticipated that such proceedings might well be instituted) had appointed Mr Bruce Harris as their arbitrator
h in respect of the same dispute, to meet the contingency that the existing arbitration would be declared defunct. This appointment was made within the limitation period for claiming under the charterparty, always assuming, however, that the appropriate period was the six years relative to a claim for breach of contract, rather than the one-year period prescribed by the Hague Rules.

j The originating summons was listed for hearing on 22 March 1982. At that time the authorities were in the following state. Bremer Vulkan Schiffbau Und Maschinenfabrik v South India Shipping Corp [1981] 1 All ER 289, [1981] AC 909 had been decided by the House of Lords, André & Cie SA v Marine Transocean Ltd, The Splendid Sun [1981] 2 All ER 993, [1981] QB 694 had been decided by the Court of Appeal and Paal Wilson & Co A/S v Partenreederei Hannah Blumenthal, The Hannah Blumenthal [1983] 1 All ER 34, [1983] 1 AC

854 had been heard at first instance (see [1982] 1 All ER 197, [1981] 1 AC 854). These authorities appeared to establish that, although a prolonged period of inactivity on both sides probably could not amount to a repudiation by the claimant of the agreement to arbitrate, such delay could in appropriate circumstances bring about either a frustration of the contract or a rescission by mutual abandonment. By coincidence, at the time when the case was awaiting argument, *The Hannah Blumenthal* [1982] 3 All ER 394, [1983] 1 AC 854 had reached the Court of Appeal and was due for judgment in only three days' time. It was accordingly decided to adjourn the argument to see how the law stood in the light of the new judgments. In the event, the decision of the Court of Appeal largely confirmed the position as I have just summarised it. It did not, however, prove possible to restore the present case to the list until November 1982, when by a further coincidence *The Hannah Blumenthal* was in the course of argument in the House of Lords. Information as to the way in which the matter had been developing suggested a strong probability that frustration would disappear as a medium of discharge by long delay, but that mutual rescission would remain a possibility, subject, however, to one important new qualification, to which I shall later refer. Against this background, it seemed sensible to keep the hearing in being until after the speeches had been delivered in the House of Lords. Accordingly, all the issues not directly affected by *The Hannah Blumenthal* were argued to a conclusion, and the case was then once again adjourned. In the event, the forecasts of what the speeches would contain proved to be substantially correct and when the matter was restored to the list during March 1983 attention was confined to the question of discharge by mutual abandonment, the alternative pleas of repudiation being treated as untenable, at least before a judge of first instance.

At the same time as this intermittent hearing a series of other proceedings had been brought into existence and debated, for the purpose of exploring the practical consequences of various alternative solutions to the main question. To a considerable extent, subsequent developments have caused these to be of no more than academic interest, and I will not encumber this judgment by explaining them. There was, however, one which remained a live issue, namely whether the effect of incorporating the clauses paramount into the charterparty was to produce a limitation of one year for claims of the kind now brought by the charterers, or whether the claims remained subject to the normal period of six years. The relevance was this. One possible outcome of the present proceedings was a decision that the individual reference to the arbitrament of the two named arbitrators had been cancelled by mutual abandonment, but that this abandonment had left untouched the charterers' cause of action and the agreement contained in the arbitration clause to refer disputes to arbitration. In such a situation there would be nothing to prevent the charterers from persisting in the arbitration called into existence by their 'protective' appointment of Mr Harris. This appointment was, however, made after the expiry of the Hague Rules time limit, if this limit applied to the charterers' claim. Thus, if it did so apply, and if the proceedings resulted in a decision to that effect either by the arbitrators in the new arbitration or by the High Court, the claim would fail, without the merits ever being entered on at all.

In these circumstances the owners asked the court to approach the problem in the following sequence. First, consider whether the existing reference is defunct, but the cause of action and the arbitration agreement are intact. Second, decide whether any claim pursued in the new arbitration would inevitably be defeated by a plea that the appointment of Mr Harris was made outside the period prescribed by the Hague Rules. Finally, if the answer to the second question is affirmative, grant an injunction to restrain the prosecution of the new arbitration, which must inevitably result in the failure of the claim.

This line of argument raised a question of great practical and theoretical importance in the law of arbitration, namely whether there exists under English law a jurisdiction which may be regarded as the obverse of proceedings under RSC Ord 14. By virtue of the latter, the court has power to give summary judgment even though the contract contains an arbitration clause, the rationale being that summary judgment is only a possiblity if there is no genuine dispute; and if there is no genuine dispute there is

a nothing to refer to arbitration. Can this argument be turned upside down so as to produce the result that, if the court is satisfied that there is no genuine claim, it can hold that there is no genuine dispute, and hence that there is nothing which can properly be referred to arbitration, so that the court should intervene by injunction to prevent the respondents from being harrassed by futile proceedings? To hold that such a jurisdiction exists would be to recognise that the court can pre-empt the decision of the arbitrator,

b even though the parties have conferred on him alone the power to adjudicate on the dispute. This would seem to accord ill with the policy expressed, in the international field, by the New York Convention on the Recognition and Enforcement of Foreign Arbitral Awards (10 June 1958; TS 20 (1976) Cmnd 6419), and domestically by the Arbitration Act 1979. On the other hand, real support for the owners' argument can be found in *Glasgow and South-Western Rly Co v Boyd and Forrest* 1918 SC (HL) 14, and the

c *Bremer Vulkan* case. In the end, it became unnecessary to decide this question, because the parties came to an agreement that the court should rule on the application of the time bar, to the effect that, if it were held that the Hague Rules limit applied, the owners should be free to rely on it in any new arbitration which might ensue. In these circumstances I think it best to express no opinion on the question of general principle.

d *Principles*

Without going in great detail into matters which have already been thoroughly explored in previous cases, including those already cited, and *Birkett v James* [1977] 2 All ER 801, [1978] AC 297, I believe that the relevant principles can now be summarised as follows.

e (1) An arbitration agreement creates mutual promises to submit to arbitration all disputes falling within the stated category, and to abide by the award of the arbitrator in respect of disputes actually referred to him.

(2) On the happening of three successive events, viz (a) the making by one party of a claim falling within the arbitration agreement and (b) the invoking of the arbitration agreement in respect of the dispute raised by that claim and (c) the appointment of an

f arbitrator in respect of the dispute, there comes into existence a series of mutual contractual relationships between the parties inter se, and between each party and the arbitrator. I will for convenience refer to the group of relationships between the parties as 'the reference'.

(3) As with any other bilateral contractual relationship, both the arbitration agreement and the reference are capable of discharge by consent.

g (4) The reference may be terminated by consent, leaving the arbitration agreement intact.

(5) A consent to discharge the reference may be inferred from prolonged inactivity on both sides.

(6) Discharge by consent inferred from inactivity may take place in two situations: (i) where each party conducts himself so as to evince to the other party an intention to treat

h the reference as ended; (ii) where the conduct of B is such as to lead A reasonably to believe that B intends to treat the reference as ended, and A alters his position in reliance on that belief. This second way of procuring a consensual discharge of the reference represents the important addition to the law brought about by the speeches in the House of Lords in *The Hannah Blumenthal* to which I have already referred.

(7) In neither of these two situations is it material to examine the actual subjective

j belief and intention of B.

(8) In situation (i), since the test is objective, it is necessary to look only at the conduct of each party actually brought to the notice of the other. But in situation (ii) the court must investigate the state of A's mind at the relevant time. The oral evidence of A will be admissible on this question. So also will be evidence of his actions at the time, even if these were not brought to the attention of B.

(9) In deciding whether the reference has been discharged by consent, the court is arriving at a conclusion of mixed fact and law, not exercising a discretion in arriving at a solution which appears just in all the circumstances of the case. The court performs a function which is quite different from that which is involved when the question is whether a High Court action should be dismissed for want of prosecution. Thus, for example, it is not necessary to consider (a) whether the claimant's delay was culpable, (b) whether it would be in the interests of justice for the reference to be terminated, (c) whether the delay is such as to make a fair trial of the dispute impossible, save only that the longer the delay the more easy it is to infer an abandonment of the reference, (d) whether the claim is time-barred, although in an indirect sense this is material, for in such a case the abandonment of the reference will mean the abandonment of the cause of action, an inference which will be less easy to draw than in a case where the cause of action will remain in being, or (e) whether the claim is large and is likely to succeed, except to the extent that where a new arbitration would be time-barred an inference of abandonment will be less easy to draw, where the claimant appears to have a good prospect of recovering a substantial sum.

Unfortunately these propositions are not sufficient to dispose of the present case, since the possibility that the claimants can begin a fresh arbitration makes it necessary to decide whether, even if the reference has been discharged by implied consent, the claimant's underlying cause of action still remains alive. This was not a matter for decision in *The Splendid Sun* or *The Hannah Blumenthal*, since in both instances a much longer period than six years had elapsed since the cause of action arose, so that abandonment of the reference ipso facto entailed abandonment of the claim. The question whether the claim itself had gone was explicitly discussed only by Eveleigh LJ in *The Splendid Sun* [1981] 2 All ER 993 at 999 ff, [1981] QB 694 at 705 ff, and in terms which did not differ significantly from the way in which the other judgments and speeches dealt with the abandonment of the reference. The present case therefore raises a novel issue.

One aspect of the problem may, I think, be taken as clear, namely that the cause of action may survive a consensual termination of the reference. Parties do from time to time agree to end an arbitration: for example, so that they can begin again before another arbitral tribunal or before the High Court. Obviously in such a case it could not be suggested that the agreement to terminate the reference was ipso facto a termination of the claim. Conversely, an express agreement to give up the arbitration might operate, in appropriate circumstances, as an agreement to terminate the dispute in all its aspects. In each case, it would be a question of interpreting what the parties said and did.

(It is convenient to mention in passing the suggestion that a similar conclusion can be arrived at by a comparison with the position in the High Court, where it is trite law that a discontinuance within the time limit does not bar a further action. This analogy is tempting, but in my judgment misleading. The discontinuance of an action is not consensual, for it is the leave of the court, not of the defendant, which is required.)

Another point is also clear, namely that on the abandonment of the cause of action the reference falls away. There is no longer any dispute in existence, and hence nothing in respect of which the arbitrator can make a binding award.

Returning to the abandonment of the claim, how can this be brought about? General principle suggests that this can take place either by an accord and satisfaction, or an estoppel. The problem with an accord and satisfaction is that there must be consideration for the abandonment of the claimant's rights, and it is not at first sight easy to see what this could be. From a practical point of view, an agreement by the respondent to cede his right to insist on the reference against him being continued seems scant recompense for the cancellation of the claim against him. Nevertheless, *The Splendid Sun* and *The Hannah Blumenthal* take it for granted that the cesser of the respondent's rights under the agreement to refer can be sufficient consideration for the claimant's cesser of his own rights under the reference, and if this is so there seems no reason in principle why it should not equally be a consideration for the claimant's agreement to abandon the totality of his rights and remedies in respect of his cause of action. Moreover, there may perhaps a be more substance in the consideration than meets the eye, for, if the reference disappears, so does the respondent's right to obtain an award in his favour on liability and, of more practical importance, an award of costs.

The idea of a consensual abandonment of the claim does therefore seem to be valid in terms of consideration, and the two leading cases also demonstrate that it is valid in terms of offer and acceptance, even though inactivity and silence would not, in the general law of contract, usually be regarded as capable of being either an offer or an acceptance.

b The difficulties of this analysis are made to seem more formidable once it is set against the background of a contract or statute which limits the time for initiating proceedings. Where the time limit is six years, no inference of abandonment can be drawn if the claimant does nothing to prosecute his claim for five years and eleven months, since this is his right under the statute. Is the position different if the claimant commences an arbitration after one year and then relapses into silence for another four years and eleven c months? Although in practical terms the difference might seem imperceptible, in theory at least I believe that one does exist. Once the arbitration has been launched, the limitation statute becomes irrelevant, and the claimant's silence cannot be explained away as a simple biding of time in accordance with his statutory rights. The court could, if it thought fit, interpret his conduct as showing that he had finally lost interest in the claim, and as either an offer to give up the claim and the reference, or as a tacit d representation that the claim and the reference would not be pursued. Accordingly, I reject that part of the charterers' argument which asserts that if the relevant time limit is held to be six years rather than one year there can be no possibility of holding that the claim has been abandoned by consent.

The facts

e As I have said, the vessel was chartered on 25 April 1975 on the New York Produce Exchange form. Clause 24 of the form provided that the contract would be subject to the terms of the Harter Act 1893, but the part of the clause which incorporated the United States clause paramount was deleted. However, by a typewritten cl 44 there were incorporated the three clauses paramount, to which I have referred. The charterparty also provided that any dispute between the owners and the charterers should be referred f to three persons at London, one to be appointed by each of the parties and the third by the two so chosen.

The vessel appears to have traded uneventfully for more than one and a half years, until disputes arose during December 1975 and March 1976 at the ports of Beaumont and Jacinto. These concerned the fitness of the vessel's holds to receive grain cargo. It was the charterers' case that the holds were affected by rust and scale, so that they had to g engage and pay specialised shore labour in order to make the holds fit for loading. In respect of these two incidents the charterers claimed $US26,303·15 for loss of time and $US25,500 for cleaning costs at Beaumont, and $US32,182·77 for loss of time and $US23,500 for cleaning costs at Jacinto. During February 1976 the charterers withheld $US51,682·82 from hire, in respect of the first incident. They made no deduction in respect of the second incident, because, by the time the relevant instalment was due, an h arrangement had been reached on the following lines: (i) the charterers would pay the amount of withheld hire, and would also pay the next instalment; (ii) the owners would not withdraw the vessel for non-payment of hire; (iii) the owners would give the charterers an irrevocable letter of credit in the amount of $US51,878; (iv) the letter of credit would be considered null and void if the charterers failed to name an arbitrator before 30 April 1976.

j In the event, the parties, by the end of April 1976, appointed Mr Cedric Barclay and Mr Donald Davies as their respective arbitrators. No third arbitrator, or umpire, as the law then required it, has ever been appointed.

Subsequently, a letter of credit was opened at the owners' request by the Bank of Nova Scotia in favour of the charterers. In summary, this document provided: (1) the charterers were authorised to draw up to $51,878·00 against (a) a certified copy of a final award of the arbitrators, or (b) a sworn statement by the parties or their agents that the parties had

settled the dispute; (2) the letter of credit would be automatically renewed from year to year, unless the bank gave written notice that they elected not to renew it; (3) if such a *a*
notice was given, the charterers could draw on the bank for the full amount of the credit, in which case the charterers were to state that the moneys drawn would be held by them in a special bank account until such time as there was either a judgment confirming an award, or the dispute had been settled. The statement was also to be accompanied by the charterers' undertaking to return to the owners any sums in excess of the award; (4) if the owners were to satisfy any award, or if the dispute was settled, the letter of credit *b*
would be cancelled.

This ingenious document provided an acceptable commercial solution to the problem of keeping the vessel in service, on the reasonable hypothesis that the charterers would pursue their claim for $110,000 and that in due course there would be either an award or a settlement. The vessel did in fact continue to perform services under the charter until it expired in May 1977. Unfortunately, the document took no account of the *c*
possibility that the charterers would do nothing at all, and this placed the owners in an unenviable position. The only way in which they could obtain the release of the letter of credit, in accordance with its terms, would be to obtain a favourable award. The arbitrators had no jurisdiction to make an award dismissing the claim for want of prosecution. The owners would therefore have to provoke the charterers to revive their claim, and fight it, solely for the purpose of having the claim dismissed. Similarly, if the *d*
owners instructed the bank not to renew the credit, the charterers would be entitled to call for payment and the owners would then need to revive the arbitration in order to obtain the return of their money. Neither of these alternatives was attractive. The only other possibility was to go on renewing the credit from year to year until sufficient time had elapsed to justify the intervention of the court, always assuming that the court had jurisdiction to intervene. This is what the owners have in fact done, at the cost of a *e*
renewal fee amounting to $259·39 per annum.

Abandonment

It follows from what I have already said that two different types of abandonment must be considered in a case such as the present. First, abandonment of the reference alone, the claimant's cause of action (if any) remaining intact and second, abandonment of both *f*
the reference and the cause of action.

I can deal with the first possibility very briefly. For the court to find an abandonment of this kind it would have to be satisfied that the charterers' silence and inactivity amounted to a representation that they wished to give up an arbitration conducted by Mr Barclay and Mr Davies and an umpire, whilst reserving the right to pursue their claim before another tribunal. I find it difficult to see how the fact that a claimant has *g*
done nothing for a long time could ever justify the inference that he intended to produce such a result and, a fortiori, how inactivity by the respondent could justify the inference that he concurred. It is not, however, necessary to go so far. For present purposes, it is ·
sufficient to say that I can see nothing in the facts of the present case on which it would be proper to find that the parties had consented to abandon the arbitration before the two named arbitrators whilst leaving the claim intact, or that there was a representation *h*
to this effect relied on by the owners.

The alternative proposition, that the claim and the reference have both come to an end, raises altogether more difficult questions. Three areas of fact must be explored. First, what were the statements and conduct of the charterers, as evinced to the owners? Second, what were the statements and conduct of the owners, as evinced to the charterers? Third, what was the owners' understanding of the charterers' intentions, and what (if *j*
any) action did they take in reliance on this understanding?

As regards the first question, I have already suggested that the size and apparent validity of the claim may on occasion have a bearing on the inference to be drawn from the claimant's inactivity. In fact the present case does not appear to me to be one of those occasions. In the light of the information now before the court, I consider that the claim is neither so obviously weak that a sensible person could be expected to drop it if his a initial approach produced no result, nor so obviously well founded that no sensible person could be expected to throw it away.

What other facts are material to the significance of the charterers' conduct? The following have been relied on.

(1) The letter of credit called for an arbitration to be commenced within 30 days, and the charterers complied.

(2) The charter terminated during May 1977, and a final account was arrived at
b without any mention of the charterers' claim.

(3) On an occasion during 1977 or 1978 (it seems safer to assume the latter) a gentleman known as 'Captain George', having some connection with the charterers, inquired of the bank whether the letter of credit would be drawn on. Pursuant to instructions given by Orion and Global Chartering Co Inc (Orion), the United States agents for the owners, he was told that it would not, and that the charterers should
c proceed with the arbitration. Shortly afterwards, Captain George made contact with Mr Lloyd Nelson, the president of Orion, apparently trying to find out about the arbitration, and seeming not even to know who were the charterers' solicitors. He was briskly sent about his business. No more was heard from him.

(4) The charterers continued to carry on other business transactions with the owners, until very recently.

d (5) The visit of Captain George was the last mention by the charterers of the arbitration or the claim until their solicitors wrote the letter of 3 August 1981.

In my judgment, this is not just a case of a 5½-year delay, significant enough as that fact would be even in isolation. There was to be a speedy commencement of the arbitration. The charterers began speedily, and then totally stopped. They did not raise the matter on the obvious occasion to do so when the time-charter accounts were
e finalised. The intervention of Captain George suggested that they were not serious about the arbitration, and they did not take Mr Nelson's hint about how to effect a recovery under the letter of credit, but instead relapsed into silence for more than three years. To my mind, this course of events can properly be interpreted as a tacit representation by the charterers that they did not intend to pursue the claim, or the associated reference.

The next stage is to consider the conduct of the owners, as evinced to the charterers.
f Apart from the type of conduct which consists of doing nothing, this had one aspect peculiar to the present case, on which the charterers have strongly relied, namely the repeated renewal of the letter of credit. Since the credit would operate only on an award or settlement, and since no settlement had been proposed, the continuance of the credit must (so it is argued) have meant that the owners foresaw that the arbitration would, however slowly, be brought to a conclusion. This is an attractive argument, but it
g overlooks the very special features of the credit. Essentially, the owners were locked into the credit, until either they or the charterers did something about the arbitration. Paying a modest sum was simply a means of allowing the arbitration to stagnate. And indeed, paradoxically, to refuse a renewal might have been less, rather than more, consistent with a belief that the arbitration had died, for it would be a recognition that the owners would have to press forward with the reference to obtain the release of the special
h account. It seems to me therefore that the dealings with the letter of credit were at the most neutral. Apart from this the owners' conduct, evinced to the charterers, consisted of a complete blank. It appears from the authorities which I have cited that this is sufficient to amount to an acceptance of a tacit offer to abandon the reference. This being so, I can see no reason why it should not also be sufficient to complete an accord and satisfaction of the claim. Accordingly, I hold that the owners' application is entitled to
j succeed.

Having reached this conclusion, it is not strictly necessary to explore the alternative argument based on an estoppel. Nevertheless I think it right to deal with it. The starting point is the same (namely a tacit representation by the charterers that they did not intend to pursue the claim) but the analysis of the owners' conduct takes an entirely different shape. Where an accord and satisfaction is in issue, what matters is how the owners acted towards the charterers, the investigation being of an entirely objective nature. The estoppel, by contrast, calls for an inquiry into the owners' subjective belief and intention, and into the steps which they took in reliance on that belief, irrespective of whether those steps were manifested to the charterers. Such an inquiry could not adequately be performed without discovery of documents and oral evidence on the owners' side, and these were duly made available for the last of the three hearings. What they revealed was as follows. As one would expect, the owners and their solicitors began to consider, quite soon after the arbitrators had been appointed, what evidence should be adduced at the hearing. They also gave some thought to the shape of the proceedings, and in particular to the question whether the charterers should be invited to take on the role of claimants. It was decided to take no action unless and until something was heard from the charterers' solicitors. In fact nothing was heard, and accordingly on 7 February 1978 Ince & Co wrote suggesting that it appeared unlikely that the proceedings would be revived, and that they should thereafter close their file. Orion replied on 16 February in the following terms:

> 'We seriously doubt if this matter will die a natural death. The letter of credit expires May 18, 1978, and this no doubt will promote some action by Charterers. Rather than close your file we would suggest that if you desire you could submit a notice of your charges to date.'

On 20 April 1978 Orion wrote to Ince & Co asking how long the owners must continue renewing the letter of credit before the charterers' claim in the arbitration was time-barred. Ince & Co did not reply in writing, although it seems that they did give some oral advice. But a year later they wrote to the effect that it appeared unlikely that the matter would proceed and asked whether they should submit a note of their charges, whilst still keeping the file open. Orion agreed and by August 1979 the owners had paid Ince & Co's fees and also a small appointment fee to their arbitrator. Ince & Co did not destroy their file, but it was placed in a repository. After that, nothing happened until the owners sought to revive the reference, during August 1981.

The documentary evidence was expanded by oral testimony from Mr Nelson. That I find this rather hard to follow is no reflection on Mr Nelson, because the concept of tacit abandonment, which is difficult enough to grapple with even in a straightforward situation, was here entangled with the conundrum created by the letter of credit. It seems clear enough that Mr Nelson did consciously address his mind to the problem of getting the letter of credit released, and I believe the gist of his evidence to be that the arbitration would technically remain alive until the six-year period expired in 1982, but that there ought to be some means of obtaining a default award. However, since the renewal fee was so small, he seems to have been content to let the matter run on, troublesome though it was. Whether Mr Nelson ever consciously formed the opinion that the charterers had finally written off the claim, or indeed whether he ever asked himself the question after February 1978, is much less clear. I think it quite probable that he did not. Nevertheless this should not, in my view, be fatal to the plea of estoppel. Where the issue is whether there was reliance by A on B having done nothing, the reliance may take the shape of A also doing nothing, and there seems no reason why, for the purposes of an estoppel, A's response should have been the result of a conscious choice. Here, the owners did spontaneously react to the charterers' silence by taking none of the steps in the way of preparing their case which would have been appropriate if the claim was still active. By this omission, at least so far as relates to the period commencing about the middle of 1978, they suffered a real detriment which, if I have correctly understood the law, is sufficient to make good the argument based on an estoppel. Accordingly, for this reason also I consider that the owners' application is entitled to succeed.

Limitation of time

A full and interesting argument was addressed on the question whether the Hague Rules time limit applied to the charterers' claim by virtue of the various clauses

a
paramount. This question would be material only if I were to conclude that, by contract or estoppel, the reference had disappeared, but the claim had survived. That this is not the correct outcome is the one aspect of this rather difficult case which does seem to me to be quite clear. The point would therefore be academic even if I were wrong about the disappearance of the claim, and, since the effect of incorporating the Hague Rules into a time charter is of considerable general importance, it is better that I should say nothing about it here, leaving it for decision where it is directly in point.

b
I cannot part from this case without observing that it demonstrates, not for the first time, the need for the creation by statute of a discretionary power, vested either in the arbitrator or in the court, to dismiss a claim in an arbitration for want of prosecution. The jurisdiction at common law, which has been the subject of the present action, is cumbersome and in all but the clearest cases unpredictable and s 5 of the Arbitration Act 1979 is far from providing a complete solution.

c   *Order for the owners accordingly.*

Solicitors: *Ince & Co* (for the owners); *Richards Butler & Co* (for the charterers).

K Mydeen Esq   Barrister.

d
President of the Methodist Conference v Parfitt

COURT OF APPEAL, CIVIL DIVISION
SIR JOHN DONALDSON MR, MAY AND DILLON LJJ
10, 28 OCTOBER 1983

e
Master and servant – Contract of service – Incidents of contract – Minister of religion – Methodist minister dismissed by the Church after disciplinary hearing – Minister alleging unfair dismissal – Whether contract between minister and Church – Whether contract of service – Whether industrial tribunal having jurisdiction to hear minister's complaint – Employment Protection (Consolidation) Act 1978.

f
The respondent, who had been a Methodist minister, was dismissed by the governing body of the Methodist Church after disciplinary proceedings had been taken against him in the Church court. He contended that he had been unfairly dismissed and applied to an industrial tribunal for relief under the Employment Protection (Consolidation) Act 1978. The Church contended as a preliminary issue that the respondent fell outside the jurisdiction of an industrial tribunal because he was not employed under a contract and especially not a contract of service. The respondent claimed that a contract of service had been created either when he was received into the Church as a minister or when he accepted the invitation to become a minister of a circuit prior to his dismissal. The industrial tribunal held that he did have a contract of service. The Church appealed to the Employment Appeal Tribunal, which dismissed the appeal, and then to the Court of Appeal.

g

h
Held – In all the circumstances, especially having regard to the doctrinal standards of the Church and the spiritual nature of both the act of his admission as a minister and the functions of a Methodist minister, it was clear that the parties had not intended to create binding legal relations either at the time the respondent was ordained or when he accepted the invitation to join the circuit of the Methodist Church. A fortiori the respondent did not have a contract of service with the Church and accordingly an industrial tribunal did not have jurisdiction to consider his complaint of unfair dismissal. The appeal would therefore be allowed (see p 752 *a* to *e* and *g h*, p 753 *d* and *h* and p 754 *h* to p 755 *d* and *g* to *j*, post).

j
Re Employment of Methodist Ministers (1912) 107 LT 143, *Re Employment of Church of England Curates* [1912] 2 Ch 563 and *Rogers v Booth* [1937] 2 All ER 751 considered.

Notes

For the nature of a contract of employment and the characteristics of the relationship of
employer and employee, see 16 Halsbury's Laws (4th edn) paras 501–502, and for cases
on the subject, see 20 Digest (Reissue) 238–255, 2302–2407.

For the dismissal of protestant noncomformist ministers, see 14 Halsbury's Laws (4th
edn) para 1409, and for cases on the subject, see 19 Digest (Reissue) 481–482, 3773–3787.

For the Employment Protection (Consolidation) Act 1978, see 48 Halsbury's Statutes
(3rd edn) 452.

Cases referred to in judgments

Church of England Curates, Re Employment of [1912] 2 Ch 563.
Edwards (Inspector of Taxes) v Bairstow [1955] 3 All ER 48, [1956] AC 14, [1955] 3 WLR
   410, HL.
Methodist Ministers, Re Employment of (1912) 107 LT 143.
Ready Mixed Concrete (South East) Ltd v Minister of Pensions and National Insurance [1968] 1
   All ER 433, [1968] 2 QB 497, [1968] 2 WLR 775.
Rogers v Booth [1937] 2 All ER 751, CA.
Winfield v London Philharmonic Orchestra Ltd [1979] ICR 726, EAT.

Case also cited

Barthrope v Exeter Diocesan Board of Finance [1979] ICR 900, EAT.

Appeal

The President of the Methodist Conference appealed against the decision of the
Employment Appeal Tribunal (M E Sunderland and E A Webb, Waterhouse J dissenting)
given on 15 November 1982 dismissing his appeal from the decision of an industrial
tribunal (P Kettley-Jackson and J Murley, Lady French dissenting) given on 13 January
1982 whereby it was held on the hearing of the preliminary issue that the respondent
applicant, Warton Parfitt, succeeded in his contention that he had been employed by the
Methodist Church under a contract of service and that therefore the industrial tribunal
had jurisdiction to consider his complaint that he had been unfairly dismissed by the
Church from his position as a minister of the Jersey (Channel Islands) circuit. The facts
are set out in the judgment of Dillon LJ.

R Moxon Browne for the appellant.
The respondent appeared in person.

Cur adv vult

28 October. The following judgments were delivered.

DILLON LJ (giving the first judgment at the invitation of Sir John Donaldson MR).
This is an appeal by the President of the Methodist Conference against a majority decision
of the Employment Appeal Tribunal, the chairman, Waterhouse J, dissenting, which
affirmed a majority decision of an industrial tribunal, the chairman, Lady French, again
dissenting.

The President of the Methodist Conference is a party to the proceedings because he is
nominated by statute to represent the Methodist Church in all legal proceedings. The
question for decision is a question of jurisdiction, namely whether the industrial tribunal
had jurisdiction to entertain a complaint of unfair dismissal lodged with it by the
respondent, Mr Parfitt, who was formerly a Methodist minister.

The jurisdiction of the industrial tribunal arises under the Employment Protection
(Consolidation) Act 1978. Under that Act every employee has the right not to be unfairly
dismissed by his employer, and a complaint may be presented to an industrial tribunal
by any person who claims that he has been unfairly dismissed by his employer. Only an
employee, however, has this right, and the word 'employee' is defined in the Act as
meaning an individual who has entered into or works under (or, where the employment

has ceased, worked under) a contract of employment. 'Contract of employment' means a

a contract of service or apprenticeship, whether express or implied, and, if express, whether oral or in writing.

The question is therefore whether the respondent had a contract of service with the Methodist Church or some body on behalf of that Church. That question has been broken down in argument in this court, as it was in both the lower courts, into two questions: did the respondent have a contract with the Church and, if so, was that

b contract a contract of service?

The important dates in the respondent's career as a minister are few. He was admitted as a minister in full connection of the Methodist Church (ie in Anglican terms he was ordained) in September 1958. He served as a minister on a number of circuits of the Church in Great Britain and ultimately in 1978 he was appointed to be a minister on the Jersey (Channel Islands) circuit and took up residence in Jersey. Nothing turns, in the

c argument, on the fact that his last appointment was in Jersey rather than in England or Wales.

Disciplinary charges were brought against the respondent in November 1980 in a local Methodist Church court, the minor synod of the Channel Islands district. That court found the charges proved and recommended to the Conference of the Methodist Church that the respondent be no longer allowed to act as a minister. The respondent appealed

d from that decision to the appeal committee of the Methodist Conference, but on 6 January 1981 that committee dismissed his appeal and confirmed the recommendation. He appealed again to the Conference itself but on 1 July 1981 the Conference confirmed the earlier decisions. In the meantime on 28 April 1981 he had made his application to the industrial tribunal. We have not been told the nature of the charges against the respondent, since they are not relevant to the question of jurisdiction of the industrial

e tribunal, nor have we had to consider the reasons why the respondent says that his dismissal was unfair.

The respondent submits that the contract of service with the Methodist Church on which he relies was made either in 1958 when he was received into full connection as a minister or in 1978 when he accepted the invitation of the circuit steward of the Jersey circuit that he should become a minister of that circuit, and the invitation and acceptance

f were approved by the stationing committee of the Conference. He says that the terms of the contract incorporate in either case the standing orders of the Methodist Church as from time to time in force. These standing orders are made by the Conference to provide for the government of the Methodist Church, and they derive their force from the original deed of union of 20 September 1932 and the enabling Act of Parliament which constituted the Methodist Church. The standing orders, the deed of union and other

g seminal documents of the Methodist Church are conveniently assembled in a loose leaf book called *Constitutional Practice and Discipline of the Methodist Church* (the CPD).

The majority of the industrial tribunal took the view that the respondent was employed by the Church under a contract of service because: (i) when he became a minister in full connection he agreed to provide his work and skill in the discharge of the responsibilities laid on him by the CPD and to abide by the conditions there laid

h down, in return for a stipend and the provision of a manse in which to live; (ii) he intended to become a servant of the Church and to be bound by its rules and subject to its discipline which amounted to a very high degree of control by the Conference as master, and (iii) all the other provisions of the contract as set forth in the CPD are consistent with its being a contract of service.

The majority of the Employment Appeal Tribunal agreed with the reasons of the

j majority of the industrial tribunal and relied in addition on certain further matters, such as the treatment of ministers as employed persons for the purposes of national insurance contributions, the deduction of income tax from ministers' stipends at source under Sch E to the Income and Corporation Taxes Act 1970, the existence of a compulsory superannuation scheme for ministers and the fact that the passage in the CPD which is concerned with ministers' holidays, although included in a section which bears the general heading 'Guidance' refers to a minister's 'entitlement' to certain holidays.

The chairman of the industrial tribunal and the chairman of the Employment Appeal Tribunal dissented largely on the ground of the essentially spiritual nature of the work that, as a minister, the respondent undertook.

In this court the respondent has supported his case with arguments commendably clear and concise which I would summarise as follows. (i) The spiritual nature of the work done by a minister and the spiritual discipline to which he is subject do not necessarily exclude a contractual relationship. (ii) Any reasonable person could do no other than conclude, looking at all the facts, that a minister, though a servant of God, is also a servant of the Church. (iii) The minister has to provide for non-spiritual matters as well as spiritual matters, and his arrangements with the Church cater for the non-spiritual matters, such as provision for his house and food and pension and provision for his wife and children, which are matters appropriate to be covered by a contract of service. (iv) There are many persons employed under contracts of service, such as the master of a ship or a journalist on the staff of a newspaper, who have to perform functions or exercise their skills in circumstances in which it would be impossible for the employer directly to control the capacity of the servant for doing the work. Such persons are none the less still employees.

The industrial tribunal is the tribunal to find the facts and an appeal lies to the Employment Appeal Tribunal, and a fortiori to this court, only on grounds of law. In the present case the majority of the industrial tribunal have found that the respondent was employed by the Church under a contract of service and the lay members of the Employment Appeal Tribunal have indorsed that finding. Is there any scope for appeal to this court? It seems to me that there is. The conclusion of the majority in each court has been based not on any special circumstances applicable to the respondent, but on their interpretation of the CPD, which applies to all ministers alike, and of the general law. It would be open to a differently constituted industrial tribunal to reach an opposite conclusion, based on the same texts of the CPD, in the case of some other minister. That would be most unsatisfactory, if no appeal lay. In my judgment this point is covered by *Edwards (Inspector of Taxes) v Bairstow* [1955] 3 All ER 48 at 59, [1956] AC 14 at 39 and not least by the comment of Lord Radcliffe that the duty of the courts—

'is no more than to examine [the] facts with a decent respect for the tribunal appealed from and, if they think that the only reasonable conclusion on the facts found is inconsistent with the determination come to, to say so without more ado.'

I turn therefore to consider the positon of a Methodist minister under the CPD. Spiritual matters are at the heart of this and it is particularly important to have in mind the doctrinal standards of the Methodist Church as set out in cl 30 of the deed of union in the CPD. I quote the following passages:

'Christ's Ministers in the Church are Stewards in the household of God and Shepherds of His flock. Some are called and ordained to this sole occupation and have a principal and directing part in these great duties but they hold no priesthood differing in kind from that which is common to all the Lord's people and they have no exclusive title to the preaching of the gospel or the care of souls ... It is the universal conviction of the Methodist people that the office of the Christian Ministry depends upon the call of God who bestows the gifts of the Spirit the grace and the fruit which indicate those whom He has chosen. Those whom the Methodist Church recognises as called of God and therefore receives into its Ministry shall be ordained by the imposition of hands as expressive of the Church's recognition of the Minister's personal call. The Methodist Church holds the doctrine of the priesthood of all believers and consequently believes that no priesthood exists which belongs exclusively to a particular order or class of men but in the exercise of its corporate life and worship special qualifications for the discharge of special duties are required and thus the principal of representative selection is recognised. The Preachers itinerant and lay are examined tested and approved before they are authorised to *a* minister in holy things. For the sake of Church Order and not because of any priestly virtue inherent in the office the Ministers of The Methodist Church are set apart by ordination to the Minister of the Word and Sacraments.'

The fundamental importance of the call of God is emphasised in s 718 of the standing orders in that each probationer, or ordinand, before he is received into full connection must be asked whether he is still as convinced of his call to the ministry as he was when he was accepted for training.

b Under the standing orders, a minister in full connection cannot unilaterally resign from the ministry. If he desires to resign he must send a notice of resignation which will be referred to an advisory committee for consideration. It is for the advisory committee to decide whether the resignation should be accepted, and, if so, from what date it should take effect.

The standing orders contain provisions under the heading 'Stationing' for the
c appointment of ministers to circuits, this being the territorial organisation of the Church. The responsibility of the minister appointed to a circuit is to preach and perform all acts of religious worship and Methodist discipline in the circuit. On reception into full connection, the newly ordained minister is for the first three years entirely at the disposal of the stationing committee, and may not accept an invitation to serve in a circuit. Thereafter he may be invited to a circuit for an initial period of five years, and that period
d may be renewed annually thereafter (see cll 543 to 547 of the standing orders). But under cl 736 reappointment to a circuit may not be renewed beyond eight years except by resolution of the Conference expressly authorising the renewal.

When a minister is appointed to a circuit the circuit is to provide a manse for him to a prescribed standard, and the standing orders include a detailed schedule of minimum requirements for the furnishing of manses. The minister is also to be paid by the circuit
e an allowance or stipend not less than the appropriate rate on the scale of minimum allowances from time to time prescribed by the Conference. In relation to payment, however, a pamphlet headed 'The Methodist Ministry', which was put before the lower courts at the respondent's request, sets out the following which is common ground between the parties:

f 'The principle which lies behind our system is this. No minister is paid for his services. He cannot be paid for that which he gives without measure in whole-hearted devotion to Christ and His Church but, as he gives himself, leaving no time or energy to provide for the material needs of himself and his family, the Church undertakes the burden of their support and provides for each man according to his requirements. There is a basic stipend which is committed to his own stewardship
g ... The Church also makes some provision for the maintenance and education of a Minister's children and for the years of retirement at the end of his ministry, in addition to that which is provided by the State. The spirit that shapes this system is that of the Christian communism of the New Testament—from each according to his ability, to each according to his needs. We should feel that to sell our services or bargain for remuneration would make us guilty of the sin of attempting to buy or
h sell the gifts of the spirit and of serving God for personal gain.'

With many professions, it would be quite impossible to suggest that, on a new entrant qualifying, a contract of service came into existence between the new entrant, barrister, solicitor, doctor or architect or whatever he may be, and the body which has recognised him as qualified and admitted him to the profession, because the admitting body is not concerned with how or where the newly qualified person carries on his profession
j provided that he does not transgress the profession's standards of conduct. With a Methodist minister newly received into full connection, the position is in this respect different in that the Conference is concerned with the stationing of the minister throughout his years as a minister and is concerned that he should receive an appropriate stipend even before he is appointed to any circuit. Even so, however, in my judgment,

the spiritual nature of the functions of the minister, the spiritual nature of the act of ordination by the imposition of hands and the doctrinal standards of the Methodist Church which are so fundamental to that Church and to the position of every minister in it make it impossible to conclude that any contract, let alone a contract of service, came into being between the newly ordained minister and the Methodist Church when the minister was received into full connection. The nature of the stipend supports this view. In the spiritual sense, the minister sets out to serve God as his master; I do not think that it is right to say that in the legal sense he is at the point of ordination undertaking by contract to serve the Church or the Conference as his master throughout the years of his ministry.

Equally I do not think it is right to say that any contract, let alone a contract of service, comes into being between the Church and the minister when the minister accepts an invitation from a circuit steward to become a minister on a particular circuit and the invitation and acceptance are approved by the stationing committee of the Conference. Despite the elaborate detail of the standing orders in relation to the manse and the furniture and fittings to be provided by the circuit for the newly appointed minister on the circuit, it seems to me that it follows, from a correct appreciation of the spiritual nature of the minister's position and relationship with the Church, that the arrangements between the minister and the Church in relation to his stationing throughout his ministry and the spiritual discipline which the Church is entitled to exercise over the minister in relation to his career remain non-contractual.

It is not in dispute that there are persons such as secretaries or caretakers who are employed by the Methodist Church or by its local circuits under contracts of service. But because of his spiritual position and functions a minister is in a very different position from such persons.

I would agree with the respondent's submissions to this extent that the spiritual nature of the work to be done by a person and the spiritual discipline to which that person is subject may not necessarily, in an appropriate context, exclude a contractual relationship under which work which is of a spiritual nature is to be done for others by a person who is subject to spiritual discipline. On any view the spiritual nature of the work and the spiritual discipline under which it is performed must be very relevant considerations when it has to be decided whether or not there is a contractual relationship.

A contract of service between a newly ordained minister and the Church could perhaps be drafted (despite the practical difficulties of having a binding contract of service for life which is not repugnant to the law as a contract of servitude), but the arrangements under such a contract would not be the same as the arrangements for ministers under the CPD and in particular under the doctrinal standards of the Methodist Church. A fortiori it would be possible to draft a legally binding offer and a legally binding acceptance between the minister and the circuit which invites him, with enforceable clauses as to the stipend and the manse and its contents and an enforceable obligation on the part of the minister to hold a particular number of services on particular days and a right in the minister to defined holidays in each year. That again, however, is not the arrangement before us in this case; a binding contract to achieve such objects would look very different from what we have to consider.

The courts have recognised that it is not practicable to lay down a hard and fast list of what is required to constitue a contract of service. There are too many variants. None the less the courts have repeatedly recognised what is and what is not a contract of service and I have no hesitation in concluding that the relationship between a church and a minister of religion is not apt, in the absence of clear indications of a contrary intention in the document, to be regulated by a contract of service.

I do not doubt that there probably are binding contracts between the Methodist Church and its ministers in relation to some ancillary matters, such as the compulsory superannuation scheme and the obligation, of which the respondent told us, on trainees to repay a proportion of the expense of their training if they do not remain in the ministry for at least ten years. These however are no part of the contract of service, either

on reception into full connection or on appointment to a circuit, which the respondent
a seeks to set up.

I derive no assistance from the treatment of ministers' stipends for income tax purposes
or from the treatment of ministers as employed persons in respect of national insurance
contributions. These treatments are based on convenience and compromise and do not
represent any binding decision in principle on the status of ministers; this is most clearly
stated in relation to the national insurance contributions.

b As for the use of the word 'entitlement' in the section of the CPD which gives guidance
on holidays for ministers, I find this all too slender a plank to bear the weight which the
respondent would put on it in arguing that he has a binding contract with the Church.
On the other hand the views of the Church in the document which I have mentioned on
the basis on which a stipend is paid to a minister are significant and are inconsistent with
any contention that the stipend is the consideration, or part of the consideration, for the
c minister's labours as a minister under his supposed contract of service with the Church.

Notwithstanding the respondent's cogent submission that any reasonable person could
do no other than conclude from all the facts that a minister is a servant of the Church or
of the Conference as well as a servant of God, and with all deference to the views of the
majority in each of the lower courts, I think that, on a proper appreciation of the position
of a minister under the CPD, the only reasonable conclusion is inconsistent with the
d determination of the lower courts that the respondent was employed by the Church
under a contract of service. I agree with Waterhouse J for the reasons which he gave and
which I have endeavoured to elaborate that there was no relevant contract between the
respondent and the Church and a fortiori no contract of service.

We were referred to a number of authorities. I have not found them of much
assistance, but would comment briefly on a few.

e Re Employment of Methodist Ministers (1912) 107 LT 143 is directly in point in that it
was a decision that Methodist ministers are not employed under contracts of service. I do
not doubt that the decision was correct, but the judgment of Joyce J is so tersely reported
that no help can be derived from it beyond the mere fact of the decision.

Re Employment of Church of England Curates [1912] 2 Ch 563 was a decision that a curate
of the Church of England holds an ecclesiastical office and so is not an employee under a
f contract. This is not relevant here since it is not suggested that a Methodist minister
holds an office. The judgment of Parker J is useful however in recognising a distinction
between the duties owed by a minister of religion to his ecclesiastical superiors and the
duties owed by a servant to his master under a contract of service.

Rogers v Booth [1937] 2 All ER 751, where a claim by a lieutenant in the Salvation
Army under the Workman's Compensation Act 1925 was rejected, turned especially on
g the fact that on being granted her commission the claimant had signed documents which
made it absolutely clear that her relationship with the army was not contractual.

The most that perhaps can be said from these authorities is that the courts have shown
themselves ready to conclude that the relationship between a minister of religion and his
Church is not founded on contract and he is not an employee of the Church. I do not for
my part see any good reason why modern economic conditions or the development of
h social security and employment protection should lead to a different conclusion now.

I would allow this appeal, discharge the order of the industrial tribunal and dismiss
the respondent's complaint.

MAY LJ. In my opinion, the first question which we have to consider in this appeal is
whether the respondent ever had any relevant contract with the Methodist Church at all.
j It is only if he did that the further question then arises, namely whether it was one of
employment, whether it was a contract of service on the one hand or for services on the
other (or indeed a contract of some other nature, perhaps sui generis).

The facts of the instant case, or facts similar to them, by their very nature only come
before the courts infrequently. Nevertheless the legal principles to be applied can be no
different just because of the unusual context in which the questions relevant to this

appeal have to be answered. First, I think that there is at least adequate evidence of the existence of an agreement between the respondent and the Methodist Church that he should act as and perform the duties of a Methodist minister. Second, in my opinion there is sufficient evidence of good consideration to support such an agreement. Nevertheless, on the question whether there ever was any contract between the respondent and the Methodist Church, I think that in the particular circumstances of this case the important consideration is whether the parties intended to create legal relations between them so as to make the agreement between the respondent and his church enforceable in the courts.

With all respect to the industrial tribunal, although it is apparent that they had this point in mind I do not think that they followed it through to any sufficient conclusion. At the beginning of para 16 of their decision they indicated that they then proposed to consider the evidence before them on this issue. They first referred to the evidence of Dr Greet on behalf of the Church: this was clearly to the effect that there had been no such intent. In para 17 the industrial tribunal turned to the respondent's evidence. He had contended that not only had there been a contract between himself and the Church but also that it had been a contract of employment. Implicit in such a contention was that there had been an intent to create legal relations, although the tribunal did not refer to this specifically. Then in para 18 of their decision the tribunal said:

> 'It is clear that the applicant did not advert to the question of contractual relations between himself and the church at the time he was appointed a minister in full connection.'

Having thus rehearsed the opposing evidence and contentions, I think that the industrial tribunal should then have made a clear finding on the particular issue. With respect, I do not think that they did so. They continued in para 18 of their decision in this way:

> 'It is also clear that the Conference disclaimed any intention to enter into contracts of employment with ministers in 1975 when the question of employed status arose. What the intention of the conference was prior to the passing of the Trade Union and Labour Relations Act 1974 is a matter of speculation. However, having examined the relevant provisions of the CPD and noted the very high degree of control that a minister must submit to in most aspects of his every day life and work, the tribunal takes the view that the parties, that is the applicant and the Conference, did, by their conduct, enter into contractual relations, the terms and conditions of such contract being clearly set forth in the deed of union and standing order, as expressed in the CPD.'

I understand the industrial tribunal to have been saying in this passage that because of the relevant provisions of the CPD and of the high degree of control by the Church to which a minister had to submit, it necessarily followed that there had been a legally binding contract between them. With all respect, I think that this begs the very question which at this point in their decision the tribunal were considering and which, as I have said, was by reason of the nature of the case of pre-eminent importance.

When this case came before the Employment Appeal Tribunal, in the first place the majority of that tribunal upheld the majority view in the industrial tribunal that a contractual arrangement had existed between the respondent and the Church. In their opinion the spiritual nature of a minister's work was not incompatible with such a legal relationship. Waterhouse J took the opposite view and it is the one with which respectfully I agree. I do not think that it is a point which permits of elaborate analysis and I gratefully adopt the relevant passage from the judgment of the Employment Appeal Tribunal in which the judge gave his reasons for disagreeing with the majority of the tribunal:

> 'I consider that the starting point of any consideration of the relationship between the Methodist Church and its ministers must be an examination of the faith and

a doctrine to which they subscribe and which they seek to further. The concept of a minister as a person called by God, a servant of God and the pastor of His local church members seems to be to be central to the relationship. In my judgment the reasoning of the Court of Appeal in *Rogers v Booth* [1937] 2 All ER 751 and of Joyce J in *Re Employment of Methodist Ministers* (1912) 107 LT 143 affords persuasive authority for rejecting the assertion that there was a contract between the respondent and the Methodist Church, and I do not consider that the concept of a Methodist
b minister's role or the interpretation of the words "a contract of service" has changed significantly since the enactment of the National Insurance Act 1911. I am unable to accept that either party to the present proceedings intended to create a contractual relationship. Moreover the elaborate code of practice and discipline of the Methodist Church, containing a wide spectrum of rules, recommendations and exhortations addressed to a variety of subsidiary organisations and persons, does not seem to me
c to be capable of formulation in terms of a contract between identifiable parties. The submission by the Methodist Church that a minister is, in effect, a person licensed by the Methodist Conference to perform the work of a minister in accordance with the doctrine of the Church and subject to its discipline is, in my judgment, the most persuasive description of his status and role.'

d However if he and I are wrong about the nature of the relationship between the respondent and the Church, and a contract enforceable at law did come into existence between them, then nevertheless I cannot accept that this was a contract of service. As Dillon LJ has said, the courts have recognised that it is not practicable to lay down precise tests of what is required to constitute a contract of service. The tasks which people carry out and the contexts in which they do so daily become so much more numerous, more diverse and more sophisticated that no one test or set of tests is apt to separate contracts
e of service and contracts for services in all cases: indeed the further one finds oneself from the more usual type of master/servant relationship, as is the situation in this present case, the more difficult it becomes to apply the tests which the courts have hitherto suggested are of help. As MacKenna J indicated in his well-known formulation of the appropriate tests in *Ready Mixed Concrete (South East) Ltd v Minister of Pensions and National Insurance* [1968] 1 All ER 433 at 439–440, [1968] 2 QB 497 at 515, the question of control by the
f putative master of his servant's performance is an important consideration. However, like all decisions, that of MacKenna J has to be considered in its context, just as the question in the instant case has to be considered in the context of a Christian Church and one of its recognised ministers (cf the judgment of the Employment Appeal Tribunal in *Winfield v London Philharmonic Orchestra Ltd* [1979] ICR 726, where the context was also not the normal industrial or commercial one but 'that of one of the world's finest
g orchestras composed of some of the world's finest musicians'). In other words, 'in deciding whether or not you are in the presence of a contract of service you look to the whole of the picture.' Looking at the whole of the picture in the present appeal I am not satisfied that if there was a contractual relationship between the respondent and the Methodist Church it was a contract of service: indeed I am quite satisfied that it was not. On this second point, therefore, I respectfully agree with the minority opinions of both
h the chairman of the industrial tribunal and the chairman of the Employment Appeal Tribunal.

For these reasons I too would allow this appeal, with the consequential results referred to by Dillon LJ.

SIR JOHN DONALDSON MR. I have had the advantage of reading the judgments
j which have been delivered by Dillon and May LJJ. I agree with those judgments and would allow the appeal.

Appeal allowed.

Solicitors: *Pothecary & Barratt* (for the appellant).

Frances Rustin   Barrister.

R v Thomas

COURT OF APPEAL, CRIMINAL DIVISION
LORD LANE CJ, MICHAEL DAVIES AND FRENCH JJ
11, 14 OCTOBER 1983

*Road traffic – Disqualification for holding licence – Disqualification after repeated offences –
Mitigating grounds justifying non-disqualification or disqualification for less than prescribed
period – Motorist convicted and sent to prison for driving while disqualified – Motorist incapable
of keeping away from motor vehicles – Sentencing policy not to impose disqualification extending
for substantial period after release of such an offender from prison – Whether sentencing policy a
'ground for mitigating the normal consequences of the conviction' – Transport Act 1981, s 19(2).*

It is accepted sentencing policy in relation to persons who are imprisoned after repeated
offences of driving while disqualified and who are incapable of leaving motor vehicles
alone that the court should not impose a period of disqualification extending for a
substantial period after their release from prison; and, for the purpose of s 19(2)[a] of the
Transport Act 1981, that policy is a 'ground for mitigating the normal consequences of
the conviction' where the conviction is for an offence involving obligatory disqualification
and there are 12 or more penalty points to be taken into account under s 19(3) (see p 757
c to *e* and p 758 *e f* and *j*, post).

Notes

For disqualification and endorsement of driving licences, see 40 Halsbury's Laws (4th
edn) paras 515–529, and for cases on the subject, see 45 Digest (Repl) 117–120, 398–430.
For the Transport Act 1981, s 19, see 51 Halsbury's Statutes (3rd edn) 1413.

Cases referred to in judgment

R v Farnes (Note) [1983] RTR 441, CA.
R v Hansel (Note) [1983] RTR 445, CA.

Appeal

On 26 April 1983 in the Crown Court at Grimsby, before his Honour Judge Geoffrey
Jones, the appellant, Kevin Thomas, pleaded guilty to two counts of driving whilst
disqualified. He was sentenced to two consecutive terms of three months' imprisonment
and was disqualified from driving for two years. He appealed against the disqualification
order. The facts are set out in the judgment of the court.

T J Spencer (assigned by the Registrar of Criminal Appeals) for the appellant.

Cur adv vult

14 October. The following judgment of the court was delivered.

LORD LANE CJ. On 26 April 1983 in the Crown Court at Grimsby the appellant
pleaded guilty to two offences of driving whilst disqualified. He was sentenced by his
Honour Judge Geoffrey Jones to three months' imprisonment in respect of each offence
to be served consecutively, a total of six months' imprisonment. In addition he was
ordered to be disqualified from driving for a period of two years.
He appeals against sentence by leave of the single judge. He makes no complaint about
his sentences of imprisonment, which he has now served. It is expressly accepted on his

---

a Section 19, so far as material, is set out at p 757 *g* to p 758 *a*, post behalf that in the circumstances of the case he could have no cause for complaint. He

a appeals solely in respect of the order for disqualification.

The appellant is now 25 years of age. His driving record is appalling. He has been convicted on many occasions. On at least four previous occasions he has been before the court for offences of driving whilst disqualified. In 1981 and again in 1982 he was sentenced to imprisonment for this offence.

On 10 September 1982, which must have been not long after he was released from

b prison, the appellant was seen by the police riding a motor scooter. He was released on bail but on 5 October he was seen riding another motor scooter. At the time of these offences he was disqualified until 21 February 1983. He has only ever held a provisional licence.

This recital amply justifies the expressed view of the trial judge that this appellant was quite arrogant in relation to the law. For his deliberate and repeated offences he had to

c be punished. Nevertheless, it is perfectly plain from the transcript of the proceedings that Judge Geoffrey Jones, who dealt with this case with the utmost care and patience, would have liked to impose a lesser period of disqualification than two years. He was influenced in this regard by what in recent years has become accepted sentencing policy in this type of case, that is that with persons like the present appellant, who seem to be incapable of leaving motor vehicles alone, to impose a period of disqualification which

d will extend for a substantial period after their release from prison may well, and in many cases certainly will, invite the offender to commit further offences in relation to motor vehicles. In other words a long period of disqualification may well be counter-productive and so contrary to the public interest. So well established has this sentencing policy become in recent years that it is not necessary to refer to a line of cases. A good recent example is *R v Farnes* [1983] RTR 441.

e As has been said, Judge Geoffrey Jones thought that this was such a case and we agree with him. However he came to the conclusion, after hearing argument, that he was precluded by the provisions of the Transport Act 1981 (the relevant part of which came into operation on 1 November 1982) from imposing a period of disqualification of less than two years.

There was no doubt that before 1 November 1982 the courts had power to do that

f which, as has already been said in this judgment, they often did. However s 19 of the 1981 Act introduced tighter restrictions on the power of a court to reduce what would otherwise be a mandatory period of disqualification.

The relevant part of s 19 of the Transport Act 1981 is as follows:

'... (2) Where a person is convicted of an offence involving obligatory or

g discretionary disqualification and the penalty points to be taken into account under subsection (3) number twelve or more, the court shall order him to be disqualified for not less than the minimum period defined in subsection (4) unless the court is satisfied, having regard to all the circumstances not excluded by subsection (6), that there are grounds for mitigating the normal consequences of the conviction and thinks fit to order him to be disqualified for a shorter period or not to order him to

h be disqualified ...

(4) The minimum period referred to in subsection (2) is—(a) six months if no previous disqualification imposed on the offender is to be taken into account; and (b) one year if one, and two years if more than one, such disqualification is to be taken into account; and a previous disqualification imposed on an offender is to be taken into account if it was imposed within the three years immediately preceding

j the commission of the latest offence in respect of which penalty points are taken into account under subsection (3) ...

(6) No account is to be taken under subsection (2) of—(a) any circumstances that are alleged to make the offence or any of the offences not a serious one; (b) hardship, other than exceptional hardship; or (c) any circumstances which, within the three years immediately preceding the conviction, have been taken into account under

that subsection in ordering the offender to be disqualified for a shorter period or not ordering him to be disqualified . . .'

a

It was conceded at the trial and before us that the appellant was caught by the provisions in that (i) his penalty points to be taken into account totalled 12 or more and (ii) more than one previous disqualification had to be taken into account.

Accordingly the court was obliged to disqualify the appellant for not less than two years, unless (and we repeat the relevant words in s 19(2))—

b

'the court is satisfied, having regard to all the circumstances not excluded by subsection (6), that there are grounds for mitigating the normal consequences of the conviction and thinks fit to order him to be disqualified for a shorter period or not to order him to be disqualified.'

Subsection (6) has already been read. Counsel for the appellant submits that none of the three exceptions which the court is required not to take account of apply to the present case. Quite clearly paras (*a*) and (*c*) do not. It has not been and could not be contended that these were not serious offences and there were no circumstances which had been taken into account on an earlier occasion for the purposes set out in sub-s (6)(*c*).

c

This leaves sub-s (6)(*b*), 'hardship, other than exceptional hardship'. It could not be said that this disqualification constituted 'exceptional hardship'; if it did, of course, the task of the trial judge and of this court would have been easy. We then have to ask ourselves whether to have regard to the principle of sentencing policy with which we have dealt is taking account of 'hardship'. If so, it would have to be excluded from consideration. In our judgment a proper construction of the statute does not lead to that result. We do not think that to have regard to the well-settled policy, in other words to the public interest, is taking account of 'hardship' any more than of 'exceptional hardship'.

d

Accordingly, returning to s 19(2), are there circumstances not excluded by s 19(6) (and as we have said the principle of sentencing policy in question is in our view not so excluded) in which the court can say that it is satisfied that there are 'grounds for mitigating the normal consequences of the conviction'?

e

Our conclusion is that the principle of sentencing policy does constitute such grounds. The judge would have been entitled in law to do that which he wished to do. However, a culpable offender like this appellant cannot expect that his period of disqualification will be no longer than the period which he is likely to spend in prison: see *R v Hansel* [1983] RTR 445, decided by this court on 17 November 1982. The period of disqualification must depend on all the facts of the particular case. In the present case we consider that the appropriate period of disqualification, reflecting sentencing policy and the circumstances of this appellant, would be not two years but one year. To that extent this appeal is allowed.

f

g

Before parting with this case, we should add that we were at one stage troubled by the apparent anomaly that a persistent offender like this appellant might escape the minimum obligatory disqualification on account of sentencing policy whilst a person of reasonably good record and character who happened to acquire the appropriate number of penalty points might find himself unable to found successfully any argument against the imposition of the minimum obligatory disqualification. We think that the answer to this apparent anomaly was provided by counsel, who pointed out that the lesser gravity of such an offender's case would no doubt be reflected in the punishment meted out to him apart from disqualification. For example, this appellant was rightly sentenced to imprisonment. A less serious offender, although he might have to be disqualified for a longer period, might well have been fined. So in our judgment the apparent anomaly is no good reason for departing from what we have indorsed as good sentencing policy, which policy we have held may still be lawfully implemented in proper cases notwithstanding the changes introduced in the 1981 Act.

h

i

Appeal allowed in part. Period of disqualification varied.

N P Metcalfe Esq   Barrister.

a

Calabar Properties Ltd v Stitcher

COURT OF APPEAL, CIVIL DIVISION
STEPHENSON, GRIFFITHS AND MAY LJJ
11, 28 JULY 1983

b   *Landlord and tenant – Repair – Landlord's covenant – Damages for breach – Measure of damages – Premises acquired as a home becoming uninhabitable due to landlord's breach of repairing covenant – Tenant having to move into alternative accommodation – Whether measure of damages the diminution in market value of the premises – Whether cost of alternative accommodation recoverable by tenant.*

c   In October 1975 the tenant acquired the lease of a flat in a block of flats with the intention of living there permanently with her husband. The lease contained a repairing covenant by the landlords requiring them to maintain the external parts of the block in good repair. In January 1976 the tenant complained to the landlords that rainwater was penetrating into the flat and causing damage to the decorative work. Despite further complaints by the tenant the landlords took the view that the dampness and damage were not their responsibility and consequently failed to carry out any external repairs to

d   the flat. The tenant and her husband remained in the flat for five years, even though the dampness caused the husband to suffer ill-health, until January 1981 when the flat became uninhabitable and the tenant and her husband were forced to rent alternative accommodation. When the landlords sued the tenant for charges due from her under the lease she counterclaimed for damages for breach of the landlords' covenant to repair but did not plead any particular head of damage, such as the cost of the alternative

e   accommodation. The tenant also sought an order requiring the landlords to repair the flat. The action was tried in December 1982. The judge found that the dampness and damage to the flat were caused by the landlords' breach of the repairing covenant and held that the measure of damages for breach of a landlord's covenant to repair was the diminution in the market value of the premises during the period between the first request to carry out repairs and the date when damages were assessed. The judge

f   accordingly ordered the landlords to repair the flat and awarded the tenant (i) special damages of £4,606·44 for diminution in the market value of the flat between January 1976 and December 1982 based, in the absence of other evidence of value, on the cost of repairs and redecoration carried out by the tenant, less a reduction of one-third of the cost to take into account the betterment resulting from the redecoration, and (ii) general damages of £3,000 for the discomfort, loss of enjoyment and ill-health suffered by herself

g   and her husband during the period they occupied the deteriorating flat. However, the judge refused to award the tenant damages either (i) for the outgoings on the flat during the period when it was uninhabitable and she and her husband had to live elsewhere, on the ground that such damages would be comparable to an award for the cost of alternative accommodation while the flat was being repaired and such an award was an irrecoverable

h   head of damage, or (ii) assuming the flat to be a marketable asset, for loss of rental value arising out of the notional loss of rent during the period it was uninhabitable, on the ground that such damage was too remote. The tenant appealed against the judge's refusal to award damages under those two heads. The landlords contended, inter alia, that no award should be made under those heads because they had not been pleaded in the counterclaim.

j

Held – (1) The fundamental principle in measuring damages payable to a tenant for breach of a repairing covenant by the landlord was that the object of the damages was to restore the tenant to the position he would have been in if there had been no breach. Thus, the diminution in the value of the premises was not necessarily the measure of the damages for breach of a landlord's repairing covenant, while, on the other hand, the cost

of alternative accommodation could be recoverable. Accordingly, where the tenant had
acquired premises for his personal occupation and intended to occupy them after the
landlord had effected the necessary repairs, the tenant was entitled to damages to
compensate him for (a) the cost of alternative accommodation if he had been forced by
the lack of repair to move out temporarily, (b) the cost of any repairs paid for by the
tenant and (c) the unpleasantness of living in deteriorating premises until they became
uninhabitable. A tenant was not entitled to damages based on the diminution in the
market value of the premises unless to the knowledge of the landlord he had acquired
the premises with the intention of reselling or subletting them or unless he was driven
out of occupation by the breach and forced to sell the premises (see p 765 a to d, p 766 g
to p 767 a and c, p 768 e to j and p 769 d and j to p 770 d, post); *Dodd Properties (Kent) Ltd
v Canterbury City Council* [1980] 1 All ER 928 applied; *Green v Eales* (1841) 2 QB 225 and
Hewitt v Rowlands [1924] All ER Rep 344 explained.

(2) Applying those principles, it followed that because the tenant had acquired the flat
as a home rather than as an investment the proper measure of her damages was the
reasonable cost of alternative accommodation while the flat was being repaired, the cost
of any repairs and redecoration done by her (without any reduction for betterment) and
compensation for the discomfort, loss of enjoyment and ill-health endured while the flat
was deteriorating. However, since the tenant had not pleaded the cost of alternative
accommodation as an item of special damage and had not contested the judge's reduction
of damages for betterment, the judge's award of damages would not be disturbed in
respect of those items. The tenant's claim for reimbursement of the outgoings on her flat
for the period it was uninhabitable failed because such outgoings were a necessary
consequence of retaining the lease of the flat and would have been offset by the outgoings
included in the award for alternative accommodation if that had been claimed. The
tenant's claim for notional loss of rent also failed because that was merely another aspect
of a claim for diminution in value of the flat as a marketable asset and such a claim was
not open to the tenant because she had bought the flat as a home rather than as a
marketable asset. In all the circumstances therefore the tenant's appeal would be dismissed
(see p 763 f to h, p 767 d to g, p 768 c to e, p 769 e and p 770 c d, post).

Notes

For a landlord's covenant to repair and damages for breach of the covenant, see 27
Halsbury's Laws (4th edn) paras 298, 307, and for cases on the subject, see 31(2) Digest
(Reissue) 600–605, 4879–4928.

Cases referred to in judgments

Dodd Properties (Kent) Ltd v Canterbury City Council [1980] 1 All ER 928, [1980] 1 WLR
　433, CA.
Green v Eales (1841) 2 QB 225, 114 ER 88.
Harbutts Plasticine Ltd v Wayne Tank and Pump Co Ltd [1970] 1 All ER 225, [1970] 1 QB
　447, [1970] 2 WLR 198, CA.
Hewitt v Rowlands (1924) 93 LJKB 1080, [1924] All ER Rep 344, CA.
Lister v Lane and Nesham [1893] 2 QB 212, [1891–4] All ER Rep 388, CA.
Lurcott v Wakely and Wheeler [1911] 1 KB 905, [1911–13] All ER Rep 41, CA.
Penbury v Lamdin [1940] 2 All ER 434, CA.
Perestrello e Cia Lda v United Paint Co Ltd [1969] 3 All ER 479, [1969] 1 WLR 570, CA.
Perry v Sidney Phillips & Son (a firm) [1982] 3 All ER 705, [1982] 1 WLR 1297, CA.

Appeal

By particulars of claim the plaintiffs, Calabar Properties Ltd (the landlords), claimed in
the Willesden County Court from the defendant, Mrs Renee Stitcher (the tenant), the
sum of £1,403·82 for ground rent, service charges and insurance premiums due from
her as the assignee of a lease of a penthouse flat known as 54 Hendon Hall Court, London
NW4. By a defence and counterclaim the tenant admitted her failure to pay the sum

claimed but sought by a counterclaim to set off against that sum a claim for damages
a against the landlords, without particularising the damages claimed, for breach of the
landlords' repairing covenant in the lease requiring them to maintain in good and
substantial repair, condition and decoration the structural parts of the block which
included the windows. The tenant alleged that the landlords' breach of covenant had
caused severe damp penetration and substantial damage to the decorations in her flat.
She also sought in the counterclaim an order requiring the landlords to repair the defects
b in the flat and to put it into a watertight condition. By an order dated 25 September 1981
the action was by consent transferred to an official referee. By a judgment given on 14
December 1982 his Honour Judge Stabb QC, sitting as an official referee, awarded the
tenant, on her counterclaim, total damages of £7,606·44 consisting of (1) £4,606·44 for
the diminution in the value of the flat to the tenant for the period from January 1976,
when she or her husband first complained to the landlord about the damp penetration,
c to 14 December 1982, the date of the judge's assessment of the damages, such damages
being based, in the absence of other evidence, on the cost to the tenant of making good
and redecorating the flat less a reduction of one-third for the element of betterment, and
(2) £3,000 for the disappointment, discomfort, loss of enjoyment and ill-health suffered
during the five years the tenant and her husband occupied the flat. The judge refused to
make any award for (a) the running costs of the flat, e g rent, rates, service charges which
d the tenant had to pay during the two years from January 1981 to the date of assessment
of damages when the flat was uninhabitable and she and her husband had to live in
alternative accommodation, on the ground that such an award was comparable to an
award for expenses incurred in taking alternative accommodation while the flat was
being repaired which the judge regarded as irrecoverable, or (b) for diminution in the
market value of the flat during that two-year period based on the capital value of the flat
e or its rack rental value, on the ground that that head of damage was too remote. From
the total award of £7,606·44 the judge deducted the amount of the landlords' claim
against the tenant, ie £1,403·82, and thus entered judgment for the tenant for £6,202·62.
The judge also ordered that the landlords carry out all necessary work to the flat to
comply with their repairing covenant. The tenant appealed on the ground that the judge
erred in law in refusing to award damages (a) to cover the consequential loss of the
f running costs of the flat incurred by the tenant for the two-year period from January
1981 when the flat was uninhabitable and/or (b) to cover consequential loss for
diminution in the value of the flat during that period based on the capital value of the
flat or its rack rental value. The landlords served a respondent's notice that the judge's
judgment should be affirmed on the additional ground that particulars of the additional
special damages claimed by the tenant on the appeal were not pleaded in her counterclaim.
g The facts are set out in the judgment of Stephenson LJ.

Peter Ralls for the tenant.
Robert Pryor QC for the landlords.

Cur adv vult

h

28 July. The following judgments were read.

STEPHENSON LJ. This is the defendant tenant's appeal against an order of his Honour
Judge Stabb QC giving judgment for her on a counterclaim against the plaintiff landlords
j for £6,202·62. Counsel on her behalf submits that the award of damages ought to have
been larger and that the judge was wrong to disallow two recoverable heads of damage,
or possibly three.
        The award was for the balance of a counterclaim for damages for breach of a landlord's
repairing covenant after deducting the admitted amount of the landlords' claim for
£1,403·82 ground rent, service charges and insurance premiums in respect of a penthouse

flat at 54 Hendon Hall Court, London NW4. The amount of the claim was set off against
the amount of £7,606·44 awarded to the tenant on the counterclaim.

 The flat was on top of a block built by the landlords in the 1960s and let by a lease
dated 9 January 1964 to a Mr Danzig for 99 years from 29 September 1963 for a premium
of £15,000 at a ground rent of £100 a year, the tenant paying also service charges,
insurance premiums, rates and taxes. In October 1975 the defendant took an assignment
of the lease for £40,000. She and her husband redecorated the flat, but as early as 8
January 1976 her husband wrote complaining of water entering the flat following weeks
of delay after a visit from a representative of the landlords, and of damage to the walls
'due to defects on the outside'. I take that to mean that the first complaint had been made
some weeks earlier.

 The landlords took the line that the damp and damage were due not to any defect or
breach of covenant for which they were responsible but to condensation, in spite of a
report, which they obtained on 22 December 1976 from an expert but did not disclose
to the tenant, attributing the dampness to 'water penetration and also the lack of sealing
compound around the window frame' and recommending that their builder 'attends to
all these defects as soon as possible'. So the main issue which the judge had to decide at
the trial of their claim against the tenant in December 1982, started in the Willesden
County Court in April 1978, was the issue of their liability. That issue the judge decided
against them. He held that the damage to the flat was caused by breaches of the landlord's
covenant to maintain in good and substantial repair and condition and decoration the
main structural parts of the block of flats including the external parts thereof, and in
addition to awarding the tenant damages he ordered the landlords to carry out all
necessary work to comply with their covenant, such work to be commenced by 15
January 1983.

 From the judge's decision on liability there is no cross-appeal by the landlords. On
damages there is no cross-appeal (or appeal) against the two items which the judge did
award. They were: (1) £4,606·44, being the cost of making good and redecorating the
flat plus 10% for supervision plus value added tax, amounting to £6,909·67 paid by the
tenant (or her husband), reduced by one-third for the element of betterment; (2) £3,000
'for the disappointment, discomfort, loss of enjoyment and bouts of ill-health which he
[the tenant's husband] suffered during the five years that he was occupying what was
supposed to be a high-class flat', and which were due to the landlords' 'persistent refusal
to take any steps to remedy the breaches of which they were made well aware'.

 The tenant's husband gave evidence, which the judge accepted, that he and the tenant
purchased the lease of the flat intending to live there permanently, but it became
uninhabitable:

> 'External woodwork was rotting, mastic sealing around the windows was
> perishing and the damp penetration was so bad that after two attacks of pleurisy and
> one of bronchitis he decided to leave the flat which he did on 23 January 1981, and
> he and his wife went to the Isle of Man where they now propose to live permanently.'

'They were forced to leave' by reason of the continuous failure of the landlords to carry
out the necessary external repairs.

 The second item, the £3,000 general damages, is not in dispute. (No distinction is
drawn between the tenant and her husband.) The first item, £4,606·44 special damages,
is also not in dispute, though no special damage was pleaded and it was awarded as the
diminution in the value of the flat to the tenant for the period from January 1976, when
the landlords were requested to repair, to 14 December 1982, the date of the judge's
assessment of damages. This award is explained by the judge in the following passage in
his judgment:

> 'One of the difficulties of assessing any diminution of value by reference to the
> value of the flat in good condition as compared with the flat in its present condition
> is that the only evidence of value was given by a Mr Lewis, a valuation consultant, a

report of whose expert opinion was not furnished to the other side in accordance
with the order for directions and accordingly if objected to by Mr Pryor [counsel for
the landlords] such evidence would not have been given. [Counsel for the landlords]
has said that if an assessment is to be based on the evidence of Mr Lewis then he
wishes to be given the opportunity of calling expert evidence on valuation. I think
that that is a perfectly reasonable request. On the other hand, I have evidence of the
cost of making good the interior of the flat which, if coupled with an order that the
plaintiffs [the landlords] should carry out the necessary external work to prevent a
recurrence of the damage, could in my view form the basis of a measure of the
difference in value comparable to such cases where the cost of remedying dilapidation
can properly be said to represent the diminution in value of the reversion.'

(It would have been open to the tenant to challenge the reduction for the element of
betterment, in reliance on the decision of this court on the point, not yet overruled by
the House of Lords, in *Harbutt's Plasticine Ltd v Wayne Tank and Pump Co Ltd* [1970] 1 All
ER 225 at 236, 240, 242, [1970] 1 QB 447 at 468, 473, 476: see *McGregor on Damages*
(14th edn, 1980) p 763, para 1120.)

The two items claimed, though not pleaded, which the judge refused to award were (I
take them from the notice of appeal):

'(i) the rates, rent and running costs, including, without limitation, the service
charges of the flat, the subject matter of the action, during the period when the said
flat was rendered uninhabitable as a result of the Plaintiffs' breach of their repairing
covenants in the lease of the said flat and (ii) consequential losses for loss of use
during the said period based on the capital value of the said flat or alternatively
based on the rack rental value of the said flat.'

The judge held that neither head of damage was recoverable, the second because too
remote, the first because it was comparable to expenses incurred in taking another house,
which he regarded as irrecoverable on the authority of *Green v Eales* (1841) 2 QB 225, 114
ER 88. Counsel for the landlords contends that the judge was right to reject these heads
of damage as irrecoverable on those grounds, and, by a respondent's notice, on the
additional ground that they were not pleaded in the tenant's defence and counterclaim.

The running costs or outgoings in respect of the tenant's flat are not, in my judgment,
recoverable. It is true that while the tenant was not living in the flat because of the
landlords' breach of contract she was not getting anything for the rates etc which were
payable under the lease. But she had not terminated the lease and had to pay outgoings
on some property, and I would regard the costs of the property which she rented as
alternative accommodation for herself and her husband in the Isle of Man as prima facie
the loss suffered by being kept out of her flat for the period of the landlords' continuing
breach of covenant, subject to the renting of that alternative accommodation being
reasonable. The judge regarded the one set of expenses as comparable to the other and so
irrecoverable on the authority of *Green v Eales*. Though accepted by counsel for the tenant
as an authority for the proposition that such expenses of alternative accommodation are
not recoverable, that decision is not binding on this court and is, in my opinion, valid
only as a decision that such expenses were not recoverable on the particular facts of that
case. As is stated in *McGregor* pp 543–544, para 777 in a passage relied on by counsel for
the tenant:

'The court pointed out that although the defendant covenanted to repair he did
not covenant to find the lessee another house while repairs were going on, but went
on to suggest that damages might be recovered in respect of the additional time that
the lessee was obliged to be in another house on account of the defendant's delay in
commencing repairs (*Green v Eales* (1841) 2 QB 225 at 238, 114 ER 88 at 93).'

The judgment of the Court of Queen's Bench (Lord Denman CJ, Patteson and Williams
JJ) was given by Lord Denman CJ. He accepted the argument for the landlord on the

fifth issue that he was not obliged to provide a house for the tenant while the repairs
were going on, and therefore the plaintiff could not claim the expenses of his residence
at Mr Lee's, which was claimed and quantified as 'expense in providing another residence
and place of trade till the [demised] premises could be made fit and safe' (see 2 QB 225 at
228, 233, 114 ER 88 at 89, 91–92) and the court must have to that extent qualified Rolfe
B's direction to the jury—

> 'that the plaintiff was entitled to recover for all his expenses, if they were
> reasonably incurred, and such as a prudent man would have taken upon him; and
> he left it to them to say whether, under the circumstances of this case, the rebuilding
> of the wall [which fell down and ought to have been repaired by the defendant
> landlord], and the removal to other premises in the mean time, were reasonable
> expenses . . .'

(See 2 QB 225 at 232, 114 ER 88 at 91.)

The jury's verdict was for the whole amount of the claim, including the quantified
items of expense of the plaintiff's residence at Mr Lee's, and the court reduced it by the
amount of those items. I have to say that I regard the court's reason given for disallowing
those items as unsound (unless it is interpreted as Griffiths LJ interprets it) and the trial
judge's direction to the jury as correct. I would have accepted the argument of counsel
for the plaintiff tenant that the judge left the question of damages properly to the jury,
and their verdict ought not to have been disturbed (see 2 QB 225 at 234, 114 ER
88 at 92).

It is, however, noteworthy that the court indicated that such items of expense might
have been recoverable if 'the time during which the plaintiff was obliged to be in another
house was indeed somewhat lengthened by the delay in commencing the repairs', and if
they had been claimed and the jury been asked to award them on that basis; for Lord
Denman CJ said 'but no calculation of that sort was made at the trial or submitted to the
jury, and we do not think it can now be fairly made'. So counsel for the tenant would
not have been prevented by this authority from claiming the expenses of alternative
accommodation. But he settled the tenant's counterclaim on 10 June 1978, when the
tenant and her husband were still living in the flat, and he simply counterclaimed
damages without particularising or quantifying them.

The other head of damage which counsel for the tenant says the judge was wrong to
disallow was another aspect of the diminution in value of the flat to the tenant, based on
some loss of capital or rental value. For this item he claims to have the support of a
decision of this court in *Hewitt v Rowlands* (1924) 93 LJKB 1080, [1924] All ER Rep 344.
He put it in the alternative: diminution in the capital value of the flat, stated, according
to the report and evidence of the expert, Mr Lewis, to be £90,000 in the condition in
which it was in November 1982, as against £100,000 at the same date with the defects
repaired and the redecoration completed; or diminution in the rack rental value which
he gave as £170 per week exclusive of rates if let furnished, and £100 per week exclusive
of rates if let unfurnished, in December 1982. Before us counsel for the tenant argued
only for the difference between the nil letting value which the unrepaired flat would
have in the open market and the £100 a week for which it would let unfurnished when
repaired.

The first objection to that submission is that it is using Mr Lewis's undisclosed report
and his evidence as a basis for assessing damage without giving counsel for the landlords
the opportunity of calling expert evidence on valuation; and I infer from the passage I
have already quoted from his judgment that, if asked, the judge would have granted
counsel for the landlords an adjournment for that purpose had he not felt able to base his
assessment of the difference in value between the flat in good condition and the flat in its
unrepaired condition on the cost of making good the interior of the flat, although that
item of special damage had not been particularised or quantified in the counterclaim, as
it should have been for reasons which I give later. I think this objection is itself fatal to
the submission of counsel for the tenant.

The second objection is that to submit that what the tenant has lost by the landlords'
a breach of covenant is the consequent diminution in the value of the flat as a marketable
asset is to ask the court to take a wholly unreal view of the facts. The reality of the tenant's
loss is the temporary loss of the home where she would have lived with her husband
permanently if the landlords had performed their covenant. She cannot increase her loss
by deciding not to return after the covenant has been performed, and she does not seek
to do so. But she can claim, as it seems to me, to be put in as good a position as she would
b have been if the landlords had performed their covenant, at least as early as they had
notice that the main structure was out of repair instead of years later. If she had bought
the lease as a speculation intending to assign it, to the knowledge of the landlords, the
alleged diminution in rental (or capital) value might be the true measure of her damage.
But she did not; she bought it for a home, not a saleable asset, and it would be deplorable
if the court were bound to leave the real world for the complicated underworld of expert
c evidence on comparable properties and values, on the fictitious assumption that what the
flat would have fetched had anything to do with its value to her or her husband. I do not
think we are bound by the authority of *Hewitt v Rowlands* or any other decision to do
something so absurd, and the second objection of counsel for the landlords must, in my
opinion, rule out any damages for difference in rental value.

Hewitt v Rowlands was a case of a statutory tenant living in a rent-controlled cottage
d without a damp course, who sued his landlord for breach of his covenant to 'keep the
cottage dry and the outside in repair'. For want of a damp course the walls of this 150-
year-old cottage had become saturated with damp, and the roof and gutters also required
repairing at an estimated cost of £600. The case came up to this court three times, first
from a judgment of Acton J for the defendant landlord, apparently on expert evidence
that the cottage was worn out and not worth the cost of repairing unless the landlord was
e under an obligation to do so. How the judge found, as he must have, that the defendant
was under no such obligation is not clear, but he may have held that a statutory tenant
could not rely on the landlord's contractual obligation. This court allowed the plaintiff's
appeal, and entered judgment for the plaintiff for damages to be assessed by the Liverpool
district registrar. The registrar assessed the damages at £30; the plaintiff appealed his
decision to the Divisional Court, who remitted the case to the registrar; the defendant
f appealed for the second time to this court, who remitted the case to the registrar for
information on how the £30 damages was arrived at. The registrar informed the court
that they were made up of several sums for damage to a piano, pictures and a carpet, and
general damages to the value of £5. The report continues (93 LJKB 1080 at 1081; cf
[1924] All ER Rep 344 at 346):

g 'He [the registrar] added that, in his opinion, it was not in the contemplation of
the parties to the agreement that the tenant should be entitled to recover from the
landlord any damages for breach of the contract to repair beyond the actual loss and/
or expense to which the tenant might by put through the landlord's default, nor
were such damages to be increased by any such act on the part of the tenant as
remaining in occupation of the premises after the tenancy had been determined by
notice. In his view, in the absence of any evidence of any other loss or damage
h beyond the first three items allowed for, the sum of £5 was adequate to allow for all
other damage, if any, which the plaintiff might have suffered in consequence of the
defendant's default. In arriving at that figure he took into consideration the fact that
the written notice of want of repair was not given until after the expiration of the
notice to quit given by the defendant.'

j The court (Bankes, Scrutton and Atkin LJJ) then sent the case back to the registrar for the
third time to assess the damages in accordance with their directions.

Bankes LJ, with whom Scrutton LJ simply agreed, stated that the registrar had gone
wrong (1) in holding that as a statutory tenant the plaintiff was not entitled to any
damages in respect of any breaches of an agreement to repair by the landlord, and (2) in
holding that the measure of damages in respect of the covenant to repair would not

include anything except what the plaintiff might pay in doing the repairs which the
landlord ought to have done. He then said (93 LJKB 1080 at 1082; cf [1924] All ER Rep
344 at 347):

> 'Prima facie the measure of damage for breach of the obligation to repair is the
> difference in value to the tenant during that period between the house in the
> condition in which it now is and the house in the condition in which it would be if
> the landlord on receipt of the notice had fulfilled his obligation to repair. In assessing
> the damages on these lines it will be necessary to consider the extent of the landlord's
> obligation—a difficult question for the Registrar to decide, but which he must
> decide on the facts. He must consider, whether, having regard to the age and
> structure of the house, the damage complained of is really the result of the landlord's
> failure to do something which he ought to have done. Apparently the main cause
> of dampness was saturation of the stone which comprises part of the house through
> the absence of a damp course, and he must consider whether, upon the facts of this
> case, it falls within that class of cases such as LISTER v. LANE ([1893] 2 QB 212, [1891–
> 4] All ER Rep 388), as explained in LURCOTT v. WAKELY ([1911] 1 KB 905, [1911–13]
> All ER Rep 41), and, to the extent to which the Registrar may find after directing
> himself with reference to those decisions, that damage due to dampness was caused
> by defects which the landlord was not bound to remedy, the defendant will not be
> responsible and that damage must be excluded from the assessment. I hope I have
> expressed sufficiently clearly the view which the Registrar must take in assessing
> these damages. Perhaps I could express it shortly in this way: that the measure of
> damages is the difference in value to the tenant of the premises, from the date of the
> notice to repair down to the date of the assessment of damages, between the premises
> in their present condition and their value, if the landlord on receipt of the tenant's
> notice had fulfilled the obligations of the covenant.'

Atkin LJ gave a judgment agreeing that the measure of damages would be that stated by
Bankes LJ and indicating that the main points argued were the statutory tenant's right in
law to enforce the landlord's obligation to repair under the tenancy agreement and the
landlord's liability in fact for the dampness and damage under that agreement.

What is plain is that, in laying down the measure of damage, the court cannot have
had the capital or rental value of the cottage as a marketable asset in mind, because a
statutory tenancy is not marketable, and the court was considering the position of a
statutory tenant who was still living in the cottage and would lose his interest in the
cottage if he ceased to live there. What the difference in value to the plaintiff of the
statutory tenancy of the cottage repaired and unrepaired may have been was not an easy
matter for the registrar to assess, but I suspect he would not have gone far wrong if he
had equated it with what the plaintiff might have to spend on performing the landlord's
covenant (assuming the landlord would not perform it himself) and substantial general
damages for inconvenience and discomfort for the period from notice to the landlord till
assessment or performance of the covenant by the plaintiff. In my judgment there is
nothing in that case which supports counsel for the tenant's claim to any such additional
sum as he claims for diminution in value to the tenant or which would disable the judge
from measuring that diminution and the tenant's damage by the amounts he has
awarded as general and special damages, and by the reasonably incurred costs of
alternative accommodation, an item which was never in issue in *Hewitt v Rowlands*
because the tenant never left the cottage he occupied.

I might add that the only case I have found in which *Green v Eales* (1841) 2 QB 225,
114 ER 88 or *Hewitt v Rowlands* (1924) 93 LJKB 1080, [1924] All ER Rep 344 has been
considered is *Pembery v Lamdin* [1940] 2 All ER 434, where both were considered but not
on any point which assists counsel or the court.

In measuring and assessing any tenant's damages for breach of a landlord's repairing
covenant the court must, I think, always start with the fundamental principle that they
are 'so far as is possible by means of a monetary award, to place the plaintiff in the

position which he would have occupied if he had not suffered the wrong complained of,
be that wrong a tort or a breach of contract'. I take that statement from the judgment of
Donaldson LJ in *Dodd Properties (Kent) Ltd v Canterbury City Council* [1980] 1 All ER 928
at 938, [1980] 1 WLR 433 at 456, a case in which this court applied that principle by
awarding the owners as damages for negligence and/or nuisance the cost of repairing a
building damaged by the defendants' operations, and the lessees of the building their loss
of profits through dislocation of their business. The diminution in the building's value
in the open market was not considered as a basis for assessing the damage of either of the
plaintiffs. That basis was, however, considered appropriate to the assessment of damages
for the negligence of a surveyor at the suit of a purchaser of the surveyed property in
Perry v Sidney Phillips & Son (a firm) [1982] 3 All ER 705, [1982] 1 WLR 1297, where the
court awarded the plaintiff the difference in price between what he paid for the property
and its market value as it should have been described at the time of purchase with interest
and damages for distress and discomfort, vexation and inconvenience, since his conduct
in the circumstances had been reasonable. So the true measure of damages for persons
owning or occupying land, whether in tort or contract, depends on the position of the
plaintiffs and all the circumstances in which they have suffered loss and damage, in the
light of the fundamental principle to which I have referred.

I would dismiss the appeal because I think that the judge applied this principle
correctly to the facts of this case in awarding what he awarded and in refusing to award
what he refused to award. He did his best, on the evidence he was asked to consider, to
assess the difference between the value to the tenant of the flat as it was and of the flat as
it would have been if the landlords had performed their repairing covenant. He did not
award anything in respect of the alternative accommodation which the tenant and her
husband found in the Isle of Man because he was not asked to. And that brings me to the
next reason for dismissing the appeal.

The notice of appeal asks us to remit the action to an official referee with a direction
for the assessment of the further damages which I would hold were rightly disallowed
by the judge; and, emboldened by the views expressed by the court in *Green v Eales*
(1841) 2 QB 225, 114 ER 88, counsel for the tenant now asks us to add a direction to
award damages for the cost of the alternative accommodation.

Counsel for the landlords submits that even if that last head of damage be recoverable,
and even if I were wrong in holding the other two heads of damage to be irrecoverable,
none of them was pleaded and remission to an official referee should be refused on that
ground.

I agree with his submission. It is trite law that special damage must be pleaded so that
a defendant may know what case he has to meet and may be in a position to meet it with
evidence and perhaps with a payment into court: see RSC Ord 18, r 12 and the notes to
that rule in *The Supreme Court Practice 1982* vol 1, esp p 330, para 18/12/29 and the cases
there cited, to some of which counsel for the landlords referred us. I refer only to what
Lord Donovan said in giving the judgment of this court in *Perestrello e Cia Lda v United
Paint Co Ltd* [1969] 3 All ER 479 at 485–486, [1969] 1 WLR 570 at 579. He there pointed
out that the test whether damage should be pleaded is not whether it is general or special
but whether fairness to the defendant requires it to be pleaded, and some general damage
must be pleaded as having been suffered, as well as special damage as having been
incurred which is capable of substantially exact calculation. In disallowing an amendment
to claim loss of profits, Lord Donovan said ([1969] 3 All ER 479 at 486, [1969] 1 WLR
570 at 580):

'What amounts to a sufficient averment for this purpose will depend on the facts
of the particular case, but a mere statement that the plaintiffs claim "damages" is not
sufficient to let in evidence of a particular kind of loss which is not a necessary
consequence of the wrongful act and of which the defendant is entitled to fair
warning.'

That is all the tenant claimed in the instant case. If she had claimed the diminution in value, capital or rack rental, the landlords could have had discovery on the subject and agreed expert evidence about it, or had an expert and an expert's report to contradict the tenant's expert evidence and reports about it. If she had claimed the costs of alternative accommodation, she would have had to amend her pleading by alleging that the flat became uninhabitable on a particular date and in consequence she and her husband went to rented accommodation in the Isle of Man. But none of that was pleaded, so the landlords were not in a position to dispute that the flat became uninhabitable, or to argue for a postponement of the date when it began to be so, or to query the reasonableness of the tenant's choice of alternative accommodation in the Isle of Man, in the light of discovery of documents relating to it. Without discovery and the opportunity of testing the evidence of the tenant or her husband, or of contradicting it by evidence of their own, the landlords would not have a fair trial of these issues as to damage.

Counsel for the tenant submits that they would now have that opportunity if we granted him the remit which he asks for. But a party must present his whole case to the court and, save in exceptional circumstances not present here, will not be given an opportunity to present a new or additional case after his first presentation of it fails or fails in part. Apart from possible injustice to the other party, it is in the public interest that there should be an end to litigation. I have come to the conclusion that it would not be right to allow the tenant to amend and reopen her case now, and for this reason also I would dismiss the appeal.

GRIFFITHS LJ. I agree that this appeal fails for the reasons given by Stephenson LJ, but I venture to add a few words of my own because it appears to me, both from the arguments at the bar and the way in which the judge expressed himself, that there may be a widely held belief by those practising in this field that when damages are claimed by a tenant for breach of a landlord's repairing covenant they must always be assessed by reference to the diminution in the open market value of the premises and that they can never include the cost of alternative accommodation while the repairs are being carried out.

The object of awarding damages against a landlord for breach of his covenant to repair is not to punish the landlord but, so far as money can, to restore the tenant to the position he would have been in had there been no breach. This object will not be achieved by applying one set of rules to all cases regardless of the particular circumstances of the case. The facts of each case must be looked at carefully to see what damage the tenant has suffered and how he may be fairly compensated by a monetary award.

In this case on the findings of the judge the landlords after notice of the defect neglected their obligation to repair for such a length of time that the flat eventually became uninhabitable. It was also clear that, unless ordered to do so by an order of the court, the landlords had no intention of carrying out the repairs. In these circumstances the tenant had two options that were reasonably open to her: either of selling the flat and moving elsewhere or alternatively of moving into temporary accommodation and bringing an action against the landlords to force them to carry out the repairs and then returning to the flat after the repairs were done.

If a tenant chooses the first option then the measure of damages would indeed be the difference in the price he received for the flat in its damaged condition and that which it would have fetched in the open market if the landlord had observed his repairing covenant. If, however, the tenant does not wish to sell the flat but to continue to live in it after the landlord has carried out the necessary structural repairs it is wholly artificial to award him damages on the basis of loss in market value, because once the landlord has carried out the repairs and any consequential redecoration of the interior is completed there will be no loss in market value. The tenant should be awarded the cost to which he was put in taking alternative accommodation, the cost of redecorating, and some award for all the unpleasantness of living in the flat as it deteriorated until it became uninhabitable. These three heads of damage will, so far as money can, compensate the tenant for the landlord's breach.

a
But it was said that the court cannot award the cost of the alternative accommodation because of the decision in *Green v Eales* (1841) 2 QB 225, 114 ER 88 and in particular the passage in the judgment of Lord Denman CJ in which he said (2 QB 225 at 238, 114 ER 88 at 93):

b

> 'We are of opinion that the defendant was not bound to find the plaintiff another residence whilst the repairs went on, any more than he would have been bound to do so if the premises had been consumed by fire.'

But I take that passage to do no more than draw attention to the fact that a landlord is not in breach of his covenant to repair until he has been given notice of the want of repair and a reasonable time has elapsed in which the repair could have been carried out. If in this case the landlords had sent workmen round to carry out the repairs promptly on receiving notice of the defect and the tenant for her own convenience had decided to
c
move to a hotel whilst the repairs were carried out she could not have claimed the cost of the hotel accommodation because the landlords would not have been in breach of the repairing covenant. That Lord Denman CJ meant no more than this is I think apparent from his observation that the tenant might have had a claim on the basis that the time he had to be in alternative accommodation had been lengthened by the delay in carrying out repairs.

d
For these reasons I do not regard *Green v Eales* as an authority for the proposition that there can be no claim for the costs of alternative accommodation, but if it did purport so to decide, it was in my view wrongly decided.

If the tenant in this case had claimed for the cost of alternative accommodation it would in principle have been an allowable head of damage. It would naturally have been closely investigated on the evidence: was her (and her husband's) true reason for leaving the flat that they found the conditions intolerable, or were there other reasons for going
e
to live in the Isle of Man?, was the cost of the alternative accommodation reasonable? and so forth. However, the claim was not made and I agree that it is now too late to put it forward.

The judge awarded the tenant part of the costs of the internal decorations which she had had to carry out as a result of the landlords' breach of covenant. In my view he
f
should have awarded the whole of the costs of the repairs. However, he deducted one-third of the cost of repairs as a betterment element because he was attempting the unreal exercise of putting a price on the diminution in value of the flat in circumstances when there was no need to do so.

The judge was, however, invited to assess damages in this way by the tenant's counsel because it was thought that the decision of the Court of Appeal in *Hewitt v Rowlands* (1924) 93 LJKB 1080, [1924] All ER Rep 344 left no other approach to the assessment.
g
That was a case in which a statutory tenant claimed damages against his landlord for breach of the landlord's duty to repair. The sums involved were very small and in giving directions to the registrar as to the basis on which damages should be assessed Bankes LJ said (93 LJKB 1080 at 1082; cf [1924] All ER Rep 344 at 347):

h

> '*Prima facie* the measure of damage for breach of the obligation to repair *is the difference in value to the tenant* during that period between the house in the condition in which it now is and the house in the condition in which it would be if the landlord on receipt of the notice had fulfilled his obligation to repair.' (My emphasis.)

Whatever Bankes LJ meant by 'the difference in value to the tenant', the one thing he cannot have meant in the circumstances of that case was the diminution in the market value of the tenancy, for it was a statutory tenancy which the tenant could not sell, and
j
thus it had no market value. In my view the difference in value to the tenant must vary according to the circumstances of the case. If the tenant is in occupation during the period of breach he is entitled to be compensated for the discomfort and inconvenience occasioned by the breach and I suspect that that is what Bankes LJ had in mind when he used the phrase 'the difference in value to the tenant' in *Hewitt v Rowlands*, for which the

judge in this case awarded £3,000. If the tenant has rented the property to let it and the landlord is aware of this, then 'the difference in value to the tenant' may be measured by his loss of rent if he cannot let it because of the landlord's breach. If the tenant is driven out of occupation by the breach and forced to sell the property then 'the difference in value to the tenant' may be measured by the difference between the selling price and the price he would have obtained if the landlord had observed his repairing covenant. But each case depends on its own circumstances and *Hewitt v Rowlands* should not be regarded as an authority for the proposition that it is in every case necessary to obtain valuation evidence.

In my view there was no need for any valuation evidence in this case. I repeat that damages in a case such as this should include the cost of the redecoration, a sum to compensate for the discomfort, loss of enjoyment and health involved in living in the damp and deteriorating flat and any reasonable sum spent on providing alternative accommodation after the flat became uninhabitable.

The tenant has not appealed against the one-third reduction of the cost of repairs; the claim for alternative accommodation was not pleaded or argued, and for the reasons given by Stephenson LJ the heads of damage for which the tenant contended in this court are not recoverable.

MAY LJ. I agree with both judgments which have been delivered and that consequently this appeal should be dismissed.

Appeal dismissed.

Solicitors: *Theodore Goddard & Co* (for the tenant); *Grangewoods* (for the landlords).

Diana Brahams   Barrister.

Titchener v British Railways Board

HOUSE OF LORDS

LORD HAILSHAM OF ST MARYLEBONE LC, LORD FRASER OF TULLYBELTON, LORD KEITH OF KINKEL, LORD ROSKILL AND LORD BRIDGE OF HARWICH

24, 25 OCTOBER, 24 NOVEMBER 1983

Negligence – Duty to take care – Railway line – Duty to fence – Entrant taking short cut through gap in fence – Entrant familiar with line and aware of dangers – Whether occupier owing entrant duty to repair fence – Occupiers' Liability (Scotland) Act 1960, s 2(1).

Negligence – Volenti non fit injuria – Knowledge of risk – Railway line – Person crossing railway line through gap in fence injured by train – Train not being driven negligently – Entrant fully aware of, and accepting, risks – Whether occupier liable – Occupiers' Liability (Scotland) Act 1960, s 2(3).

In February 1974 at about 11 pm the appellant, then aged 15, was seriously injured when she was walking across a railway line and was struck by a train belonging to the respondents. The train which injured the appellant was not driven negligently. The appellant had climbed up a slope to the embankment on which the railway ran and had then passed through a gap in the boundary fence to get onto the line. The appellant had walked across the line on previous occasions and knew of the dangers involved in so doing. The route across the line was a short cut to a housing area and a brickworks but there was no necessity to walk across the line to reach those areas. There had been gaps in the fence for some years before the accident and the respondents were aware that people passed through those gaps to walk across the line. Although it was dark at the time of the accident there was no difficulty in seeing approaching trains. The appellant brought an action against the respondents claiming damages under the Occupiers' Liability (Scotland)

Act 1960, contending that the respondents, in failing to maintain the fence along the
a railway line in a reasonable state of repair, were in breach of their duty as occupiers under
s 2[a] of the 1960 Act to take such care as was reasonable in the circumstances to see that
the appellant did not suffer injury or damage by reason of any dangers which were due
to the state of the premises or anything done or omitted to be done on them. The
respondents denied that they owed a duty to the appellant to maintain the fence in good
condition and contended that since the appellant had voluntarily accepted the risks of
b walking across the line the respondents were absolved from liability by virtue of s 2(3) of
the 1960 Act. The Lord Ordinary and the Inner House of the Court of Session upheld the
respondents' contentions and refused the appellant's claim. The appellant appealed to the
House of Lords.

Held – The appeal would be dismissed for the following reasons—
   (1) The duty owed by an occupier of premises under s 2(1) of the 1960 Act to a person
c entering on his premises was a duty to show reasonable care. What was reasonble
depended on the circumstances of the case, including the age and intelligence of the
entrant. On the facts and having regard to the facts that the appellant knew of the
existence of the railway line, that it was dangerous to walk across and along it, that she
ought to have kept a look-out for trains and that she had done so when crossing the line
on previous occasions, the respondents did not owe the appellant a duty to maintain the
d fence in a better condition than they had. Furthermore, the line was so situated that the
appellant could not possibly have strayed onto it unawares and enough fence remained
to give her further warning, if that were necessary, that she would be going onto railway
premises when she entered. However, even if a duty to maintain and repair the gaps in
the fence had been established, the respondents' failure to maintain and repair had not
caused the accident because, on the evidence, the appellant would not have been deterred
e by a post and fence wire from crossing the line (see p 772 c and e f and p 775 a to f and j
to p 776 a and g to j, post); dictum of Lord Guest in M'Glone v British Rlys Board 1966 SC
(HL) at 15 applied.
   (2) In any event, the respondents were exempted from any obligation towards the
appellant by virtue of s 2(3) of the 1960 Act because the appellant fully appreciated the
risk she took in crossing the line, and since the train which injured her had not been
f negligently driven the risk which materialised was one of the risks that the appellant had
accepted (see p 772 c to e and p 776 b to j, post); dictum of Lord Reid in M'Glone v British
Rlys Board 1966 SC (HL) at 13 applied; Slater v Clay Cross Co Ltd [1956] 2 All ER 625 and
M'Glone v British Rlys Board 1966 SC (HL) 1 distinguished.

Notes
g For an occupier's common duty of care, see 34 Halsbury's Laws (4th edn) paras 21–24,
and for cases on the subject, see 36(1) Digest (Reissue) 17–32, 34–103.
   For the defence of volenti non fit injuria, see 34 Halsbury's Laws (4th edn) paras 62–
63, and for cases on the subject, see 36(1) Digest (Reissue) 248–253, 963–989.
   Section 2(1) and (3) of the Occupiers' Liability (Scotland) Act 1960 corresponds to s 2(2)
and (5) of the Occupiers' Liability Act 1957. For s 2 of the 1957 Act, see 23 Halsbury's
h Statutes (3rd edn) 794.

Cases referred to in opinions
M'Glone v British Rlys Board 1966 SC (HL) 1.
Slater v Clay Cross Co Ltd [1956] 2 All ER 625, [1956] 2 QB 264, [1956] 3 WLR 232, CA.

Appeal
j The pursuer, Ann Marie McGinlay or Titchener, appealed against an interlocutor of an
Extra Division of the Inner House of the Court of Session in Scotland (Lord Hunter, Lord
Avonside and Lord Grieve) dated 1 December 1982 refusing a reclaiming motion by the
appellant against an interlocutor pronounced by the Lord Ordinary (Lord Ross) on 25
September 1980 whereby the Lord Ordinary granted decree of absolvitor of the defenders,

---

a   Section 2, so far as material, is set out at p 774 c to e, post the British Railways Board (the respondents), in an action pursued by the appellant against the respondents under the Occupiers' Liability (Scotland) Act 1960 for damages *a* for personal injuries sustained by the appellant as a result of being struck by a train on the respondents' railway line. The facts are set out in the opinion of Lord Fraser.

William C Galbraith QC and *P H Brodie* (both of the Scottish Bar) for the appellant.
A M Morison QC and *J W McNeill* (both of the Scottish Bar) for the respondents.

b

Their Lordships took time for consideration.

24 November. The following opinions were delivered.

LORD HAILSHAM OF ST MARYLEBONE LC. My Lords, I have read in draft the speech about to be delivered by my noble and learned friend Lord Fraser. I entirely *c* agree with his conclusion that this appeal must be dismissed, and with the train of reasoning by which he would arrive at this conclusion.

To my mind the crucial fact in this appeal was that no averment was or could have been made against the respondent board that the train which struck the appellant was being driven otherwise than in a perfectly proper manner. If such an averment had been made and proved the respondent board would have been liable on the lines of the well- *d* known passage of Denning LJ's judgment in *Slater v Clay Cross Co Ltd* [1956] 2 All ER 625 at 628, [1956] 2 QB 264 at 271. But, on the facts and evidence in this case, once it was accepted that there was no negligence on the part of the driver of the train, it seems to me that the pursuer's claim, which was based solely on the condition of the fence was doomed to failure, if only because, on her own admission, she had voluntarily accepted the risk whatever it was which she incurred by crossing the line, provided only that it *e* was a 'risk of danger from the running of the railway in the ordinary and accustomed way'.

On this analysis of the facts it is possible to formulate the result either by saying that, at the critical moment, that is when the appellant crossed the line, the respondent board owed no duty to the appellant, or that the duty they owed to the appellant had been discharged by the time she crossed the boundary fence, or that the accident was not *f* caused by any breach of duty on the part of the respondent board, or alternatively that, having assumed the risk involved, the respondent board was covered by the doctrine volenti non fit injuria.

But I must take leave respectfully to add that the condition of the boundary fence as depicted by the evidence left much to be desired. The line was a suburban line passing through a populated area. Trains crossed by at intervals of about twenty minutes. There *g* was evidence that at least one small child had been killed at approximately the same spot. Quite apart from the danger to children straying, there could well have been a danger to passengers in trains had children, animals or vandals come onto the line and created an obstruction on it. It follows that had the facts of the case been other than what they were, it would be unsafe for the respondent board to assume that they would have been immune from liability from the state of the fence from a different claimant had another *h* and different accident occurred.

LORD FRASER OF TULLYBELTON. My Lords, on 23 February 1974 about 11 pm the appellant, who was then aged 15, was struck by a train on the respondents' railway line, between Shettleston and Carntyne stations in Glasgow. She was in the company of a young man, named John Grimes, aged 16, who was also struck by the *j* train. John Grimes was killed, and the appellant suffered very serious injuries, some of which will leave permanent effects on her. In this action, the appellant sues the respondents for damages under the Occupiers' Liability (Scotland) Act 1960. Her case is that the accident was caused by the negligence of the respondents in failing to maintain the fence along their railway in a reasonable state of repair. The respondents deny that they owed a duty to the appellant to maintain the fence in good condition. They also deny liability on other grounds to which I shall return, and they pleaded that the

appellant's averments were irrelevant. A proof before answer was heard by the Lord
Ordinary (Lord Ross), who assoilzied the defenders. An Extra Division of the Inner
House (Lord Hunter, Lord Avonside and Lord Grieve) dismissed the appellant's appeal
and adhered to the Lord Ordinary's interlocutor. The appellant has now appealed to this
House.

The accident occurred at a place where the railway line runs through a built-up and
populous area of Glasgow. It runs approximately east and west, and the train which
struck the appellant was travelling westwards from Shettleston towards Carntyne. The
exact point where the accident occurred was not established, but the Lord Ordinary
found that it was about a quarter of a mile west of Shettleston station in the vicinity of a
bridge by which the line crosses over Earnside Street. Earnside Street runs approximately
north and south, and passes under the railway at right angles. For a person walking
northwards in Earnside Street towards the railway bridge, there was a fence, for which
the respondents had no responsibility, on the right-hand side. At right angles to that
fence there was another fence, for which the respondents were responsible, running
along the south side of the railway both east and west of the bridge. The latter fence was
made of sleepers standing upright in the ground, but at the time of the accident, and
apparently for some years before that, there were gaps in it. In particular there was a gap
between the sleeper fence to the east of the bridge and the fence along the east side of
Earnside Street, the gap being wide enough for a person to pass through it without
difficulty. In order to reach the gap from Earnside Street a person would have to climb a
slope up to the embankment on which the railway ran. There was a rough path up the
slope leading to the gap in the fence. Having passed through the gap a person could
either cross the railway lines, and go through any one of several gaps in the fence on the
north side of the railway or he could walk along the line in either direction. The route
across the line was used to some extent as a short cut to a housing area further to the
north. It was also used as a short cut to a brickworks which lay immediately to the north
of the railway line, and to the east of the bridge. This brickworks was a popular resort for
courting couples. There was no necessity to walk across the line in order to reach the
housing estate or the brickworks; the proper way was to continue along Earnside Street
and under the railway bridge, but that route was apparently rather longer than the short
cut and was also liable to flooding. The Lord Ordinary concluded after a careful review
of the evidence that 'there was a certain amount of passage across the railway line on both
the east and west sides of the bridge'. He also concluded that the respondents 'must have
been aware that people from time to time did cross the line in the vicinity of the bridge'.

The appellant has no recollection of the accident or of the events immediately before
it, as she suffers from post-traumatic amnesia. Her last recollection before the accident is
of events in the morning of 23 February, some twelve hours earlier. But she is familiar
with the neighbourhood of Earnside Street and she gave evidence, apparently very
frankly, about having crossed the railway line with John Grimes, on the way to and from
the brickworks, on several previous occasions. There were no eyewitnesses of the accident,
but several witnesses gave evidence of having seen the appellant and John Grimes
together earlier in the evening up till about 10 pm. The Lord Ordinary's findings about
the time and place of the accident, and how it occurred, were based partly on the evidence
of these witnesses, partly on the appellant's own evidence of her previous visits to the
brickworks and partly on the real evidence found after the accident. There was evidence
from one of the respondents' witnesses that at off-peak times there were three trains per
hour in each direction on this line.

I did not understand counsel for either party to criticise the Lord Ordinary's findings
of fact as being erroneous, but counsel for the respondents submitted to the Division,
and more briefly to this House, that they did not go far enough to entitle him to hold
that the appellant had proved her case as averred on record. This submission persuaded
Lord Hunter who held that the appellant could not succeed because the Lord Ordinary's
finding that the accident had occurred 'somewhere in the vicinity of the bridge' did not
prove her averment on record that the accident had occurred when she and Grimes were
following the particular route or short cut referred to in the pleadings, and in her
evidence, namely a route to the east of the railway bridge. Lord Grieve was inclined to

agree with Lord Hunter although he based his decision on other grounds. Lord Avonside
rejected the argument. In my opinion, with all respect to Lord Hunter and Lord Grieve, ***a***
it would not be reasonable to reach a decision adverse to the appellant merely on the
ground that she had not precisely proved her case as averred. The respondents had ample
notice that the case against them was based on the fact that the accident occurred at a part
of the line in the vicinity of the bridge where, to their knowledge, people were in the
habit of walking across it, after getting through gaps in the fence. Nothing turned on the
exact spot where the appellant was struck and it is of no consequence whether it was on ***b***
the east or the west side of the bridge. The respondents were in at least as good a position
as the appellant to identify the point of impact, as the appellant herself has no recollection
of the accident. The railway police appear to have been at the locus soon after the
accident, although none of them was called as a witness. I have no hesitation in rejecting
the argument for the respondents on what I may call the pleading point.

The duty of care owed by an occupier of premises towards a person entering thereon ***c***
is now stated in the Occupiers' Liability (Scotland) Act 1960. Section 2(1) of that Act
provides:

> 'The care which an occupier of premises is required, by reason of his occupation
> or control of the premises, to show towards a person entering thereon in respect of
> dangers which are due to the state of the premises or to anything done or omitted
> to be done on them and for which the occupier is in law responsible shall . . . be ***d***
> such care as in all circumstances of the case is reasonable to see that that person will
> not suffer injury or damage by reason of any such danger.'

Section 2(3) provides:

> 'Nothing in the forgoing provisions of this Act shall be held to impose on an
> occupier any obligation to a person entering on his premises in respect of risks ***e***
> which that person has willingly accepted as his; and any question whether a risk was
> so accepted shall be decided on the same principles as in other cases in which one
> person owes to another a duty to show care.'

These two subsections are intimately related but I shall, as far as possible, consider them
separately. I shall consider first whether the respondents as occupiers owed to the ***f***
appellant as a person entering on their premises in respect of danger due to something
done on the premises (namely the running of trains) a duty to maintain the fence in
better condition than it was at the time of the accident. Let me repeat that the fence had
gaps through which persons like the appellant could easily pass, and that the respondents
knew that persons did pass through the gaps and walk across the line.

The duty under s 2(1) was considered by your Lordships' House in M'*Glone v British* ***g***
Rlys Board 1966 SC (HL) 1 at 15 where Lord Guest said: 'The duty is not to ensure the
entrant's safety but only to show reasonable care. What is reasonable care must depend
"on all the circumstances of the case".' One of the circumstances is the age and intelligence
of the entrant. That appears from the provision in s 2(1) that the duty is to show 'such
care as in all the circumstances of the case is reasonable to see that *that person* will not
suffer injury . . .' (my emphasis). The question in each case relates to the particular person ***h***
who has entered on the premises. The submission of counsel for the respondents was
that they did more than enough to discharge their obligations to this appellant because
the fences along the north and south sides of the line, notwithstanding that they had
gaps, gave her warning that if she went on she would be entering on railway premises.
She was well aware, as she admitted, of the danger of walking across or along the line,
and she said that when doing so she normally kept a look-out for trains. By giving her ***j***
that warning, the respondents were, said counsel for the respondents, doing more than
they were obliged to do, because this appellant already knew that the railway was there,
and therefore needed no warning. Counsel accepted that the logical conclusion of this
argument was that, as the appellant had no need of a warning, the respondents could
have left their premises near the bridge completely unfenced without being in breach of
any duty towards her. A fortiori they had no duty to do more than they did.

The Lord Ordinary accepted that argument, and in the Division Lord Hunter agreed,
a although only with some hesitation.

I must emphasise that the question in this appeal is not whether the respondents, and
other operators of railways if any there be, have as a general rule a duty to the public to
maintain fences beside their lines in good condition or at all. The existence and extent of
a duty to fence will depend on the circumstances of the case including the age and
intelligence of the particular persons entering on the premises; the duty will tend to be
b higher in a question with a very young or a very old person than in the question with a
normally active and intelligent adult or adolescent. The nature of the locus and the
obviousness or otherwise of the railway may also be relevant. In the circumstances of this
case, and in a question with this appellant, I have reached the opinion that the Lord
Ordinary was well entitled to hold, as he did, that the respondents owed no duty to her
to do more than they in fact did to maintain the fence along the line. I reach that view
c primarily because the appellant admitted that she was fully aware that the line existed,
that there was danger in walking across it or along it, that she ought to have kept a look-
out for trains, and that she had done so when crossing the line on previous occasions. In
addition the following features of the case are in my opinion important. The line ran
along an embankment up which the appellant had to climb, whether she approached
from the south or the north. Accordingly, she could not possible have strayed onto the
d line unawares. Enough of the fence remained to give her further warning, if that were
necessary, that she would be going onto railway premises where (as she knew) there was
danger from the trains. For reasons explained by the Lord Ordinary, it seems that the
train which caused this accident approached from the east, that is from Shettleston, and
the line in that direction is perfectly straight and free from obstruction for at least a
quarter of a mile from the bridge over Earnside Street to Shettleston Station and for some
e distance beyond the station. There was no difficulty in seeing trains as they approached.
It was dark at the time of the accident but, even in the dark, their lights would have been
visible. There was therefore no special danger peculiar to the locus of the accident, and
no criticism was made by the appellant of the way in which the particular train was
being operated. (I shall return to the last point in a moment.) Taking all these
circumstances together I consider that the respondents did not owe the appellant a duty
f to maintain the fence in better condition that it was. If it were necessary to do so, I would
hold that they owed her no duty to provide any fence at all.

If I am right so far, that would be enough to dispose of this appeal in favour of the
respondents. But the Lord Ordinary and the Division based their decisions also on other
grounds and I ought briefly to consider those additional grounds. In the first place the
Lord Ordinary held that, even if the respondents were at fault in failing to maintain the
g fence and to repair the gaps in it, the appellant had failed to prove, as a matter of
probability, that if the respondents had performed their duty in those respects, the
accident would have been prevented. The Lord Ordinary expressed himself strongly on
this point and concluded that the appellant and her companion would not have been
stopped by anything short of an impenetrable barrier. No doubt he reached that
conclusion mainly because of the appellant's evidence in cross-examination, that the
h respondents should have put up an impenetrable barrier which would have been
'impossible to get through'. That extreme view is clearly untenable; even in M'Glone's
case 1966 SC (HL) 1 at 11, where the danger (from a transformer) was at least as great as
the danger in this case and where the injured intruder was a boy aged only 12, Lord Reid
described the suggestion that the defenders owed him a duty to surround the transformer
with an impenetrable and unclimbable fence as 'quite unreasonable'. But the appellant
j also said that even an ordinary post and wire fence would have been enough to prevent
her from crossing the line because she could not have climbed over it. This was at least
partly because she was wearing platform shoes. The Lord Ordinary disbelieved her
evidence on this point, but counsel for the appellant submitted that, in the absence of
any other evidence, he had not been entitled to do so. In my opinion the Lord Ordinary
was in no way bound to accept the appellant's evidence on this point, even though it was
uncontradicted. Having regard to the fact that the appellant, helped perhaps by her

boyfriend, was apparently able to climb up the embankment and walk across the line,
platform shoes and all, I consider that the Lord Ordinary was fully entitled to conclude
that she had failed to satisfy him that a post and wire fence would have deterred her. It
follows that the respondents' failure to maintain the fence in a reasonable condition, even
assuming that it was their duty to have done so, did not cause the accident. The
respondents aver that post and wire fencing was the type of fencing mainly relied on by
them near the locus and that it was subject to frequent vandalism, but these matters were
not explored in evidence.

Second, the Lord Ordinary held that the respondents had established a defence under
s 2(3) of the 1960 Act by proving that the appellant had willingly accepted the risks of
walking across the line. As Lord Reid said in M'Glone's case (at 13) sub-s (3) merely puts
in words the principle volenti non fit injuria. That principle is perhaps less often relied
on in industrial accident cases at the present time than formerly, but, so far as cases under
the 1960 Act are concerned, the principle is expressly stated in s 2(3) and there is no room
for an argument that it is out of date or discredited. If the Lord Ordinary was entitled to
sustain this defence, the result would be that, whether the respondents would otherwise
have been in breach of their duty to the appellant or not, the appellant had exempted
them from any obligation towards her (see *Salmond and Heuston on the Law of Torts* (18th
edn, 1981) p 467). On this matter I am of opinion, in agreement with Lord Hunter, that
the Lord Ordinary was well founded in sustaining this defence. The reasons for doing so
are in the main the same as the reasons for holding that the respondents were not in
breach of their duty. The appellant admitted that she was fully aware that this was a line
along which trains ran, and that it would be dangerous to cross the line because of the
presence of the trains. She said in cross-examination '. . . it was just a chance I took', and
the Lord Ordinary evidently accepted that she understood what she was saying. She was
in a different position from the boy in M'Glone's case who did not have a proper
appreciation of the danger from live wires (see 1966 SC (HL) 1 at 13, 18 per Lord Reid
and Lord Pearce). As I said already the appellant did not suggest that the train which
injured her had been operated in an improper or unusual way. The importance of that is
that the chance which she took was no doubt limited to the danger from a train operated
properly, in the 'ordinary and accustomed way': see *Slater v Clay Cross Co Ltd* [1956] 2 All
ER 625 at 628, [1956] 2 QB 264 at 271 per Denning LJ. Had there been evidence to show
that the train which injured the appellant was driven negligently, like the train in *Slater's*
case, the risk which materialised would not have been within the risks that the appellant
had accepted. But there is nothing of that kind here. In my opinion therefore the defence
under s 2(3) is established.

In these circumstances no question of apportioning the blame on the ground of
contributory negligence arises.

For these reasons I would dismiss the appeal.

LORD KEITH OF KINKEL. My Lords, I agree that, for the reasons set out in the
speech of my noble and learned friend Lord Fraser, this appeal should be dismissed.

LORD ROSKILL. My Lords, I have had the advantage of reading in draft the speech
delivered by my noble and learned friend Lord Fraser. For the reasons he gives I too
would dismiss this appeal.

LORD BRIDGE OF HARWICH. My Lords, for the reasons given in the speech of
my noble and learned friend Lord Fraser, with which I fully agree, I too would dismiss
this appeal.

Appeal dismissed.

Solicitors: *Asher Fishman & Co*, agents for *Allan McDougall & Co SSC*, Edinburgh (for the
appellant); *M G Baker*, agent for *W Roddie*, Edinburgh (for the respondents).

Mary Rose Plummer   Barrister.

a
Antaios Cia Naviera SA v Salen Rederierna AB
The Antaios

b
COURT OF APPEAL, CIVIL DIVISION
SIR JOHN DONALDSON MR, ACKNER AND FOX LJJ
15, 17 JUNE, 8 JULY 1983

c
Arbitration – Award – Leave to appeal to Court of Appeal against grant or refusal of leave to appeal to High Court – When leave to appeal to Court of Appeal should be granted – Principles applicable to grant of leave – Arbitrator's decision raising substantial and arguable point of law – Case important to parties or of general interest – Judge concluding arbitrator's decision probably right – Judge requiring guidance on principles applicable to grant of leave – Whether judge should grant leave – Arbitration Act 1979, s 1(6A).

d
Arbitration – Award – Leave to appeal against award – Factors to be considered by court when deciding whether to grant leave – Award affecting parties' rights and involving conflict of judicial opinion – Judge concluding that arbitrator's decision probably right and refusing leave to appeal to High Court – Whether judge right to refuse leave to appeal – Arbitration Act 1979, s 1(3)(b).

e
Contract – Breach – Waiver – Conduct amounting to waiver – Owners chartering vessel to charterers – Charterparty providing for withdrawal of vessel in event of any breach of charterparty – Charterers issuing inaccurate bills of lading – Owners indicating that charterers in breach of charterparty – Owners purporting to withdraw vessel three weeks after breach – Whether owners entitled to withdraw vessel – Whether owners exercising right of withdrawal within reasonable time – Whether owners can extend time in which it is reasonable for them to withdraw vessel.

f
By cl 5 of a time charter in the standard New York Produce Exchange from, which provided for disputes to be referred to arbitration in London, the owners were entitled to withdraw the vessel from the charterers' service in the event of 'any breach' of the charterparty by the charterers. On 7 May 1980 the owners discovered that the charterers had issued inaccurate bills of lading and indicated to the charterers on the same day that although they considered the charterers to be in breach under cl 5 they reserved the right to withdraw the vessel without prejudice to any delay in doing so. On 20 May the owners

g
did in fact purport to withdraw the vessel. The question whether the owners were entitled to do so was referred to arbitration. The arbitrators found (i) that on its true construction cl 5 only gave the owners the right to withdraw in the case of a repudiatory breach, whereas the charterers' breach was not repudiatory, and (ii) alternatively, that if the owners had acquired the right to withdraw they had lost that right by not exercising it within a reasonable time, which the arbitrators considered to be 48 hours after

h
becoming aware of the breach. The arbitrators held that there was an implied term in the charterparty that the owners had to give notice within a reasonable time. The owners applied under s 1(3)(b)[a] of the Arbitration Act 1979 for leave to appeal to the High Court, contending that, since there was a conflict of judicial opinion on the construction of cl 5 the determination of which would substantially affect the rights of the parties, leave ought to be given. The owners further contended, on the issue of withdrawal within a

j
reasonable time, that they could only lose their right to withdraw if they waived that right or were estopped from enforcing it and that their notice to the charterers on 7 May

---

a   Section 1, so far as material, provides:
     '... (3) An appeal under this section may be brought by any of the parties to the reference ...
     (b) ... with the leave of the court ...
     (6A) Unless the High Court gives leave, no appeal shall lie to the Court of Appeal from a decision
     of the High Court—(a) to grant or refuse leave under subsection (3)(b) ...'

showed that they did not intend to waive that right. The judge refused leave to appeal to the High Court, on the ground that although the construction of cl 5 gave rise to *a* substantial and arguable questions of law that issue was immaterial and did not affect the rights of the parties because, in his opinion, the arbitrators were prima facie right on the issue of withdrawal within a reasonable time. However, the judge granted the owners leave to appeal to the Court of Appeal under s 1(6A) of the 1979 Act on the question whether a judge ought to give leave under s 1(6A) where the arbitrator's decision raised a substantial and arguable point of law but the judge considered his decision was probably *b* right.

Held – (1) On the issue of leave to appeal to the Court of Appeal against a decision granting or refusing leave to appeal to the High Court, the purpose of the 1979 Act was to encourage finality in arbitration and discourage appeals, and therefore a judge ought not to grant leave where the arbitrator's decision raised a substantial and arguable point *c* of law but was probably right or further (per Sir John Donaldson MR and Fox LJ) merely because the case was important to the parties or of general interest. Although the judge at first instance had an unfettered discretion to grant leave under s 1(6A) that discretion was normally to be exercised only where the judge required guidance on the principles applicable to the grant of leave (see p 782 *a* to *d*, p 787 *a b*, p 788 *d e* and p 789 *b c*, post).

(2) On the issue of leave to appeal to the High Court under s 1(3)(*b*) of the 1979 Act, a *d* judge ought to refuse leave where he formed the view that the arbitrator's decision was probably right, regardless of the basis on which the arbitrator reached his decision or whether the Court of Appeal might, simply because it was an appellate court, take a different view. If, however, the resolution of the issue was going to affect the rights of the parties substantially and there was known to be a conflict of judicial opinion then leave ought to be given (see p 780 *e* to *j*, p 782 *d e g* to *j*, p 783 *e*, p 785 *g*, p 787 *c*, p 788 *d* *e* and p 789 *c d*, post); dictum of Lord Diplock in *Pioneer Shipping Ltd v BTP Tioxide Ltd, The Nema* [1981] 2 All ER at 1040 explained.

(3) (Ackner LJ dissenting) On the substantive issue of whether the owners had exercised their right of withdrawal within a reasonable time, the rule was that notice of withdrawal had to be given within a reasonable time after default and what was reasonable in any case was a matter for the arbitrator. Therefore, whatever the basis of *f* the rule, the owners were not entitled, merely by the unilateral assertion that delay on their part was to be without prejudice to their rights, to extend the time for withdrawal beyond what was reasonable. In any event (per Sir John Donaldson MR), the charterers were by their without prejudice notice seeking to acquire a right which they would not otherwise have had, namely the right to withdraw the vessel after the expiry of a reasonable time, and therefore they could not rely on a supposed refusal to waive their *g* right since that presupposed that they already had the right. On the facts, therefore, regardless of whether the juridical basis of the doctrine was an implied term (as found by the arbitrators) or waiver, the arbitrators were probably correct in deciding that the owners had not exercised their right of withdrawal within a reasonable time, and accordingly the judge had been right to refuse leave to appeal to the High Court (see p 783 *a b d* to *f*, p 784 *b c*, p 788 *f j* to p 789 *a d*, post); dictum of Lord Wilberforce in *h* *Mardorf Peach & Co Ltd v Attica Sea Carriers Corp of Liberia, The Laconia* [1977] 1 All ER at 552 applied; *Scandinavian Trading Tanker Co AB v Flota Petrolera Ecuatoriana, The Scaptrade* [1983] 1 All ER 301 considered.

Per Sir John Donaldson MR and Fox LJ. Since the time within which it is reasonable for shipowners to withdraw their vessel from the charterers' service may be affected by matters known only to the owners, it follows that if the owners make any problems they *j* may have known to the charterers and indicate that they are not abandoning their right of withdrawal they may thereby extend the period within which it is reasonable for them to withdraw the vessel (see p 783 *j* and p 788 *g*, post); dictum of Lloyd J in *Scandinavian Trading Tanker Co AB v Flota Petrolera Ecuatoriana, The Scaptrade* [1981] 2 Lloyd's Rep at 430 applied.

Notes

a   For appeals to the High Court from an arbitrator's award, see 2 Halsbury's Laws (4th edn) para 627.

For waiver generally, see 9 ibid para 571, and for cases on the subject, see 12 Digest (Reissue) 544–545, 3796–3806.

For promissory estoppel, see 9 Halsbury's Laws (4th edn) paras 575–579 and for cases on the subject see 21 Digest (Reissue) 8–16, 52–74.

b   For the Arbitration Act 1979, s 1, see 49 Halsbury's Statutes (3rd edn) 59, and for s 1(6A) of that Act (as inserted by the Supreme Court Act 1981, s 148(2)), see 51 ibid 672.

Cases referred to in judgments

BVS SA v Kerman Shipping Co SA, The Kerman [1982] 1 All ER 616, [1982] 1 WLR 166.

China National Foreign Trade Transportation Corp v Evlogia Shipping Co SA of Panama, The
c   *Mihalios Xilas* [1979] 2 All ER 1044, [1979] 1 WLR 1018, HL.

Italmare Shipping Co v Ocean Tanker Co Inc, The Rio Sun [1982] 1 All ER 517, [1982] 1 WLR 158, CA.

Mardorf Peach & Co Ltd v Attica Sea Carriers Corp of Liberia, The Laconia [1977] 1 All ER 545, [1977] AC 850, [1977] 2 WLR 286, HL.

Pioneer Shipping Ltd v BTP Tioxide Ltd, The Nema [1981] 2 All ER 1030, [1982] AC 724,
d   [1981] 3 WLR 292, HL.

Scandinavian Trading Tanker Co AB v Flota Petrolera Ecuatoriana, The Scaptrade [1981] 2 Lloyd's Rep 425; *affd* [1983] 1 All ER 301, [1983] QB 529, [1983] 2 WLR 248, CA.

Telfair Shipping Corp v Athos Shipping Corp SA, The Athos [1983] 1 Lloyd's Rep 127, CA; *affg* [1981] 2 Lloyd's Rep 74.

Tropwood AG v Jade Enterprises Ltd, The Tropwind [1977] 1 Lloyd's Rep 397.

e   *Tyrer & Co and Hessler & Co, Re* (1902) 86 LT 697, CA.

Cases also cited

Amherst v James Walker Goldsmith and Silversmith Ltd [1983] 2 All ER 1067, [1983] 3 WLR 334, CA.

Eximenco Handels AG v Partrederiet Oro Chief, The Oro Chief (10 May 1983, unreported),
f   QBD.

Gatoil Anstalt v Omennial Ltd, The Balder London [1980] 2 Lloyd's Rep 489.

Appeal

Antaios Cia Naviera SA (the owners) appealed with leave against the decision of Staughton J dated 5 November 1982 refusing the owners leave to appeal against the
g   award of the arbitrators, Mr Anthony Diamond QC, Mr Bruce Harris and Mr John Potter, dated 9 July 1982 whereby they held that the owners were not entitled to withdraw the vessel Antaios on 20 May 1980 from the service under a charterparty made between the owners and the respondents, Salen Rederierna AB (the charterers). The facts are set out in the judgment of Sir John Donaldson MR.

h   *Gordon Pollock QC* and *Angus Glennie* for the owners.
Mark O Saville QC and *Bernard Eder* for the charterers.

Cur adv vult

j   8 July. The following judgments were delivered.

SIR JOHN DONALDSON MR. The appellants, the owners of the Antaios, applied to the Commercial Court under s 1(3)(*b*) of the Arbitration Act 1979 for leave to appeal to the High Court against an arbitration award dated 9 July 1982. The application was heard and refused by Staughton J. Normally that would have been the end of the matter,

because s 1(6A) of the Arbitration Act 1979 bars any appeal to the Court of Appeal from
the grant or refusal of leave to appeal to the High Court, unless the High Court itself   *a*
gives leave authorising such an appeal. However in this case Staughton J gave leave to
appeal to this court and also invited us to consider whether he should have done so.

The background

Before considering that question and the substance of the appeal, I should set the scene
briefly. At all material times the vessel was under time charter to the respondents on the
New York Produce Exchange form, which provides for disputes to be referred to three   *b*
arbitrators. The arbitrators in this case were Mr Anthony Diamond QC, Mr Bruce Harris
and Mr John Potter, all of whom are very experienced in this field. A major issue in the
arbitration concerned the right of the owners to withdraw the vessel from the chartered
service on discovery that the charterers had issued bills of lading which were 'inaccurate',
to use a neutral word. This turned on whether cl 5 of the charter entitled the owners to
withdraw the vessel in the event of *any* breach of the charterparty on the part of the   *c*
charterers or only in the event of a repudiatory or some other restricted category of
breach.

The arbitrators held that the breach by these charterers was non-repudiatory and that
the clause, properly construed, gave a right of withdrawal only in the case of a repudiatory
breach. They further held that, even if they were wrong in this and the owners had   *d*
acquired a right of withdrawal, it had to be exercised within a reasonable time and that
the owners had lost that right by delaying far beyond a reasonable time before purporting
to exercise it. The arbitrators held that in all the circumstances of the case, including in
particular the fact that the owners had long suspected that the charterers were in breach
of the charterparty, a reasonable time would have expired on 9 May 1980, ie 48 hours
after the owners acquired firm knowledge of the breach, whereas the owners gave notice
of withdrawal on 20 May.   *e*

Staughton J said that if the only issue had been the true construction of cl 5 he would
have granted leave to appeal to the High Court because the arbitrators had disagreed with
a dictum of Neill J and also with a dictum of Kerr J which itself conflicted with the view
expressed by Neill J. In this I think he was right. There is a public interest in the
construction of cl 5 and some measure of uncertainty as to what is the true answer. It   *f*
thus falls within the category of case considered by Lord Diplock in *Pioneer Shipping Ltd v
BTP Tioxide Ltd, The Nema* [1981] 2 All ER 1030 at 1040, [1982] AC 724 at 743. In saying
that I think Staughton J was right, I am, of course, construing Lord Diplock's speech as if
it had read, 'But leave should not be given, even in such a case, unless the judge considered
that a strong prima facie case had been made out that the arbitrator *might well have been
wrong* in his construction' rather than 'the arbitrator *had been* wrong in his construction'.
I think that this must have been his intention as otherwise, where there are known to be   *g*
differences of judicial opinion on a matter such as this, whether leave to appeal was
granted or refused would depend on the accident of whether the judge hearing the
application did or did not take the same view as the particular arbitrator. This cannot
have been the intention of Parliament. If I am wrong in so construing Lord Diplock's
speech, then I think that this is one of those cases in which it is permissible to remind   *h*
oneself that the speeches in *The Nema* were intended to provide guidelines rather than to
remove the discretion granted to the judge hearing the application and that guidelines
by definition permit of exceptions, albeit great care must be exercised to ensure that the
exceptions do not become so numerous as to blur the edges of the guidelines or even
render them invisible.

However, despite his willingness to grant leave on the basis of the cl 5 issue, Staughton J   *j*
refused leave to appeal to the High Court because he considered that issue to be
immaterial, and thus incapable of affecting the rights of the parties substantially or at all
(see s 1(4) of the 1979 Act), unless the arbitrators were wrong in their view that the
owners had, by their own inactivity, lost any right of withdrawal. On this latter issue he
was of the opinion that the arbitrators were probably right and it would follow, applying
The Nema guidelines, that leave to appeal to the High Court should be refused.

There was also a subsidiary point on the charterers' counterclaim, the owners
a complaining that there was some logical inconsistency between two parts of the award.
So far as this was concerned Staughton J considered that the owners were plainly wrong.

Section 1(6A) of the 1979 Act: leave to appeal to the Court of Appeal
I now return to the reason why leave to appeal to this court was given by Staughton J
and I cannot do better than quote from his judgment. After adverting to s 1(6A) of the
b Arbitration Act 1979 he said:

'Parliament thus contemplated that in some cases at any rate it would be right for
a judge at first instance to grant leave to appeal to the Court of Appeal against his
own decision either granting leave to appeal from an arbitration award or refusing
leave to appeal from an arbitration award. There have been discussed in argument
c three classes of cases in which this problem might arise. Class 1 is cases like *BVS SA
v Kerman Shipping Co SA, The Kerman* [1982] 1 All ER 616, [1982] 1 WLR 166, where
Parker J laid down guidelines as to the granting of leave under the Arbitration Act
1979, or perhaps it may be said laid down a practical interpretation of the guidelines
earlier laid down in *The Nema*. It is not disputed that in such a class of case it would
be right for this court to give leave to appeal to the Court of Appeal so that the
d guidelines may be either approved or varied and have the authority of that court.
The second class of case is where the judge at first instance has decided the matter
for one reason or another as one of discretion. In such a case counsel for the
charterers submits, and I would agree, that it is not right to give leave to appeal to
the Court of Appeal. The third class of case is more difficult. That is where the issue
raised by the arbitration award is a genuine arguable point of law, but one on which
e the judge at first instance has concluded that the arbitrators, so far from being
probably wrong as they must be shown to be if leave is given in accordance with
The Nema guidelines, are, on the contrary, probably right. If a judge at first instance
comes to the conclusion on such a substantial and arguable point of law that the
arbitrators are probably right, should he nevertheless give leave to appeal to the
Court of Appeal? Most judges at first instance are occasionally wrong, and I certainly
f count myself among that number and am the first to recognise that, although I may
think that the arbitrators were probably right, the Court of Appeal might take the
view that they were probably wrong, and that therefore leave should be given in
accordance with *The Nema* guidelines. Nevertheless it seems to me that the policy of
the 1979 Act will not be best served if leave is given in such circumstances. The
judge at first instance must make up his mind; and, if he concludes, even on a
g substantial and arguable point of law, that the arbitrators are probably right, then
he must say so and must refuse leave to go to the Court of Appeal. That would be
my conclusion but for this point. In expressing that view I have in effect laid down
or attempted to lay down a principle, a principle which would benefit by being
considered, and if right adopted, by the Court of Appeal. It would be very much to
the advantage of the commercial community, as it seems to me, that the Court of
h Appeal should consider this very point, and if I were to refuse leave they would have
no opportunity of doing so. In effect this case has now become one in the first class
like *The Kerman* where I have stated what seems to me to be a principle, and the
Court of Appeal ought to consider that principle. So I conclude that in general it is
not right for a judge at first instance to grant leave to appeal under the new s 1(6A)
in a case where the arbitrators' decision raises a substantial and arguable point of law
j but the judge considers that the arbitrators were probably right on it. I say "in
general", but in this particular case I consider it right to grant leave to appeal in
order that that conclusion can itself be considered by the Court of Appeal.'

I appreciate the problem which confronted Staughton J. As he says, 'Most judges at
first instance are occasionally wrong', or, as I would prefer to put it, 'Most judges at first
instance have had the experience of taking a different view from that of an appellate

court'. They are equally aware, of course, that if the parties are sufficiently persistent there may be a further appeal in which their judgment is restored.

Parliament has made it clear that, subject to the exceptional situation contemplated by s 1(6A) of the 1979 Act, it was content and indeed required that the decision whether to grant or refuse leave to appeal to the High Court should be left exclusively to the discretion of the judges of the High Court which, in the light of RSC Ord 73, r 6, means the judges of the Commercial Court. This is understandable because of the need for speed of decision and the fact that the judges of that court are specialists in the field of arbitration.

The exceptional situation contemplated by s 1(6A) is, I think, one in which a judge of the High Court wishes to have a 'second opinion' on the principles which should guide him in the exercise of his discretion. That is this case and accordingly I consider that Staughton J was right to grant leave to appeal to this court.

Counsel for the owners submitted that leave to appeal to the Court of Appeal from the decision granting or refusing leave to appeal to the High Court should also be given where the issue raised by the award itself was of general interest or importance, of particular importance to the parties or one on which there is a difference of judicial opinion. I do not accept this submission. These factors may well have to be taken into account within the general *Nema* guidelines in deciding whether or not to grant leave to appeal to the High Court, but they do not seem to me to have any bearing on whether, a decision having been given to grant or refuse leave to appeal to that court, that decision should be open to reconsideration by the Court of Appeal.

Counsel for the owners stressed the undesirability of allowing a situation to arise in which, in relation to any particular award, one judge would grant leave because he thought that the arbitrator was prima facie wrong and another would refuse leave because he thought that the arbitrator was probably right. This, of course, I accept without reservation. But the solution is not an appeal to the Court of Appeal. It is to grant leave to appeal to the High Court. Staughton J, I think, applied this principle in deciding that if the construction of cl 5 had been the only issue he would have granted such leave.

Section 1(3) of the 1979 Act: leave to appeal to the High Court

In the light of the fact that Staughton J gave leave to appeal, we have to review his decision not to grant leave to appeal to the High Court pursuant to s 1(3) of the 1979 Act. That involves a consideration of the award with which he was concerned. However, before doing so, I should consider the general question which he asked, namely whether, where a judge has formed a firm view that the arbitrator is probably right, the fact that the Court of Appeal might take a different view is any ground for granting leave to appeal to the High Court. My answer to this question is that it is not if his appreciation that the Court of Appeal might take a different view has no more solid a basis than that this is in the nature of appellate courts and that if the Court of Appeal did take a different view and the parties were sufficiently persistent his own view might equally well be affirmed by the House of Lords. It is quite different if there are known to be differing schools of thought, each claiming their adherents amongst the judiciary, and the Court of Appeal, given the chance, might support either the school of thought to which the judge belongs or another school of thought. In such a case leave to appeal to the High Court should be given, provided that the resolution of the issue would substantially affect the rights of the parties (s 1(4) of the 1979 Act) *and* the case qualified for leave to appeal to the Court of Appeal under s 1(7) of the 1979 Act as no doubt it usually would. I add this additional qualification because there is no point in the judge giving leave when he has little doubt that the arbitrator is right and that, despite adversarial argument, he will affirm the award, unless he is also prepared to enable the Court of Appeal to resolve the conflict of judicial opinion.

I now turn to the substance of the appeal. In *Mardorf Peach & Co Ltd v Attica Sea Carriers Corp of Liberia, The Laconia* [1977] 1 All ER 545, [1977] AC 850 Lord Wilberforce,

with the agreement of Lord Salmon, said, obiter, that notice of withdrawal must be
a given within a reasonable time after the default and that what is a reasonable time is
essentially a matter for the arbitrators. As a general proposition this is hardly open to
challenge, but somewhat different views have been expressed on why this should be the
case. Two theories in particular have been aired, namely that the rule stems from an
implied term of the contract or that delay in exercising the right will amount to waiver
or create an estoppel. In the present case the owners knew of the default on 7 May 1980
b and indicated to the charterers that any delay in withdrawing the vessel would be without
prejudice to their right to do so. The arbitrators took the view that such an indication
prevented the owners' conduct amounting to a waiver of their rights or creating any
estoppel. However, they espoused the implied term explanation for the legal result
declared in *The Laconia* and held that the owners had lost any right to withdraw the
vessel.
c   Counsel for the owners submitted, in effect, that, while Staughton J might be described
in this context as 'an implied term judge', it was clear from *Scandinavian Trading Tanker
Co AB v Flota Petrolera Ecuatoriana, The Scaptrade* [1981] 2 Lloyd's Rep 425 that Lloyd J
was 'a waiver judge'. From this, he submitted, it would follow that Lloyd J would have
considered that the arbitrators were wrong in law in the conclusion which they reached
and would have given leave to appeal to the High Court.
d   I think that this argument confuses the juridical basis of the rule that a right of
withdrawal must be exercised within a reasonable time with the rule itself. What matters
in the context of deciding whether leave should be given to appeal to the High Court is
whether the arbitrators have given effect to the rights of the parties, not whether they
have correctly divined the juridical basis of those rights. Unless the arbitrators' *decision* is
wrong, the fact that their reasoning is wrong will not affect the rights of the parties
e substantially or at all.
I know of no authority for the proposition, and I do not think that I have ever heard it
suggested before, that a shipowner can extend the time for reaching a decision whether
or not to withdraw beyond what is reasonable in all the circumstances by the simple
device of announcing that his failure to decide is without prejudice to his rights. He can
certainly do so by reaching an agreement with the charterers either ad hoc or by including
f in the charterparty an anti-technicality clause. But neither occurred in the present case.
If counsel for the owners is right, and the owner can extend his option to withdraw the
vessel in this way, chaos would result. Ships would be hove to at sea or tied up in port, no
one knowing whether they were going to perform the chartered service. Counsel for the
owners answers this by saying that when the next hire comes due, or when the owner
has to accept or reject instructions from the charterers, he will have to make up his mind.
g I am not sure that this is necessarily so, because if counsel is right I do not see why he
should not continue to perform the charterparty in all respects while at the same time
proclaiming that none of this was to be taken as being an election to affirm the contract.
So far as accepting payment of hire is concerned, if this must inevitably amount to an
affirmation of the contract, it must be remembered that hire is sometimes paid only
monthly. An interval of nearly a month before the owners could be forced to elect would
h be wholly unacceptable commercially.
This is not to say that a declaration such as was made by the owners in this case can
never have any effect. As Lloyd J pointed out in *The Scaptrade* (at 430), what time is
reasonable may well be affected by matters known only to the owners. Being in ignorance
of these matters, charterers might reasonably conclude after x days that the owners were
not going to withdraw the vessel and in such circumstances I can well understand it
j being held that the owners had waived their right to withdraw or were estopped from
asserting it. If on the other hand the owners made their problems known to the charterers
or indicated that they were not abandoning their rights, they may thereby retain their
right of withdrawal for a longer period than x days, being such period as was reasonable
in all the circumstances, including the special problems which were afflicting them.
Thus waiver or an implied term are not alternatives. The implied term may well set a

limit on the owners' rights and waiver may cut down those rights, but the concept of waiver is only appropriate where the person 'waiving' is giving up some right. In the instant appeal the owners are contending that by 'waiver' they acquired something which they would not otherwise have had, namely a right to withdraw the vessel after the expiry of a reasonable time.

Counsel for the owners also relied on the subsidiary point based on an alleged logical inconsistency to which I referred earlier in this judgment. Suffice it to say that this is pure makeweight and very little weight at that.

I would dismiss the appeal for two reasons. First, in my judgment the decision was one for the discretion of Staughton J and I can detect no error in the principles which he applied. Second, if the matter had been one of my discretion, I would have exercised it in exactly the same way as he did.

ACKNER LJ. Staughton J accepted that if the only question arising out of the award concerned the proper construction of cl 5 of the charter, that is to say the owners' right to withdraw for 'any breach', he would have given leave to the owners to appeal to the Commercial Court. The charterers not only wholly accept the correctness of such a view, but in their outline written submissions, to which counsel for the charterers faithfully adhered in his cogent submissions before us, they accepted that the court should 'plainly' have given leave, if that was the only question, and for the following reasons: (1) cl 5 would have given rise to a question of law the determination of which 'would substantially effect the rights of one or more of the parties to the arbitration agreement' thereby satisfying the (negative) requirements of s 1(4) of the Arbitration Act 1979; (2) that question of law concerned the proper interpretation of a printed clause in a standard form of charter; (3) the question of law remained undetermined by the authorities: see *Telfair Shipping Corp v Athos Shipping Corp SA, The Athos* [1981] 2 Lloyd's Rep 74; *affd* [1983] 1 Lloyd's Rep 127 and *Tropwood AG v Jade Enterprises Ltd, The Tropwind* [1977] 1 Lloyd's Rep 397.

The arbitrators (Mr Anthony Diamond QC, Mr Bruce Harris and Mr John Potter) held that 'any breach' meant a repudiatory breach and therefore concluded that the owners were not entitled to withdraw the vessel from the head charter. They were almost content to base their decision on this finding, but in case they were wrong on their construction of 'any breach' they went on to consider the charterers' contention that the owners lost their right to withdraw the vessel by their own conduct and/or delay. The charterers' contention was that the owners had 'elected' to affirm the charter having had from the first week in April until 20 May to exercise their right to withdraw the vessel. This contention was rejected by the arbitrators on the ground that the duty to elect did not arise before 7 May, when the owners had knowledge of the breach, and that between 7 and 8 May the owners reserved their position and then on 20 May exercised their right to elect to *disaffirm* the contract. The arbitrators specifically rejected that there was any foundation in the evidence for a claim based on estoppel and then considered the final contention of the charterers that the period from the first week in April until 20 May was 'by itself so long that the owners lost their right to withdraw independently of all the above matters'. In support of this submission the charterers relied on the observations of Lord Wilberforce in *Mardorf Peach & Co Ltd v Attica Sea Carriers Corp of Liberia, The Laconia* [1977] 1 All ER 545 at 552, [1977] AC 850 at 872:

'The owners must within a reasonable time after the default give notice of withdrawal to the charterers. What is a reasonable time—essentially a matter for arbitrators to find—depends on the circumstances. In some, indeed many cases, it will be a short time—viz the shortest time reasonably necessary to enable the shipowner to hear of the default and issue instructions.'

As to this submission, the arbitrators concluded that the critical period was from 7 to 20 May, since, as previously stated, before 7 May the owners did not have the knowledge of the breach. The arbitrators concluded:

a 'In view of the Owners' long standing and firm belief, as from the first or second week of April, that the breach had been committed there was in our view no need on 7th May for the Owners to wait any longer, whether to obtain legal advice (which could have been obtained earlier), or to obtain further information or to make up their minds or for any other reason. In particular, there was no need for a meeting to take place at Piraeus or anywhere else to enable the Owners to decide whether or not to withdraw the vessel ... We therefore find that a reasonable time for

b withdrawing the vessel expired on 9th May, at the latest, and that the notice of withdrawal on 20th May was not given within a reasonable time.'

The arbitrators then asked themselves this question: does this finding entitle the charterers to contend successfully that the owner lost their right to withdraw the vessel? To this they replied: 'This is a question of law. We find it difficult. Though discussed at the hearing, we have had little argument upon it.'

c In the succeeding paragraphs they then explained why they found it a difficult question of law. In substance they said this. The answer to the problem must lie in the question whether Lord Wilberforce's statement that withdrawal must be effected within a reasonable time is based on the doctrine of 'election' or on the principle that a contractual option must be exercised at the time stipulated in the contract or, if none is stated, then there is an implied term that the option should be exercised within a

d reasonable time. They decided that, if the relevant principle is that of election, then there was nothing in the circumstance of the delay to indicate that the owners had elected to affirm the contract. Accordingly, if election was the correct principle, the delay after 9 May did not preclude the owners from withdrawing the vessel.

However, in their opinion Lord Wilberforce's statement in *The Laconia* was not based on election but on the implied term, although they recognised that this did not appear

e to be the view of Lloyd J in *Scandinavian Trading Tanker Co AB v Flota Petrolera Ecuatoriana, The Scaptrade* [1981] 2 Lloyd's Rep 425.

I return to the three grounds which the charterers accepted 'plainly' justified that grant of leave to appeal if the only question arising out of the award concerned the proper construction of cl 5 of the charter and I ask myself the question: why should those three grounds not equally apply to this question of law which the arbitrators found difficult?

f Before considering whether the three reasons equally apply to the waiver point, I note that neither the judge nor the charterers could have been applying the guidelines in *Pioneer Shipping Ltd v BTP Tioxide Ltd, The Nema* [1981] 2 All ER 1030, [1982] AC 724 when they accepted that leave should be given if the cl 5 point stood on its own. The relevant guideline is that leave should not be given even where it is not a 'one-off case' unless the judge considers that a strong prima facie case had been made out that the

g arbitrator had been wrong in his construction. Counsel for the charterers in fact strongly contended that the arbitrators had been wholly right in their construction of the 'any breach' clause. I infer that both the judge and counsel for the charterers were completely accepting the observation of Lord Denning MR in *Italmare Shipping Co v Ocean Tanker Co Inc, The Rio Sun* [1982] 1 All ER 517 at 521, [1982] 1 WLR 158 at 162: 'Useful as guidelines often are, nevertheless it must be remembered that they are only guidelines.

h They are not barriers.'

Ground one

There can be no dispute but that the 'waiver' question of law 'would substantially effect the rights of one or more of the parties to the arbitration agreement' thereby satisfying the (negative) requirements of s 1(4) of the Arbitration Act 1974.

j
Ground two

The judge took the view, and in my view rightly, that this was the equivalent of a 'standard terms' case. The 'election' point is a commonly recurring one not only in the context of withdrawal under a time charterparty, but also in many other situations where contractual options have to be exercised.

Ground three

The question of law does remain undetermined by the authorities. This appears clearly *a* to have been recognised by Staughton J, who said in his judgment:

> 'If one looks at the cases, Lloyd J in *Scandinavian Trading Tanker Co v Flota Petrolera Ecuatoriana, The Scaptrade* [1981] 2 Lloyd's Rep 425 at 428 cited a decision of the Court of Appeal in 1902, *Re Tyrer & Co and Hessler & Co* 86 LT 697, and in particular a judgment there of Romer LJ, who said that lapse of time was immaterial in effect unless it shows an intention on the part of shipowners to abandon their right to *b* withdraw the vessel or amounted to waiver or estoppel (at 699), and Lloyd J followed that reasoning. But there are other authorities which show to my mind quite clearly that lapse of a reasonable time does deprive the owner of the right to withdraw.'

He then quotes *The Laconia* and other cases. I accept the submission of counsel for the owners that there are, or appear to be, in the Commercial Court two schools of thought. *c* To the question, 'Can mere lapse of time defeat a right to exercise an option where that lapse of time does not give rise to any inference of an affirmation of the contract, or of an election not to exercise the option to withdraw or to an estoppel?', one school will answer in the affirmative and one in the negative. It is obviously highly desirable for commercial men and their advisers in particular to know which school is right. Any so-called guidelines which frustrate the resolution of that conflict seem to my mind to be *d* performing the function of a strait-jacket confining the commercial law to an utterly unsatisfactory position.

In the course of the argument I ventured to inject into this esoteric branch of the law the prosaic example of the conflict of decisions at first instance that existed, prior to the wearing of car seatbelts becoming mandatory, whether the failure to wear a seatbelt could form the basis of a valid plea of contributory negligence to a claim by an injured *e* driver or passenger. Counsel for the charterers was prepared frankly to accept that *The Nema* guidelines imposed such a fetter on the exercise of the judicial discretion under s 1(4) of the 1979 Act that that conflict, had it any relevance in arbitral disputes, could not have been resolved by the grant of leave to appeal unless fortuitously the application came before a judge who was a member of the opposite school of thought to that espoused by the arbitrator. *f*

It therefore seems to my mind that all the grounds which would have justified the giving of leave if the only question arising out of the award concerned the proper construction of cl 5 of the charter equally apply to the waiver point.

Counsel for the charterers submitted that the problem was of the simplest proportions. The arbitrators had decided that the owners lost their right of withdrawal because they did not exercise it within a reasonable time; this was a question of fact for the arbitrators *g* and that was an end of the matter. In my judgment that is an over-simplification. In order to decide whether or not a contracting party has exercised his right within a reasonable time you must first ask: reasonable for what purpose or reasonable by what criteria? The criterion adopted by the arbitrators was the shortest time reasonably necessary to enable the shipowner to hear of the default and issue the notice of withdrawal. It was on that basis that they held against the appellants. However, they *h* were at pains to explain that such a period of time did not in the circumstances give rise to an election to affirm, to an estoppel or to a waiver of the option. Clearly on their approach a longer period would have been required for any of those inferences to have been drawn. That is why the arbitrators, as I understand the matter, said the problem was one of law which they found difficult.

With great respect, it seems clear to me that the judge, like counsel for the charterers, *j* over-simplified the situation and concluded that once there was a finding that a reasonable time had expired there could then be only one answer, and that unfavourable to the owners. The starting point must be: for what purpose and on what basis are your seeking to assess what is a reasonable time? It is the different approach to this fundamental question which has created the two schools of thought.

As previously stated, the waiver question satisfies all the grounds which were accepted
_a_   as 'plainly' justifying the giving of leave on cl 5, if that had been the only question. With
all proper diffidence I would therefore have allowed this appeal.

I should perhaps refer to one remaining point of general application. As regards the
basis of appeals to _this court_, I agree entirely that the philosophy of the 1979 Act is to
favour finality in arbitration and therefore to discourage appeals. I therefore wholly agree
with Staughton J that, if the judge concludes, even where there is a substantial and
_b_   arguable point of law, that the arbitrators are probably right, he must say so and refuse
leave to appeal to the Court of Appeal. However, it would be wrong in my judgment to
confine the discretion given by the 1979 Act to those cases where guidelines (or their
interpretation) as to the granting of leave are in issue. As an example of another category,
where there is a conflict of judicial opinion on some important point of principle, the
commercial judge ought to give leave to appeal to enable that conflict to be resolved. It
_c_   would reflect no credit on our system, in fact the reverse, if the final outcome of a dispute
which depended on the application of a principle of law also depended fortuitously on
which particular judge chanced to try the issue.

FOX LJ. The opinion of the arbitrators was that the critical period was from 7 to 20
May 1980. Before 7 May the owners did not have knowledge of the breach. They became
_d_   aware of it on 7 May. In view of the owners' long-standing and firm belief as from the
first or second week of April that the breach had been committed, the arbitrators
concluded that by 7 May there was no need for the owners to wait any longer either to
obtain legal advice or further information or to make up their minds or for any other
reason. They therefore held that a reasonable time for withdrawing the vessel expired on
9 May at the latest.

_e_   The arbitrators then considered whether that finding entitled the charterers to claim
that the owners had lost their right to withdraw the vessel.

That, said the arbitrators, was a question of law which depended on whether the rule
as to 'reasonable time' stated by Lord Wilberforce in _Mardorf Peach & Co Ltd v Attica Sea
Carriers Corp of Liberia, The Laconia_ [1977] 1 All ER 545 at 552, [1977] AC 850 at 872 (to
which I refer later) depends on the doctrine of election or on an implied term that the
_f_   right must be exercised within a reasonable time. The 'election' theory is sometimes
called 'waiver'. Lloyd J in _Scandinavian Trading Tanker Co AB v Flota Petrolera Ecuatoriana,
The Scaptrade_ [1981] 2 Lloyd's Rep 427 at 430 said that it is the kind of waiver which is
better categorised as 'election'.

If the basis of the rule was election the arbitrators concluded that, as the owners
indicated that the delay after 7 May would be without prejudice to their right to
_g_   terminate for fundamental breach (which the arbitrators took as including the right of
withdrawal), there was nothing in the circumstances to indicate that the owners had
elected to affirm the contract. If that was correct, the arbitrators were of opinion that the
delay after 9 May did not preclude the owners from withdrawing the vessel. They were,
however, of the opinion that the rule is based on an implied term that if no specific time
is stated in the contract the contractual option to withdraw the vessel must be exercised
_h_   within a reasonable time. In accordance with their finding of fact on that matter,
therefore, the arbitrators held that the owners had lost their right to withdraw.
Staughton J was of opinion that, whatever was the correct basis of the rule (and whatever
was the correct interpretation of cl 5), the actual decision of the arbitrators was correct
and he therefore refused leave to appeal to the High Court.

Now whatever the basis of the rule, there seems no doubt as to its existence. Lord
_j_   Wilberforce's statement of it in _The Laconia_ [1977] 1 All ER 545 at 552, [1977] AC 850 at
872 is that—

'The owners must within a reasonable time after the default give notice of
withdrawal to the charterers. What is a reasonable time—essentially a matter for
arbitrators to find—depends on the circumstances. In some, indeed many cases, it

will be a short time—viz the shortest time reasonably necessary to enable the
shipowner to hear of the default and issue instructions. If, of course, the charterparty
contains an express provision regarding notice to the charterers, that provision must
be applied.   *a*

In *China National Foreign Trade Transportation Corp v Evlogia Shipping Co of Panama, The
Mihalios Xilas* [1979] 2 All ER 1044 at 1055, [1979] 1 WLR 1018 at 1030 Lord Salmon
said:
                                                                                               b
'If the vessel had not been withdrawn within a reasonable time after the charterers'
breach, the right to withdraw it would have been waived by the owners.'

Lord Scarman in that case said ([1979] 2 All ER 1044 at 1061, [1979] 1 WLR 1018 at
1037):

'The owners were bound within a reasonable time after default to give notice of   *c*
withdrawal. If they did not do so, they would be held to have waived the default.'

I do not think that the fact that doubt or dispute exists as to the basis of the rule is, by
itself, a sufficient reason for giving leave to appeal to the High Court. If the decision was
probably right, whatever the basis of the rule, it was proper to refuse leave. But if the
resolution of the question as to the basis of the rule would substantially affect the rights   *d*
of the parties, then I think it would be proper to give leave to appeal (assuming that the
case qualified for leave to appeal to the Court of Appeal under s 1(7) of the Arbitration
Act 1979, as to which qualification I agree with the observations of Sir John Donaldson
MR).

I turn then to consider what would be the consequence in this case of a resolution of
the question of the basis of the rule as stated by Lord Wilberforce in *The Laconia*.   *e*
Resolution in favour of the implied term theory would leave matters as they are since
the arbitrators proceeded on that basis. The question, therefore, is what would be the
consequence of resolution in favour of the 'election' theory.

As I understand the reasons of the arbitrators, the only materiality of the 'election' basis
is that, if it be right, the fact that the owners indicated that the delay after 7 May would
be without prejudice to their right to terminate demonstrated that there was no election   *f*
by the owners to affirm the contract.

I cannot see how the mere unilateral assertion of the owners that delay after 7 May was
to be without prejudice to their rights can affect the matter. If the owners can do that,
the rule, whatever its basis, is largely useless. I can see that there might be circumstances
in which the owners could not reasonably be expected to make up their mind at once
and that if they bring that to the notice of the charterers (who might not otherwise be   *g*
aware of it) they could reserve their position. That, however, is a quite different matter
and goes generally to the question of reasonableness. I would suppose that the question
of reasonableness must be determined in the light of all the circumstances. One does not
look at it exclusively from the point of view of either side. But, be that as it may, if the
owners' right to withdraw must be exercised within a reasonable time I do not see how
they can extend the 'reasonable time' simply by their own choice; though they could no   *h*
doubt extinguish or reduce their rights by waiver.

Apart from the 'without prejudice' point, the arbitrators, as I read the reasons, do not
suggest that the juridical basis of the rule would have affected their finding of fact on the
question of reasonable time and I do not think it would.

Thus, the arbitrators found that, by 7 May, there was no reason for the owners to wait
any longer either to obtain legal advice or fuller information or to make up their minds   *j*
or for any other reason. In particular, say the arbitrators, there was no need for a meeting
to take place at Piraeus to enable the owners to decide whether or not to withdraw the
vessel.

In the circumstances, in my opinion Staughton J was right in his view that the
arbitrators' decision was probably correct whatever the juridical basis of the doctrine.

a And I think he was right in the exercise of his discretion (on which he did not misdirect himself) to refuse leave to appeal to the High Court. I would likewise have refused leave.

I add only some observations on the question of the principles applicable to the question of giving leave to appeal from the High Court to the Court of Appeal.

I do not think that the fact that the judge of first instance may think that, so to speak, 'there is always a chance' that an appellate court might take a different view to his own is even on a substantial and arguable point sufficient reason for giving leave to appeal to the
b Court of Appeal. That in my opinion is not the spirit of sub-s (6A) of s 1 of the 1979 Act at all. The subsection, I think, must have been intended, in the interests of finality, to tilt the balance fairly heavily against appeals beyond the High Court. I think that the judge would be justified in giving leave to appeal if he wanted guidance on the principles applicable to the grant of leave. I do not think that the importance of the case to one or other of the parties or the fact that it is one of general interest are reasons for giving leave
c to appeal, though I would not doubt that they could be of importance in determining whether to give leave to appeal to the High Court where the matter could be fully investigated.

I would not, however, wish to tie the granting of leave to appeal wholly to cases where the judge requires guidance as to principles relating to leave to appeal, though I think that would be the normal case. The judge is, however, given a discretion by the statute
d and, if he is satisfied that for a special reason leave to appeal to the Court of Appeal from refusal of leave is desirable, I think he should be free to give it.

I would dismiss the present appeal.

Appeal dismissed. Leave to appeal to the House of Lords refused.

e Solicitors: *Vincent Stokes French & Brown* (for the owners); *Richards Butler & Co* (for the charterers).

Diana Procter   Barrister.

f

R v Simpson

COURT OF APPEAL, CRIMINAL DIVISION
LORD LANE CJ, MUSTILL AND LEONARD JJ
g 28 OCTOBER 1983

Criminal law – Offensive weapons – Article made or adapted for use for causing injury – Flick knife – Whether an offensive weapon per se – Prevention of Crime Act 1953, s 1(1)(4).

Criminal evidence – Judicial notice – Offensive weapons – Flick knife an offensive weapon per se
h *– Prevention of Crime Act 1953, s 1(1)(4).*

A flick knife is an offensive weapon per se for the purpose of s 1(1)[a] of the Prevention of Crime Act 1953, since it is an 'article made . . . for use for causing injury to a person' within the meaning of s 1(4) of that Act. A judge may take judicial notice of the fact that it is an offensive weapon and may direct the jury accordingly (see p 794 *a* to *c* and *g h*,
j post).
     R v Allamby [1974] 3 All ER 126, *R v Williamson* (1977) 67 Cr App R 35, *DPP v Stonehouse* [1977] 2 All ER 909, *Tudhope v O'Neill* 1982 SLT 360 and *Gibson v Wales* [1983] 1 All ER 869 considered.

_____

a   Section 1, so far as material, is set out at p 791 *b*, post

Notes

For the meaning of offensive weapon, see 11 Halsbury's Laws (4th edn) para 852, and for cases on the subject, see 15 Digest (Reissue) 900–903, 7758–7777.

For the Prevention of Crime Act 1953, s 1, see 8 Halsbury's Statutes (3rd edn) 407.

Cases referred to in judgment

DPP v Stonehouse [1977] 2 All ER 909, [1978] AC 55, [1977] 3 WLR 143, HL.
Fisher v Bell [1960] 3 All ER 731, [1961] 1 QB 394, [1960] 3 WLR 919, DC.
Gibson v Wales [1983] 1 All ER 869, [1983] 1 WLR 393, DC.
R v Allamby [1974] 3 All ER 126, [1974] 1 WLR 1494, CA.
R v Lawrence (Rodney) (1971) 57 Cr App R 64, CA.
R v Williamson (1977) 67 Cr App R 35, CA.
Tudhope v O'Neill 1982 SLT 360.

Case also cited

Woodward v Koessler [1958] 3 All ER 557, [1958] 1 WLR 1255, DC.

Appeal

On 7 January 1983 in the Crown Court at Croydon, before his Honour Judge Band QC and a jury, the appellant, Calvin Simpson, was convicted of having with him on 5 May 1982 in a public place, without lawful authority or reasonable excuse, an offensive weapon, namely a flick knife, contrary to s 1 of the Prevention of Crime Act 1953. He was sentenced to three months' imprisonment, suspended for two years, and ordered to pay a fine of £100 or, in default of payment, to serve one month's imprisonment. He appealed against conviction by leave of the single judge. The facts are set out in the judgment of the court.

David Wolchover (assigned by the Registrar of Criminal Appeals) for the appellant.
Arnold Cooper for the Crown.

LORD LANE CJ delivered the following judgment of the court. On 7 January 1983 in the Crown Court at Croydon before his Honour Judge Band QC and a jury the appellant was convicted of having with him on 5 May 1982 in a public place and without lawful authority or reasonable excuse an offensive weapon, that is to say a flick knife, contrary to the provisions of s 1 of the Prevention of Crime Act 1953. He was sentenced to three months' imprisonment suspended for two years. He was ordered to pay a fine of £100 or, in default of payment of that fine, to serve one month's imprisonment. There were other charges levelled against him, to which no reference need be made for the purpose of this decision.

It was admitted at the trial that the appellant was in possession of the flick knife and in possession of it in a public place. In the event, after submissions made to the judge which we shall describe shortly, he raised as his defence reasonable excuse for the possession of that weapon, the flick knife, on the basis that he had it in his possession for nothing more sinister than the carrying out of electrical repairs to his motor car. This defence was, as is apparent, rejected by the jury.

It was not contended before the jury by counsel for the defence that the weapon was other than one made for use for causing injury to the person. The reason for that matter was this. At the close of the prosecution case defending counsel sought an indication from the judge whether he, the judge, considered it to be open to the defendant to argue that the flick knife was not made for such use, or, as it is sometimes called, was not offensive per se. The judge held that on the authority of the decision of the Divisional Court in Gibson v Wales [1983] 1 All ER 869, [1983] 1 WLR 393 that defence was not open to the defendant.

The appellant now contends before us, through the arguments of his counsel, that the judge was in error in that conclusion and he submits that this court should not follow the decision of the Divisional Court in Gibson v Wales. That sets the scene for the appeal.

It is necessary first of all to turn to the provisions of the Prevention of Crime Act 1953,
a on the interpretation of which, in the end, the decision of this court must be based.
Section 1(1) reads:

'Any person who without lawful authority or reasonable excuse, the proof
whereof shall lie on him, has with him in any public place any offensive weapon
shall be guilty of an offence . . .'

b Section 1(4) contains a definition of 'offensive weapon', and it is in these terms:

'"offensive weapon" means any article made or adapted for use for causing injury
to the person, or intended by the person having it with him for such use by him.'

If one analyses the words of the definition, there are three possible categories of
offensive weapon. First of all the weapon made for use for causing injury to the person,
that is a weapon offensive per se as it is called, for instance a bayonet, a stiletto or a hand-
c gun. The second category is the weapon which is adapted for such a purpose; the example
usually given is the bottle deliberately broken in order that the jagged end may be
inserted into the victim's face. The third category is an object not so made or adapted,
but one which the person carrying intends to use for the purpose of causing injury to the
person.

d The question, simple to state but like most questions simple to state not so easy to
answer, is whether the flick knife comes within the first category or not; and the
subsidiary question is: if it does come within the category, in what terms should the
judge direct the jury?

The flick knife is an easily recognisable object. It has as a matter of fact been
conveniently defined in s 1(1)(a) of the Restriction of Offensive Weapons Act 1959 as—

e 'any knife which has a blade which opens automatically by hand pressure applied
to a button, spring or other device in or attached to the handle of the knife,
sometimes known as a "flick knife" or "flick gun" . . .'

We observe in passing that the 1959 Act and its 1961 counterpart (which was passed
in order to fill up a gap in the 1959 Act which was disclosed by *Fisher v Bell* [1960] 3 All
f ER 731, [1961] 1 QB 394) were designed to prohibit the importation, sale, display for
sale and so on of flick knives in this country, the reason being that there had been a whole
bevy of cases in which flick knives had been used often with lethal effect in affrays and
brawls, and the public was, not unnaturally, alarmed. Parliament acted in order to allay
such alarm. But the fact that Parliament and the public in general justifiably regarded
this weapon and its use with that alarm does not necessarily mean that they are made for
use for causing injury to the person.
g Griffiths LJ, who delivered the leading judgment in *Gibson v Wales* [1983] 1 All ER
869 at 872, [1983] 1 WLR 393 at 398, to which we have already referred, came to this
conclusion:

'. . . there is no alternative to the view that a flick knife is a dangerous weapon per
se. It is made for the purpose of causing injury to the person. It may sometimes be
h used for wholly innocent purposes, even possessed for innocent purposes, but there
will be a very heavy burden on any person in possession of a flick knife to satisfy
any court that he had it for such an innocent purpose. I would say that the justices
here on the facts of this case fell into error and that a flick knife is now to be regarded
as an offensive weapon per se for the purpose of s 1(1) of the Prevention of Crime
j Act 1953.'

McCullough J, the other member of the court, had this to say ([1983] 1 All ER 869 at
872, [1983] 1 WLR 393 at 398–399):

'Whether a flick knife is an article made for use for causing injury to the person is
a question of fact, but in my judgment it is a question which admits of only one
answer: it is. For the reasons given by Griffiths LJ I take this to have been the view

held by Parliament in 1953 and 1961 and to be beyond argument. I too would allow this appeal.'

The opposing argument put forward is based on what was said by this court in *R v Williamson* (1977) 67 Cr App R 35. That was a case of a sheath knife, where obviously very different considerations apply from those which affect the position of a flick knife. It would plainly be impossible to classify all sheath knives as either offensive per se or not offensive per se, and in those circumstances the matter was plainly a question for the jury. But does a flick knife fall within the words used in *R v Williamson* (at 38):

'But what is sometimes lost sight of is this. It is for the jury to decide these matters. It is for the jury to decide whether a weapon held by the defendant was an offensive weapon, bearing in mind the definition in the section which I have just read. Consequently whether the object in the possession of the defendant in any case can properly be described as an offensive weapon is a matter not for the judge but for the jury to decide. The jury must determine whether they feel sure that the object was made or adapted for use in causing injury to the person or was intended by the person having it with him for such use by him. There may perhaps be circumstances in which it is possible to say that there is no evidence to the contrary in a particular case. But that is not the case here.'

What has to be decided first of all is whether the flick knife falls within that exclusion which was put forward as possible in *R v Williamson*. It has first to be observed that the mere fact that a particular weapon can be, and perhaps often is, used for an innocent purpose does not necessarily take it out of the offensive per se category. That is the reason why we emphasise 'made' in the definition in the Prevention of Crime Act 1953, which I have read. For instance a bayonet may be used to poke the fire, a stiletto may be used as a letter knife, and indeed a hand-gun to shoot vermin. They remain nevertheless in the first category: they are 'made for use for causing injury to the person.'

We have had our attention drawn to an article by Captain Athelstan Popkess CBE, Chief Constable of Nottingham City Police ([1959] Crim LR 640). The passage to which our attention has been directed is in the following terms (at 641):

'As a matter of interest, flick-knives are not manufactured in this country but are all imported. The German article is generally a useful knife. The Italian one, on the other hand, has no cutting edge but is exclusively a stiletto—it is only fair to say, however, that many of these are only meant to be used as paper-knives. Few chief constables are of the opinion that workers would be seriously handicapped if the sale of the knives were banned altogether. Fishermen, on the other hand, commonly use them; as do many miners and agricultural workers. But, in general, mining, farming and fishing areas report little or no use being made of these knives by tradesmen. One chief constable points out that if their use was really essential, British manufacturers would have been making them long since.'

The second half of that passage seems to contradict the first. In any event it is the purpose for which they are made, not that for which they may be used, which is the question.

The other volume to which counsel for the appellant drew our attention was *Brownlie's Law Relating to Public Order and National Security* (1968) p 67. The passage to which our attention was drawn runs as follows:

'*What are offensive weapons?*—Section 1(4) [of the 1953 Act] defines "offensive weapon" to mean "any article made or adapted for use for causing injury to the person, or intended by the person having it with him for such use by him". The first class of articles are those *made* for the prime purpose of causing injury to the person. This includes bludgeons, clubs, bayonets, daggers, firearms (other than those commonly used for gaming), coshes, and knuckledusters. It is sometimes assumed that flick knives are within this class. [He cites (1959) 123 JP Jo 370, and (1958) 121 *a*   JP Jo 733, to which we need not refer. He goes on:] In fact, knives of this type, more properly called spring clip knives, are used extensively by farmers, fishermen, butchers and electricians.'

For that he cites as the second source the article by Captain Athelstan Popkess to which we have already referred and criticism of which we have already made.

Our attention has also been drawn to a passage in the Third Supplement to *Archbold's*
b   *Pleading, Evidence and Practice in Criminal Cases* (41st edn, 1982) para 19–250 which reads as follows:

c   'In *Gibson* v. *Wales* it was held that although the question whether a flick-knife (as defined in section 1(1)(a) of the *Restriction of Offensive Weapons Act* 1959 . . .) was made for use for causing injury to the person was a question of fact (see *R.* v. *Williamson* . . .), it was a question to which there was only one answer—such a weapon was an offensive weapon *per se*. It is submitted that this decision, not binding on the Crown Court, is unlikely to be approved by the House of Lords. There are many situations where it may be a matter of life or death for a sailor to be able to cut a rope instantly. While a sheath knife will often suffice, there are occasions, for example when wearing wet weather gear and safety harness, when a flick-knife in an outside pocket would be preferable. How the Court could say that
d   either as a matter of law or as an irresistible inference of fact a tribunal must decide that a flick-knife (perhaps constructed in a country where their sale is legal) was "made for use for causing injury to the person" is difficult to understand.'

If that paragraph is correct, then doubtless a sailor who had a flick knife in his pocket would in any event be able to establish a good defence of reasonable excuse.

e   It is interesting to note on the other side of the coin that the court in *R v Allamby* [1974] 3 All ER 126, [1974] 1 WLR 1494 assumed that the flick knife was an offensive weapon per se. It was a powerful court consisting of Roskill, James LJJ and Caulfield J. James LJ delivered the judgment of the court, in the course of which he said ([1974] 3 All ER 126 at 128, [1974] 1 WLR 1494 at 1496):

f   'The flick-knife was an offensive weapon per se in that it was made for use for causing injury to the person. The other knives were not. [There were other knives involved which were not flick knives.] If the jury found the fact to be that the defendants were jointly in possession of that knife, there was no defence to the charge.'

It seems that in that case the contrary was not argued, but that passage shows what the
g   immediate reaction of that particular court was to the proposition that we are now examining.

There is a further decision in *R v Lawrence (Rodney)* (1971) 57 Cr App R 64 where a similar assumption seems to have been made by the court.

This is one of the areas where there is great scope of unevenness in the administration of the law. If it is to be left in each case to a jury to decide whether or not a flick knife is
h   an offensive weapon per se, the identical weapon may be the subject of different decisions by different juries.

It is perhaps convenient to read a passage from *Cross on Evidence* (5th edn, 1979) p 160, which appears to be apposite to this consideration. It is under the heading, 'Judicial Notice' and under the sub-heading, 'Rationale'. It runs as follows:

j   'There are at least two reasons why we should have a doctrine of judicial notice. In the first place, it expedites the hearing of many cases. Much time would be wasted if every fact which was not admitted had to be the subject of evidence which would, in many instances, be costly and difficult to obtain. Secondly, the doctrine tends to produce uniformity of decision on matters of fact where a diversity of findings might sometimes be distinctly embarrassing.'

It is never easy to say where the line should be drawn in this type of situation. This court has held that the category into which a sheath knife falls is a matter for the jury (see *R v Williamson*) because in effect it depends on the sort of knife which was in the sheath. We think that the flick knife falls on the other side of the line and that these knives do come into the category of weapons which are offensive per se, namely the first category which is raised by the definition in s 1(4) of the 1953 Act. These weapons are plainly designed by the manufacturers to be carried conveniently in the hand or in the pocket and there concealed, to be brought into use with the minimum of delay to the assailant and the minimum of warning to the victim. There is no pause while the blade is pulled out from the handle against the spring or is removed from its sheath by hand. By their very design in this way they betray the purpose for which they were made.

We are reinforced in that view by a Scottish decision to which we have been referred, *Tudhope v O'Neill* 1982 SLT 360 at 361. In the course of the judgment the judge, who is anonymous as is the rest of the court, said:

> 'The learned advocate-depute repeated that submission, and in our view did so effectively. He acknowledged that the Crown had to rely on the submission that a flick-knife was per se an offensive weapon within the meaning of the [Prevention of Crime Act 1953], since in the circumstances neither of the other two definitions of an offensive weapon was applicable here. He maintained, however, that the nature of the weapon itself, by reason of its spring mechanism which allowed it to be used quickly in an emergency, clearly indicated that it was made for causing injury to the person. In contrast to such things as a sgian-dhubh or a kitchen knife or a penknife it has no other ostensible purpose.'

That submission was accepted by the High Court of Justiciary in Scotland.

In a commentary on *Gibson v Wales* Professor J C Smith points out that it is of importance in the Crown Court, though for obvious reasons not in the magistrates' court, to decide whether this matter should be approached by the judge on the basis that judicial notice is taken of the fact that the flick knife is offensive per se, or whether on the other hand the nature of the knife itself constitutes overwhelming evidence that it should be held to be offensive per se (see [1983] Crim LR 113). The professor points out that in *Gibson v Wales* it seems that on this particular point Griffiths LJ took the view that it was a matter of judicial notice whereas McCullough J was of the contrary view.

In the former case, if it is a matter of judicial notice, then of course the judge is entitled to direct the jury to find the weapon to be offensive per se. In the latter case, so argues Professor Smith in his commentary at any rate, on the authority of the majority speeches in the House of Lords in *DPP v Stonehouse* [1977] 2 All ER 909, [1978] AC 55 the matter must be left to the jury to reach, if they so wish, what in the circumstances appears to be a perverse verdict.

Once one reaches the conclusion, as we have done, that a knife proved to be a flick knife necessarily is one made for use for causing injury to the person, we take the view that that is a matter of which judicial notice can be taken and the jury can be directed accordingly. That is what we believe Griffiths LJ intended and we respectfully agree with his conclusion in all aspects of his judgment.

That means that the passage which we have cited from the Third Supplement to *Archbold* is misleading. The editors might like to consider making the necessary amendments to that.

Accordingly, for those reasons, this appeal must be dismissed.

Appeal dismissed.

Solicitors: *D M O'Shea* (for the Crown).

N P Metcalfe Esq   Barrister.

a

Oliver v J P Malnick & Co (a firm)

EMPLOYMENT APPEAL TRIBUNAL
BROWNE-WILKINSON J, MR T H JENKINS AND MRS M E SUTHERLAND
19 APRIL, 26 JULY 1983

b *Solicitor – Articled clerk – Employment – Clerk articled to partner in firm but doing work for benefit of firm as a whole – Whether clerk employed by firm – Whether clerk can be articled to partner and employed by firm at same time.*

In 1981 Miss O responded to an advertisement for an articled clerk and had an interview with a solicitor, one of the partners of a firm. Shortly afterwards, in a letter on the firm's headed notepaper but in the first person singular, the solicitor wrote to Miss O offering

c her the position of an articled clerk at a salary of £4,000 a year. Miss O accepted the offer and began work in December 1981. Miss O and the solicitor discussed the provisions of the deed of articles that would be executed, but before they were agreed or signed Miss O discovered that a male articled clerk, who was articled to another partner in the firm, had a salary of £4,500 a year. A claim by Miss O for equality of salary having been

d rejected, Miss O left the firm in January 1982. Miss O complained to an industrial tribunal, claiming that she had been unlawfully discriminated against contrary to s 6(1)(b)[a] of the Sex Discrimination Act 1975, and she named the firm but not the individual solicitor as respondents. The industrial tribunal found as a fact that Miss O and the other articled clerk were paid their salaries by the firm and that much of their work was for the benefit of the firm as a whole and not just for the partner to whom each

e was articled, but the tribunal went on to hold that Miss O had been employed not by the firm but by the individual solicitor. The tribunal therefore dismissed Miss O's claim. Miss O appealed to the Employment Appeal Tribunal. On the hearing of the appeal Miss O was given leave to admit further evidence from the Law Society consisting of (i) a report by a committee of the society recommending that clerks should be articled to an individual partner in a firm but employed by the firm and (ii) a specimen deed of articles

f subsequently issued by the society some of the clauses of which were required to be included in every deed of articles, including a clause stating the clerk's salary as a fixed sum 'or such larger sum as the [individual partner to whom the clerk was articled] may think appropriate' but not in terms specifying who was liable to pay the salary.

Held – It was clear from the further evidence before the appeal tribunal that, rather than

g articles of clerkship being inconsistent with employment by a firm of solicitors, the dual system involving a training contract with a principal (i e the articles of clerkship) running concurrently with a contract of employment with a firm was not only possible but the normal arrangement, and the Law Society's specimen deed of articles was not inconsistent with that because, although the deed set out the salary payable to the clerk, it did not in terms impose on the principal individually the obligation to pay it. That and the evidence

h before the tribunal all pointed to Miss O having been engaged as an articled clerk under the dual system of having been articled to the solicitor personally but employed by the firm. The only evidence the other way was the original letter offering Miss O articles and the proposal to enter into a deed of articles, but the offer letter's use of the first person singular could be explained by the fact that it dealt with the undoubtedly personal obligation of the articles and, although the deed of articles would have regulated and

j perhaps been determinative of the parties' legal relationship, the deed had in fact never been executed. It followed that on the facts Miss O, although articled to the solicitor, had

---

a   Section 6(1), so far as material, provides: 'It is unlawful for a person, in relation to employment by him at an establishment in Great Britain, to discriminate against a woman . . . (b) in the terms on which he offers her that employment . . .'

been employed by the firm. The case would therefore be remitted to the industrial tribunal to consider the claim on its merits (see p 799 *d* to p 800 *a* and *e f*, post).

Notes

For articles of clerkship, see 4 Halsbury's Laws (4th edn) paras 43–46.

For the Sex Discrimination Act 1975, s 6, see 45 Halsbury's Statutes (3rd edn) 229.

Cases referred to in judgment

Townrow v Davies (1977) 121 SJ 354, EAT.

Waterman v Herbert Franklin & Piggott (31 July 1978, unreported), industrial tribunal sitting at Reading.

Appeal

Lisa Oliver appealed against the decision of an industrial tribunal (chairman Mr M S Hunter-Jones) sitting in London North on 18 August 1982 whereby, on an originating application dated 8 April 1982 in which Miss Oliver alleged that her dismissal by J P Malnick & Co (a firm) amounted to sex discrimination contrary to the Sex Discrimination Act 1975 and unlawful victimisation of her attempts to exercise her rights under the Equal Pay Act 1970, the tribunal held that Miss Oliver was in fact employed by Mr J P Malnick and not by the firm and that accordingly s 6(3) of the 1975 Act applied to exempt Mr Malnick from liability. The tribunal accordingly dismissed Miss Oliver's claim. The facts are set out in the judgment of the appeal tribunal.

Cherie Booth for Miss Oliver.
Donald Broatch for the firm.

Cur adv vult

26 July. The following judgment was delivered.

BROWNE-WILKINSON J. This case raises a question of some importance to solicitors, namely whether a solicitor's articled clerk can have any right to bring proceedings under the Sex Discrimination Act 1975. Miss Oliver claims that because she was offered lower remuneration as an articled clerk than that offered to a male articled clerk in the same firm she has been unlawfully discriminated against contrary to s 6 of the 1975 Act. The industrial tribunal dismissed her claim. They found that she was employed, not by the firm of solicitors, but by the individual solicitor to whom she was articled (Mr Malnick). Although the firm, J P Malnick & Co, had more than five employees, Mr Malnick as an individual employed less than five people. The tribunal accordingly reached the conclusion that under s 6(3) of the 1975 Act Mr Malnick was not himself personally liable. The industrial tribunal accepted that, as a result of their decision, no articled clerk would in practice be able to bring a complaint of unlawful discrimination under the 1975 Act.

In the autumn of 1981 Miss Oliver responded to an advertisement for an articled clerk and had an interview with Mr Malnick. On 30 November Mr Malnick wrote to Miss Oliver on the headed notepaper of the firm. The letter reads as follows:

'Re: *Articles*

Further to your recent interview, I shall be glad to offer you the position as Articled Clerk subject to a probationary period of one month at an annual salary of £4,000. Would you please telephone me on receipt of this letter to let me know whether you will accept my offer and if so when you can start.'

Miss Oliver accepted the offer and started work on 8 December 1981. There were discussions between her and Mr Malnick as to the provisions of the deed of articles that would be executed, such discussions being based on the Law Society's model articles of

clerkship. However, before any articles were agreed or signed, Miss Oliver discovered
a that a male articled clerk (articled to a different partner in the same firm) had a salary of
£4,500 per annum. Miss Oliver's claim for equality of salary having been rejected, she
left the firm on 25 January 1982.

The industrial tribunal found as a fact that Miss Oliver and the other articled clerks
were paid their salaries by the firm and that a great part of their activities were for the
benefit of the firm as a whole and not just for the partner to whom each clerk was
b articled. The industrial tribunal do not specifically mention in their reasons two further
facts. First, exhibit A4 before the tribunal (which was the firm's pay record for tax
purposes, form P11) states that the firm, not Mr Malnick individually, were Miss Oliver's
employers. Second, in a letter from the firm dated 11 August 1982, the firm states that
an articled clerk's salary may be reviewed at any time 'as indeed may any other member
of our staff's'.

c Miss Oliver presented to the industrial tribunal an originating application under the
1975 Act, joining the firm as sole respondent and alleging that the firm was her
employer; Mr Malnick personally was not joined as a party. The firm entered a notice of
appearance in its own name. The notice did not challenge the allegation that Miss Oliver
was employed by the firm nor did it raise the possibility of a defence under s 6(3) of the
1975 Act.

d The matter came on for hearing before the industrial tribunal on 18 August 1982.
After counsel for Miss Oliver had started to open the case, counsel for the firm intervened
to submit that articles of clerkship were a personal contract between the clerk and the
individual partner to whom the clerk was articled and that Mr Malnick was excepted
from liability under s 6(3) of the 1975 Act since he personally employed less than five
employees. Miss Oliver was given an opportunity to amend to join Mr Malnick
e personally as a party but the offer was declined.

In a very full and closely reasoned decision the industrial tribunal held that Miss
Oliver's employer was Mr Malnick personally and not the firm. A summary cannot do
full justice to their reasoning but in outline it was this. The three strongest points in
favour of the firm being the employer were that the salary was paid by the firm, that the
articled clerk's time was spent for the benefit of the firm as a whole and, thirdly, that the
f common custom of articled clerks when asked where they are articled is to reply with
the name of the firm rather than that of the individual partner. The industrial tribunal
rightly gave little weight to this third point. As to the other two points, the industrial
tribunal felt that they had less force than at first sight appeared in that they were
compatible with the provisions of the Law Society model articles. Such articles are
expressed to be made between the clerk and the individual partner. The clerk binds
g himself to the individual solicitor for a period at 'The salary of . . . £   per annum'. The
articles do not in terms impose on the solicitor the liability to pay that salary; but the
industrial tribunal considered that on ordinary principles of construction a liability so to
do would be implied in the articles. The industrial tribunal considered that the articles
envisage that the clerk, as part of his training, will do work for other partners, that this
work would be for the benefit of the firm, and therefore that in the circumstances it was
h not unreasonable that the firm should bear the ultimate burden of the clerk's salary
although the individual solicitor was personally liable for it.

Having shown that the factors pointing to the firm being the employer were not
decisive, the industrial tribunal said:

j 'In section 82 employment is defined as "employment under a contract of service
or of apprenticeship or a contract personally to execute any work or labour." That
definition does not suggest that it would be right to look outside the words of a
written contract (unless they are patently ambiguous) to decide who are the parties
to it. Articles of Clerkship constitute a contract of employment; the concept of
employment assumes an employer and an employee. The parties to such articles are
the clerk, the employee, and the Solicitor, the employer. The tribunal feels therefore

that unless there is authority to the contrary it must find that the application fails
against the firm named as the respondents, since they were not the persons who
offered the employment as an articled clerk. That must be a matter to be decided as
a fact and it is immaterial that the notice of appearance entered in the name of the
firm had been approved and signed by Mr Malnick in the firm's name or that the
point was not taken before the hearing.'

The industrial tribunal then referred to certain decisions relating primarily to apprentices
but also to two decisions relating to articled clerks. They considered that the common
factor of all the cases was that a contract of apprenticeship is a contract of employment
between the named parties and as such is strictly personal to those parties. It was on those
grounds that the industrial tribunal held Mr Malnick, and not the firm, to be Miss
Oliver's employer.

In essence, the industrial tribunal were deciding that although there were factors
pointing to the firm being the employer, the nature of articles of clerkship generally
were such that in all cases the conclusion must be that the articled clerk is employed by
the individual solicitor to whom he is articled and not by the firm. On the hearing of the
appeal, there was an application on behalf of Miss Oliver to admit further evidence from
the Law Society. We admitted this evidence because, the point having been sprung by
surprise in the industrial tribunal, evidence from the Law Society was not reasonably
available at the time of that hearing, such evidence was obviously credible and might
have had a substantial effect on the decision reached by the industrial tribunal. In the
event, the fresh evidence is in our judgment decisive of the case.

The evidence was in the form of an affidavit from Mr Snowling, the secretary of the
education and training committee of the Law Society. Although he was cross-examined,
nothing of any materiality emerged. His evidence is that in 1977 there was a working
party set up by his committee to consider the position of articled clerks. That working
party produced a report which included the following passage (para 7.1):

'Most articled clerks, although articled to a partner in a firm, do not necessarily
spend their time working for their principal, but in effect have a dual capacity in
being articled to a partner and employed by a firm.'

The report then considered but rejected a suggestion that the clerks should be articled to
the firm. The report recommended a 'dual system', ie that the clerk should be articled to
the individual solicitor but employed by the firm. In considering the merits of the dual
system, the report says (para 7.3):

'In addition the articled clerk would, by virtue of the contract of employment
with the firm, have similar rights and obligations to other employees of that firm,
company or local authority and it could well be that his Contract of Employment
came into force before his articles. Furthermore under the dual system, the principal
has the responsibility of ensuring that the firm, company or local authority is
organised in such a way as to enable him to fulfil his obligations to the articled clerk
under the Articles of Clerkship. We therefore recommend that separate "Contract
of Employment" and "Articles of Clerkship" be entered into.'

The Law Society, pursuant to its statutory powers, subsequently issued a specimen
deed of articles and notes on offering articles. As to the deed of articles some of the clauses
are mandatory (ie they must be included in every deed of articles); others are by way of
suggestion. The specimen deed is expressed to be made between the articled clerk and
the individual solicitor ('the solicitor') who is described as 'a partner in the firm of . . .'
Amongst the mandatory clauses are a clause binding the articled clerk to the solicitor and
a separate clause which reads as follows:

'The salary of the Articled Clerk shall be £   per annum payable   in arrear
or such larger sum as the Solicitor may think appropriate upon reviewing it after
months of the period of Articles has expired.'

It is to be noted that that clause, although stating a salary, does not in terms say who is
a liable to pay the salary.

The notes on offering articles refer to a model notice setting out the terms and
conditions of employment which, it is envisaged, will be given to the articled clerk in
addition to the articles of clerkship. The introductory part of this notice provides a space
for the name of the articled clerk and the name of the principal and continues as follows:

b   'In order to comply with the provisions of the Employment Protection
       (Consolidation) Act 1978 (hereinafter called "the Act"), this statement gives
       particulars of your terms of employment with .... ("the firm") as an Articled
       Clerk as at .... in which position you will be expected to perform all such acts
       and duties as may be required of you and to comply with all reasonable directions
       from time to time given you by any superior and to observe all rules and regu-
       lations from time to time laid down by the firm [and contained in the Staff Manual].'
c
Mr Snowling in his affidavit says that that notice—

       'is drawn on the assumption that the articled clerk will be employed by the firm,
       as distinct from his Principal. Whether that is the situation in any particular case
       must depend on the individual circumstances, but it is the view of the Education
       and Training Committee of the Council of The Law Society that an articled clerk
d   will normally be employed by the firm.'

It is therefore manifest from this further evidence that in general, far from the articles
of clerkship being inconsistent with employment by the firm, the 'dual system' involving
a training contract with the principal (the articles of clerkship) running concurrently
with the contract of employment with the firm is not only possible but the normal
e arrangement. The specimen deed of articles is in no way inconsistent with this view
since, although the deed of articles must set out the salary payable to the clerk, it does not
in terms impose the obligation to pay it on the solicitor individually.

In our judgment this evidence puts the case in quite a different light and if it had been
available before the industrial tribunal they would have reached a different conclusion.
Apart from two factors, all the evidence in the case points to Miss Oliver having been
f engaged as an articled clerk under the dual system, ie articled to Mr Malnick personally
but employed by the firm. She was paid by the firm; in the firm's tax records (prepared
for the Inland Revenue) the firm was entered as being her employer; her work was
done for the firm generally; she and the other articled clerk regarded themselves as
employed by the firm; as evidenced by the notice of appearance and the letter of 11
August 1982, the firm regarded their articled clerks as employees of the firm. The only
g factors pointing the other way are the original letter offering articles (which was written
by Mr Malnick personally and couched in the first person singular) and the proposal to
enter into the deed of articles.

As to the offer letter, it was written on the firm's headed paper and since it was dealing
with the undoubtedly personal obligation of articles it is not surprising that it is expressed
in the first person.

h   As to the deed of articles, the first point to notice is that no deed was in fact ever
executed. If there had been an executed deed of articles, we would accept the view of the
industrial tribunal that such deed would regulate the parties' relationship and might be
determinative of the legal relationship between the parties. But where there is in fact no
deed the contents of the model deed can at best only be evidence of what the parties
intended to do. More important, contrary to the assumption made by the industrial
j tribunal on the evidence before them, the fresh evidence demonstrates that the fact that
the model deed lays down the salary to be paid does not necessarily require the
implication of the term that the individual partner is assuming any individual liability
to pay it. The model deed (including the mandatory clause) covers the normal case where
the firm is to be the employer and as such liable for the payment of the salary.

Therefore, in the light of the further evidence, in our judgment the only possible conclusion on all the facts of this case is that Miss Oliver, whilst articled to Mr Malnick, was employed by the firm as both she and the firm considered her to be.

We were referred to a number of the decisions which were mentioned by the industrial tribunal in their decision. We have not found the cases on apprenticeship of any assistance. As to the cases on solicitor's articled clerks, we doubt whether the unreported decision of an industrial tribunal in *Waterman v Herbert Franklin & Piggot* (31 July 1978) would have been the same if the Law Society's evidence had been before that industrial tribunal. The decision of this appeal tribunal in *Townrow v Davies* (1977) 121 SJ 354 concerned the status of a clerk articled to the sole principal in a firm. We have looked at the full transcript of the judgment and there is nothing in the decision itself which assists in this case. However, in the course of giving the judgment of the appeal tribunal, Phillips J said:

> 'The position of an articled clerk can be analysed as having two components. On the one hand, he is employed as a clerk; but in this case Mr Townrow had been a clerk before he became an articled clerk; indeed, if he had not, the industrial tribunal would not have had jurisdiction to hear the case, because his period as an articled clerk was not long enough to confer jurisdiction. As well as being an employee or clerk, the articled clerk is also a man under articles having a special relationship with the individual solicitor to whom he is articled, and the one is contractually bound to the other.'

That passage, recognising as it does the dual capacity of an articled clerk, is entirely in accordance with the Law Society's analysis of the position and accords with our own view.

Accordingly, although we are far from saying that on the material before them the industrial tribunal reached the wrong conclusion, in the light of the further evidence before us we are satisfied that their decision was wrong and that the only possible conclusion on the totality of the evidence is that Miss Oliver was employed by the firm. It follows that any defence under s 6(3) of the 1975 Act fails since the firm had more than five employees. The case must be remitted to the industrial tribunal to consider the claim on its merits.

There was one other point argued on the appeal. Before the industrial tribunal, Miss Oliver applied for leave to add a claim under the Equal Pay Act 1970. This application was refused. The industrial tribunal considered that so far as amendment was necessary it would be raising a new claim outside the time limit laid down by s 2(4) of the 1970 Act. They further ruled that if amendment was not necessary Miss Oliver could not be prejudiced by their refusal of amendment. We can see no error of law in the industrial tribunal's decision on that point.

Appeal allowed. Case remitted to industrial tribunal.

Solicitors: *Fisher Meredith & Partners* (for Miss Oliver); *J P Malnick & Co.*

K Mydeen Esq   Barrister.

End of Volume 3